PUNTOS DE PARTIDA

TENTH EDITION

Thalia Dorwick

Ana María Pérez-Gironés

Anne Becher

CONNECT ACCESS CARD INCLUDED

create.mheducation.com

ISBN-13: 9781308810140

ISBN-10: 1308810148

Contents

Online Supplements

Puntos has been the starting point for over a million students beginning to learn Spanish. The best-selling program combines digital innovations with the program's solid foundation and proven approach.

This is what *Puntos* offers that continues to set the standard for Introductory Spanish programs:

• **Comprehensive scope and sequence**

Puntos' hallmark approach to vocabulary and grammar focuses on the acquisition of vocabulary during the early stages of language learning (**Capítulo 1: Ante todo**) and then at the start of each chapter throughout the text. Grammar is introduced in thorough explanations, with careful attention given to skill development rather than grammatical knowledge alone.

To this end, the overall organization carefully progresses from formulaic expressions to vocabulary and grammar relevant to daily life and personal interests (studies, family, home, leisure activities), then goes on to prepare students for survival situations (ordering a meal, traveling), and finally branches out to broader themes (current events, social and environment issues). This forward progress is reinforced by a cyclical structure where vocabulary, grammar, and language functions are continuously reviewed and recycled.

• **Clear and effective vocabulary and grammar presentations**

The thorough, effective grammar explanations in *Puntos* are in keeping with the extensive changes made in the ninth edition. These explanations are now even more accessible to students, featuring conversational language, increased clarity, additional examples, and organization of complex, dense explanations into manageable chunks of concise grammar summary. Students will find the grammar explanations to be clear and comprehensible, and particular care has been taken to bolster those grammar points that traditionally prove difficult.

- **Integrated four-skills approach with scaffolded activities that move students from input to open-ended communication**

One of the hallmark features of *Puntos* is its careful sequencing of activities, moving students from controlled to free-form tasks. In the tenth edition, this scaffolding is improved and introduced at the individual activity level. Starting with the very first activity following the grammar explanation, additional *Pasos* have been added to give students the opportunity to use the new grammar in a controlled but more personalized way, facilitating practice and communication with their peers as soon as new concepts are introduced. The activities following each vocabulary topic and grammar point also build up to one or more free- expression activities in which students communicate more independently and creatively.

- **Inclusion of all Spanish-speaking countries**

The tenth edition of *Puntos* highlights the proven concept that introducing students to the Spanish-speaking world goes beyond asking them to simply absorb information about each country. Instead, a few key cultural insights, appearing at various moments throughout each chapter, serve to spark students' interest and, by closing with a question that asks students to reflect on cultural comparisons, encourage them to create personal connections with the cultures of the Spanish-speaking world.

Práctica y comunicación

A. Los gustos y preferencias para las vacaciones

Paso 1. Autoprueba. Complete las siguientes oraciones con -a or -an.

1. Me gust_____ nadar.
2. Por eso me gust_____ las playas caribeñas.
3. A mi familia y a mí nos gust_____ esquiar.
4. Por eso nos gust_____ las vacaciones de invierno.
5. A mi mejor amigo le gust_____ el sol.
6. Por eso siempre le gust_____ la República Dominicana para las vacaciones.
7. ¿A ti te gust_____ las vacaciones activas o relajantes (*relaxing*)?

Paso 2. Use las siguientes frases en oraciones completas para expresar sus gustos.

MODELOS: ¿viajar? → (No) Me gusta viajar.
¿los aviones? → (No) Me gustan los aviones.

1. ¿viajar?
2. ¿los viajes con mi familia?
3. ¿los vuelos?
4. ¿el calor?
5. ¿el invierno?
6. ¿las playas caribeñas?
7. ¿los aeropuertos?
8. ¿viajar en coche?

Paso 3. Ahora, en parejas, túrnense para entrevistarse sobre las ideas del Paso 2. Luego díganle al resto de la clase algo que Uds. tienen en común.

MODELO: E1: A mí me gusta viajar. ¿Y a ti?
E2: A mí también. →
A nosotros nos gusta viajar.

EL MUNDO HISPANOHABLANTE*

- El español es la lengua que más se habla* en el mundo* después del* mandarín. Más de* 500 (quinientas) millones de personas hablan español.

- Es la lengua oficial de 20 (veinte) naciones y de Puerto Rico.

*EL...The Spanish-speaking world *la...the language spoken most *world *después... after *Más...More than

ABOUT THE AUTHORS

Thalia Dorwick retired as McGraw-Hill's Editor-in-Chief for Humanities, Social Sciences, and Languages. For many years she was also in charge of McGraw-Hill's World Languages college list in Spanish, French, Italian, German, Japanese, and Russian. She has taught at Allegheny College, California State University (Sacramento), and Case Western Reserve University, where she received her Ph.D. in Spanish in 1973. She was recognized as an Outstanding Foreign Language Teacher by the California Foreign Language Teachers Association in 1978. Dr. Dorwick is the coauthor of several textbooks and the author of several articles on language teaching issues. She is a frequent guest speaker on topics related to language learning, and she was also an invited speaker at the II Congreso Internacional de la Lengua Española, in Valladolid, Spain, in October 2001. In retirement, she consults for McGraw-Hill, especially in the area of world languages, which is of personal interest to her. She is a Vice President of the Board of Trustees of Case Western Reserve University and a past President of the Board of Directors of Berkeley Repertory Theatre.

Ana María Pérez-Gironés is an Adjunct Associate Professor of Spanish at Wesleyan University, Middletown, Connecticut, where she teaches and coordinates Spanish language courses. She received a Licenciatura en Filología Anglogermánica from the Universidad de Sevilla in 1985, and her M.A. in General Linguistics from Cornell University in 1988. Professor Pérez-Gironés' professional interests include second language acquisition and the use of technology in language learning. She is a coauthor of *A otro nivel, Puntos en breve,* Second Edition, and *¿Qué tal?,* Seventh Edition. She is also a coauthor of the Student Manuals for Intermediate Grammar Review and Intensive and High Beginner Courses that accompany *Nuevos Destinos.*

Anne Becher received her M.A. in Hispanic Linguistics in 1992 from the University of Colorado—Boulder, and now coordinates the Beginning Spanish One course and teaches pedagogy and methods courses for the Department of Spanish and Portuguese there. She has taught beginning through advanced levels of Spanish since 1996, including several years teaching Modified Spanish classes for students with difficulty learning languages. She has published several reviews in *Hispania,* presents frequently at the Colorado Congress of Foreign Language Teachers (CCFLT) conferences, and has served on the boards of CCFLT and the Colorado chapter of American Association of Teachers of Spanish and Portuguese. She co-edited the bilingual literary journal *La selva subterranea* from 1987–1996.

An Invitation to

Puntos de partida

Puntos de partida
means *points of departure* in Spanish. This program will be your point of departure for learning Spanish and for learning about Hispanic cultures. With *Puntos de partida*, you will get ready to communicate with Spanish speakers in this country and in other parts of the Spanish-speaking world. To speak a language means much more than just learning its grammar and vocabulary.

To know a language is to know the people who speak it. For this reason, *Puntos de partida* will provide you with cultural information to help you understand and appreciate the traditions and values of Spanish-speaking people all over the world. Get ready for the adventure of learning Spanish!

1

Ante todo°

Ante... *First of all*

En este capítulo°

En... *In this chapter*

connect® |SPANISH

www.connectspanish.com

Zócalo (*Main Plaza*),
México, D.F., México

Parque Güell, Barcelona, España

- ¡Hola! ¿Cómo está usted?[a]
- ¿Cómo se llama?[b]
- ¿De dónde es?[c]
- ¿Cómo es usted?[d]

[a]¡Hola!... *Hello! How are you?* [b]¿Cómo... *What's your name?* [c]¿De... *Where are you from?* [d]¿Cómo... *What are you like?*

ALEJANDRA HERNÁNDEZ SOTO CONTESTA LAS PREGUNTAS.[a]

- ¡Hola! Estoy[b] muy bien. ¿Y usted?[c]
- Me llamo Alejandra Hernández Soto.
- Soy de[d] Guanajuato, México.
- ¿Cómo soy?[e] Optimista, responsable, sentimental y muy independiente. ¿Y cómo es usted?

[a]contesta... *answers the questions* [b]*I am* [c]¿Y... *And (how are) you?* [d]Soy... *I'm from* [e]¿Cómo... *What am I like?*

Saludos° y expresiones de cortesía

Greetings

Here are some words, phrases, and expressions for meeting and greeting others in Spanish. Can you tell the difference between those that are formal and those that are more informal or familiar (as on a first-name basis)?

Situaciones formales

1. ELISA VELASCO: Buenas tardes, señor Gómez.
MARTÍN GÓMEZ: Muy buenas, señora Velasco. ¿Cómo está?
ELISA VELASCO: Bien, gracias. ¿Y usted?
MARTÍN GÓMEZ: Muy bien, gracias. Hasta luego.
ELISA VELASCO: Adiós.

2. LUPE: Buenos días, profesor.
MARTÍN GÓMEZ: Buenos días. ¿Cómo se llama usted, señorita?
LUPE: Me llamo Lupe Carrasco.
MARTÍN GÓMEZ: Mucho gusto, Lupe.
LUPE: Igualmente.

Situaciones informales

3. JOSÉ: ¡Hola, Carmen!
CARMEN: ¿Qué tal, José? ¿Cómo estás?
JOSÉ: Muy bien. ¿Y tú?
CARMEN: Regular. Nos vemos mañana, ¿eh?
JOSÉ: Bien. Hasta mañana.

4. MIGUEL RENÉ: Hola. Me llamo Miguel René. ¿Y tú? ¿Cómo te llamas?
KARINA: Me llamo Karina. Mucho gusto.
MIGUEL RENÉ: Encantado, Karina. Y, ¿de dónde eres?
KARINA: Soy de Venezuela. ¿Y tú?
MIGUEL RENÉ: Yo soy de México.

> Translations of short dialogues like the ones on this page will always be at the foot of the page, but you should try to read them without the translations first!

---

1. EV: *Good afternoon, Mr. Gómez.* MG: *Afternoon, Mrs. Velasco. How are you?* EV: *Fine, thank you. And you?* MG: *Very well, thanks. See you later.* EV: *Bye.*
2. L: *Good morning, professor.* MG: *Good morning. What's your name, miss?* L: *My name is Lupe Carrasco.* MG: *Nice to meet you, Lupe.* L: *Likewise.*
3. J: *Hi, Carmen!* C: *How's it going, José? How are you?* J: *Very well. And you?* C: *OK. See you tomorrow, OK?* J: *Fine. Until tomorrow.*
4. MR: *Hello. My name is Miguel René. And you? What's your name?* K: *My name is Karina. Nice to meet you.* MR: *Nice to meet you, Karina. And where are you from?* K: *I'm from Venezuela. And you?* MR: *I'm from Mexico.*

Note the use of **red** to highlight aspects of Spanish that you should pay special attention to.

	formal		informal	
títulos	**señor (Sr.)**	Mr.		
	señora (Sra.)	Mrs., ma'am		
	señorita (Srta.)	Miss		
	profesor (*for a man*)			
	profesora (*for a woman*)			
saludos	**buenos días**	good morning	**hola**	hi
	buenas tardes	good afternoon/evening		
	buenas noches	good evening/night		
	(muy) buenas	good day (*any time*)		
preguntas (*questions*)	**¿Cómo está?**	How are you?	**¿Cómo estás?** ⎫	How are
			¿Qué tal? ⎬	you?
	¿Y usted?	And you?	**¿Y tú?** ⎭	And you?
	—**¿Cómo se llama (usted)?**		—**¿Cómo te llamas (tú)?**	
	—**Me llamo…**		—**Me llamo…**	
	"What's your name?"		"What's your name?"	
	"My name is . . ."		"My name is . . ."	
	—**¿De dónde es (usted)?**		—**¿De dónde eres (tú)?**	
	—**(Yo) Soy de…**		—**(Yo) Soy de…**	
	"Where are you from?"		"Where are you from?"	
	"I'm from . . ."		"I'm from . . ."	

¡OJO!*

There is no Spanish equivalent for *Ms.;* use **Sra.** or **Srta.**, as appropriate.

¡OJO!

Note the accent marks on Spanish words that ask questions.

Nota **cultural**

Los saludos en el mundo° hispano   *world*

Hispanics all over the world hug and kiss when they are greeting each other a lot more frequently than do non-Hispanics in this country. Younger people especially greet in this way, even when they have just met. Two men will typically hug or pat each other on the back, and if they are family, they will sometimes give a kiss on the cheek and embrace, just like women do.

¿Qué pasa, hombre? (*What's up, man?*)

 How do you greet your friends? Your relatives?

Así se dice (*That's how it's said*) introduces optional vocabulary from the Spanish-speaking world.

Así se dice

The following greetings express *What's up?, What's happening?,* or *How's it going?*

¿Qué hay? ¿Qué pasa? ¿Qué hubo? ¿Qué onda? (*Mexico*)

The phrase **por nada** is an alternative to **de nada**.

Nota **comunicativa**

Más° expresiones de cortesía   *More*

—**Encantado.** (*for a man*) ⎫		**por favor**	please (*also used to get someone's attention*)
—**Encantada.** (*for a woman*) ⎬ "Nice to meet you."		**perdón**	pardon me, excuse me (*to ask forgiveness or to get someone's attention*)
—**Mucho gusto.** ⎭			
—**Igualmente.**	"Likewise."		
Gracias.	Thanks. Thank you.	**(con) permiso**	pardon me, excuse me (*to request permission to pass by or through a group of people*)
Muchas gracias.	Thank you very much.		
De nada. / No hay de qué.	You're welcome.		

You will use these expressions in **Comunicación**.

---

*¡OJO! *means* Watch out! *or* Pay attention! *in Spanish.*

Comunicación

A. Expresiones de cortesía. How many different ways can you respond to the following greetings and phrases?

1. Buenas tardes.
2. Adiós.
3. ¿Qué tal?
4. Hola
5. ¿Cómo está?
6. Buenas noches.

7. Muchas gracias.
8. Hasta mañana.
9. ¿Cómo se llama usted?
10. Mucho gusto.
11. ¿De dónde eres?
12. Buenos días.

B. Situaciones. If the following people met or passed each other at the times given, what might they say to each other? Role-play the situations with a classmate.

1. Mr. Santana and Miss Pérez, at 5:00 P.M.
2. Mrs. Ortega and Pablo, at 10:00 A.M.
3. Ms. Hernández and Olivia, at 11:00 P.M.
4. you and a classmate, just before your Spanish class

C. Situaciones. What would you say in Spanish in the following situations?

1. Your classmate passes you a handout from the professor.
2. You need to be excused from class to go to the restroom.
3. You just dropped your drink on a friend's book.
4. Your professor thanks you for opening the door for her.
5. You need your professor's attention.

D. Más (More) situaciones. Are the people in this drawing saying **por favor, con permiso,** or **perdón?** **¡OJO!** More than one response is possible for some items.

E. Entrevista (Interview)

Paso (Step) 1. Turn to a person sitting next to you and do the following.

- Greet him or her appropriately, that is, with informal forms.
- Ask how he or she is.
- Find out his or her name.
- Ask where he or she is from.
- Conclude the exchange.

Paso 2. Now have a similar conversation with your instructor, using the appropriate formal or familiar forms, according to your instructor's request.

Pronunciación: Las vocales:° *a, e, i, o, u*   *vowels*

There is a very close relationship between the way Spanish is written and the way it is pronounced. This makes it relatively easy to learn the basics of Spanish spelling and pronunciation.

Many Spanish sounds, however, do not have an exact equivalent in English, so you can't always trust English to be your guide to Spanish pronunciation. Even words that are spelled the same in both languages are usually pronounced quite differently.

English vowels can have many different pronunciations or may be silent. Spanish vowels are always pronounced, and they are almost always pronounced in the same way. They are always short and tense. They are never drawn out with a *u* or *i* glide as in English: **lo** ≠ *low;* **de** ≠ *day.*

> **a:** pronounced like the *a* in *father,* but short and tense
> **e:** pronounced like the *e* in *they,* but without the *i* glide
> **i:** pronounced like the *i* in *machine,* but short and tense*
> **o:** pronounced like the *o* in *home,* but without the *u* glide
> **u:** pronounced like the *u* in *rule,* but short and tense

¡OJO!
The *uh* sound or schwa (which is how most unstressed vowels are pronounced in English: c*a*nal, wait*e*d, at*o*m) does not exist in Spanish.

Práctica

A. Palabras (*Words*). Repeat the following words after your instructor.

1. hasta	tal	nada	mañana	natural	normal	fascinante
2. me	qué	Pérez	Elena	rebelde	excelente	elegante
3. sí	señorita	permiso	terrible	imposible	tímido	Ibiza
4. yo	con	como	noches	profesor	señor	generoso
5. uno	usted	tú	mucho	Perú	Lupe	Úrsula

B. Nombres. Here is a table of the 10 Spanish names most frequently given to Hispanic babies (male and female) in the U.S. in 2012 (**dos mil doce**).

Los 10 nombres de bebé preferidos por los hispanos en el 2012	
Niño	**Niña**
Santiago	Sofía
Matías	Isabella
Sebastián	Valentina
Mateo	Camila
Nicolás	Valeria
Alejandro	Luciana
Samuel	Ximena/Jimena
Diego	Mariana
Daniel	María José
Benjamín	Victoria

From Fox News Latino

Paso 1. Can you find the Spanish word for *boy?* for *girl?* for the phrase *preferred by Hispanics?*

Paso 2. Working in pairs, try to give the English version of some of these names. Say the Spanish names aloud and, as you do, focus on the different pronunciation and spelling as compared to English. **¡OJO!** One name in the list is not really Spanish. After studying **El alfabeto español** on page 8, you will know which one it is.

Paso 3. In pairs, make a list of other Hispanic first names you know and say them out loud, trying to pronounce them in Spanish.

---

*The word **y** (and) is also pronounced like the letter **i**, as is the letter **y** at the end of a word: ¡**ay!**

El alfabeto español

¡OJO!

The **rr** combination occurs frequently in Spanish, but it is not a separate letter.

The Spanish *alphabet* (**el alfabeto** or **el abecedario**) is slightly different from the English alphabet.

- It has 27 letters (not 26).
- The extra letter is **ñ.**
- The letters **k** and **w** appear only in words borrowed from other languages.

Letters	Names of Letters	Examples			Pronunciation
a	a	Antonio	Ana	la Argentina	
b	be	Benito	Blanca	Bolivia	like Spanish **v**
c	ce	Carlos	Cecilia	Cáceres	**c** + **a/o/u** = like English *k*; **c** + **e/i** = like English *s* (in Spain, a *th* sound)
d	de	Domingo	Dolores	Durango	
e	e	Eduardo	Elena	el Ecuador	
f	efe	Felipe	Francisca	Florida	
g	ge	Gerardo	Gloria	Guatemala	**g** + **e/i** = like hard English *h*; **g** + **a/o/u** and **gue/gui** = like English *g* in *got*
h	hache	Héctor	Hortensia	Honduras	silent; in **ch** combination = like English *cheese*
i	i	Ignacio	Inés	Ibiza	
j	jota	José	Juana	Jalisco	like hard English *h*; similar to **g** + **e/i**
k	ca (ka)	(Karl)	(Karina)	(Kansas)	like English *k*
l	ele	Luis	Lola	Lima	like English *l*; when doubled (**ll**), like *y* in English *yes*
m	eme	Manuel	María	México	
n	ene	Nicolás	Nati	Nicaragua	
ñ	eñe	Íñigo	Begoña	España	like *ny* in English *canyon*
o	o	Octavio	Olivia	Oviedo	
p	pe	Pablo	Pilar	Panamá	
q	cu	Enrique	Raquel	Quito	
r	ere	Álvaro	Rosa	Monterrey	like *tt* in English *butter*; trilled at beginning of a word or as **rr**
s	ese	Salvador	Sara	San Juan	
t	te	Tomás	Teresa	Toledo	
u	u	Agustín	Úrsula	el Uruguay	
v	uve	Víctor	Victoria	Venezuela	like Spanish **b**
w	doble uve	(Oswaldo)	(Wilma)	(Washington)	like English *w*
x	equis	Xavier	Ximena	Extremadura	like English *x*; at beginning of a word and in **México, mexicano, x** = Spanish **j**
y	ye	Pelayo	Yolanda	el Paraguay	like *i* in English *machine*
z	ceta (zeta)	Gonzalo	Zoila	Zaragoza	like English *s* (in Spain, a *th* sound); never like English *z*

Práctica

A. Pronunciación. Match the Spanish letters with their equivalent pronunciation and pronounce the example words.

EXAMPLES/SPELLING

1. _____ mucho: **ch**
2. _____ Geraldo: **ge** (also: **gi**); Jiménez: **j**
3. _____ hola: **h**
4. _____ gusto: **gu** (also: **ga, go**)
5. _____ me llamo: **ll**
6. _____ señor: **ñ**
7. _____ profesora: **r**
8. _____ Ramón: **r** (to start a word); burro: **rr**
9. _____ nos vemos: **v**

PRONUNCIATION

a. like the *g* in English *garden*
b. similar to *tt* of *butter* when pronounced very quickly
c. like *ch* in English *cheese*
d. like Spanish **b**
e. similar to a "strong" English *h*
f. like *y* in English *yes*
g. a trilled sound, several Spanish **r**'s in a row
h. like the *ny* sound in *canyon*
i. never pronounced

B. ¿Cómo se escribe... ? *(How do you write ... ?)*

Paso 1. Pronounce these U.S. place names in Spanish. Then spell the names aloud in Spanish. All of them are of Hispanic origin: **Toledo, Los Ángeles, Montana, Colorado, El Paso, Florida, Las Vegas, Amarillo, San Francisco.**

Paso 2. Spell your own name aloud in Spanish, and listen as your classmates spell their names. Try to remember as many of their names as you can.

MODELO: Me llamo María: **M** (eme) **a** (a) **r** (ere) **í** (i con acento) **a** (a).

Nota **comunicativa**

Los cognados

As you study Spanish, note that many Spanish and English words are similar or identical in form and meaning. These related words are called *cognates* (**los cognados**). It's useful to begin recognizing and using cognates immediately; they will help you enrich your Spanish vocabulary and develop language proficiency more quickly. Here are some examples.

TO DESCRIBE PEOPLE		TO NAME PLACES AND THINGS	
cruel	optimista	banco	hotel
elegante	paciente	bar	museo
idealista	pesimista	café	oficina
importante	responsable	clase	parque
independiente	sentimental	diccionario	teatro
inteligente	terrible	estudiante	teléfono
interesante	tolerante	examen	televisión

You will practice this vocabulary throughout this chapter.

¿Cómo es usted? (Part 1)

Ángela Suárez del Pino

Ismael Figueroa García

1. —¿Quién **es usted** y cómo **es**?
— **Soy** Ángela Suárez del Pino.
Soy optimista y tolerante.

> Remember to watch for the words in red. Check the translation at the bottom of the page only if you need to.

2. —¿Quién **eres tú**?
— Me llamo Ismael Figueroa García y **soy** estudiante de universidad.
—Ismael, ¿cómo **eres**?
— **Soy** inteligente, romántico y responsable.

---

1. *"Who are you and what are you like? "I'm Ángela Suárez del Pino. I'm optimistic and tolerant."*
2. *"Who are you?" "My name is Ismael Figueroa García, and I'm a university (college) student." "Ismael, what are you like?" "I'm intelligent, romantic, and responsible."*

a verb / **un verbo** = a word that describes an action or a state of being

¡OJO!

In Spanish, subject pronouns are not always used because the verb form indicates the person. See how this works in the dialogues on page 9.

Use the following verb forms to describe yourself or another person.

Subject Pronouns / Pronombres personales*	ser (to be):† Formas singulares	
yo	soy	I am
tú	eres	you (*familiar*) are
usted	es	you (*formal*) are
él	es	he is
ella	es	she is

Comunicación

A. ¿Cómo es usted? Indique todas las palabras apropiadas (*appropriate words*).

(Yo) Soy...

_____ diligente	_____ pesimista	_____ independiente
_____ idealista	_____ materialista	_____ estudiante
_____ impaciente	_____ normal	_____ diferente
_____ extravagante	_____ profesor	_____ profesora
_____ elegante	_____ importante	_____ ¿ ?

B. ¿Quién es... ?

Paso 1. With a classmate, take turns asking and answering questions.

MODELO: arrogante →
ESTUDIANTE 1: ¿Quién es arrogante?
ESTUDIANTE 2: **Enrique Iglesias** es arrogante.

Personas

Enrique Iglesias   Selena Gómez   Penélope Cruz   ¿ ?

1. arrogante	**4.** materialista	**7.** elegante
2. independiente	**5.** impresionante	**8.** terrible
3. paciente	**6.** interesante	**9.** fascinante

Paso 2. Now describe the people in negative terms, using **no** in front of the verb.

MODELO: Enrique Iglesias **no** es arrogante.

C. Una encuesta (*A poll*)

Paso 1. Use cognates from **Nota comunicativa** (page 9) and others you have heard or seen to describe the following people and things.

MODELO: Jennifer López → Jennifer López es **independiente.**

1. Jennifer López
2. este país (*this country*)
3. _____ (programa de televisión)
4. _____ (una persona famosa)

Paso 2. Now poll 2 classmates about the same 4 items. Write their answers in the chart.

MODELO: To ask: ESTUDIANTE 1: En tu opinión, ¿cómo es Jennifer López?
To answer: ESTUDIANTE 2: Es independiente.

Estudiantes (nombre)	Jennifer López	este país	_____ (programa de televisión)	_____ (persona famosa)

---

*You will learn more about subject pronouns in **Gramática 3** (Capítulo 2) *and* **Gramática 8** (Capítulo 3).
†*You will learn more about **ser** in **Gramática 6** (Capítulo 3).

¡Aquí se habla español!

If you sometimes have the feeling that Spanish is everywhere, that's because it's true, and it may become even more so during your lifetime. Here are some interesting facts.

- Spanish is spoken as a first or second language by about 450 million people. This makes Spanish the second most widely spoken language in the world. (Chinese is the most widely spoken.) Some Spanish speakers also speak an indigenous language, like **náhuatl** in Mexico, **mapuche** in Chile, or **catalán** in Spain.
- Spanish is an official language of 20 countries.
- Over 40 million people in the United States speak Spanish, making it the fourth largest Spanish-speaking country in the world.
- Spanish is the official language (along with English) of Puerto Rico, an **Estado Libre** (*Free State*) associated with the United States.
- Spanish is present in Equatorial Guinea (where it is an official language) and in the Philippines as a heritage from the not so distant past when the islands were colonies of Spain.
- Spanish is second only to English in terms of the number of people studying it worldwide.

La Misión Basílica San Diego de Alcalá, cerca de (*near*) San Diego, California

Knowing a second language has many personal and professional advantages. If you live in a country like the United States, there is no need to explain to you why it's a good thing to study Spanish. The language and its culture are part of the country's historical and cultural past. And, from an economic standpoint, Spanish speakers provide a huge market of consumers of all kinds of goods and services, including the entertainment industry and the world of art.

Spanish is also a great asset for traveling for business or pleasure, within this country or abroad. Like all languages spoken by a large number of people, modern Spanish varies from region to region. The Spanish of Madrid is different from that spoken in Mexico City, Buenos Aires, or Los Angeles. Although these differences are most noticeable in pronunciation ("accent"), they are also found in vocabulary and special expressions used in different areas of the world. But the majority of structures and vocabulary is common to the many varieties of Spanish.

Knowing Spanish also opens the door to a fascinating culture. Actually, *cultures*, plural, would be more accurate. Spanish was the language of one of the most impressive intersections of culture and civilization the world has ever known, when a small group of Spaniards landed on an island in the Caribbean over 500 years ago. No two of the Spanish-speaking American countries that arose from that fusion of European and indigenous cultures (including those of Africans, brought to work as slaves) are alike. They offer a rich and diverse cultural panorama, one that you will learn about in every chapter of *Puntos de partida*.

So . . . welcome to the Spanish-speaking world! Actually, you know, you're already in it.

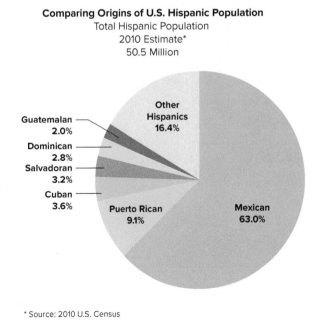

Comparing Origins of U.S. Hispanic Population
Total Hispanic Population
2010 Estimate*
50.5 Million

Other Hispanics 16.4%
Guatemalan 2.0%
Dominican 2.8%
Salvadoran 3.2%
Cuban 3.6%
Puerto Rican 9.1%
Mexican 63.0%

* Source: 2010 U.S. Census

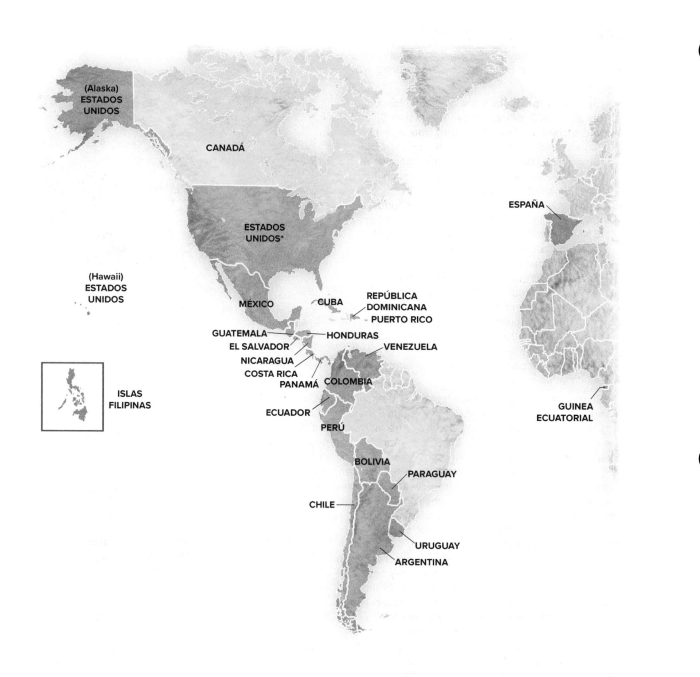

(Alaska)
ESTADOS
UNIDOS

CANADÁ

(Hawaii)
ESTADOS
UNIDOS

ISLAS
FILIPINAS

ESTADOS
UNIDOS*

MÉXICO

CUBA

REPÚBLICA
DOMINICANA
PUERTO RICO

GUATEMALA
EL SALVADOR
NICARAGUA
COSTA RICA
PANAMÁ

HONDURAS

VENEZUELA

COLOMBIA

ECUADOR

PERÚ

BOLIVIA

PARAGUAY

CHILE

URUGUAY

ARGENTINA

ESPAÑA

GUINEA
ECUATORIAL

*The United States is generally expressed as **los Estados Unidos** in Spanish. The phrase is abbreviated in a number of ways:
E.U., EE. UU. (the double vowels indicate plurality), **EEUU** (without the periods), **USA,** and **U.S.A.** (the latter pronounced as
one word). **U.S.A.** is not recommended usage. **Los Estados Unidos de América (E.U.A.)** is also used.

Los números del 0 al 30; *Hay*

En un salón de clase

Hay una profesora.
Hay cuatro estudiantes.

Los números del 0 al 30

0	cero				
1	uno	11	once	21	veintiuno
2	dos	12	doce	22	veintidós
3	tres	13	trece	23	veintitrés
4	cuatro	14	catorce	24	veinticuatro
5	cinco	15	quince	25	veinticinco
6	seis	16	dieciséis*	26	veintiséis
7	siete	17	diecisiete	27	veintisiete
8	ocho	18	dieciocho	28	veintiocho
9	nueve	19	diecinueve	29	veintinueve
10	diez	20	veinte	30	treinta

¡OJO!

uno, dos,... veinti**uno,**
  veintidós,...
but
un señor, veinti**ún**
  señores
una señora, veinti**una**
  señoras

Nota **comunicativa**

El género (*gender*) y los números

The number *one* has several forms in Spanish. **Uno** is the form used in counting. The forms **un** and **una** are used before *nouns* (**los sustantivos**). How will you know which one to use? It depends on the *gender* (**el género**) of the noun.

All Spanish nouns are either masculine or feminine. For example, the noun **señor** is masculine (*m.*) in gender, and the noun **señora** is feminine (*f.*). (As you will learn, even nouns that are not sex-linked have gender.) Here is how *one* is expressed with these nouns: **un señor, una señora.** The number **veintiuno** has similar forms before nouns: **veintiún señores, veintiuna señoras.** Just get used to using **un** and **una** with nouns now. You'll learn more about gender and number in **Capítulo 2.**

The numbers 16 to 19 and 21 to 29 can be written as one word (dieciséis... veintiuno...**) or as three words (**diez y seis... veinte y uno...**).*

Algo... Something about

Algo sobre°...

los números

In Spanish-speaking countries, hand-written numbers may look a little different than they do in the U.S.

Can you see any differences in this photo?

a noun / **un sustantivo** = a word that denotes a person, place, thing, or idea

Hay

The word **hay** expresses both *there is* and *there are* in Spanish. It can be made negative (**no hay**) and can also be used to ask a question: **¿Hay... ?** (*Is there . . . ? Are there . . . ?*)

hay = there is / there are

Hay un teatro en esta universidad, pero **no** hay museo.

There's a theater at this university, but there isn't a museum.

—¿Cuántos estudiantes hay en la clase?
—(Hay) Treinta.

"How many students are there in the class?"
"(There are) Thirty."

Práctica y comunicación

A. Una canción infantil. (*A children's song.*) This is a popular song for children from all over the Spanish-speaking world. Complete it with the missing numbers. It's basic math!

Dos y dos son _____, y ocho _____,

cuatro y dos son _____, y ocho _____,

Seis y dos son _____, y _____ treinta y dos...

B. Los números. Practique los números, según (*according to*) el modelo.

MODELO: 1 señor → Hay **un** señor.

1. 4 señoras
2. 12 pianos
3. 1 café (*m.*)
4. 21 cafés (*m.*)
5. 14 días

6. 1 idea (*f.*)
7. 21 ideas (*f.*)
8. 11 personas
9. 15 estudiantes
10. 13 teléfonos

11. 28 naciones
12. 5 guitarras
13. 1 león (*m.*)
14. 30 señores
15. 20 oficinas

C. Problemas de matemáticas. Express the following simple mathematical equations in Spanish. Note: + (**y**), − (**menos**), = (**son**).

MODELOS: $2 + 2 = 4$ → Dos y dos son cuatro.
$4 - 2 = 2$ → Cuatro menos dos son dos.

1. $2 + 4 = 6$
2. $8 + 17 = 25$
3. $11 + 1 = 12$
4. $3 + 18 = 21$
5. $9 + 6 = 15$
6. $5 + 4 = 9$
7. $1 + 13 = 14$

8. $15 - 2 = 13$
9. $9 - 9 = 0$
10. $13 - 8 = 5$
11. $14 + 12 = 26$
12. $23 - 13 = 10$
13. $1 + 4 = 5$
14. $1 + 3 - 1 = 3$

15. $8 - 7 = 1$
16. $13 - 9 = 4$
17. $2 + 3 + 10 = 15$
18. $28 - 6 = 22$
19. $30 - 17 = 13$
20. $28 - 5 = 23$
21. $19 - 7 = 12$

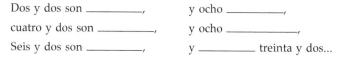

D. Intercambios (*Exchanges*)

1. ¿Cuántos (*How many*) estudiantes hay en la clase de español? ¿Cuántos estudiantes hay en clase hoy (*today*)? ¿Hay tres profesores o un profesor / una profesora?

2. ¿Cuántos días hay en una semana (*week*)? ¿Hay seis? (**No, no hay...**) ¿Cuántos días hay en un fin de semana (*weekend*)? ¿Cuántos días hay en el mes (*month*) de febrero? ¿en el mes de junio? ¿Cuántos meses hay en un año (*year*)?

3. En una universidad, hay muchos edificios (*many buildings*). En esta (*this*) universidad, ¿hay una cafetería? (**Sí, hay... / No, no hay...**) ¿un teatro? ¿un laboratorio de lenguas (*languages*)? ¿un bar? ¿una clínica? ¿un hospital? ¿un museo? ¿muchos estudiantes? ¿muchos profesores?

Los gustos° y preferencias (Part 1)*

Los... *Likes*

—¿Te gusta el fútbol?
—Sí, ¡me gusta mucho!
— Y a usted, señor, ¿también le gusta el fútbol?
— No, no me gusta el fútbol, pero sí me gusta el fútbol americano.

La selección nacional (*team*) de la Argentina, subcampeona del mundo (*world runner-up*) de fútbol en 2014 (dos mil catorce).

Use these patterns with the verb **gustar** to express likes and dislikes.

Me gusta _____.	I like _____.
No me gusta _____.	I don't like _____.
(No) Te gusta _____. (*familiar*) (No) Le gusta _____. (*formal*)	You (don't) like _____.
¿Te gusta _____? (*familiar*) ¿(A usted) Le gusta _____? (*formal*)	Do you like _____?

In the following activities you will use **el** to mean *the* with masculine nouns and **la** with feminine nouns. Don't try to memorize which words are masculine or feminine.

You will also use Spanish verbs in the infinitive form, which always ends in **-r.** Here are some examples: **estudiar** = *to study*, **comer** = *to eat*. You will be able to guess the meaning of other infinitives from context (the surrounding words).

an infinitive / **un infinitivo** = a verb form that indicates action or state of being without referring to a specific person or time

Práctica y comunicación

A. **¿Yo, tú o usted?** Indicate which pronoun you associate with each question or statement.

   1. ¿Te gusta la pizza?
   2. ¿Le gusta la Coca-Cola?
   3. Me gusta mucho el chocolate.

B. **Versión bilingüe.** Match the ideas.

   1. _____ —¿Te gusta esquiar?
 —No, no me gusta.
   2. _____ —¿Le gusta esquiar?
 —Sí, me gusta.
   3. _____ —Me gusta esquiar.
 —¿Sí? A mí no me gusta.

   a. "Do you (*formal*) like to ski?" "Yes, I like to."
   b. "I like to ski." "Yeah? I don't like to."
   c. "Do you (*familiar*) like to ski?" "No, I don't like to."

"Do you like soccer?" "Yes, I like it a lot!" "And (what about) you, sir, do you also like soccer?" "No, I don't like soccer, but I do like football."

*You will learn more about **gustar** in Gramática 22 (Capítulo 8).

C. Los gustos y preferencias

Paso 1. Make a list of six things you like and six things you don't like, following the model. You may choose items from the **Vocabulario útil** box.

MODELO: Me gusta **la clase de español.** No me gusta **la clase de matemáticas.**

> **Vocabulario útil** is not active; that is, you don't need to focus on learning it. But it will help you do this activity.

Vocabulario útil

el actor _____, la actriz _____
el café, el té, la limonada, la Coca-Cola
el/la cantante (*singer*) _____
el cine (*movies*), el teatro, la ópera, el arte abstracto, el fútbol
la música moderna, la música clásica, el *hip hop,* la música *country*
la pizza, la pasta, la comida (*food*) mexicana, la comida de la cafetería
_____ (programa de televisión)
_____ (ciudad [*city*])

¡OJO!
The word **cantante** is used for both men *and* women.

1. Me gusta _____. No me gusta _____.
2. _____
3. _____
4. _____
5. _____
6. _____

Paso 2. Now ask a classmate if he or she shares your likes and dislikes.

MODELO: ESTUDIANTE 1: ¿Te gusta la clase de español?

ESTUDIANTE 2: Sí, me gusta (la clase de español). (No me gusta la clase de español.)

ESTUDIANTE 1: ¿Y la clase de matemáticas?

ESTUDIANTE 2: Sí, también me gusta (la clase de matemáticas). (No me gusta la clase de matemáticas.)

D. Más (*More*) gustos y preferencias

Paso 1. Here are some useful verbs and nouns to talk about what you like. For each item, combine an infinitive (shaded) with a noun to form a sentence that is true for you. The verb **estudiar** is an easily recognizable cognate. Use context to guess the meaning of verbs that are not cognates.

MODELO: Me gusta _____. → Me gusta **estudiar inglés.**

1. beber	café chocolate limonada té	
2. comer	enchiladas ensalada hamburguesas pasta pizza	
3. estudiar	computación (*computer science*) español historia inglés matemáticas	
4. hablar	con mis amigos (*with my friends*) español por teléfono (*on the phone*)	
5. jugar	al basquetbol al béisbol al fútbol al fútbol americano al tenis	
6. tocar	la guitarra el piano el violín	

Paso 2. Ask a classmate about his or her likes, using your own preferences as a guide.

MODELO: ¿Te gusta **comer enchiladas**?

Paso 3. Now ask your professor if he or she likes certain things. **¡OJO!** Remember to address your professor in a formal manner if that is his or her preference.

MODELO: ¿Le gusta **jugar al tenis**?

¿Qué hora es?

Es la una.

Son las dos.

Son las cinco.

¿Qué hora es? is used to ask *What time is it?* In telling time, one says *Es la una* but *Son las dos* (las tres, las cuatro, and so on).

Es la una y { cuarto. / quince.

Son las dos y { media. / treinta.

Son las cinco y diez.

Son las ocho y veinticinco.

Note that from the hour to the half-hour, Spanish, like English, expresses time by adding minutes or a portion of an hour to the hour.

Son las dos menos { cuarto. / quince.

Son las ocho menos diez.

Son las once menos veinte.

From the half-hour to the hour, Spanish usually expresses time by subtracting minutes or a part of an hour from the *next* hour.

Nota **comunicativa**

Cómo expresar la hora

de la mañana	A.M., in the morning
de la tarde	P.M., in the afternoon (and early evening)
de la noche	P.M., in the evening
en punto	exactly, on the dot, sharp
¿a qué hora... ?	(at) what time . . . ?
a la una (las dos,...)	at 1:00 (2:00, . . .)
Son las cuatro **de la tarde en punto.**	It's exactly 4:00 P.M.
—¿**A qué hora** es la clase de español?	"What time is Spanish class (at)?"
—Es **a las** once **de la mañana.**	"It's at 11:00 A.M."

You will practice these phrases in **Práctica y comunicación.**

¡OJO!

Es la... / Son las... = to tell time
A la... / A las... = to tell *at* what time something happens

Práctica y comunicación

A. **¡Atención!** Listen as your instructor says a time of day. Find the clock face that corresponds to the time you heard and say its number in Spanish.

1.   **2.**   **3.**   **4.**

5.   **6.**   **7.**

B. **¿Qué hora es?** Express the time in full sentences in Spanish.

1. 1:00	**4.** 1:30 P.M.	**7.** 4:15 A.M.	**10.** 9:50 sharp
2. 6:00	**5.** 3:15 A.M.	**8.** 11:45 exactly	
3. 11:00	**6.** 7:45 P.M.	**9.** 9:10 on the dot	

C. **¡Atención!** With a classmate, ask and answer questions about the drawings (**los dibujos**) in **Actividad A.**

MODELO: ESTUDIANTE 1: Son las nueve y media de la mañana.

         ESTUDIANTE 2: Es el dibujo 6.

         ESTUDIANTE 1: ¡Correcto! (No es correcto.)

D. **Intercambios**

Paso 1. Read and practice pronouncing the words in **Vocabulario útil.**

Vocabulario **útil**	
¿cuándo?	when?
los días de la semana*	the days of the week
el lunes	on Monday
el martes	on Tuesday
el miércoles	on Wednesday
el jueves	on Thursday
el viernes	on Friday
el sábado	on Saturday
el domingo	on Sunday

---

*You will learn more about the days of the week in Spanish in **Capítulo 5.**

Paso 2. With a partner, take turns asking and answering questions about when the following events or activities take place, according to the schedule.

Esta (This) semana

L	M	X	J	V	S	D
español: 9 a.m.		español: 9 a.m.		español: 9 a.m.	excursión: 8:45 a.m.	
física: 11:50 a.m.	historia: 11:50 a.m.	física: 11:50 a.m.	historia: 11:50 a.m.	física: 11:50 a.m.		tenis: 10 a.m.
	laboratorio: 3:10 p.m.		laboratorio: 3:10 p.m.			concierto: 7:30 p.m.
					fiesta: 10 p.m.	

MODELO: la clase de español →
 ESTUDIANTE 1: ¿Cuándo es la clase de español?
 ESTUDIANTE 2: El lunes, el miércoles y el viernes a las nueve de la mañana.

1. la clase de español
2. la clase de física
3. la clase de historia
4. la sesión de laboratorio

5. la excursión
6. la fiesta
7. el partido (*game*) de tenis
8. el concierto

Paso 3. Now ask when your partner likes to perform the following activities on a given day.

MODELO: cenar (*to have dinner*) →
 ESTUDIANTE 1: ¿Cuándo te gusta cenar **el sábado**?
 ESTUDIANTE 2: El sábado me gusta cenar **a las seis y media**.

1. cenar
2. estudiar español
3. mirar (*to watch*) la televisión

4. ir al (*to go to the*) gimnasio
5. ir al cine
6. ir a una fiesta

E. Situaciones en la calle. Complete los diálogos con un compañero / una compañera.

Diálogo 1: Por la mañana, en la calle (*street*)
 SR. ROLDÁN: Buenos días, Sra. Valdés. ¿Cómo _____?
 SRA. VALDÉS: Muy bien. ¿_____ , Sr. Roldán?
 SR. ROLDÁN: _____. Perdón, ¿qué hora _____?
 SRA. VALDÉS: _____ las _____ (*10:30*), señor.
 SR. ROLDÁN: _____ gracias, señora.

Diálogo 2: Por la tarde
 SILVIA: ¡Hola!, muy _____, Julio. ¿Cómo _____?
 JULIO: Bien, ¿y _____? ¡Huy!, perdón, ¿qué hora _____?
 SILVIA: _____ las _____.
 JULIO: ¡Ay!, la clase de historia es a las _____ y diez. Me voy corriendo.ª ¡Hasta luego!
 SILVIA: Oye,ᵇ ¿nos vemos el sábado en la fiesta?
 JULIO: ¡Sí, sí!

ªMe... *I have to run.* ᵇHey

Salu2 desde° Los Ángeles

from

El presentador (*anchor*) Víctor Gutiérrez y la presentadora Ana García Blanco. *Salu2* es un programa sobre (*about*) la comunidad global de hispanohablantes (*Spanish speakers*).

Antes de mirar°

Antes... *Before watching*

What is a morning news and talk television show usually like? Check all of the phrases that apply.

☐ un poco (*a little*) cómico
☐ un poco serio
☐ informativo
☐ muy dramático
☐ para (*for*) una audiencia diversa
☐ solo para las personas mayores (*only for older people*)

Este° programa

This

This is the introductory program of a new morning show, based in Los Ángeles, California.

> Reading part of the script before watching each segment of *Salu2* will help you understand more of the show.

Estrategia

You will not understand every word in *Salu2*. In fact we never catch everything in any program even in our native language. But you will be able to get the gist of the show by catching some key words and phrases that you *do* know and by using context, both in the program as well as in the text and images in this section.

Fragmento del guion°

script

VÍCTOR: Muchas gracias, Laura. La presencia del español en la ciudad de Los Ángeles es impresionante, ¿no crees,[a] Ana?

ANA: Absolutamente. Y personas de todo tipo hablan español, no solo[b] los hispanos. Bueno, es hora de decir[c] adiós por hoy. Espero que les haya gustado nuestro primer programa.[d] Nos vemos muy pronto.[e]

VÍCTOR: Desde el estudio de *Salu2* en la ciudad de Los Ángeles, California, les mandamos[f] saludos a todos los telespectadores y esperamos verlos en nuestro próximo programa.[g] ¡Hasta entonces![h]

[a]¿no... *don't you think* [b]no... *not only* [c]es... *it's time to say* [d]Espero... *I hope you liked our first program.* [e]muy... *very soon* [f]les... *we send* [g]esperamos... *we hope to see you at our next program* [h]¡Hasta... *Until then!*

> These words and phrases (given in the order in which they appear in the show) will help you understand more when you watch this episode.

Vocabulario del° programa

of the

hoy les presentamos	today we're introducing . . . to all of you
un nombre	a name
antiguo	former
la ciudad	the city
el país	the country, nation
el tema	topic, subject
dentro y fuera de	within and outside of
vamos a hablar/escuchar	we're going to talk/listen to
cuarenta y ocho	forty-eight
les saludo	I'm greeting all of you
la playa	the beach
disculpa	pardon me
¿de dónde vienes?	**¿de dónde eres?**
(yo) vengo de	**(yo) soy de**
¿cuántos años tienes?	how old are you?

If you scan **Después de mirar** *before* watching the show, you will understand more of what is in the program.

Después de mirar°

Después... *After watching*

A. **¿Está claro?** ¿Cierto o falso? Corrija (*Correct*) las oraciones falsas.

	CIERTO	FALSO
1. *Salu2* es un programa matinal (*morning*) de televisión.	☐	☐
2. Es un programa informativo para un público hispanohablante diverso.	☐	☐
3. El estudio está en San Francisco.	☐	☐
4. Hay tres presentadores (*anchors*) y una reportera.	☐	☐
5. Pocas (*Few*) personas hablan español en Los Ángeles.	☐	☐

Laura Sánchez Tejada es reportera. Es de México pero hoy está en California.

B. **¿Quién lo dice? (*Who says it?*)** Indique el presentador: **A** = Ana o **V** = Víctor.

1. «...el Pueblo de Nuestra Señora la Reina de los Ángeles de Porciúncula.» _____
2. «...el nombre de Los Ángeles es un nombre español...» _____
3. «Y vamos a escuchar a personas hispanohablantes de varios países...» _____
4. «...vamos a escuchar a miembros de la comunidad hispana de Los Ángeles.» _____
5. «...es evidente que muchas personas no hispanas sí hablan español.» _____
6. «Y hoy vamos a escuchar los saludos de algunos angelinos...» _____

C. **Un poco más. (*A little more.*)** Match each person with her/his place of origin.

PERSONAS

1. _____ Ricardo

2. _____ Wally

3. _____ Jennifer

4. _____ Michelle y Amy

5. _____ Miriam y Verónica

6. _____ Rubí

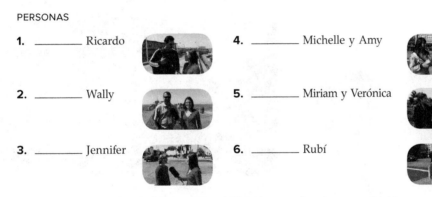

ORIGEN

a. Chicago
b. Los Ángeles
c. México
d. Puerto Rico
e. no se sabe (*not known*)

D. **Y ahora, Uds. (*And now it's your turn.*)** Practique su (*your*) pronunciación y su talento como presentador(a). Haga el papel (*Play the role*) de Laura y complete el fragmento con su propia (*your own*) información.

Buenos días a todos. ¿Cómo están ustedes? Yo estoy muy bien. Me llamo _____ y soy el reportero / la reportera del programa *Salu2*. Les saludo desde^a _____, en el estado de _____.

^aLes... *I'm speaking to you (lit. I'm greeting you from)*

Producción personal
Filme los saludos de dos o tres personas en español.

A LEER°

Estrategias

- This reading has many easily guessable cognates. In addition, the photos and the context will help you understand the meaning of the underlined words.

- As you read, notice that you will "get" a lot of information without actually knowing or understanding all the words. That happens even when you read in your own language!

- Finally, don't just read these pages once. Read them through quickly, without looking up any words, then start back at the beginning again, going paragraph by paragraph. You will be surprised by how much you will "get" the second time you read.

Una lección de geografía

La diversidad del mundo[a] hispano es fabulosa. Lea[b] el texto, mire[c] las fotos ¡y consulte los mapas al final del libro[d]!

1.
El volcán Chimborazo (en el Ecuador), en la cordillera de Los Andes. Los Andes forman la cordillera más larga[e] del mundo (ocho mil quinientos[f] kilómetros), y se extienden por[g] siete naciones de Sudamérica.

3.
Una selva[i] en México. Hay selvas también en otros países[j] en Centroamérica y Sudamérica.

2.
Una playa en la península de Samaná, República Dominicana. En el mar Caribe hay tres islas de habla española. El mundo hispano también tiene[h] costas en el océano Atlántico y en el Pacífico.

4.
El desierto de Atacama, Chile. Es el más árido[k] del mundo. También hay zonas desérticas en otros países hispanos de Norteamérica a Sudamérica: México, el Perú, Bolivia, la Argentina, Colombia. Y también en España.

[a]*world* [b]*Read* [c]*look at* [d]*al... at the back of the book* [e]*más... longest* [f]*ocho... 8,500* [g]*se... they pass through* [h]*has* [i]*jungle* [j]*naciones* [k]*más... driest*

5.
El <u>glaciar</u> Perito Moreno, en la Patagonia argentina. Chile y la Argentina tienen[l] territorio en la Patagonia y en el continente de la Antártida.

6.
Madrid, la capital de España, en Europa. Es una <u>ciudad</u> de gran[m] importancia histórica y cultural. En Latinoamérica también hay muchas ciudades grandes,[n] como la Ciudad de México, Buenos Aires, Santiago,...

[l]have [m]great [n]large

Comprensión

A. ¿Qué significa? (*What does it mean?*)

Paso 1. In pairs, decide on the meaning of the Spanish words for geographical features that are underlined in the reading.

Paso 2. With your partner, give examples of these geographical features in the U.S (or other part of the world) and in the Spanish-speaking world.

1. un volcán
2. una cordillera
3. una playa
4. una península

5. un mar
6. un océano
7. un desierto

B. Los nombres de las regiones del mundo. ¿Cómo se dice en español?

1. Latin America
2. Central America
3. North America

4. South America
5. Europe
6. Antarctica

EN RESUMEN En este capítulo

≣ILEARNSMART·

Visit **www.connectspanish.com** to practice the vocabulary and grammar points covered in this chapter.

AFTER STUDYING THIS CHAPTER I CAN . . .

☐ meet and greet others appropriately in Spanish (4–5)

☐ pronounce words in Spanish and say the alphabet (7–8)

☐ recognize the meaning of many Spanish cognates (9)

☐ describe myself and others (9–10)

☐ say numbers 0–30 and use **hay** (13–14)

☐ talk about some of my likes and dislikes (15)

☐ tell time (17)

☐ recognize/describe at least 2–3 facts about the Spanish-speaking world

Vocabulario

This is the active vocabulary for *Capítulo 1*. Be sure that you know all the words, including the meaning of the group titles, before beginning **Capítulo 2**.

Saludos y expresiones de cortesía

Buenos días. Buenas tardes. Buenas noches. (Muy) Buenas.
Hola. ¿Qué tal? ¿Cómo estás? ¿Cómo está?
Muy bien. Regular. Bien.
¿Y tú? ¿Y usted?
Adiós. Hasta mañana. Hasta luego. Nos vemos.

¿Cómo te llamas? ¿Cómo se llama usted?
  Me llamo _____.

¿De dónde eres (tú)? ¿De dónde es (usted)?
  (Yo) Soy de _____.

señor (Sr.), señora (Sra.), señorita (Srta.)
profesor, profesora

Gracias. Muchas gracias.
De nada. No hay de qué.
Por favor. Perdón. (Con) Permiso.
Mucho gusto. Igualmente. Encantado/a.

el saludo   greeting

¿Cómo es usted?

All forms of infinitives highlighted in red can be found in Appendix 5.

ser: soy, eres, es

¿Cómo es usted?   What are you like?

Los gustos y preferencias

¿Te gusta _____? ¿(A usted) Le gusta _____?
(Sí,) Me gusta _____. (No,) No me gusta _____.
los gustos   likes

Los números del 0 al 30

cero	diez	veinte
uno	once	treinta
dos	doce	
tres	trece	
cuatro	catorce	
cinco	quince	
seis	dieciséis	
siete	diecisiete	
ocho	dieciocho	
nueve	diecinueve	

¿Qué hora es?

¿qué hora es?	what time is it?
es la... , son las...	
y/menos cuarto (quince)	
y media (treinta)	
en punto	
de la mañana (tarde, noche)	
¿a qué hora... ?, a la(s)...	

Las palabras interrogativas

¿cómo?	how?; what?
¿dónde?	where?
¿qué?	what?
¿quién?	who?

Palabras adicionales

sí/no	yes/no
hay	there is/are
no hay	there is not / are not
¿hay?	is there / are there?
hoy/mañana	today/tomorrow
y/o	and/or
a	to; at (*with time*)
de	of; from
en	in; on; at
muy	very
pero	but
también	also
la palabra	word

Vocabulario personal

Use this space for other words and phrases you learn in this chapter.

ESPAÑOL	INGLÉS

An Introduction to the Rest of

Puntos de partida

Puntos de partida

Each chapter of the rest of this textbook has a chapter theme and follows a consistent organization. In addition, every chapter focuses on one or more countries of the Spanish-speaking world.

- **The opening pages of the chapter:** Here you will begin to learn about each chapter's theme and geographical focus. A Spanish speaker will provide a model of things you will be able to say after studying the vocabulary and grammar in the chapter, which are previewed in **En este capítulo.**
- **Vocabulario: Preparación:** This section presents vocabulary related to each chapter's theme.
- **Pronunciación:** Found in **Capítulos 2–4,** this section presents important aspects of Spanish pronunciation and orthography (spelling).
- **Salu2 … Segmento 1:** This section will help you to understand a segment of the *Salu2* morning show.
- **Gramática:** This section presents grammar points in context and offers many opportunities for you to practice Spanish, alone and with a partner or group. In a subsection of **Gramática** called **Un poco de todo (A bit of everything)**, you will practice all of the grammar points from the chapter

plus review important grammar topics from previous chapters.
- ***Salu2 … Segmento 2:*** Here is another segment of the show.
- **A leer** (*Let's read*)**:** In this reading section, you will learn more about the chapter's country of focus (**Lectura cultural**) and also read authentic materials from the Spanish-speaking world (**Del mundo hispano**), including literature.
- **A escuchar *(Let's listen)*:** In this section you will practice authentic listening tasks.
- **Producción personal:** In this section you will create a portfolio that showcases what you can do in Spanish: essays and other real-world writing tasks, oral and video materials, and so on.
- **En resumen: En este capítulo:** This section shows you vocabulary and grammar you need to know from each chapter.

2

En la universidad

www.connectspanish.com

En un salón de clase universitario

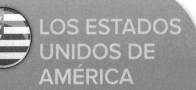

LOS ESTADOS UNIDOS DE AMÉRICA

316 (trescientos dieciséis) millones de habitantes

- En los Estados Unidos hay más de 54 (cincuenta y cuatro) millones de personas de origen hispano.

- Es el quinto[a] país del mundo por[b] número de hispanohablantes.

- En todo el territorio estadounidense, especialmente en el suroeste,[c] hay lugares[d] con nombres[e] en español.

[a]fifth [b]país... country in the world in [c]Southwest [d]places [e]names

- ¿En qué universidad estudia usted[a]?
- ¿Qué materias[b] estudia este[c] semestre/trimestre?
- ¿Cuál[d] es su[e] clase favorita? (**Mi** clase...)

[a]estudia... are you studying [b]subjects [c]this [d]Which [e]your

ALEJANDRA HERNÁNDEZ SOTO CONTESTA LAS PREGUNTAS.

- Estudio Relaciones Internacionales en la UNAM, la Universidad Nacional Autónoma de México.

- Este semestre tomo[a] seis clases: estadística, historia, geografía, economía, sistemas políticos, teorías de las relaciones internacionales. ¡Ah! Y también estudio inglés.

- ¿Mi materia favorita este semestre? No sé[b]. ¡Me gusta todo[c]!

[a]I'm taking [b]No... I don't know. [c]everything

VOCABULARIO: PREPARACIÓN

En el salón de clase

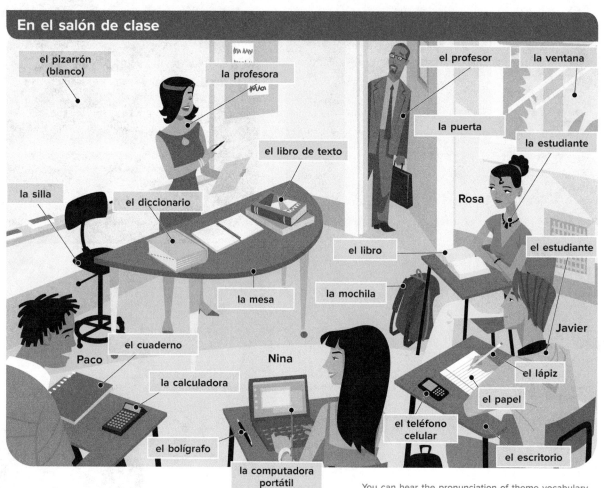

el pizarrón (blanco)

la profesora

el profesor

la ventana

la silla

el libro de texto

la puerta

la estudiante

el diccionario

Rosa

el libro

el estudiante

la mesa

la mochila

el cuaderno

Nina

Javier

Paco

la calculadora

el lápiz

el papel

el teléfono celular

el bolígrafo

el escritorio

la computadora portátil

You can hear the pronunciation of theme vocabulary words and phrases in the Connect eBook.

¿Dónde? Lugares en la universidad

la biblioteca	the library
la cafetería	the cafeteria
el edificio	the building
la librería	the bookstore
la oficina	the office
la residencia	the dormitory
el salón de clase	the classroom

¿Quién? Personas

el bibliotecario	the (male) librarian
la bibliotecaria	the (female) librarian
el compañero (de clase)	the (male) classmate
la compañera (de clase)	the (female) classmate

el compañero de cuarto	the (male) roommate
la compañera de cuarto	the (female) roommate
el consejero	the (male) advisor
la consejera	the (female) advisor
el hombre	the man
la mujer	the woman
el secretario	the (male) secretary
la secretaria	the (female) secretary

¿Qué? Objetos

la computadora (portátil)	(laptop) computer
el dinero	money
el pizarrón (blanco)	(white)board
el teléfono (celular)	(cellular) telephone

Comunicación

A. Identificaciones. ¿Es hombre o mujer?

MODELO: ¿El profesor? → Es hombre.

1. ¿La consejera?
2. ¿La estudiante?
3. ¿El secretario?
4. ¿El estudiante?
5. ¿La bibliotecaria?
6. ¿El compañero de cuarto?

B. ¿Dónde están (*are they*)? Tell where these people are and identify the numbered people and things.

MODELO: El dibujo (*drawing*) 1: **Están** en el salón de clase.
1 → la profesora, **2** → la estudiante,...

1.

2.

3.

Algo sobre...°

Algo... *Something about*

la universidad

CAA COLEGIO DE ARQUITECTOS DE LOS ANDES

En el mundo[a] hispanohablante no llaman[b] **colegio** a una institución universitaria. La palabra **colegio** se usa para referirse a[c] a la educación preuniversitaria, aunque[d] con nombres diferentes en diferentes países.[e] También se usa en el nombre de asociaciones de profesionales, como el «Colegio de Arquitectos».

¿Cómo se llama su[f] colegio?

[a]*world* [b]*no... they don't call* [c]*se... is used for talking about* [d]*although* [e]*countries* [f]*your*

Nota **cultural**

Las universidades más antiguas° del mundo hispano°

En España
- la Universidad de Salamanca, Salamanca (1220 = mil doscientos veinte)

En Latinoamérica
la Universidad Nacional Mayor de San Marcos, Lima, Perú (1551 = mil quinientos cincuenta y uno)

- la Universidad Nacional Autónoma de México (UNAM), en México, D.F. (Distrito Federal), México (1551 [mil quinientos cincuenta y uno])
- la Universidad Nacional de Córdoba, Argentina (1621 = mil seiscientos veintiuno)
- la Universidad San Francisco Xavier de Chuquisaca, Sucre, Bolivia (1624 = mil seiscientos veinticuatro)
- la Universidad de San Carlos de Guatemala, Antigua, Guatemala (1676 = mil seiscientos setenta y seis)
- la Universidad Nacional de San Antonio Abad del Cusco, Perú (1692 = mil seiscientos noventa y dos)
- la Universidad de San Jerónimo, ahora la Universidad de La Habana, Cuba (1728 = mil setecientos veintiocho)

¿Cuál[a] es la universidad más antigua de su país[b]?

°What [b]su... your country

más... *oldest* / del... *of the Spanish-speaking world*

El *campus* de la Universidad de San Marcos, en Lima, Perú

Las materias°

Las... *Subject areas*

The names for most of these subject areas are cognates. See if you can recognize their meaning without looking at the English equivalent. You should learn in particular the names of subject areas that are of interest to you.

la administración de empresas	business administration
las comunicaciones	communications
la economía	economics
el español	Spanish
la filosofía	philosophy
la literatura	literature
las matemáticas	mathematics
la sociología	sociology
las ciencias	sciences
naturales	natural
políticas	political
sociales	social
las humanidades	humanities
las lenguas (extranjeras)	(foreign) languages

la computación · el arte · la química · la física · Rosa · Javier · la sicología · la historia · el inglés

Así se dice

la administración de empresas = el comercio, los negocios (*U.S.*)
la computación = la informática (*Spain*)
el español = el castellano (*Spain, Latin America*)

Comunicación

A. Asociaciones. ¿Qué materia(s) asocia usted con (*with*) las siguientes (*following*) personas y cosas (*things*)?

1. la zoología, la botanía, la química
2. Sigmund Freud, B.F. Skinner, Dr. Phil
3. CNN, NBC, ESPN
4. la ética, la moral, la esencia de la realidad
5. Shakespeare, J.K. Rowling, Junot Díaz
6. Frida Kahlo, Pablo Picasso, Salvador Dalí
7. Apple, Microsoft, Google
8. las guerras (*wars*), las elecciones, las civilizaciones antiguas

B. ¿Qué estudia usted? Create sentences about your academic interests by using one word or phrase from each column. Can you guess the meaning of the phrases in the left-hand column? If you need help, they are translated at the bottom of the page*.

MODELOS: Deseo estudiar **español y antropología.**
Necesito estudiar **matemáticas.**

1. (No) Estudio _____.
2. (No) Deseo estudiar _____.
3. (No) Necesito estudiar _____.
4. (No) Me gusta estudiar _____.

+

español, francés, inglés
arte, filosofía, literatura, música
ciencias políticas, historia
antropología, sicología, sociología
biología, física, química
computación, matemáticas, ¿ ?

Vocabulario útil

la contabilidad	accounting
la ingeniería	engineering
el mercadeo	marketing
el periodismo	journalism

> These boxes will help you review content you already know on which new material is based.

¿Recuerda usted?°

¿Recuerda... *Do you remember?*

In **Capítulo 1,** you used a number of interrogative words to get information: **¿cómo?, ¿dónde?, ¿qué?,** and **¿quién?** Tell what those words mean in these questions. Then answer the questions.

1. ¿Cómo estás?
2. ¿Cómo es usted?
3. ¿De dónde eres?
4. ¿Qué hora es?
5. ¿Quién es la profesora?

As you listen to your instructor say questions with those words, you will notice that, in Spanish, the voice falls at the end of questions that begin with interrogative words.

¿Qué hora es?   ¿Cómo es usted?

You will learn more about interrogatives in the **Nota comunicativa** on the next page and in **Gramática 4** in this chapter.

an interrogative word / **una palabra interrogativa** = a word used to ask a question about specific information (*who?, where?,* and so on)

****1.** *I'm studying (I'm not studying)* **2.** *I want to study (I don't want to study)* **3.** *I need to study (I don't need to study)* **4.** *I like to study (I don't like to study)*

Nota **comunicativa**

Más palabras interrogativas

Use **¿qué?** to mean *what?* when you are asking for a definition or an explanation. Use **¿cuál?** to mean *what?* in all other contexts. You will learn more about using these words in **Gramática 28 (Capítulo 10).**

> **¿Qué** es un hospital? **¿Qué** es esto (*this*)?
>
> **¿Cuál** es la capital de **¿Cuál** es tu materia favorita?
> Colombia?

Guess the meaning of the following interrogatives from the context in which they appear.

1. —**¿Cuándo** es la clase? —Es mañana, a las nueve.
2. —**¿Cuánto** cuesta (*costs*) el cuaderno? —Dos dólares.

3. —**¿Cuántos** estudiantes hay en la clase? —Hay quince.
4. —**¿Cuántas** naciones hay en Centroamérica? —Hay siete.

Remember to drop your voice at the end of a question that begins with a Spanish interrogative word, the opposite of what happens in English, where the voice usually rises at the end of such questions. This feature of Spanish may cause you to "hear" a Spanish question as a statement at first, but you'll get used to it. Compare these questions.

¿Qué es un tren?	*What's a train?*
¿Cuándo es el programa?	*When is the program?*

You will use many of the preceding interrogative words in **Comunicación C.**

C. Intercambios (*Exchanges*)

¿Dónde le gusta estudiar a usted?

Paso 1. Answer the following questions. Pay attention to the words and endings in bold; you have seen most of them before and should be able to guess what they mean.

1. —¿Qué **estudias** este (*this*) semestre/trimestre?

   —**Estudio** _____.

2. —¿Cuál es **tu** (*your*) materia favorita?

   —Mi materia favorita es el/la _____.

3. —¿Quién es **tu** profesor(a) en la clase de español?

   —Es el profesor / la profesora _____.

4. —¿Cuántas horas **estudias** al día (*per day*)?

   —**Estudio** _____ horas al día.

5. —¿Dónde **estudias**?

   —**Estudio** en _____ (la residencia, la biblioteca, mi cuarto, mi apartamento, la cafetería...).

6. —¿Te **gusta** estudiar por (*in*) la mañana, por la tarde o por la noche (*at night*)?

   —Me **gusta** estudiar por _____.

Paso 2. Now practice the conversation in **Paso 1** with a classmate. Use **¿Y tú?** to ask about your partner.

MODELO: **ESTUDIANTE 1:** ¿Qué **estudias** este semestre/trimestre?
        ESTUDIANTE 2: **Estudio** matemáticas, historia, literatura y español. ¿Y tú?
        ESTUDIANTE 1: Yo **estudio** español, biología, física y arte.

«¡Qué bacán!°» Segmento 1

¡Qué... *How great!*

Antes de mirar°

Antes... *Before watching*

What do you think Víctor and Ana will talk about as they introduce the show? Check all of the phrases that apply.

_____ su (*their*) familia
_____ su concentración/carrera (*major*) en la universidad
_____ el nombre de su universidad
_____ el tráfico en Los Ángeles
_____ el costo de una educación universitaria

Este° segmento

This

Los presentadores presentan el tema (*topic*) del programa: la universidad en el mundo (*world*) hispanohablante.

Víctor y Ana, los presentadores de *Salu2*, que (*who*) hablan de sus (*talk about their*) estudios universitarios

Vocabulario **del segmento**

bienvenidos	welcome	**el país**	country
los telespectadores	TV viewers	**el/la periodista**	journalist
los universitarios	university students	**estudiaste**	did you study
los padres	parents	**pasé**	I spent
con frecuencia pagan	frequently pay for	**en el extranjero**	abroad
bien cara	quite expensive	**marca tu vida**	changes your life
la maestría	master's degree	**vamos a ver**	we're going to see

Estrategia

Before you watch the segment, be sure to read the photo caption and go over the vocabulary list. Don't expect to remember most of the words while watching; they're new and may be difficult for you. But just reading the list will enhance your comprehension, giving you ideas about what to watch for.

Después de mirar°

Después... *After watching*

A. **¿Está claro?** Empareje a (*Match*) los presentadores, Ana (**A**) y Víctor (**V**) o a **los dos** (*both*), con las carreras o concentraciones y universidades apropiadas.

LAS CARRERAS O CONCENTRACIONES   LAS UNIVERSIDADES

_____ sociología   _____ UCLA
_____ comunicación   _____ la Universidad de Panamá
_____ inglés

B. **Un poco más. (*A little more*.)** ¿Cierto o falso? Corrija (*Correct*) las oraciones falsas, según (*according to*) el video.

	CIERTO	FALSO
1. El programa no es interesante para los padres.	☐	☐
2. La universidad es cara.	☐	☐
3. Victor pasó (*spent*) un semestre en España.	☐	☐
4. Ana es de Panamá.	☐	☐

C. **Y ahora, Uds. (*And now it's your turn*.)** Practique su (*your*) pronunciación y su talento como presentador(a). Complete el fragmento con su propia (*your own*) información y con vocabulario del programa.

Buenos días desde^a _____. Soy _____. Es es un placer^b presentar un nuevo programa de *Salu2*. El tema del programa de hoy es la universidad, un tema muy _____ (adjetivo) para^c los _____ (personas) y los _____ (personas). Estamos en la Universidad de _____, donde yo estudio _____ (materias). ¡Bienvenidos!

^a*from* ^b*pleasure* ^c*for*

PRONUNCIACIÓN

Diphthongs and Linking

¿Recuerda usted?

Review what you already know about the pronunciation of Spanish vowels by saying the following names and nicknames aloud.

1. Ana **2.** Pepe **3.** Pili **4.** Momo **5.** Lulú

a diphthong / **un diptongo** = a combination of two vowel sounds in one syllable

Two successive weak vowels (**i, u**) or a combination of a strong vowel (**a, e, o**) and a weak vowel (**i, u**) are pronounced as a single syllable in Spanish, forming a *diphthong* (**un diptongo**): L**ui**s, s**ie**te, c**ua**derno.

When words are combined to form phrases, clauses, and sentences, they are linked together in pronunciation. In spoken Spanish, it is often difficult to hear the word boundaries—that is, where one word ends and another begins.

Práctica

A. Vocales. Más práctica con las vocales.

1. hablar	regular	reservar	compañera
2. trece	clase	papel	general
3. pizarrón	oficina	bolígrafo	libro
4. hombre	profesor	dólares	los
5. universidad	gusto	lugar	mujer

B. Diptongos. Practique las siguientes (*following*) palabras.

1. historia	secretaria	gracias	estudiante	materia
2. bien	Oviedo	siete	ciencias	diez
3. secretario	biblioteca	adiós	diccionario	Antonio
4. cuaderno	Eduardo	el Ecuador	Guatemala	Managua
5. bueno	nueve	luego	pueblo	Venezuela

C. Frases y oraciones (*sentences*). Practice saying each phrase or sentence as if it were one long word, pronounced without a pause.

1. el papel y el lápiz
2. la profesora y la estudiante
3. las ciencias y las matemáticas
4. la historia y la sicología
5. la secretaria y el profesor
6. el inglés y el español
7. la clase en la biblioteca
8. el libro en la librería
9. Es la una y media.
10. Hay siete estudiantes en la oficina.
11. No estoy muy bien.
12. No hay consejero aquí (*here*).

GRAMÁTICA

Grammar Tutorial 1
■ **connect**
|SPANISH
www.connectspanish.com

 ¿Recuerda usted?

As you know, in English and in Spanish, a noun is the name of a person, place, thing, or idea. You have been using nouns since the beginning of *Puntos de partida*. Remember that **el** and **la** mean *the* before nouns. If you can change the Spanish words for *the* to *one* in the following phrases, you already know some of the material in **Gramática 1.**

1. el libro   **2.** la mesa   **3.** el profesor   **4.** la estudiante

1 Naming People, Places, Things, and Ideas (Part 1)

Singular Nouns: Gender and Articles*

Gramática en acción: La lista de José María

> Note the use of red in **Gramática en acción** to indicate examples of the grammar point of focus.

(handwritten phone note:)

6:13 PM   6%

Para Español 30 / Profesor Durán
● un diccionario español-inglés
● la novela Don Quijote
● un cuaderno

Para Cálculo 2 / Profesora Lifante
● los libros de texto (2)
● una calculadora
● la tarjeta de acceso para el cuaderno electrónico
● un cuaderno

Y
● una agenda
● unos bolígrafos

Comprensión

	CIERTO	FALSO
1. La profesora de matemáticas es la profesora Durán.	☐	☐
2. Un cuaderno es para la clase de literatura.	☐	☐
3. La agenda es para la clase de matemáticas.	☐	☐

You use nouns to name people, places, things, and ideas. In Spanish, all *nouns* (**los sustantivos**) have either masculine or feminine *gender* (**el género**). This is a purely grammatical feature; it does not mean that Spanish speakers perceive things or ideas as having male or female attributes.

Since the gender of all nouns must be memorized, it is best to learn the definite article along with the noun; that is, learn **el lápiz** rather than just **lápiz**. The definite article is given with nouns in vocabulary lists in this book.

José María's list For Spanish 30 / Professor Durán ■ *a Spanish-English dictionary* ■ *the novel Don Quijote* ■ *a notebook. for Calculus 2 / Professor Lifante* ■ *the textbooks (2)* ■ *a calculator* ■ *the access card for the electronic workbook* ■ *a notebook. And* ■ *a calendar/datebook* ■ *a few ballpoint pens*

The grammar sections of Puntos de partida are numbered consecutively throughout the book. If you need to review a particular grammar point, the index will refer you to its page number.

an article / **un artículo** = a determiner that sets off a noun

a definite article / **un artículo definido** = an article that indicates a specific noun (*the*)

an indefinite article / **un artículo indefinido** = an article that indicates an unspecified noun (*a, an*)

Nouns / **Los sustantivos**				
	Masculine / **Masculino**		Feminine / **Femenino**	
Definite Articles / **Los artículos definidos**	el **hombre** el **libro**	the man the book	la **mujer** la **mesa**	the woman the table
Indefinite Articles / **Los artículos indefinidos**	un **hombre** un **libro**	a man a book	una **mujer** una **mesa**	a woman a table

Note the two-column format of grammar explanations. Explanations are on the left, examples are on the right, and red highlighting will help you see what's important.

Gender / El género

1. Masculine Nouns

Nouns that refer to male beings and most other nouns that end in **-o** are *masculine* (**masculino**) in gender.

Sustantivos masculinos

hombre, libro

2. Feminine Nouns

Nouns that refer to female beings and most other nouns that end in **-a, -ción, -sión, -xión, -tad,** and **-dad** are *feminine* (**femenino**) in gender.

Sustantivos femeninos

mujer, mesa, silla
nación, misión, conexión
libertad, universidad

3. Other Endings

Nouns that have other endings and that do not refer to either male or female beings may be masculine or feminine. The gender of these words must be memorized.

**el lápiz, el papel, el salón de clase
la clase, la noche, la tarde**

4. Spelling Changes

Many nouns that refer to people indicate gender . . .
• by changing the last vowel

OR

• by adding **-a** to the last consonant of the masculine form to make it feminine

el compañero → **la compañera**
el bibliotecario → **la bibliotecaria**

un profesor → **una profesora**

5. Some Nouns that Refer to People

Many other nouns that refer to people have a single form for both masculine and feminine genders. Gender is made clear by context or by an article.

However, a few such nouns that end in **-e** also have a feminine form that ends in **-a.**

Masculino	Femenino
el **estudiante**	la **estudiante**
el **dentista**	la **dentista**
el **presidente**	la **presidenta**
el **cliente**	la **clienta**
el **dependiente** (*clerk*)	la **dependienta**

¡OJO!

A common exception to the normal rules of gender is the word **el día,** which is masculine in gender. Many words ending in **-ma** are also masculine: **el problema, el programa, el sistema,** and so on.

Articles / Los artículos

1. Definite Articles

In English, there is only one *definite article* (**el artículo definido**): *the*.

In Spanish, there are two definite articles for singular nouns, one masculine (**el**) and one feminine (**la**).

Artículo definido: *the*

m. sing. → **el**
f. sing. → **la**

2. Indefinite Articles

In English, the singular *indefinite article* (**el artículo indefinido**) is *a* or *an*.

In Spanish, the indefinite article, like the definite article, must agree with the gender of the noun: **un** for masculine nouns, **una** for feminine nouns.

Un and **una** can mean *one* or *a/an*, depending on context.

Artículo indefinido: *a, an*

m. sing. → **un**
f. sing. → **una**

> **¡OJO!**
> Only the *indefinite* article (never the definite article) is used directly after the word **hay: Hay un** libro en la silla. Hay **unos** cuadernos en la mesa.

> One of the first two activities in **Práctica y comunicación** will always include a brief **Autoprueba** (*Self-test*). Take it to see if you understand the basics of the grammar point. The answers are at the bottom of the page.

Práctica y comunicación

A. Autoprueba. Escoja (*Choose*) el artículo definido apropiado.

1. el / la libro
2. el / la mujer
3. el / la oficina
4. el / la escritorio
5. el / la libertad
6. el / la acción

> **Gender Summary**
>
> | MASCULINO | FEMENINO |
> | --- | --- |
> | **el, un** | **la, una** |
> | -o | -a |
> | -ma | -ción, -sión, -xión |
> | | -dad, -tad |

B. Los artículos

Paso 1. Dé (*Give*) el artículo definido apropiado (**el, la**).

1. edificio
2. biblioteca
3. bolígrafo
4. mochila
5. hombre
6. diccionario
7. universidad
8. dinero
9. señora
10. nación
11. bibliotecario
12. calculadora

Paso 2. Ahora (*Now*) dé el artículo indefinido apropiado (**un, una**).

1. día
2. mañana
3. problema
4. lápiz
5. clase
6. papel
7. condición
8. programa

C. Escenas de la universidad

Paso 1. Haga una oración (*Form a sentence*) con las palabras indicadas.

MODELO: estudiante / librería → **Hay un** estudiante **en la** librería.

1. consejero / oficina
2. profesora / salón de clase
3. lápiz / mesa
4. cuaderno / escritorio
5. libro / mochila
6. bolígrafo / silla
7. palabra / papel
8. oficina / residencia
9. compañero / biblioteca
10. diccionario / librería

Paso 2. Now create new sentences by changing one of the words in each item in **Paso 1.** Try to come up with as many variations as possible.

MODELOS: Hay un estudiante en **la residencia.** Hay **una profesora** en la librería.

D. Definiciones. En parejas (*pairs*), definan las siguientes (*following*) palabras en español, según (*according to*) el modelo.

MODELO: biblioteca → ESTUDIANTE 1: ¿Qué es una biblioteca?
ESTUDIANTE 2: Es **un edificio**.

CATEGORÍAS: **edificio, materia, objeto, persona**

1. cliente
2. bolígrafo
3. residencia
4. dependienta
5. hotel (*m.*)
6. computadora
7. computación
8. inglés
9. ¿ ?

E. Nuestra (*Our*) universidad. En parejas, hagan oraciones (*form sentences*) sobre su (*about your*) universidad.

MODELOS: mi consejero/a → El profesor Márquez es mi consejero.
cafetería → Hay una cafetería. Se llama (*It's called*) Foster Hall. (No hay una cafetería.).

1. mi consejero/a
2. mi profesor(a) de _____ (materia)
3. residencia
4. biblioteca principal
5. cafetería
6. edificio de clases

Grammar Tutorial 2
connect
|SPANISH
www.connectspanish.com

2 **Naming People, Places, Things, and Ideas (Part 2)**

Nouns and Articles: Plural Forms

Gramática en acción: Un anuncio

You don't have to understand all of the words in this ad (**anuncio**) to get its general meaning. What is it an ad for?

Cursos de **Idiomas** en el **Extranjero**[a]

Financiación **SIN INTERESES** en 3, 6 ó 12 meses

Cursos para jóvenes de 7 a 17 años
Cursos para adultos a partir de 18 años
Cursos en Universidades: Idioma general y/o técnico
Minimasters en Universidades
USA, Inglaterra e Irlanda
Programa residencial en Sevilla y/o Madrid con inglés
Preparación para TOEFL, GMAT, SAT, GRE, USMLE
Cursos de idiomas en Madrid

Instituto ProLengua ofrece pagar su curso aplazado en 3, 6 ó 12 meses

INSTITUTO PROLENGUA

Infórmate **902-253 797**

[a]en... *abroad*

Comprensión

1. How many nouns (including proper nouns) can you find in the ad? Can you guess the meaning of most of them?
2. Some of the nouns in the ad are plural. Can you tell how to make nouns plural in Spanish?
3. Look for the Spanish equivalent of these words: *adults, preparation, program, courses.*
4. The word **idioma** is a false cognate; it never means *idiom*. What do you think it means?

	Singular	Plural	
Nouns Ending in a Vowel	el **libro**	los **libros**	the books
	la **mesa**	las **mesas**	the tables
	un **libro**	unos **libros**	some books
	una **mesa**	unas **mesas**	some tables
Nouns Ending in a Consonant	la universidad	las **universidades**	the universities
	un papel	unos **papeles**	some papers

1. **Plural Endings**

   Spanish nouns that end in a vowel form plurals by adding **-s.** Nouns that end in a consonant add **-es.** Nouns that end in the consonant **-z** change the **-z** to **-c** before adding **-es: lápiz → lápices.**

   Sustantivos plurales

   vowel + **-s**
   consonant + **-es**
   -z → -ces

2. **Plural of Articles**

   The definite and indefinite articles also have plural forms: **el → los, la → las, un → unos, una → unas. Unos** and **unas** mean *some, several,* or *a few.*

   Artículos plurales

   el → los   un → unos
   la → las   una → unas

3. **Groups of People**

   In Spanish, the masculine plural form of a noun is used to refer to a group that includes both males and females.

   los amigos = *the friends* (all male or both male and female)
   las amigas = *the friends* (only female)
   unos extranjeros = *some foreigners* (all male or both male and female)
   unas extranjeras = *some foreign women*

Práctica y comunicación

Plural Forms Summary

el → los   un → unos
la → las   una → unas

vowel + **-s**
consonant + **-es**
-z → -ces

A. Autoprueba. Empareje (*Match*) los sustantivos con los artículos apropiados.

1. libros	**a.** el
2. hombre	**b.** las
3. librería	**c.** unos
4. profesoras	**d.** una

B. Cambios (*Changes*)

Paso 1. Singular → plural.

1. la mesa	**4.** la oficina	**7.** una universidad
2. el papel	**5.** un cuaderno	**8.** un bolígrafo
3. el amigo	**6.** un lápiz	**9.** un teléfono

Paso 2. Plural → singular.

1. los profesores	**4.** los estudiantes	**7.** unas residencias
2. las computadoras	**5.** unos hombres	**8.** unas sillas
3. las bibliotecarias	**6.** unas tardes	**9.** unos escritorios

Prác. A: Answers, Paso 1. 1. c 2. a 3. d 4. b

C. **Identificaciones.** Nombre (*Name*) las personas, los objetos y los lugares.

MODELOS: Hay _____ en _____. → Hay **unos estudiantes** en **el salón de clase.**
Hay **un profesor** en **el laboratorio.**

1.   **2.**

D. **¡Ojo alerta!***

Paso 1. ¿Cuáles son las semejanzas (*similarities*) y las diferencias entre (*between*) los dos salones de clase? Hay por lo menos (*at least*) seis diferencias.

En el dibujo A, hay _____.
En el dibujo B, hay solo (*only*) _____.
En el escritorio del dibujo A, hay _____.
En el escritorio del dibujo B, (no) hay _____.

Paso 2. Ahora indique qué hay en su propio (*your own*) salón de clase.

MODELO: En mi salón de clase hay _____. En mi escritorio hay _____.

---

*In Spanish, activities like this one are often called **¡Ojo alerta!** = *Eagle Eye!*

¿Recuerda usted?

These sentences contain Spanish verbs that you have already used. Pick them out.

1. Soy estudiante en la Universidad de _____.
2. Este (*This*) semestre/trimestre, estudio español.
3. En el futuro, deseo estudiar francés.

If you selected **estudiar** in addition to three other words, you did very well! You will learn more about Spanish verbs and how they are used in **Gramática 3.**

3 Expressing Actions

Subject Pronouns (Part 1): Present Tense of **-ar** Verbs; Negation

Grammar Tutorial 3
connect
|SPANISH
www.connectspanish.com

Gramática en acción: ¿Una escena típica?

Manu habla enfrente de la clase porque hoy es su presentación. Pero... ¡varias personas no escuchan!

- Laila manda un mensaje por teléfono.
- Kevin y Lisa trabajan en otras materias.
- Teresa mira por la ventana.
- ¿Y Ud.? ¿También desea estar en otro lugar?

Comprensión

En la escena...

1. ¿Cuántos estudiantes hablan?
2. ¿Cuántas personas escuchan la presentación?
3. ¿Quién manda un mensaje por teléfono?
4. ¿Quién estudia chino?

Subject Pronouns / Los pronombres personales

Singular		Plural	
yo	I	**nosotros / nosotras**	we
tú	you (*familiar*)	**vosotros / vosotras**	you (*familiar, Spain*)
usted (Ud.)*	you (*formal*)	**ustedes (Uds.)***	you (*formal*)
él	he	**ellos**	they (*m., m. + f.*)
ella	she	**ellas**	they (*f.*)

a subject / **un sujeto** = the person or thing that performs the action in a sentence

a pronoun / **un pronombre** = a word that takes the place of a noun or represents a person

---

A typical scene? *Manu is talking in front of the class because today is his presentation. But . . . several people are not listening! • Laila is sending a text message on her phone. • Kevin and Lisa are working on other subjects. • Teresa is looking out the window. • And you? Do you want to be somewhere else too?*

*****Usted** *and* **ustedes** *are frequently abbreviated in writing as* **Ud.** *or* **Vd.**, *and* **Uds.** *or* **Vds.**, *respectively.*

1. Subject Pronouns

The person that performs the action in a sentence is expressed by *subject pronouns* (**los pronombres personales**).

In Spanish, many subject pronouns have masculine and feminine forms. The masculine plural form is used to refer to a group of males as well as to a group of males and females.

Manuel →	**él**	*he*
Sara →	**ella**	*she*
Manuel + Juan →	**ellos**	*they*
Manuel + Sara →	**ellos**	*they*
María + Sara →	**ellas**	*they*

2. Pronouns for *you*

Spanish has different words for *you.*

- In general, **tú** is used with a friend or a family member.
- **Usted** is used with people with whom the speaker has a more formal or distant relationship.

The situations in which **tú** and **usted** are used also vary among different countries and regions.

tú → friend, family member
usted (Ud.) → formal or distant relationship

3. Plural of *you*

In Latin American Spanish, the plural for both **usted** and **tú** is **ustedes**.
In Spain, however, **vosotros/vosotras** is the plural of **tú**, while **ustedes** is used as the plural of **usted** exclusively.

Latinoamérica

tú }
usted (Ud.) } → **ustedes (Uds.)**

España

tú → **vosotros/vosotras**
usted (Ud.) → **ustedes (Uds.)**

4. Omitting Subject Pronouns

Subject pronouns are not used as frequently in Spanish as they are in English, and they may usually be omitted. You will learn more about the uses of Spanish subject pronouns in **Gramática 8 (Cap. 3).**

Present Tense of -ar Verbs / El tiempo presente de los verbos -*ar*

1. Infinitives

As you know, the *infinitive* (**el infinitivo**) of a verb indicates the action or state of being, with no reference to who or what performs the action or when it is done (present, past, or future).

Infinitives in English are indicated by *to: to* speak, *to* eat, *to* live.

In Spanish, all infinitives end in **-ar, -er,** or **-ir.**

-ar:	**hablar**	to speak
-er:	**comer**	to eat
-ir:	**vivir**	to live

an infinitive / **un infinitivo** = a verb form that indicates action or state of being without reference to person, tense, or number

a tense / **un tiempo** = the quality of a verb form that indicates time: present, past, or future

2. Conjugating Verbs

To *conjugate* (**conjugar**) a verb means to give the various forms of the verb with their corresponding subjects: *I speak, you speak, she speaks,* and so on.

All regular Spanish verbs are conjugated by adding *personal endings* (**las terminaciones personales**) that reflect the subject doing the action. These are added to the *stem* (**la raíz**), which is the infinitive minus the infinitive ending.

Infinitive / **Infinitivo**		Stem / **Raíz**
hab**lar**	→	**habl-**
co**mer**	→	**com-**
vi**vir**	→	**viv-**

3. Present Tense Endings

The personal endings that are added to the stem of all regular **-ar** verbs to form the *present tense* (**el presente**) are listed at the right. The chart below shows those same endings attached to the stem of the infinitive **hablar** (**habl-**).

Las terminaciones -*ar* del tiempo presente

-o, -as, -a, -amos, -áis, -an

hablar (*to speak; to talk*): **habl-**					
Singular			**Plural**		
(yo)	**habl**o	I speak	(nosotros) (nosotras)	**habl**amos	we speak
(tú)	**habl**as	you speak	(vosotros) (vosotros)	**habl**áis	you speak
(Ud.) (él) (ella)	**habl**a	you speak he speaks she speaks	(Uds.) (ellos) (ellas)	**habl**an	you speak they (*m., m. + f.*) speak they (*f.*) speak

4. Important -*ar* Verbs

Here are some **-ar** verbs used in this chapter.

Los verbos -*ar*	
bailar	to dance
buscar	to look for
cantar	to sing
comprar	to buy
desear	to want
enseñar	to teach
escuchar	to listen (to)
estudiar	to study
hablar	to speak; to talk
mandar un mensaje	to (send a) text
necesitar	to need
pagar	to pay (for)
practicar	to practice
regresar	to return (*to a place*)
tocar	to play (*a musical instrument*)
tomar	to take; to drink
trabajar	to work

¡OJO!

Note that in Spanish the meaning of the English word *for* is included in the verbs **buscar** (*to look **for***) and **pagar** (*to pay **for***); *to* is included in **escuchar** (*to listen **to***).

5. Conjugated Verb + *Infinitive*

As in English, when two Spanish verbs are used in a row and there is no change of subject, the second verb is usually in the infinitive form.

Necesito mandar un mensaje.
I need to send a text (message).

Me gusta bailar.
I like to dance.

6. Tense

In both English and Spanish, conjugated verb forms also indicate the *time* or *tense* (**el tiempo**) of the action: *I speak* (present), *I spoke* (past).

Some English equivalents of the present tense forms of Spanish verbs are shown at the right.

	I speak	Simple present tense
hablo	I am speaking	Present progressive (indicates an action in progress)
	I will speak	Near future action

¡OJO!

The exact English equivalent of a Spanish verb form depends on the context in which the verb appears. In the following sentence, the word **mañana** indicates a future action, so **hablo** means *I will:* **Hablo con Juan mañana.**

Negation / La negación

In Spanish the word **no** is placed before the conjugated verb to make a negative sentence.

*subject + **no** + verb*

El estudiante no habla español.
The student doesn't speak Spanish.

No, no necesito dinero.
No, I don't need money.

Práctica y comunicación

A. Asociaciones. ¿Qué verbos asocia Ud. con las siguientes ideas? Dé (*Give*) infinitivos.

MODELO: la música → escuchar, tocar, bailar, ...

1. español
2. mucho (*a lot of*) dinero
3. en la librería
4. en el salón de clase
5. un coche (*car*)
6. a la residencia
7. Coca-Cola o café (*coffee*)
8. la música

Summary of *-ar* Verb Endings		
(yo) -o	(nosotros/as) -amos	
(tú) -as	(vosotros/as) -áis	
(Uds., el/ella) -a	(Uds., ellos/as) -an	

B. Mi compañero/a y yo

Paso 1. Autoprueba. Complete los verbos con las terminaciones apropiadas.

1. (yo) pag_____
2. (tú) toc_____
3. (ella) habl_____
4. (nosotras) compr_____
5. (Ud.) escuch_____
6. (ellos) trabaj_____

Paso 2. ¿Sí o no? Complete las oraciones de forma personal. Use **no** delante del (*in front of the*) verbo si es necesario.

MODELO: **1.** Necesit_____ un coche. → Necesito un coche. (**No** necesito un coche.)

1. Necesit___ un coche.
2. Trabaj___ en la biblioteca de la universidad
3. Cant___ en un coro (*choir*).
4. Tom___ una clase de ciencias sociales este (*this*) semester.
5. Bail___ salsa en las fiestas.
6. Habl___ inglés como (*as a*) lengua nativa.
7. Mand___ muchos mensajes todos los días (*every day*).
8. Toc___ un instrumento musical.

Paso 3. En parejas (*pairs*), hagan y contesten preguntas (*ask and answer questions*) basadas en el **Paso 2.**

MODELO: Necesito un coche. → ESTUDIANTE 1: ¿**Necesitas** un coche?

ESTUDIANTE 2: Sí, **necesito** un coche. (No, **no necesito** un coche.)

Prác. A: Answers, Paso 1. 1. pago **2.** tocas **3.** habla **4.** compramos **5.** escucha **6.** trabajan

C. Una o más personas

Paso 1. Cambie por (*Change to*) un sujeto plural.

MODELOS: Él no desea tomar café. →
        Ellos no **desean** tomar café.
        Yo no deseo tomar café. →
        Nosotros no **deseamos** tomar café.

1. Ella no desea estudiar francés (*French*).
2. Ud. baila muy bien el tango.
3. ¿Mandas muchos (*a lot of*) mensajes?
4. Escucho la radio con frecuencia.

Paso 2. Ahora cambie por un sujeto singular. En los números 2 y 4 hay más de una opción.

1. Ellas no buscan el dinero.
2. Los estudiantes no necesitan seis clases.
3. Pagamos mucho dinero de matrícula (*tuition*).
4. ¿Compran Uds. muchos libros?

D. La fiesta de Marcos

Paso 1. Complete el párrafo con las formas apropiadas de los verbos entre paréntesis.

Esta noche[a] hay una fiesta en casa de Marcos.[b] Marcos es de Guatemala y su compañero de apartamento, Julio, es de Honduras. Hay quince amigos en la fiesta. Una persona (tocar[1]) la guitarra y las otras personas (cantar[2]) o (escuchar[3]). ¡Yo solo (desear[4]) bailar!

Marta (hablar[5]) con Nati mucho tiempo.[c] Pero Nati (desear[6]) bailar con Miguel, el estudiante mexicano, porque[d] él (bailar[7]) muy bien. Eduardo, Marcos y yo (bailar[8]) en grupo.

A las once de la noche Julio (buscar[9]) pizza para todos.[e] Pero todos (pagar[10]).

¡La fiesta es fantástica! (*Yo:* Practicar[11]) español toda la noche[f] porque todos los amigos de Marcos (hablar[12]) español. ¡Eduardo y yo (regresar[12]) a casa[g] a las dos de la mañana!

¿A Ud. le gustan las fiestas?

[a]Esta... *Tonight*   [b]en... *at Marco's place (lit., house)*   [c]mucho... *for a long time*   [d]*because*
[e]*para... for everyone*   [f]toda... *all night*   [g]a... *home*

Paso 2. Comprensión. Indique si las siguientes (*following*) oraciones son **ciertas**, **falsas** o **no se sabe** (*not known*). Luego (*Then*) indique dónde está la información correcta en el texto.

	CIERTO	FALSO	NO SE SABE
1. La persona que (*who*) habla es hispanohablante.	☐	☐	☐
2. Nati baila muy bien.	☐	☐	☐
3. Marcos y Julio compran la pizza.	☐	☐	☐
4. Todos tocan la guitarra y bailan.	☐	☐	☐
5. Marta habla mucho (*a lot*) en la fiesta.	☐	☐	☐

E. Oraciones lógicas. Form eight complete logical sentences by using one word or phrase from each column. Many combinations are possible. Use the correct form of the verbs and make any sentences negative.

MODELO: Yo no estudio francés.

yo				
tú (un[a] estudiante)		buscar	la guitarra, el piano, el violín	
nosotros (los miembros de esta clase)		comprar	el edificio de ciencias	
los estudiantes de aquí		enseñar	en la cafetería, en la universidad, en casa (*at home*)	
el extranjero	**+** (no)	estudiar	en una oficina, en una librería	
un secretario		hablar	a casa muy tarde (*very late*)/temprano (*early*)	
una profesora de español		mandar **+**	a la biblioteca a las dos	
una dependienta		pagar	muchos/pocos mensajes	
		regresar	francés, alemán (*German*), italiano, inglés	
		tocar	bien el español	
		tomar	los libros de texto, la matrícula	
		trabajar	libros y cuadernos en la librería	

¡OJO!
Remember that the verb form that follows **desear** or **necesitar** is the infinitive, just as in English.

+ (no) { desear / necesitar } **+**
tomar una clase de computación
hablar bien el español
estudiar más
comprar una calculadora, una mochila
pagar la matrícula en septiembre

¡OJO!
Remember that **de la mañana (tarde, noche)** are used when a specific hour of the day is mentioned. Also, remember to use **a la una / a las dos (tres...)** to express a specific time of day.

Generalmente estudio en casa **por** la mañana.

Hoy estudio con Javier en la biblioteca **a las** diez **de** la mañana.

Nota **comunicativa**

Cómo expresar las partes del día

You can use the preposition **por** to mean *in* or *during* when expressing the part of the day in which something happens.

Estudio **por** la mañana y trabajo **por** la tarde. **Por** la noche, estoy en casa.
I study in the morning and I work in the afternoon. At night I'm at home.

You will practice these phrases in **Práctica F.**

F. Intercambios (Exchanges)

Paso 1. Use los siguientes verbos y frases para crear (*create*) cinco preguntas (*questions*) interesantes.

MODELO: ¿**Cantas** bien?

1. cantar o bailar   bien/mal (*poorly*), mucho/poco (*a little*)
2. estudiar o trabajar   muchas/pocas (*few*) horas, todos los días
3. necesitar   **+**   dinero, libros, una computadora, pagar la matrícula
4. tomar   _____ (número de clases) / café o té por la mañana
5. tomar   clases por la mañana / por la tarde / por la noche

Paso 2. En parejas, túrnense (*take turns*) para hacer y contestar (*answer*) sus (*your*) preguntas del **Paso 1.**

MODELO: **ESTUDIANTE 1:** ¿Cantas bien?
            ESTUDIANTE 2: Sí, **canto** bien. (No, **canto** mal.)

Nota **comunicativa**

El verbo *estar*

Estar is a Spanish **-ar** verb that means *to be*. You have already used forms of it to ask how others are feeling or to tell where things are located. Here is the complete present tense conjugation of **estar.** Note that the **yo** form is irregular. The other forms take regular **-ar** endings, and some have an accent to maintain the stress pattern.

(yo)	est**oy**	I am	(nosotros/as)	est**amos**	we are
(tú)	est**ás**	you are	(vosotros/as)	est**áis**	you are
(Ud.)	est**á**	you are	(Uds.)	est**án**	you are
(él/ella)	est**á**	he/she is	(ellos/ellas)	est**án**	they are

You will learn the uses of the verb **estar,** along with those of **ser** (a second Spanish verb that means *to be*) gradually, over the next several chapters. Review what you already know by answering these questions.

1. ¿Cómo está Ud. en este momento (*right now*)?
2. ¿Cómo están sus (*your*) compañeros? (**Mis** compañeros...)
3. ¿Dónde está Ud. en este momento?

You will use **estar** in **Práctica G.**

G. ¿Dónde están? Tell where these people are and what they are doing.

MODELO: **FOTO 1:** La Sra. Martínez _____. →
La Sra. Martínez **está en una oficina. Trabaja por la tarde. Necesita...**

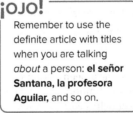

Vocabulario **útil**

buscar información	**tomar apuntes**
hablar por teléfono	to take notes
mandar un mensaje	**usar una computadora**
preparar la lección	
pronunciar las palabras	

¡OJO!

Remember to use the definite article with titles when you are talking *about* a person: **el señor Santana, la profesora Aguilar,** and so on.

1. La Srta. Martínez _____.

Trabaja por _____.

Necesita _____.

2. Estas (*These*) personas _____.

El profesor _____.

Una estudiante _____.

Muchos (*Many*) estudiantes _____.

4 Getting Information (Part 1)

Asking Yes/No Questions

Grammar Tutorial **4**

connect
|SPANISH

www.connectspanish.com

Gramática en acción: La matriculación

PENÉLOPE: ... y ahora necesito una clase más por la mañana. ¿Hay sitio en la clase de Sociología 2?

JAVIER: A ver... No, no hay.

PENÉLOPE: ¿Hay una clase de historia o de matemáticas?

JAVIER: Solo por la noche. ¿Deseas tomar una clase por la noche?

PENÉLOPE: ¡Ay, chico, es imposible! Trabajo por la noche.

JAVIER: Pues... ¿qué tal la clase de Literatura Hispana en los Estados Unidos?

PENÉLOPE: ¡Perfecto! ¡Me gusta mucho Sandra Cisneros! ¿Cuándo es la clase?

Comprensión

1. ¿Necesita Penélope dos clases más?
2. ¿Hay sitio en Sociología 2?
3. ¿Cuál es el problema con los cursos de historia y matemáticas?
4. ¿Qué curso recomienda Javier por fin?

You have been asking questions since the beginning of *Puntos de partida*, and you learned more about asking questions in **Nota comunicativa (page 32).** This section will help you review all that you know about this topic as well as learn another way to ask questions in Spanish.

---

1. **Types of Questions**

   There are two kinds of questions (**las preguntas**) in English and in Spanish.

   • *Information questions* ask for information, for facts. They typically begin with *interrogative words* (**las palabras interrogativas**). You have already learned a number of them.

   Preguntas informativas

   —¿Qué lengua habla Ud.?
   —Hablo español.

   ¡OJO!

   Remember that intonation drops at the end of an information question in Spanish, whereas it rises in English.

   • *Yes/No questions* can be answered by a simple **sí** or **no.**

   Preguntas sí/no

   —¿Habla Ud. francés?
   —No.

Registration PENÉLOPE: . . . and now I need one more class in the morning. Is there room in Sociology 2? JAVIER: Let's see . . . No, there isn't (room). PENÉLOPE: Is there a history or a math class? JAVIER: Only at night. Do you want to take a night class? PENÉLOPE: Come on, that's impossible! I work at night. JAVIER: Well . . . what about the class about Hispanic Literature in the U.S.? PENÉLOPE: Perfect! I love Sandra Cisneros! When is the class?

2. Forming Yes/No Questions

There are two ways to form this kind of question.

- *Rising intonation:* The simplest way is to make your voice rise at the end of a statement. Doing so makes the statement into a question.

- *Inversion:* Another way to form yes/no questions is to invert (transpose) the order of the subject and verb, in addition to making your voice rise at the end of the question. You can also put the subject all the way at the end of the question.

STATEMENT:	Ud. trabaja aquí todos los días. *You work here every day.*
QUESTION:	¿Ud. trabaja aquí todos los días? *Do you work here every day?*
STATEMENT:	**Ud.** trabaja aquí todos los días.
QUESTION:	¿Trabaja **Ud.** aquí todos los días?
STATEMENT:	**María** manda muchos mensajes.
QUESTION:	¿Manda muchos mensajes **María**?

Práctica y comunicación

Summary of Questions

- with interrogatives
- with intonation
- by inverting the subject and verb

A. Preguntas

Paso 1. Autoprueba. ¿Cómo se dice (*How do you say it*) en inglés?

1. ¿Habla Ud. inglés?
2. ¿Necesitan Uds. otra clase?
3. ¿Tomas biología?
4. ¿Trabajo mañana?

Paso 2. Ahora exprese las siguientes oraciones como preguntas. ¡OJO! Hay dos formas.

MODELO: Alicia toca el violín. → ¿**Toca Alicia** el violín? ¿**Alicia toca** el violín?

1. Susana toca la guitarra.
2. Los estudiantes compran muchos libros.
3. Uds. miran el teléfono en clase.
4. Diego manda mensajes en clase.
5. Uds. toman cinco clases este semestre/trimestre.

Paso 3. Ahora, en parejas, usen las oraciones del **Paso 2** para hacer y contestar preguntas. ¡OJO! No es necesario usar los pronombres **tú** y **yo** en la pregunta o en la respuesta (*answer*).

MODELO: tocar la guitarra →

> ESTUDIANTE 1: ¿**Tocas** la guitarra?
> ESTUDIANTE 2: SÍ, **toco** la guitarra. (No, no **toco** la guitarra.)

B. Una conversación inventada.
Imagine that you have just met Diego, a new person on campus. You asked him some questions and he gave you the following answers. What were the questions that you asked?

MODELO: Sí, estudio antropología. → ¿**Estudias** antropología?

1. Sí, soy estadounidense (*from the United States*).
2. Sí, estudio con frecuencia.
3. No, no toco el piano. Toco la guitarra clásica.
4. No, no deseo trabajar más horas.
5. No, no hablo francés, pero hablo italiano un poco.
6. No, no soy reservado. ¡Soy muy extrovertido!

Prác. A: Answers, Paso 1. 1. Do you speak English? 2. Do you (pl.) need another class? 3. Are you taking (a) biology (class)? 4. Do (Will) I work tomorrow?

C. Intercambios: Sus (*Your*) actividades

Paso 1. Use the following cues as a guide to form questions that you will ask a classmate. You may ask other questions as well. Write the questions on a sheet of paper. ¡OJO! Use the **tú** form of the verbs.

MODELO: escuchar música por la mañana →
¿**Escuchas** música por la mañana?

1. estudiar en la biblioteca todos los días
2. practicar español con un amigo o amiga
3. tomar mucho / un poco de (*a little bit of*) café por la mañana
4. bailar mucho en las fiestas
5. cantar en la ducha (*shower*)
6. regresar a casa muy tarde los fines de semana
7. comprar los libros en la librería de la universidad
8. mandar muchos mensajes
9. trabajar los fines de semana
10. usar (*to use*) un diccionario bilingüe online

Paso 2. Now use the questions to get information from your partner. Jot down his or her answers for use in **Paso 3.**

MODELO: **ESTUDIANTE 1:** ¿Escuchas música por la mañana?
ESTUDIANTE 2: Sí, (No, no) **escucho** música por la mañana.

Paso 3. With the information you gathered in **Paso 2,** report your partner's answers to the class. (You will use the **él/ella** form of the verbs when reporting.)

MODELO: Jenny no **escucha** música por la mañana.

D. Una encuesta (*poll*): ¿Qué clases tomas?

Paso 1. Make a list in Spanish of the classes you are taking. Ask your instructor or use a dictionary to find the names of classes you don't know how to say in Spanish. If you ask your instructor, remember to ask in Spanish: **¿Cómo se dice _____ en español?**

Paso 2. Circulate, asking yes/no questions to find classmates who are taking the same classes as you. Write down their answers.

MODELO: **ESTUDIANTE 1:** Carlos, ¿tomas una clase de matemáticas?
ESTUDIANTE 2: Sí, tomo matemáticas. Tomo Cálculo 2.

Paso 3. Report back the information you have learned to the whole class.

MODELO: Carlos y yo tomamos matemáticas. Jennie y yo... Solo yo tomo geología.

Algo... *Something about*

Algo sobre°...

los Departamentos de Estudios Latinos en las universidades de los Estados Unidos

La importancia de la población hispana en los Estados Unidos se refleja[a] en el mundo[b] académico. Muchas universidades tienen[c] departamentos o concentraciones[d] que investigan[e] y enseñan temas[f] relacionados con los latinos en los Estados Unidos. En los estados del suroeste,[g] se ofrecen[h] regularmente Estudios Chicanos, especializados en la población norteamericana de origen mexicano.

¿Hay un programa o un área de concentración de estudios especializados en los latinos en su[i] universidad?

[a]se... *is reflected* [b]*world* [c]*have* [d]*majors* [e]que... *that research* [f]*topics* [g]*Southwest* [h]se... *are offered* [i]*your*

Un poco de todo

A. Lengua y cultura: Dos universidades fabulosas... y diferentes

Paso 1. Complete the following description of two well-known universities. Give the correct form of the verbs in parentheses, as suggested by context. When the subject pronoun is in *italics,* don't use it in the sentence. When two possibilities are given in parentheses, select the correct word.

¿Cómo es la universidad perfecta? Hay muchas opciones. Por ejemplo, (hay / es[1]) dos (universidad / universidades[2]) muy famosas en los Estados Unidos. La primera[a] es (el / la[3]) Universidad de Texas, en Austin. ¡Es (un / una[4]) universidad muy grande[b]! Hay veinticuatro grupos sociales para estudiantes hispanos y una (librería / biblioteca[5]) con una colección latinoamericana fantástica, la Colección Latinoamericana Benson. (Los / Las[6]) materias más populares en la UT son: administración de empresas, ingeniería, humanidades y comunicaciones. Muchos estudiantes (tomar[7]) cursos en (el / la[8]) Instituto de Estudios Latinoamericanos y en (el / la[9]) Centro para Estudios Mexicoamericanos.

Stanford, en (el / la[10]) estado de California, es una universidad menos grande.[c] Tiene[d] una residencia para estudiantes de español, la Casa

La Colección Latinoamericana Benson, una colección comprensiva de libros, documentos, revistas (*magazines*) y periódicos (*newspapers*) relacionados con (*related to*) Latinoamérica

Zapata. Allí,[e] (los / las[11]) estudiantes (practicar[12]) español y (participar[13]) en celebraciones hispanas. Las materias más populares en Stanford son:[f] biología, economía, inglés y ciencias políticas. (El / La[14]) problema en Stanford es que los estudiantes (pagar[15]) mucho por[g] la matrícula.

¿Prefiere Ud. la UT o Stanford? ¿(*Ud.:* Desear[16]) (estudia / estudiar[17]) en California o en Texas?

[a]*La... The first one* [b]*big* [c]*menos... smaller* [d]*It has* [e]*There* [f]*are* [g]*for*

Paso 2. Comprensión. Las siguientes oraciones son falsas. Corríjalas. (*Correct them.*)

1. En la Universidad de Texas hay dos grupos sociales para estudiantes hispanos.
2. En el Instituto de Estudios Latinoamericanos hay pocos (*few*) estudiantes.
3. La Universidad de Stanford está en Texas.
4. La Casa Zapata es una biblioteca importante.

Paso 3. Ahora complete la siguiente información sobre su (*about your*) universidad.

Mi universidad est_____ en el estado de _____.

En mi universidad...
1. muchos / pocos (*many/few*) estudiantes tom_____ clases de español.
2. hay / no hay un centro o un / una programa de estudios latinoamericanos.
3. hay / no hay organizaciones de estudiantes latinos
4. las materias más populares son: _____.
5. los estudiantes pag_____ mucho / poco dinero.

B. **¿Qué pasa (*What's happening*) en la fiesta?**

Paso 1. En parejas, describan la escena.

MODELO: En la fiesta, Pilar y Ana bailan. Nora...

Vocabulario útil

descansar to rest
escuchar
fumar to smoke
hablar
mirar to watch
  una película a movie
  la tele TV
tocar
  la batería drum set
  la guitarra
  el piano
tomar refrescos soft drinks

Paso 2. Ahora comparen la escena con las fiestas en su (*your*) universidad. Usen **nosotros.**

MODELO: En las fiestas, mis amigos y yo **bailamos.**

En su° comunidad   *your*

As you know, all Spanish-speaking countries use the word **universidad** to refer to colleges or universities, big or small, public or private. But there is a lot of variation in the words that Spanish speakers use for *elementary school*, *middle school*, and *high school*. There is also variation in how the following words and phrases are expressed: (*academic*) *grade* (and the symbols used to give grades), *to pass, to fail*.

PREGUNTAS POSIBLES

- Ask someone who was raised in a Hispanic country what language is used in his or her country to express different levels of schooling and the grading system.
- Ask the person to describe his or her educational experience in the country of origin.
- If relevant, ask for a comparison with the educational system in this country.

«¡Qué bacán!°» Segmento 2

¡Qué... *How great!*

Antes de mirar°

Antes... *Before watching*

Conteste (*Answer*) las siguientes preguntas.

1. ¿Desea Ud. estudiar en un país (*country*) hispanohablante? ¿En qué país(es)?

2. En ese (*that*) país, ¿desea vivir (*to live*) con una familia o en una residencia de estudiantes?

Este° segmento

This

Desde (*From*) Lima, Perú, Laura presenta un reportaje sobre la Universidad del Pacífico, un lugar muy interesante para estudiar español.

Muchos (*Many*) estudiantes extranjeros viven (*live*) con familias peruanas hospitalarias (*welcoming*). Así (*So*), practican el español todo el tiempo (*all the time*) y aprenden (*they learn*) por experiencia la cultura de manera directa y personal.

Vocabulario del segmento

la ciudad	city	**los negocios**	business
el sitio	place, site	**la mercadotecnia**	marketing
el barrio	neighborhood	**la contabilidad**	accounting
lindo/a	pretty, cute	**pequeño/a**	small
se especializa	it specializes	**se sienten como**	feel like
la carrera	concentration, major	**miembros**	members

Fragmento del guion°

script

Esta universidad limeña[a] atrae[b] a numerosos estudiantes internacionales por varias razones.[c] Primero,[d] la universidad cuenta con[e] modernas instalaciones,[f] como la biblioteca. Segundo,[g] está muy cerca del[h] centro histórico de Lima. Pero lo más importante es que la universidad tiene[i] un estupendo Centro de Idiomas.

[a]*in Lima* [b]*attracts* [c]*por... for various reasons* [d]*First* [e]*cuenta... has* [f]*facilities* [g]*Second* [h]*está... it is very close to the* [i]*has*

Después de° mirar

Después... *After*

A. ¿Está claro? ¿Cierto o falso? Corrija (*Correct*) las oraciones falsas según (*according to*) el video.

	CIERTO	FALSO
1. La ciudad de Lima...		
a. es pequeña.	☐	☐
b. tiene (*has*) barrios modernos.	☐	☐
c. tiene sitios arquelógicos de los incas.	☐	☐
2. La Universidad del Pacífico...		
a. es rural.	☐	☐
b. es pública.	☐	☐
c. tiene un centro para estudiar lenguas.	☐	☐
d. se especializa en Humanidades.	☐	☐

B. Un poco más. Conteste las siguientes preguntas.

1. ¿En qué materias se especializa la Universidad del Pacífico?

2. ¿Cuándo hay clases para los estudiantes extranjeros, por la mañana o por la tarde? ¿Qué hay por la tarde?

C. Y ahora, Uds. En parejas, usen algunas (*some*) ideas del programa y del capítulo para hablar de su universidad.

MODELO: Esta (*This*) universidad es pública/privada. Se especializa en...

¿Hay muchos estudiantes de origen hispano en su universidad? ¿Hay organizaciones para ellos? ¿Es Ud. miembro de una organización estudiantil?

Lectura cultural: Los Estados Unidos

La presencia latina en las universidades norteamericanas

En la actualidad[a] hay muchos estudiantes latinos en las universidades de los Estados Unidos.

Las organizaciones de estudiantes latinos
La experiencia universitaria típica en los Estados Unidos incluye[b] la participación en organizaciones de estudiantes con diversos intereses. Por eso,[c] las universidades estadounidenses tienen[d] una variada representación de organizaciones latinas.

- Algunas[e] son para todos los hispanos de la universidad, como **Latinos Unidos.**
- Otras son para un grupo específico, como **Fuerza Quisqueyana** (estudiantes dominicanos) o **(La) Raza** (estudiantes mexicoamericanos o chicanos).

Las organizaciones latinas coordinan eventos sociales y académicos: bailes de gala[f] con música hispana, conferencias de escritores[g] hispanohablantes, servicios sociales, etcétera. Con frecuencia, también hay una Casa Latina, donde miembros de la organización viven juntos.[h]

[a]En... *Currently* [b]*includes* [c]Por... *For this reason* [d]*have* [e]*Some (organizations)* [f]bailes... *formal dances* [g]*writers* [h]viven... *live together*

El mural *Resurrection of the Green Planet,* del artista chicano Ernesto de la Loza, en *East Los Angeles*

Un símbolo latino en los Estados Unidos: Los murales y el arte urbano

La tradición muralista mexicana está muy presente en las comunidades latinas de los Estados Unidos, especialmente en California y los estados del Suroeste.[a] Presenta motivos indigenistas,[b] históricos y sociales. Ahora hay ejemplos del arte urbano en los grandes[c] museos, desde[d] grafitis hasta[e] murales.

[a]*Southwest* [b]motivos... *indigenous (native) themes or elements* [c]*great* [d]*from* [e]*to*

COMPRENSIÓN

Empareje (*Match*) la información de las dos columnas.

A	B
1. el Ecuador	**a.** ejemplos del arte latino
2. los murales	**b.** asociación de estudiantes dominicanos
3. bailes de gala	**c.** un país (*country*) con dos ciclos académicos
4. Fuerza Quisqueyana	**d.** ejemplo de un evento social

Y ahora, Uds.

- ¿Son Uds. miembros de organizaciones estudiantiles? ¿De cuál(es)?
- ¿Hay ejemplos del arte mural en su (*your*) ciudad?

En **otros** países° hispanos — *countries*

- **En todo el mundo**[a] **hispanohablante** Hay universidades nacionales que son gratuitas[b] o muy económicas en comparación con las universidades privadas. Las universidades nacionales son con frecuencia las más prestigiosas y antiguas[c] del país.

- **En el Ecuador** Hay dos ciclos escolares: uno para la región de la sierra, de octubre a junio, y el otro para la costa, de abril a enero.[d] Es para evitar que haya escuela en los meses de lluvia,[e] porque[f] hay peligro de inundaciones.[g]

[a]*world* [b]que... *that are free* [c]las... *the most prestigious and oldest* [d]*January* [e]para... *to avoid having school in the months of the rainy season* [f]*because* [g]peligro... *danger of flooding*

Del mundo hispano°

Del... *From the Hispanic world*

Antes de leer°

Antes... *Before reading*

What is a good way for an adult to learn another language? On the job (**el trabajo**), with friends who speak the language, in school (**una escuela**)? Can you think of other ways? Explain your answer. In a school, how many other learners would there ideally be in each class? How many days per week would the class meet? How many hours per day?

Lectura: Un anuncio° de Inglés USA

Lectura... *Reading: An ad*

Comprensión

A. Traducciones. (*Translations.*) Empareje (*Match*) las frases en español del anuncio con sus equivalentes en inglés.

1. _____ una hora de descanso
2. _____ el almuerzo
3. _____ semanas
4. _____ mayor

    a. *more*
    b. *an hour-long break*
    c. *weeks*
    d. *lunch*

B. En el anuncio. Busque (*Look for*) la siguiente información en el anuncio.

1. ¿Cómo se llama la escuela?
2. ¿Dónde está la escuela?
3. ¿Cuántos estudiantes hay en una clase?
4. ¿Qué tipo de estudiantes hay en la escuela?
5. ¿Cuántas horas de clase hay al (*per*) día?

INGLES USA ★

**CURSOS INTENSIVOS
INDIVIDUALES en
CINCINNATI, OHIO, USA.**

especial para
empresas y
altos ejecutivos[a]

Hotel y almuerzo de lunes
a sábado incluídos[b]
en el precio paquete

PROGRAMA:
7 horas diarias de clases,
lunes a sábado con
una hora de descanso
para el almuerzo con el
profesor.

Duración de
2 a 4 semanas

Para mayor información:

FUNDADA EN 1972[c]

CINCILINGUA INC.®

**322 East Fourth Street
Cincinnati, Ohio 45202 U.S.A.**
(513) 721-8782
FAX: (513) 721-8819
www.cincilingua.com

[a]para... *for business and corporate executives* [b]*included* [c]*mil novecientos setenta y dos*

Un anuncio° para los cursos de verano° de la Universidad Internacional   A... *Let's listen / ad / summer*

Antes de escuchar°   Antes... *Before listening*

What kind of information do you expect to hear in an ad for a summer course?

Vocabulario **para escuchar**			
el anuncio	ad	**la semana**	week
el verano	summer	**julio**	July
mayo	May	**agosto**	August

Después de escuchar°   Después... *After listening*

A. **Información básica.** Indique las respuestas (*answers*) apropiadas.

   1. El período de matrícula es en...

   _____ mayo   _____ junio   _____ julio   _____ agosto

   2. Hay cursos de...

   _____ 2 semanas _____ 4 semanas _____ 8 semanas _____ 10 semanas

   3. Con seguridad (*For sure*) hay cursos de... según (*according to*) el anuncio.

   _____ sociología _____ arte _____ matemáticas _____ literatura

   4. Por internet se ofrecen (*are offered*) cursos de...

   _____ alemán _____ filosofía _____ italiano _____ portugués

B. **Más información.** Según (*According to*) el anuncio, ¿cuál es el nombre de la residencia? ¿la dirección (*address*) de la página web? ¿el teléfono de contacto?

PRODUCCIÓN PERSONAL

¡Ahora, yo!

A. Use de (*as a*) modelo las preguntas y respuestas (*answers*) de la página 27 de este capítulo para hablar de sus propios estudios universitarios (*own university studies*).

B. Con las preguntas de la página 27 como modelo, filme una o dos entrevistas con compañeros de clase sobre (*about*) las materias que estudian y su especialización universitaria.

A ESCRIBIR°
Un ensayo sobre este° semestre/trimestre

A... *Let's write*

ensayo... *essay*
about this

¿Qué estudia Ud.? ¿Trabaja? ¿Es su horario (*schedule*) este semestre/trimestre muy diferente del (*from the*) horario de sus (*your*) compañeros de clase? ¿O es similar?

Preparar

Paso 1. Primero (*First*), complete la columna de la izquierda (*left-hand column*) con información personal. Luego entreviste a (*Then interview*) un compañero / una compañera y complete la columna de la derecha.

Yo	Mi compañero/a
Mi especialización[a] es / puede ser[b]:	Su[c] especialización es / puede ser:
Clases que[d] tomo este semestre/ trimestre:	Clases que toma este semestre/ trimestre:
Mi clase favorita es:	Su clase favorita es:
No trabajo. / Trabajo en...	No trabaja. / Trabaja en...
(No) Me gusta este semestre/ trimestre.	(No) Le gusta[e] este semestre/trimestre.

[a]*major* [b]puede... *might be* [c]*His/ Her* [d]*that* [e]*Le... He/She likes*

Paso 2. Ahora combine la información para escribir un ensayo. Hay más ayuda (*help*) en Connect.

Más ideas para su portafolio

- Make a list of reasons why you are studying Spanish. No reason is too silly or too small!
- Make a list of things you'd like to be able to do eventually with your Spanish. Let your imagination run wild!
- If you have been playing *Practice Spanish: Study Abroad,* in Quest 1 you saw the importance of the *plaza.* Where can *plazas* generally be found? How do people use them within their communities?

Sugerencia: You are now ready to play Quest 1 in **Practice Spanish: Study Abroad** (www.mhpractice.com).

EN RESUMEN En este capítulo

▦ILEARNSMART
Visit **www.connectspanish.com** to practice the vocabulary and grammar points covered in this chapter.

AFTER STUDYING THIS CHAPTER I CAN . . .

☐ name people, places, and things in the classroom and the university (28)

☐ name academic subject areas (30)

☐ recognize nouns and articles as masculine or feminine, singular or plural (35–36, 37–39)

☐ talk about actions with **-ar** verbs and subject pronouns (41–44)

☐ ask questions with interrogatives and yes/no questions with proper intonation (32, 48–49)

☐ recognize/describe at least two to three aspects of the Hispanic population of the U.S.

Gramática en breve

1. **Singular nouns: Gender and Articles**

   Noun Endings
   Masculine: **-o**
   Feminine: **-a, -ión, -dad, -tad**
   Masculine or feminine: **-e**

2. **Nouns and Articles: Plural Forms**

   Plural Endings
   -o $\rightarrow$ -os
   -a $\rightarrow$ -as
   -e $\rightarrow$ -es
   z $\rightarrow$ -ces
   consonant   +-es

Definite Articles		**Indefinite Articles**	
Masculine **el** $\rightarrow$ **los**		**un** $\rightarrow$ **unos**	
Feminine **la** $\rightarrow$ **las**		**una** $\rightarrow$ **unas**	

3. **Subject Pronouns; Present Tense of
   -ar Verbs; Negation**

   Subject Pronouns
   yo, tú, Ud., él, ella, nosotros/as, vosotros/as, Uds., ellos/as

   Regular -ar Verb Endings
   -o, -as, -a, -amos, -áis, -an

4. **Asking Yes/No Questions**

   • Rising intonation
   • Inversion of word order:
   subject **+** *verb* $\rightarrow$ *verb* **+** *subject*

Vocabulario

¡OJO!

• Infinitives listed in colored text in **Vocabulario** lists are conjugated in all tenses and moods in Appendix 5.
• Be sure that you know the meaning of the group headings in addition to the meaning of the words in each group.
• If you are not sure of the meaning of a word, you can look it up in the end-of-book Spanish-English Vocabulary.)

Los verbos

bailar	to dance
buscar	to look for
cantar	to sing
comprar	to buy
desear	to want
enseñar	to teach
escuchar	to listen (to)
estar (estoy, estás,...)	to be
estudiar	to study
hablar	to speak; to talk
hablar por teléfono	to talk on the phone
mandar un mensaje	to (send a) text
necesitar	to need
pagar	to pay (for)
practicar	to practice
regresar	to return (*to a place*)
regresar a casa	to go home
tocar	to play (*a musical instrument*)
tomar	to take; to drink
trabajar	to work

Las personas

el/la amigo/a	friend
el/la bibliotecario/a	librarian
el/la cliente/a	client
el/la compañero/a (de clase)	classmate
el/la compañero/a de cuarto	roommate
el/la consejero/a	advisor
el/la dependiente/a	clerk
el/la estudiante	student
el/la extranjero/a	foreigner
el hombre	man
la mujer	woman
el/la secretario/a	secretary

Repaso: el/la profesor(a)

> **Repaso** (*Review*) indicates vocabulary listed as active in this chapter that you learned in previous chapters.

Los lugares

el apartamento	apartment
la biblioteca	library
la cafetería	cafeteria
el cuarto	room
el edificio	building
la fiesta	party
la librería	bookstore
el lugar	place
la oficina	office
la residencia	dormitory
el salón de clase	classroom
la universidad	university

Los objetos

el bolígrafo	pen
la calculadora	calculator
la computadora	computer
la computadora portátil	laptop (computer)
el cuaderno	notebook
el diccionario	dictionary
el dinero	money
el escritorio	desk
el lápiz (*pl.* lápices)	pencil
el libro (de texto)	(text)book
la mesa	table
la mochila	backpack
el papel	paper
el pizarrón (blanco)	(white)board
la puerta	door
la silla	chair
el teléfono (celular)	(cell) phone
la ventana	window

Las materias

la administración de empresas	business administration
la ciencia	science
la computación	computer science
la física	physics
la materia	subject area
la química	chemistry
la sicología	psychology

Cognados: el arte, las ciencias naturales/políticas/ sociales, las comunicaciones, la economía, la filosofía, la historia, las humanidades, la literatura, las matemáticas, la sociología

> **Cognado(s)** lists vocabulary you should be able to recognize because the words are close cognates of English.

Las lenguas (extranjeras)

el alemán	German
el español	Spanish
el francés	French

el inglés	English
el italiano	Italian
la lengua (extranjera)	(foreign) language

Otros sustantivos

el café	coffee
la clase	class (*of students*); class, course (*academic*)
el día	day
la matrícula	tuition

Las palabras interrogativas

¿cuál?	what?; which?
¿cuándo?	when?
¿cuánto?	how much?
¿cuántos/as?	how many?

Repaso: ¿cómo?, ¿(de) dónde?, ¿qué?, ¿quién?

¿Cuándo?

ahora	now
con frecuencia	frequently
el fin de semana	weekend
por la mañana/tarde	in the morning/afternoon
por la noche	at night, in the evening
tarde/temprano	late/early
todos los días	every day

Los pronombres personales

yo	I
tú	you (*fam. sing.*)
Ud.	you (*form, sing.*)
él	he
ella	she
nosotros/as	we
vosotros/as	you (*fam., plural*)
Uds.	you (*form., plural*)
ellos/as	they

Palabras adicionales

aquí	here
con	with
en casa	at home
mal	poorly
más	more
mucho (*adverb*)	much; a lot
poco (*adverb*)	(a) little
un poco (de)	a little bit (of)
solo	only

Repaso: no

> **Vocabulario personal**
> Use this space for other words and phrases you learn in this chapter.
>
> | ESPAÑOL | INGLÉS |
> |---|---|

3

La familia

connect
|SPANISH

www.connectspanish.com

Una familia mexicana, en una celebración especial

MÉXICO

120 (ciento veinte) millones de habitantes

- El nombre oficial de México es Estados Unidos Mexicanos. Hay 31 estados mexicanos.

- Es el primer país del mundo por[a] número de hispanohablantes.

- Un 64% (sesenta y cuatro por ciento) de los hispanos de los Estados Unidos de América son de origen mexicano.

[a]*el... the number one country in the world by*

- ¿Cómo es su[a] familia, grande[b] o pequeña[c]? (**Mi** familia...)
- ¿Cuántas personas hay en su familia más cercana[d]?
- ¿Cómo se llama su padre[e]/madre? (**Mi** padre/madre...)
- ¿Le gusta celebrar su cumpleaños[f] con sus amigos? (...con **mis** amigos) ¿con su familia? (...con **mi** familia)

[a]*your* [b]*big* [c]*small* [d]*más... closest* [e]*father* [f]*birthday*

ALEJANDRA HERNÁNDEZ SOTO CONTESTA LAS PREGUNTAS.

- Mi familia más cercana es pequeña porque[a] soy hija única.[b]

- Pero mi familia extendida es muy grande: tengo seis tías[c] y tíos y doce primos.[d]

- Mi padre se llama Juan y mi madre se llama Susana. Yo me llamo como mi abuela[e] materna.

- Me gusta celebrar mi cumpleaños con mis padres y también con mis amigos pero ¡por separado!

[a]*because* [b]*hija... an only child* [c]*aunts* [d]*cousins* [e]*grandmother*

VOCABULARIO: PREPARACIÓN

LS

You can hear the pronunciation of theme vocabulary words and phrases in the Connect eBook.

La familia y los parientes°

relatives

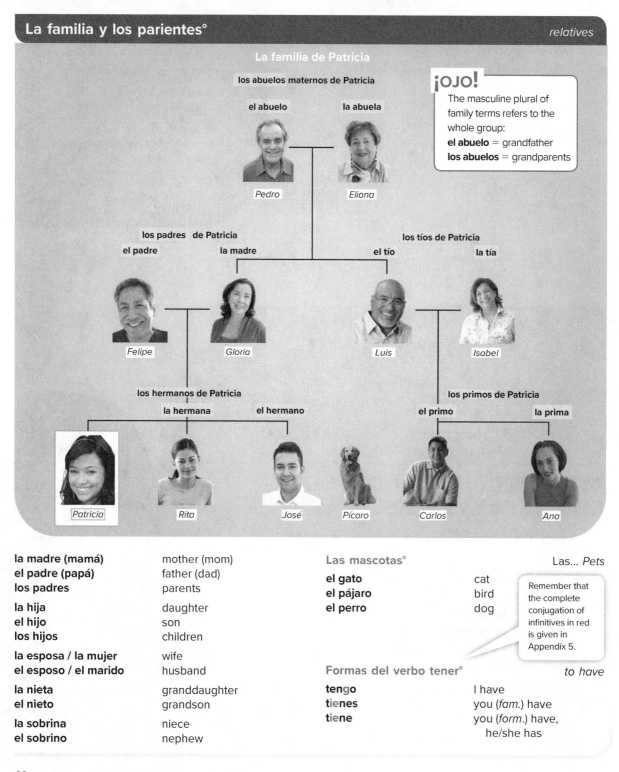

La familia de Patricia

los abuelos maternos de Patricia

el abuelo — la abuela

Pedro — *Eliana*

¡OJO!
The masculine plural of family terms refers to the whole group:
el abuelo = grandfather
los abuelos = grandparents

los padres de Patricia
el padre — la madre

los tíos de Patricia
el tío — la tía

Felipe — *Gloria*

Luis — *Isabel*

los hermanos de Patricia
la hermana — el hermano

los primos de Patricia
el primo — la prima

Patricia — *Rita* — *José* — *Pícaro* — *Carlos* — *Ana*

la madre (mamá)	mother (mom)
el padre (papá)	father (dad)
los padres	parents
la hija	daughter
el hijo	son
los hijos	children
la esposa / la mujer	wife
el esposo / el marido	husband
la nieta	granddaughter
el nieto	grandson
la sobrina	niece
el sobrino	nephew

Las mascotas° — Las... *Pets*

el gato	cat
el pájaro	bird
el perro	dog

Remember that the complete conjugation of infinitives in red is given in Appendix 5.

Formas del verbo tener° — *to have*

tengo	I have
tienes	you (*fam.*) have
tiene	you (*form.*) have, he/she has

Learn as many of the following terms for additional family relationships as you need to describe your own family as completely as possible. Write the terms you learn in **Vocabulario personal** (page 97).

el padrastro / la madrastra	stepfather / stepmother
el hijastro / la hijastra	stepson / stepdaughter
el hermanastro / la hermanastra	stepbrother / stepsister
el medio hermano / la media hermana	half-brother / half-sister
el suegro / la suegra	father-in-law / mother-in-law
el yerno / la nuera	son-in-law / daughter-in-law
el cuñado / la cuñada	brother-in-law / sister-in-law
...(ya) murió	...has (already) died

Comunicación

A. La familia de Patricia. Mire (*Look at*) el árbol (*tree*) genealógico de Patricia en la página 62 (sesenta y dos). Indique si las siguientes oraciones son ciertas o falsas. Corrija (*Correct*) las oraciones falsas.

	CIERTO	FALSO
1. José es el hermano de Ana.	☐	☐
2. Eliana es la abuela de Patricia.	☐	☐
3. Ana es la sobrina de Felipe y Gloria.	☐	☐
4. Patricia y José son (*are*) primos.	☐	☐
5. Gloria es la tía de José.	☐	☐
6. Carlos es el sobrino de Isabel.	☐	☐
7. Pedro es el padre de Luis y Gloria.	☐	☐
8. Isabel y Gloria son las esposas de Luis y Felipe, respectivamente.	☐	☐

B. ¿Quién es?

Paso 1. Complete las siguientes oraciones lógicamente.

1. La madre de mi (*my*) padre es mi _____.
2. El hijo de mi tío es mi _____.
3. La hermana de mi padre es mi _____.
4. El esposo (marido) de mi abuela es mi _____.

Paso 2. Ahora defina la relación de estas (*these*) personas, según (*according to*) el modelo de las oraciones del **Paso 1.**

MODELOS: El _____ de mi _____ es mi _____.
La _____ de mi _____ es mi _____.

1. prima   **2.** sobrino   **3.** tío   **4.** abuelo

C. Intercambios. Find out as much as you can about the family of a classmate, using the following dialogue as a guide.

MODELO: E1:* ¿Cuántos hermanos tienes?
E2: Bueno,[a] tengo dos hermanos.
E1: ¿Cómo se llaman tus hermanos?
E2: Se llaman Dixon y Lisa.
E1: ¿Y cuántos primos tienes?
E2: ¡Uf! Tengo un montón.[b] Más de[c] veinte.
E1: ¿Tienes una mascota?
E2: Sí, tengo un perro. Se llama Bear.

[a]*Well* [b]*bunch* [c]*Más... More than*

*From this point on in the text, ESTUDIANTE 1 *and* ESTUDIANTE 2 *will be abbreviated as* **E1** *and* **E2,** *respectively.*

Así se dice

The terms **mamá/mami** and **papá/papi** are used to speak *to* one's parents.

Many Spanish speakers use the terms **abuelito/tata** and **abuelita/nana** to speak *to* their grandparents.

Here is vocabulary for referring to non-traditional types of families:

- **una familia reconstituida** (family whose parents were previously married and have other children with previous spouses)
- **una unión civil**
- **una pareja de hecho** (non-married couple with formalized status)
- **un matrimonio entre personas del mismo sexo**

¡OJO!

¿cuántos? (*with male relatives*)
¿cuántas? (*with female relatives*)

En esta credencial para votar, de México, están el nombre y los dos apellidos de la persona: primero, los apellidos y después (*next*), el nombre.

Nota cultural

El sistema hispano de apellidos°

last names

En los países hispanos las personas llevan sistemáticamente dos apellidos oficiales. Típicamente, el primer[a] apellido es el del[b] padre y el segundo,[c] el de la madre.

PADRE	MADRE
Antonio **Lázaro** Ochoa	Marina **Aguirre** Salmero

HIJOS
Marta **Lázaro Aguirre**
Jacobo **Lázaro Aguirre**

Según el sistema hispano, ¿cómo se llamaría Ud.?[d]

[a]*first* [b]*el... that of the* [c]*second* [d]*¿cómo... what would your name be?*

Los números del 31 al 100

Continúe las secuencias:

- treinta y uno, treinta y dos...
- ochenta y cuatro, ochenta y cinco...

31	treinta y uno	**40**	cuarenta
32	treinta y dos	**50**	cincuenta
33	treinta y tres	**60**	sesenta
34	treinta y cuatro	**70**	setenta
35	treinta y cinco	**80**	ochenta
36	treinta y seis	**90**	noventa
37	treinta y siete	**100**	cien
38	treinta y ocho		
39	treinta y nueve		

setenta y ocho años
cincuenta y cinco años
treinta y nueve años
cuarenta y cinco años
cuarenta y siete años
ochenta y cinco años
«El abuelito Pedro tiene 85 años.»
«La abuelita Eliana tiene 78 años.»

Beginning with 31, Spanish numbers are *not* written in a combined form. **Treinta y uno,**[*] **cuarenta y dos, sesenta y tres,** and so on, must be three separate words.

Cien is used before nouns and in counting.

cien casas	a (one) hundred houses
noventa y ocho, noventa y nueve, cien	ninety-eight, ninety-nine, one hundred

Comunicación

A. **Más problemas de matemáticas.** Recuerde (*Remember*): + **y,** − **menos,** = **son.**

1. $30 + 50 = 80$
2. $45 + 45 = 90$
3. $68 − 28 = 40$
4. $77 + 23 = 100$
5. $100 − 40 = 60$
6. $55 + 15 = 70$

---

*Remember that when **uno** is part of a compound number (**treinta y uno**, and so on), it becomes **un** before a masculine noun and **una** before a feminine noun: **setenta y un hombres; cincuenta y una mesas.**

B. Un directorio de teléfonos de la clase. Interview five classmates to find out their full names, Spanish-style, and phone numbers. Follow the model of this directory from **México**: last name, last name, first name. **¡OJO!** In many Hispanic countries phone numbers are said with an initial single digit, then in groups of two, as in the model.

MODELO: **E1:** ¿Cómo te llamas y cuál es tu número de teléfono?

E2: Me llamo **Smith Wiliams, John** y mi número (de teléfono) es **el 215-8194** (dos-quince-ochenta y uno-noventa y cuatro).

LAZARO AGUIRRE, A. –Schez Pacheco, 12	413 0146
LAZCANO DEL MORAL, A. –Ibiza, 2	472 6868
LEAL ANTON, J. –Pozo, 6	222 3944
LOPEZ BARTOLÓME, J. –Palma, 61	323 2027
LOPEZ CABRA,J. –E. Solana, 113	407 5807
LOPEZ GONZALEZ, J. A. –Ibiza, 21	409 5225
LOPEZ GUTIERREZ, G. –5. Cameros, 1	486 8494
LOPEZ MARIN, V. –Illescas, 31	218 6630
LOPEZ MARIN, V. –Valmojado, 321	722 2823
LOPEZ NUÑEZ. J. –Pl. Pinazo, s/n	796 0051
LOPEZ NUÑEZ, M. –Rocafort, Bl. 289	768 5387
LOPEZ RODRIGUEZ, C. –Pl. Jesus, 9	429 3250
LOPEZ TRAPERO, A. –Cam. Ingenieros, 5	462 9253
LOPEZ VEGA, J. – M. Santa Ana, 7................	231 3121
LORENZO MARTINEZ, A. –P. Laborde, 53	771 2800
LOSADA MIRON, M. –Padilla, 31	276 3973

Nota **comunicativa**

Cómo expresar la edad:° *tener... años*   *age*

In Spanish, age is expressed with the phrase **tener... años** (literally, *to have . . . years*).

NORA: ¿Cuántos **años tienes**, abuela?
ABUELA: Setenta y ocho. ¿Y cuántos **años tienes** tú?
NORA: Yo **tengo** ocho.

You will practice telling how old people are in **Comunicación C**.

C. Hablemos (*Let's talk*) de la edad (*age*)

Paso 1. Complete las siguientes oraciones.

1. Yo tengo _____ años.
2. La persona mayor (*oldest*) de mi familia es **mi** _____. Tiene _____ años.
3. La persona más joven (*youngest*) de mi familia es **mi** _____. Tiene _____ años.
4. En mi opinión, una persona es vieja (*old*) cuando tiene _____ años.
5. La edad ideal para casarse (*for getting married*) es a los _____ años.
6. La edad ideal para tener hijos es a los _____ años.

Paso 2. Ahora haga (*form*) preguntas basadas en las oraciones del **Paso 1** y haga (*conduct*) una encuesta (*poll*) entre (*with*) un mínimo de seis compañeros de clase.

Estrategia

En el **Paso 2**, cambie (*change*) la palabra **mi (en negrilla)** para formar las preguntas, según el modelo:

mi → tu

MODELO: **2. E1:** ¿Quién es la persona mayor de **tu** familia? ¿Cuántos años tiene?

E2: Es **mi** abuela. Tiene noventa y siete años.

Paso 3. Finalmente, presente sus (*your*) resultados a la clase.

Algo sobre...

los estados[a] mexicanos

El escudo (símbolo) de los Estados Unidos Mexicanos es un águila sobre un nopal.

México tiene 32 entidades federativas: 31 estados y 1 distrito federal, que[b] es la capital, la Ciudad de México. Los mexicanos la llaman[c] el D.F.

¿Cuántos estados hay en los Estados Unidos? La capital, Washington D.C., ¿es un estado?

[a]*states* [b]*which* [c]*la... call it (i.e., the capital)*

guapo	handsome, good-looking
bonito	pretty
feo	ugly
grande	large, big
pequeño	small
simpático	nice, likeable
antipático	unpleasant, unlikeable
corto	short (*in length*)
largo	long
bueno	good
malo	bad
listo	smart, clever
tonto	silly, foolish
trabajador	hardworking
perezoso	lazy
rico	rich
pobre	poor
delgado	thin, slender
gordo	fat

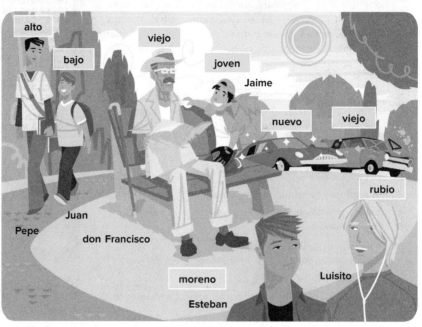

To describe a masculine singular noun, use **alt**o, **baj**o, and so on; use **alt**a, **baj**a, and so on for feminine singular nouns.

Comunicación

A. Descripciones

Paso 1. En parejas, describan estas (*these*) imágenes opuestas (*opposite*).

MODELO: Un _____ es y _____ el otro es _____.

1.   2.   3.   4.

Paso 2. Ahora describan a estas personas e* ideas.

MODELO: fumar (*to smoke*) → Fumar es malo. No es bueno.

1. bailar
2. Stephen Hawkins
3. Bill Gates
4. estudiar toda la noche
5. el edificio Empire State
6. Frankenstein
7. un átomo

B. ¿Cómo es?
Describe a famous male personality, using as many adjectives as possible so that your classmates can guess who the person is. Use cognate adjectives that you have seen in **Capítulos 1** and **2.**

MODELO: Es un hombre importante; controla una compañía de *software* muy importante. Es muy trabajador y muy rico. → Bill Gates

---

Notice that the word **y** becomes **e** before a word that starts with the sound **i**: **español e inglés,
matemáticas e historia.**

«Padres modernos» Segmento 1

Antes de mirar°

Antes... *Before watching*

¿Tiene Ud.... ?

_____ abuelos que viven cerca (*who live nearby*)
_____ muchos parientes
_____ hijos
_____ padrinos (*godparents*) (un padrino / una madrina)
_____ ahijados (*godchildren*) (un ahijado / una ahijada)

Este° segmento

This

Ana García Blanco y Víctor Gutiérrez presentan un programa sobre (*about*) la familia. También hablan de personas importantes en su vida familiar (*their family life*).

Hoy Víctor toma una taza grande (*big cup*) de café. ¿Por qué?

Vocabulario **del segmento**

disfrutar	to enjoy	**cuidar a**	to take care of
enfermo/a	sick	**¡Vivan las abuelas!**	Hooray for grandmothers!
cansado/a	tired	**los amigos íntimos**	very close friends

Estrategia

Before you watch, scan **Actividades A** and **B** in **Después de mirar.** Knowing what tasks you need to do after watching will help you focus on information to pay attention to as you watch the segment.

Después de mirar°

Después... *After watching*

A. ¿Está claro? Empareje (*Match*) las personas con las relaciones familiares del segmento.

LAS PERSONAS
____ **1.** Víctor
____ **2.** la abuela
____ **3.** Sarita
____ **4.** Marina
____ **5.** Ana
____ **6.** Leticia

LAS RELACIONES FAMILIARES
a. la esposa de Víctor
b. la mamá de Víctor
c. la hija de Víctor
d. la tía y madrina de Leticia
e. la sobrina de Ana
f. el papá de Sarita

B. Un poco más. ¿Cierto o falso? Corrija las oraciones falsas, según el video.

	CIERTO	FALSO
1. Víctor toma aspirinas porque (*because*) está cansado.	☐	☐
2. Víctor está enfermo.	☐	☐
3. La esposa de Víctor cuida a Sarita hoy.	☐	☐
4. Los padrinos y los amigos íntimos son (*are*) personas importantes y fundamentales en muchas familias.	☐	☐

C. Y ahora, Uds. Practique su (*your*) pronunciación y su talento como presentador(a). Complete el fragmento con su propia (*your own*) información y con vocabulario del programa.

Muy buenos días desde nuestro estudio en _____. ¿Cómo están Uds.? Yo estoy _____ hoy. El tema del programa de hoy es la familia. ¿Qué personas son[a] muy importantes en su[b] familia, además de[c] los padres? ¿Son importantes también los _____ (personas)? En mi caso, mi _____ y mi _____ son personas fundamentales. ¡Viva mi _____ ! ¡Vivan mis _____ !

[a]*are* [b]*your* [c]*además... besides*

PRONUNCIACIÓN

Stress and Written Accent Marks (Part 1)

Some Spanish words have *written accent marks* over one of the vowels. That mark is called **el acento (ortográfico).** It means that the syllable containing the accented vowel is stressed when the word is pronounced, as in the word **bolígrafo (bo-LÍ-gra-fo),** for example.

Although all Spanish words of more than one syllable have a stressed vowel, most words do not have a written accent mark. Most words have the spoken stress exactly where native speakers of Spanish would predict it. These two simple rules tell you which syllable is stressed when there is no written accent on the word.

¡OJO!

You will learn about words that have a written accent mark in **Capítulo 4.**

1. Las palabras llanas, words ending in a vowel, **-n,** or **-s**

Las palabras llanas have the word stress on the *second-to-last syllable* (**la penúltima sílaba**). When they end in a vowel, **-n,** or **-s,** they don't need a written accent mark. This is the largest group of Spanish words; it includes most nouns and adjectives as well as their plurals, most verb forms, and so on. Here are some examples.

 me-sa   me-xi-ca-no   e-xa-men   gra-cias   e-res

2. Las palabras agudas, words ending in a consonant other than **-n** or **-s**

Las palabras agudas have the word stress on the *last syllable* (**la última sílaba**). When they end in consonants other than **-n** or **-s** (typically **-d, -l,** and **-r**), they don't need a written accent mark. This group includes all infinitives and many common words that end in **-dad, -or,** and **-al.** Here are some examples.

 us-ted   es-pa-ñol   pro-fe-sor   es-tar   doc-tor

Práctica

A. Tipos de palabras: ¿Llanas o agudas? None of these words needs a written accent mark. Categorize each one as **llana** or **aguda,** then pronounce the word.

1. can-tan	**5.** me-sa	**9.** se-ñor
2. ar-te	**6.** es-pa-ñol	**10.** na-tu-ral
3. cla-se	**7.** a-mi-gos	**11.** com-pu-ta-do-ra
4. mu-jer	**8.** us-ted	**12.** bai-las

B. Vocales. Indicate the stressed vowel in the following words.

1. mo-chi-la	**4.** i-gual-men-te	**7.** li-be-ral
2. me-nos	**5.** E-cua-dor	**8.** hu-ma-ni-dad
3. re-gu-lar	**6.** e-le-gan-te	

Estrategia

llana (ends in a vowel, **-n,** or **-s**) = stress on the second-to-last syllable

aguda (ends in a consonant other than **-n** or **-s**) = stress on the last syllable

GRAMÁTICA

Grammar Tutorial 5

connect
|SPANISH
www.connectspanish.com

5 Describing

Adjectives: Gender, Number, and Position

Gramática en acción: Un poema sencillo

Amigo
Fiel
Amable
Simpático
¡Lo admiro!

Amiga
Fiel
Amable
Simpática
¡La admiro!

¿Y Ud.?

According to their form, which of the following adjectives can be used to describe each person? Which can refer to you?

Marta:
Mario: { fiel   amable   simpática   simpático

Adjectives (**Los adjetivos**) are words used to talk about nouns or pronouns. Adjectives may describe or tell how many of something there are.

> *an adjective* / **un adjetivo** = a word used to describe a noun or a pronoun

> ***large*** desk   ***few*** desks
>
> ***tall*** woman   ***several*** women

You have been using adjectives to describe people since **Capítulo 1.** In this section, you will learn more about describing the people and things around you.

Adjectives with *ser* / Los adjetivos con *ser*

In Spanish, forms of **ser** are used with adjectives that describe basic, inherent qualities or characteristics of the nouns or pronouns they modify. **Ser** establishes the "norm," that is, what is considered basic reality: *snow is cold, water is wet.*

Tú eres **amable.**
You're kind. (You're a kind person.)

El diccionario es **grande.**
The dictionary is big.

Mi hermana es **trabajadora.**
My sister is hardworking.

A simple poem *Friend Loyal Kind Nice I admire him/her!*

Forms of Adjectives / Las formas de los adjetivos

Spanish adjectives "agree" with the noun or pronoun they modify. This agreement is shown in two ways:

- gender agreement (masculine or feminine): **una amiga alta**
- number agreement (singular or plural): **los amigos ricos**

For this reason, Spanish adjectives have more than one form.

> *agreement* / **la concordancia** = when one word "agrees," or must be coordinated, with an aspect of another (for example, *he + speaks* but *you + speak*)

1. Adjectives Ending in -o

Adjectives that end in **-o (alto)** have four forms, showing gender and number.

Adjetivos con 4 formas

	Masculino	Femenino
Singular	amigo alto	amiga alta
Plural	amigos altos	amigas altas

2. Adjectives Ending in -e or a Consonant

Adjectives that end in **-e (amable)** or in most consonants (**fiel**) have only two forms, a singular and a plural form. The plural of adjectives is formed in the same way as that of nouns, by adding **-s** or **-es**.

Adjetivos con 2 formas

	Masculino	Femenino
Singular	amigo amable amigo fiel	amiga amable amiga fiel
Plural	amigos amables amigos fieles	amigas amables amigas fieles

> **¡OJO!**
>
> When the adjective **joven** is made plural, an accent mark is added to retain the original stress: **joven → jóvenes**.

3. Adjectives Ending in -dor

Like adjectives that end in **-o**, these adjectives also have four forms.

Adjetivos con 4 formas

	Masculino	Femenino
Singular	amigo trabajador	amiga trabajadora
Plural	amigos trabajadores	amigas trabajadoras

4. Nationality Adjectives

Many adjectives of nationality have four forms.

	Masculino	Femenino
Singular	el doctor mexicano español	la doctora mexicana española
Plural	los doctores mexicanos españoles	las doctoras mexicanas españolas

> **¡OJO!**
>
> Nationality adjectives ending in **-e** generally have only two forms: **estadounidense(s)** (from the United States), **canadiense(s).**

5. Names of Languages

The names of many languages—which are masculine in gender—are the same as the masculine singular form of the corresponding adjective of nationality.

Lengua	Adjetivo
el inglés	inglés, inglesa, ingleses, inglesas
el francés	francés, francesa, franceses, francesas
el italiano	italiano, italiana, italianos, italianas
el alemán	alemán, alemana, alemanes, alemanas

> **¡OJO!**
>
> Note that in Spanish the names of languages and adjectives of nationality are not capitalized, but the names of countries are: **el español, española,** but **España.**

> **¡OJO!**
>
> When the last syllable of an adjective has a written accent mark (**inglés, alemán**), the accent is dropped in the feminine and plural forms, as shown in the box above.

Position of Adjectives / La posición de los adjetivos

As you have probably noticed, adjectives do not always precede the noun in Spanish as they do in English. Note the following rules for adjective placement.

1. Adjectives of Quantity

Like numbers, adjectives of quantity *precede* the noun, as do the interrogatives **¿cuánto/a?** and **¿cuántos/as?**

> **¡OJO!**
>
> **Otro/a** is an adjective of quantity. By itself it means *another* or *other*. The indefinite article is never used with **otro/a**.

Hay **muchas sillas** y **dos escritorios.**
There are many chairs and two desks.

¿Cuánto dinero necesitas?
How much money do you need?

Busco **otro coche.**
I'm looking for another car.

2. Adjectives of Quality

Adjectives that describe the qualities of a noun and distinguish it from others generally *follow* the noun. Adjectives of nationality are included in this category.

un **perro listo**
un **dependiente trabajador**
una **mujer delgada** y **morena**
un **profesor español**

3. *Bueno* and *malo*

The adjectives **bueno** and **malo** may *precede or follow* the noun they modify. When they precede a masculine singular noun, they shorten to **buen** and **mal,** respectively.

un **buen perro** / un **perro bueno**
una **buena perra** / una **perra buena**

un **mal día** / un **día malo**
una **mala noche** / una **noche mala**

4. *Grande*

The adjective **grande** may also *precede or follow* the noun.

- When it precedes a singular noun—masculine or feminine—it shortens to **gran** and means *great* or *impressive*.
- When it follows the noun, it means *large* or *big*.

Nueva York es una **gran ciudad.**
New York is a great (impressive) city.

Nueva York es una **ciudad grande.**
New York is a large city.

Forms of *this/these* / Formas de *este/estos*

1. *This/These*

The adjective *this/these* has four forms in Spanish.* Learn to recognize them when you see them.

este hijo	this son
esta hija	this daughter
estos hijos	these sons
estas hijas	these daughters

2. *Esto*

You have already seen the neuter demonstrative **esto.** It refers to something that is as yet unidentified.

¿Qué es **esto**?
What is this?

---

*You will learn all forms of this type of adjective (*this, that, these, those*) in* **Gramática 9 (Cap. 4).**

Práctica y comunicación

A. La familia

Paso 1. Autoprueba. Complete los adjetivos con la forma apropiada.

1. El padre es alt_____ y trabajador_____.
2. La madre es baj_____ y amabl_____.
3. Los abuelos son viej_____ y simpátic_____.
4. Las hijas son pequeñ_____ y adorabl_____.
5. Hay much_____ parientes en la familia.
6. La familia tiene buen_____ amigos.

Paso 2. Ahora complete las siguientes oraciones según la familia de Ud.

1. Mi padre/hermano/tío es _____ y _____.
2. Mi madre/hermana/tía es _____ y _____.
3. Mis abuelos son (*are*) _____ y _____. (Mi abuelo/a es _____ y _____.)
4. _____ (nombre) y _____ (nombre) son buen_____ amigos/amigas de mi familia

Paso 3. Ahora, en parejas, túrnense para hacer y contestar (*take turns asking and answering*) preguntas sobre su (*about your*) familia. Usen las oraciones del **Paso 2** como modelo.

MODELO: **E1:** Mis abuelos son mexicanos y simpáticos.
¿Y tus abuelos?
E2: Mis abuelos son estadounidenses y viejos.

B. Descripciones

Paso 1. Haga oraciones con los siguientes adjetivos para describirse (*to describe yourself*). **¡OJO!** Use la forma apropiada del adjetivo.

Soy...
No soy...

1. alto
2. trabajadora
3. estadounidense
4. rico
5. rubia
6. fiel
7. simpático

8. europeo
9. gordo
10. hispana (latina)*
11. dedicado
12. social
13. estudiosa
14. listo

Paso 2. Ahora haga oraciones para describir a su (*your*) padre/madre, a su esposo/a o a su mejor amigo/a (*best friend*).

MODELOS: Mi mejor amiga es moren**a**, simpátic**a** y pobre.
Mi esposo es alt**o**, trabaja**dor** y muy dedica**do**.

*Hispano/a *is a general term used by most Hispanics to refer to themselves. The term* latino/a *is often used by Hispanics born in this country.*

Prác. A, Paso 1: Answers: 1. alto, trabajador (no change) 2. baja, amable 3. viejos, simpáticos 4. pequeñas, adorables 5. muchos 6. buenos

C. **La familia de Carlos.** Estos son los parientes de Carlos (página 62). Complete las oraciones con los adjetivos apropiados según su forma.

1. **El tío Felipe** es _____. (trabajador / alto / nueva / gran / amable)
2. **Los abuelos** son _____. (rubio / antipático / inteligentes / viejos / religiosos / sinceras)
3. **Mi tía Gloria,** la madre de Patricia, es _____. (rubio / elegante / sentimental / buenas / gordas / simpática)
4. **Mis primos** son _____. (trabajadores / morenos / lógica / bajas / mala)

D. **¡Dolores es igual!** Cambie (*Exchange*) **Diego** por **Dolores.**

Diego es un buen estudiante. Es listo y trabajador y estudia mucho. Es estadounidense de origen mexicano, y por eso[a] habla español. Desea ser profesor de antropología. Diego es moreno, guapo y atlético. Le gustan las fiestas grandes y tiene buenos amigos en la universidad. Tiene parientes estadounidenses y mexicanos. Diego tiene 20 años.

[a]por... *for that reason*

Nota **comunicativa**

Otras nacionalidades

You learned some nationality adjectives on page 70. Here are some more. If you don't find the adjective(s) you need to describe yourself and your family, ask your instructor. Write the adjectives you need in **Vocabulario personal** (page 97).

Norteamérica	Centroamérica y el Caribe	Sudamérica		Europa y Asia	
canadiense	costarricense	argentino/a	ecuatoriano/a	chino/a	japonés, japonesa
mexicano/a	cubano/a	boliviano/a	paraguayo/a	coreano/a	pakistaní (*pl.* pakistaníes)
	dominicano/a	brasileño/a	peruano/a	indio/a	palestino/a
	guatemalteco/a	chileno/a	uruguayo/a	israelí (*pl.* israelíes) ruso/a	
	hondureño/a	colombiano/a	venezolano/a	iraní (*pl.* iraníes)	tailandés, tailandesa
	nicaragüense			iraquí (*pl.* iraquíes) vietnamita	
	panameño/a				
	salvadoreño/a				

You will use many of these adjectives in **Práctica E.**

E. **Países (*Countries*) y nacionalidades del mundo (*world*)**

Paso 1. Diga (*Tell*) la nacionalidad de las siguientes personas.

1. Monique es de Francia; es _____.
2. Piero y Andri son del Uruguay; son _____.
3. Indira y su (*her*) hermana son de la India; son _____.
4. Ronaldo y Ronaldinho son del Brasil; son _____.
5. Saji es un hombre del Japón; es _____.
6. La familia Musharraf es de Pakistán; son (*they are*) _____.
7. Paul es de Inglaterra; es _____.
8. Samuel y su (*his*) hermana son de Guatemala; son _____.
9. Sonia es de la Argentina; es _____.
10. Ramón y José son de Colombia; son _____.
11. Jimena es de Costa Rica; es _____.
12. Bill y Susan son de California; son _____.

¡OJO!

Recuerde (*Remember*): Los adjetivos de nacionalidad y los nombres de las lenguas no comienzan con letra mayúscula (*capital letter*).

Paso 2. En parejas, hagan oraciones con las nacionalidades hispanas, según el modelo. Busquen (*Look for*) los nombres de las naciones hispanas en el mapa de la página 12.

MODELO: E1: ¿Una mujer de Costa Rica?
E2: Es **costarricense.** ¿Y un hombre?
E1: Es **costarricense.** ¿Una mujer de El Salvador?
E2: Es...

F. Una mujer sorprendente (*surprising*)

Paso 1. Complete con las terminaciones apropiadas la siguiente descripción de una mujer muy especial.

Sor (*Sister*) Juana Inés de la Cruz, 1651 – 1695 (mil seiscientos cincuenta y uno hasta mil seiscientos noventa y cinco)

Sorª Juana Inés de la Cruz es una mujer religios___¹ mexican___² del siglo^b XVII. Es una gran___³ poeta y una mujer muy inteligent___⁴ y muy ilustrad___ᶜ⁵ para su^d época. Es muy famos___⁶ internacionalmente. Escribió^e much____⁷ poemas important____⁸ de la literatura hispan___⁹.

ªSister ^bcentury ^cilustrado/a = *educated* ^dpara... *for her* ^eShe wrote

Paso 2. Comprensión. ¿Cierto o falso? Corrija las oraciones falsas.

	CIERTO	FALSO
1. Sor Juana es de Nicaragua.	☐	☐
2. Escribió poemas en español.	☐	☐
3. Es famosa solamente en México.	☐	☐

G. Asociaciones. En grupos, hablen (*talk*) de las personas o cosas (*things*) que (*that*) asocian con las siguientes frases. Expresen acuerdo (*agreement*) o desacuerdo (*disagreement*) con **(No) Estoy de acuerdo.**

MODELO: un gran hombre →
E1: Creo que (*I believe that*) **mi padre** es un gran hombre.
E2: No estoy de acuerdo.

1. un mal restaurante
2. un buen programa de televisión
3. una gran mujer, un gran hombre
4. un buen libro (¿una novela?), un libro horrible
5. un buen coche
6. una buena computadora

H. Descripciones. En parejas, describan a su (*your*) familia, haciendo (*forming*) oraciones completas con estas palabras, con cualquier (*any*) otro adjetivo que conozcan (*that you may know*) y con los adjetivos de nacionalidad. **¡OJO!** Cuidado (*Be careful*) con la forma de los adjetivos.

MODELO: Mi familia no es grande. Es pequeña. Mi padre tiene 50 años. Es pakistaní de nacimiento (*by birth*).

mi familia
mi padre/madre
mi esposo/esposa
mi ¿ ? (otro pariente)
mi perro/gato

+ (no) es **+**
+ tiene...
años

agresivo	famoso	pequeño
amable	grande	sensible (*sensitive*)
animado (*lively*)	(im)paciente	sentimental
antipático	importante	serio
bueno	inteligente	simpático
cariñoso (*affectionate*)	interesante	tolerante
comprensivo (*understanding*)	malo	travieso (*mischievous*)
difícil (*difficult*)	nuevo	viejo

Grammar Tutorial 6
■ connect®
|SPANISH
www.connectspanish.com

6 Expressing *to be*

Present Tense of *ser;* Summary of Uses (Part 2)

Gramática en acción: Presentaciones

Lea lo que dice Francisco y luego complete su descripción de su esposa.

— Hola. Me llamo Francisco Durán Ferrer, pero todos me llaman Pancho.

- Soy profesor de la universidad.
- Soy alto y moreno.
- Soy de Guanajuato, México.

—¿Y Lola Benítez Velasco, mi esposa?

- Es _____ (profesión).
- Es _____ y _____ (descripción).
- Es de _____ (origen).

> **Vocabulario útil**
>
> guapa, pesimista, muy inteligente
> Jalisco (un estado de México)
> médica en el Hospital Central, profesora también

ser (to be)			
(yo)	soy	(nosotros/as)	somos
(tú)	eres	(vosotros/as)	sois
(Ud.)		(Uds.)	
(él)	es	(ellos)	son
(ella)		(ellas)	

As you know, two Spanish verbs mean *to be:* **ser** and **estar.** They are not interchangeable; the meaning the speaker wants to convey determines their use. Here, you will review the uses of **ser** that you already know and learn some new ones. Remember to use **estar** to express location and to ask how someone is feeling. You will learn more about **estar** in **Gramática 15–16 (Cap. 6).**

Some basic uses of **ser** are presented on the following pages. You have used or seen all of them already in this and previous chapters.

Introductions *Read what Francisco says and then complete his description of his wife. Hello! My name is Francisco Durán Ferrer, but everyone calls me Pancho.* ■ *I'm a university professor.* ■ *I'm tall and brunet.* ■ *I'm from Guanajuato, Mexico. And Lola Benítez, Velasco, my wife?* ■ *She's _____.* ■ *She's _____ and _____.* ■ *She's from _____.*

Identification / La identificación

To *identify* people (including their profession) and things

> **¡OJO!**
> Note that the indefinite article is not used after **ser** before unmodified (undescribed) nouns of profession: **Carmen es profesora.** *but* **Carmen es una buena profesora.**

Yo **soy estudiante.**
Alicia y yo **somos hermanas.**
La doctora Ramos **es profesora.**
Esto **es un libro.**

Description / La descripción

To *describe* people and things*

Soy sentimental.
I'm sentimental (a sentimental person).

El coche **es muy viejo.**
The car is very old.

Origin / El origen

With **de,** to express *origin*

Somos de Chile, pero nuestros padres **son de la Argentina. ¿De dónde es** Ud.?
We're from Chile, but our parents are from Argentina. Where are you from?

Generalizations / Las generalizaciones

To express *generalizations* (with **es** + *adjective*)

> **¡OJO!**
> Note that **es** + *adjective* is followed by an infinitive in this context, just like in English.

Es necesario estudiar. Por eso no **es posible** mirar la televisión todos los días.
It's necessary to study. For that reason (That's why) it's not possible to watch television every day.

Here are two basic functions of **ser** that you have not yet practiced.

Possession / Las posesiones

With **de,** to express *possession,* to whom something belongs.

> **¡OJO!**
> Note that there is no **'s** in Spanish.

—Este **es** el perro **de Carla.** ¿De quién son las gatas?
—**Son** las gatas **de Jorge.**
"This is Carla's dog. Whose are those (fem.) cats?"
"They're Jorge's cats."

The masculine singular article **el** contracts with **de** to form **del.** (No other article contracts with **de.**)

Esta **es** la casa **del** abuelo.
Esta **es** la casa **de la** abuela.

Use **¿de quién es... ?** to ask to whom something belongs.

—**¿De quién es** esta casa?
—**Es del** abuelo.
"Whose house is this?"
"It's grandfather's."

> **¡OJO!**
> The subject pronoun **él** never contracts with **de: Es la casa de él.**

Destination / El destino

With **para,** to tell for whom or what something *is intended*

¿Romeo y Julieta? **Es para** la clase de inglés.
Romeo and Juliet? It's for English class.

—**¿Para** quién son los regalos?
¿Para mi nieto?
"Who are the presents for?" For my grandson?"

---

*You practiced this use of **ser** in **Gramática 5** in this chapter.

Práctica y comunicación

A. Así es mi familia (*That's what my family is like*)

Paso 1. Autoprueba. Complete las frases con las formas apropiadas del verbo **ser**.

1. yo _____
2. tú _____
3. Ud. _____
4. Pedro _____
5. tú y yo _____
6. Pedro y Alicia _____
7. Ud. y sus (*your*) amigos _____
8. tú y tus amigos _____

Paso 2. Complete las siguientes oraciones con formas del verbo **ser** y el adjetivo o frase apropiados.

1. Yo _____ miembro de una familia grande / pequeña.
2. Mi familia _____ de origen (*f.*) _____ (adjetivo de nacionaliad).
3. Mi familia más cercana (*closest*) y yo _____ del estado / país de(l) _____.
4. Otros parientes de mi familia _____ de _____ (estado o país).
5. Mi abuelo paterno / materno / abuela paterno / materna _____ de_____ (estado o país).
6. En mi familia, (no) _____ normal celebrar fiestas familiares / bailar en las fiestas familiares / estar en contacto con frecuencia...

Paso 3. Ahora use formas del verbo **ser** y las ideas del **Paso 2** para entrevistar (*interview*) a un compañero o una compañera.

1. ¿_____ miembro de una familia grande o pequeña?
2. ¿De qué nacionalidad _____ tu familia?
3. ¿De qué estado o país _____ tu familia y tú?
4. ¿De dónde _____ otros de tus parientes?
5. ¿De dónde _____ tu abuelo paterno/materno / tu abuela paterna/materna?
6. En tu familia, ¿_____ normal _____?

B. Nacionalidades

Paso 1. ¿De dónde son, según los nombres, apellidos y ciudades?

MODELO: João Gonçalves, Lisboa → João Gonçalves **es de** Portugal.

1. John Doe, Nueva York
2. Karl Lotze, Berlín
3. Graziana Lazzarino, Roma
4. Mongkut, Bangkok
5. María Gómez, San Salvador
6. Claudette Moreau, París
7. Timothy Windsor, Londres
8. Hai Chow, Beijing

Paso 2. Ahora, dé su (*your*) información personal. ¿De dónde es Ud.? ¿De este estado / una metrópoli / un área rural? ¿Es de otro país?

C. Personas extranjeras

Paso 1. ¿Quiénes son, de dónde son y dónde trabajan ahora?

MODELO: **Teresa:** actriz / de Madrid / en Cleveland →
Teresa **es** actriz. **Es** de Madrid. **Ahora trabaja** en Cleveland.

1. **Carlos Miguel:** médico / de Cuba / en Milwaukee
2. **Pilar:** profesora / de Barcelona / en Miami
3. **Mariela:** dependienta / de Buenos Aires / en Nueva York
4. **Juan:** dentista* / de Lima / en Los Ángeles

Paso 2. Ahora hable sobre (*talk about*) un amigo o pariente, según el modelo del **Paso 1**.

---

*A number of professions end in **-ista** in both masculine and feminine forms. The article indicates gender: **el/la dentista**, **el/la artista**, and so on.

Prác. A, Paso 1: Answers: 1. soy 2. eres 3. es 4. es 5. somos 6. son 7. son 8. sois/son

D. ¿De quién es? Las siguientes cosas (*things*), ¿son de la rica actriz Jennifer Sánchez o de Martín Osborne, el estudiante (pobre, naturalmente)? En parejas, hagan y contesten preguntas. Las respuestas pueden (*can*) variar.

MODELO: la mochila →
    E1: ¿De quién es la mochila?
    E2: Es la mochila **del** estudiante. (La mochila es **del** estudiante.)

Estrategia

Use **son** with plural items:
¿De quién son los... ? Son...

1. la casa grande
2. la computadora
3. la limosina
4. los libros de texto
5. el Óscar
6. los exámenes
7. los ex esposos
8. el teléfono celular
9. los mensajes

E. ¡Somos como una familia!

Paso 1. Complete el párrafo con las formas correctas de **ser** o con **hay**.

M e llamo Antonia y _____[1] de Chicago. (Yo) _____[2] estudiante de ingeniería en la Universidad de Illinois. En mis clases _____[3] estudiantes de todas partes[a] y muchos de ellos _____[4] hispanos. Mi familia _____[5] de origen mexicano y aunque nunca he vivido[b] en México, hablo bastante bien[c] el español. Me gusta hablar español con mi amigo Javier. Javier _____[6] de Costa Rica y estudia ingeniería también. Javier y yo _____[7] los asistentes del profesor Thomas; por eso pasamos mucho tiempo juntos.[d] Javier _____[8] muy guapo y simpático, pero nosotros solo _____[9] buenos amigos. Javier _____[10] el novio[e] de mi mejor[f] amiga.

[a]*places* [b]*aunque... although I have never lived* [c]*bastante... rather well* [d]*pasamos... we spend a lot of time together* [e]*boyfriend* [f]*best*

Paso 2. Comprensión. ¿Cierto o falso? Corrija las oraciones falsas.

	CIERTO	FALSO
1. Antonia es una persona muy sociable.	☐	☐
2. Es de México.	☐	☐
3. Antonia y Javier son novios.	☐	☐

Nota **comunicativa**

Cómo dar° explicaciones: Porque y para + *infinitive*   *to give*

porque *because*

—¿Por qué trabajas tanto?
—¡**Porque** necesitamos dinero!

"Why do you work so much?"
"Because we need money!"

para + *inf.* *in order to* (*do something*)

—¿Por qué necesitamos una televisión nueva?
—Pues... **para** mirar el partido de fútbol...
  ¡Es la Copa Mundial!

"Why do we need a new TV set?"
"Well ... (in order) to watch the soccer game ... It's the World Cup!"

¡OJO!

Note: **porque** (one word, no accent) versus the interrogative **¿por qué?** (two words, accent on **qué**), meaning *why?*

You will practice using these words in **Práctica F.**

F. El regalo ideal

Paso 1. Look at Diego's list of gifts and what his family members like. With a partner, decide who receives each gift and why. A sample item is done for you.

MODELO: la camiseta (*t-shirt*) de la selección (*team*) nacional de México →
    E1: **¿Para quién** es la camiseta de la selección nacional de México?
    E2: **Es para** la prima.
    E1: **¿Por qué?**
    E2: **Porque** le gusta (*she likes*) el fútbol.

LOS REGALOS DE DIEGO

1. _____ una calculadora grande
2. _____ unas entradas (*tickets*) para un concierto
3. _____ un teléfono celular
4. _____ la última (*latest*) novela de Isabel Allende
5. _____ una suscripción para un canal de fútbol
6. _____ dinero

LOS MIEMBROS DE LA FAMILIA DE DIEGO

a. el primo: Desea estudiar en el extranjero (*abroad*).
b. el padre: Le gusta mucho mirar el fútbol.
c. los abuelos: Les gusta mucho la música clásica.
d. el hermano: Estudia ingeniería y toma clases de matemáticas
e. la hermana pequeña: Tiene 11 años y no tiene teléfono propio (*of her own*).
f. la madre: Le gusta mucho leer (*to read*).

Paso 2. With a partner, exchange ideas about good gifts for members of your family and also about good gifts for you.

MODELO: Para mi mamá, deseo comprar ropa, porque ella necesita ropa nueva. Yo necesito ropa nueva también.

G. ¿Qué opina Ud.? Exprese opiniones originales, afirmativas o negativas, con estas palabras como base.

MODELO: En mi opinión, **es importante hablar español en la clase de español.**

(no) es importante	
(no) es muy práctico	
(no) es necesario	mirar la televisión todos los días
(no) es absurdo	hablar español en la clase
(no) es fascinante **+**	tener muchas mascotas
(no) es una lata (*pain, drag*)	llegar (*to arrive*) a clase puntualmente
(no) es posible	tomar café en el salón de clase

mirar la televisión todos los días
hablar español en la clase
tener muchas mascotas
llegar (*to arrive*) a clase puntualmente
tomar café en el salón de clase
hablar con los animales / las plantas
tomar mucho café y fumar cigarrillos
trabajar dieciocho horas al día
tener muchos hermanos
ser amable con todos los miembros de la familia
estar mucho tiempo (*a lot of time*) con la familia

Vocabulario útil

el coche
el radio
la ropa clothing

¿Recuerda Ud.?

You have already learned one way to express possession in Spanish: **de** + *noun*. Express these ideas in Spanish.

1. Juan's house
2. Jorge and Estela's grandfather
3. the man's niece
4. the student's book

You will learn another way to express possession in **Gramática 7.**

7 Expressing Possession

Unstressed Possessive Adjectives (Part 1)*

Gramática en acción: Invitación y posesión

los señores Ortega

los señores Gil

Juanita

Joaquín

A. «¡Pasen, por favor! Nuestra casa es su casa.»

B. «¡No son tus juguetes! ¡Son mis juguetes!»

Comprensión

En el dibujo A:
1. ¿De quién es la casa?
2. ¿Quiénes visitan la casa?

En el dibujo B:
3. ¿De quién son los juguetes?
4. ¿Quién desea jugar (*to play*) con los juguetes?

Possessive adjectives (**Los adjetivos posesivos**) are words that tell *to whom* or *to what* something belongs: *my* (book), *his* (sweater). You have already seen and used several possessive adjectives in Spanish. Here is the complete set.

Possessive Adjectives / Los adjetivos posesivos

my	mi hijo/hija	our	nuestro hijo	nuestra hija
	mis hijos/hijas		nuestros hijos	nuestras hijas
your (*fam.*)	tu hijo/hija	your (*fam.*)	vuestro hijo	vuestra hija
	tus hijos/hijas		vuestros hijos	vuestras hijas
your (*form.*), his, her, its	su hijo/hija / sus hijos/hijas	your (*form.*), their	su hijo / hija / sus hijos / hijas

a possessive adjective / **un adjetivo posesivo** = an adjective that expresses who owns or has something

1. Agreement with Person or Thing Possessed

In Spanish, the ending of a possessive adjective agrees in form with the person or thing owned, not with the owner or possessor. Note that these possessive adjectives are placed before the noun.

$$\text{Es} \begin{Bmatrix} \text{mi} \\ \text{tu} \\ \text{su} \end{Bmatrix} \text{hermano.} \quad \text{Son} \begin{Bmatrix} \text{mis} \\ \text{tus} \\ \text{sus} \end{Bmatrix} \text{hermanos.}$$

The possessive adjectives **mi(s)**, **tu(s)**, and **su(s)** show agreement in number only (as seen in the chart above). **Nuestro/a/os/as** and **vuestro/a/os/as**, like all adjectives that end in **-o**, show agreement in both number and gender.

$$\text{Es} \begin{Bmatrix} \text{nuestra} \\ \text{vuestra} \\ \text{su} \end{Bmatrix} \text{familia.} \quad \text{Son} \begin{Bmatrix} \text{nuestras} \\ \text{vuestras} \\ \text{sus} \end{Bmatrix} \text{familias.}$$

Invitation and Ownership A. "Come in, please! Our house is your house." ***B.*** "They're not your toys! They're my toys!"

Another kind of possessive is called the stressed possessive adjective. *It can be used as a noun. You will learn more about using stressed possessive adjectives in* **Capítulo 17.**

2. Su(s)

As you have seen, the word **su(s)** has several equivalents in English: *your* (sing.), *his, her, its, your* (pl.), and *their*. Usually its meaning is clear in context. When the meaning is not clear, the construction **de** + *pronoun* is used to indicate possession.

su **hijo** = **el** hijo **de**	Ud., Uds.
	él/ella
	ellos/ellas

sus **hijos** = **los** hijos **de**	Ud., Uds.
	él/ella
	ellos/ellas

3. Su(s) versus vuestro/a/os/as

The forms **vuestro/a/os/as** are the possessives that correspond to the subject pronoun **vosotros.** They are only used in Spain.

Latin America	Spain
Uds. ⟶ su, sus	vosotros ⟶ vuestro/a/os/as
	Uds. ⟶ su, sus

Práctica y comunicación

A. Las posesiones

Paso 1. Autoprueba. Complete la tabla con los posesivos apropiados. ¡OJO! Preste atención a (*Pay attention to*) las personas y los sustantivos. ¿Son masculinos o femeninos? ¿singulares o plurales? Siga (*Follow*) el modelo del número 1.

Personas	Adjetivos posesivos	Sustantivos
1. yo	mi	compañero de clase
2. nosotros = mi compañero/a y yo		computadoras
3. Ud.		mesa
4. los otros compañeros de clase		escritorios
5. tú		teléfono celular
6. Luisa		profesoras

Paso 2. Ahora indique los sustantivos posibles para cada (*each*) adjetivo posesivo según su forma.

1. su: problema primos dinero tías escritorios familia
2. tus: perro idea hijos profesoras abuelo examen
3. mi: ventana médicos cuarto coche abuela gatos
4. sus: animales oficina nietas padre hermana abuelo
5. nuestras: guitarra libros materias lápiz sobrinas tía
6. nuestros: gustos consejero parientes puertas clases residencia

Paso 3. Ahora, en parejas, indiquen tres sustantivos para cada uno de los siguientes adjetivos posesivos.

MODELO: tu ⟶ **computadora, tía, perro**

Adjetivos posesivos (personas)	Tres sustantivos
1. mis	
2. su (de los compañeros de clase)	
3. sus (del profesor / de la profesora)	
4. nuestras (de nosotros dos)	

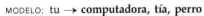

Summary of possessive Adjectives

mi(s) nuestro/a(s)
tu(s) vuestro/a(s)
su(s)

B. ¿Cuáles son sus hijos? Empareje (*Match*) las fotos de padres e hijos.

LOS PADRES

LOS HIJOS

1. Su hija es _____.

a. David

2. Sus hijos son _____.

b. Sara

3. Sus hijas son _____.

c. Maribel y Julia

4. Su hijo es _____.

d. Joaquín y Rosa

C. David y su familia

David

Paso 1. Describa a la familia de David.

MODELO: familia / pequeño →
    Su familia **es** pequeña.

1. hijo / guapo
2. perro / feo
3. hija / rubio
4. padre / viejito
5. esposa / bonito

Estrategia

You must provide a possessive adjective for the noun, then a verb, as in the model. Then be sure that the adjective agrees with the noun!

Paso 2. Ahora imagine que Ud. es David y modifique (*change*) las respuestas (*answers*).

MODELO: familia / pequeño →
    Mi familia es pequeña.

Paso 3. Ahora imagine que Ud. es la esposa de David. Hable por (*Speak for*) Ud. y por su esposo. Modifique solo las respuestas del 1 al 3.

MODELO: familia / pequeño →
    Nuestra familia es pequeña.

D. ¿Sí o no? Are the following things or people in your classroom right now? In these items, **su(s)** = *your* (**de Ud.**).

MODELOS: ¿su libro? → Sí, **mi** libro está en mi mochila. (No, **mi** libro está en casa.)
        ¿los amigos de Uds.? → No, **nuestros** amigos no están en el salón de clase. Están en la cafetería.

Estrategia

Remember to use forms of **estar** to express location.

1. ¿su computadora portátil?
2. ¿los libros de Uds.?
3. ¿el profesor / la profesora de Uds.?
4. ¿la computadora del profesor / de la profesora de Uds.?
5. ¿los teléfonos celulares de Uds.?
6. ¿su silla?
7. ¿sus padres? / ¿su esposo/a?
8. ¿la mochila de otro estudiante?
9. ¿su dinero? (la cartera = *wallet*)

E. Intercambios

Paso 1. With a partner, take turns asking and answering questions about your families. Talk about what family members are like, their ages, some things they do, and so on. Use the model as a guide. Take notes on what your partner says.

MODELO: tu abuela →
>E1: Mi abuela es alta. ¿Y tu abuela? ¿Es alta?
>E2: Bueno, no. Mi abuela es baja.
>E1: ¿Cuántos años tiene?...

1. tu familia en general
2. tus padres
3. tus abuelos
4. tus hermanos/hijos
5. tu esposo/a / compañero/a de cuarto/casa

Paso 2. Tell the class one thing that you and your partner have in common.

MODELO: Nuestras abuelas tienen 75 años.

¿Recuerda Ud.?

The personal endings used with **-ar** verbs share some characteristics with **-er** and **-ir** verbs, which you will learn in **Gramática 8**. Review the present tense endings of **-ar** verbs by telling which subject pronoun(s) you associate with each of these endings.

1. -amos   **2.** -as   **3.** -áis   **4.** -an   **5.** -o   **6.** -a

---

8 Expressing Actions
Present Tense of -er and -ir Verbs; Subject Pronouns (Part 2)

Grammar Tutorial 8
connect
|SPANISH
www.connectspanish.com

Gramática en acción: Un estudiante típico

- Se llama Samuel Flores Toledo.
- Estudia en la UNAM (Universidad Nacional Autónoma de México).
- Vive con su familia en la Ciudad de México, el D.F. (Distrito Federal).
- Come pizza y tacos con frecuencia.
- Bebe café por la mañana.
- Recibe muchos e-mails de sus primos del Canadá.
- Lee y escribe mucho para su especialización.
- Aprende inglés porque desea visitar a su familia en Ontario.

¿Y Ud.? Complete las oraciones con formas verbales que terminan en **-o** (= **yo**) y con información personal.

1. Yo (no) vivo con mi familia.
2. (No) Com_____ muchos tacos.
3. Recib_____ muchos e-mails de _____.
4. Le_____ y escrib_____ mucho para mi clase de _____.
5. Aprend_____ español en esta clase.

Samuel Flores Toledo

A typical student ■ *His name is Samuel Flores Toledo.* ■ *He studies at UNAM (the National Autonomous University of Mexico).* ■ *He lives with his family in Mexico City,* **el D.F.** *(Federal District).* ■ *He frequently eats pizza and tacos.* ■ *He drinks coffee in the morning.* ■ *He gets a lot of e-mails from his cousins in Canada.* ■ *He reads and writes a lot for his major.* ■ *He's learning English because he wants to visit his family in Ontario.*

1. Present Tense Endings

The present tense of **-er** and **-ir** verbs is formed by adding personal endings to the stem of the verb (the infinitive minus its **-er/-ir** ending). The personal endings for **-er** and **-ir** verbs are the same except for the first and second person plural.

¡OJO!

Only the endings for **nosotros** and **vosotros** are different for **-er** and **-ir** verbs.

Las terminaciones **-er/-ir** del tiempo presente			
-er		**-ir**	
-o	-emos	-o	-imos
-es	-éis	-es	-ís
-e	-en	-e	-en

comer (*to eat*)				**vivir** (*to live*)			
(yo)	**com**o	(nosotros/as)	**com**emos	(yo)	**viv**o	(nosotros/as)	**viv**imos
(tú)	**com**es	(vosotros/as)	**com**éis	(tú)	**viv**es	(vosotros/as)	**viv**ís
(Ud.) (él) (ella)	**com**e	(Uds.) (ellos) (ellas)	**com**en	(Ud.) (él) (ella)	**viv**e	(Uds.) (ellos) (ellas)	**viv**en

2. Important *-er/-ir* Verbs

These are the frequently used **-er** and **-ir** verbs you will find in this chapter.

comer

beber

leer

escribir

-er verbs		**-ir** verbs	
aprender	to learn	**abrir**	to open
aprender +**a** + *inf.*	to learn how to (*do something*)	**asistir (a)**	to attend, go to (*a class, a function*)
beber	to drink		
comer	to eat	**escribir**	to write
comprender	to understand	**recibir**	to receive
creer (en)	to think; to believe (in)	**vivir**	to live
deber + *inf.*	should, must, ought to (*do something*)		
leer	to read		
vender	to sell		

- **Deber,** like **desear** and **necesitar,** is followed by an infinitive.

- **Aprender** + **a** +*infinitive* means *to learn how to (do something).*

Debes leer tus e-mails todos los días.
You should read your e-mails on a daily basis.

Muchos niños **aprenden a hablar** español con sus abuelos.
Many children learn to speak Spanish with their grandparents.

3. English Equivalents of the Present Tense

Remember that the Spanish present tense has a number of present tense equivalents in English. It can also be used to express future meaning.

como = *I eat, I am eating, I will eat*

Uses of Subject Pronouns / Los usos de los pronombres personales

In English, a verb must have an expressed subject (a noun or pronoun): *the train arrives*, *she says*. In Spanish, however, as you have probably noticed, an expressed subject is not required. Verbs are accompanied by a subject pronoun only for clarification, emphasis, or contrast.

- *Clarification:* When the context does not make the subject clear, the subject pronoun is expressed. This happens most frequently with third person singular and plural verb forms.

Unclear: Escribe cartas. Nunca **escribe** cartas. →
Ella escribe cartas. **Él** nunca escribe cartas.
She writes letters. He never writes letters.

- *Emphasis:* Subject pronouns are used in Spanish to emphasize the subject when in English you would stress it with your voice.

—¿Quién debe pagar?   *"Who should pay?"*
—¡**Tú** debes pagar!   *"**You** should pay!"*

- *Contrast:* Contrast is a special case of emphasis. Subject pronouns are used to contrast the actions of two individuals or groups.

Ellos leen mucho; **nosotros** leemos poco.
They *read a lot;* ***we*** *read little.*

¡OJO!

Avoid using subject pronouns in Spanish when they are not necessary. The overuse of subject pronouns sounds overbearing to native speakers of Spanish.

Unnecessary: Yo soy de Tampa. **Yo** soy estudiante universitario. **Yo** vivo con mi familia.

Natural: (Yo) Soy de Tampa. Soy estudiante universitario. Vivo con mi familia.

Práctica y comunicación

A. Asociaciones. Empareje las ideas y cosas (*things*) con el verbo más lógico. Luego (*Then*) dé otras ideas para cada (*each*) verbo.

MODELO: 1. abrir → e: abrir **una puerta** También: abrir **una ventana**...

Summary of -er/-ir Verb Endings	
(yo) **-o**	(nosotros/as) **–emos / -imos**
(tú) **-es**	(vosotros/as) **-éis / -ís**
(Uds., el/ella) **-e**	(Uds., ellos/as) **-en**

VERBOS		IDEAS Y COSAS	
1. abrir	**6.** deber	**a.** una revista (*magazine*)	**e.** una puerta
2. aprender	**7.** escribir	**b.** una com-posición	**f.** un concierto
3. asistir a	**8.** leer	**c.** un té	**g.** tacos
4. beber	**9.** vivir	**d.** las materias	**h.** estudiar más
5. comer			**i.** en un apar-tamento

Algo sobre...

la comida[a] de México

El maíz[b] es el producto esencial en la comida de los mexicanos y otros pueblos[c] americanos desde[d] 1500 a. C. (mil quinientos antes de Cristo). Es la base para las tortillas y los tamales. El tamal consiste en masa[e] de maíz con otros ingredientes, envuelta[f] y cocida[g] en hojas[h] de maíz (u* hojas de otras plantas, como el plátano[i]).

 En su opinión, ¿qué ingrediente(s) son esenciales en la comida de su país de origen?

[a]*food* [b]*corn* [c]*peoples* [d]*since* [e]*dough* [f]*wrapped* [g]*steamed* [h]*leaves* [i]*plantain*

Un delicioso tamal mexicano

Notice that the word **o becomes **u** before a word that starts with the sound **o**: inglés **u** otra materia, pesimista **u** optimista. In Algo sobre... above, the word **hoja** starts with the sound **o**, since the letter **h** is silent in Spanish.*

Paso 1. Autoprueba. Complete los verbos con las terminaciones apropiadas.

1. yo: com_____ , viv_____
2. tú: aprend_____ , escrib_____
3. él: cre_____ , abr_____
4. nosotros: le_____ , asist_____
5. Uds.: comprend_____ , recib_____

Paso 2. Ahora use las siguientes ideas para expresar acciones que Ud. hace (*do*) o no hace en la clase de español.

MODELO: comer en clase —→ **Como** en clase. (No **como** en clase.)

1. escribir respuestas en el libro de texto
2. aprender palabras nuevas
3. asistir a clase todos los días
4. beber café en clase
5. comprender las instrucciones para las actividades
6. abrir regalos

Paso 3. Ahora, en parejas, túrnense para hacer y contestar preguntas basadas en el **Paso 2.** Luego (*Then*) digan (*tell*) a la clase algo (*something*) que Uds. tienen en común.

MODELO: escribir respuestas en el libro texto —→
    E1: ¿Escribes respuestas en el libro de texto?
    E2: No, no escribo respuestas en el libro de texto.
    E2: Yo tampoco. (*Me neither.*) (Yo sí.)
EN COMÚN: Nosotros/as dos (no) escribimos respuestas en el libro de texto.

C. Diego habla de su padre. Complete el siguiente párrafo con la forma correcta de los verbos entre paréntesis.

M i padre (vender[1]) coches y trabaja mucho. Mis hermanos y yo (aprender[2]) mucho de papá. Según mi padre, los jóvenes (deber[3]) (asistir[4]) a clase todos los días, porque es su obligación. Papá también (creer[5]) que no es necesario mirar la televisión por la noche. Es más interesante (leer[6]) el periódico,[a] una revista o un buen libro. Por eso (*nosotros:* leer[7]) o (escribir[8]) por la noche y no miramos la televisión. Yo admiro a mi papá y (creer[9]) que él (comprender[10]) la importancia de la educación.

[a]*newspaper*

Comprensión. ¿Cierto o falso? Corrija las oraciones falsas.

	CIERTO	FALSO
1. Diego y sus hermanos venden coches.	☐	☐
2. Diego mira mucho la televisión.	☐	☐
3. El padre de Diego lee mucho.	☐	☐

Una escena típica de una tamalada

D. Este domingo, tamalada

Paso 1. Una tamalada consiste en hacer (*making*) y comer tamales. Hay familias que hacen una tamalada en ocasiones especiales.

Complete las siguientes oraciones con la forma apropiada de un verbo de **Vocabulario útil**. El número 2 entre paréntesis indica que Ud. debe usar el verbo dos veces (*twice*) en las oraciones.

¡OJO!

Hay verbos de todos tipos en la lista: **-ar, -er, -ir,** irregular.

Vocabulario útil

aprender, asistir, beber, celebrar, comprender, creer, deber, leer (2), mirar, preparar, ser (2), vivir

1. Hoy todos nosotros _____[1] el cumpleaños (*birthday*) de mi abuela y, como es domingo, hay una tamalada.
2. Toda la familia _____[2] a la tamalada en nuestra casa.
3. Mis padres y mis tíos _____[3] los tamales, con la ayuda (*help*) de las mujeres de la familia.
4. Después de comer (*After eating*), los adultos _____[4] café.
5. Muchos _____[5] la tele y mi padre _____[6] el periódico.
6. Yo _____[7] un libro a los niños pequeños. Mi prima Lucy _____[8] descansar (*rest*) porque solo tiene 2 años.
7. Mi primo Rudy, que (*who*) _____[9] en Oklahoma, no _____[10] todo porque su español no _____[11] perfecto. Pero _____[12] rápido.
8. Yo _____[13] que todos en mi familia _____[14] cocineros (*cooks*) excelentes.

Paso 2. Comprensión. Complete las oraciones con información del **Paso 1.**

1. _____ es un ejemplo de una fiesta familiar.
2. Esta familia celebra _____ de la abuela.
3. _____ preparan los tamales; _____ ayudan (*help*).
4. Después de comer, unos _____ y _____.
5. La persona que narra la historia (*story*) _____.
6. Rudy no _____ bien el español.

Nota **comunicativa**

Cómo expresar la frecuencia de las acciones

AT THE BEGINNING OR END OF A SENTENCE		AT THE BEGINNING OF A SENTENCE	
a veces	sometimes, at times	**casi nunca**	almost never
con frecuencia	frequently	**nunca**	never
siempre	always		
todos los días	every day		
una vez a la semana	once a week		

Hablo con mis amigos **todos los días.** Hablo con mis padres **una vez a la semana. Casi nunca** hablo con mis abuelos. Y **nunca** hablo con mis tíos que viven en Italia.

You will use these expressions in **Práctica E.**

Algo sobre...

una gran ciudad mexicana

Más de[a] 21 millones de personas viven en el área metropolitana de la Ciudad de México, o el Distrito Federal. Los mexicanos lo llaman[b] simplemente el D.F.

México, D.F.

 ¿Cuántos habitantes hay en su ciudad?

[a]Más... *More than* [b]lo... *call it*

E. ¿Con qué frecuencia?

Paso 1. Indique con oraciones completas la frecuencia con que Ud. hace (*do*) las siguientes actividades.

EXPRESIONES DE FRECUENCIA:

todos los días   con frecuencia   a veces   casi nunca   nunca

MODELO: 1. recibir un e-mail de **sus** padres/abuelos →
Todos los días recibo e-mails de **mis** abuelos. / **Nunca recibo** un e-mail de **mis** abuelos.

1. recibir un e-mail de sus padres/abuelos
2. escribir en su Facebook
3. usar la computadora en una clase
4. comer pizza
5. leer revistas
6. beber café
7. comprar cosas por (*on the*) internet
8. vender sus libros al final del semestre/trimestre

 Paso 2. Ahora compare sus oraciones con las (*those*) de dos compañeros/as. Luego (*Then*) digan (*tell*) a la clase algo (*something*) que Uds. tienen en común.

MODELO: 1. recibir un e-mail de **sus** padres/abuelos →
EN COMÚN: Todos los días los/las tres recibimos un e-mail de **nuestros** abuelos. (Nunca recibimos un e-mail de **nuestros** abuelos.)

F. Intercambios. Use las siguientes frases para entrevistar a un compañero o una compañera. Use expresiones de frecuencia cuando sea (*it is*) apropiado. Luego (*Then*) digan (*tell*) a la clase algo (*something*) que Uds. tienen en común.

MODELO: leer + novelas de horror
→ Carmen, ¿lees novelas de horror a veces?
EN COMÚN: Los/Las dos leemos novelas de horror a veces. (Nunca leemos novelas de horror.)

(nombre de estudiante), tú
tus padres/hijos
tus abuelos
tu mejor (*best*) amigo/a

+

abrir
beber
comprender
escribir
leer
recibir
vender
vivir
¿ ?

+

mucho / poco

la situación / los problemas de los estudiantes
Coca-Cola/café antes de (*before*) la clase
tu ropa (*clothing*), un estéreo viejo
la puerta a (*for*) las mujeres / los hombres

novelas de ciencia ficción / de horror
el periódico / una revista todos los días
muchas/pocas cartas, novelas, revistas
muchos/pocos ejercicios, libros, regalos

en una casa / un apartamento / una residencia
en otra ciudad / en otro estado/país
en un cuaderno / con un bolígrafo/lápiz

+ deber

+ mirar mucho la televisión
llegar a casa temprano

Un poco de todo

A. Lengua y cultura: Las familias

Paso 1. Complete the following paragraphs about families. Give the correct form of the words in parentheses, as suggested by context.

¿Existe la familia hispana típica? La idea de que las familias hispanas son muy (grande[1]) es un estereotipo del pasado,[a] especialmente en las (grande[2]) ciudades. Ahora, la norma (ser[3]) una familia con dos o tres hijos. Es difícil tener (mucho[4]) hijos cuando el padre y la madre (trabajar[5]) fuera de la casa,[b] y cuando los abuelos o tías no (vivir[6]) en casa para cuidar[c] a los niños.

A pesar de[d] la reducción en el número de hijos, los hispanos (creer[7]) que la familia es su institución (principal[8]). Muchos hispanos mantienen[e] relaciones con parientes que (estar[9]) en otro país y muchos les mandan[f] dinero y regalos para ayudarlos.[g] En las reuniones (familiar[10]) también es frecuente incluir a parientes de (vario[11]) generaciones.

En su opinión, ¿hay (mucho[12]) diferencias entre su familia y las familias hispanas que conoce[h]?

Una familia mexicana que celebra un día especial

[a]*past* [b]fuera... *outside the home* [c]cuidar... *care for* [d]A... *In spite of* [e]*keep up, maintain* [f]les... *send to them* [g]*help them* [h]*you know*

Paso 2. Comprensión. ¿Cierto o falso? Corrija (*Correct*) las oraciones falsas.

	CIERTO	FALSO
1. Todas las familias hispanas son grandes.	☐	☐
2. Por lo general (*Generally*), las familias urbanas son pequeñas.	☐	☐
3. Para los hispanos, la familia es una institución social fundamental.	☐	☐

Paso 3. Ahora, en parejas, contesten la pregunta del final de **Lengua y cultura:** «¿Hay muchas diferencias entre su familia y las familias hispanas que conoce?» Deben escribir 3–4 oraciones para expresar su opinión. Usen las oraciones de **Lengua y cultura** como modelo y hagan los cambios (*changes*) necesarios. **¡OJO!** No es necesario usar todo el texto original.

MODELOS: En **nuestra** opinión (no) hay muchas diferencias entre **nuestras** familias y las familias hispanas.
No estamos de acuerdo. Yo creo que... pero mi compañera cree...
En la familia típica estadounidense/mexicana, hay...

B. Una fiesta. There is a Spanish saying, **«Una fiesta se hace** (*is made*) **con tres personas: una canta, otra baila y la otra toca.»** Working in groups of four, use this saying as a model to tell what the following things are "made of."

MODELO: una clase ⟶ Una clase se hace con un profesor o una profesora. Esta persona enseña la clase. También hay unos estudiantes. Desean aprender la materia y estudian mucho. Leen su libro de texto y escriben informes (*papers*). También hay un salón de clase, un pizarrón...

¿Cómo se hace... ?

1. una clase de español
2. una fiesta en esta universidad
3. una universidad
4. una familia

Estrategia

Use...

• all of the **-ar/-er/-ir** verbs that you know
• the irregular verbs **ser** and **estar**
• forms of **tener: tengo, tienes, tiene**
• the verb form **hay**

En **su** comunidad

Entreviste a (*Interview*) una persona hispana de su universidad o ciudad sobre (*about*) su familia.

PREGUNTAS POSIBLES

• ¿Tiene esta persona una familia grande o pequeña? ¿Cuáles son los miembros de la familia?

• ¿Cuál es el país de origen de los abuelos de la persona? ¿Viven solos (*alone*) o con un pariente?

• ¿Los parientes se reúnen (*get together*) con frecuencia? ¿En qué ocasiones?

«Padres modernos» Segmento 2

Antes de mirar°   Antes... *Before watching*

Conteste las siguientes preguntas.

1. ¿De dónde es su familia?
2. ¿Tiene parientes en ese (*that*) país?
3. ¿Cree que su familia es muy unida (*close*)?

Este segmento

Laura entrevista (*interviews*) a los miembros de una familia mexicana que vive en Los Ángeles.

Las hermanas Minerva (de blanco [*in white*]) y Araceli Rubio, con sus hijos. Todos extrañan (*miss*) a los parientes que están en México.

Vocabulario **del segmento**

único/a	unique; only
una vida mejor	a better life
mil novecientos noventa y nueve	1999
mayor	oldest
estar solo/a	to be alone
han crecido juntos	they've grown up together
dejar atrás	to leave behind

Fragmento del guion°   *script*

El año pasado hubo[a] una celebración especial en México. Una sobrina de Minerva y Araceli cumplió 15 años.[b] Mine fue[c] a México para estar en la celebración de la quinceañera[d] de su prima. Fue[e] una buena oportunidad de estar cerca del[f] resto de su familia y ver[g] a todos los parientes: abuelos, tíos, primos. ¡Fue una fiesta fantástica!

[a]El... *Last year there was* [b]cumplió... *turned 15* [c]*went* [d]*fifteenth birthday* [e]*It was* [f]cerca... *close to the* [g]*to see*

Después de mirar°   Después... *After watching*

A. ¿Está claro? ¿Cierto o falso? Corrija las oraciones falsas según el video.

	CIERTO	FALSO
1. Minerva tiene dos hijas.	☐	☐
2. Las hijas de Minerva viven en California.	☐	☐
3. Araceli tiene 3 hijos.	☐	☐
4. Los hijos de Araceli y de Minerva no son unidos.	☐	☐

B. Un poco más. Conteste las siguientes preguntas.

1. ¿Qué miembros de esta familia viven en los Estados Unidos?
2. ¿Qué celebración importante para la familia de Minerva y Araceli hubo en México?

C. Y ahora, Uds. En grupos, hablen de (*talk about*) la familia. ¿Es importante la familia extendida en su caso? ¿Qué parientes incluye? ¿Incluye a parientes que viven en otro país? ¿Cómo es su familia? ¿Es tradicional? ¿patriarcal? ¿matriarcal?

A LEER°

Antes de leer

¿Es normal para los jóvenes estadounidenses vivir con su familia cuando tienen 20 años o más? Si Ud. vive con su familia, ¿le gusta? ¿Le gusta vivir cerca de (*close to*) su familia?

Lectura cultural: México

La institución de la familia en México

or tradición,[a] las familias en México son muy unidas. Esto tiene ventajas[b] para los niños y adolescentes: tienen el apoyo[c] de sus padres, hermanos y parientes cercanos.[d] Pero hay personas que creen que esta unión familiar presenta problemas. Cuando los jóvenes viven con sus padres hasta que[e] son adultos, pueden perder[f] parte de su identidad individual. Muchos jóvenes viven con su familia hasta que contraen matrimonio.[g] Y si no contraen matrimonio, siempre viven en casa de sus padres.

Aquí hay unas cifras para pensar.[h]

- El 90,5% (noventa coma cinco por ciento) de los hogares[i] mexicanos es de tipo familiar, es decir,[j] entre[k] las personas que los forman[l] existe una relación familiar.
- El 18,5% de los hogares familiares es monoparental. Las mujeres son responsables de su familia[m] en el 84% de los hogares monoparentales.
- México, D.F. tiene la mayor[n] proporción de hogares monoparentales en el país: el 24,3%.

[a]Por... *Traditionally* [b]*advantages* [c]*support* [d]*close* [e]hasta... *until* [f]pueden... *they can lose* [g]hasta... *until they marry* [h]cifras... *numbers to think about* [i]*homes* [j]es... *that is* [k]*among* [l]los... *make them up* [m]responsables... *the heads of the household* [n]*greatest*

La Pirámide del Sol (*Sun*) en la antigua ciudad de Teotihuacán, cerca de (*close to*) la Ciudad de México. Tiene 63,5 metros de altura (*height*).

Un símbolo mexicano: Los centros arqueológicos

Hay muchos por todo el país, pero los más importantes son las ruinas mayas de Chichén Itzá (cerca de[a] Cancún), el complejo[b] de Teotihuacán (cerca del D.F.) y las ruinas zapotecas (cerca de Oaxaca).

[a]cerca... *close to* [b]*building complex*

COMPRENSIÓN

¿Cierto o falso? Identifique la parte de los textos donde aparece la información.

	CIERTO	FALSO
1. La unidad de la familia mexicana tiene aspectos positivos para los hijos.	☐	☐
2. Para los jóvenes, vivir con la familia es siempre ideal.	☐	☐
3. La estructura familiar mexicana es única en el mundo hispanohablante.	☐	☐
4. En México hay ruinas de solo una cultura indígena.	☐	☐

En **otros** países hispanos

En todo el mundo hispanohablante Es impresionante cómo los hispanos de todos los países coinciden en cuanto a[a] la importancia de la familia. También es típico en todo el mundo hispano que los hijos se independicen tarde.

[a]en... *with regards to*

Y ahora, Uds.

- ¿Creen Uds. que la unión familiar es una ventaja o una desventaja?
- ¿Hay ejemplos de ruinas arqueológicas en su estado?

Del mundo hispano

Antes de leer°

Antes... *Before reading*

Match the sentences with the numbers given in **Números útiles**. If you don't know, guess! ¡OJO! In Spanish, decimals are marked with a comma: 3.4 = **3,4 (tres coma cuatro).**

Números útiles: 1,32; 1,65; 2; 2,06; 2,2; 3; 4; 5; 6; 8; 40

1. _____: número de semanas de un embarazo (*pregnancy*) normal
2. _____: número de bebés, si son mellizos o gemelos (*twins*)
3. _____: número de bebés, si son octillizos
4. _____: número de bebés, si son quintillizos
5. _____: número de bebés, si son trillizos
6. _____: número de libras (*pounds*) en 1 kilogramo
7. _____: promedio (*average number*) de hijos por mujer en Puerto Rico
8. _____: promedio de hijos por mujer en España
9. _____: promedio de hijos por mujer en los Estados Unidos

Lectura: Un parto° excepcional en la República Dominicana

birth

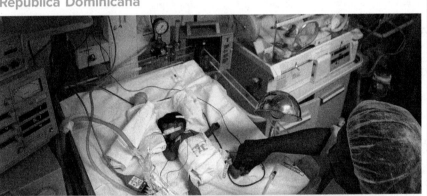

Uno de los sextillizos dominicanos
27 de diciembre, Hospital Plaza de la Salud, Santo Domingo, República Dominicana: Máxima Pérez y su esposo Emilio Figueroa son ahora los padres de sextillizos. Pérez se sometió aª un tratamiento de fertilidad y dio a luzᵇ mediante una cesárea. Los bebés nacieron trasᶜ 29 semanas de embarazo y pesaronᵈ entre 800 y 1.000 gramos. Es la primera vezᵉ que en el país se produce un parto de seis criaturas.

ªse... *went through* ᵇdio... *gave birth* ᶜnacieron... *were born after* ᵈ*they weighed* ᵉla... *the first time*

Comprensión

A. Resumen de la noticia (*Summary of the news item*).
Para resumir la información de la noticia, complete las oraciones con las palabras apropiadas.

esposo fertilidad padres República seis sextillizos

Noticias de la _____[1] Dominicana:

La Sra. Máxima Pérez y su _____,[2] el Sr. Emilio Figueroa, son ahora los _____[3] de _____[4] hijos, gracias a un tratamiento de _____.[5] No hay otro caso de _____[6] en la historia del país.

B. En el texto. Encuentre (*Find*) las siguientes ideas y palabras en la noticia.

1. *birth*
2. *babies* (2 *words*)
3. *through a C-section*
4. *fertility treatment*

La familia de Lucía Jiménez Flores

A... Let's listen

la escuela	school
la cuñada	sister-in-law
travieso/a	troublemaker
las mellizas	twins
juntas	together

Antes de escuchar

¿Tiene Ud. hermanos casados (*married*)? ¿Tiene buenas relaciones con sus cuñados (*in-laws*)? ¿Tiene padrinos (*godparents*) o es padrino o madrina de un niño?

Después de escuchar°

Después... After listening

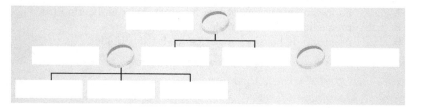

A. **El árbol genealógico de la familia.** Complete el árbol genealógico con los nombres de los miembros de la familia.

B. **¿Quién es quién?** Complete las oraciones.

1. La cuñada de Lucía se llama _____.
2. El cuñado de José se llama _____.
3. Lucía tiene tres _____.
4. La abuela de Camila tiene _____ años.
5. El nombre del padre de Lucía es _____.
6. La familia de Lucía es de _____ (ciudad).
7. En México, Lucía tiene muchos _____.

PRODUCCIÓN PERSONAL

¡Ahora, yo!

A. Use de (*as a*) modelo las preguntas y respuestas de la página 61 de este capítulo para hablar de su propia (*own*) familia.

B. Con las preguntas de la página 61 como modelo, filme una o dos entrevistas con personas que hablan de sus familias.

A ESCRIBIR

Un ensayo sobre° la familia

ensayo... *essay about*

¿Cómo es la familia «moderna» estadounidense? ¿Es diversa? ¿complicada? ¿Hay una familia estereotípica? ¿Qué une (*unites*) a los miembros de una familia?

Preparar

Paso 1. Use las siguientes preguntas para entrevistar a varios compañeros de clase. Sus respuestas le darán (*will give you*) información específica para defender sus ideas en su ensayo. Repase (*Review*) el vocabulario de **Más parientes** (pág. 63) antes de empezar.

- ¿Viven tus padres en el mismo domicilio (*same residence*)?
- ¿Cuántos hermanos tienes?
- ¿Tienes padrastro / madrastra / hermanastro/a(s) / hijastro/a(s) / medio/a(s) hermano/a(s) / ?
- ¿Viven tus abuelos en el mismo estado?
- ¿Cuál es el país de origen de tu familia?
- _____ (una pregunta propia [*of your own*])

Paso 2. Ahora use sus opiniones y las respuestas de sus compañeros para escribir un ensayo sobre la familia moderna. Hay más ayuda (*help*) en Connect.

Más ideas para su portafolio

- Busque (*Look for*) una fotografía de su familia y seleccione un adjetivo especial para cada persona de la foto.
- Escriba un breve poema sobre (*about*) una persona de su familia que es muy especial para Ud. Aquí está el modelo de la página 69.

Amigo	Amiga
Fiel	Fiel
Amable	Amable
Simpático	Simpática
¡Lo admiro!	¡La admiro!

- Dé tres palabras favoritas de este capítulo para Ud. ¿Por qué son interesantes para Ud.? ¿Con qué las asocia Ud. (*do you associate them*)?
- Si ha estado jugando (*have been playing*) Practice Spanish: Study Abroad, en Quest 2 Ud. conoció (*met*) a un fantasma (*ghost*) que se llama la Mancarita. Dibuje (*Draw*) a la Mancarita y luego escriba 4 oraciones describiéndola (*describing her*).

Sugerencia: You are now ready to play Quest 2 in **Practice Spanish: Study Abroad** (www.mhpractice.com).

EN RESUMEN En este capítulo

Visit **www.connectspanish.com** to practice the vocabulary and grammar points covered in this chapter.

AFTER STUDYING THIS CHAPTER I CAN . . .

☐ name family members (62–63)

☐ count from 31 to 100 (64)

☐ describe people, places, things, and ideas using adjectives and the verb **ser** (66, 69–71)

☐ also use **ser** to identify and to expres origin, generalizations, possession, and destination (75–77)

☐ use possessive adjectives to distinguish what's mine and what belongs to others (80–81)

☐ talk about more actions with **-er** and **-ir** verbs (83–85)

☐ avoid subject pronouns but use them to clarify or emphasize the subject (85)

☐ recognize/describe at least 2–3 aspects of Mexican cultures

Gramática en breve

5. Adjectives: Gender, Number, and Position

Adjective Endings

Singular	Plural
-o	-os
-a	-as
-e	-es
-[consonant]	-[consonant] + -es

6. Present Tense of *ser;* Summary of Uses

ser: soy, eres, es, somos, sois, son

Uses of **ser:** identification, description, origin, generalizations, possession, destination

de + el → del

7. Unstressed Possessive Adjectives

yo → mi(s)   nosotros → nuestro/a(s)
tú → tu(s)   vosotros → vuestro/a(s)
Ud., él, → su(s)   Uds., ellos, → su(s)
  ella   ellas

8. Present Tense of *-er* and *-ir* Verbs; Subject Pronouns

Regular -er Verb Endings

-o, -es, -e, -emos, -éis, -en

Regular -ir Verb Endings

-o, -es, -e, -imos, -ís, -en

When to use subject pronouns: for clarification, emphasis, and contrast

Vocabulario

Los verbos

abrir	to open
aprender	to learn
aprender a + *inf.*	to learn how to (*do something*)
asistir (a)	to attend, go to (a *class, a function*)
beber	to drink
comer	to eat
comprender	to understand
creer (en)	to think; to believe (in)
deber + *inf.*	should; must; ought to (*do something*)
escribir	to write
leer	to read
llegar	to arrive
mirar	to look at; to watch
mirar la tele(visión)	to watch television
recibir	to receive
ser (soy, eres,...)	to be (I am, you are . . .)
vender	to sell
vivir	to live

La familia y los parientes

el/la abuelo/a	grandfather/grandmother
los abuelos	grandparents
el/la esposo/a	husband/wife
el/la hermano/a	brother/sister
los hermanos	siblings
el/la hijo/a	son/daughter
los hijos	children
la madre (mamá)	mother (mom)
el marido	husband
la mujer	wife
el/la nieto/a	grandson/granddaughter
el/la niño/a	small child; boy/girl
el padre (papá)	father (dad)
los padres	parents
el pariente	relative
el/la primo/a	cousin
los primos	cousins
el/la sobrino/a	nephew/niece
el/la tío/a	uncle/aunt
los tíos	aunts and uncles

Las mascotas

el gato	cat
la mascota	pet
el pájaro	bird
el perro	dog

Otros sustantivos

la carta	letter
la casa	house, home
la ciudad	city
el coche	car
el estado	state
el/la médico/a	(medical) doctor
el mundo	world
el país	country
el periódico	newspaper
el regalo	present, gift
la revista	magazine

Los adjetivos

alto/a	tall
amable	kind; nice
antipático/a	unpleasant, unlikeable
bajo/a	short (*in height*)
bonito/a	pretty
buen, bueno/a	good
corto/a	short (*in length*)
delgado/a	thin, slender
este/a	this
estos/as	these
feo/a	ugly
fiel	faithful
gordo/a	fat
gran, grande	large, big; great
guapo/a	handsome, good-looking
joven	young
largo/a	long
listo/a	smart; clever
mal, malo/a	bad
moreno/a	brunet(te)
mucho/a	a lot (of)
muchos/as	many
nuevo/a	new
otro/a	other, another
pequeño/a	small
perezoso/a	lazy
pobre	poor
rico/a	rich
rubio/a	blond(e)
simpático/a	nice, likeable
todo/a	all; every
tonto/a	silly, foolish
trabajador(a)	hardworking
viejo/a	old

Cognados: hispano/a, inteligente, necesario/a, posible

Los adjetivos de nacionalidad

alemán/alemana	German
español(a)	Spanish
estadounidense	U.S.
inglés/inglesa	English
mexicano/a	Mexican

Los adjetivos posesivos

mi(s)	my
tu(s)	your (*fam. sing.*)
nuestro/a(s)	our
vuestro/a(s)	your (*fam. pl., Sp.*)
su(s)	his, hers, its; your (*form. sing.*); their; your (*form. pl.*)

Los números del 31 al 100

treinta, cuarenta, cincuenta, sesenta, setenta, ochenta, noventa, cien

¿Con qué frecuencia... ?

a veces	sometimes, at times
casi	almost
casi nunca	almost never
nunca	never
siempre	always
una vez a la semana	once a week

Repaso: con frecuencia, todos los días

Palabras adicionales

¿de quién?	whose?
del (de + el)	of the, from the
estar de acuerdo / no estar de acuerdo	to agree / to disagree
esto	this (*neuter*)
para	(intended) *for*
para + *inf.*	in order to (*do something*)
por eso	for that reason
¿por qué?	why?
porque	because
que	that, which; who
según	according to
tener... años (tengo, tienes, tiene)	to be . . . years old

Repaso: ¿de dónde es Ud.?

Vocabulario personal

Remember to use this space for other words and phrases you learn in this chapter.

ESPAÑOL	INGLÉS

4

De compras°

De... *Shopping*

www.connectspanish.com

En este capítulo

En un mercado (*market*), en
Tecpán, Guatemala

GUATEMALA

15 millones de habitantes

- Guatemala es el centro de la civilización maya. También hay población maya en Honduras, México, El Salvador y Belice.

HONDURAS

8 millones de habitantes

- Honduras tiene una población afroindígena[a] muy grande: los garífunas, que viven a lo largo del[b] Golfo de Honduras, de Belice a Nicaragua.

[a]*native African* [b]*a... along the*

- ¿Qué tipo de ropa[a] le gusta llevar[b] con más frecuencia, ropa formal o informal?
- ¿Prefiere usar ropa de muchos colores o prefiere la ropa de colores muy básicos, como el blanco y el negro[c]? (**Prefiero...**)
- ¿Le gusta ir de compras[d] o prefiere comprar por[e] internet? Cuando va[f] de compras, ¿va a centros comerciales o a pequeñas tiendas[g] locales? (**Voy...**)

[a]*clothing* [b]*to wear* [c]*el... white and black* [d]*ir... to go shopping*
[e]*on the* [f]*you go* [g]*shops*

ALEJANDRA HERNÁNDEZ SOTO CONTESTA LAS PREGUNTAS.

- Me gusta todo tipo de ropa. Para ir[a] a la universidad todos los días, llevo ropa cómoda:[b] *jeans*, camisetas[c] y suéteres grandes, zapatos bajos o deportivos.[d] Pero me gusta la ropa elegante para ocasiones especiales.
- Me gusta mucho combinar el negro con el blanco y colores vivos,[e] como el rojo[f] y el turquesa.
- Prefiero ir de compras. Con frecuencia voy a un centro comercial. Pero a veces, voy a tiendas pequeñas en el centro que tienen cosas un poco diferentes. ¡Nunca compro por internet!

[a]*go* [b]*comfortable* [c]*T-shirts* [d]*zapatos... low or sporty shoes*
[e]*strong, vibrant* [f]*red*

De compras: La ropa°

De... *Shopping: Clothing*

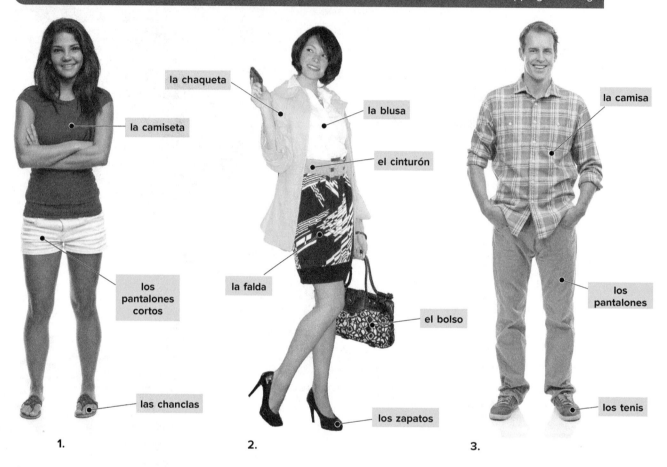

la chaqueta

la blusa

la camiseta

el cinturón

la camisa

los pantalones cortos

la falda

el bolso

los pantalones

las chanclas

los zapatos

los tenis

1. 2. 3.

You can hear the pronunciation of theme vocabulary words and phrases in the Connect eBook.

Los verbos

comprar	to buy
llevar	to wear; to carry; to take
regatear	to haggle; to bargain
usar	to wear; to use
vender	to sell
venden de todo	they sell (have) everything

Los lugares

el almacén	department store
el centro	downtown
el centro comercial	shopping mall

el mercado	market (place)
la plaza	plaza
la tienda	shop, store

¿Cuánto cuesta(n)?

la ganga	bargain
el precio	price
el precio fijo	fixed (set) price
las rebajas	sales, reductions
barato/a	inexpensive
caro/a	expensive
cómodo/a	comfortable

Otras palabras y expresiones útiles

el abrigo	coat	las sandalias	sandals
los aretes	earrings	el sombrero	hat
las botas	boots	la sudadera	sweatshirt
los calcetines	socks	el suéter	sweater
la cartera	wallet; handbag	el traje	suit
la chaqueta	jacket (*for a woman or a man*)	el traje de baño	bathing suit
la corbata	tie	el vestido	dress
las gafas de sol	sun glasses	de cuadros (lunares, rayas)	plaid (polka-dot, striped)
la gorra	baseball cap	Es de (algodón, cuero, lana, oro, plata, seda)*	it is made of (cotton, leather, wool, gold, silver, silk)
el impermeable	raincoat		
los *jeans*	blue jeans, jeans		
las medias	stockings	Es de última moda.	It's trendy (hot).
el reloj	watch	Está de moda.	
la ropa interior	underwear		

Comunicación

A. La ropa

Paso 1. ¿Qué ropa llevan estas personas?

1.   **2.**   **3.**

Vocabulario **útil**	
el chico	guy
la chica	girl
el hombre	
la mujer	

Paso 2. De estas personas, ¿quién trabaja hoy? ¿Quién probablemente no trabaja en este momento? ¿Quién va a (*is going to*) una fiesta?

---

*Note another use of **ser** + **de**: to tell what material something is made of.*

B. Asociaciones. Complete las siguientes oraciones lógicamente con palabras de **De compras: La ropa.**

1. Un _____ es una tienda grande, con muchos departamentos.

2. No es posible _____ cuando hay precios fijos.

3. En la librería, _____ de todo: textos y otros libros, cuadernos, lápices,...

4. Hay grandes _____ en las tiendas al final de la temporada (*season*), en las cuales (*in which*) todo es muy barato.

5. Siempre hay *boutiques* en los _____.

6. El _____ de una ciudad es con frecuencia la parte histórica.

7. Esta ropa es para fiestas formales: _____.

8. La ropa de _____ (materia) es muy elegante.

C. El estilo personal. Complete las siguientes oraciones lógicamente para hablar de sus preferencias con relación a la ropa.

1. Para ir a la universidad, llevo _____.

2. Para ir a las fiestas con los amigos, llevo _____.

3. Para pasar un día en la playa (*beach*), me gusta llevar _____.

4. Para estar en casa todo el día, me gusta llevar _____.

5. Nunca uso _____.

6. No puedo vivir sin (*I can't live without*) ___ y ___.

Nota **comunicativa**

Preguntas coletilla (*tag*)

Tag phrases can change statements into questions.

| Aquí venden de todo, | ¿no? ¿verdad? | They sell everything here, right? (don't they?) |
| No necesito impermeable hoy, **¿verdad?** | | I don't need a raincoat today, do I? |

¿Verdad? is found after affirmative or negative statements; **¿no?** is usually found after affirmative statements only.

You will practice using tag phrases in **Comunicación D.**

D. Intercambios. En parejas, usen las coletillas **¿no?** y **¿verdad?** para intercambiar (*exchange*) información de sus hábitos y preferencias sobre (*about*) las compras.

MODELO: Hay un buen centro comercial cerca de (*close to*) tu casa. →
E1: Hay un buen centro comercial cerca de tu casa, ¿no? (¿verdad?)
E2: Sí, hay un centro comercial muy grande a cinco millas (*five miles away*) de mi casa. (No, no hay un buen centro comercial cerca de mi casa.)

1. Hay un buen centro comercial cerca de tu casa.
2. Te gusta la ropa deportiva (*sports*) más que la ropa elegante.
3. Tienes muchos zapatos.
4. Te gusta llevar ropa de moda.
5. No compras en las tiendas de ropa usada (*used*).
6. Compras muchas cosas (*things*) por internet.
7. No hay muchos mercados en esta ciudad.

Los colores: ¿De qué color es?

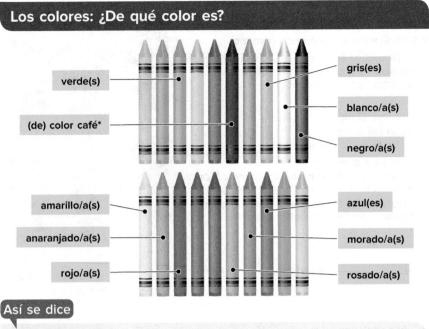

verde(s)

(de) color café*

gris(es)

blanco/a(s)

negro/a(s)

amarillo/a(s)

anaranjado/a(s)

rojo/a(s)

azul(es)

morado/a(s)

rosado/a(s)

¡OJO!

The names of colors are masculine, like the word **color: el rojo, el azul,** and so on. Note that three colors (**azul, gris, verde**) have only one singular form for masculine and feminine: **el traje azul, la camisa azul.**

Así se dice

anaranjado = naranja
(de) color café = marrón, pardo
morado = (de) color violeta, púrpura, purpúreo
rosado = (de) color rosa, rosa

Note that some Spanish speakers use **marrón** for objects and **pardo** for animals. Brown hair and eye color are often expressed with **castaño.**

Comunicación

A. Un cuadro colorido (*colorful painting*). Hay muchos colores en este cuadro de Edwin Guillermo. ¿Cuáles son?

El cortejo (Courting), de Erwin Guillermo

Algo sobre...

un artista guatemalteco

Erwin Guillermo (1951– [mil novecientos cincuenta y uno]) vive y trabaja en la Ciudad de Guatemala. Su estilo es representativo del arte contemporáneo guatemalteco: es muy expresivo y simbólico. Con frecuencia, como se ve[a] en este cuadro,[b] las figuras de Guillermo tienen una forma estilizada y sensual, con muchos colores.

¿Le gusta el estilo del cuadro de Guillermo? ¿Qué pintor(a) le gusta mucho a Ud.?

[a]*se... is seen* [b]*painting*

---

*The expression (de) **color café** *is invariable;* that is, it does not show gender or number agreement with the noun it modifes: **el sombrero (de) color café, la falda (de) color café, los pantalones (de) color café.**

Nota cultural

La ropa tradicional en el mundo hispano

La ropa tradicional en el mundo hispano es muy diversa, porque hay muchos países y regiones diferentes. Algunas prendas[a] son ahora conocidas[b] en todo el mundo:

- la guayabera[c] (Caribe)
- el poncho (los Andes)
- el traje de flamenco (España)

En los países de cultura maya

En estos países hay tejidos muy bellos y coloridos.[d] Varían según la región y forman parte de la ropa habitual de las mujeres indígenas. Una prenda distintiva es el huipil, una especie de blusa, que varía de región a región.

 ¿Hay ropa tradicional en este país?

[a]articles of clothing [b]known [c]elegant short-sleeved shirt worn outside the pants [d]tejidos... beautiful and colorful textiles

Una mujer guatemalteca que hace tejidos (is weaving)

B. **Asociaciones.** ¿Qué asocia Ud. con los siguientes colores?

1. gris
2. verde
3. blanco y negro
4. amarillo
5. rojo
6. azul

C. **¡Ojo alerta! ¿Escaparates (Window displays) idénticos?** These window displays are almost alike . . . but not quite! Can you find at least nine differences between them?

MODELO: En el dibujo A hay _____, pero en el dibujo B hay _____.

A. **B.**

D. ¿De qué color es?

Paso 1. Describa el color de la ropa y de las cosas (*things*) de sus compañeros.

MODELO: El bolígrafo de Anita es amarillo. Un libro de Anita es azul...

Paso 2. Ahora describa la ropa que lleva una persona de la clase sin decir (*without saying*) su nombre. Sus compañeros tienen que (*have to*) identificar a la persona de la descripción.

MODELO: E1: Lleva botas negras, una camiseta blanca y *jeans*.
E2: Es Anne.

Los números a partir del 100°   a... *from 100 on*

Continúe las secuencias:

- noventa y nueve, cien, ciento uno...
- mil, dos mil...
- un millón, dos millones...

100	cien, ciento	**700**	setecientos/as
101	ciento uno/una	**800**	ochocientos/as
200	doscientos/as	**900**	novecientos/as
300	trescientos/as	**1.000**	mil
400	cuatrocientos/as	**2.000**	dos mil
500	quinientos/as	**1.000.000**	un millón
600	seiscientos/as	**2.000.000**	dos millones

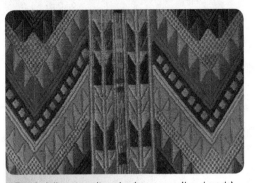

Este huipil guatemalteco hecho a mano (*hand-made*) cuesta 750 (setecientos cincuenta) quetzales.

- **Cien** is used in counting and when referring to exactly one hundred of something: **cien** dólares.
- **Ciento** is used in combination with numbers from 1 to 99 to express the numbers 101 to 199: ...noventa y nueve, cien, **ciento** uno, **ciento** dos...
- **Cien** is used before numbers greater than 100: **cien mil, cien millones.**
- When counting, the masculine form of words containing **cientos** is used: ...**doscientos uno, doscientos dos...**
- When the numbers 200 to 900 modify a noun, they must agree in gender: **doscientos veintiún dólares, quinientas ocho sillas.**
- **Mil** means *one thousand* or *a thousand*. It does not have a plural form in counting, but **millón** does. When followed directly by a noun, **millón (dos millones,** and so on) must be followed by **de.**

mil gracias	
3.000 habitantes	**tres mil habitantes**
14.000.000 *de* habitantes	**catorce millones *de* habitantes**

- Years are expressed like regular numbers in Spanish.

1899	**mil ochocientos noventa y nueve**
2008	**dos mil ocho**

¡OJO!

In many parts of the Spanish-speaking world, a period (**punto**) is used where a comma (**coma**) is used in English and viceversa.
$1.500 $1.000.000 $10,45   65,9%

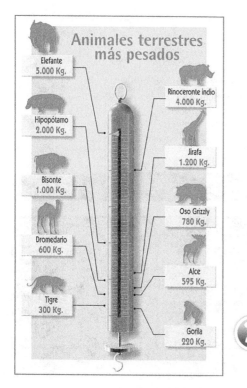

Animales terrestres más pesados

- Elefante 5.000 Kg.
- Rinoceronte indio 4.000 Kg.
- Hipopótamo 2.000 Kg.
- Jirafa 1.200 Kg.
- Bisonte 1.000 Kg.
- Oso Grizzly 780 Kg.
- Dromedario 600 Kg.
- Alce 595 Kg.
- Tigre 300 Kg.
- Gorila 220 Kg.

Estrategia

un kilo = 2.2. libras (aproximadamente)

Comunicación

A. ¿Cuánto cuestan? Exprese los siguientes precios en dólares en español.

1. unos *jeans* de moda: $100
2. unos tenis tipo NBA: $150
3. un anillo (*ring*) de diamantes: $1.200
4. unos aretes (*earrings*) de oro: $225
5. una tela (*fabric*) de artesanía local de excelente calidad: $400
6. un cinturón de cuero de un diseñador (*designer*) famoso: $330
7. un coche europeo: $75.000
8. una casa grande en una zona residencial muy exclusiva: $2.000.000
9. un edificio de apartamentos: $15.800.000

B. ¿Cuánto pesan? (*How much do they weigh?*)

Paso 1. Estos son los animales terrestres más grandes. ¿Cuánto pesan en kilos? ¡OJO! Use el artículo masculino para todos los nombres, menos para (*except for*) **jirafa.**

MODELO: El elefante pesa cinco mil kilos.

Paso 2. Ahora, en parejas, calculen cuánto pesan aproximadamente en kilos o en libras (*pounds*) los siguientes animales y objetos.

MODELO: E1: ¿Cuánto crees que pesa un perro grande?
E2: Creo que pesa más de (*more than*) 25 kilos.
E1: Estoy de acuerdo. (No estoy de acuerdo. Creo que pesa más de 30 kilos.)

1. un perro/gato
2. su mochila con los libros
3. un coche
4. su libro de español
5. el animal más grande del mundo

C. Más o menos

Paso 1. With a classmate, determine how much the following items probably cost, using **¿Cuánto cuesta(n)... ?** Keep track of the prices that you decide on. Follow the model.

MODELO: una chaqueta de cuero →
E1: ¿Cuánto cuesta una chaqueta de cuero?
E2: Cuesta doscientos dólares.

1. un iPhone de último (*latest*) modelo
2. un coche nuevo/usado
3. una computadora portátil de último modelo
4. la matrícula de esta universidad
5. un reloj de oro muy elegante
6. unos tenis (¡OJO! **cuesta**n)
7. una casa en esta ciudad

Paso 2. Now compare the prices you selected with those of others in the class. What is the most expensive thing on the list? (**¿Cuál es la cosa más cara** [*most expensive*]**?**) What is the least expensive? (**¿Cuál es la más barata?**)

D. Fechas (*Dates*) importantes. Exprese las siguientes fechas en español.

1. este año, el año pasado y el próximo (*next*) año
2. el año de su nacimiento (*birth*)
3. 1821, el año de la independencia de Guatemala y Honduras (de España)
4. 1776, el año de la independencia de los Estados Unidos (de Inglaterra)

«¡Moda,° moda, moda!» Segmento 1

Fashion

Antes de mirar

¿Qué estilo de ropa prefiere Ud.? Indique sus preferencias después de leer (*after reading*) la descripción del estudio de Vilma (foto).

_____ siempre ropa cómoda e informal
_____ ropa elegante de alta costura y de tiendas exclusivas
_____ ropa variada, a veces informal, a veces elegante
_____ ropa muy juvenil y deportiva (*youthful and sporty*)

Este segmento

El tema de este programa es la moda. El segmento incluye una entrevista (*inverview*) con una diseñadora (*designer*) puertorriqueña.

«En el estudio de Vilma, vemos (*we see*) vestidos (*costumes*) de épocas históricas para obras de teatro (*plays*), vestidos de alta costura (*designer*) y su nueva línea de prendas (*garments*) reversibles de cuero.»

Vocabulario del segmento

te ves	you look	**acá/allá**	here/there
no creas	don't get the idea	**mismo/a**	same
el significado	meaning	**la marca**	brand, label
Cuéntanos.	Tell us (about it).	**hablé**	I spoke
primero vamos	first let's go	**Ropajes**	Apparel
el clima	climate	**desarrollamos**	we develop
la playa	beach	**la enseñanza**	teaching
Colón llegó	Columbus arrived	**todo el mundo**	everybody
el segundo viaje	second voyage		

Estrategia

You can pick up vocabulary that will be in the segment by reading the photo caption, **Este segmento,** and **Vocabulario del segmento,** doing **Antes de mirar,** and scanning **Después de mirar** before you watch the segment!

Después de mirar

A. ¿Está claro? Las siguientes oraciones son falsas. Corríjalas (*Correct them*), según el video.

1. Ana y Víctor están hoy en Puerto Rico.
2. Víctor lleva una camiseta hoy porque va (*he's going*) a la playa.
3. Solo hay influencia de España en Puerto Rico.
4. El estilo de Ropajes Inc. es juvenil e informal.

B. Un poco más. Empareje (*Match*) las ideas de la **Columna A** con la forma correcta de una palabra de la **Columna B.**

COLUMNA A
1. _____ el clima de Puerto Rico
2. _____ las playas de Puerto Rico
3. _____ la apariencia de Víctor hoy, en camiseta
4. _____ la diseñadora Vilma Martínez
5. _____ las prendas de cuero de la nueva línea

COLUMNA B
a. bonito
b. relajado (*relaxed*)
c. reversible
d. fundador (*founder*)
e. suave (*mild*)

C. Y ahora, Uds. En parejas, imaginen que son los presentadores del programa de hoy sobre la ropa y la moda. Sigan el modelo de este segmento y hagan una breve introducción al programa, incluyendo (*including*):

- un saludo + una presentación personal + el lugar donde Uds. están
- un comentario informal sobre la ropa de uno de Uds. o su estilo (o sobre la ropa que Uds. llevan hoy o su propio [*own*] estilo). (Usen vocabulario de **Antes de mirar** y de **Vocabulario: Preparación.**)
- una breve introducción al próximo (*upcoming*) reportaje sobre la moda o sobre una tienda en particular

PRONUNCIACIÓN

Stress and Written Accent Marks (Part 2)

¿Recuerda Ud.?

In the **Pronunciación** section of **Capítulo 3**, you learned that most Spanish words do not need a written accent mark because their pronunciation is completely predictable. Review the two basic rules of Spanish word stress in words that do not have a written accent mark by looking at the examples and completing the rules. The stressed syllable is underlined.

- Examples: **li̱bro, me̱sa, exa̱men, ima̱gen, e̱res, gra̱cias**

  A word that ends in a _____, _____, or _____ is stressed on the next-to-last syllable.

- Examples: **baila̱r, uste̱d, pape̱l, esto̱y**

  A word that ends in _____ is stressed on the last syllable.

In Spanish, the written accent mark is used in the following situations.

1. A written accent mark is needed when a word does not follow the two basic rules reviewed in **¿Recuerda Ud.?**

Look at the words in this group.

ta-bú	a-le-mán	in-glés
ca-fé	na-ción	es-tás

The preceding words end in a vowel, **-n,** or **-s,** so one would predict that they would be stressed on the *second-to-last syllable* (**la penúltima sílaba**). But the written accent mark shows that they are in fact accented on the *last syllable* (**la última sílaba**).

Now look at the words in this group.

lá-piz   dó-lar   ál-bum   á-gil   dó-cil

The preceding words end in a consonant (other than **-n** or **-s**), so one would predict that they would be stressed on the last syllable. But the written accent mark shows that they are in fact accented on the next-to-last syllable.

2. All words that are stressed on the *third-to-last syllable* (**la antepenúltima sílaba**) must have a written accent mark, regardless of which letter they end in. These are called **palabras esdrújulas.**

bo-lí-gra-fo   ma-trí-cu-la   ma-te-má-ti-cas

3. When two consecutive vowels do not form a diphthong (see **Pronunciación, Cap. 2**), the weak vowel (**i, u**) that receives the spoken stress will have a written accent mark. This pattern is very frequent in words that end in **-ía.**

Ma-rí-a	po-li-cí-a	as-tro-no-mí-a
dí-a	bio-lo-gí-a	

¡OJO!

Contrast the pronunciation of those words with the following words in which the vowels **i** and **a** *do* form a diphthong: **Patricia, Francia, infancia, distancia.**

4. Some one-syllable words have accents to distinguish them from other words that are pronounced the same but have different meanings. This type of accent does not follow the general rules of accentuation; it is called the *diacritic accent* (**el acento diacrítico**). Here are some of the most common examples.

él (*he*)/el (*the*)
sí (*yes*)/si (*if*)
tú (*you*)/tu (*your*)
mí (*me*)/mi (*my*)

5. Interrogative and exclamatory words have a written accent on the stressed vowel. For example:

¿quién?
¿dónde?
¡Qué ganga! (*What a bargain!*)

6. Accent marks are also added to preserve the original stress of a word when the word is changed in some way, for example, when it becomes plural. Here are some examples:

joven → jóvenes   examen → exámenes

You will learn about other situations in which accents are added for this reason in upcoming chapters.

¡OJO!

As you know, the accent mark is sometimes dropped when a word is made plural.

pantalón	pantalones
francés	franceses
nación	naciones

Práctica

A. **Sílabas.** The following words have been separated into syllables for you. Read them aloud, paying careful attention to where the spoken stress should fall. Don't worry about the meaning of words you haven't heard before. The rules you have learned will help you pronounce them correctly.

1. a-quí	pa-pá	a-diós	bus-qué
2. prác-ti-co	mur-cié-la-go	te-lé-fo-no	ar-chi-pié-la-go
3. Ji-mé-nez	Ro-drí-guez	Pé-rez	Gó-mez
4. si-co-lo-gí-a	so-cio-lo-gí-a	sa-bi-du-rí-a	e-ner-gí-a
5. his-to-ria	te-ra-pia	Pre-to-ria	me-mo-ria

B. **Reglas.** *(Rules.)* Indicate the stressed vowel of each word in the following list. Give one of the three reasons from the list to explain the stressed vowel of each word.

1. exámenes	**9.** Están
2. lápiz	**10.** hombre
3. necesitar	**11.** peso
4. perezoso	**12.** mujer
5. actitud	**13.** plástico
6. acciones	**14.** María
7. dólares	**15.** Rodríguez
8. francés	**16.** Patricia

GRAMÁTICA

¿Recuerda Ud.?

You learned the four forms of the demonstrative adjective **este** in **Gramática 5 (Cap. 3).** Review them now by completing these phrases.

1. est____ pantalones   **2.** est____ falda   **3.** est____ blusas   **4.** est____ abrigo

9 Pointing Out People and Things
Demonstrative Adjectives (Part 2) and Pronouns

Grammar Tutorial 9
connect
|SPANISH
www.connectspanish.com

Gramática en acción: Suéteres a buenos precios

el vendedor

Jorge   Susana

Susana busca un suéter con su amigo Jorge.

SUSANA: ¿Cuánto cuesta este suéter?

VENDEDOR: Bueno, ese que Ud. tiene en la mano cuesta 800 quetzales. Este aquí cuesta 700 quetzales.

SUSANA: ¡Qué caros!

VENDEDOR: Es que todos son de pura lana. Mire aquellos suéteres de rayas sobre aquella mesa. Solo cuestan 300 quetzales. Son acrílicos.

SUSANA: Muchas gracias.

Comprensión

¿Quién habla, Susana, su amigo Jorge o el vendedor?

1. «Estos suéteres de rayas son bonitos. Y solo cuestan 300 quetzales.»
2. «Los suéteres en aquella mesa no son de pura lana.»
3. «Compro este suéter. Me gusta la ropa de lana.»
4. «Estos suéteres acrílicos son más baratos que aquellos de lana.»

Demonstrative Adjectives / Los adjetivos demostrativos

Singular		Plural		Adverbs / **Los adverbios**
this	**este** abrigo **esta** gorra	these	**estos** abrigos **estas** gorras	**aquí** = here
that	⎰ **ese** abrigo **esa** gorra ⎱ **aquel** abrigo **aquella** gorra	those	⎰ **esos** abrigos **esas** gorras ⎱ **aquellos** abrigos **aquellas** gorras	**allí** = there **allá** = way over there

an adverb / **un adverbio** = a word (such as *very* and *quickly*) that modifies a verb, adjective, or another adverb

¡OJO!

Note that the final -e in the singular forms **est**e and **es**e changes to an -o- in the plural: **est**os, **es**os.

Sweaters at good prices   *Susana is looking for a sweater with her friend Jorge.* SUSANA: *How much is this sweater?* SALESMAN: *Well, that one that you have in your hand costs 800 quetzales. This one here costs 700 quetzales.* SUSANA: *(They're) So expensive!* SALESMAN: *It's because they're all made of pure wool. Take a look at those striped sweaters on that table (over there). They only cost 300 quetzales. They're acrylic.* SUSANA: *Thanks a lot.*

1. Agreement

Demonstrative adjectives are used to indicate a specific noun or nouns. In Spanish, **los adjetivos demostrativos** precede the nouns they modify. They also agree in number and gender with the nouns.

> *a demonstrative adjective* / **un adjetivo demostrativo** = an adjective used to indicate a particular person, place, thing, or idea

2. Using *este* and *ese*

Forms of **este** (*this, these*) and **ese** (*that, those*) are used just like *this/these* and *that/those* in English.

- When two people are speaking, forms of **este** are used to refer to nouns that are close to the speaker in space or time.
- Forms of **ese** refer to nouns that are close to the person spoken *to*.
- When the noun is distant from both speakers, forms of **ese** are used.

3. Using *ese* and *aquel*

There are two ways to say *that/those* in Spanish.

- Forms of **ese** refer to nouns that are not close to the speaker(s) (point 2).
- Forms of **aquel** refer to nouns that are even farther away from the speaker(s).

¿Esos pantalones?

No, aquellos allá.

In the chart on page 110, the *adverbs* (**los adverbios**) **aquí, allí,** and **allá** are associated with the forms of **este, ese,** and **aquel,** respectively. However, it is not obligatory to use these words with the demonstrative adjectives.

Este niño es mi hijo. **Ese** joven allí es mi hijo también. Y **aquel** señor allá es mi esposo.

This boy is my son. That young man there is also my son. And that man way over there is my husband.

Demonstrative Pronouns / Los pronombres demostrativos

1. Demonstrative Pronouns

In English, the *demonstrative pronouns* are the demonstrative adjective + the word *one(s)*, as in the examples to the right. In Spanish, **los pronombres demostrativos** are the same as demonstrative adjectives, except that the noun is not used and there is no direct equivalent for English *one(s)*.*

—¿Te gusta **aquella** casa allá?
—¿Cuál?
—**Aquella,** la de las ventanas grandes.
—¡Ah, **aquella**! Sí, me gusta mucho. Mucho más que **esta**...

*"Do you like **that** house way over there?"*
"Which one?"
*"**That one,** the one with the big windows."*
*"Oh, **that one!** Yes, I like it a lot. A lot more than **this one** . . ."*

2. Agreement

In Spanish, demonstrative pronouns agree in gender and number with the noun they are replacing: **ese libro, en la mesa** $\longrightarrow$ **ese, en la mesa.**

3. Neuter Demonstrative Pronouns

Use the neuter demonstrative pronouns **esto, eso,** and **aquello** to refer to as yet unidentified objects or to a whole idea, concept, or situation.

¿Qué es **esto**?
What is this?

Eso es todo.
That's it. / That's all.
¡**Aquello** es terrible!
That's terrible!

¡OJO!

Esto es una mochila. (to identify in general)
This is a backpack.

Esta es mi mochila. (to identify one out of a group)
This (one) is my backpack.

---

*Some Spanish speakers to use accents on demonstrative pronouns: **este coche y ése, aquella casa y ésta.** However, it is correct in modern Spanish, according to the **Real Academia Española** in Spain, to omit the accent on these forms when context makes the meaning clear (see Appendix 2).

Gramática

near	este/a, estos/as, esto
far	ese/a, esos/as, eso
farther	aquel(la), aquellos/as, aquello

Práctica y comunicación

A. Una cuestión de perspectiva

Paso 1. Autoprueba. Empareje las palabras con su significado apropiado en inglés.

1. estas
2. aquellos
3. ese
4. esas
5. este

a. *that*
b. *those (over there)*
c. *these*
d. *this*
e. *those*

Paso 2. Autoprueba. Ahora empareje los siguientes demostrativos con los objetos apropiados.

1. esta _____
2. estas _____
3. este _____
4. aquel _____
5. aquellos _____
6. esos _____

Paso 3. Ahora, en parejas, desde el lugar donde Uds. están, usen los siguientes demostrativos para identificar los objetos de la clase.

1. estos _____ y esta _____
2. ese _____ y esas _____
3. aquel _____ y aquellos _____

B. Cambios (*Changes*)

Paso 1. Cambie (*Change*) las formas de **este** por **ese** y añada (*add*) **también,** según el modelo.

MODELO: Este abrigo es muy grande. →
Ese abrigo **también** es muy grande.

1. Esta falda es muy pequeña.
2. Este diccionario es muy largo.
3. Este libro es muy bueno.
4. Esta corbata es muy fea.

Paso 2. Ahora cambie **este** por **aquel** y añada **allá** también.

MODELO: Este abrigo es muy grande. →
Aquel abrigo **allá también** es muy grande.

Paso 3. Finalmente, cambie las oraciones del singular al plural.

MODELO: Este abrigo es muy grande. →
Est**os** abrigos **son** muy grandes.

Prác. A: Answers, Paso 1. 1. c 2. b 3. a 4. e 5. d
Answers, Paso 2. 1. gorra 2. chanclas 3. traje de baño 4. suéter 5. zapatos/tenis 6. pantalones

C. Situaciones. Empareje (*Match*) cada (*each*) situación de la columna A con un comentario de la columna B.

A

1. _____ Aquí hay un regalo para Ud.
2. _____ Ocurre un accidente de coche.
3. _____ No hay clases mañana.
4. _____ La matrícula cuesta más este semestre/ trimestre.
5. _____ Ud. tiene A en su examen de español.

B

a. ¡Eso es un desastre!
b. ¡Eso es magnífico!
c. ¿Qué es esto?
d. ¡Eso es terrible!

D. En una tienda

Paso 1. Complete el siguiente diálogo con los demostrativos apropiados. Asuma (*Take*) el punto de vista (*point of view*) del vendedor y el cliente.

VENDEDOR: ¿Qué suéter le gusta?

¿_____¹ rojo que está aquí?

CLIENTE: No, el rojo no.

VENDEDOR: ¿_____² suéter amarillo?

CLIENTE: No, tampocoᵃ el amarillo.

¡Me gusta _____³

anaranjado de allá!

ᵃNo... *No, not* [*the yellow one*] *either*

Paso 2. Ahora indique el demostrativo apropiado para los pantalones de cada maniquí, según la perspectiva de los dos hombres.

1. _____ pantalones negros
2. _____ pantalones azules
3. _____ pantalones color kaki

E. En la alcoba (*bedroom*) de Ernesto. Working with a partner, imagine that you are the person depicted in the drawing, who is looking into Ernesto's bedroom. Some objects and items of clothing are close to you, some are a bit farther away, and some are at the other end of the room. Describe them as accurately as you can, using the appropriate demonstrative adjectives and all of the vocabulary you have learned so far.

MODELOS: _____ gato es blanco y
_____ gato es negro.
_____ libro es verde.

Vocabulario **útil**	
la cama	bed
el estante	book shelf
la mesita	nightstand

F. En el salón de clase

Paso 1. En parejas, usen demostrativos para identificar cinco pares (*pairs*) de personas o cosas en el salón de clase.

MODELO: Esta chica es rubia. Aquella chica cerca de la puerta es morena.

Vocabulario **útil**	
cerca de	near
lejos de	far from

Paso 2. Ahora compartan (*share*) sus oraciones con el resto de la clase. Sus compañeros deben adivinar (*guess*) a qué personas u objetos Uds. se refieren.

You began using the singular forms of the verb **tener** in **Capítulo 3.** Review them by completing the following verb forms.

1. tú t___nes
2. yo te____o
3. Julio t___ne

You will learn about similar patterns in **Gramática 10.**

Grammar Tutorial 10
connect
|SPANISH
www.connectspanish.com

10 Expressing Actions and States

Tener, venir, poder, preferir, querer;
Some Idioms with **tener**

Gramática en acción: Un mensaje telefónico

Hola, Jorge. Soy Jaqui. Esta tarde tengo que comprar un regalo para Miguel y no quiero ir sola. ¿Vienes conmigo? Podemos encontrarnos en ese centro comercial que está cerca de tu casa. O si prefieres, puedo pasar por ti antes. ¡Llámame!

Comprensión

Ahora vuelva a contar (*retell*) el mensaje de Jaqui. Estas formas verbales son como **tiene.**

1. Jaqui tien_____que comprar un regalo.
2. Quier_____ir de compras con Jorge.
3. Pued_____encontrarse con Jorge en el centro comercial.
4. O si Jorge prefier_____, Jaqui pued_____pasar por la casa de él.

Tener, venir, poder, preferir, querer

> Remember that infinitives in red are conjugated in their entirety in Appendix 5.

tener (to have)		venir (to come)		poder (to be able, can)		preferir (to prefer)		querer (to want)	
tengo	tenemos	vengo	venimos	puedo	podemos	prefiero	preferimos	quiero	queremos
tienes	tenéis	vienes	venís	puedes	podéis	prefieres	preferís	quieres	queréis
tiene	tienen	viene	vienen	puede	pueden	prefiere	prefieren	quiere	quieren

---

A phone message *Hello, Jorge. It's Jaqui. This afternoon I have to buy a gift for Miguel, and I don't want to go alone. Will you come with me? We can meet at that shopping center that's near your house. Or if you prefer, I can come by for you ahead of time. Call me!*

114 ■ ciento catorce

Capítulo 4 De compras

The five verbs shown on the preceding page share a number of characteristics.

- The **yo** forms of **tener** and **venir** are irregular.
- In other forms of **tener** and **venir,** and in **preferir** and **querer,** when the stem vowel **e** is stressed, it becomes **ie.**
- Similarly, the stem vowel **o** in **poder** becomes **ue** when stressed.
- Like **deber**, **desear**, and **necesitar**, the verbs **poder, preferir,** and **querer** can be followed by an infinitive.

Verbs like these are called *stem-changing verbs.* You will learn more verbs of this type in **Gramática 13 (Cap. 5).**

tener: yo **tengo,** tú **tienes** (e → ie)...
venir: yo **vengo,** tú **vienes** (e → ie)...

preferir, querer: (e → ie)

poder: (o → ue)

In vocabulary lists, these changes are shown in parenthesis after the infinitive: **poder (puedo).**

¿**Puedes correr** muy rápido?
Can you run very fast?

¿Qué **quieres/prefieres** hacer hoy?
What do you want/prefer to do today?

Prefiero **no ir** a la biblioteca el sábado por la noche.
I prefer not to go to the library Saturday night.

¡OJO!
The **nosotros** and **vosotros** forms of these verbs do not have changes in the stem vowel because it is not stressed.

¡OJO!
You will learn to use the verb **hacer** (*to do or to make*) in **Gramática 12 (Cap. 5).** Learn to recognize it in questions and direction lines.

Some Idioms with tener / Algunos modismos con *tener*

1. Conditions or States

Many ideas expressed in English with the verb *to be* are expressed in Spanish with *idioms* (**los modismos**) that use **tener.**

Idioms are often different from one language to another. For example, in English, *to pull Mary's leg* usually means *to tease her*, not *to grab her leg and pull it.* In Spanish, *to pull Mary's leg* is **tomarle el pelo a Mary** (lit., *to take hold of Mary's hair*).

You already know one **tener** idiom: **tener... años.** Here are some more **tener** idioms. They all describe a condition or state. Based on the drawings, can you guess what these idioms mean?

*an idiom / **un modismo** =* an expression whose meaning cannot be inferred from the literal meaning of the words that form it

| tener **sueño** | tener **prisa** | tener **razón** | no tener **razón** | tener **miedo (de)** |

Note that **de** (in **tener miedo de**) can be followed by an infinitive or a noun.

Tengo miedo **de estar** solo aquí. ¡Tengo miedo **de la oscuridad**!
I'm afraid of being alone here. I'm afraid of the dark!

2. *Tener* Idioms + *Infinitive*
Other **tener** idioms include the following:

tener ganas de + *infinitive* = to feel like (*doing something*)

tener que + *infinitive* = to have to (*do something*)

¡OJO!

Note that the English equivalent of the infinitive in expressions with **tener ganas** is expressed with *-ing*, not with the infinitive as in Spanish.

Tengo ganas de comer.
I feel like eating.

¿No tiene Ud. que leer este capítulo?
Don't you have to read this chapter?

Summary of Verbs

tener: tengo, tienes...
venir: vengo, vienes...
poder: puedo...
preferir: prefiero...
querer: quiero...

Práctica y comunicación

A. Esta semana

Paso 1. Autoprueba. Complete los siguientes verbos.

1. p_____do, p_____des, p_____demos
2. pref_____ro, pref_____mos, pref_____ren
3. qu_____ro, qu_____re, qu_____remos
4. t_____o, t_____nes, t_____nemos
5. v _____o, v_____ne, v_____nimos

Paso 2. Ahora complete las siguientes oraciones con uno de los verbos o frases. Debe añadir (*add*) información de sus actividades esta semana y el nombre de un día de la semana. Solo debe repetir el verbo **tener.**

Verbos: poder   preferir   querer   tener   tener ganas   venir

Esta semana yo...

1. _____ clase de _____ (materia) el _____.
2. (no) _____ que estudiar mucho el _____.
3. (no) _____ estudiar en la biblioteca el _____.
4. _____ (no) estudiar en la biblioteca el _____ por la noche.
5. (no) _____ de mirar _____ (programa de televisión) el _____.
6. (no) _____ a la universidad el _____ / todos los días.

Paso 3. Finalmente, en parejas, usen sus oraciones del **Paso 2** como base para hacer y contestar preguntas. Luego (*Then*) digan (*tell*) a la clase algo (*something*) que Uds. tienen en común.

MODELO: 1. Tengo clase de chino el martes. ⟶
  E1: ¿**Tienes** clase de chino el martes?
  E2: No, no estudio chino. Pero **tengo** clase de química el martes.

B. Situaciones. Empareje las situaciones con las respuestas apropiadas.

SITUACIONES

1. _____ El niño es muy pequeño.
2. _____ En esa casa, hay un perro furioso.
3. _____ Son las tres de la mañana.
4. _____ Pablito: «Dos y dos son... seis».
5. _____ Pablito: «Buenos Aires es la capital de la Argentina».
6. _____ Tenemos que estar en el centro a las tres y ya son (*it's already*) las tres menos cuarto.
7. _____ Mañana tengo un examen.

RESPUESTAS

a. Tengo mucho sueño.
b. Yo tengo miedo de ese perro.
c. Solo tiene dos años.
d. Tiene razón.
e. Por eso tengo que estudiar mucho.
f. No tiene razón.
g. Por eso tenemos mucha prisa.

Prác. A, Paso 1: Answers: 1. puedo, puedes, podemos **2.** prefiero, preferimos, prefieren **3.** quiero, quiere, queremos **4.** tengo, tienes, tenemos **5.** vengo, viene, venimos

Nota **comunicativa**

Mucho y poco

In this chapter, you learned that words like **aquí, allí,** and **allá** are *adverbs* (**los adverbios**), words that modify a verb (*run **quickly***), an adjective (***very** smart*), or another adverb (***very** quickly*). One very common Spanish adverb that you have used frequently is **muy** (*very*).

In the first chapters of *Puntos de partida,* you have used the words **mucho** and **poco** as both adjectives and adverbs. In English and in Spanish, adverbs are invariable in form. Spanish adjectives, however, agree in gender and number with the words they modify, as you know.

ADVERBIOS:	**mucho**	Rosa estudia **mucho.**	*Rosa studies a lot.*
	poco	Julio come **poco.**	*Julio doesn't eat much.*
ADJETIVOS:	**mucho/a(s)**	Rosa tiene **mucha** ropa.	*Rosa has a lot of clothes.*
		Tiene **muchos** zapatos.	*She has a lot of shoes.*
	poco/a(s)	Julio come **poca** pasta.	*Julio doesn't eat much pasta.*
		Come **pocos** postres.	*He eats few desserts.*

You will use these words in **Práctica C, D,** and **E.**

C. En mi armario (*closet*)

Paso 1. Haga rápidamente una lista aproximada de su ropa y complementos (*accessories*). Escriba (*Write*) **muchos, muchas, pocos, pocas** o **no tengo,** según sea (*is*) apropiado.

	MUCHOS/AS	POCOS/AS	NO TENGO
camisas/blusas			
camisetas			
pantalones largos			
pantalones cortos			
faldas			
vestidos			
chaquetas			
zapatos (de todo tipo)			
botas			
complementos			

Paso 2. Ahora, en parejas, túrnense para hacer y contestar preguntas sobre cuánta ropa tienen y de qué tipo.

MODELO: E1: ¿Tienes muchas camisas?
　　　　E2: No, no tengo muchas camisas. Solo tengo dos o tres. ¿Y tú?
　　　　E1: Yo tengo más de 6.

Paso 3. Para terminar, hagan una evaluación mutua de su vestuario (*wardrobe*). ¿Qué es obvio que prefieren llevar o no llevar? ¿Tienen su propio (*own*) estilo? ¿Qué tienen en exceso? ¿Qué tienen que comprar?

Vocabulario **útil**

demasiados/as	too many
deportivo/a	sporty
más/menos	more/less
de + *number*	than

D. Circunstancias personales

Paso 1. Choose a partner, but before working with him or her, try to predict the choices he or she will make in each of the following cases.

MODELO: tener muchos / pocos libros en su cuarto →
Mi compañero tiene pocos libros en su cuarto.

1. estudiar mucho / poco este semestre/trimestre
2. querer tomar muchas / pocas clases de ciencias en la universidad
3. venir en coche / en autobús / a pie (*on foot*) a la universidad todos los días
4. preferir estudiar en la biblioteca / casa / la residencia
5. tener muchas / pocas cosas con el logotipo (*logo*) de la universidad
6. poder correr (*run*) una milla en menos / más de (*than*) cinco minutos
7. tener muchas ganas de estudiar / bailar esta noche
8. tener mucha / poca ropa
9. preferir el verde / rojo / amarillo
10. preferir usar botas / zapatos / sandalias / tenis / chanclas

Paso 2. Now, using tag questions (*preguntas coletilla*), ask your partner questions to find out if you guessed correctly in **Paso 1**.

MODELO: **E1:** Tienes muchos libros en tu cuarto, ¿verdad?
E2: Sí, tengo muchos libros en mi cuarto. (No, tengo pocos libros.)

E. Intercambios. En parejas, túrnense para entrevistarse sobre los siguientes temas. Deben añadir (*add*) una pregunta original para cada (*each*) verbo.

VERBO INICIAL	OPCIONES
preferir	¿los gatos o los perros? ¿mirar una película (*movie*) en casa o en el cine (*movie theater*)? ¿la ropa elegante o la ropa cómoda? ¿ ?
tener	¿mucho dinero o muchas deudas (*debts*)? ¿una familia grande o pequeña? ¿sueño en clase con frecuencia? ¿ ?
venir	¿a clase tarde o temprano? ¿de una familia anglosajona, hispana o de otro origen? ¿a clase todos los días? ¿ ?
(¿qué?) querer	¿comprar esta semana? ¿comprar en el futuro? ¿mirar en la tele esta noche? ¿ ?
poder	¿hablar una lengua extranjera? ¿vivir sin (*without*) dinero? ¿escribir poemas? ¿ ?

11 Expressing Destination and Future Actions

Ir; The Contraction **al**; **Ir** + **a** + Infinitive

Gramática en acción: ¿Adónde vas?

El Mercado Central, Ciudad de Guatemala

Rosa y Casandra son compañeras de casa.

CASANDRA: ¿Adónde vas?

ROSA: Voy al Mercado Central.

CASANDRA: ¿Qué vas a comprar allá?

ROSA: Voy a comprar unos regalos para mi familia en Nueva Jersey.

CASANDRA: ¿Vas a viajar a los Estados Unidos pronto?

ROSA: Sí, en quince días. ¿Por qué no vienes conmigo al Mercado?

CASANDRA: ¡Sí! Vamos.

Comprensión

¿Cierto o falso? Corrija las oraciones falsas.

	CIERTO	FALSO
1. Rosa va a estudiar.	☐	☐
2. Rosa va a comprar regalos.	☐	☐
3. Casandra va a los Estados Unidos.	☐	☐

The Verb **ir** / El verbo *ir*

ir (*to go*)			
(yo)	voy	(nosotros/as)	vamos
(tú)	vas	(vosotros/as)	vais
(Ud., él, ella)	va	(Uds., ellos/as)	van

Ir is the irregular Spanish verb used to express *to go*.

Rosa va al centro.
Rosa is going downtown.
¿Adónde vas tú?
Where are you going?

The first person plural of **ir, vamos** (*we go, are going, do go*), is also used to express *let's go*.

Vamos a clase ahora mismo.
Let's go to class right now.

The Contraction **al** / La contracción *al*

As you can see in the preceding examples, the verb **ir** is often used with the preposition **a** to indicate where someone is going (to).

When **a** is followed by **el**, it contracts to **al**, just as de + el → **del** (Capítulo 3). **Al** and **del** are the only *contractions* (**las contracciones**) in Spanish.

a + **el** → **al**

Voy al centro comercial.
I'm going to the mall.

Vamos a la tienda.
We're going to the store.

Where are you going? Rosa and Casandra are housemates. **CASSANDRA:** *Where are you going?* **ROSA:** *I'm going to the Central Market.* **CASSANDRA:** *What are you going to buy there?* **ROSA:** *I'm going to buy some presents for my family in New Jersey.* **CASSANDRA:** *Are you going to travel to the United States soon?* **ROSA:** *Yes, in two weeks. Why don't you come to the Market with me?* **CASSANDRA:** *Yes! Let's go.*

Using *ir* to Talk About the Future / El uso de *ir* para hablar del futuro

You can use the verb **ir** + **a** + *infinitive* to talk about the future in Spanish.

¡OJO!

This structure is like **aprender** + **a** + *infinitive*, which you learned in **Gramática 8 (Cap. 3).**

¡OJO!

This use of **a** is different from the use of **a** to indicate where someone is going.

Voy al centro para comer.
I'm going downtown *to eat.*

Van a venir a la fiesta esta noche.
They're coming to the party tonight.
Voy a comer en un restaurante en el centro.
I'm going to eat at a downtown restaurant.

Práctica y comunicación

A. Mañana

Summary of *ir*

voy, vas...
ir + a + infinitivo

Paso 1. Autoprueba. Complete las siguientes frases con formas del verbo **ir**.

1. tú _____
2. nosotros _____
3. yo _____
4. Uds. _____
5. Ud. _____

Paso 2. Ahora use las siguientes frases para expresar lo que (*what*) Ud. va a hacer o no hacer mañana.

MODELO: estudiar → Mañana **no voy a** estudiar.

1. ir a un centro comercial
2. comer en la cafetería de la universidad
3. estudiar en la biblioteca
4. escribir e-mails
5. venir a la clase de español
6. poder hacer toda mi tarea (*homework*)
7. bailar en una discoteca

Paso 3. Ahora use las frases del **Paso 2** para entrevistar a un compañero o una compañera.

MODELO: estudiar → ¿**Vas a** estudiar mañana?

B. ¿Adónde van de compras? Haga oraciones completas, usando (*using*) **ir**. **¡OJO!** a + el → al.

MODELO: Marta / el centro → Marta **va al** centro.

1. tú y yo / la *boutique* Regalitos
2. Francisco / el almacén Goya
3. Juan y Raúl / el centro comercial
4. (tú) / el Mercado Central
5. Ud. / la tienda Gómez
6. yo / ¿ ?

C. ¿Adónde va Ud. si... ? ¿Cuántas oraciones puede hacer?

Vocabulario útil

el cine movie theater
el mercadillo flea market

Me gusta **+**

leer.
ir de compras.
buscar gangas y regatear.
hablar con mis amigos.
comer en restaurantes.
mirar programas de detectives.
ver películas (*movies*).

+ Por eso voy a _____.

Prác. A, Paso 1: Answers: 1. *vas* 2. *vamos* 3. *voy* 4. *van* 5. *va*

D. Intercambios

Paso 1. En parejas, túrnense para hacer y contestar preguntas sobre sus planes para el fin de semana. Aquí hay unas actividades posibles. Traten de obtener (*Try to get*) mucha información. **¡OJO!** **¿adónde?** = *where to?*

MODELO: ir de compras → **¿Vas a ir** de compras **este fin de semana? ¿Adónde** vas a ir? **¿Por qué** vas a ese centro comercial? **¿Qué** vas a comprar?

1. ir de compras
2. leer una novela
3. asistir a un concierto
4. estudiar para un examen
5. ir a una fiesta

6. escribir una carta
7. ir a bailar
8. escribir un enayo (*essay*)
9. practicar un deporte (*sport*)
10. mirar mucho la televisión

Paso 2. Ahora digan (*tell*) al resto de la clase un plan que Uds. tienen en común y otra actividad para la que (*which*) tienen distintos planes.

Un poco de todo

Algo sobre...

las compras en Guatemala y Honduras

Igual que[a] en los Estados Unidos, en el mundo hispano abundan[b] los centros comerciales. De hecho,[c] en algunos[d] países, como en Guatemala y Honduras, se llaman «malls». Algunos centros comerciales están en el centro de la ciudad y otros en las afueras.[e] En las tiendas de los centros comerciales los precios son siempre fijos.

¿Hay grandes centros comerciales en el centro de su ciudad? ¿O están en las afueras?

[a]Igual... *Similar to* [b]*there are many* [c]De... *In fact* [d]*some* [e]en... *in the outskirts*

City Mall, San Pedro Sula, Honduras. Es probablemente el centro comercial más grande y moderno de todo el país.

A. Lengua y cultura: Pero, ¿no se puede* (*can't one*) regatear?

Paso 1. Complete the following paragraphs about shopping. Give the correct form of the words in parentheses, as suggested by context. When two possibilities are given in parentheses, select the correct word.

¿A Ud. le gusta ir de compras? En (los / las[1]) ciudades hispanas, hay una (grande[2]) variedad de tiendas para (ir[3]) de compras. Hay almacenes, centros comerciales y *boutiques* (elegante[4]), como en (este[5]) país, en donde los precios son siempre (fijo[6]).

También hay tiendas que (vender[7]) un solo[a] producto. Por ejemplo,[b] en una zapatería solo hay zapatos. En español el sufijo **-ería** se usa[c] para (formar[8]) el nombre de la tienda. ¿Dónde (creer[9]) Ud. que venden papel y (otro[10]) artículos de escritorio[d]? ¿A qué tienda (ir[11]) a ir Ud. a comprar fruta?

Finalmente, vamos (a / de[12]) mencionar los mercados porque hay muchos en el mundo hispano. En (este[13]) mercados hay (pequeño[14]) tiendas permanentes o temporales[e] donde Ud. (poder[15]) encontrar[f] desde comida[g] típica hasta artesanías[h] locales o ropa interior. Allí los compradores[i] (regatear[16]) los precios, porque el primer[j] precio casi siempre (ir[17]) a ser muy alto.

[a]*single* [b]Por... *For example* [c]se... *is used* [d]artículos... *writing implements* [e]*temporary* [f]*find* [g]*food* [h]*arts and crafts* [i]*shoppers, buyers* [j]*first*

---

*Note that sometimes placing the word **se** before a verb changes its meaning slightly: **puede** = *he/she/you can*; **se puede** = *one can*. You will learn how to use this structure in **Capítulo 8**.

Una zapatería, en Quetzaltenango, Guatemala

Paso 2. Comprensión. Complete las oraciones.

1. En las ciudades hispanas hay *boutiques*, tiendas, _____, _____ y _____.

2. El nombre de muchas tiendas especializadas en un tipo de producto termina en _____.

3. Una tienda de zapatos se llama una _____.

4. Si a Ud. le gusta practicar español y regatear, debe ir a _____.

Paso 3. En parejas, hagan una lista de los lugares para ir de compras que hay en la ciudad donde Uds. estudian. No olviden (*Don't forget*) su propio *campus*. ¿Hay muchas opciones o pocas? ¿Son fijos los precios en todos los lugares? ¿Tienen una tienda favorita entre todas? Luego (*Then*) comparen sus respuestas con las (*those*) de otras parejas. ¿Hay una tienda favorita de toda la clase?

B. Encuesta *(Poll)*

Paso 1. Entreviste a (*Interview*) un mínimo de seis compañeros de clase para saber (*to find out*) la siguiente información. Apunte (*Write down*) sus respuestas.

- un aspecto de la moda actual (*current*) que tiene ganas de tener o llevar
- algo (*something*) dictado por la moda que cree que es absurda

---

Vocabulario útil

un agujero (hole) **en la nariz** (nose) / **la lengua** (tongue)
unos aretes de oro
unos *jeans* **de Ralph Lauren o Narciso Rodríguez**
llevar faldas muy cortas/largas
llevar la gorra de atrás para adelante (backwards)
llevar los pantalones muy bajos (low) / **estrechos** (tight)
los tatuajes

Paso 2. Organice los resultados de su encuesta para presentarlos al resto de la clase. **¡OJO! nadie** = *no one*.

MODELO: Seis estudiantes quieren tener tatuajes. Nadie quiere comprar aretes de oro. Tres estudiantes creen que es bueno llevar faldas muy, muy cortas. Uno/a cree...

En su comunidad

Entreviste a (*Interview*) una persona hispana de su universidad o ciudad para informarse de (*find out about*) sus preferencias con respecto a las compras y la moda.

PREGUNTAS POSIBLES

- ¿Cuáles son las tiendas favoritas de esta persona para comprar comida (*food*)? ¿para comprar ropa?
- ¿Hay mercados en su país de origen? ¿Qué venden en los mercados? ¿Se puede regatear allí?
- En su opinión, ¿dónde hay más preocupación por la ropa, en este país o en su país de origen?

SALU2 «¡Moda, moda, moda!» Segmento 2

Antes de mirar

Conteste las siguientes preguntas.

1. ¿Prefiere Ud. las camisetas o con diseños o mensajes (*messages*) o sin nada? ¿Tiene una camiseta muy especial?
2. En general, ¿hay algunas marcas (*brands*) que Ud. prefiere? ¿Qué le gusta especialmente de esas marcas? ¿los diseños? ¿los colores? ¿el precio?

Este segmento

En este segmento del programa, Laura entrevista a otro diseñador puertorriqueño y los presentadores hablan del tipo de ropa de su preferencia.

Javier Claudio es dueño (*owner*) de la tienda Icónica, que se especializa en diseños (*designs*) de camisetas.

Fragmento del guion

Yo creo que en Puerto Rico por la condición del Caribe, que es un clima tropical y es caluroso,[a] pues los jóvenes universitarios mayormente andan[b] siempre en *T-shirts* y mahones,[c] quizás[d] andan también en pantalones cortos, ¿no? y tenis. De hecho, eso fue lo que me llevó a mí a hacer[e] la marca Icónica.

[a]*hot* [b]*mayormente... mostly wear* [c]*jeans (only in Puerto Rico)* [d]*maybe* [e]*De... In fact, that's what motivated me to create*

Vocabulario del segmento

se hace	becomes	**nos recuerda**	it reminds us
como dice el nombre	as the name suggests	**importantísimos**	very important
nos representan	respresents us	**¡Ay, mi'jo!**	Oh, boy!
la venta	sale	**en todas partes**	everywhere
¡Bien padres!	Very cool!	**vestida impecablemente**	impeccably dressed

Después de mirar

A. **¿Está claro?** ¿Quién dice (*says*) las siguientes oraciones? Conteste con la inicial del nombre de la persona: Ana (**A**), Javier (**J**), Laura (**L**) o Víctor (**V**).

1. «...donde el viejo San Juan se hace global con los diseños de camisetas.»
2. «...como dice el nombre, son íconos de la cultura popular, ... »
3. «Icónica es otro ejemplo (*example*) de globalización, en este caso de productos hispanos.»
4. «Nos recuerda que en el mundo de la alta costura (*high fashion*) hay nombres hispanos importantísimos, ... »
5. «El próximo segmento nos lleva a una tienda aquí en Los Ángeles.»

B. **Un poco más.** Conteste las siguientes preguntas.

1. ¿Cómo se llama la tienda de Javier? ¿Por qué se llama así (*like that*)?
2. ¿Qué diseñadores importantes nombra Ana?
3. ¿Dónde compra ropa Ana?

C. **Y ahora, Uds.** En parejas, hablen de los estilos o marcas de ropa que se mencionan en el programa y de los estilos o marcas que Uds. prefieren. Expliquen por qué. Luego digan (*tell*) a la clase una cosa que Uds. tienen en común o una en que son muy diferentes.

A LEER

¿Hay mercados de artesanías (*arts and crafts*) en la zona donde Ud. vive? ¿Son fijos los precios en esos mercados?

Lectura cultural: Guatemala y Honduras

Los mercados

En Guatemala y Honduras hay mercados donde se puede comprar artículos de artesanía a buen precio. Son famosos los mercados guatemaltecos de las ciudades de Guatemala, Antigua, Chichicastenango y Quezaltenango. En estos mercados existe la costumbre[a] del «regateo»: el comprador[b] de un artículo debe negociar el precio con el vendedor.[c] Los vendedores invitan a los compradores a regatear y con frecuencia se escucha decir:[d] « ...pero tiene rebaja, ofrezca un precio[e]».

En Guatemala, los tejidos[f] de tradición maya son especialmente populares entre los turistas por su colorido y belleza.[g] En Honduras, además de[h] artesanías, los turistas también compran café, ron,[i] vainilla, cerámica y puros.[j]

[a]*custom* [b]*buyer, customer* [c]*seller* [d]*se... one hears people say* [e]*pero... but a discount is possible, make an offer* [f]*weavings* [g]*por... for their colors and beauty* [h]*además... besides* [i]*rum* [j]*cigars*

Los gemelos (*twins*) Hunahpú y Xbalanqué, que juegan a la pelota (*play a ball game*) en Xibalba, el otro mundo (*underworld*) de los mayas, según el *Popol Vuh*

En **otros** países hispanos

- **En todo el mundo hispanohablante** En los países hispanohablantes es común encontrar[a] ropa con tallas[b] similares a las[c] de los Estados Unidos (XS, S, M, L y XL). Pero si la ropa es hecha[d] en un país hispano, se usan con frecuencia las iniciales de los adjetivos en español:

      CH = chico (México y Latinoamérica)
      P = pequeño (España)
      M = mediano
      G = grande
      EG = extra grande
      EEG = extra extra grande

- A la talla de los zapatos se le llama[e] «número». En España y en muchos países latinoamericanos, los números de zapatos para los adultos van del 35 al 46. Los números 37, 38 y 39 son muy comunes para las mujeres y, para los hombres, los números 41, 42 y 43 son muy populares.

- **En los países andinos** En estos países hay una lana[f] excelente que viene de los camélidos[g] de la región: la llama, la vicuña, la alpaca y el guanaco. La lana de estos animales es de excelente calidad y se utiliza para hacer[h] suéteres, gorras,[i] guantes,[j] ponchos, mantas,[k] etcétera.

[a]*to find* [b]*sizes* [c]*those* [d]*made* [e]*A... Shoe size is called a* [f]*wool* [g]*camel-like animals* [h]*making* [i]*knitted caps* [j]*gloves* [k]*blankets*

Un símbolo guatemalteco y hondureño: El *Popol Vuh*

La cultura maya es el sustrato fundamental de Guatemala y Honduras. El *Popol Vuh* es el libro sagrado[a] de los mayas, escrito en el siglo XVI.[b] Es la historia de la creación del mundo, según las creencias[c] mayas.

[a]*sacred* [b]*escrito... written in the 16th century* [c]*beliefs*

COMPRENSIÓN

Conteste las siguientes preguntas.

1. ¿En qué ciudades de Guatemala hay mercados de artesanías?
2. ¿Qué es el regateo?
3. ¿Cómo se indica la talla de la ropa y de los zapatos en el mundo hispanohablante?
4. ¿Dónde hay muchos productos de lana?
5. ¿En dónde se describe la creación del mundo, según los mayas?

Y ahora, Uds.

- ¿Qué productos compran los turistas en la zona donde Uds. viven?
- ¿Cuál es el libro sagrado de su religión o la religión de su familia? ¿En qué lengua se escribió (*was it written*) originalmente?

Del mundo hispano

Antes de leer

Conteste las siguientes preguntas.

1. ¿Qué significa para Ud. la frase «ropa activa»?

2. ¿Cuándo y dónde es buena idea usar «ropa activa»? ¿Tiene Ud. ropa de este tipo?

3. Para Ud., ¿es importante que la ropa tenga (*have*) las siguientes cualidades? Explique por qué sí o por qué no.

- Repeler los mosquitos.
- Servir para proveer (*provide*) protección solar.
- Ser impermeable.
- Neutralizar malos olores (*odors*).

Lectura: Un artículo sobre la ropa

Algo[a] más que ropa
por Gregori Dolz

➔ Desde[b] las calles[c] de Manhattan a las colinas nevadas[d] de Aspen, Exofficio proporciona[e] a sus clientes algo más que ropa activa. Parte de sus beneficios ayudan a[f] causas medioambientales[g] como la Conservation Alliance o World Concern, que auxilian[h] a comunidades necesitadas[i] de todo el mundo. Además,[j] sus prendas[k] proporcionan protección contra los insectos, contra el sol[l] y el agua, contra los olores corporales[m] y muchas otras inconveniencias.

» www.exofficio.com

[a]*Something* [b]*From* [c]*streets* [d]*colinas... snowy hills* [e]*offers* [f]*ayudan... help* [g]*environmental* [h]*help* [i]*needy* [j]*In addition* [k]*ropa* [l]*sun* [m]*bodily*

Comprensión

A. Un resumen del artículo. Las tres oraciones del artículo «Algo más que ropa» describen tres de las características de la compañía Exofficio y de la ropa que vende. Empareje (*Match*) las tres oraciones del artículo con los siguientes resúmenes.

_____ **a.** La compañía dona (*donates*) parte de sus ganancias (*earnings*) a organizaciones conservacionistas y humanitarias.

_____ **b.** La ropa de Exofficio protege (*protects*) contra diversos inconvenientes.

_____ **c.** Uno puede usar la ropa de Exofficio en muchos lugares diferentes.

B. Ud. y Exofficio

Indique la importancia que tienen para Ud. las siguientes características de Exofficio y la ropa que produce. Luego explique sus respuestas.

	MUY IMPORTANTE	IMPORTANTE	POCO IMPORTANTE	NADA IMPORTANTE
1. La compañía dona parte de sus ganancias a varias causas.	☐	☐	☐	☐
2. Es ropa protectora.	☐	☐	☐	☐
3. Es «ropa activa» que uno puede usar en muchas situaciones.	☐	☐	☐	☐

Antes de escuchar

¿Espera Ud. (*Do you wait for*) las rebajas para ir de compras? ¿Para comprar qué tipo de cosas (*things*) busca Ud. rebajas? ¿para comprar ropa? ¿objetos electrónicos?

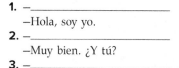

> **Vocabulario para escuchar**
>
> | | | | |
> |---|---|---|---|
> | **la llamada** | (telephone) call | **empiezan** | they start |
> | **¿Qué onda?** | What's up? (*Mexico*) | **¡Qué padre!** | Great! (*Mexico*) |
> | **conmigo** | with me | | |

Después de escuchar

A. **¿Cierto o falso?** Las siguientes oraciones son falsas. Corríjalas (*Correct them*).

1. Las rebajas empiezan hoy.
2. Cristina tiene clases mañana por la mañana.
3. Lidia no tiene clases mañana.
4. Cristina y Lidia van a encontrarse (*meet up*) en la universidad.
5. Lidia no tiene hermanos.

B. **Intercambios.** Invente la parte que falta (*is missing*) de los intercambios, usando expresiones del diálogo.

1. —_____
   —Hola, soy yo.
2. —_____
   —Muy bien. ¿Y tú?
3. —_____
   —Perfecto. En Zara, a las 7.

PRODUCCIÓN PERSONAL

¡Ahora, yo!

A. Use de (*as a*) modelo las preguntas y respuestas de la página 99 de este capítulo para hablar de su ropa favorita y su propio (*own*) estilo de vestir.

B. Con las preguntas de la página 99 como modelo, filme una o dos entrevistas con personas que hablan de su estilo de vestir y de sus tiendas de ropa favoritas.

A ESCRIBIR

Un ensayo sobre los estilos en el *campus*

¿Cree Ud. que hay un estilo de ropa que llevan los estudiantes universitarios en general o hay más de un estilo? En su opinión, ¿se ven (*are seen*) en este *campus* las tendencias de la moda (*fashion*) que predominan en el resto del país?

Preparar

Paso 1. En parejas, hagan una lista del estilo o los estilos de moda típicos en su universidad. Para cada estilo, hagan una lista de la ropa más característica del estilo, con una descripción básica (por ejemplo: pantalones negros muy estrechos...). La siguiente tabla va a ayudarles (*help you*) a organizar sus ideas. ¡Deben incluir a los profesores también! Pónganle (*Give*) un nombre a cada (*each*) estilo si no lo tiene todavía (*yet*). ¡Sean (*Be*) originales!

	Primer (*1st*) lugar en popularidad en el *campus*	Segundo (*2nd*) lugar en popularidad	Tercer (*3rd*) lugar en popularidad
¿Nombre del estilo?			
Personas (estudiantes, profesores, personal administrativo...)			
Descripción de la ropa			

Paso 2. Ahora use sus ideas para escribir un ensayo sobre la moda en su universidad. Incluya unas oraciones sobre su propio (*own*) estilo. Hay más ayuda (*help*) en Connect.

Más ideas para su portafolio

- Busque (*Find*) una fotografía reciente de Ud. llevando (*wearing*) ropa bonita o interesante en una ocasión especial y descríbala (*describe it*).

- Busque la página web de su tienda o marca favorita y determine si tiene una página en español. Si la tiene (*If it has one*), incluya (*include*) unos detalles de la página.

- Si ha estado jugando (*have been playing*) Practice Spanish: Study Abroad, en Quest 2 Ud. pasó su primer día (*spent your first day*) en el Instituto de Lenguas y tuvo que aprender sobre (*had to learn about*) sus clases y el campus. Ahora cree un folleto (*brochure*) para estudiantes nuevos sobre la universidad a la que asiste Ud. Incluya (*Include*) detalles (*details*) sobre las clases y las actividades que ofrece (*that it offers*).

Sugerencia: You are now ready to play Quest 2 in **Practice Spanish: Study Abroad** (www.mhpractice.com).

ILEARNSMART

Visit **www.connectspanish.com** to practice the vocabulary and grammar points covered in this chapter.

AFTER STUDYING THIS CHAPTER I CAN . . .

☐ name items of clothing and use color adjectives (100–101, 103)

☐ talk about shopping (100)

☐ count beyond 100 and express years (105)

☐ use demonstratives to describe people and things at different distances (110–112)

☐ talk about more actions with a different kind of **-er** and **-ir** verbs (114–115)

☐ use very frequent expressions with **tener** (115–116)

☐ talk about where I'm going and what I'm going to do in the near future, using the verb **ir** (119–120)

☐ recognize/describe at least 2–3 aspects of Guatemalan and Honduran cultures

Gramática en breve

9. **Demonstrative Adjectives and Pronouns**

this → *these* *that/those* *that/those (over there)*

este → estos ese →esos aquel → aquellos
esta → estas esa →esas aquella → aquellas
neuter: **esto** neuter: **eso** neuter: **aquello**

10. *Tener, venir, poder, preferir, querer;* **Some Idioms with** *tener*

   tener: **tengo, tienes, tiene, tenemos, tenéis, tienen**

   venir: **vengo, vienes, viene, venimos, venís, vienen**

   poder: **puedo, puedes, puede, podemos, podéis, pueden**

   preferir: **prefiero, prefieres, prefiere, preferimos, preferís, prefieren**

   querer: **quiero, quieres, quiere, queremos, queréis, quieren**

   Idioms with **tener:**
   tener miedo de / prisa / razón / sueño
     no tener razón
   tener ganas de + *inf.* / **que** + *inf.*

11. *Ir;* **The Contraction** *al; Ir* + *a* + *inf.*

   ir: **voy, vas, va, vamos, vais, van**

   a + el → al

Vocabulario

Remember that changes like **e ⟶ ie** and **o ⟶ ue** will be shown like this in vocabulary lists.

Los verbos

ir (voy, vas,...)	to go
ir a + *inf.*	to be going to (*do something*)
poder (puedo)	to be able, can
preferir (prefiero)	to prefer
querer (quiero)	to want
tener (tengo, tienes,...)	to have
venir (vengo, vienes,...)	to come

La ropa

llevar	to wear; to carry; to take
usar	to wear; to use
el abrigo	coat
los aretes	earrings
la blusa	blouse
el bolso	purse
las botas	boots
los calcetines	socks
la camisa	shirt
la camiseta	T-shirt
la cartera	wallet; handbag
las chanclas	flip-flops
la chaqueta	jacket
el cinturón	belt
la corbata	tie
la falda	skirt
las gafas de sol	sun glasses
la gorra	baseball cap
el impermeable	raincoat
las medias	stockings
los pantalones	pants
los pantalones cortos	shorts
el reloj	watch
la ropa	clothing
la ropa interior	underwear
las sandalias	sandals
el sombrero	hat
la sudadera	sweatshirt
el traje	suit
el traje de baño	swimsuit
el vestido	dress
los zapatos	shoes

Cognados: los *jeans,* **el suéter, los tenis**

De compras

ir (voy, vas...) de compras	to go shopping
regatear	to haggle; to bargain

Repaso: comprar, vender

la ganga	bargain
el precio (fijo)	(fixed, set) price
las rebajas	sales, reductions
¿cuánto cuesta(n)?	how much does it (do they) cost?
de todo	everything
Es de última moda. } Está de moda. }	It's trendy (hot).

Las materias

de...	
cuadros	plaid
lunares	polka-dot
rayas	striped
es de...	it is made of . . .
algodón (m.)	cotton
cuero	leather
lana	wool
oro	gold
plata	silver
seda	silk
la materia	material

Los lugares

el almacén	department store
el centro	downtown
el centro comercial	shopping mall
el mercado	market(place)
la tienda	shop, store

Cognado: la plaza

Los colores

amarillo/a	yellow
anaranjado/a	orange
azul	blue
blanco/a	white
(de) color café	brown
gris	gray
morado/a	purple
negro/a	black
rojo/a	red
rosado/a	pink
verde	green

Otros sustantivos

el/la chico/a	guy/girl
el examen	exam, test

Los adjetivos

barato/a	inexpensive
caro/a	expensive
cómodo/a	comfortable
poco/a	little, few

Repaso: mucho/a

Los números a partir del 100

ciento, ciento uno, ciento dos... ciento noventa y nueve, doscientos/as, trescientos/as, cuatrocientos/as, quinientos/as, seiscientos/as, setecientos/as, ochocientos/as, novecientos/as, mil, un millón (de)

Repaso: cien

Las formas demostrativas

aquel, aquella, aquellos/as	that, those ([way] over there)
aquello (neuter)	that ([way] over there)
ese/a, esos/as	that, those
eso (neuter)	that

Repaso: este/a, esto (neuter), estos/as

Palabras adicionales

¿adónde?	where (to)?
al (a + el)	to the
allá	(way) over there
allí	there
si	if
sobre	about
tener...	
ganas de + inf.	to feel like (doing something)
miedo (de)	to be afraid (of)
prisa	to be in a hurry
que + inf.	to have to (do something)
razón	to be right
sueño	to be sleepy
no tener razón	to be wrong
vamos	let's go
¿no?, ¿verdad?	right, don't they (you, and so on)?

Repaso: aquí, mucho (adv.), poco (adv.), tener... años

Vocabulario personal

5

En casa

En este capítulo

www.connectspanish.com

Casas de muchos colores en una calle (*street*) del centro de Granada, Nicaragua

EL SALVADOR

6.3 (punto tres) millones de habitantes

- El Salvador es el país más pequeño de Centroamérica, pero tiene la densidad de población más alta de la América continental.

NICARAGUA

6 millones de habitantes

- Nicaragua tiene diecisiete volcanes y dos lagos inmensos.

- ¿Dónde vive Ud.? ¿En qué parte de la ciudad? ¿en el centro, en la zona universitaria o en una zona residencial? ¿Vive en una residencia, en una casa o en un apartamento?
- ¿Cómo es su alcoba,[a] grande o pequeña? ¿Tiene un cuarto de baño propio[b]?
- ¿Cómo se siente Ud.[c] cuando está en casa? (**Me siento...**)

[a]*bedroom* [b]*un... your own bathroom* [c]*se... do you feel*

MANUEL GIL DEL VALLE CONTESTA LAS PREGUNTAS.

- Vivo en Managua, en un apartamento en una zona residencial que está a 5 kilómetros del centro de la ciudad.
- Es un apartamento muy cómodo, con tres alcobas y dos baños. Mi mujer y yo tenemos la alcoba de matrimonio,[a] que es muy amplia y luminosa y tiene su propio[b] baño. La alcoba de mis hijas también está muy bien, pero no tiene cuarto de baño propio. La otra alcoba es más pequeña y funciona como un estudio.
- Me gusta mucho estar en casa. Allí me siento bien porque puedo descansar y relajarme.[c] Pero sobre todo[d] porque en mi casa estoy con mi mujer y mis hijas, que son lo más importante en mi vida.[e]

[a]alcoba... *master bedroom (lit., of the marriage)* [b]*own* [c]descansar... *rest and relax* [d]sobre... *especially* [e]lo... *the most important thing in my life*

Los muebles,° los cuartos y otras partes de la casa
Los... *Furniture*

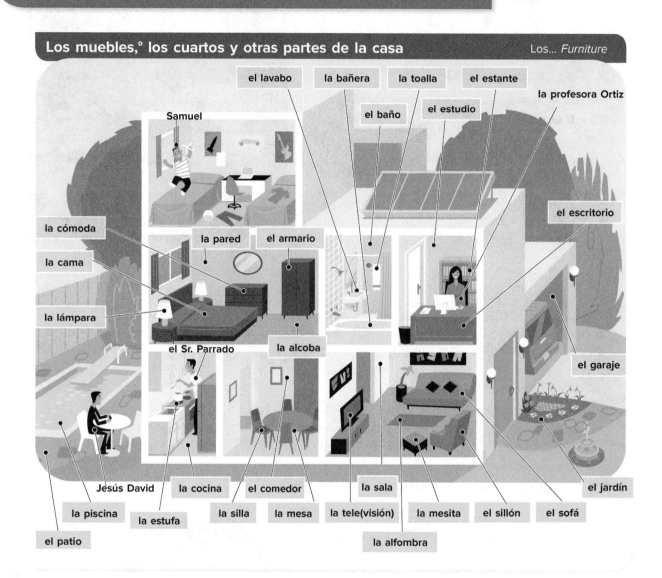

el lavabo — la bañera — la toalla — el estante

la profesora Ortiz

el baño — el estudio

Samuel

la cómoda

la cama

la pared — el armario

el escritorio

la lámpara

el Sr. Parrado — la alcoba

el garaje

Jesús David — la cocina — el comedor — la sala — el jardín

la piscina

la estufa — la silla — la mesa — la tele(visión) — la mesita — el sillón — el sofá

el patio

la alfombra

You can hear the pronunciation of theme vocabulary words and phrases in the Connect eBook.

Así se dice

el armario = el ropero
la bañera = la tina
el estudio = el despacho (*Sp.*)
el lavabo = la pileta (*L.A.*)

la piscina = la alberca (*Mex.*), la pileta (*Arg.*)
la sala = el living
la televisión = el televisor

There is great variation in the ways in which Spanish-speakers refer to the bedroom. It is called **la habitación** (also a synonym for any room of a house) by many native speakers, **el dormitorio** by Argentines, and **la recámara** by Mexicans.

*This is the first group of words you will learn for talking about where you live and the things found in your room, house, or apartment. You will learn additional vocabulary for those topics in **Capítulos 10** and **12**.*

Comunicación

A. Asociaciones. ¿Qué cuarto(s) o lugar de la casa asocia Ud. con estas actividades? **¡OJO! se** + *verb* = *"one (does something)"*.

1. Es donde se trabaja en la computadora.
2. Es donde se come con toda la familia.
3. La parte de la casa para el coche.
4. Allí se nada (*one swims*).
5. Allí se duerme (*one sleeps*).
6. Es donde se prepara la comida (*food*).

B. Asociaciones

Paso 1. En parejas, hagan y contesten preguntas para hacer una lista de los muebles o partes de la casa que Uds. asocian con las siguientes actividades.

1. estudiar para un examen
2. dormir la siesta (*to take a nap*) por la tarde
3. pasar (*to spend*) una noche en casa con la familia
4. celebrar con una comida (*meal*) especial
5. lavar (*to wash*) el perro
6. hablar de temas (*topics*) serios con los amigos (padres, esposo/a, hijos)

Paso 2. Ahora comparen sus respuestas con las (*those*) del resto de la clase. ¿Tienen todos las mismas costumbres (*same customs*)?

C. Esta casa

Paso 1. En parejas, identifiquen las partes de esta casa y lo que (*what*) hay en cada (*each*) una. Usen colores también.

MODELO: E1: El número 1 corresponde al **garaje.**
E2: ¿Qué hay en el garaje?
E1: Hay **un coche verde** y...

Vocabulario **útil**

la bicicleta
las cortinas
la planta

Paso 2. Ahora expandan el plano de esta casa para incorporar dos partes más. Deben pensar (*think*) en la utilidad (*purpose*) que tienen esas partes y poner (*put in*) los muebles apropiados. Luego (*Then*) prepárense para describir sus cambios.

Paso 3. Describan al resto de la clase las nuevas partes de la casa sin (*without*) leer.

MODELO: Las nuevas partes de nuestra casa son... En el/la _____ hay...

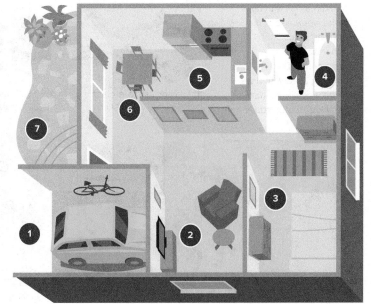

Nota **cultural**

Las casas en el mundo hispano

La palabra **casa** se usa de manera genérica en español para significar hogar,[a] como en estos ejemplos.

ir/regresar a casa	to go/return home
estar en casa	to be at home
Estás en tu casa.	Welcome. (*Lit.* You're in your home.)

Hay una gran variedad de tipos de casas en el mundo hispano y no se puede decir que haya[b] «una casa típica». Las construcciones dependen del[c] uso, de la zona (rural o urbana), del clima y de las tradiciones históricas y culturales. Y, por supuesto,[d] del factor económico.

En las ciudades, la mayoría de las personas no vive en casas sino[e] en apartamentos. Otras palabras para apartamento son **piso** (España) y **departamento** (México, Argentina).

[a]*home* [b]*decir... say that there is* [c]*on the* [d]*por... of course* [e]*but rather*

El Museo Casa Natal de Rubén Darío, en Ciudad Darío, Nicaragua

En su ciudad, ¿es más común vivir en un apartamento o en una casa? En su estado o país, ¿hay un estilo de casas predominante o tradicional?

¿Qué día es hoy?

lunes

1. Javier asiste a clase el lunes a las ocho.

martes

2. Javier mira la televisión el martes.

miércoles

3. Javier va al gimnasio el miércoles.

jueves

4. Javier trabaja cuatro horas el jueves.

viernes

5. El viernes va al mercado con unos amigos.

el fin de semana (sábado y domingo)

6. El fin de semana juega al basquetbol con sus amigos.

Hoy es viernes (domingo,...).	Today is Friday (Sunday, . . .).
Mañana es sábado (lunes,...).	Tomorrow is Saturday (Monday, . . .).
Ayer fue martes (miércoles,...).	Yesterday was Tuesday (Wednesday, . . .).
el fin de semana	the weekend
pasado mañana	the day after tomorrow
anteayer	the day before yesterday
el próximo jueves (viernes,...)	
el jueves (viernes,...) que viene	next Thursday (Friday, . . .)
la próxima semana	
la semana que viene	next week

- In Spanish-speaking countries, the week usually starts with **lunes.**
- The days of the week are not capitalized in Spanish.
- The words **sábado** and **domingo** have plural forms: **sábados, domingos.** All other days of the week end in **-s**; they use the same form for the plural as they do for the singular. See examples in **Nota comunicativa.**

Nota **comunicativa**

Cómo expresar *on* **con los días de la semana**

The definite article (singular or plural) is used to express **on** with the days of the week in Spanish.

el + *day* = on (Monday, Tuesday . . .)

Esta semana, tengo que ir al mercado **el** lunes.

This week, I have to go to the market on Monday.

los + *day* (plural form, if any) = on (Mondays, Tuesdays . . .)

Por lo general voy al mercado **los** viernes o **los** sábados.

I generally go to the market on Fridays or on Saturdays.

You will use **el** and **los** with days of the week in **Comunicación A** and **B**.

Comunicación

A. La semana

Paso 1. Complete las oraciones.

1. Hoy es _____. Mañana es _____.

2. Ayer fue _____ y anteayer fue _____.

3. Si hoy es sábado, mañana es _____. Ayer fue _____.

4. Si ayer fue domingo, hoy es _____ y mañana es _____.

5. Hay clase de español los _____, _____ y _____.

6. No tengo clases los _____ ni (*nor*) los _____.

7. Mi próximo examen de _____ es este _____.

8. Trabajo los _____ por la mañana/tarde/noche.

9. Los _____ por la tarde nunca estudio en la biblioteca.

10. Casi todos los _____ salgo (*I go out*) con mis amigos.

Paso 2. En parejas, intercambien (*exchange*) la información de los números 6–10. Luego digan (*tell*) a la clase las actividades que tienen en común.

B. Mi semana. Primero (*First*), indique lo que Ud. va a hacer **el** (lunes...) que viene. Luego indique una actividad típica de todos **los** (lunes...). Siga los modelos.

MODELOS: **El lunes** tengo que ir al gimnasio. (Voy a ir al gimnasio **el lunes.**)
Por lo general (Generalmente) voy al gimnasio **los lunes.**

Estrategia

Remember to use an infinitive after **ir a** if you want to use a verb. To express a place after **ir a,** remember to form the contraction **al** if necessary. The infinitive is used after all of the other verbs in the middle column.

| lunes
martes
miércoles
jueves
viernes
sábado
domingo | **+** | ir a + *place*
ir a + *inf.*

deber
desear
necesitar
poder
preferir
tener ganas de
tener que | **+** | el bar
la biblioteca
el centro
el cine (*movies*)
el gimnasio
el museo
el parque
¿ ?

descansar (*to rest*) en cama hasta
 muy tarde
jugar (*to play*) al (tenis, golf, voleibol,
 basquetbol)
¿ ? |

¿Cuándo? • Las preposiciones (Part 1)*

1. Antes de la fiesta, Rosa prepara la ensalada.

2. Durante la fiesta, Rosa baila y baila hasta el final.

3. Después de la fiesta, Rosa limpia la sala.

a preposition / **una preposición** = a word or phrase that specifies the relationship of one word to another

Prepositions link words or phrases to other words or phrases. The prepositions are indicated in the following sentences. Can you tell what words or phrases are linked by them?

1. The book is **on** the table.
2. The homework is **for** tomorrow.
3. Los sábados siempre descanso **hasta** muy tarde.
4. Voy a mirar la tele **después de** comer.

---

*You will learn prepositions that express spatial relationships in the **Vocabulario: Preparación** section of **Capítulo 6.**

You have already used many common Spanish prepositions, including: **a, con, de, en, hasta** (as in **hasta mañana**), **para**, and **por** (*in*, *during*, as in **por la mañana**).

In English, prepositions are often followed by the *-ing* form of a verb. However, in Spanish, the infinitive is the only verb form that can follow a preposition. You learned this with the expressions **para** + *inf*. and **ir a** + *inf*.

¿Adónde vas **después de** estudiar?

Where are you going after studying (after you study)?

Tengo ganas de comer **antes de mirar** la tele esta noche.

I feel like eating before watching TV (before I watch TV) tonight.

Comunicación

A. ¿Cuándo?

Paso 1. Complete las siguientes oraciones lógicamente. Puede usar sustantivos, infinitivos, días de la semana, etcétera.

1. Por lo general, prefiero estudiar antes de / después de las nueve de la noche.
2. Siempre tengo mucho sueño durante la clase de _____.
3. Voy a la clase de español antes de / después de la clase de _____.
4. Los _____ (día o días), estoy en la universidad hasta _____ (hora).
5. No puedo ir a fiestas durante la semana. Voy los _____ (día o días).
6. Tengo que estudiar en esta universidad hasta el año _____.

Paso 2. Ahora entreviste (*interview*) a un compañero o una compañera, usando (*using*) las oraciones del **Paso 1.**

MODELOS:: ¿Prefieres estudiar antes de las nueve de la noche?
¿Prefieres estudiar antes o después de las nueve de la noche?
¿Cuándo prefieres estudiar, antes o después de las nueve de la noche?

B. Intercambios. En parejas, túrnense para entrevistarse. Hagan sus preguntas, usando una palabra o frases de cada columna.

estudiar	antes de	tu programa favorito de televisión
hablar por teléfono	después de	las clases
leer	durante	las conferencias (*lectures*) de _____
trabajar	hasta	los viernes por la noche, los domingos por la mañana...
¿ ?		estudiar, mirar la tele,...
		las tres de la mañana, medianoche (*midnight*), muy tarde,...
		¿ ?

«Vivir con la familia» Segmento 1

«Bueno, mientras (*while*) asisto a la universidad vivo con mis padres. Lo mejor (*The best part*) de vivir con mis padres es la convivencia (*living together*) con ellos y lo peor (*the worst thing*) es que tengo que acatar sus reglas (*follow their rules*).»

Antes de mirar

Conteste las siguientes preguntas.

1. ¿Dónde vive Ud. ahora mientras (*while*) asiste a la universidad? ¿En una residencia universitaria? ¿en un apartamento compartido (*shared*) con otros estudiantes? ¿con su familia?

2. ¿Dónde vive la mayoría (*majority*) de los estudiantes de su universidad?

Este segmento

El tema del reportaje (*report*) de este segmento es dónde viven los estudiantes universitarios estadounidenses y mexicanos.

Estrategia

Remember to go over everything on this page before watching the segment for the first time. As you watch, make a mental note of words or expressions that are repeated in the segment. What are they?

Vocabulario del segmento

les vuelven a dar la bienvenida	welcome you again
¡En efecto!	You're so right!
lejos de	far from
en cambio	in contrast
no deja su hogar	don't leave home
la colonia	neighborhood (*Mex.*)
lo más céntrico	very centrally located
el apoyo que me dan	the support they give me
la novia	girlfriend
los familiares	relatives
las facilidades	facilities, conveniences

Después de mirar

A. ¿Está claro? Complete las siguientes oraciones según el video.

   1. Según Víctor, muchos/pocos estudiantes estadounidenses asisten a una universidad que está lejos de su casa.
   2. La mayoría de los estudiantes entrevistados (*interviewed*) vive/no vive con su familia.
   3. Según unos estudiantes, uno tiene que/no tiene que acatar las reglas de la familia.
   4. Para estos estudiantes, la compañía o convivencia es/no es importante.
   5. Según un estudiante, cuando uno vive con la familia, no es necesario pagar las facilidades/la matrícula.

B. Un poco más. Conteste las siguientes preguntas.

   1. Según los estudiantes mexicanos entrevistados, ¿qué es lo mejor de vivir con la familia? ¿Y lo peor?
   2. Según Víctor, ¿por qué es caro asistir a la universidad en los Estados Unidos?

C. Y ahora, Uds. En grupos, expresen sus opiniones sobre la idea de vivir con la familia mientras uno asiste a la universidad. ¿Qué es lo mejor y lo peor?

GRAMÁTICA LS

12 Expressing Actions
Hacer, oír, poner, salir, traer, ver

Grammar Tutorial 12
McGraw Hill Education **connect**
|SPANISH
www.connectspanish.com

Gramática en acción: Aspectos de la vida de Rigoberto

1. Traigo muchos libros al salón de clase.
2. No oigo bien. Por eso hago muchas preguntas en clase.
3. Pongo la tele y veo mi programa favorito.
4. Salgo con Elena los fines de semana.

Comprensión

1. ¿Qué trae Rigoberto al salón de clase?
2. ¿Por qué hace muchas preguntas en clase? ¿Ve bien? ¿Oye bien?
3. ¿A qué hora pone la tele? ¿Por qué prefiere mirar la tele a esa hora?
4. ¿Con quién sale?

hacer (to do; to make)		oír (to hear)		poner (to put; to place)		salir (to leave; to go out)		traer (to bring)		ver (to see)	
hago	hacemos	oigo	oímos	pongo	ponemos	salgo	salimos	traigo	traemos	veo	vemos
haces	hacéis	oyes	oís	pones	ponéis	sales	salís	traes	traéis	ves	veis
hace	hacen	oye	oyen	pone	ponen	sale	salen	trae	traen	ve	ven

Aspects of Rigoberto's life **1.** *I bring a lot of books to class.* **2.** *I don't hear well. That's why I ask a lot of questions in class.* **3.** *I turn on the TV and watch my favorite program.* **4.** *I go out with Elena on weekends.*

1. *hacer*

Hacer expresses English *to do* or *to make* in many contexts.

Pero, Julio, ¿qué **haces**?
But, Julio, what are you doing?

Siempre **hago** la tarea en la cafetería.
I always do my homework in the cafeteria.

Hacer is also used in a number of common idioms.

hacer un viaje
hacer una pregunta

Quieren **hacer un viaje** al Perú.
They want to take a trip to Peru.

Los niños siempre **hacen** muchas **preguntas**.
Children always ask a lot of questions.

Hacer is also used to express *to do* with physical and academic exercises. Note that the singular **ejercicio** is used to express *to exercise* in a gym, but the plural **ejercicios** is used for aerobics.

Hace ejercicio en el gimnasio, pero **hace ejercicios aeróbicos** en casa.
She exercises in the gym but does aerobics at home.

Alicia **hace los ejercicios** en el cuaderno.
Alicia does the exercises in the notebook.

---

2. *oír*

Oír means *to hear*.
The command forms of **oír** are used to attract someone's attention in the same way that English uses *Listen!* or *Hey!*

    oye (tú)   **oiga** (Ud.)   **oigan** (Uds.)

¡OJO!

oír = to hear
escuchar = to listen to
Some native speakers of Spanish use **oír** to mean *to listen to* things like music or the news. But **escuchar** can never mean *to hear*.

No **oigo** bien a la profesora.
I can't hear the professor well.

Oye, Juan, ¿vas a la fiesta?
Hey, Juan, are you going to the party?

¡Oigan! ¡Silencio, por favor!
Listen! Silence, please!

Oímos/Escuchamos música en clase.
We listen to music in class.

No **oigo** bien por el ruido.
I can't hear well because of the noise.

---

3. *poner*

Poner means *to put* or *to place*. Many Spanish speakers use **poner** with appliances to express *to turn on*.

Voy a **poner** la televisión.
I'm going to turn on the TV.

Siempre **pongo** leche y mucho azúcar en el café.
I always put milk and a lot of sugar in my coffee.

---

4. *salir*

Salir means *to leave* or *to go out*. Note in the examples at the right how different prepositions are used with it to express different meanings.

salir de + *place*
salir con + *person*
salir para + *destination*

Here's another useful expression: **salir bien/mal,** which means *to turn/come out well/poorly, to do well/poorly.*

Salgo con el hermano de Cecilia.
I'm going out with / dating Cecilia's brother.

Salimos para la sierra pasado mañana.
We're leaving for the mountains the day after tomorrow.

Todo va a **salir bien**.
Everything is going to turn out OK (well).

Salen de la clase ahora.
They're leaving class now.

No quiero **salir mal** en esta clase.
I don't want to do poorly in this class.

5. traer

Traer means *to bring*.

¡OJO!

Traer and **llevar** are somewhat related in meaning, but they are actually antonyms, like *bring* and *take* in English. **Traer** expresses *to bring* as in *to have* something *with* or *on* one. It also expresses *to bring* something *to* the person who is speaking. **Llevar** means *to take* someone or something *to* a place.

¿Por qué no **traes** ese radio a la cocina?
Why don't you bring that radio to the kitchen?

¿Cuánto dinero **traes** hoy?
How much money do you have (on you, did you bring) today?
¿Por qué no me **traes** una de las sillas del comedor?
Why don't you bring me one of the chairs from the dining room?
Este año voy a **llevar** a mi familia a Nicaragua.
This year I'm going to take my family to Nicaragua.

6. ver

Ver means *to see*. It can also mean *to watch* as in watching television or a movie, which is also expressed with the verb **mirar**.

¡OJO!

Mirar never expresses *to see* (except with movies). It only means *to watch, look at.*

No **veo** bien sin mis lentes.
I don't see well without my glasses.

Los niños **ven/miran** una película.
The kids are watching a movie.

Práctica y comunicación

A. Mi rutina

Paso 1. Autoprueba. Dé la forma indicada para cada verbo.

1. hacer: yo
2. oír: ellos
3. poner: yo
4. salir: yo
5. traer: yo
6. ver: yo

Verb Summary		
hacer,		
oír,		
poner	= -g-,
salir,		
traer		
oír	= -y-
ver	veo	

Paso 2. Ahora complete las siguientes oraciones lógicamente usando los verbos del **Paso 1** solo una vez. Añada (*Add*) una expresión de tiempo a cada oración y la palabra **no,** si es necesario.

Expresiones de tiempo

Before or after the verb: **los lunes/martes/..., los fines de semana, (casi) todos los días, a veces...**

Before the verb: **(casi) siempre, (casi) nunca**

1. _____ ejercicio en el gimnasio_____.
2. _____ a mis amigos los _____ por la _____.
3. _____ de casa antes de las _____ de la mañana.
4. _____ mi libro de texto a la clase de español _____.
5. _____ las noticias (*news*) por la tele _____.
6. _____ la ropa en la cómoda y el armario _____ .

Paso 3. Ahora, en parejas, túrnense para hacer y contestar preguntas basadas en las oraciones del **Paso 2.** Luego digan (*tell*) a la clase algo (*something*) que Uds. tienen en común o que hacen de manera muy diferente o peculiar.

MODELO: Hago ejercicio en el gimnasio casi todos días. →
¿Con qué frecuencia haces ejercicio en el gimnasio? (¿Haces ejercicio en el gimnasio todos los días?) →
Hannah y yo casi nunca hacemos ejercicio en el gimnasio.

Prác. A, Paso 1: Answers: hago 2. oyen 3. pongo 4. salgo 5. traigo 6. veo

B. Lógicamente

Paso 1. Complete las siguientes oraciones con la forma apropiada de **hacer, oír, poner, salir, traer** o **ver.** Use **no** cuando es necesario para que (*so that*) las oraciones sean (*will be*) apropiadas para Ud.

MODELO: Los estudiantes de esta clase _____ mucha tarea. →
Los estudiantes de esta clase **hacemos/hacen** mucha tarea.

1. (Yo) _____ la tele por la noche.
2. Siempre (tú) _____ los sábados por la noche con tus amigos.
3. (Nosotros) _____ el libro de texto de español a clase.
4. Muchas personas no _____ ejercicio.
5. Los hispanos _____ mucho la radio.
6. Yo _____ azúcar (*sugar*) en mi café.
7. Mi amigo va a _____ un viaje a Nicaragua en diciembre.
8. En general, (yo) _____ bien en los exámenes.
9. Me gusta _____ películas extranjeras.

Paso 2. Use las respuestas del **Paso 1** para hacerle preguntas a un compañero ouna compañera. ¿Está siempre de acuerdo con Ud. su compañero/a?

MODELO: Los estudiantes de esta clase **hacemos** mucha tarea. →
¿**Crees que** los estudiantes de esta clase hacemos mucha tarea?

C. Los nuevos verbos

Paso 1. Lea (*Read*) el siguiente afiche (*poster*), que ilustra una expresión idiomática.

LOS TRES MONOSᵃ **SABIOS**

NO OÍR, NO VER, NO HABLAR

ᵃmonos... *smart monkeys*

1. ¿Qué dicen los monos sabios en inglés?
2. ¿Qué diría (*would say*) cada mono en español hablando (*speaking*) en primera persona?
3. ¿Dónde sería (*would it be*) apropiado colgar (*to hang*) un afiche como este?

Paso 2. Los nuevos verbos se usan en más expresiones idiomáticas. Pero el significado (*meaning*) de los modismos no es siempre transparente. ¿Puede Ud. emparejar cada expresión con su significado?

EXPRESIONES

1. _____ poner un granito de arena (*sand*)
2. _____ poner en duda
3. _____ poner un límite a
4. _____ traer algo (*something*) entre manos (*hands*)
5. _____ salir en las noticias
6. _____ hacer un papel (*role*)
7. _____ ver para creer

SIGNIFICADOS

a. ¡tener sus 15 minutos de fama!
b. decir (*to say*) que algo (*something*) es cuestionable
c. necesitar la observación personal para aceptar que una cosa es verdad
d. hacer una pequeña contribución
e. decidir hasta dónde queremos llegar
f. tener un plan
g. actuar en una película o una obra de teatro (*play*)

Algo sobre...

los lagos de Nicaragua

En Nicaragua hay dos lagos inmensos: el lago de Nicaragua (o Cocibolca) y el lago de Managua (o Xolotlán). Los dos están unidos por el río[a] Tipitapa. El Cocibolca es el lago más grande[b] de Centroamérica y, después del lago Titicaca en Bolivia, es el lago más grande de Latinoamérica. En el Cocibolca hay volcanes e islas.

¿Cómo se llama el lago más grande de este país? ¿y el río más grande?

[a]*river* [b]*más... biggest*

El lago de Nicaragua, con el volcán Maderas al fondo (*in the background*)

D. **Consecuencias lógicas.** En parejas, indiquen acciones lógicas o consecuencias relacionadas con cada situación. No se limiten a usar los verbos de esta sección del libro. ¡Sean (*Be*) creativos y audaces (*daring*)!

1. Me gusta nadar (*to swim*) en los lagos. Por eso...
2. Todos los días usamos este libro en la clase de español. Por eso...
3. Mis hijos / compañeros de cuarto hacen mucho ruido en la sala. Por eso...
4. La televisión no funciona. Por eso...
5. Hay mucho ruido en el salón de clase. Por eso...
6. Estoy en la biblioteca y ¡no puedo estudiar más! Por eso...
7. Queremos bailar y necesitamos música. Por eso...
8. No comprendo la lección. Por eso...
9. Me gusta hacer ecoturismo y hablar español. Por eso...

Vocabulario útil

gritar «¡silencio!»	to shout "silence!"
hacer una cita	to make an appointment
los vecinos	neighbors

E. **Intercambios**

Paso 1. En parejas, hagan y contesten las siguientes preguntas.

EN CASA

1. ¿Qué pones en el armario? ¿y en la cómoda? ¿en el cajón (*drawer*) del escritorio?
2. ¿Pones la televisión con frecuencia cuando estás en casa? ¿Qué programa(s) ves todos los días? ¿Qué programa muy popular no ves nunca? (**Nunca veo...**) ¿Cuál es el canal de televisión que más miras? ¿Por qué te gusta tanto (*so much*)?
3. ¿Pones el radio con frecuencia? ¿Prefieres oír las noticias por radio o verlas (*to see them*) en la televisión? ¿Cuál es la estación de radio que más escuchas? ¿Por qué te gusta tanto?

(Continúa.)

4. ¿Qué haces los _____ (día) por la noche? ¿Cuándo sales con los amigos? ¿Adónde van cuando salen juntos (*together*)?

5. ¿Te gusta hacer ejercicio? ¿Haces ejercicios aeróbicos? ¿Dónde haces ejercicio?

PARA LAS CLASES

6. Generalmente, ¿qué traes a clase todos los días? ¿Crees que traes más cosas (*things*) que tus compañeros o menos? ¿Sales a veces para la clase sin tu libro de texto? ¿sin dinero? ¿Qué trae tu profesor(a) de español a clase?

7. ¿A qué hora sales para las clases los lunes? ¿A qué hora sales de clase los viernes?

8. ¿Cuándo haces la tarea? ¿Por la mañana? ¿Dónde haces la tarea? ¿En casa? ¿Haces la tarea mientras (*while*) ves la televisión? ¿mientras oyes música?

9. ¿Siempre sales bien en los exámenes? ¿En qué clase no sales bien? ¿Qué haces si sales mal en un examen?

Paso 2. Ahora digan (*tell*) a la clase dos o tres cosas que Uds. tienen en común.

MODELO: Jim y yo nunca ponemos la ropa en el armario. Hacemos ejercicio todos los días: Jim hace ejercicios aeróbicos y yo voy al gimnasio. Los dos vemos el programa _____ los lunes por la noche; es nuestro programa favorito.

Algo sobre...

las casas tradicionales centroamericanas

En Centroamérica y en otros países latinoamericanos hay casas de bajareque, un tipo de construcción tradicional de origen precolombino.[a] Se usan materiales locales y económicos: paredes sostenidas por palos[b] y rellenas de barro y cañas.[c] Las casas de bajareque son generalmente humildes,[d] pero también son construcciones ecológicas y sismorresistentes,[e] una característica importante para una región de alta actividad sísmica como es Centroamérica.

En los Estados Unidos, ¿es la construcción de las casas típicas del norte diferente de la (*that*) de las casas del sur?

[a]*pre-Columbian* [b]*sostenidas... held up by sticks or logs* [c]*rellenas... filled with mud and reeds* [d]*humble* [e]*resistant to earthquakes*

Una casa de bajareque, en Nicaragua

¿Recuerda Ud.?

The change in the stem vowels of **preferir**, **querer**, and **poder** was presented in **Gramática 10**. Review the forms of **preferir**, **querer**, and **poder** now.

poder: o → ¿ ?

p__do	podemos
p__des	podéis
p__de	p__den

preferir: e → ¿ ?

pref__ro	preferimos
pref__res	preferís
pref__re	pref__ren

querer: e → ¿ ?

qu__ro	queremos
qu__res	queréis
qu__re	qu__ren

If you could complete those verb forms correctly, you already know most of the important information in **Gramática 13**.

Present Tense of Stem-changing Verbs (Part 2)

Gramática en acción: ¿Una fiesta exitosa?

Es la noche del sábado y todos están en una fiesta en casa de Ernesto.

- Aurora duerme en el sofá.
- Samuel juega a las cartas... a solas.
- Ernesto sirve las bebidas. Kevin pide una Coca-Cola.
- Noemí sale y vuelve con más amigas.
- ¿Es una fiesta exitosa? ¿Qué piensa Ud.? ¿Por qué?

¿Y Ud.? ¿Qué hace en las fiestas?

1. ¿Duerme Ud. en el sofá?
2. ¿Juega a las cartas?
3. ¿Sirve las bebidas?
4. ¿Pide Coca-Cola?
5. ¿Sale y vuelve con más amigos?

e → ie: pensar (to think)		o → ue: volver (to return)		e → i: pedir (to ask for; to order)	
pienso	pensamos	vuelvo	volvemos	pido	pedimos
piensas	pensáis	vuelves	volvéis	pides	pedís
piensa	piensan	vuelve	vuelven	pide	piden

1. **Stem-changing Verbs**

   You have already used three *stem-changing verbs* **(los verbos que cambian el radical): poder, preferir,** and **querer.** And you also know two other verbs that are similar (**tener** and **venir**), but whose first person singular forms are irregular.

A successful party? *It's Saturday night and everybody is at a party at Ernesto's house.* • *Aurora is sleeping on the couch.* • *Samuel is playing cards ... alone.* • *Ernesto is serving beverages. Kevin asks for a Coke.* • *Noemí leaves and comes back with more friends.* • *Is it a successful party? What do you think? Why?*

2. Stem Vowel Changes

There are three groups of stem-changing verbs. You already know about the first two.

- verbs like **preferir** and **querer,** in which the stem vowel **e** becomes **ie** in stressed syllables
- verbs like **poder,** in which the stem vowel **o** becomes **ue** in stressed syllables

Here is the third group.

- verbs in which the stem vowel **e** becomes **i**

The stem-changing pattern of all three groups is shown at the right. The stem vowels are stressed (and so they change) in all present tense forms except **nosotros** and **vosotros.** All three groups follow this regular pattern, which looks like a boot.

Las vocales que cambian el radical

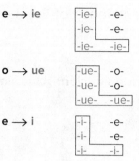

e → ie	-ie-	-e-
	-ie-	-e-
	-ie-	-ie-

o → ue	-ue-	-o-
	-ue-	-o-
	-ue-	-ue-

e → i	-i-	-e-
	-i-	-e-
	-i-	-i-

¡OJO!

Nosotros and **vosotros** forms *do not* have a stem vowel change.

---

3. Important Stem-changing Verbs

Some stem-changing verbs practiced in this chapter include the following.

e → ie

cerrar (cierro)

cerrar (cierro)	to close
empezar (empiezo)	to begin, start
entender (entiendo)	to understand
pensar (pienso)	to think
perder (pierdo)	to lose; to miss (*an event*)

o (u) → ue

dormir (duermo)

almorzar (almuerzo)	to have lunch
dormir (duermo)	to sleep
jugar (juego)	to play (*a game, sport*)
volver (vuelvo)	to return (*to a place*)

¡OJO!

Jugar *is the only* **u → ue** *stem-changing verb in Spanish.* **Jugar** *is usually followed by* **al** *when used with the name of a sport:* **Juego al tenis.** *Some Spanish speakers, however, omit the* **al.** *Just* **a** *is used before the names of other games:* **Juego a las cartas.**

e → i

servir (sirvo) (para)

pedir (pido)	to ask for; to order
servir (sirvo)	to serve; to be used (*for*)

As you learned with **poder, preferir,** and **querer,** stem-changing verbs will be indicated in vocabulary lists with the **yo** form in parentheses, as shown here.

4. *Verb + **a** + Infinitive*
Like **aprender** and **ir,** the stem-changing verbs **empezar** and **volver** are followed by **a** before an infinitive.

Uds. **empiezan a hablar** muy bien el español.
You're starting to speak Spanish very well.

The meaning of **empezar** does not change in this structure, but **volver a** + *infinitive* expresses *to do* (*something*) *again.*

¿Cuándo **vuelves a jugar** al tenis?
When are you going to play tennis again?

---

5. *Conjugated Verb + Infinitive*
Like other verbs you already know (**desear, necesitar, deber,...**), **pensar** can be followed directly by an infinitive. In that case, it expresses *to intend, plan.*

¿Cuándo **piensas** almorzar?
When do you plan to eat lunch?

The phrase **pensar en** can be used to express *to think about.*

—¿**En** qué **piensas**?
—**Pienso en** las cosas que tengo que hacer el domingo.
"What are you thinking about?"
"I'm thinking about the things I have to do on Sunday."

Pensar de indicates one's opinion about someone or something. The answer to a question with **pensar de** usually starts with **Pienso que...**

—¿Qué **piensas de** esa situación?
—¡**Pienso que** es un desastre!
"What do you think about that situation?"
"I think (that) it's a real mess!"

—¿Qué **piensas del** nuevo apartamento de Cristina?
—**Pienso que** es elegante. . . pero ¡muy caro!
"What do you think of/about Cristina's new apartment?"
"I think (that) it's fancy. . . but very expensive!"

---

6. Present Tense Equivalents
Remember that the Spanish present tense has a number of present tense equivalents in English. It can also be used to express future meaning.

cierro = *I close, I am closing, I will close*

Práctica y comunicación

A. Asociaciones

Paso 1. Dé por lo menos un infinitivo que asocia con las siguientes ideas y cosas.

1. una bebida	**10.** la cocina
2. una lección	**11.** una siesta
3. a casa	**12.** un favor
4. una cama	**13.** las cartas
5. una hamburguesa	**14.** una palabra o frase
6. el tenis	**15.** la música
7. una opinión	
8. una puerta	
9. las llaves (*keys*)	

> **Stem-Change Summary**
>
> empezar (empiezo)
> volver (vuelvo)
> jugar (juego)
> pedir (pido)

Paso 2. Explique para qué sirven las siguientes cosas.

MODELO: las cartas → **Sirven para** jugar.

1. las llaves	**4.** un menú
2. una cama	**5.** un diccionario
3. una bandeja (*tray*)	**6.** el cerebro (*brain*)

B. La vida (*Life*) en la universidad

Paso 1. Autoprueba. Dé la forma de cada verbo para **yo** y para **nosotros**.

1. almorzar
2. entender
3. pedir
4. perder
5. dormir
6. jugar
7. pensar
8. volver

Paso 2. Ahora complete las siguientes oraciones lógicamente usando los verbos del **Paso 1** solo una vez. Añada (*Add*) una expresión de tiempo y/o la palabra **no,** si es necesario.

Expresiones de tiempo

Before or after the verb: **los lunes/martes/... , los fines de semana, (casi) todos los días, a veces...**

Before the verb: **(casi) siempre, (casi) nunca**

1. _____ la siesta _____.
2. _____ en la cafetería _____.
3. _____ pizza para almorzar _____.
4. _____ a las cartas con mi familia _____.
5. _____ en mis notas (*grades*) _____.
6. _____ mi carnet de identificación de la universidad _____.
7. _____ a casa de mis padres / de mi familia _____.
8. _____ muchas cosas en mi clase de _____ (materia).

 Paso 3. Ahora, en parejas, túrnense para hacer y contestar preguntas basadas en las oraciones del **Paso 2.** Luego digan (*tell*) a la clase algo (*something*) que Uds. tienen en común o que hacen de manera muy diferente o peculiar.

MODELOS: Duermo la siesta casi todos días. →
      ¿Con qué frecuencia duermes la siesta? (¿Duermes la siesta todos los días?) →
      Jacob y yo dormimos la siesta casi todos los días.

C. Una tarde típica en casa. ¿Cuáles son las actividades de todos? Haga oraciones completas, usando una palabra o frase de cada columna.

yo		descansar, dormir
mi padre/madre	almorzar	solo/a
mi esposo/a	dormir	en un sillón / en la cocina
los niños	empezar a	toda la tarde / la siesta
mi amigo/a _____ y yo	entender	su pelota (*ball*), sus llaves, su mochila
el perro/gato	jugar a	tarde/temprano a casa
mi compañero/a	pedir	en el patio / en la piscina / afuera (*outside*)
(no)	pensar	el golf (tenis, voleibol...), las cartas
	pensar en	las películas viejas/recientes
	perder	mis notas, mis clases, los exámenes
	preferir	la lección, la oración
	volver	hablar bien el español
	volver a	ver una película con frecuencia
	¿ ?	¿ ?

yo + (no) + [verbo] + [frase]

D. Una semana ideal... ¡y posible!

Paso 1. ¿Qué va a hacer Ud. la semana que viene? Organice la próxima semana en la siguiente agenda. Escriba frases con el infinitivo, por ejemplo: **ver la televisión.** Incluya actividades que tiene que hacer, pero también algunas (*some*) que tiene ganas de hacer.

	por la mañana	por la tarde	por la noche
lunes			
martes			
miércoles			
jueves			
viernes			
sábado			
domingo			

Paso 2. En parejas, hablen de su horario (*schedule*) para esta semana, basándose (*based on*) en la agenda del **Paso 1.** Luego digan (*tell*) algunas (*some*) respuestas interesantes a la clase.

MODELO: ver la televisión →
　　　　E1: ¿Qué **piensas** hacer el domingo por la tarde?
　　　　E2: **Pienso** ver la televisión. Y tú, ¿qué haces el domingo?
　　　　E1: El domingo **juego** al tenis con mi amigo Alex.

Estrategia

e → ie
o → ue
e → i

E. Intercambios. En parejas, túrnense para hacer y contestar preguntas sobre los temas siguientes con las frases sugeridas (*suggested*).

MODELOS: almorzar (¿dónde? ¿con quién? ¿a qué hora?) →
　　　　Por lo general, ¿dónde **almuerzas** de lunes a viernes?
　　　　¿Con quién **vas a almorzar** hoy?
　　　　¿A qué hora **piensas almorzar** el domingo?

1. almorzar (¿dónde? ¿con quién? ¿a qué hora?)
2. perder (¿qué? ¿dónde? ¿con frecuencia? ¿siempre?)
3. dormir (¿cuántas horas? ¿mucho o poco? ¿siestas frecuentes o infrecuentes? ¿largas o cortas?)
4. jugar (¿juegos de mesa [*board games*]? ¿cuáles? ¿con quién? ¿dónde?)

Estrategia

generalizations: present tense
future: **ir** + **a** + *inf.*
definite plans: **pensar** + *inf.*

¿Recuerda Ud.?

In **Capítulo 1,** you learned how to ask what someone's name is and express your own name by using phrases with the verb **llamar.** Show what you remember by completing the following phrases.

1. (yo) _____ llamo　　**2.** (tú) _____ llamas　　**3.** Ud. _____ llama

The words with which you completed those phrases are part of a pronoun system that you will learn about in **Gramática 14.**

14 Expressing *-self/-selves*
Reflexive Pronouns (Part 1)*

Gramática en acción: La rutina diaria de Andrés

La rutina diaria de Andrés empieza a las siete y media.

1.   2.   3.   4.

(1) Me despierto a las siete y media y me levanto en seguida. Primero, (2) me ducho y luego (3) me cepillo los dientes. (4) Me peino, (5) me pongo la bata y (6) voy al cuarto a vestirme. Por fin, (7) salgo para la universidad. No tomo nada antes de salir porque, por lo general, ¡tengo prisa!

5.   6.   7.

¿Y Ud.? ¿Cómo es su rutina diaria?

1. Yo me levanto a las _____ .
2. Me ducho por la mañana / noche.
3. Me visto en el baño / mi cuarto.
4. Me peino antes de / después de vestirme.
5. Antes de salir para las clases, tomo / no tomo el desayuno (*breakfast*).

Verbs Used Reflexively / Los verbos que se usan con pronombres reflexivos

bañarse (*to take a bath, bathe*)

(yo)	me **baño**	I take a bath	(nosotros)	nos **bañamos**	we take a bath
(tú)	te **bañas**	you take a bath	(vosotros)	os **bañáis**	you take a bath
(Ud.)	se **baña**	you take a bath	(Uds.)	se **bañan**	you take a bath
(él)		he takes a bath	(ellos)		they take a bath
(ella)		she takes a bath	(ellas)		they take a bath

Andrés's daily routine *Andrés's daily routine begins at seven-thirty. (1) I wake up at seven-thirty and I get up right away. First, (2) I take a shower and then (3) I brush my teeth. (4) I comb my hair, (5) I put on my robe, and (6) I go to my room to get dressed. Finally, (7) I leave for the university. I don't eat or drink anything before leaving because I'm generally in a hurry!*
You will learn how to use reflexive pronouns to express each other *in* **Gramática 32 (Cap. 11).**

1. Reflexive Pronouns

In Spanish, some verbs are used reflexively, that is, with reflexive pronouns that indicate that the subject is doing something *to* or *for* *himself, herself, itself,* and so on. The reflexive pronouns that correspond to the subject must accompany the verb, coming before it: **yo** → **me**; **tú** → **te**; **él, ella, Ud.** → **se**; **nosotros** → **nos**; **vosotros** → **os**; **ellos, ellas, Uds.** → **se**.

The pronoun **-se** at the end of an infinitive indicates that the verb is used reflexively: **bañarse** (to take a bath; to bathe oneself).

Los pronombres reflexivos

yo	me	myself
tú	te	yourself (*fam., sing.*)
Ud./él/ella	se	himself, herself, itself; yourself (*form. sing.*)
nosotros/as	nos	ourselves
vosotros/as	os	yourselves (*fam. pl. Sp.*)
Uds./ellos/as.	se	themselves; yourselves (*form. pl.*)

me baño = I take a bath (bathe myself)
me ducho = I shower (take a shower)

¡OJO!
Verbs used reflexively often do not have an exact parallel in English, and there is not always a reflexive pronoun in the translation.

2. Important Verbs Used Reflexively

Many English verbs that describe parts of one's daily routine—to get up, to take a bath, and so on—are expressed in Spanish with a reflexive construction. Here are some that are frequently used.

¡OJO!
Notice that some of these reflexive verbs also have stem changes: **e** → **ie, o** → **ue, e** → **i**.

| despertarse (me despierto) | ducharse | afeitarse | vestirse (me visto) | sentarse (me siento) |

Note the **-se** on the end of these infinitives. This is how reflexive verbs will be shown in vocabulary lists.

acostarse (me acuesto)	to go to bed	**ducharse**	to take a shower
afeitarse	to shave	**levantarse**	to get up (out of bed); to stand up
bañarse	to take a bath, bathe	**llamarse**	to be called
cepillarse los dientes	to brush one's teeth	**peinarse**	to brush/comb one's hair
despertarse (me despierto)	to wake up	**ponerse (me pongo)**	to put on (*an article of clothing*)
divertirse (me divierto)	to have a good time, enjoy oneself	**quitarse**	to take off (*an article of clothing*)
		sentarse (me siento)	to sit down
dormirse (me duermo)	to fall asleep	**vestirse (me visto)**	to get dressed

¡OJO!
After **ponerse** and **quitarse**, the definite article, not the possessive as in English, is used with articles of clothing.

Me siento y **me quito** los zapatos. Luego **me quito** los pantalones y la camisa y **me pongo** la bata.
I sit down and take off my shoes. Then I take off my pants and shirt and put on my bathrobe.

3. Placement of Reflexive Pronouns

Reflexive pronouns are placed before a conjugated verb. In a negative sentence, they are placed between the word **no** and the conjugated verb: **No se bañan.**

When a conjugated verb is followed by an infinitive that is used reflexively, the reflexive pronouns may either precede the conjugated verb or be attached to the infinitive.

¡OJO!

The reflexive pronoun must be repeated with each verb in a series of verbs.

Me **levanto** temprano todos los días.
I get up early every day.
No me **levanto** temprano todos los días.
I do not get up early every day.

Me **tengo** que levantar temprano.
Tengo que **levantarme** temprano.
I have to get up early.

Debo **acostarme** más temprano.
Me **debo** acostar más temprano.
I should go to bed earlier.

Me **levanto** a las siete, me **ducho** y me **visto** antes de **peinarme.**
Mi esposo se **baña,** yo me **ducho** y los dos nos **peinamos** antes de las seis.

4. Nonreflexive Use of Verbs

All of these verbs can also be used nonreflexively, often with a different meaning. Some examples of this appear at right.

dormir = to sleep	**dormirse** = to fall asleep
poner = to put, place	**ponerse** = to put on

Algo sobre...

la costa centroamericana

Los países centroamericanos tienen costa en los océanos Pacífico y Atlántico (el mar Caribe), excepto El Salvador, que solo tiene costa en el Pacífico. El Salvador es un poco más pequeño que el estado de Massachusetts. Así que aunque[a] solo tiene costa en el Pacífico, ¡el mar nunca está muy lejos[b] para ir a bañarse!

¿Tiene su estado (o país) costa marítima? ¿En qué océano o mar?

[a]Así... *So although* [b]*far*

Playa la Paz, El Salvador, un lugar ideal para bañarse y hacer *surfing*

Práctica y comunicación

A. Asociaciones. Dé todas las palabras que pueda (*you can*) asociar con los siguientes infinitivos. Piense (*Think*) en grupos de palabras que Ud. ya conoce (*you already know*): los cuartos de una casa, los muebles, la ropa, otros verbos, los adverbios, etcétera.

Reflexive Pronoun Summary	
yo	→ me
tú	→ te
Ud., él, ella	→ se
nosotros/as	→ nos
vosotros/as	→ os
Uds., ellos, ellas	→ se

1. llamarse
2. levantarse
3. bañarse
4. sentarse
5. ponerse
6. despertarse
7. divertirse
8. acostarse

B. Su rutina diaria

Paso 1. Autoprueba. Empareje los pronombres reflexivos con los verbos apropiados.

PRONOMBRES

1. me _____
2. te _____
3. se _____
4. nos _____

VERBOS

a. acuesta
b. baño
c. ponemos
d. duermen
e. despierta
f. vistes

Paso 2. Complete las siguientes oraciones lógicamente con verbos en la primera persona singular (**yo**) y **no** si es necesario. Luego indique si Ud. hace las acciones **los lunes, los sábados** o los dos días. No repita los verbos.

VERBOS: acostarse, despertarse, divertirse, ducharse, levantarse, ponerse

1. _____ con el reloj despertador (*alarm clock*).
2. _____ antes de salir de casa.
3. _____ muy tarde después de una fiesta con mis amigos.
4. _____ mucho durante toda la tarde con amigos.
5. _____ ropa deportiva (*sports*) y tenis.
6. No _____ inmediatamente después de despertarme.

Paso 3. Ahora, en parejas, túrnense para hacer y contestar preguntas basadas en las oraciones del **Paso 2.** Luego digan (*tell*) a la clase algo (*something*) que Uds. tienen en común o que hacen de manera muy diferente o peculiar.

MODELOS: 1. Me despierto con el reloj despertador los lunes. →
¿Te despiertas con el despertador los lunes? →
Sam y yo nos despertamos con el reloj despertador los lunes.

Nota comunicativa

Cómo expresar una secuencia de acciones

The following adverbs and expressions will help you indicate the sequence of actions or events.

primero	first	**finalmente**	finally
luego, después	then, later, next	**por fin**	finally
en seguida	immediately		

Primero, me ducho y me visto. **Luego,** tomo un café y leo el periódico. **Después,** me cepillo los dientes. **Finalmente,** salgo para el trabajo.

You will use these words and phrases in **Práctica C.**

C. Un día típico

Paso 1. Complete las siguientes oraciones lógicamente para describir su rutina diaria. Use el pronombre reflexivo cuando sea necesario. ¡OJO! Use el infinitivo después de las preposiciones.

1. Me levanto después de _____.
2. Primero, (yo) _____ y luego _____.
3. Me visto antes de / después de _____.
4. Luego me siento a la mesa para _____.
5. Me gusta estudiar antes de _____ o después de _____.
6. Por la noche me divierto y luego _____.
7. Me acuesto antes de / después de _____ y finalmente _____.

Paso 2. Con las oraciones del **Paso 1,** describa los hábitos de su esposo/a, su compañero/a de cuarto/casa, sus hijos...

Prác. B, Paso 1: Answers: 1. b 2. f 3. a, d, e 4. c

D. El día de Ángela. Ángela es dependienta en una tienda de ropa para jóvenes en El Paso. ¿Cómo es un día normal de trabajo para ella? Complete la narración con los verbos apropiados, según los dibujos. **¡OJO!** Algunos (*Some*) verbos se usan más de una vez (*more than once*).

1.

2.

3.

4.

5.

6.

1. Me despierto a las nueve de la mañana y _____ en seguida. (Yo) _____ rápidamente y salgo de casa sin _____. Llego a la tienda a las diez menos diez de la mañana con mis compañeras de trabajo. Primero (yo) _____ mi trabajo, ordenando (*putting in order*) la ropa. La ropa de la tienda _____ muy bonita.
2. A las diez abren la tienda y los clientes _____ a llegar.
3. Mis compañeras no _____ español. Por eso yo siempre atiendo a los clientes hispanos.
4. (Yo) _____ a las doce y media con mi amiga Susie, que trabaja en una zapatería. Generalmente podemos _____ en la pizzería San Marcos y casi siempre _____ pizza.
5. Luego, (yo) _____ a la tienda y _____ a trabajar. Nunca _____ la siesta.
6. Por fin, la supervisora _____ la tienda a las seis en punto. Luego yo _____ a casa. _____ la ropa de trabajo (*work clothes*) y _____ un vestido y zapatos elegantes. _____ salir a bailar con unos amigos... ¡y no pienso ir a _____ hasta muy, muy tarde!.

E. Intercambios: Su rutina

Paso 1. En parejas, túrnense para entrevistarse. Hagan preguntas, usando las ideas de las tres columnas y otras de su imaginación. Usen una palabra o frase de cada columna y traten de (*try to*) explicar sus acciones.

(Continúa.)

MODELO: **E1:** ¿A qué hora te acuestas?

E2: Siempre me acuesto muy tarde porque trabajo hasta las once de la noche en un restaurante. Luego tengo que estudiar un poco.

| ¿a qué hora?
¿con quién?
¿cuándo?
¿dónde?
¿durante _____ ?
¿hasta qué hora? | **+** | acostarse
afeitarse
cepillarse los dientes
despertarse
dormirse
ducharse/bañarse
levantarse
peinarse
sentarse
vestirse/ponerse _____
volver | **+** | los días de la
   semana
los fines de semana
los lunes (martes...)
todos los días
tarde/temprano
solo/a |

Paso 2. Ahora digan (*tell*) a la clase un detalle (*detail*) interesante, raro o indiscreto de la vida (*life*) de su compañero/a.

MODELO: Sebastián se duerme a la una todas las noches con su perro y con sus dos gatos. ¡Debe tener una cama muy grande!

Un poco de todo

A. Lengua y cultura: Una tradición extendida: El Día de la Cruz (*Cross*)

Paso 1. Complete the following paragraphs about a special holiday. Give the correct form of the words in parentheses, as suggested by context. When two possibilities are given in parentheses, select the correct word.

Nicaragua y El Salvador tienen tradiciones que reflejan su mezcla[a] étnica y cultural. Una de estas tradiciones es la fiesta (del / de la[1]) Día de la Cruz, una fiesta religiosa que se celebra el 3 de mayo en El Salvador, en Nicaragua y en (otro[2]) países hispanohablantes, incluyendo España. ¿(Por qué / Porque[3]) es una tradición tan[b] extendida la celebración del Día de la Cruz? Porque todos son países en donde muchas personas (pero no todas) observan las (tradición[4]) católicas.

En algunos[c] pueblos y (ciudad[5]) hay procesiones[d] que (salir[6]) por los barrios.[e] Muchas familias salvadoreñas (poner[7]) una cruz en su patio. Las (cruz[8]) están adornadas con mucha fruta y con fruta y flores[f] (con / de[9]) papel. Las personas (vestirse[10]) con ropa especial y (celebrar[11]) el día con comidas y bebidas típicas, con (su[12]) familia y con sus amigos.

En El Salvador la celebración del 3 de mayo (unir[g][13]) el culto a la cruz de los cristianos con el culto a la tierra[h] de los indígenas. En el mes de mayo se cosecha[i] la fruta y también (empezar[14]) las lluvias.[j] (Por / Para[15]) eso es un (bueno[16]) momento para dar gracias[k] a la tierra. Además,[l] los campesinos (pedir[17]) una buena cosecha para el año entrante,[m] según la tradición indígena. Esto es solo *un* ejemplo de cómo la influencia indígena y la española se unen en las tradiciones latinoamericanas.

[a]reflejan... *show their mixture* [b]*so* [c]*some* [d]*religious parades, processions* [e]*por... out from (individual) neighborhoods* [f]*flowers* [g]*to join, unite* [h]*earth* [i]*se... is harvested* [j]*rains* [k]*dar... thank* [l]*Besides* [m]*coming*

El Día de la Cruz en Panchimalco, El Salvador

Paso 2. Comprensión. ¿Cierto o falso? Corrija las oraciones falsas.

	CIERTO	FALSO
1. Nicaragua y El Salvador tienen mucho en común.	☐	☐
2. El Día de la Cruz es una celebración política.	☐	☐
3. No hay comidas y bebidas especiales para el Día de la Cruz.	☐	☐
4. En la celebración del Día de la Cruz, se unen las tradiciones cristianas con las indígenas.	☐	☐

Paso 3. Conteste las siguientes preguntas con un compañero o una compañera.

1. ¿Hay fiestas religiosas en esta ciudad o en este estado? ¿Cuáles son?

2. En este país, ¿celebramos la cosecha (*harvest*)? ¿Cómo se llama en inglés la fiesta con que se celebra?

B. Hábitos

Paso 1. Todos tenemos nuestros hábitos. Indique en qué cuarto o parte de la casa Ud. hace las siguientes actividades. También debe especificar qué muebles y objetos usa.

MODELO: Por lo general, estudio en la alcoba, en mi escritorio. Pero a veces también leo y hago la tarea en la cama. Uso...

1. estudiar
2. dormir la siesta o acostarse por la noche
3. quitarse los zapatos
4. bañarse o ducharse
5. desayunar
6. vestirse
7. divertirse
8. ser desorganizado/a o ser muy organizado/a

Paso 2. Ahora, en parejas, túrnense para hacer y contestar preguntas basadas en las acciones del **Paso 1.**

MODELO: **E1:** ¿Dónde estudias, por lo general?
E2: Por lo general, estudio en la alcoba, en mi escritorio y a veces también en la cama. ¿Y tú?

Paso 3. Finalmente, digan (*tell*) a la clase algo (*something*) que tienen en común o que hacen de manera muy diferente.

MODELO: Maribel y yo estudiamos en la alcoba, por lo general. Pero preferimos hacer la tarea en la cama, no en el escritorio porque...

En **su** comunidad

Entreviste a (*Interview*) una persona hispana de su universidad o ciudad sobre las viviendas (*housing*) de su país de origen.

PREGUNTAS POSIBLES

- ¿En qué tipo de vivienda vive la mayoría de las personas en su país de origen?
- ¿Hay un tipo o estilo de casa «típico»? ¿Cómo es?
- ¿Dónde vive su familia?

«Vivir con la familia» Segmento 2

Antes de mirar

Conteste las siguientes preguntas.

1. ¿Piensa Ud. pasar un tiempo en otro país mientras (*while*) completa sus estudios universitarios? ¿A qué país piensa ir? ¿Por qué quiere ir a ese país?

2. ¿Cuáles son las ventajas (*advantages*) y desventajas de vivir con una familia en otro país?

Este segmento

Desde México, D.F., Laura ofrece un reportaje sobre una mujer que espera recibir (*hopes to house*) a estudiantes extranjeros en su casa.

Lorena Campus Verduzco quiere rentar un cuarto en su casa a un estudiante extranjero, porque su hija se va a casar (*get married*) y no quiere quedarse sola (*to be left alone*).

Vocabulario del segmento

bienvenidos	welcome	por lo regular	generally
mostrarnos	showing us	la carrera	university studies
el próximo curso	next academic year	hasta que no se casan	until they get married
disfrutar	to enjoy	la costumbre	custom
la actual habitante	the current inhabitant	grandes	adults
debido a que	due to (the fact) that	la gente	people
la luz	light	el hogar	home
cuentas con	you have	hasta cierto punto	up to a point
se la va a pasar	he/she is going to be	nos despedimos	we'll say good-bye

Fragmento del guion

Bueno,[a] aquí en casa va a tener todas las comodidades[b] como si estuviera[c] en su propia[d] casa. Porque a mí me gusta tener ordenado el cuarto,[e] entonces no va a haber necesidad de que él vaya a pagar lavandería,[f] aquí mismo lo podemos hacer. Va a comer comida casera[g] muy rica.[h] Y aparte[i] va a tener compañía...

[a]*Well* [b]*comforts* [c]*como... as if he were* [d]*own* [e]*tener... to have the room tidy* [f]*entonces... so there is no need for him to pay for laundry* [g]*homemade* [h]*muy... very tasty* [i]*besides*

Después de mirar

A. ¿Está claro? ¿Cierto o falso? Corrija las oraciones falsas.

	CIERTO	FALSO
1. Lorena y su familia viven en Guadalajara, México.	☐	☐
2. Lorena tiene tres hijos.	☐	☐
3. La hija de Lorena que se va a casar se llama Luisa.	☐	☐
4. Por lo general, los jóvenes mexicanos viven con sus padres durante y después de sus estudios universitarios.	☐	☐

B. Un poco más. Describa el cuarto para un estudiante extranjero. ¿De quién es ahora el cuarto? ¿Cómo es? ¿Qué tiene?

C. Y ahora, Uds. En parejas, imaginen que son los presentadores de *Salu2*. Preparen un cierre (*closing*) diferente para este segmento, incluyendo:

- una idea general como resumen del segmento
- una despedida (*sign-off*) con el nombre del programa y la ciudad de origen
- un anticipo (*preview*) del próximo programa (¡tienen libertad de imaginar!)

Antes de leer

¿Vienen sus amigos a su apartamento o casa con frecuencia? ¿Es formal o familiar (*relaxed*) su actitud?

Lectura cultural: El Salvador y Nicaragua

La vivienda[a]

Como en todo el mundo, la vivienda en El Salvador y Nicaragua puede variar mucho. Hay lujosas[b] mansiones para las personas ricas y casas muy pobres y humildes[c] con un solo cuarto para toda una familia. En las ciudades principales hay edificios de apartamentos, como en cualquier[d] otro país.

En las ciudades de León y Granada, en Nicaragua, hay hermosas[e] casas de la época colonial. Estas casas cuentan con[f] muchos cuartos y tienen techos de tejas,[g] un jardín en medio de la casa y un patio trasero.[h]

[a]*La... Housing* [b]*luxurious* [c]*humble, simple* [d]*any* [e]*beautiful* [f]*cuentan... tienen* [g]*techos... tiled roofs* [h]*out back*

El volcán Izalco, también llamado «el Faro (*Lighthouse*) del Pacífico», todo un símbolo salvadoreño

En otros países hispanos

En todo el mundo hispanohablante Los hispanos en general tienen un concepto muy generoso de la hospitalidad en su hogar[a] y les gusta ofrecer algo[b] de comer y beber a sus invitados.[c] Otra característica es que la hospitalidad en los hogares hispanos es más formal que en los Estados Unidos, una formalidad que los hispanos comprenden bien. Por ejemplo, es una falta[d] de respeto abrir el refrigerador en la casa de un amigo sin su permiso, aun si[e] se trate de[f] la casa de un amigo íntimo.

[a]*home* [b]*ofrecer... to offer something* [c]*guests (in their home)* [d]*lack* [e]*aun... even if* [f]*se... it involves*

COMPRENSIÓN

Conteste las siguientes preguntas.

1. ¿En qué son similares las viviendas en El Salvador y Nicaragua a las (*those*) del resto del mundo?
2. En general, ¿cómo es la hospitalidad de los hispanos?
3. ¿Por qué se consideran los volcanes un símbolo del país en Nicaragua y El Salvador?

Y ahora, Uds.

- En la zona donde Uds. viven, ¿qué tipo de vivienda es más común?
- En su región o estado, ¿qué se destaca (*stands out*) en la geografía? ¿Volcanes o montañas? ¿ríos (*rivers*)? ¿la costa?

Un símbolo de El Salvador y Nicaragua: Los volcanes

Los volcanes son una imagen representativa en estos dos países, que están dentro del llamado[a] Arco[b] Volcánico Centroamericano. En Nicaragua solamente,[c] hay diecisiete volcanes. Por eso, los escudos de las banderas[d] nicaragüense y salvadoreña muestran[e] una cordillera[f] con cinco volcanes.

[a]*dentro... inside the so-called* [b]*Rim, Arch* [c]*En... In Nicaragua alone* [d]*flags* [e]*show* [f]*mountain range*

Del mundo hispano

Antes de leer

¿Cómo es su casa? Piense en la casa de su familia o en el lugar donde vive ahora y dé la siguiente información.

1. Número de alcobas y de baños
2. Área en pies cuadrados (*square feet*), aproximadamente
3. ¿Tiene cocina? ¿patio? ¿jardín? ¿garaje? (¿Para cuántos coches?)
4. ¿Qué otras comodidades (*facilities*) tiene? (piscina, gimnasio, etcétera)

Lectura: Anuncios de bienes raíces°   Anuncios... *Real estate ads*

RESIDENCIAL
Santa Fe

$1'450,000

3rec, 3baños, 2plantas
109m2C, 126m2T
Cocina integral[a] amplia,
closet, cuarto de servicio,[b]
cochera 2 autos, jardín
exterior, patio interior,
acabados de primera[c]

Tel. 11372885
ID. 52*131133

TUZANIA

Zapopan
3 Recs, 1 Baño, 1 planta,
89mts construcción, 89mts
terreno, Bonita Casa
$449.000   Tel. 3629 6555

CULTURA
Inmobiliaria

PROVIDENCIA

Departamento en Torre
Ontario, planta baja, 232m2
terreno, 238m2 const., 2
niveles, 3 recámaras, 3,5
baños, jardín común,
cochera 2 autos, seguridad
24hrs $4.200.000
37002053 • 15683392

www.culturainmobiliaria.com.mx

[a]Cocina... *kitchen with built-in cabinets and kitchen appliances* [b]cuarto... *servant quarters* [c]acabados... *first-class finishing touches*

Comprensión

A. Características de las viviendas mexicanas. Para cada vivienda, busque (*look for*) la siguiente información:

1. número de recámaras
2. número de baños
3. tamaño (*size*) de la construcción (**C**) y del terreno (**T**)
4. capacidad para coches
5. precio
6. otros atractivos

B. Estas viviendas. Conteste las siguientes preguntas.

1. ¿Cuál es la vivienda más grande (*biggest*)? ¿más pequeña? ¿más cara?
2. ¿Cuántos dígitos tienen los números de teléfono en esta ciudad?
3. ¿Cuál es la vivienda más apropiada para las siguientes personas: una familia con 3 hijos, una pareja sin hijos, una persona que vive sola? Explique su respuesta.
4. ¿Cuál es la vivienda más apropiada para Ud.? Explique su respuesta.

Vocabulario **para escuchar**

amueblar	to furnish
ya	already
la plasma	flat-screen TV

Antes de escuchar

¿Qué es más usual entre los estudiantes universitarios: alquilar (*to rent*) un apartamento amueblado o uno sin amueblar (*furnished or unfurnished*)? ¿Tiene Ud. muchos muebles propios (*of your own*) donde Ud. vive? En su cuarto, casa o apartamento, ¿qué cosas son de Ud.?

Después de escuchar

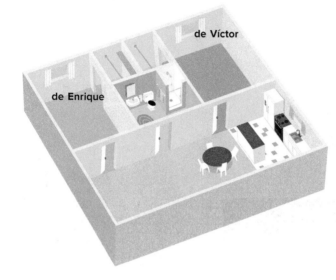

de Víctor

de Enrique

A. **¿Qué necesitan?** Enrique y Víctor acaban de alquilar (*have just rented*) un apartamento que tiene muy pocos muebles, pero no importa porque ellos tienen varias cosas. Dibuje (*Draw*) o escriba en el plano del apartamento el nombre de los muebles y cosas que ellos ya tienen para cada cuarto.

B. **Más detalles.** Conteste las siguientes preguntas.

1. ¿Qué cosas tienen que comprar Víctor y Enrique para sus alcobas?
2. ¿Qué parte de la casa no mencionan en la conversación?
3. ¿Qué muebles no necesitan comprar para la sala comedor?
4. ¿Cuántos televisores tienen entre los dos?

PRODUCCIÓN PERSONAL

¡Ahora, yo!

A. Use de (*as a*) modelo las preguntas y respuestas de la página 131 de este capítulo para hablar de su casa y su alcoba.

B. Con las preguntas de la página 131 como modelo, filme una o dos entrevistas con estudiantes de su universidad que hablan del lugar donde viven mientras (*while*) asisten a la universidad.

A ESCRIBIR

Un ensayo sobre una semana típica de los estudiantes universitarios

¿Cree Ud. que los estudiantes universitarios en general tienen una manera típica de vivir? Y, en particular, ¿los estudiantes de su universidad? ¿Por qué?

Preparar

Paso 1. En una hoja de papel aparte, complete una tabla como la siguiente con información sobre 5 o 6 actividades que Ud. hace de lunes a viernes y durante el fin de semana en una semana típica. Luego entreviste (*interview*) a dos compañeros de clase sobre sus actividades y complete la tabla con su respectiva información.

	de lunes a viernes	fines de semana
Ud.		
compañero/a A		
compañero/a B		

Paso 2. Ahora use la información para escribir un ensayo sobre la semana típica de los estudiantes de su universidad, si cree que es posible hablar de una semana típica. Hay más ayuda (*help*) en Connect.

Más ideas para su portafolio

- Incluya (*Include*) una foto de su cuarto o alcoba y descríbalo (*describe it*).
- Describa con muchos detalles la casa de sus sueños (*dreams*).
- Describa un día ideal para Ud. ¿Qué día de la semana es, dónde está Ud. y qué hace durante todo el día?
- Si ha estado jugando (*have been playing*) Practice Spanish: Study Abroad, en Quest 3 Ud. almorzó (*had lunch*) en la casa de su familia colombiana. ¿Cómo es la casa? Dibuje el plano (*Draw the floorplan*) de la casa de su familia colombiana, incluyendo (*including*) todos los cuartos que Ud. recuerde (*that you remember*). Luego, nombre (*name*) dos actividades que se hacen (*are done*) en cada cuarto.

Sugerencia: You are now ready to play Quest 3 in **Practice Spanish: Study Abroad** (www.mhpractice.com).

EN RESUMEN En este capítulo

LEARNSMART

Visit **www.connectspanish.com** to practice the vocabulary and grammar points covered in this chapter.

AFTER STUDYING THIS CHAPTER I CAN. . .

☐ name the parts of a house or apartment and furniture (132)

☐ use the names of the days of the week as well as other time expressions (134–135)

☐ use some words and expressions that put actions in sequence (136–137, 153)

☐ use important irregular and stem-changing verbs (139–141, 145–147)

☐ talk about my daily routine and other actions that require reflexive pronouns (150–152)

☐ recognize/describe at least 2–3 aspects of Salvadoran and Nicaraguan cultures

Gramática en breve

12. Present Tense of *hacer, oír, poner, salir, traer, ver*

hacer: hago, haces, hace, hacemos, hacéis, hacen

oír: oigo, oyes, oye, oímos, oís, oyen

poner: pongo, pones, pone, ponemos, ponéis, ponen

salir: salgo, sales, sale, salimos, salís, salen

traer: traigo, traes, trae, traemos, traéis, traen

ver: veo, ves, ve, vemos, veis, ven

13. Present Tense of Stem-changing Verbs

Stem-changing Patterns

e → ie		o → ue		e → i	
-ie-	-e-	-ue-	-o-	-i-	-e-
-ie-	-e-	-ue-	-o-	-i-	-e-
-ie-	-ie-	-ue-	-ue-	-i-	-i-

14. Reflexive Pronouns

yo → me	nosotros/as → nos
tú → te	vosotros/as → os
Ud./él/ella → se	Uds./ellos/ellas → se

Vocabulario

Los verbos

almorzar (almuerzo)	to have lunch
cerrar (cierro)	to close
descansar	to rest
dormir (duermo)	to sleep
dormir la siesta	to take a nap
empezar (empiezo)	to begin, start
empezar a + *inf.*	to begin to (*do something*)
entender (entiendo)	to understand
hacer	to do; to make
hacer ejercicio	to exercise
hacer un viaje	to take a trip
hacer una pregunta	to ask a question
jugar (juego) (a; al)	to play (*a game; a sport*)
oír (oigo, oyes,...)	to hear; to listen to (*music, the radio*)
pedir (pido)	to ask for; to order
pensar (pienso) (en)	to think (about)
pensar de/que	to think of, have an opinion about/that
pensar + *inf.*	to intend, plan to (*do something*)
perder (pierdo)	to lose; to miss (*an event*)
poner (pongo)	to put; to place; to turn on (*an appliance*)
salir (salgo) (de)	to leave (*a place*)
salir bien/mal	to turn/come out well/badly; to do well/poorly
salir con	to go out with, date
salir para	to leave for (*a place*)
servir (sirvo)	to serve
servir para	to be used for
traer (traigo)	to bring
ver (veo)	to see; to watch (*a program, movie*)
volver (vuelvo)	to return (*to a place*)
volver a + *inf.*	to (*do something*) again

Los verbos que se usan con pronombres reflexivos

acostarse (me acuesto)	to go to bed
afeitarse	to shave
bañarse	to take a bath, bathe
cepillarse los dientes	to brush one's teeth
despertarse (me despierto)	to wake up
divertirse (me divierto)	to have a good time, enjoy oneself
dormirse (me duermo)	to fall asleep
ducharse	to take a shower
levantarse	to get up (out of bed); to stand up
llamarse	to be called
peinarse	to brush/comb one's hair
ponerse (me pongo)	to put on (*an article of clothing*)
quitarse	to take off (*an article of clothing*)
sentarse (me siento)	to sit down
vestirse (me visto)	to get dressed

Los cuartos y otras partes de una casa

la alcoba	bedroom
el baño	bathroom
la cocina	kitchen
el comedor	dining room
el estudio	office (in a home)
el jardín	garden
la pared	wall
el patio	patio; yard
la piscina	swimming pool
la sala	living room

Cognado: el garaje

Repaso: la casa, el cuarto

Los muebles y otras cosas de una casa

la alfombra	rug
el armario	armoire, free-standing closet
la bañera	bathtub
la cama	bed
la cómoda	bureau; dresser
el estante	bookshelf
la estufa	stove
la lámpara	lamp
el lavabo	(bathroom) sink
la mesita	end table
el mueble	piece of furniture
el sillón	armchair
la toalla	towel

Cognado: el sofá

Repaso: el escritorio, la mesa, la silla, la tele(visión)

Otros sustantivos

la bebida	drink
el cine	movies; movie theater
la cosa	thing
el diente	tooth
el ejercicio	exercise
la llave	key
la nota	grade
las noticias	news
la película	movie
la pregunta	question
el ruido	noise
la rutina	routine
la tarea	homework
el viaje	trip

Los adjetivos

cada inv.*	each, every
diario/a	daily
siguiente	following
solo/a	alone

Las preposiciones

antes de	before
después de	after
durante	during
sin	without

Repaso: a, con, de, en, hasta, para, por (in, during)

¿Qué día es hoy?

los días de la semana:
   lunes, martes, miércoles, jueves, viernes, sábado, domingo

anteayer	the day before yesterday
ayer fue (miércoles...)	yesterday was (Wednesday. . .)
el lunes (martes...)	on Monday (Tuesday. . .)
los lunes (los martes...)	on Mondays (Tuesdays. . .)
pasado mañana	the day after tomorrow
el próximo (martes...)	next (Tuesday. . .)
la próxima semana	next week
la semana (el lunes...) que viene	next week (Monday. . .)

Repaso: el día, el fin de semana, hoy, mañana

Palabras adicionales

después adv.	then, later, next
en seguida	immediately
finalmente	finally
lo que	what, that which
luego	then, later, next
por fin	finally
por lo general	generally
primero	first

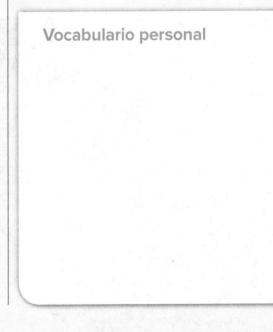

Vocabulario personal

---

*The abbreviation inv. means invariable, unchanging (in form). The adjective **cada** is used with masculine and feminine nouns (**cada libro, cada mesa**), and since its meaning (each) is singular, it is never used with plural nouns.

6

Las estaciones y el tiempo°

Las... *Seasons and the weather*

www.connectspanish.com

En este capítulo

Una catarata (*waterfall*) del río Celeste, en el Parque National Volcán Tenorio, Costa Rica

Mar Caribe

MÉXICO

BELICE

GUATEMALA   HONDURAS

EL SALVADOR

NICARAGUA

Lago de Nicaragua

OCÉANO
PACÍFICO

COSTA RICA   Parque Nacional
la Amistad

San José   PANAMÁ

0   100   200 Millas

0   100   200 Kilómetros

COSTA RICA

**4.8 (punto ocho)
millones de habitantes**

- La Constitución de Costa Rica
prohíbe la organización de fuerzas
armadas.[a]

- El ecoturismo es fundamental para
la economía de Costa Rica y para
preservar sus **bosques**[b] y **selvas**,[c]
que cubren[d] un 30% (por ciento) de
su territorio.

[a]fuerzas... *armed forces* [b]*forests*
[c]*jungles* [d]*cover*

- ¿Cómo es el clima de su país?
- ¿Qué le gusta hacer cuando el tiempo[a] es bueno?
- ¿Cuál es su estación[b] favorita?

[a]*weather* [b]*season*

MANUEL GIL DEL VALLE
CONTESTA LAS PREGUNTAS.

- El clima de Managua es poco variado. Solo hay
dos estaciones, una lluviosa[a] y otra seca.[b] La
temperatura diaria varía poco: alrededor de[c] 30
grados de máxima y 21 de mínima. Es decir,[d]
hace calor[e] todo el año.

- Bueno,[f] no hago nada[g] en especial, porque no
hay una estación de calor y otra de frío.[h]

- Prefiero la estación seca. Es que[i] puede llover[j]
mucho durante la estación lluviosa y no me gusta
estar mojado.[k]

[a]una... *a rainy one* [b]otra... *a dry one* [c]alrededor... *around*
[d]*Es... That is* [e]hace... *it's hot* [f]*Well* [g]no... *I don't do anything* [h]*cold*
[i]*Es... That's because* [j]*rain* [k]*wet*

¿Qué tiempo hace hoy?°

¿Qué... *What's the weather like today?*

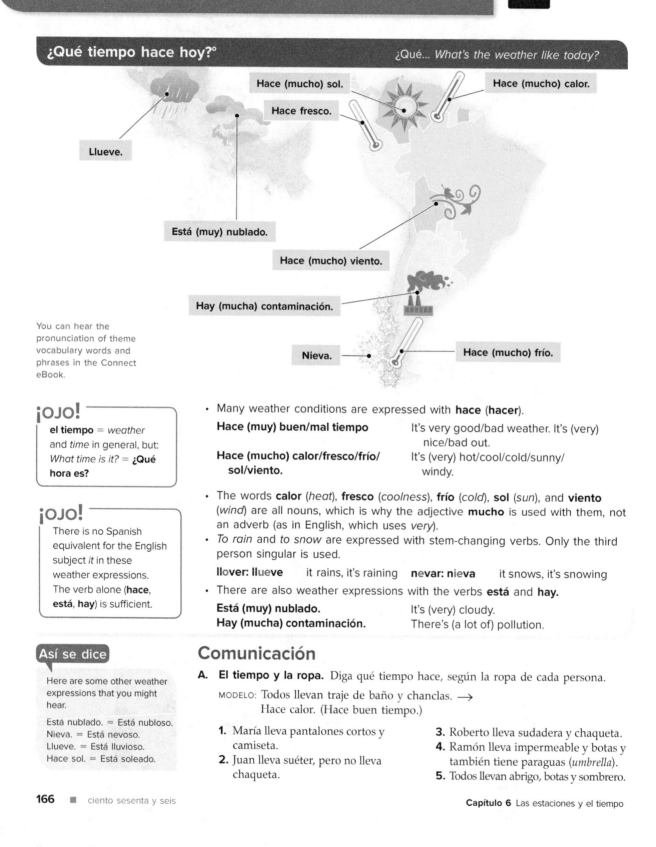

Llueve.

Hace (mucho) sol.

Hace fresco.

Hace (mucho) calor.

Está (muy) nublado.

Hace (mucho) viento.

Hay (mucha) contaminación.

Nieva.

Hace (mucho) frío.

You can hear the pronunciation of theme vocabulary words and phrases in the Connect eBook.

¡OJO!

el tiempo = *weather* and *time* in general, but: *What time is it?* = **¿Qué hora es?**

¡OJO!

There is no Spanish equivalent for the English subject *it* in these weather expressions. The verb alone (**hace, está, hay**) is sufficient.

- Many weather conditions are expressed with **hace (hacer)**.

  Hace (muy) buen/mal tiempo It's very good/bad weather. It's (very) nice/bad out.

  Hace (mucho) calor/fresco/frío/ sol/viento. It's (very) hot/cool/cold/sunny/ windy.

- The words **calor** (*heat*), **fresco** (*coolness*), **frío** (*cold*), **sol** (*sun*), and **viento** (*wind*) are all nouns, which is why the adjective **mucho** is used with them, not an adverb (as in English, which uses *very*).
- *To rain* and *to snow* are expressed with stem-changing verbs. Only the third person singular is used.

  llover: llueve it rains, it's raining **nevar: nieva** it snows, it's snowing

- There are also weather expressions with the verbs **está** and **hay**.

  Está (muy) nublado. It's (very) cloudy.
  Hay (mucha) contaminación. There's (a lot of) pollution.

Así se dice

Here are some other weather expressions that you might hear.

Está nublado. = Está nubloso.
Nieva. = Está nevoso.
Llueve. = Está lluvioso.
Hace sol. = Está soleado.

Comunicación

A. El tiempo y la ropa. Diga qué tiempo hace, según la ropa de cada persona.

MODELO: Todos llevan traje de baño y chanclas. →
Hace calor. (Hace buen tiempo.)

1. María lleva pantalones cortos y camiseta.
2. Juan lleva suéter, pero no lleva chaqueta.
3. Roberto lleva sudadera y chaqueta.
4. Ramón lleva impermeable y botas y también tiene paraguas (*umbrella*).
5. Todos llevan abrigo, botas y sombrero.

B. El clima en el mundo

Paso 1. ¿Qué clima o condición asocia Ud. con las siguientes ciudades?

1. Seattle, Washington
2. Los Ángeles, California
3. San José, Costa Rica

4. Buffalo, Nueva York
5. Waikikí, Hawái
6. Chicago, Illinois

Paso 2. ¿Qué clima o condición asocia Ud. con los siguientes lugares?

1. un desierto
2. una playa (*beach*)
3. una montaña muy, muy alta
4. una ciudad grande

5. la Antártida
6. una zona tropical
7. una zona templada
8. Londres

C. El tiempo y las actividades. Haga oraciones completas, indicando una actividad apropiada para cada situación. Es necesario conjugar los verbos a la derecha (*right*).

cuando hace buen/mal tiempo cuando hace calor cuando hace frío cuando hay mucha contaminación cuando llueve cuando nieva	**+** (no) **+**	jugar al basquetbol/voleibol con mis amigos almorzar afuera (*outside*) / en el parque divertirse en el parque / en la playa con mis amigos salir de casa volver a casa trabajar o estudiar quedarse (*to stay*) en casa

Nota **comunicativa**

Otras expresiones con *tener*

Other conditions are expressed in Spanish with **tener** idioms—not with *to be*, as in English.

tener **(mucho) calor**	to be/feel (very) warm, hot
tener **(mucho) frío**	to be/feel (very) cold

These expressions are used to describe people or animals only. *To be comfortable*—neither hot nor cold—is expressed with **estar bien.**

You will use these expressions in **Comunicación D.**

D. ¿Tienen frío o calor? ¿Están bien? En parejas, describan el tiempo que hace en cada dibujo. También deben indicar cómo están las personas. Si Uds. creen que no tienen ni (*neither*) frío ni (*or*) calor, pueden decir (*say*): «Está(n) bien».

1.
2.
3.
4.
5.
6.

Los meses y las estaciones° del año *seasons*

**Las cuatro estaciones
en el hemisferio norte**

el invierno

diciembre

enero

febrero

la primavera

marzo

abril

mayo

el otoño

septiembre

octubre

noviembre

el verano

junio

julio

agosto

Así se dice

Other ways to ask what day
it is include:

¿Qué día es hoy?
¿A cuántos estamos?

In the last sentence, **cuántos**
is masculine because it
refers to **días** (*m.*).

¿Cuál es la fecha de hoy?
¿Qué fecha es hoy? }   What's today's date?

(Hoy) Es el primero de abril.   (Today is) It's the first of April.
(Hoy) Es el cinco de febrero.   (Today is) It's the fifth of February.

- The ordinal number **primero (1°)** is used to express the first day of the month. Cardinal numbers (**dos, tres,** and so on) are used for other days.
- The definite article **el** is used before the date. However, when the day of the week is expressed, **el** is omitted: **Hoy es jueves, 3 de octubre.**
- As you know, **mil** is used to express the year (**el año**) after 999.

  1950 mil novecientos cincuenta   2011 dos mil once

Comunicación

A. ¿Cuántos días hay en cada mes? Piense en el poema que se usa en inglés para recordar (*remember*) el número de días en cada mes: *Thirty days* . . . Aquí está el poema en español. Para completarlo (*complete it*), Ud. tiene que hacer rimar los dos primeros versos (*lines*).

Treinta días tiene _____,
Con abril, _____ y _____.
De veintiocho solo hay uno,
Y los demás,ª treinta y uno.

ªlos... *the rest*

B. Las fechas

Paso 1. Exprese estas fechas en español. ¿En qué estación caen (*do they fall*)?

MODELO: February 15 → Es el quince de febrero. Cae (*It falls*) en invierno.

1. March 7
2. August 24
3. December 1
4. June 5
5. September 19, 1997
6. May 30, 1842
7. January 31, 1660
8. July 4, 1776

Paso 2. ¿Cuándo se celebran (día y mes)?*

1. el Día del Año Nuevo
2. el Día de los Enamorados (de San Valentín)
3. la Navidad (*Christmas*)
4. el Día de los Inocentes (*Fools*), en los Estados Unidos
5. su cumpleaños (*birthday*)
6. el cumpleaños de su novio/a (*boyfriend/girlfriend*), esposo/a, mejor (*best*) amigo/a,...

Nota **cultural**

El clima en el mundo hispano

El mundo hispanohablante es inmenso. Se extiende en las Américas desde los Estados Unidos hasta la Argentina. Por eso, el clima de los países hispanohablantes es muy variado.

- No todos los países tienen cuatro estaciones. Costa Rica y otros países centroamericanos y sudamericanos solo tienen dos: una estación seca[a] y otra húmeda, con mucha lluvia. Esto es normal en los países de la zona tropical.
- El Niño, un fenómeno meteorológico, afecta directamente a varios países hispanos. Está caracterizado por temperaturas más calientes de lo normal[b] en la zona ecuatorial del océano Pacífico. El fenómeno se llama El Niño porque se presenta típicamente alrededor de[c] Navidad, época en que nace el Niño Jesús.[d]

[a]*dry* [b]*más... warmer than normal* [c]*alrededor... around* [d]*nace... the Baby Jesus is born (Christian faiths)*

La costa del Perú, donde se descubrió (*was discovered*) el fenómeno de El Niño en el siglo (*century*) XIX

¿Cómo es el clima de su estado o país? ¿Están las estaciones bien diferenciadas?

C. Intercambios

Paso 1. En parejas, túrnense para entrevistarse sobre los siguientes temas. Deben obtener detalles interesantes y personales de su compañero/a.

MODELO: la fecha de su cumpleaños →
¿Cuál es la fecha de tu cumpleaños? ¿Qué tiempo hace, generalmente, ese día? ¿Cómo celebras tu cumpleaños?

1. la fecha de su cumpleaños
2. su signo del horóscopo
3. su estación favorita
4. una estación que no le gusta

Paso 2. Digan a la clase lo que Uds. tienen en común.

MODELO: Nosotras tenemos el cumpleaños en abril. La fecha de María es el 16 y mi fecha es el 18. Nuestro signo es Aries. Las dos (*Both of us*) preferimos la primavera. ¿Por qué? Porque nuestro cumpleaños es en primavera y es una estación muy bonita.

Los signos del horóscopo

Aries	Libra
Tauro	Escorpión
Géminis	Sagitario
Cáncer	Capricornio
Leo	Acuario
Virgo	Piscis

---

*Remember that the word **se** before a verb changes the verb's meaning slightly. **¿Cuándo se celebran?** = When are they celebrated? You will see this construction throughout **Puntos de partida**. You will learn about this usage in **Capítulo 8**.

¿Dónde está? Las preposiciones (Part 2)

Pablito está **a la derecha** de Teresa.

Teresa está **entre** Carmen y Pablito.

El libro **está encima de** la mesa.

La mochila está **debajo de** la mesa.

La maestra habla: «Todos los estudiantes están **delante de mí**».

Nueva York está **al norte de** Miami. México está **al sur de** los Estados Unidos.

cerca de	close to	**al lado de**	alongside of	**a la derecha de**	to the right of
lejos de	far from	**entre**	between, among	**a la izquierda de**	to the left of
debajo de	below	**delante de**	in front of	**al norte/sur/**	to the north/south/
encima de	on top of	**detrás de**	behind	**este/oeste de**	east/west of

¡OJO!

Note that **mí** has a written accent, but **ti** does not. This diacritical accent (**Capítulo 4**) distinguishes the object of a preposition (**mí**) from the possessive adjective (**mi**).

- In Spanish, the *pronoun objects of prepositions* (**los pronombres preposicionales**) are identical in form to the subject pronouns, except for **mí** and **ti**.

Julio está *delante de mí*.	Julio is in front of me.
María está *detrás de ti*.	María is behind you.
Me siento *a la izquierda de ella*.	I sit on her left.

- The pronouns **mí** and **ti** combine with the preposition **con** to form **conmigo** (*with me*) and **contigo** (*with you*), respectively.

—¿Vienes *conmigo*?	"Are you coming with me?"
—Sí, voy *contigo*.	"Yes, I'll go with you."

Comunicación

A. En el salón de clase

Paso 1. Describa a las personas o cosas de su clase en relación con Ud. Siga el modelo. Use **nadie** (*no one*) cuando sea (*it's*) necesario.

MODELO: está cerca de la puerta. → **Jaime** está cerca de la puerta.

Una persona o una cosa que...
1. está cerca/lejos de la puerta.
2. está detrás de la mesa del profesor / de la profesora.
3. está delante del pizarrón.
4. está a su izquierda/derecha.
5. habla con Ud. en la clase.
6. hoy trabaja con Ud.

(Continúa.)

Paso 2. Con un compañero / una compañera, escoja (*choose*) a una persona o un objeto en el salón de clase. Luego, sin nombrarlo/la (*without naming him/her/it*), use las preposiciones de lugar para explicar dónde está. Su compañero/a va a adivinar (*guess*) qué persona, objeto o mueble es.

MODELO: Está a la derecha de Paul ahora, pero generalmente se sienta detrás de mí. Siempre llega a clase conmigo. ¿Quién es?

B. ¿De qué país se habla?

Paso 1. Escuche la descripción de un país de Sudamérica que da (*gives*) su profesor(a). ¿Cuál es ese país?

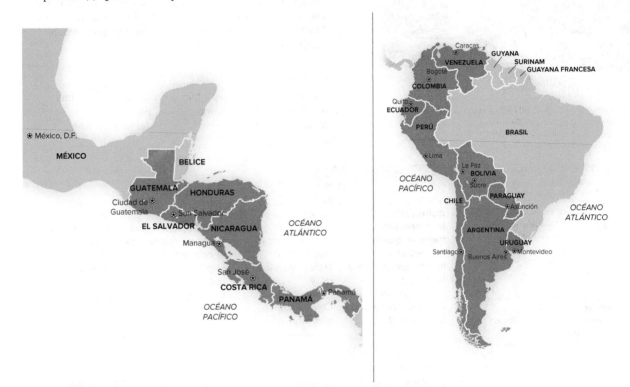

Paso 2. Ahora describa un país de Sudamérica. Sus compañeros de clase van a decir cuál es. Siga (*Follow*) el modelo, usando todas las frases que sean (*are*) apropiadas.

MODELO: Este país está al norte/sur/este/oeste de _____. También está cerca de _____. Pero está lejos de _____ . Está entre _____ y _____. Su capital es _____. ¿Cómo se llama?

C. Intercambios. Find out as much information as you can about the location of each others' hometown or state, or country of origin. You should also tell what the weather is like.

MODELO: E1: ¿De dónde eres?
E2: Soy de Tylertown.
E1: ¿Dónde está Tylertown?
E2: Está en el estado de _____, al oeste de _____.
E1: ¿Cómo es el clima?

SALU2

«En la Mitad del Mundo°» Segmento 1

Mitad... *Middle of the World*

El monumento a la Mitad del Mundo: «Aquí turistas ecuatorianos y de todos los países vienen a poner un pie (*foot*) en cada hemisferio.»

Antes de mirar

Indique todas las opciones que son ciertas para Ud.

- ☐ Donde yo vivo hay cuatro estaciones.
- ☐ Me gusta el clima cálido (*warm*) y seco (*dry*). ¡Me gusta el sol!
- ☐ Prefiero el invierno porque me gusta el frío y la nieve (*snow*).
- ☐ Llueve mucho aquí. Afortunadamente me gusta mucho la lluvia (*rain*).

Este segmento

Este segmento incluye un reportaje sobre aspectos del clima y la geografía del Ecuador. Para empezar, los presentadores intercambian comentarios sobre el clima del país de Ana, Panamá.

Estrategia

This segment includes a lot of vocabulary that you learned in **Vocabulario: Preparación.** You will understand the segment more easily if you review that vocabulary before watching. Consider adding some additional weather-related vocabulary to **Vocabulario personal** (at the end of the chapter).

Vocabulario del segmento

rico/a	beautiful	**reflejar**	to reflect
disfrutando	enjoying	**olvidar**	to forget
la temporada	season	**montañoso/a**	mountainous
mejor te quedas	you better stay	**atravesar (atravieso)**	to cross
me gustaría	I would like	**el corazón**	heart
la infatigable viajera	tireless traveler	**segundo/a**	second
lluvioso/a	rainy	**rodear**	to surround
a nivel del mar	at sea level	**contrarrestar**	to react (with),
el grado centígrado	Celsius degree		counteract
la humedad	humidity		

Después de mirar

A. ¿Está claro? Las siguientes oraciones son falsas. Corríjalas. (*Correct them.*)

1. A Ana no le gusta la nieve.
2. El clima de Panamá es muy diferente del clima del Ecuador.
3. La Mitad del Mundo es una ciudad del Ecuador.
4. En los países tropicales hay dos temporadas, una cálida y otra fría.
5. En Quito no llueve mucho.

B. Un poco más. Conteste las siguientes preguntas.

1. ¿Es muy cálido el clima en todas las zonas tropicales del mundo? Dé un ejemplo.
2. ¿Qué factor geográfico afecta el clima del Ecuador?

C. Y ahora, Uds. En parejas, hablen sobre si les gustaría (*you would like*) vivir en un lugar con un clima como el (*like that*) de Quito o como el de la costa ecuatoriana, que es mucho más cálido. Expliquen por qué.

MODELO:: Me gustaría vivir en un lugar con un clima similar al (*to that*) de Quito porque me gusta la lluvia...

Grammar Tutorial 15
connect
|SPANISH
www.connectspanish.com

15 *¿Qué están haciendo?*

Present Progressive: **Estar + -ndo**

Gramática en acción: ¿Qué está haciendo Elisa esta tarde?

Elisa es periodista. Por eso escribe y habla mucho por teléfono en su trabajo. Pero ahora mismo no está trabajando. Está descansando en casa. Está oyendo música, leyendo una novela y tomando un café.

¿Y Ud.?

En el salón de clase, ¿quién está haciendo las siguientes cosas en este momento? **¡OJO!** **nadie** = *nobody.*

1. _____ está hablando en su teléfono celular.
2. _____ está leyendo un periódico.
3. _____ está tomando un café.
4. _____ está mandando mensajes.
5. _____ está escuchando su iPod.

The Progressive / **El progresivo**			
estoy		I am	
estás		you (*fam.*) are	
está	tomando	he, she, it, you (*form.*) are	drinking
estamos	comiendo	we are	eating
estáis	abriendo	you (*pl. fam.*) are	opening
están		they, you (*pl. form.*) are	

Uses of the Progressive / Los usos del progresivo

1. **The Progressive**

   Spanish and English form the *progressive* (**el progresivo**) in similar ways, as you can see in the preceding chart, but the use of the progressive is not the same in both languages.

> *the progressive / **el progresivo** = a verb form that expresses continuing or developing action*

What's Elisa doing this afternoon? *Elisa is a journalist. That's why she writes and talks a lot on the phone in her job. But she's not working right now. She's resting at home. She's listening to music, reading a novel, and having a cup of coffee.*

2. Uses of the Progressive

As shown in the example sentences, English uses the present progressive to tell:

- what is happening *right now* (1)
- what is happening *over a period of time* (2)
- what is *going to* happen (3)

However, in Spanish, the present progressive is used primarily to express an action that *is happening right now* (1).

To express actions that are happening over a period of time, Spanish generally uses uses the simple present tense (2).

To express actions that are going to happen, Spanish uses the simple present tense or **ir** + **a** + *infinitive* (3), but never the progressive.

1. *Ramón is eating right* now.
Ramón **está comiendo** ahora mismo.

2. *Adelaida is studying chemistry this semester.*
Adelaida **estudia** química este semestre.

3. *We're buying the house tomorrow.*
Compramos (Vamos a comprar) la casa mañana.

Forming the Present Progressive / La formación del presente progresivo

1. Spanish Present Progressive

The Spanish *present progressive* (**el presente progresivo**) is formed with **estar** plus the *present participle* (**el gerundio**).

The present participle is formed by adding **-ando** to the stem of **-ar** verbs and **-iendo** to the stem of **-er** and **-ir** verbs.

The present participle never varies; it always ends in **-o.**

> *a present participle* / **un gerundio** = the verb form that ends in *-ing* in English

estar + *present participle*

tomar $\rightarrow$ **tom**ando		taking; drinking
comprender $\rightarrow$ **comprend**iendo		understanding
abrir $\rightarrow$ **abr**iendo		opening

¡OJO!

Unaccented **i** represents the sound [y] in the participle ending **-iendo: comiendo, viviendo.** Unaccented **i** between two vowels becomes the letter **y.**

leer: le + iendo $\rightarrow$ leyendo
oír: o + iendo $\rightarrow$ oyendo

---

2. Present Participle of *-ir* Stem-changing Verbs

-Ir stem-changing verbs also have a stem change in the present participle.

- The stem vowel **e** changes to **i.**
- The stem vowel **o** changes to **u.**

As you can see, sometimes that change is the same as in the present tense (as in **pedir**) and sometimes it is different (as in **preferir** and **dormir**).

The verbs you have learned so far that show this second change are: **divertirse, dormir(se), pedir, preferir, servir,** and **vestirse.**

preferir (prefiero) (i) $\rightarrow$ prefiriendo
pedir (pido) (i) $\rightarrow$ pidiendo
dormir (duermo) (u) $\rightarrow$ durmiendo

Note that (**duermo**) shows you the present tense stem change for **dormir: o $\longrightarrow$ ue.** The (**u**) shows you the change in the present participle of **dormir: o $\longrightarrow$ u (durmiendo).**

In vocabulary lists from this point on in *Puntos de partida,* this second stem change will be shown in parentheses after the first person singular form of the verb.

---

3. Position of Reflexive Pronouns

Reflexive pronouns can be attached to a present participle or precede the conjugated form of **estar.** Note the accent that is added to the present participle when pronouns are attached.

Pablo **se está** bañando.
Pablo está **bañándose.** } *Pablo is taking a bath.*

¡OJO!

When a verb used reflexively follows expressions like **empezar a,** the pronoun is usually placed at the end of the infinitive: **Estoy empezando a vestirme.**

Práctica y comunicación

A. Un sábado típico

Paso 1. Autoprueba. Complete el gerundio de los siguientes verbos con una de las siguientes terminaciones.

a. -ando   **b.** -iendo   **c.** -yendo

1. acost_____
2. bañ_____
3. durm_____
4. hac_____
5. le_____

6. pid_____
7. prefir_____
8. divirt_____
9. cre_____
10. empez_____

Paso 2. Ahora piense en su rutina de un sábado típico. Indique dos acciones que es posible que Ud. esté (*might be*) haciendo a las siguientes horas. Hay una lista de **Frases útiles**, pero Ud. puede modificarlas (*change them*) o añadir otras.

MODELO: a las ocho de la mañana →
A las ocho de la mañana estoy durmiendo o duchándome.

1. a las 8 de la mañana
2. a las 10:30 de la mañana
3. al mediodía (*noon*)
4. a las 4 de la tarde
5. a las 9 de la noche
6. a la medianoche (*midnight*)

> **Frases útiles**
>
> | | |
> |---|---|
> | almorzar | levantarse |
> | despertarse | oír música |
> | dormir (la siesta) | pedir una pizza |
> | ducharse | ver una película |
> | estudiar | volver a casa |
> | hacer ejercicio | |

Paso 3. Ahora, en parejas, túrnense para determinar si hacen las mismas (*same*) cosas a la misma hora.

MODELO: E1: A las ocho de la mañana los sábados, ¿estás durmiendo?
E2: No, a esa hora estoy trabajando.

B. Hoy, en casa de Lola.

Hoy no es un día como todos los días para la familia de Lola, porque su tío de Costa Rica está de visita. Complete las siguientes oraciones para expresar lo que está pasando (*happening*).

MODELO: Casi siempre, Lola almuerza con su hija. Hoy Lola...
(almorzar con su tío en un restaurante) →
Hoy Lola **está almorzando** con su tío en un restaurante.

1. Generalmente, Lola pasa la mañana en la universidad. Hoy Lola... (pasar el día con su tío Ricardo)
2. Casi siempre, Lola toma un café en la cafetería después de sus clases. Hoy Lola y su tío... (tomar un café en casa)
3. De lunes a viernes, Marta, la hija de Lola, va a la escuela (*school*) por la tarde. Pero esta tarde ella... (jugar con Ricardo)
4. Generalmente, la familia cena (*has dinner*) a las nueve. Esta noche todos... (cenar a las diez)

Prác. A, Paso 1: Answers: 1. a **2.** a **3.** b **4.** b **5.** c **6.** b **7.** b **8.** b **9.** c **10.** a

Algo sobre...

los valores[a] de los costarricenses

El Parque Nacional Rincón de la Vieja, parte de la importante industria ecoturística de Costa Rica

Dos cualidades caracterizan el país de Costa Rica. Una es la paz.[b] Esta nación no tiene fuerzas armadas[c] desde 1948. Hay una expresión que ilustra este sentimiento nacional: «Donde haya[d] un costarricense, habrá[e] paz.» La segunda[f] característica es la importancia que la ecología tiene para el país. Costa Rica no solo preserva su biodiversidad; también la explota.[g]

¿Qué cualidades caracterizan este país? ¿Es la paz un valor estadounidense?

[a]*values* [b]*peace* [c]*fuerzas... armed forces* [d]*Donde... Wherever there is* [e]*there will be* [f]*second* [g]*la... she uses it*

C. En casa con la familia Duarte

Paso 1. Describa lo que pasa en cada dibujo, explicando quién está haciendo la acción —el padre, la madre, la hija, los gemelos (*twins*), el perro— y a qué hora. Use los verbos de la lista u otros verbos, si desea. Puede hacer más de (*than*) una oración para cada dibujo, si quiere. **¡OJO!** Hay verbos reflexivos en las listas.

MODELO: salir de la ducha (*shower*) ⟶ El padre **está saliendo** de la ducha a las seis de la mañana.

Por la mañana: A las seis de la mañana

Verbos

dormir todavía (*still*)
leer el periódico
levantarse
salir de la ducha
tomar un café

Más tarde: A las ocho de la mañana

Verbos

desayunar
leer sus e-mails
pensar en el examen que tiene hoy
salir para la universidad
trabajar en la oficina
vestirse

Por la tarde: A las seis y media de la tarde

Verbos

hacer la tarea
jugar
leer un libro de texto
preparar la cena (*dinner*)
quitarse la ropa

Paso 2. Ahora explique qué hacen Ud. y otros miembros de su familia o sus compañeros de cuarto/casa a la misma hora que ve en los dibujos.

Nota comunicativa

El gerundio con otros verbos

As in English, the Spanish present participle (**el gerundio**) can be used with verbs other than **estar**. The following verbs are commonly used with the present participle.

- **pasar tiempo** + *present participle* — *to spend time* (doing something)

  ¿**Pasas** mucho tiempo **haciendo** la tarea? — *Do you spend a lot of time doing homework?*

- **seguir (sigo) (i) / continuar (continúo)*** + *present participle* — *to continue* (doing something)

  Sigue lloviendo mucho. — *It continues to rain / raininig a lot.*

- **divertirse (me divierto) (i)** + *present participle* — *to enjoy* (doing something)

  ¿Te **diviertes** mucho **bailando** salsa? — *Do you have a good time dancing salsa?*

You will use these verbs in **Comunicación D** and **E**.

> Remember that the letter in parentheses indicates the change in the present participle of the verb, which in this case would be **siguiendo**.

> **¡OJO!**
> Note the present tense forms of **continuar**, which have an accent on the **u** when it is stressed (like the boot pattern of stem-changing verbs):
>
> | | |
> |---|---|
> | continúo | continuamos |
> | continúas | continuáis |
> | continúa | continúan |

> **¡OJO!**
> If the second verb in these constructions is reflexive, its reflexive pronoun must agree with the subject.
>
> Me divierto **bañándome** en el mar.
> *I enjoy bathing in the sea.*

D. Intercambios

Paso 1. Use las siguientes ideas para hacer cinco oraciones sobre sus hábitos.

continuar/seguir
divertirse
estar
pasar más tiempo
pasar mucho/poco tiempo

+

infinitivo ⟶ gerundio

bailar hasta la medianoche
estudiar / leer / ¿ ?
hablar español después de la clase
mandar mensajes
mirar la tele / **oír** música
ser amigo/a de mi mejor (*best*) amigo/a de la escuela primaria
trabajar (en ¿ ?)
¿ ?

Paso 2. Ahora, en parejas, túrnense para entrevistarse sobe los mismos temas. Luego compartan (*share*) con la clase algo (*something*) que tienen en común.

MODELOS: ¿Pasas mucho tiempo mirando la tele? ¿Cuántas horas al (*per*) día?
¿Cuál es tu programa favorito?

E. ¿Qué están haciendo?

Imagine lo que están haciendo las siguientes personas ahora mismo. Use una palabra o frase de cada columna y la forma progresiva.

yo
mi mejor amigo/a
mis padres
mi equipo (*team*) deportivo favorito
el/la líder (*leader*) de este país
el profesor / la profesora de español
_____ (un compañero / una compañera que está ausente hoy)

+

descansar, dormir(se),
escribir, hacer,
jugar (al), leer,
practicar, trabajar, ¿ ?

divertirse + *inf.*, seguir + *inf.*,

+

fútbol/basquetbol
un libro / una novela
a los estudiantes / a sus consejeros
la tarea / un informe
ejercicio físico
¿ ?

¿Recuerda Ud.?

You have been using forms of **ser** and **estar** since **Capítulo 1.** The following section will help you consolidate everything you know so far about these two verbs, both of which express *to be* in Spanish. You will learn a bit more about them as well.

Before you begin **Gramática 16,** think in particular about the following questions: **¿Cómo está Ud.? ¿Cómo es Ud.?** What do these questions tell you about the difference between **ser** and **estar**?

Grammar Tutorial 16
connect
|SPANISH
www.connectspanish.com

16 ¿Ser o estar?

Summary of the Uses of **ser** and **estar**

Gramática en acción: Una conversación a larga distancia

Aquí hay un lado de la conversación entre una esposa que **está** en un viaje de negocios y su esposo, que **está** en casa. Habla el esposo.

Aló. [...] ¿Cómo **estás**, querida? [...] ¿Dónde **estás** ahora? [...] ¿Qué hora **es** allí? [...] ¡Huy!, **es** muy tarde. Y el hotel, ¿cómo **es**? [...] Oye, ¿qué **estás** haciendo ahora? [...] Ay, lo siento. **Estás** muy ocupada. ¿Con quién tienes cita mañana? [...] ¿Quién **es** el dueño de la compañía? [...] Ah, él **es** de Costa Rica, ¿verdad? [...] Bueno, ¿qué tiempo hace allí? [...] Muy bien. Hasta luego, ¿eh? [...] Adiós.

Comprensión

Complete las oraciones con **es** o **está.**

1. El esposo _____ en casa.
2. La esposa _____ una mujer de negocios.
3. La esposa _____ en un viaje de negocios.
4. No sabemos (*We don't know*) cómo _____ el hotel.
5. _____ muy tarde donde _____ la esposa.
6. La esposa _____ trabajando ahora.
7. El dueño de la compañía _____ de Costa Rica.

A long-distance conversation Here is one side of a conversation between a wife who is on a business trip and her husband, who is at home. The husband is speaking. Hello . . . How are you, dear? . . . Where are you now? . . . What time is it there? . . . Wow, it's very late. And how's the hotel? . . . Hey, what are you doing now? . . . Gosh, I'm sorry. You're very busy. Who do you have an appointment with tomorrow? . . . Who's the owner of the company? . . . Ah, he's from Costa Rica, isn't he? . . . Well, what's the weather like there? . . . Great. See you later, OK? . . . Good-bye.

Summary of the Uses of ser / Resumen de los usos de ser

• To *identify* people (including their profession) and things	Ella es **doctora.** Tikal es **una ciudad maya.**
• To express *nationality;* with **de** to express *origin*	Son **cubanos.** Son **de** La Habana.
• With **de** to tell of what *material* something is made	Este bolígrafo es **de plástico.**
• With **de** to express *possession*	Es **de** Carlota.
• With **para** to tell *for whom something is intended*	El regalo es **para** Sara.
• To tell *time* and give the *date*	Son **las once.** Es **la una y media.** Hoy es **martes,** tres de octubre.
• With *adjectives* that describe *basic, inherent characteristics*	Ramona es **inteligente.**
• To form many *generalizations* or *impersonal expressions* (only **es**)	Es **necesario** llegar temprano. Es **importante** estudiar.

Summary of the Uses of estar / Resumen de los usos de estar

• To tell *location*	El libro está **en la mesa.**
• To describe *health*	Estoy muy **bien,** gracias.
• With *adjectives* that describe *conditions*	Estoy muy **ocupada.**
• In a number of *fixed expressions*	**(No)** Estoy **de acuerdo.** Está **bien.** (*It's fine, OK.*)
• With *present participles* to form the *progressive tense*	Estoy **estudiando** ahora mismo.

Ser and *estar* with Adjectives / *Ser y estar con adjetivos*

1. *Ser* = Fundamental Characteristics

Ser is used with adjectives that describe the *fundamental qualities* (**las características fundamentales**) of a person, place, or thing.

Esa mesa es muy **baja.**
That table is very short.

Sus calcetines **son morados.**
His socks are purple.

Este sillón es **cómodo.**
This armchair is comfortable.

Sus padres **son cariñosos.**
Their parents are affectionate people.

2. *Estar* = Conditions

Estar is used with adjectives to express *conditions* (**las condiciones**) or observations that are true at a given moment but that do not describe inherent qualities of the noun. The adjectives on the next page are generally used with **estar.**

Temporary Conditions / **Las condiciones temporales**

abierto/a	open	desordenado/a	messy	ocupado/a	busy	
aburrido/a	bored	enfermo/a	sick	ordenado/a	neat	
alegre	happy	furioso/a	furious, angry	preocupado/a	worried	
cansado/a	tired	limpio/a	clean	seguro/a	sure, certain	
cerrado/a	closed	loco/a	crazy	sucio/a	dirty	
congelado/a	frozen; very cold	molesto/a	annoyed	triste	sad	
contento/a	content, happy	nervioso/a	nervous			

3. *Ser* or *estar*?

Many adjectives can be used with either **ser** or **estar,** depending on what the speaker intends to communicate. In general, when *to be* implies *looks, feels,* or *appears,* **estar** is used. Compare the use of **ser** and **estar** in the sample sentences.

Daniel **es guapo.**
Daniel is handsome. (He is a handsome person.)
Daniel **está muy guapo** esta noche.
Daniel looks very nice (handsome) tonight.

Amalia **es muy simpática,** pero hoy **está muy seria.**
Amalia is very nice, but she's very serious today.

Algo sobre...

la democracia en Costa Rica

Costa Rica se considera un país modelo en el mundo hispano. Lleva disfrutando de paz[a] y democracia desde 1948, un período muy largo en comparación con otros países hispanohablantes. Ese año, hubo[b] una rebelión después de unas elecciones problemáticas. Entonces[c] se creó[d] una nueva constitución con una asamblea[e] democráticamente elegida.[f] José Figueres Ferrer, el líder de la rebelión, fue el primer presidente elegido bajo[g] la nueva constitución. Es considerado un héroe nacional.

¿Cuánto tiempo lleva su país disfrutando de la democracia? ¿Quién es considerado un héroe / una heroína nacional en su país?

[a]Lleva... *It has been enjoying peace* [b]*there was* [c]*Then* [d]*se... was created* [e]*assembly* [f]*elected* [g]*under*

Luis Guillermo Solís Rivera, presidente de Costa Rica desde 2014

Práctica y comunicación

Summary of *ser* and *estar*

ser = inherent qualities
    identification
    nationality, origin
    material
    possession
    for whom
    time, date
    generalizations

estar = conditions
    location
    present progressive
    fixed expressions

A. ¿Soy o estoy?

Paso 1. Autoprueba. ¿**Ser** o **estar?** ¿Cuál es el verbo apropiado para cada caso?

___ **1.** to describe a health condition
___ **2.** to tell time
___ **3.** to describe inherent characteristics
___ **4.** to tell where a thing or person is located
___ **5.** to tell someone's profession
___ **6.** to say who something belongs to
___ **7.** to tell where someone is from
___ **8.** to describe a temporary condition
___ **9.** to make a generalization
___ **10.** to tell what something is intended for

Prác. A Paso 1: **Answers: 1.** *estar* **2.** *estar* **3.** *ser* **4.** *estar* **5.** *ser* **6.** *ser* **7.** *ser* **8.** *estar* **9.** *ser (es)* **10.** *ser*

Paso 2. Ahora complete las siguientes oraciones con **estoy** o **soy.** También identifique la razón para usar cada verbo, usando los números de las explicaciones del **Paso 1.**

RAZÓN DEL **PASO 1**

a. _____ bien. _____
b. _____ simpático/a. _____
c. _____ contento/a de tomar español este semestre. _____
d. _____ estudiante universitario/a. _____
e. _____ de (ciudad, estado o país). _____

Paso 3. Ahora, en parejas, túrnense para hacer y contestar preguntas basadas en el **Paso 2.** Luego digan a la clase algo (*something*) que Uds. tienen en común.

MODELO: a. Estoy bien. →
  E1: ¿Cómo estás?
  E2: Estoy muy bien. ¿Y tú?
  EN COMÚN: Los dos estamos bien hoy.

B. **Un regalo estupendo.** Use **es** o **está** para describir el siguiente regalo que los padres de su compañero/a de cuarto acaban de comprarle (*just bought for him/her*).

La computadora...

1. _____ en la mesa del comedor.
2. _____ un regalo de cumpleaños.
3. _____ para mi compañero de cuarto.
4. _____ de la tienda Computec.
5. _____ en una caja (*box*) verde.
6. _____ de los padres de mi compañero.
7. _____ un regalo muy caro, pero estupendo.
8. _____ de metal y plástico gris.
9. _____ una IBM último modelo.
10. _____ muy fácil (*easy*) de usar.

Nota **comunicativa**

El uso de adjetivos + *por*

Por often expresses *because of* or *about (*as in *due to)*, especially with adjectives such as **contento/a, furioso/a, nervioso/a,** and **preocupado/a.**

Amalia está preocupada **por** los exámenes finales.
Amalia is worried about her final exams.

You will use **por** in this way in **Práctica C** and **D.**

C. **¿Quiénes son?** En parejas, hagan oraciones con **ser** o **estar,** inventando detalles para describir a las personas y cosas que se ven en la foto.

1. ¿quiénes?
2. ¿de qué país?
3. simpáticos/antipáticos / ¿ ?
4. en este momento, contentos/tristes / ¿ ?
5. molestos/cansados por el viaje / ¿ ?
6. aquí por un mes / una semana / ¿ ?
7. ¿ ?

nuestros primos de San José

Gabriela   Julio

D. Publicidad

Paso 1. Complete el siguiente anuncio (*ad*) con la forma apropiada de **ser**, **estar** o **hay**, según el contexto.

Costa Rica... belleza[a] natural

Una heliconia

¿(*Tú:* _____[1]) de una gran ciudad? ¿(*Tú:* _____[2]) una persona aventurera? ¿(_____[3]) la naturaleza una gran atracción en tu vida[b]? ¿(_____[4]) preocupado/a por los cambios[c] en el clima global? Entonces,[d] Costa Rica (_____[5]) el país para ti. Imagina: (_____[6]) en un lugar cerca del mar[e] en donde (_____[7]) increíbles especies de animales y plantas: iguanas, caimanes, orquídeas, heliconias...

(*Nosotros:* _____[8]) los expertos en turismo natural en Costa Rica. Todos nuestros guías[f] (_____[9]) costarricenses de nacimiento,[g] pero (*ellos:* _____[10]) contentos de conocer[h] a personas de todo el mundo y hacer nuevos amigos. Con sus conocimientos,[i] con su gran paciencia, con su español, (*ellos:* _____[11]) como profesores... pero sus clases (_____[12]) mucho más interesantes que las clases académicas... ¡y menos difíciles!

No (_____[13]) necesario viajar[j] a Costa Rica en una estación específica. (_____[14]) bueno viajar a Costa Rica en cualquier[k] mes del año. ¡Ven![l] ¡Costa Rica (_____[15]) esperándote[m]!

[a]*beauty* [b]*life* [c]*changes* [d]*Then* [e]*sea, ocean* [f]*guides* [g]*de...by birth* [h]*de... to meet* [i]*knowledge* [j]*to travel* [k]*any* [l]*Come (to visit)!* [m]*waiting for you*

Paso 2. Comprensión. ¿Cierto o falso? Corrija las oraciones falsas.

	CIERTO	FALSO
1. En Costa Rica, la naturaleza tiene mucha importancia para el turismo.	☐	☐
2. El turista no va a ver animales exóticos allí.	☐	☐
3. El turista puede aprender español allí.	☐	☐
4. No todas las estaciones son apropiadas para el turismo.	☐	☐

E. Una conversación entre esposos

Paso 1. En parejas, organicen el diálogo entre el marido de la página 178 (**Columna A**) y su esposa (**Columna B**), que está en un viaje de negocios. Primero, emparejen los elementos de las dos columnas. El esposo empieza el diálogo, contestando el teléfono.

A

1. _____ Aló.
2. _____ Bien. ¿Cómo estás tú, querida?
3. _____ ¿Dónde estás ahora?
4. _____ ¿Qué hora es allí?
5. _____ ¡Huy!, es muy tarde. Y el hotel, ¿cómo es?
6. _____ Oye, ¿qué estás haciendo ahora?
7. _____ Ay, lo siento. Estás muy ocupada. ¿Con quién tienes cita mañana?
8. _____ ¿Quién es el dueño de la compañía?
9. _____ Ah, él es de Costa Rica, ¿verdad?
10. _____ Bueno, ¿qué tiempo hace allí?
11. _____ Bueno. Mañana hablamos más. Buenas noches.

B

a. _____ muy moderno y _____ muy limpio.
b. Sí, pero ahora _____ trabajando en Nueva York.
c. _____ las once de la noche.
d. Hola, querido. ¿Qué tal?
e. El señor Cortina.
f. _____ leyendo unos informes para la reunión de mañana. _____ que leer uno más todavía.
g. Sí. Hasta mañana.
h. _____ en el hotel, en Nueva York.
i. _____ un poco cansada por el viaje y _____ sueño.
j. _____ fresco y _____ nublado.
k. Con un señor de Computec.

Paso 2. Ahora completen las oraciones de la señora con la forma correcta de **estar, hacer, ser** o **tener**. Luego practiquen la conversación completa.

F. Una tarde terrible

Paso 1. Hoy es un día desastroso para la familia Castañeda. Ud. va a describir su casa en el **Paso 2.** Para prepararse, repase (*review*) primero unos adjetivos, cambiando (*exchanging*) las palabras rosadas por antónimos en las siguientes oraciones.

1. No hace buen tiempo; hace _____.
2. El bebé no está bien; está _____.
3. El gato no está limpio; está _____.
4. El esposo no está tranquilo; está _____ por el bebé.
5. El garaje no está cerrado; está _____.
6. Los niños no están tranquilos; están _____, porque tienen miedo.
7. La esposa no está contenta; está _____ por el tiempo.
8. El baño no está ordenado; está _____.

Paso 2. Ahora use los adjetivos del **Paso 1** y otros que Ud. conozca (*you know*) para expresar lo que *están haciendo* todos los miembros de la familia *en este momento*. Póngales (*Give*) nombres a todos y exprese su *estado de ánimo* (*their feelings*) o sus deseos. ¡Use su imaginación! Si puede, diga también lo que *usualmente hacen* estas personas a esta hora.

Estrategia

lo que están haciendo =
   el presente progresivo

el estado de ánimo =
   el presente simple

lo que usualmente hacen =
   el presente simple

Vocabulario útil

la cena	dinner	**ladrar**	to bark
cenar	to have dinner	**llorar**	to cry
cocinar	to cook	**los truenos y**	thunder and
conducir (conduzco)*	to drive	**relámpagos**	lightning

Only the first person singular of the verb* **conducir *is irregular, as noted. The other forms of the present tense are regular:* **conduces, conduce...**

G. Ana y Estela. Conteste las preguntas para describir el siguiente dibujo de un cuarto de dos estudiantes. ¡OJO! Invente otros detalles necesarios.

1. ¿Quiénes son las dos compañeras de cuarto?
2. ¿Dónde estudian? ¿Qué estudian?
3. ¿De dónde son?
4. ¿Cómo son?
5. ¿Dónde están en este momento?
6. ¿Qué hay en el cuarto?
7. ¿Cómo está el cuarto?
8. ¿Son ordenadas las dos o desordenadas?

H. Intercambios. ¿Cómo están Uds. en estas situaciones? En parejas, túrnense para hacer y contestar preguntas, según el modelo.

MODELO: cuando / tener mucha tarea →
    E1: ¿Cómo estás cuando **tienes** mucha tarea?
    E2: Estoy cansado y estresado, como ahora. ¿Y tú?
    E3: Yo también.

1. cuando / tener mucha tarea / una tarea fácil/difícil
2. cuando / no tener trabajo académico
3. cuando / sacar (to get) A/D en un examen
4. en verano/invierno
5. cuando llueve/nieva
6. los lunes por la mañana / los domingos por la tarde / los...
7. después de una fiesta / un examen
8. durante la clase de _____
9. ¿ ?

Gramática en acción: Buenos Aires y San José

El centro de Buenos Aires, Argentina

- Buenos Aires es más grande que San José.
- Tiene más edificios altos que San José.
- Generalmente, en Buenos Aires no hace tanto calor como en San José.

Pero...
- San José es menos antigua que Buenos Aires.
- No tiene tantos habitantes como Buenos Aires.
- Sin embargo, los costarricenses son tan simpáticos como los argentinos.

¿Y Ud.?

1. Mi ciudad/pueblo...
   - (no) es tan grande como Chicago.
   - es más/menos cosmopolita que San Francisco.

2. Me gusta _____ (nombre de mi ciudad/pueblo)...
   - más que _____ (nombre de otra ciudad).
   - menos que _____ (nombre de otra ciudad).
   - tanto como _____ (nombre de otra ciudad).

El centro de San José, Costa Rica

Algo sobre...

San José y Buenos Aires

San José
- Fundada en 1738 y capital de Costa Rica desde 1823
- Población: 288.000 habitantes
- Clima: 2 estaciones; 23° C promedioª todo el año

Buenos Aires
- Fundada en 1580 y capital de la Argentina desde 1853
- Población: 2.891.000 habitantes
- Clima: 4 estaciones; 26° C de máximas temperaturas (diciembre–febrero) y 14° C de mínimas (junio–agosto).

La ciudad donde Ud. vive, ¿es una ciudad capital? ¿Cuántos habitantes tiene, aproximadamente? ¿Cuántas estaciones hay?

ªaverage

In English *comparisons* (**las comparaciones**) are formed in a variety of ways. Equal comparisons are expressed with the word *as*. Unequal comparisons are expressed with the adverbs *more* or *less*, or by adding *-er* to the end of the adjective.

as cold as
as many as

more intelligent,
less important
taller, smarter

a comparative / **un comparativo** = a form of or structure with nouns, adjectives, and adverbs used to compare nouns, qualities, or actions

---

Buenos Aires and San José *Buenos Aires is bigger than San José. • It has more tall buildings than San José. • It is not as hot in Buenos Aires as it is in San José, generally. But . . . San José is newer (lit., less ancient) than Buenos Aires. • It doesn't have as many inhabitants as Buenos Aires. • Nevertheless, Costa Ricans are as nice as Argentines.*

Comparatives / **Los comparativos**

Inequality / **La desigualdad**				Equality / **La igualdad**	
más... que	more . . . than	**menos... que**	less . . . than	**tan... como**	as . . . as
más que	more than	**menos que**	less than	**tanto/a/os/as... como**	as much/many . . . as
				tanto como	as much as

Inequality / **La desigualdad: más/menos... que, más/menos que**

1. Comparing Adjectives, Adverbs, and Verbs

Elena habla: «Juan es más
alto que yo. Y corre más
rápido que yo.»

Para describir

más/menos + *adjective* + que

$\left.\begin{array}{l}\textit{more/less} + \textit{adjective} \\ \textit{adjective} + \textit{-er}\end{array}\right\} + \textit{than}$

Juan es **más alto** que Elena.
Juan is taller than Elena (is).

Elena es **menos alta** que Juan.
Elena is shorter than Juan (is).

Para describir cómo se hace una acción

más/menos + *adverb* + que

$\left.\begin{array}{l}\textit{more/less} + \textit{adverb} \\ \textit{adverb} + \textit{-er}\end{array}\right\} + \textit{than}$

Juan corre **más rápido** que Elena.
Juan runs faster (more quickly) than Elena (does).

Elena corre **menos rápido** que Juan.
Elena runs slower (less quickly) than Juan (does).

> **¡OJO!**
> While the repetition of a verb is optional in English, as shown in the examples with (*is*) and (*does*), the second verb is *never* repeated in Spanish.

Para expresar la frecuencia o intensidad de una acción

verb + más/menos que

verb + *more/less than*

Juan **corre** más que Elena.
Juan runs more than Elena (does).

Elena **corre** menos que Juan.
Elena runs less than Juan (does).

---

2. Comparing Nouns

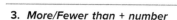

Carmen habla: «Rigoberto tiene **más
coches que** yo.»

Para comparar la cantidad

más/menos + *noun* + que

more/less (fewer) + noun + than

Rigoberto tiene **más coches** que Carmen.
Rigoberto has more cars than Carmen (does).

Carmen tiene **menos coches** que Rigoberto.
Carmen has fewer cars than Rigoberto (does).

---

3. *More/Fewer than + number*

Juan habla: «Elena tiene
menos lápices que yo.»

> **¡OJO!**
> The preposition **de** is used instead of **que** when the comparison is followed by a number.

Para expresar una cantidad

más/menos de + *number* + *noun*

more/fewer than + number + noun

Juan tiene **más de dos** lápices.
Juan has more than two pencils.

Elena tiene **menos de dos** lápices.
Elena has fewer than two pencils.

Equality / La igualdad: tan... como, tanto como, tanto/a/os/as... como

1. Comparing Adjectives, Adverbs, and Verbs

Ernesto
Patricia

¡OJO!

Remember that the second verb, indicated in parentheses, optional in English, is *never* repeated in Spanish.

Patricia habla: «Ernesto es **tan alto** y **tan delgado como** yo»

Para describir

tan + *adjective* + como

as + adjective + as

Patricia es **tan alta** como Ernesto. También es **tan delgada** como él.
Patricia is as tall as Ernesto (is). She's also as thin as he (is).

Para describir cómo se hace una acción

tan + *adverb* + como

as + adverb + as

Patricia juega al tenis **tan bien** como Ernesto. También juega **tan agresivamente** como él.
Patricia plays tennis as well as Ernesto (does). She also plays as aggressively as he (does).

Para expresar la frecuencia o intensidad de una acción

verb + tanto como

verb + as much as

Patricia **juega** al tenis **tanto como** Ernesto. También **gana tanto como** él.
Patricia plays tennis as much as Ernesto (does). She also wins as much (often) as he (does).

Ernesto

MARTES

JUEVES

SÁBADO

Ernesto habla: «Patrica juega **tan agresivamente como** yo. También juega **tanto como** yo.»

---

2. Comparing Nouns

Ernesto   Patricia

¡OJO!

Like all adjectives, **tanto** must agree in gender and number with the noun it modifies: **tanto dinero, tanta prisa, tantos abrigos, tantas hermanas.**

Para comparar la cantidad

tanto/a/os/as + *noun* + como

as much/many + noun + as

Ernesto tiene **tantos trofeos** como Patricia. También tiene **tantas raquetas de tenis** como ella.
Ernesto has as many trophies as Patricia (does). He also has as many tennis rackets as she (does).

Patricia y Ernesto tienen **tantas hermanas como** hermanos.
Patricia and Ernesto each have as many sisters as (they have) brothers.

Ernesto

Patricia habla: «Ernesto tiene **tantos hermanos como** yo.»

Gramática   Patricia

Irregular Forms / Las formas irregulares

- **bueno/a/os/as** *adj.* → mejor, mejores (que)

  Estos coches son **buenos,** pero esos son **mejores** (que estos).
  These cars are good, but those are better (than these).

- **bien** *adv.* → mejor (que)

  Yo hablo español **bien,** pero mi amigo Dennis lo habla **mejor** (que yo).
  I speak Spanish well, but my friend Dennis speaks it better (than I [do]).

- **malo/a/os/as** *adj.* → peor, peores (que)

  La nueva película de este director es **mala,** pero su primera es **peor.**
  This director's new movie is bad, but his first one is worse.

- **mal** *adv.* → peor (que)

  La profesora canta **mal,** pero yo canto **peor** (que ella).
  The professor sings badly, but I sing worse (than she [does]).

- **viejo/a/os/as** → mayor, mayores (que)

  La abuela es **viejita,** pero el abuelo es **mayor** *que* ella.
  Grandmother is old, but grandfather is older than she (is).

- **joven, jóvenes** → menor, menores (que)

  Delia es **joven,** pero su esposo es todavía **menor** que ella.
  Delia is young, but her husband is even younger than she (is).

Comparison Summary

| más... que
más que/de | menos... que
menos que/de | tan... como
tanto/a/os/as...
como tanto como |

Práctica y comunicación

A. Comparaciones

Paso 1. Autoprueba. Complete las frases con la palabra comparativa apropiada.

a. como   **b.** que

1. más + _____
2. tantos + _____
3. peor + _____
4. tan + _____
5. menos + _____
6. tanta + _____

Paso 2. Ahora compárese *(compare yourself)* con su mejor amigo/a, haciendo oraciones con los siguientes verbos y las formas comparativas del **Paso 1** u otras.

MODELO: tener años → Tengo **tantos años como** mi mejor amiga. (Soy [un año] **mayor/menor que** mi mejor amiga.)

1. tener años
2. tomar cursos
3. bailar
4. tener dinero
5. ser inteligente
6. tener pasión por el/la

Paso 3. Ahora, en parejas, usen las oraciones del **Paso 2** para entrevistarse. Luego digan a la clase algo *(something)* que tienen en común.

MODELO: E1: Tengo tantos años como mi mejor amiga. ¿Y tú?
E2: Sí, tengo tantos años como mi mejor amiga. (No, soy [un año] mayor que mi mejor amiga.)
EN COMÚN: Las dos tenemos tantos años como nuestras mejores amigas. (Las dos no tenemos tantos años como nuestras mejores amigas.)

Prác. A, Paso 1: Answers: 1. b 2. a 3. b 4. a 5. b 6. a

B. Alfredo y Gloria

Alfredo
San José, Costa Rica
Profesor universitario
Casado. (*Married*) Vive en una casa
    cerca del *campus*.
Dos hijos

Gloria
Punta Arenas, Chile
Estudiante universitaria
Vive en una casa en el centro
    con ocho compañeros.
No tiene hijos.

Paso 1. ¿Quién probablemente tiene más de las siguientes cosas y cualidades y quién tiene menos? **¡OJO!** Los dos son similares en los números 4, 5 y 6.

1. botas de invierno
2. camisas de manga (*sleeves*) corta
3. chanclas
4. inteligencia
5. parientes
6. camisetas

Paso 2. ¿Quién probablemente hace más o hace menos? **¡OJO!** Los dos son similares en los números 4, 5 y 6.

1. ganar (*to earn*) dinero
2. salir con sus amigos
3. dormir
4. levantarse temprano
5. hacer ejercicio
6. trabajar

Paso 3. Use los comparativos irregulares para hablar de Alfredo y Gloria.

1. Es obvio que Alfredo tiene más años: es _____ _____ Gloria.
2. Los padres de Alfredo tienen más de 65 años. Sin duda, los padres de Gloria son _____ _____ los padres de Alfredo.
3. Gloria toma clases de danza. Así que (*So*), Gloria baila _____ _____ Alfredo.

C. Opiniones

Paso 1. Escriba oraciones completas para expresar su opinión.

MODELO: el cine / la televisión : ser / interesante →
        El cine **es más** interesante **que** la televisión.

1. el fútbol / el fútbol americano: ser / divertido
2. la clase de historia / la clase de español: ser / interesante
3. en esta universidad, las artes / los deportes (*sports*): ser / importante
4. el español / el inglés: ser / difícil
5. mis amigos / mis padres: divertirse con
6. los niños / los adultos: dormir
7. los profesores / los estudiantes: trabajar
8. en primavera / en otoño: llover

Paso 2. Ahora en parejas, comparen sus respuestas y expliquen sus opiniones. Luego digan a la clase una idea que los dos comparten (*share*).

D. Más opiniones

Paso 1. Compare las siguientes personas y cosas para expresar su opinión sobre ellas. Puede añadir (*add*) más palabras si quiere.

MODELO: el basquetbol y el golf: interesante, rápido, fácil de aprender →
        El basquetbol es **menos** interesante **que** el golf.

1. Meryl Streep y Cameron Díaz: joven, bonito, tener premios Óscar, actriz
2. Ud. y sus padres (hijos): joven, conservador, tener experiencia, desordenado
3. un Prius y un Cadillac: grande, barato, gastar (*to use*) gasolina, elegante
4. los perros y los gatos: independiente, inteligente, cariñoso, activo
5. Texas y Delaware: grande, tener habitantes, petróleo, estar lejos de California

(Continúa.)

Paso 2. En parejas, comparen sus opiniones. Traten de (*Try to*) explicar sus razones. Luego digan a la clase algo (*something*) que tienen en común.

MODELO: el basquetbol y el golf: interesante, rápido →
　　　E1: El basquetbol es **menos** interesante **que** el golf.
　　　E2: No estoy de acuerdo. El basquetbol es **más** interesante **que** el golf porque es **más** rápido.

E. Comparaciones. Complete las siguientes oraciones según su experiencia personal.

1. En mi familia, yo soy mayor que _____ y menor que _____.
2. En esta clase, _____ estudia tanto como yo.
3. En esta universidad, los estudiantes _____ más que _____.
4. _____ es más guapo que Juanes.
5. _____ es más guapa que Shakira.
6. _____ tiene tanto talento como Carlos Santana.

F. La familia de Lucía y Miguel

Paso 1. En parejas, miren la foto e identifiquen a los miembros de la familia de Lucía. Piensen en la edad (*age*) de cada persona.

MODELO: Sancho es mayor que sus hermanos.

Paso 2. Comparen a cada miembro de la familia con otra persona.

MODELO: Amalia es menor que Sancho pero es más alta que él.

Paso 3. Ahora comparen a los miembros de su propia (*own*) familia. Haga por lo menos cinco declaraciones.

MODELOS: E1: Mi hermana Mary es mayor que yo, pero yo soy más alto que ella.
　　　　E2: Mi abuela es mayor que mi abuelo, pero ella es más activa que él.

el abuelo Jaime　Lucía　Miguel　la abuela Lucía　Amalia

Lucía, con su esposo, sus padres y sus hijos
Sami　Sancho

G. La rutina diaria... en invierno y en verano

Paso 1. ¿Es diferente nuestra rutina diaria en cada estación? Complete las siguientes oraciones sobre su rutina.

	EN INVIERNO	EN VERANO
1. me levanto a _____ (hora)		
2. almuerzo en _____		
3. me divierto con mis amigos / mi familia en _____		
4. estudio _____ horas todos los días		
5. estoy / me quedo en _____ (lugar) por la noche		
6. me acuesto a _____ (hora)		

Paso 2. En parejas, comparen sus actividades de invierno con las de verano.

MODELO: E1: En invierno, ¿te levantas más temprano que en verano?
　　　　E2: No, en invierno, me levanto tan temprano como en verano.
　　　　　　(No, en invierno, me levanto a la misma hora que en verano.)

Paso 3. Ahora digan a la clase una o dos cosas que Uds. tienen en común.

MODELO: Nosotros nos levantamos más tarde en verano que en invierno. En verano no hay clases y, por lo general, nos acostamos más tarde.

Un poco de todo

A. Lengua y cultura: Dos hemisferios

Paso 1. Complete the following paragraphs with the correct forms of the words in parentheses, as suggested by context. When two possibilities are given in parentheses, select the correct word.

¿Sabe Ud.[a] algo de las diferencias entre los hemisferios del norte y del sur? Hay (mucho[1]) diferencias entre el clima del hemisferio norte y el del hemisferio sur.

Cuando (ser / estar[2]) invierno en este país, por ejemplo, (ser / estar[3]) verano en la Argentina, en Bolivia, en Chile... Cuando yo (salir[4]) para la universidad en enero, con frecuencia tengo que (llevar[5]) abrigo y botas. En (los / las[6]) países del hemisferio sur, un estudiante (poder[7]) asistir (a / de[8]) un concierto en febrero llevando solo pantalones (corto[9]), camiseta y sandalias.

En muchas partes de este país, (antes de / durante[10]) las vacaciones de diciembre, casi siempre (hacer[11]) frío y a veces (nevar[12]). En (grande[13]) parte de Sudamérica, al otro lado del ecuador, hace calor y (muy / mucho[14]) sol durante (ese[15]) mes. A veces en los periódicos, hay fotos de personas que (tomar[16]) el sol y nadan[b] en las playas sudamericanas en enero.

Es diciembre en Buenos Aires. ¿Qué tiempo hace?

Tengo un amigo que (ir[17]) a (hacer / tomar[18]) un viaje a Buenos Aires. Él me dice[c] que allí la Navidad[d] (ser / estar[19]) una fiesta de verano y que todos (llevar[20]) ropa como la que[e] llevamos nosotros en julio. Parece[f] increíble, ¿verdad?

[a]¿Sabe... *Do you know* [b]*are swimming* [c]*Él... He tells me* [d]*Christmas* [e]*la... that which* [f]*It seems*

Paso 2. Comprensión. ¿Probable o improbable?

	PROBABLE	IMPROBABLE
1. Los estudiantes argentinos van a la playa en julio.	☐	☐
2. Muchas personas sudamericanas hacen viajes de vacaciones en enero.	☐	☐
3. En Santiago (Chile) hace frío en diciembre.	☐	☐

Paso 3. En parejas, lean el anuncio (*ad*) del inicio del año escolar (*school*) en el Perú (página 192). Luego conteste las siguientes preguntas.

1. ¿En qué mes cae (*occurs*) el inicio del año escolar en los Estados Unidos? ¿En qué estación cae?
2. ¿En qué mes empieza en el Perú? ¿En qué estación cae?
3. ¿Por qué la escuela empieza en meses diferentes en los dos países?
4. ¿Cuándo son las vacaciones de verano en los Estados Unidos?
5. ¿Cuándo creen Uds. que empiezan las vacaciones de verano en el Perú?

Buen inicio del año escolar

10 de marzo

B. Expresiones

Paso 1. Las comparaciones se usan mucho en refranes y expresiones populares e idiomáticas. En parejas, lean las siguientes expresiones. ¿Tienen equivalentes en inglés?

1. pesar (*to weigh*) menos que un mosquito
2. ser más pesado (*overbearing, boring*) que el matrimonio
3. ser más bueno que el pan (*bread*)
4. ser más largo que un día sin pan
5. estar más claro que el agua (*water*)
6. ser más alto que un pino (*pine tree*)
7. ser tan rápido como un chisme (*rumor*)

Paso 2. Ahora, en parejas, inventen por lo menos cuatro expresiones que se parecen a las (*resemble those*) del **Paso 1.** Pueden cambiar la terminación de las expresiones del **Paso 1** (**pesar menos que...** ¿ ?) o crear expresiones originales (**ser tan divertido como...** , **ser más larga que una semana sin...**).

Al crear (*When you are creating*) las expresiones, piensen en cosas y cualidades que, en la cultura de este país, son generalmente positivas o negativas. En las expresiones del **Paso 1,** por ejemplo, se usa la palabra **pan** dos veces. ¿Cómo se presenta el pan en la cultura hispana en estas expresiones, como una cosa muy positiva o negativa?

En su comunidad

Entreviste (*Interview*) a una persona hispana de su universidad o ciudad sobre el clima de su país de origen y los horarios (*schedules*) de clases durante el año.

PREGUNTAS POSIBLES

- ¿Hay en su país cuatro estaciones o solo dos?
- ¿Coinciden con las estaciones del lugar donde Ud. vive ahora?
- ¿Cómo es el clima en cada estación?
- ¿En qué mes empiezan las clases en las escuelas? ¿Y en qué mes terminan?
- ¿Es igual para los ciclos de la universidad?

«En la Mitad del Mundo» Segmento 2

Antes de mirar

Indique todas las palabras que Ud. asocia con las artesanías (*crafts*).
¿Tiene otras asociaciones?

_____ la tradición
_____ mercados al aire
libre (*open air*)
_____ la gente (*people*)
mayor

_____ su país
_____ la modernidad
_____ centros comerciales
_____ la gente joven
_____ otros países

Este segmento

Laura presenta un reportaje sobre la tradición artesanal textil en la
ciudad ecuatoriana de Otavalo y habla con un maestro tejedor.

El Sr. José Cotocachi, maestro tejedor (*master weaver*) de tercera (*third*) generación que mantiene (*maintains*) la tradición textil de su familia

Fragmento del guion

LAURA: La lengua materna de José es el quechua, la lengua que
hablaban[a] los incas y que hoy siguen hablando
muchas personas desde Ecuador hasta Chile. José nos
enseñó[b] cómo él mismo[c] hace los tintes[d] para la lana
que usa en los tejidos de su taller.[e] Estos tintes son
completamente naturales y los colores son increíbles.
Vemos cómo un insecto tan pequeño, la cochinilla,
produce un intenso color rojo.

JOSÉ: Si es que le guardo[f] un año o dos años mejor todavía
más fuerte[g]... y bueno un poco de ácido natural...
llegó [a ser] un poquito claro.[h]

[a]*used to speak* [b]*nos... showed us* [c]*él... he himself* [d]*dyes* [e]*tejidos... fabrics of his shop* [f]*Si... If I keep it* [g]*todavía... even stronger* [h]*llegó... it got lighter*

Vocabulario del segmento

rodeado/a de	surrounded by
sobre todo	especially
la bufanda	scarf
tuve	I had
la transmite	he teaches it
era	it was
duro/a	hard, difficult
no ha cambiado	has not changed
la venta masiva	mass distribution
nos explicó	explained to us
los negocios	businesses
la feria	fair
trabajábamos	used to work
ya salíamos	we were already leaving
ya no es así	it's not that way any more

Después de mirar

A. ¿Está claro? Las siguientes oraciones son falsas. Corríjalas
(*Correct them*) según el video.

1. Otavalo está en la costa del Ecuador.
2. Allí hace mucho calor.
3. Otavalo es famosa por su gran centro comercial.
4. La ciudad no tiene población indígena.
5. José es el único (*only*) tejedor en su familia.

B. Un poco más. Conteste las siguientes preguntas.

1. Además del (*Besides*) español, ¿qué otra lengua se habla en el Ecuador?
2. ¿Qué prendas (*articles of clothing*) textiles producen los artesanos otavaleños?
3. ¿Qué pasa en una feria?

C. Y ahora, Uds. En parejas, preparen un resumen informativo de este segmento
de *Salu2*. Deben crear (*create*) un texto que pudiera (*could*) ser útil a turistas.

A LEER

¿Es muy variado el clima en el país donde Ud. vive?

Lectura cultural: Costa Rica
El clima de Costa Rica

Se puede decir[a] que el clima de Costa Rica es tropical. Esto significa que propiamente[b] no tiene una estación de invierno. Lo que sí tiene son dos temporadas:[c] una seca[d] y otra lluviosa.[e] En la mayor parte del país, esta última[f] ocurre entre mayo y noviembre. En las zonas más lluviosas del país, las lluvias son muy copiosas[g] y llegan a ocasionar muchas inundaciones.[h]

Sin embargo, el clima de Costa Rica es muy diverso. Esto llama mucho la atención de los turistas, ya que[i] en pocas horas se puede pasar de un clima lluvioso en las montañas a uno caluroso[j] en la playa.

[a]*say* [b]*really* [c]*seasons* [d]*dry* [e]*rainy* [f]*last one (i.e., last season)* [g]*heavy* [h]*llegan... they cause a lot of floods* [i]*ya... since* [j]*uno... a warm one (i.e., warm climate)*

Una carreta de Sarchí, Costa Rica

En **otros** países hispanos

- **En Chile** En este país se encuentra[a] el desierto de Atacama, el más seco del mundo.

- **En España** La diversidad climática y geográfica de este país europeo es espectacular para su tamaño.[b] La zona más caliente de Europa (el área de Córdoba y Sevilla) coexiste con una de las cordilleras[c] más altas del continente (la Sierra Nevada). Hasta hay[d] una zona desértica (en Almería).

[a]*se... is found* [b]*size* [c]*mountain ranges* [d]*Hasta... There's even*

COMPRENSIÓN

Conteste las siguientes preguntas.

1. ¿Por qué no tiene el clima costarricense cuatro estaciones?
2. ¿Cuáles son los meses secos en Costa Rica?
3. ¿Dónde está el desierto de Atacama?
4. ¿Qué aspecto del clima y la geografía de España es interesante?
5. ¿Para qué sirve una carreta?

Un símbolo costarricense: La carreta

Como método de transporte tradicional, las carretas no son exclusivas de Costa Rica. Allí su uso se asocia con las plantaciones de café. Sin embargo, sí es puramente costarricense decorar las carretas con bellos diseños[a] y colores. Por eso, las carretas son un símbolo nacional del trabajo y la cultura costarricense. La ciudad de Sarchí, al norte de la capital, es el centro artesanal de estas carretas.

[a]*bellos... beautiful designs*

Y ahora, Uds.

Uds. ya saben (*know by now*) muchos detalles sobre la geografía y el clima del mundo hispanohablante. En grupos, seleccionen un país de ese mundo donde les gustaría (*you would like*) vivir. También deben escribir una lista de razones que justifiquen su decisión, para presentar a la clase.

Del mundo hispano

Antes de leer

Conteste las siguientes preguntas.

Vocabulario para leer

guardar	to save, keep
promover	to promote, encourage
el reciclaje	recycling

1. ¿Qué tipo de calendario(s) usa Ud.?
2. Mire el calendario que aparece en esta lectura. ¿Qué día de la semana se representa con la X? ¿Por qué cree que se usa la X?
3. ¿Cuál es el primer día de la semana en los calendarios de los países hispanos?

Lectura: Un calendario especial

CURIOSIDADES   ¿Se pueden usar calendarios de otros años?

ENERO	FEBRERO	MARZO
L M X J V S D	L M X J V S D	L M X J V S D
1 2 3 4	1	1
5 6 7 8 9 10 11	2 3 4 5 6 7 8	2 3 4 5 6 7 8
12 13 14 15 16 17 18	9 10 11 12 13 14 15	9 10 11 12 13 14 15
19 20 21 22 23 24 25	16 17 18 19 20 21 22	16 17 18 19 20 21 22
26 27 28 29 30 31	23 24 25 26 27 28	23/30 24/31 25 26 27 28 29

ABRIL	MAYO	JUNIO
L M X J V S D	L M X J V S D	L M X J V S D
1 2 3 4 5	1 2 3	1 2 3 4 5 6 7
6 7 8 9 10 11 12	4 5 6 7 8 9 10	8 9 10 11 12 13 14
13 14 15 16 17 18 19	11 12 13 14 15 16 17	15 16 17 18 19 20 21
20 21 22 23 24 25 26	18 19 20 21 22 23 24	22 23 24 25 26 27 28
27 28 29 30	25 26 27 28 29 30 31	29 30

JULIO	AGOSTO	SEPTIEMBRE
L M X J V S D	L M X J V S D	L M X J V S D
1 2 3 4 5	1 2	1 2 3 4 5 6
6 7 8 9 10 11 12	3 4 5 6 7 8 9	7 8 9 10 11 12 13
13 14 15 16 17 18 19	10 11 12 13 14 15 16	14 15 16 17 18 19 20
20 21 22 23 24 25 26	17 18 19 20 21 22 23	21 22 23 24 25 26 27
27 28 29 30 31	24/31 25 26 27 28 29 30	28 29 30

REPETIMOS CADA 28 AÑOS

¿Alguien[a] guarda el calendario de hace 28 años? Si la respuesta es afirmativa, es el momento de sacarlo,[b] ya que[c] coincide día por día con el de este año 2010. Esa ha sido[d] la curiosa iniciativa que la asociación ecologista más importante de Italia, Legambiente, ha puesto en marcha[e] para promover el reciclaje. Resulta que, cada 28 años, los calendarios se repiten, siendo iguales en todas sus fechas. La explicación es que cada año solo puede comenzar en un día de la semana, por lo que existirían[f] 7 calendarios posibles... si no existieran años bisiestos.[g] Según los cálculos, al repetirse los años bisiestos cada 4 años, y los normales cada 7, el ciclo dura 28 años.

Y la próxima...
¿Cuándo nació la corbata?

[a]Anyone [b]take it out [c]ya... since [d]ha... has been [e]ha... has put in motion [f]por... in which case, there would be [g]años... leap years

Comprensión

A. Según el texto. Conteste las siguientes preguntas.

1. ¿Cómo se llaman los años de 366 días?
2. ¿Con qué frecuencia se repiten los calendarios?
3. ¿Qué es Legambiente?
4. ¿Qué acción recomienda Legambiente?
5. Además de (*Besides*) servir para el año 2010, ¿para qué otros años del pasado y del futuro puede servir el calendario de la Lectura?

B. Comentario. ¿Cree Ud. que es buena idea seguir la recomendación de Legambiente? ¿Es algo práctico y fácil de hacer? Explique sus razones.

A ESCUCHAR

El pronóstico° del tiempo en la Argentina   *report*

Vocabulario **para escuchar**

despejado	clear, no clouds	**el granizo**	hail
los grados	degrees	**la borrasca**	storm
soleado	sunny	**la bajada**	dip, lowering
la franja	coastal area	**bajo**	below

Antes de escuchar

¿Mira Ud. el pronóstico del tiempo todos los días? ¿Le gustan los pronósticos con muchos detalles o solo quiere saber (*know*) la información básica, como la temperatura máxima y mínima y si va a hacer sol o va a llover?

Después de escuchar

A. Temperaturas y condiciones atmosféricas.
Complete los espacios en blanco (*blanks*) en el mapa con las temperaturas máximas y mínimas. También dibuje (*draw*) el símbolo correspondiente a las condiciones atmosféricas que se mencionan.

Se espera nieve.   Se espera lluvia.

Se espera granizo.   Se espera sol.

B. El pronóstico en general. Conteste las siguientes preguntas.

1. ¿Qué tiempo va a hacer el domingo en la mayoría de las regiones argentinas?

2. ¿Qué estación es hoy en la Argentina?

PRODUCCIÓN PERSONAL

¡Ahora, yo!

A. Use de modelo las preguntas y respuestas de la página 165 de este capítulo para hablar del clima donde Ud. vive y de su estación del año favorita y lo que le gusta hacer en esa estación.

B. Mire el pronóstico del tiempo de su ciudad para los próximos tres días y filme su propio informe metereológico. Puede tener un tono serio o cómico.

A ESCRIBIR
Un ensayo sobre sus preferencias climáticas

Preparar

Paso 1. Piense en la estación del año que Ud. prefiere. ¿Por qué prefiere esa estación? ¿Con qué la asocia (*do you associate it*)? ¿Cuál es la estación del año que menos le gusta? ¿Por qué?

Paso 2. Entreviste a dos compañeros de clase sobre la estación del año que más les gusta y la que (*that which*) menos les gusta. También debe preguntarles por qué. Complete el cuadro con su respectiva información y también con sus propias (*your own*) respuestas a las preguntas.

nombre	estación preferida	estación que menos le gusta	¿por qué?
yo			
compañero/a 1			
compañero/a 2			

Paso 3. Ahora use sus opiniones y las respuestas de sus compañeros para escribir su ensayo. Hay más ayuda (*help*) en Connect.

Más ideas para su portafolio

- Incluya una imagen del mapa del tiempo de una ciudad donde Ud. desea vivir. Explique por qué le gusta (o no le gusta) el tiempo de esta ciudad.

- Dé tres palabras que Ud. asocia con el clima del estado donde vive y tres palabras que asocia con el clima del estado o país donde le gustaría (*you would like*) vivir en el futuro. Incluya una foto que represente el clima de su estado o el clima del país de su futuro.

- Si ha estado jugando (*have been playing*) Practice Spanish: Study Abroad, en Quest 4 Ud. participó (*participated*) en una telenovela (*soap opera*) sobre una compañía que se especializa en (*specializes in*) la moda. Hay muchos diseñadores (*designers*) de ropa y modelos hispanos famosos, por ejemplo Carolina Herrera, Paloma Picasso, Narciso Rodríguez, Oscar de la Renta, Cristóbal Balenciaga y Manolo Blahnik. Busque información en el internet sobre dos hispanos famosos en la industria de la moda y escriba por lo menos 6 oraciones comparándolos (*comparing them*). Incluya (*Include*) una foto de cada uno y escriba 2-3 oraciones sobre la ropa que llevan en la foto.

Sugerencia: You are now ready to play Quest 4 in **Practice Spanish: Study Abroad** (www.mhpractice.com).

EN RESUMEN En este capítulo

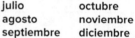

Visit **www.connectspanish.com** to practice the vocabulary and grammar points covered in this chapter.

AFTER STUDYING THIS CHAPTER I CAN . . .

☐ talk about the weather (166)

☐ talk about months and seasons of the year and express dates (168)

☐ use prepositions and cardinal points to locate people, places, and things (170)

☐ use the present progressive to express what I'm doing right now (174–174)

☐ use the verbs **ser** and **estar** correctly, especially with adjectives (178–180)

☐ compare people, places, things, and actions (185–188)

☐ recognize/describe at least 2–3 aspects of Costa Rican cultures

Gramática en breve

15. Present Progressive   estar + -ndo

-ar ⟶ -ando
-er/-ir ⟶ -iendo

Unaccented **-i-** ⟶ **-y- (leyendo)**

-ir Stem-changing Verbs: e ⟶ i **(pidiendo)**
o ⟶ u **(durmiendo)**

16. Summary of the Uses of *ser* and *estar*

ser	estar
inherent qualities, characteristics	mental, physical, health conditions
identification (including profession)	location
nationality, origin	present progressive
material	fixed expressions
possession	
for whom intended	
time and date	
generalizations	

Idioms with tener (expressing *to be*)

tener (mucho) calor, (mucho) frío

17. Comparisons

Comparisons of Inequality

más/menos... que
más/menos que
más/menos de +
   número
mayor/menor que
mejor/peor que

Comparisons of Equality

tan... como
tanto/a/os/as**... como**

VOCABULARIO

Los verbos

celebrar	to celebrate
continuar (continúo)	to continue
pasar	to spend (*time*); to happen
quedarse	to stay, remain (*in a place*)
seguir (sigo) (i)	to continue, to follow
Repaso: divertirse (me divierto) (i)	

 Remember that the parenthetical letter gives you the stem change for the present participle.

¿Qué tiempo hace?

el clima	climate
el tiempo	weather; time
está (muy) nublado	it's (very) cloudy, overcast
hace...	it's ...
(muy) buen/mal tiempo	(very) good/bad weather (very) nice out
(mucho) calor	(very) hot
(mucho) fresco	(very) cool
(mucho) frío	(very) cold
(mucho) sol	(very) sunny
(mucho) viento	(very) windy
hay (mucha) contaminación	there's (lots of) pollution
llover: llueve	to rain: it rains, it's raining
nevar: nieva	to snow: it snows, it's snowing
¿qué tiempo hace?	what's the weather like?

Los meses del año

el año	year
la fecha	date (*calendar*)
el mes	month
¿Cual es la fecha de hoy? ¿Qué fecha es hoy?	What's today's date?
el primero de	the first of (*month*)

enero	abril	julio	octubre
febrero	mayo	agosto	noviembre
marzo	junio	septiembre	diciembre

Las estaciones del año

la estación	season
la primavera	spring
el verano	summer
el otoño	fall, autumn
el invierno	winter

Los lugares

la capital	capital city
la playa	beach

Otros sustantivos

el cumpleaños	birthday
la medianoche	midnight
el mediodía	noon
el/la novio/a	boyfriend/girlfriend
la respuesta	answer

Los adjetivos

abierto/a	open
aburrido/a	bored
alegre	happy
cansado/a	tired
cariñoso/a	affectionate
cerrado/a	closed
congelado/a	frozen; very cold
contento/a	content, happy
desordenado/a	messy
difícil	hard, difficult
enfermo/a	sick
fácil	easy
furioso/a	furious, angry
limpio/a	clean
loco/a	crazy
mismo/a	same
molesto/a	annoyed
nervioso/a	nervous
ocupado/a	busy
ordenado/a	neat
preocupado/a	worried
querido/a	dear
seguro/a	sure, certain
sucio/a	dirty
triste	sad

Las comparaciones

más/menos de + number	more/fewer than + *number*
más/menos que	more/less than
más/menos... que	more/less (-er) . . . than

(comparaciones, continued)

tan... como	as . . . as
tanto como	as much as
tanto/a(s)... como	as much/many . . . as
mayor (que)	older (than)
mejor (que)	better (than); best
menor (que)	younger (than)
peor (que)	worse (than)

Las preposiciones

a la derecha de	to the right of
a la izquierda de	to the left of
al lado de	alongside of
cerca de	close to
debajo de	below
delante de	in front of
detrás de	behind
encima de	on top of
entre	between; among
lejos de	far from

Los puntos cardinales

el norte, el sur, el este, el oeste

Palabras adicionales

afuera	outdoors
ahora mismo	right now
conmigo	with me
contigo	with you (*fam.*)
esta noche	tonight
está bien	it's fine, OK
estar bien	to be comfortable (*temperature*)
mí (*obj. of prep.*)	me
por	about; because of
sin embargo	nevertheless
tener (mucho) calor	to be (very) warm, hot
tener (mucho) frío	to be (very) cold
ti (*obj. of prep.*)	you (*fam.*)
todavía	still

Vocabulario personal

7

¡A comer!

¡A... Let's eat!

www.connectspanish.com

En este capítulo

Una frutería, en la Ciudad de Panamá, Panamá

PANAMÁ

3.8 (punto ocho) millones habitantes

- Vasco Núñez de Balboa fue[a] el primer europeo que vio[b] el océano Pacífico en 1514, desde una colina[c] de Panamá. Este descubrimiento[d] cambió[e] la comprensión[f] de la geografía de nuestro planeta.

- El arroz con pollo[g] es uno de los platos panameños más típicos. Es también típico el sancocho, un tipo de sopa que muestra[h] la influencia de varias culturas: la indígena, la hispana, la africana y la afroantillana.[i]

[a]*was* [b]*saw* [c]*hill* [d]*discovery* [e]*changed* [f]*understanding* [g]*arroz... chicken with rice* [h]*shows* [i]*Afro-Caribbean*

Map labels:
- NICARAGUA
- COSTA RICA
- Mar Caribe
- Ciudad de Panamá
- PANAMÁ
- David
- COLOMBIA
- OCÉANO PACÍFICO
- 0 100 200 Millas
- 0 100 200 Kilómetros

- ¿Cuál es su comida[a] favorita?
- ¿Cuáles son algunos[b] de los platos[c] típicos de su país?
- ¿Dónde y a qué hora almuerza y cena[d] Ud., por lo general?

[a]*food* [b]*some* [c]*dishes* [d]*have dinner*

MANUEL GIL DEL VALLE CONTESTA LAS PREGUNTAS.

- Eso es difícil de contestar porque me gusta comer bien y me gusta casi todo. Pero si tengo que elegir un plato, elijo la paella de mariscos.[a]

- Los «nacatamales» son muy populares. Son tamales muy grandes, rellenos de carne, verduras, arroz, ciruelas[b] y otros ingredientes más. Una bebida típicamente nicaragüense es el pinolillo, una especie de horchata hecha de harina de maíz.[c] Pero en Nicaragua también son populares las comidas originarias de otros países, como la española, italiana, mexicana, china, etcétera.

- Trabajo en el centro de Managua. Así que,[d] por lo general, almuerzo en uno de los muchos restaurantes pequeños que hay en el centro. La hora siempre depende del trabajo, pero con frecuencia almuerzo al mediodía. ¿Y la cena? Casi siempre cenamos en casa con toda la familia, a eso de[e] las ocho. Mi esposa es una cocinera[f] estupenda.

[a]*paella... seafood paella* [b]*rellenos... stuffed with meat, vegetables, rice, cherries* [c]*hecha... made with corn flour* [d]*Así... So* [e]*a... around* [f]*cook*

La comida y las comidas°

La... *Food and meals*

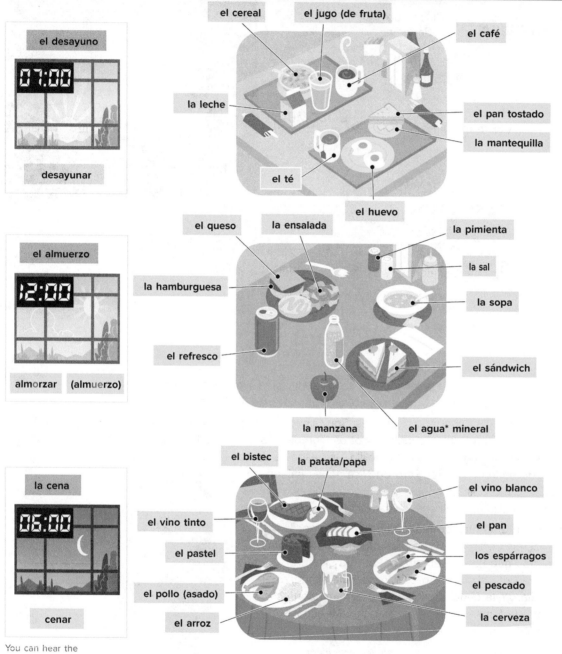

el desayuno

07:00

desayunar

el cereal

el jugo (de fruta)

el café

la leche

el pan tostado

la mantequilla

el té

el huevo

el almuerzo

12:00

almorzar (almuerzo)

el queso

la ensalada

la pimienta

la hamburguesa

la sal

la sopa

el refresco

el sándwich

el agua* mineral

la manzana

el bistec

la patata/papa

el vino blanco

la cena

06:00

cenar

el vino tinto

el pan

el pastel

los espárragos

el pescado

el pollo (asado)

el arroz

la cerveza

You can hear the pronunciation of theme vocabulary words and phrases in the Connect eBook.

*The noun **agua** (water) is feminine, but the masculine articles are used with it in the singular: el **agua**. Adjectives that modify it are feminine: el **agua fría**. This occurs with all feminine nouns that begin with a stressed **a** sound, for example, el/un **ama de casa** (homemaker).

Otras frutas

la **banana**	banana
la **naranja**	orange

Otras verduras

el **aguacate**	avocado
las **arvejas**	green peas
la **cebolla**	onion
los **champiñones**	mushrooms
los **frijoles**	beans
los **garbanzos**	chickpeas
la **lechuga**	lettuce
el **pepino**	cucumber
el **tomate**	tomato
la **zanahoria**	carrot

Otras carnes

la **barbacoa**	barbeque
la **chuleta (de cerdo)**	(pork) chop
el **jamón**	ham
el **pavo**	turkey
la **salchicha**	sausage; hot dog

Otros pescados y mariscos

el **atún**	tuna
los **camarones**	shrimp
la **langosta**	lobster
el **salmón**	salmon

Otros postres

los **dulces**	sweets; candy
el **flan**	(baked) custard
la **galleta**	cookie
el **helado**	ice cream

Otras comidas

el **aceite (de oliva)**	(olive) oil
el **azúcar**	sugar
la **salsa**	salsa
el **yogur**	yogurt

Los verbos

desayunar	to have (eat) breakfast
almorzar (almuerzo)	to have (eat) lunch
cenar	to have (eat) dinner, supper
cocinar	to cook

Así se dice

There is great variety in the words used to refer to foods in the Spanish-speaking world. The following are only a few of the most common ones.

las arvejas = los guisantes (*Sp.*)
los camarones = las gambas (*Sp.*)
el jugo = el zumo (*Sp.*)

la papa = la patata (*Sp.*)
el refresco = la gaseosa, la soda (**¡OJO!** = *soda water* in some areas)

There are many ways to express **la tienda de comestibles** (*grocery store*): **la abacería, el almacén** (which you have learned means *department store* in most areas), **la bodega** (popular in the Caribbean), **la pulpería** (*C.A., S.A.*), **la trucha** (*C.A.*).

Nota **comunicativa**

Más vocabulario para hablar de la comida

tener (mucha) hambre	to be (very) hungry
tener (mucha) sed	to be (very) thirsty
merendar (meriendo)	to snack
la **merienda**	snack
la **cocina**	cuisine
los **comestibles**	groceries, foodstuff
el **plato**	dish (*food prepared in a particular way*); course
el **plato principal**	main course
caliente	hot (*in temperature, not taste*)
frito/a	fried
picante	hot, spicy
rico/a	tasty, savory; rich (*in calories*)

La merienda (typically a late afternoon snack) is a traditional custom in those countries where the dinner hour is quite late, such as Spain, for example, where people may have dinner at 10:00 or 11:00 P.M. or even later. **La merienda** tides people over until the late evening meal.

You will use these words and phrases in **Comunicación A** and **B.**

Comunicación

A. ¿Qué quiere tomar? Empareje las descripciones con las comidas.

DESCRIPCIONES

1. _____ una sopa fría, langosta, espárragos, ensalada de lechuga y tomate, vino blanco y, para terminar, un pastel
2. _____ jugo de fruta, huevos con jamón, pan tostado y café
3. _____ un vaso (*glass*) de leche y unas galletas
4. _____ pollo asado, arroz, arvejas, agua mineral y, para terminar, una manzana
5. _____ una hamburguesa con patatas fritas, un refresco y un helado

COMIDAS

a. un menú ligero (*light*) para una dieta
b. una comida rápida
c. una cena elegante
d. un desayuno estilo estadounidense
e. una merienda

B. Definiciones

Paso 1. Dé las palabras definidas.

1. un plato de lechuga y tomate
2. una bebida alcohólica blanca o roja
3. una verdura anaranjada
4. una carne típica para una barbacoa en este país
5. la comida favorita de los ratones (*mice*)
6. una verdura que se come frita con las hamburguesas
7. una fruta roja o verde

Paso 2. Ahora, en parejas, túrnense para crear (*create*) definiciones de comidas y bebidas, según el modelo del **Paso 1.** Una persona da (*gives*) la definición y la otra da la palabra correspondiente.

Nota cultural

La comida del mundo hispano

No se puede hablar de una sola comida hispana, porque en el mundo hispanohablante hay una gran variedad culinaria.

- La comida cambia de país a país, dependiendo de los productos locales y de influencias nativas y externas. Sin embargo, sí hay productos de origen americano que se utilizan[a] en prácticamente todas las cocinas latinoamericanas: el maíz, las papas, los frijoles, los tomates, los aguacates.
- El arroz es también fundamental, pero es de origen asiático. Fue introducido en América por[b] los españoles.

Una de las influencias básicas en la cocina de todos los países latinoamericanos es la cocina española. Se combina con la tradición culinaria indígena de cada región y, en algunos[c] países, también con la tradición culinaria africana, gracias a la influencia de los esclavos[d] que fueron traídos[e] a América.

El maíz, uno de los ingredientes básicos de casi todos los países latinoamericanos

¿Cuáles son los ingredientes básicos de la cocina de su familia o su país?

[a]se... *are used* [b]*by* [c]*some* [d]*slaves* [e]fueron... *were brought*

C. Consejos (*Advice*) a la hora de comer. ¿Qué puede comer o beber su compañero/a en las siguientes situaciones? Déle consejos, según el modelo.

MODELO: Tengo mucha/poca hambre (sed). →
     E1: Tengo mucha hambre.
     E2: Puedes comer un bistec con papas fritas.

1. Tengo mucha/poca hambre (sed).
2. Tengo hambre a las cuatro de la mañana, después de una fiesta.
3. Estoy a dieta.
4. Estoy de vacaciones en Maine (Texas, California, la Florida,...).
5. Es hora de merendar. Estoy en casa (la universidad).
6. Soy vegano/a.

D. Las preferencias gastronómicas

Paso 1. Complete las siguientes oraciones para describir lo que Ud. come y no come.

1. Por la mañana siempre como _____.
2. En el desayuno me gusta comer _____.
3. Para cenar, prefiero comer _____.
4. Nunca como _____ y nunca bebo _____.
5. No me gusta comer _____, pero lo/la como (*I eat it*) en casa de mis padres/hijos/abuelos.

Paso 2. Haga una lista de los tres tipos de cocinas que Ud. prefiere.

Paso 3. Entre todos, comparen las listas. ¿Cuáles son los platos, lugares para comer y cocinas favoritos de la clase? ¿Cuáles son los ingredientes más necesarios para cocinar sus platos favoritos?

¿Qué sabe Ud. y a quién conoce?

As you know, two Spanish verbs express *to be:* **ser** and **estar.** They are not interchangeable, and their use depends on the meaning the speaker wishes to express. Similarly, two Spanish verbs express *to know:* **saber** and **conocer.** Note their uses in the drawings and text below. Also note that **conocer** is frequently used with the word **a** when referring to a person (as in the phrase **¿a quién conoce?** from the title of this section).

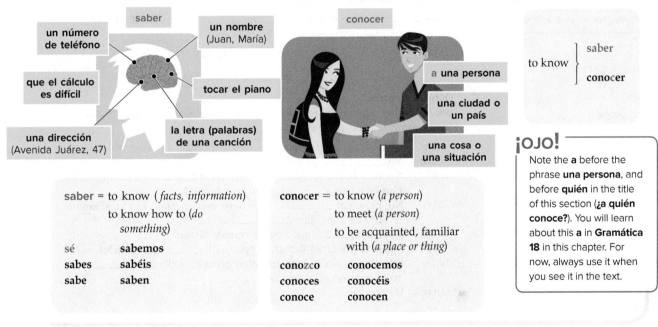

saber

un número de teléfono
un nombre (Juan, María)
que el cálculo es difícil
tocar el piano
una dirección (Avenida Juárez, 47)
la letra (palabras) de una canción

conocer

a una persona
una ciudad o un país
una cosa o una situación

to know { saber conocer }

¡OJO!

Note the **a** before the phrase **una persona,** and before **quién** in the title of this section (**¿a quién conoce?**). You will learn about this **a** in **Gramática 18** in this chapter. For now, always use it when you see it in the text.

saber = to know (*facts, information*) to know how to (*do something*)	**conocer** = to know (*a person*) to meet (*a person*) to be acquainted, familiar with (*a place or thing*)

sé	sabemos
sabes	sabéis
sabe	saben

conozco	conocemos
conoces	conocéis
conoce	conocen

Comunicación

A. ¿Cuánto sabe Ud. de Panamá?

Paso 1. ¿Cierto o falso? Complete las oraciones con la forma **yo** del verbo **saber** o **conocer**. Luego diga si las oraciones son ciertas o falsas para Ud.

		CIERTO	FALSO
1.	_____ Panamá.	☐	☐
2.	_____ dónde está Panamá.	☐	☐
3.	_____ el nombre de la capital de Panamá.	☐	☐
4.	_____ a una persona panameña famosa.	☐	☐
5.	_____ quién es Rubén Blades.	☐	☐
6.	_____ la música de Blades.	☐	☐
7.	_____ la letra de una canción de Blades.	☐	☐
8.	_____ bailar salsa.	☐	☐
9.	_____ un restaurante panameño.	☐	☐

Paso 2. Ahora, en parejas, túrnense para hacer y contestar preguntas basadas en las oraciones del **Paso 1.**

MODELO: **E1:** ¿Conoces Panamá?
　　　　 E2: No, no conozco Panamá. ¿Y tú?
　　　　 E1: Yo sí. / Yo tampoco. (*Me neither.*)

B. Los usos de *saber* y *conocer*

Paso 1. Llene (*Fill in*) los espacios en blanco con la forma apropiada de **saber**. Luego dé su equivalente en inglés.

—¿(Tú) _____[1] la dirección de un restaurante panameño?

—¡Cómo no![a] Hay uno en la calle[b] Park. El chef, Felipe, _____[2] hacer unos platos muy originales.

—¿(Tú) _____[3] a qué hora abren los sábados?

—No (yo) _____[4] exactamente. ¡Pero _____[5] la dirección electrónica!

[a]¡Cómo... *Of course!* [b]*street*

Paso 2. Ahora llene los espacios en blanco con la forma apropiada de **conocer**. Luego dé su equivalente en inglés.

—¿(Tú) _____[1] ese restaurante panameño que está en la calle Park?

—Sí, y también (yo) _____[2] al chef, Felipe.

—¿Ah sí? Yo lo[a] quiero _____[3]. Es muy famoso.

[a]*him*

C. ¿Dónde cenamos?

Paso 1. Lola y Manolo quieren salir a cenar. Complete su diálogo con las formas apropiadas de **saber** o **conocer**.

LOLA: ¿(Tú) _____[1] adónde quieres ir a cenar?
MANOLO: No _____.[2] ¿Y tú?
LOLA: No, pero hay un restaurante nuevo en la calle Betis. Creo que se llama Guadalquivir. ¿_____[3] el restaurante?
MANOLO: No, pero (yo) _____[4] que tiene mucha fama. Es el restaurante favorito de Pepa. Ella _____[5] al dueño.[a]
LOLA: ¿(Tú) _____[6] qué tipo de comida tienen?
MANOLO: No, pero podemos llamar a Pepa. ¿(Tú) _____[7] su teléfono?
LOLA: Está en mi celular. Llámala[b] y pregúntale[c] si ella _____[8] si aceptan reservaciones o no.
MANOLO: De acuerdo.

[a]*owner* [b]*Call her* [c]*ask her*

Paso 2. Comprensión. Conteste las siguientes preguntas.

1. ¿Saben Lola y Manolo dónde quieren cenar?
2. ¿Conocen el nuevo restaurante?
3. ¿Saben qué tipo de comida se sirve allí?
4. ¿Saben el número de teléfono de Pepa?
5. ¿Conocen al dueño del restaurante?

D. ¿Sabe Ud. mentir (*to lie*) bien?

Paso 1. Escriba dos oraciones con **saber** sobre algunas (*some*) cosas que sabe hacer y dos oraciones con **conocer** sobre personas interesantes que conoce. Algunas oraciones deben ser falsas. **¡OJO!** No olvide (*Don't forget*) usar la **a** con **conocer**.

Paso 2. En grupos de tres, túrnense para presentar sus oraciones. Los compañeros que escuchan deben adivinar (*guess*) cuáles son las oraciones falsas.

> **Vocabulario útil**
>
> **la mentira**   lie, falsehood

> **¡OJO!**
> **Conozco** a **Brad Pitt.**

E. Encuesta (*Poll*) sobre los talentos especiales de la clase

Paso 1. Haga una lista de tres cosas interesantes que Ud. sabe hacer bien. Use infinitivos, según el modelo.

MODELO: tocar el acordeón, hacer paella, esquiar

Paso 2. Ahora haga una encuesta entre los compañeros de clase para ver si los talentos de Ud. son únicos o comunes en su clase. Si sus compañeros tienen un talento que Ud. también tiene, deben firmar (*sign*) en el espacio indicado.

MODELO: tocar el acordeón ⟶ ¿**Sabes** tocar el acordeón? Si **sabes, firma** aquí.

Talento 1: _____	Talento 2: _____	Talento 3: _____

F. Intercambios

1. ¿Qué restaurantes conoces en esta ciudad? ¿Cuál es tu restaurante favorito? ¿Por qué es tu favorito? ¿Es buena la comida allí? ¿Qué tipo de comida sirven? ¿Te gusta el ambiente (*atmosphere*)? ¿Comes allí con frecuencia? ¿Llamas para hacer reservaciones?

2. ¿Qué platos sabes hacer? ¿Tacos? ¿enchiladas? ¿pollo frito? ¿hamburguesas? ¿Te gusta cocinar? ¿Cocinas con frecuencia? ¿Qué ingredientes usas con más frecuencia? ¿Tienes una receta (*recipe*) favorita?

Ana saluda, tomando café: «Me entusiasmé (*I became a fan*) con el café cubano durante los meses que viví (*I lived*) en Miami. Y va muy bien con el primer segmento de hoy... »

Antes de mirar

Indique con qué comida del día se relacionan las siguientes comidas y bebidas. Y si le gusta mucho una comida o bebida, ¡indíquela (*mark it*) con una estrella (*star*) también! Si no conoce una comida o bebida, escriba **no sé.**

D = el desayuno   **A** = el almuerzo   **C** = la cena   **M** = la merienda

1. _____ el café	**5.** _____ el jamón
2. _____ la leche	**6.** _____ el queso
3. _____ el chocolate	**7.** _____ las tapas
4. _____ el arroz	**8.** _____ los mariscos

Este segmento

En este segmento Laura va a Miami y después a Barcelona para hablar de comidas... ¡y de bebidas!

Vocabulario **del segmento**

fuerte	strong
¡a mí me encanta!	I love it!
la calle	street
cortado/a con	diluted, cut with
un poquito de	a little bit of
yo no sabía nada	I didn't know anything
Se ve bien rico.	It looks great (very delicious).
estuvo	was
dicen	(they) say

la sartén	frying pan
se cocina	it is cooked
vine	I came
para que la vean	for you to see
no es nada barato	not at all cheap
una auténtica delicia	a true delicacy
algo dulce	something sweet
espeso/a	thick, dense
¡Riquísimo!	Very delicious!

Después de mirar

A. **¿Está claro?** Empareje las palabras de las dos columnas para describir las comidas que se mencionan en el segmento.

1. _____ la «medianoche»	**a.** una tapa
2. _____ los churros	**b.** el chocolate
3. _____ la paella	**c.** los mariscos
4. _____ el jamón serrano	**d.** un sándwich cubano

B. **Un poco más.** Conteste las siguientes preguntas.

1. ¿Qué adjetivos usan los presentadores para hablar del café cubano?
2. ¿Qué ingredientes varían en la paella? ¿Cuál es la paella favorita de Laura?
3. ¿Cómo es el chocolate español? Según Laura, ¿cuándo se toma un chocolate con churros?

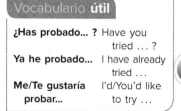

C. **Y ahora, Uds.** En parejas, hablen de las comidas y bebidas que se presentan en el segmento. ¿Son Uds. gourmets o se resisten a probar (*trying*) cosas nuevas?

MODELO: E1: Ya he probado el café cortado.
E2: ¿Te gusta?
E1: ¡Me encanta! Es intenso.

Vocabulario **útil**

¿Has probado... ?	Have you tried ... ?
Ya he probado...	I have already tried ...
Me/Te gustaría probar...	I'd/You'd like to try ...

GRAMÁTICA

Grammar Tutorial 18
connect
|SPANISH
www.connectspanish.com

18 Expressing *what* or *who(m)*

Direct Objects; The Personal **a**; Direct Object Pronouns

Gramática en acción: La pirámide alimenticia

[Pirámide alimenticia con los siguientes niveles:]

Dulces
Carnes rojas

ALGUNAS VECES[a] AL MES
Pollo   Huevos   Legumbres[b]

Pescado

ALGUNAS VECES A LA SEMANA
Leche   Aceite   Queso   Yogures

Frutas   Verduras   Patatas

Pan   Cereales   Pasta   Arroz

TODOS LOS DÍAS

[a]Algunas... *Sometimes* [b]Vegetales *Vegetables*

¿Y Ud.?

Indique cuáles de estas declaraciones expresan lo que Ud. hace.

1. el pollo
- Lo como todos los días. Por eso tengo que comprarlo con frecuencia.
- Lo como de vez en cuando (*once in a while*). Por eso no lo compro a menudo (*often*).
- Nunca lo como. No necesito comprarlo.

2. la fruta
- La como todos los días. Por eso tengo que comprarla con frecuencia.
- La como de vez en cuando. Por eso no la compro a menudo.
- Nunca la como. No necesito comprarla.

3. los refrescos
- Los bebo todos los días. Por eso tengo que comprarlos con frecuencia.
- Los bebo de vez en cuando. Por eso no los compro a menudo.
- Nunca los bebo. No necesito comprarlos.

4. las bananas
- Las como todos los días. Por eso tengo que comprarlas con frecuencia.
- Las como de vez en cuando. Por eso no las compro a menudo.
- Nunca las como. No necesito comprarlas.

Direct Objects / Los complementos directos

In English and in Spanish, the *direct object* (**el complemento directo**) of a sentence answers the question *what?* or *who(m)?* in relation to the subject and verb.

> *the direct object /* **el complemento directo** = the noun or pronoun that receives the action of the verb

SUBJECT (S)	VERB (V)	DIRECT OBJECT (DO)
Ana	is preparing	**dinner.**
They	can't hear	**the waiter.**

What is Ana preparing? → **dinner**
Who(m) can't they hear? → **the waiter**

Indicate the subjects, verbs, and direct objects in the following sentences.

1. *I don't see Betty and Mary here.*
2. *We don't have any money.*
3. No veo a Betty y María aquí.
4. No tenemos dinero.
5. Julio va a poner la sopa en la mesa.
6. ¿Necesitas el libro y un bolígrafo?

The Personal a / La a personal

In Spanish, the word **a** immediately precedes the direct object of a sentence when the direct object refers to a specific person or persons. This **a**, called the *personal a* (**la a personal**), has no equivalent in English.*

Vamos a visitar **a nuestros abuelos.**
We're going to visit our grandparents.
but
Vamos a visitar **la casa de nuestros abuelos.**
We're going to visit our grandparents' house.

Necesitan **a sus padres.**
They need their parents.
but
Necesitan **el coche de sus padres.**
They need their parents' car.

The personal **a** is not used when the direct object is a nonspecific person or an unknown person.

Conozco **a un buen chef.**
I know a great chef.
but
Necesito **un buen chef para una fiesta.**
I need a great chef for a party.

Pets (but not all animals) are treated like people and take the personal **a.**

¿Ves **a Bear,** mi perro?
Do you see Bear, my dog?
but
¿Ves **el perro** allí?
Do you see the dog over there?

¡OJO!
The personal **a** is used before the interrogative words **¿quién?** and **¿quiénes?** when they function as direct objects.

¿**A quién** llamas? ¿**al** camarero?
Who(m) are you calling? The waiter?

¡OJO!
The English verbs *to listen* **to** / *look* **at** / *look* **for** / *wait* **for** are all followed by prepositional phrases (a *preposition* + *noun* or *pronoun*). However, the Spanish equivalents of those verbs (**escuchar, mirar, buscar,** and **esperar**) are not followed by prepositions. They *are* followed by the personal **a** before a specific person or pet. Compare these pairs of sentences.

Miro el menú. *I'm looking at the menu.*
Miro **al** niño. *I'm looking at the boy.*

Espero el autobús. *I'm waiting for the bus.*
Espero **al** niño. *I'm waiting for the boy.*

¡OJO!
Don't confuse the personal **a** with other uses of the word **a** that you have learned so far.
- **a** = the preposition *to*
- **a** = used after some verbs before an infinitive

Voy **a** la universidad.
En esta clase **aprendemos a** hablar español.
Vamos a salir mañana.

---

*The personal **a** is not generally used with* **tener** *or* **hay**: *Tenemos cuatro hijos. Hay tres niños en la sala.*

me	me	nos	us
te	you (*fam. sing.*)	os	you (*fam. pl.*)
lo	you (*form. sing.*), him, it (*m.*)	los	you (*form. pl.*), them (*m., m. + f.*)
la	you (*form. sing.*), her, it (*f.*)	las	you (*form. pl.*), them (*f.*)

1. Direct Object Pronouns

Like direct object nouns, *direct object pronouns* (**los pronombres del complemento directo**) are the first recipient of the action of the verb.

If the direct object noun were repeated in the English answer to the right, it would sound very repetitive: *"Where are the carrots?" "Do you need the carrots right now?"* Direct object pronouns avoid that kind of unnecessary repetition: *"Do you need **them** right now?"*

—¿Dónde están **las zanahorias**?
—¿**Las** necesitas ahora mismo?
*"Where are **the carrots**?"*
*"Do you need **them** right now?"*

2. Placement of Direct Object Pronouns

Direct object pronouns are placed:
- before a conjugated verb
- after the word **no** when it appears

—¿Conoces a **Diego**?
—No, no **lo** conozco.
"Do you know Diego?"
"No, I don't know him."
—¿Quién **te** llama más por teléfono?
—Mi madre **me** llama más.
"Who calls you the most?
"My mother calls me the most."

3. With Infinitives or Present Participles

When the conjugated verb is followed by an infinitive or a present participle, the pronouns either precede the conjugated verb *or* follow (and are attached to):
- the infinitive
- the present participle

Las tengo que leer. ⎫
Tengo que **leerlas.** ⎬ *I have to read them.*

Lo estoy comiendo. ⎫
Estoy **comiéndolo.** ⎬ *I am eating it.*

¡OJO!

When the pronoun is added to the end of a present participle, an accent mark is added to retain the original stress: **mirando** ⟶ **mirándolo.**

4. Multiple Meanings of *lo/la/los/las*

Note that the direct object pronouns **lo/la/los/las** have different meanings depending on the context. In the first sentence to the right, it is impossible to know what **lo** means.

Notice how the meaning of **lo** is clear in the three sentences that follow.

No **lo** veo por la niebla.

I don't see ⎰ *it* / *him* / *you (form.)* ⎱ *because of the fog.*

¿El coche? No lo veo por la niebla. (**lo** = *it*)
¿El niño? No lo veo por la niebla. (**lo** = *him*)
¿Ud.? No lo veo por la niebla. (**lo** = *you* [*form.*])

5. The Pronoun *lo*

Note that the direct object pronoun **lo** can refer to actions, situations, or ideas in general. When used in this way, **lo** expresses English *it* or *that.*

Lo comprende muy bien.
He understands it (that) very well.

No **lo** creo.   Lo sé.
I don't believe it (that).   *I know (it).*

Práctica y comunicación

Summary of Direct Object Pronouns

yo	→	me
tú	→	te
Ud., él	→	lo
Ud., ella	→	la
nosotros/as	→	nos
vosotros/as	→	os
Uds., ellos	→	los
Uds., ellas	→	las

A. Correspondencias

Paso 1. Autoprueba. Complete las siguientes oraciones. ¡OJO! Use la **a** personal cuando sea (*whenever it is*) necesaria.

Conozco...

1. una persona famosa
2. la ciudad de Nueva York
3. el estado de Montana
4. el profesor / la profesora de _____
5. los padres de mi compañero/a de cuarto

Necesito...

6. el libro de texto en esta clase
7. más clases para graduarme
8. mi familia
9. mis buenos amigos
10. mi perro/gato

Paso 2. Ahora complete las oraciones del **Paso 1** con el pronombre del complemento directo apropiado.

MODELO: Conozco... al profesor de historia latinoamericana. → **Lo** conozco.

Paso 3. Ahora, en parejas, túrnense para hacer y contestar preguntas usando las oraciones del **Paso 2**.

MODELO: Conozco... al profesor de historia latinoamericana. →
　　　E1: ¿Conoces al profesor de historia latinoamericana?
　　　E2: Sí, **lo** conozco. (No, no **lo** conozco.) ¿Y tú?
　　　E1: Yo sí/también. / Yo tampoco. (*Me neither.*)

B. Más correspondencias.
Empareje los pronombres del complemento directo con las personas. A veces hay más de una correspondencia posible.

PRONOMBRES

1. _____ los
2. _____ la
3. _____ te
4. _____ lo
5. _____ las
6. _____ nos

PERSONAS

a. Ana
b. tú
c. Pedro y Carolina
d. María y yo
e. Jorge
f. Elena y Rosa
g. Uds.
h. Ud.

C. ¿Qué comen los vegetarianos?
Aquí hay una lista de diferentes comidas. ¿Cree Ud. que las come un vegetariano? Conteste según los modelos.

MODELOS: el bistec → No **lo** come.
　　　　　la banana → **La** come.

1. las patatas
2. el arroz
3. las chuletas de cerdo
4. las zanahorias
5. las manzanas
6. los camarones
7. los champiñones
8. los frijoles
9. la ensalada

D. La cena de Lola y Manolo

Paso 1. La siguiente descripción de la cena de Lola y Manolo es muy repetitiva. Combine las oraciones, según el modelo.

MODELO: El camarero (*waiter*) trae un menú. Lola lee el menú. →
　　　　　El camarero trae un menú y Lola **lo** lee.

1. El camarero trae una botella de vino tinto. Pone la botella en la mesa.
2. Lola quiere la especialidad de la casa. Va a pedir la especialidad de la casa.
3. Manolo prefiere el pescado fresco (*fresh*). Pide el pescado fresco.
4. Lola quiere una ensalada también. Por eso pide una ensalada.
5. El camarero trae la comida. Sirve la comida.
6 «¿La cuenta (*bill*)? El dueño está preparando la cuenta para Uds.»
7. Manolo quiere pagar con tarjeta (*card*) de crédito. Pero no trae su tarjeta.
8. Por fin, Lola toma la cuenta. Paga la cuenta.

Prác. A, Paso 1: Answers: 1. a una **2.** a **3.** a **4.** al / a la **5.** a los **6.** ø **7.** ø **8.** a **9.** a **10.** a

Paso 2. Las siguientes oraciones describen la cena de Lola y Manolo. Diga en español a qué se refieren los pronombres indicados. Luego diga quién hace cada acción.

1. Lo pide.

2. La sirve.

3. No **la** trae.

4. La paga.

E. Minidiálogos

Paso 1. Complete los siguientes minidiálogos con los pronombres del complemento directo que faltan (*are missing*).

1. —¿Me quieres (*do you love*)?

—¡_____ quiero muchísimo!

2. —Voy a Panamá y tengo un boleto (*ticket*) de avión gratis. ¿Me acompañas?

—¡Claro que _____ acompaño! ¿Cuándo nos vamos?

3. —Buenas noches, señor. ¿_____ atienden ya (*Is someone already helping you*)?

—No, todavía no, gracias.

— Perdón. Entonces (*Then*) voy a atender_____ yo.

4. —¡Mi hija nunca me llama por teléfono!

— ¡Tu hija solo tiene 19 años! Seguro que _____ llama si necesita dinero.

5. —¿Cuándo van a visitar a Uds. sus primos panameños?

—_____ van a visitar este verano.

6. —Buenos días, señora. ¿En qué puedo ayudar_____ (*to help*)?

—Buenos días. Busco una blusa negra de mi talla (*size*).

7. —¡Qué perro tan bonito (*What a beautiful dog*) tienes!

—Si quieres, puedes tocar_____ (*to touch*).

Paso 2. Las siguientes oraciones añaden (*add*) un intercambio más a cada minidiálogo del **Paso 1.** Emparéjelos e identifique en cada caso a quién se refiere el pronombre del complemento directo.

a. ¿Desde cuándo lo tienes?

b. ¿Qué desea tomar?

c. ¡Y yo te adoro!

d. ¿La quiere de algodón o de seda?

e. Pues yo quiero conocerlos también.

f. La primera semana de julio.

g. Sí, eso es lo que hace.

Nota **comunicativa**

Cómo expresar una acción muy reciente: *acabar* + de + *infinitivo*

To talk about what you have *just* done, use the phrase **acabar** + **de** + *infinitive*.

Acabo de almorzar con Beto.	*I just had lunch with Beto.*
Acabas de celebrar tu cumpleaños, ¿verdad?	*You just celebrated your birthday, didn't you?*

Note that the infinitive follows the preposition **de.**

You will practice talking about what you have *just* done in **Práctica F.**

F. **¡Acabo de hacerlo!** Imagine that a friend is pressuring you to do the following things. With a classmate, tell him or her that you just did each one, using either of the structures in the model.

MODELO: E1: ¿Por qué no haces la ensalada? →
E2: Acabo de hacer**la**. (**La** acabo de hacer.)

1. ¿Por qué no preparas las chuletas para la fiesta?
2. ¿Vas a comprar la fruta hoy?
3. ¿Por qué no pagas los cafés?
4. ¿Vas a cocinar la comida para la cena?
5. ¿Quieres ayudarme?
6. ¿Por qué no me invitas a cenar?

G. **¡Ayuda! (*Help!*)**

Paso 1. Todos necesitamos ayuda alguna vez (*at some point*), ¿no? ¿Quién ayuda a Ud. en los siguientes casos?

MODELO: con el coche → **Mi padre me** ayuda con el coche.

1. con las cuentas (*bills*)
2. con la tarea
3. con la matrícula
4. con el horario de clases
5. con el español
6. pagar las deudas (*debts*)
7. estudiar para los exámenes
8. resolver los problemas personales

Paso 2. Ahora, en parejas, túrnense para hacer y contestar preguntas basadas en el **Paso 1.**

MODELO: con el coche →
E1: ¿Quién **te** ayuda con el coche?
E2: Generalmente, **mis padres me** ayudan un poco. A veces también **me** ayudan **mis abuelos.**

H. **Intercambios.** En parejas, túrnense para hacer y contestar preguntas sobre los alimentos (*foods*) que consumen y con qué frecuencia. Expliquen por qué tienen esos hábitos. Luego digan a la clase algo (*something*) que tienen en común.

MODELO: E1: ¿Comes pan sin gluten?
E2: No, no **lo** como porque no soy celiaco.

Vocabulario útil

la cafeína	ser **bueno/a para la salud** (health)
las calorías	ser **celiaco/a**
el colesterol	
la grasa fat	**me pone(n) nervioso/a** it/they make me nervous
estar **a dieta**	**me sienta(n) mal** it/they don't agree with me
ser **alérgico/a a**	**lo/la/los/las detesto**

1. pan sin gluten
2. refrescos sin azúcar
3. productos bajos en sodio
4. frutas y verduras orgánicas
5. pescados y mariscos
6. hamburguesas
7. bebidas alcohólicas
8. café
9. productos lácteos (*milk*)
10. comidas congeladas (*frozen*)

19 Expressing Negation
Indefinite and Negative Words

Grammar Tutorial 19
connect
|SPANISH
www.connectspanish.com

Gramática en acción: ¿Un refrigerador típico?

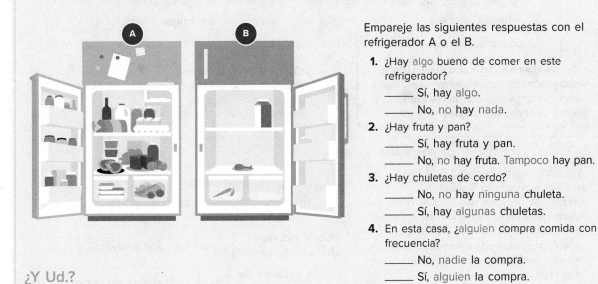

Empareje las siguientes respuestas con el refrigerador A o el B.

1. ¿Hay algo bueno de comer en este refrigerador?

_____ Sí, hay algo.

_____ No, no hay nada.

2. ¿Hay fruta y pan?

_____ Sí, hay fruta y pan.

_____ No, no hay fruta. Tampoco hay pan.

3. ¿Hay chuletas de cerdo?

_____ No, no hay ninguna chuleta.

_____ Sí, hay algunas chuletas.

4. En esta casa, ¿alguien compra comida con frecuencia?

_____ No, nadie la compra.

_____ Sí, alguien la compra.

¿Y Ud.?

¿Cuál de los dos refrigeradores se parece (*resembles*) más al refrigerador de su casa o apartamento? ¿Cuál se parece más al típico refrigerador de los estudiantes? ¿de una familia con hijos? ¿de jóvenes profesionales?

Indefinite and Negative Words / Las palabras indefinidas y negativas

Los adverbios indefinidos y negativos		
siempre	always	Siempre estudio en casa. Estudio en casa siempre.
nunca, jamás	never	Nunca estudio en la biblioteca. No estudio nunca en la biblioteca.
también	also	Yo también sé preparar una paella. Yo sé preparar una paella también.
tampoco	neither, not either	Tampoco sé preparar una paella. Yo no sé preparar una paella tampoco.

A typical refrigerator? **1.** *Is there something good to eat in this refrigerator? Yes, there is something. No, there is nothing.* **2.** *Is there (some) fruit and bread? Yes, there is (some) fruit and bread. No, there is no fruit. There isn't any bread either.* **3.** *Are there pork chops? No, there aren't any chops. (Lit., No, there is no chop.) Yes, there are some chops.* **4.** *In this house, does anyone buy food frequently? No, no one buys it. Yes, someone buys it.*

Los sustantivos indefinidos y negativos

alguien	someone, anyone	En esta clase alguien habla chino.
nadie	no one, nobody, not anybody	En esta clase nadie habla chino.
		En esta clase no habla chino nadie.
		Conozco **a** alguien en esa fiesta.
		No conozco **a** nadie en esa fiesta.
algo	something, anything	Sé algo de la cocina panameña.
nada	nothing, not anything	No sé nada de la cocina panameña.

> **¡OJO!**
> The personal **a** is used with **alguien** and **nadie** when they function as direct objects, as in the examples.

Pronunciation Hint: Pronounce the **d** in **nada** and **nadie** as a fricative, that is, like the *th* sound in *the*: [na-d̶a], [na-d̶ie].

Los adjetivos indefinidos y negativos

algún, alguna, algunos/as	some, any	algún tomate, algunas chuletas
ningún, ninguna	no, not any	ningún tomate, ninguna chuleta

> **¡OJO!**
> Note how **alguno** and **ninguno** shorten (**algún, ningún**) before masculine singular nouns. You've seen something similar with **uno (⟶ un), bueno (⟶ buen),** and **grande (⟶ gran).**

algún / ningún problema
alguna / ninguna cosa
algunos problemas
algunas cosas

The Double Negative / La negativa doble

A double negative is avoided in English but is often necessary in Spanish.
- When the negative word comes *before* the conjugated verb, that is all that is needed.
- When the negative word comes *after* the conjugated verb, another negative word—usually **no**—must be placed before the verb.

negative word + verb
no + *verb + negative word*

¿**Nadie estudia?**
¿**No estudia nadie?** } *Isn't anyone studying?*

Nunca estás en clase.
No estás en clase **nunca.** } *You're never in class.*

Tampoco quieren cenar aquí.
No quieren cenar aquí **tampoco.** } *They don't want to have dinner here either.*

The Adjectives algún and ningún / Los adjetivos *algún* y *ningún*

Algún (Alguna/os/as) and **ningún (ninguna)** are adjectives. Unlike the other indefinite and negative words you have learned (which are nouns or adverbs), **algún** and **ningún** must agree with the noun they modify. **Ningún (Ninguna)** is rarely used in the plural.

—¿Hay **algunos recados** para mí hoy?
—Lo siento, pero hoy no hay **ningún recado** para Ud.
"Are there any messages for me today?"
"I'm sorry, but there are no messages for you today."
(*"There is not a single message for you today."*)

Summary of Indefinite and Negative Words

algo	nada
alguien	nadie
algún/alguna/os/as	ningún, ninguna
siempre	nunca, jamás
también	tampoco

Práctica y comunicación

A. Cosas esenciales

Paso 1. Autoprueba. Dé la palabra negativa correspondiente.

1. siempre **2.** también **3.** algo **4.** alguien **5.** alguna

Paso 2. Complete las siguientes oraciones.

1. Siempre tengo _____ (algo) en mi cuarto y también tengo _____ (otra cosa).
2. Nunca _____ (una acción) temprano por la mañana. Tampoco _____ (otra acción que no me gusta hacer).
3. Algo que siempre hay en mi refrigerador es _____. Algo que nunca hay es _____.
4. Para mí, no hay nada tan importante como mi(s) _____ (alguien).
5. En este momento, nadie es tan importante en mi vida (*life*) como mi(s) _____.

Paso 3. Ahora, en parejas, comparen sus oraciones del **Paso 2** y digan a la clase algo que tienen en común.

MODELO: Para nosotros/as dos, no hay nada tan importante como nuestras familias.

B. ¿Qué pasa esta noche en esta casa?

Paso 1. Complete las siguientes oraciones con la palabra indefinida o negativa apropiada según el dibujo.

1. Hay _____ cantando en el baño.
2. Hay _____ niños jugando en su alcoba.
3. Hay _____ en la mesa del comedor.
4. Hay _____ comida en la barbacoa.
5. Hay _____ personas en la sala.
6. No hay _____ en la cocina.
7. No hay _____ plato en la mesa del comedor.

Estrategia

Remember that **ninguno** is always used in the singular and that it shortens to **ningún** before a masculine, singular noun.

Paso 2. Ahora haga otras oraciones ciertas, pero contrarias a las (*those*) del **Paso 1**.

MODELO: **1.** No hay **nadie** cantando en **el jardín**.

C. ¡Nadie come allí! Exprese negativamente, usando la negativa doble.

MODELO: Hay alguien en el restaurante. → **No** hay **nadie** en el restaurante.

1. Hay algo interesante en el menú.
2. Tienen algunos platos típicos.
3. El profesor cena allí también.
4. Mis amigos siempre almuerzan allí.
5. Preparan algo especial para grupos.
6. Siempre hacen platos nuevos.
7. Y también sirven paella, mi plato favorito.

Prác. A, Paso 1: Answers: 1. nunca 2. tampoco 3. nada 4. nadie 5. ninguna

D. Extremos

Paso 1. Modifique las siguientes declaraciones para hacerlas negativas.

MODELO: Hay muchas personas antipáticas en mi familia. →
No hay **ninguna persona** antipática (**No** hay **nadie** antipático) en mi familia.

1. Tengo muchos planes interesantes para este fin de semana.
2. Todas mis clases este semestre/trimestre son maravillosas (*wonderful*).
3. Me gusta toda la comida de la cafetería.
4. Hay muchos programas interesantes en la tele últimamente (*lately*).
5. Siempre estudio en la biblioteca.
6. Todos los estudiantes de esta universidad son internacionales.

Paso 2. Ahora modifique las oraciones del **Paso 1** para que expresen (*so that they express*) su opinión.

MODELOS: Hay muchas personas antipáticas en mi familia. →
No hay ninguna persona antipática en mi familia.
En mi familia hay algunas personas antipáticas, pero muy pocas.

Paso 3. Ahora, en parejas, túrnense para hacer y contestar preguntas basadas en las oraciones del **Paso 2.**

MODELO: En mi familia hay algunas personas antipáticas, pero muy pocas. →
E1: En tu familia ¿hay alguna persona antipática (alguien antipático)?
E2: Sí, mi tío Gerry es muy antipático. (No, no hay nadie antipático.)

E. Intercambios

Paso 1. En parejas, túrnense para entrevistarse sobre los siguientes temas. Deben obtener detalles interesantes y personales de su compañero/a.

MODELO: E1: ¿Tienes alguna buena excusa para no ir al gimnasio esta semana?
E2: No, no tengo ninguna buena excusa esta semana. (Sí, tengo una buena excusa. ¡No tengo tiempo!)

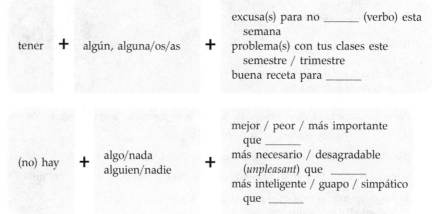

tener + algún, alguna/os/as + excusa(s) para no _____ (verbo) esta semana
problema(s) con tus clases este semestre / trimestre
buena receta para _____

(no) hay + algo/nada alguien/nadie + mejor / peor / más importante que _____
más necesario / desagradable (*unpleasant*) que _____
más inteligente / guapo / simpático que _____

Paso 2. Ahora digan a la clase una respuesta interesante o peculiar.

MODELOS: Algo interesante de Jim es que tiene una excusa muy buena para no hacer la tarea esta noche. Va a...
Algo interesante de Aurora es que, en su opinión, no hay nada más desagradable que la arrogancia.

Algo sobre...

los emberás

Unas casas típicas de los emberás

Los emberás son un pueblo amerindio del este de Panamá y también de la región noroeste de Colombia y del Ecuador. Tradicional-mente viven en la selva,ª junto a ríos,ᵇ en zonas donde llueve todo el año. Por eso sus casas están en alto.ᶜ Están cubiertasᵈ de hojasᵉ de palma.

 ¿Hay algún pueblo indígena en su estado? ¿Qué sabe de ellos?

ªjungle ᵇrivers ᶜen... raised up
ᵈcovered ᵉleaves

¿Recuerda Ud.?

Review what you already know about irregular first person present tense forms by giving the **yo** form of the following infinitives. You will need to know this information in **Gramática 20.**

1. salir _____   **3.** conocer _____   **5.** hacer _____   **7.** perder _____
2. tener _____   **4.** pedir _____   **6.** dormir _____   **8.** traer _____

20 Influencing Others

Commands (Part 1): Formal Commands

> **Grammar Tutorial** 20
> **connect**
> |SPANISH
> www.connectspanish.com

Gramática en acción: Receta para guacamole

El guacamole

1 aguacate
1 diente de ajo,[a]
  prensado[b]
1 tomate
jugo de un limón[c]
sal
un poco de cilantro
  fresco[d]

Cómo se prepara

Corte el aguacate y
el tomate en trozos[e] pequeños. Añada el jugo del limón, el
ajo, el cilantro y la sal a su gusto. Mezcle bien todos los
ingredientes y sírvalo con tortillas de maíz[f] fritas.

En español, los mandatos se usan con frecuencia en las recetas. Los siguientes verbos se usan en forma de mandato en esta receta. ¿Puede encontrarlos?

añadir	to add
cortar	to cut
mezclar	to mix
servir (sirvo) (i)	

¿Y Ud.?

¿Le gusta el guacamole? ¿Lo hace con frecuencia? ¿Con qué lo sirve?

[a]diente... *clove of garlic* [b]*crushed* [c]*lime* [d]*fresh* [e]*pieces* [f]*corn*

Formal Command Forms / Los mandatos formales (Ud., Uds.)

In *Puntos de partida* you have seen formal commands in the direction lines of activities since the beginning of the text: **haga, complete, conteste,** and so on.

Commands (imperatives) are verb forms used to tell someone to do something. In Spanish, *formal commands* (**los mandatos formales**) are used with people whom you address as **Ud.** or **Uds.**[*] Here are some of the basic forms.

> *a command or imperative / un mandato = a verb form used to tell someone to do something*

	hablar	comer	escribir	volver	poner
Ud.	hable	coma	escriba	vuelva	ponga
Uds.	hablen	coman	escriban	vuelvan	pongan
English	*speak*	*eat*	*write*	*come back*	*put, place*

1. Regular Verbs

Most formal command forms can be derived from the **yo** form of the present tense.

Note that the "opposite" vowel is used:

   -ar → e
   -er/-ir → a

> *-ar:* -o → -e, -en   *-er/-ir:* -o → -a, -an
>
> hablo → hable   como → coma
>   hablen   coman
>   escribo → escriba
>   escriban

2. Stem-changing Verbs

Formal commands for stem-changing verbs show the stem change, since the stem vowel is stressed. Base the command on the **yo** form to get the stem change right.

> **pensar (pienso)** → **piense** Ud., **piensen** Uds.
> **volver (vuelvo)** → **vuelva** Ud., **vuelvan** Uds.
> **pedir (pido)** → **pida** Ud., **pidan** Uds.

---

*You will learn how to form informal (**tú**) commands in **Gramática 36 (Cap. 13).**

3. Verbs Ending in -car, -gar, -zar

These verbs have a spelling change to preserve the -c-, -g-, and -z- sounds of the infinitives.

c → qu	**buscar: busque** Ud., **busquen** Uds.
g → gu	**pagar: pague** Ud., **paguen** Uds.
z → c	**empezar: empiece** Ud., **empiecen** Uds.

¡OJO!

From this chapter on, these three spelling changes for verbs in formal commands will be indicated in parentheses in vocabulary lists. If these three verbs were active in this chapter, they would be listed in the end-of-chapter vocabulary list as follows: **buscar (qu)**, **pagar (gu)**, **empezar (empiezo) (c)**.

4. Verbs with Irregular Present Tense *yo* Forms

Verbs that have an irregular **yo** form in the present tense will keep the irregularity in the **Ud./Uds.** commands.

conocer: **conozco**	→ **conozca** Ud., **conozcan** Uds.
decir* (*to say, tell*): **digo**	→ **diga** Ud., **digan** Uds.
hacer: **hago**	→ **haga** Ud., **hagan** Uds.
oír: **oigo**	→ **oiga** Ud., **oigan** Uds.
salir: **salgo**	→ **salga** Ud., **salgan** Uds.
tener: **tengo**	→ **tenga** Ud., **tengan** Uds.
traer: **traigo**	→ **traiga** Ud., **traigan** Uds.
venir: **vengo**	→ **venga** Ud., **vengan** Uds.
ver: **veo**	→ **vea** Ud., **vean** Uds.

5. Irregular Formal Commands

A few verbs have irregular **Ud./Uds.** command forms.

dar* (*to give*)	→ **dé** Ud., *but* **den** Uds.
estar	→ **esté** Ud., **estén** Uds.
ir	→ **vaya** Ud., **vayan** Uds.
saber	→ **sepa** Ud., **sepan** Uds.
ser	→ **sea** Ud., **sean** Uds.

Position of Pronouns / El lugar de los pronombres

1. Pronouns with Affirmative Commands

Direct object pronouns and reflexive pronouns must *follow* affirmative commands and are attached to them. In order to maintain the original stress of the verb form, an accent mark is added to the stressed vowel if the original command has two or more syllables.

una palabra:	*mandato + pronombre*
Pídalo Ud.	*Order it.*
Siéntese, por favor.	*Sit down, please.*

2. Pronouns with Negative Commands

Direct object and reflexive pronouns must *precede* the verb form in negative commands.

tres palabras:	**no** + *pronombre + mandato*
No lo pida Ud.	*Don't order it.*
No se siente.	*Don't sit down.*

¡OJO!

Now that you know how to form formal commands, be sure to use them carefully when speaking to native speakers of Spanish. Commands are strong forms in any language. It is wise to soften formal commands with **por favor** and by using a polite tone, just as you would in English. Example: **Abra la puerta, por favor.**

---

*Decir *and* dar *are used primarily with indirect objects. Both of these verbs and indirect object pronouns will be formally introduced in* **Gramática 21 (Cap. 8).**

Práctica y comunicación

A. Mandatos de esta clase

Paso 1. Autoprueba. Complete los siguientes mandatos formales de **Ud.** con las terminaciones apropiadas. **¡OJO!** Es necesario escribir más de una letra en algunos casos.

1. habl_____
2. escrib_____
3. lleg_____
4. aprend_____
5. cierr_____
6. duerm_____
7. le_____
8. ha_____
9. empie_____
10. bus_____

Paso 2. Cambie las siguientes frases en mandatos lógicos y típicos de una clase de español. **¡OJO!** Pueden ser afirmativos o negativos.

MODELO: abrir los libros en la página x ⟶
Abran los libros en la página x.

1. cerrar los libros
2. traer la tarea mañana
3. sentarse en círculo
4. dormirse
5. leer el texto
6. hacer preguntas
7. hablar en inglés
8. repetir (*like* pedir) más alto (*louder*)

Paso 3. En parejas, indiquen cuáles de los mandatos del **Paso 2** se oyen en su clase de español. Luego añadan (*add*) otros tres mandatos típicos de su clase.

B. El mundo al revés (*The world upside down*)

Paso 1. Hoy, los estudiantes son los «jefes» (*bosses*)... pero ¡solo por un día! Cambie las siguientes acciones en mandatos «lógicos» para todos sus profesores, no solo para su profesor(a) de español. Haga mandatos afirmativos y negativos.

1. llegar a tiempo
2. venir a la universidad
3. pedir la tarea
4. volver a casa
5. poner música de _____
6. pensar en _____
7. traer _____ (¿comida?) a clase
8. sentarse en _____
9. hacer _____
10. dar _____ a los estudiantes

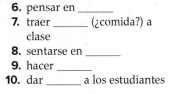

Vocabulario útil

el examen
la nota grade (*academic*)
la prueba quiz

Paso 2. ¿Qué otros mandatos pueden dar a sus profesores hoy? En parejas, inventen tres mandatos para ellos.

C. ¡Pobre Sr. Casiano!

Paso 1. El Sr. Casiano no se siente (*feel*) bien. Lea la descripción que él da de las cosas que hace.

Trabajo[1] muchísimo[a] —¡me gusta trabajar! En la oficina, soy[2] impaciente y critico[3b] bastante[c] a los otros. En mi vida personal, a veces soy[4] un poco impulsivo. Fumo[5d] bastante y también bebo[6] cerveza y otras bebidas alcohólicas, a veces sin moderación... Almuerzo[7] y ceno[8] fuerte,[e] y desayuno[9] poco. Por la noche, con frecuencia salgo[10] con los amigos —me gusta ir a las discotecas— y vuelvo[11] tarde a casa.

[a]*a great deal* [b]critico ⟶ criticar [c]*a good deal* [d]Fumo ⟶ fumar (*to smoke*) [e]*a lot*

Prác. A, Paso 1: Answers: 1. hable 2. escriba 3. llegue 4. aprenda 5. cierre 6. duerma 7. lea 8. haga 9. empiece 10. busque

(*Continúa.*)

Paso 2. Comprensión. ¿Cierto o falso?

	CIERTO	FALSO
1. El Sr. Casiano es una persona muy simpática.	☐	☐
2. Tiene algunos hábitos malos.	☐	☐
3. Por la noche, siempre está en casa.	☐	☐

Paso 3. ¿Qué *no* debe hacer el Sr. Casiano? Aconséjelo (*Advise him*) y dígale (*tell him*) lo que no debe hacer. Use los verbos en rosado o cualquier (*any*) otro.

MODELOS: **1.** Trabajo → Sr. Casiano, **no trabaje** tanto.
    2. soy → **No sea** tan impaciente.

D. Estrategias para adelgazar (*lose weight*). ¿Qué debe o no debe comer y beber una persona que quiere adelgazar? En parejas, imaginen una conversación entre esa persona y su médico.

MODELOS: ensalada → **E1:** ¿Ensalada? postres → **E1:** ¿Postres?
      E2: Cóm**al**a.   **E2:** No **los** coma.

1. bebidas alcohólicas   **5.** leche entera (*whole*)
2. verduras   **6.** hamburguesas con queso
3. pan   **7.** frutas frescas
4. dulces   **8.** refrescos dietéticos

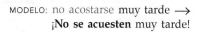

E. ¡Qué desastre! Imagine los mandatos que esta madre va a darles a sus hijos adolescentes. ¿Le resultan (*Do they sound*) familiares a Ud. estos mandatos?

MODELO: no acostarse muy tarde →
    ¡No se acuesten muy tarde!

1. levantarse más temprano
2. bañarse todos los días
3. quitarse esa ropa sucia
4. ponerse ropa limpia
5. no divertirse todas las noches con los amigos
6. ir más a la biblioteca y estudiar más
7. ¿ ?

Vocabulario útil

la boca	one's mouth
llena	full
la cuchara	spoon
el cuchillo	knife
la mano	hand
la servilleta	napkin
el tenedor	fork
masticar (qu)	to chew
servirse (me sirvo) (i) a uno mismo	to help one's self
despacio	slowly

F. Consejos sobre los buenos modales (*good manners*) en la mesa

Paso 1. Use las siguientes ideas para dar consejos en forma de mandatos formales sobre cómo se debe comer en una ocasión formal. **¡OJO!** Algunos consejos son normas de los buenos modales en los países hispanos y *no* coinciden con los modales que se practican en este país. ¿Puede decir cuáles son los modales hispanos?

1. poner las dos manos en la mesa
2. no poner los codos (*elbows*) en la mesa
3. para cortar, agarrar (*to hold*) el tenedor con la mano izquierda y el cuchillo con la derecha
4. cortar solo el pedazo (*piece*) de comida que puede poner en la boca
5. no cambiar (*to change*) de mano el tenedor para llevar la comida a la boca
6. no eructar (*to burp*) en público

Paso 2. Ahora, en grupos, inventen por lo menos (*at least*) cuatro consejos más.

Un poco de todo

A. Lengua y cultura: La cocina panameña

Paso 1. Complete the following paragraphs with the correct form of the words in parentheses, as suggested by context. When two possibilities are given in parentheses, select the correct word. **¡OJO!** As you conjugate the verbs in this activity, note that you will make formal commands with some infinitives.

El arroz con pollo, un típico plato panameño

¿Creen Uds. que la comida panameña es similar a la[a] de México y que los tacos y las tortillas (ser / estar[1]) parte de la comida típica de los panameños? Si creen eso, entonces[b] no (*Uds.:* saber / conocer[2]) (algo / nada[3]) de la comida de (este[4]) nación. (*Uds.:* Seguir[5]) (leer[6]), porque van a aprender mucho.

La influencia (extranjero[7]) en la comida de la cosmopolita Ciudad de Panamá es muy visible. Hay (mucho[8]) restaurantes que (servir[9]) comida italiana, china, (francés[10]), etcétera.

Sin embargo, los panameños no (perder[11]) su identidad nacional, y frecuentemente (preferir[12]) la comida tradicional. En la cocina panameña hay muchos platos de mariscos y pescados, entre ellos **el ceviche.** Las personas vegetarianas no (tener[13]) problema (también / tampoco[14]) porque hay una variedad de platos (preparado[15]) con arroz y verduras. El arroz es un ingrediente importante en la comida de Panamá. Si Ud. desea (saber / conocer[16]) cuál es el plato nacional de Panamá, los panameños (contestar[17]): «el arroz con pollo.» (*Ud.:* Pedirlo[18]). Le va a gustar.

[a]*a... to that* [b]*then*

Paso 2. Comprensión. Conteste las siguientes preguntas.

1. ¿Cómo se sabe que la Ciudad de Panamá es cosmopolita?
2. ¿Cuál es el plato que representa mejor la cocina panameña?
3. ¿Qué ingredientes son comunes en la comida de Panamá?

Paso 3. En parejas, imaginen que un extranjero busca donde comer. Quiere saber dónde preparan de manera excelente las siguientes comidas, que son típicas de algunas partes de los Estados Unidos. Denle recomendaciones en forma de consejos o mandatos. Luego comparen sus recomendaciones con las (*those*) del resto de la clase para ver si todos están de acuerdo.

1. la mejor barbacoa
2. los mejores mariscos
3. la mejor comida china
4. la mejor comida hispana
5. el mejor queso
6. la mejor langosta

B. Publicidad. Como se ve en este anuncio de un periódico argentino, en español (como en inglés) los mandatos se usan con frecuencia en los anuncios y en la publicidad en general. En parejas, creen (*create*) un anuncio publicitario para un lugar de su universidad o de su ciudad, como un restaurante, un estadio, un cine, etcétera. El humor es siempre apreciado por sus compañeros.

ᵃ*grows*   ᵇacercarse = *to approach, draw near*

En su comunidad

Entreviste a una persona hispana de su universidad o ciudad sobre la cocina y la comida de su país.

PREGUNTAS POSIBLES

- ¿Cuáles son los ingredientes más importantes?
- ¿Puede encontrar estos ingredientes en los supermercados de aquí?
- ¿Cuál es la comida principal del día? ¿Comen un desayuno fuerte (*heavy*)?
- ¿Cuáles son algunos de los platos típicos?
- ¿Hay muchos restaurantes especializados en la comida de su país en este estado? ¿Cuál es su favorito?

Antes de mirar

Conteste las siguientes preguntas.

1. ¿Hay restaurantes de comida hispana donde Ud. vive? ¿En qué tipo de cocina se especializan?

2. ¿Se puede comprar comida en la calle (*street*) donde Ud. vive? ¿Hay muchos *food trucks*?

Este segmento

Los presentadores introducen un reportaje sobre la comida que se puede comprar en la calle (*street*). Luego cierran el programa haciendo planes para almorzar.

«Sin duda (*Undoubtedly*), los tacos son la comida callejera (*street*) por excelencia. Los hay de muchos tipos: al pastor, de carne, de pescado, etcétera. En efecto, cualquier alimento sabroso envuelto (*any tasty food wrapped*) en tortillas de esta manera puede llamarse taco.»

Fragmento del guion

¡Esa paella! Este reportaje de Laura me ha abierto el apetito.[a] El castellano[b] y la comida son la herencia[c] más positiva que nos dejó[d] la colonización española. Y lo mejor es que la comida española se adaptó fácilmente[e] a los ingredientes locales de cada país. Y se mezcló[f] con las tradiciones indígenas y también con las africanas que llegaron con los esclavos.[g] Y para qué hablar[h] del efecto de los productos americanos en la cocina de España y de toda Europa.

[a]me... *has whet my appetite* [b]*Spanish language* [c]*heritage, inheritance* [d]nos... *gave (lit. left) to us* [e]se... *easily adapted itself* [f]se... *it mixed* [g]llegaron... *arrived with the slaves* [h]para... *what can we say*

Vocabulario del segmento

neoyorquino/a	de Nueva York
el chorizo	type of sausage
la empanada	turnover
relleno/a	stuffed
el horneado de puerco	pork roast
me dijo	told me
el vendedor ambulante	street vendor
ya se imaginarán	you can imagine
cuidado con	(be) careful with
me muero de hambre	I'm starving
te apetece	do you feel like
la pupusa	filled corn tortilla
nos despedimos	that's all
¡No se lo pierdan!	Don't miss it!
¿Nos acompañan?	Won't you come with us?

Después de mirar

A. **¿Está claro?** Empareje las siguientes comidas con su lugar de origen.

COMIDAS	LUGARES DE ORIGEN
1. _____ el horneado de puerco	a. la Argentina
2. _____ el choripán	b. América
3. _____ el chocolate y el tomate	c. el Ecuador
4. _____ el taco	d. El Salvador
5. _____ la pupusa	e. México

B. **Un poco más.** Conteste las siguientes preguntas.

1. ¿Qué es el choripán? ¿Cuál es el origen de su nombre?

2. ¿Cuál es la comida callejera por excelencia en México?

3. ¿Cómo se siente (*feels*) Víctor al final del programa? ¿Por qué?

 C. **Y ahora, Uds.** En parejas, preparen un cierre del programa similar al (*to that*) de este segmento, usando algunas de las expresiones que usan los presentadores e información sobre la comida hispana de su ciudad.

¿Cuáles son algunos de los platos típicos de su país? ¿Hay alguna comida típica de su ciudad o estado?

Lectura cultural: Panamá
La comida panameña

El arroz con pollo al estilo panameño es uno de los platos más típicos de Panamá. Otro plato típico es el sancocho, una sopa que también es parte de la cocina de otros países caribeños y que lleva algún tipo de carne, verduras y legumbres.[a] Y es necesario mencionar también las frituras, es decir,[b] la comida frita. Hay gran variedad de frituras: la yuca frita, las carimañolas (unas bolas de masa[c] de yuca con carne dentro[d]), los patacones (rebanadas[e] de plátano frito), las empanadas[f] al estilo panameño, etcétera.

De beber, se debe probar[g] las chichas, que son refrescos naturales de frutas panameñas, como el coco, la guanábana y el maracuyá.[h]

[a]*beans* [b]*es... that is* [c]*bolas... balls of dough* [d]*inside* [e]*slices* [f]*see* **En otros países** [g]*try* [h]*coco... coconut, soursop, and passion fruit*

En **otros** países hispanos

- **En todo el mundo hispanohablante** Las empanadas son probablemente la constante culinaria más notable de todos los países hispanohablantes. Consisten en una masa de pan[a] rellena[b] de algo dulce o salado.[c] Pueden ser pequeñas e individuales o grandes para ser compartidas.[d] Las empanadas son de procedencia española... y los españoles las heredaron[e] de los árabes. ¡Una larga y deliciosa tradición!

- **En los Estados Unidos** La comida latina es omnipresente en los Estados Unidos hoy día. La cocina mexicana es muy popular, como también lo es su variante Tex-Mex, genuinamente estadounidense. Pero también se puede encontrar la comida de casi todas las otras cocinas hispanas: las pupusas[f] salvadoreñas, la tortilla[g] española (con papas y cebollas), el arroz con gandules[h] puertorriqueño, el dulce de leche[i] (una comida panhispana), etcétera.

[a]*masa... bread dough* [b]*filled* [c]*salty* [d]*shared* [e]*inherited* [f]*corn masa stuffed with cheese, refried beans, or meat, then fried like a tortilla* [g]*omelet* [h]*pigeon peas* [i]*dulce... caramel*

El Canal de Panamá: 48 millas de canales y esclusas (*locks*)

Un símbolo panameño: El canal de Panamá

Es una de las obras[a] de ingeniería más importantes del mundo por su impacto en el transporte mundial. Une el mar Caribe con el océano Pacífico. Fue inaugurado[b] en 1914. Antes de su existencia, los barcos tenían que dar la vuelta por el Estrecho de Magallanes.[c] La ruta del canal fue descubierta[d] en 1514 por el explorador español Vasco Núñez de Balboa. Desde entonces[e] los españoles tuvieron[f] la idea de construir un canal. Pero su construcción no se hizo[g] realidad hasta principios del siglo XX.[h] En la actualidad,[i] el canal se está ampliando.[j]

[a]*works* [b]*opened* [c]*tenían... had to go around the Straight of Magellan* [d]*discovered* [e]*Desde... Since then* [f]*had* [g]*no... didn't become* [h]*principios... the beginning of the 20th century* [i]*En... Currently* [j]*se... is being enlarged*

COMPRENSIÓN

1. ¿Qué son las frituras panameñas?
2. ¿Qué es la chicha?
3. ¿Qué comida es muy típica de todo el mundo hispano?
4. ¿Qué cocina genuinamente estadounidense es de origen hispano?
5. ¿Cuándo empezó (*began*) a funcionar el Canal de Panamá? ¿Cuándo empezaron los españoles a pensar en hacer un canal?

Y ahora, Uds.

- ¿Cuáles son los platos más tradicionales de la cocina de los Estados Unidos? Escojan entre los/las dos el plato más representativo de este país y luego comparen su respuesta con las (*those*) de otros grupos o parejas.

- ¿Hay alguna obra de ingeniería muy importante en su país? ¿Por qué es importante?

Del mundo hispano

Antes de leer

Piense en la lasaña, un plato italiano tradicional. ¿Qué ingredientes contiene una lasaña típica? ¿pollo, aceite de oliva, papas, pimienta, pasta, tomates, sal, champiñones, tortillas, frijoles, agua, salchicha, lechuga, queso?

Lectura: Una receta

Lasaña de tortillas Para 6 porciones

INGREDIENTES

18 tortillas de maíz[a] en cuadrados[b]
480 gramos de queso ricotta
60 gramos de espinacas[c]
60 gramos de cebolla picada[d]
60 gramos de tomates en cuadrados
2 cucharadas[e] de mantequilla
Sal y pimienta

Salsa de tomate
4 tomates
1/2 cebolla
1 diente de ajo[f]
2 cucharadas de mantequilla
100 gramos de puré de tomate
100 mililitros de agua
Sal, pimienta y orégano al gusto[g]

Variación

PREPARACIÓN

Salsa de tomate
1. Corte los tomates y la cebolla en cuadrados y póngalos a hervir en una cacerola[h] con el agua, el puré de tomate, el ajo y el orégano. Licúelo[i] todo.
2. Vuelva a calentarlo[j] con la mantequilla y sazone con sal y pimienta.

Lasaña
1. Lave las espinacas y póngalas a hervir en un poco de agua; después, séquelas y saltéelas en una sartén[k] con la mantequilla, sal y pimienta.
2. En una fuente,[l] ponga la mitad de la salsa de tomate en el fondo[m] y encima[n] coloque las tortillas, el queso, las espinacas, el tomate y la cebolla en capas[ñ] hasta formar dos capas de todo. Después, cúbralo[o] con el resto de la salsa de tomate.
3. Meta la lasaña al horno[p] 30 o 40 minutos a 180° centígrados.

[a]*corn* [b]*squares* [c]*spinach* [d]*minced* [e]*tablespoons* [f]*diente... clove of garlic* [g]*al... to taste* [h]*póngalos... boil them in a pot* [i]*Blend it* [j]*Vuelva... Reheat it* [k]*séquelas... dry them (the spinach leaves) and sauté them in a frying pan* [l]*serving dish* [m]*bottom* [n]*on top* [ñ]*layers* [o]*cover it* [p]*oven*

Comprensión

A. Los mandatos de la receta. Todos los verbos para preparar esta receta son mandatos formales. Empareje los siguientes mandatos con su traducción en inglés, según el contexto de la receta.

MANDATOS
1. _____ corte
2. _____ sazone
3. _____ lave
4. _____ coloque
5. _____ meta

TRADUCCIONES
a. *put (into)*
b. *wash*
c. *place, arrange*
d. *cut*
e. *season*

B. Paso por *(by)* paso. Ponga en orden cronológico (de 1 a 4) los siguientes pasos para la lasaña, según la receta.

_____ Cocinar la lasaña en el horno.
_____ Hervir las espinacas y luego cocinarlas en una sartén.
_____ Preparar la salsa de tomate.
_____ Poner en una fuente, en capas, todos los ingredientes preparados para formar la lasaña.

Los señores Roble piden la cena

Antes de escuchar

¿Sale con frecuencia a comer en restaurantes? ¿Tiene algún restaurante favorito? ¿En qué se especializa?

Vocabulario para escuchar

la carta	menu	**mixto/a**	mixed (with **paella** = having
los entrantes	starters, first courses		both meat and seafood)
el segundo plato	main course	**cómo no**	of course

Después de escuchar

A. ¿Qué desean? Los señores Robles cenan esta noche en un restaurante elegante. ¿Qué piden?

    1. El Sr. Robles:

       Entrante _____ Segundo plato _____

    2. La Sra. Robles:

       Entrante _____

       Segundo plato _____

    3. De beber:

       _____

B. Más detalles. Conteste las siguientes preguntas.

    1. ¿Qué platos tienen fama en este restaurante?
    2. ¿Cuándo van a pedir el postre los Sres. Robles?

PRODUCCIÓN PERSONAL

¡Ahora, yo!

A. Use de modelo las preguntas y respuestas de la página 201 de este capítulo para hablar de la comida de su país y de sus preferencias culinarias.

B. Filme un programa culinario en el que (*which*) presente al menos dos platos o ingredientes tradicionales de una cocina nacional o regional.

A ESCRIBIR
La comida de las cafeterías de esta universidad

Preparar

Paso 1. ¿Qué piensan Uds. de la comida que sirven en las cafeterías de su universidad?

En parejas, compartan (*share*) sus ideas sobre este tema. Usen las siguientes preguntas de guía (*as a guide*). La conversación los/las ayudará (*will help you*) a clarificar sus propias (*own*) ideas y determinar un enfoque para su ensayo.

- ¿Ofrecen las cafeterías una buena variedad de comidas? Ejemplos: platos vegetarianos, comida baja en calorías
- ¿Cuáles son los platos que más piden los estudiantes?
- En general, ¿es rica la comida? ¿Es cara o barata?
- ¿Hay alguna cafetería mejor que otra?

Paso 2. Ahora use sus opiniones y las (*those*) de su compañero/a (no olvide citarlo/la [*quote him or her*] para escribir su ensayo). Escoja (*Choose*) un enfoque desde el principio (*from the beginning*) para organizar bien su texto. Hay más ayuda en Connect.

Más ideas para su portafolio

- Incluya una lista de sus comidas y bebidas favoritas. Incluya los lugares (restaurantes, la casa de alguien) donde las come o las bebe porque son mejores.
- Incluya una receta familiar favorita.
- Entreviste a un(a) hispanohablante sobre los platos más tradicionales de su cultura y pídale (*ask him/her for*) una receta fácil.
- Si ha estado jugando (*have been playing*) Practice Spanish: Study Abroad, en Quest 4 Ud. participó (*participated*) en una telenovela (*soap opera*) sobre una compañía que se especializa en (*specializes in*) la moda. En grupo, escriban una escena (*scene*) de una telenovela que tenga lugar (*that takes place*) en un restaurante. Usen vocabulario de este capítulo ¡y sean creativos (*be creative*)! Después, ustedes pueden interpretar (*act out*) su escena para la clase.

Sugerencia: You are now ready to play Quest 4 in **Practice Spanish: Study Abroad (www.mhpractice.com).**

LEARNSMART

Visit **www.connectspanish.com** to practice the vocabulary and grammar points covered in this chapter.

AFTER STUDYING THIS CHAPTER I CAN. . .

☐ talk about food and the meals of the day (202–203)

☐ use the verbs **saber** and **conocer** to express *to know* (205)

☐ use direct object pronouns to avoid repetition in conversation (209–211)

☐ use negative and indefinite words (215–216)

☐ give and understand formal commands (219–220)

☐ recognize/describe at least 2–3 aspects of Panamanian cultures

Gramática en breve

18. Direct Object Pronouns

me, te, lo/la, nos, os, los/las

19. Indefinite and Negative Words

algo	nada
alguien	nadie
algún (alguna/os/as)	ningún (ninguna)
siempre	nunca, jamás
también	tampoco

no + verb + negative word
negative word + verb

20. Formal Commands

-ar ⟶ -e(n)
-er/-ir ⟶ -a(n)

Affirmative: command + pronoun (1 word)
Negative: no + pronoun + command (3 words)

Vocabulario

Los verbos

acabar de + *inf.*	to have just (*done something*)
ayudar	to help
ayudar a + *inf.*	to help to (*do something*)
conocer (conozco)	to know, to be acquainted, familiar with; to meet
contestar	to answer
esperar	to wait (for); to expect
invitar	to invite
llamar	to call
saber (sé)	to know
saber + *inf.*	to know how to (*do something*)

La comida

cenar	to have/eat dinner, supper
cocinar	to cook
desayunar	to have/eat breakfast
merendar (meriendo)	to have a snack
preparar	to prepare

Repaso: almorzar (almuerzo) (c)

> Remember that this letter indicates the spelling change that happens in the formal commands of verbs that end in **-car, -gar,** or **-zar.**

el aceite (de oliva)	(olive) oil
el aguacate	avocado
el arroz	rice
las arvejas	green peas
el atún	tuna
el azúcar	sugar
el bistec	steak
los camarones	shrimp
la carne	meat
la cebolla	onion
los champiñones	mushrooms
la chuleta (de cerdo)	(pork) chop
la comida	food
los dulces	sweets; candy
los espárragos	asparagus
el flan	(baked) custard
los frijoles	beans
la galleta	cookie
los garbanzos	chickpeas
el helado	ice cream
el huevo	egg
el jamón	ham
la langosta	lobster
la lechuga	lettuce
la mantequilla	butter
la manzana	apple
los mariscos	shellfish
la naranja	orange
el pan	bread
el pan tostado	toast
la papa (frita)	(French fried) potato
el pastel	cake; pie
el pavo	turkey
el pepino	cucumber
el pescado	fish
la pimienta	pepper
el pollo (asado)	(roast) chicken
el postre	dessert
el queso	cheese
la sal	salt
la salsa	salsa; sauce
la salchicha	sausage; hot dog
la sopa	soup
las verduras	vegetables
la zanahoria	carrot

Cognados: la banana, la barbacoa, el cereal, la ensalada, la fruta, la hamburguesa, el salmón, el sándwich, el tomate, el yogur

Las bebidas

el agua (but *f.*) (mineral)	(mineral) water
la cerveza	beer
el jugo (de fruta)	(fruit) juice
la leche	milk
el refresco	soft drink
el vino (blanco, tinto)	(white, red) wine

Cognado: el té

Repaso: la bebida, el café

Las comidas

el almuerzo	lunch
la cena	dinner, supper
la comida	meal
el desayuno	breakfast
la merienda	snack

En un restaurante

el/la camarero/a	waiter/waitress
la cuenta	check, bill
el plato	dish; course
el plato principal	main course

Cognado: el menú

Otros sustantivos

la ayuda	help
la canción	song
la cocina	cuisine
los comestibles	groceries, foodstuff
el consejo	(piece of) advice

la dirección	address
el/la dueño/a	owner
la letra	(*song*) lyrics
el mandato	command
el nombre	name
la receta	recipe
la tarjeta de crédito	credit card

Los adjetivos

asado/a	roast(ed)
caliente	hot (*in temperature, not taste*)
fresco/a	fresh
frito/a	fried
ligero/a	light, not heavy
picante	hot, spicy
rico/a	tasty, savory; rich (*in calories*)
tostado/a	toasted

Las palabras indefinidas y negativas

algo	something, anything
alguien	someone, anyone
algún (alguna/os/as)	some, any
jamás	never
nada	nothing, not anything
nadie	no one, nobody, not anybody
ningún (ninguna)	no, not any
tampoco	neither, not either

Repaso: nunca, siempre, también

Palabras adicionales

estar a dieta	to be on a diet
tener (mucha) hambre	to be (very) hungry
tener (mucha) sed	to be (very) thirsty

Vocabulario personal

8

De viaje°

De... *On a trip, Traveling*

www.connectspanish.com

En este capítulo

En la zona colonial de Santo Domingo, República Dominicana

OCÉANO ATLÁNTICO

CUBA

HAITÍ

REPÚBLICA DOMINICANA

*Santo Domingo

PUERTO RICO

Mar Caribe

| 0 | 125 | 250 Millas |
| 0 | 125 | 250 Kilómetros |

LA REPÚBLICA DOMINICANA

10.4 (punto cuatro) millones de habitantes

- La República Dominicana comparte[a] la isla de La Española (*Hispaniola*, en inglés) con el país de Haití.

- La ciudad de Santo Domingo, capital del país, fue fundada[b] por el hermano de Cristóbal Colón en 1496. Es la más antigua de todas las ciudades fundadas por los europeos en América.

[a]*shares* [b]*founded*

- ¿Dónde le gusta pasar las vacaciones? ¿En la playa? ¿en las montañas? ¿visitando una ciudad o un país que Ud. no conoce? (¿una nueva ciudad o un nuevo país?)

- ¿Qué le gusta hacer cuando está en la playa? ¿nadar[a]? ¿tomar el sol[b]? ¿hacer *surfing* u otros deportes[c]?

- ¿Qué es lo peor[d] de hacer un viaje? ¿hacer la maleta,[e] el viaje mismo[f] o volver a casa?

[a]*swim* [b]*tomar... sunbathe* [c]*sports* [d]*lo... the worst part* [e]*hacer... packing* [f]*el... the trip itself*

CECILIA FIGUEROA MARTÍN CONTESTA LAS PREGUNTAS.

- Prefiero ir de viaje a otros países y también visitar a mis parientes en los Estados Unidos. Como[a] soy de Puerto Rico y tengo el mar[b] y el calor todo el tiempo, me gusta ir de vacaciones a lugares con un clima diferente. ¡Me encanta[c] ver la nieve!

- Cuando voy a la playa, me gusta nadar y estar en la arena[d] leyendo.

- Para mí, lo peor de un viaje es tener que trasladarse.[e] Odio[f] especialmente los viajes en avión.[g] Pero si el viaje es muy divertido,[h] ¡odio volver!

[a]*Since* [b]*ocean* [c]*¡Me... I love* [d]*sand* [e]*change locations* [f]*I hate* [g]*en... by plane* [h]*muy... a lot of fun*

De viaje°

De... *On a trip, Traveling*

en el aeropuerto · el maletero · el asistente de vuelo · la piloto · el piloto · la asistente de vuelo · Vuelo 33 · Salida 10:35 · el equipaje · la maleta · Jorge · Anita · Alejandro · Javier · Josefina · la agente (el agente) · Juana · el pasajero · la pasajera · facturar el equipaje · el mostrador

You can hear the pronunciation of theme vocabulary words and phrases in the Connect eBook.

Los medios de transporte

la cabina	cabin (*on a ship*)
el crucero	cruise (ship)
la estación	station
de autobuses	bus station
de trenes	train station
el puerto	port
la sala de espera	waiting room
la sala de fumar /	smoking area
de fumadores	
el vuelo	flight
ir en...	to go/travel by . . .
autobús	bus
avión	plane
barco	boat, ship
tren	train

El viaje

el asiento	seat
el billete (*Sp.*) /	ticket
el boleto (*L.A.*)	
de ida	one-way ticket
de ida y vuelta	round-trip ticket
el billete/boleto	e-ticket
electrónico	
la demora	delay
la llegada	arrival
el pasaje	fare, price (*of a transportation ticket*)
el pasaporte	passport
la puerta de embarque	boarding gate
la salida	departure
la tarjeta de embarque	boarding pass

anunciar	to announce	**ir al extranjero**	to go abroad
bajarse (de)	to get down (from); to get off (of) (*a vehicle*)	**pasar por la aduana**	to go/pass through customs
estar atrasado/a	to be late	**el control de seguridad**	security (check)
facturar el equipaje	to check baggage		
guardar (un puesto)	to save (a place [*in line*])	**quejarse (de)**	to complain (about)
		salir/llegar (gu) a tiempo	to depart/arrive on time
hacer cola	to stand in line		
hacer escala/parada	to make a stop	**subir (a)**	to go up; to get on (*a vehicle*)
hacer la(s) maleta(s)	to pack one's suitcase(s)	**viajar**	to travel
hacer un viaje	to take a trip	**volar (vuelo) en avión**	to fly; to go by plane

Comunicación

A. Hablando de medios de transporte. ¿Con qué medio de transporte relaciona Ud. las siguientes personas y cosas? Hay más de una respuesta posible en algunos casos.

1. un crucero
2. un(a) asistente de vuelo
3. un puerto
4. una estación
5. una cabina

6. una agencia de viajes
7. un asiento
8. un(a) piloto
9. un capitán / una capitana
10. la llegada

B. Un viaje al extranjero

Paso 1. Use los números del 1 al 9 para organizar un viaje de manera lógica.

a. _____ subir al avión cuando se anuncia el vuelo
b. _____ pasar por el control de seguridad
c. _____ hacer cola para obtener la tarjeta de embarque y facturar el equipaje
d. _____ pedir un taxi y llegar al aeropuerto
e. _____ oír el anuncio de la salida del vuelo
f. _____ hacer la maleta y poner el pasaporte en el bolso
g. _____ esperar en la puerta de embarque mandando mensajes
h. _____ sentarse en el asiento junto a la ventanilla (*window*)
i. _____ llegar al aeropuerto de destino (*destination*) y pasar por el control de inmigración y la aduana

Paso 2. Ahora narre la secuencia en primera persona (**yo**).

C. Definiciones

Paso 1. Dé las palabras definidas.

1. Es necesario pasar por este control al llegar a otro país.
2. Es la cosa que se compra antes de hacer un viaje.
3. Es el antónimo de **subir a.**
4. Se va allí cuando se hace un viaje en avión.
5. Se va allí cuando se hace un viaje en tren.
6. Es la persona que nos ayuda durante un vuelo.

Paso 2. Ahora prepare dos definiciones para leer a toda la clase. Sus compañeros van a dar (*give*) la palabra que Ud. define.

Frases útiles del Paso 1: Es necesario para... Es la cosa que... Se va allí... Es la persona que... Es el antónimo de...

Otras frases útiles: Es el sinónimo de... Es el lugar donde... Es cuando... Es lo que...

---

*The words **la entrada** and **la localidad** are used to refer to tickets for movies, plays, or other events.

Así se dice

El autobús is expressed in a variety of ways in different parts of the Spanish-speaking world. Here are a few of the most common ones.

el camión (*Mex.*)
el bus (*C.A.*)
la guagua (*Cuba, P.R.*)
el colectivo (*Arg.*)

Here are some other common travel-related variations.

la maleta = la valija (*Arg.*), la petaca (*Mex.*)

El boleto is generally understood to express ticket* throughout the Spanish-speaking world. The word **el tiquete** is heard in Mexico and Central America, as well as in this country, and **el billete** is used in Spain.

D. En el aeropuerto. En parejas, nombren o describan las cosas y
acciones representadas en este dibujo.

De vacaciones°

De... *On vacation*

el *camping*	campground
el mar	sea
el océano	ocean
estar de vacaciones	to be on vacation
hacer *camping*	to go camping
ir de vacaciones a...	to (go on) vacation to/in . . .
pasar las vacaciones en...	to spend one's vacation in . . .
salir de vacaciones	to leave on vacation
tomar unas vacaciones	to take a vacation

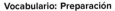

> **Así se dice**
>
> la camioneta = la ranchera, la rubia, el coche rural, el coche familiar, el monovolumen (*Sp.*)
>
> el *camping* = el campamento
>
> hacer *camping* = acampar
>
> sacar fotos = tomar fotos
>
> la tienda de campaña = la tienda de acampar, la carpa, la casa de campaña

Comunicación

A. ¿Qué hace Ud.?

Paso 1. Diga si las siguientes declaraciones son ciertas o falsas para Ud. Corrija las declaraciones falsas.

	CIERTO	FALSO
1. Cuando estoy de vacaciones, tomo el sol.	☐	☐
2. Prefiero ir de vacaciones a las montañas.	☐	☐
3. Duermo muy bien en una tienda de campaña.	☐	☐
4. Saco muchas fotos cuando estoy de vacaciones.	☐	☐
5. Es fácil ir a playas bonitas desde (*from*) aquí.	☐	☐
6. Escribo muchas tarjetas postales.	☐	☐

Paso 2. En parejas, túrnense para hacer y contestar preguntas basadas en las oraciones del **Paso 1.**

Nota **cultural**

Tipos de turismo en el mundo hispano

En el mundo hispano hay ciudades y lugares impresionantes que visitar y playas maravillosas donde pasar las vacaciones. Pero hay también una gran variedad de lugares de destino para las personas que desean disfrutar de[a] unas vacaciones excepcionales.

- **El ecoturismo**
  Consiste en visitar lugares poco explotados por los seres[b] humanos. La selva costarricense y la selva amazónica (en el Ecuador y el Perú) son destinos populares, así como[c] la Patagonia (en la Argentina y Chile) y las Islas Galápagos. En el norte de España, muchos caminantes[d] de todas partes del mundo hacen el Camino de Santiago.[e] Su origen fue como un camino de peregrinación,[f] pero ahora muchas personas lo hacen sin motivo religioso. Es una actividad física no extrema que le permite a uno[g] hacer compañeros de viaje interesantes y variados.

- **El agroturismo**
  Este tipo de vacaciones implica pasar las vacaciones en un lugar rural. Los turistas pueden quedarse[h] en casas renovadas que ofrecen la experiencia de hacer trabajo agrícola y excursiones educativas. En la isla chilena de Chiloé, por ejemplo, hay ofertas agroturísticas interesantes.

- **El aventurismo**
  Es para aquellos[i] que buscan aventuras emocionantes y físicas. Se puede esquiar en los Andes o en las montañas españolas, hacer ciclismo de montaña, navegar en rápidos, etcétera.

Un grupo de estudiantes en una excursión ecoturística en la selva (*jungle*) amazónica, Perú

¿Practica Ud. alguno de estos tipos de turismo? ¿Dónde lo hace?

[a]disfrutar... *to enjoy* [b]*beings* [c]así... *as are* [d]*hikers* [e]Camino... *St James's Trail, Way* [f]un... *a (religious) pilgrimage* [g]le... *allows one* [h]*stay, be lodged* [i]*those (people)*

B. Intercambios

Paso 1. Complete el siguiente párrafo sobre sus vacaciones típicas y sus vacaciones más memorables.

En mis vacaciones típicas, voy a _____^{1} en _____^{2} (medio de transporte) en el mes de _____.^{3} Voy con _____^{4} (personas) y esto es lo que hago: _____.^{5}

En mis vacaciones más memorables, fui^a a _____^{6} en _____^{7} en el mes de _____.^{8} Fui con _____.^{9} Hice^b las siguientes actividades: _____^{10} (infinitivos).

^{a}*I went* ^{b}*I did*

Paso 2. Ahora, en parejas, túrnense para hacer y contestar preguntas basadas en las ideas del **Paso 1.** Obtengan (*Get*) mucha información de su compañero/a.

MODELOS: ¿Adónde vas para tus vacaciones, generalmente? ¿Hay un lugar que siempre visitas para las vacaciones? ¿Vas allí todos los años? ¿Por qué vas allí? Y para tus vacaciones más memorables, ¿a qué lugar fuiste (*did you go*)?

Algo sobre...

el colmado dominicano

Un colmado dominicano

En todo el mundo hispanohablante hay tiendas en los barrios^a donde se venden comestibles, bebidas y las cosas que en este país se compran en los supermercados. En la República Dominicana, estas tiendas se llaman «colmados». Un colmado es un punto de encuentro^b para la gente^c del barrio. A veces es como un bar-discoteca, donde se baila merengue y bachata^d y otros tipos de música.

¿Existe en el lugar donde Ud. vive alguna tienda similar a los colmados? ¿Qué se hace allí?

^{a}*neighborhoods* ^{b}*punto... meeting place* ^{c}*people* ^{d}*dance music (typically Dominican but danced in all Spanish-speaking countries)*

Nota **comunicativa**

Otro uso de la palabra *se*: para expresar acciones impersonales

If there are native Spanish speakers living in your area, you probably have seen signs like the one in the photo: **Se habla español.** The word **se** in front of the verb (rather than a specific subject, like **Juan** or **ellos**) changes the English equivalent of the verb. In English, **se habla español** can mean: *Spanish is spoken here. They speak Spanish here. People speak Spanish here.* You have already seen this use of **se** in direction lines and readings in *Puntos de partida.*

Here are some additional examples of this use of **se** to talk about things that "people," rather than specific individuals, do.

Se va al aeropuerto para tomar un vuelo.	*One goes / People go / You go to the airport to catch a flight.*
Se aprende mucho viajando.	*One learns / People learn / You learn a lot by traveling.*

Be alert to this use of **se** in *Puntos de partida* as well as in real-life Spanish; it is very frequent and you need to understand it. You will practice it in **Comunicación C.** You will also see (and hear) plural verbs, but you will not practice using them in this text.

C. **¿Dónde se hace esto?** Indique el lugar (o los lugares) donde se hacen las siguientes actividades.

MODELO: Se come. → Se come en un restaurante, en casa, en la cafetería...

1. Se factura el equipaje y se anuncia el vuelo.
2. Se hace la maleta.
3. Se compra un boleto.
4. Se espera el avión.
5. Se pide una bebida.

6. Se mira una película.
7. Se nada y se toma el sol.
8. Se habla francés.
9. Se habla portugués.
10. Se viaja en barco.

D. La publicidad. En parejas, lean este anuncio de una aerolínea latinoamericana y contesten las preguntas. ¡Piensen como expertos en *marketing*!

1. ¿Cómo se llama la aerolínea?
2. ¿A qué tipo de persona va dirigido (*directed*) el anuncio?
3. ¿Por qué se usa un plato con comida en el anuncio?
4. ¿Qué se ve en el plato? ¿Qué representa?
5. ¿En qué tipo de publicación creen Uds. que se encuentra (*is found*) este anuncio?

En LAN convertimos Latinoamérica en una gran red para tus negocios.
Vuela directo con el mejor servicio, a todas las capitales de América del Sur.

¿Recuerda Ud.?

In **Gramática 18 (Cap. 7),** you learned how to use direct object pronouns to avoid repetition. Can you identify the direct object pronouns in the following exchange? To what or to who(m) do these pronouns refer?

ROBERTO: ¿Tienes los boletos?

ANA: No, no los tengo, pero mi agente de viajes ya los tiene listos (*ready*).

ROBERTO: Si quieres, te acompaño a la agencia.

ANA: Encantada. Casi nunca te veo.

SALU2

«¡De viaje!» Segmento 1

![waterfall photo]

Un arcoíris (*rainbow*) en las Cataratas (*Falls*) del Iguazú: «La caída (*plunging*) de agua desde una altura de ochenta metros es simplemente indescriptible... Hay que estar allí para oír el rugido (*roar*) de las cataratas, sentir (*to feel*) el vapor del agua... »

Antes de mirar

¿Qué espera Ud. ver en un programa de viajes?

- ☐ la gente (*people*) del lugar que se visita
- ☐ el ambiente en las calles (*the atmosphere in the streets*)
- ☐ la naturaleza (selvas [*jungles*], animales autóctonos [*native*])
- ☐ la comida
- ☐ otras cosas: _____

Estrategia

So far you have talked almost exclusively about the present time. What verb tense do you think a traveler would use to talk about a trip?

Este segmento

Este segmento introduce un programa que muestra (*shows*) videos filmados por telespectadores sobre sus viajes favoritos a lugares de Latinoamérica. El primer video es sobre la Argentina.

Vocabulario del segmento

la elección	choice	visité	I visited	me pareció	it seemed
estar listo/a	to be ready	enterrado/a	buried	impresionante	impressive
la voz	voice	me encantó	I loved	me gustó	I liked
hice	I took, made	fui/encontré	I went / I found	estuve	I was
el año pasado	last year	el puesto	stall, stand		
llegué	I arrived	vi	I saw		

Después de mirar

A. ¿Está claro? Empareje los lugares con las descripciones de Jaime.

LUGARES

1.

3.

2.

4.

DESCRIPCIONES DE JAIME

a. _____ la tumba de Eva Perón en el Cementerio de la Recoleta

b. _____ un espectáculo (*show*) de gauchos en la Feria de Mataderos

c. _____ las increíbles Cataratas del Iguazú

d. _____ la famosa Plaza de Mayo

B. Un poco más. Las siguientes oraciones son falsas. Corríjalas, según el video.

1. Ana y Víctor recibieron (*received*) más de mil videos para este programa.
2. El video que se ve en este segmento es sobre Chile.
3. El turista solo fue (*went*) a las Cataratas del Iguazú.
4. Los gauchos son similares a los tucanes.

C. Y ahora, Uds. En parejas, escojan un lugar que a los dos les gustaría (*you would both like*) visitar. Luego completen la siguiente descripción del viaje.

En el futuro, nos gustaría[a] ir a _____ en el/la _____ (estación del año) porque nos gusta _____ (infinitivos). Nos gustaría ir con _____ y pasar _____ (período de tiempo) allí.

[a]nos... *we would like*

GRAMÁTICA

21 **Expressing** *to who(m)* **or** *for who(m)*
Indirect Object Pronouns; **Dar** and **decir**

Grammar Tutorial 21

www.connectspanish.com

Gramática en acción: En el aeropuerto

En el mostrador
—¿**Me** puede dar un asiento de
  ventanilla, por favor?
—Lo siento, pero ya no hay. Pero sí
  puedo asignar**le** un asiento de pasillo.

En el control de seguridad
—¿**Le** enseño la tarjeta de embarque?
—No es necesario, señorita.
—¿**Le** enseño el pasaporte?
—Tampoco es necesario.

Comprensión

¿Dónde se oye, en el mostrador o en el control de seguridad?

1. «¿Puede enseñar**me** (*show me*) lo que hay en su bolso?»
2. «No **me** gusta sentarme en el asiento de en medio (*middle*).»
3. «En un momento **le** doy la nueva tarjeta de embarque.»
4. «¿**Me** enseña el pasaporte, por favor?»

Indirect Object Pronouns / Los pronombres del complemento indirecto

me	to/for me	nos	to/for us
te	to/for you (*fam. sing.*)	os	to/for you (*fam. pl.*)
le	to/for you (*form. sing.*), him, her, it	les	to/for you (*form. pl.*), them

the indirect object / **el complemento indirecto** = the noun or pronoun that indicates *to who(m)* or *for who(m)* an action is performed

¡OJO!
Note that indirect object pronouns have the same form as direct object pronouns, except in the third person: **le, les.**

At the airport **At the counter:** *"Could you please give me a window seat?" "I'm sorry, but there aren't any more (available). But I can give you an aisle seat."* **At the security check:** *"Do I show you my boarding pass?" "That's not necessary, miss." "Do I show you my passport?" "That isn't necessary either."*

Gramática

1. Indirect Objects

Indirect object nouns and pronouns are the second recipient of the action of the verb. They usually answer the question *to who(m)?* or *for who(m)?* in relation to the verb. The word *to* is frequently omitted in English.

	INDIRECT	DIRECT	
Ana is preparing	**them**	dinner.	
I'll give	**her**	the gift	tomorrow.

For who(m) is Ana preparing dinner? → **(for) them**
To who(m) am I giving the gift? → **(to) her**

Indicate the direct and indirect objects in the following sentences.

1. *He'll give me the car tomorrow.*
2. *Please tell me the answer now.*
3. *Me va a dar el coche mañana.*
4. Dígame la respuesta ahora, por favor.
5. El profesor nos va a hacer algunas preguntas.
6. ¿No me compras una revista ahora?

---

2. Placement of Indirect Object Pronouns

Like direct object pronouns, *indirect object pronouns* (**los pronombres del complemento indirecto**) can precede the conjugated verb.

When the conjugated verb is followed by an infinitive or a present participle, the pronouns either precede the conjugated verb *or* follow (and are attached to):

• the infinitive
• the present participle

Remember to add an accent mark to the present participle when you attach a pronoun to it.

No, no **te presto** el coche.
No, I won't lend you the car.

Voy a **guardarte** el asiento.
Te voy a guardar el asiento.
I'll save your seat for you.

Le estoy escribiendo una carta a Marisol.
Estoy **escribiéndole** una carta a Marisol.
I'm writing Marisol a letter.

---

3. With Commands

As with direct object pronouns, indirect object pronouns:

• are attached to the affirmative command form
• precede the negative command form.

Remember to add an accent to most affirmative commands when you attach a pronoun.

Sírvanos un café, por favor.
Serve us some coffee, please.

No me dé su número de teléfono ahora.
Don't give me your phone number now.

---

4. Redundancy of the Indirect Object

Even when a sentence has a third person indirect object *noun*, it must also have a third person indirect object *pronoun*. The noun object is preceded by **a,** which expresses *to* or *for*. This redundancy may sound repetitive to you, but it is what happens in Spanish most of the time.

Vamos a **mandarle** un mensaje a **Juan.**
Let's send Juan a message.
(Lit., *Let's send **to him** a message **to Juan**.*)

¿**Les** guardo los asientos a **los niños?**
Shall I save the seats for the kids?
(Lit., *Shall I **for them** save the seats **for the kids**?*)

---

5. Multiple Meanings of *le(s)*

Le and **les** can have several different meanings. When context does not make the meaning clear, the meaning is clarified with a prepositional phrase: **a** + *pronoun object of a preposition.* This redundancy is appropriate in Spanish.

Voy a **mandarle** un telegrama. = meaning of **le** unclear unless specified
Voy a mandarle un telegrama a **Ud.** / ...a **él.** / ...a **ella.**
I'm going to send you/him/her a telegram.

¡OJO!
Object of prepositions = subject pronouns, except for **mí** and **ti**.

---

6. Clarification or Emphasis of Indirect Object Pronouns

To clarify or emphasize the indirect object pronouns **me, te, nos,** and **os,** a phrase with **a** + *object pronoun* is also used. English accomplishes this by tone of voice, but Spanish does it with redundancy.

¿Ud. **me** habla a **mí**?
*Are you talking to **me**?*

Pedro **te** dio el pasaporte a **ti,** no a **mí.**
*Pedro gave **you** the passport, not (to) **me.***

---

7. Verbs Often Used with Indirect Objects

Here are some verbs frequently used with indirect objects. You already know the meaning of the ones marked with*.

contar (cuento)	to tell; to narrate	***pedir (pido) (i)**	to ask for
entregar (gu)	to hand in	**preguntar**	to ask (*a question*)
***escribir**	to write	**prestar**	to lend
explicar (qu)	to explain	**prometer**	to promise
***hablar**	to speak	**recomendar (recomiendo)**	to recommend
***mandar**	to send	**regalar**	to give (*as a gift*)
mostrar (muestro)	to show	***servir (sirvo) (i)**	to serve
ofrecer (ofrezco)	to offer		

Dar and decir

dar (*to give*)		decir (*to say; to tell*)	
doy	damos	digo	decimos
das	dais	dices	decís
da	dan	dice	dicen

Juan **dice** que tiene muchos gastos (*expenses*) en la universidad. Por eso Juan les **dice** a sus padres que necesita dinero.

Sus padres le **dan** un cheque.

1. dar

Dar means *to give*. It is almost always used with indirect object pronouns.

> **¡OJO!**
> Another Spanish verb expresses *to give* as a gift: **regalar**.

Mis profesores **nos dan** mucha tarea en todas las clases.
My professors give us a lot of homework in all my classes.

Mis abuelos **me regalan** dinero para mi cumpleaños.
My grandparents give me money for my birthday.

---

2. decir

Decir means *to say* or *to tell*. When **decir** means *to tell*, it is almost always used with indirect object pronouns, like **dar**.

> **¡OJO!**
> Other verbs related to speaking are used to express different meanings.
>
> | **hablar** | to speak |
> |---|---|
> | **contar (cuento)** | to tell; to narrate |

Mi profesor **dice** que la historia es fascinante.
My professor says that history is fascinating.

Y **nos dice** que tenemos mucho que aprender de la historia.
And he tells us that we have a lot to learn from history.

El profesor **habla** varias lenguas.
The professor speaks several languages.

A veces **nos cuenta** algunas de sus experiencias en Latinoamérica.
At times he tells us some of his experiences in Latin America.

---

3. Formal Commands of dar and decir

As you know, **dar** and **decir** also have irregular formal command forms. There is a written accent on **dé** to distinguish it from the preposition **de**.

Mandatos formales
dar → **dé, den**
decir → **diga, digan**

Práctica y comunicación

A. Asociaciones. ¿Qué verbos asocia Ud. con los siguientes objetos y situaciones?

1. un coche, el dinero
2. la comida en un restaurante
3. las fotos
4. hacer algo por (*for*) alguien
5. la gramática, un profesor
6. la tarea, un informe (*report, paper*)
7. algo para un cumpleaños
8. un restaurante, una película, un libro
9. flores (*flowers*), un e-mail
10. un secreto, un chiste (*joke*)

B. Dar y recibir

Paso 1. Autoprueba. Complete las siguientes oraciones con el pronombre del objeto indirecto apropiado.

1. _____ presto el coche a ti, Carolina, no a tu hermano.
2. Los señores Gómez _____ mandan saludos a su amigo dominicano.
3. No _____ dé más galletas a los niños, por favor.
4. ¿_____ pasas el pan, por favor? Está muy lejos de mí.
5. Profesora, no podemos terminar el examen si no _____ da más tiempo.
6. El tío Juan siempre _____ dice a mis hermanos y a mí que la ciudad de Santa Domingo es muy bonita.

Paso 2. Complete las siguientes declaraciones sobre su vida (*life*) con el pronombre del objeto indirecto apropiado. Si la oración no es cierta para Ud., hágala negativa usando **no** u otras palabras negativas.

1. Todos los años _____ doy una tarjeta de cumpleaños a mi mejor amigo/a.
2. Todos los años mi mejor amigo/a _____ da una tarjeta de cumpleaños.
3. Todos los días _____ escribo un mensaje a mis padres o a mis abuelos.
4. Todos los días mis padres o mis abuelos (mis hijos) _____ mandan un mensaje.
5. Todos mis profesores _____ cuentan chistes en clase con frecuencia.
6. Con frecuencia, _____ cuento historias a mis profesores y compañeros de clase.
7. Mis abuelos _____ regalan dinero con frecuencia.
8. _____ regalo dinero a mis abuelos con frecuencia.

Paso 3. Ahora, en parejas, túrnense para hacer y contestar preguntas, usando las oraciones del **Paso 2**. Luego díganle al resto de la clase algo que Uds. tienen en común. ¡OJO! Hagan los cambios necesarios, según el modelo.

MODELO: Todos los años _____ doy una tarjeta de cumpleaños a mi mejor amigo/a. →

> E1: ¿Todos los años **le das** una tarjeta de cumpleaños a **tu** mejor amiga?
> E2: No, nunca **le doy** una tarjeta de cumpleaños a **mi** mejor amiga. ¿Y tú?
> E1: Yo tampoco. →

> Nosotros nunca **les damos** una tarjeta de cumpleaños a **nuestras** mejores amigas.

C. De vuelta (*Returning*) a la República Dominicana

Paso 1. Unos amigos dominicanos necesitan ayuda para arreglar (*arrange*) su vuelta (*return*) a casa. Explíqueles cómo Ud. los puede ayudar.

MODELO: imprimir (*to print*) el boleto electrónico → **Les** imprimo el boleto electrónico.

1. llamar un taxi
2. bajar (*to carry down*) las maletas de su habitación
3. guardar (*to keep an eye on*) el equipaje
4. guardar un puesto en la cola
5. comprar una revista
6. por fin dar un abrazo (*hug*)

Prác. B, Paso 1: Answers: 1. Te 2. le 3. les 4. Me 5. nos 6. nos

Paso 2. Ahora describa las acciones, pero desde el punto de vista (*point of view*) de sus amigos.

MODELO: imprimir el boleto electrónico → **Nos** imprimes el boleto electrónico.

D. **¿Qué hacen estas personas?** Complete las siguientes oraciones lógicamente con un verbo y un pronombre del complemento indirecto.

MODELO: El vicepresidente _____ consejos al presidente.

→ El vicepresidente **le ofrece** consejos al presidente.

1. Romeo _____ flores a Julieta.
2. Snoopy _____ besos (*kisses*) a Lucy... ¡Y a ella no le gusta!
3. Eva _____ una manzana a Adán.
4. Los psicólogos _____ consejos a la gente (*people*) que los necesita.
5. Los bancos _____ dinero a las personas que quieren comprar una casa.
6. Los asistentes de vuelo _____ bebidas a los pasajeros.
7. Yo siempre _____ la verdad a todos.

> **Vocabulario útil**
>
> dar
> decir
> **ofrecer (ofrezco)**
> **prestar**
> **regalar**
> **servir (sirvo) (i)**

E. **En un restaurante.** Explíquele al pequeño Benjamín, que solo tiene 4 años, lo que se hace en un restaurante. Llene los espacios en blanco con pronombres del complemento indirecto.

Primero el camarero _____¹ ofrece una mesa desocupada.ᵃ Luego tú _____² pides el menú al camarero. También _____³ haces preguntas sobre los platos y las especialidades de la casa y _____⁴ dices lo que quieres comer. El camarero _____⁵ trae la comida. Por fin tu papá _____⁶ pide la cuenta al camarero. Si tú quieres pagar, _____⁷ pides dinero a tu papá y _____⁸ das el dinero al camarero.

ᵃ*vacant*

F. **Intercambios.** En parejas, túrnense para entrevistarse sobre los siguientes temas. Traten de (*Try to*) continuar la conversación.

hacer buenos regalos →

MODELO: E1: **¿Quién te** hace buenos regalos?
E2: Mis padres siempre me hacen buenos regalos.
E1: **¿Qué te** regalan, por ejemplo?
E2: Bueno, me regalan dinero, CDs, cosas para mi apartamento...

1. hacer buenos / interesantes regalos / regalar cosas feas
2. decir la verdad / mentiras (*lies*)
3. contar secretos / los secretos de otras personas
4. hacer favores / recomendaciones / la cena
5. escribir e-mails / poemas de amor / tarjetas postales cuando están de vacaciones
6. mostrar las fotos de sus vacaciones / las notas (*grades*) de sus exámenes
7. servir la comida / bebidas
8. pedir / dar ayuda / consejos
9. prestar dinero / ropa / su coche
10. prometer cosas que luego no hace
11. recomendar películas / restaurantes / clases en la universidad
12. ¿ ?

> **Algo sobre...**
>
> **el casabe**
>
>
>
> El casabe, un producto que representa la cultura de la República Dominicana
>
> El casabe es una especie de tortilla que se hace con la yuca.ᵃ Es un producto básico de alimentaciónᵇ de los dominicanos. Como comida, el casabe es una tradición que viene de los taínos, los indígenas de la isla de La Española (hoy día, Haití y la República Dominicana).
>
> En su cultura, ¿qué alimento se puede comparar con el casabe?
>
> ᵃ*manioc, cassava root* ᵇ*diet, what people eat*

Grammar Tutorial 22
connect
|SPANISH
www.connectspanish.com

22 Expressing Likes and Dislikes

Gustar (Part 2)

Gramática en acción: Vacaciones en la República Dominicana

En la República Dominicana se puede hacer de todo en las vacaciones.

- A algunas personas les gusta relajarse en la playa.
- A otras personas les gustan las vacaciones que les permiten hacer actividades deportivas (*sporting*).
- A algunos turistas les gustan los museos y los monumentos históricos.
- A mucha gente le gusta hacer de todo un poco.

¿Y a Ud.?

¿Qué le gusta hacer en sus vacaciones? ¿Le gusta ir a un sitio donde hace buen tiempo? ¿Le gustan las actividades deportivas o las culturales (*cultural ones*)?

Using gustar / Los usos de *gustar*

Spanish	English Phrasing	Literal Equivalent
Me gusta <u>la playa</u>.	*I like the beach.*	The beach is pleasing to me.
No le gustan <u>sus cursos</u>.	*He doesn't like his courses.*	His courses are not pleasing to him.
Nos gusta <u>esquiar</u>.	*We like to ski.*	Skiing is pleasing to us.

You have been using the verb **gustar** since the beginning of *Puntos de partida* to express likes and dislikes. However, **gustar** does not literally mean *to like,* but rather *to be pleasing.*

Me gusta viajar.
Traveling is pleasing to me. (I like to travel.)

Me gustan los viajes de aventura.
Adventure trips are pleasing to me. (I like adventure trips.)

---

1. Gustar + Indirect Object Pronouns

Gustar is always used with an indirect object pronoun: Something is pleasing to someone. The verb agrees with the subject of the sentence = the thing that is pleasing. In the first two examples, **gusta** is used with the singular noun **asiento, gustan** with the plural **asientos.**

¡OJO!

An infinitive is a singular subject in Spanish. **Gusta** is used even if there are two or more infinitive subjects.

(no) *indirect object pronoun* + **gusta(n)** + *subject*

Me gusta **este asiento** de pasillo.
This aisle seat is pleasing to me. (I like this aisle seat.)

No **me** gustan **los asientos** de ventanilla.
Window seats are not pleasing to me. (I don't like window seats.)

Me gusta mucho **volar** en avión.
Flying is really pleasing to me. (I really like to fly.)

Me gusta nadar y **tomar** el sol.
I like to swim and sunbathe.

2. Redundancy of Indirect Object

When the person pleased is a noun or a proper name, the indirect object pronoun is still used. This redundancy (repetition) is the same concept you learned with *le* and *les* in **Gramática 21**.

¡OJO!

Remember: The indirect object pronoun *must* be used with **gustar** even when the prepositional phrase **a** + *noun* or *pronoun* is used.

a + *noun* + **(no) le / les gusta(n)** + *subject*
(no) le / les gusta(n) + *subject* + **a** + *noun*

Al niño no **le** gustan los aviones.
No **le** gustan los aviones **al niño.**
The child doesn't like airplanes.

A Raquel y a Arturo les gusta viajar juntos.
Les gusta viajar juntos a **Raquel y Arturo.**
Raquel and Arturo like to travel together.

3. Clarification or Emphasis

A phrase with **a** + *pronoun* is often used for clarification or emphasis. The prepositional phrase can appear before the indirect object pronoun or after the verb.

¡OJO!

Remember that subject pronouns (**Ud., él, ella...**) are used as the object of prepositions, except for **mí** (accent) and **ti** (no accent). (Exceptions: **conmigo, contigo.**)

CLARIFICATION
¿**Le** gusta a **Ud.** viajar? ¿**A Ud. le** gusta viajar?
Do you like to travel?

¿**Le** gusta a **él** viajar? ¿**A él le** gusta viajar?
Does he like to travel?

EMPHASIS
A mí me gusta viajar en avión, pero **a mi esposo le** gusta viajar en coche. Y **a ti,** ¿en qué **te** gusta viajar?
I like to travel by plane, but my husband likes to travel by car. How do you like to travel?

4. Gustar + determiner + noun

When the thing liked is a noun, it is always preceded by a determiner of some kind: an article, an adjective of quantity (like **muchos**), a possessive, or a demonstrative.

¡OJO!

In English, the definite article is omitted with the verb *like.* The definite article is *never* omitted with **gustar** unless another determiner is used.

Me gusta **el** chocolate. Me gustan **los** dulces.
I like chocolate. I like sweets.

Me gustan **muchas** canciones de Shakira.
I like many of Shakira's songs.

Me gustan **tus** sugerencias, pero no me gusta **ese** tipo de vacaciones.
I like your suggestions, but I don't like that type of vacation.

Would Like / Wouldn't Like = Gustaría

To express what you *would* or *would not* like to do, use **gustaría** + *infinitive* with the appropriate indirect objects.

A mí me gustaría viajar a Colombia.
I would like to travel to Colombia.

No nos gustaría hacer camping este verano.
We would not like to go camping this summer.

Práctica y comunicación

A. Los gustos y preferencias para las vacaciones

Paso 1. Autoprueba. Complete las siguientes oraciones con **-a** or **-an.**

1. Me gust_____ nadar.
2. Por eso me gust_____ las playas caribeñas.
3. A mi familia y a mí nos gust_____ esquiar.
4. Por eso nos gust_____ las vacaciones de invierno.
5. A mi mejor amigo le gust_____ el sol.
6. Por eso siempre le gust_____ la República Dominicana para las vacaciones.
7. ¿A ti te gust_____ las vacaciones activas o relajantes (*relaxing*)?

Paso 2. Use las siguientes frases en oraciones completas para expresar sus gustos.

MODELOS: ¿viajar? —→ (No) Me **gusta** viajar.
¿los aviones? —→ (No) Me **gustan** los aviones.

1. ¿viajar?
2. ¿los viajes con mi familia?
3. ¿los vuelos?
4. ¿el calor?
5. ¿el invierno?
6. ¿las playas caribeñas?
7. ¿los aeropuertos?
8. ¿viajar en coche?

Paso 3. Ahora, en parejas, túrnense para entrevistarse sobre las ideas del **Paso 2.** Luego díganle al resto de la clase algo que Uds. tienen en común.

MODELO: **E1:** A mí me gusta viajar. ¿Y a ti?
E2: A mí también. —→
A nosotros nos gusta viajar.

B. ¿Cómo van a organizar las vacaciones los Soto?

Paso 1. Los Soto tienen gustos muy diversos: ¡a cada uno le gusta solo una cosa! Explique el gusto de cada persona con oraciones completas. Luego nombre una actividad que probablemente le gusta hacer en las vacaciones.

MODELO: 1. la madre: las novelas de Julia Álvarez —→

A la madre le gustan las novelas de Julia Álvarez. **Seguro que le gusta** leer en la playa.

1. la madre: las novelas de Julia Álvarez
2. el padre: los deportes (*sports*) acuáticos
3. los abuelos: el arte
4. Lucas: la naturaleza (*nature*)
5. Elena, la hija adolescente: la música pop
6. los mellizos (*twins*) de 11 años: jugar en la piscina

Paso 2. Ahora, en parejas, nombren un lugar al que a cada una de esas personas les gustaría ir para las vacaciones.

MODELO: A la madre le **gustaría** ir a una playa tranquila.

Paso 3. Finalmente, escojan un destino en el que (*which*) todos los miembros de la familia puedan (*can*) hacer algo que les gusta.

Prác. A, Paso 1: Answers: 1. gusta 2. gustan 3. gusta 4. gustan 5. gusta 6. gusta 7. gustan

C. ¿Conoce bien a... ?

Paso 1. ¿Cree Ud. que conoce bien a su profesor(a) de español? Haga oraciones completas para decir si a él/ella le gustan o no las siguientes cosas.

MODELO: **1.** la música clásica →
(No) Le gusta la música clásica.

1. la música clásica
2. bailar salsa
3. los niños pequeños
4. las canciones de los años 80
5. viajar
6. los destinos exóticos
7. el arte surrealista
8. ¿ ?

Paso 2. Ahora entreviste a su profesor(a) para saber si le gustan las cosas del **Paso 1** o no.

MODELOS: ¿A Ud. le gusta la música clásica?
A Ud. le gusta la música clásica, ¿verdad?

Paso 3. Ahora entreviste a un compañero o una compañera sobre las mismas cosas.

MODELO: **E1:** ¿Te gusta la música clásica?
E2: Sí. ¿Y a ti?

D. Perfiles personales. En parejas, inventen con detalles las preferencias de las siguientes personas.

> ### Vocabulario **útil**
>
> la música *rap*, *hip hop*
> **ju**gar (**jue**go) (**gu**) a los videojuegos
> **patinar en monopatín** to skateboard

1. Toño

2. los Sres. Sánchez

3. Memo

Nota **comunicativa**

Otras maneras de expresar los gustos y preferencias

Here are some ways to express intense likes and dislikes.

INTENSE LIKES

- **mucho/muchísimo** (with **gustar**)

  Me gusta **mucho/muchísimo**.   *I like it a lot / a whole lot.*

- **encantar** (*like* **gustar**), **interesar** (*like* **gustar**)

  Me encantan las películas extranjeras.   *I love foreign films.*

  Me interesa aprender otras lenguas.   *I'm interested in learning other languages.*

> Verbs that are used like **gustar** will be noted in vocabulary lists with the parenthetical note (like **gustar**).

INTENSE DISLIKES

- **no... (para) nada** (with **gustar**)

  No me gusta **(para) nada** la comida japonesa. *I don't like Japanese food at all.*

- **odiar**

  Unlike **encantar** and **interesar,** which are used like **gustar, odiar** is conjugated like regular **-ar** verbs. It is a transitive verb, that is, a verb that can take a direct object.

  Odio los champiñones.   *I hate mushrooms.*

  Mi madre **odia** viajar sola.   *My mother hates traveling alone.*

Use as many of these verbs and expressions as you can in **Práctica E**.

E. Intercambios. En parejas, túrnense para describir lo que les gusta y lo que odian cuando están en las siguientes situaciones. Inventen los detalles necesarios.

MODELO: en la playa → Cuando estoy en la playa, me encanta nadar en el mar, pero no me gusta el sol ni me gusta la arena (*sand*). Por eso odio pasar todo el día en la playa. Prefiero nadar en una piscina.

> **Situaciones**
>
> | | |
> |---|---|
> | en un autobús | en el salón de clase |
> | en un avión | en el coche |
> | en la biblioteca | en una discoteca |
> | en una cafetería | en una fiesta |
> | en casa con mis amigos | en un parque |
> | en casa con mis padres/hijos | en la playa |
> | en un centro comercial | en un tren |

¿Recuerda Ud.?

You have already learned one of the irregular past tense verb forms that is presented in **Gramática 23**. Review it now by telling what day yesterday was: **Ayer...**

23 Talking About the Past (Part 1)

Preterite of Regular Verbs and of **dar, hacer, ir,** and **ser**

Gramática en acción: Un viaje a la República Dominicana

Elisa es reportera. Hace poco, fue a la República Dominicana para escribir un artículo sobre la isla de La Española. Habla Elisa.

- Hice el viaje en avión.
- El vuelo fue largo porque el avión hizo escala en Miami.
- Pasé una semana entera en la Isla.
- Visité muchos sitios de interés turístico e histórico.
- Comí mucha comida típica del Caribe.
- Tomé el sol, nadé en el mar y escribí muchas tarjetas postales.
- ¡Lo pasé muy bien!

Comprensión

¿Cierto o falso? Corrija las oraciones falsas.

	CIERTO	FALSO
1. Elisa fue a la República Dominicana para pasar sus vacaciones.	☐	☐
2. El avión hizo escala en los Estados Unidos.	☐	☐
3. Elisa no visitó ningún lugar importante de la Isla.	☐	☐
4. No lo pasó bien en la playa.	☐	☐

So far, you have almost always talked in the present tense. In this section, you will use forms of the preterite, one of the past tenses in Spanish.

To talk about the past in Spanish, there are two simple tenses:* the preterite and the imperfect. In this chapter, you will learn the regular forms of the preterite and those of four irregular verbs: **dar, hacer, ir,** and **ser.** Then in **Capítulos 9, 10,** and **11,** you will learn more about both tenses.

Preterite: Regular Verbs / El pretérito: Los verbos regulares

-*ar* Verbs		-*er/-ir* Verbs			
hablar		**comer**		**vivir**	
hablé	I spoke (did speak)	comí	I ate (did eat)	viví	I lived (did live)
hablaste	you spoke	comiste	you ate	viviste	you lived
habló	you/he/she spoke	comió	you/he/she ate	vivió	you/he/she lived
hablamos	we spoke	comimos	we ate	vivimos	we lived
hablasteis	you spoke	comisteis	you ate	vivisteis	you lived
hablaron	you/they spoke	comieron	you/they ate	vivieron	you/they lived

---

A trip to the Dominican Republic *Elisa is a reporter. A little while ago, she went to the Dominican Republic to write an article about the island of Hispaniola. Here's Elisa.* ■ *I made the trip by plane.* ■ *The flight was long because the plane made a stop in Miami.* ■ *I spent a whole week on the Island.* ■ *I visited a lot of interesting tourist and historical sites.* ■ *I ate a lot of typical Caribbean food.* ■ *I sunbathed, swam in the ocean, and wrote a lot of postcards.* ■ *I had a really good time!*

*Simple tenses are those formed without an auxiliary or "helping" verb. Examples of simple tenses in English: I ate, I saw. Examples of tenses with an auxiliary: I have eaten, I have seen.

1. Uses of the Preterite

As you saw in the chart on p. 251, the *preterite* (**el pretérito**) has several English equivalents.

The preterite is used to report finished, completed actions or states of being in the past. If the action or state of being is viewed as completed—no matter how long it lasted or took to complete—it will be expressed with the preterite. A two-month period is specified in the first example sentence; that period is over. No time span is specified in the second sentence, but the action is clearly over since it took place *last summer.*

hablé = I spoke, I did speak

Pasé dos meses en el Caribe.
I spent two months in the Caribbean.

El verano pasado **hicimos** camping en Puerto Rico.
Last summer we went camping in Puerto Rico.

2. *Nosotros* forms

Note that the **nosotros** forms of regular preterites for **-ar** and **-ir** verbs are the same as the present tense forms. Context usually helps determine meaning. If the translation were not available, what words would tell you that the first **hablamos** means *we spoke* and the second one *we're speaking*?

Ayer **hablamos** del viaje con nuestros amigos. Hoy, más tarde, **hablamos** con el agente de viajes a las dos de la tarde.
Yesterday we spoke about the trip with our friends. Today, later on, we'll speak with the travel agent at 2:00 P.M.

3. Accent Marks

Note the accent marks on the first and third person singular of the preterite tense. These accent marks are not used in the conjugation of **ver: vi, vio.**

bailé, bailó

bebí, bebió

asistí, asistió

but

vi, vio

4. Verbs ending in *-car*, *-gar*, and *-zar*

These verbs show a spelling change in the first person singular (**yo**) of the preterite. This is the same change you have already learned to make in formal commands, **Gramática 20 (Cap. 7).**

-car → qu buscar	busqué	buscamos
	buscaste	buscasteis
	buscó	buscaron
-gar → gu pagar	pagué	pagamos
	pagaste	pagasteis
	pagó	pagaron
-zar → c empezar	empecé	empezamos
	empezaste	empezasteis
	empezó	empezaron

5. Unstressed *-i-*

An unstressed **-i-** between two vowels becomes **-y-.** Also, note the accent on the **í** in the **tú, nosotros,** and **vosotros** forms.

creer		leer	
creí	creímos	leí	leímos
creíste	creísteis	leíste	leísteis
creyó	creyeron	leyó	leyeron

6. *-ar* and *-er* Stem-changing Verbs

Stem-changing verbs that end in **-ar** and **-er** are completely regular in the preterite. However, the preterite of **-ir** stem-changing verbs is not regular. You will learn the preterite of those verbs in **Gramática 25 (Cap. 9).**

despertar (despierto): desperté, despertaste,...
volver (vuelvo): volví, volviste,...

Irregular Forms / Las formas irregulares

1. Dar

The preterite endings for **dar** are the same as those used for regular **-er/-ir** verbs, except that the accent marks are dropped.

dar	
di	dimos
diste	disteis
dio	dieron

2. Hacer

All forms of **hacer** are irregular in the preterite, especially the third person singular, **hizo,** which is spelled with a **z** rather than a **c** to keep the [s] sound of the infinitive.

hacer	
hice	hicimos
hiciste	hicisteis
hizo	hicieron

3. Ir and ser

These verbs have identical forms in the preterite. Context will make the meaning clear. For example, in the first sentence to the right, the word **a** is a clue that **Fui** means *I went*, since forms of the verb **ir** are often followed by **a**. In the second sentence, **Fui** is followed directly by a noun; forms of **ir**/*to go* are never *directly* followed by a noun, so **fui** must mean *I was*.

ir/ser	
fui	fuimos
fuiste	fuisteis
fue	fueron

Fui a la playa el verano pasado.
I went to the beach last summer.

Fui agente de viajes.
I was a travel agent.

Práctica y comunicación

A. El verano pasado

Paso 1. Autoprueba. Dé la forma apropiada del pretérito para cada sujeto.

1. **tú:** comprar, ir, acostarse, beber, hacer
2. **Ud.:** comprender, empezar, creer, afeitarse, dar
3. **nosotros:** hacer, ser, ir, pagar, leer
4. **ellas:** asistir, volver, terminar, despertarse, salir

Paso 2. Complete las siguientes oraciones sobre el verano pasado con las terminaciones apropiadas de la primera persona singular (**yo**). Si es necesario, use **no** para hacer oraciones que son ciertas para Ud.

El verano pasado...

1. tom_____ clases en la universidad.
2. asist_____ a un concierto en otra ciudad.
3. trabaj_____ mucho y gan_____ mucho dinero. (**ganar** = to earn)
4. hi_____ *camping* con unos amigos.
5. viv_____ todo el tiempo con mi familia.
6. me qued_____ trabajando y estudiando en la universidad.
7. fu_____ a la playa.
8. me levant_____ tarde casi todos los días.

Paso 3. Ahora, en parejas, túrnense para entrevistarse sobre las ideas del **Paso 2.** Luego díganle a la clase dos cosas que Uds. tienen en común.

MODELO: tomé clases en la universidad. →
　　　　E1: El verano pasado, ¿**tomaste** alguna clase en la universidad?
　　　　E2: No, ¿y tú?
　　　　E1: Yo tampoco. →

Nosotros no **tomamos** ninguna clase el verano pasado.

B. El viernes pasado por la tarde

Paso 1. Narre la secuencia de las acciones que hizo Julio el viernes pasado por la tarde. ¡OJO! **Julio** es el sujeto de muchas oraciones, pero no de todas. A veces el sujeto es **ellos** (Julio y su amigo Roberto).

El viernes por la tarde, Julio...

1. volver a casa después de trabajar todo el día

2. llamar a su amigo Roberto y los dos: decidir ir al cine juntos

3. ducharse y afeitarse

4. salir de casa rápidamente e ir al cine en autobús

5. los dos: hacer cola para comprar las entradas y comprar palomitas (*popcorn*)

6. entrar en la sala y sentarse

7. ver la película pero no gustarles nada

8. ir a un restaurante a cenar y quedarse conversando hasta muy tarde

Paso 2. Comprensión. ¿Cierto, falso o no lo dice?

	CIERTO	FALSO	NO LO DICE
1. El amigo de Julio se llama Roberto.	☐	☐	☐
2. Son compañeros de clase.	☐	☐	☐
3. A los dos amigos les interesa el cine.	☐	☐	☐
4. Vieron una película extranjera.	☐	☐	☐
5. Odiaron la película.	☐	☐	☐
6. Comieron después de la película.	☐	☐	☐
7. Julio regresó a casa en autobús.	☐	☐	☐

Paso 3. Ahora, en parejas, vuelvan a contar la historia, usando las siguientes palabras en su narrativa: **primero, segundo** (*second*), **después, luego, finalmente.**

Algo sobre...

las hermanas Mirabal

Un billete^a de 200 pesos dominicanos con fotos de las hermanas Mirabal

Patria (1924–1960), Minerva (1926–1960) y María Teresa (1935–1960) Mirabal son heroínas dominicanas que

lucharon contra la terrible dictadura^b de Rafael Trujillo. (Se conocen también como las Mariposas.^c) Las tres fueron brutalmente asesinadas por orden del dictador. La hermana sobreviviente,^d Dedé, dedicó el resto de su vida a preservar la memoria de sus hermanas. Ahora hay una provincia dominicana con el nombre de Hermanas Mirabal. Las Mariposas también aparecen^e en los billetes de 200 pesos dominicanos.

La Asamblea General de las Naciones Unidas designó el día de la muerte^f de las Mirabal como el Día Internacional de la No Violencia Contra la Mujer.

¿Cuáles son algunos de los héroes y heroínas nacionales más importantes de su país? ¿Por qué son importantes?

^abill ^bdictatorship ^cButterflies ^dsurviving ^eappear ^fdeath

C. El día de ayer de dos compañeras

Paso 1. Teresa y Liliana son compañeras de apartamento en la universidad. Haga oraciones completas según el modelo para describir su día.

MODELO: 7:30 **levantarse** → **Se levantó a** las siete y media.

TERESA
1. 8:00 ducharse y desayunar
2. 9:00 salir de casa / ir a la universidad
3. 10:00 estudiar toda la mañana
4. 12:00 almorzar con unos compañeros de la universidad
5. 1:00 hacer experimentos en el laboratorio de química
6. 3:15 volver a casa

LILIANA
7. 9:45 despertarse, pero no levantarse pronto
8. 10:30 desayunar y empezar a hacer la tarea de matemáticas
9. 12:30 terminarla y ver la tele
10. 2:00 empezar a hacer un pastel para el cumpleaños de Miriam
11. 2:30 mandar unos e-mails.
12. 4:30 terminar el pastel / decorarlo

TERESA Y LILIANA
13. 5:00 ir al gimnasio cerca de su apartamento / allí hacer ejercicio por una hora
14. 6:30 volver a casa / ducharse y hablar de la fiesta de Miriam
15. 9:30 ir a casa de Miriam / cantarle «Cumpleaños feliz» / darle su regalo y comer el pastel

¿Quién es, Teresa o Liliana? ¿Cómo lo sabe?

Paso 2. En parejas, túrnense para hacer y contestar preguntas basadas en las oraciones del **Paso 1**.

MODELO: E1: ¿**Te duchaste** a las ocho, como Teresa?
E2: No, **me duché** por la noche. ¿Y tú?
E1: No **me duché**. Me bañé.

D. **Un semestre en la República Dominicana.** Cuente la siguiente historia desde el punto de vista de la persona indicada, usando el pretérito de los verbos.

MODELO: *yo:* viajar a la República Dominicana el año pasado →
Viajé a la República Dominicana el año pasado.

1. *yo:* pasar todo el semestre en Santo Domingo
2. mis padres: pagarme el vuelo
3. *yo:* trabajar para ganar el dinero para los otros gastos (*expenses*)
4. vivir con una familia dominicana
5. aprender mucho sobre la la cultura dominicana
6. visitar muchos sitios de interés turístico e histórico
7. mis amigos: escribirme con frecuencia
8. *yo:* mandarles muchas tarjetas postales
9. comprarles recuerdos (*souvenirs*) a todos
10. volver a Denver a fines de agosto

E. **La última (*last*) vez**

Paso 1. Conteste las siguientes preguntas. Añada más detalles si puede.

MODELO: La última vez que Ud. fue a una fiesta, ¿le llevó un regalo al anfitrión / a la anfitriona (*host/hostess*)? →
Sí, **le** llevé flores / una botella de vino. (No, no **le** llevé nada.)

La última vez que Ud....

1. hizo un viaje, ¿le mandó una tarjeta postal a algún amigo o amiga?
2. tomó el autobús/metro, ¿le ofreció su asiento a una persona mayor?
3. vio a su profesor(a) de español en público, ¿le habló en español?
4. comió en un restaurante, ¿le recomendó algún plato a su compañero/a?

5. entró en un edificio, ¿le abrió la puerta a otra persona?
6. voló en avión, ¿le pidió algo a uno de los asistentes de vuelo?
7. le regaló algo a alguien, ¿le gustó el regalo a la persona?
8. le prometió a alguien hacer algo, ¿lo hizo?
9. se quejó de algo, ¿a quién habló?

Paso 2. Ahora, en parejas, túrnense para hacer y contestar preguntas basadas en las oraciones del **Paso 1.**

Paso 3. Ahora díganle a la clase dos cosas interesantes sobre su compañero/a.

F. **Intercambios**

Paso 1. Escriba una lista de diez de las acciones que Ud. hizo ayer. Use los siguientes verbos y añada cuatro más de su preferencia. Haga oraciones completas.

MODELO: levantarse → Ayer **me levanté** a las seis de la mañana.

1. levantarse	4. dar	7. ¿ ?	9. ¿ ?
2. empezar	5. hacer	8. ¿ ?	10. ¿ ?
3. leer	6. ir		

Paso 2. En parejas, túrnense para entrevistarse sobre las acciones de su lista del **Paso 1.**

MODELO: E1: Ayer **me levanté** a las seis de la mañana. ¿A qué hora **te levantaste tú**?
E2: **Me levanté** a las diez.

Paso 3. Ahora díganle a la clase en qué acciones los dos coincidieron ayer.

G. **Más intercambios**

Paso 1. En parejas, túrnense para entrevistarse sobre su último viaje. Deben obtener información relacionada con las siguientes preguntas.

1. ¿cuándo?
2. ¿adónde?
3. ¿en qué medio de transporte?
4. ¿cuántos días?
5. ¿con quién?

Paso 2. Ahora díganle a la clase los detalles esenciales del viaje de su compañero/a.

MODELO: Susie fue a Puerto Rico el verano pasado. Hizo el viaje en avión. Se quedó en Puerto Rico una semana. Viajó con su novio y su familia.

Un poco de todo

A. Lengua y cultura: Mi abuela dominicana

Paso 1. Complete the following paragraphs with the correct form of the words in parentheses, as suggested by context. When two possibilities are given in parentheses, select the correct word. **¡OJO!** The verbs in the paragraphs will be present tense or preterite; the context will indicate which tense to use.

Ayer llegó de visita mi abuela Manuela. Ella vive en Santo Domingo, con mi tía Zaira, la (hermana / sobrina[1]) de mi mamá. (*Nosotros:* Ir[2]) a recibir(la / le[3]) al aeropuerto y nos (*ella:* dar[4]) un abrazo[a] muy fuerte. (Mi / Mí[5]) abuela va a (a / de[6]) pasar dos meses con nosotros en Connecticut, y luego (ir[7]) a quedarse un mes con el tío Julián en Nueva York. Así es la vida[b] de muchas abuelas con hijos en otro país.

A mi abuela le (gusta / gustaría[8]) tener a todos sus hijos y (nietos / sobrinos[9]) en Santo Domingo y siempre (ser / estar[10]) muy triste cuando (volver[11]) a la República Dominicana (antes de / después de[12]) visitarnos. Pero también (le / la[13]) gusta mucho la vida en los Estados Unidos. (*Ella:* Decir[14]) que aquí se vive muy bien y que las casas (ser / estar[15]) muy buenas. (El / La[16]) problema es que no le (gustan / gustarían[17]) los inviernos de (este / esto[18]) país. ¡Es lógico! A ella le (gusta / gustan[19]) las playas y las palmeras, porque es lo que (conoce / sabe[20]) bien.

Cuando mi abuela regresa a Santo Domingo, (les / los[21]) mandamos con ella muchos regalos a nuestros (padres / parientes[22]). Casi todos los años mi familia (viaje / viaja[23]) a la República Dominicana, porque mis padres (vivir[24]) allá hasta que (ir[25]) a estudiar a la Universidad de Massachusetts. ¡(A / —[26]) mí me encanta ir de vacaciones a la República Dominicana!

[a]*hug* [b]**Así...** *Such is the life*

Una abuela con su hija y su nieta

Paso 2. Comprensión. Conteste las siguientes preguntas.

1. ¿Quién habla en la narración? ¿Se sabe si es hombre o mujer?
2. ¿Dónde vive la tía Zaira?
3. ¿Qué le gusta de la vida en los Estados Unidos a la abuela?
4. ¿Qué no le gusta?
5. ¿Cuándo emigraron a los Estados Unidos los padres del narrador / de la narradora?

Paso 3. La gran mayoría de estadounidenses es descendiente de inmigrantes; muchos son inmigrantes recientes. En parejas, túrnense para saber algo de la historia de la familia de su compañero/a, haciéndole las siguientes preguntas.

1. ¿Tienes un pariente que nació (*was born*) en otro país? ¿Quién(es)?
2. ¿Cuándo llegó a los Estados Unidos?
3. ¿Vino solo/a? ¿A quién(es) dejó (*did he/she leave behind*) en su país de origen?
4. Si ese pariente vive todavía, ¿visita a veces su país de origen? Si ya murió (*he/she is already deceased*), ¿volvió a visitar su país de origen antes de morir (*die*)? ¿Cuántas veces fue?

B. Humor viajero. En parejas, lean el dibujo y contesten las preguntas.

HUMOR VIAJERO

-¿Y cómo pasó...?
-No sé... Te juro que no lo vi venir.

David Sebastián Ojeda, Pasaje Blanco 1662, Morón, prov. de Buenos Aires, tel. 4697-6858; artepiero@hotmail.com

¿El piloto o Superhombre? ¿Quién...

1. no vio el avión?
2. no vio a Superhombre?
3. sufrió un accidente?
4. juró (*swore*) algo?
5. no llegó a su destino?
6. va a ir al hospital?
7. hizo un informe (*report*) sobre el accidente?

En **su** comunidad

Entreviste a una persona hispana de su universidad o ciudad sobre sus últimas (*last*) vacaciones y los lugares más populares de su país para ir de vacaciones.

PREGUNTAS POSIBLES

- ¿Cuándo fue de vacaciones a su país la última vez? ¿Con quién fue? ¿Cuánto tiempo pasó allá? ¿Se quedó en casa de su familia o en un hotel? ¿Con cuánta frecuencia va de vacaciones a su país?

- ¿Cuáles son los lugares de vacaciones más famosos de su país? ¿Los visitan solo los turistas extranjeros o los nacionales también? ¿Cuál es su lugar favorito? ¿Por qué?

 **«¡De viaje!» Segmento 2**

Antes de mirar

¿Le gustaría visitar el Perú? ¿Por qué? ¿Qué sabe del país?

Este segmento

Este segmento muestra otro video filmado por un telespectador de *Salu2*. Este turista hizo un viaje inolvidable (*unforgettable*) al Perú.

«Primero estuvimos (*we were*) varios días en Cusco, la antigua capital del Imperio inca. Está a más de 3.000 metros de altitud, y esta altitud puede provocar malestar (*discomfort*) físico. ¡Pero el malestar no es nada comparado a la belleza (*beauty*) de la ciudad!»

Vocabulario **del segmento**

con razón	rightly so	**el fuerte**	fort
la piedra	stone	**al final**	at the end
rodeado/a de	surrounded by	**la fuente**	fountain
permanecer	to remain	**el espectáculo**	show
oculto/a	hidden	**no dejen de**	don't miss out
descubrir	to discover	**visitar**	on visiting

Fragmento del guion

De Cusco nos fuimos al Valle Sagrado[a] de los Incas para visitar un santuario de llamas. Estuvimos[b] con personas de esta comunidad mientras hacían tejidos tradicionales.[c] Es un arte que ha pasado[d] de generación en generación y un gran ejemplo de la hermosa[e] artesanía peruana. Pero lo mejor[f] del viaje fue Machu Picchu, considerada una de las siete maravillas del mundo actual.[g]

[a]Valle... *Sacred Valley* [b]*We were* [c]mientras... *while they made traditional weavings* [d]ha... *has been passed down* [e]*beautiful* [f]lo... *the best part* [g]*modern*

Después de mirar

A. ¿Está claro? Ponga los lugares que visitó el turista en el orden de su visita. Luego empareje cada lugar con las frases del video.

LUGARES

1. _____ Machu Picchu
2. _____ Cusco
3. _____ Lima
4. _____ el Valle Sagrado de los Incas

FRASES DEL VIDEO

a. «la ciudad más visitada de todo Perú»
b. «el nuevo Parque de las Fuentes»
c. «un santuario de llamas»
d. «una de las siete maravillas del mundo actual»

B. Un poco más. Conteste las siguientes preguntas.

1. ¿Por qué se puede sentir (*feel*) malestar físico en Cusco?
2. ¿Qué tipo de artesanía hacen en el Valle Sagrado de los Incas?
3. ¿Por qué es misterioso Machu Picchu?

C. Y ahora, Uds. En parejas, preparen un resumen de este segmento de *Salu2*, contando lo que hizo este turista e incluyendo algo interesante que vio o aprendió en cada sitio. También deben decir lo que más le gusto a él.

MODELO: Primero fue a la ciudad de Cusco. Allí...

A LEER

¿Es el turismo un sector económico muy importante en su ciudad o estado?

Lectura cultural: La República Dominicana

El turismo en la República Dominicana

El turismo es el sector económico más importante de la República Dominicana. Es un país que ofrece lugares de interés para cualquier[a] visitante: bosques,[b] parques nacionales, ríos, lagos, playas, ciudades y zonas rurales. Uno de los destinos turísticos más populares es Punta Cana, al este del país. Allí se puede disfrutar de[c] un clima tropical y de bellas[d] playas de arena[e] blanca y fina. Santo Domingo, la capital del país, tiene una hermosa[f] zona colonial con museos, casas antiguas y otros monumentos históricos. En 1990, fue reconocida[g] como Patrimonio Cultural de la Humanidad[h] por la UNESCO.

[a]any [b]forests [c]disfrutar... enjoy [d]beautiful [e]sand [f]beautiful [g]recognized [h]Patrimonio... World Cultural Heritage site

En otros países hispanos

- **En todo el mundo hispanohablante** En muchos países hispanos, y no solo en los países tropicales, hay playas maravillosas.[a] El Uruguay, la Argentina y Chile tienen costas fabulosas sin estar en el trópico.

- **En España** La industria del turismo es un importante motor[b] de la economía española. España es el cuarto[c] país del mundo receptor de turistas extranjeros, después de China, Francia y los Estados Unidos.

- **En los Estados Unidos** Gran parte del actual[d] territorio estadounidense fue antes territorio español. Así que podría[e] visitar lugares históricos en Florida, Texas, California, etcétera, para saber de la historia del mundo hispano... ¡sin salir de este país!

[a]wonderful [b]engine [c]fourth [d]present-day [e]Así... So you could

Un grupo de merengueros dominicanos

COMPRENSIÓN

1. ¿Cuáles son dos de los lugares turísticos importantes en la República Dominicana?
2. ¿Qué país hispanohablante está muy alto en la lista de países receptores de turistas?
3. ¿Por qué se puede decir que en los Estados Unidos es muy importante la presencia histórica de los países hispanos?
4. ¿En qué países hispanos no tropicales hay playas fabulosas?
5. ¿Qué es el merengue?

Un símbolo dominicano: El merengue

El merengue es un tipo de música de origen dominicano. Sin embargo, se conoce y se baila en todo el mundo hispano. Empezó a tocarse[a] con instrumentos de cuerda,[b] pero se incorporó el acordeón (de influencia europea), el güiro[c] (de origen taíno) y la tambora[d] (de origen africano). Hoy se incluyen el piano y los instrumentos de viento.

[a]Empezó... It was first played [b]string [c]percussion instrument made of the gourd of the calabash tree [d]bass drum

Y ahora, Uds.

Escojan un destino turístico en los Estados Unidos o en su país de origen e indiquen todas las razones para visitarlo, incluyendo el clima y un poco de su historia.

Del mundo hispano

Antes de leer

En la **Nota cultural** (pág. 237) de este capítulo se describen varios tipos de turismo, incluyendo el aventurismo. ¿A Ud. le interesa esta forma de turismo? ¿Por qué? En su opinión, ¿cómo son las personas que practican este estilo de viajar? ¿Conoce a algunos «aventuristas»?

Lectura: I love viajes

Norte de África en 4x4[a]
Explora el Marruecos[b] más desconocido[c] y aventúrate[d] en 4x4 entre las dunas del Sahara. Descubre oasis perdidos[e] en lo más profundo[f] del desierto y disfruta de una flora que no esperarías[g] encontrar en estas latitudes. ¡Pon rumbo a[h] la aventura!

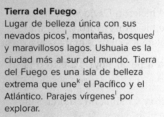

Tierra del Fuego
Lugar de belleza única con sus nevados picos[i], montañas, bosques[j] y maravillosos lagos. Ushuaia es la ciudad más al sur del mundo. Tierra del Fuego es una isla de belleza extrema que une[k] el Pacífico y el Atlántico. Parajes vírgenes[l] por explorar.

Safari por África
El espectacular parque natural del delta del Okavango (Botsuana) es una gran concentración de animales salvajes. Visita las Cataratas[m] Victoria (en Zimbabue) donde observarás[n] la cortina[o] de agua más caudalosa[p] del mundo. ¡Refréscate![q]

[a]four-wheel drive [b]Morocco [c]unknown [d]venture out, go exploring [e]lost [f]lo... the deepest part [g]no... you wouldn't expect [h]¡Pon... Get ready for [i]nevados... snowy peaks [j]forests [k]conecta [l]Parajes... Virgin expanses, territories [m]Falls [n]vas a observar [o]curtain [p]más... fastest flowing [q]Cool off!

Comprensión

A. ¡Sea agente de viajes! ¿Adónde deben ir de viaje las siguientes personas? Dé una recomendación lógica para cada caso, explicando por qué hace esa sugerencia. Use **Le recomiendo...** o **Les recomiendo...** , según el caso.

> MODELO: **El profesor Legrán:** «Tengo todo el verano para viajar. Quiero escaparme del calor de Nuevo México en el verano y visitar lugares remotos.» → Le recomiendo la Tierra del Fuego, porque allí no hace calor y está en el extremo sur de Sudamérica. Hay montañas, lagos y bosques allí. También hay una ciudad interesante.

1. Los Sres. Ávila: «Queremos viajar a un lugar cálido (*warm*) y seco (*dry*) durante el invierno.»

2. El Sr. Sorkin: «A mí me gusta observar los animales, pero solo los he visto (*I've seen*) en mi estado. Este año quiero ver animales exóticos en un lugar diferente.»

3. Alejandra: «Conozco Norteamérica, Europa y África. Para mis próximas vacaciones, quiero visitar un continente totalmente nuevo para mí.»

4. Jorge y Jimena: «Somos ecologistas, especialistas en la flora tropical. Pero para estas vacaciones queremos algo diferente.»

B. Preferencias personales. En parejas, hagan y contesten las siguientes preguntas sobre los destinos turísticos que Uds. prefieren y conocen.

1. De los tres destinos que sugiere (*suggests*) la lectura, ¿cuál es el más atractivo para ti? ¿Por qué? ¿Cuál es la mejor estación del año para visitar ese lugar? ¿Por qué?

2. ¿Hay algún lugar de los tres destinos que no te gustaría visitar? ¿Por qué?

3. ¿Qué otros lugares conoces o puedes nombrar donde se pueda (*one can*) hacer el mismo tipo de turismo de los destinos mencionados en los anuncios?

Antes de escuchar

Por lo general, ¿qué hace Ud. en su tiempo libre (*free time*)? ¿Qué actividades le gusta hacer cuando va a la playa? ¿y cuando va al centro de su ciudad?

Vocabulario para escuchar

¡No me digas que... !	Don't tell me that . . . !
apagado/a	turned off
¿De veras?	Really?
corriendo	running (in a hurry)

Después de escuchar

A. **¿Qué pasó ayer?** Conteste las siguientes preguntas según la conversación telefónica para decir lo que hicieron ayer unos amigos dominicanos.

    1. ¿Qué hicieron David y Paula?
    2. ¿Qué hicieron Arturo y Cristina?
    3. ¿Cuál de los cuatros amigos hizo la actividad más relajada (*relaxing*)?

B. **¿Qué va a pasar hoy?** ¿Cierto o falso? Corrija las oraciones falsas.

	CIERTO	FALSO
1. Arturo y Cristina no quieren salir con David y Paula.	☐	☐
2. Hace viento hoy.	☐	☐
3. Van a la playa en coche.	☐	☐
4. No van a llevar nada de comer.	☐	☐

PRODUCCIÓN PERSONAL

¡Ahora, yo!

A. Use de modelo las preguntas y respuestas de la página 233 de este capítulo para hablar de sus vacaciones favoritas.

B. Haga un fotomontaje con voz en off (*voiceover*) sobre un destino turístico. Puede ser un destino que Ud. ya conoce o uno que le gustaría visitar.

A ESCRIBIR

Un ensayo sobre el verano pasado

¿Qué hizo Ud. el verano pasado? ¿Tomó vacaciones o solo trabajó?

Preparar

Paso 1. En parejas, hagan una lista de las preguntas básicas que se pueden hacer para hablar de lo que hicieron el verano pasado.

Paso 2. Ahora usen esas preguntas para entrevistarse mutuamente, buscando detalles interesantes, como por ejemplo, lo que más les gustó del verano y lo que menos les gustó.

Paso 3. Con esa información, escriba un ensayo individual sobre cómo pasaron el verano. Hay más ayuda en Connect.

Más ideas para su portafolio

- Haga una lista de seis palabras que Ud. asocia con la palabra **vacaciones**.
- Incluya una imagen de unas vacaciones memorables, explicando qué hizo durante ese tiempo.
- Ponga la foto de un lugar que le gustaría conocer y diga qué cosas se ven y se hacen allí típicamente.
- Si ha estado jugando (*have been playing*) Practice Spanish: Study Abroad, en Quest 5 Ud. fue a un mercado al aire libre en Colombia y tuvo que regatear (*had to haggle*). En parejas, conversen sobre la costumbre de regatear. ¿Dónde se hace típicamente? ¿Es aceptable regatear en el país donde viven Uds.? ¿En qué situaciones es regatear aceptable (o incluso esperado)? Luego, hagan una lista de instrucciones para una persona que quiera aprender a regatear.

Sugerencia: You are now ready to play Quest 5 in **Practice Spanish: Study Abroad** (www.mhpractice.com).

ILEARNSMART

Visit **www.connectspanish.com** to practice the vocabulary and grammar points covered in this chapter.

AFTER STUDYING THIS CHAPTER I CAN. . .

☐ talk about travel, transportation, and vacations (234–236)

☐ understand and use pronouns to explain *to* or *for who(m)* an action is done (241–243)

☐ use **gustar** and other verbs to talk about likes and dislikes in more detail (246–247)

☐ talk about actions in the past with many types of verbs (251–253)

☐ recognize/describe at least 2–3 aspects of Dominican culture

Gramática en breve

21. Indirect Object Pronouns; *Dar* and *decir*

me, te, le, nos, os, les

dar: **doy, das, da, damos, dais, dan**
decir: **digo, dices, dice, decimos, decís, dicen**

22. *Gustar*

(no) *indirect object pronoun* + **gusta** + *singular subject*
(no) *indirect object pronoun* + **gustan** + *plural subject*

Would like: **gustaría**

23. Preterite of Regular Verbs and of *dar, hacer, ir,* and *ser*

-ar Verbs: **-é, -aste, -ó, -amos, -asteis, -aron**
-er/-ir Verbs: **-í, -iste, -ió, -imos, -steis, -ieron**

dar: **di diste, dio, dimos, disteis, dieron**
hacer: **hice, hiciste, hizo, hicimos, hicisteis, hicieron**
ir/ser: **fui, fuiste, fue, fuimos, fuisteis, fueron**

Vocabulario

Los verbos

contar (cuento)	to tell; to narrate
dar (doy)	to give
decir (digo) (i)	to say; to tell
encantar (*like* **gustar**)	to like very much; to love
entregar (gu)	to hand in

explicar (qu)	to explain
gustar	to be pleasing
interesar (*like* **gustar**)	to interest (*someone*)
mostrar (muestro)	to show
odiar	to hate
ofrecer (ofrezco)	to offer
preguntar	to ask (*a question*)
prestar	to lend
prometer	to promise
recomendar (recomiendo)	to recommend
regalar	to give (*as a gift*)

Repaso: escribir, hablar, mandar, pedir (pido) (i), servir (sirvo) (i)

De viaje

de viaje	on a trip, traveling
la aduana	customs (*at a border*)
el aeropuerto	airport
el/la agente	agent
el asiento	seat
el/la asistente de vuelo	flight attendant
el autobús	bus
el avión	airplane
el barco	boat, ship
el billete (*Sp.*) / **el boleto** (*L.A.*)	ticket
de ida	one-way ticket
de ida y vuelta	round-trip ticket
electrónico	e-ticket
la cola	line (*of people*)
el control de seguridad	security (check)
el crucero	cruise (ship)
la demora	delay
el destino	destination
el equipaje	baggage, luggage
la escala	stop
la estación	station
de autobuses	bus station
de trenes	train station
la llegada	arrival
la maleta	suitcase
el maletero	porter
el medio de transporte	means of transportation
el mostrador	counter
la parada	stop
el pasaje	fare, price (*of a transportation ticket*)
el/la pasajero/a	passenger
el pasillo	aisle
la puerta de embarque	boarding gate
el puerto	port

el puesto	place (*in line*)
la sala de espera	waiting room
la sala de fumar /	smoking area
de fumadores	
la salida	departure
la tarjeta (postal)	(post)card
la tarjeta de embarque	boarding pass
la ventanilla	small window (*on a plane*)
el vuelo	flight

Cognados: el/la agente, la cabina, el pasaporte, el/la piloto, el tren

Repaso: el viaje

anunciar	to announce
bajarse (de)	to get down (from); to get off (of) (*a vehicle*)
facturar el equipaje	to check baggage
fumar	to smoke
guardar (un puesto)	to save (a place [*in line*])
hacer cola	to stand in line
hacer escala/parada	to make a stop
hacer la(s) maleta(s)	to pack one's suitcase(s)
ir al extranjero	to go abroad
ir en...	to go/travel by . . .
autobús	bus
avión	plane
barco	boat, ship
tren	train
pasar por	to go/pass through
el control de seguridad	security (check)
la aduana	customs
quejarse (de)	to complain (about)
subir (a)	to go up; to get on (*a vehicle*)
viajar	to travel
volar (vuelo) en avión	to fly, go by plane

Repaso: hacer un viaje, llegar (gu), salir

De vacaciones

de vacaciones	on vacation
el bloqueador solar	sunscreen
la camioneta	station wagon; van
el *camping*	campground
la foto(grafía)	photo(graph)
el mar	sea
la montaña	mountain
el océano	ocean
la tienda (de campaña)	tent

Repaso: la playa, el sol

estar de vacaciones	to be on vacation
hacer *camping*	to go camping
ir de vacaciones a...	to go on vacation to/in . . .
nadar	to swim
pasar las vacaciones en...	to spend one's vacation in . . .
sacar (qu) fotos	to take photos
salir de vacaciones	to leave on vacation
tomar el sol	to sunbathe
tomar unas vacaciones	to take a vacation

Otros sustantivos

el chiste	joke
la flor	flower
la gente	people
la historia	story

Los adjetivos

atrasado/a (*with* **estar**)	late
juntos/as	together

Palabras adicionales

a tiempo	on time
me gustaría (mucho)...	I would (really) like . . .
muchísimo	an awful lot
(para) nada	at all
por	through; for

Vocabulario personal

www.connectspanish.com

9

Los días festivos° Los... *Holidays*

En este capítulo

VOCABULARY
Celebrations and holidays   268
Talking about feelings and emotions   271

GRAMMAR
The preterite of more types of verbs   274, 278
Using direct and indirect object pronouns in the same sentence   282

CULTURAL FOCUS
Cuba and its cultures

El Carnaval de Santiago de Cuba, que se celebra en julio, con música, bailes y desfiles (*parades*)

CUBA

11.5 (y medio) millones de habitantes

- La isla de Cuba está a solo 150 kilómetros (90 millas) de la costa sur de Florida.

- Cuba es un destino turístico importante para europeos y canadienses.

- Es un país con una tradición musical impresionante y que también se destaca[a] en el béisbol y en la danza.

[a]se... *excels*

- ¿Cuáles son las celebraciones más importantes de su país?
- ¿Qué días celebran más Ud. y su familia? ¿Cómo los celebran Uds.?
- ¿Tuvo Ud.[a] una fiesta en su último cumpleaños? ¿Quién se la dio[b]?

[a]¿Tuvo... *Did you have* [b]se... *gave it for you*

CECILIA FIGUEROA MARTÍN CONTESTA LAS PREGUNTAS.

- En Puerto Rico celebramos las fiestas de los Estados Unidos: el Día de los Presidentes, el Cuatro de Julio, el Día de Gracias, la Navidad. Y luego hay las fiestas patronales[a] de cada ciudad.

- Para nosotros la Navidad es un día muy importante de reunión familiar. Aunque,[b] en realidad,[c] nosotros festejamos[d] en Nochebuena.[e] La familia se reúne,[f] vienen amigos, comemos, bebemos, cantamos, bailamos...

- ¡Sí! Mi marido me hizo una fiesta muy grande para mi cumpleaños. Invitó a toda la familia y a nuestros amigos. ¡Estuvimos[g] de fiesta hasta las 4 cuatro de la mañana!

[a]fiestas... *holidays of the patron saints* [b]*Although* [c]en... *actually*
[d]nosotros... *we celebrate* [e]*Christmas Eve* [f]se... *gets together* [g]*We were*

Una fiesta de cumpleaños para Javier

¡FELICITACIONES!

el anfitrión

la anfitriona

Sí, la fiesta es en casa de Javier.

Jorge

Melisa

bailar

Carmen

Pedro

los regalos

Javier

las tarjetas

el champán

las botanas / las tapas

el pastel de cumpleaños

los refrescos

las velas

20 años

Para comer y beber

las botanas (*Mex.*) / **las tapas**	appetizers

Otros sustantivos

el anfitrión / la anfitriona	host (*of an event*)
el cumpleaños	birthday
el día festivo	holiday
el invitado / la invitada	guest

Los verbos

celebrar	to celebrate
comer/beber (demasiado)	to eat/drink (too much)
cumplir años	to have a birthday
darle una fiesta (a alguien)	to give (someone) a party
divertirse (me divierto) (i)	to have a good time, enjoy oneself
faltar (a)	to be absent (from), not attend

You can hear the pronunciation of theme vocabulary words and phrases in the Connect eBook.

gastar	to spend (*money*)
hacerle una fiesta (a alguien)	to give (someone) a party; to have a party (for someone)
invitar	to invite
pasarlo bien/mal	to have a good/bad time
regalar	to give (*as a gift*)
reunirse (me reúno) con*	to get together (with)
ser + en + *place*	to take place in/at (*a place*)
¿Dónde es la fiesta?	Where is the party (at)?

Palabras adicionales

¡Felicitaciones!	Congratulations!
gracias por + *noun*	thanks for + *noun*
Gracias por el regalo.	Thanks for the present.
gracias por + *inf.*	thanks for + *verb* (*-ing*)
Gracias por invitarme.	Thanks for inviting me.

*Note the accent that occurs on **-u-** in forms of **reunirse** when the weak vowel **-u-** is stressed: **me reúno, te reúnes, se reúne, nos reunimos, os reunís, se reúnen.** This pattern is like that of stem-changing verbs (that is, the stem vowel changes when it is stressed.)

¡OJO!

Only the highlighted items are active vocabulary. Learn the Spanish names of the holidays that you need to talk about your activities and those of your family and write them in **Vocabulario personal** at the end of the chapter.

Los días festivos hispanos

el Día de los Reyes Magos	Day of the Magi (Three Kings) (Jan. 6)
la Pascua	Easter
la Pascua judía	Passover
el Día de la Raza	Columbus Day (Oct. 12)
el Día de los Muertos	Day of the Dead (Nov. 2)
el Janucá	Hanukkah
la Nochebuena	Christmas Eve
la Navidad	Christmas
la Nochevieja	New Year's Eve
la quinceañera	young woman's fifteenth birthday party

Los días festivos estadounidenses

el Día de San Patricio, el Cinco de Mayo, el Cuatro de Julio, el Día de (Acción de) Gracias

Note that **el Día de la Raza** corresponds to *Columbus Day* in the U.S. In some areas it is called *Hispanic Awareness Day*.

Algo sobre...

las parrandas cubanas

Una parranda en Remedios, Cuba

Las parrandas son grandes fiestas navideñas[a] típicas de los pueblos y ciudades de una región de la Cuba central. Las más famosas son las[b] de Remedios. La costumbre de las parrandas data del siglo XVIII.[c] Cada barrio[d] de una ciudad monta[e] una parranda y hay una competición entre los barrios para ver cuál es la mejor.[f] Estas fiestas incluyen fuegos artificiales y disfraces,[g] como las fiestas de carnaval.

¿En qué fiestas de su país hay fuegos artificiales? ¿y disfraces?

[a]*Christmas* [b]*those* [c]*data... dates back to the 18th century* [d]*neighborhood* [e]*throws, organizes* [f]*la... the best one (parranda)* [g]*fuegos... fireworks and costumes*

Así se dice

hacer una fiesta = hacer un juerga (*Sp.*), armar (un) bochinche (*Cuba*)
la quinceañera = la fiesta de quince años
el pastel = la torta, la tarta, el queque (*L.A.*)

la Pascua = la Pascua Florida
el Día de los Muertos = el Día de los Difuntos
la Navidad = las Pascuas

The figure of **Santa Claus** is a familiar one in Hispanic countries. That is what he is called in Mexico and Puerto Rico. In other parts of the Spanish-speaking world, he is more often called **Papá Noel.**

Comunicación

A. Una fiesta de cumpleaños para Javier. Conteste las siguientes preguntas sobre el dibujo de la página 268.

1. ¿Qué tipo de fiesta es? ¿Dónde es la fiesta?
2. ¿Quiénes son los anfitriones de la fiesta? ¿Quién es el invitado de honor?
3. ¿Qué hay de comer y de beber? ¿Qué hacen los invitados?
4. ¿Qué le dan los invitados a Javier, además de (*besides*) regalos?
5. ¿Quién falta a la fiesta? ¿Quién lo invita por teléfono?
6. ¿Qué le van a decir todos a Javier cuando corte (*cuts*) el pastel?
7. ¿Qué cree Ud. que Javier les va a decir a Carmen y Pedro después de la fiesta?

B. Asociaciones. ¿Qué palabras asocia Ud. con las siguientes ideas? Dé por lo menos (*at least*) dos palabras asociadas con cada idea.

1. un cumpleaños
2. una fiesta
3. los fuegos artificiales (*fireworks*)
4. un árbol (*tree*)
5. los regalos
6. una comida grande

C. Definiciones

Paso 1. Dé las palabras definidas.

1. Algo de comer o beber que se sirve en las fiestas.
2. El día en que, por tradición, algunas personas visitan los cementerios.
3. La fiesta de una muchacha que cumple 15 años.
4. Lo que uno le dice a un amigo que celebra algo.
5. Una fiesta de los judíos (*Jewish people*) que dura 8 días.

Paso 2. Ahora, en parejas, creen (*create*) por lo menos dos definiciones como las del **Paso 1.** La clase va a adivinar (*guess*) la palabra definida.

Nota **cultural**

Los días festivos importantes del mundo hispano

Algunas fiestas se celebran en casi todos los países hispanos.

- **La Nochebuena**
  Esta fiesta se celebra con una gran cena en casa. Luego los hispanos cristianos van a la Misa del Gallo,[a] un servicio religioso que se celebra a medianoche. En algunos países, los niños reciben la visita de Papá Noel, quien les deja[b] regalos.
- **La Nochevieja**
  Es una ocasión para grandes celebraciones, tanto entre familia como en lugares públicos. En España y otros países algunos siguen la tradición de comer una uva[c] por cada una de las doce campanadas[d] de medianoche.
- **El Día de los Reyes Magos**
  Esta fiesta se celebra en muchos países el 6 de enero. Los Reyes Magos son los encargados[e] de traer regalos. Muchos niños ponen sus zapatos en la ventana o balcón antes de acostarse la noche del 5 de enero. Los Reyes llegan en camellos durante la noche y llenan los zapatos con regalos y dulces.
- **El Día de la Independencia**
  Todos los países latino americanos celebran el día de la declaración de su independencia de España. Por ejemplo, Cuba celebra su independencia el 10 de octubre; México, el 16 de septiembre; Bolivia, el 6 de agosto; el Paraguay, el 15 de mayo y El Salvador, el 15 de septiembre.

[a]Misa... *Midnight Mass* [b]les... *leaves ... for them* [c]*grape* [d]*bell strokes* [e]los... *in charge*

Unos bailarines (*dancers*) durante las celebraciones del Día de los Reyes Magos, en La Habana, Cuba

- **La quinceañera**
  Esta fiesta, celebrada en muchos países latinoamericanos y en este país, celebra la llegada de las niñas a los 15 años, es decir, su transición de niña a mujer. La familia y los amigos de la joven le dan una gran fiesta, en la que[f] ella se viste de largo.[g] A veces se celebra una misa especial, pero siempre hay una cena y una fiesta con música para bailar.

¿Cuáles de estas fiestas se celebran en su familia? Si no se celebra ninguna de ellas, ¿cuáles son las fiestas familiares de más importancia para Ud.?

[f]la... *which* [g]se... *dresses up (in a gown)*

D. Hablando de fiestas

Paso 1. ¿Cuáles de estas fiestas le gustan a Ud.? ¿Cuáles no le gustan? Explique por qué. Compare sus respuestas con las (*those*) de sus compañeros de clase.

MODELO: el Cuatro de Julio → Me gusta mucho el Cuatro de Julio porque vemos fuegos artificiales (*fireworks*) en el parque y...

1. el Cuatro de Julio
2. el Día de (Acción de) Gracias
3. la Nochevieja
4. la Navidad

Paso 2. Ahora piense en su fiesta favorita. Puede ser una de la lista del **Paso 1** o una del **Vocabulario útil** de la página 269. Piense en cómo celebra Ud. esa fiesta, para explicárselo (*explain it*) luego a la clase. Debe pensar en lo siguiente.

- los preparativos que Ud. hace de antemano (*beforehand*)
- la ropa especial que lleva
- las comidas o bebidas especiales que compra o hace
- el lugar donde se celebra
- la decoración especial que hay o que Ud. pone

Paso 3. ¿Hay algún día festivo que debe existir, según Uds., pero que no existe? En grupos, inventen por lo menos dos días festivos: **el Día de...** Presenten sus días festivos originales a la clase y expliquen cómo se deben celebrar.

Las emociones y los estados afectivos° estados... *emotional states*

llorar

discutir con (alguien) por/sobre (algo)

enojarse con (alguien) por (algo)

ponerse rojo/a

Otros verbos

olvidar	to forget
portarse bien/mal	to (mis)behave
quejarse de	to complain about
recordar (recuerdo)	to remember
reírse* (me río) (i) (de)	to laugh (about)
sonreír* (sonrío) (i)	to smile

Para expresar *to become/get* y *to feel*

ponerse + *adj.*	to become/get + *adj.*
sentirse (me siento) (i) + *adj.*	to feel + *adj.*

Adjetivos: alegre, contento/a, enojado/a (*angry, upset*), **feliz** (*pl.* **felices**) (*happy*), **furioso/a, nervioso/a, tranquilo/a** (*calm*), **triste**

Comunicación

A. Asociaciones

Paso 1. ¿Con qué verbos asocia Ud. las siguientes cosas y situaciones? Use verbos de **Las emociones...** o cualquier (*any*) otro.

1. ver un bebé
2. una situación injusta
3. un número de teléfono nuevo
4. algo memorable que pasó
5. tener un examen importante
6. un chiste muy bueno
7. un perro muy joven
8. un desacuerdo (*disagreement*) con un amigo
9. conocer a una persona muy interesante
10. estar equivocado (*wrong*) en público / enfrente de una clase

---

*The verbs **reír** and **sonreír** are **e** → **i** *stem-changing verbs. An accent is required on all present tense forms of these verbs (as well as on the infinitives) to show the breaking of dipthongs io, ie, ei by stressing the weak vowel i:* (son)río, (son)ríes, (son)ríe, (son)reímos, (son)reís, (son)ríen. *No accent mark is needed on the present participle, in which the **i** is not stressed:* (son)riendo.

Paso 2. Ahora, en parejas, digan las palabras o frases que Uds. asocian con los siguientes verbos o frases.

1. recordar
2. sonreír

3. ponerse nervioso/a
4. discutir con alguien

Nota **comunicativa**

Cómo enfatizar: -*ísimo*

To emphasize the quality described by an adjective or an adverb in English, you can put *very very* or *really really* before the word: *I tried very very hard. I really really like it.* This is expressed in Spanish by adding **-ísimo** to an adverb and **-ísimo/a(os/as)** to an adjective. You already know one adverb formed like this: **muchísimo.**

- If the word ends in a consonant, **-ísimo** is added to the singular form and any accents on the original word are dropped: **difícil → dificilísimo.**

  Estas tapas son **dificilísimas** de preparar.
  These appetizers are very, very hard to prepare.

- If the word ends in a vowel, that vowel is dropped before adding **-ísimo** and any accents on the original word are also dropped.

  tarde → tardísimo   rápida → rapidísima

- There are spelling changes when the final consonant is a **c, g,** or **z.** This is the same spelling change you have learned to make in the formal command and preterite forms of verbs that end in **-car, -gar,** and **-zar.**

  rico → riquísimo   largas → larguísimas
  feliz → felicísimo

You can use adjectives and adverbs formed in this way in **Comunicación B** and **C.**

Vocabulario **útil**
avergonzado/a   embarrassed **de buen/mal humor** **contento/a** **feliz/triste** **furioso/a** **impaciente** **nervioso/a** **preocupado/a**

B.   Reacciones. ¿Cómo se pone o se siente Ud. en estas situaciones? Use los adjetivos y verbos que Ud. sabe y también algunas formas enfáticas (**-ísimo**). ¿Cuántas emociones puede Ud. describir?

MODELO: Llueve todo el día. → Me pongo / Me siento **triste/tristísima.**

1. Llueve el día de su cumpleaños.
2. Es Navidad. Alguien le hace un regalo carísimo.
3. Ud. quiere bañarse. No hay agua caliente.
4. Ud. está solo/a en casa una noche y oye un ruido.
5. Ud. da una fiesta en su apartamento. Los invitados están aburridísimos.
6. Ud. tiene un examen importantísimo pero no estudió nada la noche anterior (*before*).
7. Ud. cuenta un chiste pero nadie se ríe.
8. Ud. acaba de terminar un examen difícil. Cree que lo hizo muy mal.

C.   ¿Cuándo... ?

Paso 1. En parejas, completen las siguientes oraciones con un lugar y una acción o situación, según su experiencia. Sigan el modelo.

MODELO: Me quejo en... (lugar) cuando... (acción o situación) →
      E1: Me quejo en **el aeropuerto** cuando **tengo que hacer cola... ¡y la cola es larguísima!**
      E2: Yo también, y también me quejo en **una tienda cuando tengo que esperar demasiado tiempo.**

1. Me quejo en... cuando...
2. Me río muchísimo en... cuando...
3. Sonrío en... cuando...
4. Lloro en... cuando...
5. Mis padres se enojan en... cuando... (Mis hijos... Mi esposo/a... Mi novio/a...)

6. Los niños se portan bien/malísimo en... cuando...
7. Las mascotas se portan bien/mal en... cuando...
8. Me pongo rojo/a en... cuando...

Paso 2. Ahora comparen sus respuestas con las (*those*) del resto de la clase. ¿En qué son similares o diferentes las respuestas de todos?

«De fiesta en fiesta» Segmento 1

Antes de mirar

Indique las religiones más representadas en su comunidad.

- ☐ el budismo
- ☐ el cristianismo
    - **a.** ☐ católicos
    - **b.** ☐ evangélicos
    - **c.** ☐ protestantes
    - **d.** ☐ otros
- ☐ el Islam
- ☐ el judaísmo

Mucha gente limeña (*from Lima*) participa en la procesión del Señor de los Milagros (*Our Lord of the Miracles*). Es una imagen de un Cristo crucificado (*Christ on the cross*) muy venerada (*worshipped*) por más de cinco siglos (*centuries*).

Este segmento

En este segmento Víctor y Ana presentan datos estadísticos sobre la afiliación religiosa de los hispanos estadounidenses y hablan de las fiestas que celebran. Luego Laura presenta un reportaje desde el Perú.

Vocabulario **del segmento**

de nuevo nos encontramos	here we are again	**el/la muchacho/a**	boy/girl
aunque	although	**el/la esclavo/a**	slave
el/la seguidor(a)	follower	**el muro**	wall
atraer	to attract	**el terremoto**	earthquake
la escuela	school	**asolar**	to devastate
conocido/a	known	**rendir (rindo) (i) culto**	to worship
la fe	faith	**caminar despacio**	to walk slowly
alrededor de	circa, about	**la mantilla**	lace veil

Estrategia

The following Christian holidays are mentioned in **Segmento 1.** You do not need to know any details about them, but this list will help you recognize their names when you hear them.

- **la Navidad** (the celebration of the birth of Christ)
- **la Semana Santa** (*Holy Week* = the week leading up to Easter Sunday)
- **el Viernes Santo** (*Good Friday* = the day Christ was crucified on the cross)
- **el Domingo de Pascua de Resurrección** (*Easter Sunday* = the celebration of Christ's resurrection)

Después de mirar

A. ¿Está claro? Empareje los siguientes porcentajes con la explicación apropiada.

PORCENTAJES Y FECHAS

1. 60% (por ciento)
2. 22%
3. 12%
4. 1%

FRASES

a. población hispana cristiana pero no católica
b. población hispana religiosa pero no cristiana
c. población hispana católica
d. población hispana sin afiliación religiosa

B. Un poco más. Conteste las siguientes preguntas.

1. ¿En qué mes se celebra el Mes Morado? ¿Cuál es el origen del nombre de la celebración?
2. ¿Quién pintó la imagen del Señor de los Milagros? ¿En qué año?
3. En Panamá, ¿qué representan las fechas 3/11 y 28/11?

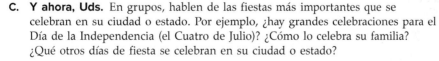

C. Y ahora, Uds. En grupos, hablen de las fiestas más importantes que se celebran en su ciudad o estado. Por ejemplo, ¿hay grandes celebraciones para el Día de la Independencia (el Cuatro de Julio)? ¿Cómo lo celebra su familia? ¿Qué otros días de fiesta se celebran en su ciudad o estado?

¿Recuerda Ud.?

You already know the irregular preterite stem and endings for **hacer.** All verbs presented in **Gramática 24** have irregular stems used with the same preterite endings as **hacer.** Review those endings by completing these forms.

1. yo: hic_____ **2.** nosotros: hic_____ **3.** Ud.: hiz_____ **4.** ellos: hic_____

24 Talking About the Past (Part 2)
Irregular Preterites

Gramática en acción: ¿Qué pasó en la fiesta de fin de año en casa de Sofía y Paco?

Jorge · Esteban · David · Luz · Sultán · Ernesto · Marina · Sofía · Patricia · Arturo · Gema · Paco

Mire con atención los verbos en rojo. Son formas del pretérito. ¿Puede Ud. dar el infinitivo?

1. ¿Quién estuvo hablando por teléfono?
2. ¿Quién dio la fiesta?
3. ¿Quién no pudo ir a la fiesta?
4. ¿Quién puso su copa sobre la televisión?
5. ¿Quién hizo mucho ruido?
6. ¿Quién no quiso beber más?
7. ¿Quién probablemente tuvo que irse temprano?

¿Y Ud.?

1. ¿Estuvo Ud. alguna vez en una fiesta de fin de año como esta? (**Estuve...**)
2. ¿Tuvo que irse temprano de la fiesta? (**Tuve...**) ¿O se quedó hasta medianoche? (**Me quedé...**)
3. ¿Recuerda qué ropa se puso para la fiesta? (**Me puse...**)

Irregular Forms / Las formas irregulares

1. Additional Irregular Forms

You have already learned the irregular preterite forms of **hacer.** The verbs to the right are also irregular in the preterite, like **hacer.**

• Their stem (shown in red) is irregular.
• They use the same preterite endings as **hacer.**

Only the first and third person singular endings are irregular (they have no accent marks). The verb **estar** is conjugated for you. The other verbs listed are conjugated like **estar.**

estar	
estuve	estuvimos
estuviste	estuvisteis
estuvo	estuvieron

¡OJO!
There are no accents on -e and -o.

estar:	estuv-
poder:	pud-
poner:	pus-
querer:	quis-
saber:	sup-
tener:	tuv-
venir:	vin-

Las terminaciones irregulares

-e	-imos
-iste	-isteis
-o	-ieron

2. Preterite of *decir* and *traer*

The irregular preterite stems of these two verbs end in **-j-**. They use the same endings as the verbs on page 274, except that the **-i-** of the third person plural is omitted: **dijeron, trajeron.**

decir: dij-
traer: traj- } -e, -iste, -o, -imos, -isteis, -eron

3. Preterite of *hay: Hubo*

Hay (*There is/are*) comes from the infinitive **haber.** Its preterite form is **hubo** = *there was/were.*

Hubo un accidente ayer en el centro.
There was an accident yesterday downtown.

Hubo muchas fiestas de Navidad el año pasado.
There were a lot of Christmas parties last year.

Changes in Meaning / Cambios de significado

The following Spanish verbs have an English equivalent in the preterite tense that is different from that of the infinitive.

Infinitive	Present Tense	Preterite Meaning
saber =	to know (*facts, information*)	to find out, learn
	Ya lo **sé.**	Lo **supe** ayer.
	I already know it.	*I found it out (learned it) yesterday.*
conocer =	to know, be familiar with (*people, places*)	to meet (*for the first time*)
	Ya la **conozco.**	La **conocí** ayer.
	I already know her.	*I met her yesterday.*
querer =	to want	to try
	Quiero hacerlo hoy.	**Quise** hacerlo ayer.
	I want to do it today.	*I tried to do it yesterday.*
no querer =	not to want	to refuse
	No quiero hacerlo hoy.	**No quise** hacerlo anteayer.
	I don't want to do it today.	*I refused to do it the day before yesterday.*

Práctica y comunicación

A. La última Nochevieja.

Paso 1. Autoprueba. Dé la forma indicada del pretérito.

1. yo: saber
2. ellos: tener
3. tú: venir
4. él: poner
5. nosotros: querer
6. Ud.: poder
7. ellos: decir
8. haber

> **Summary of Irregular Preterites**
>
> Endings: **-e, -iste, -o, -imos, -isteis, -ieron**
> Irregular stems: **dij-, estuv-, hic-, pud-, pus-, quis-, sup-, traj-, tuv-, vin-**

Paso 2. Ahora diga lo que Ud. hizo o no hizo el último día del año pasado. Haga oraciones completas con la forma apropiada del pretérito.

MODELO: 1. (no) querer hacer algo / nada especial ese día →
Quise hacer **algo** especial ese día. **No quise** hacer **nada** especial ese día.

El último día del año pasado, (yo)...

1. (no) querer hacer algo / nada especial ese día
2. (no) dar una fiesta en mi casa / apartamento
3. (no) estar con unos buenos amigos
4. (no) tener que hacer algo / nada de comida

(Continúa.)

5. (no) conocer a alguien / nadie interesante
6. (no) decirle ¡Feliz Año Nuevo! a alguien / nadie
7. (no) poder quedarme despierto/a (*awake*) hasta la medianoche
8. (no) ponerse ropa elegante esa noche

Paso 3. Ahora, en parejas, túrnense para hacer y contestar preguntas basadas en las oraciones del **Paso 2.** Luego díganle a la clase lo que tienen en común.

MODELO: E1: ¿**Quisiste** hacer algo especial ese día?
E2: No, no **quise** hacer nada especial. ¿Y tú?
E1: Yo tampoco. →
Ninguno de nosotros **quiso** hacer nada especial ese día.

B. En una fiesta. ¿Cómo se dice en inglés?

1. Conocí al primo cubano de una amiga.
2. Quise abrir una botella de champán.
3. Supe algo interesante sobre los anfitriones.
4. No quise bailar. ¡Bailo malísimo!

C. Una Nochebuena en Santiago de Cuba

Paso 1. Complete la siguiente narración sobre la celebración de la Nochebuena de una familia cubana de la ciudad de Santiago, al sur de la isla de Cuba. Habla Manuel, el padre de la familia. Use el pretérito de los verbos.

Estrategia

Not all of the verbs in this story are irregular in the preterite. As you conjugate each infinitive, first ask yourself if its preterite is regular or irregular.

El lechón (*suckling pig*) con moros (= frijoles) y cristianos (= arroz)

E l año pasado mi esposa y yo celebramos la Nochebuena en casa con toda la familia. (Estar[1]) con nosotros mi primo Andrés, de la Florida, quien (quedarse[2]) con nosotros toda la semana. (Venir[3]) mis padres, mis suegros,[a] hermanos y cuñados[b] con sus hijos. También (*nosotros:* invitar[4]) a nuestros vecinos[c] de toda la vida,[d] los Benjumea. Pero ellos no (poder[5]) asistir porque (irse[6]) a La Habana para estar con su hija, que (tener[7]) un niño en noviembre.

Mi esposa (preparar[8]) lechón asado, moros y cristianos, yuca y tostones.[e] ¡Qué sabroso todo! Mi cuñado (traer[9]) turrón[f] español y cava.[g] A las 10:30, mi hermana (decir[10]) que era[h] hora de ir a la Misa del Gallo[i] y (llevar[11]) a los abuelos a la iglesia.[j] Los demás[k] no (querer[12]) ir y seguimos armando bochinche hasta que (volver[13]) los otros. Todo (ir[14]) bien chévere.[l] Como regalo de Navidad, mi primo Andrés me (dar[15]) un álbum con fotos y cartas de mis parientes en la Florida y Nueva Jersey. Yo (ponerse[16]) tan emocionado[m] que (llorar[18]).

[a]*in-laws* [b]*brothers- and sisters-in-law* [c]*neighbors* [d]*de... long-time (lit., of one's whole life)* [e]*fried plantains* [f]*sweet Christmas candy* [g]*Spanish champagne* [h]*it was* [i]*Misa... Midnight Mass* [j]*church* [k]*Los... The others* [l]*great* [m]*touched, emotional*

Paso 2. Comprensión

1. ¿Qué tuvo de especial la Nochebuena del año pasado para Manuel?
2. ¿Por qué no pudieron asistir los Benjumea?
3. ¿Quiénes fueron a la Misa del Gallo?
4. ¿Qué comieron y bebieron todos?

Prác. A, Paso 1: Answers: **1.** supe **2.** tuvieron **3.** viniste **4.** puso **5.** quisimos **6.** pudo **7.** dijeron **8.** hubo

Paso 3. Ahora complete las siguientes oraciones basadas en lo que pasó en la celebración de la pasada Navidad, Pascua judía u otra fiesta de importancia para su familia. Conjugue los verbos en el pretérito, añadiendo el sujeto y otra información apropiada.

MODELO: celebrar _____ (fiesta) en _____ (lugar) →
        Mi familia **celebró** la Nochebuena en casa de mis abuelos.

1. celebrar _____ (fiesta) en _____ (lugar)
2. querer asistir / (no) poder
3. ir _____ (servicio religioso) antes / después de cenar
4. comer _____ (platos) y beber _____ (bebidas)
5. ponerse muy emocionado/a porque _____
6. darle un regalo a _____ (persona)

D. Hechos (Events) históricos. Describan Uds. algunos hechos históricos, usando una palabra o frase de cada columna. Usen el pretérito de los verbos. Su profesor(a) los puede ayudar con los datos (information) que no saben.

| en 1957 los rusos
en 1969 los estadounidenses
Adán y Eva
George Washington
los europeos
los aztecas
Stanley | **+** | conocer
estar
poner
saber
traer | **+** | en Valley Forge con sus soldados
a un hombre en la luna (moon)
un satélite en el espacio por primera vez
el significado (meaning) de un árbol especial
a Livingston en África
el caballo (horse) al Nuevo Mundo
a Hernán Cortés en Tenochtitlán |

E. Intercambios

Paso 1. Haga preguntas en el pretérito con los siguientes verbos. En el **Paso 2,** Ud. va a usar las preguntas para entrevistar a un compañero o una compañera de clase.

MODELO: conocer → ¿Cuándo **conociste** a tu mejor amigo/a?

1. conocer   **3.** estar   **5.** hacer
2. saber   **4.** tener   **6.** dar

Paso 2. En parejas, túrnense para hacer y contestar sus preguntas. Luego díganle a la clase algo que los/las dos tienen en común.

MODELO: conocer → Los dos **conocimos** a nuestros mejores amigos en la
        escuela secundaria.

F. La última fiesta que Ud. dio

Paso 1. Haga una lista de todos los detalles (details) que Ud. recuerda de la última fiesta a la que (which) fue. Puede ser una fiesta que Ud. organizó o que otra persona dio. Use los siguientes verbos: **conocer, dar, estar, invitar, organizar, poder, saber, ser, venir.**

MODELO: Di una fiesta para el cumpleaños de mi mejor amigo.
        Mi amigo Clark y yo organizamos la fiesta...

Paso 2. Ahora entreviste a un compañero o una compañera sobre la última fiesta que organizó él o ella. Haga preguntas con las palabras interrogativas y el pretérito.

Palabras interrogativas: ¿cuándo?, ¿dónde?, ¿quién?, ¿con quién?, ¿qué?, ¿por qué?

MODELOS: ¿**Cuándo dieron** la fiesta?
        ¿**Qué sirvieron** de comer y beber?

Paso 3. Luego díganle a la clase dos detalles interesantes sobre las fiestas que Uds. organizaron.

¿Recuerda Ud.?

You learned in **Gramática 15 (Cap. 6)** to make a change in the **-ndo** form of **-ir** stem-changing verbs. That same change occurs in some forms of the preterite of that type of verb. Review the change in the present participle by completing the following forms.

1. pedir: p___diendo   **2.** dormir: d___rmiendo

You will learn about this change in the preterite in **Grámatica 25.**

Grammar Tutorial 25

www.connectspanish.com

25 Talking About the Past (Part 3)

Preterite of Stem-changing Verbs

Gramática en acción: Una fiesta de quinceañera

Escoja las respuestas más lógicas para describir la fiesta de quinceañera de Lupe Carrasco. Al leer (*As you read*), mire con atención los verbos en rojo. Son formas del pretérito. ¿Puede Ud. dar el infinitivo de esos verbos?

1. Para su fiesta, Lupe se vistió con...
   ☐ un vestido blanco muy elegante.
   ☐ una camiseta y *bluejeans*.

2. Mientras Lupe cortaba[a] el pastel de cumpleaños, la madre de ella...
   ☐ empezó a llorar.
   ☐ se rio mucho.

3. Lupe pidió un deseo[b] al cortar[c] el pastel. Ella...
   ☐ les dijo a todos qué fue lo que pidió.
   ☐ prefirió guardarlo en secreto.

4. En la fiesta sirvieron...
   ☐ champán y refrescos.
   ☐ solo té y café.

5. Todos los invitados...
   ☐ se divirtieron mucho.
   ☐ se quejaron.

6. A las tres de la mañana, el último invitado
   ☐ se despidió.[d]
   ☐ se sonrió.

[a]Mientras... *While she was cutting* [b]*wish* [c]al... *as she cut*
[d]se... *said good-bye*

Otra costumbre de quinceañera común en Cuba: ir por la ciudad en coche, como los recién casados (*newlyweds*) en este país

¿Y Ud.?

1. ¿Recuerda Ud. qué hizo cuando cumplió 15 años?
2. ¿Qué regalos pidió? (**Pedí...**)
3. ¿Qué sirvieron en la fiesta? (**Sirvieron...**)
4. ¿Se divirtió? (**Me divertí...**)
5. ¿Cómo se sintió ese día? (**Me sentí...**)

1. Preterite of -ar and -er Stem-changing Verbs

In **Gramática 23** (**Cap. 8**) you learned that **-ar** and **-er** stem-changing verbs have no stem change in the preterite (or in the present participle).

El pretérito de los verbos en -ar/-er			
recordar (recuerdo)		perder (pierdo)	
recordé	recordamos	perdí	perdimos
recordaste	recordasteis	perdiste	perdisteis
recordó	recordaron	perdió	perdieron
recordando		perdiendo	

2. Preterite of -ir Stem-changing Verbs

-Ir stem-changing verbs *do* have a stem change in the preterite.

- The change occurs only in the third person singular and plural forms.
- The stem vowels **e** and **o** change to **i** and **u**, respectively. This is the same change that occurs in the present participle of **-ir** stem-changing verbs.

El pretérito de los verbos en -ir			
e → i		o → u	
pedir (pido) (i)		dormir (duermo) (u)	
pedí	pedimos	dormí	dormimos
pediste	pedisteis	dormiste	dormisteis
pidió	pidieron	durmió	durmieron
pidiendo		durmiendo	

¡OJO!

Remember that this change is indicated in parentheses after the infinitive in vocabulary lists: **pedir (pido) (i)**, **dormir (duermo) (u).** Now you know that it indicates two different changes: (1) in the present participle, and (2) in the third person singular and plural of the preterite.

3. Important -ir Stem-changing Verbs

You already know or have seen many of these verbs. New ones are indicated with *.

*conseguir (consigo) (i)	to get; to obtain
conseguir + *inf.*	to succeed in (*doing something*)
*despedirse (me despido) (i) (de)	to say good-bye (to)
divertirse (me divierto) (i)	to have a good time
dormir (duermo) (u)	to sleep
dormirse	to fall asleep
morir(se) ([me] muero) (u)	to die
pedir (pido) (i)	to ask for; to order
preferir (prefiero) (i)	to prefer
reírse (me río) (i) (de)	to laugh (at)
seguir (sigo) (i)	to continue; to follow
sentirse (me siento) (i)	to feel

servir (sirvo) (i)	to serve
sonreír (sonrío) (i)	to smile
sugerir (sugiero) (i)	to suggest
vestirse (me visto) (i)	to get dressed

¡OJO!

The verbs **reírse** and **sonreír** are **e** → **i** stem-changing verbs, but they drop the **e** completely in the third persons of the preterite and in the present participle.

(me reí, te reíste)	(nos reímos, os reísteis)
se rio	se rieron → riendo
(sonreí, sonreíste)	(sonreímos, sonreísteis)
sonrió	sonrieron → sonriendo

Práctica y comunicación

A. ¿Quién lo hizo?

Paso 1. Autoprueba. Complete las siguientes formas del pretérito.

1. nos divert____mos
2. se d____rmieron
3. tú s____rviste
4. se v____stió
5. yo sug____rí
6. Uds. p____dieron

Summary of the Preterite of Stem-changing Verbs

-ar / -er = no change
-ir = change in the third persons singular and plural
   e → i
   o → u

Paso 2. Ahora indique quiénes de sus compañeros de clase hicieron las siguientes acciones la semana pasada (*last week*). Use verbos en el pretérito. Si nadie lo hizo, simplemente diga **Nadie...** Si más de una persona lo hizo, use el verbo en plural.

MODELO: 1. _____ vestirse con ropa elegante / extravagante para venir a clase →
Tom **se vistió** con ropa **elegante** para venir a clase.

1. _____ vestirse con ropa elegante / extravagante para venir a clase
2. _____ dormirse en clase
3. _____ pedirle al profesor / a la profesora más tarea
4. _____ sentirse bien / mal con el resultado de un examen
5. _____ divertirse muchísimo en un concierto
6. _____ reírse a carcajadas (*out loud*)
7. _____ sugerir tener la clase afuera (*outside*)
8. _____ no recordar traer la tarea a clase
9. _____ despedirse en español de sus amigos de la clase
10. _____ morirse de vergüenza (*embarrassment*) por algo

Paso 3. Ahora, en parejas, comparen sus respuestas del **Paso 2.** Luego díganle a la clase una o dos de las respuestas que tienen en común. Mencionen el día, si lo recuerdan.

MODELO: Pensamos que Tom **se vistió** con ropa **elegante** para venir a clase **el miércoles de la semana pasada.**

B. José Martí

Paso 1. Complete la siguiente narración con formas del pretérito para saber más sobre José Martí.

José Martí (servir[1]) la causa de la independencia cubana toda su vida.[a] Siempre (pedir[2]) la libertad de Cuba, de España, y se opuso a la esclavitud.[b] Nació[c] en 1853 en Cuba, hijo de españoles. (Estudiar[3]) en España, donde (recibir[4]) el título de abogado[d] en 1874. Pero no (poder[5]) ejercer[e] esta profesión en Cuba. Luego (vivir[6]) en México, Guatemala y los Estados Unidos.

En 1876 (conocer[7]) a la mujer que luego (ser[8]) su esposa, María, y se casaron.[f] (*Ellos*: Tener[9]) un hijo, pero el matrimonio se separó y Martí (perder[10]) contacto con su hijo.

En 1895 (decidir[11]) empezar una guerra de independencia en Cuba. (Morir[12]) en acción en su querida[g] Isla.

Algunos de sus versos son especialmente famosos en todo el mundo gracias a la canción «Guantanamera».

[a]*life* [b]*slavery* [c]*He was born* [d]*título... law degree* [e]*practice* [f]*se... they got married* [g]*beloved*

Paso 2. Ahora, haga cinco preguntas usando verbos en el pretérito que se puedan contestar (*can be answered*) con información del texto.

MODELO: ¿Cuántos años vivió Martí?

C. Las historias que todos conocemos

Paso 1. Empareje los personajes (*characters*) de la columna de la izquierda con las acciones de la columna de la derecha para crear oraciones en el pretérito basadas en unos cuentos o historias muy famosos. ¿Puede adivinar (*guess*) quiénes son Caperucita Roja, la Cenicienta y Blancanieves?

(Continúa.)

Algo sobre...

José Martí

José Martí, llamado el Apóstol (*founding voice*) de la independencia cubana

José Martí fue un escritor[a] y periodista[b] cubano que se considera un héroe nacional por su lucha[c] por la independencia y por la libertad de su país. Fue uno de los grandes intelectuales hispanohablantes del siglo XIX.[d]

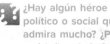 ¿Hay algún héroe político o social que Ud. admira mucho? ¿Por qué lo/la admira?

[a]*writer* [b]*journalist* [c]*fight* [d]*siglo... 19th century*

PERSONAJES	ACCIONES
1. Caperucita Roja el lobo (*wolf*)	**a.** conocer a una mujer misteriosa en un baile
	b. divertirse bailando con un joven muy guapo
2. la Cenicienta el Príncipe las hermanastras de la Cenicienta	**c.** dormirse después de comer una manzana
	d. morirse por el amor de su novia
	e. perderse en el bosque (*forest*)
	f. perder un zapato muy bonito
3. Blancanieves los siete enanos (*dwarves*)	**g.** encontrar (*to find*) un zapato de cristal (*glass*)
	h. sentirse preocupados por su amiga
4. Romeo Julieta	**i.** vestirse de (*as a*) abuela
	j. no conseguir ponerse el zapato de cristal
	k. hablar con un joven guapo desde su balcón

Paso 2. Ahora, en parejas, inventen dos acciones más en el pretérito para cada historia, pero sin incluir el nombre del personaje. La clase va a adivinar a qué personaje, cuento o historia se refieren sus oraciones.

MODELO: Una mujer **quiso** ponerse el zapato de cristal, pero no **pudo** ponérselo. ⟶ la hermanastra de la Cenicienta

D. Una entrevista indiscreta

Paso 1. Lea las siguientes preguntas y escriba una respuesta para cada una. ¡OJO! Tres de sus respuestas deben ser falsas.

1. ¿A qué hora te dormiste anoche?

2. ¿Perdiste mucho dinero alguna vez?

3. ¿Con qué programa de televisión te divertiste mucho en los días o meses pasados... pero te avergüenzas de (*you're ashamed to*) admitirlo?

4. ¿Seguiste haciendo algo después de que tu padre/madre (compañero/a, esposo/a) te dijo que no lo hicieras (*not to do it*)?

5. ¿Pediste una bebida alcohólica antes de tener 21 años?

6. ¿Qué cosa o tarea no conseguiste terminar el mes pasado?

Paso 2. En parejas, usen las preguntas del **Paso 1** para entrevistarse. Traten de (*Try to*) adivinar las respuestas falsas de su compañero/a.

Paso 3. Ahora presenten a la clase una de las respuestas interesantes de su compañero/a. La clase va a adivinar si la respuesta es cierta o falsa.

MODELO: E1: Julie, ¿a qué hora te dormiste anoche?
E2: Me dormí a las tres de la mañana.
E1: (*a la clase*): Julie se durmió a las tres de la mañana anoche.
CLASE: No es cierto.
E1: Tienen razón. No es cierto. Me dormí a las once.

E. Una fiesta de Halloween

Paso 1. En grupos, usen las siguientes ideas como guía para entrevistarse sobre la última fiesta de Halloween a la que (*which*) asistieron.

MODELO: vestirse de ⟶ E1: ¿De qué **te vestiste**?
E2: **Me vestí** de vampiro. ¿Y tú?
E3: Yo **me vestí** de bruja.

1. la fiesta: ser en _____ (lugar)

2. llegar _____ (modo de transporte)

3. vestirse de (*as*) _____ (disfraz)

4. ir con _____ (persona[s])

5. pedir / conseguir / dar _____ (comida)

6. bailar / hablar / beber / ¿ ?

7. divertirse mucho/poco

8. despedirse a la(s) _____ (hora)

9. ¿ ?

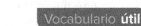

Vocabulario útil

la bruja witch
el disfraz costume
el esqueleto
el fantasma ghost
la máscara
la momia
el monstruo
el vampiro / la vampira

Paso 2. Escojan a la persona que asistió a la mejor fiesta y díganle a la clase dos cosas interesantes que esa persona hizo en la fiesta.

Grammar Tutorial 26
connect
|SPANISH
www.connectspanish.com

26 Avoiding Repetition
Expressing Direct and Indirect Object Pronouns Together

Gramática en acción: La fiesta de Anita

① Berta le hizo un pastel a Anita y **se lo** dio en la fiesta.

② Anita le prestó unos aretes a Berta.

③ Berta le sacó una foto a Anita y **se la** mostró.

Comprensión

¿Quién lo dijo? ¿De qué habla?

1. «Me lo hizo para mi cumpleaños.»
2. «Me los prestó para la fiesta.»
3. «Se la mostré en el celular.»

¿Y Ud.?

Describa los siguientes detalles de su último cumpleaños.

1. ¿Un pastel? ¿Alguien se lo hizo? **(Alguien / Nadie me...)**
2. ¿Unas fotos? ¿Alguien se las sacó?
3. ¿Algo de vestir? ¿Alguien se lo prestó?

complemento indirecto		complemento directo	complemento indirecto		complemento directo
me	+	lo / la / los / las	nos	+	lo / la / los / las
te	+	lo / la / los / las	os	+	lo / la / los / las
(le →) se	+	lo / la / los / las	(les) → se	+	lo / la / los / las

Order of Pronouns / La secuencia de los pronombres

1. Both Object Pronouns in the Same Sentence

When both an indirect and a direct object pronoun appear in the same sentence, the indirect object pronoun comes first, followed by the direct object pronoun. You can remember the order of the pronoun by thinking of **ID**.

This is the *opposite* of the order in English. In addition, while a word (like *ready*, first example) can come in between the two pronouns in English, that is not possible in Spanish.

¿El almuerzo? **Te lo** hago ahora mismo.
Lunch? I'll get it ready for you right now.

¿El trofeo? No **nos lo** dieron.
The trophy? They didn't give it to us.

2. Position of Double Object Pronouns

The placement of double object pronouns in relation to the verb is the same as for single object pronouns. The pronouns come:
- before a conjugated verb
- after an infinitive or present participle *or*

- before the conjugated verb that precedes them

- before a negative command
- after an affirmative command

¿El libro? **Me lo dio.**

¿El equipaje? Acaban de **dármelo**. Están **dándomelo** ahora mismo.

¿Los pronombres? **Te los acabo** de explicar. **Te los estoy** explicando ahora.

¿La comida? **No me la traiga** ahora.
¿Las bebidas? **Tráigamelas**, por favor.

Le(s) → se

1. Use of *se*

When both the indirect and the direct object pronouns begin with the letter **l**, the indirect object pronoun *always* changes to **se**.

This **le(s)** → **se** change only happens in third person expressions, the equivalents of English (*Give*) *it to him/her/them*; (*Give*) *them to him/her/them.*

Only four third-person pronoun combinations are possible in Spanish: **se lo, se la, se los, se las.** In these combinations:
- se = indirect object pronoun (**le** or **les**)
- lo/la/los/las = direct object pronouns (no change)

So, in third-person combinations, all you need to focus on is the gender of the direct object pronoun (**lo, la, los, las**), since **se** will always be the same.

Indirect <u>direct</u>

Les dimos <u>el coche.</u>
↓ (les lo)
Se lo dimos.
We gave them the car.
We gave it to them.

Le escribí <u>la carta</u> ayer.
↓ (le la)
Se la escribí ayer.
I wrote her the letter yesterday.
I wrote it to her yesterday.

Le regaló <u>esos zapatos.</u>
↓ (le los)
Se los regaló.
He gave him those shoes.
He gave them to him.

Les mandamos <u>las invitaciones.</u> (les las)
Se las mandamos.
We sent them the invitations.
We sent them to them.

2. Clarifying *se*

Since **se** can stand for **le** (*to/for you* [sing.], *him, her*) or **les** (*to/for you* [pl.], *them*), it is often necessary to clarify its meaning by using **a** plus the prepositional pronoun.

You learned to clarify the indirect object pronouns **le** and **les** in this way in **Capítulo 8.** This is exactly the same thing, since **se** represents **le** and **les.**

¿La carta de recomendación? Voy a escribír**sela.**
(meaning of **se** unclear unless specified)

¿La carta de recomendación? Voy a escribír**sela a Ud. / a Uds.**
a él / a ellos.
a ella / a ellas.

The letter of recommendation? I'm going to write it for you (sing.) / you (pl.).
for him / for them (m. or m. and f.).
for her / for them (f.).

Práctica y comunicación

A. Oraciones «familiares»

Paso 1. Autoprueba. Complete las siguientes oraciones con los pronombres apropiados del complemento directo e indirecto: **se lo, se la, se los, se las.**

1. Le dieron el libro. → _____ _____ dieron.
2. Les sirvieron la paella. → _____ _____ sirvieron.
3. Le di las direcciones. → _____ _____ di.
4. Les trajo los boletos. → _____ _____ trajo.

Paso 2. Indique cuáles pueden ser los complementos posibles en las siguientes oraciones. Para cada oración, escoja un complemento indirecto y otro directo. **¡OJO!** A veces hay solo una posibilidad. A veces hay varias.

	COMPLEMENTOS INDIRECTOS	COMPLEMENTOS DIRECTOS
1. Se lo digo.	a mí	un consejosobre algo
2. Me la hacen.	a ti	el dinero
3. Se los hago.	a mis parientes	los favores
4. Me lo dan.	a mis amigos	la fiesta de cumpleaños
5. «¡Te lo dije!»		«Te quiero».

Paso 3. Ahora, en parejas, digan si alguno de Uds. (u otras personas) hace las siguientes acciones con frecuencia.

MODELO: decirle «te quiero» a algún miembro de la familia →
     E1: ¿**Le dices** «te quiero» a algún miembro de tu familia?
     E2: Sí, **se lo digo a mi madre** con frecuencia. ¿Y tú?
     E1: Yo **se lo digo a mi madre** también.

1. decirle «te quiero» a un miembro de la familia
2. hacerle una fiesta de cumpleaños a alguien
3. decirle «¡te lo dije!» a alguien
4. darle dinero a alguien
5. hacerle favores a alguien

B. En la mesa.
Ud. todavía tiene hambre. Pida más comida, según el modelo. Preste atención al uso del tiempo presente para pedir algo de manera informal.

MODELO: ensalada → ¿Hay más **ensalada**? ¿Me **la** pasas, por favor?

1. pan
2. tortillas   **4.** fruta   **6.** jamón
3. tomates   **5.** vino

C. En el aeropuerto.
Cambie los sustantivos por pronombres para evitar (*avoid*) la repetición.

MODELO: ¿La maleta? Van a prestarme la maleta mañana. →
     Van a prestár**mela** (**Me la** van a prestar) mañana.

1. ¿La hora de la salida? Acaban de decirnos la hora de la salida.
2. ¿El horario (*schedule*)? Sí, léame el horario, por favor.
3. ¿Los boletos? No, no tiene que darle los boletos aquí.
4. ¿El equipaje? ¡Claro que le guardo el equipaje!
5. ¿Los boletos? Ya te compré los boletos.
6. ¿El puesto? No te preocupes. Te puedo guardar el puesto.

D. ¿Una madre típica?
La madre de Aurora le recuerda (*reminds*) a su hija todo lo que debe hacer. Conteste las preguntas afirmativamente por Aurora, usando pronombres del complemento directo e indirecto.

MODELO: ¿Le diste un beso a papá antes de salir? →Sí, **se lo** di.

(Continúa.)

1. ¿Les diste las gracias a los abuelos por el regalo de cumpleaños?
2. ¿Le llevaste el ensayo al profesor de historia?
3. ¿Le mandaste las fotos a tu amiga?
4. ¿Me mandaste la cuenta de la matrícula?
5. ¿Te dio tu amiga el dinero para la blusa que le compraste?
6. ¿Les dijiste a tus amigos que están invitados para el Día de Gracias?

Algo sobre...

el son cubano

El son es un género musical cubano que dio lugar[a] al mambo, a la rumba y a la salsa, entre otros bailes. También está presente en el *latin jazz*.

El son se originó en el este de Cuba a finales del siglo XIX[b] con elementos musicales africanos y españoles. A principios[c] del siglo XX llegó a La Habana y de allí salió al mundo. Los grupos soneros originales tocaban[d] con un tres cubano (una guitarra con tres pares de cuerdas[e]), bongós y maracas. Después empezaron a usar la guitarra, el contrabajo[f] y la trompeta.

En su opinión ¿cuál es el género musical de su país que más influencia tiene en el mundo? ¿Qué sabe de esa música?

[a]dio... *gave rise, created* [b]siglo... *19th century* [c]A... *At the beginning* [d]*played* [e]*strings* [f]*string bass*

Celia Cruz (1925–2003), la gran cantante cubana que llevó el son por todo el mundo

---

E. ¿Quién le regaló eso?

Paso 1. Haga una lista de los cinco mejores regalos que Ud. ha recibido (*have received*) en su vida (*life*).

Paso 2. Ahora dele a un compañero o una compañera su lista. Él/Ella le va a preguntar: **¿Quién te regaló ?** Use pronombres en su respuesta. **¡OJO!** Preste atención a estas formas en plural **(ellos): regalaron, dieron, mandaron.**

MODELO: E1: ¿Quién te regaló **los aretes de oro**?
E2: Mis padres **me los** regalaron.

Paso 3. Ahora descríbale a la clase por lo menos uno de los regalos interesantes que recibió su compañero/a.

MODELO: Cintia recibió **unos aretes de oro** como regalo. **Se los** regalaron sus padres.

Un poco de todo

A. Lengua y cultura: La Virgen de Guadalupe, quince siglos (*centuries*) de historia

Paso 1. Complete the following paragraphs with the correct form of the words in parentheses, as suggested by context. When two possibilities are given in parentheses, select the correct word. Use the present tense or the preterite of the infinitives, according to context.

En todos los países hispanohablantes, hay festividades religiosas que son días de fiesta nacionales. Por ejemplo, el día de Navidad se (celebrar[1]) en todo el mundo hispano. Otra celebración religiosa que también (es / está[2]) una fiesta nacional en (mucho[3]) países es el 12 de diciembre. Es el día de la fiesta de la

(Continúa.)

La tilma (*shawl*) de Juan Diego en la Basílica de Nuestra Señora (*Lady*) de Guadalupe, en la Ciudad de México

Virgen de Guadalupe, una imagen venerada[a] por todo el mundo católico, especialmente en México.

La historia de la Virgen de Guadalupe (venir[4]) a México desde[b] España. En el siglo VI,[c] el Papa[d] Gregorio tenía[e] una estatua de la Virgen y (se lo / se la[5]) regaló al Obispo[f] de Sevilla. Pero luego la estatua (desaparecer[6]) durante los siglos en que los árabes ocuparon la Península. Después de la expulsión de los árabes, un pastor[g] cristiano (le / la[7]) (encontrar[8]) cerca de la ciudad de Guadalupe. Por eso la estatua (tomar[9]) el nombre de la Virgen de Guadalupe.

En lo que hoy es México, en el siglo XVI, un campesino[h] indígena, Juan Diego, se convirtió[i] al cristianismo. Un día (*él*: ver[10]) a la Virgen en un lugar llamado Tepeyac. Por un milagro,[j] la Virgen (dejar[k11]) su imagen impresa[l] en la tilma[m] de Juan Diego. Esta imagen (recibir[12]) el nombre de Virgen de Guadalupe porque Tepeyac (es / está[13]) cerca del pueblo mexicano de Guadalupe.

La tilma de Juan Diego, con la imagen de la Virgen, todavía se puede (ver[14]) en la Basílica[n] de Nuestra Señora de Guadalupe, en la Ciudad de México.

[a]imagen... *image venerated, adored* [b]*from* [c]el... *the sixth century* [d]*Pope* [e]*had* [f]*Bishop* [g]*shepherd* [h]*peasant* [i]se... *converted* [j]*miracle* [k]*to leave* [l]*imprinted* [m]*shawl* [n]*large church*

Paso 2. Comprensión. ¿Cierto o falso? Corrija las oraciones falsas.

	CIERTO	FALSO
1. La Virgen de Guadalupe española es una estatua.	☐	☐
2. El Papa Gregorio vio a la Virgen en Tepeyac.	☐	☐
3. El campesino Juan Diego era (*was*) de origen español.	☐	☐
4. La tilma de Juan Diego ya no (*no longer*) existe.	☐	☐

Paso 3. En parejas, vuelvan a contar la historia de la Virgen de Guadalupe. Primero, hagan una lista de los hechos importantes en la historia, usando infinitivos. Ejemplo: **venir de España.** Luego, cuenten la historia.

B. ¿Qué pasó cuando... ? ¿Les pasó a Uds. alguna de estas cosas este año? En parejas, túrnense para hacer y contestar preguntas. Digan cuándo ocurrió y cómo reaccionaron. Luego díganle a la clase algo interesante.

MODELO: **1.** Su compañero/a de cuarto (esposo/a...) volvió anoche a casa muy tarde haciendo mucho ruido. →
E1: ¿Tu compañero de cuarto volvió tarde alguna vez?
E2: Sí, el domingo pasado volvió a las 4 de la mañana haciendo ruido. Me puse furioso. ¿Y tu compañero?
E1: No, él nunca vuelve tarde. ¡Yo sí!

1. Su compañero/a de cuarto (esposo/a...) volvió anoche a casa muy tarde haciendo mucho ruido.
2. Un profesor le dio un examen «sorpresa».
3. Ud. perdió algo importante o de otra persona.
4. Un amigo/pariente de Ud. le dijo algo ofensivo / muy triste.
5. Ud. sacó una nota sorprendentemente (*surprisingly*) buena.
6. Ud. fue a una celebración familiar muy entrañable (*touching*).

En su comunidad

Entreviste a una persona hispana de su universidad o ciudad sobre las celebraciones tradicionales de su país y de su familia.

PREGUNTAS POSIBLES

- ¿Cuáles son los días festivos más importantes de su país? ¿Son celebraciones de origen civil o religioso? ¿Se celebran en familia? ¿También hay eventos en la ciudad?
- ¿Cuáles son las celebraciones más importantes en su familia? ¿Y sus favoritas?
- ¿Cuál fue la última fiesta que Ud. celebró en su país? ¿Cómo y con quién la celebró?

«De fiesta en fiesta» Segmento 2

Antes de mirar

¿Qué asocia Ud. con una gran fiesta nacional?

_____ música
_____ comida
_____ mucha gente
_____ banderas (*flags*)
_____ colores patrióticos
_____ celebraciones en la calle (*street*)
_____ ¿ ?

La Fiesta Broadway, una celebración que conmemora una victoria mexicana

Este segmento

Laura presenta un reportaje sobre el Cinco de Mayo, y los presentadores, Ana y Víctor, cierran el programa.

Vocabulario **del segmento**

sino	but rather	**la manzana**	(city) block
la fuerza invasora	invading force	**el escenario**	stage
ha llegado a ser	has become	**órale**	right on
en grande	in a big way		

Fragmento del guion

ANA: Bueno, con sabor a^a fiesta mexicana, despedimos^b el programa de hoy. No se olviden que nos volvemos a ver aquí muy, muy pronto.

VÍCTOR: Hasta entonces,^c cuídense mucho.^d Nos vemos pronto.

^acon... *with the taste of... in mind* ^b*we close* ^c*then* ^dcuídense... *take good care of yourselves*

Después de mirar

A. ¿Está claro? Complete las siguientes oraciones con las cifras (números) que se oyen en el segmento.

1. _____ fue el año de una victoria mexicana.
2. En la Fiesta Broadway hay _____ escenarios musicales diferentes.
3. Se calcula que _____ de personas asisten a la Fiesta Broadway.
4. La Fiesta Broadway ocupa _____ manzanas.

B. Un poco más. Conteste las siguientes preguntas.

1. ¿Dónde tiene lugar (*take place*) la Fiesta Broadway?
2. ¿Qué tiene de raro (*What's odd about*) la celebración del Cinco de Mayo?
3. ¿Qué otra fiesta muy conocida (*well known*) en los Estados Unidos está asociada con otro grupo nacional?

C. Y ahora, Uds. En parejas, preparen un segmento informativo sobre una fiesta que se celebra en su ciudad o estado. El segmento debe comenzar con un saludo a los telespectadores y la introducción de Uds., los presentadores del programa. El segmento debe cerrarse formalmente. Usen el **Fragmento del guion** como modelo para el cierre.

A LEER

Antes de leer

¿Hubo en este país alguna época de intolerancia política o religiosa?

Lectura cultural: Cuba
Dos días festivos cubanos

En Cuba se conmemoran dos días muy importantes. El primero es el 10 de octubre, que se conoce como el Día de la Independencia Nacional. En este día el patriota cubano Carlos Manuel de Céspedes declaró libres a todos los esclavos.[a] También llamó a todos los cubanos a liberarse del dominio[b] colonial de España. Esto marca el inicio[c] de la primera guerra[d] de independencia de Cuba.

El otro día festivo de mucha importancia para los cubanos es la Navidad. Como resultado del cambio[e] político de 1959 y durante muchos de los años bajo el régimen de Fidel Castro, no se les permitió a los cubanos celebrar la Navidad de manera oficial. Todo cambió[f] con la visita a Cuba del Papa[g] Juan Pablo II (Segundo) en el año 1998. Desde entonces[h] los cubanos pueden asistir a la iglesia y celebrar este día tan importante con su familia y amigos.

[a]*slaves* [b]*control* [c]*beginning* [d]*war* [e]*change (that is, the regime of Fidel Castro)* [f]*changed* [g]*Pope (Head of the Catholic Church)* [h]*Desde... Since then*

Unas palmas reales en La Habana, Cuba

Un símbolo cubano: La palma

La palma real[a] (también llamada palmera en otros países) es un ícono nacional que se encuentra por toda la Isla. Forma parte del escudo[b] nacional como símbolo del espíritu cubano: siempre alto y orgulloso.[c] José Martí la menciona en sus famosos versos[d]:

> Yo soy un hombre sincero
> De donde crece[e] la palma,
> Y antes de morirme quiero
> Echar[f] mis versos del alma.[g]

[a]*royal* [b]*coat of arms* [c]*proud* [d]*lines (of a poem)* [e]*grows* [f]*Release* [g]*soul*

En **otros** países hispanos

En todo el mundo hispanohablante Estas festividades se celebran en todas partes.

- **La Semana Santa** Así[a] se llama a la semana que va desde el Domingo de Ramos[b] hasta el Domingo de Pascua. En muchas ciudades hay procesiones[c] para conmemorar la pasión, muerte[d] y resurrección de Jesús. Coincide con el principio[e] de la primavera o el otoño, según el hemisferio.

- **El Carnaval** Esta fiesta precede al comienzo de la Cuaresma.[f] El Carnaval más famoso del mundo es el[g] de Río de Janeiro (Brasil), pero hay Carnavales hispanos que también son famosos por la exuberancia de su música, bailes y colorido, como los Carnavales de Cádiz (España), Barranquilla (Colombia) y Santiago de Cuba (Cuba).

[a]*That's how* [b]*el... Palm Sunday* [c]*street processions* [d]*la... passion (that is, suffering), death* [e]*beginning* [f]*Lent (period from Ash Wednesday to Good Friday)* [g]*that*

COMPRENSIÓN

1. ¿Cuáles son los días festivos más importantes de Cuba?
2. ¿Desde cuándo se permite celebrar la Navidad sin restricciones otra vez en Cuba?
3. ¿Cuáles son otros de los días festivos importantes del mundo hispano?
4. ¿Cuándo se celebra la Semana Santa?
5. ¿Por qué es la palma un símbolo apropiado del espíritu cubano?

Y ahora, Uds.

Piensen en los símbolos nacionales de los Estados Unidos. ¿Cuáles son? ¿Se usan en los días festivos? ¿en otros eventos? ¿Se usan símbolos nacionales similares en otras partes del mundo?

Del mundo hispano

Antes de leer

Es muy común hacer algunos propósitos (*resolutions*) cuando un año empieza. ¿Los hace Ud., generalmente? Haga una lista de cuatro propósitos que Ud. hizo en años pasados o tuvo la intención de hacer. Use infinitivos en su lista. ¿Los cumplió todos? (*Did you achieve all of them?*)

Lectura: Una declaración de propósitos

12 propósitos para el Año Nuevo

Complete la siguiente declaración:

Yo, _____ (nombre), me comprometo[a] a cumplir
_____ (número) propósitos de esta lista en los próximos 365 días.

- Leer un libro cada dos meses.
- No excederte en tus horas de trabajo.
- Comer más sano.[b]
- Asistir a una muestra[c] de cine o de arte.
- Comprar la membresía[d] de un gimnasio.
- Tomar dos litros de agua diariamente.
- Ir a una ceremonia religiosa ajena a la tuya.[e]
- Regalar sin razón.[f]
  - Desayunar bien.
  - Ir a votar.
    - Ir de excursión a un lugar remoto.
    - Separar la basura en orgánica e inorgánica.

[a]me... *I promise* [b]más... *in a more healthy manner* [c]*exhibition* [d]*membership* [e]ajena... *different from yours* [f]sin... *for no reason*

Comprensión

Una vida mejor. La gente generalmente hace propósitos para el año nuevo con la intención de mejorar (*improving*) su vida (*life*) de alguna manera. Clasifique los (*those*) de esta lectura según las tres categorías a continuación y explique por qué puso cada propósito en la categoría que Ud. escogió (*chose*). (Algunos se pueden poner en más de un grupo.)

1. Los que pueden mejorar la salud (*health*) física
2. Los que pueden mejorar la salud mental o espiritual
3. Los que pueden mejorar las relaciones con los otros y con el medio ambiente (*environment*)

El mensaje telefónico de Pilar

Antes de escuchar

¿Qué actividades generalmente se hacen en una boda (*wedding*)? Haga una lista de todas las actividades que pueda imaginar. Consulte el **Vocabulario para escuchar** al hacer (*while making*) su lista.

Vocabulario **para escuchar**

¡qué lástima!	what a shame!	**tirar**	to throw, toss
los novios	bride and groom	**lo sintió mucho**	was very sorry
cortar	to cut	**el recuerdo**	souvenir, party
ensuciarse la cara	to dirty each other's		favor
	faces		

Después de escuchar

A. **¿Quién hizo qué?** Indique quién hizo qué, emparejando las acciones con las personas que las hicieron. Hay más de una opción en algunos casos.

ACCIONES	PERSONAS
_____ **1.** bailar	**a.** Estela
_____ **2.** cortar el pastel y tirarlo	**b.** un conjunto (*group*) musical
_____ **3.** llorar	**c.** Pilar
_____ **4.** mandar un recuerdo	**d.** la mamá de Estela
_____ **5.** tocar salsa	**e.** los novios
_____ **6.** no ir a la boda	**f.** la amiga de Pilar y de Estela

B. **Más información.** ¿Qué más se sabe o deduce Ud. del mensaje?

1. La amiga de Pilar, ¿es amiga de Estela también?
2. ¿Cómo se llama el novio?
3. ¿Por qué no fue la amiga de Pilar a la boda?
4. ¿Por qué cree Pilar que su amiga no contesta su llamada (*call*)?
5. ¿Cuál es la profesión de la amiga de Pilar?

PRODUCCIÓN PERSONAL

¡Ahora, yo!

A. Use de modelo las preguntas y respuestas de la página 267 de este capítulo para hablar de los días festivos que Ud. celebra.

B. Filme una entrevista con una persona hispana no estadounidense en su universidad o su comunidad. Hágale preguntas sobre un día festivo muy especial que se celebra en su ciudad o país, pero que no se celebra en los Estados Unidos.

A ESCRIBIR

Un ensayo sobre una celebración memorable

¿Cuál es la celebración más memorable de su vida (*life*)? ¿un baile de fin de curso (*prom night*)? ¿una boda (*wedding*)? ¿un cumpleaños? ¿una fiesta de Nochevieja? ¿el bautizo (*baptism*) de una hija o un hijo? ¿Qué es memorable de esa celebración?

Preparar

Paso 1. En parejas, hagan una lista de los aspectos que su ensayo debe incluir, sin olvidar lo que más le gustó.

Paso 2. Use las ideas del **Paso 1** para escribir su ensayo. Debe expresar sus sentimientos o los (*those*) de otras personas que estuvieron o no estuvieron en la celebración. Hay más ayuda en Connect.

Más ideas para su portafolio

- Escriba una o dos oraciones sobre unos momentos emocionantes de su vida: cuándo se puso más feliz (rojo/a, triste...), cuándo lloró más desconsoladamente (*nonstop*) o se rio con más ganas (*most uproariously*), etcétera.

- Escriba unas oraciones sobre una fiesta de un país hispanohablante a la que (*which*) Ud. quiere asistir algún día.

- Si ha estado jugando (*have been playing*) Practice Spanish: Study Abroad, en Quest 6 Ud. pasó tiempo en el museo del pueblo. Si hay una galería de arte en el campus de la universidad a la que asiste Ud. (o en su ciudad), haga un afiche (*poster*) o un folleto (*brochure*) con información sobre la galería para la comunidad hispanohablante.

Sugerencia: You are now ready to play Quest 6 in **Practice Spanish: Study Abroad** (www.mhpractice.com).

LEARNSMART

Visit **www.connectspanish.com** to practice the vocabulary and grammar points covered in this chapter.

AFTER STUDYING THIS CHAPTER I CAN . . .

☐ talk about holidays (268)

☐ express more feelings and emotions (271)

☐ use more types of verbs in the preterite (274–275, 278–279)

☐ understand double object pronouns and use them to avoid repetition (282–283)

☐ recognize/describe at least 2–3 aspects of Cuban cultures

Gramática en breve

24. Irregular Preterites

Irregular Preterite Endings

estuv- pud- pus- quis- sup- tuv- vin-		-e = -iste -o	-imos -isteis -ieron	dij- traj-	-e = -iste -o	-imos -isteis -eron

hay: haber → hubo (*there was/were*)

25. Preterite of Stem-changing Verbs

Preterite Stem-changing Patterns

-ar/-er = no change

-ir = change in the third person singular and plural

    e → i

    o → u

26. Direct and Indirect Object Pronouns Together

Indirect	Direct
me/te/nos/os	
le(s) → se	⊠ lo/la/los/las

Vocabulario

Los verbos

adivinar	to guess
conseguir (*like* seguir)	to get; to obtain
conseguir +*inf.*	to succeed in (*doing something*)
despedirse (*like* pedir) (de)	to say good-bye (to)

encontrar (encuentro)	to find
morir(se) ([me] muero) (u)	to die
sugerir (sugiero) (i)	to suggest

Repaso: dormir(se) ([me] duermo) (u), pedir (pido) (i), preferir (prefiero) (i), servir (sirvo) (i), vestirse (me visto) (i)

Los días festivos y las fiestas

el anfitrión, la anfitriona	host (*of an event*)
las botanas (*Mex.*)	appetizers
el champán	champagne
el día festivo	holiday
el/la invitado/a	guest
el pastel de cumpleaños	birthday cake
las tapas	appetizers
la vela	candle

Repaso: el cumpleaños, la fiesta, el pastel, el refresco, el regalo, la tarjeta

cumplir años	to have a birthday
darle una fiesta (a alguien)	to give someone a party
faltar (a)	to be absent (from); to not attend
gastar	to spend (*money*)
hacerle una fiesta (a alguien)	to give someone a party, have a party (for someone)
pasarlo bien/mal	to have a good/bad time
reunirse (me reúno) (con)	to get together (with)
ser en + *place*	to take place in/at (*a place*)

Repaso: bailar, beber, celebrar, comer, divertirse (me divierto) (i), invitar, regalar

Las emociones y los estados afectivos

el estado afectivo	emotional state
discutir con (alguien) por/sobre (algo)	to argue with (someone) about (something)
enojarse con (alguien) por (algo)	to get angry with (someone) about (something)
llorar	to cry
olvidar	to forget (about)
ponerse + *adj.*	to become, get + *adj.*
ponerse rojo/a	to blush
portarse bien/mal	to (mis)behave
recordar (recuerdo)	to remember
reírse (me río) (i) (de)	to laugh (about)
sentirse (me siento) (i) + *adj.*	to feel (*an emotion*) + *adj.*
sonreír (*like* reír)	to smile

Repaso: quejarse (de)

Otros sustantivos

el árbol	tree
el detalle	detail
el fin de año	end of the year
el hecho	fact; event

Los adjetivos

avergonzado/a	embarrassed
enojado/a	angry; upset
feliz (*pl.* felices)	happy
festivo/a	festive, celebratory
tranquilo/a	calm
-ísimo/a	very very

Repaso: alegre, contento/a, furioso/a, nervioso/a, triste

Algunos días festivos

la Navidad	Christmas
la Nochebuena	Christmas Eve
la Nochevieja	New Year's Eve
la Pascua	Easter
la quinceañera	young woman's fifteenth birthday party

Palabras adicionales

demasiado (*adv.*)	too; too much
¡Felicitaciones!	Congratulations!
gracias por + *noun* or *inf.*	thanks for
por lo menos	at least
ya	already
-ísimo (*adv.*)	very very

Repaso: muchísimo

Vocabulario personal

10

El tiempo libre

www.connectspanish.com

En este capítulo

VOCABULARY
Leisure time activities   296
Household tasks   298

GRAMMAR
Another way to talk about the past   302
Review of interrogative words   308
How to express *the most, least ...*   310

CULTURAL FOCUS
Puerto Rico and its cultures

Un grupo de bomba en San Juan, Puerto Rico

O C É A N O
A T L Á N T I C O

REPÚBLICA
DOMINICANA

PUERTO
RICO
San Juan ⊛
Ponce ●

M a r   C a r i b e

```
0          100        200 Millas
0     100      200 Kilómetros
```

PUERTO RICO

3.6 (punto seis) millones de habitantes

- Puerto Rico es un Estado Libre Asociado a los Estados Unidos. Esto significa que Puerto Rico no es independiente, pero sí tiene autonomía interna. Los puertorriqueños son ciudadanos[a] estadounidenses.

- Los puertorriqueños tienen una gran conciencia[b] de su historia y de la importancia de su cultura. Se sienten muy orgullosos[c] de su herencia indígena, africana e hispana.

[a]*citizens* [b]*awareness* [c]*proud*

- ¿Qué le gusta a Ud. hacer en su tiempo libre? ¿Prefiere las actividades al aire libre[a]? ¿O prefiere las actividades sedentarias?

- ¿Es el baile una de sus diversiones preferidas? ¿Qué tipo de música le gusta más para bailar?

- ¿Tiene que pasar a veces parte de su tiempo libre haciendo quehaceres domésticos[b]?

[a]*al... outdoor* [b]*quehaceres... household tasks*

CECILIA FIGUEROA MARTÍN CONTESTA LAS PREGUNTAS.

- En mi tiempo libre, además de[a] descansar, me gusta hacer cosas con mi familia y con mis amigos. Algunas de las actividades que me gustan son sedentarias, como leer, ver películas, jugar al dominó y a las cartas. Pero también juego al tenis y me encanta nadar en el mar.

- ¡Claro que sí![b] Ahora no bailo tanto como cuando era[c] joven, pero me encanta bailar siempre que[d] puedo. Cualquier[e] tipo de música: pop, rock, salsa, merengue... lo que sea.[f]

- ¡Quién no! Tengo dos niños chicos.[g] Pero, en mi opinión, hacer los quehaceres domésticos no es parte del tiempo libre. ¡Es otro trabajo[h]!

[a]*además... besides* [b]*¡Claro... Of course!* [c]*I was* [d]*siempre... whenever* [e]*Any* [f]*lo... whatever* [g]*niños... small, young kids* [h]*job*

Los pasatiempos, diversiones y aficiones°

Los... *Pastimes, fun activities, and hobbies*

montar a caballo

caminar

hacer (el) yoga

esquiar (esquío), el esquí

jugar (juego) (gu) a los videojuegos

correr

dar una caminata

ir a una fiesta

You can hear the pronunciation of theme vocabulary words and phrases in the Connect eBook.

Los pasatiempos

los ratos libres	spare (free) time
dar/hacer una fiesta	to give a party
dar un paseo	to take a walk
hacer *camping*	to go camping
hacer planes para + *inf.*	to make plans to (*do something*)
hacer un *picnic*	to have a picnic
ir...	to go . . .
a un bar	to a bar
al cine	to the movies
a una discoteca	to a disco
a un museo	to a museum
al teatro / a un concierto	to the theater / to a concert
a ver una película	to see a movie
jugar (juego) (gu) a las cartas / al ajedrez	to play cards/chess
sacar (qu) fotos	to take pictures
tomar el sol	to sunbathe
aburrirse	to get bored
ser...	to be . . .
aburrido/a	boring
divertido/a	fun

Los deportes

el ciclismo	bicycling
el fútbol	soccer
el fútbol americano	football
hacer *surfing*	to surf
montar/pasear en bicicleta	to ride a bicycle
nadar	to swim
la natación	swimming
patinar	to skate

Cognados: el basquetbol, el béisbol, el golf, el hockey, el tenis, el voleibol

el equipo	team
el jugador / la jugadora	player
el partido	game, match
la pelota	ball
entrenar	to practice; to train
ganar	to win
jugar (juego) (gu) al + *sport*	to play (*a sport*)
perder (pierdo)	to lose
practicar (qu)	to participate (*in a sport*)
ser aficionado/a (a)	to be a fan (of)

Comunicación

A. El tiempo libre

Paso 1. ¿Cierto o falso? Corrija las oraciones falsas, según su opinión.

	CIERTO	FALSO
1. Es más aburrido ver un partido en la tele que en el estadio.	☐	☐
2. Lo paso mejor con mi familia que con mis amigos.	☐	☐
3. Las actividades creativas y artísticas me gustan más que las deportivas (*sport-related ones*).	☐	☐
4. Odio el béisbol tanto como el fútbol.	☐	☐
5. Los estudiantes universitarios tienen tanto tiempo libre como los (*those*) de la escuela secundaria.	☐	☐
6. La mejor actividad para un viernes por la noche es estudiar.	☐	☐
7. Jugar al ajedrez es más aburrido que jugar a las cartas.	☐	☐
8. No me gustan las actividades al aire libre (*outdoor*).	☐	☐

Así se dice

el basquetbol =
   el baloncesto (*Sp.*)
dar una caminata = hacer
   senderismo (*Sp.*)
hacer *camping* = hacer
   acampada, acampar
hacer *surfing* = hacer *surf*
   (*P.R.*), surfear
pasear en bicicleta = andar
   en bicicleta, montar en
   bicicleta
la película = el filme, el film
el voleibol = el vólibol, el
   volibol

Paso 2. Ahora haga una lista de sus pasatiempos favoritos y de los que Ud. odia o no le interesan.

Paso 3. Compare su lista con la (*that*) de un compañero o una compañera de clase con quien Ud. no habla con frecuencia. ¿Les gustan los mismos pasatiempos?

B. Definiciones

Paso 1. Dé las palabras definidas.

MODELO: entrar en un lugar para ver una película ⟶ ir al cine

1. un grupo de jugadores
2. salir bien en una competencia; salir mal
3. practicar un deporte intensamente
4. asistir a todos los partidos de un equipo en particular
5. un deporte que se practica en una piscina

Paso 2. Ahora defina las siguientes palabras, según el modelo del **Paso 1.**

1. un jugador
2. un partido
3. aburrirse
4. hacer un *picnic*
5. dar un paseo

Nota cultural

Los deportes más populares del mundo hispano

Dos deportes predominan en el panorama deportivo del mundo hispano: el fútbol y el béisbol.

- **El fútbol** Sin duda este es el rey[a] de los deportes en el mundo hispano, como en el resto del mundo. Ningún evento deportivo se compara en seguimiento[b] a la Copa Mundial de Fútbol. Se estima que mil millones de telespectadores miraron el partido final de la Copa 2014, entre Alemania y la Argentina. En todos los países hispanos, el fútbol se juega en cualquier calle,[c] plaza o espacio abierto y hay innumerables ligas[d] de todo tipo.

- **El béisbol** Un deporte inmensamente popular en los países de la costa caribeña es el béisbol. En las grandes ligas estadounidenses hay muchos jugadores de primer orden con apellidos hispanos. Muchos de estos «peloteros[e]», como se les llama[f] en muchos países, vienen de las ligas de sus respectivos países de origen, como la República Dominicana, Venezuela y México.

[a]*king* [b]*following* [c]*cualquier... any street* [d]*leagues* [e]*ball-players* [f]*se... they are called*

El equipo nacional de béisbol puertorriqueño, que celebra una victoria

- **El basquetbol, el tenis y el ciclismo** Estos deportes también tienen gran seguimiento en el mundo hispano. El basquetbol está creciendo[g] en cuanto al[h] número de espectadores y tiene dos grandes potencias[i] hispanas: España y la Argentina. Estos países tienen varios jugadores en la NBA estadounidense.

¿Qué otros deportistas hispanos puede Ud. nombrar?

[g]*growing* [h]*en... as far as the* [i]*superpowers*

Actividad	Media^a de tiempo diario (aproximada)
Estudios	
Vida^b social con los amigos (en persona o a distancia)	
Vida familiar	
Tareas domésticas	
Deportes	
Ver medios de comunicación^c	
Leer por placer	
Otras actividades	

^aAverage ^bLife ^cmedios... media

C. ¿Cómo pasa Ud. su tiempo?

Paso 1. Complete la siguiente tabla con el tiempo medio (*average*) que Ud. pasa diariamente haciendo las actividades indicadas.

Paso 2. Ahora, en parejas, hagan comparaciones sobre el tiempo que Uds. pasan haciendo las actividades de cada categoría. Díganle a la clase algo que tienen en común.

MODELO: E1: ¿Cuánto tiempo pasas en los estudios?
E2: Paso cinco horas aproximadamente. ¿Y tú?
E1: Yo paso seis horas. Yo paso más horas estudiando que tú.

Los quehaceres domésticos°

Los... *Household chores*

limpiar (la casa)°   limpiar... *to clean (house)*

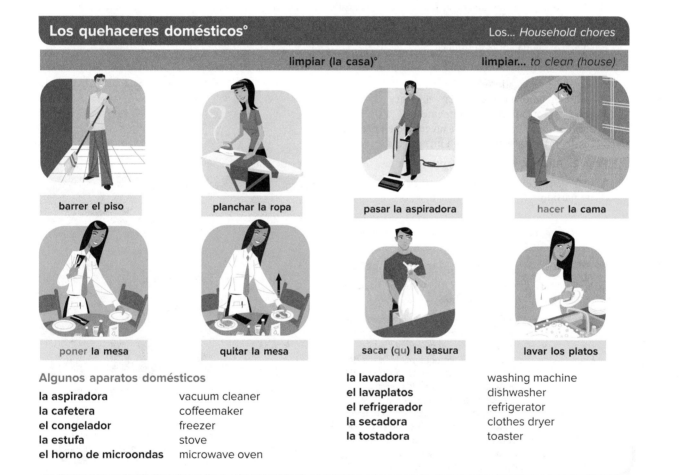

| barrer el piso | planchar la ropa | pasar la aspiradora | hacer la cama |
| poner la mesa | quitar la mesa | sacar (qu) la basura | lavar los platos |

Algunos aparatos domésticos

la aspiradora	vacuum cleaner	la lavadora	washing machine
la cafetera	coffeemaker	el lavaplatos	dishwasher
el congelador	freezer	el refrigerador	refrigerator
la estufa	stove	la secadora	clothes dryer
el horno de microondas	microwave oven	la tostadora	toaster

Comunicación

A. Los quehaceres domésticos. ¿En qué cuarto o parte de la casa se hacen las siguientes actividades? Hay más de una respuesta en muchos casos.

1. Se hace la cama en _____.
2. Se saca la basura de _____ y se pone en _____.
3. Uno se baña en _____ pero baña al perro en _____.
4. Se barre el piso del / de la _____.
5. Se pasa la aspiradora en _____.
6. Se lava y se seca la ropa en _____.
7. La ropa se plancha en _____.
8. Se usa la cafetera en _____.

B. Las marcas (*Brand names*). ¿Para qué se usan o para qué sirven los siguientes productos?

MODELO: Mr. Coffee → Mr. Coffee sirve para hacer el café.

1. Windex
2. Glad bags
3. Lysol
4. Tide
5. Cascade
6. Palmolive

C. Intercambios

Paso 1. En parejas, túrnense para hacer y contestar preguntas sobre cómo pasan Uds. el fin de semana. Basen sus preguntas en las siguientes ideas. Deben obtener detalles interesantes y personales de su compañero/a.

1. cuándo empieza el fin de semana (¿día? ¿hora?)
2. cómo se divierten
3. cuánta tarea hacen
4. cuánto duermen (¿por la noche? ¿la siesta?)
5. los quehaceres domésticos que tienen que hacer
6. cómo se sienten el domingo por la noche

Paso 2. Díganle a la clase dos detalles interesantes sobre lo que hace su compañero/a.

Algo sobre...

el coquí

Los coquíes son ranas[a] de varias especies de un género[b] nativo de Puerto Rico. Son muy pequeños (alrededor de una pulgada[c]) y viven en los árboles.[d] Su nombre es una versión onomatopéyica del sonido[e] que algunas especies de coquíes machos[f] hacen cuando cantan desde la caída del sol[g] hasta el amanecer.[h] La canción del coquí se puede oír por toda la isla y por eso esta ranita es uno de los grandes símbolos puertorriqueños. Desgraciadamente, los coquíes están en peligro[i] de extinción.

¿Qué animales son considerados símbolos de su estado o país? ¿Por qué lo representan?

[a]*frogs* [b]*genus* [c]*alrededor... about an inch* [d]*trees* [e]*sound* [f]*male* [g]*caída... sunset* [h]*dawn* [i]*danger*

Un coquí puertorriqueño

Nota **comunicativa**

Cómo expresar la obligación

You already know several ways to express the obligation to do something.

Tengo que		*I have to*	
Necesito	barrer el piso.	*I need to*	*sweep the floor.*
Debo		*I should, must*	

Of the three, **deber** + *infinitive* expresses the strongest sense of obligation, and **tener que** expresses the greatest sense of urgency or immediacy.

The concept *to be someone's turn or responsibility* (to do something) is expressed in Spanish with the verb **tocar (qu)** plus an indirect object.

—¿**A quién le toca** lavar los platos esta noche? "*Whose turn is it to wash the dishes tonight?*"

—**A mí me toca** solamente sacar la basura. Creo que **a papá le toca** lavar los platos. "*I only have to take out the garbage. I think it's Dad's turn to wash the dishes.*"

You will use these expressions in **Comunicación D** and **E**.

D. **Las tareas domésticas de esta semana**

Paso 1. ¿Tiene Ud. que hacer los quehaceres de la siguiente lista esta semana? Conteste usando los verbos de la **Nota comunicativa**. Si tiene que hacerlos, diga cuándo. Si no tiene que hacerlos, puede decir: **No me toca** _____ **(quehacer) esta semana.**

MODELO: 1. hacer la cama →
　　　　　Debo / Tengo que hacer la cama todos los días.

1. hacer la cama

2. poner la mesa

3. lavar los platos

4. lavar la ropa

5. planchar la ropa

6. sacar la basura

7. pasar la aspiradora

8. barrer el piso

9. limpiar el piso

10. ¿ ?

Paso 2. Ahora, en parejas, túrnense para entrevistarse sobre sus hábitos omésticos, basándose en el **Paso 1**. De los dos, ¿quién se preocupa más por su hogar (*home*)? ¿por la limpieza (*cleanliness*)? ¿Quién mantiene (*keeps*) más limpia la casa?

MODELO: hacer la cama →
　　　　E1: ¿Con qué frecuencia haces la cama? (¿A quién **le toca** hacer las camas en tu casa?)
　　　　E2: la hago. (Las hago a veces. En mi casa, **le toca** a mi madre hacer las camas.)

E. **Las obligaciones.** Piense en las cosas que todos tenemos que hacer, no solo las tareas domésticas. ¿Cuáles son las obligaciones que no le gustan a Ud. para nada? ¿Cuáles son las (*those*) que hace de buena gana (*willingly*)? Dígale a la clase una de las obligaciones en cada categoría.

«Deportes que mueven masas» Segmento 1

Antes de mirar

¿Qué deportes le gustan a Ud.? ¿Es Ud. aficionado/a o lo(s) practica?

☐ el basquetbol
☐ el béisbol
☐ el fútbol
☐ el fútbol americano
☐ la lucha libre (*wrestling*)
☐ otros: _____

Este segmento

Ana y Víctor introducen un programa sobre los deportes, que incluye un reportaje sobre el Museo del Deporte en Puerto Rico.

El Museo del Deporte de Puerto Rico es un lugar maravilloso (*wonderful*) para las personas de todas las edades (*ages*) y especialmente para los aficionados al béisbol, el deporte rey (*number one*) de los puertorriqueños.

Vocabulario del segmento

veamos	let's see	**de primer orden**	first rate	**el campeonato**	championship
de hecho	in fact	**el pelotero**	**el beisbolista**	**las destrezas**	skills
yo jugaba	I played	**el lanzador**	pitcher	**recaen en**	fall on, are the responsibility of
la magnitud	size	**el compromiso**	commitment		
los comienzos	beginnings	**el fuerte de enseñanza**	teaching strength	**han practicado**	have played
el lugar de nacimiento	birthplace				

Después de mirar

A. ¿Está claro? Empareje los años con los acontecimientos importantes del béisbol.

LOS AÑOS
_____ 1. 1942
_____ 2. 1898
_____ 3. 1973
_____ 4. a fines del siglo XIX (*at the end of the 19th century*)
_____ 5. la década de 1940

LOS ACONTECIMIENTOS
a. Los norteamericanos empezaron a llegar a Puerto Rico.
b. Los Estados Unidos tomó posesión de Puerto Rico después de ganar una guerra (*war*) contra España.
c. El primer pelotero puertorriqueño jugó para los Chicago Cubs en las Grandes Ligas (*Leagues*).
d. Terminó la segregación entre blancos y negros en los equipos estadounidenses de béisbol.
e. El primer beisbolista hispano entró en el Salón de la Fama.

B. Un poco más. Conteste las siguientes preguntas.

1. ¿Qué deportes le gustan a Víctor? ¿Y qué equipos?
2. ¿A qué pelotero se le otorga (*is awarded*) anualmente el Premio (*Prize*) Roberto Clemente?
3. Según el Director del Museo, ¿quiénes son las personas más importantes en la enseñanza de los jóvenes beisbolistas puertorriqueños?
4. ¿Qué tipo de visitantes recibe el museo?

C. Y ahora, Uds. En parejas, hablen sobre los deportes más populares en su universidad. ¿Cuáles son? ¿De qué manera son populares, por el número de aficionados o por el número de jugadores? ¿Eran (*Were*) esos mismos deportes los más populares en su escuela secundaria?

GRAMÁTICA   LS

¿Recuerda Ud.?

In **Capítulos 8** and **9**, you learned the forms and some uses of the preterite. Before you learn the other simple past tense (in **Gramática 27**), you might want to review the forms of the preterite in those chapters. The verbs in the following sentences are in the preterite. Can you identify any words in the sentences that emphasize the completed nature of the actions expressed by the verbs?

1. Esta mañana me levanté a las seis.
2. Ayer fui al cine con un amigo.

3. La semana pasada pinté las paredes de la cocina.

Grammar Tutorial 27
connect
|SPANISH
www.connectspanish.com

27 Talking About the Past (Part 4)

Descriptions and Habitual Actions in the Past: Imperfect of Regular and Irregular Verbs

Gramática en acción: Los indígenas taínos

Los indígenas taínos eran los habitantes originales de las Antillas Mayores, que son las islas de Puerto Rico, Cuba, Haití y la República Dominicana (que comparten la que antes fue la isla de La Española) y Jamaica. Allí vivían cuando los españoles llegaron al Caribe a finales del siglo XV. El pueblo taíno era pacífico y generoso y tenía una sociedad matrilineal. Llamaban a su jefe «cacique» y hablaban una lengua que nos ha dejado en el español palabras como *barbacoa, hamaca, canoa, tabaco* y *huracán*.

Comprensión

1. ¿De cuántas islas están formadas las Antillas Mayores? ¿De cuántos países?
2. ¿Cómo era el pueblo taíno?

¿Y Ud.?

1. ¿Qué significan en inglés las últimas palabras del párrafo?
2. ¿Conoce algunos de los pueblos que vivían en lo que hoy son los Estados Unidos, cuando llegaron los europeos?

The Taíno Indians The Taíno Indians were the original inhabitants of the Greater Antilles, which are the islands of Puerto Rico, Cuba, Haiti, and the Dominican Republic (which share what was formerly the island of Hispaniola), and Jamaica. They were living there when the Spaniards arrived in the Caribbean at the end of the fifteenth century. The Taíno people were peaceful and generous, and they had a matrilineal society. They called their chief cacique, and they spoke a language that has left us words such as barbacoa, hamaca, canoa, tabaco, and huracán in Spanish.

You have already used the *preterite* (**el pretérito**) to express events in the past. The *imperfect* (**el imperfecto**) is the second simple past tense in Spanish. The preterite is used when you view actions or states of being as begun or completed in the past. The imperfect is used when you view past actions or states of being as habitual or as "in progress." It is also used for describing the past, especially for giving background details.

Forms of the Imperfect / Las formas del imperfecto

hablar		comer		vivir	
hablaba	hablábamos	comía	comíamos	vivía	vivíamos
hablabas	hablabais	comías	comíais	vivías	vivíais
hablaba	hablaban	comía	comían	vivía	vivían

Pronunciation Hints
- The **b** between vowels, such as in the imperfect ending **-aba,** is pronounced as a fricative [b] sound.
- In **-er/-ir** imperfect forms, it is important not to pronounce the ending **-ía** as a diphthong, but to pronounce the **i** and the **a** in separate syllables. The accent mark over the **í** helps remind you of this.

Los verbos en *-ar*		Los verbos en *-er/-ir*	
-aba	-ábamos	-ía	-íamos
-abas	-abais	-ías	-íais
-aba	-aban	-ía	-ían

1. English Equivalents
As you can see at the right, the imperfect has several English equivalents. Most of them indicate that the action was still in progress (*was/were -ing*) or that it was habitual (*used to, would*).

yo hablaba = *I spoke, I was speaking, I used to speak, I would speak*

comíamos = *we ate, we were eating, we used to eat, we would eat*

él vivía = *he lived, he was living, he used to live, he would live*

¡OJO!

The simple English equivalent (*I spoke, we ate, he lived*) can correspond to either the preterite or the imperfect, but it usually corresponds to the preterite. You'll learn more about this in **Capítulo 11.**

¡OJO!

would = repeated action → imperfect

Comíamos allí todos los domingos.
We would eat there every Sunday.

2. Stem-changing Verbs and *hay*
Stem-changing verbs do not show a change in the imperfect.

almorzar (almuerzo) → almorzaba, almorzabas,...
perder (pierdo) → perdía, perdías,...
pedir (pido) (i) → pedía, pedías,...

The imperfect of **hay** is **había**. It means *there was, there were, there used to be*, and its form never changes.

Había muchos estudiantes en el salón de clase.
There were a lot of students in the class.

3. Irregular Imperfect Forms
Only three verbs are irregular in the imperfect: **ir, ser,** and **ver.**

ir		ser		ver	
iba	íbamos	era	éramos	veía	veíamos
ibas	ibais	eras	erais	veías	veíais
iba	iban	era	eran	veía	veían

4. First and Third Person Singular Forms
Note that the first and third person singular forms are identical for **-ar, -er,** and **-ir** verbs. When context does not make meaning clear, subject pronouns are used.

Los sábados **yo jugaba** al tenis y **él paseaba** en bicicleta.
On Saturdays I used to play tennis and he used to ride his bike.

If you know when to use the imperfect, it will be easy to understand when the preterite is used. When talking about the past, the preterite *is* used when the imperfect *isn't*. That's an oversimplification, but at the same time it's a general rule of thumb that will help you out at first.

The imperfect has the following uses. Notice that the first three are very clearly indicated by the English equivalents of the imperfect.

1. To describe *repeated habitual actions* in the past

used to ⎫
⎬ + *verb*
would ⎭

De niños, **siempre jugábamos** en el parque todas las tardes.
As children, we always played (used to play, would play) in the park in the afternoon.

Todos los agostos iban a la costa.
Every August they went (used to go, would go) to the coast.

2. To describe an *action that was in progress* (when something else happened)

was/were + *-ing*

Ramón **pedía** la cena (cuando Cristina **llamó**).
Ramón was ordering dinner (when Cristina called).

Los taínos **vivían** en Puerto Rico (cuando **llegó** Colón).
The Taíno Indians were living in Puerto Rico (when Colombus arrived).

3. To describe two *simultaneous past actions in progress,* with **mientras**

was/were + *-ing*

Tú **leías mientras** Juan **escribía** la carta.
You were reading while Juan was writing the letter.

Mientras yo **veía** la tele, los niños **jugaban** a las cartas.
While I was watching TV, the kids were playing cards.

4. To describe ongoing *physical, mental, or emotional states* in the past

Estaban muy **distraídos.**
They were very distracted.

La **quería** muchísimo.
He loved her a lot.

Hacía calor, pero Luis **tenía** frío.
It was hot (out) but Luis was cold.

5. To tell *time* in the past and to express *age* with **tener**

Era la una. / **Eran las dos.**
It was one o'clock. / It was two o'clock.

Tenía 18 años.
She was 18 years old.

¡OJO!

Just as in the present, the singular form of the verb **ser** is used with one o'clock, the plural form from two o'clock on.

Summary of the Uses of the Imperfect

used to, would
was/were + *-ing*
simultaneous actions (**mientras**)
physical, mental, and emotional states
time
age

Práctica y comunicación

A. Cuando yo tenía 16 años...

> **Paso 1. Autoprueba.** Dé la terminación apropiada del imperfecto para cada verbo.
>
> **1.** yo habl_____   **3.** nosotros com_____   **5.** tú ten_____
> **2.** Uds. er_____   **4.** Pedro ib_____

Paso 2. Haga oraciones basadas en las siguientes frases, usando el imperfecto para hablar de su vida a los 16 años. Si alguna oración no es cierta para Ud., use **No...** .

1. ser muy estudioso/a
2. saber conducir (*to drive*)
3. tener la licencia de conducir
4. ir a la escuela secundaria en autobús
5. levantarse muchos domingos antes de las 10
6. tocar un instrumento en la banda de la escuela
7. ver mis programas favoritos en internet
8. querer un celular mejor que el que (*the one*) tenía

Paso 3. Ahora, en parejas, túrnense para entrevistarse usando como base las oraciones del **Paso 2**. Luego díganle a la clase algo que Uds. tenían en común.

MODELO: **E1:** Cuando tenías 16 años, ¿eras muy estudioso?
 E2: No, no era nada estudioso. ¿Y tú?
 E1: Yo sí.

B. La vida a los 7 años

Paso 1. Haga oraciones sobre la vida de Tina Acevedo, que vivía en Puerto Rico cuando tenía 7 años. Use el imperfecto de los verbos.

1. Tina: vivir en Bayamón, Puerto Rico
2. asistir a una escuela católica
3. hablar español todo el tiempo
4. aprender inglés en la escuela
5. dibujar (*to draw*) mucho en clase
6. jugar con sus compañeros en el parque
7. ir a casa de sus abuelos después de la escuela
8. ver sus programas favoritos en la tele
9. sus padres: llegar por ella a las 7:30
10. sus padres: llevarla a casa

Paso 2. Ahora haga oraciones similares a las oraciones del **Paso 1** pero con información de su propia (*own*) vida a los 7 años.

MODELO: Tina: vivir en Bayamón, Puerto Rico. →
 Yo **vivía** en St. Louis, Missouri.

Nota **comunicativa**

El progresivo en el pasado

Just like the present progressive, the *past progressive* (**el imperfecto progresivo**) emphasizes that an action was happening at that very moment. The past progressive is formed with the imperfect of **estar** plus the present participle (**-ndo**) of another verb.

Cuando mi tío llamó, **estábamos cenando.**   El sábado a las 10 de la noche, ¿**estabas estudiando**?
When my uncle called, we were having dinner.   *Saturday night at 10, were you studying?*

You will use the past progressive in **Práctica C.**

Prác. A, Paso 1: Answers: 1. hablaba 2. eran 3. comíamos 4. iba 5. tenías

Vocabulario útil

el bebé	
el timbre	doorbell
gritar	to shout
ladrar	to bark
pelear	to fight
sonar	to ring;
(suena)*	to sound

Vocabulario útil

caerse†	to fall down
cuidar	to take care of
sacar (qu)	to take something out

C. El trabajo de niñera (baby-sitter)

Paso 1. El trabajo de niñera puede ser muy pesado (*difficult*). ¿Qué estaba pasando cuando la niñera perdió por fin la paciencia? Describa todas las acciones que pueda, usando **estaba(n)** + *present participle* (**-ndo**).

MODELO: El bebé **estaba llorando.**

Paso 2. De adolescentes, ¿trabajaban Uds. de niñeros/as? ¿Tenían que cuidar a sus hermanos menores? ¿a los niños de sus parientes? En parejas, túrnense para hablar de sus experiencias trabajando como niñero/a. Háganse preguntas para obtener mucha información. Si no trabajaron de niñeros/as, cuenten sus experiencias en otros trabajos o sus experiencias *con* un niñero o niñera.

MODELO: E1: Cuando yo tenía 15 años, cuidaba a mi hermano menor.
E2: ¿Lo cuidabas todos los días? ¿Cuánto te pagaban tus padres? ¿Se portaba bien tu hermano menor? ¿Te daba mucho trabajo? ¿Qué cosas malas hacía siempre?

D. Los tiempos cambian (change). Las siguientes oraciones describen aspectos de la vida de hoy. En parejas, comparen estos aspectos con el estilo de vida alrededor del (*around the*) año 1900. Luego, describan dos cambios más.

MODELO: E1: Ahora la gente se comunica electrónicamente. →
E2: Alrededor del año 1900, la gente **se comunicaba por carta.**

1. Ahora muchísimas mujeres trabajan fuera de (*outside of the*) casa.
2. Hoy día la gente lee libros en formato electrónico.
3. Ahora la gente puede escuchar música en casa todo el tiempo.
4. Hoy día las mujeres se ponen pantalones.

1900

HOY

(Continúa.)

***Sonar** *is a stem-changing verb. Remember that the stem of present participles does not change with* **-ar** *verbs* (**sonando**).

†*The present participle of* **caer** *is like that of* **leer**: **cayendo.**

5. Ahora hay hombres enfermeros (*nurses*) y maestros (*teachers*).

6. Hoy, tenemos más máquinas y por eso hacemos menos trabajo físicamente.

7. Las familias son más pequeñas.

8. Muchas parejas viven juntas sin estar casadas (*married*).

E. Intercambios

Paso 1. En parejas, túrnense para entrevistarse sobre su adolescencia y los años de la escuela secundaria. Usen las siguientes categorías para organizar su conversación. Deben obtener detalles interesantes y personales de su compañero/a.

MODELO: gustar: molestar (*to annoy*) a alguien →

    E1: Cuando tenías 15 años, ¿a quién te gustaba molestar?

    E2: Me gustaba molestar a mi hermano menor. Él a veces tomaba mis cosas sin mi permiso.

    E1: ¿Y ahora todavía te gusta molestarlo?

    E2: La verdad es que sí. (*Actually, yes.*)

1. gustar: molestar a alguien, oír un tipo de música, vestirse con un estilo de ropa

2. preferir: programas de tele, películas, materias, comidas y bebidas

3. comer: a qué hora, dónde, con quién

4. leer: revistas, novelas

5. hacer: los fines de semana, después de las clases

6. discutir: con quién, sobre qué

Paso 2. Ahora díganle a la clase dos cosas que Uds. tenían en común.

MODELO: A Frank y a mí nos gustaba oír música rock. Preferíamos ver películas de acción.

Algo sobre...

Borinquen

Borinquen es el nombre que los taínos, los habitantes originales de Puerto Rico, le daban a su isla. El pueblo taíno se extinguió[a] en el siglo XVI, como consecuencia de la colonización. Pero los puertorriqueños están muy orgullosos[b] de su origen taíno. Los términos[c] **boricua** y **borinqueño/a** se usan con frecuencia para referirse a las personas, instituciones y tradiciones de la Isla. De hecho,[d] el himno oficial[e] puertorriqueño se llama «La borinqueña».

El emblema del *Coast Guard* de Puerto Rico, que lleva dos símbolos puertorriqueños: el coquí y el nombre Borinquen

¿Sabe Ud. quiénes eran los habitantes originales de su estado? ¿Está presente su herencia en el folclore de su estado?

[a]se... *died out* [b]*proud* [c]*terms* [d]De... *In fact* [e]himno... *national anthem*

¿Recuerda Ud.?

You have been using interrogative words since the beginning of *Puntos de partida*, so not much will be new for you in **Gramática 28.** Review what you already know by telling which interrogative word or phrase you associate with the following phrases.

1. un lugar

2. la hora

3. una persona

4. la manera de hacer algo

5. una selección

6. la razón (*reason*) por algo

7. el lugar de origen de una persona

8. un destino

9. una cantidad

10. ser el dueño de algo

28 Getting Information (Part 2)
Summary of Interrogative Words

Gramática en acción: Un restaurante de Connecticut

1. ¿Cómo se llama el restaurante?
2. ¿En qué ciudad de Connecticut está?
3. ¿En qué tipo de cocina se especializa el restaurante?
4. ¿Qué grupo toca el viernes, 6 de octubre?

¿Y Ud.?

¿Cuántas preguntas más puede Ud. hacer sobre este restaurante, por (*based on*) lo que dice el anuncio?

Here are all of the interrogatives that you have learned so far. Only more information about using **¿qué?** and **¿cuál(es)?**, both of which express *what?* or *which?* in Spanish, is new.

¡OJO!

Remember that interrogative words always have an accent mark in Spanish, and that questions have two question marks: **¿ ?**

¿Cómo?	How?	**¿Dónde?**	Where?
¿Cuándo?	When?	**¿De dónde?**	From where?
¿A qué hora?	At what time?	**¿Adónde?**	Where (to)?
¿Qué?	What? Which?	**¿Cuánto/a?**	How much?
¿Cuál(es)?	What? Which one(s)?	**¿Cuántos/as?**	How many?
¿Por qué?	Why?	**¿Quién(es)?**	Who?
		¿De quién(es)?	Whose?

Uses of ¿qué? and ¿cuál? / Los usos de ¿qué? y ¿cuál?

1. **¿Qué? + es/son = Definition**
   Use **¿Qué es/son... ?** to ask for a definition.

   ¿Qué es esto?
   What is this?

   ¿Qué son las Antillas?
   What are the West Indies?

2. **¿Qué? + verb = Explanation/Identification**
   Use **¿Qué... ?** with any verb other than **ser** to ask for an identification or an elaboration.

   ¿Qué quieres?
   What do you want?

   ¿Qué tocas?
   What (instrument) do you play?

3. **¿Qué? + noun = Identification**
   The interrogative **¿qué?** can be directly followed by a noun. The question asks the listener to identify or specify information, often making a choice.

   ¿Qué deporte prefieres?
   What (Which) sport do you prefer?

   ¿Qué playa te gusta más?
   What (Which) beach do you like most?

   ¿Qué instrumento musical tocas?
   What (Which) musical instrument do you play?

4. ¿Cuál(es)? + *verb* **= Choice**
Use **¿cuál(es)?** to express *what* when it means *which one*, that is, when it calls for a choice.

¡OJO!

¿Qué?, not **¿cuál?**, is followed by a noun. Compare these sentences:

> **¿Qué libro** quieres? = *which book?*
> **¿Cuál** quieres? = *which one?*
> **¿Cuál de los dos** quieres? = *which one of the two?*

Sometimes a phrase like **de los dos (tres...**) makes the choice more obvious.

¿Cuál es la clase más grande?
What (Which [one]) is the biggest class?

¿Cuáles son tus jugadores favoritos?
What (Which [ones]) are your favorite players?

¿Cuál es tu (número de) teléfono?
What is your phone number?

¿Cuál prefieres?
Which one do you prefer?

¿Cuál de los dos coches vas a comprar?
Which of the two cars are you going to buy?

Práctica y comunicación

A. Preguntas personales

Paso 1. Autoprueba. Empareje las palabras interrogativas con la información que piden.

1. ¿Cuándo?
2. ¿Dónde?
3. ¿Qué?
4. ¿Cuánto?
5. ¿Cuál?

   a. un lugar
   b. una selección
   c. un número o una cantidad

   d. una definición
   e. la hora
   f. una explicación

> **Summary of ¿qué? Versus ¿cuál?**
>
> **¿qué? + es/son** = definition
>   **+** *verb* = explanation
>   **+** *noun*
> **¿cuál(es)? +** *verb* = choice

Paso 2. Complete las siguientes preguntas con **qué** o **cuál(es)** y contéstelas.

1. ¿Tiene Ud. un segundo nombre (*middle name*)? ¿_____ es? ¿_____ son sus dos apellidos, según el sistema hispano de apellidos?
2. ¿_____ es su número de teléfono?
3. ¿_____ es su dirección (*address*) postal? ¿_____ es su e-mail?
4. ¿_____ estado es su lugar de origen?
5. ¿_____ son las materias que Ud. toma este semestre/trimestre? ¿_____ es su favorita?
6. ¿_____ es más divertido para Ud., practicar un deporte o ir al cine?
7. ¿_____ tarea doméstica odia más?
8. ¿_____ es un equipo? ¿_____ es su equipo de fútbol americano favorito?

Paso 3. Ahora, en parejas, túrnense para hacer y contestar las preguntas del **Paso 2.** Luego díganle a la clase algo que Uds. tienen en común.

B. Intercambios

Paso 1. En parejas, túrnense para entrevistarse sobre los siguientes temas. Empiecen las preguntas con **¿Qué... ?** or **¿Cuál(es)...?** Hablen de sus preferencias actuales (*current*) o de sus preferencias de niño/a (usando el imperfecto).

MODELOS: estaciones del año →
       ¿Qué estación del año **prefieres?** (¿**Qué** estación **preferías** de niño/a?)
       ¿Cuál es / Cuál era tu estación del año favorita?

1. estilo de música
2. pasatiempos o deportes
3. programas de televisión

4. materias este semestre/trimestre
5. colores
6. tipos de comida

Paso 2. Ahora, díganle a la clase una cosa que tienen en común y otra en la que (*which*) no están de acuerdo.

¿Recuerda Ud.?

You learned how to make comparisons in **Gramática 17** (**Cap. 6**). Before you start **Gramática 29,** review what you remember about comparisons by completing the following comparative phrases with the appropriate word.

1. más dinero _______ tú
2. tan simpáticos _______ ellos
3. _______ hermanas como...
4. menos libros _______ Cecilia
5. correr _______ como Ud.
6. viejo, _______

Grammar Tutorial 29
connect SPANISH
www.connectspanish.com

29 Expressing Extremes

Superlatives

Gramática en acción: Los puertorriqueños más famosos

¿Está Ud. de acuerdo? Corrija las declaraciones falsas, según su opinión.

	CIERTO	FALSO
1. Jennifer López es la cantante puertorriqueña más conocida del mundo.	☐	☐
2. Benicio del Toro es el actor puertorriqueño más famoso del mundo.	☐	☐
3. Roberto Clemente, de origen puertorriqueño, es el mejor beisbolista hispano de todos los tiempos.	☐	☐

¿Y Ud.?

Complete las siguientes declaraciones para expresar su opinión.

1. El cantante hispano o hispana más popular del momento es _______.
2. La mejor actriz (*actress*) del momento es _______.
3. En la actualidad (*Currently*), la música más popular es _______ (la música de _______, la música de estilo _______).

Comparatives / Los comparativos	Superlatives / Los superlativos
Julio es **más** alto **que** Juanito.	Julio es el niño más alto de la clase. (Julio es el más alto de la clase.*)
El fútbol es **más** popular **que** el golf.	El fútbol es el deporte más popular del mundo. (El fútbol es el más popular del mundo.*)
La comida italiana es **buena,** pero la comida mexicana es **mejor**.	La comida mexicana es la mejor comida de todas las comidas del mundo. (La comida mexicana es la mejor de todas las comidas del mundo.*)

the superlative / **el superlativo** = an adjective or adverb that expresses an extreme

The most famous Puerto Ricans *Do you agree?* **1.** *Jennifer Lopez is the best known Puerto Rican singer in the world.* **2.** *Benicio del Toro is the most famous Puerto Rican actor in the world.* **3.** *Roberto Clemente, of Puerto Rican descent, is the best Hispanic baseball player of all time.*

Notice how adjectives can be used as nouns:* **el niño más alto *(the tallest child)* → **el más alto** *(the tallest), and so on. You can learn more about using adjectives in this way in Appendix 2, Using Adjectives as Nouns.*

Superlatives / Los superlativos

1. Forming the Superlative

To express the *most/best/least/worst,* and so on, the comparative forms are used with the definite article.

> **¡OJO!**
> in/of = **de**

el / la / los / las + *noun* + **más / menos** + *adjective* + **de**

El basquetbol es **el deporte más competitivo del** mundo.
Basketball is the most competitive sport in the world.

El golf es **el deporte menos peligroso de** todos.
Golf is the least dangerous sport of all.

2. Irregular Superlatives

Mejor and **peor** generally precede the noun.

el / la / los / las + **mejor(es) / peor(es)** + *noun* + **de**

Son **los mejores refrigeradores de** la tienda.
They're the best refrigerators in the store.

La verdad es que es **el peor jugador del** equipo.
The truth is that he's the worst player on the team.

Note that **mejor** and **peor** are often used alone (without the article or **de**).

Ana es **mi mejor** amiga.
Ana is my best friend.

¡Esa fue **tu peor** idea!
That was your worst idea!

Mayor and **menor** are often used without the noun.

Lorenzo es **el mayor de** los hermanos y Leticia es **la menor**.
Lorenzo is the oldest of the siblings and Leticia is the youngest.

Práctica y comunicación

A. Opiniones personales

Summary of Superlatives

el / la / los / las + *noun* + **más / menos** + *adjective* + **de**

el / la / los / las + { **mejor(es) / peor(es)** / **mayor(es) / menor(es)** } + *noun* + **de**

Paso 1. Autoprueba. Ordene las palabras para hacer oraciones con sentido (*meaningful*) que expresan ideas superlativas.

1. **Es...** ciudad / más / el / grande / la / parque / de
2. **Son...** clase / los / difíciles / de / niños / la / más
3. **Visité...** del / los / mundo / museos / mejores
4. **Vi...** peor / año / película / la / del

Paso 2. Use las siguientes ideas para dar su opinión sobre lo que es «más» en cada categoría.

MODELO: una estación del año (frío) ⟶ El invierno es **la** estación **más fría del** año.

1. un día festivo del año (divertido)
2. una materia de este semestre/trimestre (difícil)
3. una persona de la familia (vieja)
4. una persona de la familia (joven)
5. un mes del año (bueno)
6. un día de la semana (malo)
7. un amigo / una amiga (bueno/a)

Paso 3. Ahora, en parejas, usen las ideas del **Paso 2** para entrevistarse. Luego, díganle a la clase algo que tienen en común.

MODELO:: **E1:** ¿Cómo se llama tu mejor amigo o amiga?
E2: Mi mejor amigo es Jacobo. ¿Y tu mejor amigo?
E1: (Es) Luis.

Prác. A, Paso 1: Answers: 1. *Es el parque más grande de la ciudad.* **2.** *Son los niños más difíciles de la clase.* **3.** *Visité los mejores museos del mundo.* **4.** *Vi la peor película del año.*

B. Superlativos

Paso 1. Modifique las siguientes oraciones para hacer una forma superlativa.

MODELO: Es una estudiante muy alta. (la clase) →
Es **la** estudiante **más alta de la clase.**

1. Son unos días festivos muy divertidos. (el año)
2. Es una clase muy interesante. (todas mis clases)
3. Es una persona muy inteligente. (todos mis amigos)
4. Son ciudades muy grandes. (los Estados Unidos)
5. Es un estado muy pequeño. (el país)
6. Es un perro muy pequeño. (el mundo)
7. Es una residencia muy ruidosa (*noisy*). (la universidad)
8. Es una montaña muy alta. (el mundo)

Paso 2. Ahora repita cada oración con información verdadera.

MODELO: **Carla** es la estudiante más alta de la clase.

C. Intercambios. En parejas, túrnense para expresar sus opiniones sobre las siguientes ideas. Luego compartan (*share*) sus opiniones con la clase.

MODELO: el peor / mejor restaurante de la ciudad →
E1: Yo creo que _____ es **el peor** restaurante **de** la ciudad.
E2: En mi opinión, **el peor** restaurante **de** la ciudad es _____.
→ No estamos de acuerdo. Yo creo que _____ es **el peor** restaurante **de** la ciudad. Mi compañero/a cree que **el peor** es _____.

Estrategia

Emphatic adjectives formed with **-ísimo/a** cannot be used in a superlative construction. You can use **-ísimo/a** adjectives in this activity to describe individual nouns but not to make comparisons or superlative statements.

1. el peor / mejor restaurante de la ciudad
2. un libro interesantísimo / aburridísimo
3. un plato riquísimo / malísimo
4. un programa de televisión interesantísimo / pesadísimo
5. un lugar tranquilísimo / animadísimo / peligrosísimo (*very dangerous*)
6. la canción más bonita / fea del año
7. la mejor / peor película del año

Nota **comunicativa**

Los diminutivos

In Spanish, it is very common to add a suffix to nouns and adjectives to express littleness or affection. The most common diminutive ending is **-ito/a**.

• If the word ends in a consonant, **-ito/a** is added to the singular form (and any accent on the word is dropped): **papel → papelito, fácil → facilito.**

• If the word ends in a vowel, the final vowel is dropped before adding **-ito/a** (and any accent on the

word is dropped): **guapo → guapito, libro → librito (libros → libritos), rápido → rapidito.**

• Spelling changes occur when the final consonant is **c, g,** or **z: poco → poquito, amiga → amiguita, pedazos (chunks) → pedacitos.**

You will use diminutives in **Práctica D.**

D. ¿Diminutivos para Ud.? Los diminutivos se usan para hablar de algo con afecto y ternura (*tenderness*). ¿Usarían Uds. (*Would you use*) un diminutivo para hablar de las siguientes personas y cosas? Expliquen sus respuestas.

MODELO: **1.** ¿su cuarto? →
E1: Sí, mi **cuartito,** porque es muy pequeño / es un lugar especial.
E2: No, no quiero llamarlo **cuartito,** porque no es pequeño / no me gusta.

1. ¿su cuarto?
2. ¿su libro de español?
3. ¿su hermano/a (sobrino/a) menor?
4. ¿su gorra favorita?
5. ¿su libro favorito cuando Ud. era pequeño/a?

Un poco de todo

A. Lengua y cultura: Un poco de la historia de Puerto Rico

Paso 1. Complete the following passage with the correct form of the words in parentheses, as suggested by context. When two possibilities are given in parentheses, select the correct word. **¡OJO!** Give the preterite form of the verbs marked *P:* and the imperfect of those marked *I:*.

En la isla de Puerto Rico, como en todas las Antillas Mayores, (*I:* vivir[1]) los indígenas taínos. Cristóbal Colón (*P:* llegar[2]) a la Isla en 1493, en su segunda[a] expedición al Nuevo Mundo. (Se / Le[3]) dice que el jefe[b] de los taínos, que (*I:* tener[4]) el título de cacique, (*P:* recibir[5]) a Colón con un collar[c] de oro. (Por / Para[6]) eso Colón pensó que (*I:* haber[7]) mucho oro en la Isla, pero no tenía (razón / prisa[8]). De todas formas,[d] los españoles explotaron la Isla intensamente. En poco tiempo, la población taína prácticamente (*P:* desaparecer[e9]) debido a[f] tres factores: (el / la[10]) explotación física causada por labores intensas,[g] las rebeliones de los nativos y las enfermedades[h] que los españoles (*P:* llevar[11]) consigo,[i] que (*I:* ser[12]) nuevas para los taínos. La población africana, que los españoles llevaron a la Isla como esclavos,[j] (*P:* empezar[13]) a llegar en el siglo[k] XVI.

En el siglo XIX, por toda Latinoamérica, (*I:* haber[14]) guerras[l] contra España para obtener la independencia. Pero las Antillas no (*P:* independizarse[15]). En 1898 Puerto Rico se convirtió en[m] territorio de los Estados Unidos, después de que España (*P:* perder[16]) la guerra que en los Estados Unidos (*P:* recibir[17]) el nombre de «*the Spanish American War*» (la Guerra Hispanoamericana).

En 1917 los puertorriqueños (*P:* ser[18]) declarados ciudadanos[n] (estadounidense[19]) y, desde 1953, su país es un Estado Libre Asociado a los Estados Unidos de América. Esto significa que aunque[ñ] no es independiente, tiene plena[o] autonomía interna.

El monumento a las raíces puertorriqueñas en Dorado, Puerto Rico

[a]*second* [b]*chief* [c]*necklace* [d]*De... In any case* [e]*to disappear* [f]*debido... due to* [g]*labores... hard labor* [h]*illnesses* [i]*with them* [j]*slaves* [k]*century* [l]*wars* [m]*se... became a* [n]*citizens* [ñ]*although* [o]*full*

Paso 2. Comprensión. Conteste las siguientes preguntas.

1. ¿De qué grupo de islas forma parte Puerto Rico?
2. ¿Quiénes eran los habitantes originales de Puerto Rico?
3. ¿Cuándo llegaron los españoles a Puerto Rico por primera vez?
4. ¿Después del siglo XVI, qué otros grupos raciales había en la Isla?
5. ¿Desde cuándo es Puerto Rico territorio de los Estados Unidos?
6. ¿Cuál es la situación política actual de Puerto Rico?

Paso 3. Ahora, en parejas, den información histórica sobre su estado (o país) comparable a la información sobre Puerto Rico. Aquí hay unas sugerencias.

1. qué pueblo(s) vivía(n) en su estado (país) originalmente
2. qué otros pueblos llegaron más tarde y cuándo
3. si hubo guerra(s) con otro país y cuándo
4. si ganó su independencia de otro país y cuándo
5. cuándo se convirtió en estado de la Unión estadounidense

B. ¿Qué hizo Ricardo ayer?

Paso 1. Narre lo que Ricardo hizo ayer, usando como base los dibujos y las ideas debajo de ellos.

MODELO: despertarse temprano / ser 6:30 →
    Ricardo **se despertó** temprano. **Eran** las seis y media de la mañana.

Vocabulario **útil**

primero...
luego... y...
después... y...
finalmente (por fin)...

Estrategia

- La primera frase debajo del dibujo indica una acción. Por eso el verbo se conjuga en el **pretérito**.
- La segunda frase describe un aspecto de la situación en ese momento. Por eso el verbo se conjuga en el **imperfecto**.

1. quedarse en cama durmiendo / tener sueño

2. ducharse y vestirse rápidamente / tener prisa

3. llegar tarde a clase / la profesora: explicar el nuevo capítulo

4. almorzar con unos amigos / tener muchísima hambre

5. jugar un partido de basquetbol / haber mucha gente en el gimnasio

6. regresar a casa y preparar la cena / ser temprano todavía (*still*)

7. alguien: llamarlo por teléfono / ser su mamá

8. acostarse y dormirse inmediatamente / estar cansadísimo

Paso 2. Ahora, en parejas, hablen de su día de ayer, siguiendo las ideas del **Paso 1.** Luego díganle al resto de la clase algo que tuvieron en común.

En **su** comunidad

Entreviste a una persona hispana de su universidad o ciudad sobre lo que hace en su tiempo libre.

PREGUNTAS POSIBLES

- ¿Practica algún deporte? ¿Es su deporte favorito uno de los deportes más populares de su cultura?
- ¿Cuáles son sus pasatiempos favoritos? ¿Cuáles eran sus pasatiempos favoritos cuando era niño/a?
- ¿Hace muchos quehaceres domésticos? ¿Cuáles son? ¿Cuáles son los quehaceres que más odia? ¿Qué tareas domésticas tenía que hacer cuando tenía 12 o 13 años?

«Deportes que mueven masas» Segmento 2

Antes de mirar

Conteste las siguientes preguntas.

¿Vio Ud. recientemente la final de algún campeonato (*championship*) importante? ¿Qué equipos se disputaron (*fought for*) el campeonato? ¿Cuál ganó?

Este segmento

Laura presenta un reportaje sobre el deporte rey (*number one*) en México.

«Y muchos [mexicanos] se unen a una porra (*fan club*) para acompañar a su equipo hasta el campo de fútbol y defenderlo a gritos (*with shouts* [*of support*]).»

Vocabulario del segmento

hasta	even	el/la comentarista	commentator
chévere	great		
gritar	to yell; to scream	angloparlante	English-speaking
cualquier sitio	any place	sabio/a	wise
el asiento	seat	la cita	date; appointment
disfrutar	to enjoy	que la pasen bien	have a good time
el grito	yell; scream		
¿han escuchado?	have you heard?	que gane su equipo	may your team win

Fragmento del guion

Pero el auténtico deporte rey del planeta es el fútbol. Les voy a dar un dato[a] fascinante: se calcula que más de mil millones de personas en todo el mundo vieron la final de la Copa Mundial[b] de Fútbol del año 2010, que se disputaron[c] España y Holanda. ¡Más de mil millones!

[a]*fact* [b]*Copa... World Cup* [c]*se... was fought out by*

Después de mirar

A. ¿Está claro? Complete las oraciones con información del video.

1. El _____ por ciento de los beisbolistas de las grandes ligas es de origen hispano.
2. El deporte rey del planeta es el _____.
3. El deporte rey en México es el _____.
4. _____ ganó la Copa Mundial en 2010.
5. Los comentaristas _____ no saben gritar bien «¡gol!».

B. Un poco más. Conteste las siguientes preguntas.

1. ¿Dónde vio Ana la final de la Copa del Mundo?
2. ¿Qué hizo Ana durante el partido?
3. ¿Quién prefería ver los partidos de fútbol en español? ¿Por qué?

C. Y ahora, Uds. En parejas, escojan uno de los dos deportes de este programa (el béisbol, **Segmento 1**, o el fútbol, este **Segmento**) y hablen de la situación de este deporte en su país. ¿Es este deporte uno de los más populares? ¿Es popular por el número de espectadores o por el número de personas que lo practican? ¿Dónde se practica?

A LEER

¿Hay playas muy frecuentadas por la gente cerca de su ciudad o estado? En la zona donde Ud. vive, ¿cuáles son los lugares que más visita la gente en el tiempo libre?

Lectura cultural: Puerto Rico
El tiempo libre en Puerto Rico

A muchos puertorriqueños les gusta pasar el tiempo junto al[a] mar. Es lógico: Puerto Rico y sus islas más pequeñas, como Vieques y Culebra, están rodeadas de[b] deliciosas aguas cálidas[c] y hermosas[d] playas. Muchas son de arena[e] fina y mar tranquilo, ideales para relajarse y nadar. Otras, especialmente en el norte, son excelentes para hacer *surfing*. Y otras (al este y al sur) ofrecen el espectáculo natural de la bioluminiscencia: unos microorganismos llamados dinoflagelados iluminan el agua del mar en la noche.

Aunque[f] en Puerto Rico hace buen tiempo todo el año, es en los meses de verano (de mayo a septiembre) cuando los puertorriqueños van más a la playa. Amigos y familia, música, comida, una hamaca entre palmeras... ¿Qué más se puede pedir?

[a]*junto... next to* [b]*rodeadas... surrounded by* [c]*warm* [d]*beautiful* [e]*sand* [f]*Although*

El Fuerte de San Felipe del Morro, que guardaba el puerto (*port*) de la bahía de San Juan, Puerto Rico

Un símbolo puertorriqueño: El Viejo San Juan

Los puertorriqueños se sienten muy orgullosos[a] de su herencia cultural y de sus tradiciones, heredadas de los taínos, africanos y españoles. El Viejo San Juan representa la cultura y tradición españolas. Sus edificios coloniales, sus calles adoquinadas,[b] el Fuerte[c] San Felipe del Morro, la Catedral y otros edificios históricos representan la historia de la Isla.

[a]*proud* [b]*cobblestone* [c]*Fort*

COMPRENSIÓN

1. ¿Cuáles son los meses en que los puertorriqueño van más a la playa?
2. ¿Qué es la bioluminiscencia?
3. ¿Dónde están las mejores playas puertorriqueñas para hacer *surfing*?
4. ¿Cuáles son dos de los pasatiempos populares en algunos países hispanohablantes?
5. ¿Qué deporte es muy popular en la Argentina?
6. ¿Con qué herencia cultural se identifica el Viejo San Juan?

En otros países hispanos

- **En todo el mundo hispanohablante** Jugar al dominó y hacer la sobremesa son pasatiempos muy populares en muchos países hispanos. El dominó es un juego muy fácil de aprender, pero el juego se complica muchísimo —y también se hace más interesante— jugando en parejas. La sobremesa es el tiempo que se pasa charlando[a] en la mesa después de la comida. No es nada extraño[b] que un grupo de parientes o amigos hispanos pase dos o tres horas sentados[c] a la mesa, primero comiendo, luego tomando café y charlando, hasta unir el almuerzo con la merienda.

- **En la Argentina** En este país sudamericano hay gran afición por el deporte del polo. La Argentina domina ese deporte en el panorama mundial.

[a]*chatting* [b]*strange* [c]*seated*

Y ahora, Uds.

¿Cuáles son los pasatiempos que Uds. asocian más con la vida familiar estadounidense? ¿Son típicos en su familia también? Si no, ¿cuáles son los pasatiempos de su familia?

Del mundo hispano

Antes de leer

Piense Ud. en cómo usa Ud. su teléfono celular. ¿Cuáles son los aspectos positivos y negativos de su uso?

Lectura: Los teléfonos celulares

Volver a conectar

Aunque[a] tabletas, *smartphones* y otros dispositivos están pensados y diseñados[b] para servirnos, los estudios realizados[c] hasta ahora... constatan[d] nuestra «dependencia electrónica». Sin embargo, desconectar es posible. El psicólogo Fernando Azor nos aporta[e] algunas sugerencias:

PRIORIZAR Hay que atender[f] primero a aquellos que se dirigen a[g] nosotros en persona; después las llamadas; después los mensajes instantáneos y, por último, los correos electrónicos.

RESPONDER MÁS TARDE No responder de inmediato es un buen entrenamiento[h] para combatir la ansiedad. Ni nosotros estamos obligados a contestar al instante,[i] ni ellos pueden sentirse cuestionados[j] porque no se les escriba en el acto.[k]

ABSTENERSE[l] Ser capaz[m] de pasar un fin de semana o un día entero con el teléfono apagado es una señal[n] de sana independencia. Si este período es demasiado largo, hay que tratar de desconectar todas las redes[ñ] (si no, al menos[o] el wifi) en determinados momentos del día, por ejemplo durante la noche.

CONFIGURAR Configure su dispositivo para que los nuevos correos o mensajes instantáneos solo lleguen cuando usted actualice[p] manualmente. Evitará así[q] las constantes miradas a la pantalla en busca de notificaciones.

HUMANIZAR La tecnología crea una ilusoria sensación de intimidad y contacto. Por ello[r] es aconsejable,[s] al menos una vez a la semana, «desvirtualizar» nuestras relaciones y quedar con ese interlocutor[t] para tomar un café o dar un paseo real.

SELECCIONAR A menudo[u] mantenemos relaciones virtuales que, en realidad, no aportan[v] nada a nuestra vida,[w] o que incluso nos restan[x] energía y tiempo. Por ello, es muy saludable ser un poco más darwinistas* con nuestra agenda de contactos, y no dudar a la hora de dejar de[y] ser «amigo» de aquellas personas a las que, en el fondo, no nos une nada.[z]

[a]*Although* [b]pensados... *imagined and designed* [c]*completed* [d]*show* [e]ofrece [f]*pay attention* [g]se... *address* [h]*training* [i]al... *immediately* [j]*let down* [k]en... *immediately* [l]*Abstain* [m]*capable* [n]*sign* [ñ]hay... *it's necessary to try to disconnect the networks* [o]al... *at least* [p]*refresh, update* [q]Evitará... *That way you will avoid* [r]Por... Por eso [s]*advisable* [t]*conversation partner* [u]A... Con frecuencia [v]contribuyen [w]*life* [x]incluso... *even take away from us* [y]no... *not hesitate when it comes to stop* [z]a... *whom, in the final analysis, we have no ties with*

Vocabulario **para leer**

apagado/a	turned off
el dispositivo	device
la llamada	(phone) call
la pantalla	screen
quedar con	to meet, make a date with
saludable	healthy
sano/a	healthy

Comprensión

A. Ideas principales. ¿Cuál de las siguientes oraciones resume mejor la lectura? Señale (*Point out*) evidencia en el texto para la respuesta que seleccione.

1. Los teléfonos celulares son dispositivos esenciales para la vida moderna y no se puede vivir sin ellos.
2. La dependencia de los teléfonos celulares y otros dispositivos es un problema, pero es posible controlarla.
3. Es mejor vivir sin teléfonos celulares y otros dispositivos.

B. Aplicación personal. De las seis sugerencias que ofrece la lectura, ¿cuáles implementa Ud. ahora? ¿Cuáles quiere implementar? ¿Cuáles no son ni (*neither*) apropiadas ni (*nor*) aceptables para Ud.? Explique sus respuestas.

---

*Darwinistas *refers to Charles Darwin, the nineteenth-century theorist of biological evolution. In this context, the term refers to an action that will lead to self-preservation.*

Unos compañeros hablan de «un desastre»

Antes de escuchar

¿Qué quehaceres hace Ud. para mantener limpio su apartamento o alcoba? ¿Cuál de los quehaceres hace con más frecuencia? ¿Cuál le molesta más hacer?

Vocabulario **para escuchar**			
verdadero/a	real	**no discutamos**	let's not argue
no te preocupes	don't worry	**yo me encargo de**	I'll take care of
arreglar	to tidy up	**¡muévete!**	move it!, get a move on!

Después de escuchar

A. ¿Quién lo va a hacer? Empareje cada tarea con la persona que la va a hacer.

TAREAS

1. _____ limpiar la cocina
2. _____ limpiar el baño
3. _____ pasar la aspiradora
4. _____ sacar la basura

PERSONAS

a. Jorge
b. Hilda
c. Ana

B. Otros detalles. Conteste las siguientes preguntas según el diálogo.

1. ¿Por qué es urgente limpiar el apartamento?
2. ¿Quién está dispuesto (*willing*) a ayudar?
3. ¿Quién no tiene muchas ganas de ayudar?

PRODUCCIÓN PERSONAL

¡Ahora, yo!

A. Use de modelo las preguntas y respuestas de la página 295 de este capítulo para hablar de su tiempo libre y de sus pasatiempos favoritos.

B. Filme una entrevista con un(a) atleta hispanohablante de su universidad. Si no encuentra ninguno/a, entreviste a un(a) atleta anglohablante (*English-speaking*) y use su voz en off (*voiceover*) para traducir al español las ideas principales de lo que dice el/la atleta.

A ESCRIBIR

Un ensayo sobre los pasatiempos y diversiones

En el Bosque Nacional el Yunque, en Puerto Rico

¿Cuáles son las actividades típicas de los estudiantes de su universidad? ¿Y qué hacía Ud. cuando era más joven? ¿Era similar a lo que hace ahora? Ud. va a escribir un ensayo sobre estas ideas.

Preparar

Paso 1. En parejas, piensen en las actividades típicas de la gente de su edad (*age group*) y en concreto de los estudiantes de su universidad. La tabla sugiere (*suggests*) algunas categorías, pero Uds. las pueden ampliar o modificar.

Actividades durante el tiempo libre	La gente de nuestra edad, en general	Los estudiantes de esta universidad
Físicas		
Intelectuales		
Vida (*Life*) social		
Otras		

Paso 2. Ahora use la información del **Paso 1** para escribir un ensayo comparativo. ¿Es Ud. una persona representativa de su generación y de su universidad? Cuando Ud. era más joven, ¿hacía las mismas cosas? Hay más ayuda (*help*) en Connect.

Más ideas para su portafolio

- Si Ud. juega en un equipo o hace un deporte a nivel competitivo, incluya una foto de Ud. haciendo ese deporte. Describa su posición en el equipo y otros detalles importantes (ranking, nombre del entrenador / de la entrenadora, etcétera). Si no practica ningún deporte, describa el tipo de ejercicio físico que hace, incluyendo una foto si es posible. Y si no hace ningún tipo de ejercicio físico, explique cómo pasa su tiempo libre.

- Incluya dos imágenes de lugares favoritos o especiales que Ud. relaciona con el tiempo libre y los pasatiempos de su infancia o adolescencia. Explique por qué iba allí, y qué hacía, con quiénes, etcétera.

- Si ha estado jugando (*have been playing*) Practice Spanish: Study Abroad, en Quest 7 Ud. supo que su amigo David está leyendo *El ingenioso hidalgo don Quijote de la Mancha*, de Miguel de Cervantes Saavedra, en su tiempo libre. Busque información sobre la trama (*plot*), el autor, el contexto histórico, los personajes, etcétera, de esta novela. ¿Por qué cree Ud. que esta novela es tan famosa? ¿Ve paralelos entre los personajes de *Don Quijote* y los personajes del juego? Escriba un informe y entrégueselo a su profesor(a) o presente sus ideas en clase.

Sugerencia: You are now ready to play Quest 7 in **Practice Spanish: Study Abroad** (www.mhpractice.com).

LEARNSMART
Visit **www.connectspanish.com** to practice the vocabulary and grammar points covered in this chapter.

AFTER STUDYING THIS CHAPTER I CAN . . .

☐ talk about sports and other pastimes (296)

☐ talk about household chores (298)

☐ use the imperfect to describe past actions (302–304)

☐ use interrogatives more effectively, especially **¿qué?** and **¿cuál(es)?** (308–309)

☐ use superlatives to describe "the most" in a category (310–311)

☐ recognize/describe at least 2–3 aspects of Puerto Rican cultures

Gramática en breve

26. The Imperfect

Regular -ar Endings
-aba, -abas, -aba, -ábamos, -abais, -aban

Regular -er/-ir Endings
-ía, -ías, -ía, -íamos, -íais, -ían

Verbs Irregular in the Imperfect
ir: **iba, ibas, iba, íbamos, ibais, iban**
ser: **era, eras, era, éramos, erais, eran**
ver: **veía, veías, veía, veíamos, veíais, veían**

27. Superlatives

el/la/los/las + *noun* + **más/menos** + *adjective* + **de**
el/la/los/las + **mejor(es)/peor(es)** + *noun* + **de**

28. Interrogative Words

¿qué? } = definition, explanation
= identification: + *noun* = *what/which . . .?*
¿cuál(es)? = choice: + *verb* = *what/which (one) . . .?*

Vocabulario

Los verbos

pelear	to fight
sonar (suena)	to ring; to sound
tocarle (qu) a uno (like gustar)	to be someone's turn

Repaso: deber, necesitar, tener que

Los pasatiempos, diversiones y aficiones

la afición	hobby
la diversión	fun activity

el pasatiempo	pastime
los ratos libres	spare (free) time
el tiempo libre	free time
aburrirse	to get bored
caminar	to walk
dar una caminata	to hike; to go for a hike
dar un paseo	to take a walk
hacer un *picnic*	to have a picnic
hacer planes (*m.*) para + *inf.*	to make plans to (do something)
hacer (el) yoga	to do yoga
ir...	to go . . .
a un bar / a una discoteca	to a bar / to a disco
a un museo	to a museum
al teatro / a un concierto	to the theater / to a concert
jugar (juego) (gu) al ajedrez / a las cartas / a los videojuegos	to play chess/cards /videogames
ser...	to be . . .
aburrido/a	boring
divertido/a	fun

Repaso: dar/hacer una fiesta, hacer *camping*, ir a una fiesta / al cine / a ver una película, jugar (juego) (gu), sacar (qu) fotos, tomar el sol

Los deportes

correr	to run
entrenar	to practice; to train
esquiar (esquío)	to ski
ganar	to win
hacer *surfing*	to surf
montar a caballo	to ride a horse
montar/pasear en bicicleta	to ride a bicycle
patinar	to skate
ser aficionado/a (a)	to be a fan (of)

Repaso: jugar (juego) (gu) al + *sport,* nadar, perder (pierdo), practicar (qu)

el ciclismo	bicycling
el deporte	sport
el equipo	team
el fútbol	soccer
el fútbol americano	football
el/la jugador(a)	player
la natación	swimming
el partido	game, match
el patinaje	skating
la pelota	ball

Cognados: el basquetbol, el béisbol, el esquí, el golf, el hockey, el tenis, el voleibol

Algunos aparatos domésticos

el aparato doméstico	home appliance
la aspiradora	vacuum cleaner
la cafetera	coffeemaker
el congelador	freezer
el horno de microondas	microwave oven
la lavadora	washing machine
el lavaplatos	dishwasher
el refrigerador	refrigerator
la secadora	clothes dryer
la tostadora	toaster

Repaso: la estufa

Los quehaceres domésticos

el quehacer doméstico	household chore
barrer el piso	to sweep the floor
hacer la cama	to make the bed
lavar	to wash
limpiar (la casa)	to clean (house)
pasar la aspiradora	to vacuum
planchar	to iron
poner la mesa	to set the table
quitar la mesa	to clear the table

sacar (qu) la basura	to take out the trash

Repaso: la cama, la casa, hacer, la mesa, los platos, poner, la ropa

Otros sustantivos

la escuela	school
el/la niñero/a	baby-sitter

Los adjetivos

deportivo/a	sporting, sports (*adj.*); sports-loving
doméstico/a	domestic, related to the home
libre	free, unoccupied
pesado/a	boring; difficult
-ito/a	small, little

Palabras adicionales

al aire libre	outdoors
de adolescente	as an adolescent
de niño/a	as a child
en la actualidad	currently, right now
mientras	while

Repaso: ¿a qué hora?, ¿adónde?, ¿cómo?, ¿cuál(es)?, ¿cuándo?, ¿cuánto/a?, ¿cuántos/as?, ¿de dónde?, ¿de quién(es)?, ¿dónde?, ¿por qué?, ¿qué?, ¿quién(es)?

Vocabulario personal

11

La salud°

La... *Health*

connect®
|SPANISH

www.connectspanish.com

En este capítulo

VOCABULARY

Talking about health and wellness   324

Common illnesses and going to doctors   326

GRAMMAR

Talking about the past with two tenses   330

Connecting ideas   338

Expressing *each other*   341

CULTURAL FOCUS

Venezuela and its cultures

En un consultorio médico (*doctor's office*), en Venezuela

- ¿Cómo es su salud en general? ¿Lleva Ud. una vida sana[a]?

- ¿Hace Ud. ejercicio con frecuencia? ¿Hizo Ud. ejercicio ayer?

- ¿Cuándo fue la última vez que Ud. fue al médico? ¿Fue por algo grave o fue una visita rutinaria?

[a]healthy

CECILIA FIGUEROA MARTÍN CONTESTA LAS PREGUNTAS.

- Creo que mi salud es excelente, afortunadamente. ¡Toco madera![a] La verdad es que llevo una vida sana[b] por lo general. Como bien, no bebo mucho, no fumo nada...

- Sí, trato de[c] hacer ejercicio por lo menos tres o cuatro días a la semana: voy al gimnasio o corro tres o cuatro millas. Ayer corrí.

- La última vez que fui al médico fue el mes pasado, para mi chequeo anual.

[a]¡Toco... *Knock on wood!* [b]*healthy* [c]trato... *I try to*

*S.A. = Sociedad Anónima (*Inc.*)

La salud y el bienestar°

La... *Health and well-being*

el cuerpo humano

- el cerebro
- la oreja
- la garganta
- los pulmones
- el estómago
- la mano
- la pierna
- los dedos del pie
- el ojo
- la nariz (*pl.* narices)
- la boca
- el corazón
- el brazo
- los dedos (de la mano)
- el pie

- levantar pesas
- Laura
- llevar anteojos/lentes (*m.*)
- Enrique
- Marta
- correr
- caminar
- la caminadora

El cuerpo humano

la cabeza	head
el oído	inner ear

Para cuidar de la salud

comer comidas sanas	to eat healthy food
cuidarse	to take care of oneself
dejar de + *inf.*	to stop (*doing something*)
dormir (duermo) (u) lo suficiente	to get enough sleep

hacer ejercicio	to exercise; to get exercise
hacer...	to do . . .
ejercicios aeróbicos	aerobics
(el método) Pilates	Pilates
llevar lentes (*m.*) **de contacto**	to wear contact lenses
llevar una vida sana/tranquila	to lead a healthy/ calm life
practicar (qu) deportes	to practice, play sports
respirar	to breathe

You can hear the pronunciation of theme vocabulary words and phrases in the Connect eBook.

Así se dice

los anteojos, los lentes = las gafas (*Sp.*)
los lentes de contacto = las lentes de contacto (*Sp.*), las lentillas (*Sp.*)
la caminadora = la cinta de andar (*Sp.*), la cinta de correr, la cinta rodante, la trotadora (*P.R.*), la rueda de molino

Comunicación

A. Asociaciones

Paso 1. ¿Qué partes del cuerpo humano asocia Ud. con las siguientes palabras? ¡OJO! A veces hay más de una respuesta posible.

1. un ataque	**5.** pensar	**9.** la música
2. comer	**6.** la digestión	**10.** el perfume
3. cantar	**7.** el amor (*love*)	**11.** caminar
4. los anteojos	**8.** fumar	**12.** una flor

Paso 2. ¿Qué verbos asocia Ud. con las siguientes partes del cuerpo?

1. los ojos	**3.** la boca	**5.** el estómago
2. los dedos	**4.** el oído	**6.** los pulmones

B. Hablando de la salud. ¿Qué significan para Ud. las siguientes oraciones?

MODELOS: Se debe comer comidas sanas. →
Eso quiere decir (*means*) que es necesario comer muchas verduras, que...
También significa que no debemos comer muchos dulces o...

1. Se debe dormir lo suficiente todas las noches.
2. Hay que hacer ejercicio.
3. Es necesario llevar una vida tranquila.
4. En general, uno debe cuidarse mucho.
5. Es importante llevar una vida sana.

> **Vocabulario útil**
>
> **Eso quiere decir...**
> **Esto significa que...**
> **También...**

C. ¿Cómo vive Ud.? ¿Cómo vivía?

Paso 1. Indique las cosas que Ud. hace para mantener la salud y el bienestar.

	SÍ	NO
1. comer comidas sanas en general	☐	☐
2. no comer muchos dulces	☐	☐
3. comer muchas frutas y verduras	☐	☐
4. hacer ejercicio moderado diariamente	☐	☐
5. beber agua suficiente todos los días	☐	☐
6. dormir por lo menos ocho horas por noche	☐	☐
7. tomar bebidas alcohólicas en moderación	☐	☐
8. no beber mucho café o té	☐	☐
9. no fumar	☐	☐

Paso 2. Escriba un hábito malo que debe dejar y uno bueno que desea adquirir (*to acquire*).

Paso 3. Ahora, en parejas, entrevístense sobre los hábitos de los **Pasos 1** y **2.** Luego díganle a la clase algo que tienen en común.

MODELO: E1: Yo como comidas sanas, pero como muchos dulces. ¿Y tú?
E2: Yo también. Comer muchos dulces es un hábito que quiero dejar. →
Nosotros comemos muchos dulces y es un hábito que queremos dejar.

Algo sobre...

la harina[a] de maíz blanco

La harina de maíz blanco es el ingrediente básico para hacer dos platos típicos venezolanos: las arepas y las hallacas. Las arepas son similares al pan de pita y se pueden comer como sándwiches. Las hallacas son parecidas[a] a los tamales; son una comida tradicional de la Navidad y la Nochevieja.

¿Hay algo similar a las arepas o a las hallacas en la cocina de su familia?

[a]*flour* [b]*similar*

Una arepa

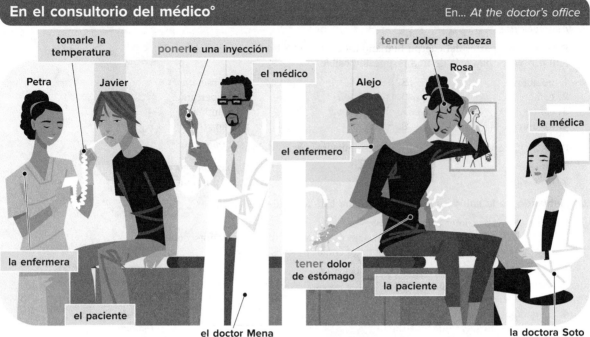

tomarle la temperatura

ponerle una inyección

el médico

tener dolor de cabeza

Rosa

Petra Javier Alejo

la médica

el enfermero

la enfermera

tener dolor de estómago

la paciente

el paciente

el doctor Mena

la doctora Soto

el antibiótico	antibiotic	**enfermarse**	to get sick
la cita	appointment; date	**estar sano/a**	to be healthy
el dolor	pain, ache	**guardar cama**	to stay in bed
el farmacéutico /	pharmacist	**molestar**	to bother
la farmacéutica		**resfriarse (me resfrío)**	to get/catch a cold
la fiebre	fever	**sacar (qu)**	to extract
la gripe	flu	**sacar la lengua**	to stick out one's tongue
el jarabe	(cough) syrup	**sacarle un diente /**	to extract (*someone's*)
la medicina	medicine	**una muela**	tooth/molar
la pastilla	pill	**sentirse (me siento) (i)**	to feel
la receta	prescription	**tener dolor de**	to have a
el resfriado	cold (*illness*)	**cabeza/**	headache/
la tos	cough	**estómago/muela**	stomachache/toothache
la vacuna	vaccination	**tener fiebre**	to have a fever
cansarse	to get tired	**toser**	to cough
doler (duele)	to hurt, ache		
		mareado/a	dizzy; nauseated
		resfriado/a	congested, stuffed-up

¡OJO!

Doler and molestar are used like gustar: **Me duele la cabeza. Me molestan los ojos.**

Así se dice

el resfriado = el catarro, el resfrío
estar resfriado/a = estar constipado/a (*Sp.*)

la gripe = la gripa
el consultorio = la consulta

¡OJO!

Use the term **el médico / la médica** to talk *about* doctors in general and **el/la dentista** for the dentist. However, when you use the doctor or dentist's name you should use the definite article plus the title: **el doctor Gómez, la doctora Velázquez.** To speak directly *to* him or her, just use the title **doctor(a).**

Comunicación

A. Estudio de palabras. Complete las siguientes oraciones con una palabra derivada de la palabra en rosado.

1. Si me resfrío, tengo _____.
2. La respiración ocurre cuando alguien _____.
3. Si me _____, estoy enfermo/a. Un(a) _____ me toma la temperatura.
4. Cuando alguien tose, es porque tiene _____.
5. Si me duele el estómago, tengo _____ de estómago.

B. Situaciones. Describa la situación de estas personas. Primero, indique dónde están y con quiénes están. Luego complete las oraciones que están al lado de de cada foto.

1. Rosa está muy sana. Nunca le duele(n) _____. Nunca tiene _____. Siempre _____. Más tarde hoy, ella va a _____.

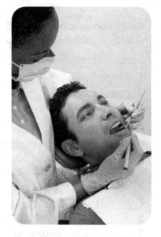

2. Anoche Martín tuvo _____. Esta mañana llamó _____ para hacer _____. El dentista va a _____. Después, Martín va a _____.

Nota **cultural**

El cuidado° médico en el mundo hispano   *care*

En el mundo hispano el cuidado médico puede ser muy variado. Depende principalmente del[a] nivel económico del país y después (como ocurre en este país) del nivel económico del individuo. Pero en todos los países hispanos hay excelentes médicos en todo tipo de especialidades, bien preparados[b] en las universidades de su país o en el extranjero. Aquí hay unos aspectos interesantes del cuidado médico en el mundo hispanohablante.

- **Los farmacéuticos y practicantes** Los hispanos consultan con frecuencia a estos profesionales cuando no pueden o no sienten la necesidad de acudir[c] a un médico. Por ejemplo, cuando uno tiene una enfermedad leve,[d] puede ir a la farmacia para pedir consejo sobre una medicina o conseguir un remedio, sin tener receta. Cuando se necesita un tratamiento simple, como ponerse una inyección, se puede llamar a un practicante, quien es más o menos como un enfermero.
- **Los remedios tradicionales o alternativos** Homeópatas, naturópatas, sanadores,[e] tiendas de botánica,[f]... Hay una importante tradición, de gran

A diferencia de las farmacias en este país, en las farmacias de muchos países hispanos, no se venden muchos productos para la higiene personal ni comestibles.

diversidad en el mundo hispanohablante, de consultar a personas que tienen conocimiento[g] de los remedios naturales o de curaciones basadas en la fe,[h] especialmente para las molestias y menores enfermedades más frecuentes.

¿A quién consulta Ud. cuando está enfermo/a?

[a]*on the* [b]*trained* [c]*go* [d]*minor, mild* [e]*healers* [f]*herbs*

[g]*knowledge* [h]*faith*

Nota **comunicativa**

Cómo expresar una cualidad general: *lo* + *adjetivo*

To describe the general qualities or characteristics of something, use **lo** with the masculine singular form of an adjective.

lo bueno/malo   lo más importante   lo mejor/peor   lo menos interesante

This structure has a number of English equivalents, especially in colloquial speech.

lo bueno = the good thing/part/news, what's good

lo más importante = the most important thing/part/news, what's most important

You will use expressions of this type in **Comunicación C.**

C. En el consultorio del médico o del dentista. En parejas, usen los siguientes adjetivos para describir una visita al médico o dentista, según el modelo.

MODELO: malo / bueno → **Lo malo** de ir al médico es la cuenta. **Lo bueno** es...

1. malo / bueno
2. peor / mejor
3. interesante / aburrido
4. curioso (*strange*) / especial
5. insoportable (*unbearable*)

D. Refranes hispanos. Empareje una frase de la columna A con otra de la columna B para formar algunos refranes muy comunes en el mundo hispano. En algunos casos lo/la puede ayudar la rima. Luego explique lo que significan los refranes. ¿Cuál es el equivalente en inglés?

COLUMNA A	COLUMNA B
1. _____ La salud no se compra:	**a.** engorda (*fattens*).
2. _____ Músculos de Sansón,	**b.** no tiene precio.
3. _____ Si quieres vivir sano,	**c.** y cerebro de mosquito.
4. _____ Para enfermedad de años,	**d.** no hay medicina.
5. _____ Ojos que no ven,	**e.** acuéstate y levántate temprano.
6. _____Lo que no mata (*doesn't kill*),	**f.** corazón que no siente.

¿Recuerda Ud.?

Since **Capítulo 8** you have been using first the preterite and then the imperfect in appropriate contexts. Indicate which tense you use to do each of the following.

	PRETERITE	IMPERFECT
1. to tell what you did yesterday	☐	☐
2. to tell what you used to do when you were in grade school	☐	☐
3. to describe background details, like physical or mental states	☐	☐
4. to tell about a completed action	☐	☐
5. to talk about the way things used to be	☐	☐
6. to describe an action that was in progress	☐	☐

If you understand these uses of the preterite and the imperfect, the summary of their uses in **Gramática 30** (page 330) will be very easy for you.

Antes de mirar

Cuando Ud. tiene problemas de salud, ¿a quién consulta? Indique a todas las personas de la lista que Ud. haya consultado (*may have consulted*) por razones de salud por lo menos una vez.

☐ mi madre/padre
☐ mi abuelo/a
☐ un médico / una médica
☐ un(a) homeópata
☐ un(a) naturópata
☐ ¿ ?

En esta botánica (*herb store*) se venden velas (*candles*), imágenes, collares (*necklaces*), rosarios, incienso, agua florida (*aromatic essences*) y mucho más. ¡Hasta (*Even*) imágenes de Buda para la buena suerte (*luck*)!

Este segmento

Laura presenta un reportaje sobre una botánica, una tienda tradicional típica del Caribe.

Vocabulario **del segmento**

desde luego	certainly
ahorrar	to save
el tratamiento	treatment
mezclarse	to mix up/in with
han visitado	have you visited
tuvo la amabilidad de concedernos	was kind enough to give us
sobar	to rub
la sávila	aloe vera
la quemada	burn
el catarro	**el resfriado**
broncear la piel	to tan (one's skin)
la tuna	cactus
el riñón	kidney
la limpieza	cleaning, cleansing
la hoja	leaf

Después de mirar

A. **¿Está claro?** Complete las siguientes oraciones con información del video.

1. Las botánicas son tiendas típicas de los países _____.
2. En una botánica se compran ingredientes naturales para hacer tés y _____ tradicionales.
3. Los viejos y los _____ van a las botánicas.
4. La tuna se usa para problemas del estómago y de los _____.

B. **Un poco más.** Conteste las siguientes preguntas.

1. ¿Por qué se llaman «botánicas» las tiendas como la (*that*) de la Sra. Santiago?
2. ¿En qué tipo de tratamientos se especializan las botánicas?
3. ¿Qué objetos se puede comprar en una botánica? ¿Para qué sirven?

C. **Y ahora, Uds.** En grupos, hablen de las comidas y bebidas que Uds. toman cuando no se sienten bien y de las cosas que hacen cuando quieren conseguir buena suerte o necesitan calmarse. Por ejemplo, ¿soban o tocan Uds. algo, como una imagen de Buda?

GRAMÁTICA

Grammar Tutorial 30

■ **connect**
|SPANISH
www.connectspanish.com

30 Talking About the Past (Part 5)
Using the Preterite and the Imperfect

Gramática en acción: En el consultorio de la Dra. Méndez

DRA. MÉNDEZ: ¿Cuándo empezó a sentirse mal su hija?

MADRE: Ayer por la tarde. Estaba resfriada, tosía mucho y se quejaba de que le dolían el cuerpo y la cabeza.

DRA. MÉNDEZ: ¿Y le notó algo de fiebre?

MADRE: Sí. Por la noche le tomé la temperatura y tenía treinta y nueve grados.*

grados centígrados	36	37	38	39	40	41
grados Fahrenheit	96.8	98.6	100.4	102.2	104	105.8

DRA. MÉNDEZ: A ver... Abre la boca, por favor.

¿Y Ud.?

1. ¿Cómo se sentía Ud. ayer por la noche?
2. ¿A qué hora se acostó?

You have already learned and used the preterite (**Capítulos 8** and **9**) and imperfect tenses (**Capítulo 10**). In this chapter you will begin to use them together to talk about the past.

Keep the following points in mind.

1. The preterite and the imperfect are both past tenses.
2. They are both used to talk about the same point in the past.

They *differ* in the point of view (aspect) about the past that they each convey. This is the same as with English usage. When you decide to say *I ran, I used to run,* or *I was going to run,* you are making a decision about the aspect of the past action that you want to communicate.

Here is a summary of the main uses of the two tenses. You will learn about them on the next pages.

Pretérito	Imperfecto
• beginning/end of an action	• habitual/repeated action
• completed action	• ongoing action
• series of completed actions	• background information
• the action on the "stage"	• the setting for the action

In Dr. Méndez's office DR. MÉNDEZ: *When did your daughter begin to feel ill?* MOTHER: *Yesterday afternoon. She was stuffed up, she was coughing a lot, and she was complaining that her body and head were hurting.* DR. MÉNDEZ: *And did you notice any fever?* MOTHER: *Yes. At night I took her temperature, and it was thirty-nine degrees.* dr. méndez: *Let's see . . . Open your mouth, please.*

Normal body temperature is 37°C (98.6°F).

Differences between the Preterite and the Imperfect /
Las diferencias entre el pretérito y el imperfecto

1. Beginning/End vs. Habitual

Use the preterite to . . . |~~~~~| |

• tell about the beginning or the end of a past action

El sábado pasado, el partido de fútbol **empezó** a la una. **Terminó** a las cuatro. El entrenador **habló** a las cinco.
Last Saturday, the soccer game began at one. It ended at four. The coach spoke (began to speak) at five.

Use the imperfect to . . . ~~~~~

• talk about the habitual nature of an action (something you always did)

Había un partido **todos los sábados.** Muchas personas **jugaban todas las semanas.**
There was a game every Saturday. Many people played every week.

2. Completed vs. Ongoing

Use the preterite to . . . | |

• express an action that is viewed as completed

El partido **duró** tres horas. **Ganaron** Los Lobos.
The game lasted three hours. The Lobos won.

Use the imperfect to . . .
~~~~~mientras~~~~~
Mientras~~~~~, ~~~~~

• tell about simultaneous events (with **mientras** = *while*)

Yo **estaba** en la cocina **mientras** todos **miraban** el partido.
I was in the kitchen while everyone was watching the game.

Mientras mi amigo **veía** el partido, **hablaba** con su novia.
While my friend was watching the game, he was talking with his girlfriend.

Use the imperfect and the preterite in the same sentence to . . .

|~~~~~ ~~~~~|

• tell what was happening when another action took place

Yo no vi el final del partido. **Estaba** en la cocina cuando **terminó.** (El partido **terminó** cuando **estaba** en la cocina.)
I didn't see the end of the game. I was in the kitchen when it ended. (The game ended while I was in the kitchen.)

3. Series of Completed Actions vs. Background Details

Use the preterite to . . . | | |

• express a series of completed actions

Durante el partido, los jugadores **corrieron, saltaron** y **gritaron.**
During the game, the players ran, jumped, and shouted.

Use the imperfect to . . . ~~~~~

• give background details of many kinds: time, location, weather, mood, age, physical and mental characteristics

Todos los jugadores **eran** jóvenes; **tenían** 17 o 18 años. ¡Y todos **esperaban** ganar!
All the players were young; they were 17 or 18 years old. And all of them hoped to win!

4. Action vs. the Setting

The preterite and imperfect are also used together in the presentation of an event.

• The imperfect sets the stage, describes the conditions that caused the action, or emphasizes the continuing nature of a particular action.

~~~~~

• The preterite narrates the actions. | |

Era un día hermoso. **Hacía** mucho sol, pero no hacía mucho calor. Como no **tenía** que trabajar en la oficina, **salí** a comprar unas flores. Luego **me puse** camiseta y pantalones cortos y **decidí** trabajar todo el día en el jardín.
It was a beautiful day. It was very sunny, but it wasn't very hot. Since I didn't have to work at the office, I went out to buy some flowers. Then I put on a T-shirt and shorts and decided to work in the garden all day.

Remember that, when used in the preterite, **saber,** **conocer,** and **querer** have English equivalents different from that of the infinitives. (See page 275.) In the imperfect, the English equivalents of these verbs do not differ from the infinitive meanings.

—¿Ya sabías que se murió el abuelo de Miguel?
—Sí, lo **supe** el mes pasado.
*"**Did** you already **know** that Miguel's grandfather passed away?"*
*"Yes, I **found out** (**learned**) about it last month."*

—Anoche **conocí** a Roberto.
—¿Anoche? Yo pensaba que ya lo conocías.
"Last night I met Roberto."
"Last night? I thought you already knew him."

—¿No querías hablar con el profesor ayer?
—Sí, **quise** llamarlo pero no estaba en su oficina.
*"Didn't you **want** to talk to the professor yesterday?"*
*"Yes, I **tried** to call him but he wasn't in his office."*

Preterite vs. Imperfect
Summary

Beginning/middle vs. habitual/repeated
Completed vs. ongoing
Actions vs. background
Action vs. setting

Práctica y comunicación

A. En la escuela secundaria

Paso 1. Autoprueba. ¿Se usa el pretérito (P) o el imperfecto (I) ?

1. para dar detalles de fondo (*background details*) y descripciones como el tiempo y la hora _____
2. para hablar de acciones habituales _____
3. para narrar acciones completadas _____
4. para hablar de hábitos personales _____
5. para hablar de una acción en progreso _____
6. para narrar una secuencia de acciones _____
7. para decir lo que pasaba cuando otra acción ocurrió _____
8. para describir condiciones y estados físicos o afectivos _____

Paso 2. ¿Cómo era su salud cuando Ud. estaba en la secundaria? ¿Sufría Ud. de alguna enfermedad física o de algún tipo de impedimento? Complete las siguientes oraciones con la forma apropiada del imperfecto o el pretérito. Use **no** cuando sea (*it's*) necesario.

Cuando estaba en la secundaria...
1. resfriarse con frecuencia
2. tener alergias
3. tener una operación
4. ir al dentista con regularidad
5. tener la gripe / mononucleosis
6. hacer mucho ejercicio
7. sufrir (*to have*) un accidente de coche
8. gustar me quedarme en casa y no ir a la escuela

Paso 3. Ahora, en parejas, túrnense para hacer y contestar preguntas basadas en las oraciones del **Paso 2.** Luego díganle a la clase algo que tienen en común.

MODELO: E1: Cuando estabas en la escuela secundaria, ¿te resfriabas con frecuencia?
E2: No, no me resfriaba con frecuencia. ¿Y tú?
E1: Yo tampoco.

Prác. A, Paso 1: Answers: 1. I 2. I 3. P 4. I 5. I 6. P 7. P 8. I

B. En el consultorio. Estos son algunos de los pacientes que el Dr. Sánchez vio ayer en el consultorio. Describa cómo se sentía cada paciente. Luego empareje cada caso con lo que hizo el Dr. Sánchez y complete esas oraciones.

LOS SÍNTOMAS DE LOS PACIENTES

1. Un paciente: tener mucho frío
2. A otro le: doler la garganta
3. Un señor: creer que estaba anémico
4. Una señora: sentirse muy mal sin saber por qué
5. Un señor mayor: querer más medicinas
6. Un niño: estar muy alto para su edad (*age*)
7. A un hombre le: doler el pecho (*chest*)

POR ESO, EL DR. SÁNCHEZ...

a. _____ hacerle muchas preguntas.
b. _____ darle una nueva receta.
c. _____ tomarle la temperatura.
d. _____ escucharle los sonidos (*sounds*) de los pulmones y del corazón.
e. _____ pedirle un análisis de sangre (*blood*).
f. _____ hacerle sacar la lengua.
g. _____ decirle que su chequeo (*check-up*) mostraba que estaba muy bien.

Nota **comunicativa**

Algunas palabras y expresiones asociadas con el pretérito y el imperfecto

Certain words and expressions are frequently associated with the preterite, others with the imperfect. Only the words that are translated are new.

Some words often associated with the **preterite** are:

ayer, anteayer, anoche (*last night*)   **de repente** (*suddenly*)
una vez, dos veces (*twice*)...   **en seguida**
el año pasado (*last*), **el lunes pasado**...

Some words often associated with the imperfect are:

todos los días, todos los lunes...   **mientras**
siempre, frecuentemente (*frequently*)   **de niño/a, de adolescente**

As you continue to practice using the preterite and imperfect, these expressions can help you determine which tense to use. These words do not *automatically* cue either tense, however. The most important consideration is the meaning that you want to express.

Ayer cenamos temprano.   *Yesterday we had dinner early.*
Ayer cenábamos cuando Juan llamó.   *Yesterday we were having dinner   when Juan called.*

Jugaba al fútbol **de niño.**   *He played soccer as a child.*
Empezó a jugar al fútbol **de niño.**   *He began to play soccer as a child.*

You will see these words and expressions in activities in the rest of this section and throughout the rest of *Puntos de partida.*

Algo sobre...

Simón Bolívar

Simón Bolívar fue un general y político venezolano que es conocido[a] en Latinoamérica como el Libertador. Fue la figura principal en el movimiento por la independencia de España de varios países latinoamericanos (Colombia, Panamá, el Perú, Bolivia y el Ecuador). Desde 1819 hasta 1830 fue presidente de la Gran Colombia, una unión de naciones hispanohablantes que se estableció después de ganar su independencia de España. La Gran Colombia solo duró[b] hasta 1831.

¿Quién es el gran héroe de la independencia de los Estados Unidos? ¿Qué cargos[c] tuvo?

[a]*known* [b]*lasted* [c]*positions*

Simón Bolívar (1783–1830), el Libertador

C. Pequeñas historias

Paso 1. Complete el siguiente párrafo con una de las palabras o frases de la lista. Antes de empezar, mire la foto que acompaña el párrafo para tener una idea general del tema de la historia.

VOCABULARIO: **íbamos, nos gustó, nos quedábamos, nos quedamos, nuestra familia decidió, vivíamos**

Cuando éramos niños, Jorge y yo _____¹ en la Argentina. Siempre _____² a la playa, a Mar del Plata, para pasar la Navidad. Allí casi siempre _____³ en el Hotel Fénix. Un año, _____⁴ quedarse en otro hotel, el Continental. No _____⁵ tanto como el Fénix y por eso, al año siguiente, _____⁶ en el Fénix otra vez.

Paso 2. Ahora, para completar la siguiente historia, debe escoger (*choose*) entre el pretérito y el imperfecto en cada caso. Antes de empezar, mire el dibujo que acompaña el párrafo.

Eran las once de la noche y yo (estaba / estuve¹) leyendo un libro, cuando de repente se (apagaban / apagaron[a2]) todas las luces[b] de la casa. (Ponía / Puse³) el libro en el suelo[c] y luego (usaba / usé⁴) mi celular para tener algo de luz. La verdad es que (tenía / tuve⁵) mucho miedo. Por eso, (salía / salí⁶) a la calle.[d] Entonces[e] (podía / pude⁷) ver que (había / hubo⁸) un apagón por todo el barrio.[f] La luz (volvía / volvió⁹) media hora después.

[a]*apagar = to go out* [b]*lights* [c]*floor* [d]*street* [e]*Then* [f]*un... a power outage in the whole neighborhood*

D. La historia afectiva de Simón Bolívar

Paso 1. Complete los siguientes párrafos con la forma apropiada de los infinitivos, en el pretérito o el imperfecto.

Simón Bolívar (1783–1830) fue el gran héroe de la independencia sudamericana. Bolívar no (tener¹) una vida[a] personal muy afortunada. (Ser²) hijo de una familia aristocrática española. (Tener³) tres hermanos mayores. Sus padres (morirse⁴) cuando Bolívar (ser⁵) muy pequeño y por eso (vivir⁶) varios años con otros parientes.

En 1798, cuando (tener⁷) 15 años, (irse⁸) a estudiar a Madrid. Allí (conocer⁹) a María Teresa, con quien (casarse[b10]) en 1802. Bolívar (regresar¹¹) a Venezuela con su joven esposa. Pero María Teresa (morir¹²) ocho meses después, víctima de la fiebre amarilla. Bolívar (empezar¹³) su carrera[c] como líder nacional viajando por Europa para soportar[d] la muerte[e] de María Teresa. Nunca (volver¹⁴) a casarse.

[a]*life* [b]*to marry* [c]*career* [d]*deal with* [e]*death*

Paso 2. Comprensión. Conteste las siguientes preguntas.

1. En la familia de Bolívar, ¿era él hermano mayor o el menor?
2. ¿Cuántos años tenía Bolívar cuando se casó con María Teresa?
3. ¿De qué murió María Teresa?
4. ¿Por qué empezó a viajar Bolívar?

E. Rubén y Soledad

Paso 1. Complete el párrafo con la forma apropiada de los infinitivos, en el pretérito o en el imperfecto.

Una merienda típicamente española: churros (*fried dough rolled in sugar*) y chocolate

Rubén estaba estudiando cuando Soledad entró en el cuarto. Ella le (preguntar[1]) a Rubén si (querer[2]) ir al cine. Rubén le (decir[3]) que sí porque (sentirse[4]) un poco aburrido de estudiar. Los dos (salir[5]) en seguida para el cine. (Ver[6]) una película cómica y (reírse[7]) mucho. Luego, como (hacer[8]) frío, (entrar[9]) en su café favorito, El Gato Negro, y (tomar[10]) churros y chocolate. (Ser[11]) las dos de la mañana cuando por fin (regresar[12]) a casa. Soledad (acostarse[13]) en seguida porque (estar[14]) cansada, pero Rubén (empezar[15]) a estudiar otra vez.

Paso 2. Comprensión. Ahora conteste las siguientes preguntas, según el párrafo.

1. ¿Qué hacía Rubén cuando Soledad entró?
2. ¿Qué le preguntó Soledad a Rubén? (**Le preguntó si...**)
3. ¿Por qué le contestó Rubén que sí?
4. ¿Les gustó la película? ¿Cómo se sabe?
5. ¿Por qué tomaron churros y chocolate después de salir del cine?
6. ¿Qué hora era cuando regresaron a casa?
7. ¿Qué hicieron cuando llegaron a casa?

Estrategia

Una pregunta *no* se contesta siempre con el mismo tiempo verbal de la pregunta. Por ejemplo, si es necesario explicar por qué ocurrió algo, se usa el imperfecto.

F. La fiesta de Roberto

Paso 1. Complete el párrafo con la forma apropiada de los infinitivos, en el pretérito, en el imperfecto o en el presente.

Durante mi segundo[a] año en la universidad, conocí a Roberto en una clase. Pronto nos (hacer[1]) muy buenos amigos. Roberto (ser[2]) una persona muy generosa que (dar[3]) una fiesta en su apartamento todos los viernes. Todos nuestros amigos (ir[4]). (Haber[5]) muchas bebidas y comida abundante, y todos (hablar[6]) y (bailar[7]) hasta muy tarde.

Una noche algunos de los vecinos[b] de Roberto (llamar[8]) a la policía porque les (parecer[c9]) que nosotros (hacer[10]) demasiado ruido. (Llegar[11]) dos policías al apartamento y le (decir[12]) a Roberto que la fiesta (ser[13]) demasiado ruidosa. Nosotros no (querer[14]) aguar la rumba,[d] pero ¿qué (poder[15]) hacer? Todos nos (despedir[16]) aunque[e] (ser[17]) solamente las once de la noche.

Aquella noche Roberto (aprender[18]) algo importantísimo. Ahora cuando (hacer[19]) una fiesta, siempre (invitar[20]) a sus vecinos.

[a]*second* [b]*neighbors* [c]*to seem* [d]*aguar... to spoil the party* [e]*although*

Paso 2. Comprensión. Las siguientes oraciones son falsas. Corríjalas.

1. A Roberto no le gustaban las fiestas.
2. Las fiestas de Roberto siempre terminaban temprano.
3. Los vecinos de Roberto nunca se quejaban del ruido de sus fiestas.
4. Roberto siempre invitaba a sus vecinos a sus fiestas.

G. Lo mejor de estar enfermo

Paso 1. Haga oraciones completas con la forma apropiada de los infinitivos, en el pretérito o el imperfecto.

1. Cuando yo (ser) niño, (pensar) que lo mejor de estar enfermo (ser) pasar el día en casa.
2. Lo peor (ser) que yo (resfriarse) con frecuencia durante las vacaciones.
3. Una vez (*yo:* ponerse) muy enfermo durante la Navidad.
4. Mi madre (llamar) al médico porque yo (tener) una fiebre muy alta.
5. El Dr. Matamoros (venir) a casa en seguida y (ponerme) una inyección de antibióticos porque yo (tener) una infección de la garganta.
6. Desgraciadamente (*Unfortunately*), mis padres (tener) que darme un baño de agua fría para bajarme la fiebre, y eso no (gustarme) para nada.
7. Tengo que decir que no (ser) la mejor Navidad de mi vida.
8. Mis primos (venir) a casa, pero yo (estar) demasiado enfermo para jugar.
9. ¡Pero esa Navidad mis abuelos (regalarme) mi primera Play Station!

Paso 2. Ahora vuelva a contar la historia desde el punto de vista (*point of view*) de la madre. Siga el modelo.

MODELO: Cuando **mi hijo era** niño, **él pensaba** que lo mejor...

H. Una historia famosa

Paso 1. La siguiente historia está narrada en el presente. Póngala en el pasado, usando los verbos en el pretérito.

La niña abre[1] la puerta y entra[2] en la casa. Ve[3] tres sillas. Se sienta[4] en la primera silla, luego en la segunda[a], pero no le gusta[5] ninguna. Por eso se sienta[6] en la tercera.[b] Ve[7] tres platos de comida en la mesa y decide[8] comer el más pequeño. Luego, va[9] a la alcoba para descansar un poco. Después de probar[c] las camas grandes, se acuesta[10] en la cama más pequeña y se queda[11] dormida.[d]

[a]*second* [b]*third* [c]*trying* [d]*asleep*

Paso 2. ¿Reconoce Ud. la historia? Es el cuento de Ricitos de Oro (lit. *Little Golden Curls*) y los tres osos (*bears*). Pero el cuento es un poco aburrido tal como está escrito (*as it is written*) en el **Paso 1.** Mejórelo (*Improve it*) con palabras de **Vocabulario útil** y dando detalles y descripciones (usando el imperfecto). También debe terminar el cuento: ¿Qué pasó al final?

MODELO: Había una vez una niña que **se llamaba** Ricitos de Oro. Un día la niña **fue...**

> #### Vocabulario útil
>
> **Había una vez...** + *imp.* Once upon a time there was ...
> **Un día...** + *pret.*
> **el bosque** forest
> **la casita** little house
> **huir** to flee*

Present tense forms of **huir** *have a* **y** (*rather than an* **i**) *in the stem-changing pattern:* **huyo, huyes...** **Y** *is also used in the preterite third person singular and plural forms (like* **leer**): **huyó, huyeron**. *The present participle is* **huyendo**.

I. Intercambios

Paso 1. ¿Cuántos años tenían Uds. cuando sus padres los dejaron hacer las siguientes cosas? Hagan y contesten preguntas sobre ese tema, según el modelo.

MODELO: te dejaron cruzar la calle (*street*) solo/a →
　　　　E1: ¿Cuántos años **tenías** cuando tus padres te dejaron cruzar la calle sola?
　　　　E2: **Tenía** 7 u 8 años cuando mis padres me dejaron cruzar la calle sola.

1. te dejaron cruzar la calle (*street*) solo/a
2. te permitieron ir de compras solo/a
3. te dejaron acostarte después de las nueve
4. te dejaron estar en casa sin niñero/a
5. te permitieron usar la estufa para cocinar
6. te dejaron ver una película para mayores de 17 años («*R*»)
7. te dejaron buscar tu primer trabajo

Paso 2. Ahora haga preguntas basadas en las ideas de la siguiente lista para saber cuántos años tenía su compañero/a cuando hizo las cosas de la lista.

MODELO: aprender a pasear en bicicleta →
　　　　¿**Cuántos años tenías** cuando aprendiste a pasear en bicicleta?

¿**Cuántos años tenías** cuando...?
1. aprender a pasear en bicicleta
2. hacer su primer viaje en avión
3. tener su primera cita romántica
4. empezar a afeitarse / teñirse el pelo (*dye his/her hair*)
5. conseguir la licencia de manejar (*driver's license*)
6. abrir una cuenta (*account*) en el banco

Paso 3. Ahora, en grupos de cuatro, comparen sus respuestas. Entre todos, ¿quién tenía los padres más estrictos? ¿los menos estrictos?

J. Experiencias memorables

Paso 1. Haga preguntas sobre una de las siguientes experiencias. En el **Paso 2,** va a usar esas preguntas para entrevistar a uno de sus compañeros de clase. Haga por lo menos cinco preguntas, usando el pretérito o el imperfecto, según el contexto.

　　EXPERIENCIAS
　　el primer trabajo
　　la primera cita / el primer beso (*kiss*)
　　algo (un incidente, una situación, un caso) que lo/la hizo ponerse rojo/a
　　el primer día de clases en la escuela primaria o en la universidad

Paso 2. Ahora, en parejas, túrnense para hacerse preguntas sobre la experiencia del **Paso 1** que Uds. escogieron. No tiene que ser la misma experiencia.

Algo sobre...

el lago de Maracaibo

El lago de Maracaibo ocupa el puesto[a] 19 entre los lagos más grandes del mundo. En la actualidad, conecta con el golfo de Venezuela en el norte, que lo hace una bahía semicerrada salobre.[b] Pero está documentado que fue originalmente un lago cerrado, uno de los más antiguos de la Tierra. Numerosos ríos[c] vierten[d] sus aguas en el lago de Maracaibo.

¿Cuál es el lago más grande de su estado? ¿Y del país?

[a]*spot* [b]*bahía... semi-closed brackish bay* [c]*rivers* [d]*empty*

El lago de Maracaibo, el más grande de toda Latinoamérica

¿Recuerda Ud.?

Que is one of the most frequently used words in the Spanish language, and it has several meanings. Review what you already know about **que** by expressing the following sentences in English.

1. ¿Qué estudias?
2. Tengo que hacer la tarea.
3. No entiendo lo que Ud. me dice.
4. Creo que la fórmula es correcta.

In **Gramática 31,** you will learn more about **que** and other related terms that you have been using for a while: **quien** and **lo que.**

Grammar Tutorial 31
connect
|SPANISH
www.connectspanish.com

31 Recognizing *que, quien*(es), *lo que*
Relative Pronouns

Gramática en acción: Tus médicos, tus mejores amigos

La Organización de Médicos Hispanohablantes: Siempre contigo

Tus médicos pueden ser tus mejores amigos.

- Son personas con quienes puedes hablar de TODO.

- Son personas que pueden ayudarte y explicarte TODO
  lo que tú necesitas saber de tu salud.

- Tienen consultorios que están CERCA de ti.

- Y además, ¡hablan ESPAÑOL!

¿Y Ud.?

Complete las oraciones con el nombre de una persona que Ud. conoce. Incluya la revlación que tiene con Ud., por ejemplo: **mi madre.**

1. Una persona que tiene mi confianza total es _____.
2. Una persona con quien hablo si necesito ayuda, no importa en qué situación, es _____.
3. Una persona que sabe todo —o casi todo— lo que pasa en mi vida es _____.

a relative pronoun / **un pronombre relativo** = a pronoun that refers back to a noun or phrase already mentioned

Relative Pronouns / Los pronombres relativos

Relative pronouns (**Los pronombres relativos**) are words that connect ideas within one sentence. Most frequently they refer back to a noun or an idea that has already been mentioned. In both English and Spanish, these words make communication more efficient and fluid because they help to avoid unnecessary repetition by linking ideas. Notice how this happens in the sentences on page 339.

Your doctors, your best friends *The Organization of Spanish-speaking Doctors: Always with you. Your doctors can be your best friends.* ■ *They're people with whom you can talk about ANYTHING.* ■ *They're people that can help you and explain (to you) EVERYTHING that you need to know about your health.* ■ *They have offices that are CLOSE to you.* ■ *And besides, they speak SPANISH!*

Conozco a una **médica**. Es de Venezuela. → Conozco a una médica **que** es de Venezuela.

I know a **doctor**. *She is from Venezuela.* → *I know a doctor* **who** *is from Venezuela.*

Spanish has a rich system of relative pronouns. You will learn only three of them in this section.

	Los pronombres relativos	
que = refers to things and people	*that, which, who*	
quien(es) = refers only to people	*who(m)*	
lo que = refers to a situation	*what, that which*	

1. Relative Pronouns

There are four principal *relative pronouns* in English: *that, which, who,* and *whom.* They are usually expressed in Spanish by the relative pronouns at the right, all of which you already know.

---

2. *que* = *that, which, who*

Que is by far the most frequently used relative pronoun in Spanish. It refers to people and things.

¡OJO!

Que cannot be used after a preposition to refer to people. See Point 3.

Tuve **una cita** con el médico **que** duró una hora.
I had an appointment with the doctor **that** *lasted an hour.*

Es **un buen médico que** tiene mucha experiencia.
He's a good doctor **who** *has a lot of experience.*

---

3. *quien, quienes* = *who(m)*

Quien and **quienes** can refer only to people. They are almost always used after a preposition.

La mujer **con quien** hablaba es mi médica.
The woman **with whom** *I was speaking is my doctor.*
(The woman I was speaking with is my doctor.)

Las enfermeras **a quienes** les dimos las flores cuidaron a mi padre.
The nurses **to whom** *we gave the flowers took care of my dad. (The nurses we gave the flowers to took care of my dad.)*

---

4. *lo que* = *what, that which, the thing that*

Lo que always refers to a whole situation or idea. It can refer to something that has been mentioned before or to something that will be referred to later in the sentence. It frequently starts sentences.

No entiendo **lo que dijo.**
I don't understand **what (that which)** *he said.*

Lo que necesito es **estudiar más.**
What (The thing that) *I need is to study more.*

¡OJO!

If you can substitute *that which* for *what* in a sentence, use **lo que,** not **que.**

---

5. Relative Pronouns versus Interrogatives

Que and **quien(es)** sound like **¿qué?** and **¿quién(es)?,** but they are not the same.

- **Que** and **quien(es)** link words within a sentence.
- **¿Qué?** and **¿quién(es)?** ask questions (and they have an accent mark to distinguish them from the relative pronouns).

—¿**Qué** es eso?
—Es una cosa **que** sirve para ver mejor.
"**What** *is this?*
"It's something **that** *helps you see better."*
—¿**Quién** es ese señor?
—Es el profesor con **quien** tengo la clase de psicología.
"**Who** *is that man?"*
"He's the professor **with whom** *I have Psychology."*

Gramática

Summary of Relative Pronouns

that, which, who = **que**
preposition + whom = **quien(es)**
what, that which, the thing that = **lo que**

Práctica y comunicación

A. **¿Que, quien(es) o lo que?**

Paso 1. **Autoprueba.** Empareje los conceptos con el pronombre relativo apropiado.

1. _____ una cosa   **a.** que
2. _____ una idea   **b.** quien
3. _____ a una persona   **c.** quienes
4. _____ con dos amigos   **d.** lo que

Paso 2. Empareje los elementos de las dos columnas. **¡OJO!** Puede repetir las personas de la Columna B.

COLUMNA A

1. _____ Es lo que me dijo mi madre antes de salir para la universidad.
2. _____ Es la persona en quien yo más confío.
3. _____ Es lo que más me importa en la vida.
4. _____ Es la persona que más me apoya (*supports*).
5. _____ Es lo que necesito hacer para graduarme.
6. _____ Es la persona que me da los mejores consejos académicos.

COLUMNA B

a. «Come bien y duerme lo suficiente.»
b. mi mejor amigo/a
c. mi familia
d. mi consejero/a
e. mi madre/padre
f. sacar notas aceptables

Paso 3. Ahora, en parejas, túrnense para hacer y contestar preguntas usando las ideas de la Columna A en el **Paso 2.**

MODELO: E1: ¿Quién es la persona **que** te da los mejores consejos académicos?
E2: (Es) Mi consejero académico. ¿Quién te los da a ti?
E1: (Es) Mi consejero también.

B. **El estrés, la condición humana.** Lea la siguiente tira cómica y complete las oraciones.

[a]cansancio... *fatigue, restlessness, worry, nervousness, (emotional) imbalance, and anxiety*

1. Lo que quiere el padre de Libertad (= la amiga de Mafalda) es _____.
2. Lo que su padre tiene es _____.
3. Según el médico, lo que tiene su padre es _____.

C. **En la preadolescencia**

Paso 1. Complete las siguientes oraciones con detalles de su vida personal.

Cuando yo tenía diez años más o menos...
1. lo que más me divertía/molestaba era _____.
2. el programa de televisión que más me gustaba era _____.
3. la persona / las personas que yo más quería (*loved*) era(n) _____.

Paso 2. Ahora, en parejas, comparen sus respuestas.

_____

PrPrác. A, Paso 1: Answers: 1. a 2. d 3. b 4. c

¿Recuerda Ud.?

Before learning how to express reciprocal actions in **Gramática 32**, review the reflexive pronouns in **Gramática 14 (Cap. 5),** then provide the correct reflexive pronouns for the following sentences.

1. ___ levanté a las ocho y media.
2. Laura ___ puso el vestido.

3. Mis amigos y yo ___ sentamos en un café.
4. ¿Prefieres duchar___ o bañar___?

32 Expressing *each other* (Part 2)
Reciprocal Actions with Reflexive Pronouns

Grammar Tutorial 32
connect
|SPANISH
www.connectspanish.com

Gramática en acción: La amistad

Los buenos amigos...

- se conocen **bien.**
- se respetan.

- se quieren.
- se recuerdan **siempre.**

En las culturas hispanas, cuando las buenas amigas se encuentran, se besan en la mejilla.

¿Y Ud.?

Cuando Ud. y sus amigos se encuentran, ¿cómo se saludan (*do you greet each other*)? ¿Se dan la mano? ¿Se besan?

Reciprocal Actions / Las acciones recíprocas

1. Reciprocal Actions

Reciprocal actions (**Las acciones recíprocas**) are actions that involve two or more people doing something *to* or *for* each other. They are usually expressed in English with *each other* or *one another*. In Spanish, reciprocal actions are expressed with pronouns that are identical to the plural reflexive pronouns.

nos = each other (**nosotros/as**)
os = each other (**vosotros/as**)
se = each other (**Uds., ellos/as**)

Nos queremos.	*We love each other.*
¿**Os** ayudáis?	*Do you help one another?*
Se miran con ternura.	*They're looking at each other tenderly.*

2. Verbs Frequently Used to Express Reciprocal Actions

Verbs frequently used in this way include those at right, but any verb to whose meaning the phrase *each other* can be added may express a reciprocal action: **hablarse, mirarse, pelearse,** and so on.

abrazarse (c)	to embrace
besarse	to kiss each other
darse la mano	to shake hands
encontrarse	to meet (*someone*
(se encuentran)	*somewhere*)
quererse	to love each other; to be fond of each other
saludarse	to greet each other

¡OJO!

Sometimes a preposition is added in English to express the meaning of these verbs: **hablarse** = *to talk to each other*, **mirarse** = *to look at each other*, **pelearse** = *to fight with each other*. But no preposition is needed in Spanish.

Most of these verbs are new. The verbs **encontrarse** and **quererse** are new to you with their reciprocal meaning.

Friendship   Good friends . . . • know each other well. • respect each other. • are fond of each other. • always remember each other. In Hispanic cultures, when close women friends meet, they kiss each other on the cheek.

Práctica y comunicación

A. Los buenos amigos

Paso 1. Autoprueba. Dé el pronombre apropiado para expresar acciones recíprocas.

1. _____ miramos   **4.** _____ llamaban
2. _____ pelearon   **5.** _____ saludamos
3. _____ conocen

Paso 2. ¿Qué hace Ud. con sus buenos amigos? Conteste usando **nos** (el pronombre recíproco). Si una oración no es cierta para Ud., use **no**.

MODELO: abrazar cuando ver → **Nos abrazamos** cuando **nos vemos.**

1. ver con frecuencia
2. conocer bien
3. respetar mucho
4. ayudar cuando necesitamos ayuda
5. mandar muchos mensajes
6. hablar por teléfono con frecuencia
7. decir la verdad siempre, lo bueno y lo malo
8. ¿ ?

Paso 3. Ahora, en parejas, túrnense para hacer y contestar preguntas basadas en el **Paso 2.** Luego, díganle a la clase algo que tienen en común.

MODELO: E1: ¿Tus amigos y tú **se abrazan** cuando **se ven**?
E2: Sí, con frecuencia **nos abrazamos** cuando **nos vemos** después de un tiempo. ¿Y Uds.?
E1: Nosotros también **nos abrazamos.**

B. ¿Qué pasa entre ellos?
Describa las siguientes relaciones familiares o sociales, haciendo oraciones completas con una palabra o frase de cada columna.

MODELO: Los buenos amigos **se conocen** bien.

| los buenos amigos
los parientes
los esposos
los padres y los niños
los amigos que no viven en la misma ciudad
los profesores y los estudiantes
los compañeros de cuarto/casa | **+** (no) **+** | visitarse con frecuencia
quererse, respetarse, necesitarse, conocerse bien
ayudarse mutuamente (en los quehaceres domésticos, cuando tienen problemas económicos o problemas personales)
verse (todos los días, con frecuencia)
llamarse por teléfono, escribirse
mirarse (con cariño [*affection*])
saludarse, darse la mano
quejarse sinceramente, escucharse |

C. Intercambios

Paso 1. Haga por lo menos una pregunta con cada una de las siguientes frases. En el **Paso 2,** va a usar esas preguntas para entrevistar a alguien de la clase sobre sus relaciones con su pareja, sus amigos, sus padres y sus parientes. Use el tiempo presente, como en el modelo.

(Continúa.)

MODELOS: besarse →¿Tu pareja y tú se besan en público?

1. verse
2. escribirse
3. mantenerse en contacto
4. llamarse por teléfono

5. abrazarse
6. besarse
7. saludarse dándose la mano
8. pelearse

Paso 2. Ahora, en parejas, túrnense para hacerse las preguntas del **Paso 1.**
Luego díganle a la clase lo que tienen en común.

Un poco de todo

A. Lengua y cultura: La leyenda del lago de Maracaibo

Paso 1. Complete the following legend with the correct form of the word in
parentheses, as suggested by context. The verbs will be in the preterite or
imperfect. When two possibilities are given in parentheses, select the correct word.

Había una vez[a] un cacique[b] indígena que se llamaba
Zapara. Este[c] tenía una hija, Maruma, que (ser[1]) muy bonita.
Al padre y a la hija (se / les[2]) (gustar[3]) pasar tiempo juntos y
caminar por el bosque.[d]

Un día Zapara (comprender[4]) que su hija ya (ser[5]) una
mujer y (se / le[6]) (decir[7]): «Debes escoger[e] esposo, pues ya
tienes edad[f] para formar una familia. Pero (su / tu[8]) esposo
debe ser guerrero,[g] como todos los hombres de nuestra
familia».

Un día, mientras su padre (estar[9]) ausente, Maruma
(salir[10]) sola a cazar[h] en el bosque. Estaba a punto de
dispararle a un ciervo[i] cuando (un / —[11]) otro cazador[j]
(matar[k12]) al animal. Maruma (ponerse[13]) muy enojada pero
el joven, (que / quienes[14]) (ser[15]) guapo y simpático, dijo: «El
ciervo es para (tú / ti[16]). Solo quiero conocerte. Me llamo
Tamaré». A partir de ese día[l] los (joven[17]) (hacerse[m18])
amigos. Pronto se enamoraron.[n]

Desgraciadamente, el joven no era un buen guerrero y por eso el padre de
Maruma (enojarse[19]) mucho cuando (saber[20]) que ella (querer[21]) casarse con él. Se
enfadó tanto[ñ] que la naturaleza reaccionó y (haber[22]) grandes terremotos[o] e
inundaciones:[p] las aguas cubrieron[q] las tierras del cacique Zapara y también a
Maruma y Tamaré, formando así el lago de Maracaibo. Zapara se convirtió en
una de sus pequeñas islas.

Una niña en su barca (*boat*), en el lago de Maracaibo

[a]Había... *Once upon a time there was* [b]*chief* [c]*He* [d]*forest* [e]*choose* [f]*ya... you're old enough* [g]*a warrior*
[h]*hunt* [i]Estaba... *She was about to shoot a deer* [j]*hunter* [k]*to kill* [l]A... *From that day on* [m]*to become* [n]se...
they fell in love [ñ]Se... *He was so angry* [o]*earthquakes* [p]*floods* [q]*covered*

Paso 2. Comprensión. Conteste las siguientes preguntas.

1. ¿Quién era Zapara?
2. ¿De quién se enamoró (*fell in love*) Maruma?
3. ¿Por qué se enojó Zapara?
4. ¿Cómo se formó el lago de Maracaibo?

Paso 3. Ahora, en grupos, inventen cuatro preguntas bien difíciles, pero posibles
de contestar, sobre la leyenda del lago de Maracaibo. Luego háganle sus preguntas
a la clase. ¿Qué grupo pudo inventar las preguntas más difíciles de contestar?

B. Caperucita Roja

Paso 1. Narre el cuento de Caperucita Roja, conjugando los verbos en la forma apropiada del imperfecto o del pretérito. Trate de adivinar (*Try to guess*) el significado de las palabras o expresiones subrayadas (*underlined*), usando el contexto.

<u>H</u>abía una vez una niña que (llamarse[1]) Caperucita Roja. Todos los animales del <u>bosque</u> (ser[2]) sus amigos y Caperucita Roja (quererlos[3]) mucho. Un día su mamá (decirle[4]): —Lleva esta <u>jarrita</u> de miel[a] a casa de tu abuelita.

En el bosque, un <u>lobo</u> (salir[5]) a hablar con la niña. Le (preguntar[6]): —¿Adónde vas, Caperucita Roja? Esta[b] (contestarle[7]): —Voy a casa de mi abuelita. Le (decir[8]) el lobo: —Pues, si vas por este sendero,[c] vas a llegar antes. Él (irse[9]) por otro <u>camino</u> más corto.

El lobo (llegar[10]) primero a la casa de la abuelita y (entrar[11]). Cuando la abuela (verlo[12]), (saltar[d13]) de la cama y (correr[14]) a esconderse.[e] Caperucita Roja (llegar[15]) por fin a la casa de la abuelita. (*ella:* encontrar[16]) a su «abuelita», que (estar[17]) en la cama. Le (decir[18]): —¡Qué dientes tan largos tienes! —Son para comerte mejor! —(decirle[19]) «su abuelita». Luego...

[a]*honey* [b]*She* [c]*path* [d]*to jump* [e]*hide herself*

 Paso 2. Ahora, en grupos, terminen el cuento de Caperucita Roja. Si no lo saben bien, no importa: inventen un final.

Vocabulario útil

el cazador	hunter
comérselo/la	to eat someone up
disparar	to shoot
huir	to flee
matar	to kill

En su comunidad

Entreviste a una persona hispana de su universidad o ciudad sobre el cuidado médico en su país de origen.

PREGUNTAS POSIBLES

- En su país de origen, ¿qué hace una persona cuando tiene una enfermedad que no es muy seria? ¿Va al médico? ¿Habla con el farmacéutico? ¿Va a alguna persona que cura con remedios naturales?

- ¿Qué alimentos se consideran muy sanos en su país? ¿Se usan algunos productos naturales? ¿Cuáles son? ¿Para qué sirven de remedio?

- ¿Cómo se dice *flu* en su país? ¿Y *cold*?

Antes de mirar

Cuando Ud. tiene resfriado, ¿va al médico generalmente? ¿Qué hace para curarse y sentirse mejor? ¿Tiene algún remedio casero? ¿Quién se lo enseñó?

Este segmento

En este segmento final del programa, una reportera española enseña un remedio casero contra el resfriado. Luego Ana y Víctor hablan de otros remedios caseros.

Un remedio casero (*homemade*) contra el catarro (resfriado): un empaste de mostaza (*mustard plaster*) con harina de trigo (*wheat flour*)

Fragmento del guion

Luego, lo que tenéis que poner es aceite de oliva, que lo frotáis[a] así en el pecho,[b] para que la masa[c]... lo coja[d] mejor. Entonces, podéis poner la pasta así directamente con la cuchara. Y así lo dejáis[e] unas horas. Luego así[f] ya te puedes ir a trabajar lo que queráis,[g] pero sobre todo no os lo quitéis.[h]

[a]*rub* [b]*chest* [c]*para... so that the paste* [d]*lo.. sticks to it* [e]*leave* [f]*this way* [g]*lo... whatever you want* [h]*no... don't take it off*

Vocabulario del segmento

la miel	honey	**tapar**	to cover
pon atención	pay attention	**ensuciarse**	to get dirty
la risa	laughter	**espero que**	I hope it works
constipado/a	**resfriado/a** (*Spain*)	**os funcione**	for you
probar (pruebo)	to try	**el ajo crudo**	raw garlic
el/la bisabuelo/a	great-grandparent	**fíjate**	look
el tercio	third part (*measure*)	**tuyo/a**	of yours
espeso/a	thick	**la planta**	sole (*of the foot*)

Después de mirar

A. ¿Está claro? ¿Cierto o falso? Corrija las oraciones falsas.

	CIERTO	FALSO
1. Es un remedio de su abuela.	☐	☐
2. El primer ingrediente del empaste es el aceite de oliva.	☐	☐
3. El empaste debe estar bastante (*rather*) espeso.	☐	☐
4. Se pone aceite de oliva en la mano.	☐	☐
5. La persona enferma debe llevar el empaste solo unos minutos.	☐	☐

B. Un poco más. Conteste las siguientes preguntas.

1. ¿Qué le pasa a Víctor hoy?
2. ¿Qué remedio casero le recomienda Ana a Víctor?
3. ¿Qué remedio prefiere Víctor? ¿Por qué?

C. Y ahora, Uds. En grupos, hablen de los remedios y productos que no necesitan receta médica que Uds. usan por razones de salud. ¿Qué tipo de remedios son? (¿farmacéuticos, herbales, homeopáticos,... ?) ¿Confían Uds. (*Do you trust*) en sus beneficios? ¿Les preocupan los posibles efectos secundarios?

Antes de leer

¿Qué tipo de seguro (*insurance*) médico tiene Ud.? ¿Tiene uno para los estudiantes de la universidad o uno a través del (*through the*) trabajo de sus padres? ¿O tiene uno de su propio (*own*) trabajo?

Lectura cultural: Venezuela

El seguro[a] médico en Venezuela

En Venezuela hay un sistema de salud público y gratuito[b] que sirve, sobre todo,[c] a la gente de la clase trabajadora que no puede pagar un seguro médico privado. Hay consultorios médicos, clínicas y hospitales que proveen de todo tipo de servicios relacionados con la salud a las personas que los necesitan.

También existe la posibilidad de tener atención médica privada a través de pólizas[d] de seguro, que se contratan generalmente a través del empleador.[e] Sin embargo, los venezolanos siempre tienen acceso al sistema público, que se paga con impuestos[f] obligatorios para la seguridad social. En general, el cuidado médico de familia, privado, es mucho más barato que en los Estados Unidos y no resulta muy caro ir al consultorio del doctor y pagar la visita sin tener un seguro. En cambio,[g] los servicios de emergencia y hospitalización son muy costosos[h] y para tenerlos es indispensable[i] un seguro médico.

[a]*insurance* [b]*free* [c]*sobre... especially* [d]*a... through policies* [e]*employer* [f]*taxes* [g]*En... On the other hand* [h]*expensive* [i]*absolutely necessary*

Un venezolano, que baila el limbo durante una fiesta, en Caracas

Un símbolo venezolano: «La rumba»

Al espíritu fiestero[a] de los venezolanos se le dice[b] «la rumba». Venezuela es el principal mercado de consumo de la música popular caribeña. Al venezolano le gusta organizar y celebrar fiestas en las cuales[c] siempre se baila salsa, merengue o cualquier otro ritmo caribeño, hasta el amanecer.[d]

[a]*party-loving* [b]*se... (it) is called* [c]*las... which* [d]*dawn*

En otros países hispanos

- **En Latinoamérica** Es muy diversa la manera en que cada país provee de asistencia sanitaria[a] a sus habitantes: a través de[b] un sistema exclusivamente gubernamental[c] o por medio[d] de una combinación de sistemas públicos y privados. El acceso al cuidado médico también varía mucho de país a país. Hay países como la Argentina, Cuba y Costa Rica que proporcionan[e] acceso a todas las personas. Desgraciadamente, en otros países hay un considerable número de personas que no tienen acceso fácil a médicos y medicinas.

- **En España** España tiene un sistema nacional de seguridad social que cubre[f] el cuidado médico de todos sus ciudadanos. Este sistema, junto con[g] otros factores, contribuye a que los españoles tengan una de las esperanzas de vida[h] más largas del mundo.

[a]*health* [b]*a... via* [c]*government-run* [d]*means* [e]*provide* [f]*covers* [g]*junto... along with* [h]*esperanzas... life expectancies*

COMPRENSIÓN

1. ¿Qué sistema de salud usa con más frecuencia la clase trabajadora venezolana?
2. ¿Cómo se paga el sistema público de salud en Venezuela?
3. ¿Los habitantes de qué país hispanohablante tienen una de las esperanzas de vida más largas del planeta?
4. ¿Qué es «la rumba» en Venezuela?
5. ¿Qué bailan los venezolanos?

Y ahora, Uds.

¿Creen Uds que las personas de los Estados Unidos tienen «espíritu de rumba»? Expliquen su opinión, dando ejemplos especificos para ilustrar su punto de vista (*point of view*).

Del mundo hispano

Antes de leer

Un epitafio es una breve inscripción que se pone en la tumba de una persona muerta (*deceased*). En su opinión, ¿cuáles de los siguientes temas son apropiados para un epitafio?

☐ datos biográficos
☐ descripción física
☐ aspectos de su profesión
☐ un símbolo de la persona
☐ sus gustos y preferencias

☐ aspectos de su personalidad
☐ la descripción de algunos de sus parientes
☐ su filosofía de la vida
☐ algo memorable que dijo una vez
☐ cómo murió

Lectura: «Epitafio», de Nicanor Parra

De estatura mediana,[a]
con una voz[b] ni delgada ni gruesa,[c]
hijo mayor de un profesor primario[d]
y de una modista de trastienda;[e]
5 flaco de nacimiento[f]
aunque[g] devoto de la buena mesa;[h]
de mejillas escuálidas[i]
Y de más bien[j] abundantes orejas;
con un rostro cuadrado[k]
10 en que los ojos se abren apenas[l]
y una nariz de boxeador mulato
baja a la boca de ídolo azteca
—todo esto bañado[m]
por una luz entre irónica y pérfida[n]—,
15 ni muy listo ni tonto de remate[ñ]
fui lo que fui: una mezcla[o]
de vinagre y de aceite de comer
¡un embutido[p] de ángel y bestia[q]!

[a]*average* [b]*voice* [c]*hearty* [d]*de escuela primaria* [e]*modista... backroom seamstress* [f]*flaco... thin since birth* [g]*although* [h]*de... to good food* [i]*mejillas... thin cheeks* [j]*más... rather* [k]*rostro... square face* [l]*hardly* [m]*bathed* [n]*treacherous* [ñ]*de... hopelessly* [o]*mixture* [p]*sausage* [q]*beast*

Comprensión

A. En este epitafio. ¿Cuáles de los posibles temas para un epitafio que se mencionaron en **Antes de leer** aparecen en este poema?

B. Preguntas

Paso 1. ¿Cierto o falso? Indiquen las palabras específicas del poema que justifiquen su respuesta.

	CIERTO	FALSO
1. Esta persona era alta.	☐	☐
2. Sus padres eran médicos importantes.	☐	☐
3. Esta persona era delgada.	☐	☐
4. Tenía orejas grandes.	☐	☐
5. Era inteligentísimo.	☐	☐
6. Su personalidad era contradictoria.	☐	☐

Paso 2. Este poema es autobiográfico; es decir (*that is*), que el poeta lo escribió acerca de sí mismo (*about himself*). ¿Qué palabras del poema revelan esto?

Antes de escuchar

¿Qué precauciones toma Ud. para no enfermarse? ¿Tuvo Ud. algún resfriado el año pasado? ¿alguna gripe? ¿Fue al médico con frecuencia durante el último año?

Vocabulario para escuchar

vacunarse	to get a shot	**la vacuna**	vaccination
la muerte	death	**de alto riesgo**	high-risk
contraer (*like* traer)	to get; to contract (*an illness*)	**embarazadas**	pregnant
		peligroso/a	dangerous

Después de escuchar

A. La gripe. Conteste las siguientes preguntas sobre esta enfermedad, según la información en el anuncio.

1. ¿Aproximadamente cuántas personas van al hospital cada año en los Estados Unidos a causa de la gripe?
2. ¿Cuántas personas mueren anualmente en los Estados Unidos a causa de la gripe, aproximadamente?
3. ¿Hay solo un tipo de virus de gripe?

B. La vacuna. Conteste las siguientes preguntas sobre la campaña de vacunación.

1. ¿Quiénes deben vacunarse contra la gripe?
2. ¿Quiénes se consideran personas de alto riesgo?
3. ¿Quiénes no pueden recibir la vacuna?

PRODUCCIÓN PERSONAL

¡Ahora, yo!

A. Use de modelo las preguntas y respuestas de la página 323 de este capítulo para hablar del tipo de vida que Ud. lleva y de su salud en general.

B. Filme a una persona que habla de un remedio casero (*homemade*) que se usa en su familia. Puede ser algo serio o cómico.

A ESCRIBIR

La historia de una enfermedad

Ud. ya ha hablado (*You've already talked*) en este capítulo de sus enfermedades. Ahora va a escribir un ensayo sobre una enfermedad que sufrió un compañero / una compañera de clase.

Preparar

Paso 1. En parejas, entrevístense sobre una enfermedad que sufrieron. Piensen en la información que van a necesitar para escribir la narración de un episodio de una enfermedad. Aquí hay algunos ejemplos. Uds. deben añadir por lo menos 3 o 4 preguntas. **¡OJO!** Usen el pretérito y el imperfecto con cuidado.

1. ¿Fue una enfermedad grave o leve (*minor*)? ¿O era crónica?
2. ¿Cuándo ocurrió? ¿Cuántos años tenías?
3. ¿Cuáles eran los síntomas?
4. ¿ ?

Paso 2. Ahora escriba la narración, usando la información que consiguió en el **Paso 1.** O, si Ud. prefiere, puede escribir sobre la enfermedad de un amigo o un pariente. Hay más ayuda en Connect.

Más ideas para su portafolio

- Incluya 5 consejos que Ud. considera fundamentales para estar bien físicamente.
- Dé un resumenwve de su historia favorita (de un libro o una película) cuando Ud. era pequeño/a.
- Si ha estado jugando (*have been playing*) Practice Spanish: Study Abroad, en Quest 8 Ud. aprendió sobre la leyenda de los dos cadejos, una leyenda que trata del equilibrio (*balance*) entre lo bueno y lo malo. ¿Conoce Ud. otras historias sobre la armonía entre el bien y el mal? Escriba un informe que resuma la leyenda de los dos cadejos y compárela con leyendas, cuentos o creencias (*beliefs*) de su propia cultura o de otras culturas que Ud. conoce sobre el bien y el mal.

Sugerencia: You are now ready to play Quest 8 in **Practice Spanish: Study Abroad** (www.mhpractice.com).

LEARNSMART

Visit **www.connectspanish.com** to practice the vocabulary and grammar points covered in this chapter.

AFTER STUDYING THIS CHAPTER I CAN. . .

☐ name many parts of the body and activities related to a healthy life (324)

☐ talk about illnesses and medical exams (326)

☐ use the preterite and imperfect together to talk about the past and tell stories (330–332)

☐ use **que, quien,** and **lo que** to avoid repetition (338–339)

☐ express the concept of "each other" with pronouns (341)

☐ recognize/describe at least 2–3 aspects of Venezuelan cultures

Gramática en breve

30. Using the Preterite and the Imperfect

Uses of the Preterite	Uses of the Imperfect
beginning/end of an action	habitual/repeated action
completed action	ongoing action
series of completed actions	background information
the action on the "stage"	the setting for the action

31. Relative Pronouns

que = refers to things and people
quien(es) = refers only to people
lo que = refers to a situation

32. Reciprocal Actions with Reflexive Pronouns

each other = **nos, os, se**

Vocabulario

Los verbos

abrazarse (c)	to embrace
besarse	to kiss each other
darse la mano	to shake hands
encontrarse (me encuentro) (con)	to meet (*someone somewhere*)
quererse	to love each other; to be fond of each other
saludarse	to greet each other

La salud y el bienestar

el bienestar	well-being
la caminadora	treadmill
la salud	health

Repaso: la comida, el deporte

cansarse	to get tired
cuidarse	to take care of oneself
dejar de + *inf.*	to stop (*doing something*)
doler (duele) (*like* gustar)	to hurt; to ache
enfermarse	to get sick
guardar cama	to stay in bed
hacer	to do
ejercicios aeróbicos	aerobics
(el método) Pilates	Pilates
levantar pesas	to lift weights
llevar una vida sana/tranquila	to lead a healthy/calm life
molestar (*like* gustar)	to bother
ponerle una inyección / una vacuna	to give (*someone*) a shot, injection / a vaccination
resfriarse (me resfrío)	to get/catch a cold
respirar	to breathe
sacar (qu)	to extract
sacar la lengua	to stick out one's tongue
sacarle un diente / una muela	to extract (*someone's*) tooth/molar
tener dolor de	to have a pain/ache in
tomarle la temperatura	to take someone's temperature
toser	to cough

Repaso: caminar, comer, correr, dormir (duermo) (u), hacer ejercicio, hacer (el) yoga, llevar (to wear), practicar (qu), sentirse (me siento) (i)

El cuerpo humano

la boca	mouth
el brazo	arm
la cabeza	head
el cerebro	brain
el corazón	heart
el cuerpo humano	human body
el dedo (de la mano)	finger
el dedo del pie	toe
el estómago	stomach
la garganta	throat
la lengua	tongue
la mano	hand
la muela	molar, back tooth
la nariz (*pl.* narices)	nose
el oído	inner ear

el ojo	eye
la oreja	(outer) ear
el pie	foot
la pierna	leg
los pulmones	lungs
la sangre	blood

Repaso: el diente

Las enfermedades y los tratamientos

los anteojos	glasses
el chequeo	check-up
el consultorio	(medical) office
el dolor (de)	pain, ache (in)
la enfermedad	illness, sickness
la fiebre	fever
la gripe	flu
el jarabe	(cough) syrup
los lentes	glasses
los lentes de contacto	contact lenses
la pastilla	pill
la receta	prescription
el resfriado	cold (*illness*)
el síntoma	symptom
la tos	cough
el tratamiento	treatment

Cognados: el antibiótico, la medicina, la temperatura

El personal médico

| el/la enfermero/a | nurse |
| el/la farmacéutico/a | pharmacist |

Cognado: el/la dentista, el/la paciente

Repaso: el/la médico/a

Otro sustantivo

| la cita | date; appointment |
| la vida | life |

Los adjetivos

mareado/a	dizzy; nauseated
pasado/a	past, last
resfriado/a	congested, stuffed up
sano/a	healthy
suficiente	enough

Repaso: tranquilo/a

Palabras adicionales

anoche	last night
de repente	suddenly
desgraciadamente	unfortunately
dos veces	twice
eso quiere decir...	that means . . .
frecuentemente	frequently
lo bueno	the good thing/news
lo malo	the bad thing/news
lo suficiente	enough

Repaso: anteayer, ayer, de adolescente, de niño/a, en seguida, lo que, mientras, que, quien(es), siempre, una vez

Vocabulario personal

12

¡Conectad@s!°

Connected!

www.connectspanish.com

En este capítulo

Una de las varias placitas (*little plazas*)
que hay en Cartagena, Colombia

Mar Caribe

Cartagena

PANAMÁ

VENEZUELA

Medellín

Río Magdalena

OCÉANO
PACÍFICO

CORDILLERA DE LOS ANDES

⊛ Bogotá

COLOMBIA

BRASIL

ECUADOR

Río Amazonas

PERÚ

| 0 | 200 | 400 Millas |
| 0 | 200 | 400 Kilómetros |

COLOMBIA

**44.7 (punto siete)
millones de habitantes**

- La diversidad natural de Colombia es magnífica. Este país comprende[a] territorio caribeño, andino[b] y amazónico.

- Además,[c] Colombia tiene muchísimos recursos naturales: petróleo, oro, platino y esmeraldas. Es uno de los principales productores y exportadores de café del mundo. También exporta flores.

[a]*includes* [b]*Andean* [c]*In addition*

- ¿Dónde vive Ud.? ¿Vive en una zona bien comunicada[a] con el resto de la ciudad?
- ¿Se mantiene Ud.[b] en contacto con sus parientes y amigos que no viven cerca? ¿Cómo lo hace?
- Después de su computadora y su celular, ¿qué aparato electrónico considera Ud. más necesario en su vida diaria? ¿Por qué?

[a]*connected* [b]¿Se... *Do you stay*

ISMAEL PÉREZ MENDIZÁBAL CONTESTA LAS PREGUNTAS.

- Mi carrera es Estudios Urbanos, en la Universidad Nacional de Colombia, en Bogotá, y vivo bastante[a] cerca de la Universidad. Vivo con mi familia en un barrio[b] que está muy bien comunicado, así que[c] puedo llegar a la universidad en bus.

- Bueno, mis abuelos y la mayoría de mis tíos viven en Bogotá, así que nos vemos con frecuencia en las reuniones familiares. Pero ahora mi hermana está estudiando en España. Por eso nos comunicamos por *Whatsapp* y nos hablamos por *Skype*.

- Pues me gusta mucho mi *Kindle*, porque me encanta leer y es más cómodo leer con el *Kindle* que con un libro tradicional.

[a]*rather* [b]*neighborhood* [c]así... *so*

VOCABULARIO: PREPARACIÓN

La ciudad y el barrio°

neighborhood

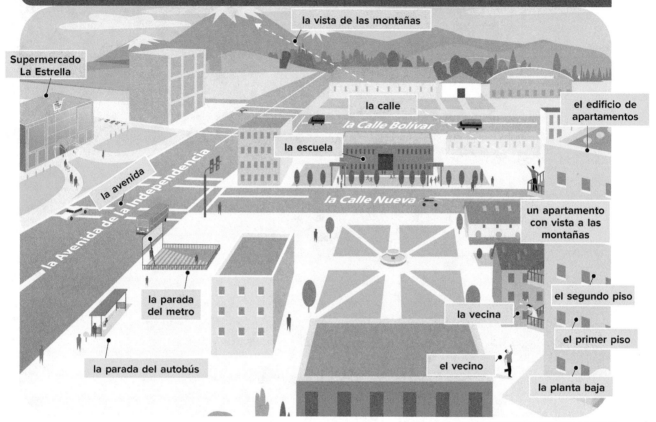

la vista de las montañas

Supermercado La Estrella

el edificio de apartamentos

la calle

la Calle Bolívar

la escuela

la avenida

la Avenida de la Independencia

la Calle Nueva

un apartamento con vista a las montañas

el segundo piso

la parada del metro

la vecina

el primer piso

la parada del autobús

el vecino

la planta baja

You can hear the pronunciation of theme vocabulary words and phrases in the Connect eBook.

La vivienda	Housing
la casa	house
la residencia de ancianos	nursing home
el dueño / la dueña	owner; landlord, landlady
el inquilino / la inquilina	tenant; renter
el portero / la portera	building manager; doorman
el ascensor	elevator
el piso	floor (*of a building*)
el primer piso	first floor (*second story*)
el segundo piso	second floor (*third story*)
la planta baja	ground floor
la vista	view

La zona	
las afueras	outskirts; suburbs
el barrio	neighborhood
la calle	street
el centro	downtown
la dirección	address
la plaza	plaza
mudarse	to move (*residences*)

Los gastos	Expenses
alquilar	to rent
el alquiler	rent
la calefacción	heat
la electricidad	electricity
el gas	gas (*residential, not for cars*)

Así se dice

el apartamento = el departamento (*Mex.*, *Arg.*), el piso (*Sp.*)
el ascensor = el elevador

El barrio is the word most generally used to express *neighborhood* in Spanish, although it is often said by Hispanics with more affection than its English counterpart. To talk about **mi barrio** is to talk about a place to which one is emotionally linked, not just the area where one lives. Many other words are used regionally and can depend on the kind of neighborhood. **La colonia** and **el fraccionamiento** are used in Mexico. Other common terms are **el vecindario** and **la zona residencial.**

¡OJO!

The word **suburbio** is a false cognate; it means *slum*. To say you live in the suburbs, say **vivo en las afueras.**

Comunicación

A. Definiciones. Defina las siguientes palabras en español, según el modelo.

MODELO: la residencia de estudiantes →
Es un lugar donde viven muchos estudiantes. Por lo general está situada en el *campus* universitario.

Vocabulario útil

Es una persona que...
Es un lugar donde...
Es una cosa que...
Es lo que...

1. el inquilino
2. el centro
3. el alquiler
4. el portero
5. la vecina

6. la dueña
7. la dirección
8. las afueras
9. el barrio
10. el ascensor

11. la avenida
12. la residencia de ancianos
13. la planta baja
14. la vista
15. la electricidad

B. Buscamos un apartamento. Lea los siguientes avisos de venta (*sale ads*) de viviendas en Bogotá y conteste las preguntas. **¡OJO!** $ = el peso colombiano

ZONA NORTE

Casa bien ubicada,[a] cerca de la Calle 170. Buenas rutas y cerca de colegios,[b] centros comerciales y supermercados. Zona de alta valorización.[c] 130 mts2.[d] Parqueadero privado con acceso directo a casa. 3 niveles;[e] 4 alcobas, 3 baños, sala-comedor, estudio y ático. $250.000.000 Celular: 3005566177

a.

BARRIO TEUSAQUILLO

Apartamento de 2 alcobas, 1 baño, cocina y sala-comedor. 3er[f] piso en edificio de 5 pisos con ascensor. Excelente ubicación cerca de bancos, supermercados, centros médicos y parque. $125.000.000 Celular: 3104488776 E-mail: micasa@gmail.com

b.

BARRIO PRADERA NORTE–TORRE[g] DE MADRID

2 habitaciones, dos baños, estudio, sala-comedor, pisos laminados, ascensor, garaje cubierto,[h] balcón. 100 mts2 4°[i] piso. Adicionales: piscina, gimnasio, sauna, cancha *squash*. $155.000.000 Tel. fijo[j] 6688775 Celular: 3169545650 E-mail: micasa@gmail.com

c.

[a]*situated, located* [b]*schools* [c]*de... high property values* [d]metros cuadrados (*square meters*) [e]*levels*
[f]tercer (*third*) [g]*Tower* [h]*covered* [i]cuarto (*fourth*) [j]*Tel.... Land line*

1. ¿Qué tipo de vivienda se vende en cada anuncio?
2. ¿Cuántas alcobas tiene cada vivienda?
3. ¿Cuál de las viviendas sería (*would be*) mejor para una familia con dos hijas adolescentes? ¿para una pareja de profesionales sin hijos y sin planes para tenerlos? ¿para una mujer profesional que ya tiene su primer trabajo, bien pagado (*well paying*)?

C. Mi situación de vivienda

Paso 1. Haga seis preguntas que Ud. puede hacerle a un compañero / una compañera de clase sobre su vivienda familiar o sobre su vivienda actual (*current*) si vive fuera de la universidad (*off campus*). Temas que se relacionan con la vivienda: **la dirección, el alquiler, el tipo de edificio, los gastos, los vecinos,...**

Paso 2. Ahora, en parejas, túrnense para entrevistarse sobre su vivienda actual, usando las preguntas del **Paso 1.** Luego hablen de dónde les gustaría vivir si el dinero se lo permitiera (*if you could financially*). Traten de (*Try to*) usar palabras y frases de los anuncios (**Comunicación B**).

MODELOS: ¿Cuántos pisos hay en la casa de tus padres?
¿Dónde te gustaría vivir, en el centro o en las afueras?

Paso 3. Díganle a la clase lo que Uds. tienen en común en cuanto a (*with regard to*) su vivienda actual y sus ideas para el futuro.

La tecnología

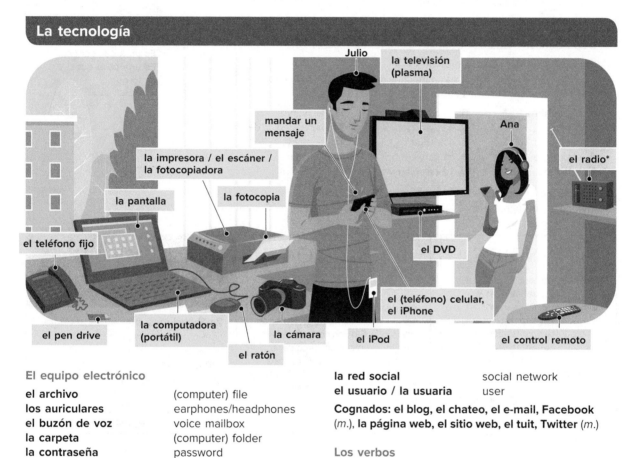

Julio — la televisión (plasma) — Ana
mandar un mensaje
la impresora / el escáner / la fotocopiadora
la fotocopia
la pantalla
el radio*
el teléfono fijo
el DVD
el pen drive
la computadora (portátil)
el ratón
la cámara
el iPod
el (teléfono) celular, el iPhone
el control remoto

El equipo electrónico

el archivo	(computer) file
los auriculares	earphones/headphones
el buzón de voz	voice mailbox
la carpeta	(computer) folder
la contraseña	password
el disco duro	hard drive
el equipo	equipment
el (espacio de) almacenamiento	storage (space)
la pantalla (grande/ plana)	(big/flat) screen (monitor)

Cognados: el android, la app, el CD, el CD-ROM, el documento, el fax, el GPS, la memoria, el módem, el video, el wifi

En internet (*m.*)

la arroba	@
el buscador	search engine
el correo electrónico	e-mail
la red social	social network
el usuario / la usuaria	user

Cognados: el blog, el chateo, el e-mail, Facebook (*m.*), la página web, el sitio web, el tuit, Twitter (*m.*)

Los verbos

almacenar	to store; to save
apagar (gu)	to turn off (*a machine*)
bajar/descargar (gu)	to download
buscar (qu) en internet	to look up on the Internet
cambiar (de canal [*m.*], de ropa...)	to change (channels, clothing . . .)
conseguir (*like* seguir)	to get, obtain
copiar/hacer (foto)copia	to copy
encender (ie), poner	to turn on (*a machine*)
entrar/estar en internet	to go/be online

---

*Usage regarding the word **radio** is changing in the Spanish-speaking world. Many countries use **el radio** for the apparatus and **la radio** for the medium of radio.

entrar/estar en Facebook	to go/be on Facebook
fallar	to "crash" (*computer*)
funcionar	to work; to function; to run (*machines*)
grabar	to record; to tape
guardar	to keep; to save (*documents*)
imprimir	to print
mandar	to send

manejar	to drive; to operate (*a machine*)
obtener (*like* tener)	to get, obtain
publicar (qu)	to post (*as on Facebook*); to publish

Cognados: conectarse, hacer clic, instalar, navegar (gu), tuitear

Comunicación

A. Lo que tenemos y lo que necesitamos

Paso 1. Haga una lista de todas las cosas electrónicas que Ud. tiene.

Paso 2. Ahora, en grupos de tres o cuatro, hablen de las cosas que todos tienen. ¿Necesita Ud. algo que está en la lista de uno de su compañeros?

Paso 3. Ahora Ud. y sus compañeros del **Paso 2** deben escoger los cinco aparatos electrónicos que Uds. consideran esenciales para los estudiantes de hoy. Luego compartan (*share*) su lista con la clase y expliquen sus decisiones.

B. Asociaciones. ¿Qué cosas asocia Ud. con los siguientes verbos?

1. mandar
2. fallar
3. conseguir
4. grabar
5. guardar
6. cambiar
7. imprimir
8. instalar

C. Definiciones

Paso 1. Dé la palabra definida. **¡OJO!** Puede haber (*There can be*) más de una respuesta en algunos casos.

1. Es un aparato que sirve para mandar documentos inmediatamente.
2. Es un aparato que hace copias de un documento.
3. Es lo que usamos para cambiar el programa de televisión sin levantarnos del sofá.
4. Este sistema recibe mensajes cuando no podemos (o no queremos) contestar el teléfono.
5. Es lo que usamos para escuchar música sin hacer ruido.
6. Esto se hace cuando hay en la tele una película que queremos ver pero que ahora mismo no podemos verla.
7. Es un sinónimo de guardar, como guardar un documento en el disco duro.

Paso 2. Ahora le toca a Ud. darles una o dos definiciones a sus compañeros de clase. Siga el modelo del **Paso 1.**

D. La tecnología y yo

Paso 1. Complete las siguientes oraciones para describir su relación con la tecnología.

1. No puedo imaginar la vida sin mi(s) _____ (aparato) porque...
2. Estoy conectado/a al internet _____ (¿con qué frecuencia?) porque...
3. Entro en internet sobre todo (*especially*) para...

Paso 2. Ahora, en parejas, comparen sus respuestas. ¿Son muy similares sus preferencias y hábitos con relación a la tecnología?

Algo sobre...

la cumbia

Un grupo folclórico de cumbia

La cumbia es un género[a] musical y un baile tradicional de la costa caribeña de Colombia y Panamá. Se cree que su origen fue una danza de cortejo[b] africana. La cumbia combina el ritmo y percusión de origen africano con instrumentos indígenas, como la gaita[c] colombiana, y europeos, como la guitarra. La cumbia es tan famosa como la salsa en algunos países de Sudamérica.

 ¿Qué géneros musicales de los Estados Unidos son populares fuera de este país? ¿Son bailables? ¿Qué tipos de instrumentos se usan?

[a]*genre, type* [b]*courtship* [c]*woodwind instrument*

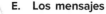

E. Los mensajes

Paso 1. En parejas, traten de descifrar (*try to decipher*) la pregunta del anuncio de VODAFONE.

La vida es móvil. Móvil es Vodafone.

Mensamanía Fin de Semana

**¿Ls fins d smana
mands mnsajs xa qdar
o qdas xa mndar mnsajs?**

Con la tarifa plana **Mensamanía Fin de Semana** de **Vodafone** podrás[a] enviar los fines de semana de abril todos los SMS[b] y MMS[c] que quieras a móviles **Vodafone** por sólo 2€. Apúntate[d] cuanto antes[e] llamando o enviando gratis FINDE ON al 136, y disfrutarás[f] de hasta cinco fines de semana de Mensamanía.

vodafone

[a]*you'll be able* [b]el servicio de mensajes cortos [c]el sistema de mensajes de multimedia [d]*sign up* [e]cuanto... *as soon as possible* [f]disfrutarás... *you'll enjoy*

Paso 2. Ahora inventen un mensaje para la clase, usando un código similar al (*to that*) del anuncio.

Paso 3. En grupos hablen de los siguientes temas y lleguen a un acuerdo (*agreement*) entre todos.

1. la edad mínima para tener un teléfono celular o móvil
2. dónde y cuándo no se debe usar el móvil
3. el número máximo de horas que uno debe pasar en internet (excluyendo investigaciones [*research*] para las clases)

Nota **cultural**

El español y la tecnología

El español ocupa el tercer[b] puesto entre las lenguas por número de internautas,[c] después del inglés y el chino, con más del 8% de los usuarios en total (según datos de 2011). El crecimiento[d]

E	Significado	Atajo de teclado[a]	E	Significado	Atajo de teclado
☺	Sonrisa	:-) :) :] =)	😉	Guiño	;-) ;)
😄	Carcajada	:-D :D =D	😕	Inseguro	:/ :-/ :\ :-\
☹	Tristeza	:-(:(:[=(	😇	Ángel	O:) O:-)
😢	Llanto	:'(	😈	Demonio	3:) 3:-)
😮	Confusión	o.O O.o	♥	Corazón	<3
😛	Sacar la lengua	:-P :P :-p :p =P	😊	Felicidad	^_^
😲	Susto	:-O :O :-o :o	😙	Beso	:-‡ :‡

en número de usuarios hispanohablantes ha sido[e] impresionante en la última década. Y el acceso y uso de internet sigue creciendo,[f] gracias a los teléfonos celulares inteligentes.

Como ocurre en inglés, la lengua española que aparece[g] en textos, redes sociales y otros sitios web es con frecuencia muy «oral» y poco pulida[h] y los emoticonos se usan con frecuencia. Aquí hay algunas características y ejemplos del español de textos y redes sociales:

- muchas abreviaturas: **que = k, q; para = p; por = x; porque = pq; besos = bss; te = t**
- onomatopeyas: **jeje, jaja, uf**
- falta de signos de puntuación y acentos: **q tal?**
- abuso[i] de las mayúsculas y signos de interrogación y admiración: **COMO??? Bien!!!!**

Por otro lado,[j] el inglés es una fuente[k] interminable de vocabulario relacionado con la tecnología, tanto para el español como para todas las otras lenguas del mundo. La lista de vocabulario de **La tecnología** (págs. 356–357) pone en evidencia[l] esta situación. Algunos de estos términos luego encuentran una traducción directa al español, como el disco duro por *hard drive*, o terminan escribiéndose y pronunciándose en una manera que es normal para el español, como **hacer clic, cliquear** o **clicar** por *to click*.

¿Usa Ud. algunas convenciones específicas cuando escribe mensajes de texto o chateo?? ¿Cuáles son?

[a]Atajo... *Key shortcut* [b]*third* [c]*internet users* [d]*growth* [e]ha... *has been* [f]*growing* [g]*appears* [h]*polished* [i]*overuse*

[j]Por... *On the other hand* [k]*source* [l]pone... *illustrates, proves*

«¡No sin mi celular!» Segmento 1

Antes de mirar

Conteste las siguientes preguntas.

1. ¿Recuerda cuándo tuvo Ud. su primer celular?
2. ¿Cuándo compró el celular que tiene ahora?
3. ¿Hay un teléfono fijo en su casa o apartamento?
4. ¿Cuáles son las compañías de telefonía móvil más usadas hoy día?

Este segmento

Este segmento trata de (*is about*) la tecnología y sobre todo de los teléfonos celulares. Laura trae un reportaje desde México sobre una compañía muy grande.

Telmex, ahora parte de América Móvil, la compañía de telefonía móvil más grande de Latinoamérica

Vocabulario del segmento

¿Qué tal han estado?	How have you been?
inconcebible	inconceivable
cierto/a	certain
a ver	let's see
que no tenga	who doesn't have
por todas partes	everywhere
tercero/a	third
el nacimiento	birth
libanés/libanesa	Lebanese
cuarto/a	fourth
sino que	but rather
estrecho/a	narrow
lleno/a	full
a pesar de	in spite of
el consumo	consumption, use

Después de mirar

A. ¿Está claro? Complete las siguientes oraciones con información del video.

1. Carlos Slim Helú es _____ pero de origen _____.
2. Slim es el _____ de Telmex.
3. México, D.F. es la _____ ciudad más grande del mundo.
4. América Móvil es la _____ compañía de telefonía móvil más grande del mundo.

B. Un poco más. Conteste las siguientes preguntas.

1. Según Laura, ¿cómo son las ciudades de México, D. F. y Guanajuato? Compárelas según la descripción de ellas.
2. ¿Cómo es Carlos Slim Helú, según el segmento?

C. Y ahora, Uds. En parejas, hablen sobre el uso de los celulares hoy día. ¿Tienen celular todos sus amigos y parientes? Si uno de sus amigos o parientes no tiene celular, ¿sabe Ud. por qué? ¿Cuáles son las desventajas del uso de los celulares?

GRAMÁTICA

¿Recuerda Ud.?

In **Gramática 20 (Cap. 7)** you learned how to form **Ud.** and **Uds.** (formal) commands with the "opposite" vowel. Remember that the commands are based on the **yo** form of the present tense of irregular and stem-changing verbs and that verbs that end in **-car, -gar,** and **-zar** have spelling changes in the command forms.

hablar → habl**e**	comer → com**an**	vivir → viv**a**
jugar → jue**guen**	poner → pon**ga**	volver → vuelv**an**

Also remember that object pronouns (direct, indirect, reflexive) must follow and be attached to affirmative commands; they must precede negative commands: **Háblele Ud. No le hable Ud.** Give the indicated command forms, affirmative and negative.

1. sentarse (Ud.)   **3.** llamarnos (Ud.)   **5.** escucharme (Uds.)
2. dárselo (Ud.)   **4.** acostarse (Uds.)   **6.** vestirse (Uds.)

You'll learn how to form informal commands in **Gramática 33**.

Grammar Tutorial 33
connect
|SPANISH
www.connectspanish.com

33 Influencing Others (Part 2)
Tú (Informal) Commands

Gramática en acción: Mandatos de la adolescencia

- Guarda la ropa limpia en tu cómoda.
- Pon la ropa sucia en el cesto.
- No te pongas esos pantalones para ir a la escuela.
- No dejes los zapatos por todas partes.
- Deja de mandar mensajes mientras te hablo. ¡Apaga eso!
- Quítate el iPod: te estoy hablando.
- ¡Estudia más! ¡Lee un libro de vez en cuando!

¿Y Ud.?

¿Oía Ud. esos mandatos cuando era adolescente? ¿Sí o no? ¿Quién se los daba? (**Me los daba mi...**)

---

a command or imperative / **un mandato** = a verb form used to tell someone to do something

In English, the command forms are the same regardless of whom you're giving them to: *Go. . . , Put. . . , Don't touch. . .* In Spanish, however, the forms for formal (**Ud., Uds.**) commands are different from those you use with a person whom you address as **tú**. And unlike **Ud.** and **Uds.** commands, whose form is the same whether affirmative or negative, the negative **tú** commands have different forms than the affirmative commands.

Commands from adolescence ■ *Put your clean clothes away in your dresser.* ■ *Put your dirty clothes in the laundry hamper.* ■ *Don't put on those pants to go to school.* ■ *Don't leave your shoes everywhere.* ■ *Stop texting while I'm talking to you. Turn that off!* ■ *Take off your iPod: I'm talking to you.* ■ *Study more! Read a book once in a while!*

Negative tú Commands / Los mandatos informales negativos

-ar → no + -es

-er/-ir → no + -as

-ar verbs		-er/-ir verbs	
No hables.	Don't speak.	No comas.	Don't eat.
No bailes.	Don't dance.	No escribas.	Don't write.
No empieces.	Don't start.	No pidas.	Don't order.
No toques.	Don't play.	No salgas.	Don't leave.
No juegues.	Don't play.	No vayas.	Don't go.

1. **Formation of Negative Informal Commands**

   Negative **tú** commands are basically the same as **Ud./Uds.** commands.

   They use the "opposite" vowel but with the **-s** that is characteristic of **tú** forms.

   All of the irregularities that you have already learned for **Ud./Uds.** commands apply to the negative **tú** commands.

   - Stem-changing verbs show the stem change: **no cierres, no vuelvas, no sirvas.**
   - Verbs that end in **-car, -gar**, and -zar have a spelling change: **no busques, no descargues, no almuerces.**
   - Verbs with irregular **yo** forms show the irregularity in the command: **no pongas, no digas.**
   - The same verbs that have irregular **Ud./Uds.** commands have irregular negative **tú** commands, identical to the **Ud./Uds.** form but with characateristic **-s** of **tú** forms.

   No lo **guardes** en esa carpeta. No **imprimas** ese documento.
   Don't save it in that folder. Don't print that document.

dar	→	no des
estar	→	no estés
ir	→	no vayas
saber	→	no sepas
ser	→	no seas

2. **Position of Pronouns**

   As with negative **Ud./Uds.** commands, object pronouns—direct, indirect, and reflexive—precede negative **tú** commands.

   No lo mires.
   Don't look at him.

   No les escribas.
   Don't write to them.

   No te levantes.
   Don't get up.

   No se lo des.
   Don't give it to them.

Affirmative tú Commands / Los mandatos informales afirmativos

-ar → -a

-er/-ir → -e

-ar verbs		-er/-ir verbs	
Habla.	Speak.	Come.	Eat.
Empieza.	Start.	Escribe.	Write.
Toca.	Play.	Pide.	Order.
Juega.	Play.	Oye.	Listen.

1. **Formation of Regular Informal Affirmative Commands**

   Most affirmative **tú** commands are identical to the third person singular (**Ud., él, ella**) form of the present tense. All stem-changes appear (because they occur in that person in the present), but there are no changes in verbs ending in **-car, -gar,** and -zar.

   Descarga otra app, por favor.
   Download another app, please.

   Enciende la computadora.
   Turn on the computer.

2. Irregular Informal Affirmative Commands

Some verbs have irregular affirmative **tú** command forms.

decir→	di	salir →	sal
hacer→	haz	ser →	sé
ir →	ve	tener→	ten
poner→	pon	venir→	ven

¡OJO!

Sé, the informal affirmative command of **ser,** has an accent mark to distinguish it from the pronoun **se.**

Sé puntual, pero **ten** cuidado.
Be there on time, but be careful.

¡OJO!

The affirmative **tú** commands for **ir** and **ver** are identical: **ve.** Context will clarify meaning. The command form of **ver** is rarely used.

¡**Ve** esa película!
See that movie!

Ve a casa ahora mismo.
Go home right now.

3. Position of Pronouns

As with affirmative **Ud./Uds.** commands, object and reflexive pronouns follow affirmative **tú** commands and are attached to them. Accent marks are necessary except when a single pronoun is added to a one-syllable command.

One pronoun: **Lé**elo. **Leván**tate. **Di**me la verdad.
Two pronouns: **Dá**selo. **Regá**lamela.

Summary of Informal Commands

Negative: -ar → -es   -er/-ir → -as
Affirmative: -ar → -a   -er/-ir → -e

Affirmative: *command + pronoun(s)*
    (1 word)
Negative: **no** + *pronoun(s) +*
    command (3 words)

Práctica y comunicación

A. Mandatos frecuentes

Paso 1. Autoprueba. Complete las siguientes oraciones con el mandato apropiado.

1. _____me qué quieres.
2. No _____ al parque sola.
3. No le _____ nada de la fiesta.
4. _____te un abrigo.
5. _____ a la tienda.
6. No _____ eso en mi cama.

a. di
b. digas
c. pon
d. pongas
e. vayas
f. ve

Paso 2. Haga mandatos informales basados en las siguientes frases.

1. buscar la información en Google
2. limpiar la cocina
3. ir al gimnasio con más frecuencia
4. aprender el vocabulario
5. salir con nosotros el viernes por la noche
6. no: regresar a casa tarde
7. no: escribir en el libro
8. no: encender el celular
9. no: decirle esta información a nadie
10. no: descargar esa app de internet

 Paso 3. Ahora, en parejas, díganse cuáles son los mandatos de la lista que se oyen con frecuencia. También deben decirse quiénes se los dicen y en qué situaciones.

B. Recuerdos de la niñez

Paso 1. Haga mandatos informales basados en las siguientes frases. ¿Oía Ud. estos mandatos cuando era niño/a? ¿Quién se los daba?

1. limpiar tu cuarto
2. hacer la tarea
3. lavarse las manos
4. decirme la verdad
5. ser bueno
6. irse a la cama
7. ¡acostarse ahora mismo!

8. no: cruzar (*to cross*) la calle solo/a
9. no: jugar con mis cosas
10. no: darles tu comida a los otros niños
11. no: decir mentiras (*lies*)
12. no: ponerse esa camiseta sucia

Paso 2. Ahora, en parejas, den los mandatos que oyen los niñitos de preescolar en las siguientes situaciones típicas. Sigan el modelo.

MODELO: Un niño está llorando. (llorar) → Por favor, **no llores.**

1. Una niña no quiere quitarse el abrigo. (quitarse)
2. Un niño deja los lápices en el piso. (dejar)
3. Es hora de sentarse en círculo, pero Kyle está corriendo. (sentarse)
4. Es la hora del recreo (*recess*), pero una niña no quiere salir afuera. (salir)
5. Una niña dice palabras feas. (decir)
6. A la hora de la siesta, un niño está haciendo ruido (*noise*). (hacer, dormirse)

Paso 3. Finalmente, en parejas, den los mandatos afirmativos y negativos que Uds. oían con frecuencia en casa o en la escuela cuando eran niños y cuando eran adolescentes. Traten de (*Try to*) recordar tres mandatos en cada categoría.

Nota **comunicativa**

Verbos derivados de *poner*, *tener* y *venir*

Many Spanish verbs are formed with a prefix (a syllable or syllables added to the beginning of a word) plus **poner, tener,** and **venir.** You already know one verb of this kind: **obtener.** Can you infer the meaning of the following infintives? **Componer** (*to compose; to form, make up*) is harder to guess, but the others should be obvious.

  poner: componer, proponer, suponer
  tener: contener, mantener
  venir: intervenir, prevenir

These verbs are conjugated just like the verbs on which they are based. The only difference is that they need an accent mark in the **tú** affirmative commands. Here are some of the forms of **componer.**

  Present: **compongo,** **compones...**

  Imperfect: **componía,** **componías...**

  Preterite: **compuse,** **compusiste...**

  Present participle: **componiendo**

  Commands: **componga Ud., compongan Uds., no compongas, compón**

You will practice some of these verbs in **Práctica C.** Recognizing and using them will increase your Spanish vocabulary. Only **obtener** is listed in the end-of-chapter **Vocabulario** list.

C. Modo avión

Paso 1. ¿Cree Ud. que estamos demasiado «conectad@s»? Compare lo que hacemos y sentimos hoy día con lo que hacía y sentía la gente a finales del siglo XX (*20th century*).

1. ¿Qué hacía la gente para obtener información sobre algo que no sabía?
2. ¿Qué hacía la gente para mantenerse en contacto con los amigos, la familia, etcétera? ¿Y ahora?
3. ¿Cree Ud. que las personas del siglo XX se sentían culpables (*guilty*) por estar desconectadas durante las vacaciones? ¿Y ahora?

Paso 2. Ahora use las siguientes ideas para dar consejos en forma de mandatos informales para vivir «en modo avión», por lo menos temporalmente (*temporarily*). Es decir (*That is*), den consejos sobre cómo usar la tecnología sin dejarse absorber por ella.

1. no tener el celular al lado de la almohada (*pillow*) toda la noche / ponerlo lejos de la cama
2. no mantener el celular encendido (*on*) todo el tiempo / desconectar a veces
3. proponer actividades físicas para hacer con los amigos en lugar de mirar una pantalla / hacer ejercicio.
4. contenerse las ganas de contestar todos los mensajes inmediatamente / ser paciente

Paso 3. Finalmente, en parejas, piensen en todas las cosas que la gente hace en público con su celular y otros aparatos electrónicos. ¿Les molestan a Ud. algunos de estos hábitos? Den consejos (en forma de mandatos informales) sobre lo que uno debe y no debe hacer.

MODELO: La gente habla muy alto (*loudly*) por teléfono. → Si estás en un lugar público, no **hables** muy alto.

D. Entre compañeros de casa. En parejas, hagan una lista de los cinco mandatos que se oyen con más frecuencia en su casa (apartamento, residencia). Piensen en los mandatos que Uds. oyen y también en los que Uds. les dan a los demás (*others*).

Vocabulario útil

apagar (gu)	no ser...	poner, encender
la computadora	así (*like that*), bobo/a (*dumb*),	(enciendo) la tele
contestar el teléfono	impaciente, impulsivo/a,	prestarme dinero
lavar los platos	loco/a, pesado/a,	sacar (qu) la basura
no hacer ruido	precipitado/a (*hasty*), tonto/a	

E. Un anuncio turístico. Los mandatos se usan con frecuencia en los anuncios, como este que nos invita a visitar Colombia. En parejas, inventen por lo menos ocho mandatos que podrían (*might*) ser útiles para un anuncio turístico sobre los Estados Unidos. ¡No repitan verbos, por favor!

F. Mandatos y preguntas

Paso 1. Imagine que estas personas son sus amigos. Deles consejos en forma de mandatos informales.

1. Su amiga Mariana trabaja demasiado. Duerme poco y bebe muchísimo café. Jamás hace ejercicio. Siempre está mirando su iPhone.
2. Su prima Sara vive sola en una casa grande en la mejor zona de la ciudad, con dos perros y dos gatos. Tiene demasiados gastos para su sueldo (*salary*). Antes, sus abuelos le mandaban dinero, pero ahora no pueden seguir mandándoselo.
3. Celia quiere salir a divertirse, especialmente los viernes por la noche. Pero su novio está muy cansado los viernes después de la semana de trabajo (*work*).

Paso 2. Ahora, en parejas, digan cómo se expresarían (*you would express yourselves*) en las siguientes situaciones. **¡OJO!** Recuerden que uno no debe usar mandatos en ciertas situaciones, incluso (*even*) con los buenos amigos y familiares.

1. A la profesora de español: Ud. no entendió lo que acaba de decir.
2. A un compañero de clase que quiere usar las respuestas de Ud. porque no hizo la tarea.
3. A una compañera de cuarto o de casa que nunca contribuye con nada para la comida... y hoy quiere tomarse la leche que Ud. tiene en el refrigerador.
4. A un señor en la calle: Ud. necesita saber dónde está la parada del autobús.
5. A un amigo en la mesa: Ud. quiere la sal.
6. A una persona joven en el *campus*: Ud. quiere saber dónde esta el edificio X.
7. A una compañera de clase: Ud. quiere saber la hora.
8. A un profesor que no puede encontrar una aplicación en la computadora: Ud. le dice cómo hacerlo.

34 Expressing Subjective Actions or States
Present Subjunctive (Part 1): An Introduction

Gramática en acción: Manuela busca apartamento

—Por supuesto, **quiero que** el apartamento esté en un buen barrio.

—Claro, por eso **es muy importante que** haya una parada del autobús cerca.

—Sí, ¡**espero que** mi sueldo sea suficiente para el alquiler y todos los gastos mensuales!

—¿El depósito? **Es probable que** mis padres me den el dinero para pagarlo.

Comprensión

Según lo que dice Manuela por teléfono, **¿es probable que...**

1. Manuela esté hablando con su mejor amiga?
2. Manuela tenga un perro?
3. Manuela no tenga coche?
4. Manuela viva en una ciudad grande?
5. los padres de Manuela estén preocupados por la situación económica de su hija?

Present Subjunctive / El presente de subjuntivo

1. Indicative Mood

Except for **Ud./Uds.** and negative **tú** commands, all the verb forms you have learned so far in *Puntos de partida* are part of the *indicative mood* (**el modo indicativo**). In both English and Spanish, the indicative is used to state facts and to ask questions; it objectively expresses what the speaker considers to be true.

El modo indicativo

Prefiero llegar temprano a casa.
I prefer getting home early.

¿**Vienes** a la fiesta, ¿verdad?
You're coming to the party, right?

Manuela is looking for an apartment —"Naturally, I want the apartment to be (*lit., that the apartment be*) in a good neighborhood." —"Of course, that's why it's really important for there to be (*lit., that there be*) a bus stop nearby." —"Yes, I hope (*that*) my salary will be enough for the rent and all the monthly expenses!" —"The deposit? It's probable that my parents will give me the money to pay it."

2. Subjunctive Mood

Spanish has another verb system called the *subjunctive mood* (**el modo subjuntivo**). The subjunctive is used to express the attitude of the speaker with respect to what he/she says. These include things that the speaker

- wants to happen or wants others to do
- reacts to emotionally
- does not yet know to be true

To sum up:

- indicative = objective reality (speaker knows it)
- subjunctive = subjective or conceptual (that is, in the mind of the speaker)

El modo subjuntivo

Prefiero que **llegues** temprano a casa.
I prefer for you to be (that you be) home early.

Espero que **vengas** a la fiesta.
I hope (that) you're coming to the party.

Es probable que **vengas** a la fiesta, ¿no?
You're probably coming (It's probable that you will come) to the party, aren't you?

3. Simple vs. Complex Sentences

In English and in Spanish, sentences may be simple or complex.

- a *simple sentence* (**una oración simple**) has one conjugated verb

Oraciones simples

Vienes a la fiesta.
You are coming to the party.

Alicia **está** en casa.
Alicia is at home.

- a *complex sentence* (**una oración compleja**) has two or more *clauses* (**las cláusulas**), each with a conjugated verb

Oraciones complejas

Ella **sabe** que **vienes** a la fiesta.
She knows (that) you're coming to the party.

Miguel **dice** que Alicia **está** en casa.
Miguel says (that) Alicia is at home.

¡OJO!

As you can see in the example sentences, in English the word *that* introduces the second clause, but it can be and is often omitted. The word **que** is never omitted in Spanish.

4. Two Types of Clauses

In English and in Spanish, there are two types of clauses: main and subordinate.

- *Main clauses* (**Las cláusulas principales**) (①in the sentences to the right) express an idea that controls the subordinate clause. These are also called independent clauses.
- *Subordinate clauses* (**Las cláusulas subordinadas**) (②in the sentences to the right) contain an incomplete thought and cannot stand alone. They require a main clause to form a complete sentence. Because they depend on the main clause, they are also called dependent clauses.

> *a clause* / **una cláusula** = a group of words that contains a subject and a verb

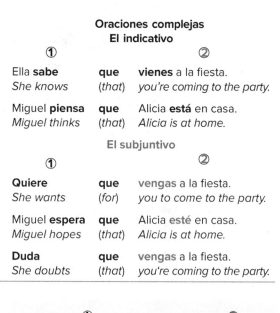

Oraciones complejas
El indicativo

①		②
Ella **sabe** *She knows*	que *(that)*	**vienes** a la fiesta. *you're coming to the party.*
Miguel **piensa** *Miguel thinks*	que *(that)*	Alicia **está** en casa. *Alicia is at home.*

El subjuntivo

①		②
Quiere *She wants*	que *(for)*	**vengas** a la fiesta. *you to come to the party.*
Miguel **espera** *Miguel hopes*	que *(that)*	Alicia **esté** en casa. *Alicia is at home.*
Duda *She doubts*	que *(that)*	**vengas** a la fiesta. *you're coming to the party.*

5. Use of the Subjunctive in Subordinate Clauses

As you can see in the sentences in Point 4, when the subjects of the clauses in a complex sentence are different, the subjunctive is often used in the subordinate clause in Spanish.

①		②
first subject = **indicative**	**que**	second subject = **subjunctive**

6. Same Subject → Infinitive

As you already know, when there is no change of subject in the sentence, the infinitive often follows the conjugated verb and no conjunction is necessary. In this type of sentence, the infinitive is the direct object of the conjugated verb.

Quiero ir a la fiesta.
I want to go to the party.

Necesitan estudiar para el examen.
They need to study for the test.

Es necesario estudiar para los exámenes.
It's necessary to study for tests.

7. Common Uses of the Subjunctive

In Spanish, the subjunctive is commonly used in the subordinate clause:

• when the main clause verb expresses *influence, emotion,* or *doubt* or *denial*

and

• when there is a different subject in the main and subordinate clauses.

You will practice all these uses of the subjunctive in this section, and learn more about them in **Gramática 38, 39,** and **40.**

Influencia: Necesito que mis padres me **den** más dinero.
Emoción: Espero que mis padres me **den** más dinero.
Duda: Dudo que mis padres me **den** más dinero.
Negación: No creo que mis padres me **den** más dinero.

Forms of the Present Subjunctive / Las formas del presente de subjuntivo

The **Ud./Uds.** and negative **tú** command forms that you have already learned are part of the subjunctive system. They are highlighted in the following box.

Terminaciones del presente de subjuntivo
-ar: -e, -es, -e, -emos, -éis, -en
-er/-ir: -a, -as, -a, -amos, -áis, -an

	-ar verbs	-er verbs	-ir verbs	stem-changing verbs	irregular verbs
	hablar: habl-	comer: com-	escribir: escrib-	volver: vuelv-	decir: dig-
Singular	hable	coma	escriba	vuelva	diga
	hables	comas	escribas	vuelvas	digas
	hable	coma	escriba	vuelva	diga
Plural	hablemos	comamos	escribamos	volvamos	digamos
	habléis	comáis	escribáis	volváis	digáis
	hablen	coman	escriban	vuelvan	digan

1. Present Indicative *yo* Stem + Present Subjunctive Endings

The personal endings of the present subjunctive are formed with the "opposite" vowel. They are added to the first person singular (**yo**) of the present indicative, minus its **-o** ending: **habl-, com-, escrib-, vuelv-, dig-,** as shown in the preceding chart.

¡OJO!
present subjunctive stem = present indicative **yo** form minus **-o**

2. *-ar* and *-er* Stem-changing Verbs

These verbs follow the stem-changing pattern of the present indicative.

pensar (pienso):

piense	pensemos
pienses	penséis
piense	piensen

poder (puedo):

pueda	podamos
puedas	podáis
pueda	puedan

3. -ir Stem-changing Verbs

The present subjunctive of **-ir** stem-changing verbs has the same stem change as that of the present indicative when the stem vowel is stressed.

- **preferir: e → ie**
- **pedir: e → i**
- **dormir: o → ue**

In addition, these verbs show a second stem change in the **nosotros** and **vosotros** forms. This change is highlighted in the verbs to the right.

- **e → i**
- **o → u**

This is *the same change* that happens in the present participle (**-ndo**) and in the third person singular and plural of the preterite of **-ir** stem-changing verbs, so you have already learned to make it.

- **preferir (prefiero) (i)**

prefiera	prefiramos
prefieras	prefiráis
prefiera	prefieran

prefiriendo / prefirió, prefirieron

- **pedir (pido) (i)**

pida	pidamos
pidas	pidáis
pida	pidan

pidiendo / pidió, pidieron

- **dormir (duermo) (u)**

duerma	durmamos
duermas	durmáis
duerma	duerman

durmiendo / durmió, durmieron

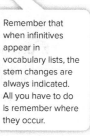

> Remember that when infinitives appear in vocabulary lists, the stem changes are always indicated. All you have to do is remember where they occur.

4. Verbs Ending in -car, -gar, and -zar

These verbs have a spelling change in *all* persons of the present subjunctive to preserve the **c**, **g**, and **z** sounds. This is the same change that happens in the **Uds./Uds.** commands, in the negative **tú** commands, and in the first person singular of the preterite of these verbs.

- **-car: c → qu**
- **-gar: g → gu**
- **-zar: z → c**

buscar (qu)		pagar (gu)		empezar (c)	
busque	busquemos	pague	paguemos	empiece	empecemos
busques	busquéis	pagues	paguéis	empieces	empecéis
busque	busquen	pague	paguen	empiece	empiecen
busque(n), no busques / busqué		pague(n), no pagues / pagué		empiece(n), no empieces / empecé	

5. Verbs with Irregular *yo* Forms

Since the present subjunctive stem is the **yo** form of the present indicative (minus **-o**), verbs with irregular **yo** forms in the present indicative show that irregularity in *all* persons of the present subjunctive.

conocer: conozca, conozcas, conozca, conozcamos, conozcáis, conozcan

decir:	**diga,...**	tener:	**tenga,...**
hacer:	**haga,...**	traer:	**traiga,...**
oír:	**oiga,...**	venir:	**venga,...**
poner:	**ponga,...**	ver:	**vea,...**
salir:	**salga,...**		

6. Irregular Verbs

A few verbs have irregular present subjunctive forms.

dar:	**dé, des, dé, demos, deis, den**
estar:	**esté,...**
ir:	**vaya,...**
saber:	**sepa,...**
ser:	**sea,...**

7. Present Subjunctive of *haber*

Remember that the infinitive form of **hay** is **haber**. The present subjunctive of **hay** is **haya**.

No creo que **haya** clases hoy.
I don't think there are any classes today.

Práctica y comunicación

Endings of the Present Subjunctive

-ar → -e
-er/-ir → -a

A. El próximo semestre/trimestre

Paso 1. Autoprueba. Dé las formas indicadas del presente de subjuntivo de los siguientes verbos. **¡OJO!** Hay unos cambios ortográficos (*spelling changes*).

1. conocer: nosotros
2. decir: Uds.

3. sacar: tú
4. entregar: ella

5. conseguir: yo
6. morir: ellos

Paso 2. Complete las siguientes oraciones con la forma apropiada de los infinitivos. En algunos casos el infinitivo es la forma apropiada, pero en otros casos es necesario usar el presente de subjuntivo. Si alguna oración es falsa para Ud., use **no** antes del verbo principal (en el indicativo).

El próximo semestre/trimestre...

1. quiero _____ (tomar) otra clase de español.
2. mi padre/madre (esposo/a, hijo/a) quiere que yo _____ (tomar) una clase de economía.
3. mi consejero/a recomienda que yo _____ (tomar) una clase de matemáticas.
4. deseo _____ (vivir) fuera del *campus*.
5. espero _____ (encontrar) un apartamento o una casa cerca del *campus*.
6. espero que mis padres _____ (ayudarme) con el alquiler.
7. deseo que mi mejor amigo/a _____ (vivir) conmigo fuera del *campus*.
8. no creo que _____ (haber) problemas en encontrar una casa o un apartamento.

Paso 3. Ahora, en parejas, entrevístense sobre las oraciones del **Paso 2** para ver si las oraciones son ciertas o falsas para Uds. Luego díganle al resto de la clase algo que Uds. tienen en común.

MODELO: **E1:** ¿Tu padre quiere que **tomes** una clase de economía el próximo trimestre?
E2: No, mi padre no quiere que **tome** una clase de economía. ¿Y tu padre?
E1: Mi padre no lo quiere tampoco. → Nuestros padres no quieren que **tomemos** una clase de economía el próximo trimestre.

B. En el trabajo (*job*). Complete las oraciones de la columna de la izquierda con la cláusula más lógica de la columna de la derecha.

1. La jefa (*boss*) quiere que ___.
2. Y duda que ___.
3. Prohíbe que ___.
4. Para ella, es importante ___.
5. Yo espero que ___.
6. Pero no creo que ___.

a. me dé un aumento de sueldo (*raise*) pronto.
b. tengamos que trabajar los sábados este mes.
c. seamos diligentes durante las horas de trabajo.
d. usemos el escáner para las cosas personales durante las horas de trabajo.
e. eso ocurra (*will happen*) este mes.
f. tener una reunión (*meeting*) semanal con todo el equipo.

C. Cosas importantes. Haga oraciones completas conectando las dos frases. En algunos casos no es necesario hacer cambios, pero en otros casos es necesario añadir la palabra **que** y conjugar el segundo verbo en el presente de subjuntivo.

MODELOS: Es necesario / saber cuáles son los gastos de electricidad y gas antes de alquilar un apartamento → Es necesario **saber** cuáles son los gastos de electricidad y gas antes de alquilar un apartamento.

Mi compañero espera / yo: saber cuáles son los gastos de un apartamento antes de alquilarlo → Mi compañero espera **que yo sepa** cuáles son los gastos de un apartamento antes de alquilarlo.

(Continúa.)

Próc. A, Paso 1: Answers: 1. conozcamos 2. digan 3. saques 4. entregue 5. consiga 6. mueran

Sobre una vivienda

1. Es importante / informarse sobre las zonas de una ciudad antes de alquilar un apartamento

2. Se recomienda / leer en internet los anuncios clasificados de viviendas

3. Todo el mundo espera / sus vecinos: ser personas amables

4. A alguna gente no le importa / haber mucho tráfico en su calle

Sobre internet y celulares

5. Mucha gente quiere / tener cientos de amigos en Facebook

6. Otros no quieren / gente desconocida (*unknown*): saber de su vida por Facebook

7. A los profesores les molesta / sus estudiantes: mandar mensajes en clase

8. Es dudoso (*doubtful*) / alguien en este país: no tener acceso a internet hoy día

D. **¿Puede Ud. substituir a su profesor(a) en el salón de clase?** Demuéstrele a su profesor(a) que Ud. lo/la conoce bien, haciendo oraciones como las que dice él/ella en clase. (Solo tiene que cambiar el infinitivo.)

| quiero que <br> espero que <br> prohíbo que <br> dudo que <br> es necesario que <br> me alegro de (*I'm glad*) que <br> no creo que <br> recomiendo que | **+** | (nombre de un[a] estudiante)
 todos Uds.
 nadie <br> alguien de la clase <br> yo | **+** | (no) | **+** | copiar en un examen <br> dormirse en clase <br> entrar en internet <br> estar en Facebook <br> estudiar <br> hacer la tarea <br> llegar a tiempo <br> saber el subjuntivo <br> sacar notas mejores <br> tener un blog
 ¿ ? |

Vocabulario útil

Es necesario/
  bueno/importante/
  esencial que...   } + subjuntivo
Recomendamos
  que...
Sugerimos que...

E. **Cómo dar una buena fiesta**

Paso 1. Haga una lista de las cosas que hay que hacer para dar una fiesta exitosa (*successful*), en su opinión. Use infinitivos en su lista.

MODELOS: llamar a los amigos con anticipación (*ahead of time*), comprar...

Paso 2. En parejas, comparen sus listas del **Paso 1** y hagan una sola lista de por lo menos diez acciones.

Paso 3. Luego conviertan la lista en una serie de recomendaciones para dar una buena fiesta.

MODELO: Recomendamos que llamen a los amigos con anticipación.

¿Recuerda Ud.?

In **Gramática 35** and in the grammar sections of **Capítulo 13,** you will learn more about the three major uses of the subjunctive. Summarize what you have learned so far by completing the following sentences.

1. In Spanish, there are _____ clauses in a sentence that contains the subjunctive.

2. The subjunctive appears in the _____ clause.

3. The indicative appears in the _____ clause.

4. The word _____ must always appear.

5. The verb subjects in each clause are _____.

35 **Expressing Desires and Requests**

Use of the Subjunctive (Part 2): Influence

Gramática en acción: ¿Quién debe hacerlo?

Comprensión

Escoja la oración que describa cada dibujo.

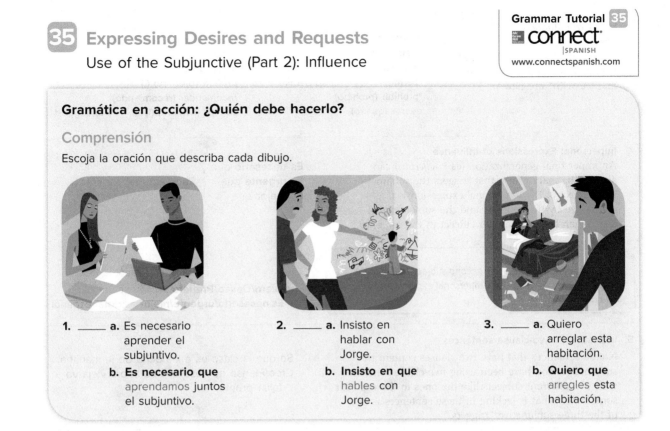

1. _____ **a.** Es necesario
aprender el
subjuntivo.

b. Es necesario que
aprendamos juntos
el subjuntivo.

2. _____ **a.** Insisto en
hablar con
Jorge.

b. Insisto en que
hables con
Jorge.

3. _____ **a.** Quiero
arreglar esta
habitación.

b. Quiero que
arregles esta
habitación.

1. Features of the Subjunctive

So far, as you know, you have learned to identify the
subjunctive by the features listed at the right.

In addition, the subjunctive is associated with three
concepts or conditions that "trigger" the use of it in
the subordinate clause: influence, emotion, and doubt
or denial.

- It is conjugated with the "opposite" vowel.
- It appears in a complex sentence, one that
  has at least two clauses and thus two
  conjugated verbs.
- It is used in the dependent clause when the
  subject of that clause is different from the
  subject of the main clause.
- It is preceded by **que.**

2. The Subjunctive after Verbs of Influence

①   ②

INFLUENCE
first subject = **indicative**   que   **second subject** = subjunctive

One trigger for the use of the subjunctive in the
subordinate clause is the concept of *influence*
(**la influencia**). The subject of the main clause
wants, prefers, insists, and so on, that the
subject of the subordinate clause do something,
expressed by a verb in the subjunctive. The verb
in the main clause is always in the indicative.

La influencia

①

Yo **quiero**
I want

②

que   tú **pagues** la cuenta.
you to pay the bill.

La profesora **prefiere**
The professor prefers

que   no **lleguemos** tarde.
that   *we don't don't
arrive late.*

3. Verbs of Influence

There are many verbs of influence, some very strong and direct, some very soft and polite. The verbs marked with* are new.

STRONG(ER)		SOFT(ER)	
*insistir en		desear	
*mandar	to order	pedir (pido) (i)	
*permitir	to permit, allow	preferir (prefiero) (i)	
*prohibir (prohíbo)		recomendar (recomiendo)	
querer (quiero)		sugerir (sugiero) (i)	to suggest

4. Impersonal Expressions of Influence

An impersonal generalization (**es** + *adjective*) can also be the main clause that triggers the subjunctive. The subject of the impersonal expression is *it* (expressed by the verb **es**), and the subjunctive is used when there is another subject in the sentence.

Es necesario que ⎫
Es urgente que ⎬ Paco **estudie** español.
Es mejor que ⎭

¡OJO!

As you know, when there is no second subject, the infinitive follows verbs of influence and impersonal expressions of influence.

Quiero/Deseo/Prefiero estudiar español.
Es necesario/urgente/mejor estudiar español.

5. Indicative in two-clause sentences

Not all sentences that have two clauses contain the subjunctive. You have been using two-clause sentences with two different subjects like the ones to the right for some time. What is lacking in these sentences is one of the three subjunctive "triggers."

Sé que la clase **es** a las ocho de la mañana.
Creo/Pienso que esa computadora vieja **va** a fallar pronto.

Summary of Influence

influence + **que** + change of subject ⟶ subjunctive

Práctica y comunicación

A. Opiniones sobre la tecnología

Paso 1. Autoprueba. Indique cuál(es) de los siguientes conceptos *no* se asocia(n) con el subjuntivo.

1. un infinitivo ☐
2. la influencia en la cláusula independiente ☐
3. dos sujetos ☐
4. dos cláusulas ☐
5. **que** para unir dos cláusulas ☐

Paso 2. Indique las oraciones que son ciertas para Ud. Indique también las oraciones con cláusulas subordinadas con el subjuntivo.

	CIERTO PARA MÍ	SUBJUNTIVO
1. Mis profesores quieren que los estudiantes tengan la computadora en clase.	☐	☐
2. Muchos profesores insisten en que desconectemos el celular en clase.	☐	☐
3. Creo que es lógico desconectar el celular en una clase.	☐	☐
4. Sé que el uso del celular puede ser una adicción.	☐	☐
5. Deseo que las multas (*fines*) por mandar mensajes mientras uno conduce (*drives*) sean más grandes.	☐	☐
6. Pienso que la gente tiene demasiadas aplicaciones inútiles (*useless*).	☐	☐

Prác. A, Paso 1: Answers: 1

Paso 3. Ahora, en parejas, entrevístense sobre las ideas del **Paso 1.**

> MODELO: **E1:** ¿Quieren tus profesores que los estudiantes tengan la computadora en clase?
>
> **E2:** Sí, mis profesores quieren eso. ¿Y tus profesores?
>
> **E1:** También.

B. Gabriel García Márquez. Complete las siguientes oraciones sobre el escritor colombiano con el verbo apropiado.

1. Dudo que muchos colombianos no (saben / sepan / saber) quién es Gabriel García Márquez.

2. El presidente de Colombia dice que García Márquez (es / sea / ser) el colombiano más famoso del mundo.

3. Todos los profesores de literatura quieren que sus estudiantes (conocen / conozcan / conocer) la obra de este escritor.

4. Los profesores de español sugieren que todo el mundo (lee / lea / leer) algo escrito (*written*) por García Márquez.

5. Mi amiga colombiana insiste en que yo (busco / busque / buscar) un cuento de García Márquez en español.

6. Pero yo prefiero (leo / lea / leer) algo traducido (*translated*) al inglés.

7. ¿Con qué novela de García Márquez me recomiendas que (yo: empiezo / empiece / empezar)?

C. Una mudanza *(move).* Imagine que Ud. y sus compañeros de casa o su familia se van a mudar. ¿Dónde van a poner las siguientes cosas? Explique por qué.

> MODELO: **Queremos que** la televisión de pantalla plana **esté** en la sala, porque nos gusta mirar la tele allí.

queremos que... es mejor que... es necesario que... es buena idea que... nos gusta que...	**+**	la televisión de pantalla plana la impresora el teléfono fijo las bicicletas el equipo de música el sofá el radio	**+**	una de las alcobas el baño la cocina, el comedor el estudio garaje, el patio la sala

D. ¿Qué quiere Ud.?

Paso 1. En parejas, hablen de cómo desean afectar las acciones de otras personas.

> MODELO: **E1:** ¿Qué quieres que haga tu padre?
>
> **E2:** **Quiero que** mi padre me **compre** una computadora.

querer preferir insistir en mandar permitir prohibir recomendar	**+**	padre/madre amigos/as hermano/a profesor(a) novio/a esposo/a compañero/a de cuarto hijo/a, hijos ¿ ?	**+**	comprarme... (una televisión, rosas, ¿ ?) visitarme... (mañana, el jueves, ¿ ?) invitarme... (al cine, a cenar, ¿ ?) (no) dar tarea... (hoy, mañana, ¿ ?) ayudarme... (a hacer la tarea, ¿ ?) salir con... (otra persona, ¿ ?) llamarme... (el viernes, ¿ ?) explicarme... (la gramática, ¿ ?) ¿ ?

Algo sobre...

Gabriel García Márquez

Gabriel García Márquez (1927–2014), un escritor[a] colombiano leído[b] y admirado en todo el mundo

Gabriel García Márquez, o «Gabo», como lo llamaban, es sin duda[c] el escritor colombiano más famoso del mundo. Su obra[d] literaria fue una de las más influyentes del siglo XX. Empezó trabajando como periodista[e] y escribió cuentos,[f] novelas y ensayos;[g] luego, en 1982, recibió el Premio Nobel de Literatura. Su obra más famosa es *Cien años de soledad*, ejemplo de un estilo literario que se llama realismo mágico. La novela narra la historia de una familia a través de[h] varias generaciones.

 ¿Puede nombrar Ud. a algunos escritores muy importantes de su país? ¿Cuál es su escritor favorito?

[a]*writer* [b]*read* [c]*sin... without a doubt* [d]*body of work* [e]*journalist* [f]*short stories* [g]*essays* [h]*a... throughout*

Paso 2. Ahora hablen de las cosas que otras personas quieren, prefieren, permiten, etcétera, que Uds. hagan.

MODELO: **E1:** ¿Qué quieren tus hijos que hagas?

E2: Quieren que yo compre una computadora nueva.

E. **El programa de radio**

Paso 1. *Te escucho* es un programa de radio que da consejos sobre todo tipo de problemas. Hoy son problemas relacionados con el uso y abuso de la tecnología. En parejas, imaginen que Uds. son los presentadores del programa. Lean lo que dicen los siguientes radioyentes (*listeners*) y preparen las respuestas que Uds. creen que los moderadores del programa deben darles.

1. **Habla Hortensia:** «Soy una chica de 20 años. Acabo de mudarme a esta ciudad y tengo pocos amigos aquí. Pero no me siento sola porque siempre estoy conectada en internet. Mi madre dice que no es normal que yo pase tantas horas en la computadora y que no salga con los amigos. ¿Qué piensan Uds.? ¿Qué me recomiendan?»

2. **Habla la Sra. Silva:** «Mi esposo es un hombre bueno y responsable. Pero la mayor parte del tiempo que pasa en casa, está en el estudio, en internet. Yo no comprendo por qué pasa tanto tiempo en eso. Estoy preocupada y también aburrida. ¿Qué me recomiendan que haga? ¿Qué le debo decir a mi esposo?»

3. **Habla Guillermo, un joven de 17 años:** «Mi hermano de 13 años está en Facebook, lo que es normal. Pero ayer descubrí que pone fotos de él y de toda la familia en internet. Yo no quiero que ponga fotos de nosotros, pero él dice que las fotos son de él. Hay una foto horrible de mi madre. No quiero decírselo a mis padres porque tengo miedo de que le quiten la computadora a mi hermano. Pero no sé qué otra cosa puedo hacer. ¿Cuáles son mis opciones? ¿Es mejor que no haga nada?

Paso 2. Ahora piensen en un problema con la tecnología que sea similar a los del **Paso 1.** Descríbanlo por escrito (*in writing*). El resto de la clase les va a hacer sugerencias sobre cómo resolverlo.

F. **Intercambios**

Paso 1. Complete las siguientes oraciones lógicamente... ¡y con sinceridad!

1. Mis padres (hijos, abuelos,...) insisten en que (yo) _____.
2. Mi mejor amigo/a (esposo/a, novio/a,...) desea que (yo) _____.
3. Prefiero que mis amigos _____.
4. No quiero que mis amigos _____.
5. Es urgente que (yo) _____.
6. Es necesario que mi mejor amigo/a (esposo/a, novio/a,...) _____.

Paso 2. En parejas, entrevístense para saber cómo completaron las oraciones del **Paso 1.** Luego díganle a la clase algo que Uds. tienen en común.

MODELO: ¿En qué insisten tus padres?

Algo sobre...

la orquídea colombiana

La orquídea cattleya trianae, más conocida[a] como «flor de mayo»

La orquídea es la flor nacional de Colombia y un símbolo del país. Pero, en realidad, no se debe hablar de la orquídea sino[b] de las orquídeas colombianas, ya que[c] en Colombia existen más de 2.700 variedades de ellas. Después del Ecuador, es el segundo país con más variedades de orquídeas en el mundo. Esta inmensa variedad de flora—y también de fauna—es una de las características de Colombia, que está entre los siete países del mundo con mayor biodiversidad.

¿Es su país uno de los países con mayor biodiversidad? ¿Sabe cuál es la flor nacional de su país? ¿Cuáles son algunos otros de los símbolos naturales del país?

[a]*known* [b]*but rather* [c]*ya... since*

Un poco de todo

A. Lengua y cultura: La ciudad de Cartagena, Colombia

Paso 1. Complete the following passage with the correct forms of the words in parentheses, as suggested by context. When two possibilities are given, select the correct word. **¡OJO!** As you conjugate the verbs in this activity, put the infinitives preceded by *I:* in the imperfect. Other verbs will be present indicative, present subjunctive, or infinitive as determined by the context.

Mayra y Joaquín son dos colombianos que viven en mi ciudad. Los dos (ser / estar[1]) de Cartagena, una (grande[2]) ciudad colombiana que (ser / estar[3]) en el mar Caribe. De niña, Mayra (I: vivir[4]) en la parte más antigua (en la / de la[5]) ciudad, el Centro Amurallado[a] colonial. La familia de Joaquín (tener[6]) un apartamento en Bocagrande, la zona (más / mejor[7]) moderna de Cartagena. Sin embargo, los dos les hacen las (mismo[8]) recomendaciones a las personas (que / quienes[9]) desean visitar la ciudad.

Mayra y Joaquín (ser / estar[10]) de acuerdo en que el Centro Amurallado tiene (mucho[11]) cosas que ver. Por eso, los dos recomiendan (que / lo que[12]) los turistas en Cartagena (dar[13]) un paseo por ese centro histórico de la ciudad. También es necesario (que / —[14]) vean y admiren las fortalezas y las murallas.[b] ¿(Saber / Conocer[15]) Uds. que algunas miden veinte metros de ancho[c]? ¡(Ser / Estar[16]) impresionantes! Además[d] (ser / haber[17]) playas muy chéveres, como la playa de La Boquilla* y el Parque Natural Corales del Rosario, en la isla Barú.† Por la noche Mayra y Joaquín (sugerir[18]) que los turistas visiten un restaurante en la Boquilla y que (pedir[19]) mariscos. Luego deben (ir[20]) a un club a bailar cumbia.

Unos edificios de apartamentos muy modernos en Bocagrande

[a]Centro... *Walled Center* [b]fortalezas... *forts and walls* [c]miden... *are 20 meters thick* [d]*In addition*

Paso 2. Comprensión

1. ¿De qué ciudad son Mayra y Joaquín?
2. ¿Qué es lo que distingue la geografía de esta ciudad?
3. ¿En qué partes de la ciudad vivían los dos de niños?
4. ¿Qué recomiendan Mayra y Joaquín que hagan los turistas que visitan Cartagena?

Paso 3. Ahora, en parejas, hagan una serie de recomendaciones a las personas que visitan su ciudad y su universidad.

VERBOS Y FRASES PARA RECOMENDAR: proponer, recomendar (recomiendo), sugerir (sugiero) (i); es recomendable, es una buena idea

IDEAS: comer, dar un paseo en/por... , ir a..., ir de compras a... subir/bajar, ver, visitar...

MODELO: (Les) Recomendamos que suban a Foss Hill porque desde allí hay una vista muy bonita de la universidad.

> **Vocabulario útil**
>
> **la colina**   hill
> **el puente**   bridge
> **la torre**   tower

*La Boquilla *is a fishing village outside of Cartagena; it has a long, secluded beach with restaurants and bars.*
†*La isla Barú *is about ten minutes by motorboat from Cartagena. It has white sand beaches, crystal clear water, and big coral reefs.*

B. Un mundo ruidoso (*noisy*)

Paso 1. En parejas, miren el siguiente dibujo y contesten las preguntas.

Vocabulario útil

la ambulancia
el claxon (car) horn
el despertador alarm clock
el megáfono loudspeaker
el ronquido snoring
la sirena
el sonido sound
el martillo mecánico
   jackhammer
el timbre ring (*on a phone, door, etc.*)

1. Según el dibujo, ¿cuáles son las cosas que causan ruido en el mundo de hoy?
2. ¿Qué otras cosas causan ruido en su vida?
3. ¿Qué ruidos les molestan más a Uds.?
4. ¿Cuáles son los lugares que Uds. consideran más ruidosos?

Paso 2. Ahora, con otro/a compañero/a, imaginen que Uds. están a cargo (*in charge*) de hacer una presentación sobre el tema del ruido. Usando mandatos de **tú,** hagan una lista de reglas (*rules*) sobre las cosas que se deben o no se deben usar y cuándo y dónde.

MODELO: Apaga tu celular antes de entrar en clase.

En su comunidad

Entreviste a una persona hispana de su universidad o ciudad sobre su ciudad de origen y el barrio donde vivía en su país.

PREGUNTAS POSIBLES

- ¿Qué tipo de ciudad es? ¿Es grande o pequeña? ¿vieja o moderna?
- ¿Hay buenas vistas desde algún punto de la ciudad? ¿Hay un buen sistema de transporte público, como autobuses o metro?
- ¿Dónde vivía su familia? ¿En el centro o en las afueras? ¿en un barrio histórico o moderno? ¿en una casa individual o en un apartamento?
- ¿Cómo es (o era) la vida del barrio? (Pida detalles.)

Antes de mirar

¿En qué sitios web y buscadores entra Ud. con frecuencia? ¿En qué proveedores de correo electrónico tiene Ud. una cuenta (*account*)?

Este segmento

Laura trae un reportaje sobre el uso de la tecnología entre los estudiantes universitarios de Quito. Para terminar, Ana y Víctor hablan de mensajes de texto.

Vocabulario del segmento

han decidido	have decided	**inalámbrico/a**	wireless
te des cuenta	you realize	**resumir**	to summarize
el uso	el hábito	**crear**	to create
la investigación	research	**la prueba**	test
los deberes	la tarea	**pertenecer**	to belong
agradar	gustar	**ni pudo**	couldn't even (do it)
la costumbre	el hábito	**anticuado/a**	antiquated, old-fashioned
¡claro!	of course!		

«Yo creo que falta desarrollar (*it's necessary to develop*) un poco lo que es el wifi aquí en Quito. Pero ha incrementado (*has increased*) bastantísimo (*a lot*) el uso del wifi en todo lo que son lugares públicos...»

Fragmento del guion

CHICO: El mundo ha sufrido[a] un gran cambio tecnológico desde que... o sea,[b] desde los últimos veinte años. Ahora nos podemos comunicar con cualquier[c] persona en el mundo en cuestión de segundos.[d] Podemos hacer videollamadas con cualquier persona al otro lado del Atlántico, podemos hablar con gente en Europa, con gente en África... Y hace diez, quince años[e] eso era casi imposible, o costaba mucho hacer una llamada internacional. Ahora es gratuito.[f]

[a]ha... *suffered* [b]o... *I mean* [c]*any* [d]en... *in a matter of seconds* [e]hace... *ten, fifteen years ago* [f]*free*

Después de mirar

A. ¿Está claro? ¿Cierto o falso? Corrija las oraciones falsas.

	CIERTO	FALSO
1. Sarita, la hija de Víctor, ya tiene un iPhone y una página de Facebook.	☐	☐
2. Facebook es la red social más popular entre los jóvenes ecuatorianos.	☐	☐
3. Estos jóvenes universitarios no pueden conectarse en la universidad.	☐	☐
4. Víctor lee los texteos con facilidad (*easily*).	☐	☐

B. Un poco más. Complete las siguientes oraciones con información del video.

1. Los sitios de internet que más visitan los estudiantes son _____.

2. En el Ecuador, hay acceso wifi en _____.

C. Y ahora, Uds. En parejas, estudien los dos mensajes de texto que aparecen en el programa y luego preparen un mensaje similar suyo (*of your own*) para el resto de la clase. ¡Inventen nuevas convenciones!

- Ola, q tal? q acs ste finde? Yamam pq es el qmple d mi hno ste finde y kiero acr 1 fiesta. Bsossssss.
- Hsta ntoncs salu2 muy cordials d td el ekipo d ste programa.

A LEER

Antes de leer

¿Conoce Ud. a sus vecinos? ¿Qué relación mantiene con ellos? ¿Hablan con frecuencia o solo se saludan?

Lectura cultural: Colombia
Los barrios colombianos

Es común que los vecinos de un barrio colombiano desarrollen[a] una relación estrecha[b] con los otros vecinos y que hasta organicen juntos fiestas y celebraciones en el barrio para fechas especiales. Es normal saber los nombres de muchos de los vecinos del barrio, no solo los[c] del edificio o de la calle donde uno vive. Con frecuencia, la gente habla de los amigos del barrio como un grupo distinto,[d] parecido[e] a los amigos del colegio,[f] de la universidad o del trabajo. En el barrio, es normal ver grupos de personas que charlan[g] juntas, en la plaza o en una esquina[h] o simplemente en la puerta de un edificio o tienda. Por eso el barrio es un lugar de intensa vida social, especialmente para las personas que no trabajan fuera de casa o para las personas mayores. Y, por supuesto,[i] para los niños.

[a]develop [b]close [c]those [d]distinct, separate [e]similar [f]school [g]are chatting [h]corner [i]por... of course

En **otros** países hispanos

- **En todo el mundo hispanohablante** Lo común es que haya una plaza central, rodeada de[a] algunos de los edificios más importantes de la ciudad, como el ayuntamiento[b] o la catedral. Estas plazas centrales frecuentemente reciben el nombre de Plaza Mayor o Plaza de Armas. Antes de la conquista de América, había plazas de este tipo en España, y cuando los españoles fundaron las ciudades en el nuevo continente, incluyeron en sus planos las plazas, así como[c] en España.

- **En México y la Argentina** Varias ciudades hispanas tienen metro, pero los de México y la Argentina son notables. El de[d] Buenos Aires es el más antiguo del Hemisferio Sur. Su construcción comenzó en 1913. Pero el más impresionante es sin duda el metro de la Ciudad de México. Es el segundo metro en longitud[e] de Norteamérica y el mayor de Latinoamérica. Por el número de pasajeros, es el quinto[f] del mundo. Su sistema para nombrar las estaciones es muy colorido y eficiente. Usa palabras y dibujos, para que las personas analfabetas[g] también puedan saber dónde están.

[a]rodeada... surrounded by [b]town hall [c]así... just as [d]El... That (i.e. el metro) [e]length [f]fifth [g]para... so that people who can't read

Un cafetal (*coffee plantation*) colombiano

Un símbolo colombiano: El café

El café colombiano es famoso en todo el mundo y tiene su propia denominación: café arábigo, que significa cien por cien[a] producido en las zonas cafeteras de Colombia. Colombia es el tercer[b] país productor de café del el mundo, y los Estados Unidos es el principal consumidor del café colombiano. Sin duda, parte de la fama del café colombiano se debe a la exitosa campaña publicitaria[c] con la figura de Juan Valdez, un personaje[d] ficticio que representa a los campesinos[e] y cafeteros[f] colombianos.

[a]cien... completely [b]third [c]exitosa... successful ad campaign [d]character [e]farm workers [f]coffee producers

COMPRENSIÓN

1. ¿Por qué es importante el barrio en la vida de una ciudad hispana?
2. ¿Por qué hay una plaza central en las ciudades latinoamericanas?
3. ¿Cuál es el metro más antiguo de Latinoamérica? ¿Y el más impresionante?
4. ¿Qué contribuye a que sea famoso el café colombiano?
5. ¿Qué país es el principal consumidor del café colombiano?

Y ahora, Uds.

¿Hay una plaza central o muy importante en su ciudad? ¿Qué edificios importantes están en esa plaza? ¿Qué hace la gente en la plaza?

Del mundo hispano

Antes de leer

Conteste las siguientes preguntas.

1. ¿Cómo es el ambiente (*environment*) en que Ud. vive ahora? ¿Y el ambiente en que vivía de niño/a?
2. ¿De qué maneras influye en Ud. el ambiente en que vive ahora (o vivía de niño/a) en cuanto a (*as far as*) las siguientes ideas?

   • sus preferencias en cuanto a la comida
   • la manera en que se viste
   • cómo pasa su tiempo libre
   • cómo se relaciona con otras personas
   • sus necesidades materiales
   • sus ideas políticas y sociales

Lectura: «Cuadrados° y ángulos», de Alfonsina Storni

Squares

Casas enfiladas,[a] casas enfiladas,
casas enfiladas.
Cuadrados, cuadrados, cuadrados.
Casas enfiladas.
5   Las gentes ya tienen el alma[b] cuadrada,
ideas en fila[c]
y ángulos en la espalda.[d]
Yo misma he vertido[e] ayer una lágrima,[f]
Dios mío, cuadrada.

[a]*in a straight row* [b]*soul* [c]*en... in single file* [d]*la... their backs* [e]*Yo... I myself shed* [f]*tear*

Comprensión

A. Elementos del poema. Identifique los siguientes aspectos del poema.

1. las palabras y frases que se repiten
2. los versos (*lines*) que describen las casas
3. el tipo de lugar descrito (*described*) en el poema
4. los versos que describen a las personas
5. los versos que se refieren a la poeta misma (*herself*)

Vocabulario útil

la arquitectura	**el sentido** sense
la monotonía	**sensible** sensitive

B. Comentario. Conteste las siguientes preguntas para expresar su opinión como lector(a) (*reader*).

1. ¿Qué efecto tiene la repetición en este poema?
2. ¿Qué relación existe entre las personas y las casas?
3. ¿Qué tipo de persona es la poeta? ¿Qué efecto tiene en ella el ambiente que describe?
4. ¿Cree Ud. que la poeta se refiere solo a un lugar determinado? ¿O cree que se refiere a un problema más grande?
5. ¿Cree Ud. que la poeta podría (*could*) ser más feliz en un ambiente diferente? ¿En cuál?

Vocabulario **para escuchar**

emitimos	we air
se trata del	we're talking about
la bienvenida	welcome
los radioyentes	radio listeners
los detalles	details
cómo no	of course
una pandemia	pandemic
la máquina	machine
conocida	known
monitorizar	to monitor
mejorar	to improve

Dos herramientas (*tools*) útiles en la lucha contra (*struggle against*) la diabetes: Un monitor continuo de glucosa y una bomba (*pump*) de insulina

Antes de escuchar

Empareje cada término médico con su definición.

1. _____ un componente necesario para el funcionamiento del cuerpo que es regulado (*regulated*) por la insulina

2. _____ un órgano del cuerpo humano

3. _____ una hormona que produce el páncreas

a. la glucosa
b. la insulina
c. el páncreas

Después de escuchar

A. La diabetes. Empareje la información de las dos columnas.

1. _____ la característica de diabetes tipo 1
2. _____ el porcentaje de la población adulta mundial que va a sufrir de diabetes en el futuro
3. _____ el nombre común de la diabetes tipo 1
4. _____ el porcentaje de pacientes diabéticos que sufren de diabetes tipo 1
5. _____ el porcentaje de la población adulta mundial que sufre de diabetes en la actualidad

a. casi el 7%
b. casi el 8%
c. el 10%
d. la diabetes juvenil
e. la ausencia total de insulina

B. Más detalles. Conteste las siguientes preguntas.

1. ¿Dónde ocurre esta conversación? ¿Cómo se llama el programa?
2. ¿Qué es el páncreas artificial? ¿Qué tipo de personas lo necesitan?
3. ¿Existe ya esa máquina?
4. ¿Por qué es un gran proyecto?

PRODUCCIÓN PERSONAL

¡Ahora, yo!

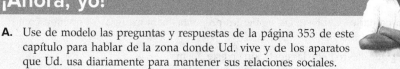

A. Use de modelo las preguntas y respuestas de la página 353 de este capítulo para hablar de la zona donde Ud. vive y de los aparatos que Ud. usa diariamente para mantener sus relaciones sociales.

B. Filme dos entrevistas con estudiantes o personal (*personnel*) de habla española en su universidad. Sus entrevistados deben hablar de los usos que hacen de la tecnología. Use como modelo las entrevistas de estudiantes ecuatorianos en el Programa 12 de *Salu2*.

A ESCRIBIR

La educación universitaria: ¿presencial o a distancia?

Preparar

Paso 1. Piensen en las opciones que existen hoy para obtener un título universitario: presencial (es decir, asistiendo a una universidad, según la manera tradicional) o a distancia, gracias al internet. ¿Cuál es el método más usado? ¿Qué ventajas y desventajas tiene cada opción? ¿Cuál fue la opción que Uds. eligieron (*chose*)? ¿Están contentos/as con su decisión? En parejas, hagan una lista de argumentos a favor y en contra de cada una de las dos opciones para obtener un título universitario: de forma presencial o a distancia. Deben incluir ejemplos específicos para apoyar (*support*) sus argumentos.

Paso 2. Ahora use las ideas del **Paso 1** para comparar las dos opciones educativas. O, si lo prefiere, puede defender una de ellas. Hay más ayuda en Connect.

Más ideas para su portafolio

- Publique algo en español en su muro (*wall*) de Facebook. Luego saque una foto de su post e inclúyala en su portafolio, con una explicación de lo que escribió.

- Incluya un anuncio de celulares en español, de internet o de una revista o periódico. Explique lo que le gusta del anuncio y del producto o servicio mismo (*itself*) y también si el producto o servicio es comparable con lo que hay en este país.

- Si ha estado jugando (*have been playing*) Practice Spanish: Study Abroad, en Quest 9 Ud. tuvo que decidir dónde quedarse cuando estaba de vacaciones en Colombia. Ahora haga un breve video dándoles consejos a los turistas que quieran visitar la ciudad donde vive Ud. ¿Dónde deben quedarse? ¿En un hotel? ¿En una tienda de campaña? ¿En una pensión (*hostel*)? ¿Con Ud.? Explique por qué. ¿Qué servicios (*amenities*) ofrece este lugar?

Sugerencia: You are now ready to play Quest 9 in **Practice Spanish: Study Abroad** (www.mhpractice.com).

AFTER STUDYING THIS CHAPTER I CAN. . .

☐ talk about my neighborhood and living arrangements (354)

☐ talk about technology and techological equipment (356–357)

☐ give informal commands and directions (360–362)

☐ form the present subjunctive and understand its main uses (365–368)

☐ use the present subjunctive to express influence (371–372)

☐ recognize/describe at least 2–3 aspects of Colombian cultures

Gramática en breve

33. *Tú* Commands

Negative **tú** commands = "opposite" vowel

-ar ⟶ -es
-er/-ir ⟶ -as

Affirmative **tú** commands = **Ud.** form of the present indicative

-ar ⟶ -a
-er/-ir ⟶ -e

34. Present Subjunctive: An Introduction

Endings: "opposite" vowel

-ar: -e, -es, -e, -emos, -éis, -en
-er/-ir: -a, -as, -a, -amos, -áis, -an

Structure:

① ②

| first subject = | **que** | second subject = |
| **indicative** | | subjunctive |

35. Uses of the Subjunctive: Influence

① ②

INFLUENCE

| first subject = | **que** | second subject = |
| **indicative** | | subjunctive |

Vocabulario

Los verbos

alegrarse (de)	to be happy (about)
dudar	to doubt
esperar	to hope
haber (*inf. of* **hay**)	(there is, there are)
insistir (en)	to insist (on)
mandar	to order
permitir	to permit, allow
prohibir (prohíbo)	to prohibit, forbid

Repaso: desear, **pedir (pido) (i), preferir (prefiero) (i), querer, recomendar (recomiendo), sugerir (sugiero) (i)**

El equipo electrónico

el archivo	(computer) file
la arroba	@
los auriculares	earphones/headphones
el buscador	search engine
el buzón de voz	voice mailbox
el canal	channel
la carpeta	(computer) folder
la contraseña	password
el correo electrónico	e-mail
el disco duro	hard drive
el equipo	equipment
el (espacio de) almacenamiento	storage (space)
la impresora	printer
la página web	web page
la pantalla (grande/plana)	(big/flat) screen (monitor)
el pen drive	memory stick
el ratón	mouse
la red social	social network
el sitio web	website
el teléfono fijo	landline

Cognados: el android, la app, el blog, la cámara, el CD, el CD-ROM, el chateo, el control remoto, el documento, el DVD, el e-mail, el escáner, Facebook (*m.*), el fax, la fotocopia, la fotocopiadora, el GPS, el internet, el iPhone, el iPod, la memoria, el módem, la televisión (plasma), el tuit, Twitter (*m.*), el video, el wifi

Repaso: la computadora (portátil), el teléfono (celular), la televisión

almacenar	to store, save
apagar (gu)	to turn off (*machine*)
bajar	to download
buscar (qu) en internet	to look up on the Internet
entrar en Facebook / en internet	to go on Facebook / online
cambiar (de)	to change

descargar (gu)	to download
encender (ie)	to turn on (machine)
fallar	to "crash" (computer)
funcionar	to work, function; to run (machines)
grabar	to record; to tape
guardar	to keep; to save (documents)
hacer (foto)copia	to copy
imprimir	to print
manejar	to drive; to operate (machine)
obtener (like tener)	to get, obtain
poner	to turn on (machine)
publicar (qu)	to post (as on Facebook); to publish

Cognados: conectarse, copiar, hacer clic, instalar, navegar (gu), tuitear

Repaso: buscar (qu), conseguir (like seguir), entrar, estar, mandar un mensaje

La ciudad y el barrio

las afueras	outskirts; suburbs
el alquiler	rent
el ascensor	elevator
la avenida	avenue
el barrio	neighborhood
la calefacción	heating
la calle	street
el/la dueño/a	landlord, landlady
el edificio de apartamentos	apartment building
el gas	gas (not for cars)
el gasto	expense
el/la inquilino/a	tenant; renter
la parada del autobús	bus stop
la parada del metro	subway stop

el piso	floor (of a building)
el primer piso	first floor (second story)
el segundo piso	second floor (third story)
la planta baja	ground floor
el/la portero/a	building manager; doorman
la residencia de ancianos	nursing home
el/la vecino/a	neighbor
la vista (a, de)	view (of)
la vivienda	housing
la zona	zone; area

Cognados: la electricidad, el supermercado

Repaso: el apartamento, la casa, el centro, la ciudad, la dirección, el/la dueño/a (owner), la escuela, la plaza

alquilar	to rent
mudarse	to move (residences)

Otros sustantivos

los/las demás	others
la mentira	lie
el trabajo	work; job
el/la usuario/a	user

Repaso: la montaña

Los adjetivos

actual	current
electrónico/a	electronic

Palabras adicionales

es urgente que + subjunctive	it's urgent that

Repaso: es mejor/necesario que + subjunctive

Vocabulario personal

13

El arte y la cultura

En este capítulo

www.connectspanish.com

Cuadros (*Paintings*) de un artista ecuatoriano en venta (*on sale*)

EL ECUADOR

15.5 (y medio) millones de habitantes

- Las Islas Galápagos, donde Darwin empezó a idear su teoría de la evolución, son territorio ecuatoriano.
- El Ecuador y Bolivia tienen una geografía impresionante, caracterizada por la cordillera de los Andes y la Amazonia.
- Los dos países tienen un alto porcentaje de población indígena y mestiza.

BOLIVIA

10.5 (y medio) millones de habitantes

- Bolivia (como el Paraguay) no tiene litoral (costa) marítimo.

- ¿Le interesa el arte en general? ¿Qué tipo de expresión artística le interesa más? ¿Le fascina la pintura, la escultura, la arquitectura, la danza, el cine, el teatro o el diseño de moda[a]? ¿O prefiere alguna otra?
- ¿Hay museos en su ciudad? ¿De qué tipo?
- ¿Hay artesanía típica de su región, como la cerámica o textiles o de otro tipo?

[a]diseño... *fashion design*

ISMAEL PÉREZ MENDIZÁBAL CONTESTA LAS PREGUNTAS.

- Bueno, la verdad es que depende. Me encanta el cine y también me interesa la literatura porque me gusta mucho leer. Y... pues, claro,[a] me gusta la música pop y para bailar. Pero las otras artes no me interesan tanto.
- Sí, claro. Hay museos muy buenos y de diferentes enfoques.[b] Por ejemplo, hay el Museo Nacional sobre la historia de Colombia. Y también está el Museo de Arte Moderno de Bogotá. Y el Museo del Oro, que tiene la mejor colección en todo el mundo de piezas metalúrgicas de la época precolombina. Y el Maloka, un museo interactivo de ciencias. ¡Es bien chévere[c]!
- En Colombia hay mucha tradición de artesanías, ya desde la época precolombina. Hay mucho trabajo textil por todo el país.

[a]*of course* [b]*emphases* [c]bien... *really cool*

Las artes*

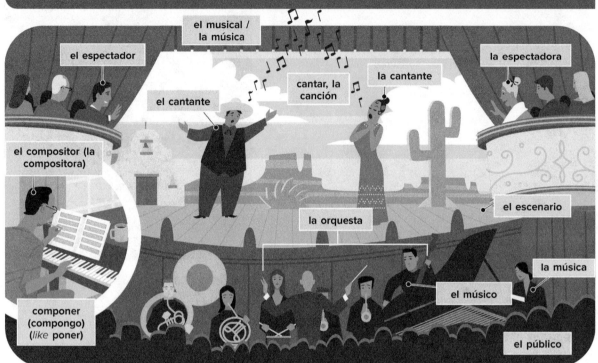

el musical / la música

el espectador

la espectadora

el compositor (la compositora)

cantar, la canción

la cantante

el cantante

el escenario

la orquesta

componer (compongo) (*like* poner)

la música

el músico

el público

La expresión artística	Los artistas	Los verbos		Las obras artísticas
la arquitectura	el arquitecto / la arquitecta	diseñar	to design	el edificio
el baile / la danza	el bailarín / la bailarina	bailar		el baile, el ballet, la danza
el cine / el teatro / la ópera	el actor / la actriz el director / la directora	actuar (actúo) dirigir (dirijo)	 to direct	la película, la obra de teatro, la ópera
el dibujo	el/la dibujante	dibujar	to draw	el dibujo
la escultura	el escultor / la escultora	esculpir	to sculpt	la escultura
la literatura	el escritor / la escritora el autor / la autora	escribir		la obra de teatro, la novela, el poema
la pintura	el pintor / la pintora	pintar		el cuadro, la pintura

You can hear the pronunciation of theme vocabulary words and phrases in the Connect eBook.

_____

*The word **arte** is both masculine and feminine. The masculine articles and adjectives are normally used with **arte** in the singular while the feminine ones are used in the plural. Note that **las artes** often refers to "the arts" in general: **Guillermo es estudiante** de arte moderno. **Me gustan mucho** las artes gráficas.

Más sobre las obras artísticas

el espectáculo	show
el guion	script
la imagen	image
el papel	role
la obra (de arte)	work (of art)
la obra de teatro	play
la obra maestra	masterpiece

Cognados: la comedia, el concierto, el drama, la escena, la fotografía, el mural

Otras personas

el dramaturgo / la dramaturga	playwright
el/la guía	guide

Cognados: el/la novelista, el/la poeta

Otras personas

crear	to create
tejer	to weave

La tradición cultural

la artesanía	arts and crafts
la cerámica	pottery; ceramics
las ruinas	ruins
los tejidos	woven goods
folclórico/a	traditional

Comunicación

A. Obras de arte

Paso 1. ¿Qué clase de arte representan las siguientes obras y qué son?

1. la catedral de una gran ciudad
2. las obras de Diego Rivera y Frida Kahlo
3. la Estatua de la Libertad
4. *El Cascanueces* (*The Nutcracker*)
5. *El Mago de Oz*
6. *La Bohème* y *La Traviata*
7. las pirámides aztecas y mayas
8. *Don Quijote* y *Hamlet*
9. *Las Meninas*, de Diego Velázquez
10. «*El cuervo* (*The Raven*)», de Edgar Allan Poe
11. las imágenes de los actores en las revistas o en internet
12. las obras de Selena Gómez o de Lady Gaga

Paso 2. Ahora dé otros ejemplos de obras en cada una de las categorías artísticas que Ud. mencionó en el **Paso 1**.

Nota **comunicativa**

Más sobre los gustos y preferencias

You already know a number of verbs for talking about what you like and don't like: **gustar, encantar, interesar, molestar.** As you know, these verbs are used with indirect object pronouns, and the verb always agrees with the thing or things liked or disliked, not with the person whose preferences are being described.

Here are some additional verbs that are used like **gustar.**

- **aburrir** **Me aburre** el baile moderno.
  Modern dance is boring to me (bores me).
- **atraer** A Juan **le atraen** las ruinas incas.
  Juan is drawn to (attracted by) Incan ruins.
- **fascinar** **Nos fascinan** las artesanías indígenas.
  We're fascinated by (We love) indigenous handicrafts.

You can use some of these verbs in **Comunicación B.**

Así se dice

Various words are used to describe comedians: **el/la comediante, el/la humorista,** or **el cómico / la cómica.**

An alternative spelling of **folclórico/a** is **folklórico/a.**

B. Encuesta (*Poll*): ¿Te gustan los eventos culturales?

Paso 1. Haga por lo menos cinco preguntas usando las siguientes ideas como base. Use verbos de la **Nota comunicativa** de la página 387.

MODELO: la ópera → ¿Te aburre la ópera?

1. el ballet clásico
2. los museos de arte moderno
3. las obras de teatro
4. los grandes museos como *The Smithsonian* o *The Natural History Museum*
5. los conciertos de música clásica
6. los recitales de poesía en algún café
7. las películas extranjeras
8. la ópera
9. ¿ ?

Paso 2. Ahora use las preguntas del **Paso 1** para entrevistar a cinco compañeros de clase para saber su opinión sobre las manifestaciones artísticas mencionadas en sus preguntas. ¿Qué puede Ud. decir sobre las tendencias culturales de la clase?

Nota **cultural**

La arquitectura en el mundo hispano

La arquitectura de los países hispanohablantes refleja la variedad de herencias[a] estéticas a través de los siglos[b]: las[c] que ya[d] estaban en el continente antes de la llegada de los españoles y las que estos[e] trajeron.

- **Los pueblos indígenas** Estos pueblos crearon obras arquitectónicas impresionantes en la época precolombina, es decir,[f] antes de la llegada de Cristóbal Colón a América. Los grandes imperios azteca, maya e inca, entre otros, construyeron edificios y ciudades que maravillaron[g] a los españoles. Algunos ejemplos: Machu Picchu, la ciudad sagrada[h] de los incas en el Perú, y los centros urbanos de Tikal en Guatemala maya y Teotihuacán en México azteca.

- **Los españoles** Como era de esperar,[i] los españoles trajeron a América los estilos artísticos europeos del momento y los aplicaron a las ciudades que inmediatamente empezaron a construir: edificios civiles y religiosos que compiten en belleza[j] con los edificios europeos. Ejemplos: la catedral de Quito (1567, el Ecuador) y la de la Ciudad de México (1571).

  Parte de la tradición estética de los españoles incluía el estilo que dejaron los musulmanes[k] durante los 800 años que ocuparon España (del siglo VIII al siglo XV). Un ejemplo de esa herencia es el uso de los azulejos,[l] muy común ahora en todo el mundo hispanohablante, para decorar las paredes y otras partes de los edificios.

- **Las ciudades modernas:** En la actualidad, la arquitectura sigue transformando ciudades a ambos[m] lados del Atlántico. La Ciudad de México, la Ciudad de Panamá, Santiago de Chile, Buenos Aires y Madrid son algunos ejemplos más sobresalientes de

La Iglesia (*Church*) de San Francisco, en Quito, Ecuador

las grandes ciudades modernas, en donde los rascacielos[n] conviven[ñ] con edificios representativos de la larga historia de cada país. Los viejos edificios se renuevan[o] y se modifican para darles nuevos usos, de tal manera que[p] siguen siendo parte activa en la vida de cada ciudad.

 ¿Cuáles son los edificios o complejos arquitectónicos más sobresalientes en su estado o ciudad?

[a]*heritages* [b]*a... across centuries* [c]*those* [d]*already* [e]*they (the Spanish)* [f]*es... that is* [g]*astonished* [h]*sacred* [i]*Como... As was to be expected* [j]*beauty* [k]*Arabs* [l]*tiles* [m]*both*

[n]*skyscrapers* [ñ]*coexist* [o]*se... are being renovated* [p]*de... so that*

C. ¿Qué hacen?

Paso 1. Haga oraciones completas, usando una palabra o frase de cada columna. **¡OJO!** Hay más de una posibilidad en algunos casos.

MODELO: La compositora compone música para una película.

el/la compositor(a) el/la artesano/a el actor / la actriz el/la director(a) el/la músico/a el bailarín / la bailarina el/la dramaturgo/a el/la pintor(a) el/la escritor(a) el/la arquitecto/a el/la poeta	**+**	bailar componer dirigir diseñar escribir esculpir hacer interpretar mirar pintar tocar trabajar	**+**	música, canciones, musicales novelas, poesía en el ballet cerámica edificios y casas papeles en la televisión guiones tejidos con actores obras de teatro cuadros instrumentos

Paso 2. Ahora, con dos o tres compañeros, dé nombres de artistas en cada categoría. ¿Cuántos artistas hispanos pueden nombrar?

D. Entrevista

Paso 1. Complete las siguientes oraciones de manera que sean ciertas para Ud.

1. Me gusta mucho _____ (una actividad relacionada con el arte).
2. El arte que más me interesa como espectador(a) es _____.
3. (No) Tengo talento artístico para _____.
4. (No) Me gusta ir a mercados y ferias de artesanía. Allí (no) compro _____.
5. En la universidad, los espectáculos que más me interesan son _____.
6. En cuanto a (*As for*) música, prefiero _____. Mi canción/artista/cantante favorito/a es _____.

Vocabulario útil

el *country*
el *hip hop*
el *jazz*
la música de los años 50 (60,...)
el *pop*
el *rap*
el *rock* (clásico)

Paso 2. Ahora, en parejas, hablen de sus preferencias artísticas, usando como base las oraciones del **Paso 1**.

Paso 3. Díganle a la clase las preferencias que Uds. tienen en común.

Algo sobre...

Oswaldo Guayasimín

El pintor y escultor Oswaldo Guayasamín (1919–1999) es un artista ecuatoriano mundialmente reconocido[a] y admirado. Era hijo de padre quechua y madre mestiza. Por eso su obra, que se considera expresionista, tiene toques[b] indigenistas. Sus pinturas y esculturas hablan del sufrimiento[c] y las injusticias que soportan[d] los seres[e] humanos.

Piense en una de sus pinturas o esculturas favoritas. ¿Qué sentimientos refleja? ¿Por qué le gusta a Ud. esa obra?

[a]mundialmente... *recognized throughout the world*
[b]*touches, elements* [c]*suffering* [d]*withstand, bear*
[e]*beings*

Ternura (Tenderness), un cuadro de la serie «Mientras viva siempre te recuerdo», que Guayasamín dedicó a su madre y a todas las madres del mundo

primer(o/a)	first	**cuarto/a**	fourth	**sexto/a**	sixth	**noveno/a**	ninth
segundo/a	second	**quinto/a**	fifth	**séptimo/a**	seventh	**décimo/a**	tenth
tercer(o/a)	third			**octavo/a**	eighth		

- Ordinal numbers are adjectives and must agree in number and gender with the nouns they modify. Ordinals usually precede the noun: **la cuarta lección, el octavo ejercicio.**
- Like **bueno,** the ordinals **primero** and **tercero** shorten to **primer** and **tercer,** respectively, before masculine singular nouns: **el primer niño, el tercer mes.**
- Ordinal numbers are frequently abbreviated with superscript letters that show the adjective ending: **las 1as lecciones, el 1er grado, el 5° estudiante.** When agreement is not needed, the ordinals are abbreviated simply as **1°, 2°,** and so on.

Comunicación

A. ¿Cultura, yo?

Paso 1. Veamos (*Let's see*) si Ud. tiene interés en la cultura o no. Ordene las siguientes actividades según sus preferencias y hábitos, empezando por **1°.**

_____ ir al cine a ver las últimas películas en inglés

_____ ver películas extranjeras dobladas (*dubbed*) o subtituladas

_____ visitar museos, preferentemente en visitas guiadas

_____ comprar o sacar de la biblioteca libros de ficción

_____ ver obras de teatro

_____ bailar en clubes y fiestas

_____ ver programas de la tele

_____ ir a conciertos de música clásica/*jazz*

_____ ir a conciertos de música pop/rock/*country*

_____ leer o escribir poesía

Paso 2. Ahora, en parejas, entrevístense sobre sus cinco actividades favoritas. Usen números ordinales.

MODELO: Mi actividad favorita es ir a ver películas extranjeras subtituladas. Mi **segunda** actividad favorita es...

B. Autorretrato (*Self-portrait*) de un(a) estudiante. Complete las oraciones.

1. Soy estudiante de _____ año.
2. Estoy en mi _____ semestre/trimestre de español.
3. Los lunes, mi primera clase es la (*that*) de _____, a la(s) _____ (hora). Mi segunda clase es la de _____, a la(s) _____.
4. Con frecuencia, soy la _____ persona en llegar a la clase de español.
5. Soy la _____ persona de mi familia que asiste a una universidad. Y soy la _____ persona de mi familia que asiste a *esta* universidad.

Antes de mirar

¿Le interesa a Ud. la arquitectura? ¿Conoce la obra de algún arquitecto importante? ¿Dónde espera Ud. encontrar arquitectura interesante?

☐ en casas y edificios de apartamentos
☐ en edificios del gobierno (*government*)
☐ en edificios de uso civil (como museos, por ejemplo)
☐ en iglesias (*churches*) y templos
☐ otro

Este segmento

En este segmento hay un reportaje sobre la obra del famoso arquitecto español Antoni Gaudí.

El templo de la Sagrada (*Sacred*) Familia, la obra inacabada (*unfinished*) del arquitecto Antoni Gaudí

Vocabulario del segmento

fines del siglo XX	the end of the 20th century
principios de	the beginning of
reconocido/a	well-known
catalán/catalana	from **Cataluña** (Catalonia, Spain)
pertenecer (pertenezco)	to belong
la naturaleza	nature
el diseño	design
fijarse en	to notice; to pay attention to
la serpiente	snake
todavía no ha terminado	is still not complete

Después de mirar

A. ¿Está claro? Las siguientes oraciones sobre el arquitecto Antoni Gaudí son falsas. Corríjalas.

1. Gaudí es un arquitecto ecuatoriano.
2. Solo construyó edificios en Barcelona.
3. Solo construyó iglesias y templos.
4. Los edificios de Gaudí incluyen muchos elementos de tipo industrial.

B. Un poco más. Conteste las siguientes preguntas.

1. ¿Qué elementos caracterizan las obras de Gaudí?
2. ¿Qué estilos combina el templo de la Sagrada Familia?
3. ¿Cuándo se comenzó a construir el templo? ¿Para qué año se espera que esté terminado?

C. Y ahora, Uds. En parejas, descríbanse mutuamente algún edificio de su interés, ya sea (*whether it be*) en su ciudad de origen o en otra. ¿Por qué les gustan esos edificios? Qué parte o aspecto de cada edificio es su favorite? ¿Son históricamente importantes los edificios? ¿Cuándo los visitaron por última vez?

GRAMÁTICA

Grammar Tutorial 36
connect
|SPANISH
www.connectspanish.com

¿Recuerda Ud.?

Review what you know about the present subjunctive by answering the following questions.

1. Is the subjunctive used in one- or two-clause sentences?
2. Is it used in the main (independent) or subordinate (dependent) clause?
3. Is it used before or after the word **que**?
4. When the subjunctive is used, is the subject the same in both clauses?
5. What verb form follows an impersonal expression when there is no change of subject?
6. Influence is one "cause" of the subjunctive. What are two more subjunctive "triggers"?

You will learn about those two subjunctive "triggers" in **Gramáticas 36** and **37.**

36 Expressing Feelings

Use of the Subjunctive (Part 3): Emotion

Gramática en acción: Diego y Lupe oyen tocar a los mariachis

México, D.F.

DIEGO: Ay, ¡cómo me encanta esta música!

LUPE: **Me alegro de que** te guste.

DIEGO: Y **yo me alegro de que** estemos aquí. ¿Sabes el origen de la palabra **mariachi**?

LUPE: No... ¿Lo sabes tú?

DIEGO: Bueno, una de las teorías es que viene del siglo XIX, cuando los franceses ocuparon México. Ellos contrataban a grupos de músicos para tocar en las bodas. Y como los mexicanos no podían pronunciar bien la palabra francesa *mariage,* pues acabaron por decir **mariachi.** Y de allí viene el nombre de los grupos.

LUPE: ¡Qué fascinante! **Me sorprende que** sepas tanto de nuestra historia.

DIEGO: Pues, todo buen antropólogo debe saber un poco de historia también, ¿no?

¿Y a Ud.?

1. ¿**Le sorprende que** la palabra mariachi venga del francés?
2. ¿**Le sorprende que** tantas personas estudien español en su universidad?
3. ¿**Se alegra de que** haya mucha información cultural en esta clase?

Diego and Lupe hear mariachis play DIEGO: *Oh, how I love this music!* LUPE: *I'm glad you like it.* DIEGO: *And I'm glad we're here. Do you know the origin of the word* **mariachi**? LUPE: *No . . . Do you?* DIEGO: *Well, one of the theories is that it comes from the nineteenth century, when the French occupied Mexico. They used to hire groups of musicians to play at weddings. And since Mexicans couldn't correctly pronounce the French word* mariage, *they ended up saying* **mariachi**. *And that's where the name of the groups comes from.* LUPE: *How fascinating! I'm surprised (that) you know so much about our history.* DIEGO: *Well, all good anthropologists should also know a bit of history, shouldn't they?*

1. The Concept of Emotion

Another "trigger" for the use of the subjunctive in the subordinate clause is the concept of *emotion* (**la emoción**). The subject of the main clause *is glad, fears, hopes*, and so on, that the subject of the subordinate clause does something, expressed by a verb in the subjunctive. The verb in the main clause is always in the indicative.

Esperamos que Ud. **pueda** asistir.
We hope (that) you'll be able to come.

Tengo miedo de que mi abuelo **esté** muy enfermo.
I'm afraid (that) my grandfather is very ill.

Es una lástima que no **den** conciertos.
It's a shame (that) they're not putting on any concerts.

---

2. Verbs of Emotion

Here are some verbs of emotion. The ones marked with * are new.

alegrarse de	to be happy about
esperar	to hope; to expect
***lamentar**	to regret; to feel sorry
***sentir (siento) (i)**	to regret; to feel sorry
***temer**	to fear, be afraid
tener miedo	to be afraid

Temo que María **se caiga** mientras baila.
I'm afraid (that) María will fall while she's dancing.

---

3. Verbs of Emotion Like *gustar*

Gustar and similar verbs are frequently used to express emotion. If there is a change of subject in the subordinate clause, the subjunctive will be used. Only the verb marked with * is new. Notice that a subordinate clause is viewed as a singular subject, so **gusta** (not **gustan**) is used in the sentences.

encantar	molestar
fascinar	*sorprender to surprise
gustar	

Me (te/le...) encanta/fascina/gusta/molesta/ sorprende que...
I'm (you're/he's ...) very glad/fascinated/pleased/ annoyed/surprised that ...

¡OJO!

Remember that these verbs are used with indirect object pronouns in Spanish.

Me molesta que las entradas del museo **sean** tan caras.
It bothers me that museum entrance fees are so expensive.

Nos sorprende que este cantante **tenga** tanto éxito.
I'm surprised that this singer is so successful.

---

4. Impersonal Expressions of Emotion

When a new subject is introduced after a generalization of emotion, it is followed by the subjunctive in the subordinate clause. Here are some general expressions of emotion.

¡OJO!

As you know, when there is no second subject, the infinitive follows verbs of emotion and impersonal expressions of emotion:

Me alegro de / Siento / Tengo miedo de estar aquí.
Es absurdo/bueno/extraño estar aquí.

es absurdo que...	it's absurd that . . .
es extraño que...	it's strange that . . .
¡qué extraño que... !	how strange that . . . !
es increíble que...	it's incredible that . . .
es mejor/bueno/ malo que...	it's better/good/ bad that . . .
es normal que...	it's normal that . . .
es terrible que...	it's terrible that . . .
es una lástima que...	it's a shame that . . .
¡qué lástima que... !	what a shame that . . . !

Es terrible que la cantante **esté** enferma.
It's awful (that) the singer is ill.

¡Qué extraño que **haya** pocos turistas en las ruinas hoy!
How strange (that) there are so few tourists at the ruins today!

Práctica y comunicación

A. Opiniones sobre el cine

Paso 1. Autoprueba. Diga si en español se debe usar el subjuntivo o el infinitivo en la cláusula subordinada de las siguientes oraciones.

MODELO: I'm surprised you're here. → **subjuntivo**

1. I'm sorry you're angry.
2. I'm sorry to anger you.
3. We're happy to get this present.
4. We're afraid the guide will change the trip.
5. It's great they want to buy the sculpture.
6. I'm not interested in working with that director.
7. I'm thrilled they're visiting us.

Paso 2. Complete las siguientes oraciones incompletas con las cláusulas principales más apropiadas para expresar su opinión.

ORACIONES INCOMPLETAS

1. _____ que muchas películas sean violentas.
2. _____ que algunos actores ganen (*earn*) tanto dinero.
3. _____ que haya más representación de actores de otras razas.
4. _____ que no haya muchos papeles interesantes para mujeres de más de 50 años.
5. _____ que gasten millones de dólares en hacer películas mientras que hay gente que se muere de hambre.
6. _____ que _____ (nombre de un actor / una actriz) sea tan famoso/a.

CLÁUSULAS PRINCIPALES

a. Me molesta
b. Es increíble/extraordinario
c. Es ridículo
d. Espero
e. Me sorprende
f. Es absurdo/ilógico

Paso 3. Ahora, en parejas, túrnense para entrevistarse sobre las ideas del **Paso 2.** Luego díganle al resto de la clase una opinión que tienen en común.

MODELO: E1: ¿Te molesta que muchas películas sean violentas?
E2: Sí, me molesta mucho. ¿Y a ti?
E2: A mí también. →

A los dos nos molesta que muchas películas sean violentas.

B. Comentarios sobre el arte

Paso 1. Complete las siguientes opiniones sobre esta pintura de María Luisa Pacheco. Use la forma apropiada de los verbos entre paréntesis.

1. Dicen que esta pintora es famosa. Me sorprende que su pintura le (gustar) a la gente. Temo que sus obras (ser) demasiado abstractas para mí. Es una lástima que (haber) tantas obras de arte que yo no comprendo.

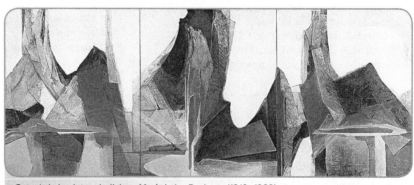

Catavi, de la pintora boliviana María Luisa Pacheco (1919–1982)

---

2. ¡Me encanta esta pintura! ¡Qué lástima que (haber) gente que no entiende el arte abstracto. Me alegro de que esta pintura (estar) en este libro, porque no yo conocía la obra de Pacheco. Me sorprende que (ella) no (tener) más fama fuera de Bolivia.

 Paso 2. Ahora, en parejas, entrevístense sobre sus opiniones de esta pintura. Deben explicar lo que les gusta más y lo que les gusta menos.

Nota **comunicativa**

Cómo expresar los deseos con *ojalá*

Ojalá is one way to express *I hope* in Spanish. It comes from the Arabic meaning *if Allah wishes*, and it is similar to English *God willing* and Spanish **si quiera Dios**.

As an expression of emotion, **ojalá** is followed by the present subjunctive. **Ojalá** is invariable in form and the use of **que** with it is optional.

Ojalá can also be used alone as an interjection in response to a question.

You will use **ojalá (que)** in **Práctica C**.

¡Ojalá (que) yo **gane** la lotería algún día!
I hope (that) I win the lottery some day!
¡Ojalá (que) **haya** paz en el mundo algún día!
I hope (that) there will be peace in the world some day!
Ojalá (que) no **pierdan** tu equipaje.
I hope (that) they don't lose your luggage.

—¿Te va a ayudar Julio a estudiar para el examen?
—¡Ojalá!

C. Una noche en la ópera. Dos amigos van a la ópera. Diga lo que temen y lo que esperan. Use **ojalá.**

MODELO: las entradas (*tickets*) / no costar mucho →
     Ojalá (que) las entradas no **cuesten** mucho.

1. los escenarios: ser fantásticos
2. haber subtítulos en inglés
3. el director (*conductor*): estar preparado
4. los músicos: tocar bien
5. nuestros asientos: no estar lejos del escenario
6. (nosotros) llegar a tiempo

D. Situaciones

Paso 1. Las siguientes personas están pensando en otra persona o en algo que van a hacer. ¿Qué emociones sienten? ¿Qué temen? Conteste las preguntas según los dibujos.

1. Jorge piensa en su amiga Estela. ¿Por qué piensa en ella? ¿Dónde está? ¿Qué siente Jorge? ¿Qué espera? ¿Qué espera Estela? ¿Espera que la visiten los amigos? ¿que le manden algo?

2. ¿Dónde quiere pasar las vacaciones Mariana? ¿Espera que alguien la acompañe? ¿Dónde espera que estén juntos? ¿Qué teme Mariana? ¿Qué espera?

 Paso 2. Ahora, en parejas, comparen sus respuestas del **Paso 1.** ¿Tuvieron los/las dos la misma impresión de los dibujos?

E. ¿Cómo es nuestra sociedad? Diga lo que Ud. opina de las siguientes declaraciones respecto a algunos de los valores de nuestra sociedad. Empiece sus opiniones con las **Expresiones** indicadas o con cualquier (*any*) otra.

MODELO: Los futbolistas profesionales ganan sueldos fenomenales →
      Es increíble que los futbolistas **ganen** sueldos fenomenales.

1. Muchas personas viven para trabajar. No saben descansar.
2. La nuestra (*Ours*) es una sociedad de consumidores.
3. Juzgamos (*We judge*) a los otros por las cosas materiales que tienen.
4. Las personas ricas tienen mucho prestigio en esta sociedad.
5. Las mujeres generalmente no ganan tanto dinero como los hombres por hacer igual trabajo.
6. Algunas obras de arte cuestan millones de dólares.
7. Para mucha gente joven, ver videos en YouTube es más atractivo que leer libros.
8. Hay discriminación contra la gente mayor en ciertas profesiones.

F. Esta universidad. Diga lo que Ud. opina de las siguientes declaraciones respecto a lo que ocurre en esta universidad. Use frases como: **Me gusta que..., Me molesta que..., Es terrible que..., Sé que...**

MODELO: Gastan mucho / poco dinero en construir nuevos edificios. →
      Me molesta que gasten mucho dinero en construir nuevos edificios.

1. Se les da mucha / poca importancia a los deportes.
2. El precio de la matrícula es exagerado / muy bajo.
3. Se ofrecen muchos / pocos cursos en mi especialización.
4. Es necesario estudiar ciencias / lenguas para graduarse.
5. Hay muchos / pocos requisitos (*requirements*) para graduarse.
6. En general, hay mucha / poca gente en las clases.

Algo sobre...

la Amazonia y los Andes

Es sorprendente que el Ecuador y Bolivia, sin tener territorios adyacentes,[a] compartan[b] tantas características geográficas. Para empezar, los dos países tienen territorio en la Amazonia, una inmensa zona que se extiende por[c] un total de nueve naciones sudamericanas. Además[d] la cordillera de los Andes cruza Bolivia y el Ecuador y hace que sus capitales sean las capitales más altas del mundo. La Paz está a 12.000 pies (3.650 metros) sobre el nivel del mar. Sucre y Quito están a más de 9.000 pies (2.800 metros).

🎨 ¿Cuáles son los factores geográficos más importantes de su país? ¿Y de su estado?

[a]*adjacent* [b]*share* [c]*through* [d]*In addition*

Dos factores geográficos que influyen en Sudamérica

Gramática en acción: El traje tradicional de las bolivianas

Unas mujeres bolivianas con su ropa tradicional, en La Paz

¿Cuánto sabe Ud. de la ropa que llevan las indígenas bolivianas? ¿Cree que son ciertas o falsas las siguientes declaraciones? Las respuestas están al pie de la página.

1. **Es verdad que** los sombreros hongo son una parte del traje tradicional de las indígenas del altiplano boliviano.

2. **Es probable que** sea muy frecuente ver a bolivianas que llevan sombrero hongo.

3. **Dudo que** los pantalones sean parte del traje tradicional de las bolivianas del altiplano.

4. **No creo que** el uso de los sombreros hongo sea una tradición inca.

5. En Bolivia, **es obvio que** llevar sombrero es una buena protección contra el sol.

¿Y Ud.?

¿Le gusta el traje tradicional de las mujeres bolivianas? ¿Cree que es hermoso (*beautiful*) y práctico? ¿Le sorprende que las bolivianas indígenas lleven sombrero?

①   ②

DOUBT/DENIAL

first subject = **indicative**   **que**   second subject = **subjunctive**

1. The Concepts of Doubt and Denial

The concepts of *doubt* (**la duda**) and *denial* (**la negación**) are also "triggers" for the use of the subjunctive in the subordinate clause. The subject of the main clause *doubts, does not believe, denies,* and so on, that the subject of the subordinate clause does something, expressed by a verb in the subjunctive. The verb in the main clause is always in the indicative.

No creo que **sean** cuadros de Goya.
I don't believe (that) they're paintings by Goya.

Es imposible que la actriz **salga** al escenario ahora.
It's impossible for the actress to go on (stage) now.

The traditional costume of Bolivian women How much do you know about the clothing that indigenous Bolivian women wear? Do you think that the following statements are true or false? The answers are at the bottom of the page. **1.** *It's true that bowler hats are a part of the traditional costume of indigenous women of the Bolivian high plateau.* **2.** *It's likely that one frequently sees Bolivian women who are wearing bowler hats.* **3.** *I doubt that pants are part of the traditional costume of women from the high plateau.* **4.** *I don't think that the use of bowler hats is an Inca tradition.* **5.** *In Bolivia, it's obvious that wearing a hat is good protection from the sun.*

Respuestas: **1.** *cierto: Muchas indígenas bolivianas lo llevan.* **2.** *cierto: Bolivia tiene el porcentaje más alto de población indígena en toda América. Por eso es muy normal ver a mujeres que llevan ropa tradicional.* **3.** *cierto: La pollera, un tipo de falda con mucho vuelo (flare) y colores, es la ropa típica de las indígenas bolivianas.* **4.** *cierto: Es una tradición colonial.* **5.** *cierto: La región del altiplano boliviano está tan alta que la exposición a los rayos solares es un problema serio. Por eso, el sombrero es una protección ideal para la cara, y también protege a los habitantes del frío.*

2. Verbs and Expressions of Doubt (versus Certainty)

Here are some verbs and expressions that imply doubt. They are followed by subjunctive in the subordinate clause if there is a change of subject. New verbs and expressions are marked with *.

verb or expression of doubt → **subjunctive** in subordinate clause with different subject

*no creer	to disbelieve
dudar	to doubt
*no estar seguro/a de	to be unsure of
no pensar (pienso)	to not think
*no es seguro que...	it's not certain / a sure thing that . . .
*(no) es posible que...	it's (not) possible that . . .
*(no) es probable/ improbable que...	it's (not) probable/ improbable that . . .

Mis padres **dudan** que yo **pueda** conseguir una entrada ahora.
My parents doubt that I can get a ticket now.

No es seguro que Emma **toque** en el concierto.
It's not certain that Emma will play in the concert.

No creo que nadie **sepa** la verdad.
I don't think (that) anyone knows the truth.

In contrast, verbs and expressions of *certainty* (**la certeza**) and *belief* (**la creencia**) are followed by the indicative in the subordinate clause when there is another subject, because they express what the speaker knows to be the reality or to be true. They express affirmation.

verb or expression of certainty → **indicative** in subordinate clause with different subject

creer	to believe
*estar seguro/a de	to be certain of
no dudar	to believe (not doubt)
pensar (pienso)	to think
*es cierto que	it's certain that
*es seguro que	it's certain / a sure thing that
*es verdad que	it's true that

Mis padres **creen / están seguros de** que puedo conseguir una entrada ahora.
My parents believe / are sure that I can get a ticket today.

Es seguro que Emma toca en el concierto.
It's certain that Emma plays in the concert.

Pienso que todo el mundo sabe la verdad.
I think everyone knows the truth.

¿**Crees** que es auténtica la pieza?
Do you think (that) the piece is authentic? (I think it's possible that it is.)

¿**Crees** que **sea** auténtica la pieza?
Do you think (that) the piece is authentic? (I'm doubtful that it is.)

¡OJO!

When used in questions, these verbs may be followed by either the indicative or the subjunctive in the dependent clause, depending on the level of certainty implied.

3. Verbs and Expressions of Denial

These are always followed by the subjunctive in the dependent clause because they negate the reality or truth of what follows them. They express negation. Only **negar** is new.

verb or expression of denial → **subjunctive** in subordinate clause with different subject

*negar (niego) (gu)	to deny
es imposible que...	it's imposible that ...
no es verdad que...	it's not true that ...

Niego / Es imposible / No es verdad que todo el mundo **sepa** la verdad.
I deny / It's impossible / It isn't true that everyone knows the truth.

4. Infinitive with no Change of Subject

All of these verbs and expressions are generally followed by the infinitive when there is no change of subject.

Creo / No creo saber la verdad.
Niego / Es imposible saber la verdad.

¡ojo!

An exception: it is very common for **creer, dudar,** and **pensar** to be followed by a conjugated verb, indicative or subjunctive, when there is no change of subject.

No creo / Dudo / No pienso que (yo) **sepa** la verdad.
Creo/Dudo/Pienso que (yo) **sé** la verdad.

Práctica y comunicación

A. Preferencias artísticas

Paso 1. Autoprueba. Indique las frases que expresan duda o negación.

___ **1.** Dudamos que...   ___ **5.** No es posible que...
___ **2.** Estoy segura de que...   ___ **6.** No creen que...
___ **3.** Niega que...   ___ **7.** No es cierto que...
___ **4.** Es cierto que...   ___ **8.** Pensamos que...

Paso 2. Exprese su opinión sobre las siguientes declaraciones. Empiece su opinión con una de las cláusulas principales de la lista y cambie el verbo de la cláusula subordinada al subjuntivo si es necesario.

MODELO: **1.** A la mayoría de la gente le gusta ir a los museos de arte. →
No creo que a la mayoría de la gente le **guste** ir a los museos de arte.

1. A la mayoría de la gente le gusta ir a los museos de arte.
2. Todos mis amigos prefieren el teatro al cine.
3. La arquitectura le fascina a muchísimas personas.
4. Me encanta regalar artesanía.
5. Voy a conciertos de música clásica con frecuencia.
6. *El Cascanueces* (*The Nutcracker*) es el ballet más famoso del mundo.
7. La música es la expresión artística más popular entre la gente joven.
8. Un vlog (un blog con video) se puede considerar una forma de arte.

Paso 3. Ahora, en parejas, túrnense para hacerse preguntas sobre sus opiniones del **Paso 2.** Luego díganle a la clase una opinión que tienen en común.

MODELO: **E1:** No creo que a mucha la gente le guste ir a los museos de arte. ¿Y tú?
E2: Yo tampoco. →
No creemos / Ninguno de nosotros dos cree que a mucha gente le guste ir a los museos de arte.

B. Una vasija (*vessel*) en el museo.
Haga oraciones completas para expresar las especulaciones de dos antropólogos sobre una nueva pieza que está en el museo.

Habla el profesor Martín:

1. «creer / que / ser una vasija de la civilización inca»
2. «ser obvio / que / estar hecha de barro (*made of clay*)»
3. «ser posible / que / el diseño (*design*): representar algo en especial»
4. «¿creer / que / ser una pieza auténtica?»

(*Continúa.*)

Summary of Doubt and Denial

doubt/denial + **que** → subjunctive

CLÁUSULAS PRINCIPALES

(No) Creo/Dudo que...
(No) Es cierto que...
(No) Estoy seguro/a de que...
(No) Es posible/probable que...

Una vasija incaica

Estrategia

primer verbo = indicativo
segundo verbo = ¿indicativo o subjuntivo?

Prác. A, Paso 1: Answers: Duda o negación: 1, 3, 5, 6, 7

Habla la profesora Figueroa:

5. «no creer / que / ser una vasija inca»

6. «ser probable / que / ser una pieza auténtica de la civilización tihuanaco»

7. «dudar / que / el diseño: simbolizar algo en especial»

Una turista en el mercado de Otavalo, Ecuador

C. En un mercado de artesanía. ¿Cómo puede reaccionar un turista en un mercado como el mercado de Otavalo, Ecuador? Complete las oraciones, pensando en los precios y en los regalos que a los turistas les gusta comprar para llevar de recuerdos (*as souvenirs*).

1. ¡Es fantástico (que)... !

2. No creo que los precios del mercado...

3. Dudo mucho que estos vendedores...

4. Estoy seguro/a de que...

5. No es muy probable que...

6. Creo que los otavaleños...

> **Vocabulario útil**
>
> **la figurita de cerámica** ceramic figurine
> **la muñeca** doll
> **el poncho de mujer**

Algo sobre...

el Lago Titicaca

Una vista del lago Titicaca en el Altiplano andino, Bolivia

El Perú y Bolivia comparten[a] el lago Titicaca, que se encuentra en los Andes centrales. Este lago es muy importante para Bolivia, ya que[b] el país no tiene salida al mar.[c] Está a 12.500 pies (3.800 metros) sobre el nivel del mar, lo que lo hace el lago navegable más alto del mundo. El lago Titicaca es el segundo lago más grande de Sudamérica, después del lago de Maracaibo.

¿Hay lagos navegables en este país? ¿Y lagos compartidos[d] con otro país?

[a]*share* [b]*ya... since* [c]*no... is landlocked* [d]*shared*

Nota **comunicativa**

Verbos que requieren preposiciones

You learned in earlier chapters that when two verbs occur in a series (one right after the other), the second verb is usually the infinitive.

Prefiero *cenar* a las siete.   *I prefer to eat at seven.*

Some Spanish verbs, however, require that a preposition or other word be placed before the second verb (still the infinitive). You have already used many of the Spanish verbs that have this feature. New vocabulary is indicated with *.

- The following verbs require the preposition **a** before an infinitive.

aprender a	**empezar (empiezo) (c) a**	**invitar a**	**venir a**
ayudar a	**enseñar a**	**ir a**	**volver (vuelvo) a**

Mis padres me **enseñaron a bailar.**   *My parents taught me to dance.*

- These verbs or verb phrases require **de** before an infinitive.

acabar de	**dejar de**	**tener ganas de**
***acordarse (me acuerdo) de**		***tratar de** (*to try to*)

Siempre **tratamos de llegar** puntualmente.   *We always try to arrive on time.*

- **Insistir** requires **en** before an infinitive.

Insisten en venir esta noche.   *They insist on coming over tonight.*

- Two verbs require **que** before an infinitive: ***hay que, tener que.**

Both of them express obligation, but only **tener que** can be conjugated in all persons. **Hay que** is invariable (like **hay**), but of course it can be used in other tenses and moods (**había, haya**).

Hay que ver el nuevo museo.   *You (One) must/should see the new museum.*

You will use these verbs in **Práctica D.**

D. En los próximos cinco años...

En parejas, hagan oraciones con una palabra o frase de cada columna para expresar lo que Uds. creen que les puede ocurrir en el futuro próximo (*near*). ¿Cuántas respuestas similares tienen Uds.?

¿INDICATIVO, SUBJUNTIVO O INFINITIVO?

(no) creo que...		ser famoso/a
(no) dudo que...		estar casado/a (*married*)
es (im)posible que...	aprender a	ganar la lotería
(no) estoy seguro/a	dejar de	jugar a la lotería
de que...	empezar a	pintar cuadros
(no) es cierto que...	**+** (yo) { ir a	**+** fumar
tengo que...	tratar de	tener hijos
	volver a	terminar mis estudios
		esculpir
		¿ ?

38 Expressing Influence, Emotion, Doubt, and Denial
The Subjunctive (Part 5): A Summary

Grammar Tutorial 38
connect |SPANISH
www.connectspanish.com

Gramática en acción: Las islas Galápagos

La iguana terrestre de islas Galápagos

- Quiero (que)...
- Espero (que)...
- Ojalá (que)...
- No me sorprende (que)...
- Dudo (que)...
- Es fascinante (que)...

+ **subjuntivo** /infinitivo

- Dicen que...
- Sé que...
- No hay duda que...
- Creo que...
- Es obvio que...

+ **indicativo**

¿Y Ud.?

Según la información de **Algo sobre...**, haga oraciones completas y verdaderas para Ud.

1. ...haya tantas especies endémicas.
2. ...las islas Galápagos están en el Pacífico.
3. ...es un lugar especial para los biólogos.
4. ...estén muy protegidas.
5. ...el Ecuador las siga protegiendo.
6. ...(yo) pueda ir a las Galápagos algún día.
7. ...visitar el Ecuador algún día.

Algo sobre...

las Islas Galápagos

Una tortuga galápago, la especie de tortuga más grande del mundo en existencia

El archipiélago de las islas Galápagos está formado por unas 19 islas y más de 40 islotes.[a] Son territorio del Ecuador, país que las protege rigurosamente. Están a casi 600 millas (1.000 km.) de la costa ecuatoriana, en el Océano Pacífico. La isla más grande es Isabela. El nombre del archipiélago le viene de las tortugas gigantes que son endémicas de estas islas. Además de[b] las tortugas galápagos, hay pingüinos, cormoranes, iguanas, leones marinos y otros animales. La variedad de especies endémicas de las Galápagos sirvió de base a la teoría de la evolución de Darwin.

¿Cuál es el archipiélago más grande de este país? ¿Por qué es conocido[c] o visitado?

[a]*islets* [b]*Además... Besides* [c]*well-known*

①	El subjuntivo	②		①	El indicativo	②
INFLUENCE EMOTION DOUBT OR DENIAL				INFORMATION CERTAINTY, BELIEF		
first subject = **indicative**	**que**	second subject = subjunctive		first subject = **indicative**	**que**	second subject = **indicative**

This section will help you review what you have already learned about using the subjunctive and when to use the indicative or the infinitive instead.

1. The Subjunctive in Two-clause Sentences

Remember that, in Spanish, the subjunctive occurs primarily in the second clause of two-clause sentences, with a different subject in each clause. If there is no change of subject, an infinitive follows the first verb.

Quiero } **sacar** una nota buena.
Es necesario }
I want } *to get a good grade.*
It's necessary }

Quiero } que **los estudiantes saquen** una buena nota.
Es necesario }
I want } *the students to get a good grade.*
It's necessary for }

2. Subjunctive "Triggers": Influence, Emotion, Doubt or Denial

The main clause must also contain an expression of *influence, emotion,* or *doubt* or *denial* for the subjunctive to occur in the subordinate clause. If there is no such expression, the indicative is used.

The verb **decir** is a subjunctive "trigger" (first sentence to the right) when it conveys an order. When **decir** conveys information rather than influence (second sentence), it triggers the indicative.

Similarly, **creer** conveys certainty or belief (third sentence) but **no creer** conveys denial (fourth sentence). When **creer** affirms rather than denies information, it is followed by the indicative.

Dicen que **cante** Carlota.
They say that Carlota should sing.

Dicen que Julio **canta** muy mal; por eso **quieren** que **cante** Carlota.
They say that Julio sings very badly; that's why they want Carlota to sing.

Yo creo que Julio **canta** muy bien.
I think that Julio sings very well.

No creo que Carlota **cante** mejor que él.
I don't think that Carlota sings better than he (does).

¡OJO!

Remember to look for the "triggers," not just for specific verbs. If you see the verbs **decir** or **creer** in the main clause, you must think about how they are used.

3. Influence + *indirect object pronoun*

Some expressions of influence are frequently used with indirect object pronouns. The indirect object pronoun in the main clause indicates the subject of the subordinate clause, as in the sample sentences: **Nos → (nosotros) vayamos.**

Nos dicen }
Nos piden } que **vayamos** al concierto.
Nos recomiendan }
They tell us to }
They ask us to } *go to the concert.*
They recommend that we }

4. Same Subject → Infinitive

Remember that verbs and expressions of influence, emotion, and doubt/denial are usually followed by an infinitive when there is no change of subject.

Es importante **practicar** todos los días.
It's important to practice every day.

Esta noche pienso **estudiar** para el examen.
Tonight I plan (intend) to study for the test.

5. Noun Clauses

The uses of the subjunctive that you have learned so far fall into the general category of the use of the subjunctive in *noun clauses* (**las cláusulas nominales**). The noun clause is the second (subordinate) clause in the sentence, the one that contains the subjunctive. It is called a noun clause because it functions like a noun in the sentence, usually as the direct object of the verb in the main clause but sometimes (with **gustar**) as the subject.

In the first two pairs of sentences to the right, the subordinate clause is the direct object of the main verb, answering the question *what?*

He wants *what?* → that they stop playing
They hope *what?* → that there will be many
　　　　　　　　　spectators

In the third pair of sentences, the subordinate clause is the subject of the verb **gustar.**

High ticket prices are not pleasing to the spectators.

A subordinate clause is viewed as a singular subject in Spanish, so **gusta** (not **gustan**) is used in the sentence.

cláusula subordinada nominal = complemento directo

—¿Qué quiere el director de la orquesta?
—Quiere **que los músicos dejen de tocar.**
"What does the orchestra director want?"
"He wants the musicians to stop playing."

—¿Qué esperan los músicos?
—Esperan **que haya muchos espectadores en el concierto.**
"What do the musicians want?"
"They hope (that) there will be many spectators at the concert."

cláusula subordinada nominal = sujeto

—¿Qué no les gusta a los espectadores?
—No les gusta **que las entradas sean muy caras.**
"What don't the spectators like?"
"They don't like tickets to be (that ticket prices are) so expensive."

Práctica y comunicación

A. Lo que deseo

Paso 1. Autoprueba. ¿Qué necesitan las siguientes cláusulas principales en la cláusula subordinada: subjuntivo, indicativo o depende?

1. El director de cine quiere que los espectadores...
2. Los artistas esperan que la gente...
3. Ojalá que...
4. Mis profesores piensan que lo más importante...
5. ¿Cree Ud. que lo más importante...?
6. Mi madre dice que...

Paso 2. Termine las frases de la Columna A con una idea de la Columna B. A veces hay que conjugar el verbo y a veces no.

COLUMNA A	COLUMNA B
1. Quiero que...	**a.** graduarme en esta universidad en cuatro años
2. Espero...	**b.** tener un buen trabajo después de graduarme
3. Ojalá (que)...	**c.** sacar una buena nota en esta clase
4. Pienso...	**d.** ganar dinero como artista algún día
5. No creo que...	**e.** mi profesor(a) de español: dar mucha tarea
6. Digo que...	**f.** hablar español con soltura (*fluently*) en el futuro
	g. mis compañeros de clase: practicar el español durante el almuerzo.

Paso 3. Ahora, en parejas, túrnense para hacerse preguntas sobre las ideas del **Paso 2.** Luego díganle a la clase una idea que tienen en común.

MODELO: **E1:** ¿Quieres que tus compañeros de clase practiquen el español durante el almuerzo?
　　　　E2: Sí, quiero que lo practiquen durante el almuerzo. →
　　　　Queremos que nuestros compañeros de clase practiquen el español durante el almuerzo.

Prác. A, Paso 1: **Answers: 1.** *subjuntivo* **2.** *subjuntivo* **3.** *subjuntivo* **4.** *indicativo* **5.** *depende* **6.** *depende*

Las meninas, de Diego Velázquez (español, 1599–1660)

B. En el Museo del Prado. Explique con oraciones completas por qué es buena idea tener la ayuda de un(a) guía en un museo.

1. Quiero que el guía...
   a. enseñarme los cuadros más famosos de Velázquez
   b. explicarme algunos detalles de los cuadros
   c. saber mucho sobre la vida del pintor
2. Me sorprende que muchos cuadros de Velázquez...
   a. tener como tema la vida cotidiana (*everyday*)
   b. estar en otros museos fuera de España
   c. ser de la familia real (*royal*) de Felipe IV
3. Es posible que el guía...
   a. recomendarme algunos libros sobre la vida y el arte del pintor
   b. preguntarle a un colega si sabe algo más sobre Velázquez
   c. no tener más tiempo para hablar conmigo

C. ¡Qué maravilla de robot! Imagine que Ud. tiene un robot último modelo que va a hacer todo lo que Ud. le diga, especialmente las cosas que Ud. detesta o le cuestan hacer (*are hard for you to do*). ¿Qué le va a mandar al robot que haga? Haga oraciones completas.

Le voy a decir que...
Le voy a mandar que...

+

escribirme el informe para la clase de historia
hacerme el proyecto de arquitectura
poner la mesa
asistir por mí a todas las clases
pagar mis cuentas
ir por mí al trabajo
¿ ?

D. El lugar ideal para vivir

Paso 1. Piense en el lugar ideal para vivir. ¿Es una casa o un apartamento? ¿Está en una ciudad grande o pequeña? ¿Qué actividades culturales ofrece la ciudad? Lea la siguiente lista de factores e indique los que son indispensables para Ud., más otros dos que no estén en la lista.

☐ casa con jardín grande
☐ apartamento grande
☐ apartamento con vista
☐ buenos museos
☐ cerca de una universidad importante
☐ buena orquesta y teatros

☐ muchos cines
☐ cerca de un gran centro comercial
☐ parques
☐ zonas naturales cerca de Ud.
☐ ¿ ?
☐ ¿ ?

Paso 2. Ahora, en parejas, describan el lugar ideal para vivir para cada uno de Uds. Usen las siguientes frases como modelo. ¿En cuántos detalles coincidieron los dos?

MODELOS: Deseo que mi casa/apartamento...
No quiero vivir en...
(No) Me importa (mucho) (que)...
Es importante que la casa / el apartamento...
(No) Es absolutamente necesario que...
Espero (que)...

Un poco de todo

A. Lengua y cultura: En un museo, contemplando una obra de Fernando Botero

Paso 1. A guide and some visitors discuss a work by Fernando Botero. Complete the following dialogue with the correct form of the words in parentheses, as suggested by context. When two possibilities are given in parentheses, select the correct word or phrase. Conjugate the verbs in the present indicative, the **Uds.** command form, the present subjunctive, or the preterite, or leave them in the infinitive, if appropriate.

GUÍA: Y ahora, vamos a ver una obra de Fernando Botero. (Pasar[1]) Uds. por aquí, por favor. También les pido que (dejar[2]) suficiente espacio para todos. Y bien, aquí estamos (delante / detrás [3]) de (este / esto [4]) cuadro (de el / del[5]) pintor y escultor colombiano Fernando Botero. Mucha gente cree que Botero (estar / ser[6]) el artista (latinoamericano / latinoamericana[7]) más reconocido[a] del mundo. Un detalle curioso sobre Botero, que mucha gente no (conocer / saber[8]): (él: empezar[9]) su vida profesional como torero.[b] Pero pronto su familia (descubrir[10]) que su vocación era la pintura. (Estar / Ser[11]) obvio que sus figuras no son una copia exacta de la realidad, ¿verdad?

Pareja bailando, de Fernando Botero, Colombia (1932 -). Botero pintó varios cuadros sobre el mismo tema y con el mismo título.

VISITANTE 1: ¿(Por qué / Porque[12]) sus figuras son tan gordas?

GUÍA: Es el estilo muy personal de Botero de representar la realidad. También (le / se[13]) gusta hacer crítica social y política con humor. Pero a veces solo representa una escena cotidiana,[c] algo trágico o íntimo. Su estilo (le / se[14]) llama el boterismo. ¿(Le / Les[15]) gusta a Uds.?

VISITANTE 1: No (yo: conocer / saber[16])... Me (gusta / gustan[17]) los colores y la escena, pero no me gusta que las figuras (ser[18]) tan obesas. Me sorprende que Botero (ser[19]) tan famoso internacionalmente.

VISITANTE 2: Pues (a mí / yo[20]) no me sorprende. Para mí, hay sensualidad y movimiento en esas figuras.

[a]*well-konwn* [b]*bullfighter* [c]*everyday*

Paso 2. Comprensión. ¿Quién pudo decir lo siguiente, el guía, la visitante 1 o el visitante 2?

	EL GUÍA	VISITANTE 1	VISITANTE 2
1. «Prefiero las figuras más realistas.»	☐	☐	☐
2. «Me encanta que estas figuras sean voluminosas y redondas (*round*).»	☐	☐	☐
3. «Es posible que Botero quiera mostrarnos la sensualidad del baile.»	☐	☐	☐
4. «Quiero que todos me sigan ahora, por favor.»	☐	☐	☐

Paso 3. Ahora, en parejas, den sus propias (*own*) opiniones sobre el cuadro.

> **Expresiones útiles**
>
> **Me gusta/sorprende/molesta que...**
> **Es interesante que...**
> **Es obvio que...**

B. Reacciones

Paso 1. Las siguientes declaraciones se refieren a temas importantes en el mundo de hoy. ¿Qué opinan Uds.? Expresen sus opiniones, usando algunas de las siguientes expresiones.

Expresiones

Dudo que...	Es probable que...
Es absurdo que...	Es terrible que...
Es bueno/malo que...	(No) Es verdad que...
Es increíble que...	No hay duda que...
Es una lástima que...	(No) Me gusta que...

MODELO: Hay mucha pobreza en el mundo. →
   Es una lástima que **haya** mucha pobreza en el mundo.

1. Los niños miran la televisión muchas horas al día.
2. Hay mucha pobreza (*poverty*) en el mundo.
3. En este país gastamos mucha energía.
4. Hay muchas escenas sexuales y violentas en la televisión y en el cine.
5. En muchas partes del mundo se come poco y mal.
6. Los temas de la música *rap* son demasiado violentos.
7. Hay mucho interés en la exploración del espacio.
8. Fumar no es malo para la salud.
9. No se permite el uso de la marihuana.
10. Los vehículos que consumen mucha gasolina son más populares cada día.

Expresiones

Es importante que...	Insisto en que...
Es mejor que...	Quiero que...
Es necesario que...	Recomiendo que...
Es urgente que...	

Paso 2. Ahora, en grupos de tres, piensen en tres deseos: uno que se relacione con Uds. personalmente, otro con algún amigo o pariente y otro con su país, con el mundo o con la humanidad en general. Expresen sus deseos con **Ojalá (que)...** o una de las **Expresiones.**

MODELO: Ojalá que no **haya** otra guerra (*war*).

Vocabulario útil

las elecciones
la gente que no tiene hogar (casa)
la guerra
el hambre
la pobreza
resolver (resuelvo)
terminar

En **su** comunidad

Entreviste a una persona hispana de su universidad o ciudad sobre el arte y la artesanía de su país de origen.

PREGUNTAS POSIBLES

- ¿Cuáles son los artistas más conocidos de su país? ¿A qué tipo de arte se dedican?
- ¿Qué tipo de artesanía se hace en su país? ¿y en su ciudad o región? ¿Tiene muestras (*examples*) de esta artesanía en su casa?
- ¿Hay muchas oportunidades de asistir a eventos culturales (por ejemplo, exposiciones en museos, conciertos, espectáculos de danza, teatro o cine) en su país? Por lo general, ¿son baratas o caras las entradas para los eventos culturales?
- ¿Cuáles son los eventos culturales que Ud. prefiere? ¿Asiste a ellos con frecuencia?

«Arte angelino» Segmento 2

Antes de mirar

¿Qué sabe Ud. de los murales como expresión artística? En su opinión, ¿son ejemplos del arte abstracto o son una expresión de mensajes políticos o sociales? ¿Hay arte mural en su *campus* o en su ciudad? ¿Dónde se puede ver? ¿Cómo es?

Este segmento

Laura presenta un reportaje sobre el movimiento muralista de la ciudad de Los Ángeles.

La Ofrenda (*Offering*), de Yreina Cervantes (1988), un tributo a la fuerza y la lucha (*struggle*) de los campesinos (*farmers*) del movimiento de la United Farm Workers, especialmente a una de sus líderes, Dolores Huerta

Vocabulario del segmento

establecer (**establezco**)	to establish
a través de	through
tener que ver	to have to do
sea	be it
el muro	wall
mide media milla	it's half a mile long
tardar... en	to take (*time*) to (*do something*)
la campaña de concientización	conciousness-raising campaign
llamar la atención	to get (*someone's*) attention
el motivo de orgullo	source of pride
se nos acabó el tiempo	our time is up

Fragmento del guion

Es muy feo cuando empiezan a marcar y rayar[a] los murales. Y eso pasa, puede ser, cada otra noche, de... No se sabe. Hay tantos[b] jóvenes que no saben la historia del muralismo y no saben que estas obras de arte les pertenecen[c] a ellos y les pertenecen a sus comunidades. Es historia de ellos. Y realmente quisiéramos[d] que ellos entiendan eso.

[a]*scratch* [b]*so many* [c]*belong* [d]*we'd like*

Después de mirar

A. ¿Está claro? ¿Cierto o falso? Corrija las oraciones falsas.

	CIERTO	FALSO
1. SPARC, el Centro Social y Público de Recursos Artísticos, está en Los Ángeles.	☐	☐
2. Pilar Castillo es una muralista angelina.	☐	☐
3. El movimiento muralista es exclusivo de la comunidad chicana/mexicana de Los Ángeles.	☐	☐
4. Baca trabajó sola en la creación de su mural *El Gran Muro*.	☐	☐

B. Un poco más. Conteste las siguientes preguntas.

1. ¿De dónde viene la influencia original del movimiento muralista angelino? ¿Cómo se adapta esta influencia a la realidad de Los Ángeles?

2. ¿Qué serio problema enfrentan (*face*) los murales? ¿Qué es necesario hacer para resolver esta situación?

C. Y ahora, Uds. En parejas, preparen un reportaje sobre un edificio de la universidad o de su ciudad que sea particularmente interesante. Mencionen cuándo se construyó, el estilo y otros detalles del edificio, como, por ejemplo, quién lo diseñó, quién lo ocupa ahora y si se construyó con otro fin (*purpose*) en otra época. No olviden decir si el edificio es un motivo de orgullo (*pride*) para la universidad o la ciudad y por qué.

¿Qué sitios culturales de su *campus*, ciudad o estado les recomienda Ud. a los turistas que visiten?

Lectura cultural: El Ecuador y Bolivia

Las artes

Tanto el Ecuador como Bolivia son países multiculturales, donde diferentes grupos étnicos contribuyen a las artes en general.

En el Ecuador, la institución encargada de apoyar y promover[a] la cultura es La Casa de la Cultura Ecuatoriana Benjamín Carrión (CCE), una red nacional de bibliotecas, cines, museos, teatros y publicaciones, con sede[b] en Quito. Su misión es de «[p]reservar, promover,[c] fomentar,[d] investigar y difundir[e] el arte, ciencia y patrimonio cultural ecuatoriano» para fortalecer[f] la identidad nacional del país.

En Bolivia, la editorial[g] Yerba Mala[h] Cartonera es una iniciativa a destacar.[i] «Publican» las obras de todo tipo de escritores locales, en libros impresos[j] en papel ordinario y con tapas[k] recicladas de las cajas de cartón que se botan[l] en los supermercados. Los autores mismos[m] venden sus libros en lugares públicos, al precio de un boliviano ($0,30, aproximadamente). Y si alguien no tiene plata,[n] se lo regalan, para difundir[ñ] la cultura.

[a]encargada... *in charge of supporting and promoting* [b]*headquarters* [c]*to promote* [d]*to encourage* [e]*to spread* [f]*strengthen* [g]*publishing house* [h]Yerba... *Weeds* [i]*highlight* [j]*printed* [k]*covers* [l]cajas... *cardboard boxes that are thrown away* [m]*themselves* [n]*dinero* [ñ]*spread*

Evo Morales, de ascendencia aymara, Presidente de Bolivia desde 2006

Un símbolo ecuatoriano y boliviano: La diversidad étnica y lingüística

El Ecuador y Bolivia son países que han logrado[a] preservar un gran porcentaje de su población indígena. Esto es sin duda una gran parte de la riqueza cultural y orgullo[b] nacional de ambos países. Además, el encuentro entre los españoles y los indígenas dio como resultado una mezcla[c] racial que hoy es el sustrato[d] más grande de la población de estos dos países (y de Latinoamérica en general).

[a]han... *have succeeded in* [b]*pride* [c]*mixture* [d]*subsection*

COMPRENSIÓN

1. ¿Qué institución está encargada de fomentar la cultura ecuatoriana?
2. ¿Cómo son los libros de la editorial Yerba Mala Cartonera?
3. ¿Cuáles son algunos de los museos famosos del mundo hispanohablante? ¿Cuál es la especialidad de cada una?
4. ¿Qué caracteriza a la mayoría de la población de Bolivia y el Ecuador?

Y ahora, Uds.

Uds. ya (*already*) saben mucho sobre varios tipos de arte en el mundo hispanohablante. En parejas, seleccionen la representación artística del **Capítulo 13** que les gusta o les interesa más y expliquen por qué. Si no pueden ponerse de acuerdo, expliquen por qué no les gusta o interesa el arte que escogió su compañero/a. Si prefieren, pueden escoger una representación artística hispana que no esté en el **Capítulo 13**.

En otros países hispanos

- **En España y México** Uno de los museos de arte más importantes del mundo es el Museo del Prado, en Madrid. Allí se puede admirar las obras de Velázquez y Goya, entre otros muchos artistas españoles y europeos anteriores al siglo[a] XX. El Museo Nacional de Antropología, en México, D.F., es uno de los mejores del mundo en su género.[b] En este museo se puede admirar y apreciar la excelencia de la artesanía y arquitectura de los pueblos indígenas mesoamericanos.

- **En los Estados Unidos** En Nueva York está el Museo del Barrio, dedicado a la obra de artistas latinos, con énfasis en el arte puertorriqueño.

[a]*century* [b]*category, genre*

Del mundo hispano

Antes de leer

Conteste las siguientes preguntas.

1. ¿Asiste Ud. a exposiciones de arte a veces?
2. ¿Hay estilos de pintura, artistas u obras de arte en particular que no le gustan nada? ¿Qué es lo que no le gusta de ellos?

Lectura: «La oportunidad de Salomón Bobadilla», de Tito Matamala

El amigo Salomón Bobadilla me lo había prometido[a] desde hacía muchos años.[b] Siempre esperó su oportunidad, y un día la oportunidad llegó, cuando la universidad pudo vanagloriarse[c] de traer a su Casa del Arte una exposición retrospectiva de Roberto
5   Matta. Y a Roberto Matta en persona para la inauguración.

    —Es mi oportunidad, repitió Salomón Bobadilla, ansioso.

    No me pregunten cómo se consiguió una chaqueta y una corbata, y menos podré[d] explicar cómo Salomón Bobadilla pudo infiltrarse entre los exclusivos asistentes al cóctel con que se abría la muestra
10   artística.

    Allí, en medio de[e] autoridades[f] civiles y militares, Salomón Bobadilla se acercó furtivamente[g] al maestro. Y cuando al fin estuvo a un metro de distancia, como si fuese[h] un invitado de largo abolengo,[i] le preguntó:

    —Don Roberto, ¿cuándo va a pasar sus pinturas en limpio[j]?

    Eso tenía[k] Salomón Bobadilla: siempre cumplía sus promesas.

[a]había... *had promised* [b]desde... *many years ago* [c]*boast* [d]menos... *even less will I be able* [e] en... *in the midst of* [f]*authorities* [g]se... *stealthily approached* [h]como... *as if he were* [i]un... *a guest used to such events* [j]pasar... *create the final version of your paintings* [k]Eso... *That's one thing you can really say about*

Vocabulario para leer

ansioso/a	anxious
el/la asistente	attendee
la exposición	exhibition
la inauguración	opening
el maestro	master
la muestra	show
cumplir una promesa	to keep a promise

Roberto Matta = un famoso pintor abstracto chileno

Comprensión

A. La exposición. ¿Qué podemos inferir (*infer*) de este microcuento?

	CIERTO	FALSO
1. Roberto Matta es un artista muy famoso.	☐	☐
2. La exposición de Matta en la Casa del Arte fue un evento importante para la universidad.	☐	☐
3. Muchas personas importantes de la sociedad asistieron a la inauguración.	☐	☐
4. Salomón Bobadilla asiste a inauguraciones de arte exclusivas con frecuencia.	☐	☐
5. Bobadilla no se vistió apropiadamente para la inauguración.	☐	☐
6. Matta no pudo asistir a la inauguración de su exposición.	☐	☐
7. Bobadilla decidió no hablar con Matta.	☐	☐

B. Preguntas sobre su opinión

1. ¿Cree Ud. que a Salomón Bobadilla le gusta el arte de Roberto Matta? ¿Y cree que fue apropiada la pregunta que Bobadilla le hizo a Matta?
2. ¿Cree Ud. que el narrador admira a Salomón Bobadilla?
3. El cuento no nos dice cuál fue la reacción de Roberto Matta ante (*to*) la pregunta de Bobadilla. ¿Cuál cree Ud. que fue la reacción de Matta?

Una reseña° de la película *La vida de Susana Jiménez*

review

Vocabulario **para escuchar**

el punto de vista	point of view
trata de	deals with
inesperada	unexpected
el argumento	plot
increíble	unbelievable
la actuación	performance
cursi	in poor taste; trite
al elegir	when she chose
recrea	it recreates

Antes de escuchar

¿Le gusta el cine? ¿Tiene un género (*genre*) preferido de películas: las de acción, de artes marciales, de aventura, de ciencia ficción, de horror, de suspenso, de guerra (*war*), las comedias, los dramas, las musicales? En su opinión, ¿qué características necesita tener una película para que (*so that*) sea interesante y/o buena? ¿Lee Ud. en el periódico o en internet reseñas de las películas antes de verlas? ¿Las lee después de verlas? ¿O no las lee nunca?

Después de escuchar

A. ¿Cierto o falso? ¿Qué dicen los críticos de la película? Corrija las oraciones falsas.

	CIERTO	FALSO
1. El hombre piensa que es una película que se debe ver.	☐	☐
2. La mujer piensa que es una película recomendable.	☐	☐
3. Los dos críticos piensan que la actriz principal es buena.	☐	☐
4. Los críticos están de acuerdo: el guion es bueno.	☐	☐

B. Más detalles. Conteste las siguientes preguntas.

1. Según la mujer, ¿cuál es el problema principal de la película?
2. ¿Cuáles son unos aspectos positivos de la película, según los críticos?

PRODUCCIÓN PERSONAL

¡Ahora, yo!

A. Use de modelo las preguntas y respuestas de la página 385 de este capítulo para hablar sobre las artes y las artesanías que a Ud. le interesan y el lugar donde se pueden ver en su ciudad.

B. Haga un fotomontaje con voz en off (*voice over*) sobre la obra de un artista hispano / una artista hispana cuya (*whose*) obra le interesa mucho a Ud.

A ESCRIBIR

Un ensayo sobre la expresión artística en las escuelas

Preparar

Paso 1. En parejas, piensen en los siguientes aspectos de la importancia del arte.

1. ¿Qué significa la palabra **arte**? ¿Cómo puede afectar el arte la vida de una persona?
2. ¿Cómo/Dónde se debe aprender las diversas formas de arte? ¿En la escuela o en el tiempo libre?
3. En general, ¿qué formas de arte se promueven (*are promoted*) y se enseñan en las escuelas públicas?

Paso 2. Luego, hagan una lista de argumentos a favor de la idea de apoyar (*supporting*) y enseñar las artes en las escuelas públicas y otra de argumentos en contra.

Unos niños en una clase de arte, en el Ecuador

Paso 3. Ahora use las ideas del **Paso 1** para escribir un ensayo a favor o en contra de la enseñanza de las artes en las escuelas públicas. Hay más ayuda en Connect.

Más ideas para su portafolio

- Incluya una imagen de una de sus obras de arte favoritas (de arquitectura, escultura, pintura, cine, música o lo que sea). Explique por qué le gusta y cómo la descubrió.

- Incluya la imagen de alguna obra artística que Ud. ya ha hecho (*have already made*) recientemente o antes de llegar a la universidad. Explique si se siente orgulloso/a (*proud*) de ella y por qué. Dé detalles sobre la obra: cuándo y por qué la hizo, dónde está o quién la tiene ahora, etcétera. Si no tiene ninguna obra suya (*of your own*) que comentar, hable de una obra hecha (*made*) por un pariente u otra persona.

- Si ha estado jugando (*have been playing*) Practice Spanish: Study Abroad, en Quest 10 Ud. aprendió sobre algunos remedios caseros (*home remedies*) tradicionales de Colombia. En parejas, escriban un diálogo en el cual una persona trata de ayudar a su amigo enfermo recomendándole unos remedios caseros populares en su país. El amigo / La amiga debe reaccionar a las sugerencias, expresando su opinión. Ensayen bien y luego presenten su diálogo a la clase.

Sugerencia: You are now ready to play Quest 10 in **Practice Spanish: Study Abroad** (www.mhpractice.com).

LEARNSMART

Visit **www.connectspanish.com** to practice the vocabulary and grammar points covered in this chapter.

AFTER STUDYING THIS CHAPTER I CAN...

☐ express the order of things (390)

☐ use the present subjunctive to express emotion (392–393)

☐ use the present subjunctive to express doubt and denial (397–398)

☐ use the indicative or the subjunctive in noun clauses (401–403)

☐ recognize/describe at least 2–3 aspects of Ecuadorian and Bolivian cultures

Gramática en breve

36. Uses of the Subjunctive: Emotion

①		②
EMOTION		
first subject = **indicative**	**que**	second subject = **subjunctive**

37. Uses of the Subjunctive: Doubt and Denial

①		②
DOUBT AND DENIAL		
first subject = **indicative**	**que**	second subject = **subjunctive**

38. The Subjunctive: A Summary

①		②
influence / emotion / doubt or denial	**que**	**subjunctive**
information / certainty or belief	**que**	**indicative**

Vocabulario

Los verbos

aburrir (*like* **gustar**)	to bore
acordarse (me acuerdo) (de)	to remember
atraer (*like* **traer**) (*like* **gustar**)	to draw, attract
fascinar (*like* **gustar**)	to fascinate
ganar	to earn (*income*)
lamentar	to regret; to feel sorry

negar (niego) (gu)	to deny
no creer	to disbelieve
no estar seguro/a de	to be unsure of
sentir (siento) (i)	to regret; to feel sorry
sorprender (*like* **gustar**)	to surprise
temer	to fear, be afraid
tratar de + *inf.*	to try to (*do something*)

Repaso: alegrarse de, creer, dudar, encantar, esperar, estar seguro/a de, gustar, molestar, pensar, tener miedo de

La expresión artística

el baile	dance
la canción	song
el cuadro	painting (*specific piece*)
la danza	dance
el dibujo	drawing
el escenario	stage; scenery
la escultura	sculpture
el espectáculo	show
la fotografía	photography
el guion	script
la imagen	image
la obra de arte	work (of art)
la obra de teatro	play
la obra maestra	masterpiece
el papel	role
la pintura	painting (*general*)

Cognados: la arquitectura, las artes (*pl.*), el ballet, la comedia, el drama, la escena, el mural, la música, el musical, la novela, la ópera, el poema

Repaso: el arte, la canción, el cine, el concierto, el edificio, la fotografía, la literatura, la película, el teatro

actuar (actúo)	to act
componer (compongo) (*like* **poner**)	to compose
crear	to create
dibujar	to draw
dirigir (dirijo)	to direct
diseñar	to design
esculpir	to sculpt
tejer	to weave

Cognado: pintar

Repaso: bailar, cantar, escribir, pintar

Las personas

el actor, la actriz (*pl.* actrices)	actor, actress
el bailarín, la bailarina	dancer
el/la cantante	singer
el/la compositor(a)	composer
el/la dibujante	drawer
el/la director(a)	director; conductor
el/la dramaturgo/a	playwright
el/la escritor(a)	writer
el/la escultor(a)	sculptor
el/la espectador(a)	spectator; *pl.* audience
el/la guía	guide
el/la músico/a	musician
la orquesta	orchestra
el/la pintor(a)	painter

Cognados: el/la arquitecto/a, el/la artista, el/la autor(a),
el/la novelista, el/la poeta, el público

La tradición cultural

la artesanía	arts and crafts
la cerámica	pottery; ceramics
los tejidos	woven goods

Cognado: la ruina

Los adjetivos

folclórico/a	traditional

Cognados: artístico/a, clásico/a, moderno/a

Los números ordinales

primer(o/a)	sexto/a
segundo/a	séptimo/a
tercer(o/a)	octavo/a
cuarto/a	noveno/a
quinto/a	décimo/a

Palabras adicionales

es... + indicative	it's . . .
cierto que	certain that
seguro que	certain/a sure thing that
verdad que	true that
es... + subjunctive	it's . . .
absurdo que	absurd that
extraño que	strange that
¡qué extraño que...!	how strange that . . . !
(im)posible que	(im)possible that
(im)probable que	(un)likely, (im)probable that
increíble que	incredible that
normal que	normal that
terrible que	terrible that
es una lástima que + subjunctive	it's a shame that
¡qué lástima que... !	what a shame that . . .!
hay que + *inf.*	it is necessary to (*do something*)
no es... + subjunctive	it's not . . .
(im)probable que	(im)probable that
posible que	possible that
seguro que...	certain / a sure thing that
ojalá (que)	I hope (that)

Repaso: es mejor/bueno/malo que

Vocabulario personal

14

Las presiones° de la vida moderna

Las... *Pressures*

www.connectspanish.com

En este capítulo

La hora punta (*Rush hour*) en Lima, Perú

COLOMBIA
ECUADOR
Río Amazonas
CORDILLERA DE LOS ANDES
BRASIL
PERÚ
Lima
•Cusco
Lago
Titicaca
OCÉANO
PACÍFICO
BOLIVIA

| 0 | 250 | 500 Millas |
| 0 | 250 | 500 Kilómetros |

CHILE

EL PERÚ

30.4 (punto cuatro) millones de habitantes

- El Perú es otro de los países andinos que tiene costa en el océano Pacífico y territorio amazónico. También tiene una zona desértica al sur.

- Lima, la capital del Perú, es una inmensa ciudad de más de 9 millones de habitantes. Es la quinta entre las ciudades más grandes de Latinoamérica y una de las treinta ciudades más grandes del mundo.

- El Perú es un país multiétnico: más del 25% de su población es amerindia, principalmente quechua, seguida después por[a] un gran porcentaje de mestizos, después blancos y, finalmente, negros, asiáticos (de origen chino y japonés) y árabes.

[a]seguida... *followed next by*

- ¿Cree Ud. que la vida moderna de hoy día es motivo de muchas presiones? ¿Y la vida estudiantil?

- En su opinión, ¿tenemos hoy más presiones en la vida diaria que hace 50 años[a]? Explique su respuesta.

- ¿Qué hace Ud. para calmarse cuando se siente muy estresado/a?

[a]que... *than 50 years ago*

ISMAEL PÉREZ MENDIZÁBAL CONTESTA LAS PREGUNTAS.

- No hay duda de que el ritmo[a] de la vida de hoy día es la causa de que suframos muchas presiones y mucho estrés, tanto si[b] estás trabajando o estudiando. A muchos jóvenes nos preocupa salir bien en la universidad porque es difícil conseguir un buen trabajo cuando terminas.

- Yo diría[c] que tenemos más presiones hoy. En realidad no creo que la vida ahora sea más difícil que hace 50 años,[d] pero sí creo que vivimos con más tensión día a día. Y también nos causan estrés las expectativas[e] que tenemos para nuestro futuro.

- Pues, hago lo normal, creo. Salgo con mis amigos para distraerme,[f] duermo una siesta si puedo. También trato de hacer deporte, como correr o levantar pesas, porque eso me hace sentirme mejor físicamente.

[a]*rhythm* [b]tanto... *regardless of whether* [c]*would say* [d]hace... *50 years ago* [e]*expectations* [f]*take my mind off things*

Las presiones de la vida académica

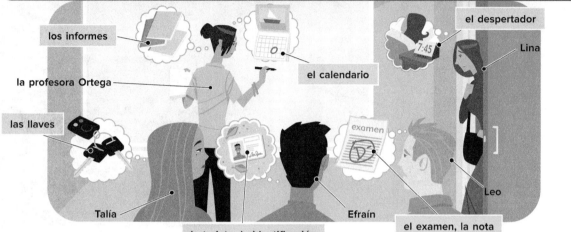

los informes

la profesora Ortega

las llaves

Talía

la tarjeta de identificación

el calendario

el examen

Efraín

el examen, la nota

el despertador

Lina

7:45

Leo

la ansiedad	anxiety
el estrés	stress
el horario	schedule
el informe (oral/escrito)	(oral/written) report
el plazo	deadline
el programa (del curso)	(course) syllabus
la prueba	quiz; test
la tarea	homework
el trabajo	job, work; report, (piece of) work
el trabajo de tiempo completo/parcial	full-time/part-time job
acordarse (me acuerdo) (de)	to remember
devolver (like volver) (algo a alguien)	to return (something to someone)
entregar (gu)	to turn/hand in
estacionar	to park
estar (muy) estresado/a	to be (very) stressed, be under (a lot of) stress

llegar (gu) a tiempo / tarde	to arrive on time/late
olvidar	to forget
pedir (pido) (i) disculpas	to apologize
recoger (recojo)*	to collect; to pick up
sacar (qu) buenas/ malas notas	to get good/bad grades
ser (in)flexible	to be (in)flexible
sufrir (de)	to suffer (from)
estar bajo / tener muchas presiones	to have/be under a lot of pressure
tomar apuntes	to take notes
Disculpa. Discúlpame.	Pardon me. I'm sorry. (fam.)
Disculpe. Discúlpeme.	Pardon me. I'm sorry. (form.)
Lo siento (mucho).	I'm (very) sorry.
Perdón.	Pardon me. I'm sorry.

Así se dice

la nota = la calificación
el plazo = la fecha límite

estacionar = aparcar (Sp.), parquear (Mex.)

la tarjeta de identificación = el carnet de identificación (Perú), el carnet de identidad (Sp.), la cédula (Col.)

---

*Note the present indicative conjugation of recoger: recojo, recoges, recoge, recogemos, recogéis, recogen.

Comunicación

A. Asociaciones

Paso 1. ¿Qué palabras asocia Ud. con los siguientes verbos? Pueden ser sustantivos o verbos, antónimos o sinónimos.

1. estacionar	**5.** sacar
2. recoger	**6.** sufrir
3. acordarse	**7.** pedir
4. entregar	**8.** llegar

Paso 2. ¿Qué palabras o situaciones asocia Ud. con los siguientes sustantivos?

1. el calendario	**8.** las llaves
2. el despertador	**9.** la tarjeta de identificación
3. las notas	**10.** las disculpas
4. las pruebas	**11.** las presiones
5. el plazo	**12.** la inflexibilidad
6. el horario	**13.** los apuntes
7. los informes	**14.** el trabajo

B. Situaciones

Paso 1. En parejas, emparejen las preguntas o comentarios con las respuestas apropiadas.

PREGUNTAS/COMENTARIOS

1. _____ —Anoche no me acordé de poner el despertador.

2. _____ —No puede estacionar el coche aquí sin permiso.

3. _____ —¿Sacaste buena nota en la prueba?

4. _____ —Ramiro se ve fatal. Algo le causa mucho estrés.

5. _____ —Discúlpeme, profesor, pero aquí tiene mi trabajo escrito sobre la Unión Europea.

6. _____ —Disculpa, pero no puedo hablar contigo ahora. Tengo que terminar el programa de curso para el semestre que viene y corregir (*grade, correct*) todos estos trabajos finales.

RESPUESTAS

a. —Siento que tengas tanto trabajo. ¿Qué crees que es más urgente que hagas en este momento?

b. —Ya lo sé, pero lo voy a dejar aquí. Estoy cansado de buscar estacionamiento por todo el *campus*.

c. —¡No te puedo creer! ¿Otra vez? ¿A qué hora llegaste al trabajo entonces (*then*)?

d. —¿Pero no se acordó de que el plazo era ayer? Es la última vez que le acepto un informe tarde.

e. —Muy buena, pero es una sorpresa. No tuve tiempo para estudiar.

f. —¡Pero, hombre! Si el pobre tiene un trabajo de tiempo completo, y además (*besides*) toma tres cursos este semestre...

Paso 2. Ahora inventen un contexto para cada diálogo. ¿Dónde están las personas que hablan? ¿En una oficina? ¿en clase? ¿Quiénes son?

MODELO: **1.** → Las personas que hablan están en el trabajo (la oficina). Probablemente están almorzando. Son compañeros de trabajo; se conocen, pero no son amigos...

C. La educación universitaria

Paso 1. Con frecuencia se oye a las personas mayores hablar de los años universitarios con nostalgia: años de libertad, sin responsabilidades, sin las presiones de la vida que vienen después. ¿Ve Ud. así la época universitaria? En parejas, comenten (*discuss*) este tema. Usen las siguientes preguntas como guía.

1. ¿Tienen muchas presiones los estudiantes universitarios?
2. ¿Qué les causa estrés a Uds.? Ordenen las causas de su estrés. (La primera causa de nuestro estrés es...)
3. ¿Son más divertidos los años universitarios que los años de la escuela secundaria? ¿Por qué?
4. ¿Les preocupa a Uds. el costo de la matrícula? ¿Es difícil para Uds. o para su familia pagarla?
5. ¿Creen Uds. que la vida va a ser mejor después de graduarse en la universidad? Expliquen su respuesta.

Paso 2. Ahora lean las siguientes citas (*quotes*) sobre la vida, la educación y el éxito (*success*) y contesten las preguntas.

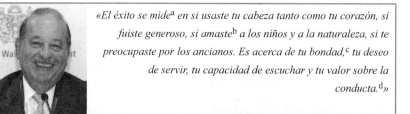

«El éxito se mide[a] *en si usaste tu cabeza tanto como tu corazón, si fuiste generoso, si amaste*[b] *a los niños y a la naturaleza, si te preocupaste por los ancianos. Es acerca de tu bondad,*[c] *tu deseo de servir, tu capacidad de escuchar y tu valor sobre la conducta.*[d]*»*

Carlos Slim Helú, hombre de negocios (*business*) mexicano

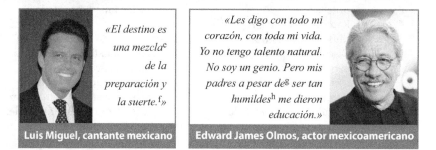

«El destino es una mezcla[e] *de la preparación y la suerte.*[f]*»*

Luis Miguel, cantante mexicano

«Les digo con todo mi corazón, con toda mi vida. Yo no tengo talento natural. No soy un genio. Pero mis padres a pesar de[g] *ser tan humildes*[h] *me dieron educación.»*

Edward James Olmos, actor mexicoamericano

[a]*se... is measured* [b]*you loved* [c]*acerca... about your kindness* [d]*valor... courage in the way you act* [e]*mix* [f]*luck* [g]*a... in spite of* [h]*poor*

1. ¿Qué creen Uds. que es más importante para triunfar en la vida, tener talento natural o preparación?
2. ¿Creen que va a ayudarles a encontrar un buen trabajo la educación que están recibiendo?
3. ¿Son importantes las buenas notas para conseguir un buen trabajo? ¿O creen que es suficiente obtener un título universitario, no importa con qué notas?
4. ¿Cómo creen Uds. que se debe medir (*measure*) el éxito individual en la vida?

SALA DE URGENCIAS

chocar (qu) con/contra

estar/ir distraído/a

caerse (me caigo)*

dolerle (duele) la cabeza

la profesora Ortega

romperse el brazo†

Enrique   lastimarse la pierna   Samuel   la madre de Samuel

Los accidentes

doler (duele) (*like* **gustar**)	to hurt, ache
equivocarse (qu) (de)	to make a mistake (about/with)
hacerse daño en	to hurt one's (*body part*)
levantarse con el pie izquierdo	to get up on the wrong side of the bed
ocurrir, pasar	to happen
pegar (gu)	to hit, strike
pegar(se) (gu) con/contra	to run/bump into/against
tener buena/mala suerte	to have good/bad luck; to be (un)lucky

¡Qué + *adjective***!**	How . . . !
distraído/a	absent-minded, distracted
¡Qué distraído!	How absent-minded!
torpe	clumsy
¡Qué torpe!	How clumsy!
¡Qué + *noun***!**	What (a) . . . !
¡Qué desastre!	What a mess! What a disaster!
¡Qué dolor!	What pain!
Fue sin querer.	I didn't mean (to do) it.

Reacciones emocionales (opcional)

- Para expresar dolor, sorpresa o compasión

¡Ay!	Ouch! Oops!	**¡No puede ser!**	No way!
¡Uy!	Oops! Oh!	**¡No me diga(s)!**	No! No way!
		¿Qué le vamos a hacer?	What can you do (about it)?

¡Cuánto lo siento!	**¡Qué maravilla!** (*How wonderful!*)
¡Qué bonito/feo/bien!	**¡Qué pena/lástima** (*shame*)**!**
¡Qué horror!	**¡Qué terrible/triste!**

- Con referencia a la suerte

¡Buena suerte!	Good luck!
¡Qué mala suerte!	Such bad luck!
¡Que te/le vaya bien!	Hope it goes well!

---

*Note that the first person singular of **caer** (to fall) is irregular: **caigo**. The present participle is **cayendo**.

†**Romper** means to break. It is generally used with **se: Se rompió la ventana.**

chocar con/contra =	hacerse daño en =
darse con/contra	lastimarse
distraído/a =	romperse =
despistado/a	quebrarse

Comunicación

A. Accidentes y tropiezos (*mishaps*)

Paso 1. ¿Le pasaron a Ud. alguna de las siguentes cosas en los últimos meses? Modifique las oraciones, usando palabras afirmativas y negativas, para que sean (*so that they are*) verdaderas para Ud.

MODELOS: Me caí por las escaleras (*stairs*) de _____.
Nunca me caí por las escaleras de **mi casa.**

1. Me caí por las escaleras de _____.
2. No me acordé de hacer la tarea para la clase de _____.
3. Me equivoqué al contestar (*when I answered*) una pregunta en clase.
4. El despertador sonó, pero no me desperté.
5. Soy un poco torpe. Rompí sin querer algo que no era mío (*mine*).
6. Choqué con algo y me hice daño.
7. Olvidé el plazo para entregar un informe.
8. Olvidé devolverle algo a alguien.
9. Iba un poco distraído/a y me equivoqué de puerta.

Paso 2. Ahora, usando las oraciones del **Paso 1** como guía, entrevístense sobre los accidentes que les han ocurrido (*have happened*) en la vida. También deben preguntarle a su compañero/a si le pasaron otros desastres.

MODELO: ¿Te caíste por las escaleras? ¿Te hiciste daño?
¿Qué (más) te pasó/ocurrió?

B. Un anuncio para un seguro. La palabra **seguro** no solo significa *sure.* También quiere decir *insurance.* Lea este anuncio de un seguro de accidentes y conteste las preguntas.

1. ¿Dónde patina el hombre?
2. ¿Qué le puede ocurrir?
3. ¿Por qué tiene buena suerte?
4. ¿Tiene Ud. un seguro de accidentes?

Un pueblo tranquilo en los Andes peruanos

Nota **cultural**

Megalópolis estresantes... y pueblitos relajantes

Muchas capitales de los países hispanohablantes son hoy día inmensas megalópolis con muchos millones de habitantes. En algunas de estas ciudades llega a concentrarse[a] más del 25% de la población total del país, como es el caso de Buenos Aires (Argentina), Lima (Perú) y Santiago (Chile).

Obviamente, el estrés causado por la congestión del tráfico en estas ciudades es altísimo. Pero el exceso de tráfico conlleva[b] el problema de encontrar aparcamiento (más estrés). Agunas de estas ciudades tienen un centro histórico muy antiguo[c] en el que[d] la circulación[e] y el aparcamiento son prácticamente imposibles. Y, por supuesto, hay que recordar el problema de la contaminación.

Para compensar el estrés de la vida urbana, mucha gente que emigró a la ciudad en busca de[f] mejores oportunidades laborales mantiene su conexión con su pueblo, su pequeña ciudad de origen. Allí vuelven con frecuencia a ver a sus parientes, a la celebración de fiestas o simplemente a relajarse.

[a]llega... *becomes concentrated* [b]*brings with it* [c]*old* [d]*el... which* [e]*driving* [f]*en... in search of*

Las ciudades hispanohablantes más grandes

Área metropolitana	población (millones)
México, D.F.	22
Buenos Aires	15
Lima	9
Bogotá	9
Madrid	8
Santiago	6
Caracas	9

¿Cuáles son las megalópolis de los Estados Unidos? ¿Cree Ud. que es estresante vivir en una? ¿Por qué?

C. ¿Qué le vamos a hacer? Indique lo que puede pasar o algo que una persona puede hacer en cada una de las siguientes situaciones. También indique algunas de las expresiones que una persona hispanohablante podría (*might*) decir en cada caso.

MODELO: Una estudiante choca contra el escritorio de un compañero de clase. →
    Lo que puede pasar: La estudiante se hace daño en la pierna o el pie y se cae. Las cosas del escritorio de su compañero también se caen.
    Se puede decir: ¡Ay¡ ¡Qué torpe soy! ¡Perdón! ¡Fue sin querer!

1. A alguien le duele mucho la cabeza.
2. Una persona que va distraída choca con otra en la cafetería.
3. Una persona torpe rompe la cámara de un amigo.
4. Un compañero de clase se equivocó en muchas preguntas en el último examen.
5. Una amiga se hizo daño mientras jubaga a su deporte favorito.
6. Un amigo se levantó con el pie izquierdo.

Nota comunicativa

Más sobre los adverbios: *adjetivo + -mente*

You already know the most common Spanish adverbs: words like **bien/mal, mucho/poco, siempre/nunca...**

Adverbs that end in *-ly* in English usually end in **-mente** in Spanish. The suffix **-mente** is added to the feminine singular form of adjectives. Note that the accent mark on the stem word (if there is one) is retained.

ADJETIVO	ADVERBIO	INGLÉS
rápida	**rápida**mente	*rapidly*
fácil	**fácil**mente	*easily*
paciente	**paciente**mente	*patiently*

You will use adverbs in **Práctica D.**

D. Intercambios

Paso 1. Modifique las siguientes acciones con un adverbio basado en los adjetivos de **Vocabulario útil.** ¡OJO! Hay más de una opción en algunos casos.

MODELO: esperar → esperar pacientemente

1. esperar
2. trabajar
3. llegar
4. hacer algo
5. relajarse (*to relax*)
6. estudiar
7. empezar algo
8. estar confundido/a

> **Vocabulario útil**
>
> | | |
> |---|---|
> | constante | posible |
> | directo/a | puntual |
> | fácil | rápido/a |
> | inmediato/a | total |
> | paciente | tranquilo/a |

Paso 2. Ahora, en parejas, túrnense para entrevistarse sobre las frases del **Paso 1.** Deben obtener información interesante y personal de su compañero/a.

MODELOS: esperar pacientemente → **¿Sabes esperar** pacientemente? **¿A quién esperas** pacientemente? **¿Cuándo esperas** pacientemente?

Paso 3. Díganle a la clase por lo menos un detalle interesante de su compañero/a.

«¡Ay, qué estrés!» Segmento 1

Este profesor opina que siempre hay algo que perturbe la mente (*bothers*) de los estudiantes, ya sea (*be it*) lo cotidiano (*everyday things*), ya sea el nivel (*level*) económico de la familia, ya sea el tránsito (*tráfico*), ya sea la presión que ejercen (*exert*) los profesores en sus materias.

Antes de mirar

¿Cree Ud. que, en general, hay muchos estudiantes estresados en su universidad? ¿Cuáles son las cosas más estresantes (*stressful*) para Ud.? ¿Qué aspectos de la vida universitaria le estresan más? ¿Qué época del año académico le provoca (*causes*) más estrés?

Este segmento

Este segmento incluye el principio del programa y un reportaje de Laura de entrevistas con estudiantes mexicanos sobre el estrés y sus causas.

Vocabulario del segmento

de nuevo	otra vez	**el apoyo**	support
restar a	to take away from	**mismo/a**	same; very
¿cómo anda...?	how is ... ?	**el/la chico/a**	young person
la seguridad	security, safety	**podría**	could
presentar	to take (*a test*)	**igual salgo**	I may even leave
el parcial	midterm (exam)	**la carga**	load
el extraordinario	make-up (exam)	**la calificación**	**la nota**
la temporada	season		

Después de mirar

A. **¿Está claro?** ¿Cierto o falso? Corrija las oraciones falsas.

	CIERTO	FALSO
1. La única presión que sufre Víctor tiene que ver (*has to do*) con el tráfico.	☐	☐
2. Ningún estudiante cree que el tráfico sea una causa de estrés.	☐	☐
3. Un profesor opina que conseguir dinero para poder pagarse los estudios genera estrés.	☐	☐
4. Varios estudiantes mencionan que sienten estrés durante la temporada de fútbol.	☐	☐

B. **Un poco más.** Conteste las siguientes preguntas.

1. ¿En qué es comparable la Ciudad de México con Los Ángeles?
2. ¿En qué época del año académico tuvieron lugar (*took place*) las entrevistas? ¿Cómo lo sabe Ud.?
3. ¿Qué presiones mencionan los estudiantes y los profesores?

C. **Y ahora, Uds.** En parejas, comparen las respuestas de los jóvenes mexicanos con la realidad de los estudiantes en su universidad. ¿En qué son semejantes y en qué son diferentes? ¿Sufren los estudiantes de su universidad algún tipo de presiones que no se menciona en el programa?

39 Telling How Long or How Long Ago Something Happened

Hace... que: Another Use of **hacer**

Grammar Tutorial 39
connect
|SPANISH
www.connectspanish.com

Gramática en acción: Cusco, una ciudad histórica

La Plaza de Armas de la bella (*beautiful*) ciudad de Cusco, con vista de la Catedral y la Iglesia de la Compañía de Jesús

Cusco, una ciudad histórica, fue la capital del imperio de los incas. Luego, durante la dominación española, fue una importante ciudad colonial.

1. La ciudad de Cusco continúa habitada desde hace más de 3.000 años. Esto la hace la ciudad más antigua de Sudamérica.

2. Hace aproximadamente 500 años que los conquistadores españoles llegaron a Cusco por primera vez. La convirtieron en una ciudad importante de su imperio.

¿Y los Estados Unidos?

¿Cuánto tiempo hace que... ?

1. son un país independiente
2. tienen cincuenta estados
3. se independizaron de Inglaterra
4. hubo elecciones presidenciales

---

con el presente: *has/have been (happening) for + time*

• **hace** + *time* + **que** + *present tense verb*
  Hace un año **que estudio** español.

• *present tense verb* + **desde hace** + *time*
  Estudio español **desde hace** un año.

I've been studying Spanish for one year.

1. Hace + *time*

In Spanish, a phrase with **hace** + *time* is used to express two very different perspectives on time.

• With the *present* tense, the **hace** phrase tells how long something *has been happening*. (English uses the present perfect progressive tense for this: *has/have been* verb + *-ing for* ...)

con el pretérito: *ago*

• **hace** + *time* + **que** + *preterite tense verb*
  Hace un año **que empecé** a estudiar español.

• *preterite tense verb* + **hace** + *time*
  Empecé a estudiar español **hace** un año.

I started studying Spanish a (one) year ago.

Hace dos años **que estudio** en esta universidad.
Estudio en esta universidad **desde hace** dos años.
I've been studying at this university for two years.

¡OJO!
Use **que** when the **hace** phrase comes before the verb, **desde hace** when it comes after.

Cusco, a historic city Cusco, a historic city, was the capital of the Inca Empire. Then, during the Spanish occupation, it was an important colonial city. **1.** The city of Cusco has been continually inhabited for more than 3,000 years. That makes it the oldest city in South America. **2.** The Spanish conquistadors arrived in Cusco for the first time about 500 years ago. They made it into an important city in their empire.

- With the *preterite*, the **hace** phrase tells how long *ago* something *happened*.

  When the **hace** phrase comes before the verb, **que** is used with it.

¡OJO!

The word **hace** is invariable with a present tense or a preterite tense verb.

Hace dos años **que me gradué** en la escuela secundaria.
Me gradué en la escuela secundaria **hace** dos años.
I graduated from high school two years ago.

Hace dos años que **vivo** en el Perú.
Hace dos años que **fui** al Perú.

---

2. Questions with *hace*

The question **¿Cuánto tiempo hace que... ?** is used with both structures, with the present and the preterite. You can answer a question of this kind just by saying the time.

- + *present tense* = to ask how long something *has been happening*
- + *preterite tense* = to ask how long *ago* something *happened*

—**¿Cuánto tiempo hace que** vives aquí?
—Dos meses.
"How long have you been living here?"
"(For) Two months."

—**¿Cuánto tiempo hace que** te mudaste aquí?
—Dos meses.
"How long ago did you move here?"
"Two months ago."

Summary of Uses of *hace*

hace + *time* + **que** + *present* *present* + **desde hace** + *time*	has/have been doing
hace + *time* + **que** + *preterite* *preterite* + **hace** + *time*	ago

Práctica y comunicación

A. Información personal

Paso 1. Autoprueba. Empareje las oraciones con el equivalente apropiado.

a. for *x* years   **b.** *x* years ago

1. _____ Hace dos años que te conozco.
2. _____ Te conocí hace dos años.
3. _____ Hace tres años que tomé cálculo.
4. _____ Hace tres años que estudio español.

Paso 2. Complete las siguientes oraciones con información personal.

1. Hace _____ que mi familia vive en el estado de _____.
2. Hace _____ que yo vivo en este estado.
3. Hace _____ que comí pizza por última vez.
4. Me duché / Me bañé hace _____.
5. Vi a mi mejor amigo/a hace _____.
6. Hace _____ que practico/hago _____ (deporte o pasatiempo).

Paso 3. Ahora, en parejas, túrnense para entrevistarse sobre las ideas del **Paso 2.** Luego díganle al resto de la clase algo que tienen en común.

MODELO: E1: ¿Dónde vive tu familia? ¿Cuánto tiempo hace que vive en ese estado?
E2: Mi familia vive en Nevada desde hace 10 años. ¿Y tu familia?
E1: Mi familia vive en Oklahoma. Vive allí desde hace 10 años también.

B. Situaciones: ¿De qué tiene ganas?

Paso 1. Lea las siguientes situaciones. Luego indique cuánto tiempo hace que existe la situación. Finalmente, explique qué tiene ganas de hacer en cada circunstancia. Siga el modelo.

MODELO: Ud. se levantó a las 8 de la mañana y es la una de la tarde. No tuvo tiempo de comer nada entre clase y clase. → **Hace** cinco horas **que** no como. **Tengo ganas de** comer.

(Continúa.)

1. Ud. está en casa. Empezó a escribir un informe a las 5 de la tarde. Ahora son las 8 de la noche y todavía sigue escribiendo.
2. Ud. llegó a una fiesta a las 9 de la noche. Son las 4 de la mañana y todavía está en la fiesta.
3. Sus padres le regalaron un coche de segunda mano, muy viejo, cuando Ud. estaba en el tercer año de la escuela secundaria. Diez años más tarde, Ud. todavía (*still*) tiene el mismo (*same*) coche.
4. Empezó a llover el miércoles. Hoy es domingo y sigue lloviendo.

Paso 2. Ahora prepare Ud. una situación similar a las (*those*) del **Paso 1** y dígasela a la clase. Sus compañeros le van a decir qué tienen ganas de hacer.

C. **Eventos históricos.** ¿Cuánto tiempo hace que pasaron los siguientes eventos? Haga oraciones completas con las palabras indicadas. Los años en que pasaron estos eventos aparecen abajo.

MODELO: el primer hombre / llegar a la luna →
Hace más de cuarenta años que el primer hombre **llegó** a la luna.

1. Cristóbal Colón / llegar a América
2. la Segunda Guerra (*War*) Mundial / terminar
3. Michael Jackson / morir
4. el presidente actual / ser elegido (*to be elected*)
5. el profesor / la profesora de español / empezar a enseñar en esta universidad

D. **Intercambios**

Paso 1. Haga preguntas basadas en las siguientes ideas. ¡OJO! Algunas requieren un verbo en el presente y otras un verbo en el pretérito.

MODELOS: vivir en esta ciudad →
¿Cuánto tiempo hace que **vives** en esta ciudad?
visitar a sus abuelos la última vez →
¿Cuánto tiempo hace que **visitaste** a tus abuelos la última vez?

1. vivir en esta ciudad
2. asistir a esta universidad
3. vivir en su apartamento/casa/residencia
4. estudiar español
5. manejar
6. conocer a su mejor amigo/a
7. visitar a sus abuelos (a ¿ ?) la última vez
8. sacar una mala nota
9. escribir el último trabajo para una de sus clases
10. llegar tarde a clase

Paso 2. Ahora use las preguntas del **Paso 1** para entrevistar a un compañero o una compañera de clase. Luego díganle a la clase un detalle interesante.

¿Recuerda Ud.?

You have learned a number of uses for the word **se**. Match each function of **se** with the appropriate sentence.

1. _____ Los niños tienen que bañarse ahora.
2. _____ Los amigos **se** quieren mucho.
3. _____ ¿El regalo? **Se** lo di a Ana ayer.
4. _____ Aquí **se** habla español.

a. to express *one* or *you*
b. to replace the indirect object pronoun **le** or **les** before **lo/ la/ los/las**
c. to express a reflexive action
d. to express a reciprocal action

In **Gramática 40** you will learn another use for the word **se**.

Prác. C: Los años: MODELO: 1969 1. 1492 2. 1945 3. 2009 4. ¿ ? 5. ¿ ?

Gramática en acción: Un día fatal

1. A Diego se le cayó la taza de café.

2. A Antonio se le olvidaron los libros.

3. A Antonio y a Diego se les olvidó apagar las luces del coche.

¿Y Ud.?

¿También pasó un día fatal ayer? Para describir su día, indique si las siguientes oraciones son ciertas o falsas.

	CIERTO	FALSO		CIERTO	FALSO
1. Se me perdió algo.	☐	☐	**3.** Se me cayeron algunas cosas.	☐	☐
2. Se me olvidó hacer algo importante.	☐	☐	**4.** Se me rompió algo de valor (*value*).	☐	☐

El *se* accidental

A + **Noun** (A + **Pronoun**)	*se*	Indirect Object Pronoun	Verb	Subject
A Antonio	**se**	le	olvidan	las llaves muchas veces.
(A Ud./él/ella)	**Se**	le	olvidó	cerrar el coche con llave.
A los estudiantes	**se**	les	olvidó	el examen.
(A mí)	**Se**	me	olvida	entregar la tarea a veces.
(A ti)	**Se**	te	olvidaba	la tarea con frecuencia cuando eras pequeño.
(A nosotros)	**Se**	nos	olvidaron	los informes ayer.
(A Uds./ellos/ellas)	**Se**	les	olvida	estudiar los fines de semana.

1. Using *se* to Express Accidental Events

Unplanned or unexpected events (*I dropped ... , We lost ... , You forgot ...*) are frequently expressed in Spanish with **se** and a third person form of the verb. The event is viewed as happening *to* someone— the unwitting "victim" of the action. This structure is called the *accidental se* (**el *se* accidental**).

Se me cayó el papel.
I dropped the paper. (The paper slipped out of my hands. [I didn't drop it on purpose.])

Se te olvidó llamar a tu hija.
You forgot to call your daughter. (Calling your daughter slipped your mind.)

Se le olvidaron las llaves.
He forgot the keys. (It slipped his mind to bring them.)

An awful day 1. *Diego dropped a cup of coffee.* **2.** *Antonio forgot his books.* **3.** *Antonio and Diego forgot to turn off the headlights on their car.*

2. Agreement with the Subject

In these kinds of sentences, as with **gustar** and similar verbs, the subject of the sentence is the thing that is dropped, forgotten, and so on. The subject usually follows the verb.

- When the subject is singular, the verb will be singular, even if the "victim" is plural.
- When the subject is plural, the verb will be plural, even if the "victim" is singular.

A los niños **se les olvid**ó **el cumpleaños** de su madre.
The children forgot their mother's birthday.

Al niño **se le olvid**ó **el cumpleaños** de su madre.
The child forgot his mother's birthday.

A Antonio **se le olvid**aron **los apuntes.**
Antonio forgot his notes.

A Antonio y Diego **se les olvid**aron **los apuntes.**
Antonio and Diego forgot their notes.

> ## ¡OJO!
> Remember that an infinitive is a singular subject: **A los niños se les olvidó llamar a su madre.**

3. Parts of the Sentence

- An accidental **se** sentence must have:

  (No) **Se** *IO pronoun   verb   subject*

  Notice that **no** comes before **se.**

- When the "victim" is specifically named (with a noun or a person's name), the sentence will also have an **a** + *name/noun* phrase: **a Tomás / a los Sres. Pérez / al gato / a los niños.**

  A + *name/noun* **(no)** **se** *IO pronoun   verb   subject*

- The indirect object pronoun can be clarified or emphasized with an **a** + *pronoun* phrase: **a mí, a ti, a Ud./él/ella, a nosotros, a vosotros, a Uds./ ellos/ellas.**

  A + *pronoun* **(no)** **se** *indirect object   verb   subject   pronoun*

Se le rompió el brazo.
He/She broke his/her arm.

No se le rompió el brazo.
He/She didn't break his/her arm.

A Ana / A la niña se **le** rompió el brazo.
Ana / The child broke her arm.

¡Y luego **a ti** se te cae el café! ¡Y luego se te cae el café **a ti!**
*And then **you** drop the coffee!*

A ella se **le** rompió el brazo.
She broke her arm.

4. Verbs Frequently Used with *se*

Here are some verbs frequently used in this construction. The verbs marked with * are new.

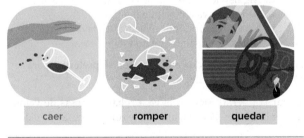

caer   romper   quedar

*acabar	to finish; to run out of
caer	to fall; to drop
olvidar	to forget
perder (pierdo)	to lose
*quedar	to remain, be left
*romper	to break

5. Accident Versus Intent

This structure is used to emphasize the accidental nature of an event. When the speaker wishes to emphasize *who* committed the act, or that the act was intentional, that person becomes the subject of the verb and the **se** structure is not used.

Se me rompió el plato.
The plate broke on me. (accidentally)

(Yo) Rompí el plato.
I broke the plate. (emphasizes either who broke the plate or the intentionality of the act)

Summary of *el se accidental*

a + *noun* + **se** + *indirect object pronoun* + *verb* + *subject*

(**a** + *pronoun*) **se** + *indirect object pronoun* + *verb* + *subject*

Práctica y comunicación

A. ¿Algo deliberado o accidental?

Paso 1. Autoprueba. Empareje las oraciones de las dos columnas.

1. _____ No encuentro las llaves.
2. _____ Tu calculadora no funciona.
3. _____ Paco no entregó la tarea.
4. _____ Necesito comprar leche.

a. Se te rompió.
b. Se me acabó.
c. Se me perdieron.
d. Se le olvidó.

Paso 2. Indique si a Ud. le pasaron las siguientes cosas o hizo algunas de ellas.

	ESO ME PASÓ.	LO HICE.
1. Se me rompió algo de otra persona sin querer.	☐	☐
2. Rompí algo de alguien, con intención de hacerlo.	☐	☐
3. Se me cayó un plato de comida sin querer.	☐	☐
4. Tiré comida a la basura porque no me gustaba.	☐	☐
5. Se me perdió algo de un ex novio / una ex novia.	☐	☐
6. Quemé (*I burned*) o rompí algo de un ex novio / una ex novia.	☐	☐

Paso 3. Ahora, en parejas, túrnense para entrevistarse sobre las acciones del **Paso 2.** Luego díganle al resto de la clase algo que tienen en común.

MODELO: E1: ¿Se te rompió algo de otra persona sin querer?
E2: Sí. ¿Y a ti se te rompió algo de otra persona sin querer?
E1: También. → A nosotros se nos rompieron cosas de otras personas sin querer.

B. ¡Qué mala memoria!

Paso 1. Hortensia es tan distraída que, cuando se fue de vacaciones al Perú, se le olvidó hacer muchas cosas importantes antes de salir. Empareje los olvidos (*lapses*) de Hortensia con las consecuencias.

OLVIDOS

1. _____ Se le olvida cerrar la puerta de su casa.
2. _____ Se le olvida pagar las cuentas.
3. _____ Se le olvida pedirle a alguien que cuidara a (*to take care of*) su perro.
4. _____ Se le olvida cancelar el correo (*mail*).
5. _____ Se le olvida pedirle permiso a su jefa (*boss*).
6. _____ Se le olvida llevar el pasaporte.
7. _____ Se le olvida hacer reserva en un hotel.

CONSECUENCIAS

a. Va a perder el trabajo.
b. No la van a dejar subir al avión.
c. Le van a suspender el servicio de la electricidad y del gas... ¡y cancelar sus tarjetas de crédito!
d. Alguien le va a robar las cosas de valor (*value*).
e. ¡«King» se va a morir de hambre!
f. No va a tener dónde alojarse (*to stay*).
g. Todos van a saber que no está en casa.

Paso 2. Ahora ponga las oraciones de las dos columnas en el pretérito, para narrar lo que le pasó a Hortensia en su viaje.

MODELO: 1. Se le olvida cerrar la puerta. Alguien le va a robar las cosas de valor.
→ Se le **olvidó** cerrar la puerta. Por eso, alguien le **robó** las cosas de valor.

C. Una mañana fatal.
Complete la siguiente descripción de lo que le pasó a Pablo ayer. ¡OJO! Use el **se** accidental.

Pablo tuvo una mañana fatal. Primero (olvidar¹) poner el despertador. Se levantó tarde y se vistió rápidamente. No cerró bien su maletín;ª por eso (caer²) unos papeles importantes. Recogió los papeles y subió al coche, pero después de cinco minutos, (acabar³) la gasolina y se le paróᵇ el coche. Dejó el coche en la calle y

(Continúa.)

ª*briefcase* ᵇ*se... (the car) stopped on him*

decidió ir a pie. Llevaba el maletín en una mano y las llaves y un documento urgente en la otra. Desgraciadamente, en el camino^c (perder⁴) el documento. Cuando llegó a la oficina, buscó a su jefe^d para entregarle el documento pero no podía encontrarlo entre sus papeles. Cansado y enojado, cerró el maletín sin cuidado y (romper⁵) los lentes.

^cen... *on the way* ^d*boss*

D. Unos dichos (*colloquial expressions*) hispanos. El **se** accidental se usa en muchos dichos en español. En parejas, traten de dar su equivalente en inglés. Luego emparejen los dichos con la situación apropiada.

DICHOS

a. Se le hace la boca agua.
b. Se le hacía tarde.
c. Se le fue el alma (*soul*) a los pies.
d. Se le fue la lengua.
e. Se le acabó la paciencia.
f. Se le cae la baba (*drool*) por (algo o alguien).

SITUACIONES

1. La clase empezaba a las dos. Eran las dos menos veinte y Raúl todavía estaba en la ducha. A Raúl _____

2. Ramón le contó a María un secreto, pero María se lo dijo a Luisa. A María _____

3. La hija de Carmen es preciosa. A Carmen _____

4. Julio tiene muchísimas ganas de comer la comida de su madre. ¡Qué rica! Solo de pensarlo, a Julio _____

5. «¡Ya no más! (*Enough already!*)», gritó (*screamed*) la madre. «Vete a tu cuarto ahora mismo.» A la madre _____

6. Una joven ha tenido (*has had*) un grave accidente. A su padre _____

E. ¡Desastres por todas partes (*everywhere*)!

Paso 1. ¿Es Ud. una persona distraída o torpe? Indique las oraciones que describen lo que le pasa a Ud. Cambie algunos de los detalles de las oraciones si es necesario. **¡OJO!** Se usa el presente para hablar de acciones típicas.

1. ☐ Con frecuencia se me caen los libros (los platos,...).
2. ☐ Se me pierden constantemente las llaves (los calcetines,...).
3. ☐ Siempre se me rompen los lentes (las lámparas,...).
4. ☐ A veces se me quedan los libros (los cuadernos,...) en la clase.
5. ☐ Se me olvida fácilmente mi horario (el teléfono de algún amigo,...).

Paso 2. ¿Es Ud. igual ahora que cuando era más joven? Complete cada oración del **Paso 1** para describir cómo era de niño/a. **¡OJO!** Use el imperfecto.

MODELO: De niño/a, (no) se me **caían** los libros con frecuencia.

Paso 3. Ahora compare sus respuestas con las de un compañero o una compañera. ¿Quién es más distraído/a o torpe ahora? ¿Quién era así de niño/a?

F. Encuesta (*Poll*): Accidentes de la semana

Paso 1. Haga una lista de cinco accidentes o cosas que ocurren con frecuencia en la vida diaria y que a nosotros nos parecen desastres. Debe usar por lo menos tres verbos diferentes.

MODELO: perder las llaves de la casa o apartamento

Paso 2. Ahora hágales cinco preguntas a cinco personas de la clase sobre los accidentes o desastres que Ud. apuntó en el **Paso 1**. Luego dígale a la clase cuál fue el accidente o desastre más común.

MODELO: perder las llaves de la casa o apartamento →
La semana pasada, ¿se te perdieron las llaves de la casa o apartamento?

Algo sobre...

el cajón

Un grupo que toca el cajón peruano

El cajón es un instrumento de percusión similar a una caja.^a Originalmente fue creado^b por los descendientes de esclavos africanos en la zona costera^c peruana. Hoy es un instrumento muy popular que se usa en la música afroperuana y también en la música de otros países, incluyendo el flamenco en España.

 ¿Qué instrumento musical considera Ud. más emblemático de su país? ¿En qué tipo de música se utiliza?

^a*box* ^b*created* ^c*coastal*

Review what you know about **por** and **para** by completing these sentences.

1. ¡Gracias para/por el regalo!
2. Esta comida es para/por ti.
3. ¿Trabajas para/por la noche?
4. Tomo cinco clases. Para/Por eso tengo mucha tarea.

5. Para/Por aprender, hay que estudiar.
6. Dame el plato, para/por favor.
7. ¡Para/Por fin conocí al novio de mi compañera!
8. El informe es para/por mañana.

You will learn more about these prepositions in **Gramática 41.**

Grammar Tutorial 41
connect
|SPANISH
www.connectspanish.com

41 *¿Por o para?*
A Summary of Their Uses

Gramática en acción: Ideas sobre la educación

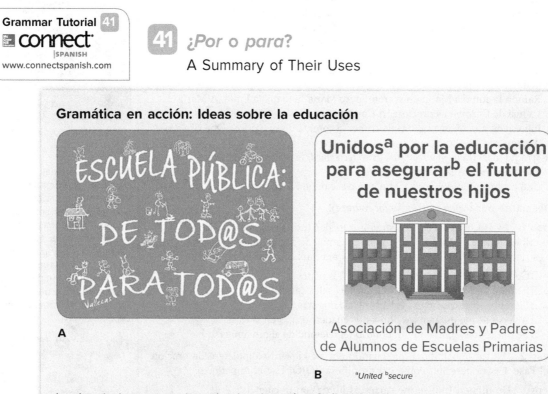

A

Unidos^a por la educación
para asegurar^b el futuro
de nuestros hijos

Asociación de Madres y Padres
de Alumnos de Escuelas Primarias

B   ^a*United* ^b*secure*

Lea los siguientes anuncios sobre la educación. ¿Cuál de los dos anuncios expresa las siguientes ideas sobre la educación?

1. La educación nos conecta.
2. La educación no debe darse solo a algunas personas.
3. Un buen sistema educativo es muy importante para el progreso de un país.
4. Los ciudadanos (*citizens*) de un país son parte del sistema educativo.
5. Un buen sistema educativo es una tarea nacional.

¿Y Ud.?

Para Ud., ¿qué otras cosas son «de tod@s y para tod@s»?

You have been using **por** and **para** since you started to study Spanish. Each preposition has some English equivalents that are unique to it, making it easy to decide between them in those cases. However, both **por** and **para** can mean *for*, depending on the context. You already know much of the information in this section.

Por

1. Unique Meanings of *por*

The preposition **por** has a number of English equivalents that are not expressed with *for* in English. (**Para** can never express these meanings.)

• *by / by means of*	El libro fue escrito **por** Mario Vargas Llosa. *The book was written by Mario Vargas Llosa.* Nos hablamos **por teléfono** mañana. *We'll talk by (on the) phone tomorrow.*
• *through/along*	Me gusta pasear **por el parque** y **por la playa.** *I like to stroll through the park and along the beach.*
• *during/in* (time of day)	Trabajo **por la mañana.** *I work in the morning.*
• *because of / due to*	Estoy nervioso **por la entrevista.** *I'm nervous because of the interview.*

2. For = *Por*

When it expresses *for,* **por** looks back at the *reason* or *cause* for something. To remember this, think of the interrogative **¿por qué?** = *why?* and the expressions **por eso...** (*that's why...*) and **gracias por...** (*thanks for...*).

• *for = for the sake of, on behalf of*	Lo hago **por ti.** *I'm doing it for you (for your sake).*
• *for = in place of*	No puedo tomar el examen **por ti.** *I can't take the exam for you (in your place).*
• *for = in exchange for*	Piden **1.000 dólares por el coche.** *They're asking $1,000 for the car.* **Gracias por todo.** *Thanks for everything.*
• *for = period of time* (often omitted)	Vivieron allí (**por**) **un año.** *They lived there for a year.*

3. Fixed Expressions with *por*

Por is used in the expressions to the right, some of which (like **por eso** and **por si acaso**) express the *reason* or *cause* of something. The expressions marked with * are new.

*por Dios	for heaven's sake
*por ejemplo	for example
por eso	that's why
por favor	please
por fin	finally
por lo general	generally, in general
por lo menos	at least
*por primera/última vez	for the first/last time
*por si acaso	just in case
*¡por supuesto!	of course!
*por todas partes	everywhere

Para

1. Unique Meaning of *para*

The preposition **para** has one English equivalent that is not expressed with *for* in English. (**Por** can never express this meaning.)

• *in order to + infinitive*

Regresaron pronto **para estudiar.**
They returned soon (in order) to study.

Estudian **para conseguir** un buen trabajo.
They're studying (in order) to get a good job.

---

2. For = *Para*

When it expresses *for*, **para** looks ahead, toward the *goal, purpose,* or *destination* of something. To remember this, think of the interrogative **¿para qué?** = *for what purpose?*

• *for = destined for / to be given to*

Todo esto es **para ti.**
All this is for you.

Le di un libro **para su hijo.**
I gave her a book for her son.

• *for = by (deadline, specified future time)*

Para mañana, estudien *por* y *para.*
*For tomorrow, study **por** and **para**.*

La composición es **para el lunes.**
The composition is for Monday.

• *for = toward / in the direction of*

Salió **para el Perú** ayer.
She left for Peru yesterday.

• *for = to be used for, purpose*

El dinero es **para la matrícula.**
The money is for tuition.

Es un vaso **para agua.**
It's a water glass.

> **¡OJO!**
> Compare the second example to **un vaso de agua** = *a glass (full) of water.*

• *for = as compared with / in relation to others*

Para mí, el español es fácil.
For me, Spanish is easy.

Para (ser) **extranjera,** habla muy bien el inglés.
For (being) a foreigner, she speaks English very well.

• *for = in the employ of, in preparation for*

Trabajan para el gobierno.
They work for the government.

Estudio **para (la carrera de) dentista.**
I'm studying to be (for a career as) a dentist.

> **Summary of *por* and *para***
>
> **por:** reason, cause
> **para:** goal, purpose, destination

Práctica y comunicación

A. ¿Por o para?

Paso 1. Autoprueba. ¿Con qué preposición asocia Ud. las siguientes frases?

1. _____ gracias
2. _____ una fecha en el futuro
3. _____ durante
4. _____ la persona que creó algo
5. _____ con el propósito (*purpose, goal*) de
6. _____ en lugar de otra persona
7. _____ a causa de
8. _____ a lo largo de (*along*)
9. _____ trabajar en una compañía
10. _____ pagar dinero
11. _____ en comparación con otros
12. _____ una carrera

Paso 2. Complete las siguientes oraciones con **por** o **para.**

1. ¿_____ qué organización o compañía trabaja tu padre/madre?
2. ¿Estudias mejor _____ la mañana o _____ la tarde?
3. ¿_____ qué calles pasas para llegar a esta clase?
4. ¿Cuánto pagaste _____ tu celular?
5. ¿_____ qué sirve hablar español en los Estados Unidos?
6. ¿_____ cuándo es la próxima tarea de español?
7. ¿_____ qué profesión estudias?
8. ¿Estás nervioso/a _____ el examen final en esta clase?

Paso 3. Ahora, en parejas, túrnense para hacer y contestar las preguntas del **Paso 2.** Luego díganle a la clase algo que tienen en común.

B. Situaciones

Paso 1. Complete las siguientes oraciones con **por** o **para.** Luego empareje las preguntas/situaciones con las respuestas apropiadas.

PREGUNTAS/SITUACIONES

1. _____ ¡Uf! Vengo de jugar un partido de basquetbol. ¡Jugamos _____ dos horas!
2. _____ ¿_____ qué quieres que llame a Pili y Adolfo? Nunca están en casa _____ la noche, mucho menos (*especially*) a estas horas.
3. _____ ¿No vas a comer nada? _____ lo menos un sándwich.
4. _____ ¡Cuánto lo siento, don Javier! Sé que llegué tarde a la cita. Discúlpeme.
5. _____ Es imposible que tome el examen hoy, _____ muchas razones.
6. _____ ¿No lo oíste? Juana acaba de tener un accidente horrible.
7. _____ ¡Pero, papá, quiero ir!
8. _____ Ay, Mariana, ¿no sabías que hubo un ciclón? Murieron más de cien personas.

RESPUESTAS

a. ¡_____ Dios! ¡Qué desgracia!
b. Te digo que no, _____ última vez.
c. No se preocupe. Lo importante es que _____ fin está aquí.
d. ¡_____ Dios! ¿Qué pasó? ¿Está bien?
e. No, gracias. No tengo mucha hambre y además (*besides*) tengo que irme en seguida.
f. ¿_____ ejemplo? Dígame...
g. Ah, _____ eso tienes tanto calor.
h. Llámalos de todas formas, _____ si acaso están en casa esta noche.

Paso 2. Ahora, en parejas, lean las preguntas/situaciones y respuestas. Luego inventen un breve contexto para cada diálogo. ¿Dónde están las personas que hablan? ¿Quiénes son? ¿Por qué dicen lo que dicen?

C. *¿Por o para?* Complete los siguientes diálogos y oraciones con **por** o **para.**

1. Los Sres. Arana salieron _____ el Perú ayer. Van en avión, claro, pero luego piensan viajar en coche _____ todo el país. Van a estar allí _____ dos meses. Va a ser una experiencia extraordinaria _____ toda la familia.
2. Mi prima Graciela quiere estudiar _____ (ser) doctora. _____ eso trabaja _____ un médico _____ la mañana; tiene clases _____ la tarde.
3. —¿_____ qué están Uds. aquí todavía? Yo pensaba que iban a dar un paseo _____ el parque.
   —Íbamos a hacerlo, pero no fuimos _____ la nieve.
4. Este cuadro fue pintado (*painted*) _____ Picasso _____ expresar los desastres de la guerra (*war*). _____ muchos críticos de arte, es la obra maestra de este artista.
5. La Asociación «Todo _____ Ellos» trabaja _____ las personas mayores, _____ ayudarlos cuando lo necesitan. ¿Trabaja Ud. _____ alguna asociación de voluntarios? ¿Qué tuvo que hacer _____ inscribirse (*sign up*)?

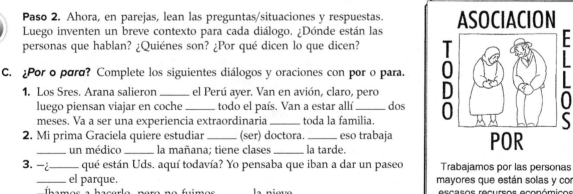

ASOCIACION TODO ELLOS POR

Trabajamos por las personas mayores que están solas y con escasos recursos económicos

AYÚDANOS, NO ES POSIBLE SIN TI

Para más información llama al teléfono 907 98 91 15, de 18.00 a 20.00 h. tardes, martes y viernes

CAJAMADRID, SUC. 1028 C/C 6000854579

TODO POR ELLOS es una asociación no gubernamental inscrita en el Registro de Asociaciones del Ministerio del Interior con el número 160.589

Mario Vargas Llosa

Mario Vargas Llosa (Arequipa, Perú, 1936–) es uno de los escritores e intelectuales de la lengua castellana[a] más famosos e influyentes de las últimas generaciones. Su reconocimiento[b] es mundial. Novelista y ensayista, Vargas Llosa ha recibido[c] numerosos premios,[d] entre ellos el Premio Nobel de Literatura. El tono de sus obras va de lo trágico a lo más cómico, pero sus obras más importantes se enfocan en el abuso del poder[e] en los gobiernos,[f] especialmente las dictaduras.

 ¿Puede Ud. nombrar a algunos escritores de su país que se consideran influyentes en todo el mundo?

[a]española [b]recognition [c]ha... has received [d]awards, prizes [e]power [f]governments

Mario Vargas Llosa, quien recibió el Premio Nobel de Literatura en 2010

D. Más sobre Mario Vargas Llosa. Complete las siguientes oraciones con la preposición apropiada para saber más sobre este importante escritor peruano.

1. Mario Vargas Llosa recibió el Premio Nobel por / para sus novelas.
2. Es obvio que para / por el año 2010 Vargas Llosa ya (*already*) era famoso.
3. Para / Por este escritor, la estabilidad democrática de Latinoamérica es muy importante.
4. Para / Por ser escritor, Vargas Llosa es muy famoso para / por mucha gente.
5. Para / Por sus ensayos, podemos saber de sus preocupaciones políticas y sociales.
6. Para / Por muchos críticos y expertos, Vargas Llosa es uno de los mejores escritores de la lengua castellana de los últimos cincuenta años.

 E. Entreviste a su profesor(a). Hágale preguntas a su profesor(a) para saber la siguiente información.

1. la tarea para mañana y para la semana que viene
2. lo que hay que estudiar para el próximo examen
3. si para él/ella son interesantes o aburridas las ciencias
4. lo que piensa de la pronunciación de Uds., para ser principiantes (*beginners*)
5. qué deben hacer Uds. para mejorar su pronunciación del español
6. cuánto tiempo deben Uds. dedicar todos los días a practicar el español

F. Preguntas con *por* y *para*

Paso 1. Complete las siguientes frases con **por** o **para**.

1. prepararse _____ una profesión
2. estar nervioso _____ algo
3. trabajar _____ una compañía
4. hablar _____ teléfono con frecuencia
5. tener algo que hacer _____ mañana
6. pasear _____ el *campus*
7. tener algo que comprar _____ su casa/apartamento/cuarto
8. la idea de pagar mil dólares _____ un abrigo
9. tener algo que hacer _____ alguien
10. la idea de vivir en un sitio _____ toda la vida

 Paso 2. Ahora, en parejas, hagan y contesten preguntas, usando las frases del **Paso 1**.

MODELO: prepararse _____ una profesión →
¿Sabes para qué profesión estás preparándote?

Un poco de todo

A. Lengua y cultura: De turismo por el Perú

Paso 1. Complete the following passage with the correct form of the words in parentheses, as suggested by context. When two possibilities are given in parentheses, select the correct word. **¡OJO!** As you conjugate the verbs in this activity, use the **tú** command when you see *comm:* in front of the infinitive. For other verbs, you will decide whether to use the present indicative or subjunctive, the preterite or imperfect, or simply the infinitive. Context will indicate which forms to use.

Machu Picchu, la ciudad imperial de los incas durante el siglo XV (1400–1500)

¿Te interesa la historia? ¿Te (gusta / gustan[1]) los lugares espirituales? Entonces,[a] (*comm:* ir[2]) a Machu Picchu. (Son / Están[3]) las ruinas de una antigua ciudad inca que (es / está[4]) en (el / la[5]) corazón de los Andes, cerca de Cusco. No es fácil (llegue / llegar[6]) a ese lugar. (Por / Para[7]) eso (se / la[8]) llaman «la ciudad perdida[b] de los incas.» En el pasado, (ser[9]) a la vez[c] lugar de refugio y de vacaciones de los reyes[d] y nobles incas. Después de la llegada de los españoles, esta ciudad fue ignorada y (estar[10]) oculta[e] hasta que Hiram Bingham, un profesor y explorador estadounidense, la (encontrar[11]) en 1911. (Hacer[12]) un siglo[f] que Machu Picchu es un sitio famoso y un atractivo destino turístico (por / para[13]) muchas personas de todas partes del mundo.

Pero Machu Picchu no (es / está[14]) el único lugar interesante que se puede visitar en el Perú. Si visitas (el / la[15]) país con tiempo suficiente, te recomendamos que (hacer[16]) una excursión (por / para[17]) la selva.[g] También (*comm:* viajar[18]) al desierto de Atacama, el lugar más árido (en el / del[19]) mundo. Además,[h] (*comm:* pasar[20]) unos días en las playas de Mancora y Cabo Blanco. (*Comm:* Hacer[21]) un viaje fabuloso que (nunca / siempre[22]) vas a olvidar. Esperamos que (*tú:* poder[23]) ir con alguien muy especial para (ti / tú[24]). (Sabemos / Conocemos[25]) que el Perú (les / los[26]) va a fascinar.

[a]*Then* [b]*lost* [c]*a... at the same time* [d]*kings* [e]*hidden* [f]*century* [g]*jungle* [h]*In addition*

Paso 2. Comprensión. Las siguientes oraciones son falsas. Corríjalas con información de la lectura.

1. El actual rey del Perú vive en Machu Picchu.
2. Es fácil llegar a Machu Picchu.
3. Hiram Bingham fue un explorador español.
4. Machu Picchu es el único sitio de interés turístico en el Perú.
5. Para los turistas, no es nada atractivo viajar al Perú.

Paso 3. Ahora, en parejas, piensen en algún lugar considerado sagrado o espiritual en su *campus*, ciudad, estado o país. ¿Quiénes lo consideran así (*that way*)? ¿Por qué? ¿Lo visita mucha gente? ¿De dónde son esos visitantes?

B. A la profesora Ortega le duele la cabeza

Paso 1. Haga oraciones completas en el siguiente diálogo. Los verbos pueden estar en el presente de indicativo, el presente de subjuntivo o el pretérito. Cuando sea necesario, añada pronombres del complemento indirecto, la palabra **que** y el **se** accidental. Use **por** o **para** según el contexto.

DOCTORA BENÍTEZ: ¿Cuánto tiempo hace / doler[1] la cabeza?

PROFESORA ORTEGA: Hace una semana / doler[2]. Tener[3] que corregir muchos exámenes hoy y ser[4] necesario / (yo) leer[5] mucho.

DOCTORA BENÍTEZ: ¿Tener[6] algún accidente? ¿Chocar[7] contra algo?

PROFESORA ORTEGA: No.

DOCTORA BENÍTEZ: ¿Cuánto tiempo hace / ir[8] al oculista[a]?

PROFESORA ORTEGA: No acordarse.[9] La verdad es / olvidarme[10] hacer una cita.

DOCTORA BENÍTEZ: Entonces[b] recomendarle[11] / ir[12] al oculista en seguida. También sugerirle[13] / dejar[14] de leer tanto (por / para)[15] unos días y / tomar[16] aspirinas (por / para)[17] el dolor de cabeza.

[a]*eye doctor* [b]*Then*

Paso 2. Comprensión. Conteste las siguientes preguntas.

1. ¿Qué problemas tiene la profesora Ortega?
2. ¿Qué cree la doctora Benítez que está causando el dolor de cabeza de su paciente?
3. ¿Por qué no fue al oculista la profesora Ortega?
4. ¿Que recomienda la doctora Benítez que haga la profesora?

Paso 3. Ahora, en parejas, inventen un diálogo sobre uno de los personajes de los dibujos de las páginas 416 o 419 o sobre una de las siguientes situaciones.

1. Rodolfo sufre muchas presiones a causa de los exámenes finales. Está muy nervioso y no puede dormir. Además (*On top of it all*), la computadora se le falló hoy.
2. Un vecinó dejó el coche delante del garaje de Laura y ahora ella no puede sacar su coche. Tiene una cita importante en el *campus*. Es posible que llegue a la universidad a pie, pero Laura no tiene tiempo de caminar.
3. Anita quiere despedirse de un amigo, porque ella tiene una cita con su novio en media hora. Pero el amigo sigue hablando y hablando. Claro, se entiende, porque a él se le murió la abuela hace poco, pero...

En su comunidad

Entreviste a una persona hispana de su universidad o ciudad sobre lo que más les causa estrés a él y a otras personas de su comunidad.

PREGUNTAS POSIBLES

- ¿Cuáles son los problemas que más les preocupan a Ud. y a su familia o a sus amigos? ¿Hay alguno que les cause más estrés que las otras?
- Si vive en una ciudad grande, ¿son el tráfico y el estacionamiento problemas para Ud.?
- ¿Qué presiones tiene la gente joven de su familia o comunidad? ¿Les preocupa su acceso a la universidad? ¿Por qué?
- ¿Qué actividades hace Ud. para relajarse (*relax*)?
- ¿Es Ud. una persona torpe o distraída? ¿Se le olvida hacer unas cosas o pierde cosas con bastante frecuencia? ¿Tiene accidentes relacionados con el estrés?

SALU2

«¡Ay, qué estrés!» Segmento 2

Antes de mirar

Indique todas las cosas que Ud. asocia con las supersticiones o creencias (*beliefs*). ¿Cree Ud. en alguna?

_____ los amuletos
_____ pasar por debajo de una escalera (*ladder*)
_____ un gato negro
_____ cruzar los dedos
_____ un trébol (*clover*) de cuatro hojas
_____ rezar (*to pray*) a Dios
_____ otro

Ana le tiene cariño a (*is fond of*) este objeto que le regaló su abuela: « ...sin darme cuenta (*without realizing it*) lo toco cuando estoy nerviosa. Y como creo que tienes envidia de mí, le pedí a mi mamá que me mandara (*to send*) uno para ti».

Este segmento

Laura entrevista a varios jóvenes mexicanos sobre sus supersticiones y creencias. Luego Ana le da un objeto especial a Víctor.

Vocabulario del segmento

podría hacerse rico/a	could become rich	**encomendarse a Dios (encomiendo)**	to entrust (oneself) to God
las horas punta	rush hours	**fuerte**	hard
dispuesto/a	ready and willing	**San Miguel Arcángel**	St. Michael the Archangel
invertir (invierto) (i)	to invest	**proteger (protejo)**	to protect
evitar	to avoid	**contra todo mal**	against all evil
mejorar	to improve		
la fe	**la religión**		
prevenir (like **venir**)	to prevent		

Fragmento del guion

Bueno, yo creo que aquí sí se van a reír porque sí tengo muchas cosas que, entre comillas,[a] me ayudan a pasar mis exámenes y dentro de ellas están los amuletos y mis creencias religiosas personales, no que... Bueno, aquí se van a percatar[b] que son bastantes[c] cosas que significan muchas cosas en chino, este, hindú, este, en hebreo, este tibetano, cristiano, este... O sea[d] viene un poquito de todo, que es como que... una protección general hacia[e] lo que... en general, no tanto para la escuela como para la vida diaria.

[a]entre... *in quotation marks* [b]*notice* [c]*quite a lot of* [d]O... *That is* [e]*toward*

Después de mirar

A. ¿Está claro? Las siguientes oraciones son falsas. Corríjalas.

1. La mayoría de los estudiantes entrevistados es supersticiosa.
2. Ninguno de los estudiantes del reportaje es religioso.
3. Es obvio que Víctor es supersticioso.
4. Ana dice que tiene un amuleto que le pertenecía (*used to belong*) a su abuela.

B. Un poco más. Haga una lista de todos los objetos, amuletos y acciones que mencionan los estudiantes supersticiosos del reportaje.

C. Y ahora, Uds. En parejas, hablen de si Uds. son supersticiosos o no. Si lo son, ¿qué amuletos tienen o qué hacen Uds. para tener buena suerte y evitar la mala suerte? Si no son supersticiosos, expliquen por qué.

A LEER

Antes de leer

¿Qué cuestiones (*topics*) sociales son motivo de ansiedad entre los estudiantes de su universidad? ¿y entre la gente de su ciudad, estado o país?

Lectura cultural: El Perú
Las preocupaciones de los peruanos

Como ocurre en todos los países, hay múltiples cuestiones que les causan ansiedad a los peruanos. El tema de la educación es una de estas cuestiones. La educación pública requiere una mayor inversión[a] de dinero para que[b] el sistema sea más efectivo y sirva a todos. Además,[c] se necesita que los maestros[d] tengan mejores salarios.

El tema de los salarios es otra de las serias preocupaciones de muchos peruanos. En el Perú existe la Remuneración Mínima, que es el salario mínimo establecido[e] por la ley.[f] Es el salario que recibe gran parte de los trabajadores[g] peruanos, pero que para muchos de ellos no resulta suficiente para cubrir[h] sus gastos cotidianos.[i]

[a]*investment* [b]*para... so that* [c]*In addition* [d]*teachers* [e]*established* [f]*law* [g]*workers* [h]*cover* [i]*daily*

En otros países hispanos

- **La emigración** Casi todos los países hispanohablantes han sufrido[a] condiciones políticas y económicas que provocaron la emigración de su gente. Con frecuencia los hispanohablantes emigran a otro país donde se habla español. Este es el caso de España. Durante la Guerra[b] Civil española (1936–1939), muchos españoles se exiliaron a México y la Argentina. En cambio,[c] en la última década del siglo[d] XX y la primera del XXI, España, por su bonanza económica, se convirtió en un país receptor de inmigrantes latinoamericanos. Sin embargo, con la crisis reciente de la economía española, muchos jóvenes españoles volvieron a mirar a Latinoamérica como una opción.

- **En todo el mundo hispanohablante** Según las creencias populares, los siguientes acontecimientos[e] traen mala suerte.
  - romper un espejo[f] (¡Esto significa siete años de mala suerte!)
  - pasar por debajo de una escalera[g]

[a]*han... have experienced* [b]*War* [c]*En... On the other hand* [d]*century* [e]*events* [f]*mirror* [g]*ladder*

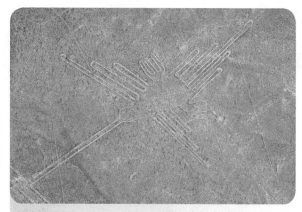

Una vista aérea de las increíbles líneas de Nazca, Perú

- derramar[h] sal (Hay un «antídoto»: tirar[i] un poco de la sal derramada por encima del hombro[j] izquierdo.)
- cruzarse con un gato negro en el camino[k]
- los el martes 13

[h]*to spill* [i]*to throw* [j]*por... over the shoulder* [k]*path*

Un símbolo peruano: La herencia indígena

El imperio inca duró aproximadamente un siglo[a] (XV). Fue el mayor dominio territorial en toda América, anterior a[b] la llegada de los españoles. Pero los incas no fueron ni[c] el primer pueblo ni el único[d] en dejar su huella[e] en lo que es hoy el Perú, como lo demuestran las impresionantes líneas de la cultura nazca (entre los siglos I y VII). Su propósito es todavía un misterio. En la actualidad, los pueblos indígenas tienen una importante presencia en el país. Se calcula que un 25% de la población peruana es amerindia. Algunas comunidades indígenas, como los quechuas y los aymaras, están extendidas por varios países andinos.

[a]*century* [b]*anterior... before* [c]*ni... ni neither ... nor* [d]*el... the only one* [e]*mark, footprint*

COMPRENSIÓN

1. ¿Qué cuestiones les causan ansiedad a los peruanos?
2. ¿Qué es la Remuneración Mínima?
3. ¿Cuáles son tres de las supersticiones que en el mundo hispano se asocian con la mala suerte?
4. ¿A qué países emigran los hispanohablantes en tiempos de necesidad?
5. Dé el nombre de dos pueblos amerindios en el Perú en la actualidad.
6. Dé el nombre de dos culturas precolombinas que existían en lo que hoy es el Perú.

Y ahora, Uds.

Ahora que saben algo de las causas del estrés entre las personas peruanas y de otros países hispanohablantes, compárenlas a las (*those*) que se sufren en este país o en su país de origen. ¿Son muy similares? Den detalles.

Del mundo hispano

Antes de leer

¿Qué opina su profesor(a) de su trabajo en la universidad? Lea las siguientes preguntas y contéstelas como Ud. cree que su profesor(a) las contestaría (*would answer*). Luego entrévistelo/la para saber lo que piensa.

1. ¿Qué aspecto de su trabajo le gusta más? ¿Cuál le gusta menos?
2. ¿Qué es lo más aburrido de su trabajo? ¿Lo más interesante?
3. ¿Se siente frustrado/a con su trabajo a veces? ¿Qué hace entonces (*then*)?

Lectura: «OH», de Mario Benedetti

Jefe[a]
usté está aburrido
aburrido de veras[b]
hace veintiocho años
5 que sabe sus asientos[c]
que comprueba los saldos[d]
y revuelve[e] el café.

Está aburrido
jefe
10 se le nota[f] en los ojos
en la voz[g]
en las órdenes

en el paso[h]
en las mangas[i]
15 en los setenta rubros[j]
de letra redondilla.[k]

Jefe
usté está aburrido
nadie lo sabe
20 nadie.

Pero ahora que está solo
ahora que no ven Ellos
desahóguese[l]
grite[m]

25 discuta[n]
diga mierda[ñ]
dé golpes[o] en la mesa
vuélvase insoportable[p]
por favor
30 diga no
diga no muchas veces
hasta quedarse ronco.[q]

No cuesta nada[r]
jefe
35 haga la prueba.[s]

[a]*Boss* [b]*de... truly* [c]*ledger entries* [d]*comprueba... you check the balance sheets* [e]*stir* [f]*se... it's obvious* [g]*voice* [h]*el... your way of walking* [i]*little errors* [j]*headings (in a spreadsheet)* [k]*rounded* [l]*let it out* [m]*scream* [n]*argue* [ñ]*shit* [o]*dé... slam your fist* [p]*vuélvase... became unbearable* [q]*quedarse... you get hoarse* [r]*No... You can do it (lit. It doesn't cost anything)* [s]*haga... give it a try*

Comprensión

A. Para comprender el poema. Seleccione la opción correcta y explique su respuesta.

1. Este poema fue escrito por / para un jefe.
2. Al jefe le gusta / no le gusta su trabajo.
3. En la segunda estrofa (*stanza*) del poema, el poeta dice que la actitud del jefe es visible / invisible.
4. En la tercera estrofa, el poeta dice que la actitud del jefe es visible / invisible.
5. El poeta le recomienda al jefe que exprese / no exprese sus sentimientos.

B. Para interpretar el poema. Conteste las siguientes preguntas según su opinión.

1. ¿Son contradictorias las estrofas 2 y 3?
2. ¿Cree Ud. que todas las personas que hacen el mismo trabajo por veintiocho años vayan a sentirse tan aburridas como este jefe? ¿Por qué sí o por qué no?
3. ¿Muestra el poeta una actitud de intolerancia o muestra compasión hacia el jefe?
4. ¿Por qué cree Ud. que el poeta le habla al jefe usando la forma **usté** en vez de **usted**?

La depresión entre los adolescentes

Antes de escuchar

Piense en una persona que Ud. conoce (o en una persona famosa) que sufre o ha sufrido (*has suffered*) de depresión. ¿Cómo se siente o sentía? ¿Qué hizo para mejorarse?

> #### Vocabulario **para escuchar**
>
> | | | | |
> |---|---|---|---|
> | **la tristeza** | sadness | **deprimido/a** | depressed |
> | **el estado de ánimo** | mood | **la desesperanza** | hopelessness |
> | **el comportamiento** | behavior | **emocionar** | to get (*someone*) excited |
> | **enfrentarse a** | to face | | about (*something*) |
> | **hacer frente a** | to face up to | **el peso** | weight |
> | **el aprendizaje** | learning | **evitar** | to avoid |
> | **el acoso** | harassment; bullying | **tratable** | treatable |

Después de escuchar

A. Hablando de la depresión. ¿Qué dice el Dr. Carvajal sobre la depresión? Todas de las siguientes oraciones son falsas. Corríjalas.

1. Todo el mundo (*Everyone*) sufre de depresión.
2. La depresión tiene solo una causa.
3. Uno de los síntomas de la depresión es querer estar siempre con los amigos y la familia.
4. La depresión es una de las enfermedades menos tratables.

B. Más detalles. Conteste las siguientes preguntas.

1. ¿Cuáles son tres de las causas de la depresión?
2. ¿Cuáles son tres de los síntomas de la depresión?
3. Según el Dr. Carvajal, ¿qué es lo primero que se debe hacer cuando un joven está deprimido?

PRODUCCIÓN PERSONAL

¡Ahora, yo!

A. Use de modelo las preguntas y respuestas de la página 415 de este capítulo para hablar de las presiones que Ud. sufre y lo que hace para reducir su nivel de estrés.

B. Filme dos entrevistas con personas de su universidad (estudiantes, profesores o personal universitario) que hablan del estrés que sufren y sus causas.

A ESCRIBIR

Un ensayo sobre las presiones de la vida estudiantil

A lo largo de este capítulo ha habido (*there have been*) muchas oportunidades para hablar de las causas del estrés que sufren las personas. Ahora Ud. va a concentrarse en las presiones de los estudiantes de su universidad, para escribir un artículo para el periódico universitario.

Preparar

Paso 1. Llene (*Fill in*) la siguiente tabla con las presiones que Ud. cree que lo/la afectan más. Luego entreviste a dos compañeros para saber las opiniones de ellos.

Las presiones...	académicas	sociales	financieras	familiares
Ud.				
compañero/a 1				
compañero/a 2				

Paso 2. Ahora, analice la información del **Paso 1,** saque algunas conclusiones y dé algunos consejos. ¿Cómo es que las presiones pueden afectar los estudios y la vida de un estudiante? ¿Qué pueden o deben hacer los estudiantes para prepararse o para aliviar estas presiones? Hay más ayuda en Connect.

Más ideas para su portafolio

- Incluya la imagen de un lugar al que (*to which*) Ud. puede volar con su mente para escaparse temporalmente (*temporarily*) de la realidad. Diga dónde está y descríbalo. ¿Lo conoce en personal o solo es un lugar que desea visitar?

- Haga una lista de las cosas que Ud. asocia con la buena suerte en su vida. Si Ud. no es nada supersticioso/a, puede hablar de las palabras que Ud. asocia con tres momentos agradables de su vida. Piense en eventos importantes o familiares, en canciones o lugares especiales, etcétera.

- Si ha estado jugando (*have been playing*) Practice Spanish: Study Abroad, en Quest 10 Ud. ayudó a su amigo cuando se cayó y se hizo daño en el brazo. Ahora imagine una situación parecida (*similar*) y escriba un guion entre un(a) médico/a y un(a) paciente que ha tenido otro tipo de accidente. ¿Qué pasó? ¿Cuáles son las heridas del paciente? ¿Qué consejos recibe? Interprete la situación en clase con un compañero o una compañera.

Sugerencia: You are now ready to play Quest 10 in **Practice Spanish: Study Abroad** (www.mhpractice.com).

EN RESUMEN En este capítulo

≣ILEARNSMART

Visit **www.connectspanish.com** to practice the vocabulary and grammar points covered in this chapter.

AFTER STUDYING THIS CHAPTER I CAN . . .

☐ talk about the typical things that cause stress in life (416)

☐ talk about accidents (420)

☐ use **hace** + time to express how something has been happening or how long ago it happened (423–424)

☐ express some actions as unexpected or unintended events (426–427)

☐ use **por** and **para** accurately in more contexts (430–432)

☐ recognize/describe at least 2–3 aspects of Peruvian cultures

Gramática en breve

33. Hace + time

hace = has/have been doing
> **hace** + time + **que** + present
> present + **desde hace** + time

hace = ago
> **hace** + time + **que** + preterite
> preterite + **hace** + time

34. Accidental se

a + noun + **se** + indirect object pronoun + verb + subject

(**a** + pronoun) **se** + indirect object pronoun + verb + subject

35. ¿Por o para?

por = reason, cause
> by / by means of   through/along
> because of / due to   during/in (time of day)
>
> for = in exchange for, for the sake of / on behalf of, in place of, for (period of time)

para = goal, purpose, destination
> in order to + inf.
>
> for = destined for / to be given to, by (future time), toward / in the direction of, to be used for, as compared with / in relation to others, in the employ of, in preparation for

Vocabulario

Los verbos

acabar	to finish; to run out of
quedar	to remain, be left

Repaso: olvidar, perder (pierdo)

Las presiones de la vida académica

la ansiedad	anxiety
los apuntes	notes (academic)
el despertador	alarm clock
el estrés	stress
el horario	schedule
el informe (oral/ escrito)	(oral/written) report
el plazo	deadline
la presión	pressure
el programa (del curso)	(course) syllabus
la prueba	quiz; test
la tarjeta de identificación	identification card
el trabajo	report, (piece of) work
el trabajo de tiempo completo/parcial	full-time/part-time job

Cognado: el calendario

Repaso: el examen, la llave, la nota, la tarea, el trabajo (work; job), la vida

devolver (like volver) (algo a alguien)	to return (something to someone)
estacionar	to park
estar bajo muchas presiones	to be under a lot of pressure
recoger (recojo)	to collect; to pick up
sacar (qu)	to get (grades)
sufrir (de)	to suffer
tener muchas presiones	to have a lot of stress

Repaso: acordarse (me acuerdo) (de), entregar (gu), llegar (gu) a tiempo / tarde, olvidar, tomar

Los accidentes

caer (caigo)	to fall; to drop
caerse	to fall down
chocar (qu) con/contra	to run into, bump against
equivocarse (qu) (de)	to make a mistake (with)
estar/ir distraído/a	to be distracted
hacerse daño	to hurt oneself
hacerse daño en	to hurt one's (body part)
lastimarse	to hurt (a body part)
levantarse con el pie izquierdo	to get up on the wrong side of the bed

ocurrir	to happen
pedir (pido) (i) disculpas	to apologize
pegar (gu)	to hit, strike
pegarse (gu) con/ contra	to run, bump into/against
romper(se)	to break
tener buena/mala suerte	to have good/bad luck, be (un)lucky

Repaso: doler (duele), pasar

Disculpa. Discúlpame.	Pardon me. I'm sorry. (*fam.*)
Disculpe. Discúlpeme.	Pardon me. I'm sorry. (*form.*)
Fue sin querer.	I didn't mean (to do) it.
Lo siento (mucho).	I'm (very) sorry.

Repaso: perdón

Los adjetivos

distraído/a	absentminded, distracted
escrito/a	written
estresado/a	stressed out, under stress
torpe	clumsy
último/a	last, final
universitario/a	(of the) university

Cognados: académico/a, (in)flexible, oral

Otros sustantivos

el desastre	disaster
las escaleras	stairs
la luz (*pl.* luces)	light
la taza	cup

Palabras adicionales

hace + *time* + **que** + *preterite* *preterite* + **hace** + *time*	} ago
hace + *time* + **que** + *present* *present* + **desde hace** + *time*	} to have been (*doing something*) for (*time*)
-mente	-ly (*adverbial suffix*)
por	by
por Dios	for heaven's sake
por ejemplo	for example
por primera/última vez	for the first/last time
por si acaso	just in case
¡por supuesto!	of course!
por todas partes	everywhere
¡qué + *adj.*!	how + *adj.*!
¡qué + *noun*!	what (a) + *noun*!

Repaso: gracias por, para, por (because of; through; in; for), **por eso, por favor, por fin, por la mañana/ tarde/noche, por lo general, por lo menos, por teléfono**

Vocabulario personal

15

La naturaleza y el medio ambiente° La... *Nature and the environment*

www.connectspanish.com

En este capítulo

La Pampa, la inmensa pradera (*grassland*) que se extiende por varias provincias de la Argentina, el Uruguay y el Brasil

PARAGUAY

Río Paraná

Cataratas del Iguazú

BRASIL

ARGENTINA

• Córdoba

Mendoza •

URUGUAY

Buenos* Aires

• Montevideo

LA PAMPA

Río de la Plata

CHILE

OCÉANO ATLÁNTICO

Cabo de Hornos

OCÉANO PACÍFICO

LA ARGENTINA

41 millones de habitantes

EL URUGUAY

3,5 (tres y medio) millones de habitantes

- La Argentina y el Uruguay son dos países del Cono Sur, el triángulo de territorio sudamericano que está al sur del Trópico de Capricornio.

- El Uruguay y la Argentina están unidos por la historia y la cultura. Las capitales de estos países están en el inmenso estuario del Río de la Plata.

- ¿Cómo llega Ud. al *campus*? ¿Necesita Ud. un coche para llegar a la universidad o al trabajo?

- ¿Le gusta a Ud. estar en contacto con la naturaleza? ¿Qué actividades hace cuando está al aire libre?

- ¿Hay mucha contaminación en el área donde Ud. vive? ¿Es la contaminación un problema que le preocupa?

GABRIELA ROMANO ACOSTA CONTESTA LAS PREGUNTAS.

- Voy en colectivo[a] al trabajo. Trabajo en la Facultad de Farmacia y Bioquímica de la Universidad de Buenos Aires, que está en la Ciudad Universitaria. Es más práctico llegar en transporte público porque el estacionamiento[b] es un problema.

- ¡Me encanta estar en contacto con la naturaleza! Mis abuelos tienen una finca[c] cerca de la ciudad de Córdoba. Cuando los visito, paso mucho tiempo al aire libre, haciendo tareas agrícolas[d] o simplemente caminando y disfrutando[e] del aire limpio.

- ¡Claro! En Buenos Aires hay problemas de contaminación porque es una ciudad inmensa. Y sí, la contaminación me preocupa, especialmente la calidad del aire que respiramos todos los días.

[a]autobús [b]parking [c]farm [d]agricultural [e]enjoying

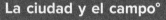
La ciudad y el campo° — *countryside*

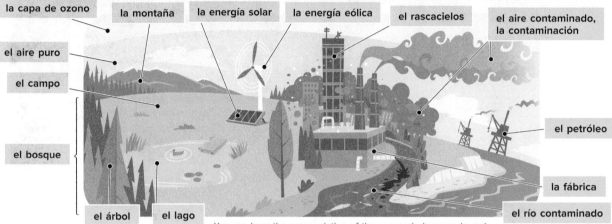

la capa de ozono · la montaña · la energía solar · la energía eólica · el rascacielos · el aire contaminado, la contaminación

el aire puro · el campo · el bosque · el árbol · el lago

el petróleo · la fábrica · el río contaminado

You can hear the pronunciation of theme vocabulary words and phrases in the Connect eBook.

Los recursos naturales° — Los... *Natural resources*

la energía	energy
eólica	wind
renovable	renewable
el medio ambiente	environment
la naturaleza	nature
el reciclaje	recycling
la Tierra	Earth

Cognados: la energía eléctrica/nuclear/solar, el planeta

bello/a	beautiful
contaminado/a	contaminated, polluted
puro/a	pure

Los animales

la ballena	whale
el caballo	horse
la especie (en peligro de extinción)	(endangered) species
el gato	cat
el pájaro	bird
el perro	dog
el pez (*pl.* peces)	fish
el toro	bull
la vaca	cow

Cognados: el elefante, el gorila

doméstico/a	domesticated, tame
salvaje	wild

El desarrollo° — El... *Development*

el agricultor / la agricultora	farmer
la agricultura	farming, agriculture
el campesino / la campesina	peasant
el delito	crime
la finca	farm
la falta	lack; absence
el gobierno	government
la población	population
el ritmo de la vida	pace of life
el servicio	service
el transporte	transportation
acelerado/a	fast, accelerated
denso/a	dense
público/a	public
acabar	to finish, run out (of); to use up completely
conservar	to save, conserve
construir*	to build
contaminar	to pollute
desarrollar	to develop
destruir (*like* construir)	to destroy
fabricar (qu)	to manufacture
proteger (protejo)	to protect
reciclar	to recycle

---

*Note the present indicative conjugation of construir: **construyo, construyes, construye, construimos, construís, construyen.**

Comunicación

A. ¿En la ciudad o en el campo?

	LA CIUDAD	EL CAMPO
1. El aire es más puro; hay menos contaminación.	☐	☐
2. La naturaleza es más bella.	☐	☐
3. El ritmo de la vida es más acelerado.	☐	☐
4. Hay más delitos.	☐	☐
5. Los servicios profesionales (financieros, legales...) son más accesibles.	☐	☐
6. Hay pocos medios de transporte públicos.	☐	☐
7. Hay menos densidad de poblacion.	☐	☐
8. Hay falta de viviendas.	☐	☐

Así se dice

la fábrica = la factoría
la finca = la granja, el rancho, la estancia

El árbol is also called **el palo** in Mexico, Central America, and the Caribbean. The names of at least two California cities contain the word **palo:** Palo Alto and Palos Verdes.

B. Definiciones. Defina las siguientes palabras en español.

MODELO: el agricultor → Es el dueño de una finca.

1. la fábrica   **4.** la finca   **7.** el río
2. el campesino   **5.** la naturaleza   **8.** el rascacielos
3. la falta   **6.** la población   **9.** el agricultor

Nota **cultural**

Programas medioambientales

En muchos países del mundo es necesario equilibrar[a] la protección del medio ambiente con los objetivos del desarrollo económico. En muchos casos, la explotación de recursos naturales es la mayor fuente de ingreso[b] para la economía de un país. Los gobiernos latinoamericanos están conscientes de la necesidad de proteger el medio ambiente y de conservar los recursos naturales. Los siguientes son algunos de los muchos programas medioambientales que existen en los países hispanohablantes.

- En las grandes ciudades de varios países (Bolivia, Chile, Colombia, el Ecuador, Honduras, México y Venezuela, entre otros) se han establecido[c] programas de restricción vehicular, que tratan de regular la cantidad de tráfico en determinadas horas o días. Se basan en un sistema que limita el uso de un vehículo según su placa.[d] Además de[e] reducir el tráfico diario en la ciudad, estos programas pueden mejorar[f] la calidad del aire.
- En muchos países hispanohablantes (la Argentina, el Uruguay, España y México, entre otros) existen programas de reciclaje, basados en sistemas de separación de basura. Es decir que, según su clase, los materiales se depositan en contenedores[g] de colores diferentes: el papel y el cartón[h] en un

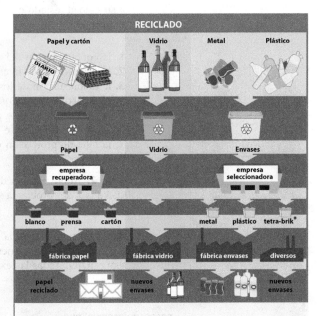

contenedor; el vidrio,[i] el metal y el plástico en otro; y en algunos casos los desperdicios de materia orgánica,[j] en otro.

🗣 **¿Qué programas medioambientales hay en su ciudad o estado?**

[a]to balance [b]fuente... source of income [c]se... have been established [d]license plate [e]Además... Besides [f]improve [g]containers, receptacles [h]cardboard

[i]glass [j]los... organic waste matter

---

*Tetra-brik *is a type of carton packaging used for beverages such as milk and fruit juices. It is a regional term, used in Spain, Argentina, and other parts of the Spanish-speaking world.*

C. **¿Cuánto sabe de los animales?**

En parejas, clasifiquen los siguientes animales según las categorías de la tabla. ¡OJO! Algunos pueden estar en más de un grupo. Luego traten de añadir otros animales en cada categoría.

Los animales:
el águila, el camello, el cocodrilo, el cóndor, la cucaracha, el delfín, el hipopótamo, el jaguar, la jirafa, el león, el mosquito, el orangután, la ostra, la rata, el rinoceronte, el tigre

Animales...			
domésticos	**salvajes**	**en peligro de extinción**	**insectos**

D. **Problemas medioambientales**

Paso 1. En parejas, indiquen cuáles de los siguientes problemas y temas afectan a su ciudad, estado o país. Añadan por lo menos un tema que Uds. consideren importante.

AFECTA A...	MI CIUDAD	MI ESTADO	MI PAÍS
1. la contaminación del aire	☐	☐	☐
2. la destrucción de la capa de ozono	☐	☐	☐
3. la deforestación de los bosques	☐	☐	☐
4. el desarrollo de energías renovables	☐	☐	☐
5. la falta de transporte público adecuado	☐	☐	☐
6. el ritmo acelerado de la vida	☐	☐	☐
7. la falta de protección de los espacios naturales	☐	☐	☐
8. ¿ ?	☐	☐	☐

Paso 2. Ahora escojan dos de estos temas y explíquenle a la clase una de las causas del problema y una de las cosas que es necesario hacer para resolverlo.

E. **Opiniones.** Con toda la clase, comenten las siguientes opiniones. Pueden usar las siguientes expresiones para aclarar (*clarify*) su posición con respecto a cada tema. ¡OJO! Todas las expresiones requieren el uso del subjuntivo.

> **Vocabulario útil**
>
> **Es / Me/Nos parece** { necesario/esencial que...
> importantísimo que...
> absurdo que... }
> **Me opongo / Nos oponemos a que...** I am / We are against . . .
> **No creo/creemos que...**

1. Para conservar energía debemos reciclar todo lo posible.

2. Es mejor calentar (*to heat*) las casas con estufas de leña (*wood stoves*) que con gas o electricidad.

3. Se debe crear más parques urbanos, estatales y nacionales.

4. La protección del medio ambiente no debe impedir la explotación de los recursos naturales.

5. Para evitar la contaminación urbana, debemos limitar el uso de los coches a ciertos días de la semana.

6. El gobierno debe ponerles multas (*fines*) muy graves a las compañías e individuos que causan la contaminación.

F. Anuncios medioambientales

Paso 1. Lea los siguientes anuncios y conteste las preguntas.

ᵃ*water heater*

1. ¿Qué cosa sugieren los anuncios que ahorremos?
2. ¿Puede Ud. explicar el uso de la imagen de la bombilla (*lightbulb*) en el anuncio de la izquierda?
3. ¿Qué significa en inglés «MAYOR AHORRO = MEJOR PLANETA»? ¿Con qué palabras juega el anuncio?
4. ¿Qué imagen predomina en el anuncio de Plan Solar? ¿Por qué es apropiada esta imagen?

Paso 2. En grupos, hablen de lo que Uds. hacen personalmente para conservar los recursos naturales. Deben considerar las siguientes ideas y añadir otras. Luego díganle a la clase algunas de las ideas interesantes de su grupo.

1. el reciclaje
2. apagar/endender las luces
3. caminar en vez de manejar (*instead of driving*)
4. pasear en bicicleta
5. consumir lo que se produce localmente
6. usar menos papel

Algo sobre...

la Pampa

La Pampa es una inmensa región sudamericana de praderasᵃ que abarcaᵇ desde el sur del Brasil, casi todo el Uruguay y parte considerable del territorio argentino. La palabra «pampa», que viene de la lengua quechua, significa llanura.ᶜ

La Pampa se divide en subregiones según el clima y la ubicación.ᵈ Pero en general es una zona dedicada a la explotaciónᵉ del ganadoᶠ y de la agricultura, especialmente de granos como la soja, el trigoᵍ y el maíz.

¿Qué zona de este país se dedica especialmente a la explotación del ganado y al cultivo de granos?

ᵃ*grasslands* ᵇ*includes* ᶜ*plain* ᵈ*location* ᵉ*development*
ᶠ*cattle* ᵍ*wheat*

La Pampa

La Pampa: un territorio multinacional

Los vehículos

la gasolinera / la estación de servicio

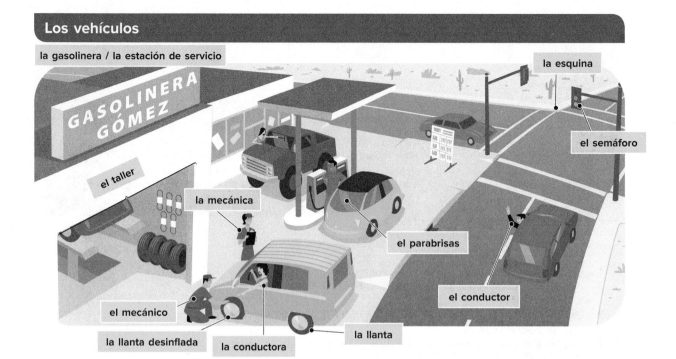

- la esquina
- el semáforo
- el taller
- la mecánica
- el parabrisas
- el conductor
- el mecánico
- la llanta
- la llanta desinflada
- la conductora

la acera	sidewalk	arrancar (qu)	to start up (a car)
la autopista	freeway, interstate	arreglar	to fix, repair
la avenida	avenue	chocar (qu) con	to run into, collide (with)
la calle	street	estacionar	to park
la camioneta	(mini)van	gastar (mucha/	to use (a lot of / little gas)
la carretera	highway	poca gasolina)	
la circulación, el tránsito	traffic	llenar	to fill (up)
el coche/carro (descapotable, híbrido, todoterreno)	(convertible, hybrid, all-terrain) car	manejar, conducir (conduzco)*	to drive
		obedecer (obedezco)*	to obey
el estacionamiento	parking place/lot	parar	to stop
los frenos	brakes	revisar el aceite	to check the oil
la licencia de manejar/conducir	driver's license	tocar (qu) la bocina	to honk the horn
la moto(cicleta)	motorcycle	Cognado: reparar	
el tanque	tank		

Cognados: el auto(móvil), la bicicleta, la gasolina, el SUV, el tráfico

Así se dice

el estacionamiento = el aparcamiento, el parking
la licencia de manejar/conducir = el carnet
   de conducir, el permiso de manejar
la llanta = la rueda

arrancar = encender el motor
doblar = voltear
estacionar = aparcar (Sp.), parquear (Col., Mex.)

There are many ways to express *car* in Spanish. You already know **el coche. El carro** is frequently used. **El automóvil,** or simply **el auto,** is perhaps the most generic word, understood in all parts of the Spanish-speaking world.

---

*Like the verb **cono**cer, **condu**cir and **obede**cer have a spelling change in the **yo** form of the present indicative: **cono**zco, **condu**zco, **obede**zco. This spelling change is also used in all forms of the present subjunctive.

Comunicación

A. Definiciones

Paso 1. Empareje las definiciones con las palabras y frases.

DEFINICIONES	PALABRAS Y FRASES
1. _____ Se pone en el tanque.	**a.** los frenos
2. _____ Se llenan de aire.	**b.** la batería
3. _____ Lubrica el motor.	**c.** una llanta desinflada
4. _____ Es necesaria para arrancar el motor.	**d.** la gasolina
5. _____ Es necesario cambiarla cuando no tiene aire suficiente.	**e.** las llantas
f. el aceite
g. la licencia
6. _____ Se usan para parar el coche.
7. _____ El policía nos la pide cuando nos para el coche.

Paso 2. Ahora, siguiendo el modelo de las definiciones del **Paso 1**, dé una definición de las siguientes palabras.

1. el semáforo
2. la circulación
3. estacionar
4. el conductor
5. la gasolinera
6. la autopista
7. la carretera
8. el taller

B. Entrevista: Un conductor responsable

Paso 1. Entreviste a un compañero o una compañera para saber con qué frecuencia hace las siguientes cosas.

1. dejar la licencia en casa cuando va a manejar
2. acelerar (*to speed up*) cuando ve a un policía
3. tomar bebidas alcohólicas y después manejar
4. respetar el límite de velocidad o excederlo
5. estacionar el coche donde dice «Prohibido estacionar»
6. revisar el aceite y la batería
7. seguir todo derecho (*straight*) a toda velocidad cuando no sabe llegar a su destino
8. rebasar (*to pass*) tres carros a la vez (*at the same time*)
9. mandar mensajes electrónicos mientras maneja
10. no parar cuando el semáforo está en rojo

Paso 2. Ahora, con el mismo compañero o compañera, haga una lista de diez de las cosas que debe hacer —o no debe hacer— un conductor responsable. Pueden usar frases del **Paso 1**, si quieren.

MODELOS: Es importante que el conductor **respete** el límite de velocidad.
No exceda el límite de velocidad.
Respetar / No exceder el límite de velocidad.

Paso 3. Ahora analice Ud. sus propias (*own*) costumbres y cualidades como conductor(a). ¡Diga la verdad! ¿Es Ud. un conductor o una conductora responsable?

C. Intercambios.
En parejas, hagan y contesten preguntas sobre su coche o el (*that*) de su familia o de un amigo.

1. la marca (*make*) y el modelo de su coche y la placa (*license plate*) que tiene
2. dónde lo estaciona
3. cuánto tiempo hace que lo tiene y cuánto tiempo más piensa tenerlo
4. si el coche expresa su personalidad o si es solo un medio de transporte para Ud.
5. si el coche tiene nombre

Nota **comunicativa**

D. En el centro de Montevideo

Paso 1. Complete las siguientes instrucciones sobre cómo llegar a varios sitios en Montevideo.

Centro de Montevideo

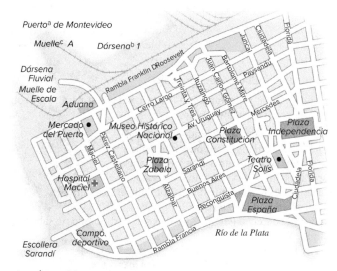

ᵃPort ᵇDock ᶜPier

1. **Del Museo Histórico Nacional al Mercado del Puerto:** Salga del Museo y vaya a la derecha / a la izquierda. Siga todo recto por / Doble en la Avenida Uruguay hasta la calle Pérez Castellano. Allí doble a la derecha / a la izquierda y siga / doble hasta la calle Cerro Largo. El Mercado está enfrente.
2. **Del Mercado del Puerto hasta la Plaza Zabala:** Saliendo del Mercado, tome la calle Pérez Castellano y doble / siga todo recto hasta llegar a la calle Mercedes. Allí, doble a la derecha / a la izquierda y siga hasta llegar a la Plaza.

Paso 2. Ahora dé Ud. las instrucciones sobre cómo llegar de la Plaza Zabala a la Plaza de la Constitución y de esa plaza a la Plaza España.

E. ¿Cómo se llega a... ?

Paso 1. En parejas, escriban o den verbalmente direcciones para ir desde su *campus* a los siguientes lugares. Usen mandatos con **tú**.

1. a un cine que está cerca del *campus*
2. al centro de la ciudad
3. a un centro comercial popular
4. a un restaurante bien conocido (*well-known*)

Paso 2. Ahora lean las direcciones del **Paso 1** a la clase pero sin dar el nombre del destino. La clase va a tratar de adivinar (*guess*) el destino.

 «EcoSalu2» Segmento 1

Antes de mirar

Mucha gente toma medidas (*measures*) para reducir el consumo de energía en su casa. Indique cuáles de las siguientes medidas toma Ud. o su familia.

☐ usar bombillas (*light bulbs*) de bajo consumo
☐ mantener baja la temperatura de la calefacción en la casa
☐ mantener apagadas (*turned off*) las luces que no son necesarias
☐ no calentar (*to heat*) el agua de la piscina (alberca)
☐ instalar páneles solares en la casa

Laura enseña esta casa que fue remodelada para producir menos impacto medioambiental.

Este segmento

En este segmento Víctor y Ana introducen el tema del medio ambiente y Laura presenta un reportaje sobre una casa que fue remodelada para hacerla más ecológica.

Vocabulario del segmento

el nivel	level	**no ha pagado**	has not paid one
mejorar	to improve	**ni un centavo**	penny
en cuanto a	as far as . . . is concerned	**contar (cuento) con**	to rely on
lograr	to achieve	**asegurar**	to ensure
el techo	roof	**el ahorro**	saving
quedan cubiertas	are covered	**el hogar**	home, household

Después de mirar

A. ¿Está claro? Las siguientes oraciones son falsas. Corríjalas.

1. La casa está al norte de Colorado.
2. Es una casa nueva.
3. Las casas viejas nunca son estructuralmente sólidas.
4. Los páneles solares no son suficientes para cubrir (*cover*) las necesidades de esta familia
5. Esta familia paga poco dinero a la compañía eléctrica.

B. Un poco más. Conteste las siguientes preguntas.

1. ¿Qué le pasa a Ana hoy?
2. Según Víctor, ¿dónde no debe vivir Ana?
3. ¿Qué medidas de ahorro energético ha tomado (*has taken*) la familia de la casa remodelada?

 C. Y ahora, Uds. En parejas, hablen sobre las medidas de ahorro energético que ha tomado (*has taken*) su universidad. ¿Son suficientes? ¿Qué otras medidas son recomendables para su *campus*?

¿Recuerda Ud.?

As you know, the Spanish present participle, like its English equivalent, does not change according to the subject of a sentence. Give the English equivalent of the following:

cantar: cantando   **beber: bebiendo**   **dormir: durmiendo**

Cecilia
Juan } está cantando, bebiendo, durmiendo.

In both English and Spanish, there is another kind of participle: the past participle. Like the present participle, it does not change its form when used as a verb. But it can also be used as an adjective. A number of adjectives you learned to use with **estar** are actually past participles.

Here are some past participle adjectives. Can you explain how they are formed?

1. **-ar** verbs: **cansado/a, cerrado/a, encantado/a, pasado/a, resfriado/a**
2. **-er/-ir** verbs: **aburrido/a, divertido/a, querido/a**
3. irregular verbs: **abierto/a, escrito/a**

You will learn more about past participles and how they are used in **Gramática 42** and **43**.

Grammar Tutorial 42
McGraw Hill connect
|SPANISH
www.connectspanish.com

42 *Más descripciones*
Past Participle Used As an Adjective

Gramática en acción: Algunos refranes y dichos en español

a. En boca cerrada no entran moscas.

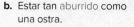

b. Estar tan aburrido como una ostra.

c. Cuando está abierto el cajón, el más honrado es ladrón.

Comprensión

Empareje estas oraciones con el refrán o dicho que explican.

1. _____ Es posible que una persona honrada caiga en la tentación de hacer algo malo si la oportunidad se le presenta.
2. _____ Hay que ser prudente. A veces es mejor no decir nada para evitar (*avoid*) problemas.
3. _____ Ejemplifican el aburrimiento (*boredom*) porque llevan una vida tranquila... siempre igual.

A few Spanish proverbs and sayings a. Into a closed mouth no flies enter. b. To be as bored as an oyster. c. When the drawer is open, the most honest person is (can become) a thief.

The Past Participle / El participio pasado

verbos en -ar	verbos en -er/-ir
hablar → hablado spoken	comer → comido vivir → vivido eaten lived

> *the past participle / **el participio pasado** = the form of a verb used with to have in English to form the perfect tenses (I have written)*

Forming the Past Participle / Cómo se forma el participio pasado

1. Regular Forms

The past participle of most English verbs ends in -ed: to walk → walked, to close → closed. Many, however, are irregular: to sing → sung, to write → written.

In Spanish, the *past participle* (**el participio pasado**) is formed by adding **-ado** to the stem of regular **-ar** verbs, and **-ido** to the stem of regular **-er** and **-ir** verbs.

    An accent mark is used on the past participle of **-er/-ir** verbs with stems ending in **-a**, **-e**, or **-o**.

El participio pasado
- -ar → -ado
- -er/-ir: → -ido

Pronunciation hint: -d- = [ð], like English th

caer → **caído**	oír → **oído**
creer → **creído**	(son)reír → (son)**reído**
leer → **leído**	traer → **traído**

2. Irregular Forms

Some Spanish verbs have irregular past participles.

¡OJO!

The past participle of most compound verbs (such as **descubrir**) that have an irregular root verb (in this case, **cubrir**) have the same irregularity in the past participle: **(des)cubierto.**

abrir:	abierto	**morir:**	muerto
cubrir:*	cubierto	**poner:**	puesto
decir:	dicho	**resolver:***	resuelto
descubrir:*	descubierto	**romper:**	roto
escribir:	escrito	**ver:**	visto
hacer:	hecho	**volver:**	vuelto

The Past Participle As an Adjective / El participio pasado como adjetivo

1. Used As an Adjective

In both English and Spanish, the past participle can be used as an adjective to modify a noun. Like other Spanish adjectives, the past participle must agree in number and gender with the noun modified.

Viven en **una casa construida** en 1920.
They live in a house built in 1920.

El español es solo una de **las lenguas habladas** en los Estados Unidos.
Spanish is only one of the languages spoken in the United States.

2. With *estar*

The past participle is frequently used with **estar** to describe conditions that are the result of a previous action.

¡OJO!

English past participles often have the same form as the past tense.

I **closed** the book.
The thief stood behind the **closed** door.

The Spanish past participle is never identical in form or use to a past tense.

El lago **está contaminado.**
The lake is polluted.

Todos los peces **estaban cubiertos** de crudo.
All the fish were covered with crude oil.

Cerré la puerta. Ahora la puerta está **cerrada.**
I **closed** the door. Now the door is **closed.**

Resolvieron el problema. Ahora el problema está **resuelto.**
*They **solved** the problem. Now the problem is **solved.***

New verbs: **cubrir = to cover, **descubrir** = to discover, **resolver** (**resuelvo**) = to solve, resolve*

Summary of Past Participle

-ar: + -ado/a
-er/-ir: + -ido/a

Práctica y comunicación

A. En este momento

Paso 1. Autoprueba. Dé el infinitivo de los siguientes participios pasados.

1. estudiadas
2. leído
3. vistos
4. dicha
5. abiertas
6. bebido

Paso 2. Use uno de los participios entre paréntesis en la forma apropiada para describir las siguientes cosas y personas del salón de clase.

1. la puerta y las ventanas del salón de clase (cerrado / abierto)
2. los libros de texto de los estudiantes (cerrado / abierto)
3. las luces (apagado / encendido)
4. el proyector (apagado / encendido)
5. los estudiantes (sentado / parado [de pie])
6. el/la profesor(a) (sentado / parado [de pie])

Paso 3. Ahora, en parejas, den ejemplos de las siguientes ideas.

MODELO: 1. algo contaminado → El aire de Los Ángeles está contaminado.

1. algo contaminado
2. un edificio del campus bien diseñado
3. algo que puede estar cerrado o abierto y que no está en el salón de clase
4. el transporte público más usado en su ciudad
5. algo deseado por muchos estudiantes
6. el mejor libro escrito en inglés
7. una cosa rota en su casa/cuarto

B. ¿Cuánto sabe de la Argentina y del Uruguay? Para saber más, complete las siguientes oraciones con el participio pasado de uno de los siguientes infinitivos.

VERBOS: **acelerar, celebrar, conquistar (*to conquer*), desarrollar, escribir, establecer (*to establish*), preferir, reconocer (*to recognize*), separar, traer**

1. La Argentina y el Uruguay son dos países muy _____.
2. Los dos países están _____ por el estuario del Río de la Plata.
3. El gaucho es una figura _____ como símbolo nacional.
4. En la Pampa, hay grandes fincas _____ en la época colonial.
5. El mate es la bebida _____ de los argentinos y uruguayos.
6. Los guaraníes son un pueblo indígena _____ por los españoles.
7. Muchos guaraníes murieron a causa de enfermedades _____ por los europeos.
8. «El Aleph» es un cuento _____ por el famoso escritor argentino Jorge Luis Borges.
9. El carnaval de Montevideo, _____ por cuarenta días, es una de las celebraciones más largas en el mundo.
10. En Buenos Aires y Montevideo, el ritmo de la vida es muy _____.

Algo sobre...

el mate

El mate, una tradición en la Argentina y el Uruguay

El mate es también conocido como la yerba[a] mate. Es un tipo de infusión[b] inmensamente popular en la Argentina y el Uruguay. Se toma tradicionalmente en un recipiente[c] también llamado «mate», hecho de una calabaza,[d] y con una bombilla, que es una pajilla[e] de metal para sorber[f] la infusión. El mate con frecuencia se comparte entre familiares y amigos.

En su opinion, ¿cuál es la bebida más popular de este país? ¿Cuál es la bebida que Ud. prefiere?

[a]*small plant, grass* [b]*herbal tea* [c]*container* [d]*gourd* [e]*straw* [f]*suck*

Capítulo 15 La naturaleza y el medio ambiente

C. Comentarios sobre el mundo de hoy. Complete cada párrafo con el participio pasado de los verbos de cada lista.

VERBOS: **desperdiciar (*to waste*), destruir, hacer, reciclar**

Todos los días, Ud. tira[a] a la basura aproximadamente media libra[b] de papel. Todo ese papel _____[1] constituye un gran número de árboles _____.[2] Esto es un buen motivo para que Ud. empiece un proyecto de recuperación de papeles hoy en su oficina. Ud. puede completar el ciclo del reciclaje únicamente si compra productos _____[3] con materiales _____.[4]

[a]*throw* [b]*media... half a pound*

VERBOS: **acostumbrar, agotar (*to use up*), apagar, bajar, cerrar, limitar**

Las fuentes[a] de energía no están _____[5] todavía. Pero estas fuentes son _____.[6] Desgraciadamente, todavía no estamos _____[7] a conservar energía diariamente. ¿Qué podemos hacer? Cuando nos servimos la comida, la puerta del refrigerador debe estar _____.[8] Cuando miramos la televisión, algunas luces de la casa deben estar _____.[9] El regulador termómetro debe estar _____[10] cuando nos acostamos.

[a]*sources*

D. ¡Ojo alerta! Las cocinas de los dibujos A y B se diferencian (*differ*) en por lo menos siete aspectos. En parejas, encuéntrenlos todos. Usen participios pasados como adjetivos si pueden.

A.   **B.**

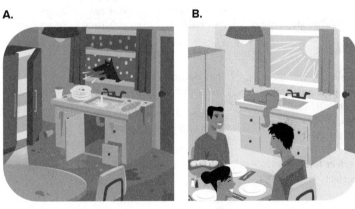

Vocabulario útil

el grifo	faucet
agitar	
cortar	
(des)ordenar	

E. ¿Hecho o por hacer todavía (*yet to be done*)?

Paso 1. Haga oraciones completas que sean verdaderas para Ud. Use un participio pasado como adjetivo, según el modelo. Si Ud. no tiene ninguna de estas cosas, diga «**No tengo...** », según el modelo.

MODELOS: una tarea para la clase de _____ →
Mi tarea para la clase de inglés **ya** está escrita.
Mi tarea para la clase de inglés **no** está escrita **todavía.**
No tengo que hacer ninguna tarea escrita para ninguna clase.

1. un informe (oral/escrito) para la clase de _____
2. una presentación oral para la clase de _____
3. los problemas para la clase de matemáticas _____
4. ¿ ?

Vocabulario útil

escribir	
investigar (gu)	to research
organizar (c)	
preparar	
resolver (resuelvo)	

Paso 2. Ahora, en parejas, comparen sus respuestas. Díganle a la clase algo que tienen en común.

43 *¿Qué has hecho?*

Perfect Forms: Present Perfect Indicative
and Present Perfect Subjunctive

Gramática en acción: Una llanta desinflada

¿Qué ha pasado? ¡Ay, no! ¡Una llanta desinflada! ¡Nunca he cambiado una llanta desinflada!

¿Y Ud.?

Alguna vez...

1. ¿le ha cambiado una llanta desinflada a un carro? (**he...** / **nunca he...**)
2. ¿le ha revisado el aceite al coche?
3. ¿le ha reparado otras cosas al coche?
4. ¿ha tenido un accidente automovilístico?
5. ¿ha excedido el límite de velocidad en la autopista?

Present Perfect Indicative / El presente perfecto de indicativo

haber + *past participle* (-ado/-ido)

he **habl**ado	I have spoken	hemos **habl**ado	we have spoken
has **habl**ado	you have spoken	habéis **habl**ado	you have spoken
ha **habl**ado	you have spoken, he/she has spoken	han **habl**ado	you/they have spoken

1. Present Perfect Indicative

In English, to say *I have (written, spoken . . .)*, you use a present tense form of *to have* plus the past participle. This compound tense is called the *present perfect*. The Spanish equivalent, **el presente perfecto**, is formed with present tense forms of **haber** plus the past participle.

   In general, the Spanish present perfect tense is used just like the English present perfect.

No **hemos estado** aquí antes.
We haven't been here before.

Me **he divertido** mucho.
I've had a very good time.

Ya le **han escrito** la carta.
They've already written her the letter.

¡OJO!

Haber is the only verb that can be used with the past participle to form the Spanish present perfect, which is never formed with **tener**. However, **tener** *can* be conjugated in the present perfect, using **haber** of course.

He **tenido** muchos exámenes este semestre.
I have (I've) had a lot of exams this semester.

2. Form and Placement

Note the following about **el presente perfecto**.
• The form of the past participle never changes. Only the masculine singular is used.

Ella **ha cambiado** llantas varias veces.
She's changed tires several times.

• **Haber** and the past participle are never separated and their order never changes.

¿Por qué **has estacionado** tú allí?
   Es el estacionamiento del jefe.
*Why have **you** parked there?*
   It's the boss's parking spot.

A flat tire What has happened? Oh, no! A flat tire! I've never changed a flat tire!

- **No** and object pronouns always come before the form of **haber**.

Todavía **no** han escrito la carta.
They haven't written the letter yet.

Todavía **no le** han escrito la carta al presidente.
They haven't written the letter to the president yet.

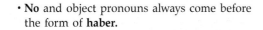

¡OJO!

Remember that **acabar** + **de** + *infinitive*—not the present perfect tense—is used to state that something *has just happened.*

Acabo de mandar la carta.
I've just mailed the letter.

3. Present Perfect of *hay*

The present perfect form of **hay** is **ha habido**. It is invariable, and it expresses both *there has been* and *there have been*.

Ha habido mucha discusión sobre este tema.
There has been a lot of discussion about this topic.

Ha habido muchos accidentes en esta esquina.
There have been many accidents at this corner.

Present Perfect Subjunctive / El presente perfecto de subjuntivo

To express *I have written* (*spoken* …) in a context that requires the subjunctive, use the present subjunctive forms of **haber** to form the *present perfect subjunctive* (**el presente perfecto de subjuntivo**).

The English equivalent of the Spanish present perfect subjunctive will vary according to the context, as shown in the examples. It can be either the simple past (*built, came, did*) or the present perfect (*have built, have come, have done*).

haya **hablado**	hayamos **hablado**
hayas **hablado**	hayáis **hablado**
haya **hablado**	hayan **hablado**

Es bueno que lo **hayan construido**.
It's good (that) they built (have built) it.

Me alegro de que **hayas venido**.
I'm glad (that) you've come (you came).

Es posible que lo **haya hecho**.
It's possible (that) he may have done (he did) it.

Práctica y comunicación

A. ¿Una vida interesante?

Summary of Present Perfect

Indicative: **he, has, ha, hemos, habéis, han** + *past participle*
Subjunctive: **haya, hayas, haya, hayamos, hayáis, han** + *past participle*

Paso 1. Autoprueba. Dé la forma indicada de **haber**.

INDICATIVO:
1. yo _____
2. tú _____
3. nosotros _____

SUBJUNTIVO:
4. Ud. _____
5. ella _____
6. ellos _____

Ahora dé el participio pasado de los siguientes verbos.

7. arrancar _____
8. conducir _____
9. conservar _____
10. construir _____
11. obedecer _____
12. proteger _____
13. morir _____
14. romper _____
15. ver _____

Paso 2. Diga si Ud. ha hecho las siguientes cosas o no. Siga el modelo.

MODELO: hacer un viaje al extranjero →
(No) He hecho un viaje al extranjero.

1. hacer un viaje al extranjero
2. montar en camello
3. comprar un auto nuevo
4. ocupar un puesto (*position*) político
5. tener una mascota
6. ver una película en español
7. escribir un poema
8. romperse el brazo o la pierna

(*Continúa.*)

Prác. A, Paso 1: Answers: 1. he 2. has 3. hemos 4. ha 5. ha 6. han 7. arrancado 8. conducido 9. conservado 10. construido 11. obedecido 12. protegido 13. muerto 14. roto 15. visto

Paso 3. Ahora, en parejas, hagan y contesten preguntas sobre las acciones del **Paso 2.** Luego díganle al resto de la clase una o dos acciones que tienen en común.

MODELO: hacer un viaje al extranjero →

E1: ¿**Has hecho** un viaje al extranjero?
E2: Sí, **he viajado** a México. ¿Y tú?
E1: Yo también **he viajado** a México. →
       Los/Las dos **hemos viajado** a México.

B. El auto de Carmina. Carmina acaba de comprarse un auto usado. Describa lo que le ha pasado a Carmina, según el modelo.

MODELO: ir a la agencia de compra-venta →
       Ha ido a la agencia de compra-venta.

1. pedirle ayuda a un amigo
2. ver diferentes coches y comparar los
3. mirar uno baratísimo
4. revisarle las llantas
5. conducirlo para probarlo
6. pensarlo y regresar a la agencia
7. decidir comprarlo
8. comprarlo
9. volver a casa
10. llevar a sus amigas al cine en su coche

C. ¡No lo creo!

Paso 1. Complete las siguientes oraciones con la forma apropiada del presente perfecto (indicativo o subjuntivo). Luego indique cuál de las oraciones de cada par expresa su opinión sobre sus compañeros de clase. Después su profesor(a) va a hacerles preguntas a todos para saber cuál es la verdad en cada caso.

1. Creo que alguien en esta clase _____ las pirámides de Egipto. (ver) ☐
    Es dudoso que alguien _____ las pirámides de Egipto. (ver) ☐
2. Estoy seguro/a de que por lo menos uno de mis compañeros _____ ☐
    una montaña alta. (escalar)
    No creo que nadie _____ una montaña alta. (escalar) ☐
3. Creo que alguien _____ autostop en un viaje. (hacer) ☐
    Dudo que alguien _____ autostop en un viaje. (hacer) ☐
4. Creo que alguien _____ en paracaídas. (saltar) ☐
    Es improbable que alguien _____ en paracaídas. (saltar) ☐
5. Estoy seguro/a de que alguien _____ el metro en Nueva York. (tomar) ☐
    No creo que nadie _____ el metro neoyorquino. (tomar) ☐

Paso 2. Ahora complete las siguientes ideas sobre las actividades de sus compañeros esta semana. **¡OJO!** Hay que usar el indicativo o el subjuntivo.

1. (No) Creo que todos _____ un examen. (tener)
2. (No) Estoy seguro/a de que todos mis compañeros _____ varios mensajes. (escribir)
3. (No) Dudo que muchos compañeros _____ un video en YouTube. (ver)
4. Es probable que nadie _____ un hueso (*bone*). (romperse)
5. Es obvio que nadie _____. (morir)

Vocabulario **útil**	
escalar	to climb
hacer autostop	to hitchhike
el paracaídas	parachute
saltar	to jump

D. Opiniones sobre el medio ambiente

Paso 1. ¿Qué se ha hecho en los últimos años para proteger el medio ambiente? En parejas, hagan oraciones completas en el presente perfecto de indicativo. Sus oraciones pueden ser afirmativas o negativas, según su opinión.

MODELO: este país: desarrollar nuevas formas de energía renovable →
Este país (no) **ha desarrollado** nuevas formas de energía renovable.

1. este país: desarrollar la energía eólica/solar
2. la población de esta ciudad: reciclar el papel, el plástico y el vidrio (*glass*) con regularidad
3. los seres humanos (*humans*): proteger muchas especies de animales
4. varios países: destruir zonas naturales para construir más viviendas
5. el aire de esta ciudad: contaminarse más
6. este estado: construir muchas carreteras nuevas

Paso 2. Ahora añadan un comentario personal a sus oraciones del **Paso 1.** Puede ser una explicación (con el indicativo) o una reacción personal (con el subjuntivo).

MODELOS: Este país no ha desarrollado nuevas formas de energía renovable
porque tenemos mucho petróleo.
Es terrible que este país no **haya desarrollado** nuevas formas de energía renovable todavía.

E. Entrevista: ¿Lo has hecho o no?

Paso 1. Indique si Ud. ha hecho o no las siguientes cosas, según el modelo. Añada una cosa interesante que Ud. ha hecho ya y otra que no ha hecho todavía, pero que quiere hacer.

MODELOS: visitar la Argentina o el Uruguay →
He visitado la Argentina una vez.
Nunca **he visitado** la Argentina, pero sí **he visitado** el Uruguay.

1. bailar el tango
2. manejar un Alfa Romeo
3. escribir un poema
4. actuar en una obra teatral

5. conocer a una persona famosa
6. caerse de la bicicleta/moto(cicleta)
7. ¿ ?
8. ¿ ?

Paso 2. Ahora, usando como base las actividades del **Paso 1,** complete las siguientes oraciones con referencia a sus compañeros de clase o a su profesor(a). **¡OJO!** Tiene que decidir si va a usar el indicativo o el subjuntivo en estas oraciones.

MODELO: Creo que... → Creo que **la profesora ha manejado** un Alfa Romeo.

1. Creo que...
2. Dudo que...
3. Es probable que...
4. Estoy seguro/a de que...
5. Ojalá que...

Paso 3. Lea sus oraciones del **Paso 2** a la clase entera. La persona nombrada en la oración va a decir si la oración es cierta o falsa.

Algo sobre...

el tango

Una pareja que baila un tango en Buenos Aires

El tango es sin duda uno de los bailes hispanos más conocidos en todo el mundo. Es netamente[a] argentino y uruguayo, ya que[b] nació[c] en la zona del Río de la Plata. Es un baile muy sensual que se baila en pareja. Con frecuencia la letra de los tangos es sentimental: habla de conflictos amorosos o de tristes memorias de los años pasados. El instrumento básico del tango, y el más tradicional, es el bandoneón, un tipo de acordeón.

¿Le gusta a Ud. bailar en pareja? ¿Qué baila? *¿algún* baile latino?

[a]*distinctly* [b]*ya... since* [c]*it originated*

F. ¿Verdad o mentira?

Paso 1. Invente Ud. tres declaraciones sobre cosas que ha hecho y no ha hecho en su vida. Dos deben ser verdaderas y una, mentira.

MODELOS: **He hecho** un viaje a Sudamérica.
Nunca **he conocido** a nadie famoso.
He visto muchas películas en español.

Paso 2. Léale sus declaraciones a la clase. Sus compañeros/as van a tratar de encontrar la mentira.

MODELO: **Creo** que **has hecho** un viaje a Sudamérica y que **has visto** muchas películas en español. **Dudo** que no **hayas conocido** a nadie famoso.

Nota **comunicativa**

El pluscuamperfecto: *había + participio pasado*

Use the past participle with the imperfect form of **haber** (**había, habías,...**) to talk about what you had—or had not—done before a given time in the past. This form, called the *past perfect* (**el pluscuamperfecto**), is used like its English equivalent.

Antes de graduarme en la escuela secundaria, no **había estudiado** español.	*Before graduating from high school, I hadn't studied Spanish.*
Antes de 1995, **habíamos vivido** en Kansas todo el tiempo.	*Before 1995, we had always lived in Kansas.*

You will use the past perfect in **Práctica G.**

G. Intercambios

Paso 1. En parejas, hagan y contesten preguntas basadas en las siguientes frases. Inventen por lo menos una pregunta original.

MODELO: ¿qué cosa? / no haber aprendido a hacer antes del año pasado →
E1: ¿Qué cosa no **habías aprendido** a hacer antes del año pasado?
E2: Pues... no **había aprendido** a nadar. Aprendí a nadar este año en la clase de natación.

1. ¿qué cosa? / no haber aprendido a hacer antes de este semestre/trimestre
2. ¿qué materia? / no haber estudiado antes de venir a esta universidad
3. ¿qué deporte? / (no) haber practicado mucho antes de cumplir 12 años
4. ¿qué libro clásico o importante? / no haber leído antes de venir a esta universidad
5. ¿qué decisión? / no haber tomado antes de cumplir 18 años
6. ¿a quién de las personas importantes en su vida? / no haber conocido antes de venir a la universidad
7. ¿ ?

Paso 2. Ahora indiquen las cosas importantes para Uds. que ya habían o no habían hecho para las siguientes fechas. Use **ya** o **no... todavía,** según el modelo.

MODELO: para septiembre del 2015 →
Para septiembre del 2015 **ya había empezado** / **no había empezado todavía** a estudiar en esta universidad. ¿Y tú?

1. para septiembre del 2015
2. para enero del 2000
3. para el verano del 2013
4. para la primavera del 2014
5. para el verano pasado

Paso 3. Ahora díganle a la clase algo de su historia personal que Uds. tienen en común. Si no tienen nada en común, cada uno debe contarle a la clase algo interesante de la vida de su compañero/a.

Un poco de todo

A. Lengua y cultura: El Parque Nacional los Glaciares

Paso 1. Complete the following paragraphs with the correct form of the words in parentheses, as suggested by context. When two possibilities are given, select the correct word. Form adverbs with **-mente,** as needed. **¡OJO!** *PP:* = present perfect (indicative or subjunctive) *P/I:* = preterite or imperfect. Other infinitives are either present subjunctive or must remain in the infinitive form.

Algunos aspectos de la cultura y de la geografía de la Argentina son bien conocidos por todos. Seguro que Uds. (*PP:* ver[1]) bailar el tango, porque es un baile que se (*PP:* hacer[2]) muy popular (reciente[3]) entre los bailes de salón.[a] Y casi todos (saben / conocen[4]) qué es la Pampa y quiénes (son / estar[5]) los gauchos.

El Cerro (*Mt.*) Fitz Roy, en la Patagonia

Pero es fácil (olvidar[6]) que la Argentina es un país larguísimo que se extiende desde la selva[b] tropical en la frontera[c] con el Brasil hasta la Antártida. (Por / Para[7]) eso el país tiene una increíble variedad climática y geográfica.

Si Ud. es aficionado/a al ecoturismo, (se / le[8]) aconsejamos que (visitar[9]) el Parque Nacional los Glaciares, en (el / la[10]) región de la Patagonia, al sur del país. El gobierno argentino (*P/I:* crear[11]) el parque en 1937, y en 1982 la UNESCO (lo / la[12]) (*P/I:* declarar[13]) Patrimonio Natural de la Humanidad. Allí, en las 600.000 hectáreas[d] del parque, los visitantes pueden explorar impresionantes glaciares. Es posible (escalar[14]) montañas de hielo[e] con grandes precipicios, que es un desafío[f] aun[g] para los (mejor[15]) escaladores.[h]

[a]bailes... *ballroom dances* [b]*jungle* [c]*border* [d]*hectares (1 hectare = 2.47 acres)* [e]*ice* [f]*challenge* [g]*even* [h]*climbers*

Paso 2. Comprensión. Conteste las siguientes preguntas.

1. ¿Qué aspectos de la cultura argentina son bien conocidos?
2. ¿Por qué hay gran variedad climática y geográfica en la Argentina?
3. ¿En qué región está el Parque Nacional Los Glaciares?
4. ¿Por qué es tan (*so*) bueno el Parque para el alpinismo (*mountain climbing*)?

Paso 3. Ahora, en parejas, comparen la Argentina con los Estados Unidos (o con su país de origen) en cuanto a (*with regard to*) la diversidad geográfica y climática. ¿Son comparables? ¿Cómo y por qué? Den ejemplos específicos.

B. Dos dibujos, un punto de vista. Los dibujos A y B comentan aspectos del mismo tema.

B

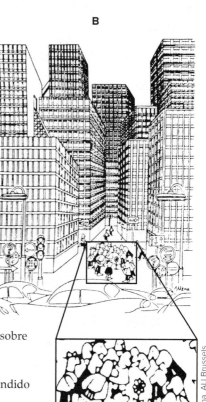

Vocabulario útil

el arado plow	**la flor**	**la mula**
el burro	**la gente**	**el tractor**
la deshumanización	**la mecanización**	

A

SÍ, CLARO, MÁS MODERNO, PERO... ¿CON QUIÉN COMENTAS TU VIDA?

Paso 1. Conteste las siguientes preguntas sobre el dibujo A.

1. ¿Qué se ha comprado el agricultor de la izquierda? ¿Qué es probable que haya vendido para comprarlo?
2. ¿Qué es «más moderno», según el otro agricultor?
3. ¿Qué desventaja tiene el tractor?

Paso 2. Conteste las siguiente preguntas sobre el dibujo B.

1. Describa la ciudad que se ve en el dibujo.
2. ¿Qué ha descubierto la gente? ¿Por qué mira con tanto interés?
3. ¿Qué hicieron primero antes de construir esta ciudad? ¿Qué destruyeron?

Paso 3. Ahora, en parejas, expliquen su opinión personal sobre estos dos dibujos. ¿Son chistosos (*funny*)? ¿serios? ¿Es probable que los dos artistas estén de acuerdo sobre algunos aspectos del mundo de hoy? ¿Sobre qué aspectos?

En **su** comunidad

Entreviste a una persona hispana de su universidad o ciudad sobre cuestiones medioambientales relacionados con su país de origen.

PREGUNTAS POSIBLES

- ¿Hay problemas de contaminación en su ciudad o país de origen? ¿Qué los causa?
- ¿Qué está haciendo el país para preservar los recursos naturales? ¿Y para disminuir la contaminación?
- ¿Ve un cambio en la actitud de las personas de su país o ciudad con relación a la conservación de los recursos naturales?
- ¿Hay programas de reciclaje? ¿Cree que son efectivos?

«EcoSalu2» Segmento 2

Antes de mirar

Indique las oraciones que, en su opinión, son ciertas en relación con su ciudad.

1. _____ Hay buenos carriles (*lanes*) para las bicicletas.
2. _____ Hay suficiente estacionamiento para las bicicletas.
3. _____ Hay demasiado tráfico.
4. _____ Hay suficiente estacionamiento para los coches.
5. _____ Hay un buen sistema de transporte público.

Este segmento

Laura presenta un reportaje sobre la iniciativa de muchas ciudades para promover (*encourage*) el uso de las bicicletas y reducir el uso de los coches. Al final, Ana y Víctor cierran el programa.

La Avenida de la Reforma en México D.F., ocupada por cientos de ciclistas un domingo

Vocabulario del segmento

qué hacer	what to do	**de manera que**	so that
el gobierno	government	**quedarse atrás**	to lag behind
a corto plazo	(in the) short term	**experimentar**	to experience
no solo... sino que	not only . . . but	**mejorar**	to improve
reportar	to create, produce	**la calidad**	quality
la red vial	road system	**ilimitado/a**	unlimited
la bici	la bicicleta	**por muy buen camino**	in the right direction

Fragmento del guion

En el Distrito Federal, el programa se llama Ecobici. Por solo 300 pesos[a] anuales, menos de 30 dólares, puedes alquilar bicicletas de manera ilimitada por períodos de menos de 45 minutos. La ciudad cuenta con[b] 90 cicloestaciones, es decir, lugares donde estacionar la bici de forma práctica y segura.

[a]*Mexican currency* [b]tiene

Después de mirar

A. **¿Está claro?** Complete las siguientes oraciones según el programa.

1. Bicing es una iniciativa en Barcelona / Buenos Aires.
2. Hay iniciativas similares en otras ciudades españolas / españolas y europeas.
3. Ecobici es un programa para alquilar / comprar bicicletas.
4. En el D.F. hay muchos / pocos carriles para las bicicletas.
5. Los domingos la Avenida de la Reforma se abre a las bicicletas y a los coches / se cierra a los coches.

B. **Un poco más.** Conteste las siguientes preguntas.

1. ¿Qué se ha construido en Barcelona para facilitar el uso de las bicicletas?
2. ¿Qué opciones incluye la iniciativa Bicing? ¿y la iniciativa Ecobici?
3. ¿Por qué son muy positivas estas iniciativas sobre el uso de la bicicleta?

C. **Y ahora, Uds.** En grupos, hablen de las iniciativas que presenta Laura para la reducción de tráfico. ¿Hay alguna iniciativa similar en este país? ¿Y en su ciudad? Si no la tiene, ¿creen Uds. que la necesita? Justifiquen sus respuestas.

Antes de leer

¿Qué ejemplos de bellezas (*beauties*) naturales hay en la zona donde Ud. vive?

Lectura cultural: La Argentina y el Uruguay

Dos países con gran belleza natural

Tanto el Uruguay como la Argentina son países orgullosos[a] de la diversidad de su naturaleza.

De norte a sur y de este a oeste, la Argentina tiene formidables atracciones naturales. Al norte, en la frontera con el Brasil y el Paraguay, están las cataratas[b] del Iguazú, una de las maravillas del mundo natural. Al sur se encuentra el impresionante glaciar Perito Moreno. Al oeste, en la frontera con Chile, la cordillera[c] de los Andes ostenta[d] el pico[e] más alto de todo el continente americano: el monte Aconcagua, de 6.962 metros (22.841 pies) de altura. En el centro, en un territorio compartido[f] con el Uruguay, se encuentra la Pampa, una interminable planicie[g] de tierras para el ganado[h] y el cultivo de granos. Al sur profundo, la Argentina continúa más allá del Estrecho de Magallanes[i] hasta la misma Antártida.

Por su parte, el Uruguay contiene los Humedales de Santa Lucía y del Este. Son tierras cubiertas de agua que mantienen ecosistemas de gran valor[j] medioambiental y el mayor parque de ombúes[k] del mundo.

[a]*proud* [b]*waterfalls* [c]*mountain range* [d]*is proud to show off* [e]*summit* [f]*shared* [g]*plain* [h]*cattle* [i]Estrecho... *Straight of Magellan* [j]*value* [k]*large shade trees*

Vista aérea de Buenos Aires y el Rio de la Plata

Un símbolo argentino y uruguayo: El Río de la Plata

El Río de la Plata es un río formado por la confluencia de dos ríos: el río Paraná y el río Uruguay. Este río se convierte en un gran estuario al entrar en el Atlántico. Es la frontera natural entre el Uruguay y la Argentina, y las capitales de estos países están junto a[a] estas aguas. El adjetivo derivado del Río de la Plata, «rioplatense», se usa para referirse a las personas y cosas de esta región de las dos naciones, que es una zona cultural y lingüística.

[a]junto... *next to*

COMPRENSIÓN

1. ¿Qué destino turístico se destaca (*stands out*) en la Argentina?
2. ¿Qué región es parte tanto de la Argentina como del Uruguay?
3. ¿Qué países hispanos se clasifican como megadiversos? ¿Por qué lo son?
4. ¿Qué tipos de energías renovables son importantes en España ahora?
5. ¿Cuál es la frontera natural entre la Argentina y el Uruguay?

En otros países hispanos

- **En Costa Rica, Colombia, el Ecuador, México, el Perú y Venezuela** Estas naciones están entre los diecisiete países megadiversos identificados por el Centro de Monitoreo de Conservación Ambiental, un organismo[a] del Programa de las Naciones Unidas para el Medio Ambiente (el PNUMA). Los países megadiversos, en su mayoría tropicales, son países que tienen el mayor porcentaje de biodiversidad en el planeta.

- **En España** En la actualidad, este país europeo está invirtiendo[b] en el desarrollo de las energías eólica y solar, ya que[c] el país disfruta de[d] innumerables horas de sol y buenas zonas de viento.

[a]*agency* [b]*investing* [c]ya... *since* [d]disfruta... *enjoys*

Y ahora, Uds.

Es evidente que la Argentina y el Uruguay tienen muchas afinidades geográficas y culturales. ¿Ocurre lo mismo entre los Estados Unidos y sus países vecinos? Den ejemplos específicos para justificar su respuesta.

Del mundo hispano

Antes de leer

Haga una lista de los aparatos que Ud. usa diariamente, sin los cuales no podría (*without which you couldn't*) vivir. Luego haga otra lista de los aparatos que no son importantes ni útiles para Ud.

Lectura: «Apocalipsis, I», de Marco Denevi

La extinción de la raza de los hombres se sitúa aproximadamente a fines del siglo XXXI.[a] La cosa sucedió así:[b] las máquinas habían alcanzado[c] tal perfección que los hombres no necesitaban comer, ni dormir, ni leer, ni escribir, ni siquiera[d] pensar. Les bastaba apretar[e] un botón y las máquinas lo hacían todo por ellos.

Gradualmente fueron desapareciendo las mesas, los teléfonos, los Leonardo da Vinci, las rosas té, las tiendas de antigüedades,[f] los discos con las nueve sinfonías de Beethoven, el vino de Burdeos, las golondrinas,[g] los cuadros de Salvador Dalí, los relojes, los sellos[h] postales, los alfileres,[i] el Museo del Prado, la sopa de cebolla, los transatlánticos, las pirámides de Egipto, las Obras Completas de don Benito Pérez Galdós.[j] Sólo había máquinas.

Después, los hombres empezaron a notar que ellos mismos iban desapareciendo paulatinamente[k] y que en cambio[l] las máquinas se multiplicaban. Bastó poco tiempo para que el número de los hombres quedase reducido a la mitad[m] y el[n] de las máquinas aumentase al doble y luego al décuplo.[ñ] Las máquinas terminaron[o] por ocupar todo el espacio disponible.[p] Nadie podía dar un paso, hacer un simple ademán[q] sin tropezarse con[r] una de ellas. Finalmente los hombres se extinguieron.[s]

Como[t] el último se olvidó de desconectar las máquinas, desde entonces[u] seguimos funcionando.

[a] *a... at the end of the 31st century* [b] *La... It happened like this* [c] *habían... had achieved* [d] *ni... not even* [e] *Les... It was enough to push* [f] *antiques* [g] *swallows* [h] *stamps* [i] *pins* [j] *19th century Spanish novelist* [k] *little by little* [l] *en... in contrast* [m] *Bastó... It only took a little while for the number of men to be reduced to half* [n] *that (the number)* [ñ] *tenfold* [o] *ended up* [p] *available* [q] *gesture* [r] *sin... without running into* [s] *se... died out* [t] *Since* [u] *desde... since then*

Comprensión

A. ¿Cierto o falso? Corrija las oraciones falsas.

	CIERTO	FALSO
1. Las máquinas llegaron a ser perfectas.	☐	☐
2. Los hombres lo hacían todo por las máquinas.	☐	☐
3. A las máquinas les gustaban las cosas más finas y artísticas del mundo y por eso conservaban el vino de Burdeos, las pirámides de Egipto, etcétera.	☐	☐
4. El número de hombres incrementaba mientras disminuía el número de máquinas.	☐	☐
5. Finalmente no hubo más máquinas.	☐	☐
6. El narrador de este microcuento es una máquina.	☐	☐

B. «Gradualmente fueron desapareciendo... » Conteste las siguientes preguntas.

1. ¿Cuáles de las cosas que fueron desapareciendo (segundo párrafo del cuento) reconoce Ud.?

2. ¿Qué tienen en común esas cosas?

3. ¿Para quiénes son más importantes esas cosas, para los hombres o para las máquinas? ¿Son importantes para Ud.? ¿Por qué?

A ESCUCHAR

Una campaña° para Greenpeace en la radio

campaign

Vocabulario **para escuchar**

hacer **campaña**	to have a campaign
el partido político	political party
pilas	batteries

¡OJO!

En la Argentina y el Uruguay, así como en muchos países centroamericanos, se usa el pronombre personal **vos** en vez del (*instead of the*) pronombre **tú.** Los mandatos informales con **vos** tienen formas diferentes de los mandatos con **tú.** En el programa de radio, Ud. va a escuchar algunos de estos mandatos.

escuchá = escucha
pensá = piensa
unite = únete
hacete = hazte
ayudá = ayuda
andá = anda (*go*)
defendé = defiende

Antes de escuchar

¿Qué problemas medioambientales le preocupan a Ud.? ¿Le preocupan más los problemas locales o los internacionales? ¿Es Ud. miembro/a de alguna organización dedicada a la protección del medio ambiente?

Después de escuchar

A. ¿Cierto o falso? Indique si las siguientes oraciones son ciertas o falsas. Corrija las falsas.

	CIERTO	FALSO
1. Greenpeace tiene una organización en la Argentina.	☐	☐
2. Greenpeace recibe dinero de varios gobiernos.	☐	☐
3. Greenpeace solo se preocupa de los problemas de la contaminación del aire y el agua.	☐	☐
4. Greenpeace solo busca miembros que contribuyan con dinero a la organización.	☐	☐

B. Más detalles. Conteste las siguientes preguntas.

1. ¿Cómo se llama el programa? ¿En qué tipo de estación de radio se presenta?

2. ¿Para qué tipo de oyentes es este programa? ¿Por qué piensa Ud. eso?

3. ¿Cómo trata de convencer el locutor (*host*) del programa a sus oyentes de que es importante hacerse miembro de Greenpeace?

4. ¿Cuáles son dos de los temas que preocupan a Greenpeace?

PRODUCCIÓN PERSONAL

¡Ahora, yo!

A. Use de modelo las preguntas y respuestas de la página 445 de este capítulo para hablar de sus preocupaciones por el medioambiente (si las tiene) y de su necesidad del coche o de su uso en su vida diaria.

B. Filme un corto (*short segment*) o haga un fotomontaje en defensa de su propia (*own*) posición sobre un tema de interés. Puede ser a favor o en contra de alguna medida (*measure*) o iniciativa. Puede entrevistar a algunos expertos, tomar datos de otras fuentes (*sources*) y usar su voz en off.

A ESCRIBIR

Un ensayo sobre los efectos del cambio climático

Como Ud. sabe, hay un debate internacional sobre el cambio (*change*) climático y lo que las naciones deben hacer para cambiar esta situación. En este capítulo, va a escribir un ensayo en el que (*which*) defiende su postura (*position*) personal sobre el tema.

Preparar

Paso 1. En parejas, piensen en el tema del cambio climático. ¿Hay más de una postura con respecto al tema? Según algunos científicos, ¿cuáles son las causas del cambio climático? ¿Cuáles son sus efectos? ¿Qué opinan las personas que no están de acuerdo con la idea del cambio climático?

Hagan una lista de cuatro o cinco efectos del cambio climático que, en su opinión, son más problemáticos. También hagan una lista de los argumentos de los defensores del cambio climático, y otra, de los que se oponen a este concepto.

Paso 2. Ahora defina su postura personal y defiéndala en un su ensayo. Hay más ayuda en Connect.

Más ideas para su portafolio

- Incluya una lista de las cosas que Ud. ha hecho en su vida de las que se siente más orgulloso/a (*proud*) y otra lista de las cosas que no ha hecho todavía pero que desea hacer.

- Lo más... Incluya una lista de las cosas más raras o extraordinarias ¡o peores! que Ud. ha visto (hecho, comido...) en su vida.

- Si ha estado jugando (*have been playing*) Practice Spanish: Study Abroad, en Quest 9 Ud. aprendió sobre tres medios de transporte público en Colombia: el minibús, el autobús y el superbús. ¿Cuál es la diferencia entre ellos? ¿Ha tomado Ud. el autobús en un país hispanohablante o en el país donde vive Ud.? Escriba un párrafo sobre su experiencia. Si Ud. ha tomado el autobús en ambos (*both*) lugares, haga una comparación entre las dos experiencias.

Sugerencia: You are now ready to play Quest 9 in **Practice Spanish: Study Abroad** (www.mhpractice.com).

EN RESUMEN En este capítulo

LEARNSMART

Visit **www.connectspanish.com** to practice the vocabulary and grammar points covered in this chapter.

AFTER STUDYING THIS CHAPTER I CAN . . .

☐ talk about natural and urban environments (446)

☐ talk about cars and driving (450)

☐ describe with adjectives that are also past participles (454–455)

☐ use the present and past perfect to express what *has* and *had happened* (458–468, 462)

☐ recognize/describe at least 2–3 aspects of Argentine and Uruguayan cultures

Gramática en breve

42. Past Participle Used As Adjective

Regular Past Participles

-ar ⟶ -a**do**/a
-er/-ir ⟶ -i**do**/a

Irregular Past Participles

abierto/a, cubierto/a, descubierto/a, dicho/a, escrito/a, hecho/a, muerto/a, puesto/a, resuelto/a, roto/a, visto/a, vuelto/a

43. Present Perfect Indicative and Subjunctive

Present Perfect Indicative		**Present Perfect Subjunctive**	
present indicative of **haber** + past participle		present subjunctive of **haber** + past participle	
he	hemos	haya	hayamos
has	habéis	hayas	hayáis
ha	han	haya	hayan

Past Perfect Indicative

imperfect of **haber** + past participle

había	habíamos
habías	habíais
había	habían

Vocabulario

Los verbos

cubrir	to cover
descubrir	to discover
evitar	to avoid
resolver (like volver)	to solve, resolve

Los recursos naturales

el bosque	forest
la energía (eólica, renovable)	(wind, renewable) energy
el lago	lake
el medio ambiente	environment
la naturaleza	nature
el reciclaje	recycling
el recurso natural	natural resource
el río	river
la Tierra	Earth

Cognados: el aire, la energía eléctrica/nuclear/solar, el petróleo, el planeta

Repaso: el árbol, la montaña

conservar	to save, conserve
construir	to build
contaminar	to pollute
desarrollar	to develop
destruir (*like* construir**)**	to destroy
fabricar (qu)	to manufacture
proteger (protejo)	to protect
reciclar	to recycle

Repaso: acabar

El desarrollo

el/la agricultor(a)	farmer
la agricultura	farming, agriculture
el/la campesino/a	peasant
el campo	field; countryside
la capa de ozono	ozone layer
el delito	crime
el desarrollo	development
la fábrica	factory
la falta	lack; absence
la finca	farm
el gobierno	government
la población	population
el rascacielos	skyscraper
el ritmo de la vida	pace of life
el servicio	service

Repaso: la ciudad, la contaminación, el transporte

Los animales

la ballena	whale
la especie (en peligro de extinción)	(endangered) species
el pez (*pl.* **peces)**	fish
el toro	bull
la vaca	cow

Cognados: el elefante, el gorila

Repaso: el caballo, el gato, el pájaro, el perro

Los vehículos

la estación de servicio	gas station
los frenos	brakes
la gasolinera	gas station
la llanta (desinflada)	(flat) tire
el/la mecánico/a	mechanic
el parabrisas	windshield
el taller	(repair) shop
el tanque	tank

Cognados: el auto(móvil), la batería, el carro, la gasolina, la moto(cicleta), el SUV

Repaso: el aceite, la bicicleta, la camioneta, el coche el vehículo

arrancar (qu)	to start up (*a car*)
arreglar	to fix, repair
gastar	to use (*gas*)
llenar	to fill (up)
revisar	to check

Cognado: reparar

En la carretera

la acera	sidewalk
la autopista	freeway, interstate
la bocina	horn (*car*)
la carretera	highway
la circulación	traffic
el/la conductor(a)	driver
la esquina	(street) corner
el estacionamiento	parking place/lot
la licencia de manejar/ conducir	driver's license

el límite de velocidad	speed limit
el/la policía	police officer
el semáforo	traffic signal
el tránsito	traffic

Cognado: el tráfico

Repaso: la avenida, la calle

conducir	to drive
doblar	to turn
obedecer (obedezco)	to obey
parar	to stop
seguir (sigo) (i)	to keep on going
tocar (qu)	to honk

Repaso: chocar (qu) (con), estacionar, manejar

(todo) derecho/recto	straight ahead

Repaso: a la derecha, a la izquierda, por (through)

¿cómo se llega a... ?	how do you get to . . . ?

Los adjetivos

acelerado/a	fast, accelerated
bello/a	beautiful
contaminado/a	contaminated, polluted
descapotable	convertible
doméstico/a	domesticated, tame
renovable	renewable
salvaje	wild
todoterreno (*inv.*)	all-terrain

Cognados: denso/a, híbrido/a, público/a, puro/a

Vocabulario personal

16

La vida social y afectiva

www.connectspanish.com

En este capítulo

¡Viva el amor! (en Asunción, Paraguay)

- ¿Tiene Ud. pareja? ¿novio o novia? ¿esposo o esposa? ¿O sale con alguien?

- En este momento, ¿cuál es la relación social más importante de su vida? ¿Es una relación romántica o una de amistad? ¿O es su relación con su familia?

- ¿Cree Ud. en el amor a primera vista? ¿Y en el amor para toda la vida? En su opinión, ¿qué es necesario para que[a] haya una relación feliz y duradera[b] entre una pareja?

[a]*para... so that* [b]*lasting*

GABRIELA ROMANO ACOSTA CONTESTA LAS PREGUNTAS.

- Sí, tengo pareja. Bueno, es algo reciente. Empecé a salir con un chico de la universidad hace un mes más o menos. No es nada serio... por ahora. Pero está bien. Es lindo.[a]

- En este momento, mi familia y mis amigos de siempre son lo más importante. En el futuro, espero tener un compañero e hijos y que ellos sean lo más importante de mi vida. Pero, por ahora, es pronto para eso.

- ¡Ay, no sé! Creo que uno puede enamorarse[b] a primera vista, pero no creo que eso sea suficiente para que el amor dure[c] para siempre. Es difícil que el amor dure toda la vida, ¿no? Pero es bonito pensar que puede ser. Y para eso es necesario que las dos personas de la pareja se comprendan y se apoyen[d] mutuamente.

[a]*Es... It's nice* [b]*fall in love* [c]*lasts* [d]*se... support each other*

Las relaciones sentimentales

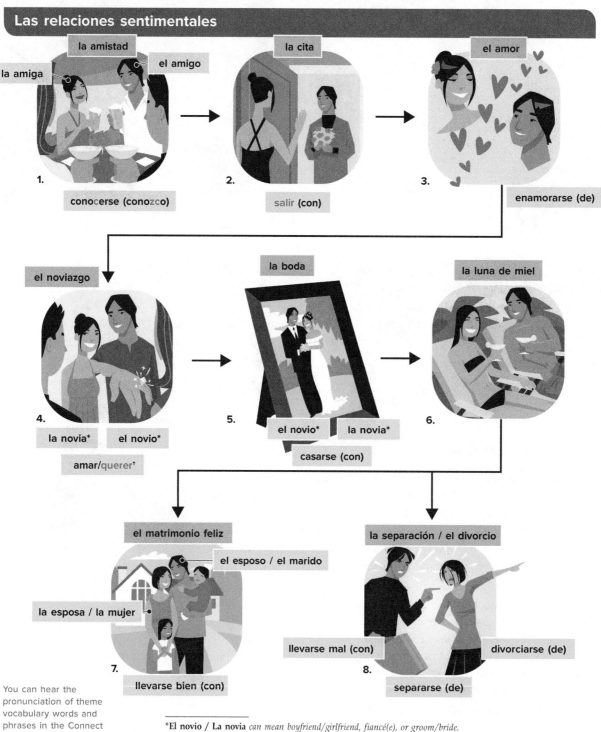

la amistad
la amiga
el amigo

la cita

el amor

1.
conocerse (conozco)

2.
salir (con)

3.
enamorarse (de)

el noviazgo

la boda

la luna de miel

4.
la novia*   el novio*
amar/querer†

5.
el novio*   la novia*
casarse (con)

6.

el matrimonio feliz
el esposo / el marido
la esposa / la mujer

la separación / el divorcio

7.
llevarse bien (con)

llevarse mal (con)   divorciarse (de)

8.
separarse (de)

You can hear the pronunciation of theme vocabulary words and phrases in the Connect eBook.

El novio / La novia can mean *boyfriend/girlfriend, fiancé(e),* or *groom/bride.*
†**Amar** *and* **querer** *both mean to love, but* **amar** *can imply more passion in some dialects of Spanish.*

el cariño	affection	casado/a	a married person
el matrimonio	marriage; married couple	recién casado/a	a newlywed
la pareja	(married) couple; partner	soltero/a	a single person
el viudo / la viuda	widower/widow		
pelear (con)	to fight (with)	**estar...**	
romper (con)	to break up (with)	casado/a (con)	married (to)
		divorciado/a (de)	divorced (from)
ser...		enamorado/a (de)	in love (with)
amistoso/a	friendly	separado/a (de)	separated (from)
cariñoso/a	affectionate		

Comunicación

A. **¡Usemos la lógica!** Complete las siguientes oraciones lógicamente.

1. Mi abuelo es el _____ de mi abuela, es decir, está _____ con ella.
2. Muchos novios tienen un _____ bastante (*rather*) largo antes de la boda.
3. María y Julio tienen una _____ el viernes para comer en un restaurante. Luego van a bailar.
4. La _____ de Juan y Pati es el domingo a las dos de la tarde, en la iglesia (*church*) de San Martín.
5. La _____ entre ex esposos es imposible. No pueden ser amigos.
6. ¡El _____ es ciego (*blind*)!
7. Para algunas personas, el _____ es un concepto anticuado. Prefieren vivir juntos, sin casarse.
8. Algunas personas no tienen el dinero para una _____ después de la boda.

Así se dice

la boda = el casamiento

Nota cultural

Expresiones familiares de cariño

En el mundo hispano se usan muchas palabras y frases para referirse a las personas queridas y para expresar cariño. Estas pueden ser diferentes en cada país. Las siguientes palabras son de uso común, aunque[a] algunas no se usan en todos los países.

- Entre personas unidas romántica o familiarmente: **mi amor, amorcito/a, mi vida, cielo,**[b] **corazón, querido/a, cariño, gordo/a, viejo/a, flaco/a,**[c] **negro/a**
- De hijos a padres: **viejo/a, mis viejos** (la Argentina, el Uruguay)
- Para referirse a una pareja con quien no se está casado: **mi compañero/a**
- Para referirse a los padrinos[d] de un niño o niña: **el compadre / la comadre**

La gente joven siempre tiene su propia jerga[e] en cada país, pero no siempre son palabras que se usan para dirigirse[f] a las personas mayores.

- **cuate:** una palabra del náhuatl, la lengua de los aztecas (México, Centroamérica, Bolivia)
- **pana:** significa **compañero/a** (Venezuela, Colombia, la República Dominicana y otros países)
- **compa:** derivado de **compañero**
- **negro/a:** se usa entre amigos en varios países
- **tío/a** (España)
- **buey** (México)

[a]*although* [b]*heaven* [c]*skinny* [d]*godparents* [e]*slang* [f]*address*

En un bautizo en una iglesia católica, los padrinos (*godparents*) sujetan (*hold*) al bebé. (México, D.F.)

Como se nota en la lista anterior,[g] una de las grandes diferencias entre el español y el inglés es el hecho de usar[h] como palabras cariñosas adjetivos que describen características físicas: **gordo/a, flaco/a, negro/a, viejo/a.** Estos adjetivos se aplican indistintamente[i] a cualquier[j] persona, es decir, no es necesario que la persona sea gorda o delgada, blanca o negra, joven o vieja.

 ¿Con qué palabras se dirige Ud. a sus amigos? ¿y a las personas que ama?

[g]*preceding* [h]*el... the use* [i]*indiscriminately* [j]*any*

B. Preguntas impertinentes

Paso 1. Use las siguientes palabras para hacer preguntas muy personales. Las preguntas pueden ser sobre el presente o el pasado.

MODELOS: ¿**Has roto** alguna vez con un novio / una novia?
¿De quién **estás enamorado/a** ahora mismo?

1. romper con
2. salir con
3. una cita
4. estar enamorado/a

5. amar
6. la luna de miel
7. llevarse mal con
8. estar divorciado/a

Paso 2. Ahora, en parejas, hagan y contesten las preguntas del **Paso 1.** Si creen que alguna pregunta es demasiado personal, pueden contestar cortésmente: «**Prefiero no contestar esa pregunta.**» También pueden contestar sin cortesía: «**¿Y a ti qué te importa?**»

Paso 3. Díganle a la clase las cosas que Uds. tienen en común.

Nota **comunicativa**

Cómo expresar los mandatos con el infinitivo

You have already learned how to use formal (**Ud./Uds.**) and informal (**tú**) commands in Spanish. Another very common way to communicate a command in Spanish, especially in signs, lists, written instructions, and recipes, is to use the infinitive. Object pronouns always follow the infinitive in an infinitive command.

No estacionar. **No pisar** el césped (*grass*).
Llamar a los padres. **Invitarlos** a cenar.

You will use infinitive commands in **Paso 1** of **Comunicación C**.

C. Receta para unas buenas relaciones.
En su opinión, ¿cuáles son los ingredientes necesarios para un buen matrimonio o una buena amistad?

Paso 1. Haga una lista de los cinco ingredientes esenciales en forma de mandatos con el infinitivo.

Paso 2. Compare su lista con las (*those*) de otros tres estudiantes. ¿Han seleccionado algunos de los mismos ingredientes? Hablen de todos los ingredientes y hagan una lista de los cinco más importantes.

Paso 3. Ahora comparen los resultados obtenidos por todos los grupos.

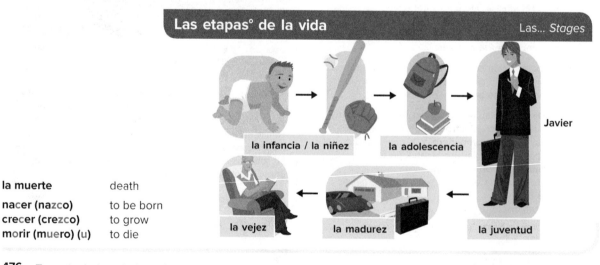

Las etapas° de la vida   Las... *Stages*

la infancia / la niñez   la adolescencia   Javier

la vejez   la madurez   la juventud

la muerte	death
nacer (nazco)	to be born
crecer (crezco)	to grow
morir (muero) (u)	to die

Comunicación

A. Etapas de la vida

Paso 1. Relacione las siguientes palabras y frases con las distintas etapas de la vida de una persona. ¡OJO! Hay más de una relación posible en algunos casos.

1. el amor
2. los nietos
3. los juguetes (*toys*)
4. no poder comer sin ayuda
5. los hijos en la universidad
6. los granos (*pimples*)
7. la universidad
8. la boda

Paso 2. Ahora dé una definición o descripción de las siguientes etapas de la vida. Pueden ser descripciones serias o divertidas.

MODELOS: La infancia es cuando una persona tiene menos de dos años.
La infancia es la etapa de la vida en que solo te importa comer, dormir y jugar.

1. la niñez   2. la adolescencia   3. la madurez   4. la vejez

B. Etapas de su vida

Paso 1. Describa lo que Ud. hacía, hace o piensa hacer, y sus sentimientos, en cada etapa de su vida.

MODELO: mi niñez → **Vivía** en Oklahoma. **Tuve** una niñez feliz. Siempre...

1. mi niñez
2. mi adolescencia
3. mi juventud
4. mi madurez
5. mi vejez

Paso 2. Ahora, en parejas o en grupos, comparen sus descripciones. Luego díganle a la clase lo que Uds. tienen en común.

Estrategia

Para hablar de cada etapa de la vida, es apropiado usar diferentes tiempos verbales. Ejemplos:

- **el pasado:** el pretérito, el imperfecto, el presente perfecto
- **la época actual:** el presente, el presente progresivo
- **el futuro:** ir + a + *infinitive*

Algo sobre...

el Gran Chaco

El Gran Chaco es un inmensa altiplanicie[a] aluvial[b] formada por los ríos Paraguay y Pilcomayo. Ocupa gran parte del Paraguay, además de[c] parte de Bolivia, la Argentina y el Brasil. Su nombre, que viene del quechua, significa tierra de caza.[d] Es una región poco poblada, pero curiosamente hay varias ciudades fundadas por colonias menonitas, alemanas y rusas que llegaron en la década de 1920.

¿Hay en este país alguna región transnacional, es decir, que va más allá de las fronteras nacionales?

[a]*high plateau* [b]*alluvial, formed by river deposits* [c]*además... in addition to* [d]*hunting*

¿Recuerda Ud.?

Before studying **Gramática 44,** review the indefinite and negative words that you learned in **Gramática 19 (Cap. 7).** Remember that **alguien** and **nadie** take the personal **a** when they are used as direct objects.

Busco **a alguien** de la familia.   *I'm looking for someone from the family.*
No veo **a nadie** en el salon   *I don't see anyone in the dance hall.* de baile.

Give the opposite of the following words.
1. nada   2. algunos   3. alguien

« ...él siempre me apoya (*supports*) en todo lo que yo quiera hacer. Y sin él, la verdad,... ya no soy completa».

«Cosas del amor» Segmento 1

Antes de mirar

¿Qué sabe Ud. de la historia romántica de sus padres o de sus abuelos? Conteste las siguientes preguntas.

1. ¿Dónde y cómo se conocieron?
2. ¿Fue amor a primera vista?
3. ¿Cuánto tiempo llevan de casados (*have they been married*)? ¿O cuánto tiempo llevan juntos?
4. ¿Cree Ud. que hacen una buena pareja? ¿Por qué?

Este segmento

Este segmento incluye unas entrevistas que Laura les hace a varias parejas para saber cómo se conocieron. El segmento termina con la historia de Víctor y su esposa.

Vocabulario del segmento

¡Qué asco!	How disgusting!
maravilloso/a	wonderful
acudir	to attend, go to
casualmente	by chance
coincidir	to be (*somewhere*) at the same time by chance
cerquita de	very near to
inesperado/a	unexpected
nos dimos la mirada	**nos miramos**

Después de mirar

A. ¿Está claro? Empareje cada pareja con la descripción de cómo se conocieron.

LAS PAREJAS

1. _____ primera pareja
2. _____ segunda pareja
3. _____ tercera pareja
4. _____ Víctor y su esposa

¿CÓMO SE CONOCIERON?

a. Trabajaron juntos en un proyecto en la comunidad.
b. Se conocieron en una fiesta.
c. Se conocieron en un baile en Ciudad Delicias, donde él tocaba.
d. Se vieron cuando ella estaba haciendo fotocopias.

B. Un poco más. Conteste las siguientes preguntas.

1. ¿Dónde viven todas las parejas que se ven en el segmento?
2. La mayoría de las parejas, ¿creen o no en el amor a primera vista?
3. ¿Está casada Ana? ¿Por qué cree Ud. eso?

C. Y ahora, Uds. En parejas, hablen de la idea del amor a primera vista. ¿Creen en ello (*that concept*)? ¿Han tenido esa experiencia alguna vez? Expliquen sus respuestas y, si pueden, den ejemplos específicos.

GRAMÁTICA

44 ¿Hay alguien que... ? ¿Hay un lugar donde... ?

The Subjunctive (Part 6): The Subjunctive After Nonexisting and Indefinite Antecedents

Grammar Tutorial **44**
■ connect·
|SPANISH
www.connectspanish.com

Gramática en acción: Los buenos padres

¡Feliz Día del P...
papá!

¡Te quiero mucho!

- Un buen padre, así como una buena madre, es alguien que quiere a sus hijos de manera incondicional, se preocupa por su formación y les enseña a ser personas útiles en la vida.
- Todos los niños **necesitan** padres **que** los quieran incondicionalmente, los eduquen y los cuiden.

¿Y Ud.?

Complete las siguientes oraciones.

1. No hay nadie que me quiera más que mi(s) _____.
2. Mi padre/madre es la persona que me enseñó a _____.
3. La persona que se preocupa más por mí en la actualidad es mi _____.

	①		②
definite/existing antecedent	que		indicative
indefinite/nonexisting antecedent	que		subjunctive

> *the antecedent / **el antecedente** = a word or phrase modified by an adjective clause*

1. Adjective Clauses and Antecedents

As you know, noun clauses function like nouns in a sentence. Adjective clauses function like adjectives: they modify/describe a noun or a pronoun. In the sentences to the right, the nouns *car* and *house* (*for sale*) are modified by dependent adjective clauses. The noun that is modified is called the *antecedent* (**el antecedente**) of the dependent clause.

I have a **car that gets good gas mileage.**

Is there a **house for sale that is closer to the city**?

Good parents ■ *A good father, just like a good mother, is someone who loves his/her children unconditionally, worries about their education, and teaches them to live useful lives (i.e. be useful in life).* ■ *All children need parents who love them unconditionally, educate them, and take care of them.*

2. Indicative with Existing Antecedents

The indicative is used in the adjective clause when it refers to or modifies something that the speaker knows exists.

DEFINITE/EXISTING ANTECEDENT: INDICATIVE

He visto un coche que me **gusta** y que no **es** caro.
I've seen a car (that) I like and that's not expensive.

Hay algo aquí que **quiero** ver.
There's something here that I want to see.

Estoy buscando un libro que **estaba** aquí.
I'm looking for a book that was here.

3. Subjunctive with Nonexisting and Indefinite Antecedents

Sometimes the antecedent of an adjective clause is something that does not exist from the point of view of the speaker, or something whose existence is indefinite, uncertain, or just not yet identified. In these cases, the subjunctive must be used in the adjective (dependent) clause in Spanish.

INDEFINITE/NONEXISTING ANTECEDENT: SUBJUNCTIVE

No hay nadie aquí que **hable** guaraní.
There is no one here who speaks Guaraní.

Busco a alguien que **hable** guaraní.
I'm looking for someone who speaks Guaraní. (That person may exist, but I don't know for sure.)

No conozco a nadie que **hable** guaraní.
I don't know anyone who speaks Guaraní.

Necesito un coche que no **gaste** mucha gasolina.
I need a car that doesn't use much gas. (The car may exist, but I haven't identified it yet.)

4. Adjective Clauses That Describe a Place

When the adjective clause describes a place, the word **donde** (rather than **que**) introduces the adjective clause.

INDEFINITE ANTECEDENT: SUBJUNCTIVE

Buscamos un restaurante donde sirvan comida chilena auténtica.
We're looking for a restaurant where they serve authentic Chilean food.

5. Questions Versus Answers with Adjective Clauses

The *subjunctive* is used in the dependent clause in a question about something that the speaker does not know exists for certain. However, the indicative or the subjunctive may be used in the answer, depending on whether the person who answers the question is sure of the existence of the antecedent or not.

QUESTION: SUBJUNCTIVE

—¿**Hay algo** aquí que te **guste**?
"Is there anything here that you like?"

DEFINITE ANTECEDENT: INDICATIVE

—Sí, **hay varios bolsos** que me **gustan.**
"Yes, there are several purses that I like."

NEGATIVE ANTECEDENT: SUBJUNCTIVE

—No, **no hay nada** aquí que me guste.
"No, there's nothing here that I like."

6. Use of the Personal *a*

Remember that the personal **a** is used only before specific persons or animals. It is not used before unknown or nonspecific persons.

UNKNOWN PERSON: SUBJUNCTIVE

Busco **un señor** que **sepa** francés.
I'm looking for a man who knows French. (I don't know of any.)

KNOWN PERSON: INDICATIVE

Busco **al señor** que **sabe** francés.
I'm looking for the man who knows French. (I know there's one in our office.)

DIRECT OBJECT

¿Conoces **a** alguien que sepa francés?
Do you know someone who speaks French?

NOT DIRECT OBJECT

No hay **nadie** aquí que sepa francés.
There's no one here who speaks French.

¡OJO!

The personal **a** is always used before **alguien** and **nadie** when they are direct objects.

Práctica y comunicación

A. Hablando de la gente que conocemos

Paso 1. Autoprueba. Indique cuáles de las siguientes oraciones expresan antecedentes indefinidos o inexistentes.

1. A friend is looking for a counselor who speaks Spanish.
2. I have a friend who is a marriage counselor.
3. I don't know of a good counselor who has an office downtown.
4. I'm looking for the counselor who helped us the last time.

Summary of Nonexisting and Indefinite Antecedents

existing, definite ⟶ indicative
nonexisting, indefinite ⟶ subjunctive

Paso 2. Indique las oraciones que sean verdaderas para Ud. y cambie las otras para que (*so that*) sean verdaderas.

MODELO: Conozco a alguien que va a casarse este año. ⟶
No conozco a **nadie** que **vaya** a casarse este año.

	CIERTO	FALSO
1. Conozco a alguien que va a casarse este año.	☐	☐
2. Tengo un amigo íntimo / una amiga íntima que está casado/a.	☐	☐
3. Conozco a alguien que está recién casado.	☐	☐
4. Tengo un pariente cercano (*close*) que se está divorciando.	☐	☐
5. Tengo un buen amigo que es viudo.	☐	☐
6. Conozco a una estudiante de mi año que está en su viaje de luna de miel.	☐	☐
7. No conozco a nadie que haya roto con su novio/a este año.	☐	☐
8. Sé de alguien que sale con una persona famosa.	☐	☐

Paso 3. Ahora, en parejas, entrevístense sobre las oraciones del **Paso 2**. Luego díganle a la clase la coincidencia que Uds. consideren más curiosa.

B. Hablando de bodas

Paso 1. Complete las siguientes oraciones según lo que se ve en el dibujo.

1. Hay un hombre que está / esté sacando una foto.
2. Hay una persona que está / esté llorando.
3. Hay un hombre que está / esté sonriendo.
4. Hay dos niñas que están / estén peleando.
5. No hay nadie que está / esté cantando.
6. ¿Hay alguien que está / esté tirando (*throwing*) arroz?

Prác. A, Paso 1: Answers: 1, 3

Paso 2. Ahora complete las siguientes oraciones según su experiencia. Use el indicativo o el subjuntivo, según el caso.

En las bodas que yo he visto,...

1. hay / no hay mucha gente de otros estados que... (asistir)
2. hay personas / no hay nadie que... (dar buenos regalos)
3. hay / no hay una ceremonia que... (ser en la iglesia)
4. hay gente / no hay nadie que... (tirar arroz)
5. siempre hay alguien / nunca hay nadie que... (llorar)
6. ¿ ?

C. Una encuesta (*poll*). ¿Qué sabe Ud. de los compañeros de su clase de español? Pregúnteles si saben hacer lo siguiente o a quién le ocurre lo siguiente. Deben levantar la mano solo los que puedan contestar afirmativamente. Luego la persona que hizo la pregunta debe hacer un comentario apropiado. Siga el modelo.

MODELO: hablar chino →
    En esta clase, ¿hay alguien que **hable** chino?
    (*Nadie levanta la mano.*) No hay nadie que **hable** chino.
    (*Alguien levanta la mano.*) Hay una (dos) persona(s) que **habla(n)** chino.

1. hablar ruso / japonés
2. saber tocar la viola / el violín
3. conocer a un actor / una actriz
4. saber preparar comida vietnamita/tailandesa
5. celebrar su cumpleaños hoy / nunca celebrar su cumpleaños
6. cantar en la ducha / la ópera
7. bailar tango/salsa
8. ¿ ?

D. Intercambios

Paso 1. Complete las siguientes declaraciones de acuerdo con su vida real y sus deseos.

1. Tengo un amigo / una amiga que...
2. No conozco a nadie que...
3. Este verano quiero tener un trabajo que...
4. Este verano no quiero hacer nada que...
5. Busco un compañero / una compañera en la vida que...
6. En este mundo, no hay nada que sea más importante que...
7. Este semestre/trimestre tengo cursos que...
8. El próximo semestre/trimestre quiero tomar cursos que...

Paso 2. Ahora, en parejas, hagan y contesten preguntas basadas en las declaraciones del **Paso 1.** Luego díganle a la clase las coincidencias o diferencias más interesantes que Uds. tienen.

Algo sobre...

la represa[a] de Itaipú

La represa de Itaipú es una obra de ingeniería impresionante. Es la central[b] hidroeléctrica que genera más electricidad en el mundo. Es el resultado de un proyecto binacional entre el Paraguay y el Brasil que explota el Río Paraná, la frontera[c] natural entre los dos países. La represa, que se abrió en 1984, provee[d] casi toda la energía que necesita el Paraguay y un cuarto de la energía que consume el Brasil.

¿Cuáles son algunas de las obras de ingeniería más importantes de los Estados Unidos?

[a]*dam* [b]*power station* [c]*border* [d]*provides*

La represa de Itaipú, entre el Paraguay y el Brasil

45 *Lo hago para que tú...*

The Subjunctive (Part 7): The Subjunctive After
Conjunctions of Purpose and Contingency

Grammar Tutorial **45**

connect
|SPANISH
www.connectspanish.com

Gramática en acción: Relaciones familiares y sociales

A.　　　　**B.**　　　　**C.**

¿A qué dibujo corresponde cada una de las siguientes oraciones? ¿Quién las dice?

1. ____ «Aquí tienes la tarjeta de crédito, pero úsala solo **en caso de que** haya una emergencia, ¿eh?»

2. ____ «Deja ya de jugar. No te permito que juegues **antes de que** termines la tarea. ¿Me entiendes?»

3. ____ «Quiero casarme contigo **para que** estemos siempre juntos y no salgas más con Raúl.»

¿Y Ud.?

¿Alguien...

1. le ha dado dinero para que Ud. pague la matrícula de la universidad?

2. le ha ofrecido un trabajo fabuloso antes de que Ud. se gradúe?

3. le ha dicho que quiere casarse con Ud. con tal de que (*provided that*) Ud. lo/la ame?

---

①　　　　　　　　　　②

indicative　conjunction of contingency or purpose　**subjunctive**

> *a conjunction /* **una conjunción** = a word or phrase that connects other words, phrases, or clauses

1. Conjunctions of Purpose and Contingency

The conjunctions at the right express *purpose* (**el propósito**) or *contingency* (**la contingencia**), that is, when one action depends on another = *I'll do X unless Y occurs.* The dependent clauses introduced by them function as adverbs in the sentence.

When there is a change of subject, the Spanish subjunctive is *always* used in the dependent clause introduced by these conjunctions.

Las conjunciones de propósito y contingencia

a menos que	unless
antes (de) que	before
con tal (de) que	provided (that), as long as
en caso de que	in case
para que	so that, in order that
sin que	without; unless

Family and social relationships To which drawing does each of the following sentences correspond? Who is saying them? **1.** *"Here's the credit card, but use it only in case there's an emergency, OK?"* **2.** *"Stop playing right now. I don't allow you to play before you finish your homework. Do you understand me?"* **3.** *"I want to marry you so that we can always be together and (so that) you don't go out with Raúl again."*

Note in the examples:
- Each conjunction contains the word **que,** which is obligatory in Spanish but optional in some cases in English.
- There is a change of subject in the dependent clause (the one introduced by the conjunction).

Voy **con tal (de) que** ellos me **acompañen.**
I'm going, provided (that) they go with me.

En caso de que llegue Juan, dile que ya salí.
In case Juan arrives, tell him (that) I already left.

No voy a la fiesta **sin que** tú me **acompañes.**
I won't go to the party unless you go with me.

2. Order of the Clauses
An adverbial clause that expresses purpose and contingency may precede or follow the main clause, separated by a comma, just as in English. Here are the sentences from Point 1 with the adverbial clause in a different position.

Con tal (de) que ellos me acompañen, voy.
Dile a Juan que ya salí, **en caso de que** llegue.
Sin que tú me acompañes a la fiesta, yo no voy.

3. Same Subject = *preposition + infinitive*
When there is no change of subject, a *preposition + infinitive* phrase is often used to express purpose or contingency, rather than a *conjunction + subjunctive.* Only a **menos que** does not have a prepositional equivalent.

para Estoy aquí **para aprender.** (subject = **yo**)
but: Estoy aquí **para que** Uds. **aprendan.**
(subjects = **yo, Uds.**)

antes de Coma Ud. algo **antes de salir.** (subject = **Ud.**)
but: Coma Ud. algo **antes de que** salgamos.
(subjects = **Ud., nosotros**)

PREPOSITIONS: **antes de, con tal de, en caso de, para, sin** + infinitive
CONJUNCTIONS: **antes (de) que, con tal (de) que, en caso de que, para que, sin que** + subjunctive

con tal de Podemos salir **con tal de tener** tiempo.
(subject = **nosotros**)
but: Podemos salir **con tal de que** tengas tiempo.
(subjects = **nosotros, tú**)

sin Es difícil salir con los amigos **sin gastar** dinero.
(subject = **impersonal**)
but: Es difícil salir con los amigos **sin que** gastemos dinero.
(subjects = **impersonal, nosotros**)

Summary of Conjunctions of Purpose and Contingency

a menos que, antes (de) que, con tal (de) que, en caso de que, para que, sin que + change of subject → subjunctive

Práctica y comunicación

A. ¿Buenos amigos y buenas parejas?

Paso 1. Autoprueba. Empareje las conjunciones con su significado en inglés.

1. _____ para que
2. _____ antes (de) que
3. _____ con tal (de) que
4. _____ a menos que
5. _____ en caso de que
6. _____ sin que

a. without, unless
b. unless
c. before
d. provided (that), as long as
e. in case
f. so that

Paso 2. Complete las siguientes oraciones con la conjunción o preposición apropiada en cada caso. ¡OJO! Algunas conjunciones necesitan **que** y otras no.

1. _____ que sea posible, les hago favores a mis amigos cuando me los piden.
2. Intento escuchar y comprender a mis amigos _____ juzgarlos (*judging them*).
3. Llevo a mis amigos a casa cuando beben demasiado _____ no conduzcan.
4. Nunca les miento a mis amigos, _____ que sea necesario para su beneficio.
5. _____ tener problemas personales, busco el apoyo de mis mejores amigos.
6. Nunca les doy consejos a mis amigos _____ me los pidan.

(Continúa.)

Paso 3. Ahora, en parejas, túrnense para entrevistarse sobre las ideas del **Paso 2.** Luego díganle a la clase algo que tienen en común o en que son radicalmente diferentes.

MODELO: **E1:** ¿Les haces favores a tus amigos con tal de que sea posible?
  E2: Sí. ¿Y tú?
  E1: Yo también. → Les hacemos favores a nuestros amigos con tal de que sea posible.

B. Un fin de semana romántico

Paso 1. Un matrimonio está planeando hacer una escapada (*getaway*) de fin de semana para esquiar. Combine las siguientes ideas para explicar sus planes.

MODELO: Quieren pasar tres días esquiando (con tal de / con tal de que) su hija no se enferme. →
  Quieren pasar tres días esquiando **con tal de que** su hija no se enferme.

1. Desean ir sin su hija (para / para que) poder celebrar su aniversario de boda de una manera especial.
2. Van a pasar el fin de semana esquiando (con tal de / con tal de que) los abuelos puedan quedarse con la niña.
3. No pueden ir (sin / sin que) los abuelos se queden con la niña.
4. El plan es salir temprano el sábado (menos / a menos que) estén muy cansados el viernes por la noche.
5. Es importante que lleguen a la estación de esquí (antes de / antes de que) empiece a nevar.
6. Llevan cadena (*chains*) para las llantas (en caso de / en caso de que) haya mucha nieve en las montañas.
7. Piensan regresar el lunes (antes de / antes de que) sea de noche.

Paso 2. Diga si las siguientes oraciones son ciertas o falsas o si no se menciona la infomación, según el **Paso 1.**

	CIERTO	FALSO	NO SE MENCIONA
1. Los esposos acaban de casarse.	☐	☐	☐
2. Casi siempre salen de vacaciones con su hija.	☐	☐	☐
3. Los dos se preocupan mucho por su hija.	☐	☐	☐
4. Piensan que va a ser muy fácil llegar a la estación de esquí y regresar a casa.	☐	☐	☐

Nota **comunicativa**

¿Para qué? / para (que)... and ¿por qué? / porque...

These words are all close in meaning, but they are used for different purposes. Their use is similar to the use of their English equivalents.

¿Para qué?	What for? For what purpose?	**¿Por qué?**	Why? For what reason?
para que (*conj.*) **para** (*prep.*)	so that (in order) to	**porque...**	because . . .

Compare the use of these words in the following sentences.

—¿**Para qué** necesitas ahora la lista de invitados a la boda?
— **Para** confirmar el número de invitados que van a asistir. Y **para que** el dueño del restaurante sepa exactamente cuántos invitados van a venir.

—¿**Por qué** estás tan nervioso?
—¡**Porque** me caso en una semana!

You will use these words and phrases in **Práctica D.**

Estrategia

cambio de sujeto → subjuntivo

sin cambio de sujeto → infinitivo

Algo sobre...

el té paraguayo

El tereré, la bebida nacional del Paraguay

El té paraguayo o tereré es una bebida que tiene como base la yerba mate. Como en la Argentina y el Uruguay, se bebe en un tipo de taza[a] que tradicionalmente se hace de una calabaza,[b] aunque[c] hoy día se hace de muchos otros materiales. En el Paraguay esta taza se llama una «guampa». A diferencia del mate argentino y uruguayo, el tereré paraguayo se prepara con agua fría o jugo de fruta.

¿Hay bebidas que Ud. relacione con ciertos países? ¿Qué bebida asocia con los Estados Unidos?

[a]*cup* [b]*gourd* [c]*although*

C. **Relaciones sociales.** Hay relaciones sociales de muchos tipos en donde unos dependen de otros. Complete las siguientes oraciones con el presente de subjuntivo para describir algunas de ellas.

1. Los abuelos miman (*spoil*) a sus nietos con tal de que los padres... (permitirlo)
2. Los padres esperan que los padrinos (*godparents*) cuiden a sus hijos en caso de que ellos... (morirse)
3. Los buenos amigos siempre saben lo que uno necesita antes de que... (decírselo)
4. Los amigos paraguayos se reúnen afuera para tomar el tereré con tal de que... (hacer buen tiempo)
5. Los estudiantes no estudian sin que los profesores... (darles tarea)
6. Las parejas se llevan bien a menos que... (haber entre ellos una gran diferencia de opiniones)
7. Los padres trabajan para que sus hijos... (tener lo que necesitan)

D. **Razones para hacer las cosas que hacemos**

Paso 1 Empareje las frases de las dos columnas para hacer oraciones completas.

¡OJO!

¿Por qué... ? / Porque...
 → *indicative*
Para... + *infinitive*
Para que... →
 subjunctive

1. _____ Las universidades tienen cursos que son requisitos para...
2. _____ Los profesores corrigen (*correct*) tareas para...
3. _____ Estudiamos español para...
4. _____ Trabajamos en parejas en clase para...
5. _____ Los profesores organizan actividades en grupo en clase para que...

a. los estudiantes tengan más oportunidad de hablar español.
b. poder comunicarnos con mucha más gente.
c. que los estudiantes tengan un conocimiento amplio del mundo.
d. darles a los estudiantes más ayuda.
e. hablar más en clase.

Paso 2. Ahora, en parejas, den explicaciones sobre la razón de las siguientes situaciones.

1. Estudiamos en la universidad para (que) / porque...
2. La universidad cuesta mucho dinero para (que) / porque...
3. Los profesores les dan tarea a los estudiantes para (que) / porque...
4. Los estudiantes quieren sacar buenas notas para (que) / porque...

E. **Intercambios**

Paso 1. Complete las siguientes oraciones usando una conjunción de contingencia y propósito o una preposición: **a menos que, antes de (que), con tal de (que), en caso de (que), para (que), sin (que).**

MODELO: Voy a graduarme en esta universidad... → Voy a graduarme en esta universidad en dos años a **menos que saque malas notas en varias clases.**

1. Voy a graduarme en esta universidad...
2. (No) Voy a casarme con mi novio/a actual... (Mi hijo/a [no] va a casarse con su novio/a actual...)
3. Espero tener un buen trabajo en dos o tres años...
4. Deseo tener hijos/nietos...
5. Voy a quedarme en este estado...

Paso 2. Ahora, en parejas o grupos, comparen sus oraciones. Luego díganle a la clase cuáles de sus ideas son muy similares o muy diferentes.

Un poco de todo

A. Lengua y cultura: ¿Cómo se divierten los hispanos?

Paso 1. Complete the following description of the favorite pastimes of Hispanic youths. Give the correct form of the words in parentheses, as suggested by context. When two possibilities are given in parentheses, select the correct word. ¡OJO! Context will help you choose what to do with the infinitives. If verbs don't remain in the infinitive form, these are your choices.

INDICATIVO: el presente, el presente perfecto, el pretérito, el imperfecto
SUBJUNTIVO: el presente, el presente perfecto

La hermosa y moderna ciudad de Asunción, Paraguay, que tiene una población metropolitana de más de dos millones de habitantes y muchos sitios para pasear

Como es obvio, hay algunas diferencias entre las culturas norteamericana e hispana. Pero en cuanto a[a] la manera en que los jóvenes se divierten, la verdad es que hay (mucho[1]) puntos en común. A los jóvenes hispanohablantes, que se (*ellos:* llamar[2]) chicos y chicas en el Paraguay, gallos y gallas en Chile, patojos y patojas en Guatemala, pelados y peladas en Colombia, (les / se[3]) (encantar[4]) la música. (Por / Para[5]) eso, no es extraño que (*ellos:* ir[6]) a las discotecas donde (bailar[7]) hasta el amanecer.[b] (A los / Los[8]) muchachos en especial (le / les[9]) (interesar[10]) los eventos deportivos.

En los últimos años, el concepto del centro comercial se (desarrollar[11]) en las ciudades hispanas. Como en este país, (a menos / con tal de[12]) que (haber[13]) tiendas de moda juvenil y electrónica, así como[c] restaurantes económicos, (este[14]) centros atraen[d] (a / –[15]) los jóvenes. También puede haber[e] cines y hasta[f] supermercados en los centros comerciales.

Una cosa que sí distingue[g] a los países hispanos es la costumbre[h] del paseo, que consiste en (caminar[16]) por distracción.[i] Es una manera de pasar un rato con amigos o familiares y es una actividad (por / para[17]) personas de cualquier[j] edad. El paseo no se considera una actividad deportiva sino social. En este sentido, no es comparable de ninguna forma[k] con el *hiking* en la cultura angloparlante.

[a]*en... as far as* [b]*dawn* [c]*así... as well as* [d] *attract* [e]*puede... there can be* [f]*even* [g]*differentiates* [h]*custom, tradition* [i]*amusement* [j]*any* [k]*de... in any way*

Paso 2. Comprensión. Conteste las siguientes preguntas.

1. Según la información en los párrafos, ¿cuáles son algunas de las semejanzas en la forma de divertirse entre los jóvenes hispanos y norteamericanos?
2. ¿Qué palabras se usan para expresar «muchachos y muchachas» en varios países hispanos?
3. ¿Qué es el paseo?
4. ¿Qué ventajas y desventajas ve Ud. en la costumbre hispana del paseo?

Paso 3. Y en su cultura, ¿cuáles son los pasatiempos típicos de las personas según su edad? En parejas, den por lo menos una opinión sobre cada grupo.

1. los adolescentes, hasta los 16 o 17 años
2. los jóvenes entre 18 y 30 años
3. los adultos entre 30 y 60 años
4. las personas mayores
5. las reuniones familiares, con personas de diferentes generaciones

B. Ahora y en el futuro

Paso 1. Complete las siguientes oraciones sobre sus preferencias y expectativas para el futuro.

MODELOS: (No) Me gustan las personas que _____.
→ Me gustan las personas que **son sinceras.**
No me gustan las personas que **no sean sinceras.**

Preferencias
1. (No) Me gustan las personas que _____.
2. (No) Me gustan los profesores que _____.
3. (No) Quiero amigos que _____.
4. No tengo ningún amigo o amiga que _____.

Expectativas para el futuro
5. Este semestre, no dudo que ...
6. Voy a graduarme en _____, a menos que...
7. Algún día, espero tener un(a) _____ que...
8. Este verano voy a _____, con tal de (que)...
9. En el futuro, espero tener _____ hijos, a menos que...
10. No voy a _____ sin (que) ...

Paso 2. Ahora, en parejas, entrevístense sobre las ideas del **Paso 1.** Luego díganle al resto de la clase algo que tienen en común y algo en lo que tienen ideas muy diferentes.

En **su** comunidad

Entreviste a una persona hispana de su universidad o ciudad sobre las relaciones afectivas en su país.

REGUNTAS POSIBLES

- ¿Qué palabras cariñosas se usan con más frecuencia entre padres e hijos en su país de origen? ¿Y entre esposos o novios? ¿entre amigos?

- ¿Cómo se celebra una boda típica en su país?

- ¿Cuál es el porcentaje de divorcios? ¿Es más alto que el de este país o más bajo? Comparado con lo que era hace veinte o treinta años, ¿ha cambiado recientemente?

 **«Cosas del amor» Segmento 2**

Antes de mirar

¿Conoce Ud. a alguien que haya encontrado pareja a través de (*through*) un servicio de internet? ¿Ha usado Ud. este tipo de servicio alguna vez? ¿Qué pasó? Si no ha usado tal (*such a*) servicio, ¿usaría (*would you use*) uno de estos en el futuro?

Este segmento

En este segmento, se muestran los videos de una mujer y dos hombres que buscan pareja. Ana y Víctor les piden a los telespectadores que escojan a uno de los dos hombres para que salga con la mujer.

«...estoy convencida de que en la vida es necesario un equilibrio entre lo profesional y lo personal».

Vocabulario **del segmento**

la carrera	career	a pesar de mi	despite my physical
conversador(a)	conversationalist	físico	appearance
sería el sueño de	would be my	cansarse de	to get tired of
toda mi vida	life's dream	¿A qué esperas?	What are you waiting for?
ponerse en contacto	to get in contact	el aspecto	appearance
aburrirse como	to be bored	el sentido del humor	sense of humor
una ostra	to death	formar un hogar	to settle down
no me falta trabajo	I don't lack for work	disponible	available
reconocer (reconozco)	to recognize	el/la concursante	contestant
la ropa interior	underwear	diremos	we'll tell

Fragmento del guion

Nuestros tres participantes colocaron[a] sus perfiles[b] en un sitio de internet para buscar pareja y los tres nos dieron permiso para mostrar sus videos y participar en este programa. Aquí están.

[a]*placed* [b]*profiles*

Después de mirar

A. **¿Está claro?** Complete las siguientes oraciones según el programa.

1. *El juego del amor* es la versión en español de _____.
2. Los participantes en *El juego del amor* se llaman _____.
3. _____ va(n) a escoger una pareja.

B. **Un poco más.** Conteste las siguientes preguntas.

1. ¿Cuál es la profesión de los tres participantes que buscan pareja?
2. ¿Qué observación sobre Víctor les hace Ana a las telespectadoras, a manera de chiste (*as a joke*)?

 C. **Y ahora, Uds.** En grupos de 4 o 5, debatan sobre cuál de los hombres es mejor para Yolanda. Después voten y presenten sus resultados al resto de la clase, ofreciendo argumentos a favor y en contra de los dos hombres.

A LEER

Hay relaciones sentimentales de muchos tipos. ¿Qué expresiones usa Ud. en inglés para referirse a los diferentes tipos de relaciones entre parejas?

Lectura cultural: El Paraguay
El concepto de noviazgo

En el Paraguay, como en casi todo el mundo hispanohablante, el concepto de noviazgo es un poco diferente del de[a] este país. «Tener novio/a» o «estar de novio/a» indica que una relación es seria y formal, con miras al[b] futuro. **Novio** y **novia,** además,[c] son los términos que se aplican a las personas que se casan durante la ceremonia de la boda. Como el noviazgo ya señala un compromiso,[d] no es tan frecuente usar la palabra **prometido/a**[e] para referirse a los novios que van a casarse.

Cuando las relaciones entre dos personas son informales, se dice que **andan**[f] o **salen** juntos, o simplemente que la persona tiene un amigo o amiga. Con frecuencia se usa la palabra **pareja** para referirse a una persona que convive[g] con otra sin casarse. Por ejemplo, se dice: «Te presento a mi pareja.»

[a]del... *from that of* [b]con... *(one that is) looking ahead to the* [c]*in addition* [d]señala... *indicates a commitment* [e]*fiancé/fiancée* [f]*lit., are walking* [g]*cohabits*

La moneda (*currency*) oficial del Paraguay es el guaraní. Su símbolo es el ₲.

Un símbolo paraguayo: La cultura guaraní

Los guaraníes, un pueblo originario de la región amazónica, se asentaron[a] en lo que hoy es el Paraguay (y zonas adyacentes[b] de Bolivia, el Brasil y la Argentina) varios siglos[c] antes de la llegada de los españoles. La cultura guaraní continúa muy presente en la actualidad. El Paraguay es uno de los países racialmente más homogéneos de Latinoamérica, debido a que[d] la inmensa mayoría de la población es mestiza, de ascendencia guaraní y española. Además,[e] más del 80% de la población del país es bilingüe: habla español y guaraní. Se puede decir que el Paraguay es un país ejemplar[f] en cuanto a[g] la conservación e integración de su herencia ancestral con la más reciente cultura española.

[a]se... *settled* [b]*adjacent, nearby* [c]*centuries* [d]debido... *due to the fact that* [e]*In addition* [f]*exemplary* [g]en... *in terms of*

COMPRENSIÓN

1. ¿En qué es diferente el concepto de novio/a del (*from that*) de *boyfriend/girlfriend*?
2. ¿Qué palabra se refiere a las personas que conviven en una relación amorosa sin estar casados?
3. ¿Por qué es normal que los jóvenes demuestren su cariño en público?
4. ¿Qué costumbre de este país no es común entre los jóvenes españoles?
5. ¿Por qué es homogénea la población paraguaya?

En **otros** países hispanos

- **En todo el mundo hispanohablante** Es muy común ver demostraciones de afecto entre una pareja en parques, plazas y calles, lo cual[a] a veces resulta chocante[b] a algunas personas de otras culturas. Pero es necesario recordar que la mayoría de los jóvenes vive con su familia y no tiene muchas oportunidades de intimidad.[c]

- **En España y otros países** El concepto de «la cita» no es común entre los jóvenes. Para muchos jóvenes españoles, la idea de tener una cita les suena[d] demasiado formal. Desde que[e] los chicos empiezan a salir sin sus padres, lo típico es salir en grupos, en los cuales[f] se forman parejas. Pero todavía prefieren salir en grupo a tomar algo en un bar por la noche o a tomar un café por la tarde.

[a]lo... *which* [b]*shocking* [c]*privacy* [d]les... *sounds to them* [e]Desde... *From the time that* [f]en... *in which*

Y ahora, Uds.

En grupos, hablen del concepto de ser novios en este país. ¿Cuándo se considera que una pareja va en serio? ¿Es cuestión de tiempo? ¿De otros factores?

Del mundo hispano

Antes de leer

¿Cuáles son algunas de las ventajas de conocer a la gente por internet? ¿Tiene esto sus desventajas también? ¿Cuáles son?

Vocabulario **para leer**

la belleza	beauty	**el espíritu**	spirit
cibernauto/a	**por internet**	**la mirada**	view, opinion
encendido/a	passionate	**proponer** (like **poner**)	to propose
enriquecer (enriquezco)	to enrich	**la réplica**	response
enviar (envío)	**mandar**	**el sufrimiento**	suffering

Lectura: «Amor cibernauta», de Diego Muñoz Valenzuela

Se conocieron por la red.[a] Él era tartamudo[b] y tenía un rostro[c] de neanderthal: cabeza enorme, frente abultada,[d] ojos separados, redondos[e] y rojos, dientes de conejo[f] que sobresalían[g] de una boca enorme y abierta, cuerpo endeble[h] y barriga[i] prominente. Ella estaba inválida del cuello hacia abajo[j] y dictaba los mensajes al computador con una voz hermosa, pausada[k] y clara que no parecía tener nada que ver[l]
5   con ella; tenía el cuerpo de una muñeca maltratada.[m] Fue un amor a primer intercambio de mensajes: hablaron de la armonía del universo y de los sufrimientos terrestres, de la necesidad del imperio[n] de la belleza y de los abyectos afanes[ñ] de los mercaderes de la guerra,[o] de la abrumadora[p] generosidad del espíritu humano que contradice la miseria[q] de unos pocos. Leían incrédulos[r] las réplicas donde encontraban una mirada equivalente del mundo, no igual, similar aunque[s] enriquecida por historias y
10   percepciones diferentes. Durante meses evitaron hablar de sí mismos,[t] menos aún de[u] la posibilidad de encontrarse en un sitio real y no virtual. Un día él le envió la foto digitalizada de un galán.[v] Ella le retribuyó con la imagen de una bailarina. Él le escribió encendidos versos de amor que ella leyó embelesada.[w] Ella le envió canciones con su propia voz,[x] él lloró de emoción al escuchar esa música maravillosa. Él le narraba con gracia[y] su agitada vida social, burlándose agudamente[z] de los mediocres.
15   Ella le enviaba descripciones pormenorizadas[aa] de sus giras[bb] por el mundo con compañías famosas. Ninguno de los dos jamás propuso encontrarse en el mundo real. Fue un amor verdadero, no virtual, como los que suelen acontecernos[cc] en ese lugar que llamamos realidad.

[a]internet [b]Él... He stuttered [c]face [d]frente... a bulging forehead [e]round [f]rabbit [g]protruded [h]rickety [i]belly [j]inválida... paralyzed from the neck down [k]slow [l]no... didn't seem to have anything in common [m]una... a beat-up doll [n]reign [ñ]ambitions [o]los... the merchants of war [p]overwhelming [q]stinginess [r]sin creer [s]although [t]evitaron... they avoided talking about themselves [u]menos... even less about [v]un... un hombre muy atractivo [w]entranced [x]su... her own voice [y]con... gracefully [z]burlándose... pointedly making fun [aa]detailed [bb]tours [cc]los... those that tend to happen to us

Comprensión

A. Un resumen del cuento. Seleccione la opción apropiada, según el cuento.

1. El hombre del cuento es muy feo / muy guapo.
2. La mujer tiene / no tiene una discapacidad (*disability*) física.
3. Primero, los dos mandan mensajes sobre temas románticos / la vida y el mundo.
4. Por su intercambio de mensajes, sienten mucha / poca armonía entre sí (*between them*).
5. Cuando por fin se comunican detalles sobre su apariencia y su vida, envían información falsa / verdadera.
6. Los dos eventualmente / nunca se conocen en persona.

B. ¿Qué piensa Ud.? Conteste las siguientes preguntas.

1. ¿Por qué cree Ud. que se dijeron mentiras sobre sí mismos? ¿Era eso necesario?
2. El autor del cuento dice que su relación fue «un amor verdadero». ¿Está Ud. de acuerdo? Explique.
3. ¿Por qué el hombre y la mujer del cuento no tienen nombres?

A ESCUCHAR — Un anuncio para Naranjas, un servicio *online*

Antes de escuchar

¿Cómo se puede encontrar a la pareja ideal? Según su experiencia, ¿es difícil conocer a personas que podrían (*could*) ser su pareja? ¿Qué es necesario o fundamental para que haya una buena relación entre una pareja?

Vocabulario para escuchar

la media naranja	better half		lograr	to achieve
el éxito	success		duradero/a	long-lasting
el cuestionario	questionnaire		los valores	values
los pilares	pillars, bases		la afinidad	compatibility
cualquier	any		elegir	to select
los terapeutas	therapists		inscríbete gratis	register for free
los investigadores	researchers		el perfil	profile
los compatibles	las personas compatibles		la soledad	loneliness
comprobado/a	demonstrated			

Después de escuchar

A. La información correcta. Las siguientes oraciones son falsas. Corríjalas.

1. El cuestionario de Naranjas se hace con papel y lápiz.
2. El éxito de este sitio está basado en las reuniones con los terapeutas.
3. La afinidad de valores e intereses no es importante para una buena relación entre dos personas.
4. Es necesario pagar para inscribirse.

B. Más detalles. Conteste las siguientes preguntas.

1. ¿Qué ventajas ofrece Naranjas sobre otros sitios?
2. ¿Por qué es importante el cuestionario de Naranjas?
3. ¿Qué ofrece gratis Naranjas?
4. ¿Cuál es la oferta para los nuevos miembros?
5. ¿Por qué cree Ud. que este sitio se llama Naranjas?

PRODUCCIÓN PERSONAL

¡Ahora, yo!

A. Use de modelo las preguntas y respuestas de la página 473 de este capítulo para hablar de sus relaciones personales y sus creencias (*beliefs*) sobre el amor.

B. Filme una entrevista que Ud. le hace con una pareja en la que (*which*) hablen de cuándo y cómo se conocieron y cuánto tiempo hace que están juntos.

A ESCRIBIR

Consejos sentimentales

En este capítulo Ud. va a escribir una columna de consejos sobre las relaciones personales. Para empezar, decida si quiere escribir sobre relaciones románticas o amistosas.

Preparar

Paso 1. En parejas, hablen de las cualidades más importantes para mantener una buena amistad o una relación amorosa. Hablen también de los problemas más comunes con que se enfrentan (*are faced*) los amigos o las parejas.

Paso 2. Ahora use las ideas del **Paso 1** para desarrollar su ensayo. Hay más ayuda en Connect.

> ## Más ideas para su portafolio
>
> - Incluya la foto de alguien con quien tiene una relación especial. Explique lo que esta persona representa para Ud. y dé otros detalles: las cualidades que Ud. admira de esta persona, cómo se conocieron, qué les gusta hacer juntos, etcétera.
>
> - Escriba un párrafo sobre una pareja especial en su vida (sus padres, sus abuelos, unos amigos...). Describa la relación entre ellos: su historia, cómo han influido en la vida de Ud., por qué son muy importantes para Ud. Si es posible, incluya una foto de la pareja.
>
> - Si ha estado jugando Practice Spanish: Study Abroad, en Quest 11 Ud. supo que fue la poesía de Pablo Neruda que inspiró a Doña Jiménez a escribir. Busque y lea el poema «Oh Tierra, espérame» de Neruda y después haga un breve análisis literario. ¿De qué se trata el poema? ¿Cómo describe el poema la relación entre el ser humano y la naturaleza? Escriba su propio poema que contenga sus ideas y sus sentimientos sobre el medio ambiente.

Sugerencia: You are now ready to play Quest 11 in **Practice Spanish: Study Abroad** (www.mhpractice.com).

EN RESUMEN En este capítulo

AFTER STUDYING THIS CHAPTER I CAN. . .

☐ talk about relationships (474–475)

☐ talk about the stages of one's life (476)

☐ use the indicative or subjunctive after antecedents to describe things and people in complex sentences (479–480)

☐ express contingency and purpose in complex sentences using the subjunctive (483–484)

☐ recognize/describe at least 2–3 aspects of Paraguayan cultures

Gramática en breve

44. The Subjunctive After Nonexisting and Indefinite Antecedents

①		②
definite/existing antecedent	**que**	**indicative**

Hay alguien/algo que...

①		②
indefinite/non-existing antecedent	**que**	subjunctive

No hay nadie/nada que...
¿Hay alguien/algo que... ?

45. The Subjunctive After Conjunctions of Purpose and Contingency

①		②
indicative	conjunction of purpose or contingency	subjunctive

Conjunctions: **a menos que, antes (de) que, con tal (de) que, en caso de que, para que, sin que**

Vocabulario

Las relaciones sentimentales

amar	to love
casarse (con)	to marry
conocerse (conozco)	to meet
enamorarse (de)	to fall in love (with)
llevarse bien/mal (con)	to get along well/poorly (with)
querer	to love

romper (con)	to break up (with)

Repaso: estar (con), pelear con, salir (con)
Cognados: divorciarse (de), separarse (de)

la amistad	friendship
el amor	love
la boda	wedding (ceremony)
el cariño	affection
la iglesia	church
la luna de miel	honeymoon
el matrimonio	marriage; married couple
la novia	fiancée; bride
el noviazgo	engagement
el novio	fiancé; groom
la pareja	(married) couple; partner
el/la viudo/a	widower/widow

Cognados: el divorcio, la separación

Repaso: el/la amigo/a, la cita, el/la esposo/a, el marido, la mujer (*wife*), **el/la novio/a** (*boy/girlfriend*)

amistoso/a	friendly
enamorado/a (de)	in love (with)
recién casado/a	newlywed
soltero/a	single (person)

estar casado/a (con)	to be married (to)
ser casado/a	to be a married person

Cognados: divorciado/a (de), separado/a (de)
Repaso: cariñoso/a, feliz (*pl.* **felices**)

Las etapas de la vida

la etapa	stage, phase
la infancia	infancy; childhood
la juventud	youth
la madurez	middle age
la muerte	death
la niñez (*pl.* **niñeces**)	infancy; childhood
la vejez	old age

Cognado: la adolescencia

Repaso: la vida

crecer (crezco)	to grow
nacer (nazco)	to be born

Repaso: morir (muero) (u)

Las conjunciones

a menos que	unless
antes (de) que	before
con tal (de) que	provided (that), as long as
en caso de que	in case
para que	so that, in order to
sin que	without; unless

Las preposiciones

con tal de	provided
en caso de	in case

Repaso: antes de, para, sin

Palabras adicionales

bastante	rather, sufficiently; enough
¿para qué... ?	for what purpose?, what for?

Repaso: para, ¿por qué?, porque

Vocabulario personal

www.connectspanish.com

17

¿Trabajar para vivir o vivir para trabajar?

En este capítulo

VOCABULARY

Professions and careers   498

The working world   500

Money matters   501

GRAMMAR

Talking about the future   505

Talking about the future in another way   511

CULTURAL FOCUS

Chile and its cultures

Durante la cosecha (*harvest*) de uvas Chardonnay, en Chile

PERÚ

BOLIVIA

BRASIL

*OCÉANO
PACÍFICO*

Antofagasta

PARAGUAY

CHILE   ARGENTINA   URUGUAY

Valparaíso
Santiago
Concepción

Isla de Pascua
(CHILE)

*OCÉANO
ATLÁNTICO*

0   125   250 Millas

0   125   250 Kilómetros

Punta Arenas

CHILE

**17.4 (punto cuatro)
millones de habitantes**

- Chile es un país muy largo y angosto[a] que tiene casi todos los tipos de climas, con excepción del tropical. Se extiende desde el desierto de Atacama, el lugar más seco[b] del mundo, hasta la Antártida.

- La minería, especialmente del cobre,[c] representa una gran parte del Producto Nacional Bruto[d] de Chile.

- Los vinos chilenos, producidos en la zona central del país, están entre los mejores del mundo. De hecho,[e] Chile ocupa el cuarto lugar entre los mayores exportadores de vino a los Estados Unidos.

[a]*narrow* [b]*más... driest* [c]*copper* [d]*Producto...
Gross National Product* [e]*De... In fact*

- En este momento de su vida, ¿trabaja Ud. y estudia o solo estudia?
- Si ha trabajado, ¿cómo ha sido su experiencia laboral? ¿Qué trabajos ha tenido?
- ¿Qué condiciones y beneficios laborales considera Ud. importantes? ¿un seguro[a] de salud? ¿un horario flexible? ¿muchos días de vacaciones al año? ¿la posibilidad de viajar o trabajar desde la casa?

[a]*insurance*

GABRIELA ACOSTA ROMANO CONTESTA LAS PREGUNTAS.

- Estoy trabajando como asistente de laboratorio desde que[a] terminé la carrera de química el año pasado. Pero el curso[b] próximo voy a empezar una maestría.[c]

- Aparte de[d] trabajar en el laboratorio, he sido tutora de niños y, antes, en el verano trabajaba en la finca de mis abuelos haciendo labores agrícolas[e] o empacando[f] las verduras para la venta.[g]

- Supongo[h] que las normales: un buen horario, un mes de vacaciones pagadas, seguro de salud... El trabajo de laboratorio no se puede hacer en casa. Pero sí es posible tener flexibilidad de horario.

[a]*desde... since* [b]*año académico* [c]*master's (degree)* [d]*Aparte... Besides*
[e]*labores... agricultural work, chores* [f]*packing* [g]*sale* [h]*I suppose*

Las profesiones y los oficios°

trades

el maestro (la maestra) (de escuela)

la médica (el médico)

el plomero (la plomera)

la cocinera (el cocinero)

el peluquero (la peluquera)

la mujer soldado (el soldado)

You can hear the pronunciation of theme vocabulary words and phrases in the Connect eBook.

Las profesiones

el abogado / la abogada	lawyer
el bibliotecario / la bibliotecaria	librarian
el consejero / la consejera	counselor
el contador / la contadora	accountant
el enfermero / la enfermera	nurse
el hombre / la mujer de negocios	businessperson
el ingeniero / la ingeniera	engineer
el/la periodista	journalist
el sicólogo / la sicóloga	psychologist
el/la siquiatra	psychiatrist
el trabajador social / la trabajadora social	social worker
el traductor / la traductora	translator

Cognados: el/la analista de sistemas, el/la artista, el/la asistente de vuelo, el/la astronauta, el/la dentista, el diseñador gráfico / la diseñadora gráfica, el fotógrafo / la fotógrafa, el/la militar, el profesor / la profesora, el programador / la programadora, el secretario / la secretaria, el veterinario / la veterinaria

Los oficios

el amo/ama de casa	housewife/husband
el cajero / la cajera	(check-out) cashier; (bank) teller
el camarero / la camarera	waiter/waitress
el dependiente / la dependienta	clerk
el obrero / la obrera	worker, laborer
el técnico / la técnica	technician
el vendedor / la vendedora	salesperson

Cognados: el/la electricista, el mecánico / la mecánica

¡OJO!

If the vocabulary needed to describe your (intended) career is not listed here, look it up in a dictionary or ask your instructor.

Comunicación

A. ¿A quién necesita Ud.?

Paso 1. ¿A quién se debe llamar o con quién se debe consultar en estas situaciones? **¡OJO!** Hay más de una respuesta posible en algunos casos.

1. La tubería del agua (*plumbing*) de la cocina no funciona bien.
2. Ud. acaba de tener un accidente automovilístico; el conductor del otro coche dice que Ud. tuvo la culpa (*blame*).
3. Por las muchas presiones de su vida profesional y personal, Ud. tiene serios problemas afectivos.
4. Ud. es el dueño o la dueña de un restaurante y necesita a alguien que haga la comida.
5. Ud. quiere que alguien le construya un muro (*wall*) en el jardín.
6. Ud. conoce los detalles de un escándalo local y quiere divulgarlos.

Paso 2. Ahora, en parejas, inventen situaciones como las del **Paso 1.** Luego léanlas a otros estudiantes para que ellos digan a quién deben consultar.

B. Asociaciones. ¿Qué profesiones u oficios asocian Uds. con estas frases? Consulten la lista de profesiones y oficios y usen el **Vocabulario útil**.

1. creativo/rutinario
2. muchos/pocos años de preparación o experiencia
3. buen sueldo / sueldo regular
4. mucha/poca responsabilidad
5. mucho/poco prestigio
6. flexibilidad / «de nueve a cinco»
7. mucho/poco tiempo libre
8. peligroso (*dangerous*) / seguro
9. en el pasado, solo para hombres/mujeres
10. todavía solo para hombres/mujeres

Así se dice

el/la contador(a) =
  el/la contable (*Sp.*)
el/la periodista =
  el/la reportero/a
el/la plomero/a =
  el/la fontanero/a (*Sp.*)

Vocabulario útil

actor/actriz	policía /
arquitecto/a	mujer
camarero/a	policía
cantinero/a	político/a
(*bartender*)	presidente/a
carpintero/a	sacerdote
chófer	(*priest*),
detective	pastor(a),
niñero/a	rabino/a
pintor(a)	senador(a)
poeta	

Nota **cultural**

Nuevas tendencias del español para evitar el sexismo lingüístico

Con el incremento de posiciones y cargos[a] ocupados por mujeres en todos los ámbitos[b] profesionales y de poder,[c] el debate por eliminar el sexismo en la lengua española se ha intensificado.

- Se evita usar exclusivamente la forma masculina para designar a las personas de los dos sexos.
- Se usan palabras que incluyen a personas de los dos sexos, como las siguientes:

  el estudiantado[d] = estudiantes (hombres y mujeres)
  el profesorado[e] = profesores y profesoras
  la infancia = niños y niñas
  la tercera edad, las personas mayores = ancianos y ancianas

- En muchos ambientes laborales, se evita dar el tratamiento de «señorita» a todas las mujeres y se prefiere el de «señora», para no hacer distinción entre las mujeres solteras y las casadas, al igual que[f] esta distinción no se hace entre los hombres.
- La aplicación de la forma femenina a algunos cargos importantes, títulos y profesiones se ha estabilizado a medida que[g] las mujeres han conquistado estos puestos: **jefa, médica, ministra, presidenta.**

[a]*posts* [b]*arenas* [c]*power* [d]*student body, the students* [e]*faculty, the professors* [f]*al... just as* [g]*a... as*

Michelle Bachelet, Presidenta de Chile por segunda vez y anteriormente Ministra de Salud y de Defensa

- Para integrar en una sola[h] palabra las formas masculina y femenina, se ha empezado a usar el símbolo de la arroba: @. Por ejemplo, **chic@s = chicos y chicas.** La limitación de esta forma es que es solo un recurso gráfico.[i]

Aunque queda mucho por hacer[j] para eliminar el sexismo en la lengua española, se han dado grandes pasos en todos los países y a todos los niveles.

 ¿Conoce Ud. algún ejemplo de sexismo en su lengua materna?

[h]*single* [i]*un... a graphic solution* [j]*Aunque... Although much remains to be done*

las **comunicaciones**
la **contabilidad**
  accounting
el **derecho** law
la **gerontología**
la **ingeniería**
el **marketing/**
  mercadeo
la **organización**
  administrativa
la **pedagogía/**
  enseñanza
la **retórica** speech
la **sociología**

C. **¿Qué preparación se necesita para ser... ?** En parejas, piensen en las carreras (*majors*) y materias específicas que se deben o se pueden estudiar para prepararse para cada profesión de la siguiente lista.

MODELO: profesor(a) de una lengua extranjera ⟶ Debe estudiar por lo menos dos lenguas extranjeras o lingüística. Es necesario que hable una de las lenguas perfectamente. También debe estudiar literatura, historia y geografía.

1. traductor(a) en la ONU (Organización de las Naciones Unidas)
2. reportero deportivo / reportera deportiva en la televisión
3. contador(a) para un grupo de abogados
4. periodista para una revista de ecología
5. trabajador(a) social, especializado/a en los problemas de los ancianos
6. maestro/a de primaria, especializado/a en la educación bilingüe

D. **Intercambios**

Paso 1. En parejas, túrnense para hacer y contestar preguntas para averiguar (*find out*) la siguiente información de su compañero/a.

1. lo que hacían sus abuelos
2. la profesión u oficio de sus padres
3. si tiene un amigo o pariente que tenga una profesión extraordinaria o interesante y el nombre de esa profesión
4. lo que los padres de su compañero/a quieren que él/ella sea y lo él/ella quiere ser
5. la carrera que estudian algunos de sus amigos (los hijos de sus amigos)

Paso 2. Ahora díganle a la clase dos detalles interesantes sobre su compañero/a.

El mundo laboral

hacer/tener una entrevista
la Sra. Alonso
la entrevistadora (el entrevistador)
el Sr. Cardozo
el currículum
el entrevistado (la entrevistada)

el/la **aspirante**	job candidate
el **empleo/trabajo**	job; position
bien/mal **pagado**	well-/poorly paying
de tiempo **completo/** **parcial**	full-/part-time
la **empresa**	corporation; business
el **gerente** / la **gerente**	manager
el **puesto**	position
el **salario**	pay, wages (*often per hour*)
la **solicitud**	job application
el **sueldo**	salary
conseguir (*like* seguir) un empleo	to get a job
despedir (*like* pedir)	to let (*someone*) go; to fire (*someone*) (*from a job*)
graduarse (me gradúo) **(en)**	to graduate (from)
jubilarse	to retire (*from a job*)
llenar (un formulario)	to fill out (a form)
renunciar (a)	to resign (from)
solicitar	to apply for (*a job*)

Así se dice

el trabajo de tiempo parcial = la jornada de tiempo parcial
el empleo = el puesto, el trabajo

Comunicación

A. Definiciones. Defina las siguientes palabras y frases en español.

MODELO: la empresa →
una compañía grande, como la IBM o Ford

1. el currículum
2. renunciar
3. la aspirante
4. el gerente
5. el sueldo
6. llenar una solicitud

B. En busca (*search*) de un empleo

Paso 1. Haga una lista de todos los pasos, en orden, que con frecuencia se dan para conseguir un empleo. Use el vocabulario de **El mundo laboral** y el **Vocabulario útil.**

Paso 2. Ahora, en parejas, narren lo que hicieron para conseguir su empleo actual o el último empleo que han tenido. Si alguno/a de Uds. no tiene trabajo, esa persona debe narrar lo que va a hacer para conseguirlo.

MODELO: Necesitaba un trabajo de tiempo parcial en la universidad. Por eso fui al centro de orientación profesional de la universidad....

> **Vocabulario útil**
>
> **los avisos clasificados** classified ads
> **los beneficios**
> **la carta de recomendación**
> **el centro de orientación profesional**
> career center
> **el/la recepcionista**

Estrategia

una secuencia de acciones = el pretérito
los detalles de fondo (*background*) = el imperfecto.

Una cuestión de dinero

el interés	interest
el préstamo	loan
el presupuesto	budget
el recibo	receipt
ahorrar	to save (*money*)
cargar (gu) a una cuenta	to charge to an account
cobrar	to cash (*a check*); to charge (*someone for an item or service*)
depositar	to deposit
ganar	to earn
gastar	to spend (*money*)
pagar (gu) a plazos / con cheque / en efectivo	to pay in installments / by check / in cash
pedir (pido) (i) prestado/a	to borrow
prestar	to lend
sacar (qu)	to withdraw, take out

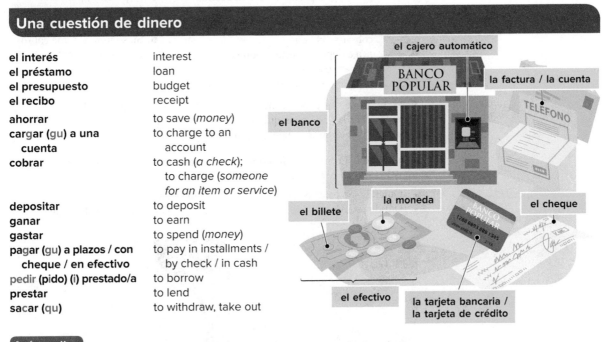

el cajero automático

BANCO POPULAR

la factura / la cuenta

TELÉFONO

el banco

el billete

la moneda

el cheque

el efectivo

la tarjeta bancaria / la tarjeta de crédito

Así se dice

depositar dinero = ingresar dinero, poner dinero en una cuenta
pagar en efectivo = pagar al contado

Comunicación

A. El mes pasado. Piense en sus finanzas personales del mes pasado. ¿Fue un mes típico? ¿Tuvo dificultades al final del mes o todo le salió bien?

Un cajero automático del Banco de Santander, Chile: ¿Hay uno donde Ud. vive?

Paso 1. Indique las respuestas apropiadas, según su experiencia.

	SÍ	NO
1. Hice un presupuesto al principio (*beginning*) del mes.	☐	☐
2. Deposité más dinero en el banco del que (*than what*) saqué.	☐	☐
3. Saqué dinero del cajero automático más de tres veces.	☐	☐
4. Pagué todas mis cuentas a tiempo.	☐	☐
5. Les pedí un préstamo a mis padres.	☐	☐
6. Almorcé en casa para economizar un poco.	☐	☐
7. Gasté mucho dinero en divertirme.	☐	☐
8. Le presté dinero a un amigo.	☐	☐
9. Usé la tarjeta de crédito solo un par de veces.	☐	☐
10. Dejé de comprar café.	☐	☐

Paso 2. Pensando todavía en sus respuestas, diga tres cosas que Ud. debe hacer para mejorar su situación económica.

MODELO: Debo hacer un presupuesto mensual (*monthly*).

B. Diálogos

Paso 1. Empareje las preguntas de la izquierda con las respuestas de la derecha.

1. _____ ¿Cómo prefiere Ud. pagar?

2. _____ ¿Hay algún problema con la cuenta?

3. _____ Me da una identificación, por favor. Necesito verla para que Ud. pueda cobrar su cheque.

4. _____ ¿Va a depositar este cheque o prefiere cobrarlo?

5. _____ ¿Le pongo el recibo en la bolsa (*bag*)?

a. Deposítelo, por favor.
b. No, mejor me lo da a mí.
c. Voy a pagar en efectivo.
d. Sí, señora. Ud. me cobró demasiado por el postre.
e. Aquí la tiene.

Paso 2. Ahora, en parejas, inventen un contexto posible para cada diálogo. ¿Dónde están las personas que hablan? ¿En un banco? ¿en una tienda? ¿Qué hacen? ¿Quiénes son? ¿Clientes? ¿cajeros? ¿dependientes?

C. Situaciones. En parejas, describan lo que pasa en los siguientes dibujos. Usen estas preguntas como guía.

- ¿Quiénes son estas personas?
- ¿Dónde están?
- ¿Cómo van a pagar?
- ¿Qué van a hacer después de pagar?

1.

2.

Nota comunicativa

Más pronombres posesivos

In Spanish, *stressed possessives* (**las formas tónicas de los posesivos**) come after the noun, which is always preceded by a definite or indefinite article.

Es **un** amigo **mío**.	*He's a friend of mine.*

Stressed possessives are often used in Spanish to contrast one thing with another.

Esta es **la** cuenta **mía** y esa es **la suya**.	*This is my bill and that's (that one is) yours (his, hers, yours).*

As you can see in the preceding example (**la suya**) and in the following one, stressed possessives can also be used without the noun. Sometimes the article is omitted.*

—¿De quién es este libro?	*"Whose book is this?"*
—Es **mío**.	*"It's mine."*

Here are the forms of the stressed possessives.

mío/a(s)	my, (of) mine	**nuestro**/a(s)	our, (of) ours
tuyo/a(s)	your, (of) yours	**vuestro**/a(s)	your, (of) yours
suyo/a(s)	your, (of) yours, his, of (his), her, (of) hers	**suyo**/a(s)	your, (of) yours their, (of) theirs

You will use stressed possessives in **Comunicación D** and **E.**

> ### ¡OJO!
> The **nosotros/as** and **vosotros/as** forms are identical to the possessives you already know.

D. Comparaciones. Compare los siguientes aspectos de su vida con lo que pasa en general.

1. Las clases de esta universidad son fáciles / regulares / difíciles. Creo que las mías...
2. Las clases aquí son grandes / pequeñas. Pienso que la nuestra...
3. En esta ciudad, los alquileres son altos / regulares. Creo que...
4. La familia es un apoyo (*support*) / una molestia cuando uno tiene problemas. En general...
5. Muchas ciudades modernas tienen / no tienen serios problemas con la contaminación. ...
6. Las finanzas son fáciles / difíciles de manejar. ...

E. Información personal

Paso 1. En parejas, túrnense para hacer y contestar preguntas, usando posesivos en sus respuestas según el modelo.

MODELO: Mi banco es... → Mi banco es University Bank. **¿Y el tuyo?**

1. Mi banco es...
2. Mis facturas mensuales (*monthly*) para los gastos de vivienda (no) son muy altas.
3. Hoy (no) tengo mucho dinero en mi cuenta corriente.
4. Mi celular es un...
5. Mi consejero/a académico/a es...
6. Un amigo mío / Una amiga mía juega en un equipo de...

Paso 2. Ahora díganle a la clase una cosa interesante sobre su compañero/a.

---

*See Appendix 3 for more information about using the stressed possessive forms.

«Los hispanos que admiramos» Segmento 1

Proporcionar (*To provide*) cuidado médico a todas las personas que lo necesiten es un compromiso (*commitment*) personal y un orgullo (*pride*) tanto para (*as much for*) esta doctora como para (*as for*) el resto del personal de su clínica.

Antes de mirar

Las personas que Ud. más admira, ¿son famosas? ¿A qué se dedican? (*What do they do?*) Puede indicar más de una categoría, pero no las indique todas. Limítese a cuatro.

1. ☐ médico/a, dentista o enfermero/a
2. ☐ maestro/a o profesor(a)
3. ☐ hombre/mujer de negocios
4. ☐ ama/o de casa
5. ☐ deportista
6. ☐ actor/actriz, cantante o artista de otro tipo
7. ☐ trabajador(a) social
8. ☐ político/a
9. ☐ otro: _____

Este segmento

El programa está dedicado a las personas hispanas que son admiradas por otros hispanos. Este segmento incluye una entrevista con una doctora que trabaja en una clínica de Los Ángeles.

Vocabulario del segmento

en respuesta a nuestra petición	responding to our request	diría	I would say
efectivamente	actually	si no estuviéramos	if we weren't
los seres queridos	loved ones	acudirían	they would come
acudir	venir	dar gusto	to give pleasure
proporcionar	dar	disfrutar	to enjoy
la gente necesitada	needy people	el seguro	insurance
la amabilidad	kindness	la meta	goal
ya que	since	tener confianza	creer
		lograr	to achieve

Después de mirar

A. ¿Está claro? Complete las siguientes oraciones con información del programa.

1. Los telespectadores nombraron a las personas que admiran por medio de (*via*) _____.
2. El programa recibió _____ de nombres de personas admiradas.
3. La Dra. Zaragoza-Kaneki es una angelina de origen _____.
4. En su clínica, más del _____ por ciento de los pacientes es de origen hispano, y el _____ por ciento de todos los pacientes no habla inglés.
5. Su deseo para la clínica es obtener recursos federales para _____ .

B. Un poco más. Conteste las siguientes preguntas.

1. ¿Entre qué horas está abierta la clínica?
2. ¿Por qué escogió la Dra. Zaragoza-Kaneki su profesión?
3. ¿Cuál es una de las metas importantes para la doctora?

C. Y ahora, Uds. En parejas, imaginen que tienen la oportunidad de entrevistar a la Dra. Zaragoza-Kaneki. Hagan una lista de cinco preguntas que les gustaría hacerle.

GRAMÁTICA

¿Recuerda Ud.?

Before studying the future tense in **Gramática 46,** review **Gramática 3 (Cap. 2)** and **Gramática 11 (Cap. 4),** where you learned ways of expressing future actions. Then indicate which of the following sentences can be used to express a future action.

1. ☐ Trabajé hasta las dos.
2. ☐ Trabajo a las dos.
3. ☐ Voy a trabajar a las dos.

4. ☐ Trabajaba a las dos.
5. ☐ Estoy trabajando.
6. ☐ He trabajado a las dos.

Grammar Tutorial 46
connect SPANISH
www.connectspanish.com

46 Talking About the Future
Future Verb Forms

Gramática en acción: ¿Cómo será su futuro?

- Seré rica y famosa porque escribiré un blog que tendrá millones de seguidores.
- Todo el mundo en Middletown me conocerá.
- Viajaré mucho con mi mejor amiga y con mi familia.
- Viviré en Nueva York, Londres y París.

¿Y Ud.?
1. ¿Será Ud. rico/a y famoso/a algún día? ([No] Seré...)
2. ¿Dónde vivirá en 10 años?
3. ¿Viajará mucho?

Alicia, 10 años

So far, you have been expressing future actions in Spanish mostly with the present tense or with **ir** + **a** + *infinitive*. But Spanish also has a future tense, like English (*I will . . . , you will . . .*). In Spanish the *future* (**el futuro**) is used to express strong intentions and dreams.

Future of Regular Verbs / El futuro de los verbos regulares

hablar		comer		vivir	
hablaré	hablaremos	comeré	comeremos	viviré	viviremos
hablarás	hablaréis	comerás	comeréis	vivirás	viviréis
hablará	hablarán	comerá	comerán	vivirá	vivirán

What will your future be like? • *I'll be rich and famous because I'll write a blog that will have millions of followers.* • *Everyone in Middletown will know me.* • *I'll travel a lot with my best friend and with my family.* • *I'll live in New York, London, and Paris.*

1. Future Tense Endings

In English the *future* (**el futuro**) is a compound tense, formed with the auxiliary (helping) verbs *will* or *shall*: *I will speak, you **shall** do what I say,* and so on. The Spanish future is a simple verb form (only one word). It is formed by adding the identical set of future endings to **-ar, -er,** and **-ir** infinitives. No auxiliary verbs are needed.

Las terminaciones del futuro

	-é	-emos
infinitivo +	-ás	-éis
	-á	-án

2. Irregular Future Forms

Here are the most common Spanish verbs that are irregular in the future. The future endings are attached to their irregular stems.

Note that the future of **hay (haber)** is **habrá** (*there will be*).*

decir: **diré, dirás, dirá, diremos, diréis, dirán**

decir:	dir-	
haber (hay):	habr-	
hacer:	har-	-é
poder:	podr-	-ás
poner:	pondr-	-á
querer:	querr-	-emos
saber:	sabr-	-éis
salir:	saldr-	-án
tener:	tendr-	
venir:	vendr-	

3. Ways to Express the Future

As you know, the future tense is not the only way to express future actions in Spanish. Other ways to express the future, especially the near future, include:

• the simple present indicative

Nos vemos mañana a las ocho.
We'll see each other tomorrow at 8:00.

• **ir + a +** infinitive

Voy a llevar una chaqueta para la entrevista.
I will wear (am going to wear) a jacket to the interview.

• the simple present subjunctive

No creo que **consiga** ese puesto.
I don't think (that) she'll get that job.

The Spanish future tense is mostly used to express serious goals and projects farther into the future, as when expressing dreams and aspirations, as seen in **Gramática en acción.**

Trabajaré mucho y **me haré** rico.
I'll work very hard, and I'll get rich.

4. Expressing Willingness

When the English *will* refers not to future time but to the *willingness* of someone to do something, Spanish does not use the future but rather the verbs **querer** or **poder,** or simply the present tense of any verb. In this context, **querer** has almost the force of a command.

¿Quieres/Puedes cerrar la puerta, por favor?
Will/Could you please close the door?

¿Cierras la puerta, por favor?
Can you close the door, please?

---

*The future forms of the verb **haber** are used to form the future perfect tense (**el futuro perfecto**), which expresses what will have occurred at some point in the future: **Para mañana, ya habré hablado con Miguel.** (By tomorrow, I will have already spoken with Miguel.) You will find a more detailed presentation of these forms in Appendix 4, Additional Perfect Forms (Indicative and Subjunctive).

Práctica y comunicación

A. Un sábado típico

Paso 1. Autoprueba. Dé la forma apropiada del futuro de los siguientes verbos.

1. yo vivir_____
2. ella dir_____
3. ellos saldr_____

4. Uds. vendr_____
5. nosotros comer_____
6. tú querr_____

Paso 2. Haga oraciones sobre cómo será su vida en los próximos 10–15 años, usando el tiempo futuro y las siguientes frases. Añada detalles y use la palabra **no** cuando cree que es necesario.

MODELO: ser _____ (profesión) →
    (No) **Seré** profesor universitario / profesora universitaria.

1. ser _____ (profesión)
2. conseguir una maestría (*masters*) o un doctorado (*Ph.D.*)
3. vivir en un país hispanohablante
4. conducir un coche deportivo
5. tener _____ (número) hijos.
6. participar activamente en la política (local, estatal o nacional)
7. casarse a los _____ años.

Paso 3. Ahora, en parejas, entrevístense sobre las ideas del **Paso 2.** Luego díganle a la clase algo que tienen en común o en lo que son muy diferentes.

MODELO: ser _____ (profesión) →
    E1: ¿**Serás** profesora universitaria?
    E2: No, **seré** analista de sistemas.
    E2: Pues yo sí **seré** profesor universitario.

B. ¿Qué harán?
Explique lo que harán las siguientes personas en su trabajo futuro. Luego, para cada grupo, diga qué profesión se describe.

MODELO: yo / darles consejos a los estudiantes →
    Les **daré** consejos a los estudiantes.

1. yo
- hablar bien el español
- pasar mucho tiempo en la biblioteca
- escribir artículos sobre la literatura latinoamericana
- enseñar clases en español

2. tú
- trabajar en una oficina y en la corte
- ganar mucho dinero
- tener muchos clientes
- cobrar por muchas horas de trabajo

3. Felipe
- ver a muchos pacientes
- resolver muchos problemas mentales
- leer a Freud y a Jung
- hacerle un sicoanálisis a un paciente

4. Susana y Juanjo
- pasar mucho tiempo sentados
- usar el teclado (*keyboard*) constantemente
- inventar nuevos programas
- mandarles mensajes electrónicos a todos los amigos

Prác. A, Paso 1: **Answers: 1.** *viviré* **2.** *dirá* **3.** *saldrán* **4.** *vendrán* **5.** *comeremos* **6.** *querrás*

C. Este mes

Paso 1. Describa lo que Ud. hará o no hará este mes en cuanto a (*as far as*) sus finanzas.

MODELO: (no) gastar más/menos este mes → (No) **Gastaré** menos este mes.

1. (no) gastar más/menos este mes
2. (no) pagar a tiempo todas mis cuentas
3. (no) hacer un presupuesto y / pero (no) seguirlo
4. (no) depositar mucho / poco dinero en mi cuenta
5. (no) cobrar un cheque de mi empleo / un pariente
6. (no) seguir usando mis tarjetas de crédito
7. (no) pedirles dinero a mis amigos / padres / hijos
8. (no) buscar un trabajo de tiempo completo / parcial

Paso 2. Ahora, en parejas, comparen sus respuestas. Díganle a la clase si Uds. son responsables en cuanto a asuntos de dinero, siguiendo los modelos. También díganle a la clase las cosas que tienen en común.

MODELOS: Dylan y yo somos muy responsables con nuestro dinero porque…
Dylan es muy responsable con su dinero, pero yo tengo que aprender a ser más responsable con el mío porque…

D. El horóscopo

Paso 1. ¿Creen Uds. en la astrología? Es posible que no, pero eso no importa para esta actividad. En parejas, hagan una lista de los temas y verbos que con frecuencia aparecen en los horóscopos.

Paso 2. Ahora escojan dos signos del Zodiaco y escriban predicciones para los próximos siete días basadas en cada uno de esos dos signos. ¡Sean creativos y demuestren su sentido del humor!

MODELO: Miércoles: Conocerás a una persona muy interesante en una clase o en una fiesta.

Paso 3. Finalmente, lean a la clase las predicciones para los signos que escogieron. ¿Cuáles son las reacciones de sus compañeros de clase ante (*to*) sus predicciones?

E. El mundo del año 2100

Paso 1. ¿Cómo será el mundo del futuro? En parejas, hagan una lista de cosas que Uds. creen que van a ser diferentes para el año 2200 (por ejemplo: el transporte, la comida, la vivienda). Piensen también en temas globales (por ejemplo: la política, los problemas que presenta la capa de ozono).

Vocabulario útil

la colonización	el transbordador espacial space shuttle
el espacio	la vida artificial
la estación espacial	
los OVNIs (Objetos Voladores No Identificados)	diseñar
	eliminar
la pobreza poverty	
el robot	intergaláctico/a
el satélite	interplanetario/a
	sintético/a

Paso 2. A base de su lista, hagan una serie de predicciones para el futuro.

MODELO: La gente **comerá** (**Comeremos**) comidas sintéticas.

Nota **comunicativa**

Cómo expresar probabilidad con el futuro

Estela, en el aeropuerto

Cecilia, en la carretera

—¿Dónde **estará** Cecilia? ¿Qué le **pasará**?

"*I wonder where Cecilia is.*" ("*Where can Cecilia be?*") "*I wonder what's up with her.*" ("*What can be wrong?*")

—**Estará** en un lío de tráfico.

"*She's probably (must be) in a traffic jam.*" ("*I bet she's in a traffic jam.*")

In Spanish, the future can also be used to express probability or conjecture about what is happening now. This use of the future is called the *future of probability* (**el futuro de probabilidad**). Note in the preceding examples that the English cues for expressing probability (*probably, I bet, must be, I wonder, Where can . . . ?,* and so on) are not directly expressed in Spanish. Their sense is conveyed in Spanish by the use of the future form of the verb.

You will use the future of probability in **Práctica F.**

Algo sobre...

«Gracias a la vida»

La canción «Gracias a la vida» es famosa en todo el mundo hispanohablante. Fue compuesta por la cantautora y folclorista chilena Violeta Parra (1917–1967). Es un himno[a] a la vida que habla de las cosas importantes y cotidianas[b] que muchas veces olvidamos. Muchos cantantes de todo el mundo han cantado esta canción, incluyendo la folclorista estadounidense Joan Baez y, más recientemente, Michael Bublé.

Aparte del[c] himno nacional, ¿hay alguna canción que Ud. considere un símbolo de su país? ¿Cuál es?

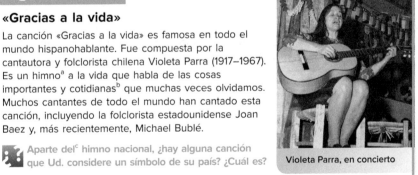

Violeta Parra, en concierto

[a]*hymn, anthem* [b]*daily* [c]*Aparte... Besides the*

F. Predicciones. ¿Quiénes serán las personas en las siguientes fotos? ¿Qué estarán haciendo? ¿Dónde estarán? En parejas, usen lo que saben de Chile e inventen todos los detalles que puedan.

1.

2.

¿Recuerda Ud.?

In **Gramática 45 (Cap. 16),** you learned about a series of adverbial conjunctions that always require the use of the subjunctive in the dependent clause. There are six such conjunctions. Complete the following phrases to name them all.

1. a _____ que = *unless*
2. _____ (de) que = *before*
3. con _____ (_____) que = *provided that, as long as*
4. en _____ de que = *in case*
5. _____ que = *so that*
6. _____ que = *without; unless*

You will learn more about using one of these conjunctions and about others like it in **Gramática 47.**

Gramática en acción: Planes para el futuro

1. Después de graduarme, tendré que buscar trabajo. **Tan pronto como** tenga trabajo, ganaré mucho dinero y pagaré los préstamos de la universidad.

2. **En cuanto** me jubile, jugaré al golf por lo menos tres veces por semana. ¡Pero desgraciadamente quedan quince años **hasta que** me jubile!

3. Cuando trabajaba, siempre estaba cansado. Ahora me siento mejor que nunca. ¡Y voy a jugar al golf **hasta que** tenga 100 años!

¿Y Ud.?

1. ¿Buscará trabajo antes de graduarse o después de graduarse?
2. ¿Tendrá que pagar préstamos cuando se gradúe?
3. Cuando tenga un trabajo, ¿estará más cansado/a que ahora?

	①		②
FUTURE/PENDING ACTION: (present, future, command)	**indicative**	adverbial conjunction of time	**subjunctive**

	①		②
HABITUAL/COMPLETED ACTION: (present, past)	**indicative**	adverbial conjunction of time	**indicative**

1. Adverbial Conjunctions of Time

Future events are often expressed in Spanish in two-clause sentences in which the dependent clause is introduced by a conjunction of time. The most common ones are listed at the right.

Las conjunciones de tiempo			
antes (de) que	before	**en cuanto**	as soon as
cuando	when	**hasta que**	until
después (de) que	after	**tan pronto como**	as soon as

Plans for the future 1. After I graduate, I'll have to look for a job. As soon as I have a job, I'll earn lots of money, and I'll pay off my university loans. 2. As soon as I retire, I'll play golf at least three times a week. But unfortunately it'll be fifteen more years until I retire! 3. When I was still working, I was always tired. Now I feel better than ever. And I'm going to play golf until I'm 100 (years old)!

2. Use of the Subjunctive After Time Conjunctions

The subjunctive is used when the dependent clause introduced by a time conjunction describes an event that is pending. This happens even when there is no change of subject in the dependent clause, as in the examples.

¡OJO!

When the present subjunctive is used in this way to express pending future actions, the *main-clause* verb is in the present indicative or future, or is a command.

This use of the subjunctive is very frequent in Spanish in clauses that begin with **Cuando**...

MAIN CLAUSE: PRESENT INDICATIVE OR FUTURE

Debo depositar el dinero **tan pronto como** lo **reciba.**
I should deposit the money as soon as I get it.

Pagaré las cuentas **en cuanto** reciba mi cheque.
I'll pay the bills as soon as I get my check.

Pague Ud. las cuentas **en cuanto** las **reciba.**
Pay bills as soon as you get them.

Cuando sea grande/mayor...   **Cuando** tenga tiempo...
When I'm older . . .   *When I have the time . . .*

3. Use of the Indicative After Time Conjunctions

The indicative is used when the dependent clause introduced by a time conjunction describes a habitual action (present or past) or a completed event in the past.

HABITUAL ACTIONS: INDICATIVE

Siempre pago las cuentas **en cuanto recibo** mi cheque.
I always pay bills as soon as I get my check.

Siempre depositaba el dinero **tan pronto como** lo **recibía.**
I always deposited the money as soon as I got it.

COMPLETED PAST ACTION: INDICATIVE

El mes pasado pagué las cuentas **en cuanto recibí** mi cheque.
Last month I paid my bills as soon as I got my check.

Cuando recibí el cheque, lo deposité.
When I got the check, I deposited it.

4. Antes (de) que + subjunctive

As you know, the subjunctive is always used after the time conjunction **antes (de) que**. You can review this usage in **Gramática 45 (Cap. 16).**

No puedo comprar nada **antes de que** me **paguen.**
I can't buy anything until they pay me.

5. Preposition + infinitive

When there is no change of subject, the prepositions **antes de, después de,** and **hasta** are often used instead of the conjunctions **antes (de) que, después (de) que,** and **hasta que.**

¡Claro que no puedo depositar el dinero **antes de recibir** el cheque!
Of course I can't deposit the money before receiving the check!

Summary of Time Conjunctions

FUTURE/PENDING

antes de que	subjunctive
all other conjunctions of time	subjunctive

HABITUAL/PAST

antes de que	subjunctive
all other conjunctions of time	indicative

Práctica y comunicación

A. ¿Futuro o presente?

Paso 1. Autoprueba. Indique cuáles de las siguientes oraciones indican una acción futura, que debe ser expresada con el subjuntivo en español.

ACCIÓN FUTURA
1. I'll call as soon as I get home.   ☐
2. We always interview applicants after we check their references.   ☐
3. Some people apply for graduate school as soon as they   ☐
   enter their senior year.
4. They won't deposit the check until you sign it.   ☐

Prác. A, Paso 1: Answers 1, 4

Paso 2. Indique si las siguientes oraciones expresan una acción habitual (**H**) o futura (**F**). Luego complételas e indique las (*those*) que son verdaderas (**V**) para Ud.

	H	F	V
1. Estudio muchos días hasta que (ser) las dos de la mañana.	☐	☐	☐
2. Mañana voy a estudiar hasta que (ser) las dos de la mañana.	☐	☐	☐
3. Necesito actualizar (*update*) mi currículum tan pronto como (tener) tiempo.	☐	☐	☐
4. Generalmente actualizo el currículum cuando (terminar) el año académico.	☐	☐	☐
5. No voy a buscar empleo hasta que (graduarse).	☐	☐	☐
6. Voy a buscar empleo antes de (graduarse).			
7. En cuanto (*yo:* tener) un rato libre esta semana, voy a ir al centro de orientación profesional.	☐	☐	☐

Paso 3. Ahora, en parejas, entrevístense sobre las oraciones del **Paso 2.**

MODELO: **E1:** ¿Estudias muchos días hasta que son las dos de la mañana?
E2: Sí, y algunos días hasta que son las tres.
E1: Yo también.

B. Decisiones económicas

Paso 1. Lea las siguientes oraciones sobre Rigoberto e indique si se trata de (*each is about*) una acción habitual (**H**) o de una acción futura (**F**). Luego escoja la frase que complete mejor cada oración.

H   F

☐ ☐ **1.** _____ Rigoberto se va a comprar un auto en cuanto...
a. ahorre suficiente dinero.   **b.** ahorra suficiente dinero.

☐ ☐ **2.** _____ Siempre usa su tarjeta de crédito cuando...
a. no tenga dinero en efectivo.   **b.** no tiene dinero en efectivo.

☐ ☐ **3.** _____ Pagará su préstamo estudiantil tan pronto como...
a. consiga un trabajo.   **b.** consigue un trabajo.

☐ ☐ **4.** _____ No puede pagar sus cuentas este mes hasta que...
a. su hermano le devuelva el dinero que le prestó.
b. su hermano le devuelve el dinero que le prestó.

Paso 2. Ahora diga cómo maneja Ud. sus propios (*own*) asuntos económicos. Indique si la oración describe una acción habitual (**H**) o una acción futura (**F**).

H   F

☐ ☐ **1.** En cuanto el banco me dé un préstamo, voy a comprarme _____.
☐ ☐ **2.** Cuando no tengo dinero en efectivo, siempre uso _____.
☐ ☐ **3.** Tan pronto como consiga un trabajo, voy a _____.
☐ ☐ **4.** Este mes, voy a _____ antes de que se me olvide.
☐ ☐ **5.** En cuanto _____, empezaré a buscar trabajo.

Estrategia

Use un sustantivo en las oraciones 1 y 2. Use un infinitivo en las oraciones 3 y 4. En la oración 5, debe usar o el indicativo o el subjuntivo.

C. Cosas de la vida. Las siguientes oraciones describen algunos aspectos de la vida de Mariana. Complételas con la forma apropiada de los infinitivos.

1. Hace cuatro años, cuando Mariana (graduarse) en la escuela secundaria, sus padres (darle) una computadora. El año que viene, cuando (graduarse) en la universidad, (darle) un carro.

2. Cuando (ser) niña, Mariana (querer) ser actriz. Cuando (tener) 18 años, (decidir) ser enfermera. Cuando (terminar) su carrera este año, (poder) encontrar un buen empleo.

3. Antes Mariana siempre (pagar) sus cuentas con cheque. Ahora las (pagar) por internet en cuanto le (*ellos:* depositar) el sueldo en su cuenta.

4. Mariana (tener) que comprar un regalo para la boda de unos amigos. No puede comprarlo hasta que su hermana le (devolver) el dinero que Mariana le (prestar).

D. Los planes de David

Paso 1. David va a graduarse en sociología en la Universidad de Chile, en Santiago. Describa sus planes, haciendo oraciones completas con las siguientes frases y usando las conjunciones de tiempo en **negrilla**.

MODELO: querer tener un buen empleo / **tan pronto como** / graduarse ⟶ David **querrá** tener un buen empleo tan pronto como **se gradúe**.

1. estar buscando un empleo / **antes de** / graduarse
2. independizarse de sus padres / **en cuanto** / ser posible
3. **cuando** / ahorrar dinero, / poder viajar a la Patagonia con su novia
4. **después de** / trabajar por un tiempo, / estudiar para obtener un doctorado
5. estudiar el mapudungun, la lengua de los mapuches, / **hasta que** / poder hablarlo bien
6. pero /**antes de que** / todo esto ser realidad, / necesitar estudiar mucho

Paso 2. Ahora use las ideas apropiadas del **Paso 1** para hablar de sus propios planes para el futuro. Haga los cambios necesarios.

MODELO: querer tener un buen empleo / **tan pronto como** / graduarse ⟶

Querré tener un buen empleo tan pronto como **me gradúe**.

E. Descripciones. En parejas, completen la oración que está debajo de cada escena. Luego completen las oraciones con información personal.

1. Esta noche, Pablo va a estudiar hasta que...

   ¿Y Uds.?
   • Esta noche, voy a estudiar hasta que...
   • Siempre estudio hasta que...
   • Anoche estudié hasta que...

2. Los Sres. Castro van a cenar tan pronto como...

   ¿Y Uds.?
   • Esta noche, voy a cenar tan pronto como...
   • Generalmente ceno cuando / antes de (que)...
   • Anoche cené tan pronto como / después de (que)...

F. Intercambios

Paso 1. Invente preguntas que a Ud. le gustaría hacerles a sus compañeros de clase sobre el futuro en general y sobre el futuro de ellos en particular.

MODELO: ¿Cuántos años tendrás... ? / cuando / jubilarse →
   ¿Cuántos años tendrás cuando **te jubiles**?

| ¿Cómo será tu vida... ?
 ¿Dónde vivirás... ?
 ¿Qué harás... ?
 ¿Cuántos años tendrás... ? | **+** | cuando | **+** | la humanidad: colonizar otros planetas <br> los científicos: descubrir una cura para casi todos los casos de cáncer <br> las mujeres: tener igualdad de oportunidades, de verdad <br> haber paz en todas partes del mundo
 ¿ ?

 graduarse <br> tener suficiente dinero para casarse / tener hijos / ¿ ?
 jubilarse
 ¿ ? |

Paso 2. En parejas, entrevístense usando las preguntas que crearon en el **Paso 1.** Luego díganle a la clase algo interesante de su conversación.

MODELO: E1: ¿Cuántos años tendrás cuando te jubiles?
   E2: Probablemente tendré más de 65 años cuando me jubile. Voy a ser maestro y creo que no voy a ganar mucho dinero. Por eso no voy a poder jubilarme antes.

Un poco de todo

A. Lengua y cultura: Trabajos para estudiantes universitarios

Paso 1. Complete the following paragraphs with the correct form of the words in parentheses, as suggested by context. When two possibilities are given in parentheses, select the correct word. *P/I:* will show you when to use the preterite or the imperfect. Conjugate all other infinitives in the future, present indicative, or subjunctive, or leave them in the infinitive form.

La necesidad de dinero es un problema para muchos estudiantes en todas partes del mundo. En la mayoría de los países hispanohablantes, (el / la[1]) sistema universitario es gratuito. Además,[a] es natural que los estudiantes (vivir[2]) con sus familias, (por qué / porque[3]) la mayoría no (irse[4]) a (estudiar[5]) a otras ciudades. (*Ellos:* Estudiar[6]) en (el / la[7]) universidad más cercana.[b]

Sin embargo, muchos estudiantes no buscan trabajo hasta que (*ellos:* terminar[8]) sus estudios universitarios. Y, así como en este país, hay estudiantes que (conseguir[9]) trabajo de tiempo parcial antes de (terminar / terminen[10]) la escuela secundaria. A continuación se puede leer las experiencias laborales de algunos estudiantes durante la época universitaria.

Una joven paraguaya: «Desde los 16 años, (*yo:* trabajar[11]) en una oficina. Así puedo (cobrar / pagar[12]) la matrícula en la universidad y mi ropa y gastos personales y también (*yo:* poder[13]) colaborar un poquito con la economía familiar.»

[a]*Besides* [b]*más... nearest*

(Continúa.)

Universidad de Chile, en Santiago

Un joven chileno: «Cuando (P / I: *yo:* ser / estar[14]) estudiante universitario, (P / I: *trabajar*[15]) como fotógrafo. (P / I: *Yo:* Sacar[16]) fotos en bodas, bautizos y primeras comuniones. Era un (bueno[17]) trabajo (por / para[18]) un estudiante, porque (P / I: *yo:* tener[19]) (de / que[20]) trabajar los fines de semana pero casi nunca los días de clase.»

Una estudiante uruguaya de la escuela secundaria: «Tan pronto como las clases (terminar[21]) este verano, (*yo:* empezar[22]) a trabajar en la tienda de mi tía y (ganar[23]) un poco de dinero. No quiero que mis padres (tener[24]) que pagarlo todo cuando yo (estar[25]) en la universidad.»

Paso 2. Comprensión. Conteste las siguientes preguntas.

1. ¿Qué necesidad comparten los estudiantes de todo el mundo?
2. ¿Es caro o barato el sistema universitario de los países hispanos?
3. ¿Dónde vive la mayoría de los estudiantes hispanos?
4. ¿Qué trabajos se describen en estos párrafos?

Paso 3. Ahora, en parejas, hablen de los trabajos que tienen los estudiantes universitarios en este país mientras que estudian. ¿Cuáles son los más comunes? Hablen también de sus propios trabajos si es que trabajan.

B. ¿Dinero en el extranjero? ¡No es problema!

Paso 1. Complete las siguientes ideas sobre las ventajas de los cajeros automáticos cuando uno está en un país extranjero. ¡OJO! Considere el contexto temporal al (*when you*) escoger el tiempo verbal: el presente de indicativo o subjuntivo, el pretérito o el imperfecto, el futuro.

1. **En el pasado,** cuando una persona (necesitar) dinero en efectivo, (tener) que entrar en un banco para sacar dinero. Si uno (ir) a un país extranjero, antes de salir (deber) cambiar su dinero a la moneda del su país de destino. Muchas personas (llevar) cheques de viaje, que (cobrar) en el extranjero.
2. **Hoy día,** todo es mucho más fácil. Un turista en el extranjero (poder) ir a un cajero automático y (sacar) dinero local de la cuenta que tiene en su país de origen.
3. **Este año,** antes de salir para Chile en viaje de estudios, los estudiantes de esta universidad (depositar) dinero suficiente en la cuenta que tienen aquí en su banco. Una vez que[a] (*ellos:* llegar) a Chile, (poder) sacar dinero, usando su tarjeta de débito en uno de los muchos cajeros automáticos que (haber) en ese país.

[a]Una... *Once*

Paso 2. En parejas, hablen de la posibilidad de vivir por un tiempo en otro país. ¿Para estudiar antes de graduarse? ¿Para trabajar? ¿Qué tipo de trabajo les gustaría tener? ¿Dónde? ¿Por cuánto tiempo? Incluyan todos los detalles que puedan.

MODELOS: Creo que (no) viviré en otro país porque...
(No) Me gustaría estudiar/trabajar en otro país cuando... / porque...
Mi futura profesión (no) me permitirá trabajar en el extranjero porque...

En **su** comunidad

Entreviste a una persona hispana de su universidad o ciudad sobre algunos temas laborales.

PREGUNTAS POSIBLES

- ¿A qué se dedica? (¿Cuál es su trabajo?) ¿Cuánto tiempo hace que se dedica a eso? ¿Le gusta su trabajo? ¿Por qué?
- ¿Vino a este país por razones de trabajo?
- ¿Cómo es la situación laboral en su país de origen?
- ¿Qué piensa de la situación laboral en este país hoy día? ¿Cree que es mejor que cuando llegó a este país o peor?

 **«Los hispanos que admiramos» Segmento 2**

Antes de mirar

¿Cuánto sabe Ud. de la música de los países hispanohablantes? Relacione los siguientes tipos de música con el país que más se asocia con ellos y con los instrumentos con que se toca.

MÚSICA	LUGAR	INSTRUMENTOS
la música andina (de los Andes) el flamenco la salsa	Puerto Rico el Perú España	el piano, el cajón (*box-shaped percussion instrument*), la flauta, el *shaker*, las castañuelas (*castanets*), el charango (*stringed instrument*), la guitarra

Este segmento

Ana y Víctor entrevistan al compositor de la música de *Salu2*, Nico Barry, quien habla del proceso creativo y de la música autóctona (*indigenous*) de varios países.

Vocabulario del segmento

de mayor	as a grown-up
ponerle una cara a	to put a face with
Es todo un honor.	It's a great honor.
investigar (gu)	to research
el ritmo	rhythm
o sea	that is
suceder	to take place
el montuno	*rhythmic coda of many Cuban songs*
vas llevando	[with it] you carry
relleno/a de	filled with
así	like this
grabar	to record
los termino reemplazando	I end up replacing them
evitar	to avoid

Nico Barry en su estudio, con su charango: «Los instrumentos, los toco todos yo... »

Fragmento del guion

Obviamente, el flamenco es la música, parte de la música autóctona de España. Usaría[a] muchas guitarras españolas; como percusión usaría el cajón o las castañuelas. O en países como... totalmente diferentes, como Perú, usaría mucho el charango, que es más andino. Los ritmos, usaría muchísimos de los ritmos andinos; usaría más flautas, o bombos legüeros,[b] que son unos bombos muy grandes hechos con piel de vaca.[c]

[a]*I would use* [b]*bombos... bass drums* [c]*piel... cowhide*

Después de mirar

A. ¿Está claro? Complete las siguientes oraciones con información del programa.

1. De pequeña, Ana quería ser _____.
2. De pequeño, Víctor quería ser _____.
3. Nico compone música para _____.
4. El *shaker* de Nico está relleno de _____.

B. Un poco más. Conteste las siguientes preguntas.

1. ¿Por qué admiran Ana y Víctor a Nico Barry?
2. ¿Qué hace Nico para componer la música de *Salu2*?

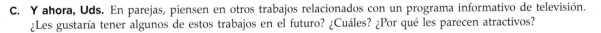 **C. Y ahora, Uds.** En parejas, piensen en otros trabajos relacionados con un programa informativo de televisión. ¿Les gustaría tener algunos de estos trabajos en el futuro? ¿Cuáles? ¿Por qué les parecen atractivos?

A LEER

Antes de leer

¿Cree Ud. que hay muchas personas preocupadas por la seguridad de su empleo hoy día? ¿Por qué existe esta preocupación?

Lectura cultural: Chile

El mundo del trabajo en Chile

Chile es uno de los países del mundo en donde la gente más trabaja. Como ocurre en otras partes del mundo, parte del problema es que algunos necesitan más de un trabajo para sobrevivir.[a] Pero existe también una minoría que tiene salarios altos. La realidad es que hay una brecha[b] salarial en el país. Según un reciente Informe de Salarios de la Organización Internacional del Trabajo, un trabajador chileno que cobra un sueldo alto gana casi 8 veces más que un trabajador que cobra uno bajo. Los abogados, médicos, ingenieros, empresarios, ejecutivos de bancos y congresistas[c] tienen las profesiones mejor pagadas. Y los obreros, maestros, trabajadores agrícolas y empleados públicos están entre las ocupaciones que no tienen buena remuneración.

[a]*survive* [b]*gap* [c]*congressional representatives*

Los majestuosos Andes, que cruzan todo Chile de norte a sur

Un símbolo chileno: Los Andes

Esta gran cordillera[a] es una imagen constante en la diversa geografía chilena y representa su frontera natural con Bolivia y la Argentina. Los Andes son muy visibles porque el territorio de Chile es tan angosto[b] que en su punto más ancho[c] de este a oeste solo mide 180 kilómetros.[d]

[a]*mountain range* [b]*narrow* [c]*más... widest* [d]*180... 111.85 miles*

COMPRENSIÓN

1. ¿Cómo es la brecha salarial en Chile?
2. ¿Qué significa la palabra **trabajólico/a**?
3. ¿De qué beneficios disfrutan los trabajadores españoles por ley?
4. ¿En qué dirección la cordillera de los Antes atraviesa Chile?
5. ¿Cómo es Chile, un país ancho o estrecho (*narrow*)?

En **otros** países hispanos

- **En algunos países hispanohablantes** La Real Academia Española de la Lengua define la palabra «trabajólico/a» como «Que trabaja afanosa[a] y compulsivamente». Curiosamente, la Real Academia identifica este adjetivo como una expresión chilena. En general, el hecho[b] de trabajar mucho o en exceso, de ser una persona trabajólica o creer que trabajar mucho es una buena cualidad son contrarios a la manera de pensar de los hispanos. Para la mayoría de estos, hay que trabajar para vivir, pero nunca al revés.[c]

- **En España** En este país, como en muchos otros países europeos, los trabajadores disfrutan de[d] buenos beneficios laborales que están establecidos por la ley.[e] Por ejemplo, un mes de vacaciones al año es el mínimo legal. Otro ejemplo es la licencia[f] por maternidad o paternidad, que la ley garantiza[g] con cuatro meses, además de otros beneficios asociados. Además,[h] España tiene un sistema nacional de salud que cubre prácticamente a toda la población.

[a]*eagerly* [b]*act* [c]*al... the other way around* [d]*disfrutan... tienen* [e]*law* [f]*leave* [g]*guarantees* [h]*In addition*

Y ahora, Uds.

¿Qué similitudes y diferencias ven Uds. entre el mundo laboral de este país y el (*that*) de Chile y otros países hispanohablantes? ¿Creen que en el futuro estas diferencias crecerán o disminuirán? Expliquen sus respuestas.

Del mundo hispano

Antes de leer

¿Qué hacen los poetas? ¿Dónde y cuándo escriben? En su opinión, ¿es fácil o difícil ser poeta? ¿Cree Ud. que, en general, los poetas tienen otro trabajo además del de (*besides that of*) escribir poemas?

Vocabulario **para leer**

el bostezo	yawn
el esclavo	slave
salir caro	to be expensive

Lectura: «Sale caro ser poeta», de Gloria Fuertes

Sale caro, señores, ser poeta.
La gente va y se acuesta tan tranquila
—que después del trabajo da buen sueño—.[a]
Trabajo como esclavo llego a casa,
5 me siento ante[b] la mesa sin cocina,
me pongo a meditar lo que sucede.[c]
La duda me acribilla[d] todo espanta[e];
comienzo a ser comida por las sombras[f]
las horas se me pasan sin bostezo
10 el dormir se me asusta[g] se me huye[h]
—escribiendo me da la madrugada—.[i]
Y luego los amigos me organizan recitales.[j]
a los que acudo[k] y leo como tonta,
y la gente no sabe de esto nada.
15 Que me dejo la linfa[l] en lo que escribo
me caigo de la rama[m] de la rima
asalto las trincheras[n] de la angustia
me nombran su héroe los fantasmas,[ñ]
me cuesta[o] respirar cuando termino.
20 Sale caro señores ser poeta.

[a]*que... after work one gets good and sleepy* [b]*at* [c]*me... I start to medidate about what's happening* [d]*harasses* [e]*frightens (me)* [f]*shadows* [g]*se... is frightened away* [h]*se... (el dormir) flees from me* [i]*me... gets me to morning* [j]*readings (of my poetry)* [k]*a... which I attend* [l]*me... I leave my lymph glands (i.e., my heart and soul)* [m]*branch* [n]*asalto... I assail the trenches* [ñ]*me... ghosts call me their hero* [o]*me... it's hard for me*

Comprensión

A. ¿Dónde lo dice? Dé el número de los versos (*lines*) del poema donde aparece la siguiente información.

1. ¿Tiene más de un trabajo la poeta?
2. ¿Cuándo escribe su poesía?
3. ¿Pasa rápido el tiempo mientras escribe?
4. ¿Se siente tranquila cuando escribe?
5. ¿Tiene audiencia esta poeta?
6. ¿Entiende el público cuánto trabaja la poeta?
7. ¿Es fácil el trabajo de poeta, según dice la poeta misma (*herself*)?

B. Preguntas

1. ¿Qué cree Ud que significa «esto» en «la gente no sabe de esto» (verso 14)?
2. ¿Por qué cree Ud. que después de escribir sus poemas le cuesta respirar (verso 19)?
3. Si la autora cree que «sale caro ser poeta», ¿por qué se dedica a (*does she work on*) escribir poesías? ¿Le parece a Ud. lógico?

Antes de escuchar

¿Qué debe o puede hacer una persona para prepararse para una entrevista de trabajo? ¿Es normal que alguien se ponga nervioso cuando sabe que tiene una entrevista?

Vocabulario para escuchar

la petición	request		**averigüe**	find out
cualquier	any		**asegúrese**	be sure
la formación	education, training		**la cartera**	portfolio; folder
la carrera	career		**hacer falta**	to need
acerca de	about		**el agradecimiento**	thanks

Después de escuchar

A. Sugerencias específicas. Haga por lo menos una sugerencia para cada momento del proceso de una entrevista laboral.

1. varios días antes de la entrevista
2. el día antes de la entrevista
3. el mismo día, antes de la entrevista
4. durante la entrevista
5. después de la entrevista

B. El programa de radio. Conteste las siguientes preguntas.

1. ¿Por qué se repite la programación de la semana anterior?
2. Según el programa, ¿cuál es la mejor manera de reducir el estrés de una entrevista?
3. ¿Dónde se puede encontrar el texto del programa?

PRODUCCIÓN PERSONAL

¡Ahora, yo!

A. Use de modelo las preguntas y respuestas de la página 497 de este capítulo para hablar de su experiencia laboral y de las condiciones de trabajo que Ud. tiene ahora o desea tener en el futuro.

B. Filme 2–3 entrevistas en las que (*which*) los entrevistados hablen de las personas que más admiran y expliquen por qué.

A ESCRIBIR

Un trabajo ideal

En este capítulo Ud. va a describir un trabajo que, en su opinion, es ideal.

Preparar

Paso 1. En parejas, piensen en las características que debe tener un trabajo ideal. Incluyan muchos aspectos diferentes: el tipo de trabajo/profesión, el sueldo, el horario, el lugar de trabajo, etcétera. Describan el impacto que este empleo puede tener en la comunidad y en la sociedad. Hablen también de la persona ideal para ocupar ese puesto. Es posible que no estén de acuerdo en varias cosas, pero esta conversación los ayudará a planear su ensayo.

Paso 2. Ahora use las ideas del **Paso 1** para escribir su ensayo. Hay más ayuda en Connect.

Más ideas para su portafolio

- Incluya un aviso clasificado de un trabajo que le interese aunque (*even if*) esté en inglés. Puede traducirlo si quiere. Debe explicar por qué le interesa ese trabajo.

- Escriba un párrafo sobre una persona que tiene una profesión que Ud. admira. Describa el trabajo que hace y explique por qué Ud. admira a esa persona.

- Si ha estado jugando Practice Spanish: Study Abroad, en Quest 11 Ud. supo que la cattleya es la flor nacional colombiana. Busque en el internet la planta o el animal nacional de otro país hispanohablante y haga un afiche (*poster*) con una foto y su propia descripción. ¿Por qué cree Ud. que escogieron esta planta o animal como representante del país?

Sugerencia: You are now ready to play Quest 11 in **Practice Spanish: Study Abroad** (www.mhpractice.com).

EN RESUMEN En este capítulo

ILEARNSMART

Visit **www.connectspanish.com** to practice the vocabulary and grammar points covered in this chapter.

AFTER STUDYING THIS CHAPTER I CAN. . .

- ☐ name many professions (498)
- ☐ talk about finding and having a job (500)
- ☐ talk about money and finances (501)
- ☐ express future plans using the future (505–506)
- ☐ speculate about what might happen using the future (509)
- ☐ use time conjunctions to talk about actions in the past, present, and future (511–512)
- ☐ recognize/describe at least 2–3 aspects of Chilean cultures

Gramática en breve

46. The Future

Infinitive + **-é, -ás, -á, -emos, -éis, -án**

Irregular forms: **dir-, habr-, har-, podr-, pondr-, querr-, sabr-, saldr-, tendr-, vendr-** + *future endings*

47. The Subjunctive After Conjunctions of Time

	Future/Pending	Habitual/Past
most conjunctions of time	subjunctive	indicative
antes (de) que	subjunctive	subjunctive

Conjunctions: **antes (de) que, cuando, después (de) que, en cuanto, hasta que, tan pronto como**

Vocabulario

Las profesiones y los oficios

el/la **abogado/a**	lawyer
el **amo/ama de casa**	housekeeper
el/la **cajero/a**	(check-out) cashier; (bank) teller
el/la **cocinero/a**	cook; chef
el/la **contador(a)**	accountant
el **hombre / la mujer de negocios**	businessperson
el/la **ingeniero/a**	engineer
el/la **maestro/a (de escuel)**	schoolteacher
el/la **obrero/a**	worker, laborer

el/la **peluquero/a**	hairstylist
el/la **periodista**	journalist
el/la **plomero/a**	plumber
el/la **sicólogo/a**	psychologist
el/la **siquiatra**	psychiatrist
el **soldado / la mujer soldado**	soldier
el/la **técnico/a**	technician
el/la **trabajador(a) social**	social worker
el/la **traductor(a)**	translator
el/la **vendedor(a)**	salesperson

Cognados: el/la **analista de sistemas,** el/la **astronauta,** el/la **diseñador(a) gráfico/a,** el/la **electricista,** el/la **fotógrafo/a,** el/la **militar,** el/la **programador(a),** el/la **veterinario/a**

Repaso: el/la **artista,** el/la **asistente de vuelo,** el/la **bibliotecario/a,** el/la **camarero/a,** el/la **consejero/a,** el/la **dentista,** el/la **dependiente/a,** el/la **enfermero/a,** el/la **mecánico/a,** el/la **médico/a,** el/la **profesor(a),** el/la **secretario/a**

El mundo laboral

el/la **aspirante**	candidate; applicant
el **currículum**	resumé
el **empleo**	job position
bien/mal pagado	well-/poorly paid
de tiempo completo/parcial	full-/part-time
la **empresa**	corporation; business
la **entrevista**	interview
el/la **entrevistado/a**	interviewee
el/la **entrevistador(a)**	interviewer
el **formulario**	form (*to fill out*)
el/la **gerente**	manager
el **oficio**	trade (*profession*)
el **salario**	pay, wages (*often per hour*)
la **solicitud**	application (*form*)
el **sueldo**	salary

Cognado: el/la **recepcionista**

Repaso: el **puesto,** el **trabajo**

despedir (*like* pedir)	to let (*someone*) go; to fire (*someone*) (*from a job*)
graduarse (me gradúo) (en)	to graduate (from)
jubilarse	to retire
llenar	to fill out (*a form*)
renunciar (a)	to resign (from)
solicitar	to apply for (*a job*)

Repaso: **conseguir** (*like* seguir)

Una cuestión de dinero

ahorrar	to save (*money*)
cargar (gu)	to charge (*an account*)
cobrar	to cash (*a check*); to charge (*someone for an item or service*)
compartir	to share
pedir (pido) (i) prestado/a	to borrow
sacar (qu)	to withdraw, take out

Cognados: depositar, economizar (c)

Repaso: devolver (*like* volver), ganar, gastar, pagar (gu), prestar

el banco	bank
el billete	bill (*money*)
la caja	cashier window
el cajero automático	automatic teller machine (ATM)
el cheque	check
la cuenta	account
el efectivo	cash
la factura	bill
el interés	interest
la moneda	coin
el préstamo	loan
el presupuesto	budget
el recibo	receipt
la tarjeta bancaria	debit card

Repaso: la cuenta, el dinero, la tarjeta de crédito

a plazos	in installments
con cheque	by check
en efectivo	in cash

Los adjetivos

laboral	work, work-related
propio/a	own, one's own

Las formas posesivas

mío/a(s)	mine, of mine
tuyo/a(s)	yours, of yours (*fam. sing.*)
suyo/a(s)	your, of yours (*form., sing./pl.*); his, of his; hers, of hers; their, of theirs
nuestro/a(s)	ours, of ours
vuestro/a(s)	yours, of yours (*fam. pl.*)

Las conjunciones de tiempo

después (de) que	after
en cuanto	as soon as
hasta que	until
tan pronto como	as soon as

Repaso: antes (de) que, cuando

Palabras adicionales

al principio de	at the beginning of

Vocabulario personal

18

La actualidad

www.connectspanish.com

Manifestación (*Demonstration*) en la Puerta del Sol, Madrid

ESPAÑA

47 millones de habitantes

- España es un país donde muchas culturas se han encontrado a través de su milenaria[a] historia. Los fenicios, griegos, romanos y árabes son solo algunos de los más influyentes.

- El nombre del país viene de *Hispania,* el nombre en latín que los romanos le dieron al territorio español cuando era una provincia de su imperio.

- España es un país diverso en geografía, clima y culturas. De hecho,[b] existen otras tres lenguas oficiales junto al[c] español: el catalán, el gallego y el vasco.

[a]a... *throughout its thousand-year* [b]De... *In fact* [c]junto... *besides*

- ¿Es importante para Ud. estar al día[a] en cuanto a[b] lo que pasa en el mundo?

- ¿Qué medios de comunicación usa principalmente para mantenerse informado/a? ¿La radio y la televisión? ¿la prensa[c]? ¿internet?

- ¿Votó en las últimas elecciones? ¿Cree que es importante votar?

[a]al... *up to date* [b]en... *as far as* [c]press

JAVIER AGUIRRE PEREIRA CONTESTA LAS PREGUNTAS.

- Sí, para mí es importante estar al día sobre lo que pasa en mi país y en el mundo. Y también en mi ciudad, claro.

- Me mantengo informado sobre la actualidad de diferentes maneras. Normalmente, escucho las noticias[a] en el coche camino a[b] la oficina o de vuelta[c] a casa. Pero también leo el periódico impreso[d] o por internet. Y en casa vemos el telediario a la hora de cenar.

- ¡Por supuesto que sí![e] He votado en todas las elecciones desde que soy mayor de edad.[f] No siempre me gustan los candidatos, la verdad. Pero creo que votar es una responsabilidad en una democracia, no solo un derecho.[g]

[a]news [b]camino... *on the way to* [c]de... *on the way back* [d]printed [e]¡Por... *Of course!* [f]mayor... *old enough to vote* [g]right

Las noticias

la reportera — el canal de televisión — la huelga

la manifestación — la estación de radio — el reportero

el choque — la víctima — la testigo — el testigo

el quiosco de prensa — la revista — el periódico

You can hear the pronunciation of theme vocabulary words and phrases in the Connect eBook.

Los acontecimientos°	Los... *Events*
el asesinato	assassination
asesinar	to assassinate
matar	to kill
el desastre (natural)	(natural) disaster
la esperanza	hope, wish
mantener (*like* tener)	to maintain
la guerra	war
la huelga	strike (*labor*)
la lucha	fight; struggle
luchar	to fight
el medio de comunicación	medium of communication (*pl.* mass media)
la muerte	death

la paz (pl. **paces**)	peace
la prensa	press; news media

Cognados: el ataque (terrorista), el blog, la bomba, la erupción, las noticias, la radio, la televisión, el terrorismo, el/la terrorista

El noticiero°	El... *Newscast*
comunicar(se) (qu) (con)	to communicate (with)
enterarse (de)	to find out; to learn (about)
estar **al día**	to be up to date
ofrecer (ofrezco)	to offer

Cognado: informar

Comunicación

A. **En tertulia (*a gathering for* discussion).** La tertulia es la tradición hispana de reunirse regularmente con un grupo de amigos/colegas para hablar de las noticias del día y otros temas interesantes de la actualidad y comentarlos.

Paso 1. ¿De qué tipo de noticias les interesaría más a Uds. (*would it most interest you*) hablar en una tertulia?

1. ☐ las noticias sobre la política internacional
2. ☐ las noticias sobre la política nacional
3. ☐ las noticias locales de su ciudad o estado
4. ☐ las noticias sobre desastres o tragedias
5. ☐ las noticias de interés humano
6. ☐ las noticias de deportes
7. ☐ las noticias financieras o de negocios
8. ☐ las noticias sobre el arte y la cultura
9. ☐ ¿ ?

Paso 2. Ahora, en grupos de cinco o seis, comparen sus respuestas. ¿Hay temas que les interesen a casi todos los estudiantes de su grupo? ¿Hay temas que no le interesen a nadie?

Paso 3. Con toda la clase, hagan una lista de los medios de comunicación que se usan hoy en día. Luego, pónganlos en orden de popularidad en el mundo de hoy, empezando por el más popular.

B. **¿Quién sabe más?** En grupos de tres o cuatro, den un ejemplo actual o histórico de las siguientes cosas o personas.

MODELO: un reportero → Jorge Ramos Ávalo

1. un reportero / una reportera
2. un asesinato
3. una huelga o una lucha
4. una guerra
5. un desastre natural
6. otro tipo de desastre (por ejemplo, un accidente)
7. un ataque terrorista
8. un canal de televisión o estación de radio

C. **Definiciones**

Paso 1. Dé las palabras definidas.

1. un programa que nos informa diariamente de lo que pasa en el mundo
2. una muerte violenta causada intencionadamente
3. un medio de comunicación que presenta la información por escrito
4. la persona que investiga y presenta una noticia
5. una persona que emplea la violencia para causar pánico
6. cuando los obreros dejan de trabajar para protestar por su situación laboral o por su salario
7. una persona que está presente cuando ocurre algo y lo ve todo

Paso 2. Ahora, en parejas, definan las siguientes palabras en español.

1. la guerra
2. la muerte
3. el terrorismo
4. ofrecer
5. luchar
6. estar al día

Paso 3. Lean a la clase las definiciones que crearon en el **Paso 2** para que sus compañeros adivinen (*guess*) la palabra definida.

Así se dice

el acontecimiento = el evento, el hecho, el suceso
estar al día = estar al tanto, estar al corriente
la huelga = el paro

D. Ud. y los medios de comunicación. En parejas, expresen y justifiquen su opinión sobre las siguientes ideas.

1. El interés por los *reality shows* demuestra que el público no se interesa realmente en los problemas actuales del mundo.
2. La prensa de los países democráticos es con frecuencia irresponsable y parcial.
3. Ver la televisión o YouTube es una pérdida (*waste*) de tiempo.
4. Hay demasiado sexo y violencia en las películas y los programas de televisión.
5. El internet es una fuente (*source*) de información tan buena como los otros medios de comunicación.

Vocabulario útil

creer que + *indicative*
no creer que + *subjunctive*
dudar que + *subjunctive*
no dudar que + *indicative*
esperar que + *subjunctive*

estar de acuerdo con/en que + *indicative*
no estar de acuerdo con/en que + *subjunctive*
es una lástima / probable / increíble que + *subjunctive*

El gobierno y la responsabilidad cívica

la política / la candidata
el político / el candidato
el ejército
la mujer soldado
los ciudadanos
la izquierda   el centro   la derecha
el rey   la reina
el soldado

Las personas

el ciudadano / la ciudadana	citizen
los/las demás	(the) others; other
el dictador / la dictadora	dictator
el rey / la reina	king/queen

Cognados: el/la representante al congreso, el senador / la senadora

Los conceptos

el deber	responsibility; obligation
el derecho	right
la (des)igualdad	(in)equality
la dictadura	dictatorship
la discriminación	discrimination

la ley	law
el partido (político)	(political) party
la política	politics; policy
el servicio militar	miltary service

Las acciones

durar	to last
ganar	to win
obedecer (obedezco)	to obey
perder (pierdo)	to lose
postularse (para un cargo / como candidato/a)	to run (for a position / as a candidate)
votar	to vote

Así se dice

postularse (para un cargo político como candidato/a) = presentarse (como candidato/a a un cargo político)

Comunicación

A. ¿Quién sabe más de la política?

Paso 1. ¿Cuánto sabe Ud. de la política? Si puede, dé un ejemplo de las siguientes categorías.

1. un país con un rey o una reina
2. un país que tenga o haya tenido una dictadura
3. un dictador o una dictadora
4. un cargo político que dure dos/cuatro/seis años
5. el mes típico para votar en este país
6. un político o una política muy conocido/a hoy en día
7. un partido político de este país
8. un derecho esencial de todos los ciudadanos de este país
9. una causa de la desigualdad social o política

Paso 2. En parejas, comparen sus respuestas del **Paso 1.** Luego díganle a la clase cuál de Uds. pudo dar ejemplos en más categorías y qué respuestas tienen en común.

Nota **cultural**

El panorama social y político en el mundo hispano

Aquí hay algunos datos de interés sobre los países de habla española.

- **La mayoría de edad:** En el mundo hispano en general se llega a la mayoría de edad a los 18 años, que es la edad en que la ley permite consumir bebidas alcohólicas y obtener el permiso de manejar.
- **El servicio militar:** Hoy día el servicio militar es voluntario en España y la Argentina y obligatorio en la mayoría de los otros países. Sin embargo, «obligatorio» no significa que todo el mundo lo haga o que todo el mundo lo haga de manera igual.
- **Las mujeres en el ejército:** Las mujeres pueden ser militares en la Argentina, Colombia, Chile, México y España.
- **Las mujeres en la política:** A pesar de[a] la fama del machismo que existe en la cultura hispana y aunque[b] no hay igualdad en la representación de cargos del gobierno, las mujeres han llegado a ser presidentas de su país en varios países (Chile, la Argentina, Costa Rica, Nicaragua y Panamá) y también vicepresidentas y primeras ministras, incluso ministras de Defensa aun[c] siendo civiles (en Chile y en España). Además[d] hay numerosas juezas[e] y mujeres que ocupan otros cargos políticos de importancia.

Sonia Sotomayor, primera jueza hispana de la Corte Suprema de los Estados Unidos

¿En cuáles de estos datos hay grandes similaridades entre su país y los países hispanohablantes?

[a]*A... In spite of* [b]*although* [c]*even* [d]*Besides* [e]*judges*

El rey Felipe VI y la reina Letizia de España

B. El gobierno de España. Complete el siguiente párrafo sobre España con las palabras de la lista.

ciudadano	los demás	rey
ejército	monarquía	servicio militar
gobierno	políticos	vota
igualdad	reina	

España es un país democrático, con principios de _____[1] muy similares a los[a] que existen en países con democracias bien establecidas, como los Estados Unidos y el Canadá. Sin embargo, una diferencia es el tipo de _____[2]. En España existe una _____[3] parlamentaria, lo que significa que hay un _____[4] y una _____[5]. Los reyes son figuras representativas, sin poder ejecutivo. Nadie _____[6] por el rey, pero sí se vota para elegir al presidente y todos _____[7] cargos _____[8].

España tiene un _____[9] voluntario; es decir, que no hay _____[10] obligatorio para ningún _____[11].

[a]*those*

C. ¿Qué opina Ud.? En parejas, den su opinión sobre las siguientes ideas.

1. En este país, se permite que consumamos demasiado petróleo (energía, carne, azúcar).
2. Votar es un deber, no un privilegio.
3. En este país, la igualdad de todos no es una realidad todavía.
4. Es posible que una dictadura sea una buena alternativa a la democracia en algunos casos.
5. El personal a cargo (*in charge*) de los servicios básicos de un país (por ejemplo, del agua) no debe tener derecho a declararse en huelga.

Vocabulario útil

Aunque... Although ...
De hecho,... In fact ...
En mi opinión...
Por un lado... On the one hand ...
Por otro lado... On the other hand ...
Sin embargo...

¿Recuerda Ud.?

The forms of the past subjunctive, which you will learn in **Gramática 48,** are based on the third person plural of the preterite. Here is a brief review of that preterite form.

- regular **-ar** verbs: **-ar** ⟶ **-aron**
- regular **-er/-ir** verbs: **-er/-ir** ⟶ -ieron
- -ir stem-changing verbs: **e** ⟶ **i, o** ⟶ **u** in the stem: **pidieron, durmieron**
- verbs whose stem ends in a vowel (**leer, construir,** and so on): **-ieron** ⟶ **-yeron: leyeron, construyeron**
- irregular preterite stems: **quisieron, hicieron, dijeron,** and so on
- four totally irregular verbs: **ser/ir** ⟶ **fueron, dar** ⟶ **dieron, ver** ⟶ **vieron**

Give the third person plural of the preterite for these infinitives.

1. hablar	5. perder	9. estar	13. traer	17. decir
2. comer	6. dormir	10. tener	14. dar	18. creer
3. vivir	7. reír	11. destruir	15. saber	19. ir
4. jugar	8. leer	12. mantener	16. vestirse	20. poder

«¡Noticias!» Segmento 1

Antes de mirar

¿Qué medios de comunicación usa Ud. para estar al corriente (*up-to-date*) de lo que pasa en el mundo?

☐ internet
☐ los noticieros de la radio
☐ los noticieros de la televisión
☐ los periódicos
☐ otros medios impresos (*print*)
☐ otros

Este segmento

En este segmento se habla de cómo la gente se entera de las noticias en una serie de entrevistas con profesores y estudiantes universitarios mexicanos.

Como estudia comunicación, esta joven mexicana desea verse inmersa en información sobre la política y la sociedad, para saber a qué atenerse (*to pay attention to*).

Vocabulario del segmento

disfrutar	to enjoy	**el afán**	interest
apenas	hardly ever	**el temblor**	earthquake
la fuente	source	**podría**	it could
mediante	though, via	**el ámbito**	area
estar suscrito/a	to be a subscriber	**englobar**	to encompass the whole world
la cadena	(TV) station		
prender	to turn on (*an appliance*)	**la belleza**	beauty
aparte	besides	**regir (rijo) (i)**	to rule; to matter
el adelanto	advancement		

Después de mirar

A. **¿Está claro?** Las siguientes oraciones son falsas. Corríjalas.

  1. A Ana le encanta leer el periódico los domingos.
  2. Ana se entera de las noticias por la radio.
  3. El primer profesor está suscrito a un periódico.
  4. El segundo profesor cree que los estudiantes están bien informados de las noticias políticas y económicas.

B. **Un poco más.** Conteste las siguientes preguntas.

  1. ¿Qué medio de comunicación usan más los jóvenes del programa?
  2. Según el segundo profesor, ¿sobre qué temas están informados los jóvenes?

C. **Y ahora, Uds.** En grupos, hablen de cómo Uds. se enteran de las noticias. ¿Creen que están al día? ¿Qué tipos de noticias les interesan más? ¿Cómo se comparan Uds. con los jóvenes mexicanos entrevistados en el segmento?

GRAMÁTICA

Grammar Tutorial 48

Eller connect®
|SPANISH
www.connectspanish.com

48 *Queríamos que todo el mundo votara*
The Subjunctive (Part 9): The Past Subjunctive

Gramática en acción: Las últimas elecciones

Indique las condiciones que eran verdaderas para Ud. sobre las últimas elecciones en su país o estado.

En las últimas elecciones...

1. ☐ yo no tenía edad para votar.
2. ☐ yo tenía edad para votar, pero no voté.
3. ☐ para mí era importante que votara mucha gente.
4. ☐ yo dudaba que ganara uno de los candidatos que yo apoyaba, ¡pero sí ganó!
5. ☐ no se postuló ningún candidato que me convenciera o me entusiasmara de verdad.
6. ☐ en mi estado/provincia no hubo clases para los niños, para que las escuelas primarias sirvieran de centros electorales.

BORICUA[a]
¡INSCRIBETE[b] **Y VOTA!**
QUE NADA
NOS DETENGA[c]
1-800-596-VOTA

[a]Puertorriqueño/a [b]*Register* [c]*Que... Let nothing stop us*

Although Spanish has two simple indicative past tenses (preterite and imperfect), it has only one simple subjunctive past tense, the *past subjunctive* (**el imperfecto de subjuntivo**). Generally speaking, this tense is used in the same situations as the present subjunctive but to talk about past events. The exact English equivalent depends on the context in which it is used.

Past Subjunctive of Regular Verbs / El imperfecto de subjuntivo de los verbos regulares					
hablar: hablarø̸n̸		**comer: comierø̸n̸**		**vivir: vivierø̸n̸**	
hablara	habláramos	comiera	comiéramos	viviera	viviéramos
hablaras	hablarais	comieras	comierais	vivieras	vivierais
hablara	hablaran	comiera	comieran	viviera	vivieran

The last elections *Indicate the conditions that were true for you about the last elections in your country or state. In the last elections...* **1.** *I wasn't old enough to vote.* **2.** *I was old enough to vote, but I didn't vote.* **3.** *it was important to me that many people vote.* **4.** *I doubted that one of the candidates that I supported would win, but he did win!* **5.** *no candidate ran who won me over or about whom I got really enthusiastic.* **6.** *in my state/province there were no classes for children, so that elementary schools could serve as voting sites.*

Forms of the Past Subjunctive / Las formas del imperfecto de subjuntivo

1. Past Subjunctive Endings

As you can see in the chart on page 532, the past subjunctive endings are identical for **-ar, -er,** and **-ir** verbs. Those endings are added to the past subjunctive stem: the third person plural of the preterite minus **-on**. For this reason, the forms of the past subjunctive reflect all of the irregularities of the third person preterite (points 2–4, below).

Las terminaciones del imperfecto de subjuntivo*	
-a	-amos
-as	-ais
-a	-an

2. The Past Subjunctive of Stem-changing Verbs

• **-ar** and **-er** verbs: no change

empezar: empezar**ø̸n** → **empezara, empezaras,...**

volver: volvier**ø̸n** → **volviera, volvieras,...**

• **-ir** verbs: All persons of the past subjunctive have the vowel change of the third person plural of the preterite.

> Remember that the stem change for the third person preterite of **-ir** verbs is shown in parentheses in vocabulary lists. It is this change that occurs in *all* persons of the past subjunctive.

pedir (pido) (i): pidier**ø̸n** →

pidiera	pidiéramos
pidieras	pidierais
pidiera	pidieran

dormir (duermo) (u): durmier**ø̸n** →

durmiera	durmiéramos
durmieras	durmierais
durmiera	durmieran

3. The Past Subjunctive of Verbs with Spelling Changes

All persons of the past subjunctive reflect the change from **i** to **y** between two vowels.

Other preterite spelling changes (**c** → **qu, g** → **gu, z** → **c**) do not occur in the past subjunctive because those changes do not appear in the third person plural of the preterite: **bus**c**aron, pa**g**aron, empe**z**aron.**

i → **y** (caer, construir, creer, destruir, leer, oír)

creer: creyer**ø̸n** →

creyera	creyéramos
creyeras	creyerais
creyera	creyeran

4. The Past Subjunctive of Verbs with Irregular Preterites

The same formula (endings are added to the third person plural of the preterite) applies to all irregular verbs.

dar: dier**ø̸n** →

diera	diéramos
dieras	dierais
diera	dieran

dar:	dier**ø̸n** → **diera,...**		**poner:**	pusier**ø̸n** → **pusiera,...**	
decir:	dijer**ø̸n** → **dijera,...**		**querer:**	quisier**ø̸n** → **quisiera,...**	
estar:	estuvier**ø̸n** → **estuviera,...**		**saber:**	supier**ø̸n** → **supiera,...**	
haber:	hubier**ø̸n** → **hubiera,...**		**ser:**	fuer**ø̸n** → **fuera,...**	
hacer:	hicier**ø̸n** → **hiciera,...**		**tener:**	tuvier**ø̸n** → **tuviera,...**	
ir:	fuer**ø̸n** → **fuera,...**		**traer:**	trajer**ø̸n** → **trajera...**	
poder:	pudier**ø̸n** → **pudiera,...**		**venir:**	vinier**ø̸n** → **viniera,...**	

---

*An alternative form of the past subjunctive ends in **-se: hablase, hablases, hablase, hablásemos, hablaseis, hablasen.** This form will not be practiced in Puntos de partida.

Uses of the Past Subjunctive / Los usos del imperfecto de subjuntivo

1. Expressing Past Events

The past subjunctive usually has the same uses as the present subjunctive, but for talking about the past. Compare the pairs of sentences at the right. The first sentence in each pair is in the present tense, the second in the past.

Quiero que **se enteren** esta tarde.
I want them to find out this afternoon.
Quería que **se enteraran** por la tarde.
I wanted them to find out in the afternoon.

Siente que no **puedan** estar allí esta noche.
He's sorry (that) they can't be there tonight.
Sintió que no **pudieran** estar allí anoche.
He was sorry (that) they couldn't be there last night.

Dudamos que **mantengan** la paz.
We doubt (that) they will keep the peace.
Dudábamos que **mantuvieran** la paz.
We doubted (that) they would keep the peace.

2. Subjunctive "Triggers"

Remember that the subjunctive is used after:

(1) expressions of influence, emotion, and doubt

(1) ¿**Era necesario** que **regatearas**?
Was it necessary for you to bargain?

(1) **Sentí** que no **pudieran** ir a Granada.
I was sorry (that) they couldn't go to Granada.

(1) **No creía** que **hubiera** tiempo para hacerlo.
I didn't think (that) there was time to do it.

(2) nonexistent and indefinite antecedents

(2) **No había nadie** que **pudiera** resolverlo.
There wasn't anyone who could (might have been able to) solve it.

(3) conjunctions of contingency and purpose, as well as those of time

(3) Los padres **trabajaron** mucho **para que** sus hijos **asistieran** a la universidad.
The parents worked hard so that their children could (might) go to the university.

(3) Anoche, **íbamos** a salir **en cuanto llegara** Felipe.
Last night, we were going to leave as soon as Felipe arrived.

3. Past Subjunctive of *querer* to Express Requests

The past subjunctive of the verb **querer** is often used to make a request sound more polite.

Quisiéramos hablar con Ud. en seguida.
We would like to speak with you immediately.

Quisiera un café, por favor.
I would like a cup of coffee, please.

Summary of the Imperfect Subjunctive

Third person plural of the preterite minus **-on** +
-a, -as, -a, -amos, -ais, -an

Práctica y comunicación

A. Cuando era adolescente

Paso 1. Autoprueba. Dé la forma del pasado de subjuntivo de los siguientes verbos.

1. quise	**4.** supe	**7.** pedí
2. tuve	**5.** estuve	**8.** leí
3. salí	**6.** traje	

Prác. A, Paso 1: Answers: 1. quisiera **2.** tuviera **3.** saliera **4.** supiera **5.** estuviera **6.** trajera **7.** pidiera **8.** leyera

Paso 2. Complete las oraciones con el pasado de subjuntivo para que sean verdaderas para Ud. cuando Ud. tenía más o menos 13 años.

(No) Era obligatorio que yo...

1. ir a un servicio religioso (en la iglesia, la sinagoga, la mezquita...)
2. sacar buenas notas para poder recibir el estipendio (*allowance*) semanal
3. poner la mesa con frecuencia
4. leer casi todos los días
5. mantener mi cuarto ordenado

Mis padres no querían que... / A mis padres no les importaba que...

6. *yo:* tener novio o novia
7. *yo:* estar solo/a en casa
8. *yo:* mirar la tele o cualquier (*any*) pantalla por más de dos horas al día
9. *yo:* comer demasiada (*too much*) comida rápida
10. mis amigos: venir a casa cuando ellos no estaban

Paso 3. Ahora, en parejas, entrevístense sobre las ideas del **Paso 2.** Luego díganle a la clase algo que tenían en común o que era muy diferente para cada uno de Uds.

MODELO: E1: Cuando tenías 13 años, ¿era necesario que fueras a un servicio religioso?
E2: No, para mí no era necesario. ¿Y para ti?
E1: Para mí tampoco. / Para mí sí.

B. Noticias

Paso 1. Empareje cada idea de la **Columna A** con una de la **Columna B.** Luego conjugue el verbo de la **Columna B** en el presente de subjuntivo para formar una oración completa y lógica.

COLUMNA A

1. _____ El Presidente pide que la Guardia Nacional...
2. _____ El Congreso ha votado una nueva ley para que...
3. _____ La policía va de puerta en puerta buscando a alguien que...
4. _____ La Ministra de Defensa dice que espera que...
5. _____ La Corte Suprema proclama que no es legal que...
6. _____ Los bomberos (*firefighters*) van a rescatar (*rescue*) a la víctima antes de que...

COLUMNA B

a. saber algo del crimen
b. caerse el edificio
c. haber más ayuda económica para los estudiantes
d. ir al lugar del desastre natural
e. los sospechosos estar detenidos sin pruebas (*proof*)
f. la intervención militar ser corta

Paso 2. Ahora ponga las oraciones del **Paso 1** en el pasado, usando el pretérito del verbo principal y haciendo otros cambios necesarios.

MODELO: Para no ir a la huelga, los obreros exigen que la compañía les dé un aumento de sueldo. →
Para no ir a la huelga, los obreros **exigieron** que la compañía les **diera** un aumento de sueldo.

Una sesión en el Congreso español, una institución similar al Congreso de los Estados Unidos

C. **Escenas históricas**

Paso 1. Complete las siguientes oraciones con la forma correcta del imperfecto de subjuntivo de uno de los verbos de la lista. Si puede, nombre un grupo al que puede referirse cada oración.

haber   poder   practicar   seguir   tener

1. Las leyes del país de origen de este grupo no permitían que _____ libremente su religión.
2. Estas personas esperaban que _____ oro y plata en América.
3. El rey no quería que estos criminales _____ viviendo en este país.
4. Estos inmigrantes buscaban un país donde _____ tener paz y prosperidad.
5. Este grupo buscaba un país donde no _____ que pasar hambre.

Paso 2. Ahora exprese algunos acontecimientos de la historia de los Estados Unidos, haciendo oraciones completas con los siguientes elementos. **¡OJO!** El verbo en la primera cláusula debe estar en el pasado.

1. Inglaterra: desear / que / los colonos: conseguir más tierras en Norteamérica
2. los indígenas americanos: temer / que / los colonos: quitarles sus tierras
3. el rey de Inglaterra: querer / que / los colonos: pagar impuestos (*taxes*)
4. los estadounidenses: ir a la guerra / para que / México: darles parte de su territorio
5. los estados del sur: no gustarles / que / los estados del norte: controlar las leyes
6. los abolicionistas: desear / que / todas las personas del país: tener los mismos derechos

Paso 3. Ahora, en parejas, contesten la siguiente pregunta: ¿Qué buscaban los primeros inmigrantes que llegaron a lo que es hoy los Estados Unidos?

Buscaban un lugar donde...

D. **Hace más de cien años.** Combine ideas de las dos columnas para describir cómo era la vida a finales del siglo XIX y principios del siglo XX.

COLUMNA A

Las leyes prohibían que...
Los padres esperaban que sus hijas...
Las mujeres tenían que aceptar esposos que...
Los hombres buscaban esposas que...
No había muchas personas que...

COLUMNA B

casarse jóvenes
tener muchos hijos
personas de razas diferentes: casarse
personas de origen africano: ser candidatos políticos
las mujeres: votar
tomar todas las decisiones
aceptar sus decisiones
poder imaginar ¿ ? (un derecho o una situación actual)

Algo sobre...

el flamenco

El flamenco no es la música típica de todas las regiones españolas, pero es sin duda la música que más se asocia con España a nivel internacional. Tiene su origen en Andalucía, la región más al sur, y lleva la marca indeleble del pueblo gitano.[a]

El flamenco es un género musical de gran diversidad que va desde canciones muy lentas y tristes a muy animadas y alegres. Los cantantes de flamenco se llaman cantaores y el instrumento tradicional es la guitarra acompañada de las palmas.[b] Los bailaores, que son los bailarines de flamenco, también hacen música con el taconeo[c] de sus zapatos.

¿Hay algún género musical en este país que incluya instrumentos musicales, canciones y bailes al mismo tiempo?

[a]*gypsy* [b]*acompañada... accompanied by clapping* [c]*stamping*

Un espectáculo de flamenco, con una bailaora, un cantaor que toca las palmas (de las manos) y un guitarrista

---

E. Una encuesta (*poll*)

Paso 1. Haga cinco oraciones completas con elementos de cada columna. Trate de no repetir muchos elementos.

MODELO: Cuando yo era niña, mi hermana mayor no permitía que yo jugara con sus videojuegos.

cuando yo era niño/a cuando yo era adolescente (13 o 14 años) cuando yo estaba en el último año de la escuela secundaria	(yo) mi madre/padre mis padres mi mejor amigo/a mi hermano/a mis hermanos (no) era necesario/imposible ¿ ?	tener miedo de (que)... (no) querer (que)... necesitar un trabajo para (que)... prohibir que... (no) permitir que... (no) gustar (que)... ¿ ?

Paso 2. Ahora convierta sus oraciones del **Paso 1** en preguntas generales sobre los temas que Ud. escogió. Use las preguntas para encuestar (*interview*) a cinco compañeros de clase para ver si tuvieron experiencias similares.

MODELO: Cuando eras niño, ¿te permitían tus hermanos que jugaras con sus videojuegos?

Paso 3. Dígale a la clase por lo menos dos detalles interesantes de su encuesta.

F. Con mucha cortesía

Paso 1. Lea el siguiente dibujo y conteste las preguntas.

1. ¿Dónde está el niño?
2. ¿Qué hora será?
3. ¿Tiene sed ahora el niño?
4. ¿Cómo demuestra (*shows*) el niño que es muy cortés y considerado?
5. ¿Por qué repite sus expresiones de cortesía?

—Verás, quisiera un vaso de agua. Pero no te molestes, porque ya no tengo sed. Solo quisiera saber si, en el caso de que tuviese otra vez sed, podría (*I could*) venir a pedirte un vaso de agua.

Gramática

Paso 2. Ahora, en parejas, inventen cómo pedirían (*you would ask for*) lo que necesitan en las siguientes situaciones.

1. Ud. quiere el número de teléfono de una persona que acaba de conocer. Habla con un amigo de él/ella.
2. Uds. quieren saber cuándo es el examen final en esta clase y qué va a comprender (*include*).
3. Ud. necesita una prórroga (*extension*) para el próximo examen de español.
4. Ud. necesita una carta de recomendación del profesor / de la profesora.
5. Ud. ha llamado a un amigo a las diez de la noche para invitarlo a salir, pero él ya estaba dormido y Ud. lo ha despertado.
6. Ud. llega a casa muy enfermo/a, con tos y fiebre. Debe guardar cama. Pero la persona con quien vive le ha preparado una fiesta sorpresa de cumpleaños. Todos sus amigos lo/la saludan cuando entra.

Nota **comunicativa**

Cómo expresar deseos imposibles

In **Capítulo 13,** you learned to use **ojalá (que)** + *present subjunctive* to express hopes that can become a reality.

ojalá (que) + *present subjunctive = I hope*

Ojalá (que) saque una buena nota en este curso.

Ojalá (que) encuentre trabajo tan pronto como me gradúe.

Ojalá (que) can also be used with the *past subjunctive* to express wishes about things that are not likely to occur or that are impossible.

ojalá (que) + *past subjunctive = I wish*

Ojalá (que) pudiera ir a la playa este fin de semana. (*You can't because the semester/quarter isn't over yet. And, unless you live on the East or West Coast, the beach may be far away.*)

Ojalá (que) todos los estudiantes **pudieran** pasar el verano en un país hispanohablante. (*It's obvious that that's not possible for everyone.*)

The expression **ojalá** comes from the Arabic meaning *if Allah wishes.* It is similar to English *God willing* and Spanish **si Dios quiere.**

You will use **ojalá (que)** with the past subjunctive in **Práctica G.**

La vicepresidenta del gobierno español, Soraya Sáenz de Santamaría

G. ¡Ojalá!

Paso 1. Complete las siguientes oraciones lógicamente.

1. Ojalá que (yo) tuviera...
2. Ojalá que (yo) pudiera...
3. Ojalá inventaran una máquina que...
4. Ojalá solucionaran el problema de...
5. Ojalá que en esta universidad fuera posible...

Paso 2. ¿Qué dirían (*would say*) estas personas en las siguientes situaciones?

1. el presidente / la presidenta de un país en guerra
2. un político / una política, durante una campaña electoral muy disputada
3. una persona que está muy enferma
4. un niño que quiere un juguete (*toy*) de último modelo muy caro (¡piense en lo que Ud. deseaba de niño/a!)
5. un(a) estudiante que tiene que pedir un préstamo para pagar la matrícula

¿Recuerda Ud.?

In **Gramática 49** you will learn the forms and uses of the conditional. You have already learned one conditional form: **me gustaría** (**Capítulo 8**). Review what you know by giving the English equivalent of the following sentence.

Hoy **me gustaría** ir al museo.

Knowing the future, which you studied in **Gramática 46** (**Capítulo 17**), will help you learn the conditional. Can you provide the correct future forms of the following verbs?

1. (yo) viajar
2. (ellos) beber
3. (tú) ir
4. (Ud.) venir
5. (nosotros) hacer
6. (ella) poner

49 Expressing What You Would Do

Conditional Verb Forms

Grammar Tutorial **49**

connect
|SPANISH
www.connectspanish.com

Gramática en acción: Un mundo utópico

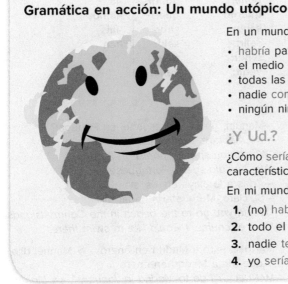

En un mundo ideal...

- habría paz en todos los países.
- el medio ambiente no estaría contaminado.
- todas las personas tendrían los mismos derechos y libertades.
- nadie cometería ningún acto criminal.
- ningún niño sufriría de hambre ni de enfermedades.

¿Y Ud.?

¿Cómo sería un mundo ideal si Ud. pudiera cambiarlo? ¿Qué más características añadiría Ud.?

En mi mundo ideal,

1. (no) habría _____.
2. todo el mundo podría _____.
3. nadie tendría _____.
4. yo sería _____ (profesión/adjetivo)

The phrase **me gustaría** expresses what you *would like* to (do, say, and so on). The verb **gustaría** is a conditional form. You will learn to form the *conditional* (**el condicional**) of all verbs in this section.

Conditional of Regular Verbs / El condicional de los verbos regulares					
hablar		**comer**		**vivir**	
hablaría	hablaríamos	comería	comeríamos	viviría	viviríamos
hablarías	hablaríais	comerías	comeríais	vivirías	viviríais
hablaría	hablarían	comería	comerían	viviría	vivirían

A perfect world *In an ideal world ... • there would be peace in all countries. • the environment would not be polluted. • everyone would have the same rights and freedoms. • no one would engage in any criminal acts. • no child would be hungry or sick.*

Gramática

1. Conditional Endings

In English the conditional, like the future, is a compound tense, formed with the auxiliary (helping) verb *would*: *I **would** speak, you **would** do,* and so on.

The Spanish *conditional* (**el condicional**), like the future, is a simple verb form (only one word). It is formed by adding the identical set of conditional endings to **-ar, -er,** and **-ir** infinitives. No auxiliary verb is needed.

Las terminaciones del condicional

$$infinitivo + \begin{cases} \text{-ía} & \text{-íamos} \\ \text{-ías} & \text{-íais} \\ \text{-ía} & \text{-ían} \end{cases}$$

2. Irregular Conditional Forms

Verbs that form the future on an irregular stem use the same stem to form the conditional.

Note that the conditional of **hay (haber)** is **habría** (*there would be*).*

decir: diría, dirías, diría, diríamos, diríais, dirían

decir:	dir- }	
haber (hay):	habr-	
hacer:	har-	-ía
poder:	podr-	-ías
poner:	pondr-	-ía
querer:	querr-	-íamos
saber:	sabr-	-íais
salir:	saldr-	-ían
tener:	tendr-	
venir:	vendr-	

3. Uses of the Conditional

Most uses of the Spanish conditional are the same as those of the conditional in English.

• to express what you *would* do in a particular situation or given a particular set of circumstances

—Manuel, ¿**hablarías** español en Portugal?
—No, **hablaría** portugués.
"Would you speak Spanish in Portugal?"
"No, I would speak Portuguese."
—¿**Irías** a la playa en las Islas Canarias?
—Sí, claro. Me **gustaría** nadar allí.
"Would you go to the beach in the Canary Islands?"
"Yes, of course. I would like to swim there."

• To report what someone said that he/she/they *was/ were going to do,* that is, to express the future from the point of view of the past

MANUEL: —Iré a Madrid en enero. → Manuel dijo que **iría** a Madrid en enero.
MANUEL: *"I'll go to Madrid in January."* → *Manuel said that he would go to Madrid in January.*
ANITA Y CARLOS: —Iremos a la manifestación esta noche. → Anita y Carlos dijeron que **irían** a la manifestación esta noche.
ANITA AND CARLOS: *"We'll go to the demonstration tonight."* → *Anita and Carlos said that they would go to the demonstration tonight.*

4. Another Way to Express *would*

Remember that *would = used to* (a habitual action) is expressed with the imperfect tense in Spanish.

Manuel **iba** a España todos los veranos.
Manuel would (used to) go to Spain every summer.

---

*The conditional forms of the verb **haber** are used to form the conditional perfect tense (**el condicional perfecto**), which expresses what would have occurred at some point in the past: **Habríamos tenido** que buscarla en el aeropuerto. (**We would have had** to pick her up at the airport.) You will find a more detailed presentation of these forms in Appendix 4, Additional Perfect Forms (Indicative and Subjunctive).

Práctica y comunicación

A. ¿Qué haría Ud. en España?

Paso 1. Autoprueba. Complete las siguientes formas del condicional.

1. salir: sal____ía
2. hacer: ha____íamos
3. querer: que____ías
4. decir: d____ían
5. tener: ten____ía
6. poder: po____ía

Paso 2. Para describir un posible viaje a España, complete las siguientes oraciones con la forma apropiada del condicional y la información indicada.

1. ir a España con _____
2. viajar en _____ (mes o estación) porque _____
3. hablar español todo el tiempo para _____
4. comer _____ (plato[s], comidas)
5. ver un espectáculo de _____
6. querer _____ (infinitivo) durante el viaje
7. gustar conocer a _____ durante mi visita
8. no poder volver a casa sin _____ (infinitivo)

> **Summary of the Conditional**
>
> Infinitive + **-ía, -ías, -ía, -íamos, -íais, -ían**

Paso 3. Ahora, en parejas, entrevístense sobre las oraciones del **Paso 1.** Luego añadan a la lista dos cosas más que harían en su viaje y díganselas a la clase.

MODELO: **E1:** ¿Con quién irías a España?
E2: Iría con mi hermana mayor, porque habla español y juntas nos divertimos mucho. ¿Y tú?

Algo sobre...

las tapas

Las tapas son pequeños platos de comida que se toman como aperitivos o en lugar del almuerzo o la cena. Es una distintiva manera española no solo de comer sino[a] de socializar en los muchos bares que existen en cualquier[b] ciudad del país. Las tapas son siempre comida salada[c] (nunca postres). Pueden ser platos fríos o calientes, simples o complicados. El concepto de las tapas ha alcanzado[d] ahora cierta popularidad en los Estados Unidos y en otros países.

En su opinión, ¿cuál es una de las comidas o tipo de comida más distintivamente estadounidense?

[a]*but also* [b]*any* [c]*con sal* [d]*achieved*

Algunas de las tapas típicas españolas: calamares (*squid*) fritos, camarones, sardinas, aceitunas (*olives*) y mejollones (*mussels*)

B. ¿Es posible escapar?

Paso 1. Cuente la siguiente fantasía de una pareja, dando la forma condicional de los verbos.

Necesitamos salir de todo esto... Pensamos que (deber[1]) ir al Caribe... No (trabajar[2])... (Poder[3]) nadar todos los días... (Tomar[4]) el sol en la playa... (Beber[5]) el agua de un coco... (Ver[6]) bellos lugares naturales... El viaje (ser[7]) ideal...

Pero... , tarde o temprano, (tener[8]) que volver a lo de siempre... a los rascacielos de la ciudad... al tráfico... al medio ambiente contaminado... al trabajo... (Poder[9]) usar tarjetas de crédito, como dice el anuncio —pero ¡(tener[10]) que pagar después!

Prác. A, Paso 1: Answers: 1. saldría 2. haríamos 3. querrías 4. dirían 5. tendría 6. podría

Paso 2. Comprensión. ¿Cierto, falso o no lo dice? Corrija las oraciones falsas.

	CIERTO	FALSO	NO LO DICE.
1. Esta pareja trabaja en una ciudad grande.	☐	☐	☐
2. No les interesan los deportes acuáticos.	☐	☐	☐
3. Pueden pagar este viaje de sueños al contado.	☐	☐	☐
4. Quisieran hacer el viaje con sus padres.	☐	☐	☐

C. ¿Qué dijo?

Paso 1. Repita lo que dijeron las siguientes personas.

MODELO: María: —Llegaré el lunes por la noche. →
María **dijo que llegaría** el lunes por la noche.

1. Tomás: —Estaré en el café a las 2.
2. Marta y Clara: —Vamos a hacer una fiesta este sábado.
3. La profesora de español: —Salgo para Madrid el 9 de junio.
4. Los padres: —Nos vemos en casa de los abuelos.
5. Ud.: —No podré ir al cine con Uds.
6. Yo: —No tener tiempo para ir de compras.

Paso 2. Ahora, en parejas, digan lo que dijeron algunas personas o noticieros recientemente, usando un elemento de cada columna.

MODELO: el pronóstico del tiempo →
El pronóstico del tiempo **dijo que** este fin de semana **haría** buen tiempo.

COLUMNA A	COLUMNA B
el pronóstico del tiempo	haber un examen el día ____
el profesor / la profesora de español	hacer buen/mal tiempo _____ (día / el fin de semana)
otro profesor / otra profesora	(no) haber un examen final
su padre/madre	(no) venir a visitarme pronto
su mejor amigo/a	ser necesario escribir un ensayo sobre _____
	querer estudiar juntos para un examen
	¿ ?

Nota **comunicativa**

Cláusulas con *si*

To express hypothetical situations, Spanish uses sentences with **si** (*if*) clauses, just like English.*

if CLAUSE	RESULT
si + *past subjunctive*	*conditional*
Si yo **pudiera,**	**iría** a España de vacaciones.
If I could,	*I would go to Spain on vacation.*
Si yo **fuera** tú,	no **haría** eso.
If I were you,	*I wouldn't do that.*

You are already familiar with **si** clauses with the present indicative. They present actions that are habitual in the present or likely to happen.

¡OJO!
The present subjunctive is never used after **si.**

Si ahorro suficiente dinero, iré de vacaciones a España.
If I save enough money, I'll go to Spain on vacation.

You will create **si**-clause sentences in **D, E,** and **G.**

These contrary-to-fact situations express speculations about the present and the future. The perfect forms of the conditional and the past subjunctive are used to speculate about the past; that is, what would have happened if a particular event had occurred: Si **hubiera tenido el dinero, **habría hecho** el viaje. (If **I had had** the money, **I would have made** the trip.) You will find a more detailed presentation of this structure in Appendix 4, Additional Perfect Forms (Indicative and Subjunctive).*

D. ¿Qué haría Ud.?

Paso 1. Complete las siguientes declaraciones lógicamente.

1. Si yo quisiera comprar comida, iría a _____.
2. Si necesitara comprar un libro, iría a _____.
3. Si necesitara consultar un libro, iría a _____.
4. Si tuviera sed en este momento, tomaría _____.
5. Si tuviera que emigrar, iría a _____.
6. Si fuera a _____, tendría que viajar en _____.
7. Si tuviera suficiente dinero, compraría _____.
8. Si pudiera, me gustaría _____.

Paso 2. Ahora, en parejas, túrnense para comparar sus oraciones del **Paso 1.** Luego díganle a la clase lo que Uds. tienen en común.

E. Situaciones

Paso 1. Empareje los siguientes dibujos con las descripciones. Luego complete las descripciones, conjugando los verbos y añadiendo los detalles necesarios.

a. b. c. d.

_____ **1.** Miriam (ir) en coche al trabajo como siempre si su coche no (tener) un serio problema con los frenos. Si su padre (vivir) cerca, (poder) arreglarlo él, pero (él)...

_____ **2.** Si el avión no (ser) tan pequeño, la Sra. Blanco no (tener) tanto miedo. (preferir) ir en coche, pero es un caso de emergencia: su hijo...

_____ **3.** Si Mariana (tener) suficiente dinero, ahora mismo (comprar) ese traje pantalón. (Ser) ideal para... (un evento o una situación)

_____ **4.** Si la compañera de casa de Julia (poder) llevarla al trabajo, Julia (seguir) durmiendo hasta las ocho por lo menos. Y Julia no (estar) tan cansada si...

Paso 2. Ahora imagine una solución para cada situación. Use el futuro para expresar lo que pasará. ¡Sea imaginativo/a!

MODELO: Mariana le pedirá dinero a... Esta persona no se lo dará / se lo dará como regalo de cumpleaños.

F. ¿En qué circunstancias lógicas... ? En parejas, hagan y contesten preguntas sobre los siguientes temas.

MODELO: comprar un coche nuevo →
> E1: ¿En qué circunstancias **comprarías** un coche nuevo?
> E2: **Compraría** un coche nuevo **si tuviera** más dinero.

1. dejar de estudiar en esta universidad
2. emigrar a otro país
3. estudiar otro idioma
4. no obedecer a tus padres / a tu jefe/a
5. votar por _____ para presidente/a
6. ser candidato/a para presidente/a
7. casarse / divorciarse
8. no decirle la verdad a un amigo / una amiga

G. ¿Qué haría si... ?

Paso 1. En parejas, inventen soluciones para los siguientes dilemas.

1. Si su mejor amigo/a le pidiera 500 dólares para algo muy urgente.
2. Si uno de sus profesores o profesoras le dijera: «Ud. me cae muy bien (*I think you're really nice*). Por eso no tiene que tomar el examen final».
3. Si su novio/a le propusiera que se casaran inmediatamente. (O si su esposo/a le propusiera que se divorciaran en seguida.)
4. Si de pronto tuviera un millón de dólares hoy.

Paso 2. Ahora inventen una situación bien difícil de resolver que la clase tiene que solucionar. ¡Sean imaginativos!

H. Una encuesta (*poll*)

Paso 1. Prepare cinco preguntas sobre temas importantes. Por ejemplo: la vida sentimental y familiar, el trabajo, el medio ambiente, etcétera.

MODELOS: ¿**Podrías** estar más de una semana sin mirar el celular?
¿**Querrías** volver a vivir con tu familia después de graduarte?

> Vocabulario **útil**
>
> **vivir permanentemente en este estado / esta ciudad**
> **tener más de dos hijos / adoptar hijos**
> **presentarse como candidato político / candidata política a nivel estatal**
> **prestar (to do) servicio militar**
> **poder vivir sin la televisión / la computadora / el celular**

Paso 2. Use sus preguntas del **Paso 1** para entrevistar a cinco compañeros de clase. Luego prepare un breve informe para toda la clase con los resultados de su encuesta.

Un poco de todo

la diversidad lingüística de España

España, por su larga y complicada historia, tiene regiones con marcadas diferencias unas de otras, incluyendo diferencias lingüísticas. No solo hay dialectos distintivos sino[a] también lenguas diferentes. El español, también llamado el castellano tanto en España como en los países latinoamericanos, es la lengua mayoritaria; se habla por todo el país. Pero hay tres lenguas oficiales más. El catalán se habla en Cataluña, y hay variedades del catalán en la región valenciana y las Islas Baleares. El gallego se habla en la región de Galicia, al noroeste de la península, haciendo frontera con Portugal. Por fin, el vasco o euskera se habla en la región vasca, que comprende[b] el País Vasco español y una región adyacente en Francia. Es interesante notar que el español, el catalán y el gallego son lenguas romances, es decir, derivadas del latín. En contraste, el vasco no lo es y es muy diferente de las otras. En la tabla, se comparan tres palabras comunes en las cuatro lenguas.

¿Cree Ud. que hay diferencias lingüísticas muy marcadas en los Estados Unidos? Si las hay, ¿puede explicar a qué se deben?

[a]*but* [b]*includes*

español o castellano	catalán	gallego	vasco
hola	hola	ola	kaixo
adiós	adéu	adeus	agur
gracias	gràcies	grazas	eskerrik asko

Mapa lingüístico de España que muestra dónde se hablan las cuatro lenguas oficiales del país

A. **Lengua y cultura: Maneras de practicar el español fuera de clase**

Paso 1. Complete the following paragraphs with the correct form of the words in parentheses, as suggested by context. When two possibilities are given, select the correct word. **¡OJO!** As you conjugate verbs, decide whether to use the subjunctive (present, present perfect, or past) or the indicative (present, present perfect, future, preterite, or imperfect). For items flagged with *comm.*, use a command. Start out in the present.

Claro está que Ud. habla español en clase. También es probable que lo (hablar[1]) con su profesor(a) cada vez que lo/la (ver[2]) en el *campus* de la universidad. Pero (por / para[3]) hablar español con soltura,[a] Ud. tiene que practicar más.

«¡Ojalá que (*yo: poder*[4]) practicar español fuera de clase!» ¿(*pres. perf.: Decir*[5]) Ud. eso alguna vez? Pues hay muchas maneras de hacerlo. Por ejemplo, los compañeros de una misma clase de español siempre pueden hablar español cuando (verse[6]) para no (perder[7]) (ninguno[8]) oportunidad de practicar. Otra idea es (mirar[9]) una telenovela[b] o (un / una[10]) programa de noticias en español. También puede escuchar la radio cuando (manejar[11]). Lo importante es dedicar un rato[c] a escuchar español auténtico con frecuencia.

Muchas personas (sentirse[12]) muy frustradas con esta actividad (por qué/ porque[13]) no pueden comprenderlo todo. Pero (haber[14]) que recordar que no es necesario entender cada una de las palabras que se oyen. Para los estudiantes principiantes,[d] es suficiente identificar (el / la[15]) tema y (alguno[16]) palabras y expresiones. Si Ud. (escuchar[17]) español habitualmente en los medios de comunicación, (aprender[18]) mucho... y rápidamente.

[a]*con... fluently* [b]*soap opera* [c]*un... a bit of time* [d]*beginning*

(Continúa.)

Una página de la edición electrónica de *El País*, un periódico de España

Otra actividad útil es leer el periódico o una revista de actualidad en español. Puesto que[e] hay muchos hispanohablantes en (este / ese[19]) país, es relativamente fácil conseguir algo que leer en español. Y si esto no (ser / estar[20]) fácil en el lugar donde Ud. vive, (*comm., Ud.:* buscar[21]) en el Internet. (Por / Para[22]) ejemplo, si le gusta viajar, (*comm., Ud.:* consultar[23]) las páginas relacionadas con el turismo en los países donde se habla español.

Finalmente, (*comm., Ud.:* recordar[24]) su propia comunidad. Es muy posible que Ud. (vivir[25]) en una ciudad o estado que tiene una comunidad hispana. Le sugerimos que (*Ud.:* visitar[26]) tiendas o supermercados hispanos para que (*Ud.:* ver[27]) las cosas que se venden allí. ¡Leer la lista de los ingredientes de cualquier producto es ya[f] un ejercicio de lectura!

[e]*Puesto... Since* [f]*actually*

Paso 2. Comprensión. Conteste las siguientes preguntas.

1. Además de (*Besides*) hablar español en clase, ¿qué cosas puede Ud. hacer para practicar el idioma fuera de la clase?
2. ¿Es buena o mala la idea de mirar la televisión en español? ¿Qué tipos de programas se recomienda ver?
3. ¿Es necesario que un estudiante entienda cada una de las palabras de lo que oye en los medios de comunicación?
4. ¿Qué tipos de lecturas puede Ud. conseguir en español para practicar más?
5. ¿Qué posibilidades de practicar español existen en la comunidad?

Paso 3. Ahora, en parejas, hablen sobre su futuro con respecto al español. Las siguientes preguntas les darán algunas ideas para su conversación.

1. ¿Van a tomar otra clase de español el próximo semestre/trimestre? ¿Por qué sí o por qué no?
2. ¿Piensan estudiar en un país hispanohablante? ¿En dónde? ¿Cuándo?
3. ¿Creen que en el futuro usarán el español en su trabajo? ¿Por qué?

B. Si el mundo fuera diferente... ¿Qué ocurriría si el mundo fuera diferente? En parejas, hablen de las siguientes circunstancias.

MODELO: Si yo fuera la última persona en el mundo... →
• **tendría** que aprender a hacer muchas cosas.
• **sería** la persona más importante —y más ignorante— del mundo.

1. Si yo pudiera tener solamente un amigo o amiga, _____.
2. Si yo tuviera que pasar un año en una isla desierta, _____.
3. Si yo fuera _____ (otra persona), _____.
4. Si el presidente / la presidenta fuera _____, _____.
5. Si yo viviera en (nombre de país), _____.

En **su** comunidad

Entreviste a una persona hispana de su universidad o ciudad sobre el gobierno de su país de origen y sobre sus preferencias políticas.

PREGUNTAS POSIBLES

• ¿Qué tipo de gobierno hay en su país? ¿Ha habido algún cambio grande en la estructura del gobierno en los últimos años? ¿Y en las últimas décadas?
• ¿Quién es el presidente o la presidenta del país? ¿Hay un congreso y un senado?
• ¿Cuáles son los partidos políticos más importantes? Si hay más de dos partidos, ¿se forman coaliciones de partidos para gobernar?
• ¿Estaba afiliado/a a algún partido en su país? ¿Votó alguna vez? ¿En qué elecciones?

Antes de mirar

¿Hace o ha hecho Ud. trabajo de voluntario? ¿En qué tipo de organización?

☐ una organización religiosa
☐ una escuela primaria, media o secundaria
☐ una residencia de ancianos
☐ un refugio para perros y gatos
☐ una organización sin fines de lucro (*non-profit*)

Este segmento

Laura presenta un reportaje sobre un programa para voluntarios extranjeros en Guatemala.

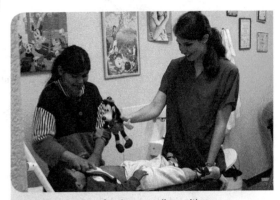

«Y al final, ¿ellos qué es lo que se llevan (*they [the volunteers] take away*)? Se llevan la sensación de haber ayudado (*having helped*), pero la mayoría se va con la idea de que ellos aprendieron más de lo que dieron.»

Vocabulario del segmento

sumo/a	great
el analfabetismo	illiteracy
mejorar	to improve
atender	to take care
el alivio	relief
colocar (qu)	to place
llenarse	to get filled up
bien satisfecho/a	very satisfied
Chinautla, Antigua	ciudades guatemaltecas
antiguo/a	former
valorar	to value
la pobreza	poverty
maravilloso/a	wonderful

Fragmento del guion

HERMANO[a] LUVÍN: Diario[b] atendemos noventa a cien ancianos, en los cuales les damos alimentación que consta[c] de un almuerzo, que para ellos es desayuno, almuerzo y cena, porque no tienen dónde más comer.[d] Fuera de eso,[e] les prestamos el servicio de baño.[f] Ellos vienen de la calle, sucios, vueltos nada.[g] Y les damos ropa, les damos el baño para que cambien y para que se bañen y queden distintos. También le[s] damos la parte espiritual, como motivación para que su autoestima[h] se eleve un poco y piensen que son importantes para la sociedad, aunque vivan en las circunstancias que viven.

[a]*Brother (in a religious order)* [b]*On a daily basis* [c]*alimentación... nourishment that consists* [d]*no... they have no where else to eat* [e]*Fuera... In addition* [f]*les... we provide them with bathing facilities* [g]*vueltos... reduced to nothing* [h]*self-esteem*

Después de mirar

A. ¿Está claro? Las siguientes oraciones son falsas. Corríjalas.

1. CCS es una compañía de negocios internacionales.
2. Los voluntarios atienden solo a ancianos.
3. CCS coloca a todos los voluntarios en la misma organización.
4. Los voluntarios de CCS no viajan.

B. Un poco más. Conteste las siguientes preguntas.

1. ¿Qué problemas endémicos tiene Guatemala?
2. Según una codirectora de CCS, ¿qué aprenden los voluntarios?
3. Además de ayudar a las personas necesitadas (*in need*), ¿qué otras actividades hacen los voluntarios?

C. Y ahora, Uds. Obviamente, no hay que ir a otro país para ayudar a las personas necesitadas. En parejas, hablen de los tipos de ayuda que uno puede dar como voluntario en este país y dónde lo puede hacer. ¿Hay áreas especialmente necesitadas en su estado? ¿Qué tipo de ayuda necesitan?

¿Cuáles son las ventajas y desventajas de que haya gran diversidad en un solo país?

Lectura cultural: España
La diversidad española

España es un país de una gran diversidad geográfica y cultural. Si bien[a] hay bastante homogeneidad racial, en el país conviven[b] regiones con identidades bien definidas a lo largo de[c] una historia milenaria.[d] Estas diferencias incluyen hasta lenguas diferentes.

Con la Constitución de 1978, España reconoce[e] esta diversidad, constituyéndose[f] como un Estado de Autonomías: diecisiete regiones que funcionan de manera descentralizada, no muy diferente del sistema federativo estadounidense.

La diversidad de España es una fuente[g] de innumerables tensiones lingüísticas, políticas, presupuestarias,[h] etcétera. Pero también es motivo de orgullo[i] general, porque con un territorio del tamaño[j] de Texas, España es un país de intensos contrastes.

[a]*Si... Although* [b]*coexist* [c]*a... throughout* [d]*thousand-year* [e]*recognizes* [f]*organizing itself* [g]*source* [h]*budgetary* [i]*pride* [j]*size*

Hay estatuas de don Quijote de la Mancha y Sancho Panza por todo el país. Estas están en la Plaza de España, en Madrid.

En todo el mundo hispano

- **En muchos países americanos hispanohablantes** En 2010, muchos países celebraron el bicentenario del proceso de su independencia de España. Esa lucha, que empezó en la mayoría de los casos en el siglo[a] XIX, duró alrededor de[b] quince años y culminó con la creación de los nuevos estados americanos.

- **En la Argentina, el Paraguay y el Uruguay** Junto con el Brasil, estos países firmaron un tratado[c] para formar el Mercado Común del Sur, o MERCOSUR. Es un acuerdo[d] que fomenta[e] la libre circulación de productos y servicios. En la actualidad MERCOSUR tiene más miembros: Bolivia, Chile, Colombia, el Ecuador y el Perú.

[a]*century* [b]*alrededor... about* [c]*firmaron... signed a treaty* [d]*agreement* [e]*encourages*

Un símbolo español: Don Quijote de la Mancha y Sancho Panza

El ingenioso hidalgo[a] *Don Qijote de la Mancha,*[b] de Miguel de Cervantes, es una de las obras cumbres[c] de la literatura mundial. Se considera la primera novela moderna y es el libro más editado y traducido del mundo, después de la Biblia.

La novela cuenta la historia de don Quijote, un señor mayor que se vuelve loco[d] y decide hacerse[e] caballero andante[f] como los de las novelas[g] que le encanta leer. Por

[a]*gentleman* [b]*region in the center of Spain* [c]*obras... masterpieces* [d]*se... goes mad* [e]*to become* [f]*caballero... knight errant* [g]*como... like the ones in the novels*

eso toma un escudero,[h] Sancho Panza, que en realidad es solo un campesino local. Sancho intenta disuadir a su señor de meterse en líos.[i] Juntos pasarán por una larga serie de aventuras que revelan la naturaleza humana. Don Quijote es un símbolo del espíritu humano que siempre lucha por algo noble, aunque[j] sean causas perdidas, mientras que Sancho Panza es símbolo de lealtad.[k]

[h]*squire* [i]*de... from getting himself into problems* [j]*although* [k]*loyalty*

COMPRENSIÓN

1. ¿Cómo está dividida España administrativamente?
2. ¿Cuántas lenguas se hablan en España?
3. ¿Qué se celebró en 2010?
4. ¿Qué es MERCOSUR?
5. ¿Por qué es importante la novela *Don Quijote de la Mancha*?
6. ¿Qué simbolizan don Quijote y Sancho?

Y ahora, Uds.

¿Cuáles son los grandes íconos humanos de su país? Pueden ser personajes (*characters*) de ficción, como don Quijote y Sancho, o personajes reales e históricos.

Del mundo hispano

Antes de leer

El Uruguay estuvo bajo una dictadura militar desde 1973 hasta 1985. Durante esta época, muchos uruguayos opuestos a ese régimen sufrieron persecusión. ¿Qué sabe Ud. de la vida bajo una dictadura? ¿Qué derechos se pierden cuando no hay democracia?

Lectura: «Celebración de la voz° humana/2», de Eduardo Galeano

voice

1   Tenían las manos atadas,[a] o esposadas,[b] y sin embargo los dedos danzaban, volaban, dibujaban palabras. Los presos[c] estaban encapuchados;[d] pero inclinándose alcanzaban a ver[e] algo, alguito, por abajo. Aunque[f] hablar estaba prohibido, ellos conversaban con las manos.

2   Pinio Ungerfeld me enseñó el alfabeto de los dedos, que en prisión aprendió sin profesor:

3   —*Algunos teníamos mala letra*— me dijo—. *Otros eran unos artistas de la caligrafía.*

4   La dictadura uruguaya quería que cada uno fuera nada más que uno, que cada uno fuera nadie: en cárceles[g] y cuarteles,[h] y en todo el país, la comunicación era delito.

5   Algunos presos pasaron más de diez años enterrados[i] en solitarios calabozos[j] del tamaño[k] de un ataúd,[l] sin escuchar más voces que el estrépito[m] de las rejas[n] o los pasos de las botas por los corredores. Fernández Huidobro y Mauricio Rosencof, condenados a esa soledad, se salvaron porque pudieron hablarse, con golpecitos,[ñ] a través de la pared. Así se contaban sueños y recuerdos, amores y desamores; discutían, se abrazaban, se peleaban; compartían certezas[o] y bellezas y también compartían dudas y culpas[p] y preguntas de esas que no tienen respuesta.

6   Cuando es verdadera, cuando nace de la necesidad de decir, a la voz humana no hay quien la pare.[q] Si le niegan la boca, ella habla por las manos, o por los ojos, o por los poros, o por donde sea. Porque todos, toditos, tenemos algo que decir a los demás, alguna cosa que merece ser por los demás celebrada o perdonada.

[a]*tied* [b]*handcuffed* [c]*prisoners* [d]*in hoods* [e]*alcanzaban… podían ver* [f]*Although* [g]*jails* [h]*military barracks* [i]*buried* [j]*cells* [k]*size* [l]*coffin* [m]*racket, noise* [n]*bars* [ñ]*little taps* [o]*certainties* [p]*feelings of guilt* [q]*no… no one can stop it*

Comprensión

A. Los detalles. Busque los siguientes detalles en el texto de Galeano.

1. las condiciones en que estaban los presos
2. los sistemas que usaban para comunicarse
3. una comparación entre uno de esos sistemas de comunicación y la palabra escrita (*writing*)
4. los temas de que hablaban

B. Interpretación. Explique con sus propias palabras las siguientes ideas del texto.

1. «La dictadura uruguaya quería que cada uno fuera nada más que uno, que cada uno fuera nadie: en cárceles y cuarteles, y en todo el país, la comunicación era delito.»
2. «Cuando es verdadera, cuando nace de la necesidad de decir, a la voz humana no hay quien la pare.»

El acueducto de Segovia, construido por los romanos y que todavía funciona

Antes de escuchar

¿Qué sabe Ud. de la historia de España? Seguro que sabe que tuvo un gran imperio, pero ¿sabía que en ese país hubo una guerra civil, como en los Estados Unidos? ¿Cómo cree que es el país en la actualidad, pobre o rico? ¿moderno o tradicional?

Vocabulario **para escuchar**

el siglo	century	**el reino**	kingdom
entonces	then	**tras**	after
autóctono/a	**indígena**	**listo/a**	ready
la huella	trace; mark	**pasar de ser**	to go from being
la caída	fall	**creciente**	growing
el imperio	empire	**milenario/a**	thousand-year
a lo largo de	throughout	**acoger**	to welcome

Después de escuchar

Estrategia

- Para indicar los siglos en español, se usan los números romanos. Por ejemplo, el siglo XV = el siglo quince (*1400s*).
- a.C. = antes de Cristo
  d.C. = después de Cristo

A. Una breve historia. Escriba el siglo a que corresponde los eventos.

1. Los griegos, fenicios y otros pueblos se establecieron en la Península Ibérica antes del siglo _____ d.C.
2. Los romanos dominaron la Península Ibérica desde el siglo _____ hasta el siglo _____.
3. La invasión de los árabes ocurrió en el siglo _____.
4. Los árabes fueron expulsados de la Península Ibérica en el siglo _____.
5. El país que hoy se conoce como España comenzó en el siglo _____.
6. El final del gran imperio español ocurrió en el siglo _____.
7. España tuvo una guerra civil en el siglo _____.

B. La España de hoy. ¿Cómo es España hoy? Use palabras de la conferencia y sus propias palabras para describir la España de hoy.

1. el gobierno
2. la economía
3. la población

PRODUCCIÓN PERSONAL

¡Ahora, yo!

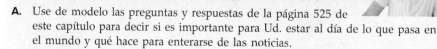

A. Use de modelo las preguntas y respuestas de la página 525 de este capítulo para decir si es importante para Ud. estar al día de lo que pasa en el mundo y qué hace para enterarse de las noticias.

B. Filme una entrevista que le hace a una persona que trabaja de voluntario/a en alguna organización local o de la universidad.

A ESCRIBIR

Un ensayo sobre la mayoría de edad

¿Cuál es su opinión sobre la mayoría de edad? ¿Está de acuerdo con la idea de que haya una edad mínima para tener derecho (*the right*) a ciertas actividades? ¿Coincide su opinión con la (*that*) de muchos de sus compañeros?

Preparar

Paso 1. En parejas, hagan una lista de los puntos que uno debe considerar para escribir un ensayo sobre el tema de la mayoría de edad. Luego preparen una serie de preguntas basadas en esas consideraciones y úsenlas para encuestar a cinco de sus compañeros.

Paso 2. Después de hacer su encuesta, use las respuestas para escribir el ensayo. Hay más ayuda en Connect.

Más ideas para su portafolio

- Haga una lista de las cosas que Ud. haría durante un viaje ideal a un país hispanohablante en las próximas vacaciones.

- Si Ud. pudiera, ¿qué cosas cambiaría en el mundo? Haga una lista de cinco o seis cosas que Ud. haría. Puede ser una lista seria o cómica.

- Si ha estado jugando Practice Spanish: Study Abroad, en Quest 12 Ud. participó en una carrera de observación que usó varios dichos y refranes de países hispanohablantes. Investigue otros refranes en español y trate de interpretarlos. Después, compárelos con refranes de su cultura de origen. ¿Hay semejanzas y correspondencias entre los refranes de diferentes culturas, o nota Ud. diferencias? ¿Qué importancia cultural tienen los refranes en general? Presente algunos refranes en clase y pídales a sus compañeros que den sus interpretaciones.

Sugerencia: You are now ready to play Quest 12 in **Practice Spanish: Study Abroad** (www.mhpractice.com).

LEARNSMART

Visit **www.connectspanish.com** to practice the vocabulary and grammar points covered in this chapter.

AFTER STUDYING THIS CHAPTER I CAN...

☐ talk about current events (526)

☐ talk about government and civic responsibilities (528)

☐ express situations in the past that require the subjunctive (532–534)

☐ talk about hypothetical events using the conditional (539–540)

☐ recognize/describe at least 2–3 aspects of Spanish culture

Gramática en breve

48. The Past Subjunctive

Third person plural preterite minus **-on** + **-a, -as, -a, -amos, -ais, -an**

49. The Conditional

Infinitive + **-ía, -ías, -ía, -íamos, -íais, -ían**
Irregular forms: **dir-, habr-, har-, podr-, pondr-, querr-, sabr-, saldr-, tendr-, vendr-** + *conditional endings*

Vocabulario

Las noticias

el acontecimiento	event, happening
el asesinato	assassination
el choque	collision, crash
la esperanza	hope, wish
la estación de radio	radio station
la guerra	war
la huelga	strike (*labor*)
la lucha	fight; struggle
la manifestación	demonstration; march
el medio de comunicación	medium of communication (*pl.* mass media)
el noticiero	newscast
la paz (*pl.* paces)	peace
la prensa	(print) press; news media
el quiosco de prensa	newsstand
el/la testigo	witness

Cognados: el ataque (terrorista), la bomba, la erupción, el/la reportero/a, el terrorismo, el/la terrorista, la víctima

Repaso: el blog, el canal (de televisión), el desastre, la muerte, las noticias, el periódico, la radio, la revista, la televisión

asesinar	to assassinate
comunicarse (qu) (con)	to communicate (with)
enterarse (de)	to find out; to learn (about)
estar al día	to be up to date
informar	to inform
luchar	to fight
mantener (*like* tener)	to maintain; to keep
matar	to kill

Repaso: ofrecer (ofrezco)

El gobierno y la responsabilidad cívica

el cargo	(political) office
el centro	center
el/la ciudadano/a	citizen
el deber	responsibility; obligation
el derecho	right
la (des)igualdad	(in)equality
el/la dictador(a)	dictator
la dictadura	dictatorship
el ejército	army
la ley	law
el partido	political party
la política	politics; policy
el/la político/a	politician
el rey / la reina	king/queen
el servicio militar	military service

Cognado: el/la candidato/a, la discriminación, el/la representante al congreso, el/la senador(a)

Repaso: los/las demás, la derecha, el gobierno, la izquierda, el soldado / la mujer soldado

durar	to last
postularse (para un cargo / como candidato/a)	to run (for a position / as a candidate)

Cognado: votar

Repaso: ganar, obedecer (obedezco), perder (pierdo)

Los adjetivos

Cognados: cívico/a, político/a
Repaso: natural

Vocabulario personal

LECTURA CULTURAL FINAL

El español en el resto del mundo

A lo largo de[a] dieciocho capítulos, se ha presentado en *Puntos de partida* el inmenso y variado mundo hispanohablante, desde[b] los Estados Unidos hasta el Cono Sur, en América y España, en Europa.

Pero el español es una lengua importante en otros países también. En África, sobrevive[c] bien arraigado[d] en la Guinea Ecuatorial, así como[e] en las ciudades norteafricanas de Ceuta y Melilla, que son territorio español. En Oceanía,* en las islas Filipinas, la lengua española es parte de su herencia[f] colonial, aunque[g] ya no es una lengua oficial en ese país. Y también hay que mencionar al Canadá, país donde hay una creciente[h] inmigración hispanohablante.

[a]*A... Throughout* [b]*from* [c]*it survives* [d]*established* [e]*así... as well as* [f]*heritage* [g]*although* [h]*growing*

---

*The term **Oceanía** refers to the islands of the tropical Pacific Ocean, including Polynesia, Australia, and New Zealand, as well as the Philippines and other island groups.*

LA GUINEA ECUATORIAL

La Guinea Ecuatorial es uno de los países más pequeños de África, pero también es uno de los más prósperos, debido a los yacimientos[a] de petróleo que se encuentran en su territorio. Fue colonia española desde[b] 1778 hasta 1968, y desde 1844 el español es una de sus lenguas oficiales, además del[c] francés y el portugués.

Aunque[d] tradicionalmente el país no se considera un país hispano, la realidad es que la mayoría de la población habla español, especialmente en la capital, Malabo. El español es también la lengua de varios escritores ecuatoguineanos, que se están abriendo camino[e] en el mundo literario hispanohablante.

La influencia de España en la Guinea Ecuatorial, así como[f] pasó en los países americanos de habla española, fue mucho más allá[g] de lo lingüístico. Es evidente en la religión (ya que[h] en el país existe una inmensa mayoría católica), en el sistema de apellidos que se usa (dos apellidos: primero el[i] del padre y luego el de la madre) y hasta[j] en la comida (entre otros platos, las empanadas).

[a]*debido... due to the fields* [b]*from* [c]*además... in addition to* [d]*Although* [e]*que... who are making a name for themselves* [f]*así... as* [g]*más... beyond* [h]*ya... since* [i]*that* [j]*even*

Malabo, la capital de la Guinea Ecuatorial

LAS ISLAS FILIPINAS

Las islas Filipinas son un archipiélago formado por más de 7000 islas en el Océano Pacífico. Fueron territorio español por más de 300 años. El fin de la colonización española ocurrió en 1898, cuando España cedió[a] el control de las Filipinas a los Estados Unidos, como consecuencia de la Guerra Hispanoamericana. Aunque[b] el español era la primera lengua oficial del país, el uso del español disminuyó[c] con la ocupación estadounidense y se perdió en la gran mayoría de la población. Sin embargo, los nombres y apellidos de muchos filipinos, así como[d] los nombres de muchos lugares y cosas de uso cotidiano[e] son españoles, testimonio de la gran influencia de la lengua española en el país.

La Universidad de Santo Tomás, fundada por los frailes dominicanos (*Dominican friars*) en 1611

La herencia de España ha quedado reflejada[f] también en la cocina filipina, en la que se combinan las influencias española, china y del sudeste asiático. En las islas Filipinas se preparan muchos platos que mantienen el nombre en español y que son adaptaciones de recetas españolas tradicionales, como la paella, el cocido,[g] el lechón asado[h] y la torta, similar a la españolísima tortilla de patatas, por solo nombrar algunos.

[a]*gave up* [b]*Although* [c]*declined* [d]*así... just like* [e]*everyday* [f]*ha... can still be seen reflected* [g]*stew* [h]*lechón... roasted suckling pig*

EL CANADÁ

Cartel (*Poster*) para la *Hispanic Fiesta* de 2010

Se estima que en el Canadá vive hoy entre medio millón y un millón de hispanohablantes, cuya mayoría[a] se concentra en la zona de las ciudades de Toronto y Hamilton. También hay comunidades hispanas importantes en el oeste del país, porque a finales[b] del siglo[c] XIX hubo una ola[d] inmigratoria de argentinos y chilenos a la provincia de Alberta.

Los hispanocanadienses disfrutan de[e] acceso a numeroso medios de comunicación en español. Además,[f] hay en el Canadá varios festivales y eventos que conmemoran la presencia hispana en el país. Uno de los más importantes es la **Hispanic Fiesta**, que se celebra anualmente en el mes de agosto en Toronto. Allí se encuentra comida de todas partes del mundo hispanohablante, se puede escuchar música andina y mexicana, entre otras formas musicales, y ver demostraciones de tango, flamenco y otros bailes.

[a]*cuya... the majority of whom* [b]*a... at the end* [c]*century* [d]*wave* [e]*disfrutan... enjoy* [f]*Besides*

COMPRENSIÓN

1. ¿En qué continentes y regiones del mundo se habla español como lengua oficial?
2. ¿En qué países tiene el español una presencia actual o histórica muy importante, aunque (*although*) no es la lengua oficial?
3. ¿Qué colonia española se independizó de España en el siglo (*century*) XX?
4. En general, ¿en qué se nota la influencia española en la Guinea Ecuatorial, las Filipinas y el Canadá?

APPENDIX 1   Glossary of Grammatical Terms

ADJECTIVE A word that describes a noun or pronoun.	una casa **grande** *a **big** house* Ana es **inteligente**. *Ana is **smart**.*
Demonstrative adjective An adjective that points out a particular noun.	**este** chico, **esos** libros, **aquellas** personas ***this** boy, **those** books, **those** people (over there)*
Interrogative adjective An adjective used to form questions.	¿**Qué** cuaderno? ***Which** notebook?* ¿**Cuáles** son los carteles que buscas? *Which ones are the posters (that) you're looking for?*
Possessive adjective (unstressed) An adjective that indicates possession or a special relationship.	**sus** coches ***their** cars* **mi** hermana ***my** sister*
Possessive adjective (stressed) An adjective that more emphatically describes possession.*	Es **una** amiga **mía**. *She's **my** friend. / She's a friend **of mine**.* Es **un** coche **suyo**. *It's **her** car. / It's a car **of hers**.*
ADVERB A word that describes an adjective, a verb, or another adverb.	Roberto es **muy** alto. *Roberto is **very** tall.* María escribe **bien**. *María writes **well**.* Van **demasiado** rápido. *They are going **too** quickly.*
ARTICLE A determiner that sets off a noun. **Definite article** An article that indicates a specific noun.	**el** país ***the** country* **la** silla ***the** chair* **las** mujeres ***the** women*
Indefinite article An article that indicates an unspecified noun.	**un** chico ***a** boy* **una** ciudad ***a** city* **unas** zanahorias *(**some**) carrots*

*See Appendix 3 on page A–7 for more information.

CLAUSE A construction that contains a subject and a verb.

Main (Independent) clause A clause that can stand on its own because it expresses a complete thought. **Busco una muchacha.**

I'm looking for a girl.

Si yo fuera rica, **me compraría una casa.**
*If I were rich, **I would buy a house.***

Subordinate (Dependent) clause A clause that cannot stand on its own because it does not express a complete thought.

Busco a la muchacha **que juega al tenis.**
*I'm looking for the girl **who plays tennis.***

Si yo fuera rica, me compraría una casa.
If I were rich, *I would buy a house.*

COMPARATIVE The form of adjectives and adverbs used to compare two nouns or actions.

Luis es **menos** hablador **que** Julián.
*Luis is **less talkative than** Julián.*

Luis corre **más rápido que** Julián.
*Luis runs **faster than** Julián.*

CONJUGATION The different forms of a verb for a particular tense or mood. A present indicative conjugation:

(yo) **hablo**	(nosotros/as) **hablamos**
(tú) **hablas**	(vosotros/as) **habláis**
(Ud.) **habla**	(Uds.) **hablan**
(él/ella) **habla**	(ellos/as) **hablan**

I speak	*we speak*
you (fam. sing.) speak	*you (fam. pl.) speak*
you (form. sing.) speak	*you (pl.) speak*
he/she speaks	*they speak*

CONJUNCTION An expression that connects words, phrases, or clauses.

Cristóbal **y** Diana
*Cristóbal **and** Diana*

Hace frío, **pero** hace buen tiempo.
*It's cold, **but** it's nice out.*

DIRECT OBJECT The noun or pronoun that receives the action of a verb.

Veo **la caja.**
*I see **the box.***

La veo.
*I see **it.***

GENDER A grammatical category of words. In Spanish, there are two genders: masculine and feminine.

	MASCULINE	FEMININE
ARTICLES AND NOUNS:	**el** disco compacto	**la** cinta
PRONOUNS:	**él**	**ella**
ADJECTIVES:	bonito, listo	bonita, lista
PAST PARTICIPLES:	El informe está **escrito**.	La composición está **escrita**.

IMPERATIVE *See* Mood.

IMPERFECT (*IMPERFECTO*) In Spanish, a verb tense that expresses a past action with no specific beginning or ending.

Nadábamos con frecuencia.
*We **used to swim** often.*

IMPERSONAL CONSTRUCTION One that contains a third person singular verb but no specific subject in Spanish. The subject of English impersonal constructions is generally *it*.

Es importante que...
It is important that . . .

Es necesario que...
It is necessary that . . .

INDICATIVE *See* Mood.

INDIRECT OBJECT The noun or pronoun that indicates *for who(m)* or *to who(m)* an action is performed. In Spanish, the indirect object pronoun is usually included, even when the indirect object is explicitly stated as a noun.

Marcos **le** da el suéter **a Raquel**. / Marcos **le** da el suéter.
*Marcos gives the sweater **to Raquel**. / Marcos gives **her** the sweater.*

INFINITIVE The form of a verb introduced in English by *to: to play, to sell, to come*. In Spanish dictionaries, the infinitive form of the verb appears as the main entry.

Luisa va a **comprar** un periódico.
*Luisa is going **to buy** a newspaper.*

MOOD A set of categories for verbs indicating the attitude of the speaker toward what he or she is saying.

Imperative mood A verb form expressing a command.

¡Ten cuidado!
***Be** careful!*

Indicative mood A verb form denoting actions or states considered facts.

Voy a la biblioteca.
***I'm going** to the library.*

Subjunctive mood A verb form, uncommon in English, used in Spanish primarily in subordinate clauses after expressions of desire, doubt, or emotion. Spanish constructions with the subjunctive have many possible English equivalents.

Quiero que **vayas** inmediatamente.
*I want you **to go** immediately.*

NOUN A word that denotes a person, place, thing, or idea. Proper nouns are capitalized names.

abogado, ciudad, periódico, libertad, Luisa
lawyer, city, newspaper, freedom, Luisa

NUMBER

Cardinal number A number that expresses an amount.

una silla, **tres** estudiantes
one chair, three students

Ordinal number A number that indicates position in a series.

la **primera** silla, el **tercer** estudiante
*the **first** chair, the **third** student*

PAST PARTICIPLE The form of a verb used in compound tenses (*see* Perfect Tenses). Used with forms of *to have* or *to be* in English and with **ser, estar,** or **haber** in Spanish.

comido, terminado, perdido
eaten, finished, lost

PERFECT TENSES Compound tenses that combine the auxiliary verb **haber** with a past participle.

Present perfect indicative This form uses a present indicative form of **haber**. The use of the Spanish present perfect generally parallels that of the English present perfect.

No **he viajado** nunca a México.
I've never **traveled** *to Mexico.*

Past perfect indicative This form uses **haber** in the imperfect tense to talk about something that had or had not been done before a given time in the past.

Antes de 2008, **no había estudiado** español.
Before 2008, I hadn't studied Spanish.

Present perfect subjunctive This form uses the present subjunctive of **haber** to express a present perfect action when the subjunctive is required.

¡Ojalá que Marisa **haya llegado** a su destino!
I hope (that) Marisa has arrived at her destination!

PERSON The form of a pronoun or verb that indicates the person involved in an action.

	SINGULAR	PLURAL
FIRST PERSON:	*I* / **yo**	*we* / **nosotros/as**
SECOND PERSON:	*you* / **tú, Ud.**	*you* / **vosotros/as, Uds.**
THIRD PERSON:	*he, she* / **él, ella**	*they* / **ellos, ellas**

PREPOSITION A word or phrase that specifies the relationship of one word (usually a noun or pronoun) to another. The relationship is usually spatial or temporal.

a la escuela
to school

cerca de la biblioteca
near the library

con él
with him

antes de la medianoche
before midnight

PRESENT PARTICIPLE The verb form that ends in *-ing* in English. Used with forms of *to be* in English and with **estar** in Spanish to form the progressive.

hablando, comiendo, pidiendo
speaking, eating, asking

PRETERITE (*PRETÉRITO*) In Spanish, a verb tense that expresses a past action with a specific beginning and ending.

Salí para Roma el jueves.
I left for Rome on Thursday.

PROGRESSIVE The verb that expresses continuing or developing action.

Julio **está durmiendo** ahora.
Julio is sleeping now.

Anita **estaba comiendo** cuando sonó el teléfono.
Anita was eating when the phone rang.

PRONOUN A word that refers to a person (I, you) or that is used in place of one or more nouns.

Demonstrative pronoun A pronoun that singles out a particular person, place, thing, or idea.

Aquí están dos libros. **Este** es interesante, pero **ese** es aburrido.
Here are two books. This one is interesting, but that one is boring.

Interrogative pronoun A pronoun used to ask a question.

¿**Quién** es él?
Who is he?

¿**Qué** prefieres?
What do you prefer?

Object pronoun A pronoun that replaces a direct object noun or an indirect object noun. Both direct and indirect object pronouns can be used together in the same sentence.

Si **me** llamas más tarde, **te** doy el número de teléfono de David.
*If you call **me** later, I'll give **you** David's phone number.*

Veo a **Alejandro. Lo** veo.
*I see **Alejandro.** I see **him.***

However, when the pronouns **le** or **les** appear before **lo, la, los,** or **las, le** or **les** changes to **se.**

Le doy **el libro** a Juana.
*I give the book **to Juana.***

Se lo doy (a ella).
*I give **it** to **her.***

Reflexive pronoun A pronoun that represents the same person as the subject of the verb.

Me miro en el espejo.
*I look at **myself** in the mirror.*

Relative pronoun A pronoun that introduces a dependent clause and denotes a noun already mentioned.

El hombre con **quien** hablaba era mi vecino.
*The man with **whom** I was talking was my neighbor.*

Aquí está el bolígrafo **que** buscas.
*Here is the pen (**that**) you're looking for.*

Subject pronoun A pronoun representing the person, place, thing, or idea performing the action of a verb.

Lucas y Julia juegan al tenis.
***Lucas and Julia** are playing tennis.*

Ellos juegan al tenis.
***They** are playing tennis.*

SUBJECT The word(s) denoting the person, place, thing, or idea performing an action or existing in a state.

Sara trabaja aquí.
***Sara** works here.*

¡**Buenos Aires** es una ciudad magnífica!
***Buenos Aires** is a great city!*

Mis **libros** y mi **computadora** están allí.
*My **books** and my **computer** are over there.*

SUBJUNCTIVE *See* Mood.

SUPERLATIVE The form of adjectives or adverbs used to compare three or more nouns or actions. In English, the superlative is marked by *most, least,* or *-est.*

Escogí **el vestido más caro.**
*I chose **the most expensive** dress.*

Ana es **la persona menos habladora** que conozco.
*Ana is **the least talkative person** I know.*

TENSE The form of a verb indicating time: present, past, or future.

Raúl **era, es** y siempre **será** mi mejor amigo.
*Raúl **was, is,** and always **will be** my best friend.*

VERB A word that reports an action or state.

Maribel **llegó.**
*Maribel **arrived.***

La niña **estaba** cansada.
*The child **was** tired.*

Auxiliary verb A verb in conjuction with a participle to convey distinctions of tense and mood. In Spanish, one auxiliary verb is **haber.**

Han viajado por todas partes del mundo.
*They **have** traveled everywhere in the world.*

Reflexive verb A verb whose subject and object are the same.

Juan **se corta** la cara cuando **se afeita.**
*Juan **cuts himself** when he **shaves** (**himself**).*

APPENDIX 2 Using Adjectives as Nouns

Nominalization means using an adjective as a noun. In Spanish, adjectives can be nominalized in a number of ways, all of which involve dropping the noun that accompanies the adjective, then using the adjective in combination with an article or other word. One kind of adjective, the demonstrative, can simply be used alone. In most cases, these usages parallel those of English, although the English equivalent may be phrased differently from the Spanish.

Article + Adjective

Simply omit the noun from an *article + noun + adjective* phrase.

> el **libro** azul → **el azul** (*the blue one*)
> la **hermana** casada → **la casada** (*the married one*)
> el **señor** mexicano → **el mexicano** (*the Mexican one*)
> los **pantalones** baratos → **los baratos**
>   (*the inexpensive ones*)

You can also drop the first noun in an *article + noun + de + noun* phrase.

> la **casa** de Julio → **la de Julio** (*Julio's*)
> los **coches** del Sr. Martínez → **los del Sr. Martínez**
>   (*Mr. Martínez's*)

In both cases, the construction is used to refer to a noun that has already been mentioned. The English equivalent uses *one* or *ones*, or a possessive without the noun.

> — ¿Necesitas el **libro** grande?
> — No. Necesito **el pequeño.**
> *"Do you need the big book?"*
> *"No. I need the small one."*

> — ¿Usamos el **coche** de Ernesto?
> — No. Usemos **el de Ana.**
> *"Shall we use Ernesto's car?"*
> *"No. Let's use Ana's."*

Note that in the preceding examples the noun is mentioned in the first part of the exchange (**libro, coche**) but not in the response or rejoinder.

Note also that a demonstrative can be used to nominalize an adjective: **este rojo** (*this red one*), **esos azules** (*those blue ones*).

Lo + Adjective

As seen in **Capítulo 11, lo** combines with the masculine singular form of an adjective to describe general qualities or characteristics. The English equivalent is expressed with words like *part* or *thing*.

lo mejor	*the best thing (part), what's best*
lo mismo	*the same thing*
lo cómico	*the funny thing (part), what's funny*

Article + Stressed Possessive Adjective

The stressed possessive adjectives—but not the unstressed possessives—can be used as possessive pronouns: **la maleta suya** → **la suya.** The article and the possessive form agree in gender and number with the noun to which they refer.

> Este es mi **banco.** ¿Dónde está el **suyo**?
> *This is my bank. Where is yours?*

> Sus **bebidas** están preparadas; las **nuestras,** no.
> *Their drinks are ready; ours aren't.*

> No es la **maleta** de Juan; es la **mía.**
> *It isn't Juan's suitcase; it's mine.*

Note that the definite article is frequently omitted after forms of **ser: ¿Esa maleta? Es suya.**

Demonstrative Pronouns

The demonstrative adjective can be used alone, without a noun. An accent mark can be added to the demonstrative pronoun (**éste, ése, aquél**) to distinguish it from the demonstrative adjectives if context does not make meaning clear.

> Necesito este diccionario y **ese (ése).**
> *I need this dictionary and that one.*

> Estas señoras y **aquellas (aquéllas)** son las
>   hermanas de Sara, ¿no?
> *These women and those (over there) are Sara's*
>   *sisters, aren't they?*

It is acceptable in modern Spanish, according to the **Real Academia Española,** to omit the accent on demonstrative pronouns when context makes the meaning clear and no ambiguity is possible.

APPENDIX 3   More About Stressed Possessives

When in English you would emphasize the possessive with your voice or with *of mine* (*of yours, of his*, and so on), you will use the *stressed possessives* (**las formas tónicas de los posesivos**) in Spanish. As the term implies, they are more emphatic than the *unstressed forms* (**las formas átonas de los posesivos**).

The stressed forms follow the noun, and the noun *must* be preceded by a definite or indefinite article or by a demonstrative adjective. The stressed forms agree with the noun modified in number and gender. In the following examples, boldface italic type in the English translations indicates voice stress.

Es **su** perro.	*It's her dog.*

But:

Es **un** perro **suyo.**	*It's **her** dog (i.e., not ours).*
	It's a dog of hers.
El perro **suyo** se llama King.	***Her** dog is named King.*
Ese perro **suyo** es bravo.	*That dog of hers is fierce.*

Es **su** maleta.	*It's **his** suitcase.*

But:

Es **una** maleta **suya.**	*It's **his** suitcase.*
La maleta **suya** está perdida.	***His** suitcase (i.e., not ours) is lost.*
Esa maleta **suya** está perdida.	*That suitcase of his is lost.*

The stressed possessives are often used as nouns. See **Appendix 2: Using Adjectives as Nouns.**

APPENDIX 4

Additional Perfect Forms (Indicative and Subjunctive)

As you know, some indicative verb tenses have corresponding perfect forms in the indicative and subjunctive moods. Here is the present tense system.

el presente:	yo hablo, como, pongo
el presente perfecto:	yo he hablado, comido, puesto
el presente perfecto de subjuntivo:	(que) yo haya hablado, comido, puesto

Other indicative forms that you have learned also have corresponding perfect indicative and subjunctive forms. Here are the most important ones, along with examples of their use. In each case, the tense or mood is formed with the appropriate form of **haber.**

El pluscuamperfecto de subjuntivo

yo:	hubiera hablado, comido, vivido, *and so on.*
tú:	hubieras hablado, comido, vivido, *and so on.*
Ud./él/ella:	hubiera hablado, comido, vivido, *and so on.*
nosotros:	hubiéramos hablado, comido, vivido, *and so on.*
vosotros:	hubierais hablado, comido, vivido, *and so on.*
Uds./ellos/ellas:	hubieran hablado, comido, vivido, *and so on.*

These forms correspond to **el pluscuamperfecto de indicativo (past perfect indicative) (Capítulo 15).** The **pluscuamperfecto de subjuntivo** is most frequently used in **si** clause sentences, along with the conditional perfect. See examples in the second column.

El futuro perfecto

yo:	habré hablado, comido, vivido, *and so on.*
tú:	habrás hablado, comido, vivido, *and so on.*
Ud./él/ella:	habrá hablado, comido, vivido, *and so on.*
nosotros:	habremos hablado, comido, vivido, *and so on.*
vosotros:	habréis hablado, comido, vivido, *and so on.*
Uds./ellos/ellas:	habrán hablado, comido, vivido, *and so on.*

These forms correspond to **el futuro (Capítulo 17)** and are most frequently used to tell what *will have already happened* at some point in the future. (In contrast, the future is used to tell what *will happen.*)

Mañana **hablaré** con Miguel.
I'll speak with Miguel tomorrow.

Para las tres, ya **habré hablado** con Miguel.
By 3:00, I'll already have spoken with Miguel.

El año que viene **visitaremos** a los nietos.
We'll visit our grandchildren next year.

Para las Navidades, ya **habremos visitado** a los nietos.
We'll already have visited our grandchildren by Christmas.

El condicional perfecto

yo:	habría hablado, comido, vivido, *and so on.*
tú:	habrías hablado, comido, vivido, *and so on.*
Ud./él/ella:	habría hablado, comido, vivido, *and so on.*
nosotros:	habríamos hablado, comido, vivido, *and so on.*
vosotros:	habríais hablado, comido, vivido, *and so on.*
Uds./ellos/ellas:	habrían hablado, comido, vivido, *and so on.*

These forms correspond to **el condicional (Capítulo 18).** These forms are frequently used to tell what *would have happened* at some point in the past. (In contrast, the conditional tells what one *would do.*)

Yo **hablaría** con Miguel.
I would speak with Miguel (if I were you, at some point in the future).

Yo **habría hablado** con Miguel.
I would have spoken with Miguel (if I had been you, at some point in the past).

Si Clause: Sentences About the Past

You have learned (**Capítulo 18**) to use the past subjunctive and conditional to speculate about the present in **si** clause sentences: what *would happen* if a particular event *were* (or *were not*) to occur.

Si **tuviera** el tiempo, **aprendería** francés.
If I had the time, I would learn French.

The perfect forms of the past subjunctive and the conditional are used to speculate about the past: what *would have happened* if a particular event *had* (or *had not*) occurred.

En la escuela superior, si **hubiera tenido** el tiempo, **habría aprendido** francés.
In high school, if I had had the time, I would have learned French.

A. Regular Verbs: Simple Tenses

Infinitive Present Participle Past Participle	INDICATIVE					SUBJUNCTIVE		IMPERATIVE
	Present	Imperfect	Preterite	Future	Conditional	Present	Imperfect	
hablar hablando hablado	hablo hablas habla hablamos habláis hablan	hablaba hablabas hablaba hablábamos hablabais hablaban	hablé hablaste habló hablamos hablasteis hablaron	hablaré hablarás hablará hablaremos hablaréis hablarán	hablaría hablarías hablaría hablaríamos hablaríais hablarían	hable hables hable hablemos habléis hablen	hablara hablaras hablara habláramos hablarais hablaran	habla tú, no hables hable Ud. hablemos hablad, no habléis hablen
comer comiendo comido	como comes come comemos coméis comen	comía comías comía comíamos comíais comían	comí comiste comió comimos comisteis comieron	comeré comerás comerá comeremos comeréis comerán	comería comerías comería comeríamos comeríais comerían	coma comas coma comamos comáis coman	comiera comieras comiera comiéramos comierais comieran	come tú, no comas coma Ud. comamos comed, no comáis coman
vivir viviendo vivido	vivo vives vive vivimos vivís viven	vivía vivías vivía vivíamos vivíais vivían	viví viviste vivió vivimos vivisteis vivieron	viviré vivirás vivirá viviremos viviréis vivirán	viviría vivirías viviría viviríamos viviríais vivirían	viva vivas viva vivamos viváis vivan	viviera vivieras viviera viviéramos vivierais vivieran	vive tú, no vivas viva Ud. vivamos vivid, no viváis vivan

B. Regular Verbs: Perfect Tenses

INDICATIVE					SUBJUNCTIVE	
Present Perfect	Past Perfect	Preterite Perfect	Future Perfect	Conditional Perfect	Present Perfect	Past Perfect
he	había	hube	habré	habría	haya	hubiera
has	habías	hubiste	habrás	habrías	hayas	hubieras
ha hablado	había hablado	hubo hablado	habrá hablado	habría hablado	haya hablado	hubiera hablado
hemos comido	habíamos comido	hubimos comido	habremos comido	habríamos comido	hayamos comido	hubiéramos comido
habéis vivido	habíais vivido	hubisteis vivido	habréis vivido	habríais vivido	hayáis vivido	hubierais vivido
han	habían	hubieron	habrán	habrían	hayan	hubieran

C. Irregular Verbs

Infinitive / Present Participle / Past Participle	INDICATIVE					SUBJUNCTIVE		IMPERATIVE
	Present	Imperfect	Preterite	Future	Conditional	Present	Imperfect	
andar andando andado	ando	andaba	anduve	andaré	andaría	ande	anduviera	anda tú, no
	andas	andabas	anduviste	andarás	andarías	andes	anduvieras	andes
	anda	andaba	anduvo	andará	andaría	ande	anduviera	ande Ud.
	andamos	andábamos	anduvimos	andaremos	andaríamos	andemos	anduviéramos	andemos
	andáis	andabais	anduvisteis	andaréis	andaríais	andéis	anduvierais	andad, no andéis
	andan	andaban	anduvieron	andarán	andarían	anden	anduvieran	anden
caber cabiendo cabido	quepo	cabía	cupe	cabré	cabría	quepa	cupiera	cabe tú,
	cabes	cabías	cupiste	cabrás	cabrías	quepas	cupieras	no quepas
	cabe	cabía	cupo	cabrá	cabría	quepa	cupiera	quepa Ud.
	cabemos	cabíamos	cupimos	cabremos	cabríamos	quepamos	cupiéramos	quepamos
	cabéis	cabíais	cupisteis	cabréis	cabríais	quepáis	cupierais	cabed, no quepáis
	caben	cabían	cupieron	cabrán	cabrían	quepan	cupieran	quepan

C. Irregular Verbs (continued)

Infinitive / Present Participle / Past Participle	INDICATIVE Present	Imperfect	Preterite	Future	Conditional	SUBJUNCTIVE Present	Imperfect	IMPERATIVE
caer / cayendo / caído	caigo	caía	caí	caeré	caería	caiga	cayera	
	caes	caías	caíste	caerás	caerías	caigas	cayeras	cae tú, no caigas
	cae	caía	cayó	caerá	caería	caiga	cayera	caiga Ud.
	caemos	caíamos	caímos	caeremos	caeríamos	caigamos	cayéramos	caigamos
	caéis	caíais	caísteis	caeréis	caeríais	caigáis	cayerais	caed, no caigáis
	caen	caían	cayeron	caerán	caerían	caigan	cayeran	caigan
creer / creyendo / creído	creo	creía	creí	creeré	creería	crea	creyera	
	crees	creías	creíste	creerás	creerías	creas	creyeras	cree tú, no creas
	cree	creía	creyó	creerá	creería	crea	creyera	crea Ud.
	creemos	creíamos	creímos	creeremos	creeríamos	creamos	creyéramos	creamos
	creéis	creíais	creísteis	creeréis	creeríais	creáis	creyerais	creed, no creáis
	creen	creían	creyeron	creerán	creerían	crean	creyeran	crean
dar / dando / dado	doy	daba	di	daré	daría	dé	diera	
	das	dabas	diste	darás	darías	des	dieras	da tú, no des
	da	daba	dio	dará	daría	dé	diera	dé Ud.
	damos	dábamos	dimos	daremos	daríamos	demos	diéramos	demos
	dais	dabais	disteis	daréis	daríais	deis	dierais	dad, no deis
	dan	daban	dieron	darán	darían	den	dieran	den
decir / diciendo / dicho	digo	decía	dije	diré	diría	diga	dijera	
	dices	decías	dijiste	dirás	dirías	digas	dijeras	di tú, no digas
	dice	decía	dijo	dirá	diría	diga	dijera	diga Ud.
	decimos	decíamos	dijimos	diremos	diríamos	digamos	dijéramos	digamos
	decís	decíais	dijisteis	diréis	diríais	digáis	dijerais	decid, no digáis
	dicen	decían	dijeron	dirán	dirían	digan	dijeran	digan

C. Irregular Verbs (continued)

Infinitive / Present Participle / Past Participle	INDICATIVE					SUBJUNCTIVE		IMPERATIVE
	Present	Imperfect	Preterite	Future	Conditional	Present	Imperfect	
estar estando estado	estoy estás está estamos estáis están	estaba estabas estaba estábamos estabais estaban	estuve estuviste estuvo estuvimos estuvisteis estuvieron	estaré estarás estará estaremos estaréis estarán	estaría estarías estaría estaríamos estaríais estarían	esté estés esté estemos estéis estén	estuviera estuvieras estuviera estuviéramos estuvierais estuviera	está tú, no estés esté Ud. estemos estad, no estéis estén
haber habiendo habido	he has ha hemos habéis han	había habías había habíamos habíais habían	hube hubiste hubo hubimos hubisteis hubieron	habré habrás habrá habremos habréis habrán	habría habrías habría habríamos habríais habrían	haya hayas haya hayamos hayáis hayan	hubiera hubieras hubiera hubiéramos hubierais hubieran	
hacer haciendo hecho	hago haces hace hacemos hacéis hacen	hacía hacías hacía hacíamos hacíais hacían	hice hiciste hizo hicimos hicisteis hicieron	haré harás hará haremos haréis harán	haría harías haría haríamos haríais harían	haga hagas haga hagamos hagáis hagan	hiciera hicieras hiciera hiciéramos hicierais hicieran	haz tú, no hagas haga Ud. hagamos haced, no hagáis hagan
ir yendo ido	voy vas va vamos vais van	iba ibas iba íbamos ibais iban	fui fuiste fue fuimos fuisteis fueron	iré irás irá iremos iréis irán	iría irías iría iríamos iríais irían	vaya vayas vaya vayamos vayáis vayan	fuera fueras fuera fuéramos fuerais fueran	ve tú, no vayas vaya Ud. vayamos id, no vayáis vayan

C. Irregular Verbs (continued)

Infinitive Present Participle Past Participle	INDICATIVE					SUBJUNCTIVE		IMPERATIVE
	Present	Imperfect	Preterite	Future	Conditional	Present	Imperfect	
oír oyendo oído	oigo oyes oye oímos oís oyen	oía oías oía oíamos oíais oían	oí oíste oyó oímos oísteis oyeron	oiré oirás oirá oiremos oiréis oirán	oiría oirías oiría oiríamos oiríais oirían	oiga oigas oiga oigamos oigáis oigan	oyera oyeras oyera oyéramos oyerais oyeran	oye tú, no oigas oiga Ud. oigamos oíd, no oigáis oigan
poder pudiendo podido	puedo puedes puede podemos podéis pueden	podía podías podía podíamos podíais podían	pude pudiste pudo pudimos pudisteis pudieron	podré podrás podrá podremos podréis podrán	podría podrías podría podríamos podríais podrían	pueda puedas pueda podamos podáis puedan	pudiera pudieras pudiera pudiéramos pudierais pudieran	
poner poniendo puesto	pongo pones pone ponemos ponéis ponen	ponía ponías ponía poníamos poníais ponían	puse pusiste puso pusimos pusisteis pusieron	pondré pondrás pondrá pondremos pondréis pondrán	pondría pondrías pondría pondríamos pondríais pondrían	ponga pongas ponga pongamos pongáis pongan	pusiera pusieras pusiera pusiéramos pusierais pusieran	pon tú, no pongas ponga Ud. pongamos poned, no pongáis pongan
querer queriendo querido	quiero quieres quiere queremos queréis quieren	quería querías quería queríamos queríais querían	quise quisiste quiso quisimos quisisteis quisieron	querré querrás querrá querremos querréis querrán	querría querrías querría querríamos querríais querrían	quiera quieras quiera queramos queráis quieran	quisiera quisieras quisiera quisiéramos quisierais quisieran	quiere tú, no quieras quiera Ud. queramos quered, no queráis quieran

Infinitive / Present Participle / Past Participle	INDICATIVE					SUBJUNCTIVE		IMPERATIVE
	Present	Imperfect	Preterite	Future	Conditional	Present	Imperfect	
saber / sabiendo / sabido	sé	sabía	supe	sabré	sabría	sepa	supiera	
	sabes	sabías	supiste	sabrás	sabrías	sepas	supieras	sabe tú, no sepas
	sabe	sabía	supo	sabrá	sabría	sepa	supiera	sepa Ud.
	sabemos	sabíamos	supimos	sabremos	sabríamos	sepamos	supiéramos	sepamos
	sabéis	sabíais	supisteis	sabréis	sabríais	sepáis	supierais	sabed, no sepáis
	saben	sabían	supieron	sabrán	sabrían	sepan	supieran	sepan
salir / saliendo / salido	salgo	salía	salí	saldré	saldría	salga	saliera	
	sales	salías	saliste	saldrás	saldrías	salgas	salieras	sal tú, no salgas
	sale	salía	salió	saldrá	saldría	salga	saliera	salga Ud.
	salimos	salíamos	salimos	saldremos	saldríamos	salgamos	saliéramos	salgamos
	salís	salíais	salisteis	saldréis	saldríais	salgáis	salierais	salid, no salgáis
	salen	salían	salieron	saldrán	saldrían	salgan	salieran	salgan
ser / siendo / sido	soy	era	fui	seré	sería	sea	fuera	
	eres	eras	fuiste	serás	serías	seas	fueras	sé tú, no seas
	es	era	fue	será	sería	sea	fuera	sea Ud.
	somos	éramos	fuimos	seremos	seríamos	seamos	fuéramos	seamos
	sois	erais	fuisteis	seréis	seríais	seáis	fuerais	sed, no seáis
	son	eran	fueron	serán	serían	sean	fueran	sean
tener / teniendo / tenido	tengo	tenía	tuve	tendré	tendría	tenga	tuviera	
	tienes	tenías	tuviste	tendrás	tendrías	tengas	tuvieras	ten tú, no tengas
	tiene	tenía	tuvo	tendrá	tendría	tenga	tuviera	tenga Ud.
	tenemos	teníamos	tuvimos	tendremos	tendríamos	tengamos	tuviéramos	tengamos
	tenéis	teníais	tuvisteis	tendréis	tendríais	tengáis	tuvierais	tened, no tengáis
	tienen	tenían	tuvieron	tendrán	tendrían	tengan	tuvieran	tengan

C. Irregular Verbs (continued)

Infinitive Present Participle Past Participle	INDICATIVE					SUBJUNCTIVE		IMPERATIVE
	Present	Imperfect	Preterite	Future	Conditional	Present	Imperfect	
traer trayendo traído	traigo	traía	traje	traeré	traería	traiga	trajera	
	traes	traías	trajiste	traerás	traerías	traigas	trajeras	trae tú, no traigas
	trae	traía	trajo	traerá	traería	traiga	trajera	traiga Ud.
	traemos	traíamos	trajimos	traeremos	traeríamos	traigamos	trajéramos	traigamos
	traéis	traíais	trajisteis	traeréis	traeríais	traigáis	trajerais	traed, no traigáis
	traen	traían	trajeron	traerán	traerían	traigan	trajeran	traigan
venir viniendo venido	vengo	venía	vine	vendré	vendría	venga	viniera	
	vienes	venías	viniste	vendrás	vendrías	vengas	vinieras	ven tú, no vengas
	viene	venía	vino	vendrá	vendría	venga	viniera	venga Ud.
	venimos	veníamos	vinimos	vendremos	vendríamos	vengamos	viniéramos	vengamos
	venís	veníais	vinisteis	vendréis	vendríais	vengáis	vinierais	venid, no vengáis
	vienen	venían	vinieron	vendrán	vendrían	vengan	vinieran	vengan
ver viendo visto	veo	veía	vi	veré	vería	vea	viera	
	ves	veías	viste	verás	verías	veas	vieras	ve tú, no veas
	ve	veía	vio	verá	vería	vea	viera	vea Ud.
	vemos	veíamos	vimos	veremos	veríamos	veamos	viéramos	veamos
	veis	veíais	visteis	veréis	veríais	veáis	vierais	ved, no veáis
	ven	veían	vieron	verán	verían	vean	vieran	vean

D. Stem-Changing and Spelling Change Verbs

Infinitive Present Participle Past Participle	INDICATIVE					SUBJUNCTIVE		IMPERATIVE
	Present	Imperfect	Preterite	Future	Conditional	Present	Imperfect	
pensar (pienso) pensando pensado	pienso piensas piensa pensamos pensáis piensan	pensaba pensabas pensaba pensábamos pensabais pensaban	pensé pensaste pensó pensamos pensasteis pensaron	pensaré pensarás pensará pensaremos pensaréis pensarán	pensaría pensarías pensaría pensaríamos pensaríais pensarían	piense pienses piense pensemos penséis piensen	pensara pensaras pensara pensáramos pensarais pensaran	piensa tú, no pienses piense Ud. pensemos pensad, no penséis piensen
volver (vuelvo) volviendo vuelto	vuelvo vuelves vuelve volvemos volvéis vuelven	volvía volvías volvía volvíamos volvíais volvían	volví volviste volvió volvimos volvisteis volvieron	volveré volverás volverá volveremos volveréis volverán	volvería volverías volvería volveríamos volveríais volverían	vuelva vuelvas vuelva volvamos volváis vuelvan	volviera volvieras volviera volviéramos volvierais volvieran	vuelve tú, no vuelvas vuelva Ud. volvamos volved, no volváis vuelvan
dormir (duermo) (u) durmiendo dormido	duermo duermes duerme dormimos dormís duermen	dormía dormías dormía dormíamos dormíais dormían	dormí dormiste durmió dormimos dormisteis durmieron	dormiré dormirás dormirá dormiremos dormiréis dormirán	dormiría dormirías dormiría dormiríamos dormiríais dormirían	duerma duermas duerma durmamos durmáis duerman	durmiera durmieras durmiera durmiéramos durmierais durmieran	duerme tú, no duermas duerma Ud. durmamos dormid, no durmáis duerman
sentir (siento) (i) sintiendo sentido	siento sientes siente sentimos sentís sienten	sentía sentías sentía sentíamos sentíais sentían	sentí sentiste sintió sentimos sentisteis sintieron	sentiré sentirás sentirá sentiremos sentiréis sentirán	sentiría sentirías sentiría sentiríamos sentiríais sentirían	sienta sientas sienta sintamos sintáis sientan	sintiera sintieras sintiera sintiéramos sintierais sintieran	siente tú, no sientas sienta Ud. sintamos sentid, no sintáis sientan
pedir (pido) (i) pidiendo pedido	pido pides pide pedimos pedís piden	pedía pedías pedía pedíamos pedíais pedían	pedí pediste pidió pedimos pedisteis pidieron	pediré pedirás pedirá pediremos pediréis pedirán	pediría pedirías pediría pediríamos pediríais pedirían	pida pidas pida pidamos pidáis pidan	pidiera pidieras pidiera pidiéramos pidierais pidieran	pide tú, no pidas pida Ud. pidamos pedid, no pidáis pidan

D. Stem-Changing and Spelling Change Verbs (continued)

Infinitive / Present Participle / Past Participle	INDICATIVE					SUBJUNCTIVE		IMPERATIVE
	Present	Imperfect	Preterite	Future	Conditional	Present	Imperfect	
reír (río) (i) / riendo / reído	río	reía	reí	reiré	reiría	ría	riera	
	ríes	reías	reíste	reirás	reirías	rías	rieras	ríe tú, no rías
	ríe	reía	rio	reirá	reiría	ría	riera	ría Ud.
	reímos	reíamos	reímos	reiremos	reiríamos	riamos	riéramos	riamos
	reís	reíais	reísteis	reiréis	reiríais	riáis	rierais	reíd, no riáis
	ríen	reían	rieron	reirán	reirían	rían	rieran	rían
seguir (sigo) (i) / siguiendo / seguido	sigo	seguía	seguí	seguiré	seguiría	siga	siguiera	
	sigues	seguías	seguiste	seguirás	seguirías	sigas	siguieras	sigue tú, no sigas
	sigue	seguía	siguió	seguirá	seguiría	siga	siguiera	siga Ud.
	seguimos	seguíamos	seguimos	seguiremos	seguiríamos	sigamos	siguiéramos	sigamos
	seguís	seguíais	seguisteis	seguiréis	seguiríais	sigáis	siguierais	seguid, no sigáis
	siguen	seguían	siguieron	seguirán	seguirían	sigan	siguieran	sigan
construir (construyo) / construyendo / construido	construyo	construía	construí	construiré	construiría	construya	construyera	
	construyes	construías	construiste	construirás	construirías	construyas	construyeras	construye tú, no construyas
	construye	construía	construyó	construirá	construiría	construya	construyera	construya Ud.
	construimos	construíamos	construimos	construiremos	construiríamos	construyamos	construyéramos	construyamos
	construís	construíais	construisteis	construiréis	construiríais	construyáis	construyerais	construid, no construyáis
	construyen	construían	construyeron	construirán	construirían	construyan	construyeran	construyan
conducir (conduzco) / conduciendo / conducido	conduzco	conducía	conduje	conduciré	conduciría	conduzca	condujera	
	conduces	conducías	condujiste	conducirás	conducirías	conduzcas	condujeras	conduce tú, no conduzcas
	conduce	conducía	condujo	conducirá	conduciría	conduzca	condujera	conduzca Ud.
	conducimos	conducíamos	condujimos	conduciremos	conduciríamos	conduzcamos	condujéramos	conduzcamos
	conducís	conducíais	condujisteis	conduciréis	conduciríais	conduzcáis	condujerais	conducid, no conduzcáis
	conducen	conducían	condujeron	conducirán	conducirían	conduzcan	condujeran	conduzcan

VOCABULARIES

This **Spanish-English Vocabulary** contains all the words that appear in the text, with the following exceptions: (1) most close or identical cognates that do not appear in the chapter vocabulary lists; (2) most conjugated verb forms; (3) diminutives ending in **-ito/a**; (4) absolute superlatives in **-ísimo/a**; (5) most adverbs ending in **-mente,** and (6) words listed or glossed in the **Vocabulario del segmento** and **Fragmento del guion** features of the **Salu2** sections. Active vocabulary is indicated by the number of the chapter in which a word or given meaning is first listed (**1** = **Capítulo 1**); vocabulary that is glossed in the text is not considered to be active vocabulary and is not numbered. Only meanings that are used in the text are given. The **English-Spanish Vocabulary** is based on the chapter lists of active vocabulary.

The gender of nouns is indicated, except for masculine nouns ending in **-o** and feminine nouns ending in **-a.** Because **ch** and **ll** are no longer considered separate letters, words beginning with **ch** and **ll** are found as they would be found in English. The letter **ñ** follows the letter **n: añadir** follows **anuncio,** for example.

Irregular verbs found in the verb charts of Appendix 5 are set all in color: andar. No changes are indicated for them in these vocabularies. Verbs with stem changes or spelling changes in the *present tense* show the **yo** form of the present tense in parentheses with the stem-vowel or spelling changes indicated in color: **sentarse (me siento); conocer (conozco); escoger (escojo); actuar (actúo).** Verbs with stem changes in the third person *preterite* and the *present participle* show the stem vowel (**i** or **u**) in parentheses after the present tense **yo** form: **preferir (prefiero) (i); morirse (me muero) (u).** Verbs with any other spelling changes in the first person *preterite* or *present subjunctive* show the change in parentheses: **buscar (qu); pagar (gu); empezar (empiezo) (c); averiguar (ü).**

The following abbreviations are used:

adj.	adjective	*inv.*	invariable form
adv.	adverb	*L.A.*	Latin America
Arg.	Argentina	*m.*	masculine
C.A.	Central America	*Mex.*	Mexico
Carib.	Caribbean	*n.*	noun
Col.	Colombia	*obj. (of prep.)*	object (of a preposition)
conj.	conjunction	*pl.*	plural
def. art.	definite article	*poss.*	possessive
d.o.	direct object	*p.p.*	past participle
f.	feminine	*prep.*	preposition
fam.	familiar	*pron.*	pronoun
form.	formal	*refl. pron.*	reflexive pronoun
gram.	grammatical term	*s.*	singular
Guat.	Guatemala	*sl.*	slang
ind. art.	indefinite article	*Sp.*	Spain
inf.	infinitive	*sub. pron.*	subject pronoun
i.o.	indirect object		
interj.	interjection		

Spanish-English Vocabulary

A

a to; at (*with time*) (1); **a base de** based on; **a causa de** because of; **a continuación** following; **a este respecto** in this regard; **a la derecha de** to the right of (6); **a la izquierda de** to the left of (6); **a la moda** in fashion, in a stylish way; **a la(s)...** at . . . (*time of day*) (1); **a menos que** unless (16); **a partir de** beyond (4); **a pesar de** in spite of; **a plazos** in installments (17); **¿a qué hora... ?** at what time . . . ? (1); **a solas** alone; **a tiempo** on time (8); **a través de** across, through; throughout; **¿a usted le gusta... ?** do you (*form. s.*) like . . . ? (1); **a veces** sometimes, at times (3); **a ver** let's see
abacería grocery store
abajo below; underneath
abandonar to abandon
abarcar (qu) to cover (*a topic*)
abarrotes *m. pl.* groceries
abecedario alphabet
abierto/a (*p.p. of* **abrir**) open (6)
abogado/a lawyer (17)
abogar (gu) to advocate
abolengo lineage
abolicionista *m., f.* abolitionist
aborto abortion
abrazar(se) (c) to embrace (11)
abrazo hug, embrace
abreviatura abbreviation
abrigo coat (4)
abril *m.* April (6)
abrir (*pp.* **abierto**) to open (3)
abrumador(a) overwhelming
absoluto/a absolute
abstenerse (*like* **tener**) to refrain
absurdo/a absurd; **es absurdo que** it's absurd that (13)
abuelo/a grandfather/grandmother (3); *m. pl.* grandparents (3)
abundante abundant
aburrido/a bored (6); **ser aburrido/a** to be boring (10)
aburrimiento boredom
aburrir (*like* **gustar**) to bore (13); **aburrirse** to get bored (10)
abuso abuse
abyecto/a wretched
acá here
acabar to finish (14); to run out of (14); **acabar de** + *inf.* to have just (*done something*) (7)
academia academy
académico/a *adj.* academic (14); **año académico** school year; **vida académica** academic life (14)

acampar to camp; **tienda de acampar** tent
acaso: por si acaso just in case (14)
acatar to obey
acceso access
accesorio accessory
accidente *m.* accident (14)
acción *f.* action; **Día** (*m.*) **de Acción de Gracias** Thanksgiving
aceite (*m.*) (**de oliva**) (olive) oil (7)
acelerado/a fast, accelerated (15)
acelerar to accelerate; to speed up
acento accent; **acento diacrítico** diacritical mark; **acento ortográfico** accent mark
acentuación *f.* accent mark
acentuado/a accentuated
aceptable acceptable
aceptar to accept
acera sidewalk (15)
acerca de *prep.* about, concerning, regarding
acercarse (qu) (a) to come near to
acertar (acierto) to guess correctly
ácido acid
acompañar to accompany
acondicionado/a: aire (*m.*) **acondicionado** air conditioning
aconsejable advisable
aconsejar to advise
acontecer to occur
acontecimiento event, happening (18)
acordarse (me acuerdo) (de) to remember (13)
acordeón *m.* accordion
acoso harassment, bullying
acostarse (me acuesto) to go to bed (5)
acostumbrarse (a) to become accustomed (to); to get used (to)
acribillar to bombard
acrílico/a acrylic
actitud *f.* attitude
actividad *f.* activity
activo/a active
acto act
actor *m.* actor (13)
actriz *f.* (*pl.* **actrices**) actress (13)
actuación *f.* performance
actual *adj.* current, present-day (12)
actualidad: de/en la actualidad currently, right now (10)
actualizar(c) to update
actuar (actúo) to act (13)
acuario aquarium; **Acuario** Aquarius
acuático/a aquatic
acudir (a) to go (to)
acueducto aqueduct

acuerdo agreement; **(no) estar de acuerdo** to (dis)agree (3)
acumular to accumulate
acusón, acusona tattler
adaptación *f.* adaptation
adaptarse (a) to adapt (to)
adecuado/a appropriate
adelante forward
adelgazar (c) to lose weight
además *adv.* moreover; **además de** *prep.* besides
adentro inside
adicción *f.* addiction
adicional additional (1)
adiós good-bye (1)
adivinar to guess (9)
adjetivo *gram.* adjective (3); **adjetivo de nacionalidad** adjective of nationality (3); **adjetivo posesivo** possessive adjective (3)
administración *f.* administration; **administración de empresas** business administration (2)
administrar to administer; to manage; to run
admiración *f.* admiration
admirar to admire
admitir to admit
adolescencia adolescence (16)
adolescente *m., f.* adolescent, teenager; **de adolescente** as an adolescent (10)
¿adónde? where (to)? (4)
adoptar to adopt
adoquinado/a cobblestoned
adorar to adore
adquirir to acquire
adquisitivo/a: poder (*m.*) **adquisitivo** purchasing power
aduana customs (*at a border*) (8); **pasar por la aduana** to go/pass through customs (8)
adulto/a adult
adverbio *gram.* adverb
adverso/a adverse
advertencia warning
adyacente adjacent
aéreo/a aerial
aeróbico/a: hacer ejercicios aeróbicos to do aerobics (11)
aerolínea airline
aeropuerto airport (8)
afán *m.* effort
afanoso/a laborious, hard
afectación *f.* affectation
afectar to affect
afectivo/a: estado afectivo emotional state (9)
afecto affection

afeitarse to shave (5)
afición *f.* hobby (10)
aficionado/a fan; **ser aficionado/a (a)** to be a fan (of) (10)
afiliación *f.* affiliation
afiliado/a (a) affiliated (with)
afín related
afinidad *f.* compatibility
afirmación *f.* statement
afirmar to affirm
afirmativo/a affirmative
afluente affluent
afortunado/a fortunate, lucky
africano/a *n., adj.* African
afroamerindo/a *n., adj.* Afro-Amerindian
afroantillano/a Afro-Antillian
afroperuano/a Afro-Peruvian
afuera *adv.* outdoors (6)
afueras *f. pl.* outskirts (12); suburbs (12)
agencia agency; **agencia de compra-venta (de coches)** used car dealership; **agencia de viajes** travel agency
agenda agenda; date book
agente *m., f.* agent (8); **agente de viajes** travel agent
ágil agile
agitar to agitate
agnóstico/a agnostic
agobiado/a overwhelmed
agosto August (6)
agotar to empty; to drain
agradable agreeable, pleasant
agradar (*like* **gustar**) to please
agradecimiento *n.* thanks
agregar (gu) to add
agresivo/a aggressive
agrícola *adj. m., f.* agricultural
agricultor(a) farmer (15)
agricultura farming, agriculture (15)
agrio/a bitter
agroturismo agritourism
agroturista *m., f.* agritourist
agroturístico/a *adj.* of rural tourism
agrupar to group
agua *f.* (*but* **el agua**) **(mineral)** (mineral) water (7)
aguacate *m.* avocado (7)
aguar (ü) to dilute; water down
agudo/a sharp
águila *f.* (*but* **el águila**) eagle
agujero hole
ahí there
ahijado/a godson/goddaughter
ahora now (2); **ahora mismo** right now (6)
ahorrar to save (*money*) (17)
ahorro savings
ahorros: cuenta de ahorros savings account

aimara *n.* Aymara
airado/a angry; annoyed
aire *m.* air (15); **aire acondicionado** air conditioning; **al aire libre** outdoors (10)
ajedrez *m.* chess; **jugar (juego) (gu) al ajedrez** to play chess (10)
ajo garlic
al (*contraction of* **a** + **el**) to the (4); **al +** *inf.* while (*doing something*); **al aire** (*m.*) **libre** outdoors (10); **al alcance** within reach; **al instante** right away; **al lado de** alongside of (6); **al menos** at least; **al principio de** at the beginning of (17)
alameda tree-lined avenue
alberca swimming pool (*Mex.*)
álbum *m.* album
alcance: al alcance within reach
alcanzar (c) to reach; to achieve
alce *m.* elk; moose
alcoba bedroom (5)
alcohol *m.* alcohol
alcohólico/a alcoholic; **bebida alcohólica** alcoholic beverage
alegrarse (de) to be happy (about) (12)
alegre happy (6)
alemán *m.* German (*language*) (2)
alemán, alemana *n., adj.* German (3)
Alemania Germany
alergia allergy
alérgico/a allergic
alerta: ojo alerta eagle eye
alfabeto alphabet
alfombra rug (5)
algo something; anything (7)
algodón *m.* cotton (4); **de algodón** *adj.* (*made of*) cotton (4)
alguien someone, anyone (7)
algún (alguna/os/as) some, any (7); **alguna vez** once; ever
alimentación *f.* diet
alimenticio/a of eating
alimento food
aliviar to alleviate
allá (way) over there (4)
allí there (4)
alma *m.* soul
almacén *m.* department store (4)
almacenamiento: espacio de almacenamiento storage space (12)
almacenar to store; to save (12)
almohada pillow
almorzar (almuerzo) (c) to have lunch (5)
almuerzo lunch (7)
¿aló? hello? (*telephone greeting*)
alojarse to lodge
alpinismo mountain climbing; **practicar (qu) el alpinismo** to mountain climb

alquilar *v.* to rent (12)
alquiler *m.* rent (12)
alrededor (de) around
alternar to take turns
alternativa *n.* alternative
alternativo/a *adj.* alternative
altiplanicie *f.* high plateau
altiplano high plateau
altitud *f.* height; altitude
alto/a tall (3); **de alta costura** high fashion; **de alto riesgo** high risk
altura altitude
alucinante incredible
alumno/a student
aluvial alluvial
amabilidad *f.* kindness
amable kind; nice (3)
amanecer *m.* dawn
amar to love (16)
amarillo/a yellow (4)
amasijo dough; mixture
Amazonas *m. s.* Amazon (River)
amazónico/a *adj.* Amazonian; **Selva Amazónica** Amazon Jungle
ambiental environmental
ambiente *m.* atmosphere; environment; **medio ambiente** environment (15)
ambigüedad *f.* ambiguity
ámbito area
ambos/as both
ambulante *adj.* traveling
América: América Latina Latin America; **Estados** (*m. pl.*) **Unidos de América** United States of America
americano/a American; **fútbol** (*m.*) **americano** football
amerindo/a *n., adj.* Amerindian
amigo/a friend (2)
amistad *f.* friendship (16)
amistoso/a friendly (16)
amo/a (*but* **el ama**) **de casa** housekeeper (17)
amoníaco ammonia
amor *m.* love (16)
amoroso/a loving
ampliar (amplío) to widen
amplio/a wide; large; spacious
amueblado/a furnished
amueblar to furnish
amuleto charm; amulet
amurallado/a walled
analfabetismo *n.* illiteracy
analfabeto/a illiterate
análisis *m. inv.* analysis
analista *m., f.* analyst; **analista de sistemas** systems analyst (17)
analizar (c) to analyze
ananá *m.* pineapple
anaranjado/a orange (4)
ancho/a wide

anciano/a *n.* old person; *adj.* old; ancient; **residencia de ancianos** nursing home (12)

Andalucía Andalusia

andaluz(a) *n., adj.* Andalusian

andante: caballero andante knight-errant

andar to walk; **andar en bicicleta** to ride a bicycle; **cinta de andar** treadmill

andino/a Andean

anécdota anecdote

anémico/a anemic

anfibio amphibian

anfitrión, anfitriona host (*of an event*) (9)

ángel *m.* angel

angelino/a *adj.* from Los Angeles; *n.* person from Los Angeles

angloparlante *adj.* English-speaking

anglosajón, anglosajona Anglo Saxon

angosto/a narrow

ángulo angle

angustia anguish

anillo ring

ánima *f. (but* **el ánima**) soul

animado/a lively; animated; **dibujos** (*m. pl.*) **animados** cartoons

animal *m.* animal (15); **animal de peluche** (*m.*) stuffed animal; **animal doméstico** pet

animar(se) to cheer up; **animarse a** to get up the courage to (*do something*)

ánimo: estado de ánimo state of mind

aniversario anniversary

anoche *adv.* last night (11)

anónimo/a anonymous

ansiedad *f.* anxiety (14)

ansioso/a anxious

antártico/a *adj.* Antarctic

Antártida Antarctica

ante *prep.* before; in front of

anteayer *adv.* the day before yesterday (5)

antecedente *m. gram.* antecedent

anteojos *m. pl.* glasses (11)

antepenúltimo/a third from the end

anterior previous, preceding

antes *adv.* before; **antes de** *prep.* before (5); **antes de Cristo (a.C.)** before Christ (B.C.); **antes (de) que** *conj.* before (16)

antibiótico antibiotic (11)

anticipar to anticipate

anticipo advance

anticuado/a antiquated

antídoto antidote

antiguo/a old; ancient; former

antillano/a *adj.* of/from the Antilles

Antillas (*f. pl.*) **Mayores** Greater Antilles

antipático/a unpleasant (3)

antojo appetizer

antónimo antonym

antropología anthropology

antropólogo/a anthropologist

anual annual

anualmente annually

anunciar to announce (8)

anuncio announcement; advertisement

añadir to add

año year (6); **año académico** school year; **año bisiesto** leap year; **el año entrante** next year; **Año Nuevo** New Year; **año pasado** last year; **el año que viene** next year; **cumplir años** to have a birthday (9); **este año** this year; **fin** (*m.*) **de año** end of the year (9); **tener... años** to be . . . years old (3)

apagar (gu) to turn off (12)

apagón *m.* blackout

aparato appliance; **aparato doméstico** home appliance (10)

aparcamiento parking place; parking lot

aparcar (qu) to park

aparecer (aparezco) to appear

apariencia appearance

apartamento apartment (2)

aparte also

apellido surname

apenas barely

aperitivo appetizer

apetecer (apetezco) (*like* **gustar**) to appeal to

apetito appetite

apio celery

aplicación *f.* application

aplicar (qu) to apply

aportar to contribute

apóstol *m., f.* apostle

apoyar to support

apoyo support; help

app *f.* app(lication) (12)

apreciar to appreciate

aprender to learn (3); **aprender a + inf.** to learn how to (*do something*) (3)

aprendizaje *m.* learning

apropiado/a appropriate

aproximadamente approximately

aproximado/a approximate

aptitud *f.* aptitude

apuntar to write down; **apuntarse** to enroll; to add one's name to the list

apuntes *m. pl.* notes (*academic*) (14)

aquel, aquella *adj.* that ([way] over there) (4); *pron.* that one ([way] over there)

aquello (*neuter pron.*) that ([way] over there) (4)

aquellos/as *adj.* those ([way] over there) (4) *pron.* those ones ([way] over there)

aquí here (2)

árabe *m.* Arabic (*language*); *n., adj. m., f.* Arab

Arabia Saudita Saudi Arabia

arábico/a *adj.* Arabic

arado *n.* plow

araña spider

árbol *m.* tree (9); **árbol genealógico** family tree

arcángel *m.* archangel

archipiélago archipelago

archivo (computer) file (12)

arco arch

ardilla squirrel

área *f. (but* **el área**) area, region

arena sand

arepa *patty made of cornmeal and flour and stuffed with different foods*

aretes *m. pl.* earrings (4)

argentino/a *n., adj.* Argentine

argumento argument; plot

árido/a arid, dry

aristocrático/a aristocratic

arma weapon

armado/a: fuerzas armadas armed forces

armar un bochinche to throw a (loud) party

armario armoire, free-standing closet (5)

armonía harmony

arpa *f. (but* **el arpa**) harp

arqueológico/a archaeological

arquitecto/a architect (13)

arquitectónico/a architectural

arquitectura architecture (13)

arraigado/a deeply rooted

arrancar (qu) to start up (*a car*) (15)

arreglar to fix; to repair (15)

arrepentido/a sorry; repentant

arriba (de) *prep.* above

arroba @ (12)

arrodillarse to kneel

arrogancia arrogance

arrogante arrogant

arroz *m.* (*pl.* **arroces**) rice (7)

arruinar to ruin

arte *m.* art (2); **artes** *f. pl.* the arts (13); **bellas artes** fine arts; **obra de arte** work of art (13)

arteria artery

arterial: presión (*f.*) **arterial** blood pressure

artesanía arts and crafts (13)

artesano/a artisan

Ártico *adj.* Arctic

artículo article; **artículo (in)definido** *gram.* (in)definite article

artista *m., f.* artist (13)

artístico/a artistic (13); **expresión** (*f.*) **artística** artistic expression (13)

arvejas *f. pl.* green peas (7)

asado/a roast(ed) (7); **lechón** (*m.*) **asado** roast suckling pig; **pollo asado** roast chicken (7)

asaltar to rob

asamblea assembly

ascendencia ancestry, descent

ascensor *m.* elevator (12)

asco: ¡qué asco! yuck!

asegurar to assure; **asegurarse (de que)** to make certain (that)

asentamiento settlement

asentarse (me asiento) to settle

asesinar to assassinate (18)

asesinato assassination; murder (18)

asesino *m., f.* murderer

así thus; so; **así como** as well as; **así que** therefore, consequently, so

asiático/a *adj.* Asian

asiento seat (8)

asignar to assign

asimismo additionally

asistencia sanitaria health care

asistente (*m., f.*) **de vuelo** flight attendant (8)

asistir (a) to attend; to go to (*a class, function*) (3)

asma *m.* asthma

asociación *f.* association

asociado/a associated; **estado libre asociado** commonwealth

asociar to associate

aspecto aspect

aspiradora vacuum cleaner (10); **pasar la aspiradora** to vacuum (10)

aspirante *m., f.* candidate; applicant (17)

aspirar to vacuum

aspirina aspirin

astronauta *m., f.* astronaut (17)

asumir to assume

asunto matter

asustar to scare

atacar (qu) to attack

ataque (*m.*) **(terrorista)** (terrorist) attack (18)

atar to tie

Atenas Athens

atención *f.* attention; **poner atención** to pay attention

atender (atiendo) to look after

atenerse (*like* **tener**) to accept

ateo/a atheist

ático attic

Atlántico Atlantic

atleta *m., f.* athlete

atmosférico/a atmospheric

átomo atom

atracción *f.* attraction

atractivo/a attractive

atraer (*like* **traer**) (*like* **gustar**) to draw; to attract (13)

atrás *adv.* back, backward; behind; **de atrás** backwards

atrasado/a (*with* **estar**) late (8)

atravesar (atravieso) to go through

atributo attribute

atún *m.* tuna (7)

audaz (*pl.* **audaces**) bold, daring

audiencia audience

auditivo/a aural

aula *f.* (*but* **el aula**) classroom

aumentar to increase

aumento raise

aun *adv.* even

aún *adv.* still, yet

aunque although

auriculares *m. pl.* headphones (12)

auscultar to listen (*with a stethoscope*)

ausencia absence

ausente absent

austeridad *f.* austerity

australiano/a *n., adj.* Australian

auténtico/a authentic

auto auto (15)

autobiográfico/a autobiographical

autobús *m.* bus (8); **estación** (*f.*) **de autobuses** bus station (8); **ir en autobús** to go/travel by bus (8); **parada del autobús** bus stop (12)

autóctono/a indigenous

autoestima self-esteem

automático/a automatic; **cajero automático** automatic teller machine (ATM) (17)

automóvil *m.* automobile

automovilístico/a *adj.* automobile (15)

automutilación *f.* self-mutilation

autonomía autonomy; region

autónomo/a autonomous

autopista freeway; interstate (15)

autoprueba self-test

autor(a) author (13)

autoridad *f.* authority

autorizado/a authorized

autorretrato self-portrait

autostop: hacer autostop to hitchhike

autosuficiencia self-sufficiency

autosuficiente self-sufficient

auxiliar to help; to assist

avance *m.* preview

avanzado/a advanced

ave *f.* (*but* **el ave**) bird

avenida avenue (12)

aventura adventure

aventurero/a adventurous

aventurismo adventure tourism

aventurista *m., f.* adventure tourist

avergonzado/a embarrassed (9)

avión *m.* airplane (8); **ir en avión** to go/travel by plane (8); **volar (vuelo) en avión** to fly; to go by plane (8)

avisar to warn

aviso warning

¡ay! *interj.* ah!; ouch!

ayer yesterday; **ayer fue (miércoles...)** yesterday was (Wednesday . . .) (5)

ayuda help (7)

ayudante *m., f.* assistant

ayudar to help (7); **ayudar a** + *inf.* to help to (*do something*) (7)

ayuntamiento local government

azteca *n., adj. m., f.* Aztec

azúcar *m.* sugar (7)

azul blue (4)

azulejo tile

B

baba saliva; **se le cae la baba por** he/she is drooling over

bacán: ¡qué bacán! fantastic!

bahía bay

bailable danceable

bailaor(a) flamenco dancer

bailar to dance (2)

bailarín, bailarina dancer (13)

baile *m.* dance (13)

bajada ebb; dip

bajar to lower; to download (12); **bajarse (de)** to get down (from) (8); to get off (of) (*a vehicle*) (8)

bajareque *n.* mud wall

bajo *prep.* under; **estar bajo muchas presiones** to be under a lot of pressure (14)

bajo/a short (*in height*) (3); low

balcón *m.* balcony

ballena whale (15)

ballet *m.* ballet (13)

baloncesto basketball

banana banana (7)

banano banana tree

bancario/a: tarjeta bancaria debit card (17)

banco bank (17)

banda band

bandeja tray

bandera flag

bandoneón *m.* large concertina

bañarse to take a bath (5)

bañera bathtub (5)

baño bathroom (5); **traje** (*m.*) **de baño** swimsuit (4)

bar *m.* bar; **ir a un bar** to go to a bar (10)

barato/a inexpensive (4)

barba beard

barbacoa barbecue (7)

barcelonés, barcelonesa of Barcelona (*Sp.*)

barco boat, ship (8); **ir en barco** to go/travel by boat, ship (8)

barra bar

barrer (el piso) to sweep (the floor) (10)

barriga belly

barrio neighborhood (12)

barro mud

basarse en to base one's ideas/opinions on

base *f.* base; **a base de** based on; **base de datos** data base; **con base en** based on

básico/a basic

basquetbol *m.* basketball (10)

bastante rather, sufficiently; enough (16)

bastar to be enough

basura trash (10); **sacar (qu) la basura** to take out the trash (10)

bata robe

batalla battle

batería drum set (15)

bautizo baptism

bebé *m., f.* baby

beber to drink (3)

bebida drink (5); **bebida alcohólica** alcoholic beverage

beca scholarship

béisbol *m.* baseball (10)

beisbolista *m., f.* baseball player

Bélgica Belgium

belleza beauty

bello/a beautiful (15); **bellas artes** (*f. pl.*) fine arts

bendecir (*like decir*) to bless; **que Dios te bendiga** God bless you

bendito/a blessed

beneficio benefit

besar to kiss; **besarse** to kiss each other (11)

beso kiss

bestia beast

Biblia Bible

biblioteca library (2)

bibliotecario/a librarian (2)

bicentenario bicentennial

bicho insect

bici *f.* bike

bicicleta bicycle; **andar en bicicleta** to ride a bicycle; **pasear en bicicleta** to ride a bicycle (10)

bien *adv.* well (1); **caerle bien a alguien** to make a good impression on someone; **empleo bien pagado** well-paid job/position (17); **está bien** it's fine, OK (6); **estar bien** to be well; to be comfortable (*temperature*) (6); **llevarse bien (con)** to get along well (with) (16); **muy bien** fine, very well (1);

pasarlo bien to have a good time (9); **portarse bien** to behave (9); **salir bien** to come/turn out well (5); to do well (5)

bienes raíces *m. pl.* real estate

bienestar *m.* well-being (11)

bienvenida *n.* welcome

bienvenido/a *adj.* welcome

bife *m.* beef

bilingüe bilingual

billete *m.* bill (*money*) (17); ticket (*Sp.*) (8); **billete de ida** one-way ticket (8); **billete de ida y vuelta** round-trip ticket (8); **billete electrónico** e-ticket (8)

binacional binational

biodiversidad *f.* biodiversity

biografía biography

biología biology

bioluminiscencia bioluminescence

bioquímica biochemistry

bisabuelo/a great-grandfather/great-grandmother

bisiesto/a: año bisiesto leap year

bisonte *m.* bison

bistec *m.* steak (7)

blanco/a white (4); **pizarrón** (*m.*) **blanco** whiteboard (2); **vino blanco** white wine (7)

blando/a soft

blog *m.* blog (12)

bloqueador (*m.*) **solar** sunscreen (8)

bloqueo de llamadas call blocker

bluejeans *m. pl.* jeans

blusa blouse (4)

boca mouth (11)

bocadillo sandwich (*Sp.*)

bochinche: armar un bochinche to throw a (loud) party

bocina horn (*car*) (15)

boda wedding (*ceremony*) (16)

bodega grocery store (*Carib.*)

bogotano/a *adj.* from Bogotá, Colombia

bola ball

bolero love song

boleto ticket (*L.A.*) (8); **boleto de ida** one-way ticket (8); **boleto de ida y vuelta** round-trip ticket; **boleto electrónico** e-ticket (8)

bolígrafo pen (2)

bolívar *m. Venezuelan currency unit*

boliviano/a *n., adj.* Bolivian

bolso purse (4)

bomba bomb (18)

bombardeo bombing

bombero/a firefighter

bombilla light bulb

bombo legüero Argentine drum

bonanza boom (*economic*)

bongó bongo

bonito/a pretty (3)

boricua *n., adj.* Puerto Rican

Borinquen *indigenous name of Puerto Rico*

borinqueño/a *adj.* Puerto Rican

borrador *m.* draft

borrasca storm

bosque *m.* forest (15); **bosque tropical lluvioso** tropical rain forest

bostezo yawn

botanas *f. pl.* (*Mex.*) appetizers (9)

botanía botany

botánico/a botanical

botar to throw out

botas *f. pl.* boots (4)

botella bottle

botón *m.* button

boxeador(a) boxer

brasileño/a *n., adj.* Brazilian

brazo arm (11)

brecha gap; **brecha digital** digital gap; **brecha salarial** wage gap

Bretaña: Gran Bretaña Great Britain

breve brief

británico/a British

bronce *m.* bronze

broncear to tan

bruja witch

brujo wizard; warlock

bruto/a: producto nacional bruto gross national product

bucear to scuba dive; to snorkel

budismo Buddhism

budista *n., adj. m., f.* Buddhist

buen, bueno/a good (3); **¡buen provecho!** enjoy your meal! **buenas noches** good night (1); **buenas tardes** good afternoon (1); **buenos días** good morning (1); **lo bueno** the good news/thing (11); **muy buenas** good afternoon/evening (1); **tener buena suerte** to have good luck; to be lucky (14)

buey *sl.* dude (*Mex.*)

bufanda scarf

burlarse de to make fun of

buscar (qu) to look for (2); **buscar en internet** to look for on the internet (12)

búsqueda search

buzón (*m.*) **de voz** voice mailbox (12)

C

caballero knight; **caballero andante** knight-errant

caballo horse (10); **montar a caballo** to ride a horse (10)

caber to fit (*into an area*)

cabeza head (11); **dolor** (*m.*) **de cabeza** headache

cabina cabin (*on a ship*) (8)

cacerola casserole dish

cacique, cacica chief

cada *inv.* each, every (5); **cada vez más** increasingly; **cada vez mayor** greater and greater

cadena chain

caer to fall; to drop (14); **caer en** to fall on (*day of the week*); **caerle bien/ mal a alguien** to make a good/bad impression on someone; **caerse** to fall down (14); **se le cae la baba por** he/she is drooling over

café *m.* coffee (2)

cafeína caffeine

cafetal *m.* coffee plantation

cafetera coffeemaker (10)

cafetería cafeteria (2)

cafetero coffee plantation worker

caída fall (*from a height*)

caimán *m.* alligator

caja box

cajero/a cashier; teller (17); **cajero automático** automatic teller machine (ATM) (17)

cajón *m.* drawer

calabaza pumpkin; squash

calabozo prison cell

calamar *m.* squid

calcetines *m. pl.* socks (4)

calculadora calculator (2)

calcular to calculate

cálculo calculus

calefacción *f.* heating (12)

calendario calendar (14)

calentador(a) *adj.* warming

calentar (caliento) to warm

calidad *f.* quality (*excellence*)

cálido/a hot

caliente hot (*temperature*) (7)

calificación *f.* grade

caligrafía calligraphy; handwriting

callar to silence

calle *f.* street (12)

callejero/a *adj.* (of the) street

calma calm

calmarse to calm down

calor *m.* heat; **hacer (mucho) calor** to be very hot (6); **tener (mucho) calor** to be (very) warm, hot (6)

caloría calorie

caluroso/a hot

cama bed (5); **guardar cama** to stay in bed (11); **hacer la cama** to make the bed (10); **tender (tiendo) la cama** to make the bed

cámara camera (12)

camarero/a waiter/waitress (7)

camarones *m. pl.* shrimp (7)

cambiar (de) to change (12)

cambio change; **cambio climático** climate change

camélidos *m. pl.* (*zool.*) Camelidae

camello camel

caminadora treadmill (11)

caminar to walk (10)

caminata: dar una caminata to hike; to go for a hike (10)

caminero/a: furia caminera road rage

camino road; path

camión *m.* truck

camioneta station wagon (8); van (8)

camisa shirt (4)

camiseta T-shirt (4)

campamento campsite

campaña campaign; **tienda de campaña** tent (8)

campeón, campeona champion

campeonato championship

campesino/a peasant (15)

camping *m.* campground (8); **hacer camping** to go camping (8)

campo field; countryside (15)

Canadá Canada; **Día** (*m.*) **del Canadá** Canada Day

canadiense *n., adj. m., f.* Canadian

canal *m.* channel (12); canal (7)

canario canary

cancelar to cancel

cáncer *m.* cancer

cancha field; court (*tennis*)

canción *f.* song (7)

candidato/a candidate (18); **postularse (para un cargo) como candidato/a** to run (for a position) as a candidate (18)

cansado/a tired (6)

cansancio fatigue

cansarse to get tired (11)

cantante *m., f.* singer (13)

cantaor(a) flamenco singer

cantar to sing (2)

cantautor(a) singer, songwriter

cantidad *f.* quantity

cantinero/a bartender

caña sugar cane

cañonazo cannon shot

capa layer (15); **capa de ozono** ozone layer (15)

capacidad *f.* capacity

capaz (*pl.* **capaces**) able

Caperucita Roja Little Red Ridinghood

capilla chapel

capital *f.* capital city (6)

capitán, capitana captain

capítulo chapter

Capricornio Capricorn

cara face

caracola large shell

característica *n.* characteristic

característico/a *adj.* characteristic

caracterizar (c) to characterize

caramañola torpedo-shaped meat pie of Colombia and Panama

cárcel *f.* jail

cardinal: punto cardinal cardinal point (6)

cardiólogo cardiologist

carga load; **carga de trabajo** workload

cargar (gu) a una cuenta to charge to an account (17)

cargo (political) office (18); **postularse para un cargo (como candidato/a)** to run for a position (as a candidate) (18)

Caribe *m.* Caribbean; **mar** (*m.*) **Caribe** Caribbean Sea

caribeño/a Caribbean

caricatura caricature

cariño affection (16)

cariñoso/a affectionate (6)

carnaval *m.* carnival

carne *f.* meat (7)

carnet (*m.*) **de identificación / de identidad** identification card

carnicería butcher's shop

caro/a expensive (4)

carpa tent

carpeta folder (12)

carpintero/a carpenter

carrera career

carreta cart, wagon

carretera highway (15)

carretilla wheelbarrow

carril *m.* lane

carro (descapotable) (convertible) car (15)

carta letter (3); card; **jugar (juego) (gu) a las cartas** to play cards (10)

cartera wallet; handbag (4)

cartón *m.* cardboard

casa house, home (3); **amo/a** (*but* **el ama**) **de casa** housekeeper (17) **casa natal** house where someone was born; **en casa** at home (2); **limpiar la casa** to clean (the) house (10); **regresar a casa** to go home (2)

casabe *m.* tortilla-type bread made of cassava

casado/a married; **estar casado/a (con)** to be married (to) (16); **recién casado/a (con)** newlywed (to) (16); **ser casado/a** to be a married person (16)

casarse (con) to marry (16)

cascanueces *m. inv.* nutcracker

caserío hamlet; farmhouse

casero/a home-made

casi *adv.* almost (3); **casi nunca** almost never (3)

caso case; **en caso de (que)** in case (16)

castaño/a brown (chestnut-colored)

castañuelas *f. pl.* castinets

castellano Spanish (language)

castigar (gu) to punish

cata (de vino) (wine) tasting

catalán *m.* Catalan (*language*); **catalán, catalana** *adj.* Catalan

catálogo catalogue

Cataluña Catalonia

catarata waterfall

catarro cold (*health condition*)

catedral *f.* cathedral

categoría category

catolicismo Catholicism

católico/a *n., adj.* Catholic

catorce fourteen (1)

caucásico/a Caucasian

causa cause; **a causa de** because of

causar to cause

cava cellar

cazador(a) hunter

cazar (c) to hunt

CD *m.* CD (compact disc) (12)

CD-ROM *m.* CD-ROM (12)

cebolla onion (7)

cédula identity card

celda cell (*prison*)

celebración *f.* celebration

celebrar to celebrate (6)

celíaco/a gluten intolerant

celos *m. pl.* jealousy

celta *n., adj. m., f.* Celtic

celular: (teléfono) celular *m.* cell phone (2)

cementerio cemetery

cena dinner, supper (7)

cenar to have (eat) dinner, supper (7)

Cenicienta Cinderella

centavo cent

centígrado Celsius

céntrico/a central

centro center (*political*) (18); downtown (4); **centro comercial** shopping mall (4)

Centroamérica Central America

centroamericano/a Central American

cepillarse los dientes to brush one's teeth (5)

cerámica pottery; ceramics (13)

cerca *adv.* near, nearby, close; **cerca de** close to (6)

cercano/a *adj.* close, near

cerdo pork; **chuleta de cerdo** pork chop (7)

cereal *m.* cereal (7)

cerebro brain (11)

ceremonia ceremony

cero zero (1)

cerrado/a closed (6)

cerrar (cierro) to close (5); **cerrarse** to close; to finish

cerro hill

certeza certainty

cerveza beer (7)

cesárea C-section

césped *m.* lawn; grass

cesto basket

ceviche *m. raw fish dish*

champán *m.* champagne (9)

champiñones *m. pl.* mushrooms (7)

chanclas *f. pl.* flip-flops (4)

chaqueta jacket (4)

charango *stringed instrument*

charco puddle

charlar to chat

chatear to chat

chateo *n.* chat (12)

chauchas *f. pl.* green beans (*Arg.*)

cheque *m.* check (17); **con cheque** by check (17)

chequeo check-up (11)

chévere *sl.* cool

chibcha *n., adj. m., f. indigenous people of the Colombian Andes*

chicha *natural fruit soft drink*

chicle *m.* gum

chico/a guy/girl (4)

chileno/a *n., adj.* Chilean

chino Chinese (*language*)

chino/a *n., adj.* Chinese

chisme *m.* gossip

chiste *m.* joke (8)

chocante shocking

chocar (qu) con/contra to run into, bump against (14)

chocolate *m.* chocolate

chofer *m., f.* driver

choque *m.* collision, crash (18)

chuleta (de cerdo) (pork) chop (7)

churro *strip of fried dough*

cibernauto/a of the internet

ciclismo bicycling (10)

ciclo cycle

ciclón *m.* cyclone

ciego/a blind

cien one hundred (3)

ciencia science (2); **ciencia ficción** science fiction; **ciencias** (*f. pl.*) **naturales** natural sciences (2); **ciencias** (*f. pl.*) **políticas** political science (2); **ciencias** (*f. pl.*) **sociales** social sciences (2)

científico/a scientist

ciento one hundred (4); **ciento dos** one hundred two (4); **ciento noventa y nueve** one hundred ninety-nine (4); **ciento uno** one hundred one (4)

cierto/a true **es cierto que** it's certain that (13)

ciervo deer; stag

cifra figure, number

cigarrillo cigarette

cinco five (1)

cincuenta fifty (3)

cine *m. s.* movies (5); movie theater (5)

cineasta *m., f.* filmmaker

cinematográfico/a *adj.* movie, film

cinta: cinta de andar/correr treadmill; **cinta rodante** treadmill

cinturón *m.* belt (4)

circulación *f.* traffic (15)

circular to circulate

círculo circle

circunstancia circumstance

cirugía surgery

cisne *m.* swan

cita date; appointment (11)

citar to cite, quote

ciudad *f.* city (3)

ciudadano/a citizen (18)

cívico/a civic; **responsabilidad** (*f.*) **cívica** civic duty (18)

civil civil; **guerra civil** civil war

civilización *f.* civilization

clarificar (qu) to clarify

claro/a clear

clase *f.* class (*of students*) (2); class, course (*academic*) (2); **compañero/a (de clase)** classmate (2); **dar clases** to teach class; **salón** (*m.*) **de clase** classroom (2)

clásico/a classic(al) (13)

clasificar (qu) to classify

cláusula *gram.* clause

clave *f. n., adj.* key

clic: hacer clic to click (12)

clicar (qu) to click

cliente/a client (2)

clima *m.* climate (6)

climático/a *adj.* climate; **cambio climático** climate change

clínica clinic

cliquear to click

clóset *m.* closet

coalición *f.* coalition

cobrar to cash (*a check*) (17); to charge (*someone for an item or service*) (17)

cobre *m.* copper

coche *m.* car (3); **agencia de compraventa (de coches)** used car dealership

cochera garage; carport

cochinilla cochineal

cocido/a *adj.* cooked

cocina kitchen (5); cuisine (7)

cocinar to cook (7)

cocinero/a cook; chef (17)
coco coconut
cocodrilo crocodile
cóctel *m.* cocktail party
codiciado/a coveted
código code
codirector(a) codirector
codo elbow
coexistir to coexist
coger (cojo) to take (*things*) (*Sp.*)
cognado *gram.* cognate
coherente coherent
cohesión *f.* cohesion
coincidencia coincidence
coincidir to coincide
cola line (*of people*) (8); **hacer cola** to stand in line (8)
colaborar to collaborate
colección *f.* collection
coleccionar to collect
colectivo bus
colega *m., f.* colleague
colegio school
colérico/a furious
colesterol *m.* cholesterol
coletilla tag (*as in tag question*)
colgar (cuelgo) (gu) to post (*on the internet*)
colina hill
collar *m.* necklace
colmado small grocery store (*Carib.*)
colocar (qu) to place
colombiano/a Colombian
colonia colony
colonización *f.* colonization
colonizador(a) colonist
colonizar (c) to colonize
colono/a settler
coloquial colloquial
color *m.* color (4)
colorado/a red-colored
colorido/a colorful
columna column
comadre *f.* godmother
combatir to combat
combinación *f.* combination
combinar to combine
comedia comedy (13)
comediante *m., f.* comedian
comedor *m.* dining room (5)
comentar to talk about
comentario comment
comentarista *m., f.* commentator
comenzar (comienzo) (c) to begin; **comenzar a** + *inf.* to begin to + *inf.*
comer to eat (3); **comerse** to eat up
comercial: centro comercial shopping mall (4)
comercio business, commerce; **libre comercio** free trade

comestibles *m. pl.* groceries, foodstuff (7)
cometa *m.* comet
cometer to commit
cómico/a funny; **tira cómica** comic strip
comida food (7); meal (7); **comida rápida** fast food
comienzo beginning
comillas *f. pl.* quotation marks
como like; as; **así como** as well as; **tan... como** as . . . as (6); **tanto como** as much as (6)
¿cómo? how?; what? (1); **¿cómo es usted?** what are you (*form. s.*) like? (1); **¿cómo está?** how are you (*form. s.*)? (1); **¿cómo estás?** how are you (*fam. s.*)? (1); **¿cómo se llama usted?** what is your (*form. s.*) name? (1); **¿cómo se llega a... ?** how do you get to . . . ? (15); **¿cómo te llamas?** what is your (*fam. s.*) name? (1)
cómoda bureau; dresser (5)
comodidad *f.* convenience
cómodo/a comfortable (4)
compacto/a: disco compacto (CD *m.*) compact disc (CD) (12)
compadre *m.* godfather
compañero/a companion; friend; **compañero/a (de clase)** classmate (2); **compañero/a de cuarto** roommate (2)
compañía company
comparación *f.* comparison (6)
comparar to compare
comparativo/a comparative
compartir to share
compasión *f.* compassion
compensar to make up for
competencia competition
competente competent
competición *f.* competition
competitivo/a competitive
complejo/a complex
complemento (in)directo *gram.* (in) direct object
completar to complete
completo/a complete; **trabajo de tiempo completo** full-time job (14)
complicación *f.* complication
componer (*like* **poner**) to compose (13)
comportamiento behavior
composición *f.* composition
compositor(a) composer (13)
compostero composter
comprador(a) buyer
comprar to buy (2)
compras: de compras shopping (4); **ir de compras** to go shopping (4)
compra-venta: agencia de compra-venta (de coches) used car dealership

comprender to understand (3)
comprensible understandable
comprensión *f.* understanding; comprehension
comprensivo/a *adj.* understanding
comprobar (compruebo) to prove
comprometido/a committed
compuesto/a composed; compound (*gram.*)
compulsivo/a compulsive
computación *f.* computer science (2)
computadora computer (2); **computadora portátil** laptop (computer) (2)
común common
comunicación *f.* communication; *pl.* communication (*subject*) (2); **medio de comunicación** medium of communication (18)
comunicarse (qu) to communicate
comunicativo/a communicative
comunidad *f.* community
comunión *f.* communion
comunitario/a *adj.* community
con with (2); **chocar (qu) con** to run into, bump against (14); **comunicarse (qu) (con)** to communicate (with) (18); **con base en** based on; **con cheque** by check (17); **con cuidado** carefully; **con frecuencia** frequently (2); **con permiso** excuse me (1); **¿con qué frecuencia... ?** how often . . . ? (3); **con respecto a** regarding; **con tal de** *prep.* provided (16); **con tal (de) que** *conj.* provided (that) (16); **darse con** to run into; **pegarse (gu) con** to run/bump into (14)
conceder to concede
concentración *f.* concentration
concentrar to concentrate
concepto concept
conciencia conscience
concienciación *f. n.* conscious-raising
concierto concert (10); **ir a un concierto** to go to a concert (10)
conciso/a concise
conclusión *f.* conclusion
concordancia *gram.* agreement
concreto: en concreto in particular
concursante *m., f.* contestant
concurso contest
condenado/a condemned
condición *f.* condition
condicional *gram.* conditional
cóndor *m.* condor
conducción *f.* driving
conducir (conduzco) to drive (15); **licencia de conducir** driver's license (15)
conductor(a) driver (15)

conectar to connect; **conectarse** to connect (12)

conector *m.* connector

conejo/a rabbit

conexión *f.* connection

conferencia lecture

confesional confessional

confianza confidence

confiar (confío) to trust

configurar to configure

confirmar to confirm

conflicto conflict

confluencia *n.* coming-together

confundido/a confused

congelado/a frozen; very cold (6)

congelador *m.* freezer (10)

congestión *f.* congestion

congresista *m., f.* member of congress

congreso congress; **representante** (*m., f.*) **al congreso** Congressional representative (18)

conjugación *f. gram.* conjugation

conjugar (gu) *gram.* to conjugate

conjunción *f. gram.* conjunction (16); **conjunción de tiempo** conjunction of time (17)

conjunto group

conllevar to involve

conmemorar to commemorate

conmigo with me (6)

Cono Sur Southern Cone

conocer (conozco) to know, be acquainted, familiar with (7); to meet (7); **conocerse** to meet (16)

conocimiento knowledge

conquista conquest

conquistador(a) conqueror

consciente conscious, aware

consecuencia consequence

consecutivo/a consecutive

conseguir (*like* **seguir**) to get; to obtain (9); **conseguir** + *inf.* to succeed in (*doing something*) (9)

consejero/a advisor (2)

consejo (piece of) advice (7)

conservación *f.* conservation

conservacionista conservationist

conservador(a) conservative

conservar to save; to conserve (15)

consideración *f.* consideration

considerar to consider

consigo with himself, herself, themselves

consiguiente: por consiguiente as a result

consistencia consistency

consistir (en) to consist (of)

constante constant

constar (de) to consist of

constatar to confirm

constipado/a: estar constipado/a to have a cold

constitución *f.* constitution

constituir (*like* **construir**) to constitute

construcción *f.* construction

construir (construyo) to build (15)

consuelo consolation

consulta consultation

consultar to consult

consultorio (medical) office (11); consultation

consumidor(a) consumer

consumir to consume

consumo consumption

contabilidad *f.* accounting

contable *m., f.* accountant (*Sp.*)

contacto contact; **lentes** (*m. pl.*) **de contacto** contact lenses (11); **mantenerse** (*like* **tener**) **en contacto** to stay in touch

contador(a) accountant (17)

contaminación *f.* pollution (6)

contaminado/a contaminated, polluted (15)

contaminar to pollute (15)

contar (cuento) to tell; to narrate (8)

contemplación *f.* contemplation

contemplar to contemplate

contemporáneo/a contemporary

contenedor *m.* container

contener (*like* **tener**) to contain

contenido contents

contento/a content, happy (6)

contestar to answer (7)

contexto context

contigo with you (*fam.*) (6)

continente *m.* continent

contingencia contingency

continuación: a continuación following

continuar (continúo) to continue (6)

contra against; **chocar (qu)/pegarse (gu) contra** to run into; to bump against (14); **darse contra** to run into

contrabajo double bass (*musical instrument*)

contradecir (*like* **decir**) to contradict

contraer (*like* **traer**) to contract

contrario contrary

contrarrestar to resist

contraseña password (12)

contrastar to contrast

contraste *m.* contrast

contrastivo/a contrasting

contribución *f.* contribution

contribuir (*like* **construir**) to contribute

control *m.* control; **control de seguridad** security (check) (8); **control remoto** remote control (12); **pasar por el control de seguridad** to go/pass through security (check) (8)

controlador(a) controller

controlar to control

convencer (convenzo) to convince

convención *f.* convention; system

conversación *f.* conversation

conversar to converse

convertir (convierto) (i) to convert

convivencia cohabitation; living together

convivir to live together

coordinar to coordinate

copa (wine) glass; **Copa del Mundo** World Cup (*soccer*); **Copa Mundial** World Cup (*soccer*)

copia copy; **hacer copia** to copy

copiar to copy (12)

copioso/a copious

coquí *m. small frog of Puerto Rico*

corazón *m.* heart (11)

corbata tie (4)

cordillera mountain range

coreano/a *n., adj.* Korean

cormorán cormorant (*aquatic bird*)

coro chorus

corona crown

corporación *f.* corporation

correcto/a correct

corregir (corrijo) (i) to correct

correo mail

correo electrónico e-mail (12)

correr to run (10); **cinta de correr** treadmill

correspondencia correspondence

corresponder (a) to correspond (to)

correspondiente *m., f.* correspondent; *adj.* corresponding

corrido *Mexican folk song*

corriente: cuenta corriente checking account; **estar al corriente** to be up to date

cortar to cut

cortejo courting

cortés *m., f.* polite

cortesía courtesy; **expresión** (*f.*) **de cortesía** courteous expression (1)

cortijo country house

cortina curtain

corto *n.* short segment

corto/a short (*in length*) (3); **pantalones** (*m. pl.*) **cortos** shorts (4)

cosa thing (5)

cosecha harvest; crop

cosechar to harvest

cosmético/a cosmetic

cosmopolita *m., f.* cosmopolitan

cosmovisión *f.* world view

costa coast

costar (cuesto) to cost

costarricense *n., adj. m., f.* Costa Rican

costero/a coastal

costo cost

costoso/a expensive

costumbre *f.* custom

costura: de alta costura high fashion

cotidiano/a daily

country *m.* country music

creación *f.* creation

crear to create (13)
creatividad *f.* creativity
creativo/a creative
crecer (crezco) to grow (16)
crecimiento *n.* rise, growth
credencial *f.* identity card
crédito credit; **tarjeta de crédito** credit card (7)
creencia belief
creer (en) to think; to believe (in) (3); **no creer** to not think/believe (13)
creíble believable
crema cream
cremoso/a creamy
creyente *m., f.* believer
criado/a servant
criatura child
crimen *m. (pl. crímenes)* crime
criollo/a *n., adj.* creole
cristal *m.* glass
cristianismo Christianity
cristiano/a *n., adj.* Christian
Cristo Christ; **antes de Cristo (a.C.)** before Christ (B.C.); **después de Cristo (a.D.)** Anno Domini (A.D.)
crítica criticism
criticar (qu) to criticize
crítico/a critic
crónica chronicle
crónico/a chronic
cronológico/a chronological
croqueta croquette
crucero cruise (ship) (8)
crudo/a raw
cruz *f. (pl. cruces)* cross; **Día** *(m.)* **de la Cruz** Day of the Cross
cruzar (c) to cross; **cruzarse con** to cross paths with
cuaderno notebook (2)
cuadrado *n.* square
cuadrado/a *adj.* square
cuadro painting *(specific piece)* (13); **de cuadros** plaid (4)
cuajar to fit in
cual: el/la cual, lo cual, los/las cuales which
¿cuál(es)? what? (2); which? (2); **¿cuál es la fecha de hoy?** what's today's date? (6); **¿cuál es tu onda?** what's your style?
cualidad *f.* quality *(characteristic)*
cualquier *adj.* any
cuando when
¿cuándo? when? (2)
cuanto: en cuanto as soon as (17); **en cuanto a** regarding
¿cuánto? how much? (2); **¿cuánto cuesta(n)?** how much does it (do they) cost? (4); **¿cuánto tiempo hace que... ?** how long ago *(did something happen)*? / for how long *(has something been happening)*?

¿cuántos/as? how many? (2)
cuáquero/a *n.* Quaker
cuarenta forty (3)
Cuaresma Lent
cuartel *m.* barracks
cuarto room (2); one-fourth; quarter (of an hour); **compañero/a de cuarto** roommate (2); **menos cuarto** a quarter to *(hour)* (1); **y cuarto** a quarter (fifteen minutes) after *(the hour)* (1)
cuarto/a *adj.* fourth (13)
cuate *sl. m., f.* buddy, pal
cuatro four (1)
cuatrocientos/as four hundred (4)
cubano/a *n., adj.* Cuban
cubanoamericano/a *n., adj.* Cuban American
cubierto/a *(p.p. of* **cubrir***)* covered
cubiertos *m. pl.* cutlery
cubrir *(p.p.* **cubierto***)* to cover (15)
cucaracha cockroach
cuchara spoon
cucharada spoonful
cuchillo knife
cuello neck
cuenta check, bill (7); **cargar (gu) a una cuenta** to charge to an account (17); **cuenta corriente** checking account
cuento story
cuerda string
cuero leather (4); **de cuero** leather (4)
cuerpo (humano) (human) body (11)
cuervo crow
cuestión *f.* question *(issue)*; matter (17)
cuestionable questionable
cuestionario questionnaire
cuidado care; *interj.* careful!; **con cuidado** carefully; **tener cuidado** to be careful
cuidar a to care for; **cuidarse** to take care of oneself (11)
culebra snake
culinario/a culinary
culminar to culminate
culpa fault; **tener la culpa** to be at fault
cultivar to cultivate
cultivo cultivation
culto cult; **rendir (rindo) (i) culto** to worship
cultrún *m.* ceremonial Mapuche drum
cultura culture
cultural cultural; **tradición** *(f.)* **cultural** cultural tradition (13)
cumbia *Colombian folk dance now popular throughout Latin America*
cumbre *f.* summit
cumpleaños *m. inv.* birthday (6); **pastel** *(m.)* **de cumpleaños** birthday cake (9)
cumplir to fulfill; **cumplir años** to have a birthday (9)

cuñado/a brother-in-law, sister-in-law
cupo quota; capacity *(space)*
cupón *m.* coupon
cura cure
curación *f.* cure
curar to cure
curativo/a curing, curative
curioso/a curious
currículum *m.* résumé (17)
cursi in poor taste; trite
curso course; **programa** *(m.)* **del curso** course syllabus (14)
cuyo/a whose

D

dama lady
danza dance (13)
daño: hacerse daño to hurt oneself (14); **hacerse daño en** to hurt one's *(body part)* (14)
dar to give (8); **dar clases** to teach class; **dar un paseo** to take a walk (10); **dar una caminata** to hike; to go for a hike (10); **dar una fiesta** to throw a party (9); **darse con/contra** to run into; **darse la mano** to shake hands (11)
darwinista *m., f.* Darwinian
datar to date back to
datos *m. pl.* data; **base** *(f.)* **de datos** data base
de of (1); from (1); **de adolescente** *adj.* adolescent (10) **de algodón** *m. (made of)* cotton (4); **de alta costura** high fashion; **de alto riesgo** high risk; **de atrás** backwards; **de compras** shopping (4); **de cuadros** plaid (4); **de cuero** leather (4); **¿de dónde eres (tú)?** where are you *(fam. s.)* from? (1); **¿de dónde es usted?** where are you *(form. s.)* from? (1); **de estatura mediana** of medium height; **de exposición** expository; **de forma presencial** in person; **de la actualidad** currently, right now (10); **de la mañana** in the morning, A.M. (1); **de la noche** in the evening, P.M. (1); **de la tarde** in the afternoon, P.M. (1); **de lana** wool (4); **de lunares** polka-dot (4); **de manera que** so that, in such a way that; **de modo que** in such a way that; **de nada** you're welcome (1); **de niño/a** as a child (10); **de oro** gold (4); **de plata** silver (4); **¿de quién?** whose? (3); **de rayas** striped (4); **de remate** hopeless(ly); **de repente** suddenly (11); **de seda** silk (4); **de todo** everything (4); **de todo tipo** of all kinds; **de vacaciones** on vacation (8); **¿de veras?** really?; **de viaje** on a trip, traveling (8); **es de...** it is made of . . . (4)

debajo de below (6)

debate *m.* debate

debatir to debate

deber *n. m.* responsibility (18); obligation (18)

deber *v. + inf.* should, must, ought to (*do something*) (3)

debido/a a due to; because of

débito debit

década decade

decadencia decadence

decente decent

decidir to decide

décimo/a tenth (13)

decimotercer(o/a) thirteenth

decir to say; to tell (8); **eso quiere decir...** that means . . . (11)

decisión *f.* decision

declaración *f.* statement

declarar to state

decoración *f.* decoration

decorar to decorate

decorativo/a decorative

dedicarse (qu) (a) to dedicate oneself (to)

dedo (de la mano) finger (11); **dedo del pie** toe (11)

deducir (deduzco) (*like* **conducir**) to deduce

defender (defiendo) to defend

defensa defense

defensor(a) defender

deficiencia deficiency

deficiente deficient

definición *f.* definition

definido: artículo definido *gram.* definite article

definir to define

degustar to taste

dejar to leave; to let, allow; to quit (17); **dejar de** + *inf.* to stop (*doing something*) (11)

del (*contraction of* **de** + **el**) of the; from the (3)

delante de in front of (6)

delegación *f.* delegation

delfín *m.* dolphin

delgado/a thin, slender (3)

deliberado/a deliberate

delicia delicacy

delicioso/a delicious

delito crime (15)

demanda demand

demás: los/las demás the rest, others (12)

demasiado *adv.* too (9)

demasiado/a *adj.* too much (9); too many (9)

democracia democracy

demócrata *m., f.* democrat

democrático/a democratic

demonio demon, devil

demora delay (8)

demostración *f.* demonstration

demostrar (demuestro) to demonstrate

demostrativo/a *gram.* demonstrative (4)

denominación *f.* denomination

densidad *f.* density

denso/a dense (15)

dentista *m., f.* dentist (11)

dentro inside; **dentro de** inside; within; in (*time*)

departamento department

dependencia dependence

depender (de) to depend (on)

dependiente/a clerk (2)

deporte *m.* sport (10); **practicar (qu)** to play (*a sport*)

deportista *m., f.* athlete

deportivo/a *adj.* sporting, sports; sports-loving (10)

depositar to deposit (17)

depósito deposit

depresión *f.* depression

deprimido/a depressed

derecha *n.* right side; **a la derecha de** to the right of (6)

derecho right (18); **(todo) derecho** straight ahead (15)

derivación *f.* branch, offshoot

derivarse (de) to derive (from)

derramar to spill

desacuerdo disagreement

desafío challenge

desagradable disagreeable

desahogarse (gu) to let off steam; to vent

desamor *m.* lack of affection

desaparecer (desaparezco) to disappear

desarrollar to develop (15)

desarrollo development (15)

desastre *m.* disaster (14)

desastroso/a disastrous

desayunar to have (eat) breakfast (7)

desayuno breakfast (7)

descansar to rest (5)

descanso rest

descapotable: carro descapotable convertible (car) (15)

descargar (gu) to download (12)

descendiente *m., f.* descendent

descentralizado/a decentralized

descifrar to decipher; to figure out

desconectar to unplug; to disconnect

desconocido/a unknown

descontento/a unhappy

descortés *m., f.* rude, impolite

describir (*p.p.* **descrito**) to describe

descripción *f.* description

descriptivo/a descriptive

descrito/a (*p.p. of* **describir**) described

descubierto/a (*p.p. of* **descubrir**) discovered

descubrimiento discovery

descubrir (*p.p.* **descubierto**) to discover (15)

desde *prep.* from; since

desear to want (2)

desempleo unemployment

deseo wish

desequilibrio imbalance

desértico/a *adj.* desert

desesperanza desperation

desfile *m.* parade

desgracia misfortune; disgrace

desgraciadamente unfortunately (11)

deshumanización *f.* dehumanization

desierto desert

designación *f.* designation

designar to appoint; to designate

desigualdad *f.* inequality (18)

desilusión *f.* disillusion

desinflado/a: llanta desinflada flat tire (15)

desocupado/a empty; available

desordenado/a messy (6)

desorganizado/a unorganized

despacio *adv.* slowly

despedida farewell

despedir (*like* **pedir**) to let (*someone*) go (17); to fire (*someone*) (*from a job*) (17); **despedirse (de)** to say good-bye (to) (9)

despejado/a clear (*sky*)

desperdiciar to waste

desperdicio waste

despertador *m.* alarm clock (14)

despertarse (me despierto) to wake up (5)

despierto/a (*p.p. of* **despertar**) awake

despistado/a absent-minded; forgetful

después *adv.* afterwards (5); **después de** *prep.* after (5); **después de Cristo (a.D.)** Anno Domini (A.D.); **después (de) que** *conj.* after (17)

destacar (qu) to emphasize; **destacarse** to stand out

destino destination (8); destiny

destrucción *f.* destruction

destruir (*like* **construir**) to destroy (15)

desventaja disadvantage

detalle *m.* detail (9)

detective *m., f.* detective

detenerse (*like* **tener**) to stop

determinación *f.* determination

determinado/a specific

determinante decisive

determinar to determine

detestar to detest

detrás de behind (6)

deuda debt

devolver (*like* **volver**) to return (*something to someone*) (14)

devoto/a devout

día *m.* day (2); **buenos días** good morning (1); **Día de Acción de**

Gracias Thanksgiving; **Día de la Cruz** Day of the Cross; **Día de la Madre** Mother's Day; **Día de los Difuntos** Day of the Dead; **Día de los Muertos** Day of the Dead; **Día de San Patricio** St. Patrick's Day; **Día de San Valentín** St. Valentine's Day; **Día del Padre** Father's Day; **día festivo** holiday (9); **Día Internacional de la No Violencia Contra la Mujer** International No Violence Against Women Day; **días de la semana** days of the week (5); **estar al día** to be up to date (18); **¿qué día es hoy?** what day is today? (5); **todos los días** every day (2)

diabetes *f. inv.* **(juvenil)** (childhood) diabetes

diabético/a diabetic

diablo devil

diacrítico/a: acento diacrítico diacritical mark

diagnosticar (qu) to diagnose

diágrafo group of letters that represent a single sound

dialecto dialect

diálogo dialogue

diamante *m.* diamond

diariamente daily

diario/a daily (5)

dibujante *m., f.* comic strip artist (13)

dibujar to draw (13)

dibujo drawing (13); **dibujos** (*m. pl.*) **animados** cartoons

diccionario dictionary (2)

dicho saying

diciembre *m.* December (6)

dictador(a) dictator (18)

dictadura dictatorship (18)

dictar to dictate

diecinueve nineteen (1)

dieciocho eighteen (1)

dieciséis sixteen (1)

diecisiete seventeen (1)

diente *m.* tooth (5); **cepillarse los dientes** to brush one's teeth (5)

dieta dieta (7); **estar a dieta** to be on a diet (7)

dietético/a *adj.* diet

diez ten (1)

diferencia difference; **a diferencia de** unlike

diferenciado/a differentiated

diferente different

difícil hard, difficult (6)

dificultad *f.* difficulty

difundir to disseminate

difunto/a dead; **Día** (*m.*) **de los Difuntos** Day of the Dead

digestión *f.* digestion

digital digital; **brecha digital** digital gap

dígito digit

dignidad *f.* dignity

dilema *m.* dilemma

diligente diligent

dimensión *f.* dimension

diminutivo *gram. n.* diminutive

Dinamarca Denmark

dinero money (2); **sacar (qu) dinero** to withdraw money

dinoflagelado *type of marine plankton*

dios *m. s.* god; **Dios** God; **por Dios** for heaven's sake (14)

diosa goddess

diptongo *gram.* diphthong

dirección *f.* address (7)

directo direct; **complemento directo** *gram.* direct object

director(a) director; conductor (13)

directorio directory

dirigir (dirijo) to direct (13) (pido) (i)

discapacidad *f.* disability

discapacitado/a disabled

disco disc; **disco duro** hard drive (12)

discoteca discotheque; **ir a una discoteca** to go to a disco (10)

discriminación *f.* discrimination (18)

disculpa apology, excuse; **pedir (pido) (i) disculpas** to apologize (14)

disculpar to excuse, pardon; **disculpa, discúlpame** pardon me (*fam. s.*) (14); I'm sorry (*fam. s.*) (14), **disculpe, discúlpeme** pardon me (*form. s.*) (14); I'm sorry (*form. s.*) (14)

discurso speech

discusión *f.* argument; discussion

discutir (con/sobre) to argue (with/about) (9)

diseñador(a) designer

diseñar to design (13)

diseño design

disfraz *m.* (*pl.* **disfraces**) costume, disguise

disfrutar (de) to enjoy

disminuir (*like* **construir**) to diminish

disparar to shoot

dispensario clinic

disponible available

disposición *f.* disposition

dispositivo device

dispuesto/a ready; prepared (*to do something*)

disputarse to compete for

distancia distance

distante distant

distinción *f.* distinction

distintivo/a distinctive

distinto/a different

distracción *f.* distraction

distraer (*like* **traer**) to distract

distraído/a absentminded; distracted (14); **ir distraído/a** to be distracted (14)

distribuido/a distributed

distrito district

disuadir to dissuade

diversidad *f.* diversity

diversión *f.* fun activity (10)

diverso/a diverse

divertido/a fun; **ser divertido/a** to be fun (10)

divertirse (me divierto) (i) to have a good time; to enjoy oneself (5)

dividirse to be divided

divorciado/a (de) divorced (from) (16)

divorciarse (de) to get divorced (from) (16)

divorcio divorce (16)

divulgar (gu) to divulge

doblar to turn (15)

doble *m.* double

doce twelve (1)

dócil docile

doctor(a) doctor

doctorado doctorate

documento document

dólar *m.* dollar

doler (duele) (*like* **gustar**) to hurt; to ache (11)

dolor (*m.*) **(de)** pain, ache (in) (11); **dolor de cabeza** headache; **tener dolor de** to have a pain/ache in (11)

doméstico/a domestic, related to the home (10); domesticated, tame (15); **animal** (*m.*) **doméstico** pet; **aparato doméstico** home appliance (10); **tarea doméstica** household chore

domicilio home

dominación *f.* domination

dominar to control; to dominate

domingo Sunday (5)

dominicano/a *n., adj.* Dominican

dominio control

don *m. title of respect used with a man's first name*

donar to donate

donde where

¿dónde? where? (1); **¿de dónde eres (tú)?** where are you (*fam. s.*) from? (1); **¿de dónde es usted?** where are you (*form. s.*) from? (1)

doña *title of respect used with a woman's first name*

dormir (duermo) (u) to sleep (5); **dormir la siesta** to take a nap (5); **dormirse** to fall asleep (5)

dormitorio bedroom

dos two (1); **dos veces** twice (11)

doscientos/as two hundred (4)

drama *m.* drama (13)

dramático/a dramatic

dramatizar(c) to dramatize

dramaturgo/a playwright (13)

droga drug

dromedario dromedary

ducha *n.* shower

ducharse to take a shower (5)

duda *n.* doubt

dudar to doubt (12)

dudoso/a doubtful

duelo duel

dueño/a landlord, landlady (12); owner (7)

dulce *adj.* sweet

dulces *m. pl.* sweets; candy (7)

duración *f.* duration

duradero/a lasting

durante during (5)

durar to last (18)

duro/a hard; **disco duro** hard drive (12)

DVD *m.* DVD (12)

E

e and (used instead of **y** before words beginning with stressed **i** or **hi**, except **hie-**)

echar to throw out

ecocasa ecological house

ecología ecology

ecológico/a ecological

ecologista *m., f.* ecologist

economía economy; *s.* economics (2)

económico/a economical

economista *m., f.* economist

economizar (c) to economize (17)

ecoturismo ecotourism

ecoturista *m., f.* ecotourist

ecoturístico/a *adj.* ecotourist

ecuador *m.* equator

ecuatoguineano/a of or from Equatorial Guinea

ecuatoriano/a Ecuadoran

edad *f.* age

edificio building (2); **edificio de apartamentos** apartment building (12)

editar to edit

editorial *f.* publishing house

educación *f.* education

educador(a) educator

educarse (qu) to be educated

educativo/a educational

efectivo cash (17); **en efectivo** in cash (17)

efectivo/a effective

efecto effect

efectuar (efectúo) to carry out, execute

eficiencia efficiency

eficiente efficient

Egipto Egypt

egoísmo selfishness

egoísta *m., f.* selfish

ejecutivo/a *n., adj.* executive

ejemplar exemplary

ejemplificar (qu) to exemplify

ejemplo example; **por ejemplo** for example (14)

ejercer (ejerzo) to apply, exercise

ejercicio exercise (5); **hacer ejercicio** to exercise (5); **hacer ejercicios aeróbicos** to do aerobics (11)

ejército army (18)

el *def. art. m. s.* the; **el cual** which; **el lunes (martes...)** on Monday (Tuesday . . .) (5); **el primero de** the first of (month) (6); **el próximo (martes...)** next (Tuesday . . .) (5)

él *sub. pron.* he (2)

elaboración *f.* elaboration

elección *f.* choice; *pl.* election

electricidad *f.* electricity (12); electric bill (12)

electricista *m., f.* electrician (17)

eléctrico/a electrical; **energía eléctrica** electrical energy (15)

electrónica electronic equipment

electrónico/a electronic; **billete** (*m.*) (*Sp.*) / **boleto** (*L.A.*) **electrónico** e-ticket (8); **equipo electrónico** electronic equipment (12)

elefante *m.* elephant (15)

elegante elegant

elegir (elijo) (i) to select; to elect

elemento element

elevado/a high

elevador *m.* elevator

elevarse to rise

eliminar to eliminate

ella *sub. pron.* she (2)

ello: por ello therefore

ellos/as *sub. pron.* they (2); *obj. (of prep.)* them (2)

e-mail *m.* e-mail (12)

embarazada pregnant

embargo: sin embargo nevertheless

embarque: puerta de embarque boarding gate (8); **tarjeta de embarque** boarding pass (8)

emberá Embera person

emblema *m.* emblem

emblemático/a emblematic

embotellamiento traffic jam

embutido sausage

emergencia emergency

emigración *f.* emigration

emigrante *m., f.* emigrant

emigrar to emigrate

emisario/a emissary

emitir to emit

emoción *f.* emotion (9)

emocionado/a excited

emocional emotional

emocionante exciting

emocionarse to get excited

emoticono emoticon

empacar (qu) to pack

empanada *turnover pie or pastry*

emparedado sandwich

emparejar to match

empezar (empiezo) (c) to begin, start (5); **empezar a** + *inf.* to begin to (do something) (5) 1

empleado/a employee

empleador(a) employer

emplear to use to employ

empleo job, position (17); **empleo bien/ mal pagado** well-/poorly paid job/ position (17); **empleo de tiempo completo/parcial** full-/part-time job/ position (17)

empresa corporation (17); business (17); **administración** (*f.*) **de empresas** business administration (2)

empresario/a businessman/woman

en in (1); on (1); at (*a place*) (1); **en casa** at home (2); **en caso de** *prep.* in case (16); **en caso de que** *conj.* in case (16); **en cuanto** as soon as (17); **en efectivo** in cash (17); **en negrilla** boldface; **en onda** in style; **en punto** on the dot (*time*) (1); **en rebaja** on sale; **en resumen** in summary; **en seguida** immediately (5); **en vez de** instead of

enamorado/a (de) in love (with) (16)

enamorarse (de) to fall in love (with) (16)

enano/a dwarf

encantado/a pleased to meet you (1); enchanted

encantar (*like* **gustar**) to like very much; to love (8)

encanto charm

encapuchado/a hooded

encarcelado/a incarcerated

encargado/a in charge

encender (enciendo) to turn on (*appliance, machine*) (12); to light

encerado blackboard

encima de on top of (6)

encomendarse (me encomiendo) a to commend yourself to

encontrar (encuentro) to find (9); **encontrarse (con)** to meet (*someone somewhere*) (11)

encuentro encounter

encuesta survey

encuestar to survey

endeble unstable

endémico/a endemic

enemigo enemy

energía energy (15); **energía eléctrica** electrical energy (15); **energía eólica** wind energy (15); **energía nuclear** nuclear energy (15); **energía renovable** renewable energy (15); **energía solar** solar energy (15)

enérgico/a energetic

enero January (6)
enfado anger
énfasis *m. inv.* emphasis
enfático/a emphatic
enfatizar (c) to emphasize
enfermarse to get sick (11)
enfermedad *f.* illness, sickness (11)
enfermero/a nurse (11)
enfermo/a sick (6)
enfilado/a in a line
enfocar (qu) to focus
enfoque *m.* focus
enfrentar(se) (a) to face
enfrente de *prep.* in front of (*across from, facing*)
englobar to encompass
engordar to gain weight; to fatten
enhorabuena congratulations
enojado/a angry (9)
enojarse (con) to get angry (with) (9)
enorme enormous
enriquecer (enriquezco) to enrich
ensalada salad (7)
ensayista *m., f.* essayist
ensayar to test
ensayo essay
enseñanza teaching
enseñar to teach (2); **enseñar a** + *inf.* to teach to (*do something*)
ensuciarse to get dirty
entender (entiendo) to understand (5)
enterarse (de) to find out; to learn (about) (18)
entero/a entire
enterrado/a buried
entidad *f.* entity
entonces then (*in that case*)
entrada entrance; ticket (*for a show*)
entrante: año entrante next year
entrañable moving, touching
entrar to enter; **entrar en internet** to go on the internet (12); **entrar en Facebook** to go onto Facebook (12)
entre *prep.* between; among (6)
entregar (gu) to hand in (8)
entrenador(a) trainer, coach
entrenamiento training
entrenar to practice, train (10)
entresemana during the week
entrevista interview (17)
entrevistado/a interviewee (17)
entrevistador(a) interviewer (17)
entrevistar to interview
entusiasmar to enthuse
envase *m.* container
envenenar to poison
enviar (envío) to send
envidia envy
envuelto/a covered
eólico/a: energía eólica wind energy (15)

episodio chapter
epitafio epitaph
época era, time (*period*)
equilibrar to balance
equilibrio balance
equipaje *m.* baggage, luggage (8); **facturar el equipaje** to check baggage (8)
equipar to equip
equipo team (10); equipment (12); **equipo electrónico** electronic equipment (12)
equivalente *m.* equivalent
equivaler (*like* **salir**) to equal
equivocarse (qu) (de) to make a mistake (about) (14)
eructar to burp, belch
erupción *f.* eruption (18)
escala stop (8); **hacer escalas** to make stops (8)
escalador(a) climber
escalar to climb
escalera staircase; *pl.* stairs (14)
escándalo scandal
escanear to scan
escáner *m.* scanner (12)
escapar(se) (de) to escape (from)
escaparate *m.* store (display) window
escaso/a scarce
escena scene (13)
escenario stage (13); scenery (13)
esclavitud *f.* slavery
esclavo/a slave
esclusa lock (*of canal*)
escoba broom
escoger (escojo) to choose; to select
escolar *adj.* school
Escorpión *m.* Scorpio
escribir (*p.p.* **escrito**) to write (3)
escrito/a (*p.p. of* **escribir**) written (14); **informe** (*m.*) **escrito** written report (14)
escritor(a) writer (13)
escritorio desk (2)
escuálido/a scrawny
escuchar to listen (to) (2)
escuela school (10); **escuela primaria** elementary school; **escuela secundaria** high school; **maestro/a de escuela** schoolteacher (17)
esculpir to sculpt
escultor(a) sculptor (13)
escultura sculpture (13)
ese/a *adj.* that (4)
esencia essence
esencial essential
esfuerzo effort
eso (*neuter pron.*) that (4); **eso quiere decir...** that means . . . (11); **por eso** for that reason; that's why (3)
esos/as *adj.* those (4)

espacial *adj.* space; **nave** (*f.*) **espacial** spaceship; **transbordador** (*m.*) **espacial** space shuttle
espacio space; **espacio de almacenamiento** storage space (12)
espacioso/a spacious
espalda back
espantapájaros *m. inv.* scarecrow
espantar to scare
español *m.* Spanish (*language*) (2)
español(a) *n.* Spaniard; *adj.* Spanish (3)
espárragos *m. pl.* asparagus (7)
especial special
especialidad *f.* specialty
especialización *f.* major (*academic*); specialization
especializarse (c) (en) to major (in)
especie *f.* species (15); **especie en peligro de extinción** endangered species (15)
especificar (qu) to specify
específico/a specific
espectacular spectacular
espectáculo show (13)
espectador(a) spectator (13); *pl.* audience (13)
especulación *f.* speculation
espejo mirror
espera wait; **llamada de espera** call-waiting; **sala de espera** waiting room (8)
esperanza hope, wish (18)
esperar to wait (for) (7); to expect (7); to hope (12)
espeso/a thick
espinaca spinach
espíritu *m.* spirit
espiritual spiritual
esplendor *m.* splendor
esposado/a handcuffed
esposo/a husband/wife (3)
esqueleto skeleton
esquema *m.* outline
esquí *m.* skiing (10)
esquiador(a) skier
esquiar (esquío) to ski (10)
esquina (street) corner (15)
esta noche tonight (6)
estabilidad *f.* stability
estable stable
establecer (establezco) to establish
estación *f.* station (8); season (6); **estación de autobuses** bus station (8); **estación de radio** radio station (18); **estación de servicio** gas station (15); **estación de trenes** train station/(8)
estacionamiento parking place/lot (15)
estacionar to park (14)
estadio stadium
estadísticas *f. pl.* statistics
estadístico/a statistical

estado state (3); **estado afectivo** emotional state (9); **estado de ánimo** state of mind; **estado libre asociado** commonwealth; **Estados** (*m. pl.*) **Unidos de América** United States of America

estadounidense *n., adj.* of the United States of America (3)

estancia stay (*in a hotel*)

estante *m.* bookshelf (5)

estar to be (2); **¿cómo está?** how are you (*form. s.*)? (1); **¿cómo estás?** how are you (*fam. s.*)? (1); **está bien** it's fine, OK (6); **está de moda** it's trendy (hot) (4); **está (muy) nublado** it's (very) cloudy, overcast (6); **estar a dieta** to be on a diet (7); **estar al corriente** to be up to date; **estar al día** to be up to date (18); **estar bajo muchas presiones** to be under a lot of pressure (14); **estar bien** to be comfortable (*temperature*) (6); **estar casado/a (con)** to be married (to) (16); **(no) estar de acuerdo** to (dis)agree (3); **estar de vacaciones** to be on vacation (8); **(no) estar seguro/a de** to (not) be sure of (13)

estatal *adj.* state, of the government

estatua statue

estatura height; **de estatura mediana** of medium height

este *m.* east (6)

este/a *adj.* this (3)

estéreo stereo

estereotípico/a stereotypical

estereotipo stereotype

estético/a aesthetic

estilizado/a slender

estilo style

estimar to estimate

estipendio stipend

estipular to stipulate

estirar to stretch

esto (*neuter pron.*) this (3)

estómago stomach (11)

estornudo sneeze

estos/as *adj.* these (3)

estrategia strategy

estrecho *n.* straight; **Estrecho de Magallanes** Strait of Magellan

estrella star

estrépito crashing

estrés *m. inv.* stress (14)

estresado/a stressed out, under stress (14)

estresante stressful

estresar to cause stress

estricto/a strict

estrofa verse (*poem*)

estructura structure

estructurar to structure

estuario estuary

estudiantado student body

estudiante *m., f.* student (2)

estudiantil *adj.* (of) student(s)

estudiar to study (2)

estudio office (*in a home*) (5); studio (*television*) pl. studies (*education*)

estudioso/a studious

estufa stove (5)

estupendo/a stupendous

etapa stage, phase (16)

etcétera etcetera

eterno/a eternal

ético/a ethical

etnia ethnicity

étnico/a ethnic

etnolingüístico/a ethnolinguistic

Europa Europe

europeo/a *n., adj.* European

euskera *m.* Basque (*language*)

evaluación *f.* evaluation

evangélico/a *n., adj.* evangelical

evangelismo evangelism

evento event

evidencia evidence

evidente evident

evitar to avoid (15)

evolución *f.* evolution

exacto/a exact

exagerado/a exaggerated

examen *m.* exam, test (4)

examinar to examine

exceder to exceed

excelencia excellence

excelente excellent

excepción *f.* exception

excepcional exceptional

excepto except

excesivo/a excessive

exceso excess

exclamar to exclaim

excluir (*like* **construir**) to exclude

exclusivo/a exclusive

excursión *f.* excursion

excusa excuse

exigente demanding

exigir (exijo) to demand

exiliarse to go into exile

existencia existence

existir to exist

éxito success; **tener éxito** to be successful

exitoso/a successful

exótico/a exotic

expandir to expand

expectativa expectation

expedición *f.* expedition

experiencia experience

experto/a expert

expiatorio/a expiatory

explicación *f.* explanation

explicar (qu) to explain (8)

exploración *f.* exploration

explorador(a) explorer

explotación *f.* exploitation

explotar to exploit

exponer (*like* **poner**) (*p.p.* **expuesto**) to display; to propose

exportador(a) exporter

exportar to export

exposición *f.* exposition; **de exposición** expository

expresar to express

expresión *f.* expression; **expresión artística** artistic expression (13); **expresión de cortesía** courteous expression (1)

expresionista expressionist

expresivo/a expressive

expulsar to expel

expulsión *f.* expulsion

exquisito/a exquisite

extender (extiendo) to extend

extensión *f.* extension

externo/a external

extinción *f.* extinction; **especie** (*f.*) **en peligro de extinción** endangered species (15)

extinguirse (me extingo) to become extinct

extracto extract

extranjero/a *n.* foreigner (2); *adj.* foreign; **ir al extranjero** to go abroad (8); **lengua extranjera** foreign language (2)

extrañar to miss

extraño/a strange; **es extraño que** it's strange that (13); **¡qué extraño que... !** how strange that . . . ! (13)

extraordinario/a extraordinary

extravagante extravagant

extremo/a extreme

extrovertido/a extrovert(ed)

F

fábrica factory (15)

fabricar (qu) to manufacture (15)

fábula fable

fabuloso/a fabulous

Facebook *m.* Facebook (12); **entrar en Facebook** to go into Facebook (12)

fácil easy (6)

facilidad *f.* ease

facilitar to facilitate

factor *m.* factor

factura bill (17)

facturar el equipaje to check baggage (8)

facultad *f.* (*university*) department

falda skirt (4)

fallar to crash (*computer*) (12)

falso/a false

falta lack (15); absence (15)

faltar (a) to be absent (from); to not attend (9)

fama fame
familia family (3)
familiar *adj.* (of the) family
famoso/a famous
fantasía fantasy
fantasma *m.* ghost
fantástico/a fantastic
farmacéutico/a pharmacist (11)
farmacia pharmacy
faro lighthouse
fascinante fascinating
fascinar (*like* **gustar**) to fascinate (13)
fastidioso/a tedious
fatal *sl.* bad, awful
fatalista *m., f.* fatalist
fauna animal species
fauno faun
favor *m.* favor; **a favor de** in favor of; **por favor** please (1)
favorito/a favorite
fax *m.* FAX (12)
fe *f.* faith
febrero February (6)
fecha date (*calendar*) (6); **¿cuál es la fecha de hoy?** what's today's date? (6); **fecha límite** deadline; **¿qué fecha es hoy?** what's today's date? (6)
federación *f.* federation
federativo/a federative
felicidades *f. pl.* congratulations
felicitaciones *f. pl.* congratulations
felicitar to congratulate
feliz (*pl.* **felices**) happy (9)
femenino/a feminine
fenicio/a Phoenician
fénix *m.* phoenix
fenomenal phenomenal
fenómeno phenomenon
feo/a ugly (3)
feria fair
feriado/a: día (*m.*) **feriado** holiday
fertilidad *f.* fertility
festejar to celebrate
festividad *f.* festival
festivo/a festive, celebratory (9); **día** (*m.*) **festivo** holiday (9)
ficción *f.* fiction; **ciencia ficción** science fiction
ficticio/a fictitious
fiebre *f.* fever (11); **tener fiebre** to have a fever
fiel faithful (3)
fiesta party (2); **dar/hacer una fiesta** to have/give/throw a party (9); **fiesta patronal** party dedicated to a patron saint
fiestero/a happy; fond of parties
figura figure
fijarse (en) to notice
fijo/a set, fixed; **precio fijo** fixed, set price (4); **teléfono fijo** landline (12)

fila line
Filadelfia Philadelphia
filantrópico/a philanthropic
Filipinas *f. pl.* Philippines
filipino/a *n., adj.* Philippine
filmar to film; to record
filosofía philosophy (2)
filosófico/a philosophical
fin *m.* end; **a fines de** at the end of; **fin de año** end of the year (9); **fin de semana** weekend (2); **por fin** finally (5); **sin fines de lucro** non-profit
final *m.* end
finalmente finally (5)
financiar to finance
financiero/a financial
finanzas *f. pl.* finances
finca farm (15)
Finlandia Finland
fino/a fine
firmar to sign
física physics (2)
físico/a physical
flaco/a skinny
flamenco *music and dance form of southern Spain*
flan *m.* (baked) custard (7)
flauta flute
flexibilidad *f.* flexibility
flor *f.* flower (8)
flora plant species
flota fleet
folclore folklore
folclórico/a traditional (13)
folclorista *m., f.* folklorist
folklórico/a traditional
fomentar to encourage; to promote
fondo background; fund; bottom
fontanero/a plumber (*Sp.*)
forma form, shape (4); way; **de forma presencial** in person
formación *f.* formation; education, training
formar to form
formato format
formidable tremendous
fórmula formula
formulario form (17)
fortalecer (**fortalezco**) to strengthen
fortaleza fort
fosforescente phosphorescent
foto(grafía) photo(graph) (8); **sacar** (**qu**) **fotos** to take photos (8)
fotocopia photocopy (12); **hacer fotocopia** to copy (12)
fotocopiadora copy machine (12)
fotocopiar to photocopy
fotografía photography (13)
fotógrafo/a photographer (17)
fotomontaje *m.* photo montage
fragmentado/a fragmented
fragmento fragment; excerpt
francés *m.* French (*language*) (2)

francés, francesa *n.* French person; *adj.* French
Francia France
franja stripe, band; border, fringe
frase *f.* phrase; sentence
fraternidad *f.* fraternity
frecuencia frequency; **con frecuencia** frequently (2); **¿con qué frecuencia... ?** how often . . . ? (3)
frecuente frequent
frecuentemente frequently (11)
frenos *m. pl.* brakes (15)
frente a facing; **hacer frente a** to face up to
fresa strawberry
fresco: hace fresco it's cool (weather) (6)
fresco/a fresh (7)
frigorífico refrigerator
frijoles *m. pl.* beans (7)
frío cold(ness); *adj.* cold; **hace (mucho) frío** it's (very) cold (*weather*); **tener (mucho) frío** to be (very) cold (6)
frito/a fried (7); **papa/patata frita** French fried potato (7)
frituras *f. pl.* fried food
frontera border
frotar to rub
frustración *f.* frustration
frustrado/a frustrated
fruta fruit (7); **jugo de fruta** fruit juice (7)
frutería fruit store, stand
frutilla strawberry
fruto fruit
fuego fire
fuente *f.* source; fountain; serving dish
fuera *adv.* outside
fuerza force; **fuerzas** (*f. pl.*) **armadas** armed forces
fumador(a) smoker; **sala de fumadores** smoking area (8)
fumar to smoke (8); **sala de fumar** smoking area (8)
funcionamiento *n.* functioning, working
funcionar to work; to function (12); to run (*machines*) (12)
fundación *f.* foundation
fundador(a) founder
fundar to found
furia rage; **furia al volante** road rage; **furia caminera** road rage
furioso/a furious, angry (6)
fútbol *m.* soccer (10); **fútbol americano** football (10)
futbolista *m., f.* soccer player
futuro *n.* future
futuro/a *adj.* future

G

gabinete *m.* cabinet
gafas *f. pl.* glasses (4); **gafas de sol** sunglasses (4)

gaita *Colombian indigenous flute*
galán *m.* handsome man
gallego Galician (*language*)
galleta cookie (7)
gallo/a rooster, hen; **Misa del Gallo** Midnight Mass
galope *m. traditional dance of Paraguay*
galopera *traditional dance of Paraguay*
gambas *f. pl.* shrimp (*Sp.*)
ganador(a) winner
ganancia earning
ganar to win (10); to earn (*income*) (13)
ganas: tener ganas de + *inf.* to feel like (*doing something*) (4)
gandules *m. pl.* pigeon peas
ganga bargain (4)
garaje *m.* garage (5)
garantizar (c) to guarantee
garbanzos *m. pl.* chickpeas (7)
garganta throat (11)
garifunas *m. pl.* Black Caribs (*descendents of Carib indigenous people and African slaves in Honduras*)
gas *m.* gas (*not for cars*) (12)
gaseosa soft drink
gasolina gasoline (15)
gasolinera gas station (15)
gastar to spend (*money*) (9); to use (*gas*) (15)
gasto expense (12)
gastronómico/a gastronomic
gato cat (3)
gaucho *Argentine cowboy*
gazpacho *cold tomato soup of southern Spain*
gemelo/a twin
genealógico/a: árbol (*m.*) **genealógico** family tree
generación *f.* generation
general general; **en general** in general; **por lo general** generally (5)
generar to generate; to create
genérico/a generic
género genre; gender
generosidad *f.* generosity
generoso/a generous
gente *f. s.* people (8)
genuinamente genuinely
geografía geography
geográfico/a geographic
geología geology
geométrico/a geometric
gerente *m., f.* manager (17)
gerundio *gram.* gerund
gigante *adj.* giant
gimnasio gym(nasium)
ginecólogo/a gynecologist
gira tour
gitano/a *n., adj.* gypsy
globalización *f.* globalization
gobernador(a) governor

gobierno government (15)
gol *m.* goal (*soccer*)
golf *m.* golf (10)
golfo gulf
golpe *m.* blow; **golpe de estado** coup d'état
gordo/a fat (3)
gorila *m.* gorilla (15)
gorra baseball cap (4)
gótico/a Gothic
GPS *m.* GPS (12)
grabadora (tape) recorder/player
grabar to record (12); to tape (12)
gracia grace
gracias thank you (1); **Día** (*m.*) **de Acción de Gracias** Thanksgiving; **gracias por** + *noun/inf.* thanks for (9); **muchas gracias** thank you very much (1)
grado grade, year (*in school*); degree (*temperature*)
graduarse (me gradúo) (en) to graduate (from) (17)
gráfico/a graphic
grafiti *m.* graffiti
gramática grammar
gramo gram
gran, grande large, big; great (3); **Gran Bretaña** Great Britain; **pantalla grande** big screen (monitor) (12)
granero barn
granizo hail
granja farm
grano grain
grasa fat
gratis *inv.* free (of charge)
gratuito/a free (of charge)
grave serious
Grecia Greece
griego/a *n., adj.* Greek
grifo faucet
gripa flu (*Mex.*)
gripe *f.* flu (11)
gris gray (4)
gritar to shout
grito shout; cry
grueso/a thick
grupo group; band
guagua bus (*Carib.*)
guaguanco *subgenre of rumba*
guampa *cup made from a hollowed bull's horn used to drink* mate; *cup used to drink* **tereré**
guanábana soursop (*tropical fruit*)
guancasco *traditional dance of the Lenca of Honduras*
guante *m.* glove
guapo/a handsome; good-looking (3)
guaraní *m. indigenous language of South America*
guardacostas *m. inv.* Coast Guard

guardar to keep (12); to save (*documents*) (12); **guardar cama** to stay in bed (11); **guardar un puesto** to save a place (*in line*) (8)
guatemalteco/a *n., adj.* Guatemalan
gubernamental governmental
guerra war (18); **guerra civil** civil war
guerrero/a warrior
guía *m., f.* guide (13)
guiado/a guided
guion *m.* script (13)
güiro *Latin American musical instrument*
guitarra guitar
guitarrista *m., f.* guitarist
gustar to be pleasing (8); **¿a usted le gusta... ?** do you (*form. s.*) like . . . ? (1); **me gustaría (mucho)...** I would (really) like . . . (8); **(no,) no me gusta** (no,) I don't like . . . (1); **(sí,) me gusta...** (yes,) I like . . . (1); **¿te gusta... ?** do you (*fam. s.*) like . . . ? (1)
gusto like preference; *pl.* likes (1); **mucho gusto** nice to meet you (1)

H

haber (*inf. of* **hay**) there is, there are; to have (*aux. verb*) (12)
habichuelas *f. pl.* beans
habilidad *f.* ability
habitación *f.* bedroom
habitante *m., f.* inhabitant
habitar to inhabit
hábito habit
hablante *m., f.* speaker
hablar to speak; to talk (2); **hablar con soltura** to speak fluently; **hablar por teléfono** to talk on the phone (2)
hacer to do; to make (5); **hace** + *time* + **que** + *present* to have been (*doing something*) for (*time*) (14); **hace** + *time* + **que** + *preterite* ago (14); *present* + **desde hace** + *time* to have been (*doing something*) for (*time*) (14); *preterite* + **hace** + *time* ago (14); **hace (muy) buen/mal tiempo** it's very good/bad weather (6); **hace (mucho) calor** it's (very) hot (weather) (6).; **hace fresco** it's cool (weather) (6).; **hace (mucho) frío** it's (very) cold (*weather*); **hacer autostop** to hitchhike; **hacer** *camping* to go camping (8); **hacer clic** to click (12) **hacer cola** to stand in line (8); **hacer (foto)copia** to copy (12); **hacer (el método) Pilates** to do Pilates (11); **hacer (el) yoga** to do yoga (10); **hacer ejercicio** to exercise (5); **hacer ejercicios aeróbicos** to do aerobics (11); **hacer escalas** to make stops (8); **hacer frente a** to face up to; **hacer la cama** to make the bed (10); **hacer la(s) maleta(s)** to pack

one's suitcase(s) (8); **hacer paradas** to make stops (8); **hacer planes** (*m.*) **para** + *inf.* to make plans to (*do something*) (10); **hacer reserva** to make a reservation; **hacer *surfing*** to surf (10); **hacer un *picnic*** to have a picnic (10); **hacer un viaje** to take a trip (5); **hacer una fiesta** to have/throw a party (9); **hacer una juerga** to throw a party; **hacer una pregunta** to ask a question (5); **hacerse daño** to hurt oneself (14); **hacerse daño en** to hurt one's (*body part*) (14); **¿qué tiempo hace?** what's the weather like? (6)

hacia *prep.* towards

hada (*but* **el hada**) fairy

hallaca *Venezuelan meat pastry*

hamaca hammock

hambre *f.* hunger; **pasar hambre** to go hungry; **tener (mucha) hambre** to be (very) hungry (7)

hamburguesa hamburger (7)

harina flour

hasta *adv.* until; even; *prep.* until; **hasta luego** see you later (1); **hasta mañana** see you tomorrow (1); **hasta pronto** see you soon; **hasta que** until (17)

hay there is/are (1); **hay que** + *inf.* it is necessary to (*do something*) (13); **no hay** there is/are not (1); **no hay de qué** you're welcome (1)

hebreo Hebrew (*language*)

hecho *n.* fact; event (9)

hecho/a (*p.p. of* **hacer**) made

hectárea *land measure equal to 2.5 acres*

helado ice cream (7)

heliconia *flowering tropical plant*

hemisferio hemisphere

herbolario/a herbalist

heredar to inherit

herencia inheritance

hermanastro/a stepbrother, stepsister

hermano/a brother/sister (3); *m. pl.* siblings (3)

hermoso/a beautiful

héroe *m.* hero

heroína heroine

hervir (hiervo) (i) to boil

híbrido/a hybrid (15)

hidalgo nobleman

hidroeléctrico/a hydroelectric

hielo ice

hierba grass

hígado liver

hijastro/a stepson, stepdaughter

hijo/a son/daughter (3); *m. pl.* children (3)

himno hymn; **himno nacional** national anthem

hipopótamo hippopotamus

hispánico/a Hispanic

hispano/a Hispanic (3)

Hispanoamérica Hispanic America

hispanoamericano/a *adj.* Hispanic American

hispanohablante *adj. m., f.* Spanish-speaking

historia history (2); story (8)

historiador (a) historian

histórico/a historical

hockey *m.* hockey (10)

hogar *m.* home

hoja leaf

¡hola! hi!; hello! (1)

Holanda Holland

hombre *m.* man (2); **hombre de negocios** businessman (17)

homeópata *m., f.* homeopath

homeopático/a homeopathic

homogeneidad *f.* homogeneity

homogéneo/a homogenous

hondureño/a *n., adj.* Honduran

honesto/a honest

hongo mushroom; toadstool; fungus; **sombrero hongo** bowler hat, derby

honor *m.* honor

honrado/a honest; honorable

hora hour; time; **¿a qué hora... ?** at what time . . . ? (1); **es hora de... ** it's time to . . . ; **hora punta** peak hour **¿qué hora es?** what time is it? (1)

horario schedule (14)

horchata *Mexican drink made from rice*

hormona hormone

horno oven; **horno de microondas** microwave oven (10)

horóscopo horoscope

horror *m.* horror

hospital *m.* hospital

hospitalario/a hospitable

hospitalidad *f.* hospitality

hospitalización *f.* hospitalization

hotel *m.* hotel

hoy today (1); **¿cuál es la fecha de hoy?** what's today's date? (6); **¿qué día es hoy?** what day is today? (5); **¿qué fecha es hoy?** what's today's date? (6)

huelga strike (*labor*) (18)

huella mark; (finger)print

huerto orchard

hueso bone

huésped *m., f.* guest

huevo egg (7)

huipil *m. traditional Mayan blouse*

huir (*like* **construir**) to flee

humanidad *f.* humanity; *pl.* humanities (2)

humanista *n., adj.* humanist

humanitario/a humanitarian

humanizar (c) to make more human

humano/a human (11); **cuerpo humano** human body (11); **ser** (*m.*) **humano** human being

humedad *f.* humidity

húmedo/a humid

humilde humble

humorístico/a humorous

huracán *m.* hurricane

I

ibérico/a *adj.* Iberian

íbero/a *n.* Iberian

icónico/a iconic

ícono icon

ida: billete (*m.*) (*Sp.*) / **boleto** (*L.A.*) **de ida** one-way ticket (8); **billete** (*m.*) (*Sp.*) / **boleto** (*L.A.*) **de ida y vuelta** round-trip ticket (8)

idealista *m., f.* idealistic

idear to think up: to conceive (*idea*)

idéntico/a identical

identidad *f.* identity; **carnet** (*m.*) **de identidad** identification card

identificación *f.* identification; **carnet** (*m.*) **de identificación** identification card; **tarjeta de identificación** identification card (14)

identificar (se) (qu) to identify (oneself)

idioma *m.* language

idiomático/a idiomatic

ídolo idol

iglesia church (16)

ignorante ignorant

ignorar to ignore

igual same; equal

igualdad *f.* equality (18)

igualitario/a egalitarian

igualmente likewise; same here (1)

ilimitado/a unlimited

ilógico/a illogical

iluminar to light up

ilusorio/a false

ilustrar to illustrate

ilustrativo/a illustrative

imagen *f.* image (13)

imaginación *f.* imagination

imaginar(se) to imagine

imaginativo/a imaginative

imitar to imitate

impaciente impatient

impacto impact

impedimento impediment

impedir (*like* **pedir**) to impede

imperfecto *gram.* imperfect

imperio empire

impermeable *m.* raincoat (4); *adj.* impermeable

impertinente impertinent
implementar to implement
implicar (qu) to imply
imponer (*like* **poner**) to impose
importancia importance
importante important
importar (*like* **gustar**) to matter; to be important
imposible impossible (13); **es imposible que** it's impossible that (13); **no es imposible que** it's not impossible (13)
impresión *f.* impression
impresionante impressive
impresionar to impress
impreso/a printed
impresora printer (12)
imprimir to print (12)
improbable unlikely (13); **es improbable que** it's unlikely, improbable that (13); **no es improbable que** it's not improbable (13)
improvisar to improvise
impuesto tax
impulsivo/a impulsive
inalámbrico/a wireless
inauguración *f.* inauguration
inca *n. m., f.* Inca; *adj. m., f.* Incan
incaico/a *adj.* Inca
incapacidad *f.* inability
incendio fire
incidente *m.* incident
incienso incense
inclinación *f.* inclination
inclinarse to lean
incluir (*like* **construir**) to include
incómodo/a uncomfortable
incompleto/a incomplete
inconcebible inconceivable
inconveniencia inconvenience
inconveniente *n. m; adj.* inconvenient
incorporar to incorporate; to include
incorrecto/a incorrect
incrédulo/a incredulous
increíble incredible (13); **es increíble que** it's incredible that (13)
incrementar to increase
incremento increment
indefinido/a indefinite; **artículo indefinido** *gram.* indefinite article; **palabra indefinida y negativa** *gram.* indefinite and negative word (7)
indeleble indelible
independencia independence
independiente independent
independizarse (c) to become independent
indescriptible indescribable
indicación *f.* instruction; direction
indicar (qu) to indicate
indicativo *gram.* indicative

índice *m.* index
Índico Indian (Ocean)
indiferente indifferent
indígena *n. m., f.* indigenous person; *adj. m., f.* indigenous
indigenista *m., f. pertaining to indigenous topics and themes*
indio/a *n., adj.* Indian
indirecto/a indirect; **complemento indirecto** *gram.* indirect object
indiscreto/a indiscreet
indispensable indispensible, essential
indistinto/a indistinct
individualidad *f.* individuality
individuo *n.* individual
individuo/a *adj.* individual
industria industry
inesperado/a unexpected
inexistente nonexistent
infancia infancy; childhood (16)
infantil *adj.* child, children's
infatigable tireless
infección *f.* infection
inferir (infiero) (i) to infer
infiltrarse to infiltrate
infinitivo *gram.* infinitive
inflexibilidad *f.* inflexibility
influencia influence
influir (*like* **construir**) to influence
influyente influential
infografía computer graphic
información *f.* information
informar to inform (18)
informática computer science
informativo/a informative
informe *m.* **(oral/escrito)** (oral/written) report (14)
infraestructura infrastructure
infrecuente infrequent
infusión *f.* infusion
ingeniería engineering
ingeniero/a engineer (17)
ingenioso/a ingenious
Inglaterra England
inglés *m.* English (*language*) (2)
inglés, inglesa *n., adj.* English (3)
ingrediente *m.* ingredient
ingresar to deposit (*in an account*)
ingreso income
inicial *f.* initial (*letter*)
iniciar to start
iniciativa initiative
inicio beginning
injusticia injustice
injusto/a unfair
inmediato/a immediate
inmenso/a immense
inmerso/a immersed
inmigración *f.* immigration
inmigrante *n., m., f.* immigrant
inmobiliario/a *adj.* real estate; property

inmóvil unmoving
innecesario/a unnecessary
innumerable countless
inocente innocent
inolvidable unforgettable
inquilino/a tenant (12); renter (12)
inscribir(se) (*p.p.* **inscrito**) **(en)** to sign up; to register (for)
inscripción *f.* inscription
inscrito/a (*p.p. of* **inscribir**) registered
insecto insect
insistir (en) to insist (on) (12)
insoportable unbearable
inspiración *f.* inspiration
instalación *f.* facility
instalar to install (12)
instantáneo/a instantaneous
instante: al instante right away
institución *f.* institution
instituto institute
instrucciones *f., pl.* instructions
instructor(a) instructor
instrumento instrument
insulina insulin
insulto insult
integración *f.* integration
integrarse to integrate oneself
intelectivo/a cognitive
intelectual intellectual
inteligencia intelligence
inteligente intelligent (3)
intención *f.* intention
intencionadamente intentionally
intensidad *f.* intensity
intensificar (qu) to intensify
intenso/a intense
intentar to attempt to
interacción *f.* interaction
interactivo/a interactive
intercambiar to exchange
intercambio exchange
interés *m.* interest (17)
interesante interesting
interesar (*like* **gustar**) to interest (*someone*) (8)
intergaláctico/a intergalactic
interior interior; inner; **ropa interior** underwear (4)
intermedio/a intermediate
interminable endless
internacional international; **Día** (*m.*) **Internacional de la No Violencia Contra la Mujer** International No Violence Against Women Day
internauta *m., f.* internet user
internet *m.* internet (12); **buscar (qu) en internet** to look for on the internet (12); **entrar en internet** to go on the internet (12)
interno/a internal
interplanetario/a interplanetary

interpretación *f.* interpretation
interpretar to interpret
interrogación: signo de interrogación question mark
interrogativo/a *gram.* interrogative (1)
interrumpir to interrupt
interrupción *f.* interruption
intervención *f.* intervention
intimidad *f.* intimacy
íntimo/a intimate; close
intolerancia intolerance
intranquilidad *f.* restlessness
introducción *f.* introduction
introducir (*like* **conducir**) to introduce
inundación *f.* flood
inútil useless
invadido/a invaded
inválido/a disabled
invasión *f.* invasion
invasor(a) *adj.* invading
inventar to invent
inversión *f.* investment
invertir (invierto) (i) to invest
investigación *f.* investigation; research
investigador(a) researcher
investigar (gu) to investigate; to research
invierno winter (6)
invitación *f.* invitation
invitado/a guest (9)
invitar to invite (7)
invocar (qu) to invoke
inyección *f.* injection (11); **ponerle una inyección** to give (*someone*) a shot (11)
iPhone *m.* iPhone (12)
iPod *m.* iPod (12)
ir to go (4); **ir a** + *inf.* to be going to (*do something*) (4); **ir a un bar** to go to a bar (10); **ir a un concierto** to go to a concert (10); **ir a una discoteca** to go to a disco (10); **ir al extranjero** to go abroad (8); **ir de compras** to go shopping (4); **ir de safari** to go on a safari; **ir de vacaciones a...** to go on vacation in/to . . . (8); **ir distraído/a** to be distracted (14); **ir en...** to go/travel by . . . (8); **ir en autobús** to go/travel by bus (8); **ir en avión** to go/travel by plane (8); **ir en barco** to go/travel by boat, ship (8); **ir en tren** to go/travel by train (8); **irse** to leave; **vamos** let's go (4)
ira al manejar road rage
iraní (*pl.* **iraníes**) *n., adj.* Iranian
iraquí (*pl.* **iraquíes**) *n., adj.* Iraqi
iridiscencia iridescence
Irlanda Ireland
irlandés, irlandesa *n., adj.* Irish
ironía irony
irónico/a ironic
irresponsable irresponsible
isla island (6)

Islandia Iceland
islote *m.* islet
israelí (*pl.* **israelíes**) *n., adj.* Israeli
Italia Italy
italiano Italian (*language*) (2)
italiano/a *n., adj.* Italian
itinerario itinerary
-ito/a *diminuitive suffix* (10)
izquierda *n.* left-hand side; **a la izquierda de** to the left of (6)
izquierdo/a *adj.* left; **levantarse con el pie izquierdo** to get up on the wrong side of the bed (14)

J

jaguar *m.* jaguar
jamaica hibiscus
jamás never (7)
jamón *m.* ham (7)
Japón *m.* Japan
japonés *m.* Japanese (*language*)
japonés, japonesa *n., adj.* Japanese
jarabe *m.* (cough) syrup (11)
jardín *m.* garden (5)
jarra jar
jazz *m.* jazz
jeans *m. pl.* blue jeans (4)
jefe/a boss
jerarquía hierarchy
jersey *m.* sweater; pullover
jirafa giraffe
jornada de tiempo parcial part-time job
joropo *folkloric music of Venezuela*
joven *n. m., f.* (*pl.* **jóvenes**) youth; *adj.* young (3); **de joven** as a youth (10)
joyería jewelry
jubilarse to retire (17)
judaísmo Judaism
juego game; **Juegos Olímpicos** Olympic Games
juerga party; **hacer una juerga** to have/throw a party
jueves *m. inv.* Thursday (5)
jugador(a) player (10)
jugar (juego) (gu) (a, al) to play (*a game, sport*) (5); **jugar a las cartas / al ajedrez / a los videojuegos** to play cards/chess/videogames (10)
jugo (de fruta) (fruit) juice (7)
juguete *m.* toy
julio July (6)
junio June (6)
junto a *prep.* near
juntos/as together (8)
jurar to swear (*oath*)
justicia justice
justificación *f.* justification
justificar (qu) to justify
justo/a fair
juvenil *adj.* youth; youthful; **diabetes** (*f.*) **juvenil** childhood diabetes
juventud *f.* youth (16)

juzgar (gu) to judge

K

kaki: color (*m.*) **kaki** khaki
kilo(gramo) kilo(gram)
kilómetro kilometer

L

la *def. art. f. s.* the; *d.o. f. s.* you (*form.*); her, it; **a la(s)...** at . . . (*time of day*) (1); **la cual** which
labor *f.* work, job
laboral *adj.* work, work-related (17)
laboratorio laboratory
lácteo/a *adj.* dairy
lado side; **al lado de** alongside of (6); **por el otro lado** on the other hand; **por un lado** on one hand
ladrar to bark
ladrón, ladrona thief
lagarto lizard
lago lake (15)
lágrima tear
lamentar to regret; to feel sorry (13)
laminado/a laminated
lámpara lamp (5)
lana wool (4); **de lana** wool (4)
langosta lobster (7)
lapicero pen
lápiz *m.* (*pl.* **lápices**) pencil (2)
largo/a long (3)
las *def. art. s. pl.* the; *d.o. f. pl.* you (*form. pl.*); **a la(s)...** at . . . (*time of day*) (1); **las cuales** which
lasaña lasagne
lástima shame; **es una lástima que** it's a shame that (13); **¡qué lástima que... !** what a shame that . . . ! (13)
lastimarse to hurt (*a body part*) (14)
lata can
latín *m.* Latin (*language*)
latino/a *adj.* Latin; **América Latina** Latin America
Latinoamérica Latin America
latinoamericano/a *n., adj.* Latin American
lavabo (bathroom) sink (5)
lavadora washing machine (10)
lavandería laundry
lavaplatos *m. inv.* dishwasher (10)
lavar to wash (10); **lavarse** to wash (oneself)
lealtad *f.* loyalty
lección *f.* lesson
leche *f.* milk (7)
lechón *m.* suckling pig; **lechón asado** roast suckling pig
lechuga lettuce (7)
lector(a) reader
lectura reading
leer (*like* **creer**) to read (3)
legislación *f.* legislation
legumbre *f.* legume

lejos *adv.* far; **lejos de** *prep.* far from (6)
lema *m.* motto
lempira *currency of Honduras*
lengua language (2); tongue (11); **lenguas extranjeras** foreign languages (2); **sacar (qu) la lengua** to stick out one's tongue (11)
lentes *m. pl.* glasses (11); **lentes de contacto** contact lenses (11)
lentillas *f. pl.* contact lenses (*Sp.*)
lento/a slow
león *m.* lion; **león marino** sea lion
leopardo leopard
letra letter (*of the alphabet*); lyrics (*song*) (7)
levantar to raise; to lift; **levantar pesas** to lift weights (11); **levantarse** to get up (out of bed) (5); to stand up (5); **levantarse con el pie izquierdo** to get up on the wrong side of the bed (14)
leve *adj.* light
ley *f.* law (18)
leyenda legend
libanés, libanesa lebanese
liberar(se) to free (oneself)
libertad *f.* freedom, liberty
libertador(a) liberator
libra pound (*measurement*)
libre free, unoccupied (10); **al aire** (*m.*) **libre** outdoors (10); **estado libre asociado** commonwealth; **libre comercio** free trade; **ratos** (*m. pl.*) **libres** spare (free) time (10); **tiempo libre** free time (10)
librería bookstore (2)
libro book (2); **libro de texto** textbook (2)
licencia license (15); **licencia de manejar/conducir** driver's license (15)
licor *m.* liqueur
licuar (licúo) to liquefy
líder *m., f.* leader
liga league
ligero/a light, not heavy (7)
lima lime
limeño/a *adj.* from Lima, Peru
limitación *f.* limitation
limitar to limit
límite *m.* limit; **fecha límite** deadline; **límite de velocidad** speed limit (15)
limón *m.* lemon
limonada lemonade
limonero lemon tree
limosina limousine
limpiar (la casa) to clean (the) house (10)
limpieza cleanliness
limpio/a clean (6)
lindo/a pretty

línea line
lingüístico/a linguistic
linterna flashlight
lío problem; trouble; **meterse en líos** to get into trouble
liquidación *f.* liquidation
líquido liquid
Lisboa Lisbon
lista list
listo/a smart; clever (3); **estar listo/a** to be ready
literario/a literary
literatura literature (2)
litoral *m.* coast
llamada call; **bloqueo de llamadas** call blocker
llamar to call (7); **¿cómo se llama usted?** what is your (*form. s.*) name? (1); **¿cómo te llamas?** what is your (*fam. s.*) name? (1); **llamarse** to be called (5); **me llamo...** my name is . . . (1) **llamarse** to be called (5)
llanero Venezuelan cowboy
llanero/a of or pertaining to the plains
llano *n.* plain
llanta (desinflada) (flat) tire (15)
llanura *n.* plain
llave *f.* key (5)
llegada arrival (8)
llegar (gu) to arrive (3); **¿cómo se llega a... ?** how do you get to . . . ? (15); **llegar a ser** to become
llenar to fill (up) (15); to fill out (*a form*) (17)
lleno/a full
llevar to wear (4); to carry (4); to take (4); **llevar una vida sana/tranquila** to lead a healthy/calm life (11); **llevarse bien/mal (con)** to get along well/poorly (with) (16)
llorar to cry (9)
llover (llueve) to rain (6); **llueve** (it's raining) (6)
lluvia rain
lluvioso/a *adj.* rainy; of rain; **bosque** (*m.*) **tropical lluvioso** tropical rain forest
lo *d.o. m. s.* you (*form.*); him; it; **lo bueno** the good news/thing (11); **lo cual** which; **lo malo** the bad news/thing (11); **lo que** what, that which (5); **lo siento (mucho)** I'm (very) sorry (14); **lo suficiente** enough (11); **por lo general** generally (5); **por lo menos** at least (9); **por lo regular** in general
lobo/a wolf
localidad *f.* ticket (*to movie, play*)
localización *f.* location
loco/a crazy (6)
locutor(a) commentator
lógico/a logical
logotipo logo

lograr to achieve
logro achievement
Londres London
longitud *f.* longitude
los *def. art. m. pl.* the; *d.o. m. pl.* you (*form. pl.*) them; **los cuales** which; **los lunes (los martes...)** on Mondays (Tuesdays . . .) (5)
lotería lottery
lubricar (qu) to lubricate
lucha fight, struggle (18)
luchar to fight (18)
lucro: sin fines de lucro non-profit
luego then, afterward, next (5); **hasta luego** see you later (1)
lugar *m.* place (2)
lujo luxury
lujoso/a luxurious
luminiscente luminescent
luminoso/a lit up
luna moon; **luna de miel** honeymoon (16)
lunares: de lunares polka-dot (4)
lunes *m. inv.* Monday (5); **el lunes** on Monday (5); **los lunes** on Mondays (5); **el lunes que viene** next Monday (5)
Luxemburgo Luxembourg
luz *f.* (*pl.* **luces**) light (14)

M

madera wood
madrastra stepmother
madre *f.* mother (3); **Día** (*m.*) **de la Madre** Mother's Day
madrileño/a of or pertaining to Madrid
madrina godmother
madrugada dawn
madurez *f.* middle age (16)
maduro/a mature
maestría master's degree
maestro/a (de escuela) schoolteacher (17); *adj.* master; **obra maestra** masterpiece (13)
Magallanes: Estrecho de Magallanes Strait of Magellan
mágico/a *adj.* magic
magnífico/a magnificent
mago wizard
mahones *m. pl.* jeans
maíz *m.* (*pl.* **maíces**) corn
mal *adv.* poorly (2); **caerle mal a alguien** to make a bad impression on someone; **empleo mal pagado** poorly paid job/position (17); **llevarse mal (con)** to get along poorly (with) (16); **pasarlo mal** to have a bad time (9); **portarse mal** to misbehave (9); **salir mal** to come/turn out badly; to do poorly (5)
mal, malo/a *adj.* bad (3); **lo malo** the bad news/thing (11); **tener mala**

suerte to have bad luck; to be unlucky (14)
maleducado/a spoiled
malestar *m.* discomfort
maleta suitcase (8); **hacer la(s) maleta(s)** to pack one's suitcase(s) (8)
maletero porter (8)
malvado/a evil
mamá mother, mom (3)
mami mom, mommy
mamífero mammal
mancha stain
mandar to send (2); to order (*someone to do something*) (12); **mandar un mensaje** to (send a) text (2)
mandarín *m.* Mandarin (*language*)
mandato command (7)
manejar to drive (12); to operate (a *machine*) (12); **ira al manejar** road rage; **licencia de manejar** driver's license (15)
manera way, manner; **de manera que** so that, in such a way that
manga sleeve
manifestación *f.* demonstration, march (18)
maniquí *m.* mannequin
mano *f.* hand (11); **darse la mano** to shake hands (11)
mansión *f.* mansion
mantener (*like* tener) to maintain; to keep (18); **mantenerse en contacto** to stay in touch
mantequilla butter (7)
manzana apple (7); (city) block
mañana tomorrow (1); **de la mañana** in the morning, A.M. (1); **hasta mañana** see you tomorrow (1); **pasado mañana** the day after tomorrow (5); **por la mañana** in the morning (2)
mapa *m.* map
mapudungun *m. language of the Mapuche people*
máquina machine
mar *m.* sea (8); **mar Caribe** Caribbean Sea
maracuyá *m.* passion fruit
maratón *m.* marathon
maravilla wonder, marvel
maravillar to delight
maravilloso/a marvelous
marca brand; label
marcar (qu) to mark
marcial martial
mareado/a dizzy (11); nauseated (11)
marido husband (3)
marihuana marijuana
marinera *folkloric dance of coastal Peru*
marino/a marine; **león** (*m.*) **marino** sea lion

mariscos *m. pl.* shellfish (7)
marítimo/a maritime; sea, marine
marketing m. marketing
marrón *adj., m., f.* brown
martes *m. inv.* Tuesday (5); **los martes** on Tuesdays (5)
Maruecos Morocco
marzo March (6)
más more (2); **cada vez más** increasingly; **más de** + *number* more than + *number* (6); **más... que** more (-er) . . . than (6)
masa mass; dough
máscara mask
mascota pet (3)
masculino/a masculine
masivo/a massive
masticar (qu) to chew
matar to kill (18)
mate *m. traditional drink of Argentina*
matemáticas *f. pl.* math (2)
materia subject area (2); material (4)
materialidad *f.* material aspect; outward appearance
materialista *m., f.* materialistic
maternidad *f.* maternity
materno/a maternal
matinal *adj.* morning
matriarcado matriarchy
matriarcal matriarchal
matrícula tuition (2)
matricularse to enroll; to register
matrimonio marriage; married couple (16)
máximo/a maximum
maya *n., adj. m., f.* Mayan
mayo May (6)
mayor older (6); oldest; greater; greatest; **Antillas** (*f. pl.*) **Mayores** Greater Antilles; **cada vez mayor** greater and greater
mayoría majority
mayoritariamente primarily
mayoritario/a *adj.* majority
mayúscula capital (letter), uppercase
me *d.o.* me; *i.o.* to/for me; *refl. pron.* myself; **me gustaría (mucho)...** I would (really) like . . . (8); **me llamo...** my name is . . . (1); **(no,) no me gusta** (no,) I don't like . . . (1); **(sí,) me gusta...** (yes), I like . . . (1)
mecánico/a mechanic (15)
mecanización *f.* mechanization
mecanografía typing
medalla medal
mediano/a: de estatura mediana of medium height
medianoche *f.* midnight (6)
mediante *prep.* by, with
medias *f. pl.* stockings (4)
medicamento medicine

medicina medicine (11)
médico/a (medical) doctor (3)
medio *n.* medium; means; *pl.* mass media (18); **medio ambiente** environment (15); **medio de comunicación** medium of communication (18); **medio de transporte** means of transportation (8)
medio/a *adj.* half; middle; average; **media naranja** better half; **y media** half past (*the hour*) (1)
medioambiental environmental
medioambiente *m.* environment
mediodía *m.* noon (6)
medir (mido) (i) to measure
meditar to meditate
megadiverso/a megadiverse
megalópolis *f.* super-city
mejor better; best (6)
mejora improvement
mejorar(se) to improve; to get better
mellizo/a fraternal twin
melódico/a melodious
memoria memory (12)
mencionar to mention
menonito/a *adj.* Mennonite
menor younger (6); youngest; less; least
menorá menorah
menos less; least; minus; **a menos que** *conj.* unless (16); **al menos** at least; **menos cuarto** a quarter to (*hour*) (1); **menos de** + *number* fewer than + *number* (6); **menos quince** fifteen minutes till (*hour*) (1); **por lo menos** at least (9)
mensaje *m.* message; **mandar un mensaje** to (send a) text (2)
mensual monthly
mente *f.* mind
mentir (miento) (i) to lie
mentira lie (12)
menú *m.* menu (7)
menudo: a menudo *adv.* often
mercadeo marketing
mercader *m., f.* merchant
mercado market(place) (4)
mercadotecnia marketing
merecer (merezco) to deserve
merendar (meriendo) to have a snack (7)
merengue *m.* dance from the Dominican Republic
merienda snack (7)
mes *m.* month (6)
mesa table (2); **poner la mesa** to set the table (10); **quitar la mesa** to clear the table (10)
meseta plateau
mesita end table (5)

mesoamericano/a *n.,* *adj.* Meso-American

mestizaje *m.* mixing of races

meta goal

metáfora metaphor

metal *m.* metal

metálico/a metallic

metalúrgico/a metallurgical

meteorológico/a meteorological

meter to put (*into*); to place; **meterse en líos** to get into trouble

método method; **hacer (el método) Pilates** to do Pilates (11)

metro subway; **parada del metro** subway stop (12)

metrópoli *f.* metropolis

metropolitano/a urban

mexicano/a Mexican (3)

mexicoamericano/a Mexican American

mezcla mix

mezclar to mix

mezclilla denim

mezquita mosque

mí *obj. of prep.* me (6)

mi(s) *poss. adj.* my (3)

microbio microbe

microcuento very short story

microondas: horno de microondas microwave oven (10)

microorganismo microorganism

miedo fear; **tener miedo (de)** to be afraid (of) (4)

miel *f.* honey; **luna de miel** honeymoon (16)

miembro/a member

mientras while (10)

miércoles *m. inv.* Wednesday (5); **ayer fue miércoles...** yesterday was Wednesday . . . (5)

mierda shit

mil (one) thousand (4)

milagro miracle

milenario/a thousand-year

mililitro milliliter

militar *n. m., f.* soldier; (17) *adj.* military; **servicio militar** military service (18)

milla mile

millón: un millón (de) one million (4)

millonario/a millionaire

mimar to spoil; to pamper

mineral: agua *f.* (*but* **el agua**) **(mineral)** (mineral) water (7)

minidiálogo minidialogue

mínimo minimum

ministerio ministry

ministro/a minister

minoría minority

minuto minute

mío/a(s) *poss. adj.* my; *poss. pron.* (of) mine (17)

mirada look

mirar to look at; to watch (3); **mirar la tele(visión)** to watch television (3)

misa mass; **misa del gallo** midnight mass

miseria misery

misil *n.* missile

misión *f.* mission

mismo/a same (6); **ahora mismo** right now (6)

misterio mystery

misterioso/a mysterious

mitad *f.* half

mixto/a mixed

moái *m. statue on Easter Island, Chile*

mochila backpack (2)

moda fashion; style; **a la moda** in fashion, in a stylish way; **es de última moda** it's trendy (hot) (4); **está de moda** it's trendy (hot) (4)

modales *m. pl.* manners

modelar to model

modelo model, example

módem *m.* modem (12)

moderación *f.* moderation

modernidad *f.* modernity

modernismo modernism

modernista *m., f.* modernist

moderno/a modern (13)

modificar (qu) to modify

modismo idiom

modista dressmaker

modo way, matter; mode; *gram.* mood; **de modo que** in such a way that

mole *m. Mexican sauce*

molestar (*like* **gustar**) to bother (11)

molestia *n.* bother

molesto/a annoyed (6)

molino: rueda de molino treadmill

momento moment

momia mummy

monarquía monarchy

monasterio monastery

moneda coin (17); currency

monedero coin purse

monitor *m.* monitor

monitoreo monitoring

monitorizar (c) to monitor

mono monkey

monolingüe *adj.* monolingual

monoparental *adj.* single-parent

monopatín *m.* skateboard

monotonía monotony

monótono/a monotonous

monovolumen *m.* minivan

monstruo monster

montaje *m.* montage

montaña mountain (8)

montañoso/a mountainous

montar to ride; **montar a caballo** to ride a horse (10); **montar en bicicleta** to ride a bicycle (10)

montón: un montón a lot

montuno *traditional hat of Panama*

monumento monument

morado/a purple (4)

morales *f. pl.* morals

morderse (me muerdo) to bite

moreno/a brunet(te) (3)

morir(se) ([me] muero) (u) (*p.p.* **muerto**) to die (9)

moro/a *n.* Moor; *adj.* Moorish

mosaico mosaic

mosca fly

mostrador *m.* counter (8)

mostrar (muestro) to show (8)

motivación *f.* motivation

motivo motive

moto(cicleta) motorcycle (15)

motor *m.* motor

mover (muevo) to move

móvil mobile

movimiento movement

muchacho/a young boy/girl

mucho *adv.* much (2); a lot (2); **lo siento mucho** I'm very sorry (14); **me gustaría mucho...** I would really like . . . (8); **muchísimo** an awful lot (8)

mucho/a a lot (of) (3); *pl.* many (3); **estar bajo muchas presiones** to be under a lot of pressure (14); **muchas gracias** thank you very much (1); **mucho gusto** nice to meet you (1); **tener (mucha) hambre** to be (very) hungry (7); **tener (mucha) sed** to be (very) thirsty (7); **tener muchas presiones** to be under a lot of stress (14); **tener (mucho) calor** to be (very) warm, hot (6); **tener (mucho) frío** to be (very) cold (6)

mudanza *n.* move

mudarse to move (*residence*) (12)

mueble *m.* piece of furniture (5)

muela molar, back tooth (11); **sacarle (qu) una muela** to extract (*someone's*) molar (11)

muerte *f.* death (16)

muerto/a (*p.p. of* **morir**) dead; **Día** (*m.*) **de los Muertos** Day of the Dead

mujer *f.* woman (2); wife (3); **Día** (*m.*) **Internacional de la No Violencia Contra la Mujer** International No Violence Against Women Day; **mujer de negocios** businesswoman (17); **mujer soldado** female soldier (17)

mula mule

mulato/a mulatto

multa fine

multilingüe multilingual

multinacional multinational

múltiple multiple
multiplicarse (qu) to multiply; to grow in number
multirracial multiracial
mundial *adj.* world; **Copa Mundial** World Cup
mundo world (3); **Copa del Mundo** World Cup (soccer)
municipio municipality
muñeca doll
mural *m.* mural (13)
muralismo muralism
muralista *m., f.* muralist
muralla city wall
murciélago bat
muro wall
músculo muscle
museo museum; **visitar un museo** to visit a museum (10)
música music (13)
musical musical (13)
músico *m., f.* musician (13)
musulmán, musulmana Muslim
mutuo/a mutual
muy very (1); **muy bien** fine, very well (1); **muy buenas** good morning/afternoon/evening (1)

N

nacer (nazco) to be born (16)
nacimiento birth
nación *f.* nation; **Organización** (*f.*) **de Naciones Unidas (ONU)** United Nations (U.N.)
nacional national; **himno nacional** national anthem; **producto nacional bruto** gross national product
nacionalidad *f.* nationality; **adjetivo de nacionalidad** adjective of nationality (3)
nada nothing, not anything (7); **de nada** you're welcome (1); **para nada** at all (8)
nadar to swim (8)
nadie no one, nobody, not anybody (7)
náhuatl *m.* Nahuatl (*language of the Aztecs*)
nana *fam.* grandma
naranja orange (7); **media naranja** better half
nariz *f.* (*pl.* **narices**) nose (11)
narración *f.* narration
narrador(a) narrator
narrar to narrate
natación *f.* swimming (10)
natal: casa natal house where someone was born
nativo/a native

natural natural; **ciencias** (*f. pl.*) **naturales** natural sciences (2); **recurso natural** natural resource (15)
naturaleza nature (15)
naturópata *m., f.* naturopath
náufrago shipwreck
nave (*f.*) **espacial** spaceship
navegable navigable
navegación *f.* navigation
navegar (gu) to navigate (12); **navegar la Red** to surf the internet
Navidad *f.* Christmas (9)
navideño/a *adj.* Christmas
neblina mist; fog
necesario/a necessary (3)
necesidad *f.* need, necessity
necesitar to need (2)
negación *f.* negation
negar (niego) (gu) to deny (13)
negativo/a negative; **palabra indefinida y negativa** *gram.* indefinite and negative word (7)
negociar to negotiate
negocio business; **hombre** (*m.*) **de negocios** businessman (17); **mujer** (*f.*) **de negocios** businesswoman (17)
negrilla: en negrilla boldface
negro/a black (4)
neoyorquino/a *adj.* pertaining to New York
nerviosismo nervousness
nervioso/a nervous (6)
neumático tire (*automobile*)
neutralizar (c) to neutralize
neutro/a neutral
nevar (nieva) to snow (6); **nieva** it's snowing (6)
nevera refrigerator
ni neither; nor; **ni... ni** neither . . . nor
nicaragüense *n., adj. m., f.* Nicaraguan
niebla fog
nieto/a grandson/granddaughter (3)
ningún (ninguna) no, not any (7)
niñero/a baby-sitter (10)
niñez *f.* (*pl.* **niñeces**) childhood (16)
niño/a small child; boy/girl (3); **de niño/a** as a child (10)
nivel *m.* level
no no (1); **no creer** to not think/believe (13); **no es seguro/(im)posible, (im)probable** it's not sure/(im)possible, (im)probable (13); **no estar de acuerdo** to disagree (3); **no estar seguro/a de** to not be sure of (13); **no hay** there is/are not (1); **no hay de qué** you're welcome (1); **no obstante** however; **no tener razón** to be wrong (4); **ya no** no longer
¿no? right, don't they (you...)? (4)

noche *f.* night; **buenas noches** goodnight (1); **de la noche** in the evening, P.M. (1); **esta noche** tonight (6); **por la noche** at night, in the evening (2)
Nochebuena Christmas Eve (9)
Nochevieja New Year's Eve (9)
nombrar to name
nombre *m.* name (7)
nopal *m.* cactus
noreste *m.* northeast
norma rule; norm
normal normal; **es normal que** it's normal that (13)
normalidad *f.* normality
noroeste *m.* northwest
norte *m.* north (6)
Norteamérica North America
norteamericano/a North American
nos *d. o. pron.* us; *i. o. pron.* to/for us; *refl. pron.* ourselves; **nos vemos** see you around (1)
nosotros/as *subj. pron.* we (2); *obj.* (*of prep.*) us (2)
nota grade (*academic*) (5); note
notar to note, to notice
noticias *f. pl.* news (5)
noticiero newscast (18)
notificación *f.* notification
novecientos/as nine hundred (4)
novela novel (13)
novelista *m., f.* novelist (13)
noveno/a ninth (13)
noventa ninety (3)
noviazgo engagement (16)
noviembre *m.* November (6)
novio/a boyfriend/girlfriend (6); fiancé(e) (16); groom/bride (16)
nube *f.* cloud
nublado/a cloudy; **está (muy) nublado** it's (very) cloudy, overcast (6)
nuclear: energía nuclear nuclear energy (15)
nuestro/a(s) *poss. adj.* our (3); *poss. pron.* ours, of ours (17)
nueve nine (1)
nuevo/a new (3); **Año Nuevo** New Year; **Nueva York** New York
numérico/a numerical
número number (1); **número ordinal** ordinal number (13)
numeroso/a numerous
nunca never (3); **casi nunca** almost never (3)
nupcial nuptial; **votos** (*m. pl.*) **nupciales** wedding vows
nutritivo/a nutritious

O

o or (1)
obedecer (obedezco) to obey (15)
obispo bishop

objetivo *n.* objective
objeto object (2)
obligación *f.* obligation
obligado/a customary
obligatorio/a obligatory
obra work; **obra de arte** work of art (13); **obra de teatro** play (13); **obra maestra** masterpiece (13); **obra teatral** play
obrero/a worker, laborer (17)
observación *f.* observation
observar to observe
obstáculo obstacle
obstante: no obstante however
obtener (*like* **tener**) to get; to obtain (12)
obvio/a obvious
ocasión *f.* occasion
ocasionar to cause
océano ocean (8); **océano Pacífico** Pacific Ocean
ochenta eighty (3)
ocho eight (1)
ochocientos/as eight hundred (4)
octavo/a eighth (13)
octillizo/a octuplet
octubre *m.* October (6)
oculista *m., f.* ophthalmologist
oculto/a hidden
ocupación *f.* occupation
ocupado/a busy (6)
ocupar to hold; to occupy
ocurrir to occur (14)
odiar to hate (8)
oeste *m.* west (6)
ofensivo/a offensive
off: voz en off voice over
oficial official
oficina office (2)
oficio trade (*profession*) (17)
ofrecer (ofrezco) to offer (8)
ofrenda *n.* offering
oído inner ear (11)
oír to hear (5); to listen to (*music, the radio*) (5)
ojalá (que) I hope (that) (13)
ojo eye (11); **ojo alerta** eagle eye; **¡ojo!** *interj.* watch out!
olímpico/a: Juegos (*m. pl.*) **Olímpicos** Olympic Games
oliva: aceite (*m.*) (**de oliva**) (olive) oil (7)
olor *m.* odor
olvidar to forget (9)
omnipresente omnipresent
once eleven (1)
onda wave; **¿cuál es tu onda?** what's your style?; **en onda** in style; **¿qué onda?** what's new/happening?
onomatopeya onomatopoeia
onomatopéyico/a onomatopoeic
ONU *f.* (**Organización** [*f.*] **de Naciones Unidas**) U.N. (United Nations)

opción *f.* option
opcional optional
ópera opera (13)
operación *f.* operation
opinar to think; to have/express an opinion
opinión *f.* opinion
oponerse (a) (*like* **poner**) to oppose
oportunidad *f.* opportunity
optar (por) to opt (for)
optimista *m., f.* optimist; *adj.* optimistic
opuesto/a opposite
oración *f.* sentence
oral oral (14); **informe** (*m.*) **oral** oral report (14)
órale *interj. sl.* wow!
orangután *m.* orangutan
órbita orbit
orden *m.* order
ordenado/a neat (6)
ordenador *m. Sp.* computer
ordenar to put in order
ordinal: número ordinal ordinal number (13)
ordinario/a ordinary
oreja (outer) ear (11)
orgánico/a organic
organismo organism
organización *f.* organization
organizar (c) to organize
órgano organ
orgullo pride
orgulloso/a proud
orientación *f.* orientation
oriental eastern
origen *m.* origin
originario/a native
originarse to come from
oriundo/a native
oro gold (4); **de oro** gold (4)
orquesta orchestra (13)
orquídea orchid
ortografía spelling
ortográfico/a: acento ortográfico accent mark
oscuridad *f.* darkness
oso/a bear
ostra oyster
otavaleno/a resident of Otavalo (*Ecuador*)
otoño fall, autumn (6)
otorgar (gu) to grant
otro/a other, another (3); **otra vez** again; **por el otro lado** on the other hand
oveja sheep
ozono: capa de ozono ozone layer (15)

P

paciencia patience
paciente *n. m., f.* patient (11); *adj.* patient

pacífico/a Pacific; **océano Pacífico** Pacific Ocean
padrastro stepfather
padre *m.* father (3); *m. pl.* parents (3); **Día** (*m.*) **del Padre** Father's Day
padrino godfather
paella *Spanish dish made with rice, shellfish, and often chicken, and flavored with saffron*
pagado/a: empleo bien/mal pagado well-/poorly paid job/ position (17)
pagar (gu) to pay (for) (2)
página page; **página web** webpage (12)
país *m.* country (3)
pájaro bird (3)
Pakistán Pakistan
pakistaní *m., f.* Pakistani
palabra word (1); **palabra indefinida y negativa** *gram.* indefinite and negative word (7)
palacio palace
palestino/a Palestinian
palma palm tree
palmera palm tree
palo stick
palomitas *f. pl.* popcorn
pampa plain (*geography, Arg.*)
pan *m.* bread (7); **pan tostado** toast (7)
panadería bakery
panameño/a *n., adj.* Panamanian
páncreas *m. inv.* pancreas
pandemia pandemic
pandilla gang
pánel (*m.*) **solar** solar panel
panhispano/a Pan-Hispanic
pánico panic
panorama *m.* panorama
pantalla (grande/plana) (big/flat) screen (monitor) (12)
pantalones *m. pl.* pants (4); **pantalones cortos** shorts (4)
pañuelo handkerchief
papa (frita) (French fried) potato (7)
papá *m.* father, dad (3); *m. pl.* parents
papel *m.* paper (2); role (13)
papi *m.* dad, daddy
par *m.* pair
para (intended) for; in order to (3); **para +** *inf.* (*do something*) (10); **para nada...** at all (8); **para que** so that (16)
parabrisas *m. inv.* windshield (15)
paracaídas *m. inv.* parachute
paracaidismo skydiving
parada stop (8); **hacer paradas** to make stops (8); **parada del autobús** bus stop (12); **parada del metro** subway stop (12)
paraguayo/a *n., adj.* Paraguayan
parar to stop (15)

parcial partial; **empleo de tiempo parcial** part-time job/position (17); **trabajo de tiempo parcial** part-time job (14)

pardo/a brown

parecer (parezco) (*like* **gustar**) to seem; **parecerse (a)** to resemble

pared *f.* wall (5)

pareja (married) couple; partner (16)

paréntesis *m. inv.* parentheses

pariente *m.* relative (3)

parlamentario/a parliamentary

parque *m.* park

parqueadero parking lot

parquear to park

párrafo paragraph

parranda Christmas party *(Cuba)*

parrilla grill

parte *f.* part (5); **por todas partes** everywhere (14)

participación *f.* participation

participante *m., f.* participant

participar to participate

particular particular; unique; **en particular** particularly

partida: punto de partida starting point

partido game, match (10); political party (18)

partir: a partir de beyond (4)

pasado/a past, last (11); **el año pasado** last year; **pasado mañana** the day after tomorrow (5)

pasaje *m.* fare, price *(of a transportation ticket)* (8)

pasajero/a passenger (8)

pasaporte *m.* passport (8)

pasar to spend *(time)* (6); to happen (6); **pasar hambre** to go hungry; **pasar la aspiradora** to vacuum (10); **pasar las vacaciones en...** to spend one's vacation in . . . (8); **pasar por el control de seguridad** to go/pass through security (check) (8); **pasar por la aduana** to go/pass through customs (8); **pasarlo bien/mal** to have a good/bad time (9)

pasatiempo pastime (10)

Pascua Easter (9)

pasear to take a walk, stroll; to go for a ride; **pasear en bicicleta** to ride a bicycle (10)

paseo walk, stroll; **dar un paseo** to take a walk (10)

pasillo aisle (8)

pasión *f.* passion

paso step

pastel *m.* cake (7); pie (7); **pastel de cumpleaños** birthday cake (9)

pastilla pill (11)

pastor(a) minister

pata leg *(of an animal)*

patata (frita) (French fried) potato (7)

paternidad *f.* paternity

paterno/a paternal

patinaje *m.* skating (10)

patinar to skate (10)

patio patio (5); yard (5)

patojo/a *sl.* young man/woman *(Guat.)*

patriarcal patriarchal

Patricio: Día *(m.)* **de San Patricio** St. Patrick's Day

patrimonio patrimony

patriota *m., f.* patriot

patriótico/a patriotic

patronal: fiesta patronal *party dedicated to patron saint*

pavo turkey (7)

paz *f.* *(pl.* **paces)** peace (18)

peca freckle

pecho chest

pedazo piece

pedir (pido) (i) to ask for (5); to order (5); **pedir disculpas** to apologize (14); **pedir prestado/a** to borrow (17)

pegar (gu) to hit (14); **pegarse con/ contra** to run, bump into/against (14)

peinarse to comb/brush one's hair (5)

Pekín Peking

pelado/a *sl.* young man/woman *(Col.)*

pelear to fight (10)

pelícano pelican

película movie (5)

peligro danger; **especie** *(f.)* **en peligro de extinción** endangered species (15)

peligroso/a dangerous

pelo hair; **teñirse (me tiño) (i) el pelo** to dye one's hair; **tomarle el pelo** to pull someone's leg

pelota ball (10)

pelotero/a baseball player

peluche: animal *(m.)* **de peluche** stuffed animal

peluquero/a hairstylist (17)

pen drive *m.* memory stick (12)

pena pity

pendiente *m.* earring *(Sp.)*

península peninsula

pensar (pienso) (de/en) to think (about) (5); **pensar** + *inf.* to intend, plan to *(do something)* (5); **pensar que** to think that (5)

penúltimo/a next to last

peor worse (6)

pepino cucumber (7)

pequeño/a small (3)

percatarse to realize

percepción *f.* perception

percibir to perceive

percusión *f.* percussion

perder (pierdo) to lose; to miss *(an event)* (5)

perdón excuse me (1)

perdonar to forgive

perdurable lasting

peregrinación *f.* pilgrimage

perezoso/a lazy (3)

perfección *f.* perfection

perfecto/a perfect

pérfido/a treacherous

perfil *m.* profile

perforación *f.* drilling *(well)*

perfume *m.* perfume

periódico newspaper (3)

periodismo journalism

periodista *m., f.* journalist (17)

período period *(of time)*

permanecer (permanezco) to remain, stay

permanente permanent

permiso permission; permit; **(con) permiso** excuse me (1); **permiso de manejar** driving permit

permitir to permit, allow (12)

pero but (1)

perro dog (3)

persecución *f.* persecution

perseguir (*like* **seguir**) to chase; to pursue

persona person (2)

personaje *m.* character *(book, movie)*

personal *(m.)* **médico** medical personnel (11)

personal *adj.* personal; **pronombre** *(m.)* **personal** *gram.* personal pronoun (2)

personalidad *f.* personality

perspectiva perspective

persuasivo/a persuasive

pertenecer (pertenezco) a to belong to

perturbar to perturb, bother

peruano/a *n., adj.* Peruvian

pesado/a boring; difficult (10); heavy

pesar to weigh; **a pesar de** in spite of

pesas: levantar pesas to lift weights (11)

pescadería fish market

pescado fish (7)

pescar (qu) to fish

pesimista *m., f.* pessimistic

peso weight

pestaña eyelash

petición *f.* request

petróleo petroleum, oil (15)

petrolero/a *adj.* oil; petroleum

pez *m.* *(pl.* **peces)** fish (15)

picante hot, spicy (7)

picar (qu) to bite; to sting

picnic: **hacer un** *picnic* to have a picnic (10)

pico peak

pie *m.* foot (11); **dedo del pie** toe; **levantarse con el pie izquierdo** to get up on the wrong side of the bed (14)

piedra stone

piel *f.* skin

pierna leg (11)

pieza piece

pila battery; **ponerse las pilas** to get one's act together; to energize oneself

pilar *m.* pillar

Pilates: hacer (el método) Pilates to do Pilates (11)

píldora pill

piloto *m., f.* pilot (8)

pimienta pepper (*condiment*) (7)

pingüino penguin

pino pine (tree)

pinola *m. typical Nicaragua drink*

pintar to paint (13)

pintor(a) painter (13)

pintura painting (*general*) (13)

piña pineapple

pirámide *f.* pyramid

piraña piranha

Pirineos *m. pl.* Pyrenees

piscina swimming pool (5)

Piscis *m.* Pisces

pisco *alcoholic beverage of Peru and Chile*

piso floor (*of a building*) (12); **barrer (el piso)** to sweep (the floor) (10); **primer piso** first floor (second story) (12); **segundo piso** second floor (third story) (12)

pizarra chalkboard

pizarrón *m.* (chalk)board (2); **pizarrón blanco** whiteboard (2)

placa license plate

placer *m.* pleasure

plan *m.* plan (10); **hacer planes para** + *inf.* to make plans to (*do something*) (10)

planchar to iron (10)

planeación *f.* planning

planear to plan

planeta *m.* planet (15)

planetario/a planetary

plano map (*of a city*); blueprint

plano/a flat; **pantalla plana** flat screen (monitor) (12)

planta plant

planta baja ground floor (12)

plantación *f.* plantation

plasma: televisión plasma *f.* plasma television (12)

plástico plastic

plata *n.* silver (4); **de plata** *adj.* silver (4)

plátano plantain

platino platinum

plato dish; course (7); plate (5); **plato principal** main course (7)

playa beach (6)

plaza plaza, square (4)

plazo deadline (14); **a plazos** in installments (17)

pleno/a complete; full

plomero/a plumber (17)

pluma pen

plurinacional multinational

población *f.* population (15)

pobre poor (3)

pobreza poverty

poco (a) little (2); few (4); **un poco (de)** a little bit (of) (2)

poder *v.* to be able, can (4)

poder *n. m.* power; **poder adquisitivo** purchasing power

poderoso/a powerful

poema *m.* poem (13)

poesía poetry

poeta *m., f.* poeta (13)

poético/a poetic

polaco/a Polish

policía *m., f.* police officer (15); *f.* police (*force*); **mujer** (*f.*) **policía** policewoman

polinésico/a Polynesian

política politics; policy (18)

político/a *n.* politician (18); *adj.* political; **ciencias** (*f. pl.*) **políticas** political science (2)

pollera *indigenous skirt of the Andes*

pollo chicken (7); **pollo asado** roast chicken (7); **pollo frito** fried chicken

polvo dust

poner to put (5); to place (5); to turn on (*an appliance*) (12); **poner atención** to pay attention; **poner la mesa** to set the table (10); **ponerle una inyección** to give (*someone*) a shot (11); **ponerse** to put on (*an article of clothing*) (5); **ponerse** + *adj.* to become, get + *adj.* (9); **ponerse las pilas** to get one's act together; to energize oneself; **ponerse rojo/a** to blush (9)

popularidad *f.* popularity

por about (6); because of (6); through (8); for (8); by (14); **gracias por** + *noun/ inf.* thanks for (9); **por consiguiente** as a result; **por Dios** for heaven's sake (14); **por ejemplo** for example (14); **por el otro lado** on the other hand; **por ello** therefore; **por eso** for that reason (3); **por favor** please (1); **por fin** finally (5); **por la mañana** in the morning (2); **por la noche** at night, in the evening (2); **por la tarde** in the afternoon (2); **por lo general** generally (5); **por lo menos** at least (9); **por lo regular** in general; **por primera/última vez** for the first/ last time (14); **por si acaso** just in case (14); **por todas partes** everywhere (14); **por un lado** on one hand

porcentaje *m.* percentage

porción *f.* portion, part

pormenorizado/a detailed

poro pore

porotos *m. pl.* beans

porque because (3)

portafolio portfolio

portarse bien/mal to (mis)behave (9)

portátil portable; **computadora portátil** laptop (computer) (2); **ordenador** (*m.*) **portátil** (*Sp.*) laptop computer (12)

portero/a building manager; doorman (12)

portón *m.* front door; gate

portugués *m.* Portuguese (*language*)

portugués, portuguesa *n., adj.* Portuguese

posar to pose

posesión *f.* possession

posesivo/a possessive (17); **adjetivo posesivo** *gram.* possessive adjective (3)

posibilidad *f.* possibility

posible possible (3); **es posible que** it's possible that (13) **no es posible** it's not possible (13)

posición *f.* position

positivo/a positive

posponer (*like* **poner**) to postpone

postal: tarjeta postal postcard (8)

posterior later, subsequent

postre *m.* dessert (7)

postularse to run (18); **postularse como candidato/a** to run as a candidate (18); **postularse para un cargo como candidato/a** to run for a position as a candidate (18)

postura posture

potencia power

potencial *m.* potential; *adj.* potential

práctica practice

practicar (qu) to practice (2); **practicar el alpinismo** to mountain climb; **practicar un deporte** to play a sport

práctico/a practical

pradera meadow

preadolescencia preadolescence

precedente *m.* precedent

preceder to precede

precio (fijo) (fixed, set) price (4)

precioso/a precious

precipicio precipice

precipitado/a hasty

precisamente precisely

precolombino/a pre-Columbian

predicción *f.* prediction

predominante predominant

predominar to predominate

preescolar *adj.* preschool

preferencia preference (1)

preferir (prefiero) (i) to prefer (4)

¿por qué? why? (3)

pregunta question (5); **hacer una pregunta** to ask a question (5)

preguntar to ask (*a question*) (8)

prehistórico/a prehistoric

premio prize

prenda article of clothing
prender to fasten
prensa (print) press (18); news media (18); **quiosco de prensa** newsstand (18)
prensado/a pressed
preocupación *f.* worry
preocupado/a worried (6)
preocupar(se) to worry
preparación *f.* preparation
preparar to prepare (7); **prepararse** to prepare oneself; to get ready
preparatoria (**prepa**) pre-university study
preposición *f. gram.* preposition (5)
prescribir to prescribe
preseleccionado/a pre-selected
presencia presence
presencial: de forma presencial in person
presentación *f.* presentation
presentador(a) presenter; (television) anchor
presentar to introduce; to present
presente *m.* present (time); *gram.* present tense; *adj.* present
preservar to preserve
presidencia presidency
presidencial presidential
presidente/a president
presión *f.* pressure (14); **estar bajo muchas presiones** to be under a lot of pressure (14); **tener muchas presiones** to be under a lot of stress (14)
preso/a prisoner
prestado/a: pedir prestado/a to borrow (17)
préstamo loan (17)
prestar to lend (8)
prestigioso/a prestigious
presupuestario/a budgetary
presupuesto budget (17)
pretérito *gram.* preterite
preuniversitario/a pre-university
prevenir (*like* **venir**) to warn
primario/a primary; first; elementary; **escuela primaria** elementary school
primavera spring (6)
primer(o/a) first (5); **el primero de** the first of (*month*) (6); **primer piso** first floor (second story) (12); **por primera vez** for the first time (14)
primo/a cousin (3); *m. pl.* cousins (3)
princesa princess
principal main; **plato principal** main course (7)
príncipe *m.* prince
principiante *m., f.* beginner; novice
principio beginning; **al principio de** at the beginning of (17)

priorizar (c) to prioritize
prisa: tener prisa to be in a hurry (4)
privacidad *f.* privacy
privado/a private
privilegio privilege
probabilidad *f.* probability
probable probable (13); **es probable que** it's likely, probable that (13); **no es probable que** it's not probable (13)
probar (pruebo) to try, taste
problema *m.* problem
problemático/a problematic
procedimiento procedure
procesión *f.* procession
proceso process
proclamar to proclaim
procurar to procure
producción *f.* production
producir (*like* **conducir**) to produce
productivo/a productive
producto product; **producto nacional bruto** gross national product
productor(a) producer
profesión *f.* profession (17)
profesional *n. m., f.* professional, person with a profession; *adj.* professional
profesionista *n. m., f.* professional, person with a profession
profesor(a) professor (1)
profesorado faculty
profundidad *f.* depth
profundo/a deep
programa *m.* program; **programa (del curso)** (course) syllabus (14)
programación *f.* programming
programador(a) programmer (17)
progresivo/a progressive
progreso progress
prohibir (prohíbo) to prohibit, forbid (12)
proliferación *f.* proliferation
promedio average
promesa promise
prometer to promise (8)
prominente prominent
promover (promuevo) to promote
pronombre *m. gram.* pronoun; **pronombre personal** *gram.* personal pronoun (2); **pronombre relativo** *gram.* relative pronoun
pronosticar (qu) to forecast
pronóstico forecast
pronto soon; **hasta pronto** see you soon; **tan pronto como** as soon as (17)
prontuario guide
pronunciación *f.* pronunciation
pronunciar to pronounce
propiedad *f.* property; characteristic
propio/a own, one's own (17)
proponer (*like* **poner**) to propose
proporción *f.* proportion

proporcionar to provide
propósito purpose
prórroga extension
protagonista *m., f.* protagonist
protección *f.* protection
protector(a) protective
proteger (protejo) to protect (15)
proteína protein
protestante *n., adj. m., f.* Protestant
protestantismo Protestantism
protestar to protest
provecho: ¡buen provecho! enjoy your meal!
proveedor(a) provider
proveer (*like* **creer**) to provide
proverbio proverb
providencia providence
provincia province
provocar (qu) to cause
próximo/a next; **el próximo (martes...)** next (Tuesday . . .) (5); **la próxima semana** next week (5)
proyección *f.* projection
proyecto project
prudente prudent
prueba quiz; test (14); proof
psicología psychology
psicólogo/a psychologist
publicación *f.* publication
publicar (qu) to publish (12)
publicidad *f.* publicity
publicitario/a *adj.* advertising
público *n.* audience (13)
público/a *adj.* public (15); **transporte** (*m.*) **público** public transportation
pueblo town
puente *m.* bridge
puerco pig
puerta door (2); **puerta de embarque** boarding gate (8)
puerto port (8)
puertorriqueño/a *n., adj.* Puerto Rican
pues *conj.* well
puesto job; position; place (*in line*) (8)
pulgada inch
pulido/a polished
pulmones *m. pl.* lungs (11)
pulpería grocery store (*C.A.*)
pulpo octopus
punto point; **a punto de** + *inf.* about to + *inf.;* **en punto** on the dot (*time*) (1); **hora punta** peak hour; **punto cardinal** cardinal point (6); **punto de partida** starting point; **punto de vista** point of view
puntuación *f.* puncutation
pupusa *thick stuffed corn tortilla*
puro cigar
puro/a pure (15)
púrpura *n.* purple
purpúreo/a *adj.* purple

Q

que that, which (3); who (3); **así que** therefore, consequently, so; **hasta que** *conj.* until; **que Dios te bendiga** God bless you; **ya que** since

¿qué? what? which?; **¿a qué hora... ?** at what time . . . ? (1); **¿con qué frecuencia... ?** how often . . . ? (3); **¿por qué?** why? (3)

¡qué... ! what . . . !; **¡qué bacán!** fantastic! **¡qué yuca!** how difficult!

quebrarse (me quiebro) to break

quedar to remain; to be left (14); to stay; to remain (*in a place*) (6)

quehacer (*m.*) **doméstico** household chore (10)

quejarse (de) to complain (about) (8)

quemada *n.* burn

quemar to burn

querer to want (4); to love (16); **eso quiere decir...** that means . . . (11); **fue sin querer** I didn't mean to do it (14); **quererse** to love each other; to be fond of each other (11); **querido/a** dear (6)

querido/a dear (6)

queso cheese (7)

quetzal *currency of Guatemala*

quien who; whom

¿quién(es)? who? whom?; **¿de quién?** whose? (3)

química chemistry (2)

quince fifteen (1); **menos quince** fifteen minutes till (*hour*) (1); **y quince** fifteen minutes after (*the hour*) (1)

quinceañera *young woman's fifteenth birthday party;* young woman who is turning fifteen (9)

quinientos/as five hundred (4)

quintillizo/a quintuplet

quinto/a fifth (13)

quiosco de prensa newsstand (18)

quiropráctico/a chiropractor

quitar to remove; **quitar la mesa** to clear the table (10); **quitarse** to take off (*an article of clothing*) (5)

quizás *adv.* perhaps

R

rabia rutera road rage

ración *f.* portion

radiante bright, shining, radiant

radical *m. gram.* root

radio *m.* radio (*apparatus*) (12); *f.* radio (*medium*); **estación** (*f.*) **de radio** radio station (18)

radioyente *m., f.* radio listener; *m. pl.* radio audience

raíz *f.* (*pl.* **raíces**) root

rama branch

rana frog

ranchera *traditional music of Mexico sung by mariachis*

rancho ranch

rap *m.* rap music

rapanui *n. m., f.* indigenous person of Easter Island

rápido *adv.* quickly

rápido/a fast; **comida rápida** fast food

rápidos *m. pl.* rapids

raqueta racket

raro/a rare; strange

rascacielos *m. inv.* skyscraper (15)

rata rat

rato while, short time; **ratos libres** spare (free) time (10)

ratón *m.* mouse (12)

raya: de rayas striped (4)

rayar to scratch

raza race (*ethnic*)

razón *f.* reason; **no tener razón** to be wrong (4); **tener razón** to be right (4)

reacción *f.* reaction

reaccionar to react

real royal; real

realidad *f.* reality

realismo realism

realista *m., f.* realistic

realizar (c) to achieve; to attain

rebaja sale, reduction; *pl.* sales, reductions (4); **en rebaja** on sale

rebanada slice

rebasar to pass (*vehicle*)

rebelde *n. m., f.* rebel; *adj.* rebellious

rebelión *f.* rebellion

recado message

recámara bedroom

recepción *f.* reception

recepcionista *m., f.* receptionist

receptor *m.* receiver; recipient

receta recipe (7); prescription (11)

recetar to prescribe

recibir to receive (3)

recibo receipt (17)

reciclaje *m.* recycling (15)

reciclar to recycle (15)

recién recently; **recién casado/a (con)** newlywed (to) (16)

reciente recent

recipiente *m.* container

recíproco/a reciprocal

recitar to recite

recoger (recojo) to collect (14); to pick up (14)

recomendable recommendable

recomendación *f.* recommendation

recomendar (recomiendo) to recommend (8)

reconocer (like **conocer**) to recognize

reconocimiento recognition

reconquista reconquest

reconstituido/a remarried; hybrid (*of a family*)

reconstituir (*like* **construir**) to reconstitute; to reconstruct

recordar (recuerdo) to remember (9)

recrear to recreate

recreo recess

recto/a straight; **(todo) recto** straight ahead (15)

rector(a) university president

recuerdo memory

recuperación *f.* recuperation

recuperador(a) recuperative

recuperar to recuperate

recurso resource; **recurso natural** natural resource (15)

red *f.* network; internet; **navegar (gu) la Red** to surf the internet; **red social** social network (12)

redacción *f.* editing

redactar to write; to edit

reducción *f.* reduction

reducir (*like* **conducir**) to reduce

reemplazar (c) to replace

referencia reference

referirse (me refiero) (i) (a) to refer (to)

refinado/a refined

reflejar to reflect

reflexivo/a reflexive; **verbo reflexivo** *gram.* reflexive verb (5)

reforma change

refrán *m.* saying, proverb

refresco soft drink (7)

refrigerador *m.* refrigerator (10)

refrigeradora refrigerator

refugio refuge

regalar to give (*as a gift*) (8)

regalo present, gift (3)

regatear to haggle; to bargain (4)

regateo bartering

reggae *m.* reggae

régimen *m.* regime

región *f.* region

regir (rijo) (i) to govern

registración *f.* registration

registrar to register

registro register; record

regla rule

regresar to return (*to a place*) (2); **regresar a casa** to go home (2)

regulador(a) regulator

regular *adj.* so-so (1); **por lo regular** in general; *v.* to regulate

regularidad *f.* regularity

reina queen (18)

reinar to reign

reino kingdom

reírse (río) (i) (de) to laugh (about) (9)

reiterar to reiterate

reivindicación *f.* vindication

reivindicar (qu) to reclaim

reja bar (*of prison*)

relación *f.* relation; relationship;
  relación sentimental emotional
  relationship (16)

relacionar to relate

relajado/a relaxed

relajante relaxing

relajarse to relax

relámpago lightning

relativo/a: pronombre (*m.*) **relativo**
  gram. relative pronoun

relevante relevant

religión *f.* religion

religioso/a religious

relleno/a filled

reloj *m.* watch (4)

remarcar (qu) to remark

remate: de remate hopeless(ly)

remedio remedy

remodelado/a remodeled

remoto/a: control (*m.*) **remoto** remote
  control (12)

remuneración *f.* remuneration

renovable renewable (15); **energía**
  renovable renewable energy (15)

renovar (renuevo) to renew

rentar to rent (*Mex.*)

renunciar (a) to resign (from) (17)

reparar to repair (15)

repasar to review

repaso review

repeler to repel

repente: de repente suddenly (11)

repetición *f.* repetition

repetir (repito) (i) to repeat

repetitivo/a repetitive

reportaje *m.* report (*on a news
  show*)

reportar to report

reportero/a reporter (18)

represa dam

representación *f.* representation

representante *n. m., f.* representative ;
  representante al congreso
  Congressional representative (18)

representar to represent

representativo/a *adj.* representative

reprobar (repruebo) to fail

república republic

republicano/a republican

requerir (requiero) (i) to require

requisito requirement

rescatar to rescue

reseña review (*book, movie*)

reserva reserve; reservation (*Sp.*); **hacer**
  reserva to make a reservation

resfriado *n.* cold (11)

resfriado/a *adj.* congested, stuffed
  up (11)

resfriarse (me resfrío) to catch/get a
  cold (11)

residencia dormitory (2); **residencia de**
  ancianos nursing home (12)

residencial *m.* building (*housing*)

residente *m., f.* resident

residuos *m. pl.* waste

resistente resistant; strong

resistir to resist

resolver (resuelvo) (*p.p.* **resuelto**) to
  solve; to resolve (15)

respectivo/a respective

respecto: a este respecto in this
  regard; (**con**) **respecto a** regarding

respetar to respect

respeto respect

respiración *f.* breathing

respirar to breathe (11)

responder to respond

responsabilidad *f.* responsibility (18);
  responsabilidad cívica civic
  duty (18)

responsable responsible

respuesta answer (6)

restablecimiento re-establishment;
  restoration

restaurante *m.* restaurant (7)

resto rest, remainder

restricción *f.* restriction

resuelto/a (*p.p. of* **resolver**) resolved

resultado result

resumen *m.* summary; **en resumen** in
  summary

resumir to summarize

resurrección *f.* resurrection

retribuir (*like* **contribuir**) to reward

retrospectivo/a retrospective

retumbar to resound

reunión *f.* meeting

reunirse (me reúno) (con) to get
  together (with) (9)

revelar to reveal

revés: al revés backwards

revisar to check (15)

revista magazine (3)

revolucionario/a revolutionary

revolver (*like* **volver**) to stir

rey *m.* king (18)

rezar (c) to pray

Ricitos de Oro Goldilocks

rico/a rich (3); tasty, savory; rich (7)

ridículo/a ridiculous

riesgo risk; **de alto riesgo**
  high risk

rígido/a rigid

rima rhyme

rimar to rhyme

rincón *m.* corner

rinoceronte *m.* rhinoceros

riñón *m.* kidney

río river (15)

rioplatense *adj., m., f.* from the **Río de la**
  Plata area

riqueza richness

risa laughter

ritmo rhythm; **ritmo de la vida** pace of
  life (15)

rito rite; ritual

robar to rob; to steal

robo theft; robbery

rodante: cinta rodante treadmill

rodeado/a (de) surrounded (by)

rodear to go around

rojo/a red (4)

Roma Rome

romano/a Roman

romántico/a romantic

romper(se) (*p.p.* **roto**) to break (14);
  romper (con) to break up
  (with) (16)

ron *m.* rum

ropa clothing (4); **ropa interior**
  underwear (4)

ropero wardrobe

rosa rose; **rosa té** tea rose

rosado/a pink (4)

rosario rosary

rostro face

roto/a (*p.p. of* **romper**) broken

rotulador *m.* felt-tipped pen

rubio/a blond(e) (3)

rueda wheel, tire; **rueda de molino**
  treadmill

ruido noise (5)

ruidoso/a noisy

ruina ruin (13)

ruso Russian (*language*)

ruso/a *n., adj.* Russian

ruta route

rutero/a: rabia rutera road rage

rutina routine (5)

rutinario/a *adj.* routine

S

sábado Saturday (5)

saber to know (7); **saber + inf.** to know
  how to (*do something*) (7)

sabiduría wisdom

sabio/a wise

sabor *m.* flavor

sabroso/a tasty

sacar (qu) to extract (11); get (*grades*)
  (14); to withdraw, take out (17); **sacar**
  dinero to withdraw money; **sacar**
  fotos to take photos (8); **sacar la**
  basura to take out the trash (10);
  sacar la lengua to stick out one's
  tongue (11); **sacarle un diente / una**
  muela to extract (*someone's*) tooth/
  molar (11)

sacerdote *m.* priest

safari: ir de safari to go on a safari

Sagitario Sagittarius
sagrado/a sacred
sal *f.* salt (7)
sala living room (5); **sala de espera** waiting room (8); **sala de fumadores/ de fumar** smoking area (8); **sala de urgencias** emergency room
salarial: brecha salarial wage gap
salario pay, wages (*often per hour*) (17)
salchicha sausage; hot dog (7)
salida departure (8)
salir (de) to leave (*a place*) (5); **salir bien/mal** to come/turn out well/ badly; to do poorly/well (5); **salir (con)** to go out (with) (5); **salir de vacaciones** to leave on vacation (8); **salir (para)** to leave (for) (*a place*) (5)
salmón *m.* salmon (7)
salón (*m.*) **de clase** classroom (2)
salsa sauce (7); salsa (*music*)
salsero/a *adj.* salsa (*music*)
saltar to jump
salud *f.* health (11)
saludable healthy
saludarse to greet each other (11)
saludo greeting (1)
salvadoreño/a *n., adj.* Salvadoran
salvaje wild (15)
salvar to save
san, santo/a *n.* saint; **Día** (*m.*) **de San Patricio** St. Patrick's Day; **Día** (*m.*) **de San Valentín** St. Valentine's Day
sanador(a) healer
sancocho *stew made with meat, cassava, and plantains*
sandalias *f. pl.* sandals (4)
sandía watermelon
sándwich *m.* sandwich (7)
sangre *f.* blood (11)
sangriento/a bloody
sanitario/a health; **asistencia sanitaria** health care
sano/a healthy (11); **llevar una vida sana** to lead a healthy life (11)
santo saint
santo/a holy
santuario sanctuary
sarcástico/a sarcastic
sartén *f.* skillet
satélite *m.* satellite
satírico/a satirical
satisfacción *f.* satisfaction
satisfactorio/a satisfactory
satisfecho/a satisfied
Saudito/a: Arabia Saudita Saudi Arabia
sazonar to season
secadora clothes dryer (10)
secar(se) (qu) to dry (oneself)
sección *f.* section
seco/a dry
secretario/a secretary (2)
secreto *n.* secret

secreto/a *adj.* secret
secuencia sequence
secundario/a secondary; **escuela secundaria** high school
sed *f.* thirst; **tener (mucha) sed** to be (very) thirsty (7)
seda silk (4); **de seda** *adj.* silk (4)
sedentario/a sedentary
seducir (*like* **conducir**) to seduce
segmento segment
seguida: en seguida immediately (5)
seguidor(a) follower
seguimiento following
seguir (sigo) (i) to follow (6); to keep on going (15)
según according to (3)
segundo/a second (13); **segundo piso** second floor (third story) (12)
seguridad *f.* security; safety; **control** (*m.*) **de seguridad** security (check) (8); **pasar por el control de seguridad** to go/pass through security (check) (8)
seguro *n.* insurance
seguro/a *adj.* sure, certain (6); **es seguro que** it's a sure thing that (13) **no es seguro** it's not sure (13); **no estar seguro/a de** to not be sure of (13)
seis six (1)
seiscientos/as six hundred (4)
selección *f.* selection; choice
seleccionador(a) *adj.* selection
seleccionar to select; to choose
selva jungle; **Selva Amazónica** Amazon Jungle
selvático/a *adj.* jungle
semáforo traffic signal (15)
semana week; **días** (*m. pl.*) **de la semana** days of the week (5); **fin** (*m.*) **de semana** weekend (2); **la próxima semana** next week (5); **la semana que viene** next week (5); **una vez a la semana** once a week (3)
semanal *m., f.* weekly
sembrar (siembro) to sow, plant
semejante similar
semejanza similarity
semestre *m.* semester
semi-cerrado/a semiclosed
semilla seed
senado senate
senador(a) senator (18)
sencillo/a simple
senda path
senderismo *n.* hiking
sendero path
sensación *f.* sensation
sensibilidad *f.* sensitivity
sensible sensitive
sentarse (me siento) to sit down (5)
sentido sense
sentimental: relación (*f.*) **sentimental** emotional relationship (16)

sentimiento feeling, emotion
sentir (siento) (i) to regret; to feel sorry (13); **lo siento (mucho)** I'm (very) sorry (14); **sentirse** to feel (*an emotion*) (9)
señalar to note; to point out
señor (Sr.) *m.* man; Mr.; sir (1)
señora (Sra.) woman; Mrs.; ma'am (1)
señorita (Srta.) young woman; Miss; Ms. (1)
separación *f.* separation (16)
separar(se) (de) to separate (from) (16)
septiembre *m.* September (6)
séptimo/a seventh (13)
ser to be (1); **ayer fue (miércoles...)** yesterday was (Wednesday . . .) (5); **¿cómo es usted?** what are you (*form. s.*) like? (1); **¿de dónde eres (tú)?** where are you (*fam. s.*) from? (1); **¿de dónde es usted?** where are you (*form. s.*) from? (1); **de última moda** it's trendy (hot) (4); **eres** you are (1); **es** he/she is, you (*form. s.*) are (1); **es absurdo que** it's absurd that (13); **es cierto que** it's certain that (13); **es de...** it is made of . . . (4); **es extraño que** it's strange that (13); **es (im)posible que** it's (im)possible that (13); **es (im)probable que** it's (un) likely, (im)-probable that (13); **es increíble que** it's incredible that (13); **es la una** it's one o'clock (1); **es normal que** it's normal that (13); **es seguro que** it's a sure thing that (13); **es terrible que** it's terrible that (13); **es una lástima que** it's a shame that (13); **es urgente que** + *subj.* it's urgent that (12); **fue sin querer** I didn't mean to do it (14); **llegar (gu) a ser** to become; **no es seguro/(im)posible, (im)probable que** + *subj.* it is not sure/(im)possible, (im)probable that (13); **pasar de ser** to go from being; **¿qué hora es?** what time is it? (1); **ser aburrido/a** to be boring (10); **ser aficionado/a (a)** to be a fan (of) (10); **ser casado/a** to be a married person (16); **ser divertido/a** to be fun (10); **ser en** + *place* to take place in/at (*a place*) (9); **son las...** it's . . . o'clock (1); **(yo) soy de...** I am from . . . (1)
ser (*m.*) **humano** human being
serie *f.* series
serio/a serious
serpiente *f.* snake
servicio service (15); **estación** (*f.*) **de servicio** gas station (15); **servicio militar** military service (18)
servilleta napkin
servir (sirvo) (i) to serve (5); **servir para** to be used for (5)

sesenta sixty (3)

sesión *f.* session

setecientos/as seven hundred (4)

setenta seventy (3)

sevillano/a of or pertaining to Seville

sexismo sexism

sexo sex

sextillo/a sextuplet

sexto/a sixth (13)

si if (4); **por si acaso** just in case (14)

sí yes (1); **sí, me gusta...** yes, I like . . . (1)

sicología psychology (2)

sicólogo/a psychologist (17)

siempre always (3)

sierra mountain

siesta nap; **dormir la siesta** to take a nap

siete seven (1)

siglo century

significado meaning

significar (qu) to mean

significativo/a significant

signo sign

siguiente following (5)

sílaba syllable

silencio silence

silla chair (2)

sillón *m.* armchair (5)

simbólico/a symbolic

simbolizar (c) to symbolize

símbolo symbol

similaridad *f.* similarity

similitud *f.* similarity

simpático/a nice, likeable (3)

sin without (5); **fue sin querer** I didn't mean to do it (14); **sin duda** without a doubt; **sin embargo** nevertheless (6); **sin que** *conj.* without; unless (16)

sinagoga synagogue

sinceridad *f.* sincerity

sincero/a sincere

sino but (rather); **sino que** *conj.* but (rather)

sinónimo synonym

sintético/a synthetic

síntoma *m.* symptom (11)

siquiatra *m., f.* psychiatrist (17)

sísmico/a seismic

sismorresistente earthquake resistant

sistema *m.* system; **analista** (*m., f.*) **de sistemas** systems analyst (17)

sistemático/a systematic

sitio place, location; **sitio web** website (12)

situación *f.* situation

situado/a situated

situarse (me sitúo) to situate oneself; to be placed (*in time*)

snowboard *m.* snowboarding

soberano/a sovereign

sobre *prep.* about (4); on; on top of; over

sobremesa after-dinner conversation

sobrenatural *adj.* supernatural

sobresaliente outstanding

sobresalir (like **salir**) to stand out

sobreviviente *adj., m., f.* surviving

sobrevivir to survive

sobrino/a nephew/niece (3)

social social; **ciencias** (*f. pl.*) **sociales** social sciences (2); **red** (*f.*) **social** social network (12); **trabajador(a) social** social worker (17)

socialismo socialism

socialista *n., adj. m., f.* socialist

socializar (c) to socialize

sociedad *f.* society

socioeconómico/a socioeconomic

sociología sociology (2)

sodio sodium

sofá *m.* couch (5)

soja soybean

sol *m.* sun; **gafas** (*f. pl.*) **de sol** sunglasses (4) **hace (mucho) sol** it's (very) sunny (6.); **tomar el sol** to sunbathe (8)

solar solar; **bloqueador** (*m.*) **solar** sunscreen (8); **energía solar** solar energy (15); **pánel** (*m.*) **solar** solar panel

solas: a solas alone

soldado soldier (17); **mujer** (*f.*) **soldado** female soldier (17)

soleado/a sunny

soledad *f.* solitud

soler (suelo) to tend to

solicitante *m., f.* applicant

solicitar to apply for (*a job*) (17)

solicitud *f.* application (*form*) (17)

sólido/a solid

solitario/a solitary, lonely

solo *adv.* only (2)

solo/a *adj.* alone (5)

soltero/a single (*not married*) (16)

soltura: hablar con soltura to speak fluently

solución *f.* solution

sombra shadow; shade

sombrero hat (4); **sombrero hongo** bowler hat, derby

sonar (sueno) to ring; to sound (10)

sonido sound

sonreír (like **reír**) to smile (9)

sopa soup (7)

soportar to bear

sor *f.* sister (*religious*)

sorber to absorb

sorprendente surprising

sorprender (like **gustar**) to surprise (13)

sorpresa surprise

sospechoso/a suspicious

sostenible sustainable

sostenido/a held

su(s) *poss. adj.* his, her, its, your (*form. s.*); their, your (*form. pl.*) (3)

suave pleasant

subir (a) to go up; to get on (*a vehicle*) (8)

subjuntivo *gram.* subjunctive

subordinado/a: cláusula subordinada *gram.* subordinate clause

subregión *f.* subregion

substituir (*like* **construir**) to substitute

subtítulo subtitle

suburbio suburb

suceder to occur; to happen

suceso happening

sucesor(a) successor

sucio/a dirty (6)

sudadera sweatshirt (4)

Sudamérica South America

sudamericano/a South American

Suecia Sweden

sueco/a Swedish

suegro/a father-in-law, mother-in-law

sueldo salary (17)

suelo floor

sueño dream; **tener sueño** to be sleepy (4)

suerte *f.* luck (14); **tener buena/mala suerte** to have good/bad luck; to be (un)lucky (14)

suéter *m.* sweater (4)

suficiente enough (11); **lo suficiente** enough (11)

sufijo *gram.* suffix

sufrimiento suffering

sufrir (de) to suffer (from, with) (14)

sugerencia suggestion

sugerir (sugiero) (i) to suggest (9)

suicidio suicide

suizo/a Swiss

sujeto *gram.* subject

sumo/a supreme

superar to overtake

superhombre *m.* superman

superlativo *gram.* superlative

supermercado supermarket (12)

superstición *f.* superstition

supersticioso/a superstitious

supervisor(a) supervisor

suplemento supplement

suponer (*like* **poner**) to suppose

supremo/a supreme

supuesto: ¡por supuesto! of course! (14)

sur *m.* south (6)

sureste *m.* southeast

surfear to surf

surfing: **hacer *surfing*** to surf (10)

suroeste *m.* southwest

surrealismo Surrealism

surrealista *adj. m., f.* surrealist

suscripción *f.* subscription

suspender to suspend

suspenso suspense

sustantivo *gram.* noun (2)
sustrato essence
sutil subtle
SUV *m.* SUV (15)
suyo/a(s) *poss. adj.* your (*form. s., pl.*); his, her, its, their; *poss. pron.* (of) your, yours (*form. s., pl.*); (of) his, her, its, their; (of) theirs (17)

T

tabaco tobacco
tabla table; chart
tableta tablet
tabú *f.* taboo
tacón *m.* heel
taconeo heel tap
tailandés, tailandesa Thai
Tailandia Thailand
taíno/a *pre-Columbian culture of the Caribbean*
tal such, such a; **con tal de** provided (16); **con tal (de) que** *conj.* provided (that) (16); **¿qué tal?** how are you? (1); **tal como** just as; **tal vez** perhaps
taladro drill
talento talent
talla size
taller *m.* (repair) shop (15)
tamal *m.* tamale
tamalada *get-together to make and eat tamales*
tamaño size
también also (1)
tambor *m.* drum
tambora African drum
tampoco neither, not either (7)
tan *adv.* so; as; **tan... como** as . . . as (6); **tan pronto como** as soon as (17)
tanque *m.* tank (15)
tanto/a *adj.* as much, so much; such (a); *pl.* so many; as many; **tanto como** as much as (6); **tanto/a(s)... como** as much/many . . . as (6)
tapa lid
tapar to cover
tapas *f. pl.* appetizers (9)
tapir *m.* tapir
taquigrafía shorthand
tardar to be long / take (a long) time
tarde *adv.* late (2)
tarde *f.* afternoon; **buenas tardes** good afternoon (1); **de la tarde** in the afternoon, P.M. (1); **por la tarde** in the afternoon (2)
tarea homework (5); **tarea doméstica** household chore
tarjeta card (8); **tarjeta bancaria** debit card (17); **tarjeta de crédito** credit card (7); **tarjeta de embarque** boarding pass (8); **tarjeta de identidad** identification card; **tarjeta de identificación**

identification card (14); **tarjeta postal** postcard (8)
tarta cake
tartamudo/a stutterer
tata *fam.* grandpa
tatuaje *m.* tattoo
taza cup (14)
té *m.* tea (7); **rosa té** tea rose
teatral theatrical; **obra teatral** play
teatro theater; **ir al teatro** to go to the theater (10); **obra de teatro** play (13)
techo roof
teclado keyboard
técnico/a technician (17)
tecnología technology
tecnológico/a technological
teja tile
tejedor(a) weaver
tejer to weave (13)
tejido weaving; *pl.* woven goods (13); textiles
tela cloth
tele *f.* T.V.
telediario news program
telefonear to phone
telefonía telephone systems
telefónico/a *adj.* telephone
teléfono phone (2); **hablar por teléfono** to talk on the phone (2); **teléfono celular** cell phone (2); **teléfono fijo** landline (12)
telegrama *m.* telegram
telenovela soap opera
telespectador(a) television viewer
televidente *m., f.* television viewer
televisión (*f.*) (**plasma**) (plasma) television (12); **mirar la tele(visión)** to watch television (3)
televisor *m.* television set
tema *m.* theme, topic
temblar (tiemblo) to tremble
temblor *m.* trembling
temer to fear; to be afraid (13)
temperatura temperature (11); **tomarle la temperatura** to take (*someone's*) temperature (11)
templo temple
temporada season (*hunting, fashion, etc.*)
temporal temporary
temprano *adv.* early (2)
tendencia tendency
tender (tiendo): tender la cama to make the bed
tenedor *m.* fork
tener to have (4); **no tener razón** to be wrong (4); **tener... años** to be . . . years old (3); **tener buena/mala suerte** to have good/bad luck; to be (un)lucky (14); **tener cuidado** to be careful; **tener dolor de** to have a pain/ache in (11); **tener éxito** to be successful; **tener fiebre** to have a

fever; **tener ganas de** + *inf.* to feel like (*doing something*) (4); **tener la culpa** to be at fault; **tener miedo (de)** to be afraid (of) (4); **tener (mucha) hambre** to be (very) hungry (7); **tener (mucha) sed** to be (very) thirsty (7); **tener muchas presiones** to be under a lot of stress (14); **tener (mucho) calor** to be (very) warm, hot (6); **tener (mucho) frío** to be (very) cold (6); **tener prisa** to be in a hurry (4); **tener que** + *inf.* to have to (*do something*) (4); **tener razón** to be right (4); **tener sueño** to be sleepy (4)
tenis *m. inv.* tennis (10); *pl.* tennis shoes (4)
tensión *f.* tension; **tensión arterial** blood pressure
tentación *f.* temptation
tentempié *m.* snack
teñirse (me tiño) (i) el pelo to dye one's hair
teoría theory
terapeuta *m., f.* therapist
terapia therapy
tercer(o/a) third (13)
tereré *m.* traditional Paraguayan drink
terminación *f. gram.* ending
terminal *m.* station, terminal
terminar to finish
término term
termómetro thermometer
ternura tenderness
terraza terrace
terremoto earthquake
terreno piece of land
terrestre *adj.* earth
terrible terrible (13); **es terrible que** it's terrible that (13)
territorio territory
terrorismo terrorism (18)
terrorista *m., f.* terrorist (18); **ataque** (*m.*) **terrorista** (terrorist) attack (18)
tertulia get-together
tesis *f. inv.* thesis
testigo *m., f.* witness (18)
testimonio testimony
texteo text (message)
textil *adj.* textile
texto text; **libro de texto** textbook (2)
ti (*obj. of prep.*) you (*fam.*) (6)
tibetano/a Tibetan
tiempo weather; time (6); *gram.* tense; **a tiempo** on time (8); **conjunción** (*f.*) **de tiempo** conjunction of time (17); **empleo de tiempo completo/parcial** full-/part-time job/position (17); **hace (muy) buen/mal tiempo** it's (very) good/bad weather (6); **jornada de tiempo parcial** part-time job; **¿qué tiempo hace?** what's the weather like? (6); **tiempo libre** free time (10); **trabajo**

de tiempo completo/parcial full/part-time job (14)
tienda shop, store (4); **tienda de acampar** tent; **tienda (de campaña)** tent (8)
tierra land
Tierra Earth (15)
tigre *m.* tiger
tihuanaco/a Tiwanakan (*of or pertaining to the pre-Columbian Tiwanaku civilization of Bolivia*)
tilma poncho; shawl
timbre *m.* doorbell
tímido/a shy
tina bathtub
tinieblas *f. pl.* darkness
tinto/a: vino tinto red wine (7)
tío/a uncle/aunt (3); *m. pl.* aunts and uncles (3)
típico/a typical
tipo type, kind; **de todo tipo** of all kinds
tira cómica comic strip
tirar to throw
tiritar to shiver
títere *m.* puppet
título title
toalla towel (5)
toallero towel rack
tocar (qu) to touch; to play (*a musical instrument*) (2); to honk (15); **tocarle a uno** to be someone's turn (10)
tocineta bacon
todavía still (6)
todo *n.* everything; **de todo** everything (4); **de todo tipo** of all kinds
todo/a *adj.* all (3); every (3); **por todas partes** everywhere (14); **todo derecho/recto** straight ahead (15); **todos los días** every day (2)
todoterreno *inv.* all-terrain (15)
tolerante tolerant
tomar to take (2); to drink (2); **tomar el sol** to sunbathe (8); **tomar unas vacaciones** to take a vacation (8); **tomarle la temperatura** to take (*someone's*) temperature (11); **tomarle el pelo** to pull (*someone's*) leg
tomate *m.* tomato (7)
tono tone
toque *f.* touch
tonto/a silly, foolish (3)
torno: en torno a around
toro bull (15)
torpe clumsy (14)
torre *f.* tower
torta sandwich (*Mex.*)
tortilla potato omelet (*Sp.*); *thin unleavened cornmeal or flour pancake* (*Mex.*)
tortuga turtle

tos *f.* cough (11)
tosco/a rustic; crude
toser to cough (11)
tostado/a toasted (7); **pan** (*m.*) **tostado** toast (7)
tostadora toaster (10)
tostones *m. pl.* crispy fried plantain slices
totalidad *f.* totality
trabajador(a) *adj.* hardworking (3)
trabajador(a) *n.* worker; **trabajador(a) social** social worker (17)
trabajar to work (2)
trabajo work; job (12); report, (piece of) work (14); **carga de trabajo** workload; **trabajo de tiempo completo/parcial** full-/part-time job (14)
trabajólico/a workaholic
trabalenguas *m. inv.* tongue twister
tractor *m.* tractor
tradición *f.* tradition; **tradición cultural** cultural tradition (13)
tradicional traditional
traducción *f.* translation
traducir (*like* **conducir**) to translate
traductor(a) translator (17)
traer to bring (5)
tráfico traffic (15)
tragedia tragedy
trágico/a tragic
traje *m.* suit (4); **traje de baño** swimsuit (4)
trámite *m.* step; procedure
tranquilo/a calm (9); **llevar una vida tranquila** to lead a calm life (11)
transatlántico *n.* ocean liner
transbordador (*m.*) **espacial** space shuttle
transformar to transform
transición *f.* transition
tránsito traffic (15)
transmitir to pass on; to transmit
transnacional international
transporte *m.* transportation; **medio de transporte** means of transportation (8); **transporte público** public transportation
tras *prep.* after
trasero/a back, rear
trasladarse to move
trastienda back room (*of a store*)
tratable treatable
tratado treaty
tratamiento treatment (11)
tratar de + *inf.* to try to (*do something*) (13); **tratar de** + *noun* to deal with + *noun*
través: a través de across; through; throughout
travieso/a mischievous

trayectoria trajectory; path
trébol *m.* clover
trece thirteen (1)
treinta thirty (1); **y treinta** thirty minutes past (*the hour*) (1)
tren *m.* train (8); **estación** (*f.*) **de trenes** train station (8); **ir en tren** to go/travel by train (8)
tres three (1)
trescientos/as three hundred (4)
triángulo triangle
tribu *f.* tribe
tributo tribute
trigo wheat
trillizo/a triplet
trilogía trilogy
trimestre *m.* trimester
triste sad (6)
tristeza sadness
triunfar to triumph
trofeo trophy
trompeta trumpet
tropical tropical; **bosque** (*m.*) **tropical lluvioso** tropical rain forest
trópico *n.* tropics
tropiezo mistake
trotadora treadmill
trozo piece
trucha trout
trueno thunder
tú *subj. pron.* you (*fam. s.*) (2); **¿de dónde eres (tú)?** where are you (*fam. s.*) from? (1); **¿y tú?** and you (*fam. s.*)? (1)
tu(s) your (*fam. s.*) (3)
tuit *m.* tweet (12)
tuitear to tweet
tumba tomb
tuna cactus fruit
turismo tourism
turista *n. m., f.* tourist
turístico/a *adj.* tourist
turnarse to take turns
turno shift (*on a job*)
turrón *m. type of candy traditionally eaten at Christmas*
tutor(a) tutor
tuyo/a(s) *poss. adj.* your (*fam. s.*); *poss. pron.* yours; of yours (*fam. s.*) (17)
Twitter *m.* Twitter (12)

U

u or (*used instead of* **o** *before words beginning with* **o** *or* **ho**)
ubicación *f.* placement, location
ubicar (qu) to locate
ucraniano/a Ukranian
¡uf! *interj.* oof!; whew!
último/a last, final (14); **es de última moda** it's trendy (hot) (4); **por última vez** for the last time (14)

ultramoderno/a ultramodern

un, uno/a one (1); *ind. art.* a, an; **un millón (de)** one million (4); **un poco (de)** a little bit (of) (2); **una vez a la semana** once a week (3)

unánime unanimous

único/a *adj.* only; unique

unidad *f.* unity

unido/a united; **Estados** (*m. pl.*) **Unidos de América** United States of America; **Naciones** (*f. pl.*) **Unidas** United Nations; **Organización** (*f.*) **de Naciones Unidas (ONU)** United Nations (U.N.)

unificar (qu) to unify

unión *f.* union

unir to join (together); to unite; **unirse a** to join (*a cause, organization*)

universidad *f.* university (2)

universitario/a *adj.* (of the) university (14)

universo universe

urbanístico/a *adj.* of urban development

urbano/a urban

urgencias: sala de urgencias emergency room

urgente urgent (12); **es urgente (que)** + *subj.* it's urgent (that) (12)

uruguayo/a *n., adj.* Uruguayan

usar to wear; to use (4)

uso use

usted (Ud., Vd.) *sub. pron.* you (*form. s.*) (2); *obj.* (*of prep.*) you (*form. s.*) (2); **¿a usted le gusta... ?** do you (*form. s.*) like . . . ? (1); **¿cómo es usted?** what are you (*form. s.*) like? (1); **¿cómo se llama usted?** what is your (*form. s.*) name? (1); **¿de dónde es usted?** where are you (*form. s.*) from? (1); **¿y usted?** and you (*form. s.*)? (1)

ustedes (Uds., Vds.) *sub. pron.* you (*form. pl.*); *obj.* (*of prep.*) you (*form pl.*) (2)

usuario/a user (12)

útil useful

utilidad *f.* utility

utilizar (c) to use; to utilize

uva grape

¡uy! *interj.* oh!; ah!

V

vaca cow (15)

vacaciones *f. pl.* vacation; **de vacaciones** on vacation (8); **estar de vacaciones** to be on vacation (8); **ir de vacaciones a...** to go on vacation in/to . . . (8); **pasar las vacaciones en...** to spend one's vacation in . . . (8); **salir de vacaciones** to leave on vacation (8); **tomar unas vacaciones** to take a vacation (8)

vacuna vaccine (11)

vacunación *f.* vaccination

vacunarse to get a shot

vainilla vanilla

valenciano/a Valencian

Valentín: Día (*m.*) **de San Valentín** St. Valentine's Day

valiente courageous

valioso/a valuable

valle *m.* valley

vallenato *Colombian folk music*

valor *m.* value

valorar to value

valorización *f.* appreciation

vals *m. inv.* waltz

vampiro vampire

vanagloriarse to brag

vandalismo vandalism

vapor *m.* mist

vaquero/a cowboy/cowgirl

variación *f.* variation

variante variant

variar (varío) to vary

variedad *f.* variety

varios/as several

vasco/a *n., adj.* Basque

vasija earthenware pot; vessel

vaso (drinking) glass

vasto/a vast

vecindario neighborhood

vecino/a neighbor (12)

vegano/a *n., adj.* vegan

vegetariano/a *n., adj.* vegetarian

vehículo vehicle (15)

veinte twenty (1)

veinticinco twenty-five

veinticuatro twenty-four

veintidós twenty-two

veintinueve twenty-nine

veintiocho twenty-eight

veintiséis twenty-six

veintisiete twenty-seven

veintitrés twenty-three

veintiún, veintiuno/a twenty-one

vejez *f.* (*pl.* **vejeces**) old age (16)

vela candle (9)

velocidad *f.* speed; **límite** (*m.*) **de velocidad** speed limit (15)

vena vein

vendedor(a) salesperson (17)

vender to sell (3)

Venecia Venice

venerar to revere; to venerate

venezolano/a *n., adj.* Venezuelan

venir to come (4); **el año que viene** next year; **el lunes** (*m.*) **que viene** next Monday (5); **la semana que viene** next week (5)

venta sale

ventaja advantage

ventana window (2)

ventanilla small window (*on a plane*) (8)

ver (*p.p.* **visto**) to see (5); **a ver** let's see; **nos vemos** see you around (1)

verano summer (6)

veras: ¿de veras? really

verbo *gram.* verb (2); **verbo reflexivo** *gram.* reflexive verb (5)

verdad *f.* truth; **es verdad que** it's true that (13)

¿verdad? right, don't they (you...)? (4)

verdadero/a true; real

verde green (4)

verdura vegetable (7)

vergonzoso/a shameful

vergüenza embarrassment

verificar (qu) to verify

versión *f.* version

verso verse; line of a poem

verter (vierto) (i) to spill; to shed (*a tear*)

vestido dress (4)

vestir (visto) (i) to dress; **vestirse** to get dressed (5)

veterano/a *n.* veteran

veterinario/a veterinarian (17)

vez *f.* (*pl.* **veces**) time; **a veces** sometimes, at times (3); **alguna vez** once; ever; **cada vez más** increasingly; **cada vez mayor** greater and greater; **dos veces** twice; **en vez de** instead of; **otra vez** again; **por primera/última vez** for the first/last time (14); **tal vez** perhaps; **una vez** once; **una vez a la semana** once a week (3)

viajar to travel (8)

viaje *m.* trip (5); **agencia de viajes** travel agency; **agente de viajes** travel agent; **de viaje** on a trip, traveling (8); **hacer un viaje** to take a trip (5)

viajero/a traveler

vial *adj.* road

vicepresidente/a vice president

víctima victim (18)

victoria victory

vicuña vicuna (llama)

vida life (11); **vida académica** academic life (14); **llevar una vida sana/ tranquila** to lead a healthy/calm life (11); **ritmo de la vida** pace of life (15)

video video (12)

videocasetera video cassette recorder

videojuego videogame; **jugar (juego) (gu) a los videojuegos** to play videogames (10)

videollamada video call

videoturismo videotourism

vidrio glass

viejo/a old (3)

viento wind (6); **hace (mucho) viento** it's (very) windy (6)

viernes *m. inv.* Friday (5)

vietnamita *n., adj. m., f.* Vietnamese

vikingo/a Viking

vinagre *m.* vinegar

vino (blanco, tinto) (white, red) wine (7)

violación *f.* violation

violencia violence; **Día** (*m.*) **Internacional de la No Violencia Contra la Mujer** International No Violence Against Women Day

violento/a violent

violín *m.* violin

Virgen *f.* Virgin (Mary)

virreinato viceroyalty

virus *m. inv.* virus

visión *f.* vision

visita visit

visitante *m., f.* visitor

visitar to visit (10); **visitar un museo** to visit a museum (10)

víspera eve

vista view (12); **punto de vista** point of view

viudo/a widower/widow (16)

vivienda housing (12)

vivir to live (3)

vivo/a lively; bright (*of colors*)

vocabulario vocabulary

vocal *f.* vowel

voga: en voga in vogue

volante *m.* steering wheel; **furia al volante** road rage

volar (vuelo) to fly; **volar en avión** to fly; to go by plane (8)

volcán *m.* volcano

volcánico/a volcanic

voleibol *m.* volleyball (10)

voltear to turn (over)

volumen *m.* volume

voluntario/a volunteer

volver (vuelvo) (*p.p.* **vuelto**) to return (*to a place*) (5); **volver a** + *inf.* to (*do something*) again (5)

vos *subj. pron.* you (*fam. s. C.A., S.A.*)

vosotros/as *sub. pron.* you (*fam. pl. Sp.*); *obj.* (*of prep.*) you (*fam. pl. Sp.*) (2)

votación *f.* vote; voting

votante *m., f.* voter

votar to vote (18)

votos (*m. pl.*) **nupciales** wedding vows

voz *f.* (*pl.* **voces**) voice; **voz en off** voice over

vudú *m.* voodoo

vuelo flight (8); **asistente** (*m., f.*) **de vuelo** flight attendant (8)

vuelta: billete *m.* (*Sp.*) / **boleto** (*L.A.*) **de ida y vuelta** round-trip ticket (8)

vuelto/a (*p.p. of* **volver**) returned

vuestro/a(s) your (*fam. pl. Sp.*) (3); *poss. pron.* your (*fam. pl. Sp.*) (17)

vulnerar to violate; to hurt

W

web: página web webpage (12); **sitio web** website (12)

Y

y and (1); **y cuarto** a quarter (fifteen minutes) after (*the hour*) (1); **y media** half past (*the hour*) (1); **y quince** fifteen minutes after (*the hour*) (1); **y treinta** thirty minutes past (*the hour*) (1)

ya already (9); **ya no** no longer; **ya que** since

yacimiento deposit (*mineral*)

yerba herb

yerno son-in-law

yo *sub. pron.* I (2); **yo soy de...** I am from . . . (1)

yoga *m.* yoga; **hacer (el) yoga** to do yoga (10)

yogur *m.* yogurt (7)

yuca cassava, manioc; **¡qué yuca!** how difficult!

Z

zalamería flattery

zampoña *South American panpipe*

zanahoria carrot (7)

zancudo mosquito

zapatería shoe store

zapato shoe; *pl.* shoes (4)

zarzuela *traditional Spanish operetta*

zócalo central plaza (*Mex.*)

Zodíaco Zodiac

zona zone, area (12)

zoología zoology

zumo juice (*Sp.*)

VOCABULARIES

English-Spanish Vocabulary

A

@ **arroba** (12)
A.M. **de la mañana** (1)
able: to be able **poder** (4)
about **por** (6); **sobre** (4)
abroad: to go abroad **ir al extranjero** (8)
absence **falta** (15)
absent: to be absent (from) **faltar (a)** (9)
absentminded **distraído/a** (14)
absurd: it's absurd that **es absurdo que** (13)
academic **académico/a** (14); academic life **vida académica** (14)
accelerated **acelerado/a** (15)
accident **accidente** m. (14)
according to **según** (3)
account **cuenta** (17); to charge to an account **cargar (gu) a una cuenta** (17)
accountant **contador(a)** (17)
ache n. (in) **dolor (de)** (11); v. **doler (duele)** (like **gustar**) (11); to have an ache in **tener dolor de** (11)
acquainted: to be acquainted with **conocer (conozco)** (7)
act v. **actuar (actúo)** (13)
activity: fun activity **diversión** f. (10)
actor **actor** m. (13)
actress **actriz** f. (pl. **actrices**) (13)
additional **adicional** (1)
address **dirección** f. (7)
adjective gram. **adjetivo** (3); adjective of nationality **adjetivo de nacionalidad** (3); possessive adjective **adjetivo posesivo** (3)
administration: business administration **administración** (f.) **de empresas** (2)
adolescence **adolescencia** (16)
adolescent: as an adolescent **de adolescente** (10)
advice (piece of) **consejo** (7)
advisor **consejero/a** (2)
aerobics: to do aerobics **hacer ejercicios aeróbicos** (11)
affection **cariño** (16)
affectionate **cariñoso/a** (6)
afraid: to be afraid (of) **tener miedo (de)** (4), **temer** (13)
after prep. **después de** (5), conj. **después (de) que** (17)
afternoon: good afternoon **buenas tardes** (1); **muy buenas** (1); in the afternoon **de la tarde** (1), **por la tarde** (2)
afterward **luego** (5); afterwards **después** (5)
agent **agente** m., f. (8)
ago **hace** + time + **que** + preterite (14); preterite + **hace** + time (14)
agree **estar de acuerdo** (3)
agriculture **agricultura** (15)
ahead: straight ahead **(todo) derecho** (15), **todo recto** (15)
air **aire** m. (15)
airplane **avión** m. (8)
airport **aeropuerto** (8)
aisle **pasillo** (8)
alarm clock **despertador** m. (14)
all **todo/a** (3)
all-terrain **todoterreno** inv. (15)
allow **permitir** (12)
almost **casi** inv. (3); almost never **casi nunca** (3)
alone **solo/a** (5)
alongside of **al lado de** (6)
already **ya** (9)
also **también** (1)
always **siempre** (3)
am: I am **soy** (1); I am from **soy de** (1)
America: of the United States of America n., adj. **estadounidense** (3)
among prep. **entre** (6)
analyst: systems analyst **analista** (m., f.) **de sistemas** (17)
and **y** (1); and you? **¿y tú?** fam. s. (1), **¿y usted?** form. s. (1)
android **android** m. (12)
angry **enojado/a** (9); **furioso/a** (6); to get angry (with) **enojarse (con)** (9)
animal **animal** m. (15)
announce **anunciar** (8)
annoyed **molesto/a** (6)
another **otro/a** (3)
answer n. **respuesta** (6); v. to answer **contestar** (7)
antibiotic **antibiótico** (11)
anxiety **ansiedad** f. (14)
any **algún (alguna/os/as)** (7)
anybody: not anybody **nadie** (7)
anyone **alguien** (7)
anything **algo** (7); not anything **nada** (7)
apartment **apartamento** (2); apartment building **edificio de apartamentos** (12)

apologize **pedir disculpas** (14)
app(lication) **app** f. (12)
appetizers **botanas** f. pl. (Mex.) (9); **tapas** f. pl. (9)
apple **manzana** (7)
appliance: home appliance **aparato doméstico** (10)
applicant **aspirante** m., f. (17)
application (form) **solicitud** f. (17)
apply for (a job) **solicitar** (17)
appointment **cita** (11)
April **abril** m. (6)
architect **arquitecto/a** (13)
architecture **arquitectura** (13)
am: you (fam. s.) are **eres** (1); you (form. s.) are **es** (1)
area **zona** (12); smoking area **sala de fumadores/de fumar** (8)
argue (with/about) **discutir (con/por/sobre)** (9)
arm **brazo** (11)
armchair **sillón** m. (5)
armoire **armario** (5)
army **ejército** (18)
arrival **llegada** (8)
arrive **llegar (gu)** (3)
art **arte** m. (2); arts and crafts **artesanía** (13); the arts **artes** f. pl. (13); work of art **obra de arte** (13)
artist **artista** m., f. (13)
artistic **artístico/a** (13); artistic expression **expresión** (f.) **artística** (13)
as: as . . . as **tan... como** (6); as a child **de niño/a** (10); as a youth **de adolescente** (10); as much as **tanto como** (6); as much/many . . . as **tanto/a(s)... como** (6); as soon as **en cuanto** (17), **tan pronto como** (17)
ask (a question) **hacer una pregunta** (5), **preguntar** (8); to ask for **pedir** (5)
asleep: to fall asleep **dormirse** (5)
asparagus **espárragos** m. pl. (7)
assassinate **asesinar** (18)
assassination **asesinato** (18)
astronaut **astronauta** m., f. (17)
at **en** (1); at . . . (time of day) **a la(s)...** (1); at all **(para) nada** (8); at home **en casa** (2); at least **por lo menos** (9); at the beginning of **al principio de** (17);

at times **a veces** (3); at what time . . . ? **¿a qué hora... ?** (1)

attack: terrorist attack **ataque** (*m.*) **terrorista** (18)

attend (*class, function*) **asistir (a)** (3); to not attend **faltar (a)** (9)

attendant: flight attendant **asistente** (*m., f.*) **de vuelo** (8)

attract **atraer** (*like* **traer**) (*like* **gustar**) (13)

audience **espectadores** *m. pl.* (13); **público** (13)

August **agosto** (6)

aunt **tía** (3); aunts and uncles **tíos** *m. pl.* (3)

author **autor(a)** (13)

auto **auto** (15)

automatic teller machine (ATM) **cajero automático** (17)

automobile **auto(móvil)** *m.* (15)

autumn **otoño** (6)

avenue **avenida** (12)

avocado **aguacate** *m.* (7)

avoid **evitar** (15)

awful: an awful lot **muchísimo** (8)

B

baby-sitter **niñero/a** (10)

back tooth **muela** (11)

backpack **mochila** (2)

bad **mal, malo/a** (3); (very) bad (weather) out **(muy) mal tiempo** (6); the bad news/thing **lo malo** (11); to have a bad time **pasarlo mal** (9); to have bad luck **tener mala suerte** (14)

badly: to come/turn out badly **salir mal** (5)

baggage **equipaje** *m.* (8); to check baggage **facturar el equipaje** (8)

baked custard **flan** *m.* (7)

ball **pelota** (10)

ballet **ballet** *m.* (13)

banana **banana** (7)

bank **banco** (17)

bar: to go to a bar **ir a un bar** (10)

barbecue **barbacoa** (7)

bargain *n.* **ganga** (4); *v.* **regatear** (4)

baseball **béisbol** *m.* (10); baseball cap **gorra** (4)

basketball **basquetbol** *m.* (10)

bath: to take a bath **bañarse** (5)

bathroom **baño** (5); bathroom sink **lavabo** (5)

bathtub **bañera** (5)

battery **batería** (15)

be **estar** (2); **ser** (1), (3); to be . . . years old **tener... años** (3); to be a fan (of) **ser aficionado/a (a)** (10); to be a married person **ser casado/a** (16); to be able **poder** (4); to be absent (from) **faltar (a)** (9); to be afraid **temer** (13); to be afraid (of) **tener miedo (de)** (4); to be born **nacer (nazco)** (16); to be (very) cold **tener (mucho) frío** (6); to be

be comfortable (*temperature*) **estar bien** (6); to be distracted **ir distraído/a** (14); to be fond of each other **quererse** (11); to be fun **ser divertido/a** (10); to be happy (about) **alegrarse (de)** (12); to be (very) hungry **tener (mucha) hambre** (7); to be in a hurry **tener prisa** (4); to be left **quedar** (14); to be lucky **tener buena suerte** (14); to be married (to) **estar casado/a (con)** (16); to be on a diet **estar a dieta** (7); to be on vacation **estar de vacaciones** (8); to be right **tener razón** (4); to be sleepy **tener sueño** (4); to be (very) thirsty **tener (mucha) sed** (7); to be under a lot of pressure **estar bajo muchas presiones** (14); to be unlucky **tener mala suerte** (14); to be up to date **estar al día** (18); to be used for **servir (sirvo) (i) para** (5); to be (very) warm, hot **tener (mucho) calor** (6); to be wrong **no tener razón** (4)

beach **playa** (6)

beans **frijoles** *m. pl.* (7)

beautiful **bello/a** (15)

because **porque** (3); because of **por** (6)

become + *adj.* **ponerse** + *adj.* (9)

bed **cama** (5); to get out of bed **levantarse** (5); to get up on the wrong side of the bed **levantarse con el pie izquierdo** (14); to go to bed **acostarse (me acuesto)** (5); to make the bed **hacer la cama** (10); to stay in bed **guardar cama** (11)

bedroom **alcoba** (5)

beer **cerveza** (7)

before *prep.* **antes de** (16); *conj.* **antes (de) que** (16)

begin **empezar (empiezo) (c)** (5); to begin to (*do something*) **empezar a** + *inf.* (5)

beginning: at the beginning of **al principio de** (17)

behave **portarse bien** (9)

behind *prep.* **detrás de** (6)

believe (in) **creer (en)** (3); to not believe **no creer** (13)

below *prep.* **debajo de** (6)

belt **cinturón** *m.* (4)

beside **al lado de** (6)

best **mejor** (6)

better **mejor** (6)

between *prep.* **entre** (6)

beyond **a partir de** (4)

bicycle **bicicleta** (10); to ride a bicycle **montar en bicicleta** (10); **pasear en bicicleta** (10)

bicycling **ciclismo** (10)

big **gran, grande** (3); big screen (monitor) **pantalla grande** (12)

bill **cuenta** (7); **factura** (17); electric bill **electricidad** *f.* (12); (*money*) **billete** *m.* (17)

bird **pájaro** (3)

birthday **cumpleaños** *m. inv.* (6); birthday cake **pastel** (*m.*) **de cumpleaños** (9); to have a birthday **cumplir años** (9)

black **negro/a** (4)

blog **blog** *m.* (12)

blond(e) **rubio/a** (3)

blood **sangre** *f.* (11)

blouse **blusa** (4)

blue **azul** (4)

blue jeans **jeans** *m. pl.* (4)

blush *v.* **ponerse rojo/a** (9)

board **pizarrón** *m.* (2)

boarding: boarding gate **puerta de embarque** (8); boarding pass **tarjeta de embarque** (8)

boat **barco** (8); to go/travel by boat **ir en barco** (8)

body: human body **cuerpo humano** (11)

bomb **bomba** (18)

book **libro** (2); textbook **libro de texto** (2)

bookshelf **estante** *m.* (5)

bookstore **librería** (2)

boots **botas** *f. pl.* (4)

bore **aburrir** (*like* **gustar**) (13)

bored **aburrido/a** (6); to get bored **aburrirse** (10)

boring **pesado/a** (10); to be boring **ser aburrido/a** (10)

born: to be born **nacer (nazco)** (16)

borrow **pedir prestado/a** (17)

bother **molestar** (*like* **gustar**) (11)

boy **niño** (3); **chico** (4)

boyfriend **novio** (6)

brain **cerebro** (11)

brakes **frenos** *m. pl.* (15)

bread **pan** *m.* (7)

break **romper(se)** (14); to break up (with) **romper (con)** (16)

breakfast **desayuno** (7); to have (eat) breakfast **desayunar** (7)

breathe **respirar** (11)

bride **novia** (16)

bring **traer** (5)

brother **hermano** (3)

brown **(de) color café** (4)

brunet(te) **moreno/a** (3)

brush one's hair **peinarse** (5); to brush one's teeth **cepillarse los dientes** (5)

budget **presupuesto** (17)

build **construir** (15)

building **edificio** (2); apartment building **edificio de apartamentos** (12); building manager **portero/a** (12)

bull **toro** (15)

bump against/into **chocar (qu) con/ contra** (14); **pegarse (gu) con/ contra** (14) bureau **cómoda** (5)

bus **autobús** *m.* (8); bus station **estación** (*f.*) **de autobuses** (8); bus stop **parada del autobús** (12); to go; to travel by bus **ir en autobús** (8)

business **empresa** (17); business administration **administración** (*f.*) **de empresas** (2)

businessman **hombre** (*m.*) **de negocios** (17)

businesswoman **mujer** (*f.*) **de negocios** (17)

busy **ocupado/a** (6)

but **pero** (1)

butter **mantequilla** (7)

buy **comprar** (2)

by **por** (14); by check **con cheque** (17)

C

cabin (*on a ship*) **cabina** (8)

cafeteria **cafetería** (2)

cake **pastel** *m.* (7); birthday cake **pastel de cumpleaños** (9)

calculator **calculadora** (2)

calendar **calendario** (14)

call **llamar** (7); to be called **llamarse** (5)

calm **tranquilo/a** (9); to lead a calm life **llevar una vida tranquila** (11)

camera **cámara** (12)

campground **camping** *m.* (8)

camping: to go camping **hacer camping** (8)

candidate (*for a job*) **aspirante** *m., f.* (17); (*political*) **candidato/a** (18); to run as a candidate **postularse como candidato/a** (18); to run for a position as a candidate **postularse para un cargo como candidato/a** (18)

candle **vela** (9)

candy **dulces** *m. pl.* (7)

cap (baseball) **gorra** (4)

capital city **capital** *f.* (6)

car **coche** *m.* (3); **carro** (15); convertible car **carro descapotable** (15)

card: (post)card **tarjeta** (**postal**) (8); credit card **tarjeta de crédito** (7); debit card **tarjeta bancaria** (17); identification card **tarjeta de identificación** (14); to play cards **jugar** (**juego**) (**gu**) **a las cartas** (10)

cardinal point **punto cardinal** (6)

care: to take care of oneself **cuidarse** (11)

carrot **zanahoria** (7)

carry **llevar** (4)

case: in case *prep.* **en caso de** (16); *conj.* **en caso de que** (6); just in case **por si acaso** (14)

cash (*a check*) **cobrar** (17); *n.* **efectivo** (17); in cash **en efectivo** (17)

cashier **cajero/a** (17)

cat **gato** (3)

catch a cold **resfriarse** (**me resfrío**) (11)

CD **CD** *m.* (12)

CD-ROM **CD-ROM** *m.* (12)

celebrate **celebrar** (6)

celebratory **festivo/a** (9)

cell phone **teléfono celular** (2)

center (*political*) **centro** (18)

ceramics **cerámica** *s.* (13)

cereal **cereal** *m.* (7)

certain **seguro/a** (6); it's certain that **es cierto que** (13)

chair **silla** (2)

champagne **champán** *m.* (9)

change **cambiar** (**de**) (12)

channel **canal** *m.* (12)

charge (*someone for an item or service*) **cobrar** (17); to charge to an account **cargar** (**gu**) **a una cuenta** (17)

chat *n.* **chateo** (12)

check (*bank*) **cheque** *m.* (17); (*restaurant*) **cuenta** (7); by check **con cheque** (17); *v.* **revisar** (15); to check baggage **facturar el equipaje** (8)

check-up **chequeo** (11)

cheese **queso** (7)

chef **cocinero/a** (17)

chemistry **química** (2)

chess: to play chess **jugar** (**juego**) (**gu**) **al ajedrez** (10)

chicken **pollo** (7); roast chicken **pollo asado** (7)

chickpeas **garbanzos** *m. pl.* (7)

child: as a child **de niño/a** (10)

childhood **infancia** (16); **niñez** *f.* (16)

children **hijos** *m. pl.* (3)

chop: (pork) chop **chuleta** (**de cerdo**) (7)

chore: household chore **quehacer** (*m.*) **doméstico** (10)

Christmas **Navidad** *f.* (9)

Christmas Eve **Nochebuena** *f.* (9)

church **iglesia** (16)

citizen **ciudadano/a** (18)

city **ciudad** *f.* (3)

civic duty **responsabilidad** (*f.*) **cívica** (18)

class (*of students*) **clase** *f.* (2); (*academic*) **clase** *f.* (2)

classic(al) **clásico/a** (13)

classmate **compañero/a** (**de clase**) (2)

classroom **salón** (*m.*) **de clase** (2)

clean *adj.* **limpio/a** (6); to clean (the) house **limpiar** (**la casa**) (10)

clear the table **quitar la mesa** (10)

clerk **dependiente/a** (2)

clever **listo/a** (3)

click *v.* **hacer clic** (*m.*) (12)

client **cliente/a** (2)

climate **clima** *m.* (6)

clock: alarm clock **despertador** *m.* (14)

close **cerrar** (**cierro**) (5)

close to *prep.* **cerca de** (6)

closed **cerrado/a** (6)

closet (*free-standing*) **armario** (5)

clothes dryer **secadora** (10)

clothing **ropa** (4)

cloudy: it's (very) cloudy **está** (**muy**) **nublado** (6)

clumsy **torpe** (14)

coat **abrigo** (4)

coffee **café** *m.* (2)

coffeemaker **cafetera** (10)

cognate **cognado** (2)

coin **moneda** (17)

cold (*illness*) **resfriado** *n.* (11); it's (very) cold (*weather*) **hace** (**mucho**) **frío** (6); to be (very) cold **tener** (**mucho**) **frío** (6); to catch/get a cold **resfriarse** (**me resfrío**) (11)

collect **recoger** (**recojo**) (14)

collision **choque** *m.* (18)

color **color** *m.* (6)

comb one's hair **peinarse** (5)

come **venir** (4); to come out badly **salir mal** (5); to come out well **salir bien** (5)

comedy **comedia** (13)

comfortable **cómodo/a** (4); to be comfortable (*temperature*) **estar bien** (6)

coming (*time*) **que viene** (5)

command **mandato** (7)

communicate (with) **comunicarse** (**qu**) (**con**) (18)

communication (*subject*) **comunicaciones** *f. pl.* (2); medium of communication **medio de comunicación** (18)

comparison **comparación** *f.* (6)

complain (about) **quejarse** (**de**) (8)

compose **componer** (*like* **poner**) (13)

composer **compositor(a)** (13)

computer **computadora** (2); computer file **archivo** (12); computer science **computación** *f.* (2); laptop (computer) **computadora portátil** (2)

concert **concierto** (10); to go to a concert **ir a un concierto** (10)

conductor **director(a)** (13)

congested (*with a cold*) *adj.* **resfriado/a** (11)

congratulations! **¡felicitaciones!** (9)

Congressional representative **representante** (*m., f.*) **al congreso** (18)

conjunction *gram.* **conjunción** *f.* (17); conjunction of time **conjunción** (*f.*) **de tiempo** (17)

connect **conectarse** (12)

conserve **conservar** (15)

contact lenses **lentes** (*m. pl.*) **de contacto** (11)

contaminated **contaminado/a** (15)

content *adj.* **contento/a** (6)

continue **continuar** (**continúo**) (6); **seguir** (**sigo**) (**i**) (6) control: remote control **control** (*m.*) **remoto** (12)

convertible car **carro descapotable** (12)

cook *v.* **cocinar** (7); *n.* **cocinero/a** (17)

cookie **galleta** (7)

cool: it's cool (weather) **hace fresco** (6)

copy *n.*: copy machine **fotocopiadora** (12); *v.* **copiar** (12); **hacer (foto)copia** (12)

corner (*street*) **esquina** (15)

corporation **empresa** (17)

cost: how much does it (do they) cost? **¿cuánto cuesta(n)?** (4)

cotton **de algodón** *adj.* (4)

couch **sofá** *m.* (5)

cough *n.* **tos** *f.* (11); cough syrup **jarabe** *m.* (11); *v.* **toser** (11)

counter **mostrador** *m.* (8)

country **país** *m.* (3)

countryside **campo** (15)

couple (*married*) **pareja** (16); **matrimonio** (16)

course (*academic*) **clase** *f.* (2); (*of a meal*) **plato** (7); course syllabus **programa** (*m.*) **del curso** (14); main course **plato principal** (7); of course! **¡por supuesto!** (14)

courteous expression **expresión** (f.) **de cortesía** (1)

courtesy **cortesía** (1)

cousin **primo/a** (3); *pl.* **primos** (3)

cover **cubrir** (*p.p.* **cubierto**) (15)

cow **vaca** (15)

craft: arts and crafts **artesanía** (13)

crash *n.* **choque** *m.* (18); *v.* (*computer*) **fallar** (12)

crazy **loco/a** (6)

create **crear** (13)

credit card **tarjeta de crédito** (7)

crime **delito** (15)

cruise (ship) **crucero** (8)

cry **llorar** (9)

cucumber **pepino** (7)

cuisine **cocina** (7)

cultural **cultural** (13); cultural tradition **tradición** (f.) **cultural** (13)

cup **taza** (14)

current *adj.* **actual** (12)

currently **en la actualidad** (10)

custard: baked custard **flan** *m.* (7)

customs (*at a border*) **aduana** (8); to go/ pass through customs **pasar por la aduana** (8)

D

dad **papá** *m.* (3)

daily **diario/a** (5)

dance *n.* **baile** *m.* (13); **danza** (13); *v.* **bailar** (2)

dancer **bailarín, bailarina** (13)

date **cita** (11); (*calendar*) **fecha** (6); to be up to date **estar al día** (18); what's today's date? **¿cuál es la fecha de hoy?** (6), **¿qué fecha es hoy?** (6)

daughter **hija** (3)

day **día** *m.* (2); day after tomorrow **pasado mañana** (5); days of the week **días** (*m. pl.*) **de la semana** (5); every day **todos los días** (2); the day before yesterday **anteayer** (5); what day is today? **¿qué día es hoy?** (5)

deadline **plazo** (14)

dear **querido/a** (6)

death **muerte** *f.* (16)

debit card **tarjeta bancaria** (17)

December **diciembre** *m.* (6)

delay **demora** (8)

demonstration **manifestación** *f.* (18)

demonstrative *gram.* **demostrativo/a** (4)

dense **denso/a** (15)

dentist **dentista** *m., f.* (11)

deny **negar (niego) (gu)** (13)

department store **almacén** *m.* (4)

departure **salida** (8)

deposit **depositar** (17)

design **diseñar** (13)

designer: graphic designer **diseñador(a) gráfico/a** (17)

desk **escritorio** (2)

dessert **postre** *m.* (7)

destination **destino** (8)

destroy **destruir** (*like* **construir**) (15)

detail **detalle** *m.* (9)

develop **desarrollar** (15)

development **desarrollo** (15)

dictator **dictador(a)** (18)

dictatorship **dictadura** (18)

dictionary **diccionario** (2)

die **morir(se) ([me] muero) (u)** (9)

diet: to be on a diet **estar a dieta** (7)

difficult **difícil** (6); **pesado/a** (10)

dining room **comedor** *m.* (5)

dinner **cena** (7); to have (eat) dinner **cenar** (7)

direct **dirigir (dirijo)** (13)

director **director(a)** (13)

dirty **sucio/a** (6)

disagree **no estar de acuerdo** (3)

disaster **desastre** *m.* (14)

disc: compact disc (CD) **disco compacto (CD** *m.*) (12)

disco: to go to a disco **ir a una discoteca** (10)

discover **descubrir** (*p.p.* **descubierto**)

discrimination **discriminación** *f.* (18)

dish **plato** (7)

dishwasher **lavaplatos** *m. inv.* (10)

distracted **distraído/a** (14); to be distracted **ir distraído/a** (14)

divorce *n.* **divorcio** (16); *v.* **divorciarse (de)** (16)

divorced (from) **divorciado/a (de)** (16)

dizzy **mareado/a** (11)

do **hacer** (5); do you like . . . ? **¿a usted le gusta… ?** *form. s.* (1); to (*do something*) again **volver a** + *inf.* (5); to do aerobics **hacer ejercicios** (*m. pl.*) **aeróbicos** (11); to do Pilates **hacer (el método) Pilates** (11); to do poorly **salir mal** (5); to do well **salir bien** (5); to do yoga **hacer (el) yoga** (10)

doctor (*medical*) **médico/a** (3)

dog **perro** (3)

domestic (*related to the home*) **doméstico/a** (10)

domesticated **doméstico/a** (15)

don't they (you…)? **¿no?** (4), **¿verdad?** (4)

door **puerta** (2)

doorman **portero/a** (12)

dormitory **residencia** (2)

dot: on the dot (*time*) **en punto** (1)

doubt **dudar** (12)

download **bajar** (12); **descargar (gu)** (12)

downtown **centro** (4)

drama **drama** *m.* (13)

draw **dibujar** (13); (*attract*) **atraer** (*like* **traer**) (*like* **gustar**) (13)

drawer **dibujante** *m., f.* (13)

drawing **dibujo** (13)

dress **vestido** (4)

dressed: to get dressed **vestirse (me visto) (i)** (5)

dresser **cómoda** (5)

drink *n.* **bebida** (5); soft drink **refresco** (7); *v.* **beber** (3); **tomar** (2)

drive *n.*: hard drive **discoduro** (12); *v.* **manejar** (12); **conducir (conduzco)** (15)

driver **conductor(a)** (15); driver's license **licencia de conducir/manejar** (15)

drop **caer** (14)

drum set **batería** (15)

dryer: clothes dryer **secadora** (10)

during **durante** (5)

duty: civic duty **responsabilidad** (f.) **cívica** (18)

DVD **DVD** *m.* (12)

E

e-mail **e-mail** *m.* (12); **correo electrónico** (12)

e-ticket **billete** (*m.*) (*Sp.*) / **boleto** (*L.A.*) **electrónico** (8)

each **cada** *inv.* (5)

ear **oreja** (11); inner ear **oído** (11)

ear/head phones **auriculares** *m. pl.* (12)

early *adv.* **temprano** (2)

earn (*income*) **ganar** (13)

earrings **aretes** *m. pl.* (4)

Earth **Tierra** (15)

east **este** *m.* (6)

Easter **Pascua** (9)

easy **fácil** (6)

eat **comer** (3); to eat breakfast **desayunar** (7); to eat dinner, supper cenar (7); to eat lunch **almorzar (ue) (c)** (5)

economics **economía** (2)

economize **economizar (c)** (17)

economy **economía** (2)

egg **huevo** (7)

eight **ocho** (1)

eight hundred **ochocientos/as** (4)

eighteen **dieciocho** (1)

eighth **octavo/a** (13)

eighty **ochenta** (3)

either: not either **tampoco** (7)

electric bill **electricidad** *f.* (12)

electrical **eléctrico/a** (15); electrical energy **energía eléctrica** (15)

electrician **electricista** *m., f.* (17)

electricity **electricidad** *f.* (12)

elephant **elefante** *m.* (15)

elevator **ascensor** *m.* (12)

eleven **once** (1)

embarrassed **avergonzado/a** (9)

embrace **abrazarse (c)** (11)

emotion **emoción** *f.* (9)

emotional **afectivo/a** (9); emotional relationship **relación** *(f.)* **sentimental** (16); emotional state **estado afectivo** (9)

end of the year **fin** *(m.)* **de año** (9)

end table **mesita** (5)

endangered species **especie** *(f.)* **en peligro de extinción** (15)

energy **energía** (15); electrical energy **energía eléctrica** (15); nuclear energy **energía nuclear** (15); renewable energy **energía renovable** (15); solar energy **energía solar** (15); wind energy **energía eólica** (15)

engagement **noviazgo** (16)

engineer **ingeniero/a** (17)

English *(language)* **inglés** *n. m.* (2); *n., adj.* **inglés, inglesa** (3)

enjoy oneself **divertirse (me divierto) (i)** (5)

enough **bastante** (16), **suficiente** (11); **lo suficiente** (11)

environment **medio ambiente** (15)

equality **igualdad** *f.* (18)

equipment **equipo** (12); electronic equipment **equipo electrónico** (12)

eruption **erupción** *f.* (18)

evening: good evening **buenas noches** (1); **muy buenas** (1); in the evening **de la noche** (1); **por la noche** (2)

event **acontecimiento** (18); **hecho** (9)

every **cada** *inv.* (5); **todo/a** (3); every day **todos los días** (2)

everything **de todo** (4)

everywhere **por todas partes** (14)

exam **examen** *m.* (4)

example: for example **por ejemplo** (14)

excuse me **(con) permiso** (1), **perdón** (1)

exercise *n.* **ejercicio** (5); *v.* **hacer ejercicio** (5)

expect **esperar** (7)

expense **gasto** (12)

expensive **caro/a** (4)

explain **explicar (qu)** (8)

expression (phrase) **expresión** *f.* (1); artistic expression **expresión artística** (13)

extinction **extinción** *f.* (15)

extract **sacar (qu)** (11); to extract *(someone's)* tooth/molar **sacarle (qu) un diente / una muela** (11)

eye **ojo** (11)

F

Facebook **Facebook** *m.* (12); to go into Facebook **entrar en Facebook** (12)

fact **hecho** (9)

factory **fábrica** (15)

faithful **fiel** (3)

fall *(season) n.* **otoño** (6); *v.* **caer** (14); to fall asleep **dormirse** (5); to fall down **caerse** (14); to fall in love (with) **enamorarse (de)** (16)

familiar: to be familiar with **conocer (conozco)** (7)

family **familia** (3)

fan: to be a fan (of) **ser aficionado/a (a)** (10)

far from **lejos de** (6)

fare **pasaje** *m.* (8)

farm **finca** (15)

farmer **agricultor(a)** (15)

farming **agricultura** (15)

fascinate **fascinar** (like **gustar**) (13)

fast **acelerado/a** (15)

fat **gordo/a** (3)

father **padre** *m.* (3), **papá** *m.* (3)

FAX **fax** *m.* (12)

fear *n.* **miedo** (4); *v.* **temer** (13)

February **febrero** (6)

feel **sentir** (13); *(an emotion)* **sentirse** (9); to feel like *(doing something)* **tener ganas de** + *inf.* (4); to feel sorry **lamentar** (13)

female housekeeper **ama** *(f.) (but* **el ama**) **de casa** (17)

female soldier **mujer** *(f.)* **soldado** (17)

festive **festivo/a** (9)

fever **fiebre** *f.* (11)

few **poco/a** (11)

fiancé **novio** (16)

fiancée **novia** (16)

field **campo** (15)

fifteen **quince** (1); fifteen minutes till *(hour)* **menos cuarto/quince** (1); young woman's fifteenth birthday party **quinceañera** (9)

fifth **quinto/a** (13)

fifty **cincuenta** (3)

fight *n.* **lucha** (18); *v.* **luchar** (18), **pelear** (10)

file *(computer)* **archivo** (12)

fill (up) **llenar** (15); to fill out *(a form)* **llenar** (17)

final **último/a** (14)

finally **por fin** (5), **finalmente** (5)

find **encontrar (encuentro)** (9); to find out (about) **enterarse (de)** (18)

fine **muy bien** (1); it's fine **está bien** (6)

finger **dedo (de la mano)** (11)

finish **acabar** (14)

fire *(someone) (from a job)* **despedir** *(like* **pedir)** (17)

first *adv.* **primero** (5); *adj.* **primer(o/a)** (13); first floor (second story) **primer piso** (12); for the first time **por primera vez** (14); the first of *(month)* **el primero de** (6)

fish *(cooked)* **pescado** (7); *(live)* **pez** *m. (pl.* **peces)** (15)

five **cinco** (1)

five hundred **quinientos/as** (4)

fix **arreglar** (15)

fixed price **precio fijo** (4)

flat: flat screen *(monitor)* **pantalla plana** (12); flat tire **llanta desinflada** (15)

flexible **flexible** (14)

flight **vuelo** (8); flight attendant **asistente** *(m., f.)* **de vuelo** (8)

flip-flops **chanclas** *f. pl.* (4)

floor *(of a building)* **piso** (12); first/second floor (second/third story) **primer/segundo piso** (12); ground floor **planta baja** (12); to sweep the floor **barrer el piso** (10)

flower **flor** *f.* (8)

flu **gripe** *f.* (11)

fly by plane **volar (vuelo) en avión** (8)

folder *(computer)* **carpeta** (12)

follow **seguir (sigo) (i)** (6)

following *adj.* **siguiente** (5)

fond: to be fond of each other **quererse** (11)

food **comida** (7)

foodstuff **comestibles** *m. pl.* (7)

foolish **tonto/a** (3)

foot **pie** *m.* (11)

football **fútbol** *(m.)* **americano** (10)

for **para** (3); **por** (8); for example **por ejemplo** (14); for heaven's sake **por Dios** (14); for that reason **por eso** (3); for what purpose? **¿para qué... ?** (16); what for? **¿para qué... ?** (16)

forbid **prohibir (prohíbo)** (12)

foreign **extranjero/a** (2); foreign language **lengua extranjera** (2)

foreigner **extranjero/a** (2)

forest **bosque** *m.* (15)

forget **olvidar** (9)

form **forma** (4); *(to fill out)* **formulario** (17)

forty **cuarenta** (3)

four **cuatro** (1)

four hundred **cuatrocientos/as** (4)
fourteen **catorce** (1)
fourth *adj.* **cuarto/a** (13)
free (*unoccupied*) **libre** (10); free time **ratos** (*m. pl.*) **libres** (10), **tiempo libre** (10)
freeway **autopista** (15)
freezer **congelador** *m.* (10)
French (*language*) **francés** *m.* (2); French fried potato **papa/patata frita** (7)
frequently **con frecuencia** (2), **frecuentemente** (11)
fresh **fresco/a** (7)
Friday **viernes** *m. inv.* (5)
fried **frito/a** (7); French fried potato **papa/patata frita** (7)
friend **amigo/a** (2)
friendly **amistoso/a** (16)
friendship **amistad** *f.* (16)
from **de** (1); from the **del** (3); I am from . . . **(yo) soy de...** (1); where are you from? **¿de dónde eres (tú)?** *fam. s.* (1); **¿de dónde es usted?** *form. s.* (1)
front: in front of **delante de** (6)
frozen **congelado/a** (6)
fruit **fruta** (7); fruit juice **jugo de fruta** (7)
full-time job **empleo de tiempo completo** (17)
fun activity **diversión** *f.* (10); to be fun **ser divertido/a** (10)
function **funcionar** (12)
furious **furioso/a** (6)
furniture (*piece*) **mueble** *m.* (5)

G

game **partido** (10)
garage **garaje** *m.* (5)
garden **jardín** *m.* (5)
gas (*not for cars*) **gas** *m.* (12)
gas station **estación** (*f.*) **de servicio** (15), **gasolinera** (15)
gasoline **gasolina** (15)
gate: boarding gate **puerta de embarque** (8)
generally **por lo general** (5)
German (*language*) **alemán** *m.* (2); *n., adj.* **alemán, alemana** (3)
get **obtener** (*like* **tener**) (12); how do you get to . . . ? **¿cómo se llega a... ?** (15); to get **conseguir** (*like* **seguir**) (9); to get (*grades*) **sacar (qu)** (14); to get a cold **resfriarse (me resfrío)** (11); to get along poorly (with) **llevarse mal (con)** (16); to get along well (with) **llevarse bien (con)** (16); to get angry (with) **enojarse (con)** (9); to get down (from) **bajarse (de)** (8); to get dressed **vestirse (me visto) (i)** (5); to get off (of) (*a vehicle*) **bajarse (de)** (8); to get on (*a vehicle*) **subir (a)** (8); to get sick

enfermarse (11); to get tired **cansarse** (11); to get together (with) **reunirse (me reúno) (con)** (9); to get up (out of bed) **levantarse** (5); to get up on the wrong side of the bed **levantarse con el pie izquierdo** (14)
gift **regalo** (3)
girl **chica** (4), **niña** (3)
girlfriend **novia** (6)
give **dar** (8); to give (*as a gift*) **regalar** (8); to give someone a party **darle/hacerle una fiesta a alguien** (9); to give (*someone*) a shot/vaccination **ponerle una inyección/una vacuna** (11)
glasses **anteojos** *m. pl.* (11), **lentes** *m. pl.* (11)
go **ir** (4); let's go **vamos** (4); to be going to (*do something*) **ir a** + *inf.* (4); to go abroad **ir al extranjero** (8); to go by boat/ship **ir en barco** (8); to go by bus **ir en autobús** (8); to go by plane **ir/ volar (vuelo) en avión** (8); to go by train **ir en tren** (8); to go camping **hacer** *camping* (8); to go for a hike **dar una caminata** (10); to go home **regresar a casa** (2); to go onto Facebook **entrar en Facebook** (12); to go on the internet **entrar en internet** (12); to go on vacation in/to . . . **ir de vacaciones a...** (8); to go out (with) **salir (con)** (5); to go shopping **ir de compras** (4); to go through customs **pasar por la aduana** (8); to go through security (check) **pasar por el control de seguridad** (8); to go to (*a class, function*) **asistir (a)** (3); to go to a bar **ir a un bar** (10); to go to a concert **ir a un concierto** (10); to go to a disco **ir a una discoteca** (10); to go to bed **acostarse (me acuesto)** (5); to go to the theater **ir al teatro** (10); to go to a museum **ir a un museo** (10); to go up **subir (a)** (8); to go/travel by train **ir en tren** (8)
gold **oro** (4); **de oro** (4)
golf **golf** *m.* (10)
good **buen, bueno/a** (3); good afternoon **buenas tardes** (1); good afternoon/evening **muy buenas** (1); good morning **buenos días** (1); good night **buenas noches** (1); the good news/thing **lo bueno** (11); it's (very) good weather out **hace (muy) buen tiempo** (6); to have a good time **pasarlo bien** (9), **divertirse (me divierto) (i)** (5); to have good luck **tener buena suerte** (14)
good-bye **adiós** (1); to say good-bye (to) **despedir(se)** (*like* **pedir**) **(de)** (9)
good-looking **guapo/a** (3)
goods: woven goods **tejidos** *m. pl.* (13)

gorilla **gorila** *m.* (15)
government **gobierno** (15)
GPS **GPS** *m. inv.* (12)
grade (*academic*) **nota** (5)
graduate (*from*) **graduarse (me gradúo) (en)**
granddaughter **nieta** (3)
grandfather **abuelo** (3)
grandmother **abuela** (3)
grandparents **abuelos** *m. pl.* (3)
grandson **nieto** (3)
graphic designer **diseñador(a) gráfico/a** (17)
gray **gris** (4)
great **gran, grande** (3)
green **verde** (4)
green peas **arvejas** *f. pl.* (7)
greet each other **saludarse** (11)
greeting **saludo** (1)
groceries **comestibles** *m. pl.* (7)
groom **novio** (16)
ground floor **planta baja** (12)
grow **crecer (crezco)** (16)
guess **adivinar** (9)
guest **invitado/a** (9)
guide **guía** *m., f.* (13)

H

haggle **regatear** (4)
hairstylist **peluquero/a** (17)
half past (*the hour*) **y media** (1)
ham **jamón** *m.* (7)
hamburger **hamburguesa** (7)
hand **mano** *f.* (11); to shake hands **darse la mano** (11)
hand in **entregar (gu)** (8)
handbag **cartera** (4)
handsome **guapo/a** (3)
happen **pasar** (6); **ocurrir** (14)
happening **acontecimiento** (18)
happy **alegre** (6), **contento/a** (6); **feliz** (*pl.* **felices**) (9); to be happy (about) **alegrarse (de)** (12)
hard **difícil** (6)
hard drive **disco duro** (12)
hardworking **trabajador(a)** (3)
hat **sombrero** (4)
hate **odiar** (8)
have **tener** (4); (*auxilliary verb*) **haber** (12); to have a bad time **pasarlo mal** (9); to have a birthday **cumplir años** (9); to have a good time **divertirse (me divierto) (i)** (5), **pasarlo bien** (9); to have (a lot of) stress **tener muchas presiones** (14); to have a pain/ache in **tener dolor de** (11); to have a picnic **hacer un** *picnic* (10); to have a snack **merendar (meriendo)** (7); to have bad luck **tener mala suerte** (14); to have been (*doing something*) for (*time*) **hace** + *time* + **que** + *present* (14); *present* + **desde hace** + *time* (14);

to have breakfast **desayunar** (7); to have dinner, supper **cenar** (7); to have good luck **tener buena suerte** (14); to have just (*done something*) **acabar de** + *inf.* (7); to have lunch **almorzar (almuerzo) (c)** (5); to have to (*do something*) **tener que** + *inf.* (4)

he *sub. pron.* **él** (2); he is **es** (1)

head **cabeza** (11)

health **salud** *f.* (11)

healthy **sano/a** (11); to lead a healthy life **llevar una vida sana** (11)

hear **oír** (5)

heart **corazón** *m.* (11)

heating **calefacción** *f.* (12)

heaven: for heaven's sake **por Dios** (14)

hello! **¡hola!** (1)

help *n.* **ayuda** (7); *v.* **ayudar** (7); to help to (*do something*) *v.* **ayudar a** + *inf.* (7)

her *poss. adj.* **su(s)** (3); her, (of) hers *poss. adj., poss. pron.* **suyo/a(s)** (17)

here **aquí** (2)

hi! **¡hola!** (1)

highway **carretera** (15)

hike: to go for a hike **dar una caminata** (10)

his *poss. adj.* **su(s)** (3); his, of his *poss. adj., poss. pron.* **suyo/a(s)** (17)

Hispanic **hispano/a** (3)

history **historia** (2)

hit **pegar (gu)** (14)

hobby **afición** *f.* (10)

hockey **hockey** *m.* (10)

holiday **día** (*m.*) **festivo** (9)

home *n.* **casa** (3); at home **en casa** (2); nursing home **residencia de ancianos** (12); to go home **regresar a casa** (2); *adj.* (*related to the home*) **doméstico/a** (10)

home appliance **aparato doméstico** (10)

homework **tarea** (5)

honeymoon **luna de miel** (16)

honk **tocar (qu)** (15)

hope **esperanza** (18); I hope (that) **ojalá (que)** (13); to hope **esperar** (12)

horn (*car*) **bocina** (15)

horse: to ride a horse **montar a caballo** (10)

host (*of an event*) **anfitrión, anfitriona** (9)

hot (*spicy*) **picante** (7); (*temperature*) **caliente** (7); it's (very) hot (weather) **hace (mucho) calor** (6); it's hot (trendy) **está de moda** (4); **es de última moda** (4); to be (very) hot **tener (mucho) calor** (6)

hot dog **salchicha** (7)

house **casa** (3)

household chore **quehacer** (*m.*) **doméstico** (10)

housekeeper: female housekeeper **ama** (*f.*) (*but* **el ama**) **de casa** (17); male housekeeper **amo de casa** (17)

housing **vivienda** (12)

how + *adj.*! **¡qué** + *adj.*! (14); how strange that . . . ! **¡qué extraño que... !** (13)

how? **¿cómo?** (1); how are you ? **¿cómo está(s)?** (1); **¿qué tal?** (1); how do you get to . . . ? **¿cómo se llega a... ?** (15); how many? **¿cuántos/as?** (2); how much? **¿cuánto?** (2); how much does it (do they) cost? **¿cuánto cuesta(n)?** (4); how often . . . ? **¿con qué frecuencia... ?** (3)

human **humano/a** (11); human body **cuerpo humano** (11)

humanities **humanidades** *f. pl.* (2)

hungry: to be (very) hungry **tener (mucha) hambre** (7)

hurry: to be in a hurry **tener prisa** (4)

hurt **doler (duele)** (*like* **gustar**) (11); to hurt oneself **hacerse daño** (14); to hurt (*a body part*) **lastimarse** (14); to hurt one's (*body part*) **hacerse daño en** (14)

husband **esposo** (3), **marido** (3)

hybrid **híbrido/a** (15)

I

I *sub. pron.* **yo** (2); I am **soy** (1); I am from . . . **(yo) soy de...** (1); I didn't mean to do it **fue sin querer** (14); I hope (that) **ojalá (que)** (13); I would (really) like . . . **me gustaría (mucho)...** (8); I'm sorry/ pardon me **disculpa, discúlpame** *fam. s.* (14); **disculpe, discúlpeme** *form. s.* (14); I'm (very) sorry **lo siento (mucho)** (14)

ice cream **helado** (7)

identification card **tarjeta de identificación** (14)

if **si** (4)

illness **enfermedad** *f.* (11)

image **imagen** *f.* (13)

immediately **en seguida** (5)

impossible **imposible** (13); it's impossible that **es imposible que** (13) it's not impossible **no es imposible** (13)

improbable **improbable** (13); it's improbable that **es improbable que** (13); it's not improbable **no es improbable** (13)

in **en** (1); in case **en caso de (que)** (16); in cash **en efectivo** (17); in front of **delante de** (6); in love (with) **enamorado/a (de)** (16); in order to (*do something*) **para** + *inf.* (10); in the afternoon **de la tarde** (1); in the evening **de la noche** (1); in the morning **de la mañana** (1); in the morning/afternoon/evening **por la mañana/tarde/noche** (2)

incredible **increíble** (13); it's incredible that **es increíble que** (13)

indefinite and negative word *gram.* **palabra indefinida y negativa** (7)

inequality **desigualdad** *f.* (18)

inexpensive **barato/a** (4)

infancy **infancia** (16), **niñez** *f.* (16)

inflexible **inflexible** (14)

inform **informar** (18)

injection **inyección** *f.* (11)

inner ear **oído** (11)

insist (on) **insistir (en)** (12)

install **instalar** (12)

installments: in installments **a plazos** (17)

intelligent **inteligente** (3)

intended for **para** (3)

interest *n.* **interés** *m.* (17); *v.* to interest (*someone*) **interesar** (*like* **gustar**) (8)

internet **internet** *m.* (12); to go on the internet **entrar en internet** (12); to look for on the internet **buscar (qu) en internet** (12)

interrogative *gram.* **interrogativo/a** (2); interrogative word **palabra interrogativa** (2)

interstate **autopista** (15)

interview **entrevista** (17)

interviewee **entrevistado/a** (17)

interviewer **entrevistador(a)** (17)

invite **invitar** (7)

iPhone **iPhone** *m.* (12)

iPod **iPod** *m.* (12)

iron *v.* **planchar** (10)

island **isla** (6)

issue **cuestión** *f.* (17)

it is... (*time*) **es la...** (1), **son las...** (1)

Italian (*language*) **italiano** (2)

its *poss. adj.* **su(s)** (3); (of) its *poss. adj., poss. pron.* **suyo/a(s)** (17)

J

jacket **chaqueta** (4)

January **enero** (6)

jeans **jeans** *m. pl.* (4)

job **empleo** (17), **trabajo** (12); full-time job **empleo de tiempo completo** (17), **trabajo de tiempo completo** (14); part-time job **empleo de tiempo parcial** (17), **trabajo de tiempo parcial** (14); poorly paid job **empleo mal pagado** (17); well-paid job **empleo bien pagado** (17)

joke **chiste** *m.* (8)

journalist **periodista** *m., f.* (17)

juice **jugo** (7); fruit juice **jugo de fruta** (7)

July **julio** (6)

June **junio** (6)

just in case **por si acaso** (14)

K

keep **guardar** (12); **mantener** (*like tener*) (18); to keep on going **seguir (sigo) (i)** (15)
key **llave** *f.* (5)
kill **matar** (18)
kind **amable** (3)
king **rey** *m.* (18)
kiss: to kiss each other **besarse** (11)
kitchen **cocina** (5)
know **conocer (conozco)** (7); **saber** (7); to know how to (*do something*) **saber + inf.** (7)

L

laborer **obrero/a** (17)
lack **falta** (15)
lake **lago** (15)
lamp **lámpara** (5)
landlady **dueña** (12)
landline **teléfono fijo** (12)
landlord **dueño** (12)
language **lengua** (2); foreign language **lengua extranjera** (2)
laptop (computer) **computadora portátil** (2)
large **gran, grande** (3)
last **pasado/a** (11); **último/a** (14); for the last time **por última vez** (14); last night *adv.* **anoche** (11); to last **durar** (18)
late *adj.* **atrasado/a** (8); *adv.* **tarde** (2)
later: see you later **hasta luego** (1)
laugh **reírse (de)** (9)
law **ley** *f.* (18)
lawyer **abogado/a** (17)
layer: ozone layer **capa de ozono** (15)
lazy **perezoso/a** (3)
lead a calm/healthy life **llevar una vida tranquila/sana** (11)
learn **aprender** (3); to learn (about) **enterarse (de)** (18); to learn how to (*do something*) **aprender a + inf.** (3)
least: at least **por lo menos** (9)
leather *adj.* **de cuero** (4)
leave (*a place*) **salir (de)** (5); to leave for (*a place*) **salir para** (5); to leave on vacation **salir de vacaciones** (8)
left: to the left of **a la izquierda de** (6); to be left **quedar** (*like gustar*) (14)
leg **pierna** (11)
lend **prestar** (5)
lenses: contact lenses **lentes** (*m. pl.*) **de contacto** (11)
less than **menos que** (6); less... than **menos... que** (6); less than + *number* **menos de +** *number* (6)
let (*someone*) go **despedir** (*like pedir*) (17)
let's go **vamos** (4)
letter **carta** (3)
lettuce **lechuga** (7)

librarian **bibliotecario/a** (2)
library **biblioteca** (2)
license: driver's license **licencia de conducir/manejar** (15)
lie **mentira** (12)
life **vida** (11); academic life **vida académica** (14); pace of life **ritmo de la vida** (15)
lift weights **levantar pesas** (11)
light *n.* **luz** *f.* (*pl.* **luces**) (14); *adj.* light (*not heavy*) **ligero/a** (7)
like *n.* **gusto** (1); do you like . . . ? **¿te gusta... ?** *fam. s.* (1); **¿a usted le gusta... ?** *form. s.* (1); I would (really) like . . . **me gustaría (mucho)...** (8); (no,) I don't like . . . **(no,) no me gusta** (1); to like **gustar** (8); to like very much **encantar** (*like gustar*) (8); what are you like? **¿cómo es usted?** *form. s.* (1); yes, I like . . . **sí, me gusta...** (1)
likeable **simpático/a** (3)
likely: it's likely that **es probable que** (13)
likewise **igualmente** (1)
limit: speed limit **límite** (*m.*) **de velocidad** (15)
line (*of people*) **cola** (8); to stand in line **hacer cola** (8)
listen to (*music, the radio*) **oír** (5); to listen (to) **escuchar** (2)
literature **literatura** (2)
little *adv.* (a) little **poco** (2); (adjective suffix) **-ito/a** (10); a little bit (of) **un poco (de)** (2); *adj.* **poco/a** (4)
live **vivir** (3)
living room **sala** (5)
loan **préstamo** (17)
lobster **langosta** (7)
long **largo/a** (3)
look at **mirar** (3); to look for **buscar (qu)** (2); to look for on the internet **buscar (qu) en internet** (12)
lose **perder (pierdo)** (5)
lot: a lot *adv.* **mucho** (2); a lot (of) **mucho/a** (3); an awful lot **muchísimo** (8); there's lots of **hay mucho/a** (6)
love *n.* **amor** *m.* (16); *adj.* in love (with) **enamorado/a (de)** (16); *v.* **amar** (16); **querer** (16); **encantar** (*like gustar*) (8); to fall in love (with) **enamorarse (de)** (16); to love each other **quererse** (11)
luck: to have bad/good luck **tener mala/buena suerte** (14)
lucky: to be lucky **tener buena suerte** (14)
luggage **equipaje** *m.* (8)
lunch *n.* **almuerzo** (7); to have lunch **almorzar (almuerzo) (c)** (5)
lungs **pulmones** *m. pl.* (11)
-ly (*adverbial suffix*) **-mente** (14)
lyrics **letra** (7)

M

ma'am **señora (Sra.)** (1)
machine: automatic teller machine (ATM) **cajero automático** (17)
made: it is made of . . . **es de...** (4)
magazine **revista** (3)
mailbox: voice mailbox **buzón** (*m.*) **de voz** (12)
main course **plato principal** (7)
maintain **mantener** (*like tener*) (18)
make **hacer** (5); to make a mistake (about) **equivocarse (qu) (de)** (14); to make plans to (*do something*) **hacer planes** (*m.*) **para + inf.** (10); to make stops **hacer escalas/paradas** (8); to make the bed **hacer la cama** (10)
male housekeeper **amo de casa** (17)
mall: shopping mall **centro comercial** (4)
man **hombre** *m.* (2); business man **hombre de negocios** (17)
manager **gerente** *m., f.* (17); building manager **portero/a** (12)
manufacture **fabricar (qu)** (15)
many **muchos/as** (3); as many . . . as **tanto/a(s) ... como** (6); how many? **¿cuántos/as?** (2)
march **manifestación** *f.* (18)
March **marzo** (6)
market(place) **mercado** (4)
marriage **matrimonio** (16)
married: to be a married person **ser casado/a** (16); to be married (to) **estar casado/a (con)** (16)
marry **casarse (con)** (16)
mass media **medios** *m. pl.* (18)
masterpiece **obra maestra** (13)
match (*game*) **partido** (10)
material **materia** (4)
math **matemáticas** *f. pl.* (2)
matter **cuestión** *f.* (17)
May **mayo** (6)
me *obj. of prep.* **mí** (6); with me **conmigo** (6)
meal **comida** (7)
mean: I didn't mean to do it **fue sin querer** (14); that means . . . **eso quiere decir...** (11)
means of transportation **medio de transporte** (8)
meat **carne** *f.* (7)
mechanic **mecánico/a** (15)
medical **médico/a** (11); medical office **consultorio** (11); medical personnel **personal** (*m.*) **médico** (11)
medicine **medicina** (11)
medium of communication **medio de comunicación** (18)
meet **conocerse (conozco)** (16); nice to meet you **mucho gusto** (1); to meet (*someone somewhere*) **encontrarse (me encuentro) (con)** (11)

memory **memoria** (12)
memory stick **pen drive** *m.* (12)
menu **menú** *m.* (7)
messy **desordenado/a** (6)
Mexican **mexicano/a** (3)
microwave oven **horno de microondas** (10)
middle age **madurez** *f.* (16)
midnight **medianoche** *f.* (6)
military *adj.* **militar** (18); military service **servicio militar** (18)
milk **leche** *f.* (7)
million: one million **un millón (de)** (4)
mine, (of) mine *poss. adj., poss. pron.* **mío/a(s)** (17)
mineral water **agua** (*f.;* but **el agua**) **mineral** (7)
minute: fifteen minutes till (*hour*) **menos quince** (1); thirty minutes past (*the hour*) **y treinta** (1)
misbehave **portarse mal** (9)
miss (*an event*) **perder (pierdo)** (5)
Miss **señorita (Srta.)** (1)
mistake: to make a mistake (*about*) **equivocarse (qu) (de)** (14)
modem **módem** *m.* (12)
modern **moderno/a** (13)
molar **muela** (11)
mom **mamá** (3)
Monday **lunes** *m. inv.* (5); next Monday **el lunes que viene** (5); on Monday **el lunes** (5); on Mondays **los lunes** (5)
money **dinero** (2)
monitor **pantalla** (12); big screen monitor **pantalla grande** (12); flat screen monitor **pantalla plana** (12)
month **mes** *m.* (6)
moped **moto(cicleta)** (15)
more **más** (2); more than **más que** (6); more . . . than **más... que** (6); more than + *number* **más de** + *number* (6)
morning: good morning **buenos días** (1); in the morning **por la mañana** (2); **de la mañana** (1)
mother **madre** *f.* (3); **mamá** (3)
motorcycle **moto(cicleta)** (15)
mountain **montaña** (8)
mouse **ratón** *m.* (12)
mouth **boca** (11)
move (*residence*) **mudarse** (12)
movie **película** (5); movie theater **cine** *m. s.* (5); movies **cine** *m. s.* (5)
Mr. **señor (Sr.)** *m.* (1)
Mrs. **señora (Sra.)** (1)
Ms. **señorita (Srta.)** (1)
much **mucho** (2); as much . . . as **tanto/a(s)... como** (6); as much as **tanto como** (6); how much? **¿cuánto?** (2); how much does it (do they) cost? **¿cuánto cuesta(n)?** (4)
mural **mural** *m.* (13)

museum **museo** (10); to visit a museum **visitar un museo** (10)
mushrooms **champiñones** *m. pl.* (7)
music **música** (13)
musical *n. m.* **musical** (13)
musician **músico/a** (13)
must (*do something*) **deber** + *inf.* (3)
my *poss. adj.* **mi(s)** (3); *poss. adj., poss. pron.* **mío/a(s)** (17)

N

name **nombre** *m.* (7); my name is . . . **me llamo...** (1); what is your name? **¿cómo se llama usted?** *form. s.* (1); **¿cómo te llamas?** *fam. s.* (1)
nap: to take a nap **dormir duermo (u) la siesta** (5)
narrate **contar (cuento)** (8)
nationality **nacionalidad** *f.* (3); adjective of nationality **adjetivo de nacionalidad** (3)
natural **natural** (15); natural resource **recurso natural** (15); natural sciences **ciencias** (*f. pl.*) **naturales** (2)
nature **naturaleza** (15)
nauseated **mareado/a** (11)
navigate **navegar (gu)** (12)
neat **ordenado/a** (6)
necessary **necesario/a** (3); it is necessary to (*do something*) **hay que** + *inf.* (13)
need **necesitar** (2)
negative: indefinite and negative word *gram.* **palabra indefinida y negativa** (7)
neighbor **vecino/a** (12)
neighborhood **barrio** (12)
neither **tampoco** (7)
nephew **sobrino** (3)
nervous **nervioso/a** (6)
network: social network **red** (*f.*) **social** (12)
never **jamás** (7), **nunca** (3); almost never **casi nunca** (3)
nevertheless **sin embargo** (6)
new **nuevo/a** (3)
New Year's Eve **Nochevieja** *f.* (9)
newlywed **recién casado/a** (16)
news **noticias** *f. pl.* (5); news media **prensa** (18); the bad news **lo malo** (11); the good news **lo bueno** (11)
newscast **noticiero** (18)
newsstand **quiosco de prensa** (18)
newspaper **periódico** (3)
next *adv.* **luego** (5); *adj.* **próximo/a** (5); next (Tuesday . . .) **el próximo (martes...)** (5); next Monday **el lunes** (*m.*) **que viene** (5); next week **la próxima semana** (5), **la semana que viene** (5)
nice **amable** (3), **simpático/a** (3); nice to meet you **mucho gusto** (1); (very) nice out **(muy) buen tiempo** (6)

niece **sobrina** (3)
night: at night **de la noche** (1), **por la noche** (2); last night *adv.* **anoche** (11)
nine **nueve** (1)
nine hundred **novecientos/as** (4)
nineteen **diecinueve** (1)
ninety **noventa** (3)
ninth **noveno/a** (13)
no **no** (1); **ningún (ninguna)** (7); no, I don't like . . . **(no,) no me gusta** (1)
no one **nadie** (7)
nobody **nadie** (7)
noise **ruido** (5)
noon **mediodía** *m.* (6)
normal **normal** (13); it's normal that **es normal que** (13)
north **norte** *m.* (6)
nose **nariz** *f.* (*pl.* **narices**) (11)
not any **ningún (ninguna)** (7)
notebook **cuaderno** (2)
notes (*academic*) **apuntes** *m., pl.* (14)
nothing **nada** (7)
noun *gram.* **sustantivo** (2)
novel **novela** (13)
novelist **novelista** *m., f.* (13)
November **noviembre** *m.* (6)
now **ahora** (2); right now **ahora mismo** (6)
nuclear energy **energía nuclear** (15)
number **número** (1); ordinal number *gram.* **número ordinal** (13)
nurse **enfermero/a** (11)
nursing home **residencia de ancianos** (12)

O

o'clock: it's . . . o'clock **son las...** (1)
obey **obedecer (obedezco)** (15)
object **objeto** (2)
obligation **deber** *m.* (18)
obtain **obtener** (*like* **tener**) (12); **conseguir** (*like* **seguir**) (9)
ocean **océano** (8)
October **octubre** *m.* (6)
of **de** (1); of course! **¡por supuesto!** (14); of the **del** (3)
off: to turn off **apagar (gu)** (12)
offer **ofrecer (ofrezco)** (8)
office **oficina** (2); (*in a home*) **estudio** (5); (*medical*) **consultorio** (11); (*political*) **cargo** (18)
often: how often . . . ? **¿con qué frecuencia... ?** (3)
oil (*cooking*) **aceite** *m.* (7); (*fuel*) **petróleo** (15)
OK: it's OK **está bien** (6)
old **viejo/a** (3); old age **vejez** *f.* (16)
older (than) **mayor (que)** (6)
olive oil **aceite** (*m.*) **de oliva** (7)
on **en** (1); on a trip **de viaje** (8); on Monday **el lunes** (5); on the dot (*time*) **en punto** (1); on top of **encima de** (6);

on Tuesdays **los martes** (5); on vacation **de vacaciones** (8)

once a week **una vez a la semana** (3)

one **uno** (1); it's one o'clock **es la una** (1)

one hundred **cien** (3); (*used with* 101–199) **ciento** (4)

one hundred ninety-nine **ciento noventa y nueve** (4)

one hundred one **ciento uno** (4)

one hundred two **ciento dos** (4)

one million **un millón (de** + *noun*) (4)

one thousand **mil** (4)

onion **cebolla** (7)

only *adv.* **solo** (2)

open *v.* **abrir** (*p.p.* **abierto**) (3); *adj.* **abierto/a** (6)

opera **ópera** (13)

operate (*a machine*) **manejar** (12)

or **o** (1)

oral **oral** (14); oral report **informe** (*m.*) **oral** (14)

orange *n.* **naranja** (7); *adj.* **anaranjado/a** (4)

orchestra **orquesta** (13)

order **mandar** (12); (*in a restaurant*) **pedir** (**pido**) (**i**) (5); in order to (*do something*) **para** + *inf.* (3)

ordinal number *gram.* **número ordinal** (13)

other **otro/a** (3); others **los/las demás** (12)

ought to (*do something*) **deber** + *inf.* (3)

our *poss. adj.* **nuestro/a(s)** (3); our, of ours *poss. adj., poss. pron.* **nuestro/a(s)** (17)

outdoors *adv.* **afuera** (6); **al aire libre** (10)

outer ear **oreja** (11)

outskirts **afueras** *f. pl.* (12)

overcast: it's (very) overcast **está (muy) nublado** (6)

own, one's own **propio/a** (17)

owner **dueño/a** (7)

ozone layer **capa de ozono** (15)

P

P.M. **de la noche** (1); **de la tarde** (1)

pace of life **ritmo de la vida** (15)

pack one's suitcase(s) **hacer la(s) maleta(s)** (8)

page: webpage **página web** (12)

paid: well/poorly paid job/position **empleo bien/mal pagado** (17)

pain (in) **dolor** *m.* **(de)** (11); to have a pain in **tener dolor de** (11)

paint **pintar** (13)

painter **pintor(a)** (13)

painting (*general*) **pintura** (13); (*specific piece*) **cuadro** (13)

pants **pantalones** *m. pl.* (4)

paper **papel** *m.* (2)

pardon me **con permiso** (1), **disculpa**, **discúlpame** *fam. s.* (14); **disculpe**, **discúlpeme** *form. s.* (14)

parents **padres** *m. pl.* (3)

park **estacionar** (14)

parking lot/place **estacionamiento** (15)

part **parte** *f.* (5)

part-time job/position **empleo de tiempo parcial** (17), **trabajo de tiempo parcial** (14)

partner **pareja** (16)

party **fiesta** (2); (political) party **partido (político)** (18); to throw a party **dar/hacer una fiesta** (9)

pass: boarding pass **tarjeta de embarque** (8)

pass through customs **pasar por la aduana** (8); to pass through security (check) **pasar por el control de seguridad** (8)

passenger **pasajero/a** (8)

passport **pasaporte** *m.* (8)

password **contraseña** (12)

past **pasado/a** (11)

pastime **pasatiempo** (10)

patient **paciente** *n. m., f.* (11)

patio **patio** (5)

pay *n.* (*often per hour*) **salario** (17); *v.* to pay (for) **pagar** (**gu**) (2)

pea: green peas **arvejas** *f. pl.* (7)

peace **paz** *f.* (*pl.* **paces**) (18)

peasant **campesino/a** (15)

pen **bolígrafo** (2); pen drive **pen drive** *m.* (12)

pencil **lápiz** *m.* (*pl.* **lápices**) (2)

people **gente** *f. s.* (8)

pepper (*condiment*) **pimienta** (7)

permit **permitir** (12)

person **persona** (2)

personal pronoun *gram.* **pronombre** (*m.*) **personal** (2)

personnel: medical personnel **personal** (*m.*) **médico** (11)

pet **mascota** (3)

petroleum **petróleo** (15)

pharmacist **farmacéutico/a** (11)

phase **etapa** (16)

philosophy **filosofía** (2)

phone **teléfono** (2); cell phone **teléfono celular** (2); to talk on the phone **hablar por teléfono** (2)

photo(graph) **foto(grafía)** (8); to take photos **sacar** (**qu**) **fotos** (8)

photocopier **fotocopiadora** (12)

photocopy **fotocopia** (12)

photographer **fotógrafo/a** (17)

photography **fotografía** (13)

physics **física** (2)

pick up **recoger** (**recojo**) (14)

picnic: to have a picnic **hacer un** *picnic* (10)

pie **pastel** *m.* (7)

piece: piece of advice **consejo** (7); piece of furniture **mueble** *m.* (5)

Pilates: to do Pilates **hacer (el método) Pilates** (11)

pill **pastilla** (11)

pilot **piloto** *m., f.* (8)

pink **rosado/a** (4)

place *n.* **lugar** *m.* (2); (*in line*) **puesto** (8); parking place **estacionamiento** (15); *v.* **poner** (5)

plaid **de cuadros** (4)

plan **plan** *m.* (10); to make plans to **hacer planes para** (10)

plane **avión** *m.* (8); to fly; to go/travel by plane **volar** (**vuelo**) **en avión** (8); **ir en avión** (8)

planet **planeta** *m.* (15)

plasma television **televisión** (*f.*) **plasma** (12)

plate **plato** (5)

play (*dramatic*) *n.* **drama** *m.* (13), **obra de teatro** (13); (*a game, sport*) *v.* **jugar** (**juego**) (**gu**) (**a, al**) (5); (*a musical instrument*) **tocar** (**qu**) (2); to play cards **jugar** (**juego**) (**gu**) **a las cartas** (10); to play chess **jugar** (**juego**) (**gu**) **al ajedrez** (10); to play videgames **jugar** (**juego**) (**gu**) **a los videojuegos** (10)

player **jugador(a)** (10)

playwright **dramaturgo/a** (13)

plaza **plaza** (4)

pleasantry **expresión** (*f.*) **de cortesía** (1)

please **por favor** (1)

pleased to meet you **encantado/a** (1), **mucho gusto** (1)

pleasing: to be pleasing **gustar** (8)

plumber **plomero/a** (17)

poem **poema** *m.* (13)

poet **poeta** *m., f.* (13)

point: cardinal point **punto cardinal** (6)

police officer **policía** *m., f.* (15)

policy **política** (18)

political: political office **cargo** (18); political party **partido** (18); political science **ciencias** (*f. pl.*) **políticas** (2)

politician **político/a** (18)

politics **política** *s.* (18)

polka-dot **de lunares** (4)

pollute **contaminar** (15)

polluted **contaminado/a** (15)

pollution: there's (lots of) pollution **hay (mucha) contaminación** *f.* (6)

pool **piscina** (5)

poor **pobre** (3); poorly paid job/position **empleo mal pagado** (17); to do poorly **salir mal** (5); to get along poorly (with) **llevarse mal (con)** (16)

poorly **mal** (2)

population **población** *f.* (15)

pork chop **chuleta (de cerdo)** (7)

port **puerto** (8)

porter **maletero** (8)

position **empleo** (17); full-time / part-time position **empleo de tiempo completo / parcial** (17), **trabajo de tiempo parcial** (14); poorly paid position **empleo mal pagado** (17); to run for a position (as a candidate) **postularse para un cargo (como candidato/a)** (18); well-paid position **empleo bien pagado** (17)

possessive **posesivo/a** (17); possessive adjective *gram.* **adjetivo posesivo** (3)

possible **posible** (3); it's not possible **no es posible que** (13); it's possible that **es posible que** (13)

post (*as on Facebook*) **publicar (qu)** (12)

postcard **tarjeta postal** (8)

potato **papa/patata** (7); French fried potato **papa/patata frita** (7)

pottery **cerámica** (13)

practice (*play*) **practicar (qu)** (2); (*train*) **entrenar** (10)

prefer **preferir (prefiero) (i)** (4)

preference **preferencia** (1)

prepare **preparar** (7)

preposition *gram.* **preposición** *f.* (5)

prescription **receta** (11)

present **regalo** (3)

press **prensa** (18)

pressure **presión** (14); to be under a lot of pressure **estar bajo muchas presiones** (14)

pretty **bonito/a** (3)

price (*of a transportation ticket*) **pasaje** *m.* (8); fixed, set price **precio fijo** (4)

print **imprimir** (12)

printer **impresora** (12)

probable **probable** (13); it's not probable **no es probable que** (13); it's probable that **es probable que** (13)

profession **profesión** *f.* (17)

professor **profesor(a)** (1)

programmer **programador(a)** (17)

prohibit **prohibir (prohíbo)** (12)

promise **prometer** (8)

pronoun: personal pronoun *gram.* **pronombre** (*m.*) **personal** (2)

protect **proteger (protejo)** (15)

provided **con tal de** (16); provided (that) **con tal (de) que** (16)

psychiatrist **siquiatra** *m., f.* (17)

psychologist **sicólogo/a** (17)

psychology **sicología** (2)

public *n.* **público** (13); *adj.* **público/a** (15)

publish **publicar (qu)** (12)

pure **puro/a** (15)

purple **morado/a** (4)

purpose: for what purpose? **¿para qué?** (16)

purse **bolso** (4)

put **poner** (5); to put on (*an article of clothing*) **ponerse** (5)

Q

quarter: a quarter (fifteen minutes) after (*the hour*) **y cuarto/quince** (1); a quarter to (*hour*) **menos cuarto/quince** (1)

queen **reina** (18)

question **pregunta** (5); to ask a question **hacer una pregunta** (5), **preguntar** (8)

quit **dejar** (17)

quiz **prueba** (14)

R

radio (apparatus) **radio** *m.* (12); radio station **estación** (*f.*) **de radio** (18)

rain **llover (llueve)** (6); it's raining **llueve** (6)

raincoat **impermeable** *m.* (4)

rather **bastante** (16)

read **leer** (*like* **creer**) (3)

reason: for that reason **por eso** (3)

receipt **recibo** (17)

receive **recibir** (3)

recipe **receta** (7)

recommend **recomendar (recomiendo)** (8)

record **grabar** (12)

recycle **reciclar** (15)

recycling **reciclaje** *m.* (15)

red **rojo/a** (4); red wine **vino tinto** (7)

reflexive verb *gram.* **verbo reflexivo** (5)

refrigerator **refrigerador** *m.* (10)

regret **lamentar** (13), **sentir (siento) (i)** (13)

relationship: emotional relationship **relación** (*f.*) **sentimental** (16)

relative **pariente** *m.* (3)

remain (*in a place*) **quedarse** (6); to remain; to be left **quedar** (14)

remember **acordarse (me acuerdo) (de)** (13); **recordar (recuerdo)** (9)

remote control **control** (*m.*) **remoto** (12)

renewable **renovable** (15); renewable energy **energía renovable** (15)

rent *n.* **alquiler** *m.* (12); *v.* to rent **alquilar** (12)

renter **inquilino/a** (12)

repair **arreglar** (15), **reparar** (15); repair shop **taller** *m.* (15)

report **informe** (14), **trabajo** (14); oral report **informe** (*m.*) **oral** (14); written report **informe** (*m.*) **escrito** (14)

reporter **reportero/a** (18)

representative: Congressional representative **representante** (*m., f.*) **al congreso** (18)

resign (from) **renunciar (a)** (17)

resolve **resolver (resuelvo)** (15)

resource: natural resource **recurso natural** (15)

responsibility **deber** *m.* (18), **responsabilidad** *f.* (18)

rest **descansar** (5)

restaurant **restaurante** *m.* (7)

résumé **currículum** *m.* (17)

retire (*from a job*) **jubilarse** (17)

return (*something to someone*) **devolver** (*like* **volver**) (14);

(*to a place*) **regresar** (2), **volver (vuelvo)** (5); to return home **regresar a casa** (2)

review **repaso** (2)

rice **arroz** *m.* (7)

rich (*wealthy*) **rico/a** (3); (*tasty*) **rico/a** (7)

ride: to ride a bicycle **montar en bicicleta** (10); **pasear en bicicleta** (10); to ride a horse **montar a caballo** (10)

right (*legal*) **derecho** (18); **¿no?** (4), **¿verdad?** (4); right now **ahora mismo** (6); right now (*currently*) **en la actualidad** (10); to be right **tener razón** (4); to the right of **a la derecha de** (6)

ring **sonar (suena)** (10)

river **río** (15)

roast(ed) **asado/a** (7); roast chicken **pollo asado** (7)

role (*in a play, an event*) **papel** *m.* (13)

room **cuarto** (2); waiting room **sala de espera** (8)

roommate **compañero/a de cuarto** (2)

round-trip ticket **billete** *m.* (*Sp.*) / **boleto** (*L.A.*) **de ida y vuelta** (8)

routine **rutina** (5)

rug **alfombra** (5)

ruin **ruina** (13)

run **correr** (10); to run against/into **chocar (qu) contra/con** (14); **pegarse (gu) con/contra** (14); to run as a candidate **postularse como candidato/a** (18); to run for a position **postularse para un cargo** (18); (*machines*) **funcionar** (12); to run out of **acabar** (14)

S

sad **triste** (6)

sake: for heaven's sake **por Dios** (14)

salad **ensalada** (7)

salary **sueldo** (17)

sales **rebajas** *f. pl.* (4)

salesperson **vendedor(a)** (17)

salmon **salmón** *m.* (7)

salt **sal** *f.* (7)

same **mismo/a** (6); same here (likewise) **igualmente** (1)

sandals **sandalias** *f. pl.* (4)

sandwich **sándwich** *m.* (7)

Saturday **sábado** (5)

sauce **salsa** (7)

sausage **salchicha** (7)

save **conservar** (15); (*a place in line*) **guardar un puesto** (8); (*documents*) **almacenar** (12), **guardar** (12); (*money*) **ahorrar** (17)

savory **rico/a** (7)

say **decir** (8); to say good-bye (to) **despedirse** (*like* **pedir**) **(de)** (9)

scanner **escáner** *m.* (12)

scene **escena** (13)

scenery **escenario** (13)

schedule **horario** (14)

school **escuela** (10)

schoolteacher **maestro/a de escuela** (17)

science **ciencia** (2); computer science **computación** *f.* (2); natural sciences **ciencias** (*f. pl.*) **naturales** (2); political science **ciencias** (*f. pl.*) **políticas** (2); social sciences **ciencias** (*f. pl.*) **sociales** (2)

screen **pantalla** (12); big screen (monitor) **pantalla grande** (12); flat screen (monitor) **pantalla plana** (12)

script **guion** *m.* (13)

sculpt **esculpir** (13)

sculptor **escultor(a)** (13)

sculpture **escultura** (13)

sea **mar** *m.* (8)

season (of the year) **estación** *f.* (6)

seat **asiento** (8)

second **segundo/a** (13); second floor (third story) **segundo piso** (12)

secretary **secretario/a** (2)

security (check) **control** (*m.*) **de seguridad** (8); to go/pass through security (check) **pasar por el control de seguridad** (8)

see **ver** (5); see you around **nos vemos** (1); see you later **hasta luego** (1); see you tomorrow **hasta mañana** (1)

sell **vender** (3)

senator **senador(a)** (18)

send a text **mandar un mensaje** (2)

separate (from) **separarse (de)** (16)

separated from **separado/a (de)** (16)

separation **separación** *f.* (16)

September **septiembre** *m.* (6)

serve **servir (sirvo) (i)** (5)

service **servicio** (15); military service **servicio militar** (18)

set price **precio fijo** (4)

set the table **poner la mesa** (10)

seven **siete** (1)

seven hundred **setecientos/as** (4)

seventeen **diecisiete** (1)

seventh **séptimo/a** (13)

seventy **setenta** (3)

shake hands **darse la mano** (11)

shame **lástima** (13); it's a shame that **es una lástima que** (13); what a shame that . . . ! **¡qué lástima que... !** (13)

shape **forma** (4)

share **compartir** (17)

shave **afeitarse** (5)

she *sub. pron.* **ella** (2); she is **es** (1)

shellfish **mariscos** *m. pl.* (7)

ship **barco** (8); cruise ship **crucero** (8); to go/travel by ship **ir en barco** (8)

shirt **camisa** (4)

shoes **zapatos** *m. pl.* (4)

shop **tienda** (4); repair shop **taller** *m.* (15)

shopping **de compras** (4); shopping mall **centro comercial** (4); to go shopping **ir de compras** (4)

short (*in height*) **bajo/a** (3); (*in length*) **corto/a** (3)

shorts **pantalones** (*m. pl.*) **cortos** (4)

shot: to give (*someone*) a shot **ponerle una inyección** (11)

should (*do something*) **deber** + *inf.* (3)

show *n.* **espectáculo** (13); *v.* **mostrar (muestro)** (8)

shower: to take a shower **ducharse** (5)

shrimp **camarones** *m., pl.* (7)

siblings **hermanos** *m. pl.* (3)

sick **enfermo/a** (6); to get/become sick **enfermarse** (11)

sickness **enfermedad** *f.* (11)

sidewalk **acera** (15)

silk *adj.* **de seda** (4)

silly **tonto/a** (3)

silver *adj.* **de plata** (4)

sing **cantar** (2)

singer **cantante** *m., f.* (13)

single (*not married*) **soltero/a** (16)

sink: bathroom sink **lavabo** (5)

sir **señor (Sr.)** *m.* (1)

sister **hermana** (3)

sit down **sentarse (me siento)** (5)

six **seis** (1)

six hundred **seiscientos/as** (4)

sixteen **dieciséis** (1)

sixth **sexto/a** (13)

sixty **sesenta** (3)

skate *v.* **patinar** (10)

skating **patinaje** *m.* (10)

ski **esquiar (esquío)** (10)

skiing **esquí** *m.* (10)

skirt **falda** (4)

skyscraper **rascacielos** *m. inv.* (15)

sleep **dormir (duermo) (u) (u)** (5)

sleepy: to be sleepy **tener sueño** (4)

slender **delgado/a** (3)

small **pequeño/a** (3); (*adjective suffix*) **-ito/a** (10); small child **niño/a** (3)

smart **listo/a** (3)

smile **sonreír** (*like* **reír**) (9)

smoke **fumar** (8)

smoking area **sala de fumadores/ de fumar** (8)

snack **merienda** (7); to have a snack **merendar (meriendo)** (7)

snow **nevar (nieva)** (6); it's snowing **nieva** (6)

so that **para que** (16)

so-so **regular** (1)

soccer **fútbol** *m.* (10)

social: social network **red** (*f.*) **social** (12); social sciences **ciencias** (*f. pl.*) **sociales** (2); social worker **trabajador(a) social** (17)

sociology **sociología** (2)

socks **calcetines** *m. pl.* (4)

soft drink **refresco** (7)

solar energy **energía solar** (15)

soldier **militar** *m., f.* (17); **soldado** (17); female soldier **mujer** (*f.*) **soldado** (17)

solve **resolver (resuelvo)** (15)

some **algún (alguna/os/as)** (7)

someone **alguien** (7)

something **algo** (7)

sometimes **a veces** (3)

son **hijo** (3)

song **canción** *f.* (7)

soon: as soon as **en cuanto** (17), **tan pronto como** (17)

sorry: to feel sorry **lamentar** (13), **sentir (siento) (i)** (13); I'm (very) sorry **lo siento (mucho)** (14)

sound **sonar (suena)** (10)

soup **sopa** (7)

south **sur** *m.* (6)

space: storage space **espacio de almacenamiento** (12)

Spanish (*language*) **español** *m.* (2); *n., adj.* **español, española** (3)

spare (free) time **ratos** (*m. pl.*) **libres** (10)

speak **hablar** (2)

species **especie** *f.* (15); endangered species **especie en peligro de extinción** (15)

spectator **espectador(a)** (13)

speed **velocidad** *f.* (15); speed limit **límite** (*m.*) **de velocidad** (15)

spend (*money*) **gastar** (9); (*time*) **pasar** (6); to spend one's vacation in . . . **pasar las vacaciones en...** (8)

spicy **picante** (7)

sport **deporte** *m.* (10)

sporting **deportivo/a** (10)

sports, sports-loving *adj.* **deportivo/a** (10)

spring (*season*) **primavera** (6)

square **plaza** (4)

stage **escenario** (13); (*phase*) **etapa** (16)

stairs **escaleras** *f. pl.* (14)

stand up **levantarse** (5); to stand in line **hacer cola** (8)

start **empezar (empiezo) (c)** (5); to start up (*a car*) **arrancar (qu)** (15)

state **estado** (3); emotional state **estado afectivo** (9)

station **estación** *f.* (8); bus station **estación de autobuses** (8); gas station **estación de servicio** (15); radio station **estación de radio** (18); station wagon **camioneta** (8); train station **estación de trenes** (8)

stay **quedarse** (6); to stay in bed **guardar cama** (11)

steak **bistec** *m.* (7)

stick out one's tongue **sacar (qu) la lengua** (11)

still **todavía** (6)

stockings **medias** *f. pl.* (4)

stomach **estómago** (11)

stop *n.* **escala** (*in a trip*) (8), **parada** (*to board transportation*) (8); bus stop **parada del autobús** (12); subway stop **parada del metro** (12); to make stops **hacer escalas** (8), **hacer paradas** (8); to stop **parar** (15); to stop (*doing something*) **dejar de +** *inf.* (11)

storage (space) **(espacio de) almacenamiento** (12)

store *n.* **tienda** (4); *v.* (*computer*) **almacenar** (12)

story **historia** (8)

stove **estufa** (5)

straight ahead **(todo) derecho** (15), **todo recto** (15)

strange: how strange that . . . ! **¡qué extraño que... !** (13); it's strange that **es extraño que** (13)

street **calle** *f.* (12)

street corner **esquina** (15)

stress **estrés** *m.* (14); to have a lot of stress **tener muchas presiones** (14); under stress, stressed out **estresado/a** (14)

strike (*labor*) **huelga** (18)

striped **de rayas** (4)

struggle **lucha** (18)

student **estudiante** *m., f.* (2)

study **estudiar** (2)

stuffed up (*with a cold*) **resfriado/a** *adj.* (11)

subject area **materia** (2)

suburbs **afueras** *f. pl.* (12)

subway stop **parada del metro** (12)

succeed in (*doing something*) **conseguir** (*like* **seguir**) **+** *inf.* (9)

suddenly **de repente** (11)

suffer **sufrir (de)** (14)

sufficiently **bastante** (16)

sugar **azúcar** *m.* (7)

suggest **sugerir (sugiero) (i)** (9)

suit **traje** *m.* (4)

suitcase **maleta** (8); to pack one's suitcase(s) **hacer la(s) maleta(s)** (8)

summer **verano** (6)

sunbathe **tomar el sol** (8)

Sunday **domingo** (5)

sunglasses **gafas** (*f. pl.*) **de sol** (4)

sunny: it's (very) sunny **hace (mucho) sol** (6)

sunscreen **bloqueador** (*m.*) **solar** (8)

supermarket **supermercado** (12)

supper **cena** (7); to have (eat) supper **cenar** (7)

sure **seguro/a** (6); it's a sure thing that **es seguro que** (13); it's not sure **no es seguro que** (13); to not be sure of **no estar seguro/a de** (13)

surf **hacer** *surfing* (10)

surprise **sorprender** (*like* **gustar**) (13)

SUV **SUV** *m.* (15)

sweater **suéter** *m.* (4)

sweatshirt **sudadera** (4)

sweep (the floor) **barrer (el piso)** (10)

sweets **dulces** *m. pl.* (7)

swim **nadar** (8)

swimming **natación** *f.* (10); swimming pool **piscina** (5)

swimsuit **traje** (*m.*) **de baño** (4)

syllabus **programa** (*m.*) **del curso** (14)

symptom **síntoma** *m.* (11)

systems analyst **analista** (*m., f.*) **de sistemas** (17)

T

T-shirt **camiseta** (4)

table **mesa** (2); to clear the table **quitar la mesa** (10); to set the table **poner la mesa** (10)

take **tomar** (2); **llevar** (4); to take a bath **bañarse** (5); to take a nap **dormir (duermo) (u) la siesta** (5); to take a shower **ducharse** (5); to take a trip **hacer un viaje** (5); to take a vacation **tomar unas vacaciones** (8); to take a walk **dar un paseo** (10); to take care of oneself **cuidarse** (11); to take off (*an article of clothing*) **quitarse** (5); to take out **sacar (qu)** (17); to take out the trash **sacar (qu) la basura** (10); to take photos **sacar (qu) fotos** (8); to take place at/in (*a place*) **ser en +** *place* (9); to take someone's temperature **tomarle la temperatura** (11)

talk **hablar** (2); to talk on the phone **hablar por teléfono** (2)

tall **alto/a** (3)

tame **domesticado/a** (15)

tank **tanque** *m.* (15)

tape **grabar** (12)

tasty **rico/a** (7)

tea **té** *m.* (7)

teach **enseñar** (2)

teacher: school teacher **maestro/a de escuela** (17)

team **equipo** (10)

technician **técnico/a** (17)

teeth: to brush one's teeth **cepillarse los dientes** (5)

television: (plasma) television **televisión** (*f.*) **(plasma)** (12); to watch television **mirar la tele(visión)** (3)

tell **contar (cuento)** (8); **decir** (8)

teller **cajero/a** (17); automatic teller machine (ATM) **cajero automático** (17)

temperature **temperatura** (11); to take someone's temperature **tomarle la temperatura** (11)

ten **diez** (1)

tenant **inquilino/a** (12)

tennis **tenis** *m.* (10)

tennis shoes **tenis** *m. pl.* (4)

tent **tienda (de campaña)** (8)

tenth **décimo/a** (13)

terrible **terrible** (13); it's terrible that **es terrible que** (13)

terrorism **terrorismo** (18)

terrorist **terrorista** *m., f.* (18); terrorist attack **ataque** (*m.*) **terrorista** (18)

test **examen** *m.* (4); **prueba** (14)

text (*electronic*) **mensaje** *m.* (2); to (send a) text **mandar un mensaje** (2)

textbook **libro de texto** (2)

than: less . . . than **menos... que** (6); less than + *number* **menos de +** *number* (6); more . . . than **más... que** (6); more than + *number* **más de +** *number* (6); older than **mayor que** (6); younger than **menos que** (6)

thank you (very much) **(muchas) gracias** (1); thanks for **gracias por +** *inf./ noun* (9)

that *conj.* **que** (3); that *adj., pron.* **ese/a** (4); *neuter pron.* **eso** (4); that ([way] over there) *adj., pron.* **aquel, aquella** (4); that ([way] over there) *neuter pron.* **aquello** (4); that means . . . **eso quiere decir...** (11); that which **lo que** (5)

theater **teatro** (10); to go to the theater **ir al teatro** (10)

their *poss. adj.* **su(s)** (3); (of) theirs *poss. adj., poss pron.* **suyo/a(s)** (17)

them *obj.* (*of prep.*) **ellos/as** (2)

then **luego** (5)

there **allí** (4)

there: (way) over there **allá** (4)

there is/are **hay** (1); is there / are there? **¿hay?** (1); there is/are not **no hay** (1); there's (lots of) **hay (mucho/a[s])** (6); infinitive form of **hay haber** (12)

these *adj., pron.* **estos/as** (3)

they *sub. pron.* **ellos/as** (2)

thin **delgado/a** (3)

thing **cosa** (5); the bad thing **lo malo** (11); the good thing **lo bueno** (11)

think **creer (en)** (3); to not think **no creer** (13); to think (about) **pensar (pienso) (de/en)** (5); **pensar que** to think that (5)

third **tercer(o/a)** (13)

thirsty: to be (very) thirsty **tener (mucha) sed** (7)

thirteen **trece** (1)

thirty **treinta** (1); thirty minutes past (*the hour*) **y treinta** (1)

this *adj., pron.* **este/a** (3); *neuter pron.* **esto** (3) those *adj., pron.* **esos/as** (4); those ([way] over there) *adj., pron.* **aquellos/as** (4)

three **tres** (1)

three hundred **trescientos/as** (4)

throat **garganta** (11)

through **por** (8)

throw: to throw a party **dar/hacer una fiesta** (9)

Thursday **jueves** *m. inv.* (5)

ticket **billete** *m.* (*Sp.*) / **boleto** (*L.A.*) (8); one-way ticket **billete/bolleto de ida** (8); round-trip ticket **billete/boleto de ida y vuelta** (8)

tie **corbata** (4)

time **tiempo** (6); at what time . . . ? **¿a qué hora... ?** (1); at times **a veces** (3); conjunction of time **conjunción** (*f.*) **de tiempo** (17); for the first/last time **por primera/última vez** (14); free time **tiempo libre** (10); on time **a tiempo** (8); free time **ratos** (*m. pl.*) **libres** (10); to have a bad time **pasarlo mal** (9); to have a good time **divertirse (me divierto) (i)** (5); **pasarlo bien** (9); what time is it? **¿qué hora es?** (1)

tire **llanta** (15); flat tire **llanta desinflada** (15)

tired **cansado/a** (6); to get tired **cansarse** (11)

to **a** (1); to the **al** (4); to the left of **a la izquiera de** (6); to the right of **a la derecha de** (6)

toast **pan tostado** (7)

toasted **tostado/a** (7)

toaster **tostadora** (10)

today **hoy** (1); what day is today? **¿qué día es hoy?** (5); what's today's date? **¿cuál es la fecha de hoy?** (6), **¿qué fecha es hoy?** (6)

toe **dedo del pie** (11)

together **juntos/as** (8)

tomato **tomate** *m.* (7)

tomorrow **mañana** (1); see you tomorrow **hasta mañana** (1); the day after tomorrow **pasado mañana** (5)

tongue **lengua** (11); to stick out one's tongue **sacar (qu) la lengua** (11)

tonight **esta noche** (6)

too much **demasiado** *adv.* (9)

tooth **diente** *m.* (5); back tooth **muela** (11); to brush one's teeth **cepillarse los dientes** (5)

top: on top of **encima de** (6)

towel **toalla** (5)

trade (*profession*) **oficio** (17)

tradition: cultural tradition **tradición** (*f.*) **cultural** (13)

traditional **folclórico/a** (13)

traffic **circulación** *f.* (15), **tráfico** (15), **tránsito** (15); traffic signal **semáforo** (15)

train **tren** *m.* (8); to go/travel by train **ir en tren** (8); to train **entrenar** (10); train station **estación** (*f.*) **de trenes** (8)

translator **traductor(a)** (17)

transportation: means of transportation **medio de transporte** (8)

trash **basura** (10); to take out the trash **sacar (qu) la basura** (10)

travel **viajar** (8); to travel by bus **ir en autobús** (8); to travel by boat/ship **ir en barco** (8); to travel by plane **ir en avión** (8)

traveling **de viaje** (8)

treadmill **caminadora** (11)

treatment **tratamiento** (11)

tree **árbol** *m.* (9)

trendy: it's trendy **está de moda** (4), **es de última moda** (4)

trip **viaje** *m.* (5); on a trip **de viaje** (8); to take a trip **hacer un viaje** (5)

true: it's true that **es verdad que** (13)

try to (*do something*) **tratar de + *inf.*** (13)

Tuesday **martes** *m. inv.* (5); on Tuesdays **los martes** (5)

tuition **matrícula** (2)

tuna **atún** *m.* (7)

turkey **pavo** (7)

turn **doblar** (15); to be someone's turn **tocarle (qu) a uno** (10); to turn on (*appliance, machine*) **encender (enciendo)** (12); to turn on (*appliance, machine*) **poner** (12); to turn off (*appliance, machine*) **apagar (gu)** (14); to turn out badly **salir mal** (5); to turn out well **salir bien** (5)

tweet *n.* **tuit** *m.* (12); *v.* **Twitear** (12)

twelve **doce** (1)

twenty **veinte** (1)

twice **dos veces** (11)

Twitter **Twitter** *m.* (12)

two **dos** (1)

two hundred **doscientos/as** (4)

U

ugly **feo/a** (3)

uncle **tío** (3); aunts and uncles **tíos** *m. pl.* (3)

under stress **estresado/a** (14); to be under a lot of stress **tener muchas presiones** (14)

understand **comprender** (3); **entender (entiendo)** (5)

underwear **ropa interior** (4)

unfortunately **desgraciadamente** (11)

United States: of the United States of America *n., adj.* **estadounidense** (3)

university *n.* **universidad** *f.* (2); *adj.* **universitario/a** (14)

unless **a menos que** (16); **sin que** (16)

unlikely: it's unlikely that **es improbable que** (13)

unlucky: to be unlucky **tener mala suerte** (14)

unoccupied **libre** (10)

unpleasant **antipático/a** (3)

until *prep.* **hasta** (1); *conj.* **hasta que** (17)

up: to be up to date **estar al día** (18)

urgent **urgente** (12); it's urgent (that) **es urgente que** (12)

us *obj.* (*of prep.*) **nosotros/as** (2)

use **usar** (4); (*gas*) **gastar** (15); to be used for **servir (sirvo) (i) para** (5)

user **usuario/a** (12)

V

vacation: on vacation **de vacaciones** (8); to be on vacation **estar de vacaciones** (8); to go on vacation in/to . . . **ir de vacaciones a...** (8); to leave on vacation **salir de vacaciones** (8); to spend one's vacation at/on/in . . . **pasar las vacaciones en...** (8); to take a vacation **tomar unas vacaciones** (8)

vaccination **vacuna** (11)

vacuum cleaner **aspiradora** (10); to vacuum **pasar la aspiradora** (10)

van **camioneta** (8)

vegetables **verduras** *f. pl.* (7)

vehicle **vehículo** (15)

verb *gram.* **verbo** (2); reflexive verb *gram.* **verbo reflexivo** (5)

very *adv.* **muy** (1); very much **muchísimo** (8); very very **-ísimo** (9); very well **muy bien** (1)

veterinarian **veterinario/a** (17)

victim **víctima** (18)

video **video** (12); videogame **videojuego** (10); to play videogames **jugar (juego) (gu) a los videojuegos** (10)

view **vista** (12)

visit a museum **visitar un museo** (10)

voice mailbox **buzón** (*m.*) **de voz** (12)

volleyball **voleibol** *m.* (10)

vote **votar** (18)

W

wages (*often per hour*) **salario** (17)

wait (for) **esperar** (7)

waiter/waitress **camarero/a** (7)

waiting room **sala de espera** (8)

wake up **despertarse (me despierto)** (5)

walk **caminar** (10); to take a walk **dar un paseo** (10)

wall **pared** *f.* (5)

wallet **cartera** (4)

want **desear** (2); **querer** (4)

war **guerra** (18)

was **fue** (5)

wash **lavar** (10)

washing machine **lavadora** (10)

watch *n.* **reloj** *m.* (4); *v.* **mirar** (3); to watch television **mirar la tele(visión)** (3) water **agua** *f.* (*but* **el agua**) (7); mineral water **agua mineral** (7)

way over there **allá** (4)

we *sub. pron.* **nosotros/as** (2)

wear **llevar** (4), **usar** (4)

weather **tiempo** (6); what's the weather like? **¿qué tiempo hace?** (6); it's (very) good/bad weather **hace (muy) buen/ mal tiempo** (6)

weave **tejer** (13)

webpage **página web** (12)

website **sitio web** (12)

wed: newly wed **recién casado/a** (16)

wedding (*ceremony*) **boda** (16)

Wednesday **miércoles** *m. inv.* (5)

week **semana** (5); days of the week **días** (*m. pl.*) **de la semana** (5); next week **la próxima semana** (5), **la semana que viene** (5); once a week **una vez a la semana** (3)

weekend **fin** (*m.*) **de semana** (2)

weight: to lift weights **levantar pesas** (11)

welcome: you're welcome **de nada** (1), **no hay de qué** (1)

well **bien** (1); very well **muy bien** (1); to come/turn out well **salir bien** (5); to do well **salir bien** (5)

well-being **bienestar** *m.* (11)

well-paid job/position **empleo bien pagado** (17)

west **oeste** *m.* (6)

whale **ballena** (15)

what (that which) **lo que** (5)

what? **¿cómo?** (1); **¿cuál?** (2); **¿qué?** (1); at what time? **¿a qué hora...?** (1); for what purpose? **¿para qué...?** (16); what (a) + *noun*! **¡qué** + *noun*! (14); what a shame that . . . ! **¡qué lástima que...!** (13); what are you like? **¿cómo es usted?** *form. s.* (1); what day is today? **¿qué día es hoy?** (5); what for? **¿para qué...?** (16); what is your name? **¿cómo se llama usted?** *form. s.* (1); **¿cómo te llamas?** *fam. s.* (1); what time is it? **¿qué hora es?** (1); what's the weather like? **¿qué tiempo hace?** (6); what's today's date? **¿cuál es la fecha de hoy?** (6), **¿qué fecha es hoy?** (6)

when? **¿cuándo?** (2)

where? **¿dónde?** (1); where (to)? **¿adónde?** (4); where are you from? **¿de dónde eres (tú)?** *fam. s.* (1); **¿de dónde es usted?** *form. s.* (1)

which *conj.* **que** (3)

which? **¿cuál?** (2)

while **mientras** (10)

white **blanco/a** (4); white wine **vino blanco** (7)

whiteboard **pizarrón** (*m.*) **blanco** (2)

who *rel. pron.* **que** (3)

who? **¿quién?** (1)

whose? **¿de quién?** (3)

why? **¿por qué?** (3)

widow **viuda** (16)

widower **viudo** (16)

wife **esposa** (3), **mujer** *f.* (3)

wifi **wifi** *m.* (12)

wild **salvaje** (15)

win **ganar** (10)

wind **viento** (6); wind energy **energía eólica** (15)

window **ventana** (2); small window (*on a plane*) **ventanilla** (8)

windshield **parabrisas** *m. inv.* (15)

windy: it's (very) windy **hace (mucho) viento** (6)

wine (white, red) **vino (blanco, tinto)** (7)

winter **invierno** (6)

wish **esperanza** (18)

with **con** (2); with me **conmigo** (6); with you *fam. s.* **contigo** (6)

withdraw (*from an account*) **sacar (qu)** (17)

without **sin** (5); **sin que** (16)

witness **testigo** *m., f.* (18)

woman **mujer** *f.* (2); business woman **mujer de negocios** (17)

wool **de lana** (4)

word **palabra** (1); indefinite and negative word *gram.* **palabra indefinida y negativa** (7); interrogative word **palabra interrogativa** (2)

work (labor) **trabajo** (12); (piece of) **trabajo** (14); to work (function) **funcionar** (12); to work (at a job) **trabajar** (2); work of art **obra de arte** (13); *adj.* **laboral** (17)

worker **obrero/a** (17); social worker **trabajador(a) social** (17)

world **mundo** (3)

worried **preocupado/a** (6)

worse **peor** (6)

woven goods **tejidos** *m. pl.* (13)

write **escribir** (*p.p.* **escrito**) (3)

writer **escritor(a)** (13)

written **escrito/a** (*p.p. of* **escribir**) (14); written report **informe** (*m.*) **escrito** (14)

wrong: to be wrong **no tener razón** (4); to get up on the wrong side of the bed **levantarse con el pie izquierdo** (14)

Y

yard **patio** (5)

year **año** (6); (*in school*) **grado** (10); end of the year **fin** (*m.*) **de año** (9); to be . . . years old **tener... años** (3)

yellow **amarillo/a** (4)

yes **sí** (1)

yesterday **ayer** (5); yesterday was . . . **ayer fue...** (5); the day before yesterday *adv.* **anteayer** (5)

yoga: to do yoga **hacer (el) yoga** (10)

yogurt **yogur** *m.* (7)

you *sub. pron.* **tú** *fam. s.* (2); **usted (Ud.)** *form. s.* (2); **vosotros/as** *fam. pl. (Sp.)* (2); **ustedes (Uds.)** *form. pl.* (2); *obj. of prep.* **ti** *fam. s.* (6); **usted** *form. s.;* **ustedes (Uds.)** *form. pl.* (6); and you? **¿y tú?** *fam. s.* (1); **¿y usted?** *form. s.* (1); how are you? **¿cómo está(s)?** (1), **¿qué tal?** (1); with you *fam. s.* **contigo** (6); you are *fam. s.* **eres** (1), *form. s.* **es** (1)

young **joven** (3); young woman **señorita (Srta.)** (1)

younger (than) **menor (que)** (6)

your *poss. adj.* **tu(s)** *fam. s.* (3); **su(s)** *form. s., pl.* (3); **vuestro/a(s)** *fam. pl. (Sp.)* (3); your, (of) yours *poss. adj., poss. pron.* **tuyo/a(s)** *fam. s.* (17); **suyo/a(s)** *form. s., pl.* (17); **vuestro/a(s)** *fam. pl. (Sp.)* (17)

you're welcome **de nada** (1), **no hay de qué** (1)

youth **juventud** *f.* (16); as a youth **de adolescente** (10)

Z

zero **cero** (1)

zone **zona** (12)

CREDITS

Photo Credits

Front Matter
Page iii: © Hero/Corbis/Glow Images

Chapter 1
Opener: (road) © Rodrigo Torres/Glow Images RF; p. 2 (Barcelona): © John Kellerman/Alamy; p. 2 (Mexico City): © Mark Lewis/Getty Images RF; p. 3: © Onoky Photography/SuperStock RF; p. 4 (teacher and student): © Tom Fowlks/Getty Images; p. 4 (greeting): © GoGo Images Corporation/Alamy RF; p. 5: © Hola Images/age fotostock RF; p. 8: © dynamicgraphics/Jupiterimages RF; p. 9 (woman): © Kevin Peterson/Getty Images RF; p. 9 (man): © Andersen Ross/Getty Images RF; p. 11: © America/Alamy RF; p. 13 (class): © Jamie Grill/Tetra Images/Getty Images; p. 13 (signs): © Julio López Saguar/Getty Images RF; p. 15: © Bob Thomas/Popperfoto/Getty Images; p. 20-21 (all): © McGraw-Hill Education/Klic Video Productions; p. 22 (mountain): © Guy Edwardes/Getty Images; p. 22 (beach): © Pixtal/age fotostock RF; p. 22 (forest): © Adalberto Rios Szalay/Sexto Sol/Getty Images RF; p. 22 (desert): © NicoElNino/Shutterstock.com; p. 23 (glacier): © Image Source RF; p. 23 (Madrid): © Pixtal/age fotostock RF; p. 25: © Rodrigo Torres/Glow Images RF.

Chapter 2
Opener: © Simon Jarratt/Corbis/Photolibrary RF; p. 27: © Onoky Photography/SuperStock RF; p. 30: © David R. Frazier Photolibrary, Inc./Alamy; p. 32: © Lifesize/Getty Images RF; p. 33: © McGraw-Hill Education/Klic Video Productions; p. 45: © Tom Merton/Caia Image/Glow Images; p. 47 (woman): © Tetra images RF/Getty Images RF; p. 47 (students): © Digital Vision/Getty Images RF; p. 48: © Digital Vision RF; p. 51: © David A. Tietz/Editorial Image, LLC; p. 53: © McGraw-Hill Education/Klic Video Productions; p. 54: © David Peevers/Lonely Planet Images/Getty Images; p. 56: © Onoky Photography/SuperStock RF; p. 57: © McGraw-Hill Education.

Chapter 3
Opener: © UpperCut Images/Alamy RF; p. 61: © Onoky Photography/SuperStock RF; p. 62 (abuelo): © Jack Hollingsworth/Getty Images RF; p. 62 (abuela): © DreamPictures/Pam Ostrow/Blend Images LLC; p. 62 (padre): © Seth Joel/Getty Images; p. 62 (madre): © Caia Image/Glow Images; p. 62 (tio): © John Lund/Marc Romanelli/Blend Images; p. 62 (tia): © John Henley/Blend Images/Getty Images RF; p. 62 (Patricia): © Glow Images/SuperStock RF; p. 62 (hermana): © Getty Images/Digital Vision RF; p. 62 (hermano): © Daniel Ernst/123RF; p. 62 (dog): © G.K. & Vikki Hart/Getty Images RF; p. 62 (primo): © Ryan McVay/Getty Images RF; p. 62 (prima): © Michael Matisse/Getty Images RF; p. 64 (abuela): © DreamPictures/Pam Ostrow/Blend Images LLC; p. 64 (padre): © Seth Joel/Getty Images; p. 64 (madre): © Caia Image/Glow Images; p. 64 (tio): © John Lund/Marc Romanelli/Blend Images; p. 64 (tia): © John Henley/Blend Images/Getty Images RF; p. 64 (abuelo): © Jack Hollingsworth/Getty Images RF; p. 64 (Patricia): © Glow Images/SuperStock RF; p. 65: © Don Hammond/Design Pics; p. 67: © McGraw-Hill Education/Klic Video Productions; p. 69: © SuperStock/Purestock RF; p. 72: © Van Vechten Collection, Library of Congress, LC-USZ62-42516; p. 73: © McGraw-Hill Education/Klic Video Productions; p. 74: © DEA/G Dagli Orti/age fotostock; p. 75 (man): © Corbis/SuperStock RF; p. 75 (woman): © Lifesize/Getty Images RF; p. 82 (1): © moodboard/SuperStock RF; p. 82 (2): © Terry Vine/Blend Images LLC RF; p. 82 (3): © Monashee Frantz/age fotostock RF; p. 82 (4): © BananaStock/age fotostock; p. 82 (a): © McGraw-Hill Education; p. 82 (b): © Blend Images/Alamy RF; p. 82 (c): © Hero/Corbis/Glow Images RF; p. 82 (d): © Image Source RF; p. 83: © McGraw-Hill Education/Klic Video Productions; p. 85: © Sergio Salvador/Getty Images RF; p. 87: © Charlie Neuman/U-T San Diego/ZUMA Wire/Alamy; p. 88: © Pixtal/age fotostock RF; p. 89: © Ann Summa/Corbis; p. 91: © McGraw-Hill Education/Klic Video Productions; p. 92: © Anuska Sampedro/Getty Images RF; p. 93: © AP Photo/Ramon Espinosa; p. 94: © Onoky Photography/SuperStock RF; p. 95: © McGraw-Hill Education.

Chapter 4

Opener: © Danny Lehman/Corbis; p. 99: © Onoky Photography/SuperStock RF; p. 100 (young woman): © drbimages/Getty Images RF; p. 100 (woman): © Glowimages RM/Alamy; p. 100 (man): © Peopleimages/Getty Images RF; p. 101 (man): © Andresr/Getty Images RF; p. 101 (woman): © drbimages/Getty Images RF; p. 101 (couple): © 4x6/Getty Images RF; p. 103 (crayons): © Nicemonkey/Alamy RF; p. 103 (art): Artwork courtesy of La Antigua Galería de Arte Antigua Guatemala, www.artintheamericas.com; p. 104: © Barry Barker/McGraw-Hill Education; p. 105: © brianlatino/Alamy RF; p. 107: © McGraw-Hill Education/Klic Video Productions; p. 114: © Onoky Photography/SuperStock RF; p. 117: © Lissa Harrison RF; p. 119: © Diego Lezama/ Lonely Planet Images/Getty Images; p. 121: © Miami In Focus, Inc.; p. 122: © Apriori, LLC/Getty Images; p. 123: © McGraw-Hill Education/Klic Video Productions; p. 124: © Dorling Kindersley/ Getty Images RF; p. 126: © Onoky Photography/SuperStock RF; p. 127 (woman in library): © Fancy Collection/Fancy Collection/SuperStock RF; p. 127 (man with skateboard): © Blue Jean Images/Corbis RF; p. 127 (woman in dress): © Ed Suter/Africa Media Online/The Image Works; p. 127 (woman in coat): © pbnj productions/SuperStock RF; p. 127 (man in suit): © Kelly Redinger/ Design Pics RF; p. 127: © McGraw-Hill Education.

Chapter 5

Opener: © Jon Arnold Images Ltd/Alamy; p. 131: © Purestock/Getty Images RF; p. 134: © John Mitchell/Alamy; p. 138: © McGraw-Hill Education/Klic Video Productions; p. 142: © Jan Stromme/ Alamy; p. 143: © Paul Taylor/Getty Images; p. 144: © BrazilPhotos.com/Alamy; p. 152: © Nicholas Gill/Alamy; p. 155: © Alex Peña/LatinContent/Getty Images; p. 157: © McGraw-Hill Education/ Klic Video Productions; p. 158: © Image Source RF; p. 160: © Purestock/Getty Images RF; p. 161 (library): © Andersen Ross/Blend Images LLC RF; p. 161 (gym): © Erik Isakson/Blend Images LLC RF; p. 161 (class): © Purestock/Alamy RF; p. 161 (café): © UpperCut Images/Glow Images RF; p. 161 (steps): © Caia Image/Glow Images RF; p. 161 (video): © McGraw-Hill Education.

Chapter 6

Opener: © Paul Souders/The Image Bank/Getty Images; p. 165: © Purestock/Getty Images RF; p. 168 (all): © Bill Brooks/Alamy RF; p. 169: © DEA/S. Buonamici/Getty Images; p. 172: © McGraw-Hill Education/Klic Video Productions; p. 173: © Janis Christie/Getty Images RF; p. 175: © imagebroker/Alamy RF; p. 178 (man): © Stockbyte/Getty Images RF; p. 178 (woman): © XiXinXing/Getty Images RF; p. 180: © Rodrigo Guerrero/LatinContent/Getty Images; p. 181: © Paul Burns/Blend Images/Getty Images; p. 182: © Jenni Kirk/McGraw-Hill Education; p. 185 (Buenos Aires): © Image Source/PunchStock RF; p. 185 (San Jose): © mtcurado/Getty Images RF; p. 189 (man): © John Lund/Sam Diephuis/Blend Images LLC RF; p. 189 (woman): © Pixtal/ age fotostock RF; p. 190: © Jack Hollingsworth/Getty Images RF; p. 191: © Alamy; p. 192 (boy left): © Paul Bradbury/age fotostock RF; p. 192 (boy middle): © Ariel Skelley/Getty Images; p. 192 (girl): © JGI/Jamie Grill/Blend Images LLC RF; p. 193: © McGraw-Hill Education/Klic Video Productions; p. 194: © Jenni Kirk/McGraw-Hill Education; p. 196: © Purestock/Getty Images RF; p. 197: © McGraw-Hill Education.

Chapter 7

Opener: © Elmer Martinez/AFP/Getty Images; p. 201: © Purestock/Getty Images RF; p. 204: © Nicholas Gill/Alamy; p. 206: © John Parra/Getty Images; p. 208: © McGraw-Hill Education/Klic Video Productions; p. 213: © Image Source RF; p. 218: © Lissa Harrison RF; p. 219: © Purestock/ Getty Images RF; p. 223: © JJM Stock Photography/Alamy RF; p. 225: © McGraw-Hill Education/Klic Video Productions; p. 226: © Gonzalo Azumendi/The Image Bank/Getty Images; p. 227: © Nathan King/Alamy; p. 228: © Purestock/Getty Images RF; p. 229: © McGraw-Hill Education.

Chapter 8

Opener: © Christian Kober/Robert Harding World Imagery/Alamy; p. 233: © Rafael Guerrero/ Photolibrary/Getty Images; p. 237: © Michael J. Doolittle/The Image Works; p. 238 (se habla...): © Elena Rooraid/PhotoEdit; p. 238 (colmado): © Jane Sweeney/AWL Images/Getty Images; p. 240 (all): © McGraw-Hill Education/Klic Video Productions; p. 245: © Alea Image/iStock/Getty Images RF; p. 251: © Reinhard Dirscherl/WaterFrame/Getty Images; p. 255 (bill): © Studio Works/Alamy; p. 255 (woman): © Tetra Images/Getty Images RF; p. 257: © MedioImages RF; p. 259: © McGraw-Hill Education/Klic Video Productions; p. 260: © Jon McLean/Alamy; p. 261 (camel): © Ingram Publishing/SuperStock RF; p. 261 (lake): © Lissa Harrison RF; p. 261 (falls): © Exactostock/SuperStock RF; p. 262: © Rafael Guerrero/Photolibrary/Getty Images; p. 263 (hikers): © Aurora Open/SuperStock RF; p. 263 (café): © Image Source RF; p. 263 (beach): © Purestock/Superstock RF; p. 263 (library): © Fancy/Veer/Corbis/Glow Images RF; p. 263 (camping): © Brand X Pictures/age fotostock RF; p. 263 (video): © McGraw-Hill Education.

Chapter 9

Opener: © Evelyn Paley/Alamy; p. 267: © Rafael Guerrero/Photolibrary/Getty Images; p. 269: © Adalberto Roque/AFP/Getty Images; p. 270: © AP Photo/Dado Galdieri; p. 273: © McGraw-Hill Education/Klic Video Productions; p. 276: © Boston Globe/Getty Images; p. 278: © C Bockermann/CHROMOR/agefotostock; p. 280: © Carl DeAbreu/Alamy; p. 285: © Frans Schellekens/Redferns/Getty Images; p. 286: © Beren Patterson/Alamy; p. 287: © McGraw-Hill Education/Klic Video Productions; p. 288: © Purestock/Superstock RF; p. 290: © Rafael Guerrero/Photolibrary/Getty Images; p. 291 (formal): © moodboard/Alamy RF; p. 291 (wedding): © Purestock/Superstock RF; p. 291 (dinner): © Cultura Creative/Alamy RF; p. 291 (pinata): © Ariel Skelley/Blend Images LLC RF; p. 291 (video): © McGraw-Hill Education.

Chapter 10

Opener: © Sylvain Grandadam/Robert Harding Picture Library/age fotostock; p. 295: © Rafael Guerrero/Photolibrary/Getty Images; p. 296 (riding): © Comstock Images/Alamy RF; p. 296 (walking): © David Planchet RF; p. 296 (yoga): © Ingram Publishing/SuperStock RF; p. 296 (skiing): © Randy Lincks/Alamy; p. 296 (family playing): © Chris Ryan/age fotostock RF; p. 296 (running): © Mark Anderson/Getty Images RF; p. 296 (hiking): © kurhan/Shutterstock; p. 296 (clubbing): © Chris Ryan/age fotostock RF; p. 297: © Beck Diefenbach/Reuters/Corbis; p. 299: © Geordie Torr/Alamy; p. 301: © McGraw-Hill Education/Klic Video Productions; p. 307: United States Coast Guard; p. 310 (Lopez): © Stephane Cardinale/Sygma/Corbis; p. 310 (del Torres): © Stefanie Keenan/WireImage/Getty Images; p. 310 (Walker): © Focus on Sport/Getty Images; p. 313: © Helen H. Richardson/Denver Post/Getty Images; p. 313: © Glyn Genin/Alamy; p. 315: © McGraw-Hill Education/Klic Video Productions; p. 316: © Medioimages/Photodisc/Getty Images RF; p. 318: © Rafael Guerrero/Photolibrary/Getty Images; p. 319 (waterfall): © Hola Images/Getty Images RF; p. 319 (video): © McGraw-Hill Education.

Chapter 11

Opener: © ZUMA Press, Inc/Alamy; p. 323: © Rafael Guerrero/Photolibrary/Getty Images; p. 325: © Nehomar Efren Hernandez Navas/123RF; p. 327 (runner): © Royalty Free/Corbis RF; p. 327 (doctor): © Mike Watson/moodboard/Corbis RF; p. 327 (farmacia): © David R. Frazier Photolibrary, Inc./Alamy; p. 329: © McGraw-Hill Education/Klic Video Productions; p. 330: © Marty Granger/McGraw-Hill Education; p. 333: © DEA/M. Seemuller/De Agostini/Getty Images; p. 334: © Imagesource/Photolibrary RF; p. 335 (food): © Boston Globe/Getty Images; p. 335 (party): © Image Source/age fotostock RF; p. 337: © Jacques Jangoux/Alamy; p. 341: © Tommy Kay/Corbis; p. 343: © Keith Dannemiller/Corbis; p. 345: © McGraw-Hill Education/Klic Video Productions; p. 346: © Paula Bronstein/Getty Images; p. 348: © Rafael Guerrero/Photolibrary/Getty Images; p. 349: © McGraw-Hill Education.

Chapter 12

Opener: © Radius/SuperStock RF; p. 353: © Daniel Ernst/iStock/Getty Images RF; p. 357: © Jose Miguel Gomez/Reuters/Corbis; p. 359: © McGraw-Hill Education/Klic Video Productions; p. 363: © Mark Dierker/McGraw-Hill Education; p. 365: © Glow Images/Superstock RF; p. 373: © Ulf Andersen/Getty Images; p. 374: © Brand X Pictures/PunchStock RF; p. 374: © Daniel Russell Ripplinger/123RF; p. 375: © Dave G. Houser/Corbis; p. 377: © McGraw-Hill Education/Klic Video Productions; p. 378: © Jane Sweeney/The Image Bank/Getty Images; p. 380 (insulin): © James R Clarke/Alamy; p. 380 (man): © Daniel Ernst/iStock/Getty Images RF; p. 381: © McGraw-Hill Education.

Chapter 13

Opener: © Bernai Velarde; p. 385: © Daniel Ernst/iStock/Getty Images RF; p. 388: © mediacolor's/Alamy; p. 389: © age fotostock/Alamy; p. 391: © McGraw-Hill Education/Klic Video Productions; p. 392: © Doug Berry/E+/Getty Images; p. 394: Blanton Museum of Art, The University of Texas at Austin, Barbara Duncan Fund, 1975. Photo by Rick Hall; p. 397: © Melanie Stetson Freeman/The Christian Science Monitor via Getty Images; p. 399: Aryballos-shaped vessel (ceramic), Incan/Museo Regional de Cuzco, Peru/Bildarchiv Steffens Henri Stierlin/The Bridgeman Art Library; p. 400 (market): © Nigel Pavitt/AWL Images/Getty Images; p. 400 (lake): © Christophe Boisvieux/Hemis/Alamy; p. 401 (tortoise): © Cleveland Metroparks Zoo/McGraw-Hill Education; p. 401 (iquana): © FAN Travelstock/Alamy RF; p. 404: © DEA/G Dagli Orti/Getty Images; p. 405: © Iberfoto/Iberfoto/Superstock; p. 407: © McGraw-Hill Education/Klic Video Productions; p. 408: © Aizar Raldes/AFP/Getty Images; p. 410: © Daniel Ernst/iStock/Getty Images RF; p. 411 (children): © SuperStock/age fotostock; p. 411 (video): © McGraw-Hill Education.

Chapter 14

Opener: © Mariana Bazo/Reuters/Corbis; p. 415: © Daniel Ernst/iStock/Getty Images RF; p. 418 (Slim): © Gillianne Tedder/Bloomberg via Getty Images; p. 418 (Miguel): © Carlos Alvarez/Getty Images; p. 418 (Olmos): © Michael Tran/FilmMagic/Getty Images; p. 420: © tose/iStock/Getty Images RF; p. 422: © McGraw-Hill Education/Klic Video Productions; p. 423: © Yadid Levy/ Robert Harding World Imagery/Getty Images; p. 425: © Ernesto Benavides/AFP/Getty Images; p. 429: © Xinhua/Alamy; p. 434: © Jonathan Nackstrand/AFP/Getty Images; p. 435: © Photographer's Choice/Getty Images RF; p. 437: © McGraw-Hill Education/Klic Video Productions; p. 438: © Glowimages/Getty Images; p. 440: © Daniel Ernst/iStock/Getty Images RF; p. 441: © McGraw-Hill Education.

Chapter 15

Opener: © Paul Stead/Alamy Stock Photo; p. 445: © Daniel Ernst/iStock/Getty Images RF; p. 453: © McGraw-Hill Education/Klic Video Productions; p. 456: © Viviane Ponti/Lonely Planet Images/Getty Images/Getty Images; p. 461: © Daniel Garcia/AFP/Getty Images; p. 463: © Digital Vision/Getty Images RF; p. 465: © McGraw-Hill Education/Klic Video Productions; p. 466: © Cristian Lazzari/iStock/Getty Images RF; p. 468: © Daniel Ernst/iStock/Getty Images RF; p. 469: © McGraw-Hill Education.

Chapter 16

Opener: © Jorge Adorno/Reuters/Corbis; p. 473: © Daniel Ernst/iStock/Getty Images RF; p. 475: © Frans Lemmens/SuperStock; p. 478: © McGraw-Hill Education/Klic Video Productions; p. 479: © Dmitrii Shironosov/123RF; p. 482: © Mike Goldwater/Alamy; p. 485: © EPA European Pressphoto Agency b.v./Alamy; p. 487: © mtcurado/iStock/Getty Images RF; p. 489: © McGraw-Hill Education/Klic Video Productions; p. 490: © Studio Works/Alamy; p. 492 (orange): © I. Rozenbaum/PhotoAlto; p. 492 (woman): © Daniel Ernst/iStock/Getty Images RF; p. 493: © McGraw-Hill Education.

Chapter 17

Opener: © Paul Harris/AWL Images/Getty Images; p. 497: © Daniel Ernst/iStock/Getty Images RF; p. 499: © Marcelo Hernandez/LatinContent/Getty Images; p. 502: © Ronald Patrick/Bloomberg via Getty Images; p. 504: © McGraw-Hill Education/Klic Video Productions; p. 507: © Mago World Image/age fotostock RF; p. 509: © El Mercurio de Chile/Newscom; p. 510 (statues): © Michael Snell/Robert Harding Picture Library/SuperStock; p. 510 (wine): © Lee Foster/Alamy; p. 514: © Martin Bernetti/AFP/GettyImages; p. 515: © Jon Arnold Images Ltd/Alamy; p. 517: © McGraw-Hill Education/Klic Video Productions; p. 518: © Marcelo Hernandez/LatinContent/ Getty Images; p. 520: © Daniel Ernst/iStock/Getty Images RF; p. 521: © McGraw-Hill Education.

Chapter 18

Opener: © Pablo Blazquez Dominguez/Getty Images; p. 525: © PhotoAlto/Eric Audras/Brand X Pictures/Getty Images RF; p. 529: © People and Politics/Alamy; p. 530: © Gerard Julien/AFP/ Getty Images; p. 531: © McGraw-Hill Education/Klic Video Productions; p. 535: © Evrim Aydin/ Anadolu Agency/Getty Images; p. 537: © Patrick Forget/age fotostock; p. 538: © Pierre-Philippe Marcou/AFP/Getty Images; p. 541: © Image Source RF; p. 546: © Hermes Mereghetti Studio/ Alamy; p. 547: © McGraw-Hill Education/Klic Video Productions; p. 548: © Pixtal/age fotostock RF; p. 550 (aqueduct): © Corbis RF; p. 550 (man): © PhotoAlto/Eric Audras/Brand X Pictures/ Getty Images RF; p. 551: © McGraw-Hill Education; p. 554: © Backyard Productions/Alamy; p. 555: © Francis R. Malasig/EPA/Newscom.

Text Credits

Chapter 1
Page 7 (table): From *Fox News Latino*; p. 11 (bottom): Source: 2010 U.S. Census; p. 12 (left – table): Source: 2006 U.S. Census.

Chapter 2
Page 55 (bottom right): From Cincilingua International Language Center, Cincinnati, Ohio.

Chapter 3
Page 64 (top left): From Instituto Nacional Electoral, Mexico; p. 65 (bottom): From Mexican Government.

Chapter 4
Page 106 (top): From Quo, HF Revistas; p. 125 (middle): Gregori Dolz, "Algo mas que ropa" in *Nexos Magazine* - © Ink-Global.

Chapter 5
Page 159 (middle): From Bienes Raíces Avisos de Ocasión.

Chapter 6
Page 195 (middle): From La U El Diario de Kampussia.

Chapter 7
Page 209 (top): From www.cnpp.usda.gov; p. 224 (middle): From CONABIP.

Chapter 8
Page 239 (middle): From En Lan; p. 246 (right): www.godominicanrepublic.com; p. 258 (cartoon): From David Sebastian Ojeda, Pasaje Blanco, 1662 Moron, prov. De Buenos Aires, artepiero@hotmail.com; p. 261 (middle): © I Love Viajes - www.iloveviajes.com.

Chapter 10
Page 308 (top): From Restaurant El Boricua.

Chapter 11
Page 340 (cartoon): © Joaquín Salvador Lavado (QUINO) Toda Mafalda - Ediciones de La Flor, 1993; p. 347 (middle): Nicanor Parra, "Epitafio", POEMAS Y ANTIPOEMAS © 1954, Nicanor Parra. Used by permission.

Chapter 12
Page 358 (top): From Vodafone; p. 364 (right): From Colombia Government - Industria y turismo; p. 379 (middle): "Cuadrados y angulos" by Alfonsina Storni, 1904.

Chapter 13
Page 409 (middle): Tito Matamala, "La opportunidad de Salomón Bobadilla" in *Con pocas palabras. Muestra de microcuentos*. Used with permission.

Chapter 14
Page 433 (bottom): From Asociacion todo ellos por; p. 439 (middle): Mario Benedetti, Poem **Oh** in *Poemas de la oficina* © Fundacion Mario Benedetti, c/o Schavelzon Graham Agencia Literaria, www.schavelzongraham.com.

Chapter 15
Page 449 (top right): © UTE; 464 (cartoon - left): © Joaquín Salvador Lavado (QUINO) ¡Cuánta bondad! - Ediciones de La Flor, 1999; p. 464 (cartoon - right): Cartoon by MENA, ALI Brussels; p. 467 (middle): "Apocalipsis, I" by Marco Denevi from *Falsificaiones*.

Chapter 16
Page 491 (middle): Diego Muñoz Valenzuela, *Amor cibernauta*. Used with permission.

Chapter 17
Page 519 (middle): © Fundación Gloria Fuertes.

Chapter 18
Page 537 (cartoon): From Antonio Mingote; p. 549 (middle): Eduardo Galeano, Celebración de la voz humana/2 in *El libro de los abrazos* © Siglo XXI DE ESPAÑA EDITORES. Used by permission; p. 555 (bottom): www.hispanicfiesta.com.

INDEX

Note: The notation "n" after a page number indicates that it is a footnote.

McGraw-Hill Connect®
Learn Without Limits

Connect is a teaching and learning platform that is proven to deliver better results for students and instructors.

Connect empowers students by continually adapting to deliver precisely what they need, when they need it, and how they need it, so your class time is more engaging and effective.

Course outcomes improve with Connect.

Exam Scores — 80.4% / 74.7%
Pass Rates — 93.7% / 72.9%
Attendance Rates — 92.9% / 74.5%
Retention Rates — 87.5% / 71.1%

With Connect / Without Connect

Using **Connect** improves passing rates by **10.8%** and retention by **16.4%**.

88% of instructors who use **Connect** require it; instructor satisfaction **increases** by 38% when **Connect** is required.

Analytics

Connect Insight®

Connect Insight is Connect's new one-of-a-kind visual analytics dashboard that provides at-a-glance information regarding student performance, which is immediately actionable. By presenting assignment, assessment, and topical performance results together with a time metric that is easily visible for aggregate or individual results, Connect Insight gives the user the ability to take a just-in-time approach to teaching and learning, which was never before available. Connect Insight presents data that empowers students and helps instructors improve class performance in a way that is efficient and effective.

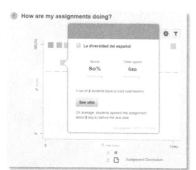

How are my assignments doing?

La diversidad del español

Score **80%**   Time spent **6m**

1 out of 2 students have scored submissions

See who

On average, students opened this assignment about 2 day(s) before the due date.

Assignment Distribution

Adaptive

AN ADAPTIVE VOCABULARY AND GRAMMAR PRACTICE EXPERIENCE DESIGNED TO TRANSFORM THE WAY STUDENTS LEARN

More students earn **A's** and **B's** when they use McGraw-Hill Education **Adaptive** products.

LearnSmart®

Proven to help students study more efficiently and improve grades, LearnSmart is an adaptive learning program that provides each student a fully customized vocabulary and grammar practice experience. By identifying the student's strengths and weaknesses and responding with personalized instruction that guides the learner to understand and retain the foundational vocabulary and grammar of the language, LearnSmart helps the student learn and master this critical course content.

LearnSmart delivers—with target precision—the content needed, exactly when it's needed.

Fueled by the Proven and Adaptive LearnSmart Engine

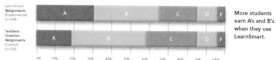

LearnSmart Assignments (Experimental) (n=358)   A | B | C | D | F

Testbank Question Assignments (Control) (n=312)   A | B | C | D | F

More students earn A's and B's when they use LearnSmart.

Over **4 billion questions** have been answered, making McGraw-Hill Education products more intelligent, reliable, and precise.

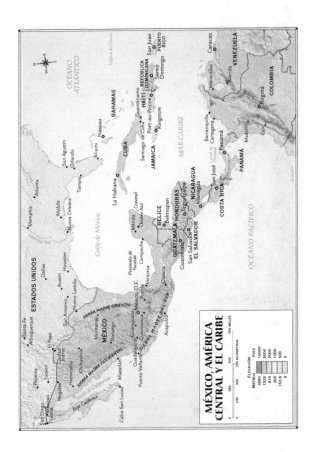

MÉXICO, AMÉRICA
CENTRAL Y EL CARIBE

AMÉRICA DEL SUR

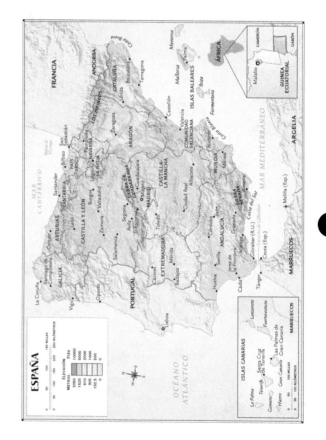

ESPAÑA

Credits

Online Supplements

Online Supplements

Connect Online Access for Puntos de partida, 10th Edition

McGraw-Hill Connect is a digital teaching and learning environment that improves performance over a variety of critical outcomes. With Connect, instructors can deliver assignments, quizzes and tests easily online. Students can practice important skills at their own pace and on their own schedule.

HOW TO REGISTER

Using a <u>Print Book</u>?
To register and activate your Connect account, simply follow these easy steps:
1. **Go to the Connect course web address provided by your instructor or visit the Connect link set up on your instructor's course within your campus learning management system.**
2. **Click on the link to register.**
3. **When prompted, enter the Connect code found on the inside back cover of your book and click Submit. Complete the brief registration form that follows to begin using Connect.**

Using an <u>eBook</u>?
To register and activate your Connect account, simply follow these easy steps:
1. **Upon purchase of your eBook, you will be granted automatic access to Connect.**
2. **Go to the Connect course web address provided by your instructor or visit the Connect link set up on your instructor's course within your campus learning management system.**
3. **Sign in using the same email address and password you used to register on the eBookstore. Complete your registration and begin using Connect.**

Note: Access Code is for one use only. If you did not purchase this book new, the access code included in this book is no longer valid.

Need help? Visit mhhe.com/support